Contemporary American Composers:
A Biographical Dictionary

Compiled by
E. Ruth Anderson

G. K. HALL & CO., 70 LINCOLN STREET, BOSTON, MASSACHUSETTS

Library of Congress Cataloging in Publication Data

Anderson, Ruth.
   Contemporary American composers.

   1. Composers, American--Biography. I. Title.
ML390.A54   780'.92'2 [B]   76-2395
ISBN 0-8161-1117-0

This publication is printed on permanent/durable acid free paper
MANUFACTURED IN THE UNITED STATES OF AMERICA

Preface

In the early 1940's when Deems Taylor was intermission commentator for the New York Philharmonic Radio Broadcasts, he received letters from two listeners on opposite sides of the continent, both putting forth the theory that music thrives and composers abound in a country that is unhappy in its government. Perhaps the present proliferation of composers can be attributed not to the state of our government (or the world, for we are not alone in this musical abundance), but to the development and practice of the Schillinger System of Musical Composition combined with a more relaxed definition of music, and also to the tremendous increase in government and private foundation grants. The large number of 20th century composers listed in this directory is testimony to all of these factors and more.

When in 1970 I began listing contemporary American composers found in some old Schwann catalogs, I had no idea that I was getting involved in a major project that would dominate my life for five years. By the time I had recorded over seven hundred names, I thought the task was almost completed. In fact, the number of composers identified reached over 6,000 with the addition of names from the College Music Society's list of composers; the American Society of University Composers; the Southeastern Composers' League; the National Association of American Composers and Conductors; the American Society of Composers, Authors and Publishers; Baker's Biographical Dictionary of Musicians; The Directory of American Women Composers; Bull's Index to Biographies of Contemporary Composers; Central Opera Service Bulletin; publisher's lists; recording company lists; concert announcements in The New York Times and elsewhere; Schwann catalogs; and the many names supplied by composers to whom I sent questionnaires. Of the 6,000 names gathered, approximately one-third that number either did not meet the criteria established for inclusion in this volume or were unlocatable.

The criteria for inclusion were: birth date no earlier than 1870; American citizenship or extended residence in the United States; and at least one original composition published, commercially recorded, performed in an urban area, or selected for an award in composition. Because of sheer numbers, composers who wrote teaching pieces only, jazz only (with a few exceptions), popular only, rock or folk were not included. Those who received two questionnaires and did not reply were omitted unless they also appeared in publishers' sources such as lists and concert announcements.

Concentrating on 20th century American composers allowed the listing for the lesser known, unknown, and minor composers of this period. Information given in returned questionnaires was accepted as presented with a minimum of verification. An asterisk preceding an entry indicates that the information included is not based upon a completed questionnaire, but gathered from other sources such as concert announcements, publishers' lists and recordings. It is possible that some composers included in this category are in fact Canadians or other nationalities, or pen names, which have eluded identification. Because of the increased interest in women composers a separate list appears on page 511.

* * * * * *

Thanks are due to all composers who suggested names of colleagues, and special thanks to those who provided more than 25 names: Donald Aird, J. Ross Albert, Sy Brandon, David Cope, Festival of Northwest Composers, Eusebia Hunkins, Virginia Kendrick, H. Owen Reed, Halsey Stevens, Nancy Van de Vate, and Walter R. Watson. I am grateful for the cooperation of the American Conference of Cantors; the American Society of Composers, Authors and Publishers; the MacDowell Colony; the Yaddo Colony; and many publishing and recording companies. I should like to acknowledge the help of John Watts of Composers' Theatre and Nicholas Slonimsky, who graciously sanctioned my using <u>Baker's Biographical Dictionary</u> as a source and in addition supplied several dates that he had received too late for inclusion in his 1971 supplement. Vera and William Filby also helped enormously with just about every composer who ever set foot in Maryland. I am particularly grateful for the cooperation of all the composers who graciously completed and returned questionnaires.

Contents

Biographical Dictionary

ABBINANTI, FRANK
b. Chicago, Ill., 24 Nov. 1949. Self-taught in music, he has been co-director of Modern Music Workshop, 1969-71, and Mixed Media Workshop, 1971-   , both in Chicago.
WORKS: Konzert for, any instrument, 1970; Rebus, percussion solo, 1971; Oracle, any pitched instrument, 1971; Derbies, black and white, any instrument, 1972; Piano piece, 1972; Liberation song, mixed media, 1972.
5955 N. Glenwood, Chicago, IL 60660

ABEL, PAUL LOUIS
b. Clarksdale, Mich., 23 Nov. 1926. Studied at Eastman School of Music with John LaMontaine and A. I. McHose. He was on the faculty of Univ. of Montana, 1950-54, and Louisiana State Univ., 1954-   .
WORKS: Cyrano de Bergerac, symphonic poem for band, 1954; Mass in honor of St. Louis, King of France, chorus and organ, 1959; Vignette for orchestra, 1962, received Edward Benjamin Award; Symphony for five winds, 1970; Gloria, sing praise to God, a capella chorus, premiere, Baton. Rouge, 2 Dec. 1973.
389 Kay Drive, Baton Rouge, LA 70815

ABRAMOWITZ, DAVID G.
b. Brooklyn, N. Y., 18 Nov. 1950. Studied with Malcolm Williamson, Westminster Choir Coll., B. M. E. 1972; with Paul E. Karvonen, Mankato State Coll. He was choral director, Maxson School, Plainfield, N. J., 1973-74.
WORKS: Orchestra: Fantasy in d, string orch.; Chamber music: trio for viola, flute, trombone; Fanfare and melody, 4 euphoniums; 4 character pieces, piano; Lower East Side scherzo, piano; Chorus: Shma Yisroael; Variations on Merrial.
1015 Avenue N, Brooklyn, NY 11230

ABRAMSON, ROBERT M.
b. Philadelphia, Pa., 23 Aug. 1928. Is a graduate of Manhattan School of Music, B. M. 1965, M. M. 1966, and had advanced study in composition with Peggy Glanville-Hicks, Max Wald, Donald Lynbert, David Diamond; harpsichord and baroque music with Edith Weirs-Mann, and conducting with Pierre Monteux. His awards include Nat. Film

(ABRAMSON, ROBERT M.)
Board Award and Edinburgh Fest. Award, both for The ages of time, 1962, a Rockefeller grant, MacDowell and Fulbright fellowships, and in 1973, Outstanding Educator of America Award. In the U.S. Army, 1952-54, he was director and conductor of the orchestra, band, and chorus at Ft. Sam Houston, Tex. Faculty positions included Westminster Choir Coll., Princeton, N. J., 1962-64; Hartford Conservatory of Music, 1964-69; Hunter Coll. 1969-   ; Manhattan School of Music, 1969-   . He has been director of The Music Workshop, New York, since 1960 and in the summers of 1965-67 he was consultant to the U.S. Govt. Title III Project Acorn for Children K-3. He has given many lecture demonstrations and seminars on eurhythmic techniques in music education.
WORKS: Opera: Dr. Faustus lights the lights, 1956; Rapunzel, 1956; The floating geezel, 1958; The donkey's tale, 1958; The return of Agamemnon, 1967; Ballet: Night piece No. 1, 1952; In the evening, 1958; Touch and go, 1969; Menage a trois, tape, piano, and Saracen, 1973; Other stage works: Countess Kathleen, on W. B. Yeats, 1957; The cat and the moon, on Yeats, 1960; many film and television scores; Orchestra: Dance variations for piano and orchestra, 1965; Chamber music: Landscapes, string quartet, 1950; Night piece No. 2, flute and percussion, 1956; Two nocturnes, cello and piano, 1960; piano trio, 1968; woodwind quintet, 1968; string quartet, 1968; many songs with varying accompaniments; piano pieces.
250 West 94 St., New York, NY 10025

*ACHRON, ISIDOR
b. Warsaw, Poland, 24 Nov. 1892; to U.S. c. 1920; d. New York, N. Y., 12 May 1948. Brother of Joseph Achron, was accompaniest of Jascha Heifetz for about 10 years, then resumed his career as a concert pianist.
WORKS: Orchestra: Suite grotesque; piano concerto; and piano pieces.

*ACHRON, JOSEPH
b. Lozdzieje, Lithuania, 13 May 1886; U.S. citizen 1930; d. Hollywood, Calif., 29 Apr. 1943. Brother of Isidor Achron, eventually settled in

(ACHRON, JOSEPH)
Hollywood as a film composer.
WORKS: Orchestra: 3 violin concertos; Hebrew melody, violin and orch., 1911; Hazan, cello and orch., 1912; other works for orchestra and for chamber groups.

ADAIR, JAMES
b. Quincy, Ill., 21 Sep. 1909. Studied violin with Jacques Gordon in Chicago and Hugo Kortschak in New York, and composition with Leo Sowerby, Howard Hanson, Paul Hindemith, and Darius Milhaud. His career as a violinist began with the Denver Symphony on his 14th birthday and he has played with the St. Louis Symphony, Chicago Little Symphony, and the Rochester Philharmonic. He was on the faculty of Stephens Coll., Columbia, Mo., to 1947, and joined the staff at California State Univ., Sacramento, in 1949. He has appeared in concerts of his own compositions in the United States and abroad.
WORKS: 3 operas, 2 symphonies, 5 violin concertos, sonatas for all the standard orchestral instruments, 3 string quartets, numerous woodwind compositions, songs, and incidental works. His composition style is described as contrapuntal, melodic, with conservative 20th century dissonance.
82 Sandburg Drive, Sacramento, CA 95819

*ADAMS, ERNEST
b. Waltham, Mass., 16 July 1886; d. Newton, Mass., 25 Dec. 1959. Studied piano with his mother, harmony with Benjamin Cutter, and organ at the New England Conservatory with Henry Dunham. His published works, chiefly for piano or voice, included a piano suite, In the flower garden, published at age 18. His many unpublished works include a piano concerto, a piano concertino, 5 sonatas, and a string quartet.

*ADAMS, GEORGE
b. Budapest, Hungary, 12 June 1904; U. S. citizen. Composed piano sonata, 1959; and songs.

ADAMS JOHN
b. Worcester, Mass., 15 Feb. 1947. Studied composition at Harvard Univ. with Leon Kirchner, Earl Kim, and Roger Sessions, taking his B. A. (Magna cum laude) 1969, M. A. 1971. He studied conducting with Mario di Beneventura. He was awarded the Julius Stratton Prize by the Friends of Switzerland in 1969, and in 1970 was composer in residence at the Marlboro Festival. In 1972 he joined the faculty of the San Francisco Conservatory of Music and also became director of the New Music Ensemble. In the latter capacity he has commissioned new works by American and English composers and conducted West Coast premieres of new works.
WORKS: Instrumental: Electric wake, 1968, Piano quintet, 1970, American standard, 1973, Mary Lou - a routine, 1973, Ktaadn, mixed chorus, 1973; Electronic: Heavy metal, 1971, Hockey seen, tape, slides, and dancers, 1972, Etudes and a continuum, tape and solo amplified clarinet.

(ADAMS, JOHN)
San Francisco Conservatory of Music
1201 Ortega St., San Francisco, CA 94122

ADAMS, LESLIE
(b. Cleveland, Ohio, 30 Dec. 1932. Studied at Oberlin Conservatory, Manhattan School of Music, Juilliard School, California State Univ., Long Beach, and Ohio State Univ., with teachers Herbert Elwell, Joseph Wood, Vittorio Giannini, Robert Starer, Leon Dallin, and Marshall Barnes. His works were twice selected for performance at the Kansas Univ. Symposium of Contemporary American Music; a program of his works was presented by the Ira Aldridge Society of New York, and he holds a composition award from the Nat. Asso. of Negro Musicians. After several positions as music director at various schools and churches, in 1970 he joined the faculty of Univ. of Kansas, Lawrence, Kans.
WORKS: Ballet: A kiss in Xanadu, in 3 acts; Orchestra: Piano concerto; Chamber music: violin sonata, cello sonata, horn sonata, Pastorale for violin; Chorus: Psalm 121, a capella choir, Madrigal, Hosanna to the Son of David, Tall tales, Harlem love song, Vocalize for voices, Under the greenwood tree; Songs: Prayer, Drums of tragedy, Since you went away, Night song, Creole girl; Piano: Three preludes.
9409 Kempton Ave., Cleveland, OH 94101

*ADDISON, JOHN
b. 1920. Concerto for trumpet and strings; Divertimento for 2 trumpets, horn, trombone.

ADELBERG-RUDOW, VIVIAN. See RUDOW, VIVIAN ADELBERG

*ADLER, CLARENCE
b. Cincinnati, Ohio, 10 Mar. 1886; d. New York, 24 Dec. 1969. Concert pianist; published piano pieces.

ADLER, SAMUEL
b. Mannheim, Germany, 4 Mar. 1928, came to the U.S. in 1939. He studied at Boston Univ., B. M. 1948; Harvard Univ. M. A. 1950; and received an honorary doctorate in music from Southern Methodist Univ. in 1969. Composition teachers were Walter Piston, Randall Thompson, Paul Hindemith, Aaron Copland, and Herbert Fromm. His many awards include the Dallas Symphony Prize from Univ. of Texas, 1953; 6 first prizes of the Texas Composers Guild, 1955, 1957-63; first Lazare Saminsky Memorial Award, 1959; a Rockefeller grant; a Ford grant; and many commissions. In 1950 he joined the U. S. Army and was sent to Germany, where he organized the 7th Army Symphony Orchestra and toured Germany with a repertory of more than 100 major works. For this he received the Medal of Honor for benefit to cultural relations. Returning to the U. S., he was director of music for Temple Emanu-El, Dallas, 1953-66; professor of composition, North Texas State Univ., 1958-66; organized and conducted Dallas Chorale, 1954-56; and conducted Dallas Lyric Theater, 1955-57. In 1966 he was appointed to the faculty at Eastman School of Music and has been chairman of the composition

(ADLER, SAMUEL)
department since 1973. He was eastern regional director of the contemporary music project sponsored by the Music Educators National Conference and the Ford Found., 1967-69.

WORKS: Opera: The outcasts of Poker Flat, 1959; The wrestler, 1971; Orchestra: 4 symphonies, 1953, 1957, 1960, 1967; Toccata, 1954; Summer stock, overture, 1955; Jubilee, prelude, 1958; Requiescat in pace, in memory of J. F. Kennedy, 1963; Rhapsody, violin and orchestra, 1961; Song and dance, viola and orchestra, 1965; City by the lake, a portrait of Rochester, N. Y., 1968; The feast of lights, 1955; Concerto for organ, 1970; Sinfonietta, 1970; Concerto for orchestra, 1970; Elegy, string orchestra, 1962; Lament, baritone and chamber orchestra, 1968; Band: Southwestern sketches, 1961; Festive prelude, 1965; Concerto for winds, brass, and percussion, 1968; Brass choir: Concert piece, 1946; Praeludium, 1947; Divertimento, 1948; 5 Vignettes, 12 trombones, 1968; Brass fragments, 20 part choir, 1970; Histrionics, with percussion; Chamber music: 5 string quartets; 3 violin sonatas; horn sonata; piano sonata; unaccompanied cello sonata; piano trio; woodwind quintet; brass quintet; Introduction and capriccio, harp solo; Music for eleven, 6 woodwinds, 5 percussion, 1964; Toccata, recitation, and postlude, organ, 1959; Two meditations, organ, 1955, 1964; Miscellany, serenade for mezzo soprano, English horn, string quartet, 1956; 7 Epigrams, woodwind sextet, 1966; Songs with words, soprano and woodwind quintet, 1967; 7 Cantos, solo instruments or small ensembles, 1970-71; Chorus: The binding, oratorio, 1967; B'shaaray Tefilah, Sabbath service for baritone, choir, organ or orchestra, 1963; A whole bunch of fun, secular cantata, 1969; numerous songs and choral works, both secular and sacred; many children's songs and choruses, and an operetta. The ring of Solomon.
Eastman School of Music
26 Gibbs St., Rochester, NY 14604

ADOLPHUS, MILTON
b. New York, N. Y., 27 Jan. 1913. Moved to Philadelphia in 1935 and studied composition with Rosario Scalero at Curtis Institute of Music. He was for a while head of the Philadelphia Music Center. Since 1938 he has held an administrative position in the Dept. of Labor and Industry, Commonwealth of Pennsylvania at Harrisburg. While not engaged in music professionally, he has been an exceedingly industrious composer, producing 13 symphonies, 1931-54; 28 string quartets, 1935-73; and opus numbers up to 113 that include orchestral and chamber music, instrumental solos, and songs. String quartet #28, written in April 1973, won honorable mention in a competition sponsored by the Catgut Acoustical Society for a composition for mezzo, alto, tenor, and baritone stringed instruments which were developed by the Society.
3920 Chamber Hill Road, Harrisburg, PA 17111

AGAY, DENES
b. Budapest, Hungary, 10 June 1911. Studied piano and composition at the Liszt Acad. of Music and received his Ph. D. from the Univ. of Budapest. In the United States since 1939 (citizen 1943) he has held positions with several music publishing firms as composer, editor, and educational consultant. In 1973 he became instructor at Hunter Coll., New York. In addition to a long list of compositions for piano, he has written works for orchestra, band, chorus, and solo voice.
1391 Madison Ave., New York, NY 10029

AHLSTROM, DAVID
b. Lancaster, N. Y., 22 Feb. 1927. Studied at Cincinnati Conservatory of Music and Eastman School of Music with Alan Hovhannes, Henry Cowell, and Bernard Rogers. In 1965 he was awarded a Danforth Found. grant to compose and to study electronic music. He was visiting lecturer at Northwestern Univ., 1961-62; associate professor at Southern Methodist Univ., 1962-67; and associate professor at Eastern Illinois Univ. 1967- .

WORKS: Three sisters who are not sisters, a melodrama in 3 acts, libretto by Gertrude Stein, 1953, revised 1962; Scherzo for trumpet, winds, and percussion; Toccatas and passacaglias for percussion, piano-celesta, string bass, and speaking voices, 1961; Sonata No. 4 in 8 scenes, for clarinet and piano, 1963; Sonata No. 8, for bass solo, 4 dancers, electronic tape and electronic manipulation, 1966, performed 17 August 1969 on CBS-TV Look up and live.
62 Oakwood St., #4, San Francisco, CA 94110

AHNELL, EMIL
b. Erie, Pa., 6 Apr. 1925. Studied at New England Conservatory, Northwestern Univ., and Univ. of Illinois with David Barnett, Anthony Donato, Wallingford Riegger, and Burrill Phillips. In 1965 he received the Centennial Choral Composition Award from the Univ. of Kentucky. His faculty positions have been Houghton Coll., 1951-52; Univ. of Illinois, 1952-57; Toledo Museum of Art, 1957-58; and Kentucky Wesleyan Coll., 1958- .

WORKS: Chamber music: flute sonata; Antigone for brass instruments; piano trio; Three pieces for cello; Five sketches for flute, violin, cello; a number of unpublished orchestral, choral, and small chamber works.
Kentucky Wesleyan College
Owensboro, KY 42301

AHRENDT, KARL
b. Toledo, Ohio, 7 Mar. 1904. Studied composition at Cincinnati Conservatory with Carl Grimm, in Paris with Jean Rivier, and at Eastman School of Music with Bernard Rogers and Howard Hanson. He received the Philadelphia Arts Alliance Eurydice Choral Award, 1954; Univ. of Illinois Contemporary Festival Orchestral Performance Award, 1950; Ohio Music Teachers' Asso. composition award, 1972; and won co-first prize in the Nat. School Orch. Asso. competition, 1973. He

AHRENDT, KARL

(AHRENDT, KARL)
was on the faculty of Florida State Univ.,
1937-44; director of the School of Music,
Augustana Coll., Rock Island, Ill., 1946-50, and
Ohio Univ., 1950-57; professor of music, Ohio
Univ., 1967-   ; named Distinguished Professor
in June 1973.
WORKS: Orchestra: Johnny Appleseed; Dance
overture; Montage; Chamber music: Concerto for
oboe and strings; 3 movements for string quartet;
piano trio; Chorus: The Lord Sun, cantata for
chorus, orchestra, soloists, and narrator; 67th
Psalm for women's voices and piano; Voice:
Song cycle, Poems from a calendar.
School of Music, Ohio University
Athens, OH 45701

AHROLD, FRANK
b. Long Beach, Calif., 12 Dec. 1931. Studied at
the Univ. of California, Los Angeles, with John
Vincent and Lukas Foss. He has had commissions
from the Oakland Symphony Orchestra, Amer. Guild
of Organists, Vocal Arts Ensemble, and others.
Along with private teaching, he has been conductor of the Long Beach Civic Chorus, 1962-67, and
Camerata de Musici, 1964-67; and assistant music
director of the Long Beach Civic Light Opera,
1967-69.
WORKS: Opera: The view, 1 act; Ballet:
The spider and the fly; Orchestra: Piano concerto; Concerto for string orchestra; Second
coming, for tenor and large orchestra; Chamber
music: 3 songs on poems of Sylvia Plath, for
soprano and chamber orchestra; flute sonata;
3 piano sonatas.
3163 Mission St., San Francisco, CA 94110

AIKEN, KENNETH
b. Deerfield, Mich., 21 June 1885; d. Detroit,
Mich., 24 July 1970. Was educated at Boston
Univ. and the New England Conservatory, studying
with Ernest Hutcheson. He was on the faculty of
the Detroit Inst. of Musical Art and a private
teacher until retirement in 1968. He was also
author of two pedagogical books on piano teaching: Modern technique for the student of piano
and The child and his study of the piano. His
compositions were chiefly choral works, the best
known being the anthem, For Christ is born.

AIRD, DONALD BRUCE
b. Provo, Utah, 24 May 1924. Studied at Univ.
of California, Berkeley, with Charles Cushing,
Edward Lawton, Roger Sessions; and at Univ. of
Southern California with Ingolf Dahl. He received the Helen S. Armstead Award in Composition
in 1960. He has held faculty positions at Stanford Univ., Univ. of Minnesota, Univ. of California, and California State Univ., San Francisco.
He is director of the Berkeley Chambers Singers.
WORKS: Psalm 33, full orchestra and double
chorus; Psalm 150, chamber orchestra and 6-part
chorus; Chamber concerto; Symphonia concertante,
violin, viola, chamber orchestra; Songs for
Carol, mezzo soprano, 2 flutes, viola, cello,
piano; Oboe quartet; Songs for Ian Partridge;

(AIRD, DONALD BRUCE)
Movements and Interludes, for one piano with 1,
2, or 3 players, 7 movements.
252 Stanford Ave., Kensington, CA 94708

AITKEN, HUGH
b. New York, N. Y., 7 Sep. 1924. Studied at the
Juilliard School with Vincent Persichetti,
Bernard Wagenaar, and Robert Ward. After graduation in 1950 he joined the faculty at Juilliard
until 1970 when he went to William Paterson
State Coll., Wayne, N. J., as chairman of the
music department.
WORKS: Ballet: The Moirai; Orchestra:
Piano concerto; Chamber music: oboe quintet;
8 pieces for wind quintet; quintet for clarinet
and strings; Montages, solo bassoon; suite for
solo bass; suite for solo cello; suite for solo
clarinet; 4 partitas for various groups; Chorus:
sacred choruses; 5 cantatas; songs and piano
pieces.
William Paterson College, Wayne, NJ 07470

ALBAM, MANNY
b. Dominican Republic, 24 June 1922. Became a
United States citizen in 1945. He studied composition privately with Tibor Serly. He is co-
director of the Arrangers' Laboratory Workshop,
Eastman School of Music; project specialist at
Glassboro State Coll.; musical director for
Solid State Records; arranger-composer for other
record companies; member of the Board of Governors and Board of Trustees, Nat. Acad. of Recording Arts and Sciences.
WORKS: Film scores: Four clowns, Dancers
in May, The black pearl; Chamber music: brass
quintets, woodwind quintets, string quintets;
Chorus: The horns and voices of a dilemma,
choir, jazz ensemble, wind ensemble; Sisterhood
is powerful, women's chorus and jazz band. He
has also composed for the TV series: Glory
trail, Artists USA, Legacy.
850 Seventh Ave., New York, NY 10019

ALBERT, J. ROSS
b. Lebanon, Pa., 1 Sep. 1922. Studied at Lebanon Valley Coll., Pa., Converse Coll., S. C.,
and Univ. of North Carolina, Greensboro, with
composition teachers E. P. Rutledge, Roger
McDuffie, Jack Jarrett, and Eddie Bass. He
taught for a while in the Lebanon public schools
and then moved to Atlantic Christian Coll., Wilson, N. C., where he is chairman of the music
department.
WORKS: Prelude and fugue for string orchestra; Four Marys for band; 2 Madrigals for brass;
Shards and marbles, brass ensemble; Contradic-
tions, trio sonata for trumpet, horn, and tuba;
Classical solo sonata, flute; Piano sonata; Palm
Sunday motet, choir and organ; The beginning,
Christmas cantata; 3 song cycles: The choice
songs, The lonely songs, Five songs of the dark;
many anthems and children's anthems.
1001 Branch St., Wilson, NC 27893

ALBERT, STEPHEN
b. New York, N. Y., 6 Feb. 1941. Studied privately with Elie Siegmeister, 1956-58; with

(ALBERT, STEPHEN)
Bernard Rogers, Eastman School of Music, 1958-60;
with Joseph Castaldo, Philadelphia Musical Acad.,
B. A. 1962; and with George Rochberg, Univ. of
Pennsylvania. He received first prize, B. M. I.
Hemispheric Competition, 1961; Columbia Univ.
Bearns Prize, 1962; MacDowell fellowships, 1964,
1969; Huntington Hartford fellowship, 1965; Rome
Prize, 1965, 1966; Ford grant for composer-in-
residence with Lima, Ohio, school system and
community orchestra, 1967-68; Rockefeller grants,
1967, 1970; Guggenheim grant, 1968; ASCAP award,
1972; Fromm Found. commission, 1975. He taught
at Philadelphia Musical Acad., 1968-69; and was
guest lecturer, Stanford Univ., 1970-71.
    WORKS: Orchestra: Illuminations, brass,
percussion, pianos, and harps, 1962; Winter
songs, tenor and orch., 1965; Bacchae, narrator,
chorus, orch.; 4 movements for orch., commissioned by Chicago Symphony; Concerto for 4 quartets, 16 players; Chamber music: 2 toccatas for
piano; Supernatural songs, soprano and chamber
orch., 1964; Canons for string quartet, 1964; 5
songs for soprano and piano; Wolf time, soprano
and ensemble with amplification, commissioned by
Seattle Players.
    Sherry Road, Harvard, MA 01451

ALBERT, THOMAS RUSSEL
    b. Lebanon, Pa., 14 Dec. 1948. Studied with
William Duckworth at Atlantic Christian Coll.,
N. C., and with Paul Zonn, Morgan Powell, and
Ben Johnston at Univ. of Illinois. He won first
prize in the Atlantic Christian Coll. Contemporary Arts Festivals in 1969 and 1970. Since 1971
he has been instructor at the School of Music,
Univ. of Illinois.
    WORKS: B-flat piece for band; Chamber music:
Permutations, for horn and piano; Sound frames,
oboe, saxophone, trombone, vibraphone, in 3 movements, 1969; Five for 2 tubas; An octet, for
indeterminate ensemble; Winter monarch for soprano, flute, and piano, based on a poem by his
father, J. Ross Albert, performed at Ann Arbor,
Mich., April 1973; Chorus: Communion hymn cluster, for 3 small choirs, a simultaneous setting
of 3 hymns from the Episcopal Service, 1970.
    907 West Columbia Ave., Champaign, IL 61820

ALBERTI, SOLON
    b. Mt. Clemons, Mich., 6 Dec. 1889. Studied at
Chicago Musical Coll., B. A., and also in Paris,
Milan, and in Berlin. He taught at Chicago
Musical Coll., 1909-14, and at Kansas City Con-
servatory, 1914-19, where he founded the Kansas
City Little Symphony and conducted the Kansas
City Grand Opera Society. In 1919 he settled in
New York, achieving great success as pianist,
conductor, coach, and accompanist to many top
operatic singers. He was organist and music
director at Park Avenue Christian Church in New
York for 35 years.
    WORKS: Piano: White swan of Samarkand; The
gypsy; Four sketches from the Far East; Songs:
Trees; The hour; Oriental serenade; other songs
and anthems.
    Hotel Ansonia
    Broadway at 73 St., New York NY 10023

ALBRECHT, MOONYEEN
    b. Chicago, Ill., 31 Mar. 1936. Studied at
Northwestern Univ. with Anthony Donato. In 1963
he composed the score for the documentary film,
Kahli Nihta, Socrates, which won first prize in
the Venice International Film Festival and the
Jesse Laske award in Hollywood. He has been a
faculty member at Central Michigan Univ. since
1963.
    WORKS: Orchestra: A symphony; Three move-
ments for chamber orchestra; Chorus: Vespers of
the Blessed Virgin Mary, for chorus, soloists,
orchestra; Salve Regina; Madrigals; Organ:
Concert piece.
    108 West Orchard Ave., Shepherd, MI 48883

ALBRIGHT, WILLIAM
    b. Gary, Ind., 20 Oct. 1944. Studied at Univ.
of Michigan with Ross Lee Finney, Leslie Bassett,
at Tanglewood with George Rochberg, and in Paris
with Max Deutsch and Olivier Messiaen. His
awards include two Koussevitzky Composition
Awards, 1964, 1966; Queen Marie-Jose Prize, 1967;
Fulbright fellowship, 1968; Symphonic Composition Award of Niagara Univ., 1968; Amer. Acad.
of Arts and Letters award, 1970. Since 1970 he
has been on the faculty of Univ. of Michigan and
associate director of the Electronic Music Studio. He is also music director of the First
Unitarian Church, Ann Arbor, and has concertized
widely in the U.S., Canada, and Europe, special-
izing in new music for organ and piano.
    WORKS: Orchestra: Alliance, 1967-70; Night
procession, 1972; chamber orchestra, 1972;
Gothic suite, concerto for organ, 1973; Chamber
music: Marginal worlds, for 12 players, 1969,
New York premiere, 16 Jan. 1974; Danse macabre,
for 5 players, 1971; Stipendium peccati, 3 players, 1973; Caroms, 8 players, 1966; Take that,
4 percussionists, 1972; Beulahland rag, for
large group, 1969; Tic, for large group, 1967;
Foils, wind ensemble, 1963; Organ: Organbook I,
1967; Organbook II, 1971; Pneuma, 1966; Juba,
1965; Partita, 1963; Piano: Pianoagogo, 1965;
Novelty rags, 1969; Grand sonata in rag, 1968.
    608 Sunset, Ann Arbor, MI 48103

*ALBRITTON, SHERODD
    Eldorado for women's chorus.

ALETTE, CARL
    b. Philadelphia, Pa., 31 May 1922. Studied at
Eastman School of Music with Bernard Rogers,
Wayne Barlow, and A. I. McHose. He received an
award from the Louisville Symphony in 1955 and
many commissions. He has held faculty positions
at Univ. of Tennessee, 1951-54; State Univ. of
New York, Brockport, 1954-57; Univ. of Mississippi, 1957-68; and Univ. of Southern Alabama,
1968-   . In 1964-65 he was visiting associate
professor at Univ. of California, Los Angeles.
    WORKS: Orchestra: Resurgence; Symphony for
chamber orchestra; Chamber music: trombone
sonata; Suite for clarinet choir; Scherzo for
brass quintet; four songs.
    4584 Hawthorne Place, Mobile, AL 36608

ALEXANDER, JOSEF

ALEXANDER, JOSEF
b. Boston, Mass., 15 May 1910. Studied at the
New England Conservatory and Harvard Univ.,
B. A., M. A., with Edward Burlingame Hill and
Walter Piston, and in France with Hugo
Leichtentritt. Awards include yearly ASCAP
awards, 1960-74; John Knowles Paine, Walter
Naumberg, and Fulbright grants; Bernard Ravitch
Found. award; International Humanities award;
and two Friends of Harvey Gaul awards. He has
been on the faculty of Brooklyn Coll., City Univ.
of New York, since 1945.
    WORKS: Orchestra: 4 symphonies; piano con-
certo; Epitaphs; Celebrations; Williamsburg
suite; Band: Processional; Campus suite; Chamber music: Clockwork for strings; Three pieces
for eight; Four for five, brass quintet; Festiv-
ities, organ or piano and brass; Nocturne and
scherzo, violin and piano; Requiem and coda,
trombone; 2 Essays for 3 trombones; piano quintet; string quartet; piano trio; Chorus: Three
American episodes, mixed chorus and piano; Dialogue spirituel, soprano, chorus, orchestra;
Voice: Songs for Eve, song cycle for soprano,
harp, violin, cello, English horn; Piano: Bagatelles; Incantations; and many other instrumental and vocal works.
    229 West 78 St., New York, NY 10024

ALEXANDER, PHILIP R.
b. Texas, 11 Mar. 1944. Is an M. D. who studied
music at Curtis Institute, Philadelphia, with
de Lancie, Colucci, and Kincaid. He was music
instructor at Texas Technological Univ., Lubbock,
1966-67, and assistant instructor in internal
medicine, Baylor Coll. of Medicine, Houston,
Tex., 1972-   .
    WORKS: Orchestra: Concerto in D for oboe;
Chamber music: Voluntary in D, trumpet and
piano; Concert etude, trumpet and piano; Symphonic corral, 2 oboes and English horn; Chorus:
Chorale fantasy; Chorale prelude on Old 100th;
Piano: Serenade; Theme and variations; Rhapsody;
Organ: Toccata; Five preludes; Chaconne; Three
preludes.
    Box 1, Conroe, TX 77301

*ALEXANDER, WILLIAM P.
The monkey's paw, opera, was performed at
Edinboro State Coll., 13 Nov. 1972.
    Department of Music, Edinboro State College
    Edinboro, PA 16412

ALEXIUS, CARL JOHN
b. New Orleans, La., 30 Apr. 1928. Studied at
Louisiana State Univ. with Helen Gunderson,
Staatliche Hochschule für Musik, Stuttgart,
Germany, with Hermann Reutter, and Univ. of
Michigan with Leslie Bassett and Ross Lee Finney.
His awards include 3 awards of the Louisiana Fed.
of Music Clubs, a Fulbright fellowship, Southern
Fellowships Fund grant, Horace H. Rackham fellow-
ship and grant, and the first Sigvald Thompson
Composition Award. He has served on the faculty
of Louisiana State Univ., 1954-55; Univ. of
North Carolina, Greensboro, 1955-62; Univ. of
Michigan, 1962-   .
    WORKS: Orchestra: Theme and variations;

(ALEXIUS, CARL JOHN)
Diptych for orchestra; Incidental music: 3
television plays by Michael Casey, The story of
Momotaro, The story of Esther, Ol'Fried Dragoman;
Arnold Colbath's A crow in the heart; Bertholt
Brecht's Good woman of Setzuan; Chamber music:
Sonatina for trumpet and piano; a string quartet;
2 piano sonatas; Chorus: Christmas cantata for
women's choir and small orchestra; Organ: Six
pieces in pairs; Songs: Eight Jewish folk songs.
    1229 Traver Road, Ann Arbor, MI 48105

ALLANBROOK, DOUGLAS PHILLIPS
b. Melrose, Mass., 1 Apr. 1921. Studied at Harvard Univ. with Walter Piston, in Paris with
Nadia Boulanger. He was a pupil of Ruggero
Gerlin in early keyboard music and harpsichord.
He held Fulbright and John Knowles Paine fellowships for study in France and Italy. He was on
the faculty of Peabody Conservatory, Baltimore,
1955-57, and has been a tutor at St. John's
Coll., Annapolis, since 1952. He is a member of
the YADDO Corporation.
    WORKS: Opera: Ethan Frome, a lyric tragedy
in 3 acts; Nightmare Abbey, comic opera in 3
acts; Orchestra: 4 symphonies (the first commissioned by the Ford Found.); a violin concerto,
harpsichord concerto; Chamber music: Fantasy
for violin and piano; A set of passions for violin and harpsichord; A game for two, piano and
percussion; Chorus: The seven last words, chorus, orchestra, soprano, baritone; Psalms 130
and 131 for chorus and organ; An American miscellany for a capella chamber chorus; Songs: 3
Noble love songs, baritone and orchestra; 2 sets
of Songs to Shakespeare sonnets; Piano: 40
Changes; 12 Preludes for all seasons; Bagatelles;
Harpsichord: 2 Little sonatas; Fantasy; 5 Studies in black and white.
    6 Revell St., Annapolis, MD 21401

*ALLCOCK, STEPHEN: Credo for chorus and organ.

*ALLEN, CREIGHTON
b. Macon, Miss., 26 Mar. 1900; d. New York.
Studied with Ernest Hutcheson, Harold Bauer,
Rubin Goldmark, Juilliard School. He made his
New York debut as pianist in 1927; settled in
New York as teacher, pianist, and composer.
    WORKS: Orchestra: piano concerto; violin
concerto; many songs and piano pieces.

*ALLEN, PAUL HASTINGS
b. Hyde Park, Mass., 28 Nov. 1883; d. Boston,
Mass., 28 Sep. 1952. Studied at Harvard Univ.,
B. A. 1903; and in Italy. He received the
Paderewski prize for a symphony, 1910. During
World War I, he served in the U.S. diplomatic
corps in Italy, returning to Boston in 1920.
    WORKS: Opera: 12 operas, including O
munasterio, 1911; Il filtro, 1912; Milda, 1913;
The last of the Mohicans, 1916; Cleopatra, 1921;
La piccola Figaro, 1931; all performed in Italy;
Orchestra: 2 symphonies; Serenade, 1928; Ex
hocte, 1930; Chamber music: Suite for chamber
orch., 1928; Dans le nuit, 1928; 3 pieces, 1928;
4 string quartets; quartet for 2 clarinets,
basset horn, bass clarinet; woodwind trio; also

(ALLEN, PAUL HASTINGS)
choral works, songs, several piano sonatas, many piano pieces.

*ALLEN, ROBERT E.
b. Minneapolis, Minn., 1 Feb. 1920. String quartet, violin sonata, choral works, etc.
37 Charles St., New York, NY 10011

ALLEN, WILLIAM T.
b. Aberdeen, S. Dak., 2 June 1926. Studied with Merritt Johnson, Northern State Coll.; with Anthony Donato, Northwestern Univ.; and with Bernard Rogers at Eastman School of Music, Ph. D. 1954. He has been professor of piano and theory, Houghton Coll., 1953-   , composer-in-residence, 1968-   .
WORKS: Opera: Pride and prejudice; Ardelia; Ballet: La belle dame sans merci, performed by Eastman and Buffalo Orchestras; Orchestra: Fantasy, for piano, chorus, orch., Houghton Coll., Oct. 1973; Piano: 2 sonatas; Domestic clavier (preludes, fugues, and finale); many compositions for chamber ensembles, chorus; musicals.
17 Seymour St., Houghton, NY 14744

ALLGOOD, WILLIAM THOMAS
b. Raleigh, N. C., 28 Dec. 1939. Studied with Martin Mailman at East Carolina Univ.; with Ben Johnston at Univ. of Illinois; and with Emerson Myers at Catholic Univ. He has held faculty positions at Univ. of Illinois, 1965-66; Univ. of Maryland, 1966-69; and Western Reserve Univ., 1969-   .
WORKS: Chamber music: 2 woodwind quintets, 1964, 1965; brass quintet, 1964; trio for trumpet, bassoon, cello, 1964; Mixed media: Pentacycle, bassoon and tape, 1969; Vectors, tuba and electronic sounds, 1970; Music da camera, Repetitions, oboe, trumpet, string bass, percussion, tape, slides and film, 1971; anthem for choir and tape.
3409 West Michigan, #7, Kalamazoo, MI 49007

ALLISON, HOWARD K. II
b. Pittsburg, Kan., 19 Dec. 1948. Studied at Kansas State Coll., Illinois Wesleyan Univ., and Indiana Univ. He is director of music and a teacher in the Bradford, Ill., Unit School District, 1970-   , and director of the Curriculum Research Div., Music Materials Development Center, 1972-   .
WORKS: Opera: An improvisational opera; Orchestra: 3 symphonies; Chamber music: Suite for solo clarinet (a commissioned work); Evolution for bass trombone, works for strings, woodwinds, brasses, and percussion; Chorus: Rejoice in the Lord, chorus and organ (a commissioned work); other choral pieces; songs and piano pieces.
P. O. Box 306, Bradford, IL 61421

ALLISON, IRL
b. Warren, Tex., 8 April 1896. Studied at Baylor Univ., B. A., M. A., Columbia Univ., Univ. of Texas, Chicago Musical Coll., and holds honorary doctorates from Hardin-Simmons Univ., Southwestern Cons. (Dallas), and Houston Cons. He has

(ALLISON, IRL)
been on the faculty of Rusk Coll., 1919-21, Montezuma Coll., 1923-27. and Hardin-Simmons Univ., 1927-35. He was president and founder of the Nat. Guild of Piano Teachers and the Amer. Coll. of Musicians, 1929-70, and chief council of the Piano Guild USA, 1970-73. He has written many songs and piano pieces, the latter chiefly educational.
1500 Murray Lane, Austin, TX 78703

*ALLITSEN, FRANCES
The Lord is my light, sacred duet.

*ALMOND, CLAUDE
b. 1915, d. 1957. Faculty, Univ. of Louisville; John Gilbert: A steamboat overture for orch.

*ALTER, MARTHA
b. New Bloomfield, Pa., 1904. Studied at Vassar Coll.; with Seth Bingham, Columbia Univ.; Bernard Rogers, Eastman School of Music; and with Rubin Goldmark. Awards include several fellowships and a Vassar publication grant. She taught at Vassar and at Connecticut Coll.
WORKS: Opera: Groceries and notions, 3-act operetta; Ballet: Anthony Comstock; Orchestra: Bric-a-brac suite; Rhythmic dance; also chamber music and choral works.

*ALTMAN, ADELLA C.
Operettas, musical plays, choral works.
580 Northeast 59th St., Miami, FL 33137

AMATO, BRUNO
b. Hartford, Conn., 21 Oct. 1936. Studied at Univ. of Hartford, B. M. 1958, Manhattan School of Music, M. M. 1963, Acad. Naz. di Santa Cecilia, dip. 1967, Princeton Univ., M. F. A. 1969, Ph. D. 1973. His teachers were Arnold Franchetti, Goffredo Petrassi, Milton Babbitt, Edward Cone, Peter Westergaard, Gunther Schuller, Luciano Berio. He received the Premio d'Atri, a McCarter Theater commission, Sinfonia Found. awards, 1969, 1970, Koussevitzky award, 1969, Fulbright grant, and Tanglewood, Princeton, MacDowell, and NDEA fellowships. He was on the faculty of Ball State Univ., 1970-71, and of Indiana Univ. 1971-   .
WORKS: Theater: Incidental music to It should happen to a dog, Wolf Mankowitz, 1967; Orchestra: Andante and Scherzo, 1960; Compound, 1965; Bells and buttercups; soprano and orchestra, 1967; Aria, strings, 1969; Tiny Tin, children's story with narrator, 1969; Tiny suite, children's orchestra, 1970; Canticle, with narrator, 1972; Canticle variations, 1972; Larghetto, strings, 1973; Psalmody, antiphonal orchestras, work in progress; Chamber music: 2 string quartets, 1958, 1966; Four love songs, soprano and string trio, 1960; woodwind quartet, 1960; string quintet, 1961; piano sonata, 1964; Tre canzoni, brass quintet, 1965; Divertimento, 3 flutes, 1966; Frequencies, flute, clarinet, violin, cello, piano, 1968; Solioquy I, violin, 1968; 3 studies, piano, 1965; Study, chamber orchestra, 1966; Chinese love lyrics, tenor, flute, cello, harp percussion, 1969; Basses and

AMATO, BRUNO

(AMATO, BRUNO)
brass, 4 horns, 5 trumpets, 3 basses, 1969;
Soliloquy II, viola, 1969-72; Alleluia, 6 horns,
1972; Two together, soprano and tuba, 1971; Music
for Emily, soprano and brass quintet, 1972;
Soliloquy III, cello, 1973; 5 Bagatelles, tenor
saxophone and piano, 1973; Hommage, 1973;
Pezzetto, 3 tubas, 1973; saxophone quartet, 1973;
Chorus: Missa brevis, with organ, 1960; Ave
Maria, a capella, 1962; Sounds and silences, a
capella, 1965; Alleluia, a capella, 1969; Prayer,
Alleluia, and Chorale, boys' choir and male chorus, a capella, 1970; Alleluia, a capella, 1973;
and songs.
3630 Park Lane, Bloomington, IN 47401

*AMES, WILLIAM T.
b. Cambridge, Mass., 20 Mar. 1901. Studied at
Harvard Univ., A. B. 1924; with Nadia Boulanger
in Paris. He was appointed instructor at Eastman School in 1938.
WORKS: Orchestra: Rhapsody; 2 symphonies;
Chamber music: violin sonata; cello sonata; 2
string quartets; piano quintet; clarinet quintet; piano sonata; also choral music, songs,
many piano pieces.

AMFITHEATROF, DANIELE
b. St. Petersburg, Russia, 29 Oct. 1901; U.S.
citizen 1944. Studied with Joseph Wihtol in
St. Petersburg; with Jaroslav Krichka in Prague;
and with Ottorino Respighi in Rome. He was
assistant conductor, Augusteo Symphony, Rome,
1924-29; music director, Italian Broadcasting
Corp., 1929-37; assistant conductor, Minneapolis
Symphony, 1938-41; then settled in Hollywood as
a film composer.
WORKS: Film scores: Lassie come home; Letters from an unknown woman; Another part of the
forest; O.S.S.; The fan; Major Dundee; also
works for orchestra, chamber music, and songs.
San Marco 3242, 30124 Venice, Italy

AMIRKHANIAN, CHARLES BENJAMIN
b. Fresno, Calif., 19 Jan. 1945. Is autodidact
as a composer. He was commissioned by the Swedish Radio and Fylkingen Society in April 1972 to
produce text-sound pieces in Stockholm, and commissioned in 1973 by the Connimicut Found. for
text-sound pieces in Berkeley, Calif. In 1968-69
he was music director of Dancers Workshop Company, San Francisco, and since 1969 music director of KPFA-FM, Pacifica Radio, Berkeley.
WORKS: Compositions No. 1, 2, 3, 4, & 5 for
solo amplified rachets, 1965-67; Symphony I for
viola, 3 trumpets, trombone, clarinet, piano, and
4 percussionists playing over 200 non-instruments,
mobile stage, and electronics, 1965; Mooga Pook,
1968, and Bake and Eeet, 1969, are visual trans-
duction scores for performance in any medium or
combination of media; Words, 1-hour text-sound
composition. Other text-sound pieces all composed on tape: Spoffy nene, 1970; Oratora
konkurso rezulto: Autoro de la jaro (an Esperanto portrait of Lou Harrison) 1970; If in is,
1971; Sound nutrition, 1972; Dzarin Bess Ga
Khorim, 1972; Heavy aspirations (portrait of

(AMIRKHANIAN, CHARLES BENJAMIN)
Nicolas Slonimsky), 1973; Seatbelt seatbelt,
1973.
1639 Curtis St., Berkeley, CA 94702

AMRAM, DAVID
b. Philadelphia, Pa., 17 Nov. 1930. Learned
piano, trumpet, and French horn at an early age,
then while working toward a B. A. at George
Washington Univ. studied horn with William Klang
and Abe Kniaz of the National Symphony, where he
himself served as extra horn. On graduating in
1952, he went into the U.S. Army and was assigned
to play horn with the 7th Army Symphony Orchestra in Germany. On discharge he remained in
Europe for a year composing and playing with
jazz groups. He then returned to the U.S. and
studied with Giannini at the Manhattan School of
Music, 1955-56. Since 1950 he has led the Amram-
Barrow Jazz Quartet with George Barrow, saxophonist. He was musical director of the New
York Shakespeare Festival, 1956-68; and in 1967
was composer-in-residence with the New York
Philharmonic and made his New York debut as a
conductor at that time.
WORKS: Opera: The final ingredient, 1-act,
premiere on ABC-TV network, 11 April 1965;
Twelfth night, text adapted from Shakespeare by
Joseph Papp, premiere, Lake George Opera Festival, 1 August 1968; Incidental music: The
rivalry; 1959; Kataki, 1959; After the fall,
play by Arthur Miller; Far Rockaway, play by
Frank D. Gilroy; Heracles and J. B., plays by
Archibald MacLeish; and some 30 Shakespearean
plays; Orchestra: The American bell, with narrator; Autobiography for strings; Elegy, violin
and orchestra; bassoon concerto; horn concerto;
Shakespearean concerto, for oboe, 2 horns and
strings; triple concerto, woodwind quintet,
brass quintet, jazz quintet, and orchestra, New
York, 10 Jan. 1971; King Lear variations, wind
symphony; Chamber music: Dirge and variations,
piano trio; Discussions, flute, cello, percussion, piano; Overture and allegro, flute solo;
Zohar, alto recorder and flute; The wind and the
rain, viola and piano; Suite for solo viola;
Three songs for Marlboro, horn and cello; Three
songs for America, bass voice with piano or
string quintet and four woodwinds; piano sonata;
violin sonata (unaccompanied); violin and piano
sonata; string quartet; trio for saxophone, horn,
bassoon; quintet for winds; Fanfare and Processional for brass quintet; Chorus: A year in our
land, cantata, New York, 13 May 1965; By the
rivers of Babylon, women's voices; Let us remember, by Langston Hughes, solo voices, orchestra,
timpani, percussion, strings; May the words of
the Lord, vocal quartet and organ; Shir L'Erev
Shabat, solo tenor, chorus, organ; The passion
of Joseph D, by Paddy Chayefsky, soli, mixed
chorus a capella; film scores and many jazz
pieces. His autobiography: Vibrations: The
adventures and musical times of David Amram was
published in New York in 1968.
461 Sixth Ave., New York, NY 10011

*ANDERSEN, ARTHUR OLAF
b. Newport, R. I., 30 Jan. 1880; d. Tucson, Ariz., 11 Jan. 1958. Studied at American Cons., honorary D. M.; with Vincent d'Indy and Alexandre Guilmant in Paris; with Durra in Berlin; and with Giovanni Sgambati in Rome. His faculty posts included American Cons., 1908-33; dean of Coll. of Fine Arts and head, theory and composition department Univ. of Arizona, 1934-50. He was author of books on harmony, counterpoint, and orchestration, and a contributor to music journals.
WORKS: Theatre: Arizona hi-ho, 3-act operetta; music for The jade bracelet; Orchestra: symphony; Suite for strings; Band: 4 marches; Wind ensemble: Arizona sketches 1 and 2, brass ensemble; Chamber music: 3 string quartets; 3 string trios; piano trio; 2 woodwind quintets; quartet for flute and strings; numerous pieces for violin and piano, etc., songs and vocal duets.

*ANDERSEN, MICHAEL
b. Los Angeles, Calif., 26 Jan. 1938. Studied with Ingolf Dahl, Halsey Stevens, and Miklos Rozsa, Univ. of Southern California. He held the Alchin fellowship at the university.
WORKS: Orchestra: trumpet concerto; Concert overture; 7 songs for voice and orch; Wind ensemble: Music for brass; Chamber music: Variations on a Gregorian theme, violin and piano; viola sonata; Suite for solo viola; Serenade for 2 flutes; string quartet; 3 piano sonatinas; Film scores: The Tower of London; Wings of chance; 12 to the moon; The runaway.
6463 Blucker, Van Nuys, CA 91401

ANDERSON, BETH
b. Lexington, Ky., 3 Jan. 1950. Studied at Univ. of California at Davis, B. A. 1971, Mills Coll., M. F. A. in piano, 1973. Her composition teachers were John Barnes Chance, Kenneth Wright, Richard Swift, John Cage, Larry Austin, Terry Riley, and Nathaniel Rubin. Awards include a Biggerstaff, 1971, Elizabeth Crothers Mills, 1972, Alumni fellowship, 1972, and 2 awards in piano contests at Univ. of California, 1970 and 1971. She began playing organ and piano in church at age 10, was a private piano teacher 1964-68, taught in the Mills Coll. preparatory program, 1971-73, and was co-editor and co-publisher of EAR Magazine, a music monthly in San Francisco, and since 1975 in New York City. Ms. Anderson's music is derived numerologically and often makes use of words as sound-text. Theater and lighting are important to her conceptions and she has used dance, electronics and film.
WORKS: Opera: Queen Christina, Mills Coll., 1974; Mixed media: Peachy Keen-O, piece for four women instrumentalists who double as vocalists, tape, and four dancers bathed in peach light, Mar. 1973; Tower of power, organ, 5 speakers, and 2 tapes, Apr. 1973; Torero piece, 2 speakers and red spot lights, July 1973; Tulip clause, tape, organ, 7 instruments, commissioned by San Francisco Conservatory New Music Ensemble.
326 Spring St., New York, NY 10013

ANDERSON, DENNIS
b. Duluth, Minn., 2 Aug. 1951. Studies at California State Univ., Fullerton, with Lloyd Rodgers and Donal Michalsky.
WORKS: Percussion: Diversions, Sol centre, Attack of the jello people, Transvestite rumba.
3136 Yorba Linda Blvd., #G7
Fullerton, CA 92637

*ANDERSON, EUGENE
Studied at Univ. of Arizona; in 1975 was music director, Baltimore Actors Theatre. His Meditations for voice and chamber orchestra was performed in Baltimore, 19 Mar. 1975.

ANDERSON, GARLAND LEE
b. Union City, Ohio, 10 June 1933. Studied at Univ. of Edinburgh with Hans Gal, and Indiana Univ. with Roy Harris. He is a lecturer on American music at Earlham Coll., Richmond, Ind.
WORKS: Orchestra: A classical overture; piano concerto; piano concertino (commissioned by the Richmond Symphony Orchestra as a contest piece for children under 12); Symphony for saxophones (commissioned by Phi Mu Alpha); Chamber music: Sonata for alto sax, 1967; sonata for tenor sax, 1968; sonata for baritone sax, 1973; Sarabande for tenor sax and piano; 1967; sonata for horn, violin sonata, 1964; Elegy for violin; 2 Interludes for horn; quartet for saxophones (commissioned by Cecil Leeson); Duo for 2 flutes; Andante for 2 harps; Piano: 4 Preludes; Passacaglia; Organ: 3 Preludes on tunes of William Billings; choral works and songs.
44 N. W. 6 St., Richmond, IN 47374

ANDERSON, LEROY
b. Cambridge, Mass., 29 June 1908; d. Woodbury, Conn., 18 May 1975. Studied at New England Conservatory and Harvard Univ., B. A., magna cum laude, 1929, M. A., 1930, with teachers Spalding, Ballantine, Heilman, Hill, Enesco, and Piston. He was a tutor in music at Radcliffe Coll., 1930-32; director of the Harvard Univ. Band, 1931-35; and organist and choir director in Milton, Mass., 1929-35. Since 1931 he has been guest conductor of the Boston "Pops" Orchestra and other orchestras. Almost all his sophisticated, witty, and expertly orchestrated works have been arranged for band, symphonic band, solo instruments and small ensembles.
WORKS: Alma mater, Arietta, Balladette, Belle of the ball, Blue bells of Scotland, Blue tango, Bugler's holiday, The captains and the kings, Chicken reel, China doll, Christmas Day, A Christmas festival, Clarinet candy, Fiddle-faddle, The first day of spring, Forgotten dreams, The girl I left behind me, The girl in satin, The golden years, Home stretch, Horse and buggy, Irish suite, Irish washerwoman, Jazz legato, Jazz pizzicato, The minstrel boy, Penny whistle song, The phantom regiment, Plink, plank, plunk!, Promenade, The rakes of Mallow, Sandpaper ballet, Sarabande, Serenata, Sleigh ride, Song of Jupiter, Song of the bells, Suite of carols, Summer skies, The syncopated clock, Ticonderoga march, A trumpeter's lullaby, Turn ye to me, The

ANDERSON, LEROY

(ANDERSON, LEROY)
typewriter, The waltzing cat; Goldilocks, musical comedy, New York, 11 Oct. 1958.

ANDERSON, RUTH
b. Kalispell, Mont., 21 Mar. 1928. Studied at Univ. of Washington, B. A., magna cum laude, 1949, M. A. 1951; Manhattan School of Music, 1952; Mannes Coll. of Music, 1953-55; Princeton Univ. Graduate School (first woman admitted) 1962-63; Columbia Univ. Electronic Music Studio, 1965, 1966, 1969; New York Univ. Computer Synthesis of Music, 1967; private study with Darius Milhaud and Nadia Boulanger; flute with John Wummer and Jean Pierre Rampal. Awards include full tuition for all study, MacDowell Colony fellowships, 1955, 1957, 1965, 1971, 1972-73, Ingram-Merrill Composition Grant, 1963-64, composer residency at Yaddo, 1969. She was flute soloist with the Totenburg Instrumental Ensemble, 1951-58, has been solo flutist with the Boston "Pops" Orchestra, has been assistant in orchestration to Robert Russell Bennett at NBC, and has done free-lance orchestration and arranging. On the faculty of Hunter Coll. since 1966, she has been also director of the Electronic Studio from 1969.
    WORKS: Chamber music: Fugue for piano; Two pieces for strings; Two movements for strings; The merchant's song (Coombs); Tape and mixed media: Dump, 2-channel tape collage in mixed media collaboration with Tania; State of the Union Message, 1973, tape collage of TV commercials; Ma Belle, tape collage; Veils, piano and 4-channel tape; Christmas oratorio, (Auden), chorus, small orchestra, actors, dancers, 4 portable audio speakers. Prof. Anderson has two books assigned for publication: The descant book; and Catches and canons, glees and quodlibets.
    Electronic Music Studio, Hunter College
    New York, NY 10021

ANDERSON, THOMAS JEFFERSON, JR.
b. Coatesville, Pa., 17 Aug. 1928. Studied at West Virginia State Coll., B. M., 1950; Pennsylvania State Univ., M. Ed., 1951; Univ. of Iowa, Ph. D., 1958; and also studied composition with Scott Huston, 1954, Philip Bezanson and Darius Milhaud, 1964. Awards include MacDowell fellowships, 1960, 1961, 1963, 1968; Copley Found. award, 1964; Fromm Found. awards, 1964, 1971; Yaddo fellowships, 1970-1971; judge in B. M. I. Student Composers' Competition, 1969; chairman of honorary advisory committee, Black Music Center, Indiana Univ., 1970-71; NEA grant of $5000, 1974. Before becoming chairman of the music dept., Tufts Univ., he held positions at Morehouse Coll.; was composer-in-residence, Atlanta Symphony Orchestra; faculty, Tennessee State Univ.; Langston Univ.; and West Virginia State Univ. He was co-director with Wendell Whalum of the Afro-American Music Workshop, Morehouse Coll., which presented the premiere of Scott Joplin's opera, Treemonisha, in January 1972. The opera was orchestrated by Anderson and co-edited by Anderson and William Bolcom.
    WORKS: Orchestra: Classical symphony, 1962;

(ANDERSON, THOMAS JEFFERSON, JR.)
Symphony in three movements, 1964; Squares, commissioned by West Va. State Coll., 1965; Chamber symphony, commissioned by Thor Johnston, conductor, Nashville Symphony, 1969; In memorium Zack Walker, 1969; Intervals, commissioned for Atlanta Symphony by Robert Shaw, 1970-71; Transitions, commissioned by Berkshire Music Center and Fromm Found., 1971; Beyond silence, premiere, Cambridge, Mass., 2 Oct. 1973; Chamber music: Connections, string quintet, 1968; Variations on a theme by M. B. Tolson, 1972; Swing set, 1973; Chorus: Personals, cantata for chorus, narrator, and brass ensemble, 1966; Piano: 5 Bagatelles, 1963; Watermelon, 1971.
    Dept. of Music, Tufts University
    Medford, MA 02155

ANDREW, DAVID S.
b. Detroit, Mich., 13 July 1943. Studied at Univ. of Michigan with Ross Lee Finney, Leslie Bassett, and George Cacioppo; Washington Univ., St. Louis, Ph. D. candidate 1973. He received the Founders' Award of the Society of Architectural Historians in 1973. In 1968-71 he was instructor, Dept. of Fine Arts, Univ. of Detroit.
    WORKS: Chamber music: Sins, piano 4 hands, 1966; DMZ, for 3 pianists and winds, 1966; String music, No. 1, 12 strings, 1969; Electronic: Revival meeting, tape and film, 1965; Flying saucers have landed, film, tape, and actors, 1966; Cross country, film, tape, and actors, 1971.
    R. D. 2, Averill Park, NY 12018

ANDREWS, BRUCE
b. Chicago, Ill., 1 Apr. 1948. Studied at Johns Hopkins Univ., B. A., M. A.; and is a candidate for the Ph. D. at Harvard Univ. He has published poetry in books, magazines, and in anthologies, and in addition writes vocal and performance scores going a step beyond Gertrude Stein in their stress on the non-referential characteristics and ordering of language, e. g., foregrounding the musical elements of discrete language units as sound for live performance or tape. Rather than setting poetry to music in the traditional sense, he selects words according to sound and object-like qualities and then further underplays the referents by specification of pitch, tempi, duration, volume, etc., use of indeterminacy, multiple voices, accompaniment, movement, theatre, tape installations.
    WORKS: Multimedia: Love songs No. 1-174.
    41 West 96th St., Apt. 10D, New York NY
    New York NY 10025

ANDREWS, CARROLL THOMAS
b. Milwaukee, Wis., 27 Oct. 1918. Attended Albertus Magnus Coll., Racine, Wis., B. M., magna cum laude, 1946; Univ. of Montreal, licentiate in music, summa cum laude, 1947. He was director of music for churches in Toledo, 1946-65, and concurrently student supervisor and guest teacher for the Gregorian Inst. of America. In 1965 he became director of music for the Diocese of St. Augustine, Fla., and later St. Petersburg, Fla.
    WORKS: 8 Masses with Latin texts, 15 motets

(ANDREWS, CARROLL THOMAS)
with Latin texts; 13 Masses with English texts,
20 anthems, 4 wedding hymns, 4 choral meditations, etc.; Instrumental: 35 pieces for tower
chimes; Easter organ suite; Set of choral improvisations on Selner hymn tunes, for organ; 2
piano suites: Day at the races and Holiday in
Hawaii.
2151 Norfolk St., N.
St. Petersburg, FL 33710

ANDREWS, GEORGE
b. Winnipeg, Manitoba, 24 Jan. 1927. Became a
United States citizen in 1957. After studying
in Boston at Tufts Univ. and Berklee Coll. of
Music he went to California and studied with
Nelson Keyes, Halsey Stevens, and Donal
Michalsky, taking his degrees (B. A. 1966, M. A.
1967) at California State Univ., Fullerton. A
free lance composer and arranger from 1952, he
was also a high school music director, 1966-73,
and conductor of South Bay Chamber Players,
1973- .
WORKS: Orchestra: Symphonic variations,
1972; Brass choir: Brass sextet, 1966; Music
for 3 brass quintets, commissioned by Brass
Ensemble of Calif. State Univ., Long Beach, 1973;
Chamber music: Duet for clarinet and cello,
1966; 3 songs for chamber chorus, 1967; piano
trio, 1969; string quartet, 1971; suite for
unaccompanied cello, 1972.
3810 Shad Place, San Pedro, CA 90732

*ANDREWS, MARK
b. Gainsborough, Lincolnshire, England, 21 Mar.
1875; to U.S. 1902; d. Montclair, N. J., 10
Dec. 1939. Studied with John Thomas Ruch at
Westminster Abbey, London. On coming to the U.S.
he was church organist and choirmaster in Montclair, N. J., and was a member of the examining
committee of the American Guild of Organists.
WORKS: Chamber music: string quartet; 2
organ sonatas; Chorus: Galilee, cantata; The
highwayman, cantata; also sacred and secular
songs.

*ANDREWS, ROGER
Memorabilia for orch.
Music Department, Queens College
CUNY, Flushing, NY 11367

ANDRIX, GEORGE
b. Chicago, Ill., 15 June 1932. Studied at Univ.
of Illinois with Burrill Phillips and Robert
Palmer, and Trinity Coll. of Music, London, with
Richard Arnell and Matyas Seiber. He was on the
faculty of Ithaca Coll., N. Y., 1960-67, Morehead
State Univ., Ky., 1967-68, and is a violinist and
conductor.
WORKS: Five pieces for orchestra; Chamber
music: Sonata for percussion, 2 players; 5 Perspectives for percussion, 6 players; Free forms
for bass trombone and strings; Miniatures for
solo trumpet; 5 pieces for violin and percussion;
14 duets for violin and viola; other solo works
for violin, viola, trumpet, trombone, saxophone,
and works for brass and mixed ensembles.
Box 2198, Edson, Alberta, Canada

ANDRUS, DONALD GEORGE
b. Seattle, Wash., 13 Sep. 1935. Studied at
Western Washington State Coll., B. A. 1957, Univ.
of Washington, M. A. 1960, Univ. of Illinois,
D. M. A. 1968. Composition teachers were John
Verrall, Kenneth Gaburo, Lejaren A. Hiller, Jr.,
and Gordon Binkerd. Awards include a Fulbright
grant for study in Utrecht, 1963-64, and a Univ.
of Washington composition award, 1960. He was
instructor at Univ. of Illinois, 1966-68, and on
the faculty, California State Univ. Long Beach,
1968- .
WORKS: Orchestra piece No. 1; Chamber music:
Piano quintet, 1959; Imbrications for 4 performers; Voice: Six songs, soprano, viola, piano;
Electronic: Sound tape for Shakespeare's Macbeth, 1964; Psssh, tape, 1964; Deciduata, 4
choruses and electronics, 1968; Piece for string
bass and electronics; Piece for bass flute and
electronics, 1974.
5281 El Parque, Long Beach, CA 90815

ANGELL, WARREN M.
b. Brooklyn, N. Y., 13 May 1907. Studied at
Syracuse Univ., B. M., M. M.; Columbia Univ.,
Ed. D.; Eastman School of Music; piano in Vienna.
He has received three ASCAP awards; in 1956 the
college of which he is dean was named Warren M.
Angell Coll. of Fine Arts; in 1973 Governor Bond
of Missouri proclaimed 29 March as Dr. Warren M.
Angell Day. After two years as head of the piano
dept. at Murray State Coll., Ky., 1934-36, he
went to Oklahoma Baptist Univ. as dean of the
Coll. of Fine Arts. He has published five books
on vocal and choral techniques and has more than
53 published compositions in the choral field,
four published piano pieces, many choral arrangements, and unpublished vocal and instrumental
compositions.
1920 N. Bell, Shawnee, OK 74801

*ANTHEIL, GEORGE
b. Trenton, N. J., 8 July 1900; d. New York,
N. Y., 12 Feb. 1959. Studied with Constantin
von Sternberg, Ernest Bloch, and Clark Smith in
Philadelphia. From 1920 to 1936 he played concerts of his piano works and presented his ballets and orchestral works in Europe and New
York, then settled in Hollywood.
WORKS: Opera: Transatlantic, 1929; Helen
retires, 1933; Volpone, 1952; The brothers, 1953;
The wish, 1954; Ballet: Ballet mecanique, 1924,
required 8 pianos, an airplane propeller, sirens,
and other unorthodox instruments, New York, 1927;
The capitol of the world, 1953; Orchestra:
Zingareska, 1921; Jazz symphony, chamber orch.,
1925; piano concerto, 1926; 6 symphonies, 1926,
1937, 1942, 1943, 1947, 1948; violin concerto,
1946; Chamber music: 3 string quartets; 4 violin sonatas; 4 piano sonatas; concerto for flute,
bassoon and piano; chamber concerto for 8 instruments; violin sonatina; Crucifixion, string
orch.; McKonkey's Ferry overture; Serenade for
strings; Chorus: Cabeza de vaca, cantata, CBS
television, 10 June 1962; Film scores: Once in
a blue moon; Angels over Broadway; The plainsman;
We were strangers; In a lonely place; The

ANTHEIL, GEORGE

(ANTHEIL, GEORGE)
buccaneer; Spectre of the rose. He wrote an
autobiography: Bad boy of music, New York, 1945.

*ANTONINI, ALFREDO
b. Italy, 31 May 1901; U.S. citizen 1938.
Studied at the Royal Cons., Milan, Italy, degrees
in composition, organ, and choral work. He was
accompanist; conductor, WOR, New York; music
director, CBS Television; was chairman, music
department, St. John's Univ., Brooklyn; guest
conductor of many orchestras in U.S., Canada,
Europe; from 1957, music director, Tampa Philharmonic.
    WORKS: Orchestra: Sicilian rhapsody; Suite
for cello and orch.; La vida; Mexican sketches;
American sketches; Suite for strings; also film
scores.

ANTONIOU, THEODORE
b. Athens, Greece, 10 Feb. 1938. Studied violin,
voice, and composition at the Nat. Conservatory,
1947-58, and Hellenic Conservatory, Athens,
1958-61; Hochschule fur Musik, Munich, and
Siemens Studio for Electronic Music with J. A.
Riedle, 1961-65; attended Internat. Courses for
New Music, Darmstadt, 1963-66. Awards include
composition prizes from Hellenic Cons., 1961;
Athens Tech Inst., 1962; City of Munich, 1964;
City of Stuttgart, 1966; Greek Ministry of Education, 1967; Premio Ondas, 1970; Koussevitzky
Prize, 1972. While still a student he edited
the works of his compatriot Nikos Skalkottas,
1959-61. In 1967 he was director of the Athens
Symphony Orchestra and of the Hellenic Group of
Contemporary Music. After a year in Berlin by
invitation of the City, he came to the U.S. and
was composer-in-residence and visiting professor
of composition and orchestration at Stanford
Univ., where he was also founder and director of
the Stanford new music ensemble Alea II. At
Tanglewood in 1969 he received a commission from
the Boston Symphony and the Fromm Found. for his
work Events II. Following a year as composer-in-
residence at Univ. of Utah, he became conductor,
composer, and professor of music at Philadelphia
Music Academy. He has conducted orchestras all
around the world both with his own works and
those of others. His works have been performed
in most major cities of Europe and the U.S.
    WORKS: (composed in the U.S.) Orchestra:
Events II, 1969; Threnos, wind orch., 1972; Chamber music; Five likes, solo oboe, 1969; Four
likes, solo violin, 1972-73; Chorus: Nenikikamen,
cantata, composed on the marathon runners' victory shout, 1971; Verlein Uns Freiden for 3 a
capella choirs, 1971-72; Voice: Mairologhia for
Jani Christou, 1970; Parodies, 1970; Mixed media:
Events III, orch., tape, slides, 1969; Cassandra,
dancers, actors, choir, orch. with tapes, lights,
and projections, 1969; Protest II, 13 instruments, actors, tapes, etc., 1971; Synthesis, 4
instruments, 4 synthesizers, 1971; Chorochronoi,
4 trombones, 4 percussionists, baritone, narrator, projections, 1973.
    313 South Broad St., Attica, PA 19107

APPLEBAUM, EDWARD
b. Los Angeles, Calif., 28 Sep. 1937. Studied
with Henri Lazarof and Lukas Foss, Univ. of
California, Los Angeles, and with Ingvar Lidholm
in Stockholm. He has had grants from the
American-Scandinavian Found.; Rockefeller Found.;
Nat. Endowment for the Arts; and Creative Arts
Inst., Univ. of California. He was faculty member, California State Univ., Long Beach, 1968-71;
Univ. of California, Santa Barbara, 1971-   .
    WORKS: Opera: The frieze of life, 1-act;
Orchestra: symphony; Variations for orch.; Chamber music: ...when dreams do show thee me...,
clarinet, cello, piano, chamber orch.; piano
sonata, 1965; string trio; Montages, clarinet,
cello, piano, 1968; The face in the cameo, clarinet and piano; Shantih, cello and piano, 1969;
Foci, viola and piano, 1971; Reflections, piano
trio, 1972.
    753 Calle de Los Amigos
    Santa Barbara, CA 93105

*APPLEBAUM, STANLEY
b. Newark, N. J., 1 Mar. 1922. Studied with
Stefan Wolpe, Wallingford Riegger, and Leon
Barzin. He was arranger for dance orchestras,
records, and musicals; on staff of Warner Bros.,
1962-63; established his own publishing company.
    WORKS: Band: Spring magic; Marrakech
bazaar, suite; theme for The lost hour; Chorus:
Irish suite; An American's heritage.

APPLETON, JON HOWRAD
b. Los Angeles, Calif., 4 Jan. 1939. Studied at
Univ. of California with Andrew Imbrie; Univ. of
Oregon with Henri Lazarof and Homer Keller;
Columbia Univ. with Vladimir Ussachevsky and
Mario Davidovsky. His awards include Guggenheim
and Fulbright fellowships; Class of 1921 Prize,
Reed College; 2nd prize, Concours Internat. de
Musique Electroacoustique, 1973; and an American-
Scandinavian Found. grant. He has had teaching
posts at Univ. of Oregon, 1963-65; Columbia Univ.,
1965-66; Oakland Univ., 1966-67; faculty member
and director, Bregman Electronic Music Studio,
Dartmouth Coll., 1968-   .
    WORKS: Theatre music: The stone angel,
1963; Summer and smoke, 1964; The visit, 1964;
Dark of the moon, 1967; The ghost sonata, 1969;
Pilobolus, 1971; Orchestra: After "Nude descend-
ing a staircase, 1965; The American songs, tenor
and orchestra (or piano); Chamber music: Four
explorations, violin and piano, 1964; Two movements for wind quintet, 1963; String trio, 1963;
Six movements for wind quintet, 1964; Four inventions for 2 flutes, 1965; Chorus: The green
wave, 1964; Voice: Two songs, 1964; The dying
christian to his soul, 1965; Piano: Three lyrics,
1963; Five etudes, 1964; Piano sonata, No. 1,
1965; Piano sonata, No. 2, for Gabriel Chodos,
1968; Film scores: Nobody knows everything,
1965; Anuszkiewicz, 1968; Scene unobserved, 1969;
Computer graphics at 110 Baud, 1969; Charlie
item and double X, 1970; Glory, glory!, 1971;
Electronic: Studies No. 1-3, 1963-64; Primary
experience, Columbis study No. 1, 1965;
Infantasy, 1966; Georganna's fancy, 1966;
Spuyten Duyvil, 1967; Chef d'oeuvre, 1967;

(APPLETON, JON HOWARD)
Nyckelharpan, 1968; Second scene unobserved,
1968; The visitation, 1969; Newark Airport rock,
1969; Times Square times ten, 1969; C.C.C.P., In
memorium: Anatoly Kuznetsov, 1969; Patience,
1969; Boghosian's piece, 1969; Burdock birds,
1969; Hommage a G.R.M., 1970; Quiet piece, 1970;
Apolliana, 1970; Kungsgatan 8, 1971; Dr. Quisling
in Stockholm, 1971; Nevsehir, 1971; Mixed media:
Circus, 4 instr. and tape, 1964; Scene unobserved, 4 instr., film, tape, 1969; The Bremen
town musicians, concerto for toy piano and 12
toy instr., 1971; Double structure (with
Christian Wolff), 1971.
    6 Jones Circle, Norwich, VT 05055

*ARBATSKY, YURY
    b. Moscow, 15 Apr. 1911; to U.S. 1949; d. New
Hartford, N. Y., 3 Sep. 1963. Composed 8 symphonies and numerous chamber and choral works.

ARCHIBALD, BRUCE
    b. White Plains, N. Y., 2 May 1933. Studied at
Cornell Univ., 1951-57, with Robert Palmer,
Hunter Johnson, Karel Husa; Tanglewood, 1958,
with Aaron Copland; and Harvard Univ., 1957-62,
Ph. D., with Walter Piston and Leon Kirchner.
He received a B. M. I. prize in 1954; Friends of
Music award at Cornell, 1956; and a Fels Found.
grant, 1962-63. He was on the faculty at
Amherst Coll., 1962-63; and at Temple Univ.,
1967-   .
    WORKS: Chamber music: Four songs on
poems of e. e. cummings, soprano, string quartet,
piano, 1954; String quartet, variations, 1957;
Chorus: God's grandeur, male chorus, piano 4
hands, 1961; What the thunder said, cantata for
solo baritone and 8 instruments; Organ:
Chemquasabamticook, variations, 1971; other works
for orchestra, small ensembles, chorus, piano.
    421 Wyndon Road, Ambler, PA 19002

AREL, BULENT
    b. Istanbul, Turkey, 23 May 1919, U.S. citizen,
1973. Graduated from Ankara State Cons. in 1947.
He studied composition with Necil Kazim Akses and
Edward Zuckmayer; sound engineering with Joze
Bernard and Willfried Garret, both of Radio Dif-
fusion Francaise. His awards include a Rockefeller grant in 1959 for research at the
Columbia-Princeton Electronic Music Center, and
several commissions for instrumental and electronic music. He taught in Ankara, 1945-51;
musical director, Radio Ankara, 1951-59, 1963-65;
faculty, Yale Univ., 1961-62, 1965-70; professor
and music director of the Electronic Music Studio, State Univ. of New York, Stony Brook,
1971-   .
    WORKS: Instrumental: Short piece for
orchestra, 1967; Music for unaccompanied viola,
1962; For violin and piano, 1966; Interrupted
preludes for organ, 1967; Electronic: Music for
string quartet and tape, 1957, rev. 1962; Electronic music no. 1, 1960; Fragment, 1960; Scape-
goat suite, after Kafka's "The Trial", 1960;
Stereo electronic music no. 1, 1961; Music for a
sacred service, Prelude and postlude, 1961; Wall
Street impressions, 1962; Mimiana I: Flux, 1968;

(AREL, BULENT)
Mimiana II: Frieze, 1969; Capriccio for TV,
1969; Stereo electronic music no. 2, 1970; Out
of into, film score, 1972; Mimiana III: 6 and 7,
1973.
    37 Van Brunt Manor Road
    East Setauket, NY 11733

ARGENT, JAMES
    b. Thayer, W. Va., 15 July 1927. Studied at
Wilberforce Univ. and Chicago Cons. Coll. He is
on the faculty of Wilberforce Univ.
    WORKS: Piano: Travel suite; Suite
fantastique.
    483 East Market St., Xenia, OH 45385

*ARGENTO, DOMINICK
    b. York, Pa., 27 Oct. 1927. Studied with
Nicolas Nabakov, Vittorio Rieti, Henry Cowell,
Peabody Cons., B. M. 1951, M. M. 1954; with
Bernard Rogers, Howard Hanson, and Alan
Hovhannes, Eastman School of Music, Ph. D. 1957.
His awards include the Gustav Klemm composition
prize, 1951, 1954; teaching fellowship, Eastman
School; Fulbright fellowship for study in Italy,
1951; 2 Guggenheim fellowships, 1957, 1964;
ASCAP award, 1973; Pulitzer prize for From the
diary of Virginia Woolf, song cycle, 1975. He
was faculty member, Hampton Inst., 1952-55; professor, Univ. of Minnesota, 1958-   .
    WORKS: Opera: Sicilian lives, 1954; The
boor; Masque of angels, 1963; Christopher Sly,
based on Taming of the shrew; Postcard from
Morocco, Minneapolis, 14 Oct. 1971; Jonah and
the whale, Minneapolis, 9 Mar. 1974; Krapp's
last tape, 1-act, 1974 NEA grant for American
Bicentennial 1976; The harmful effects of to-
bacco, after Chekhov, 1-act chamber opera-
monodrama for baritone, 1975 NEA grant; The
voyage of Edgar Poe, a full length opera on the
final days of Edgar Allan Poe, commissioned by
Minnesota Opera Company, Minneapolis, 24 Apr.
1976; Orchestra: The resurrection of Don Juan,
ballet suite, 1956; Ode to the west wind, soprano and orch., 1957; Variations; Royal invitation or Homage to the Queen of Tonga, small
orch.; A ring of time; Chamber music:
Divertimento, piano and strings; Divertimento,
piano 4-hands; Letters from composers, high
voice and guitar; 6 Elizabethan songs; Chorus:
The revelation of St. John the Divine, men's
voices, brass, percussion harp, piano; A nation
of cowslips; Trio Carmina Paschalia, women's
voices, guitar and harp.
    Department of Music
    University of Minnesota
    Minneapolis, MN 55455

*ARIA, PIETRO
    Jericho Road, opera, 2 acts, Philadelphia, 12
Mar. 1968.

*ARLEN, HAROLD
    b. Buffalo, N. Y., 15 Feb. 1905. Studied with
his father, a cantor; went to New York City at an
early age as pianist and singer. He wrote songs
for Broadway musicals, then stage scores, and in
Hollywood, 1943-55, film scores. Among the most

ARLEN, HAROLD

(ARLEN, HAROLD)
popular of his popular songs were <u>Stormy weather</u> and <u>Over the rainbow</u>; Film scores: <u>Let's fall in love</u>; <u>Rio Rita</u>; <u>Gold diggers of 1937</u>; <u>The wizard of Oz</u>; <u>Star Spangled rhythm</u>; <u>Cabin in the sky</u>; and many others.

*ARMSTRONG, LOUIS
b. New Orleans, La., 4 July 1900; d. New York, 6 July 1971. Black jazz trumpeter and composer. See: autobiography, <u>Satchmo, My life in New Orleans</u>, New York, 1954; and <u>Horn of plenty, The story of Louis Armstrong</u>, by R. Goffin, New York, 1947.

ARNATT, RONALD
b. London, England, 16 Jan. 1930, U.S. citizen, 1953. Attended Trent Coll., Derbyshire, Trinity Coll. of Music, London, and Durham Univ., B. M. 1954. He was named a fellow of Trinity Coll., 1951, and of the American Guild of Organists, 1952. In 1970 he was awarded an honorary D. M. by Westminster Choir Coll. Princeton, N. J. While on the faculty of American Univ., 1951-54, he founded the Washington Cantata Chorus and directed other choruses. From 1954 to 1958 he was organist and choir master in St. Louis and then joined the faculty of Univ. of Missouri. He founded and is conductor of the St. Louis Chamber Orchestra and Chorus and has toured widely as organist and pianist.
WORKS: Many anthems, sacred solos, and organ works.
412 South Gore Ave., St. Louis, MO 63119

*ARNOLD, BYRON
b. Vancouver, Wash., 15 Aug. 1901; d. Los Angeles, Calif. Studied at Willamette Univ., B. A. 1924; with Bernard Rogers and Howard Hanson, Eastman School of Music. He taught at Univ. of Alabama, 1938-48; was professor, California State Univ., Los Angeles, 1948-71.
WORKS: Orchestra: <u>5 incapacitated preludes</u>, 1937; <u>3 fanaticisms</u>; songs and piano works.

ARNOLD, CORLISS RICHARD
b. Monticello, Ark., 7 Nov. 1926. Studied at Hendrix Coll., Ark., B. M., 1946; Univ. of Michigan, M. M., 1948; Union Theological Seminary, S. M. D., 1954; composition teachers were Normand Lockwood, Seth Bingham, and Leo Sowerby. He was awarded a Fulbright grant in 1956 and is a fellow of the American Guild of Organists. He has served colleges and churches in Arkansas, New Jersey, New York, Illinois, and Michigan. Since 1959 he has been on the faculty of Michigan State Univ. and director of music at Peoples Church, East Lansing. He is the author of <u>Organ literature: A comprehensive survey</u>. His compositions include choral and organ works.
Michigan State University
East Lansing, MI 48823

ARNOLD, HUBERT EUGENE
b. New Orleans, La., 2 Mar. 1945. Studied with H. Owen Reed, Michigan State Univ., B. M. 1966, M. M. 1970; with Hall Overton at Juilliard School. He was staff arranger, U.S. Military Acad. Band, West Point, 1969-71; free-lance arranger and composer, 1971- .
WORKS: Chamber music: sonata for 2 trumpets and piano, 1969; <u>Dithyramb</u>, saxophone quartet, 1970; <u>Fantasy</u>, clarinet and piano.
10-11 50th Ave.
Long Island City, NY 11101

ARTHUR, JAN
b. Rochester, Minn., 1 Jan. 1939. Studied at Univ. of Chicago, Sherwood School, Chicago, and North Park Coll., Chicago, B. M. E. He has been a church organist and music director since 1965; associated with Victor Music Pub., 1968-71, and Schmitt Music Centers, 1971- . He has published anthems.
5209 Hamilton Lane, Minneapolis, MN 55443

ASCHAFFENBURG, WALTER
b. Essen, Germany, 20 May 1927; U.S. citizen, 1944. Studied at Hartford School of Music with Robert Doellner; Oberlin Coll., B. A. 1951, with Herbert Elwell; Eastman School, M. A. 1952, with Bernard Rogers; and in Florence, Italy, 1956, with Dallapiccolo. He has had grants from the Fromm Found., 1953, and Guggenheim Found., 1955-56, 1973-74, and a citation and award from the Nat. Inst. of Arts and Letters, 1966. He has been on the faculty of Oberlin Coll. Cons. since 1952.
WORKS: Opera: <u>Bartleby</u>, prologue and 2 acts, opus 10; Orchestra: <u>Ozymandius, symphonic reflections</u>, op. 5; <u>Three dances</u>, op. 15; Chamber music: <u>Quintet for winds</u>, op. 16; <u>Proem</u> for brass and percussion, op. 17; <u>Duo for violin and cello</u>, op. 18; Chorus: <u>The 23rd Psalm</u>, op. 13.
49 Shipherd Circle, Oberlin, OH 44074

*ASHFORTH, ALDEN
b. 1930. <u>The unquiet heart</u>, soprano and chamber ensemble, 1968.
4211 Saugus Ave., Sherman Oaks, CA 91403

ASHLEY, ROBERT
b. Ann Arbor, Mich., 28 Mar. 1930. Studied at Univ. of Michigan, M. B. 1952; Manhattan School of Music, M. M. 1954, composition with Wallingford Riegger; Univ. of Michigan, 1961, psychoacoustics with Roberto Gerhard. Co-founder of the ONCE Festival of Contemporary Music and the Cooperative Studio of Electronic Music, both at Ann Arbor, he was also founder and director of the ONCE Group, 1963-70, a touring multimedia ensemble. He is a member (with Gordon Mumma, David Behrman, Alvin Lucier) of the Sonic Arts Union, which toured the U.S. and Europe, 1966-73. He was named to the faculty and co-director of the Center for Contemporary Music, Mills Coll. Oakland, Calif.
WORKS: Opera: <u>In memoriam Kit Carson</u>, 1963; Orchestra: <u>In memoriam Crazy Horse</u>, symphony, 1963; <u>In memoriam John Smith</u>, concerto, 1963; Chamber music: <u>In memoriam Estaban Gomez</u>, quartet, 1963; <u>Quartet for any number of instruments</u>,

(ASHLEY, ROBERT)
1965; Trios (White on white) various instruments, 1963; Chorus: She was a visitor, 1967; Piano: Sonata, 1959; Maneuvers for small hands, 1961; Details for two pianists, one piano, 1962; Electronic: The 4th of July, 1960; Something for clarinet, piano and tape, 1961; Public opinion descends on the demonstrators, 1961; Detroit divided, 1962-72; Complete with heat, 1962; Boxing, 1963; The wolfman, 1964; Kitty Hawk, an antigravity piece, 1964; Combination wedding and funeral, 1964; Joy road interchange, 1964; Orange dessert, 1965; Untitled mixes, 1965; Unmarked interchange, 1965; Night train, 1966; The trial of Anne Opie Wehrer and unknown accomplices for crimes against humanity, 1968; Purposeful lady slow afternoon, 1968; Illusion models, for hypothetical computer, 1970; Film scores: The image in time, 1957; The bottleman, 1960; Jenny and the poet, 1964; My May, 1965; Overdrive, 1968; Portraits, self-portraits and still life, 1969; Battery Davis, 1970.
Center for Contemporary Music
Mills College, Oakland, CA 94613

ASHTON, JOHN H.
b. Pittsburgh, Pa., 11 July 1938. Studied at Carnegie-Mellon Univ., B. F. A. 1960, M. F. A. 1961, with Nikolai Lopatnikoff. He has received awards from West Virginia Univ., 1961, and from the Nat. Asso. of Coll. Wind and Percussion Instructors, 1963. He played trumpet in the U.S. Naval Acad. Band, 1962-65, Savannah Symph. Orch., 1966, Radio Telefis Eireann Symph. Orch., Dublin, Ireland, 1967, and New Orleans Philharmonic, 1968. He was on the faculty of Univ. of Nebraska in 1969, and has been at Fairmont State Coll. W. Va., 1970-   .
WORKS: Orchestra: Symphonic movement, 1961; For the love of Phoebe, 1961; Band: Rhapsody, 1964; Lyric piece for brass quintet, 1972; Dulce et decorum est, baritone solo and brass choir; Chamber music: Clarinet quintet, 1960; Trumpet sonata, 1963; Trio for clarinet, bassoon, piano, 1972; A tonal trio for flute, clarinet, bassoon, and optional suspended cymbal, 1973; Voice: Songs from the unknown Eros, on texts of Coventry Patmore, 1973; Piano: Theme and five variations, 1971.
1109 Alexander Place, Fairmont, WV 26554

*ATHERTON, PERCY LEE
b. Roxbury, Mass., 25 Sep. 1871; d. Atlantic City, N. J., 8 Mar. 1944. Studied with John Knowles Paine, Harvard Univ., B. A. 1893; with Rheinberger in Munich; Sgambati in Rome; and with Widor in Paris.
WORKS: Opera: The heir apparent; The maharajah; Orchestra: Noon in the forest, symphonic poem; many songs.

*ATHEY, RALPH
Kaolin for any mixed ensemble of winds and/or strings.

ATOR, JAMES DONALD
b. Kansas City, Mo., 15 Oct. 1938. Studied at Drake Univ., B. M. E. 1960; Wichita State Univ.,

(ATOR, JAMES DONALD)
M. M. 1964; and North Texas State Univ., D. M. A. 1971. Composition teachers were Samuel Adler, Merrill Ellis, and William Latham. He has held faculty positions at North Texas State Univ., 1969-71, Millikin Univ., 1971-73, and Indiana Univ. at Fort Wayne, 1973-   .
WORKS: Orchestra: Adagio, 1969; Piece for orchestra and prepared tape, 1971; Chamber music: Woodwind quartet, 1971; Enuffispluntee, saxophone, piano, percussion, 1972; Voice: Four haiku, mezzo and piano, 1971-72.
1925 Coronet, Fort Wayne, IN 46805

*ATWELL, RICHARD
Christmas suite for organ.

*AUERBACH, NORMAN
3 choral songs.

AUSLENDER, LEONARD STANLEY
b. Los Angeles, Calif., 24 Oct. 1936. Studied at Univ. of California, Los Angeles, B. A. 1963; and California State Univ. Los Angeles, M. A. 1974. His teachers have included Leonard Stein, Roy Harris, Henri Lazarof, Boris Kremenliev, Byong-Kon Kim, Dudley Foster, and Tak Shindo. Since 1969 he has been president of Bright Star Music Pub.
WORKS: Chamber music: Four miniatures, for violin and cello; Scherzo in C for woodwind quartet; Visions in crystal, rainbows in stone, mixed chamber ensemble.
911 N. Formosa Ave., W. Hollywood, CA 90046

AUSTIN, LARRY
b. Duncan, Okla., 12 Sep. 1930. Studied at North Texas State Univ., B. M. 1951, M. M. 1952; Composition at Mills Coll. with Milhaud, 1955, and at Univ. of California, Berkeley, 1955-58; course in computer-generated music systems at Stanford Univ., 1969. Awards include MacDowell fellowships, 1961, 1962; Inst. for Creative Arts, 1964-65, 1968; 8 Univ. of Calif. grants; B. M. I. awards; many commissions. He has held posts at Univ. of Calif., Berkeley, 1956-58, and at Davis, 1958-70; chairman and professor, Univ. of South Florida, 1970-72, director of the Systems Complex for the Studio and Performing Arts, 1973-   ; editor of SOURCE magazine, 1967-   . With colleagues at Davis in 1963, Austin evolved a technique of group improvisation which he terms "open style" and applies in composition.
WORKS: Orchestra: Prosody, 1953; Improvisations for orchestra and jazz soloists, 1961; Open style for orchestra with piano soloist, 1967; Band: Fanfare and procession, 1953; Music galore: Outdoor suite, 1958; Fanfare for 9 brass instruments, 1958; Suite for massed bands, 1961; In memoriam J. F. Kennedy, 1964; Jazz ensembles: Fantasy on a theme by Berg, jazz band, 1960; Homecoming, chamber concerto for alto saxophone and jazz quintet, 1973; Chamber music: woodwind quartet, 1948; woodwind quintet, 1949; brass quintet, 1949; sonata for violin and piano, 1950; 3 violin duets, 1951; string trio, 1952; concertino, flute, trumpet, strings, 1952; 2 string quartets, 1954, 1955; Collage for a

AUSTIN, LARRY

(AUSTIN, LARRY)
variety of instruments, 1963; Continuum for 2 to 7 instruments, 1964; A broken consort, 7 instruments, 1964; Current, clarinet and piano, 1968; Chorus: Mass for chorus and orchestra, 1958-59; Triptych, chorus and string quartet, 1961; Piano: Variations, 1964; Piano set in open style, 1968; Electronic and mixed media: Roma, theatre piece in open style, 1965; Duet Amphitryon, 1967; Bass, theatre piece in open style, 1967; The maze, 1967; Changes, trombone and tape, 1967; Catharsis, open style for 2 improvisation ensembles, tapes, and conductor, 1967; Accidents, for electronically prepared piano, tape, mirrors, actions, projections, 1967; Brass, electronically prepared brass instruments, slides, and films, 1967; The magicians, 1968; Twomanshow, tape, 1968; 3 music films, Black/white study, Color study, Transmission one, all 1969; Agape, a celebration for priests, musicians, actors, and poets, 1970; Plastic surgery, electric piano, percussion, tape, film, 1970; Walter, theatre piece for viola, viola d'amore, films, and tape, 1970-71; Quartet three, Quartet four, 1971; JB, Larry, and ___, tape with saxophone, 1971; Quadrants: Event/Complex Nos. 1-7, 1971-73. He is the author of numerous magazine articles.
   10505 Orange Grove Court, Tampa, FL 33618

AVERRE, RICHARD E.
b. Trenton, N. J., 19 Jan. 1921. Studied at Juilliard School; Cincinnati Coll. Cons.; Westminster Choir Coll., B. M.; Trenton State Coll., M. M. Ed. He was music director of the Lambertville (N. J.) Music Circus, 1962-66, and the Trenton Theatre-in-Park, 1967. Since 1968 he has been associate professor at Bucks County Community Coll., Pa. He has published many sacred and secular choral compositions.
   Box 81, Washington Crossing, PA 18977

AVERITT, WILLIAM EARL
b. Paducah, Ky., 14 Nov. 1948. Studied at Murray State Univ., B. M. 1970, with James Woodward; and at Florida State Univ., M. M. 1972, D. M. 1973, with John Boda. His awards include fellowships from the NDEA, 1970-73, and the Ellen Battell Stoeckel Trust, 1972. He is a faculty member at the Shenandoah Cons. of Music.
   WORKS: Chamber music: Sonata, woodwind quintet, 1969; sonata, brass choir, 1970; trio for flute, clarinet, bassoon, 1970; Permutation, flute, harpsichord, 1971; quartet, flute, clarinet, bass, piano, 1971; Chamber variations for 9 performers, 1972; chamber symphony, 1973; Chorus: Mass for soprano, chorus, organ, 1969; Libera me, double chorus and solo quartet, 1970; Two songs of William Blake, male chorus and piano, 1970; Songs: Two songs of Poe, baritone and percussion, 1967; Nazi songs (Brock), soprano and 5 instruments, 1972; Piano: Introduction and allegro, 1970; Two motets for 2 pianos, 1972.
   1117 Franklin St., Apt. 3
   Winchester, VA 22601

*AVNI, TZVI
b. 1927. Vocalize, voice and electronics, 1964.

*AVRIL, LLOYD
Heads or tails, 1-act opera, Glassboro State Coll., 23 Feb. 1968.

*AVSHALOMOV, AARON
b. Nikolayevsk, Siberia, 11 Nov. 1894; to U.S. 1947; d. New York, 26 Apr. 1965. Studied at the Zurich Cons. In 1914 he was sent to China to avoid the draft. There he composed on Chinese themes, attempting to fuse Chinese thematic and rhythmic elements with the Western style of composition. His first opera, Kuan Yin had its premiere in Peking in 1925; was performed in Portland, Ore., 1926, and in New York, 1927. His 2nd, 3rd, and 4th symphonies were composed in the U.S.

AVSHALOMOV, JACOB
b. Tsingtao, China, 28 Mar. 1919; U.S. citizen, 1944. Studied with his father, Aaron Avshalomov; with Ernst Toch in Los Angeles, 1938; Jacques Gershkovitch at Reed Coll., 1939-41; with Bernard Rogers, Eastman School of Music, B. M. 1942, M. A. 1943; Columbia Univ., 1946. His awards include Alice M. Ditson fellowship, 1946; Ernest Bloch award 1948; Guggenheim fellowship, 1951; New York Music Critics' Circle award, 1953; Naumburg recording award, 1956; Ditson conductor's award, 1965; honorary doctorates, Univ. of Portland, 1966, Reed Coll., 1974; appointment to Nat. Council for Humanities, 1968-74. After serving as translator during World War II, he taught at Columbia Univ., 1946-54; became conductor, Portland Junior Symphony, 1954-   . He has also been visiting professor at Tanglewood and Aspen and at several universities, and guest conductor of orchestras in the northwest. He was appointed to the planning section, Nat. Endowment for the Arts, 1974.
   WORKS: Theatre: incidental music to The little clay cart; Orchestra: The taking of T'ung Kuan, 1943, rev. 1947, 1953; Slow dance, Washington, D.C., 13 Aug. 1945; Sinfonietta, 1946, rev. 1952; Evocations, clarinet and chamber orch., 1947; How long, O Lord, cantata for alto solo, chorus and orch., 1949; Suite from The Plywood Age, with unison chorus, 1955; Inscriptions at the City of Brass, chorus, female narrator and orch., 1956; Phases of the Great Land, 1958; The Oregon, symphony, Portland, Ore., 19 Mar. 1962; City upon a hill, chorus, narrator, orch., and liberty bell, 1965; Chamber music: 2 Bagatelles, clarinet and piano; Disconsolate muse, flute and piano; Evocations, clarinet or viola and piano, 1947; Sonatine for viola and piano, 1947; Chorus: Prophecy, with tenor solo and organ, 1948, rev. 1952; Proverbs of Hell, men's voices; Tom O'Bedlam, chorus, oboe, tabor and jingles, New York, 15 Dec. 1953; Whimsies, text from The New Yorker; Wonders, Blake text; I saw a stranger yestere'en, with solo violin; Psalm 100, with winds or organ and percussion, 1957; Of man's mortalitie; Praises from the corners of the Earth, 1965; songs and piano pieces.
   2741 Southwest Fairview Blvd.
   Portland, OR 97201

16

*AYRES, FREDERIC
b. Binghamton, N. Y., 17 Mar. 1876; d. Colorado Springs, Colo., 23 Nov. 1926. Studied with Edgar Stillman Kelley and Arthur Foote.
WORKS: Orchestra: From the plains, overture; Chamber music: 2 string quartets; 2 piano trios; 2 violin sonatas; cello sonata; many songs.

*BABBITT, MILTON
b. Philadelphia, Pa., 10 May 1916. Studied at Princeton Univ. His awards include the New York Music Critics citation, 1949, 1964; Guggenheim fellowship, 1961; membership, Nat. Inst. of Arts and Letters, 1965; special citation under the Koussevitzky recording award, 1972. He has been faculty member, Princeton Univ., 1938-   .
WORKS: Orchestra: Correspondences; Occasional variations, 1969; Jazz ensemble: All set, 1957; Chamber music: 4 string quartets, New York premiere of no. 4, 24 Oct. 1971; Composition for 4 instruments, 1948; Composition for 12 instruments, 1948; Composition for viola and piano, 1950; Aria da capo, chamber ensemble, New York, 25 Apr. 1974; Electronic: Vision and prayer, soprano and electronic sounds, 1961; Composition for synthesizer, 1961; Philomel, soprano and tape, 1964; Ensemble for synthesizer, 1964.
Music Department, Princeton University
Princeton, NJ 08540

*BABCOCK, JEFFREY
Mirrors, short opera with slides and projections, Univ. of California, Santa Barbara, 6 Apr. 1972.

BABCOCK, MICHAEL J.
b. Centralia, Wash., 12 June 1940. Earned a master's degree at Indiana Univ. in 1971, studying with Iannis Xenakis, Juan Orrego-Salas, Roque Cordero, and John Eaton. He was a research fellow, Center for Mathematical and Automated Music, Indiana Univ., 1969-71; director, Studio for Electronic and Experimental Music, Chicago Musical Coll., Roosevelt Univ., 1972-   .
WORKS: Minutia, 2 movements for cello and piano; Inflexaleus, 5 percussionists, Chicago, Dec. 1971.
841 West Gunnison, Chicago, IL 60640

BABER, JOSEPH
b. Richmond, Va., 11 Sep. 1937. Attended Michigan State Univ., Eastman School of Music, M. M., studying with John Powell, Mario Castelnuovo-Tedesco, and Howard Hanson. He received the Louis Lane Prize, 1965; ASCAP award for 1972; American Recorder Society prize; and first prize in a composition contest of the Illinois State Music Teachers Assoc. He was on the faculty of Southern Illinois Univ., 1967-70; composer-in-residence, Kansas Coll. Co-operative Composers Project, 1970-71; and is head of the composition-theory department, Univ. of Kentucky.
WORKS: Opera: Frankenstein, 4-acts, libretto by John Gardner; Orchestra: Rhapsody, 1965; viola concerto, Tokyo Philh., 1967; Chamber music: trio for oboe, viola, piano; string

(BABER, JOSEPH)
quartet; violin sonata; works for choir, recorders, brass instruments.
108 Arcadia Park, Lexington, KY 40506

BABIN, STANLEY
b. Latvia, 10 Oct. 1932; U.S. citizen. Studied at Curtis Inst. of Music.
WORKS: Orchestra: piano concerto; Chamber music, string quartet; woodwind quintet; Piano: 4 piano studies; 3 piano pieces; 2 sonatinas.
230 Central Park West, New York, NY 10024

*BABIN, VICTOR
b. Moscow, 12 Dec. 1908; to U.S. 1937; d. Cleveland, Ohio, 2 Mar. 1972. Studied at the Riga Cons.; with Artur Schnabel in Berlin; honorary doctorate from Univ. of New Mexico, 1961. In 1933 the 2-piano team of Vronsky and Babin began concert tours in Europe, making a New York debut in 1937. After his service in the U.S. Army in World War II, the 2-piano concerts were resumed. He was director, Cleveland Inst. of Music, 1961-72.
WORKS: Orchestra: 2 concerti for 2 pianos and orch.; Concert piece for violin and orch.; Capriccio; Chamber music: string quartet; Variations on a theme by Purcell, cello and piano; Sonata-fantasia, cello and piano; piano trio; Piano: 6 etudes for 2 pianos; Hillandale waltzes; 3 fantasias on old themes; and a song cycle, Beloved stranger.

*BABITS, LINDA (PATRICK)
b. New York, N. Y., 28 July 1940. Studied at Manhattan School of Music, B. M.; with Roger Sessions, Oberlin Cons.
WORKS: Orchestra: Western star, piano concerto; Clinton Corner Delancey; Electronic: Vocalize, voice and tape, 1964.

BACH, JAN MORRIS
b. Forrest, Ill., 11 Dec. 1937. Attended Univ. of Kansas, 1954-55, and Univ. of Illinois, M. M. 1962, studying with Robert Kelly, Kenneth Gaburo, Burrill Phillips; Yale, 1960 with Donald Martino, and at Tanglewood, 1961 with Aaron Copland and Roberto Gerhard. His awards include a B. M. I. prize, 1957; Koussevitzky award (co-recipient), 1961; City of Birmingham, Ala., composition prize, 1966; Harvey Gaul prize (co-recipient), 1973; Mannes Opera prize, 1973, with performance in Feb. 1974. He was on the faculty Univ. of Tampa, 1965-66; and Associate professor, Northern Illinois Univ., DeKalb, 1966-   .
WORKS: Opera: The system, 1-act, 1973, New York, 7 Mar. 1974; Orchestra: Toccata, 1959, Improvisos, 1968; Band: Dionysia - Dirge and dithyrambic dances, 1964; Chamber music: Divertimento, oboe and bassoon, 1956; string trio, 1956; string quartet, 1957; clarinet sonata, 1957; Partita, flute, cello, harpsichord, 1958; quintet for oboe and strings, 1958; Dance, horn and piano, 1959; Mountain, desert, soil, and sea, 11 instruments, 1960; Rondelle, violin, flute, horn, piano, 1964; Four two-bit contraptions, flute and horn, 1964; movements for viola and winds, 1966; Turkish music, solo percussionist,

BACH, JAN MORRIS

(BACH, JAN MORRIS)
1967; Skizzen, woodwind quintet, 1967; Woodwork, 4 percussionists, 1970; Laudes, brass quintet, 1971; Eisteddfod, flute, harp, viola, 1972; Chorus: Three Shakespearean songs, 1960; Three choral dances, women's voices, 1969; Dirge for a minstrel, 1969; Spectra, soloists, chorus, orchestra, tape, 1970; and songs.
  803 Hillcrest, DeKalb, IL 60115

*BACHARACH, BURT F.
  b. Kansas City, Mo., 12 May 1928. Studied with Henry Cowell and Darius Milhaud, New School for Social Research; Mannes Coll. of Music; and with Bohuslav Martinu. He has been composer, arranger, and conductor, New York, 1952- .
  WORKS: Theatre: Promises, promises, a musical; Film title songs: Wives and lovers; A house is not a home; Send me no flowers; What's new pussycat?; Promise her anything; Alfie; Butch Cassidy and the Sundance Kid; and many other popular songs; Film score: What's new pussycat?.

*BACON, ERNST
  b. Chicago, Ill., 26 May 1898. Studied at Univ. of Chicago and Univ. of California, M. A. His awards include the Pulitzer prize, 1932; Guggenheim fellowship, 1939; MacDowell and Hartford fellowships; Bispham award. He was director, School of Music, Syracuse Univ.
  WORKS: Opera: A tree on the plains; Drumlin legend; Take your choice; Orchestra: 3 symphonies; Ford's Theatre, 1943; From these States; Riolama, 1964; Great River, Enchanted island; also chamber music and many works for chorus and solo voice.

BAHMANN, MARIANNE E.
  b. Schuylkill Co., Pa., 1 Dec. 1933. Studied at Drake Univ. with Francis J. Pyle. She received the Des Moines Symph. Young Artist award in composition, 1957, and won the 1961 Capital Univ. competition for an anthem. She has taught at Drake Univ., Preparatory Dept.; at Chicago Evangelistic Inst., Oskaloosa, Iowa; was an accompanist and singer in New York, 1957-58; and a free lance performer and composer, 1959- .
  WORKS: Magnificat for solo voice and orchestra; The altar of God, choir and organ; A setting of the Lutheran Liturgy based on spirituals, for congregation, cantor, and organ; Pastorale on 'Greensleeves' and Voluntary on a theme of Tschaikowsky, both for organ.
  1611 Stanford Ave., Palo Alto, CA 94306

BAIL, GRACE SHATTUCK
  b. Cherry Creek, N.Y., 17 Jan. 1898. Graduated from Dana School of Music, Warren, Ohio, 1919, studying piano and theory; also studied violin with Michael Banner and composition with John Christopher at Meadville Coll. of Music. She has received many awards for violin solos, string trios, piano and choral works. Her compositions include symphonic works, string quartets, string trios, choral works, and pieces for violin, piano, and organ.
  873½ Beaumont Ave., Beaumont, CA 92223

*BAILEY, PARKER
  b. Kansas City, Mo., 1 Mar. 1902. Studied with David Stanley Smith, Yale Univ.; law at Cornell Univ., L. L. B. 1934. He has practiced law in New York, 1943- . Published works include a flute sonata and Toccata, ricercata, finale, for organ. He is a nephew of Horatio Parker.

*BAIRD, JAMES
  A stroll on the bottom of the sea, percussion.

*BAKALEINIKOV, VLADIMIR ROMANOVITCH
  b. Moscow, 12 Oct. 1885; to U.S. 1927; d. Pittsburgh, Pa., 5 Nov. 1953. Composed a viola concerto, 1937; 2 oriental dances for orchestra.

BAKER, DAVID A.
  b. Hamilton, Ohio, 27 Mar. 1949. Attended Univ. of Kentucky, B. A. 1971, studying composition with John Barnes Chance; Florida State Univ., M. M., D. Mus. 1974, with Carlisle Floyd and John Boda. He is an instructor at Florida State Univ.
  WORKS: Orchestra: Concerto for piano, strings, and percussion; Chamber music: Sonata concertante, saxophone and piano; Fantasy, serenade, and fugue, flute, guitar, bassoon; Prelude and dance, trombone and piano; Five pieces, for piano.
  304-1 Pennell Circle, Tallahassee, FL 32304

BAKER, DAVID N.
  b. Indianapolis, Ind., 21 Dec. 1931. Attended Indiana Univ., B. M. Ed., M. M. Ed., and studied composition with George Russell, William Russo, John Lewis, Thomas Beversdorf, Bernhard Heiden, Gunther Schuller, Norman Merrifield, Juan Orrego-Salas. He also studied tuba, trombone, cello, and bass, and holds a Lenox School of Jazz diploma. His many awards and citations include Indiana Philharmonic Gold Award, 1954; Down Beat Hall of Fame scholarship, 1959, and New Star Award, 1962; two Notre Dame Collegiate Jazz Festival awards, 1959, 1964; Nat. Assoc. of Negro Musicians award, and many commissions and appointments to boards, etc. He taught at Lincoln Univ., Jefferson City, Mo., 1956-57; Indianapolis Public Schools, 1958-59; Indiana Central Coll., 1963-64; privately, 1960-66; Indiana Univ., assistant professor and chairman of jazz studies, 1966- ; and at Tanglewood, 1968- .
  WORKS: Jazz band: Concerto for flute; concerto for trombone; concerto for bass viol; Levels, solo bass viol, jazz band, flute quartet, horn quartet, string quartet, Claremont, Calif., July 1973; Chamber music: many pieces for string orchestra; trio for alto saxophone, horn, cello; concerto for violin and jazz ensemble, 1969; The dude, cello and piano; 2 string quartets; Romanza and march, 3 trombones; sonata for piano and string quintet; sonata for 2 pianos; Passions, brass quintet; Hymn and deviation, brass quartet; Dirge and dance, brass quartet; Modality, tonality, and freedom, saxophone and instrumental ensemble; viola sonata, violin sonata; sonatina for tuba and string quartet, 1971; cello sonata, New York, 16 Feb. 1974; 3 woodwind quintets; sonata for violin and cello; The new Americans, brass

18

(BAKER, DAVID N.)
choir; Chorus: Bratitudes, chorus, dancers, narrator, orch.; Black America, to the memory of Martin Luther King, Jr., a cantata presented on Voice of America each year on the anniversary of Dr. King's death; But I am a worm, chorus, jazz ensemble, orch.; Catholic Mass for Peace and Lutheran Mass, both for chorus and jazz ensemble; Lutheran Mass, high voice and piano; Jazz Mass, chorus and jazz septet; I am poured out like water, men's voices and string orch.; I will tell of thy name, chorus, dancers, jazz ensemble, string orch.; My God, My God, chorus, jazz ensemble, string orch.; Psalm 22, oratorio; Psalm 23, chorus and organ; 5 Songs to the survival of Black children, a cappella chorus; Songs: Song cycle for tenor and piano; song cycle for soprano and piano; Film scores: NET series, Black frontier, The trial of Captain Henry Flipper; and more than 100 pieces for jazz ensemble. He is also author of many books and articles on the contemporary scene in music.
3151 Arrow Ave., Bloomington, IN 47401

BAKER, LARRY
b. Ft. Smith, Ark., 7 Sep. 1948. Studied at Oklahoma Univ. with Woodrow James and Spencer Norton; Cleveland Inst. of Music, with Donald Erb. He received the Oklahoma Fed. of Music Clubs composition award, 1970, 1971; and was a member of the Vermont Composers' Conference, 1972, 1973. He was conductor of the Performance Group, 1971-73; on the faculty at Cleveland Inst. of Music and head of the Contemporary Music Ensemble, 1973- .
WORKS: Orchestra: A game of shadows; From the worlds of the Imperium; Chamber music: Trimophony; Night ancestor I.
2496 Derbyshire, Apt. 11, Cleveland, OH 44106

*BAKER, ROBERT A.
Has published choral works.
Music Department, Washington University
St. Louis, MO 63130

BAKER, ROBERT S.
b. Illinois, 7 July 1916. Studied at Illinois Wesleyan Univ.; with Clarence Dickinson, Union Theological Seminary; with Seth Bingham, Columbia Univ.; and with T. Tertius Noble and R. Huntington Woodman in New York. He has been church organist, 1945- ; was dean, School of Music, Union Theological Seminary, 1961-73; director, Yale Inst. of Sacred Music, 1973- . He has published anthems.
Yale Institute of Sacred Music
New Haven, CT 06510

*BAKER, W. CLAUDE
b. Lenoir, N. C., 1948. Received a BMI award for Rest, heart of the world, soprano and orch., 1973.

BAKSA, ROBERT FRANK
b. New York, N. Y., 7 Feb. 1938. Studied at Univ. of Arizona with Henry Johnson and Robert McBride; at Tanglewood with Lukas Foss; but is primarily self-taught. He is a free lance music copyist.

(BAKER, ROBERT FRANK)
WORKS: Opera: Aria da capo, 1-act, text by Millay, 1968; Red carnations, 1-act, text by Hughes; Orchestra: Meditation, 1955; Chamber concerto for wind quartet and strings; Serenade for string orch.; Chamber music: Canzonas for brass quintet; trio for clarinet, cello, piano; piano trio; woodwind octet; various trios, quartets, quintets, etc; Chorus: Herrick songs; Seven anthems for Holy Week; and songs. He also composes film scores.
625 West End Ave., New York, NY 10024

BALADA, LEONARDO
b. Barcelona, Spain, 22 Sept. 1933; to U.S. 1956. Attended Cons. of Barcelona, 1953-54, Juilliard School, 1960, and Mannes Coll. of Music, 1961-62; studied composition with Aaron Copland, Alexander Tansman, Vincent Persichetti, and conducting with Igor Markevitch. His awards include the B. Martinu prize, Mannes Coll., 1962; ASCAP awards; composer-in-residence, Aspen Inst. for Humanistic Studies; and many commissions. He has held faculty positions at Walden School, N.Y., 1962-63; United Nations Internat. School, 1963-70; and has been associate professor, Carnegie-Mellon Univ., 1970-
WORKS: Orchestra: Musica tranquila, string orch., Compostela, Spain, 1960; piano concerto, 1964; guitar concerto, 1965; Guernica, New Orleans, April, 1967; Sinfonia en negro, Homenaje a Martin Luther King, Madrid, June 1969, New York, May 1970; Maria Sabina, narrator, chorus, orch., New York, April 1970; bandoneon concerto, 1970; Persistencias, guitar and orch; Steel symphony, 1972; Transparencias, 1973; Ponce de Leon, narrator and orch., New Orleans, 9 Oct. 1973; Requiem for chorus, orch., narrators, 1973; Band: Cumbres, short symphony, 1971; concerto for piano and symphonic band, New York, April 1974; Chamber music: violin sonata, 1960; concerto for cello and 9 instruments, 1962; Geometrias for 7 instruments, 1966; Geometrias, N. 2, string quartet, 1967; Cuatris, 4 instruments, New York, 1969; End and beginning, for rock and contemporary music ensemble, 1970; Mosaico, brass quintet, Aspen, July 1970; Tresis, guitar, flute, cello, New York, 22 May 1973; Sketches for guitar quartet (Ciudad de Zaragoza international music prize, 1974); Chorus: Las moradas, mixed chorus and 7 instruments, Avila, Spain, Oct. 1970; Voces no. 1, a cappella, 1971; instrumental solos and songs.
c/o Music Dept., Carnegie-Mellon University
Pittsburgh, PA 15213

*BALAMOS, JOHN
Out of the depths, chorus and organ.

BALAZS, FREDERIC
b. Budapest, 12 Dec. 1920; U.S. citizen 1956. Studied violin in Budapest winning the Remenyi Prize at age 16. He has also received awards from Internat. Society for Contemporary Music, Texas Composers competition, Alice M. Ditson fund, and is honorary member of the Mark Twain Literary Society for his "outstanding contribution to American music." He has been music

BALAZS, FREDERIC

(BALAZS, FREDERIC)
director of the Wichita Symph., 1948-52; Tucson Symph. Soc., 1952-66; Orchestra-Opera Dept., Cincinnati Cons., 1966-70; has held faculty positions at Midwestern Univ., 1948-52; Windham Coll., Vt., 1970-71; Keene State Univ., N.H., 1970-71; and has been director and conductor, Hawaiian Inst. for Orchestra and Ensemble, and concertmaster, Honolulu Symph. Orch., 1972- . He is also active as concert violinist and lecturer.

WORKS: Ballet: Pueblo Bonito, with chorus, narrator, orch., percussion; Orchestra: Two dances after David, flute and orch.; Symphony on a plain-chant fragment; An American symphony, after Walt Whitman; Passacaglia; A statement of faith; cello concerto, In memoriam to J. F. Kennedy; Chamber music: Kentuckia, violin or cello and piano, or strings; 4 string quartets, No.3, premiere, Portland, Me., 21 April 1971; Sonnets after Elizabeth Barrett Browning, voice and string quartet; Chorus: Three contrasting songs, on poems of James Boyd and Psalm XXV, chorus, brass, percussion.
1544 Kalaepohaku Place, Honolulu, HI 96816

*BALBO, G. C.
3 etchings, flute or oboe and clarinet.

BALDWIN, DAVID
b. Alliance, Ohio, 6 Dec. 1946. Obtained a B. M. at Baldwin Wallace Coll., Berea, Ohio, studying with Charles Gorham, Bernhard Adelstein, William Vacchiano, and M. M. at Yale Univ. on a scholarship. He teaches at Walsh Coll., Canton, Ohio.
WORKS: Notes for brass quintet, 1973; Concerto for three unaccompanied trumpets; Divertimento for flute and tuba; This new man for brass trio.
6 School St., Stony Creek
Branford, CT 06405

*BALDWIN, RALPH LYMAN
b. Northampton, Mass., 27 Mar. 1872; d. Canaan, N.H., 1943. Was active as organist, choir director, composer and music supervisor in Northampton and Hartford, Conn.; after 1900 was faculty member, Inst. of Music Pedagogy, Northampton. Rollins Coll., Winter Park, Fla., confers an award in his name.

BALDWIN, RUSSELL
b. Chicago, Ill., 9 Jan. 1913. Studied at American Cons. with Leo Sowerby; Univ. of Southern California with Ingolf Dahl; and with Peter Korn in Munich. He is an associate professor and head of the theory dept., San Bernardino Valley Coll., 1947- .
WORKS: Orchestra: Symphonic interlude; Chamber music: trio for horn, clarinet, piano; 4 piano pieces; Chorus: Missa brevis; Franciscan prayers.
1390 Pacific St., Redlands, CA 92373

BALENT, ANDREW
b. Washington, Pa., 23 July 1934. Attended Univ. of Michigan, B. M. 1956, M. M. 1960; and had private study in Chicago with William Russo.

(BALENT, ANDREW)
He has taught instrumental music and directed bands in New Haven, Mich., 1956-60; Utica, Mich., 1960-62; and Warren, Mich., 1962- . He has published many compositions for school concert bands.
17585 Oak Drive, Detroit, MI 48221

*BALENTINE, JAMES
Nalost for orch.

BALES, RICHARD
b. Alexandria, Va., 3 Feb. 1915. Attended Eastman School of Music, M. B. 1936; studied conducting on a fellowship at Juilliard School, 1939-41, and with Koussevitzky at Tanglewood, 1940. He has received many awards and citations for conducting; first prize of the Arts Club, Washington, D.C., for composition; and several commissions. He was conductor of the Virginia-North Carolina Symph., 1936-38; conductor, Nat. Gallery Orch., and music director, Nat. Gallery of Art, 1943- ; conductor, Eastman Chamber Orch., 1965-67; and guest conductor of some 30 other orchestras.
WORKS: Orchestra: 4 National Gallery Suites; Music for strings; Primavera; Three songs of early America; Episodes from a Lincoln ballet; Two impressions from an animated cartoon; Chorus: 3 suites for chorus, soloists, speaker and orch.: The Confederacy, The Union, The Republic; Gate of the year; Come away, Death; God's presence, a cappella choir; many songs and piano pieces.
National Gallery Orchestra
National Gallery of Art
Washington, DC 20565

*BALK, WESLEY
The newest opera in the world, optional development of story, Minneapolis, May 1974.

*BALL, ERNEST R.
b. Cleveland, Ohio, 22 July 1878; d. Santa Ana, Calif., 3 May 1927. Studied at Cleveland Cons.; was staff composer and pianist for Witmark Company, 1907-27. He wrote scores for musicals, including Macushla and The heart of Paddy Whack; many extremely popular songs such as Will you love me in December as you do in May?; Mother Machree; When Irish eyes are smiling; Dear little boy of mine; etc.

*BALLANTINE, EDWARD
b. Oberlin, Ohio, 6 Aug. 1886; d. Martha's Vineyard, Mass., 2 July 1971. Studied with Walter Spalding and Frederick Converse, Harvard Univ., 1903-07, highest honors in music; with Artur Schnabel and Rudolph Ganz in Berlin, 1907-09. He was faculty member, Harvard Univ., 1912-47, retiring as associate professor emeritus.
WORKS: Theatre: The lotus eaters, a musical play, 1907; Orchestra: Prelude to the delectable forest; From the garden of Hellas; The Eve of St. Agnes; By a lake in Russia; Chamber music: violin sonata; songs; Piano: Mary had a little lamb, a set of variations in the styles of 10 eminent composers, 1924, a 2nd

(BALLANTINE, EDWARD)
    set brought the variations up to date with the
    styles of Stravinsky, Gershwin, and others, 1943.

BALLARD, LOUIS W.
    b. Quapaw, Okla., 8 July 1931. Attended Univ.
    of Oklahoma, B. A., B. M. Ed. 1954; Univ. of
    Tulsa, M. M. 1962; honorary D. M., Santa Fe
    Coll., 1973; and studied composition with Mil-
    haud, Castelnuovo-Tedesco, Carlos Surinach. He
    has received annual ASCAP awards, the first
    Marion Nevins MacDowell award for American music,
    Ford Found. grant, Nat. Endowment for the Arts
    commission and 2 grants, Distinguished Achieve-
    ment award from Edpress All-American Awards
    competition, 1971, Distinguished Alumnus award
    of Tulsa Univ., Nat. Indian Achievement award,
    1972, etc. He has been chairman of music and
    drama, Inst. of American Indian Arts, Santa Fe,
    1967-   ; music curriculum specialist, Bureau
    of Indian Affairs, 1969-   ; consultant and
    arranger for music textbook publishers, author
    and lecturer on Indian music.
        WORKS: Ballet: Ji-Jo-Gweh, The witch water
    gull, 3-acts, 1962; Koshare, Barcelona, Spain,
    16 May 1966; The four moons, Tulsa, 28 Oct. 1967;
    Why the duck has a short tail, Osaka, Japan,
    EXPO '70; Orchestra: Devil's promenade, Tulsa,
    20 May 1973; Scenes from Indian life, 1966; Why
    the duck has a short tail, Phoenix, 8 May 1969;
    Chamber music: Ritmo Indio, woodwind quintet
    and Sioux flute; Desert trilogy, mixed octet,
    Lubbock, Tex., 28 Oct. 1971; Kateri Tekakwitha,
    double quintet and vocalists, 1973; Katcina
    dances, cello and piano; string trio; Rhapsody,
    4 bassoons; Cacega Ayuwipi, percussion ensemble;
    Pan-Indian rhythms, percussion; Chorus: The gods
    will hear, cantata, text based on poem of Indian
    poet, Lloyd H. New, Liberty, Mo., 8 Mar. 1966;
    Portrait of Will, a tribute to Will Rogers,
    cantata for soloists, chorus, narrator, dancers;
    The American Indian sings, songbook of Indian
    chants, with piano, percussion, guitar; Espiritu
    de Santiago, lyrics in Spanish and English.
        P. O. Box 4552, Santa Fe, NM 87501

*BALLASEYUS, VIRGINIA
    b. Hollins, Va., 14 Mar. 1893; d. Calif., 1969.
    Studied with Darius Milhaud. She wrote music for
    California Centenary productions and for tele-
    vision scores.

*BALLOU, ESTHER WILLIAMSON
    b. Elmira, N.Y., 17 July 1915; d. Washington,
    D.C., 12 Mar. 1973. Studied at Bennington Coll.;
    Mills Coll.; with Bernard Wagenaar, Juilliard
    School, M. A.; privately with Otto Luening and
    Wallingford Riegger. Her awards include a Mac-
    Dowell fellowship; an honorary doctorate, Hood
    Coll.; ASCAP award, 1969. She taught at Juil-
    liard and at Catholic Univ.; was associate
    professor, American Univ., 1959-73.
        WORKS: Orchestra: Concertino for oboe and
    strings, 1953; Prelude and allegro, 1955; Early
    American portrait, soprano and orch., 1961;
    Chamber music: 2 sonatas for 2 pianos, 1943,
    1959; Beguine, 2 pianos, 1951; piano trio, 1956;

(BALLOU, ESTHER WILLIAMSON)
    Suite for winds, 1957; sextet, brass and piano,
    1961; Capriccio, violin and piano, 1963; Lament,
    cello and piano; and choral works.

BALOGH, ERNO
    b. Budapest, 4 April 1897; U.S. citizen 1929.
    Attended the Royal Acad. of Music and Royal
    Cons. Budapest, diploma 1915, studying piano
    with Bela Bartok and composition with Zoltan
    Kodaly; studied later in New York with Josef
    Lhevine. His awards include a citation from the
    Nat. Assoc. of Amer. Composers and Conductors for
    performing the most contemporary American music
    in 1947. He was associate conductor of the
    Royal Opera, Budapest, 1915-18; conductor of the
    Chamber Opera, 1918-19; on the faculty of Pea-
    body Cons., Baltimore, 1947-60; concert pianist
    and accompanist to such artists as Fritz
    Kreisler and Lotte Lehmann.
        WORKS: Orchestra: Divertimento; Portrait of
    a city, a suite; Piano: Dirge of the North;
    Caprice antique; Arabesque (transcribed for
    violin and played by Kreisler); Pastorale at
    dawn; 1947; Dance infernale, 1949; La cigale
    joyeuse, 1951; Nothing but problems, 1966;
    Peasant dance, 1966; Debate, 1968; Restless,
    1968; Complaining, 1969; A short jet flight,
    1970; and many songs. He is author of magazine
    articles and one play, $25 an hour, produced on
    Broadway and many years later made into the
    movie One night of love.
        3900 Watson Place, N.W., Washington, DC 20016

*BALOUGH, GREGOR
    Studied at Chicago Musical Coll. and Syracuse
    Univ.; privately with Clifford Shaw in Louis-
    ville, Ky. He has published songs and violin
    pieces.

BAMBACH, PAUL ANTON
    b. Bay Village, Ohio, 14 Apr. 1950. Studied
    with Brian Dykstra, Wooster Coll.; with T. Scott
    Huston and Ellsworth Milburn, Cincinnati Coll.
    Cons. He has received commissions. He teaches
    clarinet and winds privately.
        WORKS: Chamber music: Fugue, string quar-
    tet, 1971; 3 dances for piano, 1971; 3 pieces
    for viola solo, 1974; trio for clarinet, viola,
    piano, 1974; Short piece for koto and percussion.
        25585 Hilliard Blvd., Westlake, OH 44145

BAMERT, MATTHIAS
    b. Ersigen, Switz., 5 July 1942; to U.S. 1969.
    Studied composition with Sandor Veress at Bern
    Cons., Jean Rivier at Paris Cons., Pierre Boulez
    at Darmstadt; conducting with Louis Fourestier
    in Paris, and George Szell in Cleveland. He re-
    ceived the composition award of Jeunesses Musi-
    cales, Geneva, 1968; the George Szell Memorial
    Award for conducting, 1971; and several commis-
    sions. He was principal oboe, Mozarteum Orch.,
    Salzburg, 1965-69; apprentice conductor, Cleve-
    land Orch., 1969-70; assistant conductor,
    American Symph. Orch., N.Y., 1970-71; assistant
    conductor, Cleveland Orch., 1971-
        WORKS: Orchestra: Septuria lunaris, Lucerne,
    Aug. 1970; Mantrajana, New York, 12 Dec. 1971;

BAMERT, MATTHIAS

(BAMERT, MATTHIAS)
Band: Inkblot, New York, July 1971; Chamber music: Rheology, Lucerne, Dec. 1971; Introduction and tarantella, flute, piano, percussion, New York, Jan. 1973; Incon-sequenza, solo tuba, Cleveland, May 1973; Organ: Organism, Oxford, England, July 1972.
2653 N. Moreland Blvd., Cleveland, OH 44120

BAMPTON, RUTH
b. Boston, Mass., 7 Mar. 1902. Attended New England Cons., diploma with advanced honors 1927, M. B. 1931; Boston Univ.; Eastman School of Music; Union Theological Seminary, M. S. M. 1933; studied in Paris with Nadia Boulanger and Marcel Dupre. She is a member of the American Guild of Organists. She taught at Vermont Coll., 1928-30; was associate professor, Beaver Coll., Pa., 1935-43; director of music, Pasadena Polytechnic School, 1943-64; and has been organist and choir director 1928-67. She has published numerous choral works for mixed choirs and women's voices, piano pieces, piano ensembles, and songs.
Apt. D.63, 900 East Harrison Ave.
Pomona, CA 91767

BANAITIS, KAZIMIERAS VIKTORAS
b. Lithuania, 1 Jan. 1896, d. New York, N.Y., 1963; to U.S. 1949. Studied in Prague, 1921, and at the Leipzig Cons., 1922-28. He was instructor, Kaunas State School of Music, 1928-37; director, Lithuanian Cons., 1937-40; private teacher, Brooklyn, N.Y., 1949-63.
WORKS: Opera: Jurate and Kastytis; Songs: 100 Lithuanian folk songs for solo voice or male chorus and piano.

BANCHZ, WILLIAM
b. Caracas, Venezuela, 8 Oct. 1948; to U.S. 1963. Studied piano with Margaret Chaloff, composition with Avram David in Boston; and is working toward a Ph. D. in composition with Earl Kim at Harvard Univ., where he was a teaching fellow 1972-73.
WORKS: Orchestra: El deseo sagrado, Caracas, 1974; Chamber music: string quartet; septet; clarinet sonata, unaccompanied; clarinet sonata in 9 movements; The Lord's Prayer, soprano, clarinet, cello; Psalm of joy, piano, Cambridge, 1973. Omega, piano, clarinet, violin, Cambridge, 1973.
295 Harvard St., Apt. 805
Cambridge, MA 02139

BANCROFT, B. RICHARD
b. White Plains, N.Y., 17 Mar. 1936. Studied at Fredonia State Univ. Coll., B. S.; with Robert Crane, Univ. of Wisconsin, M. S.; with Robert Marvel, New York Univ., Ed. D.; also with Percy Grainger and Rudolph Kolisch. He received 2 prizes in a State of Wisconsin composition contest and a grant from the New York State Education Dept. He taught in New York and Wisconsin schools, 1958-62; at Minot State Coll., 1962-64; and has been assistant professor, Westminster Coll., Pa., 1971-   .
WORKS: Orchestra: 3 songs for soprano and orch.; Chamber music: Soliloquy, solo trumpet; brass sextet; woodwind trio.
R.D. #3, Randall Drive
New Castle, PA 16105

*BANKS, ROBERT
b. 1930. The praise chorale, negro folk-gospel cantata.

*BANUL, CHRIS
Has had music performed at Chocorua 73, N.H., and at the Sonic Arts Union.

*BARAB, SEYMOUR
b. Chicago, Ill., 9 Jan. 1921. Has been cellist with several major orchestras; plays viola da gamba with New York Pro Musica Antiqua, 1957-   .
WORKS: Opera: Chanticleer, comic opera, 1954; The rajah's ruby, farce, 1954; Game of chance, comic opera, 1956; Philip Marshall, based on Dostoevski's The Idiot; Little Red Riding Hood, children's opera; Orchestra: Tales of rhyme and reason, narrator, dance pantomime and orch.; Chamber music: woodwind quintet; sextet for piano and woodwinds; Little suite for 3 flutes; 6 pieces for recorder trio, 1957; Chorus: The silver swan, a cappella, 1956; An angel-chorus, a cappella, 1956; First person feminine, women's voices; Songs: A child's garden of verses; Songs of perfect propriety; The rivals, song cycle.
2308 Broad St.
Yorktown Heights, NY 10598

BARATI, GEORGE
b. Gyor, Hungary 3 Apr. 1913; U.S. citizen 1944. Studied at Franz Liszt Cons., Budapest, and with Roger Sessions at Princeton. His honors include a Naumburg award; Guggenheim fellowship; Ditson award; and honorary doctorates from the Univ. of Hawaii and the Music and Arts Inst., San Francisco. He was principal cellist, Budapest Symph. Orch., 1936-38; taught at Princeton Univ., 1939-43; bandmaster, U.S. Army, 1944-46; cellist, San Francisco Symph., 1946-50; conductor, Honolulu Symph. and Opera, 1950-68; conductor, Santa Cruz County Symph., 1971-   .
WORKS: Opera: Noelani, 1971; Ballet: The love of Don Perlimplin, 1947; The dragon and the phoenix; Orchestra: symphony; Scherzo, 1946; Configuration, 1947; chamber concerto; cello concerto; guitar concerto; piano concerto; Polarization; Chamber music: violin sonata; 2 string quartets; harpsichord quartet, 1964; octet, 1966; Chorus: The water of Kane, festival ode for chorus and orch., 1966.
Villa Montalvo, P. O. Box 158
Saratoga, CA 95070

*BARBER, SAMUEL
b. West Chester, Pa., 9 Mar. 1910. Studied with Rosario Scalero, Curtis Inst. of Music, honorary D. M. His other awards include an honorary doctorate, Harvard Univ.; Prix de Rome, 1935; Pulitzer traveling fellowships, 1935, 1936; New York Music Critics awards, 1946, 1964; Guggenheim fellowship, 1947; Pulitzer prize, 1958, 1963; membership in Nat. Inst. of Arts and Letters and American Acad. of Arts and Letters; numerous commissions. He served in the U.S. Army Air Force, 1942-45, then settled near New York.
WORKS: Opera: Vanessa, 1956; A hand of bridge, 1-act, 1958; Antony and Cleopatra, 1966;

(BARBER, SAMUEL)
Ballet: Medea, 1946; Cave of the heart, 1945-47;
Orchestra: Overture to The school for scandal,
1933; Music for a scene from Shelley, 1935; A
stopwatch and an ordnance map, male chorus and
orch., 1940; symphony in one movement, 1936; violin concerto, 1941; Essays no. 1 and 2, 1942;
Capricorn concerto, flute, oboe, trumpet, and
strings, 1944; cello concerto, 1946; Knoxville:
Summer of 1915, soprano and chamber orch., 1948;
Prayers of Kierkegaard, soprano, chorus, orch.,
1954; Die natali, 1960; piano concerto, 1962;
Andromache's farewell, soprano and orch., 1962;
Toccata festiva, organ and orch., 1961; The
lovers, baritone, chorus, orch., 1970; Fadograph
from a yestern scene, Pittsburgh, 10 Sep. 1971;
Band: Commando march, 1943; Chamber music:
Serenade for string quartet, 1929; Dover Beach,
voice and string quartet, 1931; cello sonata,
1932; string quartet, 1936; piano sonata, 1949;
Summer music, woodwind quintet, 1956; string
quartet, Op. 45, New York, 29 Jan. 1973; Songs
Nuvoletta, 1947; Hermit songs, 1953; Despite and
still, song cycle, 1969; also choral works, piano
pieces.
Capricorn, Mt. Kisco, NY 10549

*BARBOUR, J. MURRAY
b. Chambersburg, Pa., 31 Mar. 1897; d. Homestead,
Pa., 9 Jan. 1970. Composed Childe Rowland,
symphonic poem; chamber works.

BARKER, WARREN E.
b. Oakland, Calif., 16 Apr. 1923. Studied at
Univ. of California, Los Angeles; privately with
Henri Pensis in Iowa and Mario Castelnuovo-
Tedesco in Los Angeles. He was staff music director, Warner Bros. Records, 1948-60, and a free
lance composer for television and motion pictures,
1960-70.
WORKS: Scores for the following television
series: Bewitched, Daktari, The flying nun, The
ghost and Mrs. Muir, Here come the brides, The
iron horse, Lawbreaker, Ripcord, That girl,
Follow the sun, Valentines day, The man and the
challenge, Bracken's world, My world and welcome
to it, Nanny and the professor, Room 222; and the
motion picture, Zebra in the kitchen.
Route 3, Box 3503, Red Bluff, CA 96080

BARKIN, ELAINE
b. New York, N.Y., 15 Dec. 1932. Studied at
Queens Coll. with Karol Rathaus; Brandeis Univ.
with Irving Fine, Harold Shapero, Arthur Berger;
and Berlin Hochschule für Musik with Boris
Blacher. Her awards include a Fulbright grant,
1956; Princeton Univ., Council of Humanities
junior fellowship; New York State Council on the
Arts commission, 1973. She has held faculty
positions at Queens Coll., 1964-70; Sarah Lawrence
Coll., 1969-70; Univ. of Michigan, 1970-73;
Princeton Univ., spring 1974.
WORKS: Chamber music: Refrains for 6 players, 1967; string quartet, 1969; 6 compositions
for piano, 1969; Prim cycles for 4, 1972; Plus
ca change, strings and percussion ensemble,
1971-72.
1208 Ferdon Road, Ann Arbor, MI 48104

*BARLOW, HOWARD
b. Plain City, Ohio, 1 May 1892. Studied at
Reed Coll., B. A. L. L. D.; with Frank E. Ward
and Cornelius Rybner at Columbia Univ. on
scholarship. He was conductor, CBS Symphony,
1927-43; Baltimore Symphony, 1939-42; Voice of
Firestone program, 1943-59; guest conductor, New
York Philharmonic. He composed songs: Lament;
Garden; Mother, I cannot mind my wheel; Margaret.

*BARLOW, SAMUEL L. M.
b. New York, N.Y., 1 June 1892. Studied at Harvard Univ., B. A. 1914; with Ottorino Respighi
in Rome. His honors include the French Legion
of Honor; Bohn Government Cross of Merit; election to fellowship, Internat. Acad. of Arts and
Letters. He is author of The astonished muse,
1961.
WORKS: Opera: Mon ami Pierrot, 1-act, Paris,
1935; Amanda, 1936; Eugenie; Orchestra: Cortege
from Ballo Sardo, 1928; piano concerto, 1930;
Circus overture; Babar, symphonic concerto,
1935; choral works and songs.

BARLOW, WAYNE
b. Elyria, Ohio, 6 Sep. 1912. Studied at Eastman School of Music, B. M. 1934, M. M. 1935,
Ph. D. 1937, studying with Bernard Rogers,
Howard Hanson, and Schoenberg; Univ. of Toronto,
1963-64, electronic music with Myron Schaeffer.
He received 2 Fulbright grants and many commissions. On the faculty at Eastman since 1937, he
is also associate dean for graduate research
studies and director of the Electronic Music
Studio. He has been a frequent guest lecturer,
conductor, and visiting composer.
WORKS: Ballet: Three moods for dancing,
1940; The black madonna, 1941; Orchestra: Songs
from the silence of Amor, 1939; Nocturne for
chamber orch., 1946; Rondo-overture, 1947; Sinfonietta in C, 1950; Lento and allegro, 1955;
Night song, 1957; Poems for music, soprano and
orch., 1958; Images, harp and orch., 1961;
Vistas, 1963; Intrada, fugue, and postlude, brass
ensemble, 1959; Chamber music: The winter's
passed, oboe and strings, 1938; Lyrical piece,
clarinet and strings, 1943; Prelude, air, and
variations, bassoon and string quartet, 1949;
piano quintet, 1951; Triptych for string quartet,
1954; Rota, chamber orch., 1959; Sinfonia da
camera, 1962; trio for oboe, viola, piano, 1964;
Elegy, viola and piano, 1967; piano sonata, 1947;
Dynamisms, 2 pianos, 1967; 2 Inventions for
piano, 1968; Chorus: Zion in exile, cantata for
chorus, soloists, orch., 1937; Madrigal for a
bright morning, 1942; The 23rd Psalm, with orch.,
1944; Mass in G, with orch., 1951; Missa Sancti
Tomae, 1959; Diversify the abyss, men's glee
club, 1964; We all believe in one true God, 1965;
Wait for the promise of the father, cantata, 1968;
Electronic: Dialogues for harp and tape, 1969;
Soundscapes, tape and orch., 1972.
Eastman School of Music, Rochester, NY 14604

*BARNARD, FRANCIS
The masque of Maska, 1-act opera, Cubicolo
Theatre, New York, 12 July 1974.

BARNARD, WILLIAM

BARNARD, WILLIAM
b. N. C., 19 May 1918. Studied at Univ. of Michigan with Percival Price; New York Union Theological Sem. with Harold Friedell. He has been
organist and choirmaster in New Jersey and
Houston, Tex., 1958-   . His published choral
works include a Benedictus in C.
    1117 Texas Ave., Houston, TX 77002

*BARNES, EDWARD SHIPPEN
b. Seabright, N. J., 14 Sep. 1887; d. Idyllwild,
Calif., 14 Feb. 1958. Studied with David Stanley
Smith and Horatio Parker, Yale Univ.; organ with
Louis Vierne in Paris. He was church organist
in New York, New Jersey, Philadelphia, and Santa
Monica, Calif. His compositions included 2 organ
symphonies; cantatas and other choral works;
sacred songs.

BARNES, JAMES CHARLES
b. Hobart, Okla., 9 Sep. 1949. Attended Univ.
of Kansas studying with John W. Pozdro, Edward C.
Mattila, Charles K. Hoag, and Allen I. McHose.
He was winner of the 1971 Kansas Music Teachers
Assoc. student composition contest. He is a
staff composer and arranger in the Univ. of
Kansas band department.
    WORKS: Orchestra: Silhouettes; Trilogy; a
suite; Prelude; Today, a jazz-rock overture;
Band: Rhapsodic essay; Colours for winds and
tape; Commencement festival overture; Hunter
Park, tone poem; 2 Preludes; Rapscallion,
overture-scherzo; Golden Brass, concert march;
Chamber music: Study for seven, brass; Duo,
clarinet and bassoon; string quartet.
    1433 Ohio St., #10, Lawrence, KS 66044

*BARNES, LARRY
The 800th lifetime, piano; has had works performed at Composers' Theatre, 1973, 1974.
    Department of Music, Heidelberg College
    Tiffin, OH 44883

BARNES, MARSHALL
b. Fairfield, Iowa, 2 Oct. 1921. Studied at
Univ. of Iowa with Philip Clapp, Addison Alspach;
and Juilliard School with James Friskin, Bernard
Wagenaar, Katherine Mann. He has had awards
from the Iowa Fed. of Music Clubs, Juilliard, and
Ohio Music Educators Assoc. He has held faculty
positions at Univ. of Iowa; Parsons Coll., Iowa;
Trinity Univ., Texas; and Ohio State Univ.,
1957-   , professor and chairman of theory and
composition, 1968-   .
    WORKS: A dirge of four cities, chorus and
orch.; Salt water ballads, chorus and orch.; Old
Worthington suite, flute, clarinet, piano, narrator; songs, choral works, piano pieces.
    33 Wilson Drive, Worthington, OH 43085

BARNETT, ALICE (Mrs. George Stevenson)
b. Lewiston, Ill., 26 May 1886. Studied piano
with her father, then at Chicago Musical Coll.
with Rudolph Ganz and Heniot Levy, composition
with Felix Borowski; then at American Cons.,
Chicago, and in Berlin with Hugo Kaun. In 1917
she settled in San Diego as a teacher, helped
found the San Diego Civic Symphony, Opera Guild,

(BARNETT, ALICE)
etc. She has published more than 60 songs,
including a cycle of 8 songs on the text of
Robert Browning's In a gondola; Serenade, on
text of Clinton Scollard; Chanson of the bells
of Oseney, text of Cale Young Rice; Music when
soft voices, Shelley; etc.
    4310 Randolph Terrace, San Diego, CA 92103

BARNETT, DAVID
b. New York, N. Y., 1 Dec. 1907. Studied at
Columbia Univ., B. A.; Mannes Coll. of Music
with Howard Brockway; Juilliard School with
Rubin Goldmark; Curtis Inst., with Rosario
Scalero; and at Ecole Normale de Musique, diploma. His awards include a commission from the
Harvard Musical Assoc. He has served on the faculty at Wellesley Coll., 1936-65; New England
Cons., 1946-65; Harvard Coll., 1955-59; Columbia
Univ. summer sessions, 1947-62; professor, Univ.
of Bridgeport, 1968-   .
    WORKS: Opera: Inner voices, 1-act; Chamber
music: Ballade, viola and piano; Fantasie, clarinet and piano; trio for piano, violin and cello;
Ballad, solo trombone, 3 saxophones, contrabass,
piano; Boat-song, mixed chorus; sonatina for
oboe and piano; Gallery for piano; songs and
piano pieces. He is author of the book, The
performance of Music, New York, 1972.
    Box 1304, Weston, CT 06880

*BARON, MAURICE
b. Lille, France, 1 Jan. 1889; d. Oyster Bay,
N. Y., 5 Sep. 1964. Composed more than 300
works in all forms including film scores.

*BARON, SAMUEL
Flutist and conductor, wrote Impressions of a
parade for brass ensemble.
    State University of New York
    Stony Brook, NY 11790

*BARR, AL
The coat of many colors, short opera on Biblical
text.

*BARR, JOHN
How brightly shines the morning star, organ
prelude.

BARRETT, ROGER L.
b. Skidmore, Mo., 12 May 1924. Studied with
Francis J. Pyle at Drake Univ. He received first
place in an Iowa Young Composers Contest and a
commission from the Music Educators Nat. Conf.,
1956. At St. Cloud State Coll. he was band
director, 1949-66; department chairman, 1965-70;
professor of theory and composition, 1970-   .
    WORKS: Orchestra: Suite: It's a boy; MENC
Golden Anniversary march; In the beginning, wind
ensemble; Chamber music: Nocturne, clarinet,
horn, violin, viola, cello.
    State College, St. Cloud, MN 56301

BARROW, ROBERT GEORGE
b. Washington, D.C., 9 July 1911. In his early
years studied privately in England with Ralph
Vaughan Williams and Paul Hindemith; Yale Univ.,

(BARROW, ROBERT GEORGE)
B. A., M. A., M. M., composition with Richard Donovan, piano with Bruce Simonds, organ with Harry Jepson. He received 2 Ditson fellowships. He was organist at National Cathedral in Washington, 1935-39; on faculty of Williams Coll. from 1940, professor and chairman of music department, 1949-71
WORKS: Orchestra: Suite for strings; Suite concertante for organ and strings; Divertimento for small orch.; Partita; Sinfonia concertante, English horn, trumpet, double bass, and orch.; Chamber music: 3 string quartets, 2 woodwind quintets; Chorus: The risen Christ, cantata for chorus and organ; Emanuel, cantata for chorus and organ; Three Psalms, men's voices and string orch.; Organ: Christus natus est; Three chorale-preludes.
4 Jerome Drive, Williamstown, MA 01267

*BARROWS, JOHN
b. Glendale, Calif., 12 Feb., 1913. Composed 2 string quartets, wind trio, several sonatas, a march for woodwind quintet; toured Latin America with a woodwind quintet, 1941, then played horn in Minneapolis Symphony.

BARRUS, LAMAR
b. Sugar City, Idaho, 22 July 1935. Studied at Univ. of Utah, Ph. D. 1968, with Leroy Robertson, Ned Rorem, and Alexei Haieff. He won first place in a Utah State composition contest. He was violinist in the Utah Symph. Orch., 1953-56, 1959-60, 1963-65; conductor of Idaho Falls Symph., 1965-70; on the faculty of Ricks Coll., 1960-   , chairman of the music department, 1972-   .
WORKS: Orchestra: Ode to libertad, a choral symphony; Chamber music: trio for 2 violins and viola; Elegy for viola and piano; Soliloquy and Berceuse for organ; Whispers of heavenly death, song cycle for soprano, viola, piano.
260 South 3rd East, Rexburg, ID 83440

*BARRYMORE, LIONEL
b. Philadelphia, Pa., 28 Apr. 1878; d. Van Nuys, Calif., 15 Nov. 1954. Noted actor, director, artist, also composed Farewell symphony, 1-act opera; orchestral works, piano pieces.

BARTH, HANS
b. Leipsig, Germany, 25 June 1897; d. Jacksonville, Fla., 8 Dec. 1956; U.S. citizen 1912. Studied at Leipsig Cons. on a scholarship and gave New York recitals at age 12. He made a special study of tonal and octave divisions and invented a portable quarter-tone piano (1928) on which he played in Carnegie Hall on 3 Feb. 1930, and for which he wrote extensively. He gave concerts in Europe and America, playing harpsichord, piano, and the quarter-tone piano. His concerto for the quarter-tone piano and quarter-tone strings was played by the Philadelphia, Cincinnati, and Havana orchestras with the composer as pianist. He was director, Yonkers Inst. of Musical Art and of the Nat. School for Musical Culture, New York, and taught piano at the Mannes School of Music.
WORKS: Theater: Miragia, operetta, 1928;

(BARTH, HANS)
Save me the waltz, incidental music; Orchestra: piano concerto, 1928; concerto for quarter-tone strings, quarter-tone piano, 1930; quintet for quarter-tone strings and piano, 1930; Drama symphony, 1940; Ten etudes for piano and orch., 1943; Peace symphony; Piano: 2 sonatas, 1929, 1932; and songs.

BARTHELSON, JOYCE HOLLOWAY
b. Yakima, Wash., 18 May 1908. Studied composition with Julius Gold, Otto Cesana, Roy Harris; piano with Elizabeth Quaile, Helene Barere; conducting with Antonia Brico. In 1967 she received first prize of ASCAP and the Nat. Fed. of Music Clubs for an opera. She was a vocal and ensemble coach at NBC in San Francisco, 1930-35; assistant conductor, N. Y. Women's Symph., 1935-40; composer-in-residence, Western Maryland Coll., 1942-44; director of many choruses in N. Y. area; co-founder and co-director of a music school in Scarsdale, N. Y., 1944-   .
WORKS: Opera: Feathertop, opera buffa; Chanticleer, comic fantasy; Greenwich Village, 1910; The king's breakfast, Atlantic City, April 1973; Orchestra: Overature in a; Of time and the river, a suite; The Forty-niners for soloists, chorus, orch; Spin, spin, orch. and soloists; concerto for 2 pianos; oboe concerto with chamber orch.; Savannah, overture; The tin soldier; Weather report, suite in 6 movements; many choral works including The first Palm Sunday, a cantata; and piano pieces.
25 Central Park West, New York, NY 10023

*BARTHOLOMEW, MARSHALL MOORE
b. Belleville, Ill., 3 Mar. 1885. Chiefly a choral conductor and arranger, but wrote many songs.

BARTLES, ALFRED H.
b. Nashville, Tenn., 10 Nov. 1930. Studied at Univ. of Mississippi, B. A.; Ohio Univ., M. F. A.; cello with Claus Adam, composition with Karl Ahrendt. He received 2 grants from the Waldorf Education Found. for residence and composing in Germany, 1969-71. He was a free lance musician, composer, and teacher in New York, 1954-69; on faculty, Schiller Coll., Heidelberg, Germany, 1970-73; and Tennessee Tech. Univ., 1973-   ; and taught 3 years at Sewanee Summer Music Center.
WORKS: Orchestra: Theme in three, 1954; Music for symph orch. and jazz ensemble, Nashville, 1966; Ballad for cello and chamber orch., 1968; Engadine overture, Des Moines, 1970; Excalibur, Sewanee, Tenn., 1972; Band: Music City, USA, 1964; Applachian portrait, 1965; Excalibur, Athens, Ohio, 1960; Scherzo for tuba and wind ensemble, 1969; Chamber music: trio for clarinet, cello, piano, 1954; quartet for piano, viola, clarinet, cello, 1967; Ceremonial music, trumpet and organ, 1968; Elegy, bass trombone and piano, 1969; Lament, variations, and metamorphoses, woodwind quintet, Sewanee, 1969; sonatina for trumpet, 1972; Chorus: Child Jesus,

BARTLES, ALFRED H.

(BARTLES, ALFRED H.)
1967; Jazz: Louisiana jazz suite, 1961; Ballad for trumpet and jazz ensemble, 1962.
Dept. of Music
Tennessee Technological University
Cookeville, TN 38501

*BARTLETT, FLOY
Published songs and choral works.
Burlington, IA 52601

*BARTLETT, HARRY
1922. 4 holidays for percussion.

BARTOW, NEVETT
b. New York, N. Y., 7 Nov. 1939; d. Blairstown, N. J., 21 Nov. 1973. Studied at Manhattan School of Music with Vittorio Giannini and Ludmila Ulehla; in Rome with Ildebrando Pizzeti; and in Vienna with Karl Schiske. He received the Nat. Arts Club young artists' award, 1959; nominated for Princeton Univ. distinguished teachers award for N. J., 1972; Outstanding Secondary Educator of America, 1973; He was chairman of the music department, Blair Academy, 1962-73.
WORKS: Orchestra: Summer shadow, elegy for orch.; 3 symphonic dances, Norwalk, Conn., Dec. 1973; Chamber music: flute sonata, 1970; Divertimento, woodwind quintet; 3 organ sonatas; clarinet sonata; Soliloquy, cello and piano; Variations and fugue for piano; Toccata for piano; Chorus: The tower of Babel, cantata; Christmas cantata; A Thanksgiving exultation.

BASART, ROBERT
b. South Dakota, 17 Nov. 1926. Studied at Univ. of California, Berkeley, with Andrew Imbrie; and Mills Coll. with Darius Milhaud. He received a Hertz traveling fellowship. He was lecturer, California State Univ., San Francisco, 1966-68; and associate professor, California State Univ. at Hayward, 1968-   .
WORKS: Chamber music: Fantasy, flute and piano; Variations, cello and piano; Little suite, string quartet; Excursion, chorus and tape; Kansas City dump, clarinet, violin, cello, piano, tape; Serenade, soprano, flute, clarinet, piano, tape.
2419 Oregon St., Berkeley, CA 94705

*BASNEY, ELDON E.,
Studied with Gustav Strube, Peabody Cons. His awards include a MacDowell fellowship and performances at Lincoln Center, Nat. Asso. of American Composers and Conductors, and Eastman Festival, 1968. He has published Serenade for string trio.
Music Department, Houghton College
Houghton, NY 14744

BASS, CLAUDE L.
b. Gainesville, Tex., 31 Oct. 1935. Studied at Univ. of Oklahoma with Violet Archer; North Texas State Univ. with Samuel Adler. He won 2 awards in the Broadman anthem competition, 1959 and 1962. He was a high school choral director, 1957-65; and associate professor, Oklahoma Baptist Univ., 1965-   . He composes primarily

(BASS, CLAUDE L.)
choral works and has many published anthems such as Thy boundless love and Jesus, Thou joy of loving hearts
Oklahoma Baptist University
Shawnee, OK 74801

*BASSETT, KAROLYN WELLS
b. Derby, Conn., 2 Aug. 1892; d. 2 June 1931.
Composed songs and choral works.

BASSETT, LESLIE
b. Hanford, Calif., 22 Jan. 1923. Studied at Fresno State Coll., B. A. 1947; Univ. of Michigan, M. M. 1949, D. M. 1956, with Ross Lee Finney; Ecole Normale de Musique, Paris, with Arthur Honneger; Nadia Boulanger, Paris; Roberto Gerhard, U.S.; electronic music with Mario Davidovsky. His many awards include the Pulitzer Prize, Prix de Rome, Soc. for the Publication of American Music, Nat. Inst. of Arts and Letters, Nat. Found. for the Arts, U.S. representative to UNESCO, 1966, Nat. Asso. of College Wind and Percussion Instructors, Univ. of Michigan regents citation, Guggenheim fellowship 1973-74, and many commissions. He served as trombonist and arranger in U.S. Army bands during World War II, and has been professor of composition at Univ. of Michigan since 1952.
WORKS: Orchestra: Variations for orchestra, Rome, 6 July 1963, Philadelphia, 22 Oct. 1965; Colloquy, 1969; Five movements for orch., Rome, 5 July 1962; Forces, 1972; Band: Designs, images, and textures, 1964; Brass: trombone quartet, 1949; horn sonata, 1952; trombone sonata, 1954; suite for unaccompanied trombone, 1957; Easter triptych, 1958; brass trio, 1953; Chamber music: trio for viola clarinet, piano, 1953; string quintet, 1954; clarinet duet, 1955; viola sonata, 1956; Five pieces for string quartet, 1957; woodwind quintet, 1958; cello duets, 1959; violin sonata, 1959; piano quintet, 1962; string quartet, 1962; Music for cello and piano, 1966; Nonet, winds and piano, 1967; Music for saxophone and piano, 1968; piano sextet, New York, April 1972; Sounds remembered, violin and piano, 1972; Chorus: The lamb, Blake text, 1952; Out of the depths, 1957; For city, nation, world, 1959; Moonrise, D. H. Lawrence text, 1960; Remembrance, 1960; Eclogue, encomium, and evocation, 1962; Prayers for divine service, men's voices, 1956; Psalm 64, Hear my prayer, O Lord, 1965; Notes in the silence, text by Hammarskjöld, 1966; Moon canticle, with cello and amplified narrator, 1969; Celebration in praise of Earth, 1970; Electronic: Three studies in electronic sound, 1965; Triform, 1966; Collect, chorus and tape, 1969; also songs and piano and organ pieces.
1618 Harbal Drive, Ann Arbor, MI 48105

BATEMAN, FLORENCE GOLSON. See GOLSON, FLORENCE

*BATES, DAVID
Was one of four winners in the Stowe, Vt., Inst. composer competition, 1974, and also received a Prix de Rome fellowship at the American Acad. in Rome, 1974.
Music Department, Fresno State College
Fresno, CA 93710

BATSTONE, PHILIP NORMAN
b. Boston, Mass., 4 Jan. 1933. Studied at Boston Univ. with Henry Kaufmann; Hochschule für Musik, Berlin, with Boris Blacher, Silvia Kind; Princeton Univ. with Roger Sessions, Oliver Strunk, Milton Babbitt. He has received commissions for compositions. He was on the faculty of City Coll. of New York, 1963-65; Univ. of Colorado, 1965-71; Univ. of Illinois, 1971-73.
WORKS: A 12-minute computer piece; Parvum, a music theatre piece comprising A Mother Goose primer, Fun and games, and The phoenix and turtle; John Street, for piano solo; and many others in all genres.
Box J, Pembroke, ME 04666

*BAUER, MARION EUGENIE
b. Walla Walla, Wash., 15 Aug. 1887; d. South Hadley, Mass., 9 Aug. 1955. Studied with Nadia Boulanger and Louis Campbell-Tipton in Paris; with Paul Ertel in Berlin; and with Henry Holden Huss in New York. She received an honorary M. A. from Whitman Coll., Walla Walla, Wash., 1932. She held teaching positions at Mills Coll.; Carnegie Inst. of Technology; annually at Chautauqua Inst.; New York Univ.; Juilliard School; and from 1940 at the Inst. of Musical Art. Her compositions included orchestral works, chamber music, choral works. She was also co-author and author of several books on music.

BAUMAN, JON WARD
b. Big Rapids, Mich., 7 June 1939. Studied at Univ. of Colorado, B. M. 1961, with Cecil Effinger; Univ. of Illinois, M. M. 1963, D. M. A. 1972, with J. Robert Kelly, Salvatore Martirano; in Cologne, Germany, with Bernd-Alois Zimmermann. His awards include Fulbright grant and private commissions. He taught in Chicago public schools, 1969-70, and has been an assistant professor, Frostburg State Coll., 1970-   .
WORKS: Chamber music: string quartet; saxophone quartet; brass quintet; quintet for trumpet, guitar, and 3 double basses; Dissertation, chamber choir, chamber orch., tape, 1972; Mobiles, saxophone quartet and tape, 1972. He has also composed orchestral, theater and multimedia works.
12 Beall St., Frostburg, MD 21532

*BAUMGARTNER, H. LEROY
d. 18 Sep. 1969. Published The city, choral suite; The vision, for organ.

BAUR, JOHN WILLIAM
b. St. Louis, Mo., 27 Feb. 1947. Studied at Univ. of Cincinnati with Jeno Takacs and Paul Cooper; in London under a Fulbright grant with Richard Rodney Bennett, Thea Musgrave, and Daphne Oram. He taught at Univ. of Cincinnati, 1969-72; and at Shenandoah Cons., 1973-   .
WORKS: Orchestra: Anastrophe; Alaomai I; Band: Symphonics; Sinfonia I; Chamber music: string quartet; quintet; Chamber concerto No. 1, 6 singers and ensemble; Chamber concerto No. 2; Chorus: Acquainted with the night; Praise the Lord, chorus and organ.
104 Richards Ave., Winchester, VA 22601

BAVICCHI, JOHN
b. Boston, Mass., 25 Apr. 1922. Studied engineering until entering the U.S. Navy in 1943. After active service in World War II he attended the New England Cons., B. M. 1952; and Harvard Univ., 1952-55, studying with Francis Judd Cooke, Carl McKinley, Walter Piston, Otto Gombosi, and A. T. Davison. He has received grants from the Nat. Inst. of Arts and Letters, 1959, the Amer. Symph. Orch. League, 1961, and several commissions. Since 1952 he has taught in schools and colleges in the Boston area, and conducted numerous choruses and orchestras. He joined the faculty of Berklee Coll. of Music in 1964.
WORKS: Orchestra: Tobal, 1952; Four songs, contralto with orch., Cambridge, 17 Dec. 1952; clarinet concerto, Boston, 14 May 1958; Suite No. 1, Cambridge, 16 Apr. 1961; Farewell and hail, poem by Farber, soprano, trumpet, strings, 1957; A concert overture, Boston, 5 Dec. 1957; Concertante, 1961; Three Psalms, with chorus and soloists, Boston, 23 Apr. 1963; Fantasia on Korean folk tunes, Brookline, 10 June 1969; Band: Festival symphony, Cambridge, 6 Nov. 1965; J. D. C. March, Bowdoin, Me., 20 Jan. 1968; Spring festival overture, Boston, 3 July 1970; Suite No. 3, Atlanta, 3 Feb. 1970; Large ensembles: Summer incident, Boston, 17 Nov. 1959; Fireworks, 1962; Chamber music: 7 trios for various instruments; 3 string quartets; 11 sonatas; 2 woodwind quintets; 2 saxophone quartets, vocal works, etc.
Box 182, Astor Station, Boston, MA 02123

BAYLOR, HUGH MURRAY
b. What Cheer, Iowa, 8 Apr. 1913. Studied at Univ. of Iowa with Philip Greeley Clapp, and in France with Nadia Boulanger and Robert Casadesus. He has been on the faculty of Knox Coll. since 1942, and professor and chairman of the music department, 1968-   . His compositions include songs, chamber music, and a comic opera, By Gemini.
Knox College, Galesburg, IL 61401

BAZELON, IRWIN ALLEN
b. Evanston, Ill., 4 June 1922. Attended DePaul Univ., B. A. 1945, M. A. 1946, then studied composition with Darius Milhaud at Mills Coll., and with Ernest Bloch at Univ. of California. His awards include MacDowell fellowships, several commissions, and a first prize awarded by the Cleveland Symphony. A resident of New York since 1948, he devotes full time to composition and teaches a course on music for films at the School for Visual Arts.
WORKS: Theatre: incidental music to The merry wives of Windsor and The taming of the shrew; Orchestra: Ballet Centauri 17, concert ballet, 1960; Concert overture, 1952, revised 1960; 6 symphonies: No. 1, 1960, Kansas City, 29 Nov. 1963; No. 2, Short symphony, Testament to a big city, Washington, 4 Dec. 1962; No. 3, for brass, percussion, piano, and sextet, 1963; No. 4, 1965; No. 5, Indianapolis, 1966; No. 6, Kansas City, Dec. 1970; Symphony concertante, clarinet, trumpet, marimba, and orch., 1969; Dramatic fanfare for 1970, Cleveland, 1970; Excursion for orch., Kansas City, 5 Mar. 1966;

BAZELON, IRWIN ALLEN

(BAZELON, IRWIN ALLEN)
Chamber music; 2 string quartets; suite for clarinet, cello, piano, 1947; Ballet suite for small ensemble, 1949; Movimento da camera, flute, bassoon, horn, harpsichord, 1955; chamber symphony for 7 instruments, 1957; brass quintet, 1963; string quartet with amplified contrabass, 1967; Early American suite, harpsichord and woodwind quintet; duo for viola and piano; 3 piano sonatas; Chamber concerto for 14 players, Churchill Downs, N. Y., 16 May 1971; and music for industrial, documentary, and art films.
142 East 71st St., New York, NY 10021

*BEACH, BENNIE
b. Mississippi, 1925. Studied at Delta State Coll., B. S. 1948; at George Peabody Coll., M. A., M. Ed. 1951-52. He is associate professor, Western Kentucky State Coll.; plays trumpet in the Nashville Symphony Orchestra.
WORKS: Wind ensemble: Fanfare and chorale, brass choir; quintet for brass; Chamber music: Soliloquy, chamber orch.; Lamento, tuba solo; Suite for trombone or baritone; Peace, song for soprano to Teasdale text; also band and choral works.
1670 Normal Drive, Bowling Green, KY 42101

*BEACH, BRUCE C.
b. Philadelphia, Pa., 19 July 1903; d.   .
Taught at Eastern Baptist Coll.; received Univ. of Pennsylvania award for Plaza, a ballet symphony; also composed for band, chorus, and chamber groups.

*BEACH, JOHN PARSONS
b. Gloversville, N. Y., 11 Oct. 1877; d. Pasadena, Calif., 6 Nov. 1953. Wrote 2 operas, 2 ballets, orchestral and chamber works, songs.

BEACH, PERRY W.
b. Lincoln, Neb., 24 Oct. 1917. Studied at Univ. of Nebraska with Wilbur Chenoweth, and at Eastman School of Music, Ph. D. 1953, with Bernard Rogers, Howard Hanson, and Herbert Elwell. He has held faculty positions at Union Coll., Lincoln, Neb., 1940-42; Andrews Univ., Berrien Springs, Mich., 1947-57; Loma Linda Univ., La Sierra Campus, Calif., professor, 1957-   .
WORKS: Orchestra: piano concerto, 1952; symphony movement, 1953; Chorus: Christmas spiritual; Song of Zion; Rejoice in the Lord; Then said Isaiah; O Thou Redeemer; Lament for a fallen president, chorus, snare drum, organ, 1963; Kyrie eleison, 1973; Clap your hands.
5208 Peacock Lane, Riverside, CA 92505

BEADELL, ROBERT MORTON
b. Chicago, Ill., 18 June 1925. Studied with Anthony Donato at Northwestern Univ., B. M. 1949, M. M. 1950; with Leo Sowerby at Chicago Musical Coll.; and with Darius Milhaud at Mills Coll. His awards include a Thor Johnson award, 1950; Woods fellowship, 1962-63; grants from the Ford Found., Univ. of Nebraska, Nat. Council on the Arts; ASCAP award. His faculty positions have been at Central Coll., Fayette, Mo., 1950-52; professor, Univ. of Nebraska, 1954-   .

(BEADELL, ROBERT MORTON)
WORKS: Opera: The kingdom of Caraway, operetta, 1957; The Sweetwater affair, 1960; The number of fools, 1965-66; Napoleon, 1973; Orchestra: Trilogy, 1950; Canzona, 1952; Overture to youth, 1961; symphony No. 1, 1963; Children's zoo fantasy, 1969; Children's ballet, Mayflower, 1972; Band and Brass ensemble: Introduction and allegro, 1950; Song of Normandy, 1955; Contours, solo trombone with band; Gemini, percussion and band, 1956; Adagio, 1961; Dialogue, 1964; The mercenaries, 1968; Three sketches, tuba ensemble, 1971; Chicago dance, No. 1, jazz ensemble, 1973; Chamber music: cello sonata, 1949; piano trio, 1949; woodwind quintet, 1949; Eclogue, chamber orch., 1949; Theme and variations, clarinet, cello, piano, 1959; Lyric piece, oboe, piano, 1963; Three sketches, clarinet quartet, 1963; many choral works including Elegy for a dead soldier, the U.S. entry for the Italia Prize, 1958.
7541 Old Post Road, Lincoln, NB 68508

BEALE, DAVID BROOKS
b. Martin, Tenn., 15 Jan. 1945. Studied at Duke Univ., 1963-67; Univ. of North Carolina, with Roger Hannay, 1967-68; Cornell Univ., with Karel Husa, 1970-73. He received a scholarship to Composers Conference, 1972, and a performance award, Delius Composition Contest, Jan. 1974. As a Peace Corps volunteer he was municipal band director at Abrego, Colombia, 1968-70.
WORKS: Chamber music: Prelude and allegro for strings, 1968; Spirit of St. Louis, brass quintet, 1970; Pattern studies, woodwind quartet, 1972; Martir doloroso, low brass and saxophones, 1972; Asamadaki, trombone sextet, 1973; Chorus: Ecclesiastes, a cappella, 1971.
Box 82, R. D. 1, Richford, NY 13835

*BEALE, FREDERIC FLEMING
b. Troy, Kan., 13 July 1876; d. Caldwell, Idaho, 16 Feb. 1948. Composed 3 operettas, many songs.

BEALE, JAMES
b. Wellesley Hills, Mass., 20 Jan. 1924. Attended Harvard Univ., A. B. 1945; Berkshire Music Center, 1946; Yale Univ., B. M. 1946, M. M. 1947; studied with Irving Fine, Walter Piston, Aaron Copland, Richard Donovan. He has received a Guggenheim grant, 1958-59, and the Woods-Chandler Prize, 1947. He was on the faculty at Univ. of Louisville, 1947-48, and Univ. of Washington since 1948, professor, 1968-   .
WORKS: Orchestra: Symphony for chamber orch., Cressay symphony; Music for soprano and orch; Band: Sinfonietta; Chamber music; 2 string quartets; piano trio; 8 piano sonatas; Pisces ascending, percussion and piano; Songs: How beautiful are the dwellings of peace.
4552 51st N. E., Seattle, WA 98105

BEALL, JOHN
b. Belton, Tex., 12 June 1942. Studied at Baylor Univ., B. M., M. M., with Richard Willis; Eastman School of Music, with Samuel Adler and Wayne Barlow. He was awarded the Louis Lane Prize, 1972, and the Howard Hanson Prize, 1973. He has

(BEALL, JOHN)
been on the faculty at Southwest Texas State
Univ., 1973-   .
WORKS: Orchestra: Essay for orchestra,
Dallas, 1965; Songs of Autumn, song cycle for
tenor and orch., Dallas, 1966; Lament for those
lost in the war, Rochester, 1972; Concerto for
piano and wind orch., Rochester, 1973; Piano:
Partita, 1967.
2721 North LBJ Drive, San Marcos, TX 78666

*BEAN, MABEL
Published piano solos, sacred solos, work for
narrator and orch.
Little Rock, AR 72201

BEASLEY, RULE
b. Texarkana, Ark., 12 Aug. 1931. Studied at
Southern Methodist Univ. with Jack Kilpatrick;
Juilliard School with Robert Ward; and Univ. of
Illinois with Thomas Frederickson. He won first
place in a Southeastern Composers' League contest
in 1963. He was director, School of Music, Centenary Coll. of Louisiana, 1963-66; associate
professor, North Texas State Univ., 1966-73; on
music faculty, Santa Monica Coll., Calif.,
1973-   .
WORKS: Lyric prelude for orchestra; Concerto for tuba and band; Dialogue for bassoon and
11 instruments; Music for brass, 1972; Three
studies for bassoon and piano.
2837 Dunleer Place, Los Angeles, CA 90064

*BEATON, ISABELLA
b. Grinnell, Iowa, 20 May 1870; d. Mt. Pleasant,
Henry County, Iowa, 19 Jan. 1929. Composed an
opera, a symphony, piano pieces.

*BEATTIE, HERBERT
b. 1926. Has published choral works.
Hofstra University, Hempstead, NY 11550

BEAULIEU, JOHN
b. Indianapolis, Ind., 8 Feb. 1948. Studied at
Purdue Univ., B. A. in recreation therapy, 1970,
and at Indiana Univ., composition with Franz
Kamin, Iannis Xenakis, and John Eaton. He was
president of FIASCO, Bloomington, Ind., 1972-73,
member of its board of directors, 1973-   ; and
supervisor of music therapy, Bellevue Hospital,
New York, 1973-   .
WORKS: Piano: Spots, Bacarolle, At the ballet, Gymnastique No. 1, 2, 3, variations on
Claire de lune, all 1973; Mixed media:
Crumselzer bleu, piano 2 narrators, pantomimist,
1972; Pollution for children, 4 performers, elec-
trified garbage, timer, 1972; Occupant, any number of performers, 1972; The enlightment of
Morris, 3 dancers, tuba, flute, piccolo, percussion, 2 mini-dirty sine-wave generators, soprano
and bass narrators, weight lifter, timer, 3 slide
projectionists, piano and cat house, 1972; Telephone, magnetic tape, 1973; Three preludes, for
clarinet, slide projector, and performer, 1973.
19 Leonard St., New York, NY 10013

*BEAUMONT, VIVIAN
Has published songs and piano compositions.
7025 Warwick Road, Indianapolis, IN 46220

BEAVER, PAUL H., JR.
b. Salem, Ohio, 14 Aug. 1925. Has studied with
Marion MacArtor, Garth Edmundson, Henry Leland
Clarke, Franklyn Marks, and Paul Glass. His
film scores have won two awards, 1969 and 1973,
at the Atlanta Film Festival. He has been
composer-producer and executive of Parasound,
Inc., San Francisco, 1967-
WORKS: Film scores: Breakthrough, Legend
days are over, The Baggs (educational films);
Close but free (television); Come to your senses,
The final programme (theatrical films); Ragnarok,
In a wild sanctuary, Gandharva, All good men
(extended works for the record media). He has
published Nonesuch guide to electronic music, a
syllabus, textbook, with recorded examples, 1967.
2825 Hyans St., Los Angeles, CA 90026

BECK, JOHN H.
b. Lewisburg, Pa., 16 Feb. 1933. Studied percussion at Eastman School of Music. He was percussionist, U.S. Marine Band, 1955-59; 1st
percussionist, 1959-62, timpanist, 1962-   ,
Rochester Philharmonic Orch.; faculty, Eastman
School of Music, 1962-   .
WORKS: Percussion: Rhapsody for percussion
and band; Jazz variants for percussion ensemble;
timpani sonata.
Eastman School of Music
26 Gibbs St., Rochester, NY 14604

BECK, JOHN NESS
b. Warren, Ohio, 11 Nov. 1930. Studied composition at Ohio State Univ. Since 1961 he has been
owner of a retail sheet music store in Columbus,
Ohio.
WORKS: Reflection for concert band; flute
sonata; Five carol fantasies for piano; more
than 30 sacred choral works including: Contemporary music for the church service; Hymn for
our time; Litany of thanksgiving; Upon this rock;
and vocal solos.
3841 North High St., Columbus, OH 43214

BECK, MARTHA (Mrs. G. Howard Carragan)
b. Sodaville, Ore., 19 Jan. 1902. Attended
Oberlin Coll., B. M. 1924; American Cons., M. M.
1927; Juilliard School, 1927-29; studied composition in Berlin. Her teachers included Frances
Frothingham, Adolf Weidig, Silvio Scionti, George
Whitfield Andrews, and Hugo Leichtentritt. She
received 2 Mu Phi Epsilon prizes and the Adolf
Weidig gold medal. She taught at both the Amer-
ican Cons. and North Central Coll., Naperville,
Ill., 1924-29; Emma Willard School, Troy, N. Y.,
1932-48; then privately in Troy.
WORKS: Suite in five movements for piano;
Suite for violin and piano; piano quintet; and
other piano works. She is author of The Martha
Beck Rhythm Rule Method.
Box 261, R. D. 3, Troy, NY 12180

BECK, THEODORE

BECK, THEODORE
b. Oak Park, Ill., 17 Apr., 1929. Studied at
Northwestern Univ. with Anthony Donato and Ewald
Nolte. He has been professor, Concordia Coll.,
Seward, Neb., 1953-   ; was organist and choir
director in Lincoln, Neb., 1954-56.
WORKS: Chorus: The Christmas story; Little
Christmas concert; 8 anthems for treble voices
and instruments; Instrumental: Christmas songs
for handbells; 47 hymn intonations for organ.
Concordia College, Seward, NB 68434

*BECKER, JOHN J.
b. Henderson, Ky., 22 Jan. 1886; d. Wilmette,
Ill., 21 Jan. 1961. Wrote a ballet, a lyric
drama, 3 symphonies, 2 piano concertos, horn
concerto, violin concerto, viola concerto, etc.

BECKETT, WHEELER M. A.
b. San Francisco, Calif., 7 Mar. 1898. Studied
piano in Paris with Camille Decreuse; composi-
tion with Daniel Gregory Mason at Columbia Univ.;
and conducting with Felix Weingartner in Basel,
Switzerland. He has been guest conductor of the
Berlin Philh.; Vienna Philh.; Straram Orch.,
Paris; Water Gate concerts, D.C.; Boston "Pops";
and others. He was organist-choirmaster, Grace
Cathedral, San Francisco, 1922-27; conductor of
Young People's Concerts, San Francisco, 1923-27,
Richmond, Va., 1932-36, Boston, 1938-48, New
York, 1957-58; and was appointed by the State
Dept. to found and conduct orchestras in the
Far East, 1959-62.
WORKS: Opera: The queen's mirror; Inci-
dental music: Asses ears; Rajvara; Orchestra:
Symphony in c; The mystic trumpeter; The sea at
Point Lobos; Open road; Dedication to Indonesia,
chorus, orch., and soprano vocalize; songs. He
was conductor and commentator on two albums of
records: The complete orchestra and Essential
musical knowledge widely used in music appreciation classes.
277 Walnut St., Englewood, NJ 07631

*BECKHELM, PAUL
b. Kankakee, Ill., 3 July 1906; d. Mt. Vernon,
Iowa. Studied at Northwestern Univ., B. M.;
Eastman School of Music, M. M. Ph. D.; and with
Nadia Boulanger. He taught at Sterling Coll.,
Kansas State Coll. at Fort Hays; Hood Coll.; and
at Cornell Coll. His works include Tragic march
for brass choir, and a violin sonatina.

BECKLER, S. R.
b. Escondido, Calif., 26 Dec. 1923. Studied at
Univ. of Pacific. M. A. 1951, with J. Russell
Bodley; Eastman School of Music with Wayne
Barlow; Univ of Southern California, with George
Perle. His awards include a Pi Kappa Lambda
prize, 1960, and commissions. He held a faculty
research lectureship at Univ. of the Pacific,
1970, and has been professor 1970-   .
WORKS: 3 Chamber operas: Faust, 1945; The
outcasts of Poker Flat, 1960; The catbird seat,
1973; Incidental music: Othello, 1957; Oedipus
the king, 1966; Hamlet, 1966; Orchestra: 4 symphonies, 1946, 1951, 1953, 1956; Festival overture, 1957; Etude on an old French tune, 1963;

(BECKLER, S. R.)
Dirge, 1966; The seven ages of man, 1972; Band:
Capriccio, with baritone horn, 1955; Fire water,
1967; Chamber music: Rhapsody, violin and piano,
1957; 4 woodwind quintets, 1957-68; 7 little wind
sonatas, 1958-61; string quartet, 1961; Quotations
from Mr. Agnew, oboe, viola, piano, 1969; violin sonata, 1970; cello sonata, 1971; percussion
sonata with oboe, horn, violin, cello, piano,
1973; The Stars and Stripes forawhile, violin
and percussion, 1973; Chorus: The resurrection,
oratorio, 1955; Man and divers bestiall com-
panyons, 1969; songs and piano pieces.
Conservatory Annex, University of the Pacific
Stockton, CA 95204

BECKSTEAD, JOSEPH R.
b. Pocatello, Idaho, 3 May 1907. Attended Univ.
of Wyoming, Univ. of Utah, Columbia Univ., and
Univ. of Southern California, D. M. A. 1968,
where he studied composition with Ingolf Dahl.
He has been professor at California State Univ.,
Los Angeles, since 1951. His works are chiefly
hymns, choral compositions, and arrangements for
strings.
1908 Orange Grove Ave., Alhambra, CA 91802

*BEDELL, ROBERT LEACH
b. Jersey City, N. J., 13 Feb. 1909. Studied at
Southwestern Coll., D. M.; Findlay Coll.,
Litt. D. He is church organist and choirmaster;
composer-in-residence, Passeonest Monastery.
His works include Fantasia in C for orch.;
Legende for organ; Methinks I hear, chorus.

*BEECHER, CARL MILTON
b. Lafayette, Ind., 22 Oct. 1883; d. Portland,
Ore., 21 Nov. 1968. Taught at Portland School
of Music. He wrote chiefly piano pieces.

BEELER, C. ALAN
b. St. Louis, Mo., 10 Feb. 1939. Studied at
Illinois Wesleyan Univ. with Will Ogdon, and at
Washington Univ., Ph. D. 1973, with Harold
Blumenfeld, Robert Wykes, and Robert Baker. He
was instructor at Stevens Point State Univ.,
Wis., 1967-70, and assistant professor, Eastern
Kentucky Univ., 1970-   .
WORKS: Orchestra: Quintessence II; Chamber music: oboe sonata, 1960; Piece for piano
after Roger Sessions, 1960; Chamber piece for
flute, clarinet, viola, piano, 1965; Electronic
mobile for rocks and metal, 1966.
510 Ballard Drive, Apt. 3
Richmond, KY 40475

BEERMAN, BURTON
b. Atlanta, Ga., 6 Dec. 1943. Attended Florida
State Univ., B. M., studying with John Boda and
Harold Schiffman; Univ. of Michigan, M. M.,
D. M. A. with Ross Lee Finney, Leslie Bassett,
George B. Wilson, George Cacioppo, and Eugene
Kurtz. He won first prize in the Pittsburgh
Flute Club composition contest, 1970, and was
finalist in the 1968 Gaudeamus Internat. Festi-
val, Netherlands. He has been assistant profes-
sor at Bowling Green State Univ., since 1970,
and is also director of the Electronic Music

(BEERMAN, BURTON)

Studio and associate director of the New Music Ensemble.

WORKS: <u>Frame</u> for 6 flutes, 1970; <u>Impressions of birth</u>, 16 solo voices, percussion and 2 pianos; Mixed media: <u>Mixtures for voices</u>, instruments, tape; <u>Sensations</u>, clarinet and tape; <u>Improvisations</u> for dancers, actors, various instruments, 1970; <u>Mass</u> for tenor voice, flute, harp and tape, 1968; <u>Misogamy</u>, string quartet and tape; <u>Polygraph II</u>, piano, live electronic processing, and visuals; "C" for organ, dancer, percussion, live electronics, and visuals.

#10 Springhill Apts.
Bowling Green, OH 43402

BEESON, JACK

b. Muncie, Ind., 15 July 1921. Studied with Burrill Phillips, Bernard Rogers, and Howard Hanson at Eastman School of Music, B. M. 1943, M. M. 1943, Ph.D. 1944; privately with Bela Bartok, 1943-44; conducting and musicology at Columbia Univ., 1945-47; American Acad. in Rome, 1948-50. His awards include the Rome Prize, Fulbright and Guggenheim grants, composer-in-residence at the American Acad. in Rome, 1965-66, Marc Blitzstein award, Nat. Inst. of Arts and Letters, 1968, and ASCAP awards. In addition to being a faculty member at Columbia Univ., 1945-   , and MacDowell professor of music, 1967-   , he was conductor of Columbia's Opera Workshop, 1945-50 and of the productions of Columbia Theatre Associates, 1945-52, and lecturer at Juilliard School, 1961-63.

WORKS: Opera: <u>Jonah</u>, 1950; <u>Hello out there</u>, N. Y., 27 May 1954; <u>The sweet bye and bye</u>, N. Y., 21 Nov. 1957; <u>Lizzie Borden</u>, N. Y., 25 Mar. 1965; <u>My heart's in the highlands</u>, NET, 17 Mar. 1970; <u>Captain Jinks of the Horse Marines</u>, Kansas City, Mo., 20 Sep. 1975; Orchestra: <u>Transformations</u>, 1959; a symphony, 1959; Band: <u>Fanfare</u>, 1963; <u>Commemoration</u>, band and chorus, 1960; Chamber music: 5 piano sonatas; <u>Song</u>, flute and piano, 1945; <u>Interlude</u>, violin and piano, 1945; viola sonata, 1953; <u>The Hoosier balks</u>, 10 instruments, 1967; <u>The Hawkesley blues</u>, 10 instruments; piano and organ pieces, many vocal solos and choral works including <u>The bear hunt</u>, text by Abraham Lincoln, set for tenor, baritone, and bass, N. Y. 21 April 1961. He is the author of music reviews and magazine articles and has adapted the texts of most of his operas and some of his vocal works.

445 Riverside Drive, New York, NY 10027

BEGLARIAN, GRANT

b. Tiflis, Georgian S.S.R., 1 December 1927; U.S. citizen 1954. Studied at Univ. of Michigan, D. M. A. 1957, with Ross Lee Finney; and at Tanglewood with Aaron Copland. He received the Gershwin Memorial Award, 1957, and Ford Found. Young Composers award, 1960. He taught at the U.S. Army Music School in Munich, 1952-54, and played viola in the 7th Army Symph. Orch. In 1961-68 he was director of the Ford Found. Contemporary Music Project. Then in 1969 he was named dean, School of Performing Arts, Univ. of Southern California.

(BEGLARIAN, GRANT)

WORKS: Orchestra: Symphony in 2 movements, 1950; <u>Divertimento</u>, 1957; <u>Sinfonia</u>, 1965; <u>Diversion</u> for viola, cello, and orch., 1972; Band: <u>A hymn for our time</u> for 3 bands, 1967; Chamber music: string quartet, 1948; cello sonata, 1951; 2 violin sonatas, 1949, 1955; woodwind quintet, 1966; <u>Of foibles, fables and fancies</u>, for cello, N. Y., 31 Oct. 1971; Chorus: <u>And all the hills echoed</u>, cantata, 1968; many smaller works for instrumental ensembles and chorus.

333 South Windsor Blvd.
Los Angeles, CA 90020

BEHREND, JEANNE

b. Philadelphia, Pa., 11 May 1911. Graduated from Curtis Inst., 1934; studied composition with Rosario Scalero, Reginald Owen Morris, Abram Chasins, and piano with Josef Hofmann. She received the Columbia Univ. Bearns Prize in 1936. She has held faculty positions at Curtis Inst., Western Coll. for Women, Oxford, Ohio; Juilliard School; Philadelphia Cons.; Temple Univ.; and since 1969 at the New School of Music, Philadelphia.

WORKS: Orchestra: <u>From dawn to dusk</u>, 1944; <u>Fanfare</u>, prelude to <u>The Star Spangled Banner</u>; Chamber music: <u>Quiet piece</u> and <u>Dance into space</u>, for flute; string quartet; Vocal: <u>Song cycle</u> on poems of Sara Teasdale, 1936; <u>Song of the United Nations</u>, soprano solo, soprano chorus, 2 pianos, 1945; <u>Easter hymn</u>, soprano, soprano chorus, harp, organ; other songs, chamber works, piano pieces.

2401 Pennsylvania Ave., Apt. 4A1
Philadelphia, PA 19130

BEHRENS, JACK

b. Lancaster, Pa., 25 Mar. 1935. Studied with William Bergsma, Vincent Persichetti, Peter Mennin at The Juilliard School, B. S. 1958, M. S. 1959; with Darius Milhaud at Aspen, Colo., 1962; with Stepan Wolpe, 1964, John Cage, 1965, at Emma Lake, Sask.; Leon Kirchner and Roger Sessions, Harvard Univ., Ph. D. 1973. He received 3 Juilliard scholarships; Edward Benjamin award, 1956; Copley Found. award, 1962; Canada Council Scandinavian Research grant, 1965; Simon Fraser Univ. grant, 1969; California State Coll. grant, 1971; Carnegie grants, 1972-73; and commissions. He taught at private schools, 1959-62; Univ. of Saskatchewan, 1962-66; Simon Fraser Univ., 1966-70; California State Coll., 1970-   , professor and chairman, Fine Arts department, 1973-

WORKS: Theatre: <u>Transfigured season</u>, ballet, 1960; <u>Encounters</u>, ballet, 1963; <u>Midsummer night's dream</u>, incidental music, 1964; <u>The lay of Thrym</u>, opera, Regina, Sask., 13 Apr. 1968, composer conducting; Orchestra: <u>Declaration</u>, 1964; <u>The sound of Milo</u>, with narrator, New Orleans, 4 Mar. 1970, won prize in New Orleans Philharmonic Symph. contest; Triple concerto: clarinet, violin, piano, 1971; Chamber music: <u>Introspection</u>, strings, 1956; <u>Quarter-tone quartet</u>, 1960; Concertino, trombone and 8 instruments, 1961; <u>Pentad</u>, vibraphone and piano, 1965; violin sonata, Vancouver, B. C., 3 Feb. 1970; Chorus: <u>In a manger</u>; <u>How beautiful is night</u>, 1970; Piano:

BEHRENS, JACK

(BEHRENS, JACK)
Passacaglia, 1963; A pocket size sonata, 1964;
Film score: The old order Amish, 1959.
P. O. Box 1695, Bakersfield, CA 93302

BEHRMAN, DAVID
b. Salzburg, Austria, of American parents, 16
Aug. 1937. Studied privately with Wallingford
Riegger; then with Walter Piston at Harvard Coll.,
B. A., magna cum laude, 1959; with Karlheinz
Stockhausen in Darmstadt; with Henri Pousseur in
Brussels, 1960; Columbia Univ., M. A. 1963; and
studied the IBM System/360-assembler language
programming at The New School, New York, 1971.
He received the Knight Prize, 1957-58, Bohemians
Prize, 1958-59, and John Knowles Paine fellow-
ship, 1959-60. He worked in New York and in
Cologne as translator and copyist for Stockhausen;
with Columbia Records in New York, 1965-70; was
guest lecturer and director, Electronic Music
Studio, Ohio State Univ., 1972; faculty, New
Music in New Hampshire, Chocorua, N. H. 1973;
and co-founder in 1966 of the Sonic Arts Union,
a group comprised of Robert Ashley, Behrman,
Alvin Lucier, and Gordon Mumma, that presents
programs of individual and collaborative music
using simple or sophisticated electronics (rang-
ing from amplified attache cases through homemade synthesizers to telephone link-up from a
concert space to a computer), photography, film,
and theater. The group has performed widely in
the U.S. and has made two European tours. Its
compositions are recorded.
WORKS: Instrumental: Canons, piano and percussion, 1959; Signals, 10 instruments and percussion, 1959-60; Ricercar, piano, 1961; Whistling six, 6 players with small wind instruments,
1962; From place to place, 2 pianos, 1963; northwest, chamber chorus, 5 instruments, 2 conductors, 1963; Parallel tracks, orchestra with 2
conductors; Mixed media or electronic: Milwaukee
combination, 4 wind players; each plays a 6-hole
oriental flute and a pitchpipe in addition to his
normal instrument, and also operates a tape recorder, 1964; Track, 6 winds and 6 tapes, 1965;
Players with circuits, 4 performers, 2 play
pianos, zithers, or guitars, 2 operate the electronic gear, 1966; Wave train, 2-4 performers
with guitar microphones and 2 grand pianos, 1966;
Runthrough, 4 performers with electronic music
devices, 1967; For nearly an hour, 6 channels of
tape are fed through filters and photocell mixers by 3 performers, commissioned by Merce
Cunningham for the dance Walkaround, 1968; Questions from the floor, 2 performers, speaking,
with tape and sound system wired into audience
area, based on political events in the U.S.,
1968; A new team takes over, later version of
Questions from the floor, 1969; Sinescreen, 4
performers and electronic devices, 1970; Net for
catching big sounds, 4 instruments with electronics, commissioned by San Francisco Cons.,
1974; many collaborative pieces.
Gate Hill Road, Stony Point, NY 10980

*BELL, LARRY
b. Wilson, N. C., 1952. Variations for piano,
received B. M. I. award, 1973.

BELL, LUCILLE ANDERSON
b. St. Louis, Mo., 27 Nov.   . Studied at
Chicago Musical Coll. with Alexander Raab and in
New York with Paul Creston. She has received
ASCAP awards and has been a pianist on radio in
Chicago and New York.
WORKS: Three moods, flute and piano; Run-
away slave, a song cycle; Lead us on, Thomas
Paine, march for piano.
117 West Scribner Ave., Du Bois, PA 15801

BELL, RANDY M.
b. Fort Smith, Ark., 23 May 1945. Attended Univ.
of Arkansas and Berklee Coll. of Music, Boston,
where he is on the faculty.
WORKS: ML-Moods of life, woodwind quartet;
Phantasy, flute and piano; woodwind quintet, commissioned by the Denver Symphony Orch.
c/o Berklee College of Music
1140 Boylston St., Boston, MA 02215

BELLAMY, MARIAN MEREDITH
b. Woodbury, N. J., 17 Mar. 1927. Attended
Western Maryland Coll., B. A. 1948; Drexel Univ.;
and studied composition with Matthew Colucci,
Orlando Otey, John Davison, Harold Boatriet, and
Romeo Cascarino, piano with Temple Painter and
Stafford Newhall.
WORKS: Serenade for string quartet, 1968;
Four preludes for piano, 1967-68; Pisces suite,
oboe and piano, 1970; Capricorn suite, harp and
cello, 1971; Asia, piano sonata, Three offices
for brass quintet, Philadelphia, 14 Oct. 1973.
127 Kenilworth Road, Merion, PA 19066

BELLEROSE, SR. CECILIA, C. S. C.
b. Suncook, N. H., 8 Nov. 1897. Studied at
Laval Univ., and Montreal Univ., D. M., with
Arthur Letondal, O. Pelletier, Georges Emile
Tanquay, Isabel Delorme. She was chairman of
the music department, Notre Dame Coll., Manchester, N. H., 1950-73, and also composer-in-
residence at Notre Dame and director of music
in New England schools.
WORKS: Vocal: Concert d'oiseaux, cantata;
Dieu nous voit; Gradations; Sayez bini; La
fontaine; Lux; The burning babe; Notre Dame college song; many sacred motets and piano pieces.
2321 Elm St., Manchester, NH 03104

*BELLMAN, HELEN M.
Meditation on altar windows, organ solo.

*BELLOW, ALEXANDER
b. Moscow, 22 Mar. 1912. Has taught classical
guitar in New York for many years. His works
for guitar include a sonata; 5 diversions; Prelude and rondo; Suite miniature.

BELLSON, LOUIS
b. Rock Falls, Ill., 6 July 1924. Studied drums
with his father and with Roy Knapp, Bert Winans,
and Murray Spivack. He has received Downbeat,
Metronome, Esquire, Playboy, and Columbia awards.
He has played with Benny Goodman, Tommy Dorsey,
Harry James, Duke Ellington, Count Basie, and his
own band.

(BELLSON, LOUIS)
WORKS: Percussion: jazz ballet, performed at Las Vegas Jazz Festival, 1962; Four stories, 4 complete drum sets; Percussion suite no.1, 5 players.
8433 Melvin Ave., Northridge, CA 91324

BELTON, PAUL D.
b. Memphis, Tenn., 21 Aug. 1942. Studied at Louisiana State Univ. with Helen Gunderson and Kenneth Klaus, and in Paris with Nadia Boulanger. He received a grant from L'Alliance Francaise de New York, 1964-65. His faculty positions have been at Nicholls State Univ., La., 1967-70; Louisiana State Univ., 1970-71; and assistant professor at Washington State Univ., 1972- .
WORKS: Orchestra: symphony, 1967; Chamber music: horn sonata, 1964; string quartet, 1973; Variations, clarinet and piano, 1973; Vocal: Three songs for soprano, 1964.
N. W. 1530 Turner Drive, Pullman, WA 99163

*BENAGLIA, JOHN
5 vignettes for recorder quartet.

BENCRISCUTTO, FRANK
b. Racine, Wis., 21 Sep. 1928. Studied at Univ. of Wisconsin, Madison, B. M., M. M.; Northwestern Univ.; Eastman School of Music, D. M. A.; composition with Howard Hanson and Bernard Rogers. In 1954-57 he was director of school bands in Wisconsin, since 1960 he has been band director at Univ. of Minnesota.
WORKS: Orchestra: Symphonic jazz suite for jazz combo and orch.; symphony No. 2; Band: symphony No. 1; Serenade for saxophone and band; quartet for saxophones and band; quartet for trombones and band; concertino for tuba and band; other band pieces.
3021 Churchill St., St. Paul, MN 55113

BENDER, JAN
b. Haarlem, Neth., 3 Feb. 1909; to U.S. 1960. Studied in Leipsig with Karl Straube, 1930-33; in Amsterdam with Sem Dresden, 1933-34; and in Luebeck with Hugo Distler, 1934-35. From 1934 to 1960 he was a director of church music in Germany; then joined the faculty at Concordia Teachers Coll., Seward, Neb.; since 1965 he has been associate professor at Wittenberg Univ., Springfield, Ohio.
WORKS: He has written numerous works for the Lutheran Church service, including St. Louis Cantata, 1964, and instrumental works such as a cello sonata, concerto for brass and timpani, woodwind quartet, and organ pieces.
164 West College Ave., Springfield, OH 45504

BENEDICT, DAVID
b. Philadelphia, Pa., 24 Feb. 1923. Studied piano with Lonny Epstein, Carl Friedberg, Isadore Freed; voice with May Harrow, Vitali Koretzky; and opera coaching with Leopold Sachse at Juilliard School. After four years in the Army during World War II, he resumed vocal studies and began singing in operas, oratorios, and concerts. In 1953 he was appointed cantor at Temple Israel, N. Y., and in 1960, music director. He has been

(BENEDICT, DAVID)
on the faculty at Adelphi Univ. since 1958, and at Dowling Coll., Oakdale, N. Y., since 1966. He is accompanist and coach to many opera singers.
WORKS: Chorus: Dance service for Friday evening; Psalms 121, 137, 29, 150; May the words, Matovu; Service for Saturday morning (all of the above for cantor, mixed choir, and organ); Adon Olam, choir and organ; Service in classic style; many other services and compositions.
Pound Hollow Road, Old Brookville Glen Head, NY 11545

BENJAMIN, THOMAS
b. Bennington, Vt., 17 Feb. 1940. Studied at Bard Coll., Harvard Univ., Brandeis Univ., Eastman School of Music, with Carlos Surinach, Robert Moevs, Arthur Berger, Ernst Krenek, Bernard Rogers, and Wayne Barlow. He has had 2 grants from Univ. of Houston; Louis Lane Prize, 1967; and several commissions. He has been assistant professor, Univ. of Houston, 1968- ; and taught at Nat. Music Camp, 1968-71.
WORKS: Operetta: Hammer in his hand; Orchestra: Sinfonia, 1971; violin concerto, 1967; piano concerto, 1968; Chamber music: 4 pieces for 3 flutes, 1962; Arditiana, woodwind quartet, 1963; Chanson innocentes, soprano and string quartet, 1964; Le Corbusier in America, woodwind trio, 1965; Argument, clarinet and brass quartet, 1966; After dinner pieces, 2 clarinets, 1966; On love, baritone, piano trio, 1966; Berceuse, cello and piano, 1969; Articulations, clarinet, 1972; Four by two, clarinet and bassoon, 1972; Chorus: 3 Psalm fragments, 1961; Pooh cycle, 1965; 3 songs after Frost, 1966; Adoremus Te, 1969; 3 motets, 1970; Sabbath music, 1971.
2629 Cason St., Houston, TX 77005

BENJAMIN, WILLIAM E.
b. Montreal, 7 Dec. 1944; to U.S. 1966. Attended McGill Univ., M. B. 1965; Princeton Univ., M. F. A. 1968, studying with Milton Babbitt, Edward T. Cone, Peter Westergaard, and James K. Randall. He received a B. M. I. award, 1966, and a Tanglewood fellowship, 1967. He was instructor at Wellesley Coll., 1970-72; and Univ. of Michigan, 1972- .
WORKS: Orchestra: piano concerto, 1970-73; Chamber music: Variations for 4 players, 1967; At sixes and sevens, sextet, 1968; string trio, 1972; Chorus: Mah Tovu, a cappella, 1966.
2236 Fuller Road, Apt. 208 Ann Arbor, MI 48105

*BENNARD, GEORGE
b. Youngstown, Ohio, 4 Feb. 1873; d. Reed City, Mich., 10 Oct. 1958. Was a hymn writer.

*BENNETT, CLAUDIA
3 improvisations for chamber choir and 2 pianos, to own text.

*BENNETT, DAVID
b. Chicago, Ill., 3 Sep. 1897. Has published a saxophone concerto; pieces for various small wind

BENNETT, DAVID

(BENNETT, DAVID)
ensembles; The spirit of music, chorus and
piano; etc.
Route 2, Box 159, St. Charles, IL 60174

BENNETT, ROBERT CHARLES
b. Houston, Tex., 10 Nov. 1933. Attended Univ.
of Houston, B. S., M. Ed., studying organ with
William C. Teague. He is a Fellow, Trinity Coll.,
London, and holds the performer's diploma; has
been an organist-choirmaster in Houston since
1954, and is organ instructor at both Rice Univ.
and St. Thomas Univ. He has published choral
compositions.
6004 Buffalo Speedway, Houston, TX 77005

BENNETT, ROBERT RUSSELL
b. Kansas City, Mo., 15 June 1894. Studied in
Kansas City with Carl Busch and in Paris with
Nadia Boulanger. His many awards include 2
Guggenheim fellowships, Musical America prize,
1927, RCA Victor prize, 1929, an Oscar, an Emmy,
many medals, citations, and commissions, and an
honorary L. H. D. from Franklin and Marshall
Coll. He has been composer-arranger-conductor
and one of the most noted orchestrators in
New York theaters, 1919-   , Hollywood films,
1930-   , radio networks, 1940-   , and television networks, 1951-   .
WORKS: Opera: An hour of delusion, 1-act;
Maria Malibran, N. Y., 8 Apr. 1935; The enchanted
kiss, 1944; Endymion, 1927. Orchestra: Sights
and sounds, 1926, Abraham Lincoln, 1926 (these
two works won 2 of the 5 prizes in the 1929 RCA-
Victor contest); Charleston rhapsody, 1926;
Paysage, 1928; March for 2 pianos and orch.,
1930; Early American ballade, 1932; Concerto
grosso, dance band and orch., 1932; Adagio
eroico, 1935; Hollywood scherzo, 1936; 8 etudes
for orch., 1938; 3 symphonies, 1941, 1946, 1963;
violin concerto, 1941; The four freedoms, 1943;
Classic serenade, 1945; Overture to an imaginary
drama, 1946; Dry weather legend, 1947; piano concerto, 1948; Concerto grosso for woodwind quintet, 1958; concerto for violin, piano, and orch.,
Portland, Ore., 18 Mar. 1963; Band: Symphonic
songs, 1958; Track meet, suite, 1960; Suite of
old American dances; Down to the sea in ships;
Kentucky; Ohio River suite; 3 Humoresques; West
Virginia epic; That war in Korea, 1965; Chamber
music: violin sonata, 1927; Toy symphony, 5
woodwinds, 1928; organ sonata, 1929; Water music,
string quartet, 1937; Hexapoda, violin and piano,
1940; 2 piano sonatinas, 1941, 1944; suite for
violin and piano, 1945; 5 Improvisations, trio,
1946; Sonatine, soprano and harp; 6 Souvenirs,
2 flutes and piano, 1948; Chorus: Epithalamium,
text of John Milton, with orch.; Verses No. 1, 2,
3, text by R. R. Bennett; Nietzsche variations;
He is risen; and songs.
65 West 54th St., New York, NY 10019

BENNETT, WILHELMINE
b. Carmi, Ill., 14 June 1933. Studied with
Anthony Donato at Northwestern Univ.; Wolfgang
Fortner in Germany; and Chou Wen-chung at Columbia Univ. She has received a William T. Farley
award for creative writing, a Fulbright

(BENNETT, WILHELMINE)
fellowship, 1964; and a grant from the Nat. Council on the Arts, 1966. In 1971 she was lecturer
at Univ. of California, Santa Cruz Extension.
WORKS: Orchestra: Thumbelisa, 2 symphonies;
Enola Gay; Chamber music: woodwind quintet;
Hyperbolex; La suite absurdite; 5 quick visions
of the apocalypse.
101 Riverside, Sidney, NY 13838

BENSON, BRUCE
b. Port Chester, N. Y., 4 June 1951. Studied at
Hebrew Union Coll.-Jewish Inst. of Religion,
School of Sacred Music, with Frederick Piket.
He has been cantor at Temple B'nai Israel,
Elmont, N. Y., 1972- . He has published
Ma'agal chozer - a circle without end, a folk-
rock service for Shabbat eve.
2200 Central Road, Apt. 7-M
Fort Lee, NJ 07024

BENSON, WARREN
b. Detroit, Mich., 26 Jan. 1924. Is self-taught
in composition. His awards include 2 Fulbright
teaching grants to Greece, 1950-51; Phi Mu Alpha,
Sinfonia, 1970; Lillian Fairchild award, 1971.
He was timpanist, Detroit Symphony Orch. and
Ford Orch., 1946; on faculty, Anatolia Coll.
Salonica, Greece, 1950-52; band and orchestra
director, Mars Hill Coll., N. C., 1952-53; professor and composer-in-residence, Ithaca Coll.,
1953-67; and professor of composition, Eastman
School of Music, 1967- .
WORKS: Orchestra: horn concerto; Band:
The leaves are falling; Remembrance; Night song;
Symphony for drums and wind orchestra; Aeolian
songs for saxophone and band; Wind ensemble:
Concertina, saxophone and winds; Helix, tuba and
winds; Recuerdo, oboe, English horn and winds;
Star edge, saxophone and winds; The solitary
dancer; Shadow wood, soprano and winds; Transylvania fanfare; Percussion: trio; Streams;
3 pieces; Chamber music: Nara, saxophone, flute,
piano, percussion; Capriccio, violin, viola,
cello, piano, 1971; The dream net, saxophone and
string quartet; Prologue for trumpet; Soliloquy
for horn; Aubade for trombone; Arioso for tuba;
Marche for wind quintet; Chorus: Love is; An
Englishman with an atlas.
10 Reitz Parkway, Pittsford, NY 14534

BENTLEY, BERENICE BENSON
b. Oskaloosa, Iowa, 2 Jan. 1887; d. Claremont,
Calif., 2 Apr. 1971. Studied at Grinnell Coll.,
Iowa, and with Mary Wood Chase in Chicago. She
taught at the Mary Wood Chase School and was
associated with Guy Maier in summer workshops.
Her compositions for piano include Four northern
sketches, sonatina, several albums.

*BENTZ, CECIL
b. 1916. Window games, 1-act opera, New York,
18 Nov. 1967; Choral settings of 2 poems by
Robert Frost, Nothing gold can stay and Waspish.

*BERCKMAN, EVELYN
b. Philadelphia, Pa., 1900. Has written 2 ballets, From the Odyssey and County Fair; many
works for orchestra and chamber groups.

*BEREZOWSKY, NICOLAI
    b. St. Petersburg, Russia, 17 May 1900; to U.S.
1921; d. New York, 27 Aug. 1953. Wrote an opera,
a children's opera; 4 symphonies; violin concerts; viola concerto; cello concerto; harp concerto; many chamber works.

BERG, SIDNEY
    b. Superior, Wis., 25 July 1918. Attended the
Univ. of Michigan. He has been music director
in public schools 1944-   , Norfolk, Va., City
Schools 1963-   , and assistant conductor of
the Tidewater Youth Symphony 1971-   . He has
published a timpani method and solos for percussion instruments including Holliday, Rolling
rhythms, Rambling along, South American capers,
The victor, etc.
    4043 North Witchduck Road
    Virginia Beach, VA 23455

BERGAMO, JOHN J.
    b. Englewood, N. J., 28 May 1940. Studied in
New York with Michael Colgrass, 1963-64, Easley
Smiles, 1964-65, and with Gunther Schuller at
Tanglewood 1965. He taught percussion at Univ.
of Washington, 1968-69, and at California Inst.
of the Arts, 1970-   .
    WORKS: Interactions for vibraphone and 6
percussionists, 1963; 4 pieces for timpani, 1963;
Haiku for young voices and percussion, 1964;
Tanka for solo percussion, 1964; Style studies,
a text of etudes for keyboard percussion.
    California Institute of the Arts
    24700 McBean Parkway, Valencia, CA 91355

BERGENFELD, NATHAN J.
    b. New York, N. Y., 8 Mar. 1935. Studied at
Manhattan School of Music with Vittorio Giannini,
Nicholas Flagello, and Ludmila Ulehla. He taught
in public schools, 1966-70; Brooklyn Coll.,
1971-72; and New York Univ., 1972-73.
    WORKS: Concerto barocco for 3 trumpets and
orchestra; Canzona for 3 horns; Diversions for 3
trombones.
    2725 East 22nd St., Brooklyn, NY 11235

*BERGER, ARTHUR V.
    b. New York, N. Y., 15 May 1912. Studied with
Walter Piston at Harvard Univ., M. A. 1936; with
Nadia Boulanger and Darius Milhaud in Paris. His
awards include the John Knowles Paine fellowship,
1937-39; membership in Nat. Inst. of Arts and
Letters, 1972; concert of his works given at
Carnegie Hall, New York, 1 Apr. 1973, honoring
his 60th birthday. He has held faculty posts
at Mills Coll.; Brooklyn Coll.; Juilliard School;
Brandeis Univ., 1953-71, professor, 1972-   ;
was music critic in New York, 1943-53.
    WORKS: Ballet: Entertainment piece, 1940;
Orchestra: Serenade concertante for violin,
woodwind quartet, small orch., 1945-51; Ideas of
order, 1953; Polyphony, 1956; Chamber music: 2
episodes for piano, 1933; woodwind quartet, 1941;
duo for cello and piano, 1951; Chamber music for
13 players, 1956; 3 pieces for 2 pianos; duo for
clarinet and piano, 1957; string quartet, 1958;

(BERGER, ARTHUR V.
    woodwind trio; septet for woodwind trio, string
trio, piano, 1966.
    9 Sparks St., Cambridge, MA 02138

BERGER, DAVID
    b. New York, N. Y., 30 Mar. 1949. Studied at
Ithaca Coll., B. M. 1971, with Karel Husa; Eastman School of Music with Rayburn Wright and
Manny Albam; and at Berklee Coll. of Music,
Boston. His awards have included a Downbeat
scholarship, 1966; Duke Ellington award, 1967;
and a grant from the Nat. Endowment for the Arts,
1973.
    WORKS: Jazz ensemble: Idiom '73, concerto
for Clark Terry; Influence: within and without.
    84-20 Austin St., Kew Gardens, NY 11415

*BERGER, JEAN
    b. Hamm, Germany, 27 Sep. 1909; U.S. citizen
1943. Studied at Heidelberg Univ., Ph. D. 1931;
with Louis Aubert in Paris. He held a MacDowell
fellowship, 1973. He served in the U.S. Army in
World War II; was faculty member, Middlebury
Coll., 1948-59; Univ. of Illinois, 1959-61; Univ.
of Colorado, 1961-   .
    WORKS: Orchestra: Caribbean concerto for
harmonica and orch., 1942; Creole overture, 1949;
Chamber music: 4 sonnets, voice and string quartet, 1941; Intrada, brass quartet; Chorus: Brazilian psalm, 1941; Vision of peace, 1949; The
eyes of all wait upon thee; No man is an island;
How lovely are thy tabernacles; A diversion for
chorus and dancers.
    1107 Cedar Ave., Boulder, CO 80302

*BERGH, ARTHUR
    b. St. Paul, Minn., 24 Mar. 1882; d. en route to
Honolulu, 11 Feb. 1962. Wrote an opera, 2 operettas, 2 musical melodramas, many songs and violin pieces.

*BERGSMA, WILLIAM
    b. Oakland, Calif., 1 Apr. 1921. Studied at
Stanford Univ. and at Eastman School of Music,
B. A., M. A. He has received an American Acad.
of Arts and Letters grant; 2 Guggenheim fellowships; many commissions. He was on the faculty,
Juilliard School, 1946-63; director, School of
Music, Univ. of Washington, 1963-   .
    WORKS: Opera: The wife of Martin Guerre,
1956; Ballet: Paul Bunyan, 1938; Senor Comman-
dante, 1941; Orchestra: Music on a quiet theme,
1943; The fortunate islands, string orch., 1947;
a symphony, 1949; Dance from a New England album,
small orch.; Documentary one: Portrait of a
city; Carol on 12th night, with chorus, 1954;
March with trumpets, 1957; Concerto for wind
quintet, 1958; Chameleon variations, 1960;
Toccata for the 6th day, 1962; Chamber music: 3
string quartets; Suite for brass quartet, 1940;
Fantastic variations on a theme from Tristan and
Isolde, viola and piano, 1961; Serenade, To await
the moon, chamber orch., 1965; Chorus: On the
beach at night, 1945; In a glass of water, 1946;
Wishes; Wonders; Portents; Charms; Confrontation
from the Book of Job, chorus and 22 instruments,

BERGSMA, WILLIAM

(BERGSMA, WILLIAM)
1963: The sun, the soaring eagle, the turquoise prince, the god, New York premiere, 12 Feb. 1971.
    School of Music, University of Washington
    Seattle, WA 98105

BERK, MAYNARD H.
    b. Bucyrus, Ohio, 27 July 1913. Attended Univ. of Redlands, B. M.; Union Theological Seminary, N. Y., S. M. M.; New York Univ., Ph. D.; Univ. of Southern California; and in the Netherlands. He studied with Ernest Kanitz, Philip James, Halsey Stevens, Henk Badings, and Edwin Stringham. He was the South Dakota Music Teachers Nat. Assoc. commissioned composer of the year 1972-73. He has been on the faculty of Sioux Falls Coll. since 1949 and chairman of the music department 1968-   .
    WORKS: Chorus: Kyrie elison; Sanctus; Vocalise, unison choir, instruments, organ; and many organ, piano, and vocal solos.
    Department of Music, Sioux Falls College
    Sioux Falls, SD 57101

*BERKOWITZ, LEONARD
    Divertimento for winds; Toccata, theme and variations for winds; 4 songs on poems of Emily Dickinson; Chamber music, women's chorus, on text by Robert Frost.
    Faculty, California State University
    Northridge, CA 91324

BERKOWITZ, RALPH
    b. New York, N. Y., 5 Sep. 1910. Taught at Curtis Inst. of Music 1933-42 and summers at the Berkshire Music Center; in 1947 he was named dean at the Center and executive assistant to Koussevitzky. He was manager of the Albuquerque Symph. Orch., 1958-69. He is also concert pianist, accompanist, lecturer, painter, and author of magazine articles and the book, What every accompanist knows.
    WORKS: A telephone call, voice and orchestra, with text by Dorothy Parker, premiere in Rio de Janeiro, 1957; Syncopations for piano, 1956; transcriptions and orchestrations of Bach, Purcell, Haydn, etc.
    620 Rio Grande Blvd., N. W.
    Albuquerque, NM 87104

*BERKOWITZ, SAUL (SOL)
    b. Warren, Ohio, 27 Apr. 1922. Studied at Queens Coll., CUNY; with Karol Rathaus and Otto Luening, Columbia Univ., M. A. He received a Ford Found. grant, 1956. He was professor, Queens Coll., 1946-61, 1972-   .
    WORKS: Opera: Fat Tuesday, a jazz opera, 1956; Orchestra: Diversion; Band: Paradigm, a jazz adventure in sonata form; Game of dance; Chorus: Without words, vocalize for women's voices.
    Music Department, Queens College, CUNY
    New York, NY 11367

BERLIN, DAVID N.
    b. Pittsburgh, Pa., 23 Jan. 1943. Studied at Carnegie-Mellon Univ. with Leonardo Balada, Nicolai Lopatnikoff, James Beale, and Roland

(BERLIN, DAVID N.)
Leich. In 1969 he won the Phi Mu Alpha Sinfonia, Alpha Omega Chapter, composition contest. He has been instructor, North Allegheny School District, Pittsburgh, 1965-   .
    WORKS: Orchestra: Variants; piano concerto; Band: Divertimento; Music for brass and percussion; Chamber music: octet; Fanfare, air, and scherzando, brass trio; brass quintet; Duo for trumpets; Capriccio, violin and piano; Prelude and allegro, woodwind quintet; Rondo, trumpet and piano; Introduction, andantino, and rondo, horn and piano; Theme and variations, piano; Mixed media: Three mixtures, 4 bassoons and tape; Synchronization, band and taped sounds; Interactions, flute and tape; Articulations, soprano and tape.
    4809 Baptist Road, Pittsburgh, PA 15227

*BERLIN, IRVING
    b. Temun, Russia, 11 May 1888; to U.S. 1893. Never learned to read music, but nevertheless wrote words and music for enormously successful songs for nearly four decades. His first big hit, Alexander's ragtime band, 1911, was followed by innumerable exceedingly popular songs, musicals, and film scores. He was one of the first ten inductees into the Entertainment Hall of Fame on 23 Apr. 1974.

*BERLINSKI, HERMAN
    b. Leipzig, Germany, 18 Aug. 1910; to U.S. after World War II. Was instructor, Hebrew Union Coll.; then became organist and director of music, Washington Hebrew Congregation, D.C.
    WORKS: Orchestra: Symphonic visions, 1949; Merrymount; Chamber music: 3 or 4 part canons for winds; Chorus: It hath been told thee, O man; Job, oratorio, excerpts performed in New York, 11 June 1973; Organ: The burning bush, 1956; Sinfonia #3 (Sounds and motions).
    4000 Tunlow, N. W., Washington, DC 20007

*BERNARDO, JOSE PAUL
    The child, music, dialogue and ballet, Lake George Opera Festival, State Univ. of New York, Albany, 8 Aug., 1974.

*BERNAT, ROBERT
    b. Johnstown, Pa., 3 July 1931. Faculty member, Indiana Univ. of Pennsylvania, wrote Passacaglia, In memorium: John F. Kennedy, 1966, recorded by the Louisville Orchestra.

BERNHARDT, STEPHEN
    b. Glendale, Calif., 20 Nov. 1947. Studied at California State Univ., Fullerton, with Robert Stewart and Donal Michalsky. His works include Suite for five instruments; Variations for piano.
    2401 Foxdale Ave., La Habra, CA 90631

BERNSTEIN, DAVID STEPHEN
    b. Boston, Mass., 6 Jan. 1942. Studied at Florida State Univ. with Carlisle Floyd and John Boda; and at Indiana Univ. with Juan Orrego-Salas. He taught in the Passaic, N. J. Public Schools, 1966-68; Indiana Univ., 1969-71; and

(BERNSTEIN, DAVID STEPHEN)
has been assistant professor, Univ. of Akron, 1972-   .
WORKS: Orchestra: Dialogue for double orch. and percussion; sonata for chamber orch.; Chamber music: quartet for clarinet, trumpet, cello, harpsichord; Four songs for tenor and 14 instruments; Ziz, 6 percussionists; Sette for piano.
3327 Overlook Drive, Akron, OH 44312

BERNSTEIN, ELMER
b. New York, N. Y., 4 Apr. 1922. Had scholarships for study of piano at Juilliard School 1934-49, and composition with Israel Citkowitz, Roger Sessions, Ivan Langstrogh, and Stepan Wolpe; attended New York Univ. 1939-42. His film scores have won an Academy Award, 9 Academy Award nominations, an Emmy, 2 Golden Globe awards, Western Heritage award, and Downbeat award. Except for service in the Army in World War II he was a concert pianist, 1939-50, then turned to composing film scores.
WORKS: The award winning film scores are: The man with the golden arm, 1955; The magnificent seven, 1960; Summer and smoke, 1961; Walk on the wild side, 1961; To kill a mockingbird, 1962; The making of a president - 1960, 1963; Hallelujah trail, 1965; Hawaii, 1966; Return of the seven, 1966; Thoroughly modern Millie, 1967; and the stage musical score: How now Dow Jones, Some other scores are: The Ten Commandments, 1956; Drango, 1956; Toccata for toy trains, 1957; God's little acre, 1958; Love with the proper stranger, 1962; The scalphunters, 1968; True grit, 1969; A cannon for Cordoba, 1970.
Winter River Ranch, Malibu, CA 90265

BERNSTEIN, LEONARD
b. Lawrence, Mass., 25 Aug. 1918. Studied at Harvard Univ., A. B. 1939; Curtis Inst. of Music, grad., 1941; conducting with Fritz Reiner and Serge Koussevitzky, composition with Walter Piaton and Edward Burlingame Hill; piano with Helen Coates, Heinrich Gebhard, and Isabelle Vengerova; holds a number of honorary degrees from various institutions. His numerous other honors include an Emmy for the TV Young People's Concerts, Grammy award, Sonning Prize of Denmark, election to the Nat. Inst. of Arts and Letters, N. Y. Music Critics Circle award, N. Y. Drama Critics award, etc. He was appointed assistant to Koussevitzky at the Berkshire Music Center, 1942, served on the faculty 1948-55, and from 1951 was head of the conducting department. He was assistant conductor of the N. Y. Philharmonic, 1943-44, conductor of the N. Y. City Center Orch., 1945-48, music advisor to the Israel Philharmonic, 1948-49, on faculty Brandeis Univ., 1951-56, music director and conductor, N. Y. Philharmonic, 1958-59, then appointed laureate conductor for life; named institute lecturer, M. I. T., 1974-   . He has conducted all major orchestras of the U.S. and Europe, the Metropolitan Opera, N. Y., Vienna State Opera, and was the first American to conduct at La Scala, Milan, 1953.
WORKS: Opera: Trouble in Tahiti, 1-act, to his own libretto, 1952; Ballet: Fancy free, 1944; Facsimile, 1946; Theater: On the town, 1944;

(BERNSTEIN, LEONARD)
Wonderful town, 1952; On the waterfront, (film), 1954; Candide, 1956, revision, Brooklyn, 19 Dec. 1973; New York, 5 Mar. 1974; incidental music to Peter Pan, 1956, and The lark, 1957; West Side story, Washington, 19 Aug. 1957, N. Y., 26 Sep. 1957; Mass, a theater piece for singers, players, and dancers, written for the opening of the John F. Kennedy Center for the Performing Arts, Washington, 7 Sep. 1971; Dybbuk, New York City Ballet, 16 May 1974; Orchestra: Jeremiah symphony, 1944; Symphony No. 2, The age of anxiety, piano and orch., Boston, 8 Apr. 1949; Symphony No. 3, Kaddish, for narrator, chorus, and orch., Tel Aviv, 9 Dec. 1963; Prelude, fugue, and riffs, jazz combo and orch., 1950; Serenade, violin solo, strings, percussion, 1954; Chichester Psalms, chorus and orch., N. Y. 14 July 1965; Chamber music: clarinet sonata, 1942; Seven anniversaries for piano, 1942; Four anniversaries for piano, 1964; Songs: I hate music, song cycle, 1943; La bonne cuisine, song cycle on texts of recipes from a cookbook, 1949; Two love songs, 1949; Afterthought, 1951; Silhouette, 1951. He is author of The joy of music, 1959; Leonard Bernstein's Young People's Concerts for reading and listening, 1962, revised 1970; The infinite variety of music, 1966.
205 West 57th St., New York, NY 10019

BERNSTEIN, SEYMOUR
b. Newark, N. J., 24 Apr. 1927. Studied at Mannes Coll. of Music; Juilliard School; Fontainebleau, France; with Alexander Brailowsky, Georges Enesco, Nadia Boulanger, Clifford Curzon. His awards include Griffith Artists award; N. Y. Madrigal Soc. instrumental award; Beebe Found. grant; 2 Rockefeller grants; 4 State Dept. grants; 1st prize and Prix Jacques Durand, Fontainebleau; Nat. Fed. of Music Clubs award for furthering American music abroad. His faculty positions include Chatham Square Music School, 1956-58; Hoff-Barthelson Music School, 1959-62; New York State Univ. Coll., Purchase, N. Y., 1972-   .
WORKS: Piano: Interrupted waltz, Korean bluebird, Toccata francaise, Birds, Books 1 and 2, Concerto for our time.
10 West 76th St., New York, NY 10023

BERRY, DAVID BRUCE
b. San Diego, Calif., 29 Apr. 1947. Studied at Univ. of California, Berkeley, B. A. majoring in visual communications; and at Mills Coll., M. F. A., under Robert Ashley, William Maraldo, Terry Riley, Nathan Rubin. He received the Elizabeth C. Mills award for composition in 1973. He is an assistant instructor on the Moog Buckla at Mills Coll., 1972-   , and co-producer of Thin air, a radio program on KPFA-FM, Berkeley.
WORKS: Use speakophone or fiber needles only, Buckla, 1970; Vietnam hamburger, Moog, voice, weaponry, 1973; Up-down fire music, electric Corona, flaming plastics, electronics, 1973; Elegia Squalus, flute, piano, saxophone, tape, Moog, 1973; A substratum of uncertainty, electric guitar, Moog, tape loops, 1973.
4532 Tulip Ave., Oakland, CA 94619

BERRY, WALLACE

*BERRY, WALLACE
b. La Crosse, Wis., 1928. Studied with Halsey
Stevens, Univ. of Southern California, Ph. D.
1956; and with Nadia Boulanger in Paris. His
awards include a Fulbright fellowship; distinguished faculty award, Univ. of Michigan, 1963;
first prize, Pittsburgh Flute Club competition,
1970; many commissions. He was lecturer, Univ.
of Southern California, 1956-57; professor,
Univ. of Michigan, 1957-   .
    WORKS: Orchestra: 5 pieces for small orch.;
Intonation, 1972; Wind ensemble: Divertimento,
with percussion; Chamber music: 2 string quartets; 2 canons for 2 clarinets; duo for viola
and piano; duo for flute and piano; Canto lirico,
violin and piano; duo for flute and harp; Fantasy in 5 statements, clarinet and piano; 8 20th-
century miniatures for piano; Chorus: No man is
an island.
    School of Music, University of Michigan
    Ann Arbor, MI 48105

BERTCHUME, GARY
b. St. Louis, Mo., 29 Dec. 1949. Studied at
Washington Univ. with Roland Jordan, John Perkins,
and Robert Wykes. He has received the Antoinette
Dame award.
    WORKS: Phases, chamber orchestra, St. Louis,
1 Mar. 1973; iv for piano and tape, 1973; quartet for clarinet, cello, piano, percussion, 1973.
    822 Leland, University City, MO 63130

BEST HAROLD M.
b. Jamestown, N. Y., 1 Oct. 1931. Studied in
Claremont, Calif., with Karl Kohn, and at Union
Theological Seminary with Searle Wright and Seth
Bingham. In 1956-67 he was professor at Nyack
Coll., and chairman of the music division 1967-70;
since 1970 he has been director of the Wheaton
Coll., Ill., Coll. Cons.
    WORKS: Orchestra: piano concertino; Vocal:
Psalm II, chorus; A call to service, chorus;
Song of the divine presence; Keyboard: Toccata
for 2 pianos; Scherzo for organ; 7 Voluntaries
on early American hymn tunes, organ; several
original hymn tunes.
    151 Travers, Wheaton, IL 60187

BESTOR, CHARLES
b. New York, N. Y., 21 Dec. 1924. Studied at
Yale Univ. with Paul Hindemith; Swarthmore Coll.,
B. A. 1948; Juilliard School, B. S. 1951, with
Vincent Persichetti and Peter Mennin; Univ. of
Illinois, M. M. 1952, with Burrill Phillips;
Univ. of Colorado, D. M. A. 1973. He has held
faculty and administrative positions at Juilliard
School, 1951-59; Univ. of Colorado, 1959-64;
Willamette Univ., dean chairman, professor,
1964-71; Univ. of Alabama, chairman, professor,
1971-74; Univ. of Utah, chairman and professor,
1973.
    WORKS: Ballet: Undine, New York, 1951;
Theater: incidental music for J. B., Macleish,
1961, and Measure for measure, Shakespeare,
1963; Orchestra: Concerto grosso for percussion and orch., Jacksonville, Ore., 1968; Music
for the mountain, Salem, Ore., 1972; Band: Suite
for winds and trumpet, 1962; Concertino for trumpet

(BESTOR, CHARLES)
and band, 1973; Chamber music: piano sonata,
New York, 1963; A wind in the willows, solo
flute, New York, 1964; Little suite for beginning strings, 1968; Chorus: In memoriam to
texts from The autobiography of Malcolm X, chorus, brass, percussion, reader, 1972; several a
capella choruses; Mixed media; Improvisation I,
for tape, 1971; Improvisation II, for instruments and tape, 1971; Poem, choir, soprano soloist, electronic synthesizer, 1972; Variations,
violin and piano with synthesizer, 1973.
    26 H Northwood Lake, Northport, AL 35476

*BETTS, DONALD
As the hart panteth for chorus.

*BEVELANDER, BRIAN
Piano sonata.

BEVERIDGE, THOMAS G.
b. New York, N. Y., 6 Apr. 1938. Studied at
Harvard Coll., A. B. 1959, with Walter Piston,
and at Fontainebleau with Nadia Boulanger,
1958-60.
    WORKS: He has composed chamber music, choral
works and songs including 4 song cycles: Odysseus, Prometheus, 3 serious songs, Leaves of
grass, for bass and piano; Once: In memoriam
Martin Luther King, Jr., a cantata; a total of
260 works.
    2411 Nottingham Drive
    Falls Church, VA 22043

BEVERSDORF, THOMAS
b. Yoakum, Tex., 8 Aug. 1924. Studied at Univ.
of Texas, B. M., with Kent Kennan, Arthur Kreutz,
Eric DeLamarter; Eastman School of Music, M. M.
D. M. A., with Bernard Rogers, Howard Hanson;
and at Tanglewood with Aaron Copland, Arthur
Honneger, and Serge Koussevitzky. He held a
Danforth teacher-study grant at Eastman, and has
received several commissions and composition
awards. He was first trombonist, Houston Symph.,
1946-48, Pittsburgh Symph., 1948-49; and instructor, Univ. of Houston, 1946-48; professor, Indiana Univ., 1951-   ; composer-in-residence,
Bucknell Univ., 1970-71.
    WORKS: Opera: The hooligan, 1-act, on
Chekhov's The boor, 1964-69; Orchestra: Essay
on mass production, 1946; 4 symphonies, 1946, 1950,
1958, 1960; Reflections, 1947; Mexican portrait,
1947; concerto grosso, oboe and chamber orch.,
1948; concerto for 2 pianos, 1951; Ode, 1952;
New frontiers, 1955; Serenade, 1956; violin concerto, Danforth, 1959; Variations, 1965; Generation with the torch, an overture for youth, 1965;
Divertimento concertante, 1970; Band: Cathedral
music, brass choir, 1950; 3 epitaphs in memory of
of Eric De Lamarter, brass quartet, 1955; Serenade, winds and percussion, 1957; Chamber music:
sonatas for piano, horn, tuba, trumpet, violin,
flute, cello; 2 Suites on baroque themes, clarinet, cello, piano, Prelude and fugue, woodwind
quintet, 1950; 2 string quartets, 1952, 1955;
Divertimento da camera, flute, oboe, doublebass,
harpsichord, 1968; Walruses, cheesecake, and
Morse code, tuba and piano, 1972; choral works,

(BEVERSDORF, THOMAS)
songs, piano pieces. He has written a libretto for The metamorphosis, freely adapted from Kafka, and articles on trombone technique.
R. R. #12, Box 227, Cedar Crest
Bloomington, IN 47401

BEYER, FREDERICK H.
b. Chicago, Ill., 3 Dec. 1926. Studied with Otto Luening and Jack Beeson at Columbia Univ., and with John Boda at Florida State Univ. He received the Ostwald Band Composition award, 1965. He has been associate professor at Greensboro Coll., 1966- .
WORKS: Band: symphony; overture, 1965; Chamber music: Conversations for brass trio; Man with the blue guitar, chorus and piano; several compositions using tape and live performers.
5308 Wayne Road, Greensboro, NC 27420

BEYER, HOWARD
b. Chicago, Ill., 25 Mar. 1929. Attended American Cons., Chicago, B. A., M. A., studying with Leo Sowerby. His honors include a Thor Johnson award, U.S. Army march composition award in Europe, and an ASCAP award. He was staff musician at radio station WIND, 1955-57; WCFL, 1957- ; pianist with Norm Ladd Orch., 1970- .
WORKS: Suite for brass instruments; trumpet concerto; organ prelude; and popular compositions.
3824 Grand Ave., Western Springs, IL 60558

BEZANSON, PHILIP
b. Athol, Mass., 6 Jan. 1916. Studied at Yale Univ. with David Stanley Smith and Richard Donovan, and at Univ. of Iowa with Philip Greeley Clapp. He has received a Fromm Found. grant, 1953; Nat. Assoc. Coll. Wind and Perc. Instructors Publication award, 1960; Soc. for Publication of American Music grant, 1965; Guggenheim grant, 1967. He was professor, Univ. of Iowa, 1954-64; professor and head of music department, Univ. of Massachusetts, Amherst, 1964-73, and professor, 1973- .
WORKS: Opera: Golden child, NBC-TV, Hallmark Hall of Fame, 1960; Orchestra: piano concerto, New York, 1953; Rondo-prelude, 1954; Sinfonia concertante, Iowa City, 1972; Chamber music: string quartet, 1965; Prelude and dance, brass sextet; Diversion for brass trio, 1964; other solo, chamber, vocal and orchestral works.
15 Highland Circle, Hadley, MA 01035

BIALOSKY, MARSHALL H.
b. Cleveland, Ohio, 30 Oct. 1923. Attended Syracuse Univ., B. M. 1949, Northwestern Univ., M. M., and has studied with Lionel Nowak, Ernst Bacon, Roy Harris, Robert Delaney, and with Dallapiccola in Italy. He received a Fulbright fellowship to Italy, 1954-56, Wechsler Commission at Tanglewood, 1958, Wisconsin State composers award, 1954, and a Piano Quarterly citation, 1968. He has held faculty positions at Milton Coll., Wis., 1950-54; Univ. of Chicago, 1956-61; State Univ. of New York, Stony Brook, 1961-64; and has been professor and chairman, Fine Arts

(BIALOSKY, MARSHALL H.)
Department, California State Coll., Dominguez Hills, 1964- .
WORKS: Chamber music: Two movements for brass trio; Suite for flute, oboe, clarinet; sonatina for oboe and piano; Fantasy scherzo, saxophone and piano; Vocal: There is a wisdom that is woe; A song of degrees; Of music and musicians; Be music, night; Little ghost things; Five nonsense songs about animals; An old picture; Piano: Spring song; Five western scenes.
2043 Via Visalia
Palos Verdes Estates, CA 90274

BIDDELMAN, MARK
b. Newark, N. J., 7 June 1943. Hebrew Union Coll.-Jewish Inst. of Religion, School of Sacred Music and Carnegie Inst. of Technology. He has been a cantor since 1962, and at Temple Emanuel, Westwood, N. J., 1967- .
WORKS: Shiru Ladonai Shir Chadash, a rock-folk service for the Sabbath eve.
568 Hillsdale Ave., Hillsdale, NJ 07642

BIELAWA, HERBERT
b. Chicago, Ill., 3 Feb. 1930. Studied at Univ. of Illinois with Soulima Stravinsky, Gordon Binkerd, Burrill Phillips, Robert Kelly; Univ. of of Southern California with Ingolf Dahl, Halsey Stevens, Ellis Kohs; at Aspen with Darius Milhaud, 1958. His awards include Univ. of Illinois fellowship; Aspen composition prize; BMI fellowship; MENC and Ford Found. grant, 1964-66; Music Teachers Nat. Asso. Commission; Burke Found. grant; Bay Area Synthesizer Ensemble commission. He was instructor at Bethany Coll., 1958-60, and professor at San Francisco State Univ., 1966- .
WORKS: Theatre: A bird in the bush, chamber opera, 1962; What do you care? It's beyond repair!, satirical review, 1968; Orchestra: Concert piece, 1954; Divergents, 1968; Abstractions, string orch., 1965; Band: Concert fanfare, 1964; Toccata, 1964; Chorale, 1965; Spectrum, with pre-recorded tape, 1966; Chamber music: Trumpet duo, 1960; sonatina, clarinet and piano, 1962; Electronic and mixed media: Quodlibet SF 42569, organ and electronic sounds, 1969; Additions, 1968; Discoveries, 1970; Laps, gaps, and overlaps, tape only, 1973; A Dickinson album, choir, piano, tape, guitar, and troubadour, 1973; many choral works, vocal solos and piano and organ pieces.
81 Denslowe Drive, San Francisco, CA 94132

BIGGS, JOHN
b. Los Angeles, Calif., 18 Oct. 1932. Studied at Los Angeles City Coll. with Leonard Stein; Univ. of California, Los Angeles, with Lukas Foss, Roy Harris, John Vincent; Univ. of Southern California with Halsey Stevens, Ingolf Dahl; and Royal Cons., Antwerp, with Flor Peeters. He has had awards from Phi Mu Alpha, Atwater-Kent, Ohio State Univ., Celia Buck, and a Fulbright grant, and many commissions. He has held faculty positions at Univ. of California, Los Angeles, 1961-63; Los Angeles City Coll., 1965-67; Kansas State Teachers Coll., 1967-70.

BIGGS, JOHN

(BIGGS, JOHN)
    WORKS: Orchestra: Symphony, 1964;
Concerto for viola, woodwinds, percussion,
1965; Symphonic ode, 1971; Foreground music,
35 winds and percussion, 1971; Chamber music:
Tre canzoni for 3 clarinets, 1964; Aria and
toccata, organ, 1965; Wind collage, 1972;
Mixed media: Invention for piano and tape,
1970; Invention for flute and tape, 1971;
Invention for viola and tape, 1972; Invention
for organ and tape, 1972; Invention for voices,
tape, 1971; many choral works and songs.
    1724 Garden St., Santa Barbara, CA 93101

BILIK, JERRY H.
    b. New Rochelle, N. Y., 7 Oct. 1933. Studied
at Univ. of Michigan, B. M., M. M., with Ross
Lee Finney, Leslie Bassett, and Tibor Serly.
He has received an American Legion award,
Stanley Medal, Pi Kappa Lambda award, Standard
Oil Faculty award, and an ASCAP award. He rose
from lecturer to professor at Univ. of Michigan,
1962-68; was adjunct professor, Univ. of
Michigan and Wayne State Univ., 1971-   ; and
self-employed composer and arranger, 1968-   .
    WORKS: Theatre: Brass and grass forever,
musical play, for which he wrote the book and
lyrics; Orchestra: Aspects of man, 4 essays;
Band: Symphony for band: They walked in
darkness; American Civil War fantasy;
Concertino for alto saxophone and band.
    2635 West Delhi Road, Ann Arbor, MI 48103

BILLINGSLEY, WILLIAM A.
    b. Glasgow, Mont., 28 June 1922. Studied
principally with Francis J. Pyle at Drake Univ.
He has had commissions from the Boise Tuesday
Musicale and the Spokane Symphony. He played
trumpet in the Des Moines Symphony, 1951 and
1953 and at radio station WHO, Des Moines; and
with Spokane Symphony, 1960-61. He has been on
the faculty at Univ. of Idaho, 1954-   .
    WORKS: Chamber ballet for string quartet
and two dancers, Boise, May 1968; a work for
soprano solo and orchestra was premiered during
Expo '74 in Spokane. He has composed for band,
orchestra, chamber groups, solo wind and voice.
    School of Music, University of Idaho
    Moscow, ID 83843

*BILOTTI, ANTON
    b. New York, N. Y., 17 Jan. 1906; d. New York,
10 Nov. 1963. Wrote 2 piano concertos; violin
concerto; saxophone concerto; chamber
music.

BILYEU, LANDON
    b. Lufkin, Tex., 30 Dec. 1939. Attended
Centenary Coll., La.; Univ. of Tulsa, studying
with Bela Rozsa; and Boston Univ., studying
composition with Ulysses Kay and piano with
Bela Nagy. He was on the faculty at Midwestern
Univ., 1964-71; and assistant professor, Univ.
of Idaho, 1971-   .
    WORKS: Ballet: The debutante's ball for
violin, winds, and percussion; Chamber music:
Prelude for flute and small orch.; Invention and
2 fugues for winds; Andante and allegro, flute

(BILYEU, LANDON)
    and piano; sonatina for flute and piano; piano
sonata; four 12-tone piano pieces.
    701 East 3rd St., Moscow, ID 83843

*BIMBONI, ALBERTO
    b. Florence, Italy, 24 Aug. 1882; d. New York,
18 June 1960. Wrote 3 1-act operas; piano and
organ pieces; many songs.

*BINDER, ABRAHAM WOLFE
    b. New York, 13 Jan. 1895; d. New York,
10 Oct. 1966. Wrote symphonic works, violin
pieces, songs; The legend of Ari, oratorio.

*BINGHAM, SETH
    b. Bloomfield, N. J., 16 Apr. 1882; d. New
York, 21 June 1972. Studied with Horatio
Parker at Yale Univ., B. M. 1908; organ and
composition in Paris, 1906, 1907. He received
an honorary doctorate from Ohio Wesleyan Univ.,
1952. He was instructor, Yale Univ., 1908-20;
associate professor, Columbia Univ., 1920-54;
continued to lecture at Union Theological
Seminary to 1965; organist and music director,
Madison Avenue Presbyterian Church for 35 years.
    WORKS: Orchestra: Wall Street fantasy,
1912, played by New York Philharmonic, 1916;
concerto for brass, snare drums, and organ,
1954; numerous concertos, suites; chamber music;
choral works; organ works including Baroques,
a suite, 1943; Connecticut suite for organ and
orch.; 36 hymn and carol canons in free style,
1952.

BINKERD, GORDON
    b. Lynch, Neb., 22 May 1916. Studied at
Eastman School of Music with Bernard Rogers;
Harvard Univ. with Walter Piston; and Dakota
Wesleyan Univ. with Gail Kubik and Russell
Danburg. He has received a Nat. Inst. of Arts
and Letters award, Guggenheim grant, and
commissions from St. Louis Symph., Fromm Found.,
Ford Found., Library of Congress, Quincy Symph.,
Ill., and Univ. of Illinois. He served in the
U.S. Navy, 1942-46, and has held faculty positions at Garden City Jr. Coll., Kan., 1937-38;
Franklin Coll., Ind., 1938-40; Univ. of Illinois,
1949-71.
    WORKS: Orchestra: 3 symphonies; movement
for orchestra; piece for violin and orchestra;
Wind ensemble: Canzonas for brass choir; The
battle, brass and percussion; Chamber music:
cello sonata; flute sonatina; 2 string quartets;
violin sonata, commissioned by the McKim Fund
in the Library of Congress, and performed there
2 May 1974; song cycle for mezzo-soprano and
string quartet; song cycle for mezzo-soprano
and string duo; piano sonata; choral works; solo
songs with piano; piano and organ music.
    R. R. #2, Urbana, IL 61801

*BINNEY, OLIVER
    Sonnet, violin, strings, timpani, 1966.
    Greenville, Pa., 22 July 1971.

*BIRCHALL, STEVEN
    Reciprocals II, for 2 tubas.

*BIRD, BERNARD
A musical theory on the interpretative powers of the human mind, violin and piano, 1966, won the Kodaly prize in 1971; Concert duet, violin and piano, 1972; Quartology, a study of 4 instruments, 1972; Agnus dei, double chorus, 3 violins, 3 cellos, 1972; piano pieces.
515 South Council, Muncie, IN 47302

BIRD, HUBERT C.
b. Joplin, Mo., 12 Oct. 1939. Studied in Joplin, Mo., with Merrill Ellis; at Kansas State Coll. of Pittsburg with Markwood Holmes; Univ. of Colorado with Charles Eakin. He won first prize in a contest sponsored by the D.C. Chapter, American Guild of Organists, 1973. He has been composer-in-residence and choral director, Keene State Coll., Univ. of New Hampshire, 1967-   .
WORKS: Brass ensemble: Fanfare for an uncommon child, Christmas work, 3 horns, 4 trumpets, organ, 1966; Chamber music: Dialogues, flute, clarinet, piano, 1973; Chorus: The cricket sang, 1965; Magnificat, chorus, soloists, 4 trumpets, organ, 1966; A hope for peace, cantata, chorus, soloists, orchestra, 1970; Anthem, chorus, baritone, organ, National Cathedral, Washington, 1973; Songs: Five songs on poems of Robert Graves, 1965; Songs of a singing people, texts by Langston Hughes.
RFD #1, Marlborough, NH 03455

BIRNBAUM, MARK J.
b. Geneva, Switz., of American parents, 11 Feb. 1952. Has studied at Brooklyn Coll. with Noah Creshevsky, Jacob Druckman, and Stephen Dankner.
WORKS: Orchestra: Metamorphoses; Chamber music: piano sonata; Coffee, flute, violin, piano, 1972; Survey of literature, clarinet, tenor, piano; Rhinoceros, 3 movements for flute, bass clarinet, cello, piano, percussion, 1973; string quartet, 1973.
879 East 27th St., Brooklyn, NY 11210

BISCHOFF, KURT
b. San Francisco, Calif., 24 Sep. 1949. Studied at Univ. of California at Davis with Richard Swift, Larry Austin, Arthur Woodbury; and privately with Stanley Lunetta and Robert Fylling. He is a percussion instructor.
WORKS: Mick Martin's orthopedic blues band, theatre piece for blues band electronic preachers; 1968; War piece, for projectionists, navigator, and artillery crew, 1969; AMRA/ARMA's repetition piece, variation No. 3007, for electronics wizard, cybernaut bassist, 2 droube percussionists, and a bird, 1973; Wedding song for pseudo-cosmic calypso group, 1972.
5150 Elvas Ave., Sacramento, CA 95819

*BISH, DIANE
Organ concerto performed by composer and Fort Lauderdale Symphony Orchestra, 1974.

BITGOOD, ROBERTA (Mrs. J. G. Wiersma)
b. New London, Conn., 15 Jan. 1908. Studied at Connecticut Coll. for Women; Guilmant Organ School, New York; Columbia Univ., M. A.; Union Theological Seminary, M. S. M., S. M. D.; Univ.

(BITGOOD, ROBERTA)
of Redlands; teachers included J. Lawrence Erb, Edwin Stringham, T. Tertius Noble, and Wayne Bohrnstedt. She is a fellow and choirmaster of the American Guild of Organists and has received 15 commissions for choral works. She has been organist and choirmaster since 1932, and at First Congregational Church, Battle Creek, Mich., 1969-   . She was also on the faculty at Bloomfield Coll., N. J., 1935-47.
WORKS: Her many choral compositions include: 3 cantatas, Job, Joseph, Let there be light; The power of music, choir and organ, 1972; My heart is ready, O God, 1972; Lord may we follow, 1973; Organ: On an ancient alleluia, 1958; Rejoice, give thanks, organ and 4 brasses, 1971.
643 Riverside Drive, Battle Creek, MI 49015

*BITTER, JOHN
b. New York, 8 Apr. 1909. Studied at Curtin Inst. of Music. He was conductor, Jacksonville Symphony, 1934-36; Florida Symphony, 1936-40; faculty member, Univ. of Miami, 1940-42, dean School of Music, 1951-59. His works include a suite and 3 tone poems for orchestra; a string quartet; songs, instrumental solos, etc.
5671 Southwest 98 Terrace
South Miami, FL 33143

BITZEL, CHARLES RAYMOND
b. Baltimore, Md., 10 May 1946. Attended Peabody Cons., B. M. 1968, studying composition with Howard Thatcher. He won an international composition contest sponsored by the American Accordion Musicological Soc. He taught in public schools, 1968-70, and is a member of the Maryland Symphonette, 1973-   .
WORKS: 2 symphonies; Three atonal pieces and Two caricatures for accordion.
1918 Englewood Ave., Baltimore, MD 21207

*BLACK, CHARLES
b. Augusta, Me., 24 Nov. 1903. Studied at Eastman School of Music, B. M.; Union Theological Seminary, M. S. M. He has published choral works.

*BLACKWOOD, EASLEY
b. Indianapolis, Ind., 21 Apr. 1933. Studied with Olivier Messiaen at Tanglewood; with Paul Hindemith at Yale Univ.; with Nadia Boulanger in Paris, 1954-56. His awards include a Fulbright grant; Koussevitzky Found. award, 1958; commissions from Fromm Found., 1957, G. Schirmer, Inc., 1960, Koussevitzky Found., 1960. He has been on the faculty, Univ. of Chicago, 1958-   .
WORKS: Orchestra: 3 symphonies, 1958, 1960, 1964; clarinet concerto, 1964; violin concerto, 1966; flute concerto, 1968; piano concerto, Cleveland, 7 June 1972; Chamber music: viola sonata; chamber symphony, 1955; 2 string quartets, 1957, 1960; concertino for 5 instruments, 1959; violin sonata, 1960; Fantasy, cello and piano; sonata for flute and harpsichord.
Depart. of Music, University of Chicago
Chicago, IL 60637

BLAKE, DOROTHY GAYNOR

*BLAKE, DOROTHY GAYNOR
b. St. Joseph, Mo., 21 Nov. 1893; d. Webster
Groves, Mo. Composed songs and piano pieces.

BLAKE, JAMES HUBERT (Eubie)
b. Baltimore, Md., 7 Feb. 1883. Studied in
Baltimore with Margaret Marshall and Llewelyn
Wilson, and at New York Univ. he studied the
Schillinger system with Rudolf Schramm. He has
received honorary doctorates from Brooklyn Coll.,
1973, Rutgers Univ., Dartmouth Coll., and New
England Cons., 1974. He was pianist and organist in cafes, vaudeville, and theater, and then
in 1915 joined with Noble Sissle, lyricist, in
the vaudeville team of Sissle and Blake. During
World War I, they toured in a musical show organized by James Europe from musicians in the U.S.
369th Infantry. Blake toured five years with
the USO in World War II. But the greatest suc-
cesses of the team came with the musical shows
and the songs they wrote.
    WORKS: Musicals: Shuffle along, 1921;
Chocolate dandies, 1924; Elsie, 1924; Blackbirds,
1930; and over 300 songs including I'm just wild
about Harry and Memories of you.
See Reminiscing with Sissle and Blake, Kimball
and Bolcom, 1973.
    284 A Stuyvesant Ave., Brooklyn, NY 11221

BLAKE, RAN
b. Springfield, Mass., 20 Apr. 1935. Attended
Bard Coll., B. A.; Columbia Univ.; School of
Jazz, Lenox, Mass.; and studied privately with
Ray Cassarino, Willie L. Janes, Oscar Peterson,
Mary Lou Williams, Mal Waldron, William Russo,
and Gunther Schuller. He organized the Bard Jazz
Festivals in 1957, 1958, 1959, and helped in
organizing other jazz festivals. In 1965 he won
first prize in Germany for outstanding pop-jazz
of the year. He was music critic in New York
1958-60, and has held administrative and faculty
positions at the New England Cons. 1968- .
    WORKS: Three seeds; The blue potato; The
marriage of oppression in 3rd-stream realizations; pianist and 3 narrators, Boston, 12 Apr.
1971; and piano solos.
    25 St. Stephen St., Boston, MA 02115

*BLAKLEY, D. DUANE
Jesus Christ, the crucified, a contemporary
cantata.

*BLANCHARD, ROBERT
Preludio festiva for organ.

BLAND, WILLIAM KEITH
b. Shepherdstown, W. Va., 11 Nov. 1947. Studied
at Peabody Cons., M. M. 1970, D. M. A. 1972, with
Benjamin Lees, Ernst Krenek, Richard Rodney
Bennett, and Earle Brown. He taught at Peabody
Cons. 1970-72, and has been assistant professor
at Brooklyn Coll., CUNY, 1972- . As an author
he has contributed articles on Christian Wolff,
Morton Feldman, and Earle Brown to the new edition of Grove's Dictionary.
    WORKS: Orchestra: Between moments II and
III for large orch. and solo marimba; Chamber

(BLAND, WILLIAM KEITH)
music: Speed, organ, 1969; Sonic nocturne, horn
and piano, 1969; Like a mad animal, for six
instruments and solo contrabass, 1971; Between
moments I for guitar; Five subtitled pieces,
various instruments; Cantelina and varient I
(Cocaine says), solo violin; 4 songs for guitar
and soprano, 1973; Years after morality, theater
piece for guitar, baritone, percussion; Beverly,
theater piece for poet, piano, baritone, percussion; Chorus: Songs of morality, 8-part chorus
playing percussion, 1973.
    Shepherdstown, WV 25443

BLANK, ALLAN
b. Bronx, N. Y., 27 Dec. 1925. Studied at
Juilliard School, 1945-47; New York Univ., B. A.
1948; Univ. of Minnesota, M. A. 1950; Columbia
Univ., 1955-57, 1965-66; Univ. of Iowa, 1966-67;
Princeton summer seminar, 1960. He held a conducting fellowship at Juilliard. He was violinist with the Pittsburgh Symph., 1950-52; on the
faculty, Western Illinois Univ., 1966-68; Paterson State Coll., 1968-70; and assistant professor, Lehman Coll., CUNY, 1970- .
    WORKS: Opera: Aria da capo, chamber opera;
Excitement at the circus, children's musical;
Orchestra: Music for orchestra, Milwaukee, May
1968; Mediatation; Band: Concert piece; Chamber
music: Thirteen ways of looking at a blackbird,
soprano and 6 instruments, 1964, London, 6 June
1973; Poem, soprano and 6 instruments, 1963, London, 6 June 1973; Two parables by Franz Kafka,
soprano and chamber ensemble, 1964; Two simple
canons, 2 flutes; woodwind quintet, 1970; A song
of ascents, solo viola; Variations for clarinet
and viola; Music for violin, 1961; Four bagatelles, oboe and clarinet; Music for solo trumpet; Three novelties, alto saxophone; Knock on
wood, percussion; Two studies for brass quintet;
Composition for 11 players, New York, Feb. 1966;
Esther's monologue, cantata for soprano, oboe,
viola, cello, 1970; Rotation: a study for piano,
New York, 1962; Chorus: Tell me where is fancy
bred?; Psalm V, men's voices; The frogs, double
chorus.
    Barnes St., Ossining, NY 10562

BLANKENSHIP, LYLE MARK
b. Chicago, Ill., 11 May 1943. Studied at Oklahoma Baptist Univ. with Warren M. Angell, and at
Univ. of Texas with Alexander von Kreisler. He
won the Ford composition award at Oklahoma Baptist Univ. He has been minister of music since
1966 and at the North Phoenix Baptist Church,
Ariz., 1973- . All of his published works are
religious choral compositions.
    702 East Harmont, Phoenix, AZ 85020

BLATTER, ALFRED
b. Litchfield, Ill., 24 Dec. 1937. Studied at
Univ. of Illinois with Kenneth Gaburo, Ben
Johnston, and Robert Kelly. He was an arranger
and played horn in the U.S. Army Band, Fort
Myer, Va., 1962-65, then joined the faculty at
Marshall Univ., 1966-69, and has been professor
at Univ. of Illinois, 1969- .

(BLATTER, ALFRED)
WORKS: <u>Fusions</u>, solo percussion and orchestra, Eugene, Ore., 1969; Suite for brass; <u>A study in time and space</u> for string quartet; <u>Five sketches</u>, trombone and piano; <u>A dream within a dream</u>, tenor, piano, and piano interior.
310 Pond Ridge Lane, Urbana, IL 61801

*BLEDSOE, JULES
b. Waco, Tex., 29 Dec. 1899; d. Hollywood, Calif., 14 July 1943. Baritone and composer, sang title role in Gruenberg's <u>Emperor Junes</u>. He wrote <u>African suite</u> for orchestra and songs in the style of negro spirituals.

*BLEY, CARLA
b. Oakland, Calif., 1938. Received a Guggenheim fellowship, 1972. Her works include <u>Elevator over the hill</u>, a multimedia opera, recorded by Jazz Composers of America; <u>3/4</u>, for piano and 15 players, New York, 17 Mar. 1974.
c/o Jazz Composers of America
6 West 95th St., New York, NY 10025

BLICKHAN, CHARLES TIMOTHY
b. Quincy, Ill., 9 June 1945. Studied at Northeast Missouri State Univ. with Leon Karel and Tom V. Ritchie; and at Univ. of Illinois with Paul Zonn. He received a Nat. Fed. of Music Clubs award for composition and arranging with the U.S. CONARC Band, Ft. Monroe, Va., 1972. He has been music instructor in public schools and is now teaching assistant, Univ. of Illinois.
WORKS: Band: <u>Multi-meter suite</u>, 1973; <u>Niche of time</u>, Ann Arbor, Mich., 1973; jazz compositions and works for college musical groups.
406 East Michigan #3, Urbana, IL 61801

BLISS, MILTON CLAY
b. Charlotte, N. C., 19 Apr. 1927. Studied at Univ. of North Carolina, Chapel Hill, with Jan Schinhan and Glenn Haydon. He is on the faculty of North Carolina State Univ. and at Page High School in Greensboro.
WORKS: Theater: Incidental music to <u>The gathering</u>, <u>Medea</u>, and <u>The Trojan women</u>; Orchestra: <u>Lamentation and dance</u>; Band: <u>Pastoral and march</u>; Chorus: <u>Tower of Babel</u>; <u>Sing unto the Lord a new song</u>; <u>The raven days</u>; <u>There came a wind like a bugle</u>.
2726 Van Dyke Ave., Raleigh, NC 27607

*BLISS, P. PAUL
b. Chicago, Ill., 25 Nov. 1872; d. Oswego, N. Y., 2 Feb. 1933. Wrote 3 operettas, a piano suite, songs and choruses.

*BLITZSTEIN, MARC
b. Philadelphia, Pa., 2 Mar. 1905; d. Martinique, W.I., 22 Jan. 1964. Studied at Univ. of Pennsylvania; with Rosario Scalero, Curtis Inst. of Music; with Nadia Boulanger in Paris and Arnold Schoenberg in Berlin. His awards include 2 Guggenheim fellowships; American Acad. of Arts and Letters grant; Ford Found. grant; American Aeronautical Inst. award; and commissions. He served in the U.S. Army during World War II. He wrote many works for theatre: <u>The cradle will</u>

(BLITZSTEIN, MARC)
<u>rock</u>, 1937; <u>Regina</u>, full length opera based on Lillian Hellman's <u>The Little foxes</u>, 1949; <u>The harpies</u>, 1931, was revived at Composers' Showcase, New York, 5 Dec. 1973. His <u>Airborne</u>, a cantata, was performed by the Tulsa Philharmonic under Skitch Henderson with the Metropolitan Opera's general manager Schuyler Chapin as narrator, 26 Nov. 1973.

BLOCH, ALEXANDER
b. Selma, Ala., 11 July 1881. Attended Columbia Univ. and studied with Eduard Hermann in New York, Ottakar Sevcik in Vienna, and Leopold Auer in Petrograd. He was concertmaster and soloist with the symphony orchestra in Tiflis, Russia, in the early 1900s and made his New York debut in 1913. He was teaching assistant to Leopold Auer during his residence in the U.S., and taught at Washington Coll. of Music and Rollins Coll. Cons.; was conductor of the Central Florida Symph. Orch., 1936-43; Florida West Coast Symph. Orch., 1950-62; and guest conductor, NBC Symph. and Nat. Symph. Orch. He gave many recitals in the U.S.
WORKS: <u>Roeliff's dream</u>, children's operetta, libretto by Mrs. Bloch; <u>The lone tree</u>, Christmas play with music; art songs to poems by Shelley, Edna St. Vincent Millay, and Arthur Davison Ficke. He has published various technical works for violin and magazine articles.
(summer) Springhill Farm
Hillsdale, NY 12529
(winter) 126 Garden Lane
Sarasota, FL 33581

*BLOCH, ERNEST
b. Geneva, Switz., 24 July 1880; U.S. citizen 1924; d. Portland, Ore., 15 July 1959. Studied in Geneva, Brussels, Frankfurt am Main, and Munich. He received the Coolidge prize, 1919; 1st prize, Musical America contest, 1927; New York Music Critics Circle award, 1947. He was on the faculty, Mannes School of Music, 1917-19; director, Cleveland Inst. of Music, 1920-25; director, San Francisco Cons., 1925-30; resided in Europe, 1930-39; returned to U.S. and settled in Oregon, devoting most of his time to composition.
WORKS: Opera: <u>Macbeth</u>, Paris, 1910; Orchestra: symphony, 1910; <u>Schelomo</u>, cello and orch., 1917; Concerto grosso no. 1, strings and piano, 1925; America, 1928; violin concerto, 1938; <u>Scherzo fantasque</u>, piano and orch., 1950; Concerto grosso no. 2 for strings, 1950; <u>Suite hebraique</u>, viola and orch., 1953; <u>Suite module</u>, flute and strings, 1957; works for voice and orch.; Chamber music; 4 string quartets, 1916, 1946, 1951, 1953; <u>Suite</u> for viola and piano, 1919; <u>Baal Shem</u>, violin and piano, 1923; piano sonata, 1953; and many other works.

BLOCK, ROBERT PAUL
b. Cincinnati, Ohio, 17 Aug. 1942. Studied at Roosevelt Univ. with Karel Jirak, Robert Lombardo, Robert Muczynski; and at Univ. of Iowa with Richard Hervig.

BLOCK, ROBERT PAUL

(BLOCK, ROBERT PAUL)
WORKS: Orchestra: Concerto for alto recorder and strings, 1968; Music for orchestra and timpani, 1968; Chamber music: Ein dekadenter Walzer, 4 violas or 4 cellos, 1971; 4 Fantasies for solo instruments: viola, 1967-73; cello, 1973; doublebass, 1973; violin, 1973.
629 North Linn, Iowa City, IA 52240

BLOOD, ESTA
b. New York, N. Y., 25 Mar. 1933. Attended Manhattan School of Music and studied with Malke Gottlieb in New York and Anita Meyer in Schenectady. She has two commissions from the Albany Symph. Orch. and one from Temple Beth Emeth, Albany. She has been teaching piano since 1950.
WORKS: Chamber music: Nocturne, violin and piano; Bulgarian trio, flute, violin, piano; Six traditional songs arranged for flute, violin, viola, bassoon, piano; Jack and the beanstalk, flute, violin, viola, bassoon, and narrator; Vocal: A Psalm of David, cantor and 4-part choir, keyboard accompaniment; Starsong, poem of Tagore, soprano and piano; Fall, poem by Carl J. George, soprano and piano; Piano: Balkan suite, 1969; Seven dances in Aksak rhythms, Schenectady, 4 Jan. 1973.
1218 Regent St., Schenectady, NY 12309

*BLOOM, STEPHEN
Theme and variations for woodwind quintet.

BLUMENFELD, HAROLD
b. Seattle, Wash., 15 Oct. 1923. Studied at Eastman School of Music, 1941-43; Yale Univ., B. M. 1949, M. M. 1950; Zurich Univ. and Cons., 1948; and at Salzburg and Tanglewood with Leonard Bernstein, Robert Shaw, Boris Goldovsky. He was awarded $2000 in a national composition contest, 1955; a MacDowell fellowship; 2 Yaddo fellowships, 1968, 1970; ASCAP awards. He served in the U.S. Army, 1943-46; has been professor at Washington Univ. since 1950, and is director of the University Opera Studio and the St. Louis Opera Theatre.
WORKS: Opera: Gentle boy, adapted from Hawthorne text for television, 1968; Amphitryon 4, after Moliere, 1952-56; The road to Salem, opera for television, 1973; Orchestra: Elegy for the nightingale, baritone, chorus, orch., 1954; Contrasts, 1955; Miniature overture, 1958; Songs of innocence, text by Blake, 2 choruses, 2 soli, orch., 1973; Chamber music: Transformations for piano, 1963; Expansions, woodwind quintet, 1964; Movements for brass, septet, St. Louis, Nov. 1966; Lovescapes, texts of Isabella Gardner, soprano and 8 instruments, 1970; Chorus: Three Scottish poems, texts by L. A. G. Strong, a cappella, 1949; Four tranquil poems, texts by D. H. Lawrence, a cappella, 1950; Songs of war, texts by Siegfried Sassoon, 1970. He is author of newspaper and magazine articles on music and has published a translation of the Praetorius Syntagma musicum.
General Delivery, Osage Beach, MO 65065

*BOARDMAN, HERBERT
b. Somerville, Mass., 1892. Graduated from the New England Cons., 1916. He composed chamber music and songs.

*BOATRITE, HAROLD
b. 1932. Suite for harpsichord; cello sonata. Haverford College, Haverford, PA 19041.

BOATWRIGHT, HOWARD
b. Newport News, Va., 16 Mar. 1918. Had early training in violin and piano and gave a full-length violin recital at age 14. He studied with Paul Hindemith at Yale Univ., B. M. 1947, M. M. 1948. At Yale he held Bradley-Keeler and Horatio Parker fellowships; was Fulbright lecturer in India, 1959-60; received a Rockefeller grant to study the kritis of Tyagaraja and South India violin playing; Soc. for Publication of American Music award, 1962; Yale alumni award, 1970; Fulbright grant to Romania, 1971-72. He has made many concert tours in the U.S., Mexico, and Europe, sometimes with his wife, Helen Boatwright, noted soprano; was associate professor of violin, Univ. of Texas, 1943; on Yale faculty, 1948-64; concertmaster, New Haven Symph., 1950-62; dean, School of Music, Syracuse Univ., 1964-   .
WORKS: Orchestra: A song for St. Cecilia's day, string orch.; Variations for small orch.; Sinner man, Appalachian folk hymn, baritone and orch., 1960; The false knight upon the road, baritone and orch., 1961; Canticle of the sun, chorus, soprano, orch., 1963; Movement for orchestra, 1971; Larghetto espressivo, trio scherzando, 1972; Chamber music: string quartet, 1947; trio for two violins and viola, 1948; Serenade, two strings and two winds, 1952; Canon, two violins and piano, 1953; quartet for clarinet and strings, 1958; Variations for piano, 1966; Three inventions for keyboard, 1971; suite for clarinet alone, 1973; Chorus: many works for chorus including The passion according to St. Matthew, 1962; and many songs for solo voices. He is author of Introduction to the theory of music (N. Y., 1956), A handbook for staff notation for Indian music (Bombay, 1960), and Indian classical music and the western listener (Bombay, 1960).
School of Music, Syracuse University
Syracuse, NY 13210

BOCK, FRED
b. New York, N. Y., 30 Mar. 1939. Attended Ithaca Coll., B. S. 1960; Univ. of Southern California, M. M. 1962; studied with Warren Benson, Halsey Stevens, and Robert Linn. He has received ASCAP awards annually since 1963. He has been organist and choir director, Bel Air Presbyterian Church, Los Angeles, 1964-   .
WORKS: He has composed for piano, organ, and chorus, including a cantata, Song of triumph, and a musical, One solitary life (with Paul Johnson).
5404 Topeka Drive, Tarzana, CA 91356

*BOCKMON, GUY ALAN
Professor, Univ. of Tennessee, Knoxville, has
published Te Deum, Laudamus for chorus and organ.

*BODA, JOHN
b. Boyceville, Wis., 2 Aug. 1922. Studied at
Eastman School of Music. He has been on the faculty, Florida State Univ., 1946-   .
WORKS: Orchestra: Sinfonia, 1960; Chamber
music: 2 piano sonatas; Prelude, scherzo, postlude, brass quartet; trombone sonatina; 4 Byzantine etudes for guitar; cornet sonatina; clarinet sonatina; Introduction and dance, guitar.
School of Music, Florida State University
Tallahassee, FL 32306

BOEHLE, WILLIAM RANDALL
b. Waxahachie, Tex., 1 July 1919. Studied at
Louisiana State Univ. with Helen Gunderson, and
at Univ. of Iowa with Philip Greeley Clapp. He
was professor and chairman, Division of Fine
Arts, Chadron State Coll. Neb., 1952-60; and has
been professor and chairman, Dept. of Music,
Univ. of North Dakota, 1960-   .
WORKS: Orchestra: concertino for piano;
concerto for trumpet; Chamber music: brass
suite; woodwind quintet; sonatine for two pianos;
Sonnet, voice and piano; Passacaglia and fugue
for piano; Chorus: The aviary, on 7 Ogden Nash
poems.
406 22nd Ave. South, Grand Forks, ND 58201

*BOEHMER, ALAN
Studied composition with Robert Gross at Occidental Coll. He received first prize, California
Music Teachers Asso. composition contest, 1967,
and the Eleanor Remick Warren composition award,
1967. He has published Partita for organ, and
Variations on a play tune for piano.
2121 Valdress Drive, Glendale, CA 91208

BOEHNLEIN, FRANK
b. Bedford, Ohio, 2 Feb. 1945. Studied at
Rollins Coll. with John Carter; and received his
D. M. A. from both Case Western Reserve Univ. and
Cleveland Inst. of Music in 1972, studying with
Donald Erb and Marcel Dick. Awards include
Presser Found. scholarships, 1964-66; Ralph Lyman
Baldwin award, 1967; Ford Found. grant, 1971;
Outstanding Educators of America award, 1972;
Composers' Conference, 1970, 1973; Nat. Endowment
for the Arts, 1973-74. He taught at Cleveland
Inst. of Music, 1970-71; Wichita State Univ.,
1972; was on faculty and composer-in-residence,
St. Mary of the Plains Coll., 1971-74; assistant
professor, Texas Woman's Univ., 1974-   .
WORKS: Chamber music: piano sonata, 1970;
Canto for string quartet, 1972, revised 1973;
Chorus: Missa l'homme arme, 12-part a cappella
choir, 1971; Mixed media: The death of the ball
turret gunner, chorus, chamber ensemble, theatre
media, 1967; Karma dreama, orchestra, soprano,
tape; Gog, magog, and other passions, four dancers, tape, chamber ensemble, and theatre media,
1973; Aftermath, music drama for choirs, dancers,
ensembles, orch., and octophonic tape, 1973-74;
film score: To teach yourself.
P. O. Box 962, Denton, TX 76201

BOERINGER, JAMES
b. Pittsburgh, Pa., 4 Mar. 1930. Attended Coll.
of Wooster, B. A. 1956; Columbia Univ., M. A.
1954; Union Theological Seminary, D. S. M.; and
New York Univ. His composition teachers were
Seth Bingham and Douglas Moore. He became an
associate of the American Guild of Organists,
1953, and received a grant from the Lutheran
Church in 1967. He has held faculty positions
in public schools and at Univ. of South Dakota,
Oklahoma Baptist Univ., and is now associate professor at Susquehanna Univ.
WORKS: He has composed chiefly for chorus
and organ. He is the author of many articles
and reviews in musical journals.
Susquehanna University
Selinsgrove, PA 17870

*BOESING, PAUL and MARTHA
A ballad of now, folk opera, Center Opera Company, Minneapolis, 28 Feb. 1970.

*BOHLEN, DONALD
Ismene, 2-act chamber opera, Central Missouri
State Univ., Warrensburg, 17 Feb. 1969.

BOHRNSTEDT, WAYNE R.
b. Onalaska, Wis., 19 Jan. 1923. Studied at
Northwestern Univ. with Albert Nolte and Robert
Delaney; Eastman School of Music with Herbert
Elwell and Howard Hanson. He won first prize in
the Oppenheimer Contest for Ohio composers, 1951,
and first prize Nat. Fed. of Music Clubs, 1951.
He was on the faculty, Northwestern Univ.,
1946-47; Bowling Green State Univ., 1947-53; and
professor, Univ. of Redlands, 1953-   , director, School of Music, 1968-   , and dean, Division of Fine and Performing Arts, 1973-   .
WORKS: Opera: The necklace, chamber opera;
Orchestra: Romantic overture, 1951; trumpet
concerto; symphony No. 1; concertino for timpani,
xylophone and orch.; concertino for trombone and
strings; Chorus: Mass for the people.
School of Music, University of Redlands
Redlands, CA 92373

BOLCOM, WILLIAM
b. Seattle, Wash., 26 May 1938. Entered Univ. of
Washington, School of Music at age 11, studied
composition with George F. McKay and John
Verrall. In 1958 he began study with Darius
Milhaud at Mills Coll., and later with Milhaud,
Jean Rivier, and Olivier Messiaen at the Paris
Cons., then with Leland Smith at Stanford Univ.,
D. M. A. His awards include the American Acad.
of Arts and Letters, Marc Blitzstein award, 1965;
Guggenheim grants, 1964, 1968; Kurt Weill Found.
grant, 1961; Copley grant, 1960; Creative Arts
Public Service grant, 1971; Rockefeller Found.
grants, 1963, 1965, 1969-71; Koussevitzky Found.
grant, 1974. He taught at Univ. of Washington,
1965-66; Queens Coll., CUNY, 1966-68; Brooklyn
Coll., CUNY, 1973; and has been assistant pro-
fessor, Univ. of Michigan, 1973-   .
WORKS: Opera: Dynamite tonight, New York, 21
Dec. 1963; Orchestra: 2 symphonies, Aspen, 1957,
Seattle, 1965; Oracles, Seattle, 2 May 1965-   ;
Chamber music: Sessions I-IV, Chamber orch.,
1965-   ; Concerto-serenade, violin and strings,

BOLCOM, WILLIAM

(BOLCOM, WILLIAM)
1964; Commedia, chamber orch., 1971; 9 string
quartets, no. 9, New York, 21 May 1973; Keyboard:
Frescoes, 2 keyboard performers, 1971; War in the
heavens, 2 performers; 12 etudes, 1959-66;
Hydraulics, organ, 1973; Whisper moon, Bowdoin
Coll., 10 Apr. 1973; Morning and evening poems,
New York, Jan. 1973; numerous rags for piano;
Mixed media: Black host, percussion, organ,
tape, 1967.
    3080 Whitmore Lake Road, Ann Arbor, MI 48103

*BOLIN, NICOLAI P.
    b. Ukraine, Russia, 6 Oct. 1908; to U.S. at an
early age. Studied at Univ. of California, Los
Angeles, B. S.; has won the Hollywood Bowl
Gershwin Memorial award. His works for orchestra include Symphonic sketches, a suite; Symphonie tsigane; and Los Angeles concerto, piano
and orch.

BOLLE, JAMES
    b. Evanston, Ill., 26 July 1931. Attended Har-
vard Univ., 1949-52, and studied composition with
Darius Milhaud, 1950-52. He was on the faculty
at Univ. of Saskatchewan, 1953-59, and has been
director, Monadnock Music Center, Jaffrey, N. H.
1966-   .
    WORKS: Opera: Oleum canis, after Ambrose
Bierce, 1972; Chorus: Cantata 1, Saskatoon,
1959; La catafalque des dieux, Chicago, 1966,
cantata with texts of Christopher Smart,
Monadnock, 1970; Piano: set of four Capriccios.
    Francestown, NH 03043

BOLZ, HARRIETT (Mrs. Harold A.)
    b. Cleveland, Ohio. Attended Case Western Re-
serve Univ., B. A. 1933; Ohio State Univ., M. A.
1958; and studied privately with Leo Sowerby and
Paul Creston. She has won awards from Nat. Fed.
of Music Clubs, 1965; Phi Beta Fraternity, 1968;
Nat. League of Pen Women, 1970, 1972. She has
been a private teacher of piano and composition
and lecturer and author on contemporary music.
    WORKS: Chamber music: Duo scherzando, trum-
pet and piano, 1968; sonata for string and woodwind septet; Vis-a-vis, two short pieces for
woodwind trio; Invocation, soprano and string
quartet; Polychrome patterns, clarinet and piano,
New York, 12 Apr. 1971; cello sonata; Pageant,
woodwind quintet, 1972; Chorus: Star over star,
chorus, baritone, orchestra; Not by words alone,
1970; Teach us Thy peace, 1972; Four Christmas
songs; Carol of the flowers; two madrigals for
Christmas; That I may sing; Keyboard: Floret,
piano; Break forth into joy, organ; Andante con
moto, allegro and fugue, organ; numerous other
choral works, songs, and piano pieces.
    3097 Herrick Road, Columbus, OH 43221

BOND, VICTORIA
    b. Los Angeles, Calif., 6 May 1945. Studied at
Univ. of Southern California with Ingolf Dahl
and Ellis Kohs; and has also studied with Henri
Lazaroff, Paul Glass, Darius Milhaud; and at
Juilliard School with Roger Sessions and Vladimir
Ussachevsky. She received scholarships to the
Aspen Music Festival, 1973; to Juilliard,
1972-74, and a fellowship, 1974. She is assis-
tant conductor, Contemporary Music Ensemble,

(BOND, VICTORIA)
Juilliard School, and has conducted the Cabrillo
Music Festival, 1974; White Mts. Music Festival,
and the American Symphony Orch., 1975.
    WORKS: Orchestra: Five preludes, 1972;
C-A-G-E-D, for strings, 1972; Sonata for orchestra, 1973; Chamber music: Pastorale, woodwinds,
1967; quartet, clarinet and strings, 1967; duet,
flute and viola, 1969; trio for brass, 1969;
Variations for flute, 1969; woodwind quintet,
1970; Canons, clarinet and violin, 1970; Recitative, English horn and string trio, 1970; Interludes, chamber orch., 1970; cello sonata, 1971;
Conversation piece, viola and vibraphone, New
York, 15 Aug. 1975; Songs: Cornography, soprano
and chamber ensemble, 1970; Suite aux troubadours,
soprano and chamber ensemble, 1970; Aria, soprano and strings, 1973; many other songs; Film:
Mirror of nature, 1971.
    349 West 71st St., New York, NY 10023

BONDE, ALLEN
    b. Newton, Wisc., 22 Nov. 1936. Studied at
Lawrence Univ., Wis., with James Ming; and Catholic Univ. with George Thaddeus Jones and Robert
Hall Lewis. His awards include a Rockefeller
Found. grant, 1968; and Mount Holyoke Coll. faculty grant, 1972. On the faculty at Hood Coll.,
1963-71, he rose from instructor to professor
and chairman of the Music Department; he has
been assistant professor at Mount Holyoke Coll.,
1971-   .
    WORKS: Orchestra: Fantasia for piano and
orch.; symphony; Chamber music: Romance, viola
and piano, 1961; Contrasts, violin and piano,
1965; Romance, violin and piano, 1965; string
quartet, 1967; five preludes, guitar, 1972;
Chorus: 3 masses; Magnificat, women's voices,
oboe, harpsichord, marimba; Piano: suite, 1965;
five preludes, 1972; Sonus I, Sonus II, 2 pianos,
1973; Umore, 1971; Mixed media: Kaleidoscope II,
oboe, percussion, marimba, harpsichord, metronome, dancer, 1972.
    Mount Holyoke College
    South Hadley, MA 01075

*BONDS, MARGARET
    b. Chicago, Ill., 3 Mar. 1913; d. Los Angeles,
26 Apr. 1972. Studied at Northwestern Univ.,
B. M., M. M.; with Robert Starer at Juilliard
School; privately with Roy Harris. She received
scholarships from Nat. Asso. of Negro Musicians,
Alpha Kappa Alpha, Julius Rosenwald, and Roy
Harris; and won the Rodman Wanamaker award. She
was a concert pianist; taught at American Theatre
Wing; was music director, East Side Settlement
House and the White Barn Theatre.
    WORKS: Theatre: music for Shakespeare in
Harlem and U.S.A.; Chorus: The negro speaks of
rivers; Ballad of the brown king; Songs: 3
dream portraits, on Langston Hughes texts;
Didn't it rain.

BONNEAU, GILLES YVES
    b. St. Jean, P.Q., 26 July 1941, U.S. citizen
1949. Studied at the New England Cons. Extension Div. 1967-71. His works are chiefly for
small chamber ensembles including a trio for

(BONNEAU, GILLES YVES)
guitar, flute and bassoon; woodwind quintet;
organ preludes, and songs.
10 Stevens St., Winooski, VT 05404

*BONNER, EUGENE
b. Washington, N. C., 1889. Studied at Peabody
Cons. and in London. After service in the U.S.
Army in World War I, he remained in Paris for
study until 1927. On return to the U.S. he
settled in New York and for a time was music
critic of the Brooklyn Daily Eagle.
WORKS: Opera: Barbara Fritchee, 1921;
Celui qui epousa une femme muette, 1923; The
Venetian glass nephew, 1927; The gods of the
mountain, 1936; Orchestra: Whispers of heavenly
death, chorus and orch. on texts of Walt Whitman,
1922; White nights, prelude, 1925; Chamber music:
Flutes, voice and 4 instruments, 1923; piano
quintet, 1925; Suite sicilienne, violin and
piano, 1926. In 1945 he was commissioned to
write a score for Frankie and Johnny for presentation by the New Opera Company in New York.

BOONE, CHARLES
b. Cleveland, Ohio, 21 June 1939. Studied at
the Acad. of Music, Vienna, 1960-61, with Karl
Schiske; Univ. of Southern California, B. M.
1963; San Francisco State Coll., M. A. 1968; and
privately with Ernst Krenek. He was chairman of
the San Francisco Composers' Forum, 1964-66; coordinator, Mills Coll. Tape Music Center and Performing Group, 1966-68; and has been director,
BYOP, a contemporary chamber music group, San
Francisco, 1971-   .
WORKS: Orchestra: First landscape; Second
landscape; Chinese texts, soprano and orch;
Chamber music: Raspberries, 3 drummers; Vocalise,
solo soprano; Cool glow of radiation, flute and
tape, Not now, clarinet solo; Vermilion, solo
oboe; Zephyrus, oboe and piano.
1321 Arch St., Berkeley, CA 94708

BOOZER, PATRICIA P.
b. Atlanta, Ga., 14 Mar. 1947. Studied at
Samford Univ. with Newton Strandberg, James
Jenson, and Bob Burroughs, and later Philip
Landgrave. She taught at Trusswood School of
Music, Birmingham, 1969-71, and the Samford
Univ. Preparatory Dept., 1971-73. Her published
works are for church choral groups.

*BORDEN, DAVID
Variations on America by Charles Ives, wind ensemble and electronics, 1970.
1191 East Shore Drive, Ithaca, NY 14850

BORETZ, BENJAMIN A.
b. New York, N. Y., 3 Oct. 1934. Studied at
Brandeis Univ. with Irving Fine and Arthur
Berger; at Aspen with Darius Milhaud; at Princeton Univ. with Milton Babbitt and Roger Sessions.
His awards include Fromm Composition prize, 1956;
Ingram Merrill grant, 1966; American Music Center
grant, 1967; Fulbright-Hays senior fellowship,
1970-71; and Princeton Univ., Council of the
Humanities fellowship, 1971-72. He was music
critic for The Nation, 1962-69; and has served

(BORETZ, BENJAMIN A.)
as editor, Perspectives of New Music, 1961-
and as consultant, Fromm Music Found., 1960-70.
His faculty positions have been: Brandeis Univ.,
1962-63; New York Univ., 1964-65; Columbia Univ.,
1969-72; Princeton Univ., 1967-68, 1970-71,
1972-74; Bard Coll., 1973-   .
WORKS: Orchestra: Concerto grosso for
strings, 1954; violin concerto, 1956; Group
variations for chamber orch., 1964-67; Chamber
music: Partita for piano, 1955; Divertimento,
1955; string quartet, 1957; Donne songs,
1955-61; brass quintet, 1961-62; Group variations for computer, 1968-72; Compositions 3, 4,
and 5, 1973-74.
64 Wiggins St., Princeton, NJ 08540

BORISHANSKY, ELLIOT
b. New York, N. Y., 17 Mar. 1930. Studied at
Queens Coll. with Karol Rathaus; Columbia Univ.
with Jack Beeson and Otto Luening; Hamburg Cons.
with Phillipp Jarnach; Univ. of Michigan with
Ross Lee Finney and Niccolo Castiglioni. He
received Gershwin Memorial award, 1958;
Fulbright grant, 2 years; Europa Kolleg scholarship; Denison Univ. Research Fund grant; Ford
Humanities grant. He has held faculty positions
at Rhode Island Coll.; Bucknell Univ., 1965-66;
Univ. of Wisconsin, Milwaukee, 1966; and has
been assistant professor, Denison Univ.,
1968-   .
WORKS: Music for orchestra, 1958; Chamber
music: Aus dem West - Ostlichen Divan, four
Goethe settings for soprano and piano; Two
pieces for solo clarinet; Constellations, piano;
Three mosquitoes find they are reunited after a
convention in Atlantic City, New Jersey, for 3
trumpets.
520 West Broadway, Granville, OH 43023

BORLING, THOMAS
b. Cleveland, Ohio, 27 June 1942. Studied with
Bernhard Heiden at Indiana Univ. and with
Burton Weaver at Univ. of Dayton. He was percussionist with the St. Joseph, Mo., Symphony,
1966-70; instructor, Mt. St. Scholastica Coll.,
Kan., 1966-70; and assistant professor, Univ. of
St. Thomas, 1970-72.
WORKS: Orchestra: The lure, a ballet;
Chamber music: Duet for three moons, brass quartet; timpani sonata; trombone sonata; Why not
now?, solo flute; What's happening?, variable
ensemble, theatre piece; Swiatovid, wind
instruments.
6425 Mobud Drive, Houston, TX 77036

*BORNSCHEIN, FRANZ CARL
b. Baltimore, Md., 10 Feb. 1879; d. Baltimore,
8 June 1948. Studied at Peabody Cons. and
joined the faculty in 1906.
WORKS: Orchestra: Moon over Taos, 1939,
New York, 9 Oct. 1944; Ode to the brave, Washington, D.C., 7 Nov. 1944; The earth sings, symphony, Baltimore, 21 Nov. 1944; also an operetta,
shorter works for orch., choral works.

BOROS, DAVID JOHN

BOROS, DAVID JOHN
b. New York, N. Y., 17 May 1944. Studied at
Univ. of California at Berkeley and Los Angeles,
1962-66, with David Lewin, Henri Lazarof, Seymour
Shifrin; and at Brandeis Univ., 1966-70, with
Shifrin, Martin Boykan, and Arthur Berger. He
received the Weisner Award for Creative Arts at
Univ. of California, Berkeley, 1966, and a
Fulbright-Hays grant for study with Goffredo
Petrassi in Rome. He was lecturer at Brandeis
Univ., 1973-74.
WORKS: Chamber music: 3 fables for tenor,
harp, clarinet, bassoon; trio for violin, cello,
piano; Yet once again for solo flute; Wedding
music and waltz, piano.
40 Highland Ave., Newtonville, MA 02160

*BOROWSKI, FELIX
b. Burton, England, 10 Mar., 1872; to U.S. 1897;
d. Chicago, 6 Sep. 1956. Taught at Chicago Musical Coll., 1897-1916, president, 1916-25; professor, Northwestern Univ., 1932-42. He wrote
2 ballets, 3 symphonies, piano concerto, many
other works for orch.; 3 string quartets, etc.

BORROFF, EDITH
b. New York, N. Y., 2 Aug. 1925. Studied at
American Univ., B. M. 1946, M. M. 1948, with
Irwin Fischer; and at Univ. of Michigan, Ph. D.
1958, with Ross Lee Finney. She received an
Andrew Mellon postdoctoral award, 1960-61, and a
Univ. of Wisconsin summer grant, 1964. Her faculty positions include Milwaukee-Downer Coll.,
1950-54; Univ. of Michigan, 1955-57; Hillside
Coll., 1958-62; Univ. of Wisconsin, 1962-66;
Eastern Michigan Univ., 1966-73; visiting professor, Univ. of North Carolina, 1972-73; professor, State Univ. of New York at Binghamton,
1973- .
WORKS: Orchestra: Idyll, violin and orch.;
Monologue, baritone and orch.; Chamber music:
Variations and theme, oboe and piano; horn
sonata; canons for flute and viola; string quartet; Piano: suite; Tatterdemalion, a rag.
900 Lehigh Ave., Binghamton, NY 13903

BOTTJE, WILL GAY
b. Grand Rapids, Mich., 30 June 1925. Studied
at Juilliard School with Vittorio Giannini in
composition, Georges Barrere and Arthur Lora on
flute; Eastman School, with Howard Hanson,
Bernard Rogers; in Holland with Henk Badings; in
Paris with Nadia Boulanger. He received the
Music News performance award, 1947; Thor Johnson
brass composition contest award; Composers Press
Publication award, 1952; Fulbright grant,
1952-53; Southern Illinois Univ. Creative
Research awards, 1959, 1964, 1968, 1972. He
taught at Univ. of Mississippi, 1955-57; and has
been professor, Southern Illinois Univ. 1957- .
WORKS: Opera: Altgeld, 3 acts, 1968; Root,
2 acts, 1972; Orchestra: The ballad singer,
1951; 7 symphonies, 1951-70; concerto for flute,
trumpet, strings, harp, percussion, 1955; concertino for piccolo, 1956; piano concerto, 1961;
Rhapsodic variations, viola, piano, strings, 1962;

(BOTTJE, WILL GAY)
many compositions for various chamber ensembles,
choral works, and electronic music.
914 Taylor Drive, Carbondale, IL 62901

BOWDER, JERRY L.
b. Portland, Ore., 7 July 1928. Studied at
Univ. of Washington with George F. McKay and
John Verrall; Lewis and Clark Coll. with Robert
Stoltze; and Eastman School of Music, D. M. A.
1960, with Bernard Rogers, Alan Hovhaness, and Howard Hanson. He held scholarships for his doctoral
work at Eastman, and his 2nd symphony was chosen
to represent Eastman in a symposium in 1960; he
was commissioned by Music in Maine, 1966. He
has been professor at Univ. of Maine, Portland-
Gorham, 1960- .
WORKS: Orchestra: 3 symphonies; Band:
Variation on a plain song; Brass ensemble: Folk
suite; Suite for brass, 1968; Chamber music:
string quartet; woodwind quintet; Vocal: 3
songs for baritone; Brigg Fair, chorus, continuo,
flute.
Osborne Road, Gorham, ME 04038

BOWEN, EUGENE EVERETT
b. Biloxi, Miss., 30 July 1950. Studied at
California Inst. of the Arts with Mel Powell,
Morton Subotnick, Harold Budd, James Tenney,
Leonard Stein, William Douglas. He was co-
director, Electronic Music Seminar, Univ. of
Guadalajara, Mexico, summer 1971; and has been
professor, Moorpark Coll., Calif., 1973- .
WORKS: Chamber music: Now oh friends,
piano and female voice, 1972; Chamomile, piano,
1972; Longbow angels, for 5 basses, 1973; Electronic tape: Song, 1970; Warrior, 1971; Your
dead are waiting, 1972; Wind, 1972; Mixed media:
Casida del llanto, for tape or live improvisation and two readers, 1971; Drift, for tape,
vibes, percussion, bass, ceramic bells, clarinet,
and various wind instruments, 1973.
280 South Main, Fillmore, CA 93015

*BOWERS, ROBERT HOOD
b. Chambersburg, Pa., 24 May 1877; d. New York,
29 Dec. 1941. Wrote a 1-act opera, 4 operettas.

BOWLES, PAUL
b. New York, N. Y., 30 Dec. 1910. Attended Univ.
of Virginia; studied composition with Aaron Copland in New York and Berlin, 1930-32, and with
Nadia Boulanger and Virgil Thomson in Paris,
1933-34. He received a Guggenheim fellowship,
1941, and a Rockefeller grant, 1959. He was
music critic on the New York Herald Tribune,
1942-45, then traveled and lived in Spain, North
Africa, the Antilles, South and Central America
studying and collecting folk music.
WORKS: Opera: Denmark Vesey, 1937; The
wind remains, 1943; Ballet: Yankee clipper,
1937; The ballroom guide, 1937; Sentimental
colloquy, 1944; Pastorale, 1947; Incidental
music: Dr. Faustus; My heart's in the highlands;
Love's old sweet song; Twelfth night; Watch on
the Rhine; Liberty Jones; The glass menagerie;
Jacobowsky and the colonel; Orchestra; suite,
1933; Danza Mexicana, 1941; Chamber music:

(BOWLES, PAUL)
Scenes d'Anabase, voice, oboe, piano, 1932; trio, 1936; Melodia, 9 instruments, 1937; Music for a farce, 1938; Prelude and dance, winds, bass, percussion, piano, 1947; Picnic cantata, 4 women's voices, 2 pianos, percussion, 1954; sonata for 2 pianos; preludes for piano, 1934-45; Film scores: Roots in the soil; Congo. As an author he has published The sheltering sky, a novel, 1949; and The delicate prey and other stories, 1950.
2117 Tanger Socco, Tangier, Morocco

BOWLES, RICHARD W.
b. Rogers, Ark., 30 June 1918. Studied at Indiana Univ. with Robert Sanders, and at Univ. of Wisconsin with Cecil Burleigh. He has received 4 ASCAP awards. He has held the post of band director in public schools and of the 715th AAF Band, Lockbourne Air Base, 1942-46; was church music director, 1946-47; director of music, Lafayette City Schools, 1953-58; professor, Univ. of Florida, 1958-   .
WORKS: Many concert marches for band, works for orchestra, small ensembles, and solos. His march, Burst of flame is listed in a compilation of the world's 100 most popular band marches.
827 N. W. 15th Ave., Gainesville, FL 32601

BOWMAN, CARL
b. Philomath, Ore., 14 Dec. 1913. Studied at Willamette Univ., B. M.; Univ. of Washington, M. A., with George F. McKay, Demar Irvine; Juilliard School with Vittorio Giannini; Columbia Univ. with Normand Lockwood; and New York Univ., Ph. D. He has taught at New Jersey Musical Coll., 1947-53; Brooklyn Music School, 1954-68; Kings Coll., 1961-64; Shelton Coll., 1964-65; City Univ. of New York, 1966-   .
WORKS: Orchestra: Triptych symphony; Ballad for horn and orch.; Fantasy on a carol tune, a festival piece for orchestra, or band, or brass ensemble, or chorus, or organ; Brass ensemble: Toccacciata; Nocturne; Chamber music: trio for trombone, viola, cello; Chorus: Festival of praise, chorus, and brass ensemble or organ; Magnificat, mezzo-soprano, chorus, brass ensemble or organ.
140 West 69th St., New York, NY 10023

BOYADJIAN, HAYG
b. Paris, France, 15 May 1938; U.S. citizen, 1964. Studied at the Liszt Cons., Buenos Aires, with Bestrie Balzi, but is largely self-taught as a composer.
WORKS: Chamber music: 2 duos for flute and piano; Canticles of a memory, cello and piano; Movements for piano; Capriccioso for piano; Fusion for string quartet, optional brass, and slide projection; Episodes for sextet.
43 Fern St., Lexington, MA 02173

BOYD, JACK
b. Indianapolis, Ind., 9 Feb. 1932. Studied with Samuel Adler and Cecil Effinger. He has received commissions from several colleges and churches. He has taught at Univ. of Dubuque, and is associate professor, Abilene Christian Coll.

(BOYD, JACK)
WORKS: Band: Jackson's purchase; Chamber music: Three pieces for flute and piano; Chorus: Three lyrics, with string orch.; Thus saith the preacher, a cappella; Jefferson: American, with brass; The death of Socrates, with baritone; Three Isaiac hymns, a cappella.
Abilene Christian College
Abilene, TX 79601

*BOYD, WYNN LEO
b. Gaithersburg, Md., 28 July 1902. Piano teacher and tuner; organized piano rebuilding firm. His works include choral pieces and songs on texts of Paul Lawrence Dunbar.

BOYKAN, MARTIN
b. New York, N. Y., 12 Apr. 1931. Studied with Walter Piston at Harvard Univ.; with Paul Hindemith at Univ. of Zurich and at Yale Univ. He has been on the faculty at Brandeis Univ., 1957-   , and is now associate professor.
WORKS: Chamber music: 2 string quartets, No. 1 was awarded a performance by Composers String Quartet in 1967 by Jeunesses Musicales; Concerto for 13 players, Boston, 12 Nov. 1972; Chorus: Psalm, a cappella.
155 Summer St., Newton Centre, MA 02159

BOYKIN, A. HELEN
b. River Falls, Ala., 5 Nov. 1904. Was an honor graduate of Alabama Coll., 1927; studied in Munich, 1930-33; and at Yale summer school, 1952 and 1953. She received a Nat. Fed. of Music Clubs award of merit, 1971. She taught at Alabama Coll., 1927-30, and has taught piano privately in Atlanta, 1933-65, and Montgomery, 1965-   .
WORKS: 2-piano concerto; Geechee Dance; Scherzo in b; En bateau; Seafoam; Carnival scenes; etc.
1209 South Lawrence St.
Montgomery, AL 36104

BRACALI, GIAMPAOLO
b. Rome, Italy, 24 May 1941; to U.S. 1968. Studied in Rome with Virgilis Mortari, in Paris with Nadia Boulanger, in London with Lennox Berkeley, and in New York, all on scholarships. His awards include the Bonaventura Somma, 1965; F. M. Napolitan, 1966; Lili Boulanger, 1967; and second place in the Prix Pierre de Monaco, 1968. He was on the faculty at Accademia Filarmonica Romene, 1963-65; and Manhattan School of Music, 1968-   , where he is also assistant conductor in the Opera Department.
WORKS: Orchestra: piano concerto; Three Psalms, chorus and orch.; concerto grosso for chamber orch. and orch.; Chamber music: Openings for strings; Sextuor, 3 trumpets and 3 trombones; Viajesa for guitar.
2109 Broadway, New York, NY 10023

*BRADLEY, RUTH
b. New Jersey; d.
WORKS: Printe Toto II, women's chorus, mezzo or baritone solo; Rain, women's chorus; Abraham Lincoln walks at midnight, cantata for solo voice; Bleeker Street market, for medium voice.

BRADSHAW, MERRILL

BRADSHAW, MERRILL
b. Lyman, Wyo., 18 June 1929. Attended Brigham Young Univ., A. B. 1954, M. A. 1955; and Univ. of Illinois, M. M. 1956, D. M. A. 1962. His composition teachers were Leon Dallin, Robert Palmer, Robert Kelly, Gordon Binkerd, Burrill Phillips. In 1967 he received the Karl G. Maeser Creative Arts award ($2000) and several Brigham Young Univ. grants, 1959-72. He has been professor at Brigham Young Univ., 1957-   , and composer-in-residence 1966-   . He has also been music critic, 1958-61, and author of magazine articles.
   WORKS: Orchestra: piano concerto, 1956; 4 symphonies, 1957, 1964, 1967, 1968; Facets, 1966; Feathers, for young orch., 1968; Peace memorial, 1970; Band: Divertimento for band, 1967; Fanfares and solemnities, 1967; Elegy improvisation and romp for high school band, 1971; Chamber music: 2 string quartets, 1957, 1969; violin sonata, 1957; flute sonatina, 1966; suite for oboe and piano, 1966; Piece for strings, 1967; brass quintet, 1969; Chorus: Ah, how fleeting, ah, how futile, 1963; The articles of faith, 1966; Music for the Oedipus cycle, 1967; 3 Psalms, 1969; The restoration, oratorio, 1972-73; Piano: eight piano pieces, 1971; six piano pieces, 1973, 20 piano pieces, 1972-72; and hymns, anthems, and songs.
   248 E. 3140 N., Provo, UT 84601

*BRAGGIOTTI, MARIO
   b. Florence, Italy, 29 Nov. 1909; to U.S. at an early age. Studied with Frederick Converse, New England Cons.; with Nadia Boulanger and Alfred Cortot in Paris. He played in a duo-piano team with Jacques Fray; toured in concert programs; was radio program director with U.S. occupational army, Africa and Italy, World War II; piano soloist with symphony orchestras. His compositions include a ballet, The princess; Variations on Yankee Doodle for orch.; and Lincoln's Gettysburg address, cantata for chorus.

*BRAINE, ROBERT
   b. Springfield, Ohio, 27 May 1896; d. New York, N. Y., 26 Aug. 1940. Studied at Cincinnati Coll. of Music. He was a radio conductor in New York.
   WORKS: Opera: The eternal light, 1924; Virginia, 1926; Diana, 1929; Orchestra: S. O. S., 1927; The raven, baritone and orch., 1928; The song of Hiawatha, 1930; Concerto in jazz, violin and orch., 1931; Quartet in jazz, string quartet, 1935; Barbaric sonata, piano; also songs and piano pieces.

*BRAMAN, WALLIS D.,
   Professor, Indiana Univ. of Pennsylvania, has published The Lord reigneth for organ.

*BRANCH, HAROLD: Scherzo for piano, performed, Town Hall, New York, 30 Jan. 1971; Rondo for piano, performed Carnegie Recital Hall, New York, 11 Dec. 1971.

*BRAND, MAX
   b. Lwow, Poland, 26 Apr. 1896; U.S. citizen 1945. Wrote 2 operas, orchestral works, chamber music, choral works.

BRANDON, GEORGE
   b. Stockton, Calif. 4 Feb. 1924. Attended Union Theological Seminary, School of Sacred Music, M. S. M. 1952. He was organist-choir director 1941-67, and a faculty member at midwest colleges 1957-62. His published works include about 150 choral octavos, 50 organ pieces, many hymn tunes, and choir responses.
   P. O. Box P, Davis, CA 95616

BRANDON, SY
   b. New York, N. Y., 24 June 1945. Studied at Ithaca Coll. with Warren Benson; Hofstra Univ. with Elie Siegmeister; and Univ. of Arizona with Robert McBride. He received first prize in the Kappa Gamma Psi composition contest, 1962, and was finalist in the Nat. School Orch. Assoc. contest, 1971. He was composer-in-residence, Boise State Coll. 1973-74. He has composed for orchestra, band, chorus, and chamber ensembles.
   5362 Kootenai St., Boise, ID 83705

BRANDT, DOROTHEA
   b. Frewsburg, N. Y., 1 May 1896. Studied composition with Henry P. Eames and Carl Parrish in Claremont., Calif. She has been a piano teacher in Yakima and Seattle, Wash., and Pomona, Calif. Her published works include Wagon train, 1954; Japanese print, 1955; Zapateado, 1960; Dancing Japanese marionettes, 1963; Chinese woodcutter, 1964; Little donkey in the snow, 1964; Arietta, 1968; Calico Mountain trail, 1968; all for piano, and anthems.
   2934 North Towne Ave., Claremont, CA 91711

BRANDT, WILLIAM EDWARD
   b. Butte, Mont., 14 Jan. 1920. Studied at Washington State Univ. with Russell Danburg, and at Eastman School of Music with Bernard Rogers and Howard Hanson. He was awarded performances at Eastman's American Music Festival, 1949; a Washington State Univ. grant, 1962; and a prize in an anthem contest of the Chicago Diocese, 1973. He taught at Univ. of Rochester, 1948-50; privately in Seattle, 1950-56; and has been professor, Washington State Univ., 1956-   .
   WORKS: Chamber opera: No neutral ground, after Beaumarchais; Orchestra: Sinfonietta No. 2, 1948; King Lear suite, 1948; a symphony, 1950; suite for small orch., 1960; Music for the Decalogue, narrator and orch., 1967; piano concerto, 1972; Chamber music: string quartet, 1949; flute sonata, 1953; 2 clarinet sonatas, 1960, 1973; Divertimento for woodwind trio, 1960; Lyric movement for piano, 1973; The meditation of Mary and Rachel's Lamentation for contralto and chamber ensemble; various songs.
   N. E. 1115 Indiana St., Pullman, WA 99163

BRANNING, GRACE
   b. Washington, D.C., 10 Oct. 1912. Earned a B. M. at Univ. of Pittsburgh and studied composition with Nicolai Lopatnikoff and Mildred Gardner. She received three composition awards from the Pittsburgh Piano Teachers Assoc. She taught piano at Pittsburgh Musical Inst., 1937-60; at Fillion Studios, 1960-   ; and privately, 1937-   .

(BRANNING, GRACE)
WORKS: Opera: Scene for Icelandic saga, soprano, tenor, and chorus; Chamber music: Allegro risoluto, violin; Aria and dance, flute solo; Vocal: God's world, women's voices; Songs of Foo, a cycle to own words; Gethsemane; Night song; Sea-love; Piano: Caprice in c; Ballade; Miniature suite; Capriccio, duet; Cardinals, duet.
160 Montclair Ave., Pittsburgh, PA 15237

BRANSCOMBE, GENA
b. Picton, Ont., 4 Nov. 1881; U.S. citizen 1910. Graduated from Chicago Musical Coll., where she was a Gold Medalist in composition for two successive years. She studied piano with Rudolph Ganz and Hans von Schiller; composition with Felix Borowski and Engelbert Humperdinck; conducting with Frank Damrosch, Walter Rothwell, Clifton Chalmers, and Albert Stoessel. Her many awards and citations include an honorary M. A. from Whitman Coll., 1932; selection to conduct the Golden Jubilee massed chorus of 1000 voices for the 50th anniversary of the General Fed. of Women's Clubs, 1941, and as guest conductor of her own choral and orchestral works in concert and broadcast performances throughout the U.S. and Canada. She taught piano at Chicago Musical Coll., 1902-07; was head of the piano department, Whitman Coll., 1907-09; conductor MacDowell Chorus, Mountain Lakes, N. J., 1931-43; conductor, Branscombe Choral, New York, 1933-54; etc.
WORKS: She has composed in all forms, has published more than 150 songs and 60 choral works with her own texts or translations; and orchestral and chamber works. Her compositions include: Pilgrims of destiny, a choral drama for soli, chorus, and orch., 1920, Plymouth, Mass., 1929; Quebec suite, orchestra and tenor, in three parts: Prelude, Balladine, Procession, 1927; Youth of the world, cycle for women's voices and orch., 1933; Coventry's choir, women's voices, soprano solo, and orch., New York, 1944; The Lord is our fortress, text and choral arrangement of finale of Brahms' first symphony, 1948; Prayer for song, women's voices, 1952; 91st Psalm, chorus, piano, organ, percussion, horn, 1955; Pacific suite, horn and piano, 1957; Arms that have sheltered us, chorus and band, written for Canadian Royal Navy, 1962, and sung at a special celebration by massed bands and choruses, Halifax, 1962; Bridemaid's song, women's voices, 1958, Boston Pops, 1965; A joyful litany, chorus, 1967; Introit, prayer response, and amen, written for choir of The Riverside Church, New York, 1973; Songs: The morning wind; Happiness; Hail ye tyme of holie-dayes; Across the blue Aegean Sea; I bring you heartsease; Ah love, I shall find thee; 4 song cycles: Lute of jade; Songs of the unafraid; The sun dial; Songs of childhood.
90 La Salle St., Apt. 3-E
New York, NY 10027

*BRANT, HENRY
b. Montreal, Canada, 15 Sep. 1913. Studied in Montreal and with Rubin Goldmark at Juilliard School; privately with George Antheil. His awards include the Premio Radio Television Italiana, 1955; 2 Guggenheim fellowships, 1946,

(BRANT, HENRY)
1955; Nat. Inst. of Arts and Letters grant, 1955; Dollard grant; Coolidge, Loeb, and Seligman prizes at Juilliard. He has taught at Columbia Univ., Juilliard School, Peabody Cons., and at Bennington Coll., 1957-   .
WORKS: Opera-oratorio: December, 1955; Orchestra: 2 symphonies, 1931, 1937; double bass concerto, 1932; Gallopjig colloquy, Ballad for orch., 1934; Whoopee overture, 1937; clarinet concerto, 1939; saxophone concerto, 1940; Music for an imaginary ballet, 1947; The promised land, symphony, 1948; Kingdom come, 2 orch., and organ; Origins, percussion symphony, 1952; Mythical beasts, 1958; Conversations in an unknown tongue, string orch., 1958; Atlantis, antiphonal symphony with chorus and narrator, 1960; Voyage 4, in 83 parts, 1963; Odyssey-Why not, 1965; Homage to Ives, baritone and orch., Denver, 21 Feb. 1975; Wind ensemble: Angels and devils, flute and flute orch., 1931; Millenium 2, 1953; Fire in cities, chorus, winds, and percussion, 1961; Millenium 4, brass ensemble; Chamber music: sonata for 2 pianos, 1931; oboe sonata, 1932; viola sonata, 1937; Signs and alarms, chamber ensemble, 1953; Galaxy II, chamber ensemble, 1954; Ice age, clarinet, xylophone, piano; Verticals ascending, wind and percussion ensemble; Mobiles, solo flute; Heiroglyphics 3, viola solo, mezzo soprano, and chamber ensemble; Heiroglyphics, 1966; Dialogues in the form of secret portraits, harpsichord; Crossroads, 4 violins; Music 1970; Chorus: Spanish underground, cantata; Solomon's gardens.
c/o MCA 445 Park Ave., New York, NY 10022

*BRASWELL, JOHN
Interior castle, opera on Theresa of Avila, Lenox Arts Center, Lenox, Mass., 19 July 1973.

BRATT, C. GRIFFITH
b. Baltimore, Md., 21 Nov. 1914. Studied at Peabody Cons. with Gustav Strube, Howard R. Thatcher, Katherine Lucke; and Univ. of Utah with Leroy Robertson. He has received the Idaho Governor's award for excellence in the arts; an honorary D. M. from Northwest Nazarene Coll.; Distinguished award, Peabody Cons.; 3 citations from Nat. Fed. of Music Clubs; Idaho Arts Council award of merit. He was organist-choirmaster, Baltimore, 1934-42, Washington, D.C., 1943-46, St. Michael's Cathedral, Boise, 1946-   ; on faculty, Boise State Coll., 1946-   ; chairman of music department, 1946-70; composer-in-residence, 1955-   .
WORKS: Opera: Rachel; A season for sorrow; Orchestra: 2 symphonies; Chamber music: 2 string quartets; Keyboard: a complete cycle of organ voluntaries for the church year; many other choral, chamber, vocal, and piano works for a total of over 375 compositions.
1020 North 17th, Boise, ID 83702

BRAUER, JAMES LEONARD
b. Julesburg, Colo., 29 Sep. 1938. Studied with Jan Bender, Concordia Seminary, St. Louis, and with Joseph Goodman at Union Theological Seminary, New York. He was instructor in Latin, Greek, and

BRAUER, JAMES LEONARD

(BRAUER, JAMES LEONARD)
religion, 1965-68, in music, 1968-71, and assistant professor, 1971-   , at Concordia Coll. Bronxville, N. Y.; and organist-choirmaster, St. Mark's Lutheran Church, Yonkers, 1967-   .
WORKS: He has composed for brass, strings, woodwinds, piano and chorus, including Magnificat for soprano and chorus; Nunc dimittis, tenor and chorus.
228 Midland Ave., Tuckahoe, NY 10707

BRAUNLICH, HELMUT
b. Brünn, Czechoslovakia, 19 May 1929; U.S. citizen 1954. Studied at the Mozarteum, Saltzburg, with Kornauth and Keller; Catholic Univ. with George Thaddeus Jones; and at Tanglewood with Leon Kirchner. He has been associate professor, Catholic Univ., 1961-   .
WORKS: Orchestra: concerto for oboe, strings, and brass; concerto for ten instruments; Chamber music: wind quintet; quartet for flute, viola, bassoon, piano; 3 songs with string quartet; sonatina for viola and piano.
1101 Dennis Ave., Silver Spring, MD 20901

*BRAXTON, ANTHONY
L/C-J-637 for chamber ensemble, performed 26 Jan. 1975, New York.

*BREDEMANN, DAN
Homespun, theatre piece with music, commissioned by Baby Grand Opera Company, Cincinnati.

BREHM, ALVIN
b. New York, N. Y., 8 Feb. 1925. Attended The Juilliard School and Columbia Univ., and studied composition with Wallingford Riegger. He received grants from Ford Found., New York State Council for the Arts, and many commissions. He has been artist-in-residence, State Univ. of New York at Stony Brook, 1969-   ; visiting associate professor, State Univ. of New York at Purchase, 1972-   ; and on the faculty, Manhattan School of Music, 1968-   .
WORKS: Orchestra: Hephaestus, an overture, 1966; concertino for violin and string orch.; Chamber music: Dialogues, bassoon and percussion, 1963; quintet for brass, 1967; Cycle of 6 songs for voice and ten instruments; Dialogues and consort, flute and 4 instruments; piano variations; cello variations.
302 West 86th St., New York, NY 10024

*BREIL, JOSEPH CARL
b. Pittsburgh, Pa., 29 June 1870; d. Los Angeles, Calif., 23 Jan. 1926. Wrote 2 operas, 3 comic operas.

*BRENNER, WALTER
b. Wynberg, Union of South Africa, 21 Jan. 1906; became U.S. citizen; d. Studied music in Europe and with Dominico Brescia.
WORKS: Orchestra: piano concerto; Home they brought her warrior dead, symphonic poem; The birth of Venus; Adoration; Prophecy; Capriccio; Valse symphonique; Chamber music: quintet for flute and strings; string sextet; Impromptu for accordion; Ole torero, accordion; Wanderlust,

(*BRENNER, WALTER)
accordion; Chorus: Memorial prayer; Psalm 121; Hashkivenu; God is love; Kol nidre; Organ: Glory to God; Sabbath joy; Sabbath meditation; Contemplation hassidique.

BRESNICK, MARTIN
b. New York, N. Y., 13 Nov. 1946. Studied at Univ. of Hartford with Arnold Franchetti, B. A. 1967; M. A. 1968, with Leland Smith and John Chowning; Vienna Academy with Gottfried von Einem and Friedrich Gerha, 1969-70; and at Stanford Univ., D. M. A. 1972, with Gyorgy Ligeti and Theodore Antoniou. He received a Marion A. Bills scholarship, 1965-67; NDEA IV fellowship 1967-71; Fulbright fellowship, 1969-70; Gores award for excellence in teaching, 1973; Rome prize, 1975. He was lecturer, San Francisco Cons., 1971-72; and lecturer, Stanford Univ., 1972-74.
WORKS: Orchestra: Ocean of storms, 1970, Stanford, 1971; Chamber music: piano sonata, 1963; Theme and variations, oboe solo, New York, 1964; 3 two-part pieces for piano, 1964; Trio for 2 trumpets and percussion, 1966; Tammuz, string quartet, 1968; Introit, wind ensemble, Stanford, 1969; 3 Intermezzi for cello, 1971; Chorus: Where is the way, 1970; Computer and mixed media: PCOMP, 1969; Three fables of the ant, violin, lecturer, computer, dancers, etc.; Fragment, 1971; Musica, 9 instruments and computer, San Francisco, 1972; Film scores: Man machine meets machine man, woodwind quartet, 1968; Pour, computer collage, 1969; television spots for Operation sentinel, guitar, flutes, computer.
Stanford University, Stanford, CA 94305

BREWER, RICHARD H.
b. San Diego, Calif., 12 Aug. 1921. Studied with Robert U. Nelson and Robert Stevenson at Univ. of California, Los Angeles, and with Halsey Stevens at Univ. of Southern California. He was director of choral activities, Omaha Univ., 1952-55; and has been chairman of the music department and Division of Fine Arts, Pfeiffer Coll., 1962-   .
WORKS: Chorus: My sheep hear my voice; Sing to the Lord of harvest; Rejoice and be merry; Away in a manger; Sing, sing, sing; Plaisir d'amour.
Pfeiffer College, Misenheimer, NC 28109

BRICCETTI, THOMAS
b. Mt. Kisco, N. Y., 14 Jan. 1936. Studied at Columbia Univ. and Eastman School of Music with Bernard Rogers, Samuel Barber, Peter Mennin, Alan Hovhaness, and Jean Dansereau. His awards include ASCAP, 1959; Prix de Rome, 1959; Ford Found. grants, 1960-61, 1961-62; Yaddo fellowship, 1963; Nat. Endowment commission, 1967. He was musical director, St. Petersburg Symphony Orch., 1963-67; associate conductor, Indianapolis Symphony, 1967-72; musical director, Fort Wayne Philharmonic Orch., 1970-   ; musical director and conductor, Cleveland Inst. of Music, University Circle Orch., 1972-   .
WORKS: Orchestra: Fountain of youth, overture; violin concerto; Song of Solomon, cello

(BRICCETTI, THOMAS)
and orch.; Band: Turkey Creek march; Chamber
music: Eclogue No. 2, trombone and strings;
Eclogue No. 4, tuba and winds; flute sonata;
trio from Roman sketches, violin, voila, cello;
Chorus: Psalm 150; Millaydy's madrigals; and
compositions for all media.
4912 South Harrison, Fort Wayne, IN 46807

*BRICKEN, CARL ERNEST
b. Shelbyville, Ky., 28 Dec. 1898; d. Studied
at Yale Univ., B. A. 1922; with Rosario Scalero,
Mannes School of Music; with Alfred Cortot in
Paris and Hans Weisse in Vienna. He received a
Pulitzer award, 1929; Guggenheim fellowship,
1930. He held teaching posts at Mannes School,
Univ. of Chicago, Univ. of Wisconsin; was conductor of the Seattle Symphony Orchestra,
1944-48.
WORKS: Orchestra: 3 symphonies; Daniel
Boone, legend for orch.; The prairie years; also
chamber music, choral works, songs.

BRICKMAN, JOEL I.
b. New York, N. Y., 6 Feb. 1946. Attended
Montclair State Coll.; Juilliard School; Manhattan School of Music, B. M., M. M.; studying
with Nicolas Flagello, Ludmila Ulehla, and David
Diamond. He was winner in a Manhattan School
composition contest, 1970; and an accordion work
was chosen as the 1973 Coupe Mondiale world contest solo. He is on the faculties at Manhattan
School of Music, 1971-   , and Marymount Coll.,
1972-   .
WORKS: Orchestra: symphony; Prelude and
dithyramb, concert overture; Thousands of days,
piano concerto with solo soprano; Chamber music:
saxophone sonata; Dialogue, oboe and wind ensemble; trio for flute, oboe, bassoon; suite for
woodwind quintet; Prelude and caprice, accordion;
Chorus: Of wonder, a cappella choir.
204 Denver Road, Paramus, NJ 07652

BRIECE, JACK
b. San Francisco, 28 Jan. 1945. Reports continuous and discontinuous studies in various local-
ities including the U.S.A., Mexico, Central and
South America, and Europe. His principal teachers have been William Wendlandt, John Cage, Yoko
Ono, and the Book of Changes. From 1965 to 1972
he composed for acoustic and electric instruments,
e.g.: Wonderful music for everybody, music for
non-musicians; Movies for your ears, various
instruments and ensembles; Infinity crescendos,
flutes; m.a.p., piano music for children. Since
1972 he has been engaged in situational composition: Tortoise, for performance at sunrise and
sunset by people playing stones, bamboo wind-
chimes, and Indian nose flutes; Situation
ta yu, for television receivers, stones and primitive flute; Situation kδ, for Chinese temple
bells and stones.
69 Central Ave., San Francisco, CA 94117

*BRIGGS, G. WRIGHT
b. Taunton, Mass., 17 Oct. 1916. Studied with
Walter Piston, Harvard Coll., B. A., M. A.; with
Carl McKinley, New England Cons.; and at Harvard

(BRIGGS, G. WRIGHT)
Business School. Since 1955 he has been director of radio and television, Batten, Barton,
Durstine, and Osborn, Inc., Boston. He has composed marches, chamber music and songs.

BRIGGS, RALPH
b. Bettendorf, Iowa, 4 Aug. 1901. Attended
Cincinnati Cons., B. M. 1928, M. M. 1935, study-
ing with George Leighton and Karol Liszniewski;
L'Ecole Normale de Musique, Paris, with
Mme. Henri Dumesnil. He received the national
publication award of Composers Press., Inc., in
1954. His faculty positions included Murray
State Coll., Ky., 1929-30; Southwestern Coll.,
Winfield, Kan., 1938-44; Ohio Wesleyan Univ.,
1944-45; Univ. of Oregon, 1945-46; West Virginia
Univ., 1946-50; Univ. of Texas, El Paso, 1950-71.
WORKS: Orchestra: Burlesque, Austin, Tex.,
1958; Poem; Prelude, fugue, and aria, 1960;
Piano: Moods; Facetious, 1955; Scherzo for two
pianos.
368 Shadow Mountain Drive, El Paso, TX 79912

*BRIGHT, HOUSTON
b. Midland, Tex., 21 Jan. 1916; d. Canyon, Tex.
Studied with Halsey Stevens and Ernest Kanitz,
Univ. of Southern California, Ph. D. He was pro-
fessor and composer-in-residence, West Texas
State Univ.
WORKS: Band: Concerto grosso; Passacaglia;
Prelude and fugue; Marche de concert; Legend and
canon, brass ensemble; Chamber music: 3 short
dances for wind quintet; 4 for piano; Chorus:
Vision of Isaiah, chorus and orch.; Premonition;
Seaweed; Softly flow; Soliloquy; The tale untold;
Jabberwocky, with brass, percussion, contrabass,
piano; many of the choruses are set to his own
texts.

BRINDEL, BERNARD
b. Chicago, Ill., 23 Apr. 1912. Graduated magna
cum laude from Chicago Musical Coll. studying
with Max Wald, and also studied privately with
Paul Held and Isaac Levin. He is director of
music, Temple Sholom, Chicago, and has held faculty positions at Chicago Musical Coll., 1945-54;
and Morton Coll., Cicero, Ill., 1954-   .
WORKS: Orchestra: 4 symphonies; concerto
for cello and string orch.; Chamber music: violin sonata; 3 string quartets; suite for saxophone and piano; Autumnal meditation, saxophone;
many sacred and secular choral works and songs.
2740 Lincoln Lane, Wilmette, IL 60091

BRINGS, ALLEN
b. Brooklyn, N. Y., 24 Feb. 1934. Attended
Queens Coll.; Columbia Univ., M. A. 1957; Boston
Univ., D. M. A. 1964; Princeton Univ., 1962-63;
his composition teachers were Otto Leuning,
Gardner Read, Roger Sessions, Irving Fine. He
held several scholarships and fellowships, and
won the BMI student composer radio award in 1957.
He was instructor, Bard Coll., 1959-60; teaching
fellow, Boston Univ., 1960-62; assistant professor, Queens Coll., CUNY, 1963-   ; and teacher,
Weston Music Center, Weston, Conn., 1960-   .

BRINGS, ALLEN

(BRINGS, ALLEN)
WORKS: Orchestra: symphony; concerto for orch.; Band: Variations; Essay; Chamber music: Canzone for double brass quartet; Divertimento, flute, viola, harpsichord; Burlette, flute, clarinet, trombone; sonatas for piano, violin alone, viola or clarinet and piano; 4 pieces for violin and piano; suite for woodwind quintet; Duo concertante, cello and piano; Chorus: Altaforte, mixed chorus and piano; Shall I die for Mannis sake?, women's voices; The apparition; Organ: Passacaglia, interlude, and fugue.
199 Mountain Road, Wilton, CT 06897

BRINGUER, ESTELA
b. Argentina, 3 June 1931; to U.S. 1952. Studied in Argentina with Manuel de Falla, Jaime Pahissa, and Clemens Krauss. Her awards include first municipal prize of the City of Buenos Aires; an award of the Institute of Contemporary Arts, Washington; Woman of the Year award, Buenos Aires, 1971. She has been guest conductor of the American Symphony Orch., Colon Opera House Orch., Buenos Aires, Philharmonic Orch., Buenos Aires, and others. She was to tour the U.S. and Canada in 1975 conducting the Colon Opera House Orch.
WORKS: Orchestra: 2 symphonies; piano concerto; Carnival in Humahuaca; Elegy; Cold spring; Song of my valley; Echo of Tupac. Her first symphony was played by the American Symph. Orch. in New York, and the second will be premiered on her tour with the Colon Orch. in 1975. Her piano concerto and Carnival of Humahuaca were also played by the American Symph. Orch. and recorded by the Voice of America and played in the Master Works Hour.
150 East 69th St., New York, NY 10021

*BRINK, PHILIP
Elegy after Tu Fu, high voice and piano.

BRISMAN, HESKEL
b. New York, N. Y., 12 May 1923. Attended The Juilliard School, Columbia Univ., and Yale Univ., studying with Richard Donovan, Quincy Porter, Paul Hindemith, Ernst Toch, and Luigi Dallapiccola. He received a Tanglewood fellowship and a Friends of Harvey Gaul award. In 1959-62 he was composer for the Sermi Film Co., Rome, Italy; then director, Joseph Achron Cons., Israel, 1964-67; and on the editorial staff, Carl Fischer, Inc., 1967-69.
WORKS: Opera: The three strangers, 1-act; Whirligig, 1-act; Orchestra: concerto for piano and strings; Sinfonia breve; Chamber music: Music for string quartet and harp; woodwind quintet; Chorus: Psalms.
961 East Lawn Drive, Teaneck, NJ 07666

BRITAIN, RADIE
b. Amarillo, Tex., 17 Mar. 1903. Graduated from American Cons., Chicago, then studied composition in Munich with Albert Noelte, Leopold Godowsky, Henriot Levy, R. Deane Shure, Joseph Pembauer, and organ with Pietro Yon and Marcel Depree in Paris. On returning to the U.S. she spent two seasons at the MacDowell Colony. More than 50 of her compositions have received national or

(BRITAIN, RADIE)
international awards. In 1945 she was the first woman composer to receive the Juilliard publication award for Heroic poem. She has also received an honorary doctorate from Musical Arts Cons., Amarillo, and an award of merit from the Nat. League of American Pen Women. She is a private teacher in Hollywood.
WORKS: Stage works: Happyland, operetta, 1946; Carillon, opera, 1952; The spider and the butterfly, operetta for children, 1953; Kuthara, chamber opera, Santa Barbara, 1961; Lady in the dark, Detroit, 1962; Western testament, Omaha, 1964; Wheel of life, ballet, 1933; Kambu ballet, 1963; Orchestra: Heroic poem, 1929; Rhapsodic phantasy for piano and orch., 1933; Southern symphony, 1935; Light, 1935; suite for strings, 1940; Drouth, 1939; Ontonagon sketches, 1939; Phantasy for oboe and orch., 1942; Cowboy rhapsody, 1956; Cosmic mist symphony, 1962; Les femeux douze for 12 instruments, 1966; Chamber music: Epic poem, string quartet, 1927; string quartet in 4 movements, 1934; Chipmunks, woodwind orch., 1940; Barcarola, 8 celli and soprano, 1958; In the beginning, 4 horns, 1962; Phantasy, flute and piano, 1962; Awake to life, brass quintet, 1968; Chorus: Drums of Africa, a cappella Chicago, 1935; Prayer (Quarry), Chautauqua, N. Y., 1935; Noontide, 1935; Immortality, a cappella, 1937; Nisan, women's voices, strings and piano, Detroit, 1963; Harvest heritage, 1963; Brothers of the clouds, with orch., 1964; many instrumental solos and songs including Translunar cycle of songs dedicated to NASA, 1969.
1945 North Curson Ave., Hollywood, CA 90046

*BRITTON, DOROTHY GUYVER
b. 1922. Yedo fantasy, 1956, Impressions, 1957, both for chamber orch.

*BROCK, BLANCHE KERR
b. Greenfork, Ind., 3 Feb. 1888; d. Winona Lake Ind., 3 Jan. 1958. Studied at Indianapolis Cons. and American Cons.; published songs.

BROCKMAN, JANE E.
b. Schenectady, N. Y., 17 Mar. 1949. Attended Univ. of California at Santa Barbara and Univ. of Michigan, B. M., M. M., D. M. A., studying composition with George B. Wilson, Eugene Kurtz, and Leslie Bassett. In 1973 she received the Sigvald Thompson composition award of the Fargo-Moorhead Symphony (the first woman to win this award), and was elected to honorary membership in Pi Kappa Lambda. She has been teaching at Univ. of Michigan, 1972-.
WORKS: Orchestra: Eventail, 1973; Chamber music: Finger prints, piano, 1971; August thaw, piano, 1971; horn sonata, 1972; Two vignettes, chamber ensemble, 1972; Labyrinths, chamber ensemble, 1974; string trio, 1974.
2944 Birch Hollow Drive, #1B
Ann Arbor, MI 48104

*BROCKWAY, HOWARD A.
b. Brooklyn, N. Y., 22 Nov. 1870; d. New York, 20 Feb., 1951. Wrote a suite for orchestra, a symphony, choral works, piano pieces.

CONTEMPORARY AMERICAN COMPOSERS

BRODY, JOSHUA
b. New York, N. Y., 15 Sep., 1916. Studied at
New York Univ. with Philip James and Marion
Bauer; and privately with Wallingford Riegger in
New York and Robert McBride in Tucson. He has
been accompanist for the Kadiman Dancers,
1962- ; and on the faculty, Dance Department,
Univ. of Arizona, 1972- .
    WORKS: Theatre works: Incidental music for
plays by Sholem Alechem, Tucson, 1956; Tragi-
comedy of Don Christobita and Donna Rosita, opera
after Garcia Lorca, 1963; Orchestra: Ballad,
1960; Requiem for two veterans, with narrator,
1962; Chamber music: 2 string quartets, 1940,
1953; violin sonata, 1942; woodwind quintet,
1960; Dialogue, violin and piano, 1966; piano
sonata, 1968; Wedding music, 1970; numerous
pieces for woodwinds, piano, and songs.
    1226 North Swan Road, Tucson, AZ 85712

BROEGE, TIMOTHY
b. Neptune, N. J., 6 Nov. 1947. Studied at
Northwestern Univ. with Alan Stout, M. William
Karlins, and Anthony Donato. He has received
several commissions. He has been director of
instrumental music, Broad Street School,
Manasquan, N. J., 1971- ; and organist-
choirmaster, First Presbyterian Church, Belmar,
N. J., 1972- .
    WORKS: Orchestra: Sinfonia I, orch. and
jazz-rock ensemble; Sinfonia III, 25 winds and
percussion; Sinfonia V, wind ensemble; Sinfonias
II, IV, VI, for school bands; Chamber music:
Partita I, baroque ensemble; Partita II, harpsichord; Partita III, brass quintet; Songs without
words, chamber orch.; Chorus: Alleluia, choir,
trumpets, organ; Piano: Hartford dances; 5
bagatelles.
    515 Woodland Ave., Brielle, NJ 08730

*BROEKMAN, DAVID
b. Leyden, Neth., 13 May 1902; to U.S. 1924;
d. New York, 1 Jan. 1958. Wrote 2 symphonies;
and scores for the films, All quiet on the western front and The phantom of the opera.

BROGUE, ROSLYN
b. Chicago, Ill., 16 Feb. 1919. Attended Drake
Univ.; Univ. of Chicago; Radcliffe Coll., A. M.
1943, Ph. D. 1947; studying with Walter Piston.
She plays harpsichord, piano, organ, violin,
viola, is a soprano soloist, artist and poetess
as well as composer. She has held teaching posts
in classical studies at Cambridge School of
Weston, Mass., and Tufts Univ.; was assistant
professor of music, Boston Univ., 1959-60; associate professor, Tufts Univ., 1962- .
    WORKS: Orchestra: Suite for small orch.,
Boston, 29 Apr. 1948; Andante and variations,
harpsichord and orch., 1954-56; Chamber music:
trio, oboe, clarinet, bassoon, 1946; Allegretto,
flute and piano, 1948; Suite for recorders,
Amsterdam, June 1950; quartet for piano and
strings, 1949; string quartet, 1951; Duo lirico,
violin and harpsichord, 1952; trio for violin,
clarinet, piano, 1953; Quodlibet, flute, cello,
harpsichord, 1953; Arabesque, cello and piano,
1955; sonatina, flute, clarinet, harpsichord,

(BROGUE, ROSLYN)
1957; Juggler, 1962; woodwind quintet, Tufts
Univ., 9 May 1972; Equipoise, alto saxophone,
harpsichord, piano, Tufts Univ., 6 May 1972;
and many songs for soprano voice and varying
instrumental ensembles.
    28 Bromfield Road, Somerville, MA 02144

BROOKS, JOHN BENSON
b. Houlton, Me., 23 Feb. 1917. Studied at the
New England Cons., and in New York with Joseph
Schillinger and John Cage. He has been pianist,
arranger, and composer in New York City since
1937.
    WORKS: Orchestra: Alabama concerto; The
twelves; and many popular songs including You
came a long way from St. Louis.
    c/o ASCAP, 1 Lincoln Plaza
    New York, NY 10023

BROOKS, RICHARD JAMES
b. Syracuse, N. Y., 26 Dec. 1942. Studied at
State Univ. Coll., Potsdam, N. Y., with Arthur
Frackenpohl and Myron Fink; State Univ. of New
York, Binghamton, with Karl Korte, William Klenz,
William J. Mitchell; New York Univ., with Ursula
Mamlock. He won first prize in the Potsdam MENC
Chapter composition contest, 1963; and held a
scholarship to the Composers' Conference, John-
son, Vt., 1973. He was adjunct lecturer,
Brooklyn Coll., 1971-72; and is now staff member,
Music Division (Research) New York Public
Library.
    WORKS: Opera: Rapunzel, 1-act, Binghamton,
Jan. 1971; Chamber music: trio for viola, oboe,
piano, Binghamton, Mar., 1971; string quartet,
Johnson, Vt., Aug. 1973; violin sonata, 1973;
Chorus: Te Deum, chorus, organ, piano, string
bass, percussion; Next to of course God, chorus,
brass, piano, percussion.
    69 West 87th St., New York, NY 10024

BROOKS, WILLIAM
b. New York, N. Y., 17 Dec. 1943. Studied at
Wesleyan Univ. with Richard Winslow; Univ. of
Illinois with Kenneth Gaburo, Benjamin Johnston,
Herbert Brün, and Edwin London. His awards
include B. A. cum laude, Woodrow Wilson fellow,
and Danforth Found. fellow. He was instructor,
Univ. of Illinois, 1969-73, taking one year out
to be research assistant in the Biological Computer Laboratory; and has been acting assistant
professor, Univ. of California, Santa Cruz,
1973- .
    WORKS: Chamber music: Poempiece I: white-
gold blue, solo flute, 1967; Poempiece II: How
I fooled the armies, solo bass trombone; Theatre
pieces: Untitled, 8 solo singers, 2 actors,
cello, 1972; Stages, singer, actor, dancer, recorded voice, light technician, 1972; Limits, 10
percussionists, 10 dancers. He has also an unpublished manuscript on The music of William
Billings, Charles Ives, and John Cage.
    College V, University of California
    Santa Cruz, CA 95064

BROSCH, BARRY A.

BROSCH, BARRY A.
b. Cleveland, Ohio, 5 July 1942. Studied at
Kent State Univ., B. M. 1968; Univ. of Illinois,
M. M. 1969; with Salvatore Martirano, Ben
Johnston, Gordon Mumma, Fred Coulter, Hugh
Glauser, Edwin London, Margaret Erlanger. He
was a private teacher of trumpet, 1962-67; taught
music appreciation and theory, Univ. of West
Florida 1967-68; and has been an instructor in
music courses connected with dance, Univ. of
Illinois, 1969-73; and musical advisor for
Department of Dance, 1973-   .
    WORKS: Orchestra: Beware! The vipersnap,
children's piece for orch., narrator, tape, and
dance; Chamber music: Prolations, solo cello;
Divergencies, piano; Allegatoons; Gifts; and
many more concert and dance pieces, mostly
electronic.
    1022 West Daniel St., Champaign, IL 61820

BROSH, THOMAS DENTON
b. Montrose, Colo., 25 Aug. 1946. Studied at
Univ. of Colorado with Cecil Effinger and Philip
Batstone; Univ. of Denver with Normand Lockwood.
He taught at Univ. of Denver, 1970-72; Univ. of
North Carolina, 1972-   .
    WORKS: Theatre: Incidental music to Ubu roi,
Alfred Jarry, 1972; Indians, Arthur Kopit, 1973;
Chamber music: Spectrum, mezzo soprano, flute,
oboe, 1968; Pastel, alto saxophone, wind ensemble,
percussion, 1972; Dialogue for treble instru-
ments, 1973.
    Department of Music
    University of North Carolina
    Chapel Hill, NC 27514

BROUK, JOANNA
b. St. Louis, Mo., 20 Feb. 1949. Studied at
Univ. of California, Berkeley, B. A. 1972, and at
Mills Coll. Electronic Music Studio. She has
been a radio announcer for KPFA, Berkeley,
1972-   . She composes chiefly electronic music
using Moog and Buchla synthesizers; works for
piano, gong, and flute; sound poetry pieces; and
music emphasizing a sense of serenity and relating to states of meditation.
    2420 Fulton, Berkeley, CA 94704

*BROWN, CLEMMON MAY
Received an award in the American Coll. of Musi-
cians composition contest, 1948; has published
Old Scotland and Moother Goose.

BROWN, DAVID AULDON
b. Birmingham, Ala., 6 Feb. 1943. Studied at
Curtis Inst. with Myron Fink. He won first prize
in the Composers Guild contest, Salt Lake City,
1972. He has been on the faculty, Wilmington
Music School, Del., 1967-   ; and Univ. of
Delaware, 1972-   .
    WORKS: Chamber music: Toccata for piano,
1971; sonatina for piano, 1972; 4 piano sonatas;
Rondo fantasy for piano; suite for flute and
piano; flute sonata; woodwind quintet; Variations
for string orchestra.
    2220 Marsh Road, Wilmington, DE 19810

*BROWN, EARLE
b. Lunenberg, Mass., 26 Dec. 1926. Studied
engineering at Boston Univ.; composition at the
Schillinger School in Denver. His awards
include a $3000 grant from American Acad. of
Arts and Letters, 1972; many commissions. He
taught at the Denver Schillinger School, 1950-52;
has been faculty member, Peabody Cons.,
1968-   ; was composer-in-residence, Rotterdam,
Neth., 1973-74.
    WORKS: Orchestra: Folio and 4 systems,
piano and orch., 1952; Available forms I, 18
instruments, 1961; Available forms II, 98 players, 2 conductors, 1963; Times 5; From here,
chorus and orch., Chicago, 22 Jan. 1970; Modules
I and II, American premiere, Baltimore, 3 Mar.
1971; New pieces - loops, 1972; Time spans, 1972;
Chamber music: Music for piano trio, 1952; In
25 pages, 1953; Music for cello and piano, 1955;
clarinet sonata; Prelude and fughetta, bass clarinet; Pentathis for 9 instruments, 1958;
Hodograph I, flute, piano, percussion, 1959;
Indices, 12 players, 1960; string quartet, 1965;
Corroborree, 2 or 3 pianos; Centering, solo violin and 10 instruments, London, Dec. 1973; Electronic: 2 octets for 8 magnetic tapes, 1953,
1954; Light music, for electric lights, electronic equipment, and a varying number of players, 1961.
    922 St. Paul St., Baltimore, MD 21202

BROWN, ELIZABETH BOULDIN (Mrs. J. Stanley Brown)
b. Halifax, Va., 11 Jan. 1901. Graduated from
Cincinnati Cons., 1921, studying with Edgar
Stillman Kelley; studied also with Eugene
Phillips and James Evans in Pittsburgh. Her
awards include a first prize from the Penn. Fed.
of Music Clubs, 1965; two awards from the Nat.
League of American Pen Women, 1967, 1968; and a
commission. She has published many anthems and
hymns, and has also composed for strings, flute,
piano, etc.
    762 Lebanon Ave., Mount Lebanon
    Pittsburgh, PA 15228

BROWN, ELIZABETH VAN NESS
b. Topeka, Kan., 12 June 1902. Studied at Kansas State Coll., Manhattan, B. M. 1925; Univ. of
Kansas, Lawrence, M. Ed. 1945; and at Washburn
Univ., Topeka. She was public school music
supervisor for 30 years; violinist, Topeka Symphony, 10 years; organist and choir director in
several churches.
    WORKS: Anthems for adult and children's
choirs; pieces for violin, piano, etc.
    7322 Forest Ave., Kansas City, MO 64131

BROWN, J. E.
b. Huntington, N. Y., 27 Dec. 1937. Studied with
with George Andrix and Warren Benson at Ithaca
Coll.; privately with Robert Palmer; and with
Arthur Berger at Brandeis Univ. He has received
the Lies Memorial award, Bennington Composers'
Conference scholarship, and a Brandeis fellowship. He was coordinator, New York State Dept.
of Arts and Humanities, Information Service,
1971-72; and assistant professor, Lehigh Univ.,
1973-   .

(BROWN, J. E.)
WORKS: Chamber music: Impromptu, trombone
and tape; Theme and variations, brass quintet;
Fragments, for small orch.; trio for flute, clar-
inet, cello; Cut up, for tape; Foreplay, piano;
Number one, brass quintet.
R. D. 5, Creek Road, Bethlehem, PA 18015

*BROWN, KEITH CROSBY
b. Port Maitland, Nova Scotia, 1 Sep., 1885; to
U.S. 1886; d. Newton Center, Mass., 8 Sep. 1948.
Studied at the New England Cons.; Harvard Univ.;
and in Rome. He was chairman, music department,
Mt. Ida Junior Coll.
WORKS: Operetta: Who discovered America?;
Orchestra: On the Esplanade; Bostonia suite;
Latin American suite; and songs.

BROWN, NEWEL KAY
b. Salt Lake City, Utah, 29 Feb. 1932. Studied
at Univ. of Utah with Leroy J. Robertson; Univ.
of California, Berkeley; and at Eastman School
of Music, Ph. D., with Bernard Rogers, Howard
Hanson, and Wayne Barlow. He was on the faculty
at Centenary Coll. for Women, N. J., 1961-67;
Henderson State Coll., Ark., 1967-70; North Texas
State Univ., 1970-
WORKS: Orchestra: On the third summer day,
soprano and orch.; Eulogy, cello and orch.;
Music for trumpet and orch.; Chamber music:
woodwind quintet; brass quintet; Pastorale and
dance, flute, clarinet, saxophone, trumpet, trombone; saxophone sonata; trombone sonata; Poetics,
trumpet and piano; Postures, bass trombone and
piano; 4 duets for flute and clarinet; Silhouettes, trumpet and tuba; Lyric, flute and harp;
trumpet suite; Chorus: Born today is Christ our
king; Sing noel, ring noel; The earth is the
Lord's.
North Texas State University
Denton, TX 76203

BROWN, RAYNOR
b. Des Moines, Iowa, 23 Feb. 1912. Studied at
Univ. of Southern California, M. M. 1946. He
has received 7 ASCAP awards and Ford Found.
grants for recording. He has been organist,
Wilshire Presbyterian Church, Los Angeles,
1942-   ; and professor of music, Biola Coll.,
1952-   .
WORKS: Orchestra: 3 symphonies, 1952, 1957,
1958; Variations on a hymn, 1957; 2 organ concertos, 1959, 1966; Band: Sinfonietta, 1963;
Prelude and fugue, brass and percussion, 1963;
concerto for harp, brass percussion, 1964; concerto grosso for brass and percussion, 1965; concerto for piano and band, 1966; symphony for
clarinet choir, 1968; Chamber music: 2 flute
sonatas, 1944, 1959; quartet for strings and
piano, 1947; 3 fugues for 5 flutes, 1952; string
quartet, 1953; Prelude and scherzo for 7 flutes,
1956; 2 brass quintets, 1957, 1960; trio for
flute, clarinet, viola, 1958; sonatina for flute,
1961; concertino for harp and brass quintet, 1962,
Prelude and fughetta, bass clarinet and piano,
1963; harp sonata, 1967; sonata breve, baritone
saxophone and piano, 1969; 6 fugues for horn,
trombone, tuba, 1969; Diptych, tuba and piano,

(BROWN, RAYNOR)
1969; Organ: 24 sonatinas; 19 chorale preludes;
sonatas for viola and organ, 1956, cello and
organ, 1961, oboe and organ, 1962, clarinet and
organ, 1965, flute and organ, 1969; concerto for
organ and strings, 1944; concerto for organ and
brass, 1955; concerto for organ and band, 1960;
concerto for 2 organs, brass, percussion, 1967;
and choral music and piano works.
2423 Panorama Terrace, Los Angeles, CA 90039

*BROWN, REX P.
3 Christmas carols for chorus.

BROWN, RICHARD E.
b. Gloversville, N. Y., 21 Feb. 1947. Studied
at Central Coll., Pella, Iowa, B. A. magna cum
laude, with Robert J. Rittenhouse; and at Florida
State Univ., M. M., D. M. 1974, with Charles
Carter, Carlisle Floyd, and John Boda. He was a
school band director in Wellsburg, Iowa, 1969-71.
WORKS: Orchestra: clarinet concerto;
Torment of Medea, monodrama for soprano and
orch.; Band: Divertimento for winds; Chamber
music: 2 brass quartets; Delineations for brass;
Serenata, violin and cello; Suite pastorale,
piano; Sextuplets, piano; Chorus: Kyrie eleison.
940 West Brevard, No. B3-7,
Tallahassee, FL 32304

BROWN, THOMAS A.
b. Schenectady, N. Y., 24 June 1932. Attended
Hartwick Coll., B. S., and State Univ. Coll.,
Potsdam, N. Y., M. S. He has received five ASCAP
awards. His major faculty positions include
director of music, Potsdam High School, N. Y.,
1957-61; director of music, Burnt Hills High
School, N. Y., 1964-71; assistant professor,
Coll. of St. Rose, Albany, N. Y., 1972-74;
percussion instructor at music camps and conferences. He was percussion editor, Brass and Percussion Magazine, 1973-74.
WORKS: Band: Percussionata, band accompaniment; Rock velvet, jazzrock ensemble; and many
pieces for percussion such as Mallets in mind;
Percussion trajectories; Tropicussion; Percussion particles; etc.
10 St. Stephens Lane, Scotia, NY 12302

BROWNE, DONALD KURTZ, JR.
b. Columbus, Ohio, 23 Nov. 1946. Studied at
Ohio State Univ. with Donald McGinnis, Daniel H.
Baker, and Samuel Greene. He has had awards
from the Ohio Education Asso., 1963, 1964, and
the South Florida Music Club. He has been music
director, New Albany Schools, Ohio, 1968-69;
Green Valley Schools, Orange City, Fla., 1969-70;
Ransom School, Miami, 1970-71; and Horizon School,
Miami, 1971-72. He was music director, Florida
Symphony Orch., 1970-73.
WORKS: Percussion: Three by three; Five by
five.
6980 S. W. 83rd Court, Miami, FL 33143

BROWNE, PHILIP
b. Norman, Okla., 27 July 1933. Attended Arizona State Univ., B. A.; Eastman School of Music,
M. M.; and Univ. of California, Los Angeles.

BROWNE, PHILIP

(BROWNE, PHILIP)
His composition teachers were Bernard Rogers,
Wayne Barlow, Darius Milhaud, and Roy Harris.
His awards include the $1000 Max Winkler award
for a band composition, 1973, and selection as
an Outstanding Educator of America, 1972. He
has been professor, band director, and chairman
of the music department, California State Polytechnic Univ., Pomona, 1963-   .
WORKS: Orchestra: Concerto for strings;
Serenade; Inaugural procession; Band: Windroc
overture; Ballad for trumpet; Suite, No. 2;
Sonoro and brioso for winds.
387 Golden Carriage Lane, Pomona, CA 91767

BROWNE, RICHMOND
b. Flint, Mich., 8 Aug. 1934. Studied at Michigan State Univ. with H. Owen Reed, and at Yale
Univ. with Richard Donovan. He received BMI student composer awards, 1957, 1958; Fulbright grant,
1958; and the Yale Morse grant, 1964. He was
assistant professor, Yale Univ., 1960-68; and has
been associate professor, Univ. of Michigan,
1968-   .
WORKS: Orchestra: Translations, 1964-73;
Chamber music: Trio for solo viola, commissioned,
1965; Chorus: Chortos I, speech chorus; Chortos
II, speech chorus, commissioned, 1970.
School of Music, University of Michigan
Ann Arbor, MI 48105

*BROWNING, MORTIMER
b. Baltimore, Md., 16 Nov. 1891; d. Milford,
Del., 24 June 1953. Studied at Peabody Cons.;
Chicago Musical Coll; Mannes School of Music; and
with Percy Grainger. He taught at Greensboro
Coll.; Juilliard School; Westchester Cons.;
Greenwich Music School and Chapin School in New
York; was organist and choirmaster in Baltimore
and New York.
WORKS: Orchestra: Scherzo rondo, violin and
orch.; concerto for theremin, New York, 27 Mar.
1944; Chamber music: piano trio; piano suite;
Caprice burlesque, violin and piano; also docu-
mentary film scores.

BROZEN, MICHAEL
b. New York, N. Y., 5 Aug. 1934. Studied at
Bard Coll., with Paul Nordoff; at Tanglewood
with Lukas Foss; and at Juilliard School with
Vincent Persichetti. His awards include a
Howard Hanson commission; ASCAP award; Nat.
Inst.-American Acad. of Arts and letters grant;
Ingram Merrill fellowship; Guggenheim fellowship;
special citation of the Koussevitzky Internat.
Recording Award. He was musical advisor, modern
dance department, Brooklyn Coll., 1959-60; assistant editor, Musical America, 1961-64.
WORKS: Orchestra: Canto; Dark night, gentle night, soprano, tenor, orch.; In memoriam,
soprano and string orch.; Chamber music: The
bugle moon, baritone and 9 instruments; The ways
of water, baritone and piano; Fantasy, piano.
86 Horatio St., New York, NY 10014

BRUBECK, DAVID WARREN
b. Concord, Calif., 6 Dec. 1920. Studied at
Univ. of Pacific, B. M. 1942; at Mills Coll.;

(BRUBECK, DAVID WARREN)
and privately with Darius Milhaud. He holds
honorary Ph. Ds. from Univ. of Pacific and Fairfield Univ. After military service during World
War II he formed his own band that soon became
known throughout the jazz world.
WORKS: Orchestra: Elements; Happy anniversary, a fugal fanfare; Chorus: The light in the
wilderness, oratorio; Gates of justice, cantata;
Truth is fallen cantata, commissioned by the
Midland, Mich., Symphony for the opening of the
Midland Center for the Arts on 1 May 1971; and
more than 100 jazz tunes recorded and published.
221 Millstone Road, Wilton, CT 06897

*BRUBECK, HOWARD
b. Concord, Calif., 11 July 1916. Brother of
David Brubeck, also studied with Darius Milhaud.
He is chairman, music department, Palomar Coll.
WORKS: Orchestra: Dialogue for jazz combo
and orch., 1956; also chamber music and choral
works.
2362 Royal Crest Drive, Escondido, CA 92025

BRUCE, NEELY
b. Memphis, Tenn., 21 Jan. 1944. Attended Univ.
of Alabama, B. M.; Univ. of Illinois, M. M.,
D. M. A.; and studied composition with Thomas
Canning, J. F. Goossen, David Cohen, Ben
Johnston, and Hubert Kessler. He was named associate, Center for Advanced Study, Univ. of Illinois, 1973. He has been on the faculty, now
assistant professor, Univ. of Illinois,
1965-   .
WORKS: Theatre pieces: Pyramus and Thisbe,
chamber opera, 1965; Incidental music for
Galethea, 1967, for The tempest, 1968; Au claire
de la lune, for the Kipnis Mime Troupe; The trials of Psyche, 1-act opera, Univ. of Illinois,
1971; score for film by Illinois Environmental
Protection Agency, 1972; Orchestra: concerto
for percussion and orch., 1967; Fanfare for
William Schuman, brass choir and percussion,
1963; Quodlibet on Christmas tunes, string orch.,
flute, oboe, piano, 1963; concerto for violin
and chamber orch., 1974; Chamber music: wind
quintet, 1967; Fantasy, 10 winds, percussion,
tape, 1968; Untitled piece No. 3, oboe and piano,
1969; Untitled piece No. 4, trombone and percussion, 1969; Three canons for marimba, 1969;
Grand duo, trombone and piano, 1971; Grand duo,
saxophone and piano, 1972; many choral works,
songs, piano and organ pieces.
2203 Noel Drive, Champaign, IL 61820

*BRUHNS, GEORGE F. W.
b. Bunzlau, Silesia, 10 Apr. 1874; U.S. citizen
1918; d. Cranford, N. J., 2 July 1963. Wrote a
symphonic poem, marches, songs.

BRÜN, HERBERT
B. Berlin, Germany, 1918, to U.S. 1963. Studied
at Jerusalem Cons., Israel, and at Columbia Univ.;
teachers included Stepan Wolpe and Frank Pelleg.
In 1955-61, he was engaged in research in electro-
acoustics and electronic sound production in
musical composition in Paris, Cologne, and Munich;
gave numerous lectures and seminars. In 1963 he

(BRÜN, HERBERT)
joined the staff, School of Music, Univ. of Illinois, for further research in electronic music;
associate professor, 1972-   . He was distinguished visiting professor, Coll. of the Arts,
Ohio State Univ., 1969-70.
WORKS: Electronic: Mutatis mutandis,
FORTRAN, IBM360/75, Calcomp plotter. Brün says
of this work: "Here the interpreter is invited
to begin by contemplating a graphic as traces
left by a process which moved a pen in various
directions across the plane....to construct by
thought and imagination his version of a structure that might leave the traces which the
graphic displays....He is asked to construct the
structured process by which he would like to have
generated the graphics....The interpreter is not
asked to improvise. The interpreter is asked not
to improvise. He is asked to compose."
307 South Busey, Urbana, IL 61801

BRUNELLI, LOUIS JEAN
b. New York, N. Y., 24 June 1925. Studied at
Guildhall School of Music, London; New York
Univ., B. A.; Manhattan School of Music, M. M.;
composition with Philip James, Marion Bauer, and
Vittorio Giannini. He received the 1960 American
Symph. League recording repertoire award. He was
arranger and assistant conductor, Longine Symphonette, 1949-54; staff member, Chappell and
Co., 1954-71; faculty, Manhattan School of Music,
1970-   , and director for performance,
1972-   .
WORKS: Orchestra: Burlesca; Band: In
memoriam; Arlecchino, 1971; Essay for Cyrano.
32-43 90th St., Jackson Heights, NY 11372

*BRUNSWICK, MARK
b. New York, 6 Jan. 1902; d. London, 26 May 1971.
Studied with Rubin Goldmark and Ernest Block; and
with Nadia Boulanger in Paris. He lived in
Europe, 1925-38; on returning to New York he
taught composition; was chairman, music department, City Coll. of New York, 1946-64.
WORKS: Orchestra, symphony, 1946; Eros and
death, chorus and orch., 1954; Lysistrata, suite
for orch., women's chorus, mezzo soprano, 1930;
Chamber music: 7 trios for string quartet, 1955;
Septet in 7 movements, 1957; string quartet with
contrabass, 1958; 6 bagatelles for piano, 1958.

BRUSH, RUTH J.
b. Fairfax, Okla., 7 Feb. 1910. Attended Kansas
City Cons., studying composition with Wiktor
Labunski, Gardner Read, and David Van Vactor.
She has received awards from Texas Manuscript
Society, 1952; Composers Press, 1959; Texas Com-
posers Guild, 1954, 1972; Nat. Fed. of Music
Clubs, 1972. She was pianist, radio station WHB,
Kansas City, 1940-45; head of piano faculty,
Frank Phillips Coll., 1950-54; organist Bartles-
ville, Okla., 1955-   .
WORKS: Chamber music: Valse joyeuse, violin
and piano; Two expressive pieces for organ;
Pastorale for organ; The night lights, piano;
Suite for piano; Songs: Goddess of the sun;
Twilight.
3413 Wildwood Court, Bartlesville, OK 74003

*BRYAN, CHARLES FAULKNER
b. McMinnville, Tenn., 26 July 1911; d. Helena,
Ala., 7 July 1955. Wrote orchestral works,
chamber music, songs, choral works.

BRYANT, ALLAN C.
b. Detroit, Mich., 12 July 1931. Attended
Princeton Univ. and Cologne State Music School.
WORKS: Electric guitars: Pitch out; 40
etudes; Liberate Isang Yun; Libret Almarik;
Masses, choir, organ, electric guitars; Miscellaneous: Electronic symfony, for audience and
synthesizer; Quadruple play, for rubber band
instruments.
via Angeletto 3, Roma 00184, Italy

BUBALO, RUDOLPH
b. Duluth, Minn., 21 Oct. 1927. Studied at
Chicago Musical Coll. with John Becker, Rudolph
Ganz, Vittorio Rieti, Karel Jirak, and Hans
Tischler. He has received the Cleveland arts
award in music, 1970, and ASCAP awards, 1972,
1973. He has been assistant professor and director, Electronic Music Studio, Cleveland State
Univ., 1969-   .
WORKS: Chamber music: Three pieces for
brass quintet; five pieces for brass quintet and
percussion; Mixed media: Soundscape for orchestra and tape; Concertino for saxophone, percussion, and tape; Albert's system, clarinet and
tape.
3764 Glenwood Road, Cleveland, OH 44121

BUCCI, MARK
b. New York, N. Y., 26 Feb. 1924. Studied at
the Juilliard School, B. S., with Frederick
Jacobi and Vittorio Giannini; privately with
Tibor Serly; and at Tanglewood with Aaron
Copland. His awards include Irving Berlin schol-
arship, 1948-52; Piatigorsky award, 1949;
MacDowell Colony fellowships, 1952, 1954;
Guggenheim grants, 1953, 1957; Nat. Inst. of
Arts and Letters grant, 1959; co-winner of
Italia Prize, international television award,
1966; and many commissions.
WORKS: Theatre: Cadenza incidental music,
play by Dills, 1947; Caucasian chalk circle, to
Brecht's play, 1948; The boor, 1-act opera after
Chekov, New York, Dec. 1949; The beggar's opera,
after John Gay, New York, June 1950; The Adamses,
music and lyrics to a play by Paula Jacobi, 1952;
Elmer and Lily, score to Saroyan's play, Alfred
Univ., April, 1952; Summer afternoon, original
play with music, New York, summer, 1952; The
dress, 1-act opera, New York, 8 Dec. 1953; Sweet
Betsy from Pike, 1-act opera satire, New York,
8 Dec. 1953; The thirteen clocks, music and
lyrics to Thurber's fantasy, ABC-TV, 29 Dec.
1953; The western, music and lyrics to a mime
play, Westport, Conn., summer 1954; Tale for a
deaf ear, opera after Elizabeth Enright, Tanglewood, 5 Aug. 1957; The hero, 1-act opera based
on Gilroy's Far Rockaway, NET network, 24 Sep.
1965. Orchestra: Concerto for a singing instrument, with string orch., harp, piano-celeste,
New York, 26 Mar. 1960, with Leonard Bernstein
conducting the New York Philharmonic, Anita
Darian, kazoo soloist. Nocturne, solo voice or

BUCCI, MARK

(BUCCI, MARK)
instrument and orch., Vienna, 1962; Chamber music: Introduction and allegro, 8 woodwinds, Cleveland, Jan. 1946; Divertimento, violin and piano, Basle, Switz., 1950; American folk songs, 3 voices, guitar, piano, New York, 8 Dec. 1953; Chorus: The wondrous kingdom (Flora and fauna), cantata, a cappella chorus, Tanglewood, 1962; film scores: A time to play, Polaroid movie commissioned by USIA for U.S. Pavilion at Expo 67; Seven in darkness, ABC-TV, 23 Sep. 1969; Honeymoon with a stranger, ABC-TV, 23 Dec. 1969; Echo of a massacre, 1973. He has also written plays; book and lyrics to a pop opera, Myron It's damp down here; and, in collaboration with Rod Arrants, Keyboard, a game show format.
4044 Cartwright Ave., Studio City, CA 91604

*BUCHANAN, ANNABEL MORRIS
b. Groesbeck, Tex., 22 Oct. 1888. Wrote an oratorio, choral suite, other choral works, songs.

*BUCHANAN, EDWARD L.
b. Burnside, Ky., 1918. Studied at Chicago Musical Coll., B. M. 1949; Marshall Univ., M. A. 1958. He served in the U.S. Navy in World War II; has been instructor in music, Ashland Center, Univ. of Kentucky, 1959-   .
WORKS: Opera: Boccaccio's untold tale, 1-act; Orchestra: Square dance rhapsody; Chorus: Gethesemane.
1409 Central Ave., Ashland, KY 41101

*BUCHAROFF, SIMON
b. Ukraine, 20 Apr. 1881; d. Chicago, 24 Nov. 1955. Wrote 3 operas, several symphonic poems.

*BUCHTEL, FORREST L.
b. St. Edward, Neb., 9 Dec. 1899. Joined the faculty, Vandercook Coll. of Music in 1932. He has written many works for band.
1116 Cleveland St., Evanston, IL 60202

BUCKLEY, DOROTHY PIKE
b. Glens Falls, N. Y., 26 Apr. 1911. Studied composition with Burrill Phillips and Wayne Barlow at Eastman School of Music. She won the 1969 annual composition award from the American Coll. of Musicians, Texas. She has been a teacher in Rochester since 1945.
WORKS: Chamber music: The blue waterfall, voice, flute, cello, piano; Perception, voice, flute, cello, piano; Clouds, voice and piano; Piano: Folk theme and variations, 1969; Variphonic suite; Adirondack fantasy; Tarantella; Five after five, duet.
145 Harvard St., Apt. 2, Rochester, NY 14607

BUDD, HAROLD
b. Los Angeles, Calif., 24 May 1936. Studied at California State Univ., Northridge, B. A. 1963, with Aurelio de la Vega and Gerald Strang; and at Univ. of Southern California, M. M. 1966, with Ingolf Dahl. He joined the faculty of California Inst. of the Arts in 1969.
WORKS: Instrumental: III, concert jazz for double ensemble; The edge of August, flute and piano; The candy-apple revision, 1970; Voice:

(BUDD, HAROLD)
Madrigals of the rose angel; Electronic: Coeur d'orr, 1969; Oak of golden dreams, 1970.
23149 Oakbridge Lane, Newhall, CA 91321

BUDRECKAS, LADISLAUS
b. Gomel, Belorussia, 24 Oct. 1905; U.S. citizen 1955. Got a Dip. of Theol. at Univ. of Vytautas the Great, Lith., then studied at the Cons. of Kaunas with Juozas Naujalis, earning a degree in composition of sacred music, 1948; studying at the Pontificio Instituto di Musica Sacra, Rome, 1937-39 and 1945-49, he received the Magistrum in Cantu Gregoriano, 1949. He was professor, Univ. of Vytautas the Great, 1939-44; member of the Diocesan Music Commission, Pittsburgh, 1957-59; and head of the Commission for Lithuanian Music, 1966-   .
WORKS: Chorus: Hymn for America I, Hymn for America II, both for mixed chorus or male chorus and organ, 1960; Christus vincit, 1961; Lithuanian's Hymn, 1965; Hymn in honor of St. Casimir, male chorus and organ, 1971; Two hymns in honor of Our Lady's apparition in Siluva, for one or two voices and organ.
Immaculate Heart Residence, East Island
Glen Cove, NY 11542

BUDRIUNUS, BRONIUS
b. Pabirze, Lith., 29 July 1909; U.S. citizen 1954. Studied organ, conducting, and composition at the School of Music and Cons. in Kaunas, 1925-38, in Vilnius, 1943-44; and in Germany with F. Haberl and G. V. Albrecht, 1946-49. He was a teacher and conductor in Lithuania, 1933-44, and in Germany, 1945-49; in Detroit, 1949-53. Since 1953 he has been organist and choirmaster, St. Casimir's Church, Los Angeles, and a private teacher of piano and voice.
WORKS: Chamber music: Lament, violin and piano; string quartet; piano sonata; Chorus: The land of my forefathers; Homeland; Along the road of Lithuania's light; The legend of the land of Amber; more than 60 published songs and arrangements of Lithuanian folk songs.
2620 Griffith Park Blvd.
Los Angeles, CA 90039

BUEBENDORF, FRANCIS
b. New York, N. Y., 21 Feb. 1912. Studied with Philip James, New York Univ.; with Albert Stoessel and Bernard Wagenaar, Juilliard School, 1933-37; with Douglas Moore and Paul Henry Lang, Columbia Univ., Ed. D., 1945; conducting with Pierre Monteux, 1958. At Juilliard he held fellowships in composition and conducting. He was associate professor, Trinity Univ., 1945-57; professor, Univ. of Missouri Cons., 1947-   ; conductor, Cons. Orch., 1947-57, Kansas City Civic Ballet, 1959-61, Univ. String Orch., 1962-   .
WORKS: Orchestra: Passacaglia; Fantasia - Alaeddin; Prelude and fugue, string orch; Chamber music: Scherzo, flute and piano; Three pieces, viola and piano; Theme and variations, instrumental ensemble and tape recorder; many choral and chamber works.
9716 Jarboe St., Kansas City, MO 64114

BUFFHAM, CHARLES ALLEN
  b. Grand Rapids, Mich., 23 Dec. 1940. Studied
with Marshall Barnes and Mark Walker at Ohio
State Univ., M. M. 1966. He was instructor,
Cedarville Coll., Ohio, 1965-66; instructor,
Grand Rapids Junior Coll., 1966-   .
    WORKS: Theatre: A little season, musical
drama, 1971; Instrumental: Thematic study, 1964;
Nonet for winds and strings, 1966; Jericho, trio
for brass, 1966; Symphonette, for jazz ensemble.
    18 Burr Oak N. E., Grand Rapids, MI 49505

*BUFFKINS, ARCHIE LEE
  b. Memphis, Tenn. Studied at Jackson State Coll.,
B. S.; Columbia Univ., M. A., Ed. D. He has been
head, music department, Kentucky State Coll.,
Frankfort, 1963-   .
    WORKS: Chamber music: Prelude and fugue,
clarinet, 1961; piano sonata, 1962; Toccata,
organ, 1962; string quartet, 1963; choral works.
    Music Department, Kentucky State College
    Frankfort, KY 40601

BUGATCH, SAMUEL
  b. Rogatchov, Russia, 20 June 1898; U.S. citizen
1923. Studied with Howard Thatcher, Gustave
Strube, and Franz Bornschein at Peabody Cons.
He was music director, Temple Adath Israel,
Bronx, N. Y., 25 years, and at Beth Tfiloh
Synagogue, Baltimore, 15 years, and conducted
choruses in Philadelphia, Trenton, Newark and
Lakewood, N. J. His works are chiefly vocal com-
positions, settings of such poets as Longfellow,
Walter Scott, Lord Byron, and Yiddish and litur-
gical texts, comprising some 70 published pieces.
    144-10 69th Ave., Flushing, NY 11367

BUGGERT, ROBERT W.
  b. Chicago, Ill., 25 July 1918. Attended Vandercook School of Music, B. M. 1938; Univ. of Michigan, M. M. Ed. 1947, Ph. D. 1956. He taught in
public schools, 1939-43; was associate professor,
Univ. of Wichita, 1948-51, 1952-59; professor,
Univ. of Oklahoma, 1959-61; Boston Univ., 1961-63;
Northern Illinois Univ., 1964-   , and dean,
Coll. of Fine and Applied Arts, 1971-   . He
was percussion editor of The Instrumentalist,
1955-59; and is editor of Contemporary Percussion
Library.
    WORKS: Theatre: The night Thoreau spent in
jail, DeKalb, Ill., Dec. 1970; Percussion: Introduction and fugue, piano and percussion, 1957;
Toccata No. 1, 1969; Short overture, 1969; Dialogue for solo percussion and piano, 1969; Fanfare, song, and march, solo percussion and piano,
1969; J-21557, 1969; Didiption No. 1, 1970;
Didiption No. 2, 1970. He is author of several
books of teaching methods for percussion and co-
author of The search for musical understanding,
a textbook on general musical education.
    1712 Judy Lane, DeKalb, IL 60115

*BUHRMAN, BERT
  The Bald Knobbers, 1-act Ozark folk opera, School
of the Ozarks, Point Lookout, Mo., 12 May 1968.

BULLARD, BOB
  b. Oak Park, Ill., 22 Apr. 1927. Studied at
American Cons. with Leo Sowerby. He has been
chairman, Music Department, School District No.
87, Berkeley, Ill., 1958-   .
    WORKS: Band: Cyrano de Bergerac, tone poem,
1964; Winter scene, 1969; Tahquamenon, Chicago,
May 1970; Trumpet soliloquy, Chicago, March 1973.
    5 Westleigh Court, Aurora, IL 60538

BUNGER, RICHARD
  b. Bethlehem, Pa., 1 June 1942. Has received a
Rockefeller grant; Bennington Composers Conf.
fellowship; Nat. Fed. of Music Clubs award;
Music Soc. of Santa Barbara award; selection for
Pi Kappa Lambda, Outstanding Young Men of America, and Outstanding Educators of America. He
has held faculty positions at Queens Coll.,
1965-68; Oberlin Cons., 1968-69; California State
Coll., 1970-   . He is a concert pianist spe-
cializing in contemporary American music.
    WORKS: Theatre: Oedipus Rex, singers, elec-
tronic tape; Good woman of Setzuan, singers, percussion, tape, slides; Chamber music: Syzygy,
2 pianos, organ, 5 winds, 2 strings; Variations
on a sonata, string quartet; Abacus vocamen,
tenor, baroque ensemble; Twice five for two, violin and cello; Jiuta, chorus, recorder, guitar,
percussion; Piano: Pianography, Fantasy on a
theme by Fibonacci, for amplified and ring modu-
lated piano, chord bar, tape loop; Hommage,
suite for piano; Vocal: 3 songs on poems of
e.e. cummings, mezzo soprano and piano; Three
French songs, mezzo soprano and piano.
    303 South Ave., 57, Los Angeles, CA 90042

BURCHAM, WAYNE
  b. Burlington, Iowa, 27 Aug. 1943. Studied at
Drake Univ.; Univ. of Iowa with Gerhard Krapf;
and Univ. of Minnesota with Paul Fetler and
Dominick Argento. He won first prize in the
American Guild of Organists competition, 1973.
He was director of music, Christ Church Lutheran,
Minneapolis, 1969-71; and of Holy Nativity
Lutheran Church, Minneapolis, 1971-   .
    WORKS: Orchestra: The day time began, orch.,
chorus, and soloists; Chamber music: Variations
for bass clarinet; Variations for harpsichord;
Organ: Veni Creator Spiritus, 1973.
    13008 James Ave., South
    Minneapolis, MN 55401

*BURGE, DAVID R.
  b. Evanston, Ill., 25 Mar. 1930. Studied at
Northwestern Univ., M. M. 1952; Eastman School
of Music, D. M. A. 1956. He has been faculty
member, Univ. of Colorado, 1962-   .
    WORKS: Orchestra: Serenade for musical saw
and orch., 1965; Chamber music: Eclipse II,
piano; Aeolian music, for flute, clarinet, violin, cello, piano; Sources III, clarinet and percussion; A song of sixpence, soprano.
    Department of Music, University of Colorado
    Boulder, CO 80302

BURGSTAHLER, ELTON E.
  b. Orland, Calif., 16 Sep. 1924. Studied at
Univ. of Pacific with J. Russell Bodly; Millikin

BURGSTAHLER, ELTON E.

(BURGSTAHLER, ELTON E.)
Univ. with Walter Emch; Univ. of Illinois with Gordon Binkerd. He received a Pi Kappa Lambda composition award in 1947. He was instructor, California schools, 1947-48; professor, Milliken Univ., 1949-56; professor, Southwest Missouri State Univ., 1956- ; and church choir director, 1950- .
WORKS: 3 chamber operas; a symphony; piano concerto; many band pieces; 13 saxophone quartets; 12 trombone quartets; solo pieces for all wind instruments; works for chorus including: The ballad of Christmas, cantata; The truth about Christmas, cantata.
1300 East Elm, Apt. 302
Springfield, MO 65802

BURKE, LORETTO
b. Parkersburg, W. Va., 23 May 1922. Studied at Catholic Univ. with Conrad Bernier and Thaddeus Jones. She taught in high schools in Cincinnati, Denver, Albuquerque, and Cleveland, 1952-70; has been chairman, Music Department, Coll. of Mount St. Joseph, Ohio, 1971- .
WORKS: Orchestra: Symphonic dance suite; Chamber music: Pastorale, flute, oboe, clarinet; Chorus: Valiant woman, cantata for women's voices; Psalm of praise, mixed voices and brass choir.
5776 Delhi Ave., Cincinnati, OH 45202

BURKE, RICHARD N.
b. New York, N. Y., 10 Dec. 1947. Studied at Hunter Coll. with Ulysses Kay and Ruth Anderson. He has been instructor, Lehman Coll., CUNY, 1971- .
WORKS: Orchestra: Missa l'homme arme, orch. and tape, 1973; Chamber music: Landscapes, instrumental and vocal, 1969; Trio, 1969; cello sonata, 1973; Electronic: Study No. 1, 1971; Untitled piece, 1972.
4286 Kutonah Ave., Bronx, NY 10470

*BURKLEY, BRUCE HUNSIKER,
Studied at Peabody Cons., artist's diploma 1962. He received a Ford fellowship in 1961 to write music for school ensembles in Cincinnati; composition award, West Virginia School of Music, 1959.
WORKS: Chamber music: 3 preludes for piano, 1959; violin sonata, 1960; Image, flute and strings, 1961.

*BURLEIGH, CECIL
b. Wyoming, N. Y., 17 Apr. 1885. Studied at Chicago Musical Coll.; violin in Europe. He taught violin, Univ. of Wisconsin, 1921-55. He wrote 3 symphonies, 3 violin concertos, 2 violin sonatas, violin pieces.

*BURNHAM, CARDON V.
Festival chorale for organ and brass.
Carroll College, Waukesha, WI 53186

BURROUGHS, BOB L.
b. Tazewell, Va., 10 Mar. 1937. Studied at Oklahoma Baptist Univ. with Warren M. Angell; Southwestern Baptist Theol. Seminary with Talmage W.

(BURROUGHS, BOB L.)
Dean; privately with William J. Reynolds and Ralph Carmichael. He won a first prize in the Erskine Coll. anthem competition, and in the Rochester, N. Y., Festival of Fine Arts. He was minister of music in Muskogee, Okla., 1961-63, and Abilene, Tex., 1963-70; and has been composer-in-residence, Samford Univ., 1970- .
WORKS: Many compositions in all genres including sacred songs such as: Let all creation sing; My God, I thank Thee; Come, children, lift your voices.
Samford University, Box 2275
Birmingham, AL 35209

BURT, CHARLES AYCOCK
b. Wilson, N. C., 24 Dec. 1943. Attended Atlantic Christian Coll., A. B.; Peabody Cons.; Eastman School of Music; North Carolina State Univ., Inst. in Computer Music. He has been band and choral director, Whitley High School, 1965-72; and at Ravenscroft School, 1972-
WORKS: Film scores: The goodliest land; The battle of Alamance; Tryon Palace; Popular: The battle of Senator Sam, 1973.
701 Fieldstone Court, Raleigh, NC 27609

BURT, GEORGE
b. San Francisco, Calif., 7 Oct. 1929. Studied at Univ. of California, Berkeley, with Andrew Imbrie; Mills Coll. with Darius Milhaud and Leon Kirchner; Princeton Univ. with Roger Sessions, Milton Babbitt, Edward Cone; and in Vienna with György Ligeti. He was instructor, Smith Coll., 1963-69; associate professor, Univ. of Michigan, 1969- .
WORKS: Orchestra: Chamber concerto, 1959; Introduction, 1962; Chamber music: Four short piano pieces, 1957; Three movements, string quartet, 1960; Four studies, percussion ensemble, 1965; Canzona, viola and cello, 1965; Exit music, for 12 players, 1968; Chorus: New Hampshire, double chorus of women's voices, 1965; Threnody, double chorus of men's voices, 1967; Time passes, chorus and piano, 1972; Mixed media: Music for the New York hat, synthesizer, piano, tape, and film, 1972; Improvisation II, synthesizer, piano, tape, 1972; Sam's story, synthesizer, piano, tape, and film (written and directed by composer), 1973.
School of Music, University of Michigan
Ann Arbor, MI 48105

BURT, VIRGINIA M.
b. Minneapolis, Minn., 28 Apr. 1919. Studied at Minneapolis Coll. of Music with Gerald Bales and Stanley Avery. She is a private teacher of organ, piano, and theory, and organist-choir director in Minneapolis.
WORKS: Fanfare for a festive day, chorus, organ, and brass.
4841 Drew Ave., South, Minneapolis, MN 55410

BURT, WARREN
b. Baltimore, Md., 10 Oct. 1949. Studied at State Univ. of New York at Albany, B. A. 1971, with William Thomas McKinley and Joel Chadabe;

(BURT, WARREN)
Univ. of California, San Diego, M. A. 1974, with Robert Erickson, Pauline Oliveros, and Kenneth Gaburo. He is research assistant for analog studio design and development, Center for Music Experiment, La Jolla, 1973-   .
WORKS: Drakula, orchestra, 1969; 3 Damnthings: Aardvarks I, Anteaters, Armadillos, string trio, 1970;   any small group of instruments, 1970, Promenade Theater Orch., London, 1971; Rich's genuine 1:30 down-home department store blues, Muzak system and P. A. microphone, 1971; Trilobites and aardvarks, text from Grove Press' My secret life, voice and tape, 1971; In memoriam Carl Ruggles: Aardvarks II: Mr. Natural encounters Flakey Foont, piano, 1971; Rain at dawn, Late autumn, Saranac Lake, electronic tape, 1971; Real science comix funnies #1, text-sound tape, 1972; Lullabies II, live synthesizer performance, The Kitchen, New York, 3 Jan. 1973; for Charlemagne Palestine, electronic tape, York, England, 1973
165A Del Mar Shores Terrace
Solana Beach, CA 92037

BURTON, ELDIN
b. Fitzgerald, Ga., 26 Oct. 1913. Studied at Atlanta Cons. with George Lindner; Juilliard School with Bernard Wagenaar. His awards include scholarships at Atlanta Cons.; 3 fellowships at Juilliard; 10 ASCAP awards; New York Flute Club award, 1948. He was director, Georgia Cons. 1940-41.
WORKS: Orchestra: Piano concerto; flute concerto; Chamber music: sonatina, violin and piano, 1944; quintet, piano and string quartet, 1945; Fiddlestick!, violin and piano; sonatina, flute and piano, 1946; viola sonata, 1957; Nonchalance, piano; Sarabande in G, piano.
350 West 57th St., New York, NY 10019

*BURTON, JIM
Was trained in the visual arts. He designs and builds his own instruments with springs, amplified wires (played by resined fingertips), music box parts, and other available odds and ends. His compositions tend to run a full evening in length, as: 6 solos in the form of a pair for prepared piano; Phisiks of meta-quavers, for wheels, wires, organ pipes, and instruments; Weedauwoo, Wyoming - a pastorale, in which details of a Wyoming map are projected on a screen; one performer reads the railroads, another sings the names of the towns, another plays the roads, and another plays the rivers. See New music by Tom Johnson, Musical America, Mar. 1975.

BURTON, STEPHEN DOUGLAS
b. Whittier, Calif., 24 Feb. 1943. Studied with Hans Werner Henze at the Mozarteum, Salzburg, and in Rome; and with Jean Eichelberger Ivey at Peabody Cons. His awards include Guggenheim fellowships, 1969-70; Nat. Fed. of Music Clubs award, 1968; Devora Nadworny award, 1968; Nat. Endowment for the Arts grant of $7500 to compose three 1-act operas; various commissions. He is instructor, Catholic Univ. and George Mason Univ.,

(BURTON, STEPHEN DOUGLAS)
1970-   . He has composed in all forms: opera, ballet, symphonies. His orchestral works have been performed by many of the major orchestras in the U.S. and Europe.
4410 Everett St., Kensington, MD 20795

*BUSCH, ADOLF
b. Siegen, Germany, 8 Aug. 1891; to U.S. 1939; d. Guilford, Vt., 9 June 1952. Studied violin at the Bonn and Cologne conservatories; was concertmaster, Vienna Orchestra, 1912-18; toured as violin soloist; organized Busch Quartet in 1919 and Busch Trio with his brother Hermann and son-in-law, Rudolf Serkin. In 1950 with his brother, the Moyse family, and Serkin, he founded the Marlboro Festival in Vermont. He composed for orchestra, chamber groups, and voice. His Psalm 130 for women's chorus, 2 violas, 2 cellos, and double bass, 1944, was premiered at Marlboro, 5 July 1975.

BUSH, GORDON
b. Detroit, Mich., 4 May 1943. Studied with Clifford Taylor at Temple Univ.; with Malcolm Williamson in London; with Nicholas Flagello, Manhattan School of Music. He was organist-choirmaster, U.S. Merchant Marine Acad. 1963-65; organist-choirmaster, Union Church of Bay Ridge, Brooklyn, 1971-   ; director of music, Congregation Beth Elohim, Brooklyn, 1971-   ; and music director, Bay Chamber Ensemble, 1974-   .
WORKS: Opera: The hermit, 1-act chamber opera, string quartet, piano, percussion, 4 solo voices, Brooklyn, 11 May 1973; The visitation, 1-act, organ, percussion, 3 soloists, chorus; Chorus: Revival, short music drama for 2 soloists, choir, congregation, and organ; A view of the manger, mixed voices and piano; Three songs, soprano and piano, Ambler Music Festival, 1972; Organ: Homage, St. Patrick's Cathedral, New York, June 1972; Prelude No. 1 for prepared organ.
300 9th St., Brooklyn, NY 11215

*BUSH, GRACE E.
b. Ludington, Mich., 25 Apr., 1884; d. Wrote songs and piano pieces.

BUSH, IRVING R.
b. Los Angeles, Calif., 7 Apr. 1930. Attended California State Univ., Los Angeles, B. A., M. A., and was associate professor there, 1960-72, and on the faculty, Univ. of Southern California, 1962-68. He has played trumpet in the Los Angeles Philharmonic Orch., 1962-   , and in motion picture, television, and recording orchestras.
WORKS: Brass: Fanfare, 1969; Duet sessions; Top tones for trumpet; Artistic trumpet, technique and study; To the rescue, brass quintet.
14859 Jadestone Drive
Sherman, Oaks, CA 91403

BUTLER, EUGENE SANDERS
b. Durant, Okla., 13 Jan. 1935. Studied piano with Sylvia Zaremba, voice with Orcenith Smith at Oklahoma Univ.; composition with Seth Bingham in New York and Gerald Kemner at Univ. of

BUTLER, EUGENE SANDERS

(BUTLER, EUGENE SANDERS)
Missouri. He was named Composer of the Year in 1970 by Kansas Fed. Music Clubs, and received ASCAP awards in 1972, 1973. He was director of choral activities, Rockhurst Coll., 1971-73; and choral director and chairman of theory, Johnson County Community Coll., 1973-
  WORKS: Orchestra: Cortege; When lilacs last in the dooryard bloomed, soloists, chorus, orch.; Band: Fantasia on an old French song; Paean of praise, brass sextet; Chamber music: string quartet, No. 1; Cantilena, string quartet; Chorus: Musick's empire, chorus and percussion; Praise Christ, alleluia, chorus and organ; Sing, men and angels, chorus and organ.
    9200 England, Overland Park, KS 66212

BUTLER, LOIS
  b. Stockdale, Tex., 25 May 1912. Studied at Southwestern Univ., B. M. 1932; Juilliard School, 1936-38; Peabody Cons., M. M. 1941; Schillinger House, Boston, license, 1949; Catholic Univ., M. M. 1956. Her composition teachers were Cecil Burleigh, Gustav Strube, Howard R. Thatcher, Kenneth MacKillop, Conrad Bernier, George T. Jones, and Emerson Meyers. She played violin in the Baltimore Symph. Orch., 1939-43; has held various posts as church organist, 1946- ; composer-in-residence, Washington Public Schools, 1956- ; and First Baptist Church, Silver Spring, Md., 1972-
  WORKS: Orchestra: Symphony of the hills; Chamber music: Rondo in e, violin and piano; Sonnet XLIII, by Elizabeth Browning, voice and piano; Chorus: The Christmas story; A Christmas carol.
    8712 Colesville Road, #4
    Silver Spring, MD 20910

*BUTTOLPH, DAVID
  b. New York, N. Y., 3 Aug. 1902. Studied at Inst. of Musical Art and in Vienna. From 1933 he was a composer for films.

BUTTS, CARROL M.
  b. Shenandoah, Iowa, 15 Apr. 1924. Studied at Univ. of Colorado with Cecil Effinger and Hugh E. McMillen. He received a commission from the Wyoming Music Educators Assoc. for a work for the 1973 All-State Wyoming Band. He was band director, Bayard, Neb., 1950-56; and band director, music supervisor, Torrington, Wyo., 1956- .
He has published more than 50 works for band and instrumental ensembles.
    Box 298, Torrington, WY 82240

BUYNISKI, RAYMOND J.
  b. Bridgeport, Conn., 19 Sep. 1939. Studied at Sherwood Music School, Chicago, with Florence Grandland Galajikian; and Hartt Coll. of Music, B. M. with Arnold Franchetti.
  WORKS: Orchestra: Overture, Chicago, June 1964; Chamber music: string quartet; Valse-poeme, piano; and many piano works in the neo-romantic vein.
    3589 Main St., Stratford, CT 06497

*BUYS, PETER
  b. Amsterdam, Neth., 11 Aug. 1881; to U.S. 1902; d. Hagerstown, Md., 5 Mar. 1964. Wrote overtures, fantasies and many marches for band. He also wrote History of bands in the United States.

*BYARD, JOHN A., JR. (JAKI)
  b. Worcester, Mass., 15 June 1922. Pianist, saxophonist, arranger, and composer has appeared with many noted jazz groups; toured Europe for the Berlin Jazz Festival; has given concerts also in Japan and Australia. He has taught privately 1942- ; chairman Afro-American music, New England Cons., 1972- ; faculty, City Univ. of New York.
  WORKS: Jazz ensemble: Hazy eve, 1973; Family suite, Boston, 29 Jan. 1974.
    Department of Music, City College, CUNY
    New York, NY 10031

BYERS, ROXANA
  b. San Francisco, Calif., 30 Oct. Studied at American Cons. with Adolf Weidig; Ecole Normale de Musique, Paris, with George Dandelot. She is a national honorary member of Sigma Alpha Iota and received the SAI Rose of Honor and American composers award, 1973. She was the founder of the Hawaii Cons. of Music, Honolulu, in 1926; head, piano department, Pepperdine Coll., 1945-53.
  WORKS: Songs: A woodland day, cycle of five songs for soprano; California, gem of the nation's crown; When tears flow, Composers Forum, Mar. 1974; Keyboard: Reverie for organ; Fantasie on the themes of Christmas, piano.
    6171 Barrows Drive, Los Angeles, CA 90048

CACAVAS, JOHN
  b. Aberdeen, S. D., 13 Aug. 1930. Studied at Northwestern Univ. with Paul Hindemith, Robert Delaney, and Anthony Donato. He received a Grammy award for Gallant men. He was director of publications for Chappell and Co., 1965-70, then settled in Hollywood as a film score composer.
  WORKS: Orchestra: Montage; Overture concertante; Western scenario; The day the orchestra played, with narrator; Band: La bella Roma; March of the golden brass; Overture in miniature; Rhapsody; Symphonic prelude; Trumpeters three; and some 1500 published works for orchestra, band, chamber groups, etc.
    c/o Bart/Levy Associates
    8601 Wilshire Blvd., Beverly Hills, CA 90211

CACIOPPO, GEORGE
  b. Monroe, Mich., 24 Sep. 1926. Studied with Ross Lee Finney at Univ. of Michigan, M. A. 1952, and Roberto Gerhard, 1960; and at Tanglewood with with Leon Kirchner on a Rockefeller grant. He was lecturer in composition, Univ. of Michigan, 1968-73; and has been broadcast engineer, Univ. of Michigan broadcasting station, WUOM, since 1961.
  WORKS: Nocturne: In memoriam Bela Bartok, piano solo, 1951; Music for strings and two trumpets, 1952; string trio, 1960; Bestiary I: Eingang, soprano and percussion, 1961; Two

(CACIOPPO, GEORGE)
worlds, soprano, 8 instruments and percussion, 1962; pianopieces #1, #2, #3, Cassiopeia, 1963; Mod 3, flute, double bass, percussion, 1963; Moves upon silence, large percussion orchestra and two amplified cymbals, 1963; The advance of the fungi, 8 winds, percussion, male chorus, 1964; Time on time in miracles, 4 winds, cello, piano, soprano, percussion, 1965; Holy Ghost vacuum, or America faints, 2-manual electric organ, 1966; k for electric organ, electric piano, electronic gear, 1967; Cassiopeia in New York, solo piano and tape, 1968; Cassiopeia in Grand Rapids, solo piano and tape, 1969; pianopiece #4: Informed sources, for any number of amplified pianos, 4 hands, ring modulators, filters, loudspeakers, light mixer, 1970.
2180 Medford Road, Apt. 21
Ann Arbor, MI 48104

*CADMAN, CHARLES WAKEFIELD
b. Johnstown, Pa., 24 Dec. 1881; d. Los Angeles, 30 Dec. 1946. Studied composition with Emil Paur in Pittsburgh. He received an honorary doctorate in music from the Univ. of Southern California in 1924, and in 1926 was named director of the music department. He made a study of the music of the American Indian and drew many of his themes from this source.
WORKS: Opera: Shanewis, 1918; Garden of mystery, 1918; Sunset trail, operatic cantata, 1922; Witch of Salem, 1926; Orchestra: The thunderbird, 1917; 3 moods; Dark dancers of the Mardi Gras, with piano solo, 1933; American suite, 1937; Chamber music: piano trio; violin sonata; Chorus: Vision of Sir Launfal, cantata for male voices; many songs including From the land of the sky-blue water and At dawning.

*CADZOW, DOROTHY. See: HOKANSON, DOROTHY CADZOW

*CAGAN, STEVEN
Divertissement, suite for dance, chamber ensemble.

CAGE, JOHN
b. Los Angeles, Calif., 5 Sep. 1912. Attended Pomona Coll., 1928-30; studied composition with Adolph Weiss, Henry Cowell, and Arnold Schoenberg. He received a Guggenheim fellowship in 1949 for study in Paris and an award from the Nat. Acad. of Arts and Letters for having extended the boundaries of music through his work with percussion orchestras and his invention of the prepared piano. He won first prize in the Woodstock Art Film Festival, 1951; was elected to the Nat. Inst. of Arts and Letters, 1968; received grants from the Thorne Music Found, 1967-69; and has received many commissions. He taught composition at New School for Social Research, New York, 1955-60; was music director, Merce Cunningham and Dance Company, New York, 1944-66; fellow, Center for Advanced Studies, Wesleyan Univ., 1960-61; composer-in-residence, Univ. of Cincinnati, 1967; research professor and associate, Center for Advanced Studies, Univ. of Illinois, 1967-69. In 1951 he organized a group of musicians and engineers to make music on magnetic tape; and in 1952

(CAGE, JOHN)
produced a theatrical event at Black Mountain Coll. considered by many to have been the first Happening.
WORKS: Sonata for clarinet solo, 1933; 6 short inventions for 7 instruments, 1934; Construction in metal, 1937; Double music for percussion, with Lou Harrison, 1941; Wonderful widow of 18 springs, voice and closed piano accompaniment, 1942; Music for keyboard, prepared piano, piano, toy piano, 1935-48; Amores, prepared piano and percussion, 1943; Imaginary landscape No. 1; She is asleep, voice and prepared piano, 1943; Perilous night, suite for prepared piano, 1943-44; 3 dances for 2 amplified, prepared pianos, 1944-45; Sonatas and interludes for prepared pianos, 1946-48; String quartet in 4 parts, 1950; Concerto for prepared piano and chamber orch., 1951; Williams mix, composed by throwing Chinese dice, 1952; Music for carillon, 1954; 4 minutes and 33 seconds, silent music for piano in 4 movements, 1954; 26' 1.1499'', for a string player, 1955; concerto for piano and orch., 1957-58; Indeterminacy, narrator and piano; Aria, soprano and tape, 1958; Fontana mix, soprano and tape or tape alone, 1958; Variations I, for any kind and number of instruments, 1958; Cartridge music, 1960; Variations II, 1961; Variations III, 1963; Variations IV, electronic, 1965; Solo for voice II, 1966, 1960; Atlas eclipticalis, orchestra, 1961; Winter music; Variations V, 1965; Variations VII, 1966; HPSCHD, with Lejaren Hiller, for 7 harpsichords and 52 computer generated tapes, Univ. of Illinois, 16 May 1969; Song books, solos for voice 3-92, premiered in Paris, Oct. 1970. In 1962 Edition Peters published an annotated catalogue of his works. He is author of Silence, 1961; A year from Monday, 1968; M, 1973; co-author with Hoover: The life and works of Virgil Thomson, 1958; with Knowles: Notations, 1969; with Long and Smith, Mushroom Book, 1972.
107 Bank St., New York, NY 10014

*CAILLET, LUCIEN
b. Dijon, France, 22 May 1891; U.S. citizen 1923. Studied at Dijon Cons. and at Philadelphia Musical Acad., D. M. He has been arranger and conductor; composed film scores and many works for orchestra.
8231 43rd Ave., Kenosha, WI 53140

CAIN, JAMES
b. Lake City, Fla., 21 Sep. 1942. Studied with William Hoskins at Jacksonville Univ., and with Carlisle Floyd and John Boda at Florida State Univ. He is head of Music Department, Edison Community Coll., Ft. Myers, Fla.
WORKS: Orchestra: Homage to Delius, 1966; symphony for string orch.; Chamber music: 7 preludes for piano; flute sonata, Tallahassee, 7 Feb. 1967; Chorus: The Lord is my strength, 1969; Motet from markings, 1972.
1547 Bembury Drive, Naples, FL 33940

CALABRO, LOUIS
b. Brooklyn, N.Y., 1 Nov. 1926. Studied at Juilliard School with Vincent Persichetti. His awards include Coolidge Chamber Music awards, 1952, 1953; first recipient, Richard Rodgers

CALABRO, LOUIS

(CALABRO, LOUIS)
fellowship, 1953; Guggenheim fellowships, 1954,
1959; Vermont Council of the Arts grant, 1970;
National Endowment of the Arts composer fellowship, $10,000, 1973; various Ford, Dollard, and
Huber grants and many commissions. He has been
teacher of composition, Bennington Coll.,
1955- .
WORKS: Orchestra: Symphony #3, 1964; 10
short pieces; Triple concerto, 3 cellos and orch.,
1971; Chamber music: 5 duos, clarinet and cello;
Divertimento, woodwind quintet, Environments, 12
brass and solo clarinet, 1961; string quartet,
#2, 1968; Memoirs, bassoon and percussion, 1973;
Chorus: Metaphors, 50-part chorus, a cappella,
1959; Latitude 15.09 N, longitude 108.5 E, oratorio; Songs: Macabre reflections, song cycle,
1956; Cantilena, soprano and strings, 1964;
Piano: Suite of seven; sonatina; Diversities,
1966; Variations, 1968.
Bennington Coll., Bennington, VT 05201

CALDWELL, MARY ELIZABETH (Mrs. Philip G.)
b. Tacoma, Wash., 1 Aug. 1909. Attended Univ. of
California, Berkeley, A. B.; studied composition
privately with Richard Schrey in Munich and
Bernard Wagenaar in New York; piano and organ with
Benjamin Moore in San Francisco. She is an hon-
orary member of Mu Phi Epsilon; was Performing
Artist of the Year, 1972, Pasadena Arts Council;
Outstanding Musician of the Year in Pasadena,
Sigma Alpha Iota. She has been organist-choir
director since 1933, and at San Marino Community
Church, Calif., 1948- .
WORKS: Opera: A gift of song; The night of
the star; Pepito's golden flower; Chorus: The
little lamb, text by Blake; Spring prayer, text
by Charles Hanson Towne; Go forth, an anthem; O,
Daniel, anthem; and 150 published vocal compositions for all combinations of voices.
474 South Arroyo Blvd., Pasadena, CA 91105

CALLAHAN, JAMES P.
b. Fargo, N.D., 15 Jan. 1942. Studied at St.
John's Univ., Collegeville, Minn., and Vienna
Acad. of Music, Austria. He studied composition
with Paul Fetler and Hans Jelinek. He has been
assistant professor, Coll. of St. Thomas,
1968- .
WORKS: Orchestra: Metamorphosis, an overture based on themes of Mozart, 1973; symphony
No. 2 (Markings), orch., chorus, baritone solo;
Band: Overture; Chamber music: Etude and recitative, piano, 1973; string quartet, 1974;
Chorus: Parish worship, choir, organ congregation; Lord, You are kind and full of love,
women's voices, 1972; Organ: 6 pieces based on
Gregorian themes.
3129 23rd Ave. South, Minneapolis, MN 55407

*CALLAWAY, PAUL SMITH
b. Atlanta, Ill., 16 Aug. 1909. Studied at Westminster Coll., Fulton, Mo. 1927-29, honorary doctorate 1959; also honorary doctorate, Washington
Coll., 1967. He has been organist at Washington
Cathedral (D.C.), 1939- ; was on faculty,
Peabody Cons., 1953-57.

(CALLAWAY, PAUL SMITH)
WORKS: Chorus: Hymn of heavenly love,
1935; Office of the Holy Communion, 1945; Hark!
The glad sound, 1946.
2230 Decatur Place, Washington, DC 20008

*CALVIN, SUSAN
The half-moon westers low, Housman text, for
chorus; Words of comfort, Dorothy Parker text,
chorus.

CAMPBELL, ARTHUR
b. Lexington, Mo., 4 Apr. 1922. Studied in
London with Alec Rowley; in Kansas City with
David Van Vactor; at Yale Univ. with Quincy
Porter; and at Eastman School of Music with
Bernard Rogers, Howard Hanson, Alan Hovhaness,
and Herbert Elwell. He received a Harvey Gaul
award in 1958. He taught at Monmouth Coll.,
Ill., 1949-52; and has been on the faculty, St.
Olaf Coll., 1952- .
WORKS: Orchestra: Symphony; Chorus:
Whither shall I go?, an anthem, 1966; Prayers
from the Ark, cantata for women's voices; Key-
board: 3 piano pieces; Pillars, organ and tape.
Route 1, Northfield, MN 55057

CAMPBELL, CHARLES JOSEPH
b. Cleveland, Ohio, 8 Aug. 1930. Attended
Cleveland Inst. of Music, Western Reserve Univ.,
and Univ. of Miami. His principal teachers were
Herbert Elwell and Marcel Dick. His faculty and
administrative positions included Cleveland Inst.
of Music, 1955-57; Cleveland Music School Settlement, 1958-61; Wilmington Music School, 1961-66;
Auburn Univ., 1966-68; Virginia Commonwealth
Univ., 1970-72; Univ. of Miami, 1972-   .
WORKS: Orchestra: 2 symphonies; 2 overtures; Chamber music: numerous pieces for woodwind and brass ensembles; song cycles, piano
works; solo etudes for trombone and tuba.
9781 Colonial Drive, Miami, FL 33157

CAMPBELL, HENRY
b. Osceola, Neb., 13 Nov. 1926. Studied with
Burrill Phillips and Bernard Rogers at Eastman
School of Music, B. M. 1948, M. M. 1949; with
George McKay at Univ. of Washington; and privately with Julius Gold in Los Angeles. He has
received awards from the Montana String Teachers
Assoc.; J. Fischer Bros. Centennial composition
contest; Music Teachers Nat. Assoc.; and Montana
State Music Teachers Assoc. He has been on the
faculty, now professor, Montana State Univ.
1949- .
WORKS: Orchestra: Sinfonia non troppo
serioso; Waltz - then march; Chamber music:
Diversion, clarinet, viola, piano; Many happy
returns, string quartet; piano sonata, 4 hands;
Folk song, piano and string orch.; Grass roots
ballad, tenor or baritone and piano; Chorus:
Folk song suite; Balletto; Make we joy; short
piano pieces and orchestral works.
515 South Grand Ave., Bozeman, MT 59715

*CAMPBELL-TIPTON, LOUIS
b. Chicago Ill., 21 Nov. 1877; d. Paris, 1 May
1921. Studied in Chicago, Boston, and Leipzig;
lived in Paris from 1910.

(CAMPBELL-TIPTON, LOUIS)
WORKS: Chamber music: Suite pastorale, violin and piano; Piano: Heroic sonata; Sea lyrics; The 4 seasons; a suite; and songs.

CAMPBELL-WATSON, FRANK
b. New York, N.Y., 22 Jan. 1898. Studied at Univ. of Leipzig, B. A.; Leipzig Cons., M. A., D. M.; with Max Reger, Karl Straube, Hans Sitt, Theodore Spiering, Walter Rothwell, Nicolas Elsenheimer. He was made Knight Commander, Order of St. Gregory the Great, by Pope John XXIII, 1961. He has been organist and choirmaster in New Jersey and New York, 1920-52; and organist and composer-in-residence, Church of St. Paul the Apostle (Paulist Choristers), N.Y., 1953-71. He has also been editor-in-chief Univ. Society, 1923-32; Music Publishers Holding Corp., 1932-65; Benziger Editions, 1965-68; Carl Fischer, 1968-71.
WORKS: Orchestra: 2 symphonies; Band: symphony; Cotton moon, overture; concerto for organ and symphony band; Chamber music: Divertimento, 8 woodwinds; violin sonata; Petite suite, 4 violins; Chorus: 3 Latin Masses; 3 English Masses; 15 liturgical motets; 2 extended choral and instrumental processions; 18 Mass Propers; 5 liturgical choral settings; secular works; Organ: Meditation on Salve Regina; Praeludium on Puer natus est; Praeludium on Rorate caeli; Chant du nuit; Phantomesque. He is author of a text: Modern elementary harmony.
262 Quaker Road, Pomona, NY 10970

CAMPO, FRANK
b. New York, N.Y., 4 Feb. 1927. Studied with Ingolf Dahl and Leon Kirchner in Los Angeles; with Arthur Honneger in Paris; and Goffredo Petrassi in Rome. He received a Fulbright scholarship, 1957; BMI Composers award, 1958; Screen Composers award 1966. He was lecturer in composition, Univ. of Southern California, 1965-67, and at California State Univ., Fullerton, 1966-67; chairman of composition-theory, California State Univ., Northridge, 1967- .
WORKS: Opera: The mirror, to own libretto; Orchestra: Alpine holiday overture; Symphony; Seven dialogues; Concerto grosso; Untitled: Blue; Due quadri Romani; Symphony for chamber orch.; Partita for 2 chamber orch.; Concerto for bassoon and strings; Band: Music for Agamemmon; Chamber music: Kinesis, clarinet and piano; Fanfare 1969, 8 trumpets; Concertino for 3 clarinets and piano; Madrigals, brass quintet; Times, solo trumpet; Commedie, trombone and percussion; 5 pieces for 5 winds; violin sonata; Dualidad, bass clarinet and percussion; Vocal: Seven lyrics of Catullus, bass and 8 instruments; Sic transit, cantata; The words of Agur, cantata #2; Inscriptions at the City of Brass, cantata #3.
12336 Milbank St., Studio City, CA 91604

*CANBY, EDWARD TATNALL
b. 1912. The interminable farewell, a canonic joke for chorus, 1954.

*CANDLYN, T. F. H.
b. England, 17 Dec. 1892; d. Point Lookout, N.Y., 16 Dec. 1964. Served in U.S. Army in World War I; was head of music department, State Univ. of New York at Albany, 1919-43; organist, St. Paul's Church, Albany. He published many works for chorus and for organ.

*CANNING, THOMAS
b. 1911. 3 old nursery rhymes for chorus; Fantasy on a hymn by Justin Morgan, for string quartet solo, string quartet II, and string orch.
School of Music, West Virginia University Morgantown, WV 26506

CANNON, DWIGHT
b. Pomona, Calif., 6 July 1932. Studied with Alexander Tcherepnin and Leon Stein in Chicago; and with Robert Erickson, Pauline Oliveros, Kenneth Gaburo, and Roger Reynolds in San Diego. He has played trumpet with CBS-TV in Chicago and with recording and broadcast orchestras in New York and Los Angeles; is conductor of orchestras, jazz ensembles, choirs and bands; and assistant professor, San Jose State Univ.
WORKS: Chronometers, percussion ensemble; Music for 1-13 trumpets, 4-channel tape, and 31 helium-filled balloons; Ex pluribus unum, for jazz ensemble, vocals, and dancers; C-in, jazz ensemble. These works, Mr. Cannon says, are sonic and visual designs.
Music Department, San Jose State University San Jose, CA 95192

CANTRELL, BYRON
b. Brooklyn, N.Y., 14 Nov. 1919. Studied with Clifford Megerlin, Marion Bauer, Philip James, at New York Univ., and with Lukas Foss and John Vincent at Univ. of California, Los Angeles. He studied conducting with Philip James, Leon Barzin, Emerson Buckley, and Serge Koussevitzky. He won second prize in the Los Angeles Philharmonic composition contest, 1944. His faculty positions have included Tahoe Paradise Coll., 1967-69; California State Univ., Fullerton, 1969-70; El Camino Coll., 1971-72; International Community Coll., 1972- . He has been director, Young Peoples Opera Company, Culver City, 1966- ; and music critic, editor, and annotator in the Los Angeles area.
WORKS: Theatre: music for Raisins and almonds; Orchestra: Three symphonic sketches of Mark Twain; A jubilee overture; A victory overture; piano concerto; Chorus: The land of heart's desire; Satires of circumstance; A tooth for Paul Revere; What child is this; Variations on a spiritual; Variations on General Wolfe's song; Now welcum sumer; At Casterbridge Fair; songs and piano pieces.
822 North Occidental Blvd.
Los Angeles, CA 90026

*CANTRICK, ROBERT B.
b. 1917. 3 mimes, chamber ensemble.
State University College at Buffalo, NY 14222

CAPERTON, FLORENCE TAIT

CAPERTON, FLORENCE TAIT (Mrs. G. A. Dornin)
b. Amherst Co., Va., 21 Apr. 1886. Studied
violin at Peabody Cons., and composition with D.
Alspach in Iowa City and W. Critser in Pittsburgh. She was concertmistress and soloist with
the Norfolk Symphony Orch., 1902-04. Her compositions are chiefly for chorus. Published anthems include Come, little children and Rejoice,
ye children.
137 Lafayette St., Orange, VA 22960

*CARBONARA, GERARD
b. New York, N. Y., 8 Dec. 1886; d. Sherman Oaks,
Calif., 11 Jan. 1959. Studied at the National
Cons., New York, and at Naples Cons., Italy;
also violin with Martucci Dworzak. He was opera
coach, Milan, 1910; concert violinist and opera
conductor, Europe and U.S.; then music director
and composer for film studios.
WORKS: Opera: Armand; Orchestra: Ode to
nature, symphonic poem; Concerto orientale, violin
and orch.; Chamber music: Scherzetto fantasia,
wind quintet; many violin pieces, piano pieces,
songs; Film scores: Stage coach, Academy award
1940; The Kansan; The promised land; and others.

CAREW, MICHAEL B.
b. Bronxville, N. Y., 4 Oct. 1951. Attended
Ripon Coll., B. A. 1973, studying modular electronic music and light with Erwin M. Breithaupt.
Otherwise, he is largely self-taught, using Le
Corburier's system of proportions in ordering
his electronic music and developing what he calls
continuums, which are overlapping, omnidirec-
tional harmonious patterns, to replace scales.
He uses a modular system to create time ordinations of sound, and thus breaks out of traditional metrical time altogether into a system
more integral to tape speeds. He is mainly
interested now in electronic music, but has
written classical, folk, blues, rock, acid rock,
and jazz.
WORKS: Modular work No. 1: The turning of
the age, electronic music and light; First full
cycle, electronic acid jazz; New rising sun,
electronic acid jazz.
92 Oregon Ave., Bronxville, NY 10708

*CAREY, DAVID
b. Pittsburgh, Pa., 14 Feb. 1926. Studied at
Pittsburgh Musical Inst.; Univ. of Pittsburgh;
Manhattan School of Music. He is a television
composer, conductor, pianist and arranger.
WORKS: Chamber music: Inventions for piano;
flute sonata; sonata for piano 4 hands; and popular songs.

CARFAGNO, SIMON ALBERT
b. Scottdale, Pa., 8 Jan. 1906. Studied privately with Arnold Schoenberg and Nadia Boulanger. He received a Pro Musica prize. He
was violinist with the Los Angeles Philharmonic
Orch., 1943-44; and with Eagle-Lion, Republic
Studios, 20th Century Fox, 1945-57; conductor,
Chico Symph. Orch., 1962-67; faculty, Chico State
Univ., 1962-73, professor, 1971-73.
WORKS: Orchestra: Gettysburg, 1863, cantata
for orch., chorus, soloists; Chamber music:

(CARFAGNO, SIMON ALBERT)
string trio; Salmagundi suite, violin and piano;
Toccata, piano; Nonet (dedicated to Schoenberg),
flute, oboe, clarinet, bassoon, viola, and 4
pitched drums; flute sonata.
5037 Russell Drive, Paradise, CA 95969

CARLOS, WALTER
b. Pawtucket, R.I., 14 Nov. 1939. Studied with
Ron Nelson at Brown Univ., B. M. 1962; and with
Otto Luening, Vladimir Ussachevsky, and Jack
Beeson at Columbia Univ., M. A. 1965. He was a
Seidl fellow, 1963-64, and won 3 Grammy awards
and a Gold Record for Switched on Bach, 1969.
He has been president of Trans-Electronic Prod.,
Inc., 1967-
WORKS: Opera: Noah, with organ and electric organ accompaniment, 1964-65; background
music for Kubrick's A clockwork orange, 1971;
Orchestra: piano concerto, 1961; Chamber music:
string quartet, 1963; string sextet, 1965;
Electronic: 3 pieces for instruments and tape,
piano, 1962, flute, 1963, piano, 1964; Dialogues for piano and 2 loudspeakers, 1963; Well-
tempered synthesizer; Variations for flute and
electronic sound, 1964; Timesteps, synthesizer,
1970-71; Sonic seasonings, 1971-72; and other
works for orchestra, solo instruments, and electronic tapes.
133 West 87th St., New York, NY 10024

*CARMICHAEL, HOAGY
b. Bloomington, Ind., 11 Nov. 1897. Studied law
at Indiana Univ. earning an L. L. B., but soon
abandoned law for song writing. His enormously
successful songs include Stardust, Georgia on my
mind, In the still of the night; Ole buttermilk
sky, and many others.

*CARMINES, ALVIN A. (AL)
b. Hampton, Va., 1938. Studied at Swarthmore
Coll.; Union Theological Seminary; has won 4
Obie awards (the off-Broadway Oscar); is minister, Judson Memorial Church, New York. Son of
a harmonica-playing sea captain, he has composed
more than 60 extremely successful shows since
1961; presented a Town Hall recital of his works
in April 1972. Some of his later works are:
Joan, performed as an opera, New York, Nov.-Dec.
1971, revised as a musical, opened at Circus on
the Square, 19 June 1972; A look at the fifties,
a running commentary on a basketball game, 1973;
The faggots, oratorio, New York, Apr.-May 1973;
The duel, an opera, commissioned by the Metropolitan Opera Guild, premiere, Brooklyn Acad.,
24 Apr. 1974; music for Gertrude Stein's plays:
What happened, In circles, and Listen to me, New
York, Oct. 1974; and Christmas rappings, an
annual Christmas show.

CARMONA, PAUL BERNARD
b. Los Angeles, Calif., 11 Sep. 1947. Attended
Loyola Univ., Los Angeles, B. A. 1969; Univ. of
Southern California, candidate for M. M. in
church music, studying composition with Leroy
Southers, Jr. He was organist and choirmaster
in Los Angeles, 1966-71, and at St. James Cathedral, Seattle, 1971-   .

(CARMONA, PAUL BERNARD)
WORKS: Vocal: 3 art songs for soprano and piano: Cry of a lone bird (Ashford), Gone (Sandburg), Prayers of steel (Sandburg); Mass in honor of St. James the Apostle, choir, congregation, and orchestra, Seattle, 25 Dec. 1973; Organ: Fanfare, interlude, and toccata on Lucis Creator Optime, 1970.
623 19th Ave. East, Seattle, WA 98112

*CARNEY, DAVID
Chorus: The Angel Gabriel; A child is born; Psalm 112: Louez, serviteurs.
School of Music, Boston University
Boston, MA 02215

*CARNO, ZITA
Sextet for percussion.
New York University, Education Theatre
35 West 4th St., New York, NY 10012

CARPENTER, HOWARD R.
b. Natural Bridge, N.Y., 11 Oct. 1919. Studied with Charles O'Neill at State Univ. Coll., Potsdam, N.Y., B. S. 1942; at Univ. of Alabama, B. M. 1947; with Howard Hanson, Bernard Rogers, Herbert Elwell, Wayne Barlow at Eastman School of Music, M. M. 1948, Ph. D. 1953. His Symphony in D was selected as an outstanding work at the Southeastern Composers' League symposium in 1954. He has been professor, Western Kentucky Univ., 1953-   , and head, Department of Music, 1965-   .
WORKS: Orchestra: Symphony in D; Poem; Vocal: Luke Havergal, soprano and piano; Piano: sonata; allegro.
1730 Chestnut St., Bowling Green, KY 42101

*CARPENTER, JOHN ALDEN
b. Park Ridge, Ill., 28 Feb. 1876; d. Chicago, 26 Apr. 1951. Studied with John Knowles Paine at Harvard Univ., B. A. 1897, honorary M. A. 1922; with Bernard Ziehn in Chicago and Edward Elgar in Rome. His awards include honorary doctorates from Univ. of Wisconsin and Northwestern Univ.; Nat. Inst. of Arts and Letters award, 1947. He was a business executive in Chicago, 1909-36, then devoted full time to composition.
WORKS: Ballets: Birthday of the Infanta, 1919; Krazy Kat, 1921; Skyscrapers, 1925; Orchestra: Adventures in a perambulator, 1915; concertino for piano and orch., 1916; 3 symphonies, 1917, 1940, 1942; A pilgrim vision, 1920; Patterns, piano and orch., 1932; Song of faith, chorus and orch., 1932; Sea drift, symphonic poem, 1933; Danza, 1935; violin concerto, 1936; Song of freedom, chorus and orch., 1941; The anxious bugler, 1943; The seven ages, 1945; Carmel concerto, 1948; Chamber music: violin sonata, 1912; string quartet, 1928; piano quintet, 1934; Songs: Improving songs for anxious children, 1904; Gitanjali, song cycle on poems of Tagore, 1913; Water colors, 4 Chinese songs with chamber orch., 1918; 4 negro songs.

CARPENTER, KURT
b. Ann Arbor, Mich., 15 Nov. 1948. Studied at Univ. of Michigan, B. M. 1970, M. M. 1971, with Ross Lee Finney, Leslie Bassett, and George Balch

(CARPENTER, KURT)
Wilson; and with George Crumb, Leon Barzin and Leonard Bernstein at Tanglewood. He received BMI Young Composer awards 1968, 1971; Koussevitzky Prize in composition, 1970; American Music Center Composer Alliance grant 1971. He is vice president and treasurer of The Competition Inc., and a freelance composer.
WORKS: Opera: The new harmony opera, with Russell Peck; Orchestra: Abraxas, 1970, Indianapolis, 1971; Venus Probe, 1971, Minneapolis, 1972; Who killed Cock Robin?, narrator and orchestra, with Peck and Bleich, commissioned by New Orleans Philharmonic and played 12 times by the orchestra in 1973; many piano and chamber music works and 73 songs.
4029 Clarendon Road, Indianapolis, IN 46208

CARR, ALBERT LEE
b. Wagoner, Okla., 16 June 1929. Studied at Univ. of Nebraska with Robert Beadell. He won a Pi Kappa Lambda award for a choral composition, 1959. He has been a public school music teacher, 1956-   .
WORKS: Chorus: Innocence; Three years she grew in sun and shower; Christo paremus canticum; She dwelt among untrodden ways; Why are the roses so pale; All under the willow tree.
22 Dorfmeister Court, Madison, WI 53704

*CARR, ARTHUR
b. Pontiac, Mich., 29 Feb. 1908. Oriental miniatures, 5 songs for high voice; also a comic opera, works for orchestra, chamber music.
642 North La Brea, Los Angeles, CA 90036

*CARR, MICHAEL
Springtime suite and Wintertime suite for organ.

CARRAGAN, MARTHA BECK. See BECK, MARTHA

CARREAU, MARGARET STIVER (Mrs. Robert)
b. Bedford, Pa., 23 Jan. 1899. Studied piano in New York, 1916-21. She was rehearsal and audition pianist for Irving Berlin's Music Box Revues, 1922-24; accompanist for John Charles Thomas, 1943-52. Thomas introduced her Pastures of the soul on the Bell Telephone Hour.
WORKS: Songs: Thy heart and the sea; You and I together; Sea nocturne; Comparison; Pastures of the soul; Eventide; April fool; Query; Rapture.
Oxford, MD 21654

*CARRIER, LORAN
Game opera, 1-act, Smithsonian Inst., Washington, D.C., 12 Dec. 1969.

CARROLL, FRANK M.
b. Norfolk, Va., 19 Mar. 1928. Studied at Eastman School of Music with Herbert Elwell. He won first prize in a Wisconsin composers' contest for his piano concerto. He was department chairman, Maryland State Coll., 1961-63; director, School of Music, Centenary Coll., 1969-   ; conductor, Marshall Symph. Tex., 1971-73, and Longview Symph., 1973-74.
WORKS: Theatre: Old woman and the pig, chamber opera; incidental music to Comedy of

CARROLL, FRANK M.

(CARROLL, FRANK M.)
Errors; Orchestra: piano concerto; Chamber
music: suite for violin and piano; sonatina for
cello and piano; Chorus: Mass; Piano: March
paraphrase for 8 pianos.
6106 Gaylyn Drive, Shreveport, LA 71104

CARROLL, J. ROBERT
b. Haverhill, Mass., 31 Jan. 1927. Studied at
the New England Cons. with Donald Smith, Francis
Judd Cooke, Carl McKinley, and in Paris with
Auguste Le Guennant and Paul-Marie Masson. He
was director, Department of Education, Gregorian
Inst. of America, 1953-61; professor of music,
Mary Manse Coll., 1960-64; associate professor
of French, Univ. of Toledo, 1964-   .
WORKS: Orchestra: Essay, 1947; Christmas
processional, 1968; symphony for strings and percussion, 1971; Chorus: Three anthems on Byzantine themes, 1950; Missa pastoralis, 1950;
Music for the wedding service, 1965; Four offer-
tories, 1965; Introit for Christ the King, 1967;
Songs of the heart, 1968; Music for the Ordinary
of the Mass, 1970; Music for ordinations, 1969;
Organ: Variations on a Stralsund tune; Three
plainchant studies; many masses, antiphons,
hymns, etc. He is also editor and translator of
An applied course in Gregorian chant, 1956; and
author of The technique of Gregorian chironomy,
1955; A compendium of liturgical music terms,
1961; and The Gelineau psalter, 1972.
4203 Berwick Place, Toledo, OH 43612

CARTER, CHARLES
b. Ponca City, Okla., 10 July 1926. Studied at
Ohio State Univ. with Norman Phelps, Kent Kennan;
at Eastman School of Music with Bernard Rogers,
Wayne Barlow; and at Florida State Univ. with Lee
Rigsby and Ernst von Dohnanyi. He was instructor,
Ohio State Univ., 1952-53; graduate assistant,
Florida State Univ., 1953-63, and instructor,
1963-   .
WORKS: Band: Sinfonia; Overture in clas-
sical style; Metropolis; Seminole song; Overture
for winds; Queen City suite; Motet for band;
Cakewalk; and many more.
3830 Leane Drive, Tallahassee, FL 32303

CARTER, ELLIOTT C.
b. New York, N.Y., 11 Dec. 1908. Studied at
Harvard Univ., B. A. 1930, M. A. 1932, with
Walter Piston and Gustav Holst; in Paris with
Nadia Boulanger, 1932-35, earning a doctorate at
Ecole Normale de Musique, 1935. His many honors
include a Naumberg award, 1952; 2 Guggenheim
grants, 1945, 1950; Prix de Rome, 1953; New York
Music Critics' award, 1960; 2 Pulitzer Prizes,
1960, 1973; Sibelius Medal for Music, 1961;
Brandeis Univ. Creative Arts award, 1965; Premio
delle Muse, Florence, Italy, 1968; honorary doc-
torates from New England Cons., Swarthmore Coll.,
Oberlin Coll., Princeton Univ., Harvard Univ.,
Yale Univ. He was elected a member of the Nat.
Inst. of Arts and Letters, 1956, and received the
Gold Medal for Music, 1971; and American Music
Center Letter of Distinction Award, 1973. He has
taught at Peabody Cons., 1946-48; Columbia Univ.
1948-50; Salzburg Seminars in Austria, 1958; Yale
Univ., 1960-62; several seasons at Tanglewood and

(CARTER, ELLIOTT C.)
Aspen Music School. He was composer-in-residence
at the American Academy in Rome, 1962, and at
Aspen Music School, 1973. He is on the faculty
at Juilliard School.
WORKS: Orchestra: Prelude, fanfare, and
polka, 1938; Pocahontas, suite from the ballet,
1939; Symphony No. 1, 1942; Holiday overture,
1944-61; Elegy for strings, 1946; The minotaur,
suite from the ballet, 1947; Variations for
orchestra, Louisville, 22 Apr. 1956; Double concerto, for harpsichord, piano, 2 chamber orch.,
New York, 6 Sep. 1961; piano concerto, Boston, 6
Jan. 1967; Concerto for orchestra, commissioned
by New York Philharmonic, premiered 5 Feb. 1970;
Chamber music: Pastoral, viola and piano, 1940;
Elegy, viola or cello and piano, 1943; piano
sonata, 1946; cello sonata, 1948; woodwind quintet, 1948; Eight etudes and a fantasy, woodwind
quartet, 1950; 3 string quartets, 1951, 1959,
1973 (No. 3 premiered by Juilliard Quartet, New
York, 23 Jan. 1973); Recitative and improvisation, 4 kettledrums, 1 player, 1952; sonata for
flute, oboe, cello, harpsichord, 1952; Canonic
suite, 4 clarinets, 1957; brass quintet, U.S.
premiere, Washington, D.C., 15 Nov. 1974; duo
for violin and piano, New York, 21 Mar. 1975;
Chorus: To music, a cappella, 1937; Heart not so
heavy as mine, text by Emily Dickinson, a cappella, 1938; The defense of Corinth, text by
Rabelais, for speaker, men's chorus, piano 4-
hands, 1941; The harmony of morning, text by
Mark van Doren, women's chorus and small orch.,
1944; Musicians wrestle everywhere, a cappella,
or with strings, 1945; Emblems, text by Allen
Tate, men's chorus, piano, 1947; Solo voice: 3
songs on texts by Frost, Dust of snow, The line
gang, The rose family, all 1943; Voyage, text by
Hart Crane, 1943; Warble for lilac time, text by
Whitman, 1943; incidental music to The merchant
of Venice, guitar and alto voice, 1938.
Waccabuc, NY 10597

*CARTER, JOHN
Has composed for chorus: I sing of a maiden;
The cloths of heaven; 3 canzonets on love,
women's voices; and Cantata, for high voice.
Music Department, Rollins College
Winter Park, FL 32789

*CARUSO, JOHN
Short prelude with perspectives, band.

CASCARINO, ROMEO
b. Philadelphia, Pa., 28 Sep. 1922. Was self-
taught until entering Philadelphia Cons. on a
scholarship at age 16 for study with Paul Nordoff. He won honorable mention for a tone poem,
Spring pastoral, in the Gershwin Memorial Contest, 1945; received 2 Guggenheim fellowships,
1948, 1949; honorary D. M., Combs Coll. of Music,
1960; Phi Mu Alpha, Orpheus award, 1975. He was
chief arranger and orchestrator, Army Special
Services Symphony Orch., 1945-46, and Somerset
Records, 1957-62; and head, composition department, Combs Coll. of Music, 1955-   .
WORKS: Opera: Cross and crown, 3 acts,
based on William Penn's Holy experiment;
Ballet: Pygmalion; Prospice; Orchestra: Blades

(CASCARINO, ROMEO)
of grass, tone poem for English horn and strings; The Acadian land, tone poem; Portrait of Galatea, tone poem; Band: Fanfare and march; Chamber music: sonata for bassoon and piano.
250 Ridge Pike, Lafayette Hill, PA 19444

*CASE, JAMES
b. 1932. Composed for women's chorus: Autumn; Petals; Summer; for organ: Sonnet; Ye men of Galilee.

CASSELS-BROWN, ALASTAIR K.
b. London, Eng., 3 May 1927; U.S. citizen 1961. Was an organ scholar at St. John's, Leatherhead, under L. H. B. Read; organ scholar, Worcester Coll., Oxford, M. A. 1952, studying with Wellesz, Westrup, Rubbra, and Armstrong; and studied at Toronto Univ. under Hugo Norden. He was named fellow, Royal Coll. of Organists, 1950; and won 3rd prize from American Guild of Organists and Horn Club of Los Angeles, 1962, for Jeu de cloches. He was music director, St. George's School, Newport, R.I., 1952-55; associate organist, Cathedral of St. John the Divine, New York, 1955-57; choirmaster, Grace Church, Utica, N.Y., 1957-65; assistant professor, Hamilton Coll., 1965-67; and professor of music, Episcopal Theological School, Cambridge, Mass., 1967-
    WORKS: Orchestra: Forest idyll, Providence, 1955; My song is love unknown, cantata for chorus and orch., Utica, N.Y., 1961; cello concerto, Utica, 1964; From the divide, cantata, soloists, orch., 1972; Chamber music: violin sonata #2, Boston, 1953; Little concerto, piano, flute, oboe, strings, 1961; Jeu de cloches, 1962; Chorus: Praise the Lord, O my soul, 1955; Te Deum, 1956; The Christ Child lay in Mary's lap, 1956; South Kent, hymn, 1955; Songs: Serenade to indestructible beauty, cycle for baritone to 5 poems of Sandburg, Clinton, N. Y., 1967.
99 Brattle St., Cambridge, MA 02138

CASSLER, G. WINSTON
b. Moundridge, Kan., 3 Sep. 1906. Attended McPherson Coll., A. B. 1927; Oberlin Cons. M. B. 1931, M. M. 1948; also studied church music, organ, composition, orchestration, in London, Germany, and at Eastman School of Music. He was named associate, American Guild of Organists, 1930, and member, Pi Kappa Lambda, 1948. He taught privately, 1927-42; served in the Army, 1942-47, rising from private to major; joined faculty, St. Olaf Col., 1949, professor, 1964-72; and has been organist, St. John's Lutheran Church, Northfield, Minn., 1950-   .
    WORKS: Orchestra: De institutione musica, symphony, 1949; Band: Chorale and fugue, 1972; Joy to the world, 1973; Immanuel is born, 1973; Chorus: Peace in our time, with piano or orch., 1954; The heritage of freedom, piano or orch., 1955; Now let the vault of heaven resound, orch., 1959; Built on a rock, choral cantata with brass quintet, 1962; The gospel trumpet, chorus and solo trumpet, 1971; and many published choral and organ works.
708 St. Olaf Ave., Northfield, MN 55057

CASTALDO, JOSEPH
b. New York, N.Y., 23 Dec. 1927. Studied at St. Cecilia Acad. in Rome while serving in the U.S. Army. On returning to the U.S. studied privately with Dante Fiorello; at Manhattan School of Music with Hugh Ross and Vittorio Giannini; Philadelphia Cons., B. M., M. M., with Vincent Persichetti. He has received commissions from Temple Univ., Pennsylvania Music Teachers Assoc., and the Philadelphia Orch. He was head, composition-theory department, Philadelphia Musical Acad., 1960-66, and president, 1966-
    WORKS: Orchestra: Epigrams, piano and orch.; Epiphonia; Cycles, Acad. of Music, 7 May 1970; Theoria, 15 winds, piano, percussion, Philadelphia, 22 Jan. 1973; Chamber music: string quartet; Contrasts, solo harp; Concertante, harp and string quartet; Dichotomy, woodwind quintet, 1963; Askesis, chamber ensemble, Athens, 1971; Photograph of a funeral, baritone, piano, percussion; Chorus: Flight, cantata for chorus, winds, percussion, narrator, soprano, Temple Univ., 11 May 1960; At her feet, a cappella choir; Piano: sonatina; sonata, 1961; 3 pieces; Mixed media: Protogenesis, 15 instruments, lights, film, slides, and the Zeiss planetarium instrument, written for presentation at Fels Planetarium, Philadelphia, in the May Festival, 1973.
1628 Pine St., Philadelphia, PA 19103

*CASTELNUOVO-TEDESCO, MARIO
b. Florence, Italy, 3 Apr. 1895; U.S. citizen 1946; d. Los Angeles, Calif., 16 Mar. 1968. On coming to the U.S. in 1939 settled in Hollywood. There he composed for films and also produced a prodigious amount of music for stage and concert, e.g.: 4 operas; 3 oratorios; 2 piano concertos; 3 violin concertos; cello concerto; 6 overtures to Shakespeare's plays; numerous other works for orchestra and orchestra with voice or solo instruments; many chamber works in all forms; piano pieces; songs; choral works. Tobias and the angel, oratorio on the book of Tobit, 1965, was given its premiere in Norwalk, Conn., 1 Feb. 1975, New York premiere, 2 Feb. 1975. The world premiere of his chamber opera, The importance of being Earnest, was given in concert form at City Univ. of New York, 22 Feb. 1975.

CASTILLO, JAVIER
b. Coahuila, Mex., 27 Dec. 1933; came to U.S. 1960. Studied at Univ. of California, Berkeley and Mills Coll. with Jean Claude Eloy, Darius Milhaud, and John Swackhamer. He was composer-in-residence with the San Francisco Symphony Orch., summer 1972.
    WORKS: Orchestra: Sculptures, orch. and chorus, commissioned by San Francisco Symph.; Chamber music: Three geometric pieces, woodwinds and percussion; Ravelesque, piano; The house of two, 2 pianos; Chorus: Lament on the death of a kitty; The temple, mixed chorus, percussion, and 2 trombones.
1316 Milvia, Berkeley, CA 94709

CASTLE, PATRICK

*CASTLE, PATRICK
Entrapment, percussion and 4 melodic instruments.

*CATELINET, PHILIP
Conducted the premiere of his Concerto for 5 for
symphonic band at Carnegie Hall, New York, 8
Apr. 1973.
Carnegie-Mellon University
Pittsburgh, PA 15213

CAVE, MICHAEL
b. Springfield, Mo., 17 May 1944. Attended
Washington Univ., California Inst. of the Arts,
and Univ. of Southern California, studying
piano with Johana Harris, Bernardo Segall, and
Aube Tzerko. He was organist and choirmaster,
Los Angeles, 1963-69; head of music program,
Westlake School, Los Angeles, 1968-72; instructor, Univ. of California, Los Angeles,
1972-   .
WORKS: Opera: Pandora's box, children's
opera, Los Angeles, 1971; Chamber music: Fantasie on a choral melody, soloists, choir,
chamber orch., organ, Los Angeles, 1967; Ecclesiastes, 2 sopranos, string quartet, oboe,
horn, piano, Los Angeles, 1971; By the waters of
Babylon, soprano, 2 recorders, keyboard, Los
Angeles, 1971; oboe sonata, Los Angeles, 1971;
songs, recorder trio, piano pieces.
1525 Walnut Ave., Venice, CA 90291

CAVIANI, RONALD
b. Iron Mountain, Mich., 12 Mar. 1931. Studied
with Carl Hager at Notre Dame Univ.; George Wi
Wilson at Univ. of Michigan; H. Owen Reed and
James Niblock at Michigan State Univ. He received a faculty research grant from Northern
Michigan Univ. in 1968. He was orchestra
director in public schools, Niles, Mich., and
assistant professor, Northern Michigan Univ.
1968-   .
WORKS: Band: Synthesis I for wind ensemble;
Prelude, chorale, and march; Northern suite;
Chamber music: Dance suite, clarinet and piano;
2 string quartets; Chorus: Three poems, texts
by Leonard Cohen, a cappella; pity this busy
monster manunkind not, e. e. cummings text,
small choir and synthesizer.
609 West College, Marquette, MI 49855

CAZDEN, NORMAN
b. New York, N.Y., 13 Sep. 1914. Attended The
Juilliard School, piano diploma 1930, Graduate
School, diploma 1939, studying piano with Ernest
Hutcheson, composition with Bernard Wagenaar;
City Coll., B. S. cum laude 1943; Harvard Univ.,
A. M. 1944, Ph. D. 1948, studying composition
with Walter Piston and Aaron Copland. He received scholarships for all study at Juilliard;
won Phi Beta Kappa at City Coll.; Saltonstall
fellowship, 1945; George Knight fellowship,
1945; John Knowles Paine fellowships, 1945, 1946;
Pi Kappa Lambda, 1952; 5 MacDowell Colony fellowships; 9th Pedro Paz award in composition,
Olivet Coll., 1971. He made his debut as pianist at Town Hall, New York, in 1926 at age 12;
toured as pianist and accompanist, 1924-43; was
on staff of radio stations WNYC and WLIB, New

(CAZDEN, NORMAN)
York; music director, Humphrey-Weidman Dance
Repertory Company, 1942-43; and taught privately, 1928-   ; at Juilliard, 1934-39;
Vassar Coll., 1947-48; Peabody Cons., 1948-49;
Univ. of Michigan, 1949-50; Univ. of Illinois,
1950-53; The New School, New York, 1956-58;
and Univ. of Maine, 1969-   .
WORKS: Stage works: The lonely ones,1944;
Dingle hill, 1958; The merry wives of Windsor,
1962; The tempest, 1963; Orchestra: Concerto
for 10 instruments, 1937; Preamble, 1938; On
the death of a Spanish child, 1939; Six definitions, 1930-39; Three dances, 1940; Stony Hollow,
1944; symphony, 1948; Three ballads, 1949; Songs
from the Catskills, 1950; Three times a round,
1957; Woodland Valley sketches, 1960; Adventure,
1963; Chamber concerto, clarinet and strings,
1965; Chamber music: string quartet, 1936; 3
chamber sonatas for clarinet and viola, 1938;
quartet for clarinet and strings, 1939; Three
recitations, cello and piano, 1939; Three messages, trumpet and piano, 1940; string quintet,
1941; horn sonata, 1941; Ten conversations, 2
clarinets, 1941; flute sonata, 1941; 2 woodwind
quintets, 1941, 1966; Three directions, brass
quartet, 1941; Six discussions, wind ensembles,
1942; violin suite, 1943; Four presentations,
violin and piano, 1944; brass sextet, 1951;
quintet for oboe and strings, 1960; Four favors,
violin and piano, 1964; Three charades, clarinet
and piano, 1964; Elizabethan suite No. 1, brass
quintet, 1964; Elizabethan suite No. 2, string
quartet, 1965; piano trio, 1969; sonata for
recorder and harp, 1971; Evocations, recorder
and guitar, 1971; Five intonations, 4 trumpets,
1971; Six sennets, 4 trombones, 1971; bassoon
sonata, 1971; cello sonata, 1971; Piano: 6
sonatinas, 1932, 1935, 1959 (3), 1964; Three
satires, 1933; 8 preludes, 1937; 5 sonatas,
1938, 1950 (3), 1971; and other pieces. He is
also author of many articles, music reviews, and
the books: Musical consonance and dissonance
(dissertation), Harvard, 1948; Dances from woodland, Bridgeport, Conn., 1955; The Abelard folksong book, New York, 1958; A book of nonsense
songs, New York, 1961; and co-author of musical
portions in others including: Wake up, dead man,
by Bruce Jackson, Harvard Univ. Press, 1972.
Department of Music, University of Maine
Orono, ME 04473

CEELY, ROBERT PAIGE
b. Torrington, Conn., 17 Jan. 1930. Studied at
New England Cons., B. M. 1954, with Francis Judd
Cooke; Mills Coll., M. A. 1961, with Darius Milhaud and Leon Kirchner; and Princeton Univ. with
Roger Sessions, Milton Babbitt, and Oliver
Strunk. He received the Roy Dickinson Welch
fellowship at Princeton; and a Fromm Found. commission in 1969 for Spectrum, a work performed
at Tanglewood. He was master in music, Lawrenceville School, 1960-61; music director, Robert
Coll., Istanbul, 1961-63; guest composer, RAI
Studio de Fonologia, Milan; founder and director, Boston Experimental Electronicmusic Projects, 1965-   ; technical director, Modern

(CEELY, ROBERT PAIGE)
Language Center, Harvard Univ., 1966-67; faculty member, New England Cons., 1967-
WORKS: Instrumental: String trio, 1953; Composition for 10 instruments, 1963; Logs, 2 double basses, 1968; Hymn, cello and double bass, 1970; Electronic: Elegia, 1963; Stratti, 1963; Vonce, 1967; Modules, 1968; Spectrum, tape and 12 instruments, 1969; Mitsyn music, 1971; La fleur, 1972; Slide music, 1973; Rerap, 1973.
33 Elm St., Brookline, MA 02146

CELONA, JOHN ANTHONY
b. San Francisco, Calif., 30 Oct. 1947. Studied with Henry Onderdonk at San Francisco State Coll.; with Iannis Xenakis at Indiana Univ.; and with Kenneth Gaburo at Univ. of California, San Diego. He received a B. M. I. award in 1971. He was a Ph. D. candidate, Univ. of California, San Diego, and research assistant, Center for Music Experiment in 1973.
WORKS: Orchestra: Modulo, 1970; Chamber music: Multiphony I (Transformations) for string quartet, 1970-3; Multiphony III (Gradients), tenor trombone with trigger, 1972; Multiphony IV (Velocities), wind ensemble, 1973; Electronic: Response, 2 choirs, organ, percussion, tape, 1971; Interphase, percussion and tape, 1971; Archangel, tape, 1972.
944 Sapphire St., #5
Pacific Beach, CA 92109

CERVETTI, SERGIO
b. Uruguay, 9 Nov. 1940; to U.S. 1962. Studied at Peabody Cons. with Ernst Krenek and Stefan Grove; at Columbia Univ., electronic music with Alcides Lanza. He received first prize for chamber music in the Caracas International Music Festival, 1966; a grant as composer-in-residence, West Berlin, 1969; and several commissions. He was assistant professor, Brooklyn Coll., 1970-71; instructor, New York Univ. and Pratt Inst., 1972-   ; and music consultant, Creative Arts Public Service Program, New York Council on the Arts, 1972-   .
WORKS: Orchestra: Graffiti, speaking chorus, orch., and tape; Plexus; Chamber music: Six sequences for dance, 1966; Five episodes, piano trio, 1966; Zinctum, string quartet; Concerto for trumpet and strings; Chorus: Lux lucet in tenebris, 16 voices a cappella; Electronic: Oulom...Raga III, tape.
170 Bleecker St., New York, NY 10012

CERVONE, D. DONALD
b. Meadville, Pa., 27 July 1932. Studied with Howard Hanson, Bernard Rogers, Louis Mennini at Eastman School of Music, B. M. 1955, Ph. D. 1970; and with Burrill Phillips and Gordon Binkerd at Univ. of Illinois, M. M. 1960. He received the Benjamin composition award, 1966; 3 Ford Found. grants; State Univ. of New York fellowships, 1968-69; Yale-Gordon Found. composer award, 1970; many commissions. He has been church music director, composer-in-residence, and conductor since 1960; and has held teaching posts in public schools; Hochstein Music School, Rochester, 1962-66; State Univ. of New York, Brockport, 1966-   , associate professor, 1970-   .

(CERVONE, D. DONALD)
WORKS: Opera: Melanie, 1-act, 1958; Not long ago....not far away, children's opera, 1965; Aria da capo, 1-act, libretto by Millay, 1969; incidental music to Inherit the wind, 1961, The crucible, 1967; Orchestra: Canzone II, 1966; viola concerto, 1969; Sinfonia tutti clavieri, for keyboards and orch., 1973; Chorus: Where thorn once grew, soloists, chorus, orch., 1970; These are the times, baritone, 2 choirs, orch., organ, 1971; Songs: Remembrance, cycle for contralto, piano or chamber orch., 1955; Again this year, cycle for soprano and orch., 1964; Film score: What is a college?, 1968.
3318 Brockport-Spencerport Road
Spencerport, NY 14559

CHADABE, JOEL
b. New York, N. Y., 12 Dec. 1938. Studied at Univ. of North Carolina and Yale Univ., and privately with Elliott Carter. He received a Ford Found. grant as artist-in-residence, West Berlin; ASCAP awards; and a Creative Arts Public Service Program commission. He has been a faculty member, State Univ. of New York at Albany, 1965-   .
WORKS: Instrumental: Prelude to Naples, 4 instruments; Diversions, 2 pianos; Three ways of looking at a square, piano; Electronic: Street scene, English horn, tape and projections; Drift, tape; Ideas of movement at Bolton Landing, tape; Echoes, solo instrument and tape.
339 South Manning Blvd., Albany, NY 12208

CHAITKIN, DAVID
b. New York, N. Y., 16 May 1938. Studied with Karl Kohn at Pomona Coll., B. A.; with Seymour Shifrin, Arnold Elston, Luigi Dallapiccola, Andrew Imbrie, Univ. of California, M. A.; with Max Deutsch in Paris. At Berkeley he received the Ladd Prix de Paris, 1964-66, and the Eisner Prize. He was assistant professor, Reed Coll., 1968-69; assistant professor, New York Univ., 1969-   .
WORKS: Orchestra: Music for orchestra, 1963, revised 1973; Music in five parts, composed for the film The game, 1967; Chamber music: Concert music for violin and piano, 1963; Three studies for piano, 1960, revised 1973.
208 Dean St., Brooklyn, NY 11217

CHAJES, JULIUS
b. Lvov, Poland, 21 Dec. 1910; to U.S. 1937. Studied piano in Vienna with Moriz Rosenthal, Hedwig Rosenthal, Richard Robert, Julius Isserlis, and composition with Hugo Kauder. He won the Honor Prize in the first international competition for pianists, Vienna, 1933. He was head of the piano department, Tel-Aviv Music School, 1934-36; director, music division, Jewish Community Center, Detroit, and conductor of its orchestra, 1940-   ; and on the faculty, Wayne State Univ., 1950-   .
WORKS: Opera: Out of the desert, 2 acts; Orchestra: Eros symphonic poem; Hebrew suite; Scherzo; Hatikvah; Fantasy for piano and orch., 1928; cello concerto, 1932; piano concerto, 1953; Chamber music: Hebrew suite, clarinet, piano,

CHAJES, JULIUS

(CHAJES, JULIUS)
    string quartet; piano trio; 2 string quartets;
    violin sonata; piano sonata; Chorus: 142nd
    Psalm, cantata, 1937; Zion, rise and shine, can-
    tata; The promised land, cantata; Song for Ameri-
    cans; many other choral works, songs, pieces for
    piano and other solo instruments.
        29055 Pointe O'Woods Place
        Southfield, MI 48076

CHAMBERLIN, WILLIAM FRANCIS
    b. Springfield, Mass., 27 Aug. 1939. Has stud-
    ied at the Juilliard School with Hugo Weisgall,
    Luciano Berio, Vincent Persichetti, Elliott
    Carter, and Hubert Howe; and at Hampshire Coll.
    with Robert Stern. He won the Internat.
    Gaudeamus Composers Competition, 1972, and a
    grant from the American Music Center, 1972.
        WORKS: Orchestra: Ainsworth Street,
    1970-71; Chamber music: Chamber music for 14
    players, 1968; string quartet, 1973-74.
        Kramer Road, R. D. #1, Middlebury, NY 12122

CHAMBERS, JOSEPH A.
    b. Stoneacre, Va., 25 June 1942. Studied compo-
    sition with Vincent Persichetti at Philadelphia
    Cons., 1960-61; and at American Univ., 1962-63.
    He received the Creative Artists Public Service
    grant for composition, 1972, 1973; and New Star
    Performers award from Down Beat Magazine as per-
    cussionist, 1969-1970. He is a member of Um Boom
    Repercussion, a percussion ensemble, and has
    worked with many of the major jazz bands; taught
    at Buffalo Univ., 1968-69; Kingsboro Coll., 1970.
        WORKS: Chamber music: Movements for string
    quartet; Angels and devils, brass choir;
    Almoravid; Sketches for percussion, woodwinds,
    and soprano; Jazz: Mirrors; Idle while; Dialogue;
    Hello to the wind; and others.
        533 West 112th St., #6E, New York, NY 10025

CHAMBERS, STEPHEN A.
    b. Asheville, N. C., 8 Feb. 1940. Studied clari-
    net and piano at Manhattan School and New York
    Coll. of Music; and composition at New School for
    Social Research. His teachers included Robert
    Starer, William Sydeman, Hall Overton, David
    Reck, Morton Feldman, Chou Wen-Chung, Charles
    Wittenberg, Ornette Coleman. He received 4 fel-
    lowships to the Bennington Composers' Conference,
    5 ASCAP awards; Creative Artists Public Service
    grant; and Nat. Endowment of the Arts grant,
    1973. He is lecturer, panelist, conductor, per-
    former, and taught at Pace Univ., 1970-72; and at
    Nassau Community Coll., 1971-   . He is co-
    founder and president of the Society of Black
    Composers.
        WORKS: Orchestra: Shapes, chamber orch.,
    1965; Visions of Ishwara, 1970; reflections on
    the 5th ray, with narrator, 1972; Jazz band;
    Sketchy blue-bop, 1973; Chamber music: Mutations,
    mixed quintet, 1964; Peace-mobile, woodwind quin-
    tet, 1964; Ode to silence, soprano and piano,
    1964; Titles, woodwind quartet, 1965; Currents,
    string quartet, 1967; Set-three, soprano, cello,
    piano, 1970; and many works for various ensembles;
    Chorus: Sound images, women's voices and orch.,
    1969; Tone prayers, chorus, percussion, piano,

(CHAMBERS, STEPHEN A.)
    1973. He is author of Poems on #3, a book of
    first poems published by Afro-Arts, Inc.
        599 Front St., #3F, Hempstead, NY 11550

*CHANCE, JOHN BARNES
    b. 1932, d. 1972. Was on the faculty at Univ.
    of Kentucky and was killed accidentally in 1972.
        WORKS: Band: Introduction and capriccio;
    Incantation and dance; Variation on a Korean
    folk song; Blue Lake, an overture; Elegy; also
    Credo for trumpet and piano.

CHANCE, NANCY LAIRD
    b. Cincinnati, Ohio, 19 Mar. 1931. Studied with
    Vladimir Ussachevsky, Otto Luening, and Chou
    Wen-Chung.
        WORKS: Orchestra: Lyric essays; Daysongs, 3
    short tone poems, New York, 15 Aug. 1975; Chamber
    music: Rilke songs, soprano, flute, English horn,
    cello; Darksong, soprano and chamber orch.;
    Bathsabe's song, text by George Peele, for
    speaker, alto saxophone, live and pre-recorded;
    Edensong, soprano and chamber orch.; Chorus:
    Motet for double chorus, divided, a cappella.
        P. O. Box 345, Oyster Bay, NY 11771

CHANG, G. GORDON
    b. Hamilton, Ont., 31 Mar. 1951; to U.S. 1961.
    Studied at Banff School of Fine Arts with Luigi
    Zaninelli; at Arizona State Univ. with Roland
    LoPresti and Grant Fletcher. He won a competi-
    tion sponsored by the Catgut Acoustical Society
    for new string music for the 8 new instruments
    of the violin family developed by the Society,
    1973.
        WORKS: Orchestra: The other side and
    scherzo; Chamber music: Statements for string
    quartet (mezzo, alto, tenor and baritone strings),
    1973; Theme and variations for unaccompanied
    cello; Emergence, piano sonata; A great aston-
    ishment, vocal and instrumental chamber ensemble;
    Elegy, clarinet solo and cello quartet; Music
    for percussion; Chorus: A tribute to the
    founder, text by Kingsley Amis.
        5153 North 29th Ave., Phoenix, AZ 85017

*CHANLER, THEODORE WARD
    b. Newport, R. I., 29 Apr. 1902; d. Boston, Mass.,
    27 July 1961. Studied with Arthur Shepherd in
    Boston; with Ernest Bloch at Cleveland Inst. of
    Music; and with Nadia Boulanger in Paris.
        WORKS: Opera: The pot of fat, 1955; Chamber
    music: violin sonata; sonatina for chamber en-
    semble; Chorus: Mass for 2 women's voices, 1930;
    The doves; 8 epitaphs, 2 cycles, 1937, 1940; The
    flight; 4 rhymes from peacock pie; 3 husbands;
    Piano: Calm, suite of 12 pieces; Joyful mystery,
    4-hands.

CHAPMAN, ROGER E.
    b. Los Angeles, Calif., 3 June 1916. Studied
    privately with Wesley La Violette and at Univ.
    of California, Los Angeles, with John Vincent.
    He was on the faculty, Univ. of California, Santa
    Barbara, 1954-71, from instructor to professor.
        WORKS: He has written incidental music for
    theatre, chamber music, choral and organ works,

74

(CHAPMAN, ROGER E.)
including: Music for 2 cellos; Festival overture for organ; Suite of three cities, 4 trombones.
4000 Cuervo Ave., Santa Barbara, CA 93110

*CHAPPELL, HERBERT
The Daniel jazz, chorus and piano.

CHARLES, ERNEST
b. Minneapolis, Minn., 21 Nov. 1895. Attended Univ. of Southern California. He was a singer in vaudeville and Broadway shows and composer of art songs as well as popular songs.
1210 Benedict Canyon
Beverly Hills, CA 90210

*CHARLTON, ANDREW
3 movements for 4 recorders.
2700 Associated Road, Fullerton, CA 92635

*CHASE, ALLEN
Was principal trombonist with Detroit Symphony, 15 years; on faculty, Univ. of Wisconsin, 1974. He has published Rondo for 8 trombones.

CHASINS, ABRAM
b. New York, N. Y., 17 Aug. 1903. Studied at Juilliard School, Columbia Univ., and Curtis Inst. of Music; his piano teachers were Ernest Hutcheson and Josef Hofmann; composition, Rubin Goldmark; analysis, Sir Donald Francis Tovey. He received a Peabody award for distinguished service to music and radio; 2 awards of the U.S. Treasury Dept. for service in financing World War II; Bruckner Medal; and a String Players Guild award. His brilliant career as pianist extended from 1926 to 1946, and included performances with leading orchestras of Europe and America. He taught at Curtis Inst. of Music, 1926-36, and at Tanglewood, 1939-40; was music director, radio station WQXR, New York, 1942-65; musician-in-residence, Univ. of Southern California, 1972-73, and director of development, 1973-   , heading the expansion and development program of the university's radio station, KUSC-FM.
WORKS: His more than 100 compositions include 2 piano concertos, which he introduced himself as pianist; the first at Philadelphia, 18 Jan. 1929; the second also in Philadelphia, 3 Mar. 1933. Other works are: Three Chinese pieces, piano version and orchestra version; and 24 preludes for piano.
School of Performing Arts
University of Southern California
Los Angeles, CA 90007

CHATHAM, RHYS
b. New York, N. Y. Studied with Morton Subotnick, LaMonte Young, and Pandit Pran Nath. He is a member of New York Univ. Studio for Electronic Sound, 1968-   ; co-founder of The Kitchen, an electronic sound and image theater, and director of its contemporary music series, 1971-72.
WORKS: Green-line poem, tape, 1971; Two gongs amplified, for 2 large Chinese gongs and 3 performers, 1972; Still sound in motion music for Garrett List, 2 trombones, 1973; The Black Star pilgrimage, for 2 voices, poet, and dancer, 1973.
339 East 6th St., New York, NY 10003

*CHATMAN, STEPHEN
b. Madison, Wis., 1950. Won 2 awards in the Nat. Fed. of Music Clubs 1972 young composer contest with a choral work and a work for solo voice and orchestra. He also received a BMI award in 1973 for The followers of Lien for orch.; and Charles E. Ives scholarship, 1975.

CHEETHAM, JOHN
b. Taos, N. Mex., 13 Jan. 1939. Studied with John Verrall, Gerald Kechley, and George F. McKay at Univ. of Washington. He has been assistant professor, Univ. of Missouri, Columbia, 1969-
WORKS: His published works include Scherzo for brass quintet.
1611 Colonial Court, Columbia, MO 65201

*CHENEY, TIMOTHY
b. 1913. Rhapsody, violin and piano.

*CHENOWETH, WILBUR
b. Tecumsah, Neb., 4 June 1899. Vocalize for medium voice; also choral works, piano pieces.

CHERRY, MILTON
b. South Carolina, 6 June 1908. Attended Cincinnati Cons., American Cons., Chicago Musical Coll., and studied violin privately with Hugo Kortschak in New York. His faculty positions include Louisiana State Univ., 1931-45; Ithaca Coll., 1945-50; Virginia Commonwealth Univ., 1950-
WORKS: Orchestra: violin concerto, 1953; Chamber music: string quartet, New York, 1960; flute sonata, 1965.
3014 Darnley Drive, Richmond, VA 23235

CHERTOK, PEARL
b. Laconia, N. H., 18 June 1918. Studied harp with Carlos Salzedo at Curtis Inst. of Music. She was staff harpist for CBS, 1950-70, and has taught at Manhattanville Coll.
WORKS: Her compositions are mainly harp solos and background scores for television dramas.
56 North Greenwich Road, Armonk, NY 10504

CHESLOCK, LOUIS
b. London, England, 25 Sep. 1898; U.S. citizen 1913. Studied at Peabody Cons. with Franz Bornschein, Jan van Hulsteyn, Frank Gittelson on violin, and Gustav Strube in composition. His composition awards include Peabody Alumni prize, 1921; Chicago Daily News prizes, 1922-24; Nat. Composers Clinic, 1942; New York Women's Symph., 1938; Baltimore City Coll. Hall of Fame, 1960; honorary doctorate, Peabody Cons. 1964. He was violinist with the Baltimore Symphony, 1916-31, guest conductor, 1928, 1944, 1950; and chairman. theory and composition department, Peabody Cons., 1950-68. Many of his orchestral works have been performed by the Baltimore Symphony.
WORKS: Opera: The jewel merchants, libretto by James Branch Cabell, 1940; Ballet: Cinderella, in 3 acts; Orchestra: 3 tone poems: 'Neath Washington Monument, Cathedral at sundown, At the railway station, 1923; Symphony in D, 1932; violin concerto; horn concerto; Symphonic prelude; Rhapsody in red and white, 1950; Chamber

CHESLOCK, LOUIS

(CHESLOCK, LOUIS)
music: string quartet; violin sonata; Bagatelle, cello and piano, Baltimore, May 1969; Descant, 12 tone, unaccompanied clarinet, Baltimore, 14 Jan. 1972; numerous chamber works and solo pieces.
2318 Sulgrave Ave., Baltimore, MD 21209

CHIHARA, PAUL SEIKO
b. Seattle, Wash., 9 Sep. 1938. Attended Univ. of Washington, B. A. 1960; Cornell Univ., M. A. 1961, D. M. A. 1965, studying with Robert Palmer; in between his degrees at Cornell he studied in Paris with Nadia Boulanger, in Germany with Ernst Pepping, and later at Tanglewood with Gunther Schuller. He received the Lili Boulanger award, 1963; Fulbright fellowship to Berlin, 1965; Tanglewood fellowships, 1966-68. He has appeared in concerts as performer, conductor, and composer throughout the U.S., Japan and Mexico. He has been associate professor, Univ. of California, Los Angeles, 1966-   .
WORKS: Orchestra: Forest music, Los Angeles, 2 May 1971; Wind song, cello and orch., New York, 2 Feb. 1972; Grass, for amplified double bass and orch., Oberlin, Ohio, Mar. 1972; Ceremony IV, Los Angeles Philharmonic, 18 Apr. 1974; Suite from Shinju, Claremont Festival, Aug. 1974; Chamber music: string quartet in one movement, 1965; Tree music, 3 violas and 3 trombones, Tanglewood 1966; Branches, 2 bassoons and percussion, Tanglewood, 1966; Redwood, viola and percussion, 1967; Willow, willow, amplified bass flute, tuba, percussion, New York, 20 Feb., 1968; Logs for one or more string basses, Logs XVI, amplified bass and electronic tape, 1969; Driftwood, string quartet, 1969; Ceremony, oboe, 2 celli, bass, percussion, Marlboro Festival, Aug. 1971; Chorus: The 90th Psalm, 1965; Magnificat, for treble voices; Three dream choruses, 1968; Nocturne for 24 solo voices, 1972; The 101st Psalm.
59 Navy St., Venice, CA 90291

CHILDS, BARNEY
b. Spokane, Wash., 13 Feb. 1926. Studied at Univ. of Nevada, B. A. 1949; Oxford Univ., B. A. 1951, M. A. 1955; Stanford Univ., Ph. D. in English and music 1959; composition with Leonard Ratner, 1952-53; Carlos Chavez, 1953; Aaron Copland, 1954; Elliott Carter, 1954-55. He received a Rhodes scholarship, 1949; MacDowell fellowships, 1963, 1968, 1970. He taught English, Univ. of Arizona, 1956-65; was dean, Deep Springs Coll., 1965-67; faculty member, Wisconsin Coll. Cons., Milwaukee, 1969-71; professor and composer-in-residence, Univ. of Redlands, 1971-   .
WORKS: Orchestra: 2 symphonies, 1954, 1956; clarinet concerto, 1970; Band: 6 events, 1965; Supposes: Imago mundi, 1970; Chamber music: violin sonata, 1950; 7 string quartets, 1951-68; sonata for solo clarinet, 1951; Concerto da camera, trumpet and woodwinds, 1951; 5 wind quintets, 1951-69; woodwind trio, 1952; quartet for clarinet and strings, 1953; bassoon sonata, 1953; 4 involutions, solo English horn, 1955; 5 considerations, solo horn, 1955; 7 epigrams, voice and clarinet, 1955; concerto for English horn and chamber ensemble, 1955; violin sonata, 1956; bassoon quartet, 1958; sonata for solo oboe,

(CHILDS, BARNEY)
1958; brass trio, 1959; flute sonata, 1960; sonata for solo trombone, 1961; sonata for solo alto saxophone; Interbalances I-VI, for various ensembles, 1941-64; Take 5, for any 5 instruments, 1962; Variations sur une chanson de canotier; Stances, flute and silence, 1963; quartet for flute, oboe, doublebass, percussion, 1964; Music for doublebass and friend, 1964; Music for piano and strings, 1965; Jack's new bag, 10 players, 1966; The golden bubble, contrabass sarrusophone and percussion, 1967; 5 little sound pieces, oboe; nonet, 1967; Mr. T his fancy, doublebass, 1967; Variations for D.R., for horn; Music for 2 flute players; Operation flabby sleep, any instruments, 1968; Music for 6 tubas, 1969; Maine scene, baritone voice and piano, 1970; When lilacs first in the dooryard bloomed, soprano and percussion, Milwaukee, 31 Jan. 1971; Chorus: This is the praise of created things; Heal me O Lord; Keet seel, a cappella, 1970.
864 Hartzell, Redlands, CA 92373

CHOBANIAN, LORIS OHANNES
b. Mosul, Iraq, 17 Apr. 1933; U.S. citizen. Attended Louisiana State Univ., B. M. 1964, M. M. 1966; Michigan State Univ., Ph. D. 1970; and studied privately in composition with H. Owen Reed, Kenneth Klaus; conducting with Peter Paul Fuchs; guitar with Jacques Tchakerian, and in Andres Segovia Master Class. He was assistant professor, Muskegon Connunity Coll., 1969-70; professor Baldwin Wallace Cons., 1970-   .
WORKS: Sumer and Akkad, chamber ensemble, percussion, and dancers, WMSB-TV, East Lansing, May 1969; guitar concerto, East Lansing, 4 June 1971, composer as soloist; The id, wind ensemble, Berea, Ohio, Jan. 1972; Capriccio for piano and wind ensemble, Berea, 20 Jan. 1974, conducted by the composer.
Baldwin-Wallace Conservatory of Music
Berea, OH 44017

CHORBAJIAN, JOHN
b. New York, N. Y., 2 June 1936. Studied at Manhattan School of Music, M. M. 1959, with Vittorio Giannini, Nicolas Flagello, and Ludmila Ulehla. He received a Ford Found. grant as composer-in-residence, 1961-62. He is active mostly as a private teacher of piano and composition.
WORKS: Opera: Antigone, 1-act, 1959; Orchestra: Four Christmas Psalms, cantata for chorus and orch.; The magic of music, scene for mime with orch., 1960; The crucifixion, cantata for chorus and orch., 1962; Chorus: The swing, children's chorus, flute and piano, 1966; Bitter for sweet; The Lamb; There is a silence; Dark house; numerous other choral pieces and songs.
57-36 138th St., Flushing, NY 11355

*CHOU, WEN-CHUNG
b. Chefoo, China, 29 June 1923; to U.S. 1946. Studied at New England Cons.; with Edgard Varese and Otto Luening in New York. His awards include a Guggenheim fellowship, 1957; special citation, Koussevitzky Internat. Recording award, 1970.

(CHOU, WEN-CHUNG)
He has been a member of the judging panel for the BMI Student Composer Awards. He is professor of composition and ethnomusicology, Columbia Univ.

WORKS: Orchestra: Landscapes, 1949; All in the spring wind, 1953; And the fallen petals, New York, 9 Feb. 1955; Band: Metaphors (4 seasons); Riding the wind; Chamber music: 3 folksongs, flute and harp; Suite for woodwind quintet and harp; Chamber concerto; 2 Chinese folksongs for harp; The willows are new, piano, 1957; Soliloquy of a Bhiksuni, solo trumpet, winds, percussion, 1958; Cursive, flute and piano, 1963; Yu Ko, chamber ensemble, 1965; Pien, chamber ensemble, 1966; Songs: 7 poems of the T'ang Dynasty, tenor, winds, piano, percussion.
Department of Music
Columbia University
New York, NY 10027

*CHRISTIANSEN, F. MELIUS
b. Eidsvold, Norway, 1 Apr. 1871; to U.S. 1888; d. Northfield, Minn., 1 June 1955. Studied at Augsburg Coll. and the Northwest Cons. He was chairman, music department, St. Olaf's Coll., and founder and director of the St. Olaf Choir, for which he write the St. Olaf Choir Services in 6 volumes. He also wrote cantatas and hymns.

CHRISTIANSEN, LARRY A.
b. Chicago, Ill., 10 Oct. 1941. Studied Northwestern Univ., M. M., with Anthony Donato; Boston Univ. with Daniel Pinkham; Ohio Wesleyan Univ. with Tilden Wells. He won second place in the Illinois Young Composer contest, 1964. He has held faculty positions at Culver Stockton Coll., 1964-66; Concord Coll., 1966-67; Chicago City Coll., 1967-68; Robert L. Stevenson School. Pebble Beach, Calif., 1968-70; and has been professor, Southwestern Coll., Chula Vista, Calif., 1970-   .

WORKS: Orchestra: Elegy and Dithyramb, symphony no. 2; Fragments for chamber orch.; Chamber music: trio for clarinet, cello, piano; Chorus: Voyage, chorus, brass, tympani, and strings, San Diego, 1973; Evocation and impromptu, chorus, clarinet, piano, percussion, and strings, San Diego, 1973; many choral works and compositions in all genres.
4955 Niagara, #16, San Diego, CA 92107

CHRISTIANSEN, PAUL
b. Northfield, Minn., 31 July 1914, son of F. Melius Christiansen. Graduated from St. Olaf Coll., then studied at Oberlin Coll. and Eastman School of Music, M. M. He has received honorary doctorates from Adams State Coll. and St. Olaf Coll. He has been on the faculty at Concordia Coll. and director of the Concordia Choir since 1937. The choir under his direction has been acclaimed in Europe as well as America.

WORKS: Chorus: Everyman, to his own text, with organ or piano; Prayers of steel, Sandburg text; many original choral works and arrangements.
Department of Music, Concordia College
Moorhead, MN 56560

CHRYSTAL, WILLIAM ADAMSON
b. Pittsburgh, Pa., 26 Jan. 1931. Studied at Peabody Cons., B. M. 1955, M. M. 1956, studying piano with Alexander Sklarevski and Mieczyslaw Munz, composition with Howard Thatcher; conducting with George Hurst. He has held faculty positions at Peabody Cons., 1955-56; Newkirk School of Music, Pensacola, Fla., 1958-59; and assistant professor, Department of Drama, Carnegie-Mellon Univ., 1969-   ; has been a private teacher, 1959-   .

WORKS: Incidental music: The only jealousy of Emer, Yeats, 1970; Pericles, Prince of Tyre, Shakespeare, 1971; Twelfth night, 1973.
481 McCully St., Pittsburgh, PA 15216

CIRONE, ANTHONY J.
b. New Jersey, 8 Nov. 1941. Studied at Juilliard School with Saul Goodwin on timpani and percussion, and Vincent Persichetti in composition. He has been percussionist in the San Francisco Symphony, 1965-   , and is assistant professor, California State Univ., San Jose.

WORKS: Orchestra: Double concerto for 2 percussion and orch.; Chorus: A Sacred Mass for chorus and percussion; Percussion: Overture; Percussionality; Japanese impressions; For four; Triptych; 2 symphonies; timpani sonata; sonata for trumpet and percussion; 5 items for soprano and percussion, on poems by Lou Harrison.
1601 Santa Cruz Ave., Menlo Park, CA 94025

*CITKOWITZ, ISRAEL
b. Russia, 6 Feb. 1909; U.S. citizen; d. London, England, 4 May 1974. Studied with Aaron Copland and Roger Sessions in New York; with Nadia Boulanger in Paris. He taught at the Dalcroze School of Music in New York; lived in London from 1969.

WORKS: Chamber music: string quartet; Voice: The lamb, chorus; Song cycle to words of Joyce; Strings in the earth and air, 1930; Gentle lady.

CIUS, ANTHONY B., JR.
b. Buffalo, N. Y., 11 Mar. 1938. Studied at State Univ. of New York, Fredonia, B. M. E., 1960; with John Pozdro and Edward Mattila, Univ. of Kansas, B. M., 1967, M. M. 1970; and on an exchange scholarship at Reading Univ., England, 1968-69. He taught in public schools, 1960-62; served in U.S. Navy, 1963-66; instructor, Univ. of Kansas, 1969-70, 1972-73; teacher, public schools, 1973-   .

WORKS: Orchestra: Remembrances, orch. of cellos, 1973, rescored for string orch., 1974; Chamber music: 2 movements for violin and piano, 1966; string quartet, 1966; brass octet, 1967; The seasons, song cycle for tenor and chamber group, 1967; 5 little pieces, flute and bassoon, 1968; piano sextet, 1969; Chorus: Gloria in excelsis Deo, 1960; Confiteor, with soloists and chamber orch., 1968; 2 chorales on Psalms 121 and 130, a cappella, 1973; Piano: Fantasie, 1962; Variations, 1966; Diabolus in musica, short sonata, 1966; Fugue in C, 1968; Electronic:

CIUS, ANTHONY B., JR.

(CIUS, ANTHONY B., JR.)
Children of the Earth, synthesizer, bird calls, carillon, narrators, tape, 1973.
1409 South Van Ness Ave., Apt. 5
San Francisco, CA 94110

*CLAFLIN, AVERY
b. Keene, N. H., 21 June 1898. Studied with Archibald T. Davison at Harvard Univ., but his majors and his career were in law and banking.
WORKS: Opera: The fall of Usher, 1921; Hester Prynne, 1932; La Grande Bretèche, 1947; Uncle Tom's cabin, 1964; Orchestra: Moby Dick suite, 1929; 2 symphonies; Fishhouse punch, 1948; Teen scenes, string orch., 1955; Concerto giocoso, piano and orch., 1957; Chorus: Lament for April 15th, text verbatim from the Federal Income Tax instructions; The quangle wangle's hat, nonsense verse of Edward Lear; Design for the atomic age, also from Edward Lear; by coincidence the first performance was at Oakridge, Tenn.; and chamber music.

*CLAPP, PHILIP GREELEY
b. Boston, Mass., 4 Aug. 1888; d. Iowa City, Iowa, 9 Apr. 1954. Studied at Harvard Univ., Ph. D. 1911; and in Europe as a Sheldon fellow of Harvard. He taught at Dartmouth Coll., 1915-19; then joined the faculty of Univ. of Iowa. His works include 10 symphonies, 3 symphonic poems, chamber music, choral works, and songs.

CLARK, MERRILL ROSS
b. Salt Lake City, Utah, 26 Nov. 1951. Studied at Westminster Coll., Salt Lake City, and Univ. of Utah with Ladd McIntosh and William Fowler. He was named outstanding composer-arranger at the Intermountain Collegiate Jazz Festival, 1971 and 1972, and at the American College Jazz Festival, Urbana, Ill., 1971. He has received commissions from Univ. of Utah and J. F. Kennedy Center for the Performing Arts.
WORKS: Orchestra: Concerto for electric guitar, Univ. of Utah, Jan. 1972; Dialogue for rock band and orch., Salt Lake City, 1972; Chorus: A Rock Mass, Univ. of Utah, Mar. 1972; Jazz: Creatures, Washington, D.C., 1972; Nameless as yet; Schmear, 1972
1774 South 26th East
Salt Lake City, UT 84108

*CLARK, PHILIP
No game for kids, short opera, Tougaloo Coll., Miss., 1970-71.

CLARK, ROBERT KEYES
b. Maryland, 18 Nov. 1925. Studied at Philadelphia Cons., B. M., with Vincent Persichetti; and the Juilliard School, B. S., M. S., with Bernard Wagenaar. He held a teaching fellowship at Juilliard and received the Roth Nat. Orchestral award, 1970, several ASCAP awards and several commissions. He has been conductor, Connecticut Festival Orch., 1965-   ; was instructor, Westover School, Middlebury, Conn., 1954-59; lecturer, Western Conn. State Coll., 1972; and consultant, McGraw Hill Co., 1966-68.

(CLARK, ROBERT KEYES)
WORKS: Stage: The magic trumpet, musical fairy tale for children, 1957; Music for dance, ballet for solo dancer and piano, 1949; incidental music for The wasteland, 1959; Orchestra: 3 symphonies, 1952, 1953, 1963; The antic muse, 1962; violin concerto, 1965; Any number can play, suite for young orch., 1966; Repercussions, 1969; clarinet concerto, 1971; Band: Suite, 1954; Brevities, 1962; Chamber music: 2 piano sonatas, 1949, 1956; string quartet, 1950; Divertimento, string trio, 1954; Duo for trumpet and piano, 1954; Patterns for percussion, 5 players, 1967; Lamentations for string orch., New York, 18 Apr. 1974; Chorus: Mass for four voices, Latin liturgical setting, 1961; Songs: Dirges, cycle of 3 songs for soprano and violin, 1961; Moments for mezzo, a cycle of 4 songs for mezzo-soprano and piano.
Box 304, Kent, CT 06757

CLARK, ROGIE
b. Atlanta, Ga., 4 Apr. 1917. Studied at Clark Coll., A. B.; Chicago Musical Coll.; with Douglas Moore and Normand Lockwood, Columbia Univ., M. A.; Juilliard School; and at Tanglewood. He received fellowships from Ford Found.; Tanglewood; Nat. Endowment for the Arts, 1973; the John Hay Whitney award; Nat. Assoc. of Negro Musicians award, 1973. His academic posts include director, music department, Fort Valley State Coll.; lecturer, New School for Social Research; instructor, New Music School, New York; head, music department, Jackson State Coll.; instructor, public schools, Warren, Mich.; lecturer in Black Music, Detroit public schools. He is also consultant for Black Studies programs, folklore workshops, Black Music workshops, festivals, Afro-American programs.
WORKS: Opera: Ti Yette, 1-act; The stranger; The myrtle tree; Ballet: The lonely island; Orchestra: Fete Creole; Prelude for Wednesday; Larghetto, string orch.; Band: John Henry fantasy; Chamber music: Figurine, cello and piano; Fantasia, clarinet and piano; Divertimento, string quartet; piano works, songs, many choral arrangements. He is author of magazine articles; a play; The Black bard: A study of Black folk music (mss.); and poetry.
17127 Kentucky, Detroit, MI 48211

CLARK, THOMAS SIDNEY
b. Highland Park, Mich., 23 Aug. 1949. Studied at Univ. of Michigan with George Balch Wilson, Leslie Bassett, and Eugene Kurtz. He was lecturer in theory, Indiana Univ., 1973; and instructor, Pacific Lutheran Univ., 1973-74.
WORKS: Orchestra: Animated landscapes, 1972; Band: Microscopic episodes, 1973; Chamber music: Night songs, solo trombone, 1970; Tyger, chamber ensemble, 1971; Trilogy, brass quintet, 1968; Autumn rain music, oboe and piano; Mixed media: Somniloquy, dancer, trombone, tape, 1972; Straw music, violin and tape, 1972; Film: Space hold, 1971.
Pacific Lutheran University
Tacoma, WA 98447

CLARKE, GARRY E.
b. Moline, Ill., 19 Mar. 1943. Studied at Cornell Coll., B. M. 1965, with Alf Houkom; Yale Univ., M. M. 1968, with Mel Powell and Yehudi Wyner. He has received fellowships from Ford Found., Carnegie Found., Woodrow Wilson Fund; a Nat. Endowment for the Humanities grant; Rena Greenwald composition prize; and a Bradley-Keeler fellowship. He has been associate professor and chairman, Department of Music, Washington Coll., 1968-   .
WORKS: Opera: Westchester limited, 1972; Orchestra: Peck Hill holiday, 1973; Band: Structure for band, 1971; Chamber music: string quartet, 1966; Some versions of silence, 1968; violin sonata, 1964; woodwind quintet, 1964; violin suite, 1965; Lissajous figures, 1968; Chorus: Epitaphs, 1971; Comme avant comme apres, 1973; Piano: Triptych, 1967; Montage, 1967.
Kentmere-Quaker Neck, Chestertown, MD 21620

CLARKE, HENRY LELAND
b. Dover, N. H., 9 Mar. 1907. Studied at Harvard Univ., A. B. 1928, A. M. 1929, Ph. D. 1947; and also with Nadia Boulanger, Gustav Holst, Hans Weisse, and Otto Luening. He received the John Harvard fellowship, 1929-30; American Council of Learned Societies grant, 1936; Washington Music Educators Prize award, 1964. He was assistant, New York Public Library, 1932-36; then held teaching posts at Bennington Coll., 1936-38; Westminster Choir Coll., 1938-42; Univ. of California, Los Angeles, 1947-48, 1949-58; Vassar Coll., 1948-49; and associate professor, Univ. of Washington, 1959-   .
WORKS: Opera: The loafer and the loaf, chamber opera, 1951; Orchestra: Monograph, 1952; Chamber music: 2 string quartets; Nocturne, viola and piano, 1955; Chorus: Before dawn; Happy is the man, 1935; No man is an island, 1951; Love in the world, women's chorus, 1953; Wonders are many, men's chorus, 1954; L'Allegro and Il Penseroso, on Milton text.
6500 57th Ave., N. E., Seattle, WA 98115

CLARKE, LAURENCE G.
b. Denver, Colo., 8 Feb. 1928. Studied with Roy Harris at Colorado Coll.; with Roger Sessions at Univ. of California, Berkeley; and with Darius Milhaud at Mills Coll. He received a California symphonic award, 1968; and the Artrium Composers award, 1972. He was instructor, Music and Arts Inst. of San Francisco, 1953-56; associate professor, Santa Rosa Junior Coll., 1958-   .
WORKS: Orchestra: Episodes for orchestra; Sinfonia for strings; Chamber music: sonata for flute and guitar; Variations, violin and piano; Vocal: Everyone sang, four pieces for a cappella choir; Chamber music, song cycle for solo voice.
Department of Music, Santa Rosa Junior College
Santa Rosa, CA 95401

CLARKE, REBECCA (Mrs. James Friskin)
b. Harrow, England, 27 Aug. 1886; father was a U.S. citizen. Studied composition at Royal Coll. of Music, London, with Sir Charles Stanford. In 1919 her viola sonata placed second to Ernest Bloch's entry for the Coolidge Prize in the

(CLARKE, REBECCA)
Berkshire Festival; her piano trio placed second in the same contest in 1921. She was an accomplished violinist and violist and toured Europe with the English Ensemble, a piano quartet which she organized.
WORKS: Chamber music: Rhapsody for cello and piano, 1923; Suite for clarinet and viola, Berkeley, Calif., 1942.
300 West 108th St., New York, NY 10025

CLARKE, ROSEMARY
b. Daytona Beach, Fla., 23 June 1921. Studied at Stetson Univ. with Robert Bailey; Philadelphia Musical Acad. with Rollo Maitland; Eastman School of Music with Bernard Rogers and Herbert Elwell. She holds a B. M., M. M., organ diploma, Ph. D. in composition, and is an Associate and a Fellow of the American Guild of Organists. She taught at Stetson Univ., 1942-57; founded and directed Rosemary Clarke Cons. of Music, Deland, Fla., 1949-57; was artist-in-residence, Univ. of Dubuque, 1957-62; professor and composer-in-residence, Univ. of Wisconsin-Platteville, 1962-
WORKS: Orchestra: 2 piano concertos; 2 Elegies; Wrath, soprano and orch.; Band: Fantasy, piano and band; Skyrocket; Chamber music: Trio sonata, trumpet, viola, cello; piano trio; Happening, flute and double bass; Suite of changes, 6 instruments, voice, percussion; Scherzando, 3 clarinets, 1960; Suite for piano and percussion, 1972; Sngof roh sn Goffog, saxophone and piano,, 1972; Gravadante, 3 clarinets, 1973; Mixed media: Circus caricatures, piano and dancers, 1946; Serpents-soldiers, flute, double bass, dancers, 1969; Fors a tré, tape and 2 horns, 1969; 9x2 and 6x2, tape, 1972; To beat or not to beat, tape, visuals, dancer, 1972-73; Reflections on void's progeny, tape, speaker, visuals, brass, projectionist, dancer, 1972-73; choral works, organ, piano pieces, songs.
P. O. Box 615, Dubuque, IA 52001

CLEMAN, THOMAS J.
b. Ellensburg, Wash., 5 Jan. 1941. Attended Whitman Coll., B. A.; Univ. of California, Berkeley, M. A.; Stanford Univ., D. M. A.; studied composition with William Bailey, Charles Cushing, Arnold Elston, Seymour Shifrin, David Lewin, Marius Constant, Leland Smith. He was Regents fellow in music, 1963-64, Univ. of California; post-doctoral teaching and research fellow in composition, Macalester Coll., 1968-69; assistant professor of humanities, Northern Arizona Univ., 1969-   . He is also editor of the Newsletter, American Society of University Composers, and founder and codirector, Northern Arizona Society for Contemporary Music.
WORKS: Orchestra: Music for large orchestra; Shine perishing republic, 1969; 13 at dinner, 1969; Chamber music: Variations, piano, 4 hands, 1965; Words for the wind, baritone and chamber ensemble; Music for percussion, 1967; wind quintet, 1969; Music for multiple celli and piano, 1971; Io and the ox eye daisy, voice, tamtam, harp, 1972; Film: music for 2 educational films on the Navajo and the Hopi, 1972.
409 West Havasupai Road, Flagstaff, AZ 86001

CLEMENTS, OTIS

CLEMENTS, OTIS
  b. Baltimore, Md., 5 July 1928. Studied at
Peabody Cons., composition with Nicholas Nabokov
and Theodore Chanler, theory with Renee Longy,
piano with Pasquale Tallarico; at Juilliard
School with Bernard Wagenaar. His Suite in miniature was performed by the National Symphony
Orch. in 1947, and Gala day overture, in 1949 by
the Juilliard Orchestra. He then turned to composing and arranging scores for television and
for popular recording artists. In 1970 he composed and arranged the film score for School
play, an entrant in the New Directors' division
of the Cannes Festival.
  301 East 22nd St., New York, NY 10010

*CLIFTON, CHALMERS
  b. Jackson, Miss., 30 Apr. 1889; d. New York,
19 June 1966. Studied at Cincinnati Cons.;
Harvard Univ.; and with Vincent d'Indy and
Andre Gèdalge in Paris. He was conductor of the
St. Cecilia Society, Boston, 1915-17; American
Orchestra Society, New York, 1922-30; guest con-
ductor of many major orchestras and the San Carlo
Opera Company.
  WORKS: Orchestra: The poppy, tenor and
orch.; Suite for trumpet and orch.; Chamber mu-
sic: violin sonata; 2 piano sonatas; piano pieces.

*CLOKEY, JOSEPH WADDELL
  b. New Albany, Ind., 28 Aug. 1890; d. Covina,
Calif., 14 Sep. 1961. Studied at Miami Univ.,
Oxford, Ohio, B. A. 1912; and at Cincinnati Cons.
He taught at Pomona Coll., 1926-39; at Miami
Univ., 1915-26, dean, School of Fine Arts,
1939-46. His works include 3 operas, a music
drama, orchestral works, chamber music, choral
works, songs, organ pieces.

*CLOUGH-LEITER, HENRY
  b. Washington, D.C., 13 May 1874; d. Wollaston,
Mass., 15 Sep. 1956. Attended George Washington
Univ. (then Columbian Univ.), 1887-89; then went
to Trinity Univ., Toronto, for a musical degree.
He was organist in Washington from age 15, later
in Providence, R. I.; was editor-in-chief,
E. C. Schirmer, Inc., Boston, 1921-56.
  WORKS: Orchestra: Lasca, tenor and orch.;
The Christ of the Andes, double chorus, soli,
orch.; Cantatas: The righteous branch; Christ
triumphant; Chamber music: A day of beauty,
string quintet; some 200 songs.

*COATES, GLORIA KANNENBERG
  b. Wausau, Wis., 10 Oct. 1938. Studied with
Alexander Tcherepnin, Mozarteum, Salzburg, 1962;
with Helen Gunderson and Kenneth Klaus, Louisiana
State Univ., B. M. 1963, M. M. 1965; with Jack
Beeson and Otto Luening, Columbia Univ., 1966-68.
She received Alice M. Ditson grants, 1973, 1974.
She conducted a daily television program in Baton
Rouge, 1961-62; was music critic, Baton Rouge
State Times, 1962-65; director of music, German-
American Contemporary Music Series, Munich Ameri-
can House, 1971-73; director, Music Today,
Lenbach Gallery, Munich, 1973-74; director, Eve-
ning Concert, Munich American House, 1974-   .

(COATES, GLORIA KANNENBERG)
  WORKS: Chamber music: Counterpoint counter,
chamber ensemble; Structures, piano; Trio for 3
flutes; Fantasy on How lovely shines the morningstar, viola and organ; Voice: Emily
Dickinson songs for soprano; Voices of women in
wartime, cantata for soprano, cello, piano,
timpani.
  Lincolnstrasse 48, 8 Munich 90, Germany

COBB, HAZEL
  b. Groesbeck, Tex., 15 July 1892; d. Dallas,
Tex., 8 Sep. 1973. Attended American Cons.,
B. M. 1922, M. M. 1924. From 1927 she was ac-
tive as composer and private teacher of piano in
Dallas.
  WORKS: Operettas: Daughter of Mohammed;
Lamps trimmed in burning; Chorus: The Mission
bell, cantata; many songs, piano pieces, duets,
etc.

COBINE, ALBERT STEWART
  b. Richmond, Ind., 25 Mar. 1929. Studied composition with Bernard Heiden at Indiana Univ.,
1952-54. He won the Thor Johnson award for a
suite for brass ensemble. He is a free lance
writer-arranger, band leader, and music
contractor.
  WORKS: Band: March, pastoral, and fanfare;
Suite for trumpet and concert band; Variations
on We three kings; Brass ensemble: Vermont
suite; Trilogy for brass; Jazz stage band:
That's the way I feel; Chorus: Bethlehem; Oh
Lord, help us live each day; Snow's a comin';
Tavern of loving people; Song of the earth.
  R. R. 11, Box 85, Bloomington, IN 47401

CODY, ROBERT O.
  b. Biloxi, Miss., 18 Apr. 1928. Studied at
North Texas State Univ., B. M. 1952, with Violet
Archer and Gerhart Dorn; Stanford Univ. with
Leonard Ratner; and at East Texas State Univ.,
Ph. D. 1958, with Louis Angelini. He has re-
ceived many commissions. He was chairman of the
Fine Arts Division and of the Music Department,
Henderson County Junior Coll., 1958-68; and at
Wharton County Junior Coll., 1968-   .
  WORKS: Opera: By His own hand, 1-act opera;
Brass ensemble: Reflections in brass; Chamber
music: Theatre piece for tuba and piano; trumpet
sonata; Chorus: Still moon, mixed chorus and 2
pianos; Songs: spring is like a perhaps hand;
Love is not all; When in the sessions of sweet
silent thought.
  P. O. Box 804, Wharton, TX 77488

COE, KENTON
  b. Tennessee, 12 Nov. 1932. Studied with Quincy
Porter and Paul Hindemith, Yale Univ., B. A.
1953; with Nadia Boulanger, Paris Cons., 1953-56.
He received a composition prize, Fontainebleau
Cons., 1953; French Government grants, 1954, 1955;
MacDowell fellowships, 1960, 1963; commission
from Notre Dame Cathedral, Paris, for a new liturgy service.
  WORKS: Theatre: South, full-length opera,
adapted from play by Julien Green, first performance by Opera of Marseilles, 14 Oct. 1965;

(COE, KENTON)
Le grand siecle, text by Ionesco, 1-act opera, Opera of Nantes, 1972; The white devil, opera, after play by John Webster; Rachel, opera commissioned by Tenn. Arts Commission and Tenn. Performing Arts Found. for U.S. Bicentennial celebration and the opening of the Tenn. Cultural Center Opera House, Nashville, 1976; libretto by Anne Howard Bailey; Birds in Peru, film score, 1968.
    1309 Lynnwood Drive
    Johnson City, TN 37601

*COERNE, LOUIS ADOLPHE
    b. Newark, N. J., 27 Feb. 1870; d. Boston, Mass., 11 Sep. 1922. Studied with John Knowles Paine, Harvard Univ., B. A. 1890, Ph D., 1905; with Josef Rheinberger in Munich. He was instructor at Harvard and at Smith Coll.; director, School of Music, Univ. of Wisconsin; from 1915, professor, Connecticut Coll. His works include 4 operas, a music drama, ballet, numerous works for orchestra, chamber music, choral works, etc.

COGAN, ROBERT DAVID
    b. Detroit, Mich., 2 Feb. 1930. Attended Univ. of Michigan, M. M. 1952; Princeton Univ., M. F. A. 1956, Phi Beta Kappa; his principal teachers were Ross Lee Finney, Nadia Boulanger, Aaron Copland, Roger Sessions, Philipp Jarnach. His honors include Young Composers' Radio Award, 1952; Fulbright grants, 1952-53; Chopin scholarship, 1954; German Government grant, 1958-60; 5 MacDowell fellowships; Guggenheim fellowships, 1968-69. His works have been performed throughout the U.S. and by the Hamburg Radio Orch. and RIAS Orch., Berlin. He has been chairman of graduate theoretical studies, New England Cons., 1963-   .
    WORKS: Orchestra: Fantasia, 1951; incidental music to Brecht's A man equals a man, Ann Arbor, Feb. 1952; Chamber music: string quartet, 1950; Songs on texts by Ezra Pound, 1952-54; viola sonata, 1953; 2 string trios, 1955, 1959; Sounds and variants for piano, 1961; Spaces and cries, 5 brasses, 1964; Mixed media: Whirl...ds I, voice, 44 instruments, microphonist, text by composer, Boston, 13 Dec. 1967; Whirl...ds II, 2 solo voices (or chorus) transmute vocal sounds by cupping glass jars, metal cans, round cardboard boxes, or bull horns over their mouths; text is a collage of extracts from Hopkins, Rilke, John Howard Griffin, and Oscar Lewis. He is co-author with his wife, Pozzi Escot, of Sonic design: The nature of sound and music.
    24 Avon Hill St., Cambridge, MA 02140

COGGIN, C. ELWOOD
    b. North Carolina, 13 Nov. 1914. Attended Campbell Coll. and Southern Baptist Theological Seminary. He has held posts as minister of music in Louisville, Ky., 1954-56; Walterboro, S. C., 1956-65; and Charlotte, N. C., 1965-73. He has published more than 230 sacred anthems, and also wrote a short cantata, Let us go on, for the Bicentennial celebration of Charlotte-Mecklenburg independence in 1968.
    112 Oakridge Drive, Charlotte, NC 28216

COHEN, DAVID
    b. Pulaski, Tenn., 14 Oct. 1927. Studied with Vincent Persichetti at Philadelphia Cons. and Juilliard School; and with Ingolf Dahl at Univ. of Southern California. He received the Coolidge Chamber Music Prize at Juilliard, 1952; Fulbright scholarship, 1953; IBM Graduate Research grant, 1965; and commissions. He was on the faculty, Univ. of Alabama, 1955-67; and has been associate professor, Arizona State Univ., 1967-   .
    WORKS: Orchestra: Symphony No. 2, 1970; Chamber music: woodwind quintet, 1952; piano sonata, 1955; piano trio, 1960; Divertimento for 4 flutes, 1967; Chorus: Four seasons, 1965; La maison construite par Jean, chorus and small orch., 1971; Electronic: Sound image I for recorded synthesizer, 1971.
    1045 East Loyola Drive, Tempe, AZ 85282

*COHEN, EDWARD
    b. 1940. Studied with Seymour Shifrin and Luigi Dallapiccola, Univ. of California, Berkeley; with Max Deutsch in Paris on a George Ladd traveling fellowship from Univ. of California. His Nocturne for orchestra was performed in Boston, 11 May 1973.
    Music Department, Brandeis University
    Waltham, MA 02154

COHEN, JEROME D.
    b. Spokane, Wash., 6 Feb. 1936. Studied with Jean Sharp, Eastern Washington State Coll.; and with Francis Judd Cooke, New England Cons., B. M. 1959, M. M. 1963; also studied conducting at Tanglewood and privately with Richard Burgin. He has received many commissions. He has played cello, double bass, and bassoon in orchestras since 1948; has taught in public and private schools and conducted community orchestras in New England and Spokane; was guest conductor of Boston Pops, 1959, 1972, 1973; was on managerial staff, New England Cons., 1966-73; and has been conductor, Cape Cod Symphony, 1971-   .
    WORKS: Orchestra: Concert overture #1, Boston Pops, 1959; Cape Ann, Concert overture #2, Boston Pops, 1973; Beyond mind and speech, elegiac fugue, 1973; Old folks quadrille, on Stephen Foster themes, 1971; Songs: Preludes, by T. S. Eliot, 4 songs for tenor and piano, 1958-72.
    12 Pat Road, Hanover, MA 02339

COHEN, JOSEPH M.
    b. New York, N. Y., 3 Aug. 1917. Studied with Ralph Guenther, Texas Christian Univ., B. M., M. M.; with Bernard Rogers, Howard Hanson, and Wayne Barlow, Eastman School of Music. He received 3 ASCAP awards, and 2 first prize awards in the Wisconsin Music Club competition, 1969. He has been professor, St. Norbert Coll., 1963-   .
    WORKS: Opera: Christmas carol; Ballet: Rhapsody for three; Orchestra: Concert piece; symphony; concertino for violin; Band: concerto for piano and concert band; Poem; Chorus: David and Goliath, an oratorio; There is no God.
    1374 Skylark Lane, Green Bay, WI 54303

COHEN, MICHAEL

*COHEN, MICHAEL
If I should learn, chorus on text by Millay.

*COHEN, SOL B. (pen name of VANEUF, ANDRE)
b. Urbana, Ill., 11 Jan. 1891. Studied at Chicago Musical Coll.; also in Paris and Budapest. He wrote and arranged film scores; was music director, Ruth St. Denis-Ted Shawn Ballet; conductor, Peoria Symphony; taught in various schools, 1944-62. He has written works for orchestra, for woodwind and brass instruments, and songs.
    1609 North Normandie Ave.
    Hollywood, CA 90028

COHN, ARTHUR
b. Philadelphia, Pa., 6 Nov. 1910. Studied at Combs Cons. with William Happich; Juilliard School with Rubin Goldmark, 1933-34. He held a fellowship for his study at Juilliard and a scholarship for study at Univ. of Pennsylvania. He won first prize in a contest of the American Society of Ancient Instruments, 1939; a prize in a Nat. Symphony Orchestra contest, 1956; and many ASCAP awards. He was curator, Fleisher Music Collection, Free Library of Philadelphia, 1934-52; head of classical music department, Mills Music, Inc., 1955-65; MCA Music, 1966-73; and Carl Fischer, Inc., 1973-   .
    WORKS: Orchestra: Kaddish for orchestra; Four symphonic documents; Four nature studies; Histrionics for string orch.; flute concerto; Quintuple concerto; Chamber music: 5 string quartets; violin sonata; viola suite; violin suite; music for ancient instruments; music for brass instruments; music for solo bassoon. He is author of two books; The collector's twentieth-century music in the Western Hemisphere, 1961, and Twentieth-century music in Western Europe, 1965.
    200 West 86th St., New York, NY 10024

COHN, JAMES
b. Newark, N. J., 28 Feb. 1928. Studied with Wayne Barlow at Eastman School of Music; with Roy Harris at Cornell Univ.; and with Bernard Wagenaar at Juilliard School, B. S. 1949, M. S. 1950. His awards include Nat. Fed. of Music Clubs prize for a violin sonata and piano variations, 1944; Queen Elizabeth of Belgium prize for Symphony No. 2. 1953; Ohio Univ. award for 1-act opera, The fall of the city, 1955; and an award in Florence, Italy, for his Symphony No. 4, 1960. The Detroit Symphony premiered his 3rd symphony in 1959, and Variations on The wayfaring stranger in 1962. He has been musicologist at ASCAP since 1952.
    WORKS: 1 opera, several ballets, 7 symphonies, 2 secular cantatas, 3 string quartets, many short choral works, and many sonatas.
    1125 Lexington Ave., New York, NY 10021

*COHN, JOHN
Statues in the park, chorus on text of Felicia Lamport.

COKE-JEPHCOTT, NORMAN
b. Coventry, England, 17 Mar. 1893; d. New York, N. Y., 14 Mar. 1962; to U.S. 1911. Studied with the organist of Trinity Church, Coventry, and became a fellow of the Royal College of Organists at age 18, and of the American Guild of Organists a year later. In the 1920s he studied with Paul Vidal and Charles-Marie Widor in Fontainebleau. He was an honorary fellow Royal Canadian Coll. of Organists, and of Trinity Coll. of Music, London; received an honorary doctorate from Ripon Coll. He was organist and choirmaster, Cathedral of St. John the Divine, New York, 1932-53.
    WORKS: Anthems: O love that casts out fear; Surely the Lord is in this place; The gate of the year; Variants for St. Anne; Mass of St. John the Divine; Organ: Fugue on BACH; The glory of the Lord; Symphonic toccata; Miniature trilogy; Bishop's promenade; Terzetto; and many more sacred works for choir and organ.

COKER, WILSON
b. Pinckneyville, Ill., 26 Nov. 1928. Studied at St. Louis Inst. of Music, B. M. 1949; Yale Univ., B. M. 1951, M. M. 1954; Univ. of Illinois, D. M. A. 1965; and at Tanglewood with Milton Babbitt and Aaron Copland. He received the John Day Jackson prize, 1954; Koussevitzky prize, 1959; and Society for Publication of American Music award, 1963. He was on the faculty, Hartwick Coll., 1958-60; composer-in-residence, School District of Philadelphia on a MENC-Ford Found. grant, 1960-63; staff at Lincoln Center, 1962-64; associate professor, San Jose State Coll., 1964-68; professor and chairman, Department of Music, Fresno State Coll., 1968-   .
    WORKS: Orchestra: Orestes, ballet music, 1953; symphony, 1957; Overture giocoso, 1961; Recitative and canzona, for trombone and orch.; Lyric statement, 1967; Declarative essay, 1970; Band: concerto for trombone and band, 1961; With bugle, fife, and drum, 1963; Polyphonic ode, 1969; Chamber music: 2 string quartets, 1949, 1954; string quintet; Concertino for bassoon and string trio, 1964; woodwind quintet, 1964; trio for 3 clarinets; Chorus: The dark hills, 1966; Paean, chorus and large orchestra, 1966. He is author of the book: Music and meaning, 1971.
    1619 West Robinwood Lane, Fresno, CA 93705

*COLBURN, GEORGE
b. Colton, N. Y., 25 Sep. 1878; d. Chicago, Ill., 18 Apr. 1921. Studied at American Cons. and later taught there. He wrote incidental music for several plays, orchestral works, chamber music.

*COLE, GEORGE
Maelstrom, band; 7 impressions, brass quartet.

COLE, GERALD E.
b. Topeka, Kan., 29 Aug. 1917. Studied at Univ. of Kansas with Laurel Anderson; Oberlin Cons. with Normand Lockwood; and Eastman School of Music with Wayne Barlow. He was head of the Music Department, Tarkio Coll., 1940-44; professor, Phillips Univ. 1944-49; lecturer, Univ. of

(COLE, GERALD E.)
Western Ontario, 1951-55; head, Department of Music, Western Maryland Coll., 1955- .
WORKS: His compositions include a string quartet, pieces for varied chamber ensembles, harp pieces, organ pieces, a 2-piano sonata, piano pieces, a Mass, motets, songs.
Western Maryland College
Westminster, MD 21157

COLE, ULRIC
b. New York, N. Y., 9 Sep. 1905. Studied in Los Angeles with Homer Grunn, 1913-23; Inst. of Musical Art, New York, with Percy Goetschius; and on fellowships at Juilliard Graduate School, 1924-27, 1930-32, with Rubin Goldmark and Joseph Lhevinne; in Paris with Nadia Boulanger. She received two awards from the Society for Publication of American Music, 1931, 1941. As a pianist she toured the U.S. and appeared as soloist with major orchestras; she taught at Masters School, Dobbs Ferry, N. Y., 1936-42; was on staff, New York Philharmonic Young People's Concerts, 1943-45; on editorial staff Time Magazine, 8 years.
WORKS: Orchestra: Divertimento, piano and string orch., Cincinnati Symph. Orch., composer at piano, 31 Mar. 1939; 2nd piano concerto, Cincinnati, composer as soloist, 1 Mar. 1946; Nevada, Sunlight channel, 2 pieces for string orch.; Chamber music: 2 string quartets; 2 violin sonatas, 1931; quintet for piano and strings, 1941; Piano: Above the clouds, 1924; The prairie hobgoblins, 1925; 6 Tunes and sketches in black and white, 1927; Purple shadows, 1928; 3 Vignettes, 1937; 3 Metropolitones, 1941; Fantasy sonata; Man-about-town, 2 pianos, 1942; Tschaikowski Valse, 2 pianos, 1943.
Box 284, Southport, CT 06490

COLE, VINCENT L.
b. Los Angeles, Calif., 19 July 1946. Studied at Univ. of California, Los Angeles, 1968-69, with Henri Lazarof; and at California State Univ., Northridge, 1971-73, with Aurelio de la Vega. In 1973 he was assistant, Electronic Music Laboratory, California State Univ. Northridge.
WORKS: String quartet, 1971; Concrete study, 2-channel tape, 1971; Music for oboe and tape, 1973.
19136 Sherman Way, #C, Reseda, CA 91335

COLEMAN, HENRY, JR.
b. Pensacola, Fla., 1 Sep. 1938. Studied orchestration with Joseph Wagner and composition with Aurelio de la Vega. He was instructor, California State Univ., Northridge, 1971-72.
WORKS: Chamber music: Esoterics for string quartet; Reality sandwiches, soprano and chamber ensemble; Dimentions, [sic] 4 trombones; Sonare, for brass nonette; 3 Klee impressions, chamber ensemble; Metallics, for prepared piano, 4 tympani, percussion.
12953 South Catalina, Gardena, CA 90249

*COLEMAN, ORNETTE
b. Ft. Worth, Tex., 19 Mar. 1930. Studied at the School of Jazz, Lenox, Mass. He received

(COLEMAN, ORNETTE)
a Guggenheim fellowship, 1963. He is principally a saxophonist, but also plays trumpet and violin.
WORKS: Concert jazz: Forms and sounds; Saints and sinners; Space flight; quintet for trumpet and strings, New York, 2 Oct. 1971; Joujouka, New York, 21 Apr. 1974.
131 Prince St., New York, NY 10012

COLEMAN, RANDOLPH E.
b. Charlottesville, Va., 20 July 1937. Studied at Northwestern Univ. with Anthony Donato. He received the William Faricy award, 1960; Internat. Society for Contemporary Music awards, 1962-63; Fromm Found. grant, 1964. He was assistant professor, Winthrop Coll., 1963-65; and has been associate professor, Oberlin Cons., 1965- .
WORKS: Orchestra: Soundprint I, 1971; Chamber music: Soundprint II, 4 pianos, 1972; Soundprint III, percussion players and readers, 1972; string quartet, 1973; Undesignated: Format I, 1971; Format II, 1971; Event I, 1971; Mixed media: Format III, musicians, dancers, and lights, 1973.
39 West Vine St., Oberlin, OH 44074

*COLF, DORRITT LICHT
3 pieces for 2 flutes.

*COLGRASS, MICHAEL
b. Chicago, Ill., 22 Apr. 1932. Studied with Paul Price and Eugene Weigel, Univ. of Illinois, B. M. 1956; with Lukas Foss and Darius Milhaud at Tanglewood; also with Ben Weber and Wallingford Riegger. His awards include 2 Tanglewood scholarships, 1952, 1953; 2 Guggenheim fellowships, 1964, 1968; Fromm Found. award; Rockefeller grant for study of theatre arts at Piccolo Teatro di Milano, and for study of advanced physical training for actors at the Polish Theatre Laboratory. As a free-lance percussionist he has played with the New York Philharmonic Modern Jazz Quartet, in pit orchestras for West Side Story, Bolshoi Ballet, etc. He also conducts clinics in composing, singing, acting, and dancing.
WORKS: Orchestra: Divertimento, 8 drums, piano, strings, 1960; Rhapsodic fantasy, 15 drums and orch., 1965, New York premiere, 11 May 1974; Sea shadows, 1966; As quiet as, Tanglewood, 18 Aug. 1966; Concertino for timpani; Earth's a baked apple, chorus and orch., 1968; Virgil's dream, narrator and orch., Boston, 1969; Chamber music: Percussion music, 1953; 3 brothers, percussion; Chamber music, 4 drums and string quartet, 1954; Variations, 4 drums and viola, 1956; Fantasy variations for percussion, 1961; Rhapsody, clarinet, violin, piano, 1962; Light spirit, flute, viola, guitar, percussion, 1963; New people, mezzo-soprano, viola, piano, 1969.
c/o MCA, 445 Park Ave., New York, NY 10022

COLLER, JEROME THOMAS
b. St. Paul, Minn., 6 Feb. 1929. Studied at Univ. of Minnesota, B. A. 1949, M. A. 1954, with Donald Ferguson, Paul Fetler, James Aliferis,

COLLER, JEROME THOMAS

(COLLER, JEROME THOMAS)
Paul Christianson, Elie Siegmeister; Cornell Univ., D. M. A. 1971, with Robert Palmer, Karel Husa, Elliott Carter, Hall Overton. He has been assistant professor, St. John's Univ., College-ville, Minn., 1971-   , and chairman of the music department, 1973-   .
WORKS: His compositions are mainly church music, but he has also written concerto for piano and winds, doctoral thesis, Cornell 1971; clari-net sonata; 6 piano preludes, Firmator sancte, organ suite, etc.
St. John's Abbey, Collegeville, MN 56321

*COLLETTE, WILLIAM MARCELL (BUDDY)
b. Los Angeles, Calif., 6 Aug. 1921. Studied with Ernest Kanitz in Los Angeles. He has played flute with many jazz bands and with the Los Angeles Neophonic Orchestra.
WORKS: Jazz: Blue sands; Santa Monica; and film scores.

COLLINS, THOMAS W.
b. Dayton, Ohio, 5 Jan. 1935. Studied at Miami Univ., Oxford, Ohio, with Eugene Hill; Univ. of Missouri, Kansas City, with David Gordon. He won first prize in a Miami Univ. composition contest, 1956. His faculty positions have been at Tabor Coll., 1959-67; and School of the Ozarks, 1967-   .
WORKS: Chamber music: string quartet and other chamber works; Voice: Chapel windows, cantata, 1969; Three songs, high voice and piano, 1967; Two songs, high voice and oboe, 1969; numerous short works for organ.
School of the Ozarks
Point Lookout, MO 65726

COLSON, WILLIAM
b. Kansas City, Mo., 17 July 1945. Studied at Oberlin Cons. with Walter Aschaffenburg and Richard Hoffman; Univ. of Illinois with Gordon Binkerd and Robert Kelly. He won first prize and the Devora Nadworney award, Nat. Fed. of Music Clubs contest, 1965; and in a concerto competi-tion, Univ. of Illinois, 1968. He has been assistant professor, Southwestern Baptist Theo-logical Seminary, 1971-   .
WORKS: Orchestra: My last duchess, baritone and orch.; Three Blake songs, soprano and orch., 1968; Chamber music: 3 songs from A Shropshire lad, by A. E. Housman, 1965; Six variations and a fugue, 10 instruments; Three short pieces, vio-lin and piano.
554 South Summit, #418, Fort Worth, TX 76104

COMBS, F. MICHAEL
b. Hazard, Ky., 30 May 1943. Studied at Univ. of Illinois, B. S.; Univ. of Missouri, M. A., with Jack McKenzie, Albert Payson, and Thomas Siwe. He is assistant professor, Univ. of Tennessee, Knoxville.
WORKS: Percussion: Concert snare drum solos, 1968; Gesture, for solo percussionist, 1969; Mano dance, 1971; Leatherwood, 1971
Music Department, University of Tennessee
Knoxville, TN 37916

*COMBS, RONALD
The 3 wishes, 1-act children's opera, Northwest-ern Univ., 30 Apr. 1968; The monkey's paw, 1-act opera, Univ. of Wisconsin, Stevens Point, Feb. 1974.

CONE, EDWARD T.
b. Greensboro, N. C., 4 May 1917. Studied at Princeton Univ., A. B. 1939, M. F. A. 1942, with Roger Sessions; also studied piano with K. U. Schnabel and E. Steuermann. He held a Guggenheim fellowship, 1947-48, and was Ernest Bloch lec-turer, Univ. of California, 1972. He has been on the faculty at Princeton Univ. since 1947, pro-fessor, 1960-   .
WORKS: Orchestra: symphony; piano concerto; violin concerto; Chamber music: 2 string quar-tets; 2 violin sonatas; Rhapsody, viola and piano; clarinet quintet, 1941; piano pieces; Voice: The lotus eaters, cantata, 1939-47; Excursion, chorus, 1955; Silent noon, soprano and piano, 1964.
18 College Road West, Princeton, NJ 08540

*CONFREY, EDWARD E. (ZEZ)
b. Peru, Ill., 3 Apr. 1895; d. Lakewood, N. J., 22 Nov. 1971. Studied at Chicago Musical Coll. He played with Jack Benny and with Paul Whiteman. His most popular piano works included: Kitten on the keys, 1921; Stumbling, 1921; Dizzy fingers, 1923; 3 little oddities; Valse mirage; Grand-father's clock; Sittin' on a log; Concert etude, etc. He also wrote a miniature opera, Thanksgiving.

CONLEY, DAVID
b. Gorgas, Ala., 15 Oct. 1930. Studied at North Texas State Univ. with Samuel Adler and William Latham; Eastman School of Music with Samuel Adler. He received a commission from Sigma Alpha Iota Alumni Chapter, Fort Worth, 1970. He has been associate professor, Southwestern Baptist Theological Seminary, 1959-   .
WORKS: Orchestra: Introduction, 1967; Piece for string orch., 1968; Fugal hexagon, 1971; Pieces for woodwind ensemble, 1967, 1968; Piece for brass and percussion, 1968; Chamber music: Piano piece, 1959; Duo for violin and viola, 1960; Trio for 2 violins and cello, 1964; wood-wind quartet, 1965; 12 short studies for horn, 1967; Short piece for harp, 1968; Short and suite, flute, violin, piano, 1970; Chorus: Cool tombs, Sandberg text, 1960; Crucifixion, 1961; Let all the earth fear the Lord, men's voices, 1964; Rejoice in the Lord, 1964; All revelation, women's voices, Frost text, 1970; Songs: Glass house canticle, medium voice, Sandburg text, 1970; Slaves, medium voice, James Russell Lowell text, 1970; church service music, etc.
5204 Garrick Ave., Fort Worth, TX 76133

CONLEY, JOHN
b. Prestonsburg, Ky., 25 June 1934. Studied at Cincinnati Cons. with William Naylor, Univ. of Kentucky with Kenneth Wright, Gordon Kinney, R. Bernard Fitzgerald. He won a cash award for the official AFROTC march, Ad astra, at Univ. of Kentucky. He taught at Midway Jr. Coll.,

(CONLEY, JOHN)
1961-62; Gunnison High School, Colo., 1962-63;
Fayette County Schools, Lexington, Ky, 1963-   .
    WORKS: Theatre: The legend of Daniel Boone,
background score, 1971; Orchestra: Suite, 1962;
Intermezzo; Chamber music: Dorian piece for oboe
and string quartet, 1961; 3 early sacred pieces
for brass quartet, 1964; Retrospection, piano,
1960.
    2131 Jasmine Drive, Lexington, KY 40504

CONLEY, LLOYD
b. Rogers City, Mich., 8 Mar. 1924. Studied at
Central Michigan Univ. and Michigan State Univ.
He won the Kansas Centennial composition award
in 1961 for Kansas suite for band. He has been
a teacher in public schools 1950-
    WORKS: Many works for orchestra, band,
stage band, solo instruments, ensemble, and
voice. Band: Tawas suite; Quiet valley; A symphonic invention.
    318 East 7th St., Clare, MI 48617

CONRAD, TONY
b. Concord, N. H., 7 Mar. 1940. Studied at Peabody Cons., at Harvard Coll., and privately with
Ronald Knudsen. He has received a Rockefeller
Found. grant for research and production in film,
composition and performance; and a Cassandra
Found. grant. In 1963-66, he was composer-
performer with The Theater of Eternal Music.
    WORKS: Fugue for strings, 1961; Three loops
for performers and tape recorders, Cambridge,
Mass., 1961; The tortoise, his dreams and journeys, a cooperative piece with 7 accomplices,
1963; Emergency landing, 1970; Outside the dream
syndicate, 1972; with Faust, 1972; for piano,
1974; Film scores: Flaming creatures (with Jack
Smith), 1963; The flicker, 1965; Coming attrac-
tions, with 6 others, 1970; Ten years alive on
the infinite plain, 1972.
    111 West 42nd St., New York, NY 10036

CONSOLI, MARC-ANTONIO
b. Italy, 19 May 1941, U.S. citizen 1967.
Attended New York Coll. of Music, B. M.; Peabody Cons., M. M.; Yale Univ., M. M. A. 1971;
and studied with Paul Creston, Ernst Krenek,
Hall Overton, Alexander Goehr, Gunther Schuller,
George Crumb. He received 2 Rockefeller grants;
2 Tanglewood fellowships, 1968-70; Fulbright
grant to Poland; Guggenheim grant. He taught
part-time at Univ. of Bridgeport in 1971.
    WORKS: Orchestra: Variants, Baltimore,
1 June 1968; Profiles, 1972-73; Chamber music:
Equinox I, soprano and chamber ensemble, Baltimore, 23 May 1967; Equinox II, soprano and chamber ensemble, Tanglewood, 14 Aug. 1968; Trigram
I, violin, viola, cello, double bass, solo
strings or groups, Bennington, 16 Aug. 1969;
Dialogues, double bass and string orch., 1969;
Isonic I, soprano and ensemble, Graz, Austria,
26 Oct. 1970; Pezzo, piano, Yale Univ., 13 Feb.
1971; Interactions I, 7 winds and timpani,
Tanglewood, 12 Aug. 1970; Interactions II, violin, cello, piano, Univ. of Maryland, 21 Mar.
1971; Interactions III, flute and harp, Yale
Univ. 28 Apr. 1971; Interactions IV, winds,

(CONSOLI, MARC-ANTONIO)
double bass, percussion, Yale Univ., 12 Dec.
1971; Formations, harp, 1972; Chorus: Lux
aeterna, 8-part chorus, 1972.
    95-27 239th St., Bellerose, NY 11426

CONSTANTINIDES, CONSTANTINE DINOS
b. Ioannini, Greece, 10 May 1929; U.S. citizen
1967. Studied at Greek Cons., dip. in theory
and violin; Indiana Univ., M. M., violin with
J. Gingold; Juilliard School, violin with I.
Galamian; Michigan State Univ., Ph. D., composition with H. Owen Reed. His awards include MTNA
teaching award, 1970; Louisiana State Univ.
faculty award, 1971; Outstanding Educators of
America, 1971, 1972, 1973. He was violinist
with the Athens State Symphony, 1952-57; Athens
Radio Symphony, 1961-63; Indianapolis Symphony,
1963-65; concertmaster, Baton Rouge Symphony,
1966-   , and Beaumont Civic Opera, 1967-   ;
associate professor, Louisiana State Univ.,
1966-   .
    WORKS: Theatre: Antigone, music drama on
text by Sophocles, 1973; Orchestra: symphony,
1966; concerto for violin, cello and piano,
1968; Chamber music: string quartet, 1966; trio,
1967; Improvisation, trombone and piano, 1967;
Sappho songs, 1969; 20th century studies, 2 violins, 1970; viola sonata, 1972; Exploding parallels, 1972; Theme and variations, piano, 1973;
sonata for solo violin; Designs for strings; 2
pieces for percussion quartet.
    947 Daventry Drive, Baton Rouge, LA 70808

*CONVERSE, FREDERICK SHEPHERD
b. Newton, Mass. 5 Jan. 1871; d. Westwood, Mass.,
8 June, 1940. Studied with John Knowles Paine,
Harvard Univ., B. A. 1893; with George W.
Chadwick, New England Cons.; and with Josef
Rheinberger in Munich. His awards included the
Bispham Medal, 1909; honorary music doctorate,
Boston Univ., 1933; election to membership,
American Acad. of Arts and Letters, 1937. He
taught at Harvard, 1901-07; was vice president,
Boston Opera Company, 1911-14; served in U.S.
Army, 1917-19; taught at New England Cons.,
1930-38.
    WORKS: Opera: The pipe of desire, 1906, the
first American opera to be performed at the Metropolitan Opera in New York, 18 Mar. 1909; Orchestra: 6 symphonies; Youth; Euphrosyne;
Festival of Pan; The mystic trumpeter; The sacrifice; The immigrants; Sinbad the sailor; Flivver
ten million; many other orchestral works and
works for chorus and orch.; Chamber music: 3
string quartets; violin sonata; cello sonata;
piano trio; piano pieces; songs.

*COOK, JOHN
Organ: Divinum mysterium; Fanfare; Flourish and
fugue; Scherzo, dance and reflection; Christ is
our cornerstone.
    Massachusetts Institute of Technology
    Cambridge, MA 02139

COOK, PETER FRANCIS, III
b. Morristown, N. J., 1 Sep. 1923. Studied at
Oberlin Cons., B. M. 1946, M. M. 1950; Tanglewood;

COOK, PETER FRANCIS, III

(COOK, PETER FRANCIS, III)
Aspen School; American School, Fontainebleau;
Peabody Cons., doctoral study, 1973. His teachers have included Herbert Elwell, Irving Fine,
Jacque Ibert, Darius Milhaud, Nadia Boulanger,
Louis Cheslock, Charles Haubiel. He held a
Victor RCA scholarship to Tanglewood. He has
been on the faculty at Florida State Univ.,
1946-47; Mason Coll., Charleston, W. Va.,
1955-56; Austin Peay State Univ., 1956-73.
WORKS: Orchestra: River boat fancy, piano
and orch.; Chamber music: Dialogue, flute and
piano; Forlana, piano; Loredo variations, piano;
and many published piano pieces.
21 River Road, Denville, NJ 07834

COOK, RICHARD G.
b. Dallas, Tex., 20 Oct. 1929. Studied at Texas
Christian Univ. with Ralph Guenther, and at North
Texas State Univ. with Samuel Adler. He received
grants of the Rockefeller Found. for performance
and recording of two works by the Dallas Symphony.
He taught at Handley High School, 1957-61; Univ.
of Texas, Arlington, 1962-63; and at Kansas State
Coll., Pittsburgh, 1966-   .
WORKS: Orchestra: 2 symphonies; Concertino
for orchestra; Chamber music: Three songs of
hopelessness, soprano and piano, 1963; string
quartet, 1972; woodwind quartet; brass sextet;
violin sonata; Concert piece, trumpet and piano;
sonata for unaccompanied clarinet; Chorus:
Psalm 137; Mixed media: Concert etude, bassoon,
piano, and tape; The hydrogen dog and the cobalt
cat, soprano and Moog tape, 1972; Requiem for
Mahalia, viola, piano, Moog tape, 1972; 2 suites
for Moog synthesizer; many pieces for Moog alone
or with other instruments.
402 West First, Pittsburgh, KS 66762

*COOKE, JAMES FRANCIS
b. Bay City, Mich., 14 Nov. 1875; d. Philadelphia, Pa., 3 Mar. 1960. Was president of
Theodore Presser Company, 1925-36; of John Church
Company, 1930-36; editor of the Etude for 40
years; wrote articles on music and several books
on performance techniques, great composers, etc.
His compositions were written for piano.

*COOLEY, CARLETON
b. 1898. Studied at the Philadelphia Cons.
and at Inst. of Musical Art., New York. He received an honorary music doctorate, Philadelphia
Musical Acad., 1945. He played viola many years
with the Cleveland Orchestra; was principal violist, NBC Symphony for 17 years; and with the
Philadelphia Orchestra; also played with the
Cleveland String Quartet and the NBC String Quartet. He joined the viola faculty at Peabody
Cons., 1970. His published works include Aria
and dance, viola and orch.; Concertino for viola
and piano; Etude suite, unaccompanied viola.

COOLIDGE, PEGGY STUART
b. Swampscott, Mass., 19 July   . Studied
with Quincy Porter, Heinrich Gebhard, and Raymond
Robinson. She received a Medal of the Central
House of Workers in Art, USSR; Gold medal,
Vincent Club, Boston; Medal of the Metropolitan

(COOLIDGE, PEGGY STUART)
Government of Tokyo; Diploma of Appreciation,
Hungarian Radio Symphony. She was founder and
conductor, Junior League Orchestra, Boston,
1937-42; assistant conductor and pianist, Boston
Women's Symphony.
WORKS: Theatre: incidental music for Red
roses for me by Sean O'Casey; Ballet: An evening in New Orleans; Orchestra: Rhapsody for
harp and orch.; Look to the wind, vocalise with
orch.; many piano pieces and songs; Film score:
The silken affair.
153 East 61st St., New York, NY 10021

*COOLIDGE, RICHARD
Arioso for trombone.

COOPER, DAVID S.
b. Minneapolis, Minn., 3 Oct. 1922. Studied at
Univ. of Virginia with Randall Thompson; Princeton Univ. with Roger Sessions and Oliver Strunk;
Univ. of California with Manfred Bukofzer. He
was cited by Nat. Asso. of American Composers
and Conductors for outstanding service to American music. He was chief, Music Branch, USIA,
1951-59; dean, Peabody Cons., 1959-61; vice president, Associated Music Publishers, 1961-65; executive director, Manhattan School of Music,
1965-69; executive director, American Composers
Alliance, 1969-   .
WORKS: Chorus: Time, women's voices and
piano; Sancta Maria, women's voices a cappella;
Three poems for children, women's voices and
piano; 150th Psalm, mixed chorus, organ, brass,
percussion.
225 Kelburne Ave., North Tarrytown, NY 10591

*COOPER, JOHN
An opera on American colonial days, commissioned
by the Performing Arts Society, White Plains,
N. Y., for the American Bicentennial 1976.

COOPER, PAUL
b. Victoria, Ill., 19 May 1926. Studied at Univ.
of Southern California with Ernest Kanitz,
Halsey Stevens, Roger Sessions; and in Paris with
Nadia Boulanger. He received Fulbright fellowship, 1953; Guggenheim fellowships, 1965, 1972;
Horace H. Rackham research grants in composition,
1959, 1968; Ford Contemporary Music grant, 1967;
4 ASCAP awards; Composer of the Year award,
Music Teachers Nat. Assoc. On the faculty, Univ.
of Michigan, he rose from instructor to professor, 1955-68; he has been composer-in-residence
and head, division of composition, Univ. of
Cincinnati, 1968-   .
WORKS: Orchestra: 4 symphonies; Antiphons,
solo oboe and wind ensemble, Kennedy Center,
Washington, D.C., 16 May 1973; Chamber Music: 5
string quartets; sonatas for piano and various
string and wind instruments; Chorus: Credo,
double chorus and orch.; Cantigas, double chorus
and orch. He is author of a college theory text
Perspectives in music theory, 1973; and of
articles in musical journals.
340 Warren Ave., Cincinnati, OH 45220

COOPER, ROSE MARIE
    b. Cairo, Ill., 21 Feb. 1937. Studied at Oklahoma Baptist Univ., B. M., with Warren Angell; Columbia Univ., M. M., with Henry Cowell. She received 7 ASCAP awards; and Outstanding Young Woman of North Carolina award, 1971. She was on the faculty, Greensboro Coll., 1965-67; and in 1973 was a Ph. D. candidate, Univ. of North Carolina.
    WORKS: Chorus: Lord, speak to me, men's voices; Hymn of truth, 2-part; settings of 5 haiku, mixed chorus; Morning star, cantata; many other choral works and arrangements.
    607 West Greenway North
    Greensboro, NC 27403

COOPER, WILLIAM B.
    b. Philadelphia, Pa., 14 Feb. 1920. Studied at Philadelphia Musical Acad., B. M. 1951, M. M. 1952, with Stefan Wolpe and Julius Hijman; at Union Theological Seminary, School of Sacred Music with Harold Friedell. He was instructor, Bennett Coll., 1951-53; public school teacher, New York, 1958-   ; and minister of music, St. Philip's Church, New York, 1953-74.
    WORKS: Chorus: Beatitudes, 1966; Mass of Thanksgiving, 1968; The canticles, 1972; Psalm 150, 1973; and many choral works for the church service; Organ: Chorale prelude, 1970; Rhapsody on the name, Fela Sowande, commissioned work; Jubilate deo; Bread of Heaven, etc.
    26 Knickerbocker Road, Englewood, NJ 07631

COPE, DAVID
    b. San Francisco, Calif., 17 May 1941. Studied with Grant Fletcher at Arizona State Univ., B. M. 1963; with Ingolf Dahl, George Perle, Halsey Stevens, Univ. of Southern California, M. M. 1965; and privately with I. A. MacKenzie. He received a Univ. of Houston award, 1970; ASCAP awards, 1971, 1972; commissions including MW Ensemble, Poland, 1968; Harvard Univ. Wind Ensemble, 1972; Composers Theatre, 1972. He was faculty member, Kansas State Coll., 1966-68; California Lutheran Coll., 1968-69; Cleveland Inst. of Music, 1970-73; Miami Univ. of Ohio, 1973-
He is editor of Composer magazine, author of articles in Composer and other journals; and author of 2 books: Notes in discontinuum, 1970, and New directions in music, 1971.
    WORKS: Orchestra: Tragic overture, strings, 1962; Contrasts for orchestra, 1967; Music for brass and strings, Univ. of Iowa, May 1971; Variations for piano and wind orch., Moscow, Idaho, 1972; Streams, winds and strings, Harvard Univ., 22 Mar. 1973; Chamber music: 2 string quartets; horn sonata, 1966; 5 pieces for flute, violin, bassoon; Towers, ensemble, 1968; A Christmas for dismas, chorus, 1969; Those years ago cold mornings held no fears, voice; Cycles, flute and double bass, 1969; The birds, ensemble, 1971; Obelisk for percussion; Deadliest angel revision, ensemble, 1971; BTRB, bass trombone, 1971; Angel's camp II, 1971; 3 pieces for clarinet solo, 1972; 3 pieces for bassoon solo, 1972; Probe #3, saxophone and actress, 1972; Margins, percussion, cello, trumpet, piano, New York, May 1972; Vortex, trombone, flute, percussion, piano; Ashes, voice;

(COPE, DAVID)
    Piano: 4 sonatas; Iceberg meadow, prepared piano; Electronic: Weeds; K; Cedar breaks, bass and tape; Bright angel, trumpet and tape; Spirals, tuba and tape.
    607 Brill St., Oxford, OH 54056

*COPES, V. EARLE
    b. 1920. 2 preludes for Holy Week, organ.
    Department of Music
    Birmingham Southern College
    Birmingham, AL 35204

*COPLAND, AARON
    b. Brooklyn, N. Y., 14 Nov. 1900. Studied with Rubin Goldmark in New York; with Nadia Boulanger in Paris, 1921-24. His many awards include the first Guggenheim fellowship to be awarded to a composer, 1925; $5000 RCA Victor award; Pulitzer prize, 1945; New York Music Critics Circle award, 1947; U.S. Government Medal of Freedom, 1964; honorary music doctorate, Princeton Univ., 1956; membership in the Nat. Inst. of Arts and Letters and American Acad. of Arts and Letters; special citation by Who's Who in America, 1972; Brandeis commission award, 1975. He has been lecturer, New School for Social Research; with Roger Sessions organized the Copland-Sessions Concerts, 1928-31; organized the Yaddo Festivals, 1932; was a founder of the American Composers' Alliance, 1937; lecturer, Harvard Univ. 1935, 1944, Charles Eliot Norton lecturer, 1951-52; head of composition department, Berkshire Music Center, 1940-65, faculty chairman, 1957-65; participant in many other organizations.
    WORKS: Opera: The second hurricane, play-opera for high school students, 1937; The tender land, 1954; Theatre: Sorcery to science, music for a puppet show, 1939; Quiet city, music for a play, 1939; The 5 kings, music for a play, 1939; Ballet: Grotto, 1925; Billy the Kid, 1938; Rodeo, 1942; Appalachian spring, 1944; Dance Panels, 1963; Orchestra: Music for the theatre, 1925; symphony for organ and orch., 1925, revised without organ as first symphony, 1928; Dance symphony, 1925; piano concerto, 1926; 2 pieces for string orch., 1928; Symphonic ode, 1932; Short symphony, 1933; Statements, 1935; El salón Mexico, 1937; Outdoor overture, 1938; Music for radio, a saga of the prairie, 1938; John Henry, railroad ballad, 1940; Lincoln portrait, narrator and orch., 1942; Music for movies, 1942; Danzón Cubano, 1942; Fanfare for the common man, brass and percussion, 1943; Letter from home, 1944; Variations on a theme by Eugene Goossens (with 9 other composers), 1945; Variations on a Shaker melody, wind ensemble; 3rd symphony, 1946; clarinet concerto, 1950; Preamble for a solemn occasion; Old American songs, voice and orch., 2 sets, 1950, 1954; Orchestral variations, 1957; Connotations, 1962; Music for a great city, 1964; Inscape, 1967; Chamber music: Nocturne, violin and piano, 1926; Ukelele serenade, violin and piano, 1926; Lento molto and rondino, string quartet, 1928; As it fell upon a day, soprano, flute, clarinet, 1928; Vitebsk, study on a Jewish theme, piano trio, 1928; sextet for piano, clarinet, string quartet, 1933; violin sonata,

COPLAND, AARON

(COPLAND, AARON)
1943; quartet for piano and strings, 1950; nonet for strings, 1960; Chorus: The house on the hill, women's voices; An immorality, women's voices, 1925; What do we plant?, high school chorus, 1939; Lark, 1939; Las agachadas, 1942; In the beginning, mezzo soprano and chorus, 1947; Canticle of freedom, 1955, revised 1965; Songs: 12 poems of Emily Dickinson, 1948-50; Piano: The cat and the mouse, 1919; Passacaglia, 1922; Piano variations, 1930; Sunday afternoon music and The young pioneers, 2 pieces for children, 1936; piano sonata, 1941; 4 piano blues, 1949; Piano fantasy, 1957; Organ: Episode, 1941; Film scores: Of mice and men, 1939; Our town, 1940; North star, 1943; The Cummington story, 1945; The red pony, 1948, The heiress, 1949, won Academy award. His published books include: What to listen for in music, 1937; Our new music, 1941; Music and imagination, 1952; Copland on music, 1960; The new music, 1900-60, revised, 1968.
    c/o Boosey and Hawkes
    30 West 57th St., New York, NY 10019

COPLEY, R. EVAN
b. Liberal, Kan., 22 Mar. 1930. Studied at Michigan State Univ. with H. Owen Reed. He was a faculty member at Iowa Wesleyan Coll., 1958-64; Oklahoma State Univ., 1965-68; Univ. of Northern Colorado, 1968- , associate professor, 1973- .
    WORKS: Orchestra: 3 symphonies; Band: Toccata; symphony; 2 suites; Keyboard: 12 preludes and fugues for piano; 9 piano sonatas; 48 works for organ, most published.
    1335 25th Ave., Court, Greeley, CO 80631

*COPPOLA, DON
Quartet for winds.

CORBETT, RICHARD DEAN
b. Garden City, Kan., 9 Apr. 1942. Studied at Univ. of Northern Colorado with Anthony Menk and Dale Dykins; and at Univ. of Denver with Normand Lockwood. He has been a public school music teacher since 1967.
    WORKS: Orchestra: Music for piano and orch.; Band: Divertimento; Chamber music: Concert pieces, brass quintet; Theme and variations, piano and winds; From where the sun now stands, speaker and wind ensemble; Sones, clarinet and wind ensemble; Chorus: Psalm 95.
    1653 South Benton, Lakewood, CO 80226

*CORCORAN, WILLIAM
Games of cards, 1-act opera, Baby Grand Opera Company, Cincinnati, 6 Dec. 1973; Trilogy on the quality of life, 3 1-act operas commissioned by the Baby Grand Opera Company for the American Bicentennial 1976.

CORDERO, ROQUE
b. Panama, 16 Aug. 1917; to U.S. 1966. Studied composition with Ernst Krenek, conducting with Mitropoulos, Stanley Chapple, and Leon Barzin. He received honorable mention, Reichhold Music Contest, Detroit, 1947; Guggenheim fellowship, 1949; first prize, Ricardo Miro contest, Panama,

(CORDERO, ROQUE)
1953; Caro de Boesi prize, 2nd Interamerican Music Festival, Caracas, 1957; and many commissions. He was professor, 1950-66, and director, 1953-64, Nat. Inst. of Music, Panama; conductor, Nat. Orchestra of Panama, 1964-66; professor, Indiana Univ., 1966-69; music consultant for 2 New York music publishers, 1969- ; professor of composition, Illinois State Univ., 1972- .
    WORKS: Orchestra: 2 symphonies, 1947, 1956; piano concerto, 1944; Rapsodia campesina, 1949; Introduction and allegro burlesco; 8 miniatures, 1953; Five short messages; violin concerto, 1962; Symphony on one theme and five variations; concertino, viola and strings; Musica veinte; Band: Capriccio interiorano, 1939; Chamber music: 2 string quartets; cello sonata, 1962; Film: An mar tule.
    Music Dept., Illinois State University
    Normal, IL 61761

CORIGLIANO, JOHN
b. New York, N. Y., 16 Feb. 1938. Studied at Columbia Univ., B. A. 1959, with Otto Luening; and Manhattan School of Music with Vittorio Giannini. He received first prize in the Spoleto Festival Chamber Music competition, 1964; Guggenheim fellowship, 1968; 8 ASCAP awards; many commissions. He was programmer, WQXR Radio, 1959-62; music director, WBAI Radio, 1962-64; associate producer, CBS-TV Young Poeple's Concerts, 1961-72; professor, Coll. of Church Musicians, 1966; faculty, Manhattan School of Music, 1971- ; and Lehman Coll., 1972- .
    WORKS: Opera: The naked Carmen, rock opera; Orchestra: Elegy for orchestra, 1966; Tournaments overture, 1967; piano concerto, 1968; Creations, narrator and orch.; Band: Gazebo dances; Chamber music: Pastorale, cello and piano, 1958; Kaleidoscope, 2 pianos, 1959; violin sonata, 1963; Chorus: Fern Hill, with orch., 1961; What I expected was...., chorus, brass, percussion; Two Richard Wilbur settings; Songs: The cloisters, song cycle, 1965; Poem in October, tenor and chamber orch., 1969; incidental music for several plays and for the New York Shakespeare Festival in 1970.
    160 West 73rd St., New York, NY 10023

CORINA, JOHN
b. Cleveland, Ohio, 21 Apr. 1928. Studied with John Boda at Florida State Univ., D. M. 1965. He held a fellowship at the university, and in 1967 his Concerto for symphonic band won selection by the Coll. Band Directors Nat. Assoc. He taught in public schools, 1951-60; Miami-Dade Junior Coll., 1960-66; and has been associate professor, Univ. of Georgia, 1966- . He is also oboist, organist, and choirmaster.
    WORKS: Chorus: A prophecy of peace, chorus, soprano, orch., 1969; Is it nothing to you?, Lenten cantata, chorus and brass, 1969; The Last Supper, women's chorus, piano, percussion, 1970; various chamber, vocal, and choral works.
    396 Hancock Lane, Athens, GA 30601

CORNER, PHILIP

b. Bronx, N. Y., 10 Apr. 1933. Studied with Mark Brunswick and Fritz Jahoda at City Coll. of New York, B. A.; with Otto Luening and Henry Cowell at Columbia Univ., M. A.; Paris Cons., with Olivier Messiaen; and privately with Morris Lawner and Dorothy Tansman. He won a Nat. Fed. of Music Clubs award for choral compositions in 1958. He was a public school music teacher, 1966-72; taught at The New School, 1968-70; and has been assistant professor, Livingston Coll., Rutgers Univ., 1972- .

WORKS: His instrumental compositions are usually for indeterminate ensembles, improvisatory events, meditative environments, listening events, some using electronic devices. His published works are: 4 suits, Popular entertainments, I can walk through the world as music, and various versions of OM for performers, such as OM entrance, OM emerging.

145 West 96th St., New York, NY 10025

*CORTES, RAMIRO

b. Dallas, Tex., 25 Nov. 1933. Studied with Henry Cowell in New York; with Halsey Stevens and Ingolf Dahl, Univ. of Southern California; with Goffredo Petrassi in Rome; and with Roger Sessions at Princeton Univ. 1959. He received the Gershwin Memorial award, 1954; Steinway centennial prize, 1954; BMI awards, 1954, 1958; Fulbright fellowship for study in Rome, 1956-58. He is associate professor, Univ. of Southern California; was visiting professor, Univ. of Utah, 1973.

WORKS: Opera: Prometheus, 1-act, 1960; Theatre: music for Yorca's play, Yerma, 1955; Orchestra: Sinfonia sacra, 1954; Night music, chamber orch., 1954; Xochitl, 1955; Sinfonia breve, 1955-58; Meditation, string orch.; Chamber music: Elegy, flute and piano, 1952; Divertimento, woodwind trio, 1953; piano quintet, 1953; chamber concerto, cello and 12 winds, 1958; string quartet, 1958; piano trio, 1959; 3 movements for 3 winds; duo for flute and oboe; Chorus: 3 songs to poems of Ben Jonson; Missa breve; Songs: The falcon; 3 Spanish songs; Piano: Prelude; Suite; sonata.

2262 South Carmolina Ave.
West Los Angeles, CA 90006

CORY, ELEANOR

b. Englewood, N. J., 8 Sep. 1943. Studied with Chou Wen-Chung, Bulent Arel, Benjamin Boretz, at Columbia Univ.; with Charles Wuorinen at New England Cons.; and with Meyer Kupferman at Sarah Lawrence Coll. She was on the faculty, New England Cons., 1968-70; Brooklyn Coll., 1971-72; Columbia Univ., 1971-73; and Baruch Coll. of CUNY, 1973- .

WORKS: Chamber music: Liebeslied, mezzo-soprano, chamber ensemble, 1969; Concertino, piano and chamber ensemble, 1970; Combinations, piano, 1970; septet, 1971; Tempi for clarinet and tape, 1971; Modulations, strings and percussion, 1972; solo flute piece, 1973; trio for clarinet, cello, and piano, 1973.

945 West End Ave., #8B, New York, NY 10025

CORY, GEORGE

b. Syracuse, N. Y., 3 Aug. 1920. Studied with Ernest Bloch at Univ. of California. During his army service in 1943-45, he was chapel organist at the Presidio of Monterey. He was music director, Gilbert and Sullivan Repertory Company, San Francisco; assistant to Gian-Carlo Menotti, 1946-50; arranger, conductor, pianist in San Francisco and throughout the U.S.

WORKS: Theatre: Lysistrata, musical version of Aristophane's play; Songs: The drowned wife, text by Robert Horan; Music I heard with you, text by Conrad Aiken; And this shall be for music, text by R. L. Stevenson; Another America, text Douglass Cross; Keyboard: sonatina for piano; Pastorale and toccata-finale for organ; many popular songs including: I left my heart in San Francisco (Grammy award, 1963), and Carry me back to old Manhattan.

1210 Lombard St., San Francisco, CA 94109

*COSCIA, SILVIO

b. Milan, Italy, 27 Nov. 1899. At age 8 was cantor at St. Ambrogio Cathedral, Milan; studied at Verdi Cons. On coming to the U.S. in the early 1920s, he was horn player and arranger with the Goldman Band; was first horn, Metropolitan Opera Orchestra, 1930-64; also played under Toscanini; was private vocal teacher and coach; from 1968 has taught voice at the New England Cons.

WORKS: Orchestra: Scherzo for orchestra; Heroic vision, symphonic poem; Ecce homo, tone poem, New York, 1962; Dramatic elegy, 1965; Band: 2 preludes; Songs: Kindly loving; I come tomorrow; La vida dolce; Dark hour; Love me little, love me long; also studies for horn and duets for trumpet. He is author of Yesterday and today, Bel canto; and Operative Italian diction and articulation applied to singing.

12 Riverside St., Watertown, MA 02172

COSTINESCU, GHEORGHE

b. Bucharest, Romania, 12 Dec. 1934; to U.S. 1969. Studied with Mihail Jora at Bucharest Cons., 1954-61; and later with Nadia Boulanger, Karlheinz Stockhausen, Max Deutsch, and Luciano Berio. Since 1971, he has been working with Vladimir Ussachevsky, Mario Davidovsky, and Chou Wen-Chung in a Ph. D. program at Columbia Univ. In Romania, he received 2 Jon Vides prizes, 1964-1965; George Enescu prize, Romanian Acad., 1965; Alexander Gretchaninoff prize at Juilliard School, 1970; Henry Mancini fellowship at Juilliard, 1971; MacDowell fellowships, 1970, 1972; Yaddo fellowship, 1972; research grant, Mills Coll., 1973; and was composer-in-residence, Virginia Center for the Creative Arts, 1973. In 1960-68, he was score-reader at the Romanian Composers Alliance, presenting scores of new works in piano reduction; 1970-71, organist and choirmaster, Brooklyn and Coney Island; 1973- , teaching assistant, Columbia Univ. and instructor Brooklyn Coll.

WORKS: Comme de longs nuages, tenor solo and choir, 1969; The musical seminar, musical play for electronic organ, trombone, double bass, percussion, piano, actors, electronic tape, 1970-71;

COSTINESCU, GHEORGHE

(COSTINESCU, GHEORGHE)
A la recherche du chant, musical pantomime for
15 players, commissioned by Mario di Bonaventura,
Dartmouth Coll., 1972; Invention 5-B, electronic
piece, 1973.
125 Riverside Drive, Apt. 10D
New York, NY 10024

COTEL, MORRIS
b. Baltimore, Md., 20 Feb. 1943. Studied with
William Bergsma, Vincent Persichetti, and Roger
Sessions at the Juilliard School, B. M., M. S.;
with Darius Milhaud at Aspen, Colo. He was a
fellow at the American Acad. in Rome, 1966-68,
receiving the American Rome Prize in composition
at that time. He was instructor, Rubin Acad.,
Jerusalem, Israel, 1970-72; and at Peabody Cons.,
1972-   . Cotel had composed and scored a large
4-movement symphony by age 13. His works up to
about 1966 were chiefly serial, but thereafter
became more improvisational and aleatory with
free rhythms. He has performed his piano concerto in Europe and the Middle East as well as
the U.S.
WORKS: Orchestra : Symphonic pentad, 1964,
Rome, Sep. 1967; piano concerto, Rome, Sep. 1968,
first American performance, Baltimore, 26 Feb.
1973; Variations for an infinite space, 1970,
Jerusalem, May 1971; Variations on a theme by
Haydn, 1973; Chamber music: Music for a finite
space, piano and string quartet, 1965; Suite nonsense, ensemble and narrator, 1965; sonata for
piano 4 hands, 1966; Scales and all, alto saxophone, vibes, bass, percussion, 1972; Oŏgamous,
piano, vibes, bass, percussion, 1972, Baltimore,
20 Feb. 1974; Humanoid ritual dances, prepared
piano, percussion, tape, 1971; Great Mother Goose
sweetmerge and grand foog, tape and pop-vocal,
Tel Aviv, Nov. 1971.
12 East 33rd St., Baltimore, MD 21218

COULTER, R. SCOTT, JR.
b. Baltimore, Md., 20 June 1925. Studied with
Ingolf Dahl, Univ. of Southern California; at
Univ. of Pacific, M. M.; with Karl Kohn and Gail
Kubik, Claremont Graduate School, where in 1973
he was a Ph. D. candidate. He was instructor,
Fullerton Coll., 1959-70; and associate professor
and chairman, Music Department, Stanislaus State
Coll., 1970-   .
WORKS: Chamber music: violin sonata, 1952;
Sea songs, baritone and piano, 1961; piano sonata,
1973; Peter Quint at the clavier, baritone, harpsichord, 2 recorders, 1973; Chorus: Lamentation
of David, choir, solo, 2 pianos, 1972.
1438 Sycamore St., Turlock, CA 95380

COUPER, MILDRED
b. Buenos Aires, 10 Dec. 1887; U.S. citizen 1910.
Graduated from Karlsruhe-Baden Cons.; studied
with Moritz Mosxkowski in Paris, with Sgambati in
Rome, and with Alfred Cortot in New York. She
taught at Mannes School of Music, New York,
1918-27; and at Music Acad. of the West, Santa
Barbara, 1927-40.
WORKS: Orchestra: We are seven; Seven more;
Irish washerwoman variations, played by Werner
Janssen Symphony; Songs: 2 sets of songs to

(COUPER, MILDRED)
verses of Ogden Nash; Piano: Dirge, for 2 pianos
tuned a quarter-tone apart, published by New
Music Editions, 1937. Halsey Stevens mentioned
her as an avant garde composer after World War I.
3010 Foot Hill Road, Santa Barbara, CA 93105

*COUSINS, M. THOMAS
b. Wilson, N. C., 9 Oct. 1914. Studied at
Juilliard School. He played trumpet with the
National Symphony and CBS Symphony, 1939-42; was
army bandleader in World War II; taught in public
schools; was chairman, music department, Brevard
Coll., 1958-63; conductor, Greensboro Symphony,
1963-
WORKS: Chorus: Moses, chorus and orch.;
O clap your hands; Glorious everlasting, double
chorus.

*COWELL, HENRY DIXON
b. Menlo Park, Calif., 11 Mar. 1897; d. Shady,
N. Y., 10 Dec. 1965. Studied at Univ. of Southern California; Inst. of Applied Music, New York;
and privately in Berlin. He was a bandmaster
in the U.S. Army in World War I, and during World
War II was in charge of shortwave music broadcasts for the Office of War Information. In 1927
he founded the New Music Quarterly for the publication of contemporary music and was its editor
to 1936. He also helped organize the Pan American Assoc. of Composers. It was Cowell who invented and developed the "tone cluster" technique
for the piano, a device he used in his piano concerto in 1930. He made 5 tours of Europe playing
his own works and a dozen tours in the U.S. As
author, lecturer, publisher, and performer he was
a tireless champion of little known American
music. For example, the belated recognition of
Charles Ives was largely due to Cowell's efforts.
His teaching posts included Stanford Univ., New
School for Social Research, Univ. of California,
Mills Coll., Peabody Cons., Columbia Univ. Along
with all these activities he kept up a prodigious
output in composition. By 1950 he estimated he
had written more than 800 works, and he added
another 200 in the succeeding 15 years.
WORKS: Orchestra: 19 symphonies, 1918-65;
percussion concerto; Ensemble for string orch.,
1925, revised 1956; sinfonietta, 1928; Polyphon-
ica, chamber orch., 1930; Synchrony, 1931;
Ostinato pianissimo for percussion orch., 1934;
Old American country set, chamber orch., 1939;
Persian set, chamber orch.; Ancient desert drone,
1940; Symphonic set; Toccata, vocalize for soprano and orch.; Tales of the countryside, piano
and orch., 1941; Hymn and fuguing tune #2, string
orch., 1944; Hymn and fuguing tunes, #3 and #16;
Twilight; Air and scherzo, alto saxophone and
orch.; Fiddler's jig, violin and strings; Variations on 3rds, 2 violas and chamber orch.;
Saturday night at the firehouse; Ballad, string
orch., 1954; concerto for koto and orch., 1964;
Carol for orch., a version for Western orch. of
the 2nd movement of the koto concerto; Band:
Shipshape overture, 1939; Little concerto, piano
and band; Hymn and fuguing tune #1, 1943; A curse
and a blessing; Celtic sets, 1943; Animal magic,
1944; Wind ensemble: Fanfare for the forces of

(COWELL, HENRY DIXON)
the Latin American Allies, brass ensemble; Rondo, brass ensemble; Sailor's hornpipe, 4 saxophones; Tall tale, brass sextet, 1947; Hymn and fuguing tune #12, 3 horns; Chamber music: 5 string quartets, 1916-   ; 7 paragraphs for string trio, 1926; Suite for violin and piano, 1927; Set of 5, viola, percussion, piano; Vocalize, soprano, flute, piano; Ballad, woodwind quintet; Suite, woodwind quintet; 3 pieces for 3 recorders; Movement for string quartet, 1934; Mosaic quartet for strings, 1935; Triad, trumpet and piano; 3 ostinati with chorales, clarinet and piano; violin sonata, 1945; How old is song, violin and piano; Homage to Iran, violin and piano; Gravely and vigorously, solo cello; Two-bits, flute and piano, 1944, world premiere one bit, Baltimore, 2 Mar. 1972; Hymn and fuguing tune #7, viola and piano; Hymn and fuguing tune #9, cello and piano, 1950; Hymn and fuguing tune #13, trombone and piano, 1950; Hymn and fuguing tune #16, violin and piano; Chorus: Supplication; American muse; The Irishman lilts; To America, 1946; The lily's lament; Spring at summer's end; Ballad of the 2 mothers; Day, evening, night, morning, men's voices, 1947; Do you doodle as you dawdle?; Garden hymn for Easter; The road leads into tomorrow, 1947; Lilting fancy; The morning cometh; Sweet was the song the Virgin sang; Psalm 121, 1953; Ultimo actio; Songs: Daybreak; Firelight and lamp; The donkey; Spring comes singing; St. Agnes morning; The pasture; The little black boy; Toccata, soprano, cello, flute, piano or orch.; Piano: Amerind suite; Amiable conversation; Anger dance; Antimony; Hilarious curtain opener and ritornelle; Dynamic motion; Organ: Hymn and fuguing tune #14, 1962. He also published the books, New musical resources, 1930, and Charles Ives and his music, 1955.

*COWLES, CECIL MARION
b. San Francisco, Calif., 14 Jan. 1898; d. New York, N. Y., 28 Mar. 1968. Made her piano debut at age 9; later studied composition with Carl Deis. Her compositions include Jesu bambino, a mass; for piano: Shanghai bund; Oriental sketches; Cubanita; Nocturne, etc.; and songs.

COWLES, DARLEEN
b. Chicago, Ill., 13 Nov. 1942. Studied with Leon Stein, De Paul Univ., B. M. 1966; with Anthony Donato, Northwestern Univ., M. M. 1967; with Ralph Shapey, Univ. of Chicago, Ph. D. candidate 1975. Her awards include the Faricy award for creative composition, 1967, and commissions. She was instructor, Northwestern Univ., 1967; Elmhurst Coll., 1970; De Paul Univ., 1972-   .
WORKS: Orchestra: Chamber symphony #1, 1965; Like strangers, voice and chamber orch., 1975; Band: Sonata for band, 1964; Processional and recessional for an ordination, brass quintet; Chamber music: sonatine, horn and piano, 1965; string quartet, 1966; Continuum, trumpet, vibraharp, marimba, piano, 1968; Translucent unreality #3, clarinet, horn, amplified piano, 1974; Estampie, string quartet, 1974; Translucent unreality #5, cello and amplified piano, 1975; Chorus: Be adored, God, a cappella; Offering

(COWLES, DARLEEN)
for peace, with tenor solo and orch., 1967; O sweet spontaneous, 1972; Piano: suite, 1965.
127 Elm, Park Forest, IL 60466

*COWLES, WALTER RUEL
b. New Haven, Conn., 4 Sep. 1981; d. Tallahassee, Fla., 8 Dec. 1959. Wrote a piano concerto, piano trio, and songs.

COX, RONN
b. Ft. Smith, Ark., 9 June 1942. Studied at North Texas State Univ. with Merrill Ellis. He was a research assistant, Electronic Music Center, North Texas State Univ., 1967-70, and teaching assistant, 1973-   .
WORKS: Chamber music: Opposites, trumpet and cello; Two expressions, wind ensemble with celeste, percussion, and contrabass; The...just ...and...you, soprano and trombone quartet; Mixed media: Diachronic, trombone and tape; 5TEN8+, orchestra and tape, quasi aleatory; A saxophone?, alto saxophone and tape, improvisation; Together, tape.
1114A West Hickory, Denton, TX 76201

COYNER, LOU
b. U.S., 11 Mar. 1931. Studied with S. Coveleski. He was faculty member, Berklee School of Music, 1959-60; composer-in-residence and associate professor, Chatham Coll., 1962-74.
WORKS: Orchestra: piano concerto; Dawn stone, cello quartet and chamber orch.; Chamber music: Gentle jangle; Woodenly booming along like a carved bee, piano and woodwind quintet; Dapper rapper, percussion ensemble; Away, alone, aloved, alast along the, wind quintet; Collocations, piano and percussion; Saxifrage, saxophone quartet; Omega point, string quartet; Tycho, piano, New York, 18 Jan. 1971; Noosphere, piano; Mixed media: Saral, clarinet, cello, tape; Bird, percussion solo and tape; Piva, saxophone, percussion, and tape.
5814 Murray Hill Place, Pittsburgh, PA 15217

*CRABTREE, RAY
The fool, short opera, Carnegie Recital Hall, New York, 29 Mar. 1970.

CRAIG, DALE A.
b. Illiopolis, Ill., 19 Dec. 1939. Studied with Robert Palmer and Karel Husa at Cornell Univ.; with Priaulx Rainier in London; with Leland Smith at Stanford Univ.; and privately with Lou Harrison. He has received a commission from Radio Hong Kong. He was assistant professor, Univ. of Virginia, 1968-69; lecturer, Chung Chi Coll., Hong Kong, 1969-   , chairman of department, 1972-   .
WORKS: String quartet, 1966-67; Chamber piece No. 3, 1967; Three songs on poems by Ezra Pound, baritone and piano, 1970; Three settings of old Chinese tunes and verses, low voice and piano, 1971; In a happy mood by Seung River, Er-hu (Chinese violin) and piano, Hong Kong, 2 June 1973; Mixed media: Byàn Hwà, for orch.,

CRAIG, DALE A.

(CRAIG, DALE A.)
speakers, dancers, Stanford Univ. Chamber Orch.,
1 June 1968.
Department of Music, Chung Chi College
The Chinese University of Hong Kong
Shatin, New Territories, Hong Kong

CRAM, JAMES DOUGLAS
b. Heavener, Okla., 10 May 1931. Studied at
Oklahoma Baptist Univ. with Warren Angell; Tulsa
Univ. with Bela Rozsa; and North Texas State Univ.
with Merrill Ellis and Samuel Adler. He has received annual ASCAP awards and the Texas Composers' Guild award, 1970. He is associate professor and chairman, School of Music, Hardin-
Simmons Univ.
WORKS: Chorus: Easter cantata, 1967; Welcome, all wonders, a Christmas cantata, 1970;
Three nativity poems of Richard Crashaw, mixed
chorus and orch., 1970; To believe in God, a
choral cycle, 1973; numerous choral compositions.
3505 Hunters Glen, Abilene, TX 79601

CRANDELL, ROBERT E.
b. Hornell, N. Y., 10 Jan. 1910. Studied with
Hunter Johnson at Univ. of Michigan; with Edwin
Stringham, Union Theological Seminary; and with
Nadia Boulanger in Paris. He has held church
positions as choirmaster and organist since 1935;
his faculty posts have included lecturer, Union
Theological Seminary, 1962-71; and Packer Collegiate Inst., Brooklyn, organist, 1951-71, director of music, 1962-71.
WORKS: Chorus: Benedictus es, Domine; Close
to the heart of God; January carol; The second
beatitude; O sing unto the Lord; I sing the
mighty power; Laudate Domine; Organ: Carnival
suite.
909 Capital Ave., S.W.
Battle Creek, MI 49015

*CRANE, HELEN
An elegy, cello and piano.

CRANE, JOELLE WALLACH
b. New York, N. Y., 29 June 1946. Studied with
Meyer Kupferman at Sarah Lawrence Coll., B. A.
1967; with Chou Wen-Chung and Jack Beeson at
Columbia Univ., M. A. 1969. She received a scholarship to the Composers' Conference, Johnson,
Vt., 1973. She has been a private teacher of
piano and theory.
WORKS: Orchestra: Concerto for 4 winds;
Chamber music: Duo, clarinet and cello, 1964;
2 string quartets, 1964, 1968; Trio for 3 high
winds, flute and 2 oboes, 1965; Little duet, violin and piano, 1966; quartet for winds and
strings, 1966; duo for violin and cello, 1966;
Pas de deux, flute and harpsichord, 1967; Moment,
oboe solo, 1967; trio for 3 reed instruments,
1968; Cords, soprano and 2 string basses, 1973;
Beads, solo contrabass, 1973; Songs: Deirdre,
song cycle for mezzo-soprano and piano, 1963; The
force that through the green fuse, soprano and
oboe, 1965; Piano: Piano study in open-ended
form, 1965; Three piano pieces, 1967; Prelude and
toccata, piano and tape, 1967.
3433 De Kalb Ave., Bronx, NY 10467

CRANE, JOHN THOMAS
b. New York, N. Y., 17 Sep. 1943. Attended
Columbia Univ., B. A. 1965, M. A. 1969, D. M. A.
1973; studying with Chou Wen-Chung, Jack Beeson,
Vladimir Ussachevsky. He held scholarships at
Tanglewood, 1962; Columbia Univ., 1968-69; Com-
posers' Conference, Vt., 1971, 1972. His faculty posts include Dalton School, 1969-71;
Queensborough Community Coll., 1970; Fordham
Univ., 1970-73; assistant professor, Baruch Coll.,
CUNY, 1973-   . He was assistant conductor,
Columbia Univ. Orch., 1968-69.
WORKS: Chamber music: quartet movement for
flute, oboe, clarinet, cello, 1967; Composition
for 7 instruments and percussion, 1967-68; The
quartet, soprano and cello, 1968; quintet for
recorder, oboe, viola, tuba, and harp, 1969-70.
Aria, flute solo, 1970; Chorus: Punch, brothers,
punch, 1968; Mixed media: Aulos, oboe and tape,
1969; A rhapsody in '69, tape, 1969.
3433 De Kalb Ave., Bronx, NY 10467

CRANE, ROBERT
b. Winchester, Mass., 24 Dec. 1919. Studied at
Oberlin Coll. with Normand Lockwood; Longy School
of Music, with Nadia Boulanger; Univ. of Roches-
ter with Bernard Rogers and Howard Hanson. He
received the Lili Boulanger award, 1942; Phi Mu
Alpha Sinfonia Alumni award, 1952; Knight of Mark
Twain, 1972. He has been a faculty member,
School of Music, Univ. of Wisconsin, 1950-   ,
professor, 1972-   .
WORKS: Orchestra: A dance interlude;
Exsequiarum ordo; Band: Passacaglia and fugue;
Chorale prelude on Wachet auf; Aleatory suite;
Rotunda music, for brasses; Chamber music:
octet for brass; Incantation, cello and piano;
sonatina for piano; Chorus: Peter Quince at the
clavier, cantata; The litany, soloists, chorus,
orch.; When the lamb opened the seventh seal,
cantata.
1615 Adams St., Madison, WI 53711

CRAWFORD, DAWN
b. Ellington Field, Tex., 19 Dec. 1919. Studied
with Bernard Rogers and Herbert Elwell at Eastman School of Music; attended Rice Univ., B. A.
1939; Houston Cons., B. M. 1940; Columbia Univ.,
M. A. 1954, Ph. D. candidate. She received a
commission for incidental music to Angna Enters'
Love possessed Juana, world premiere, Houston,
1946. She taught at Houston Cons., 1938-42, was
assistant director 1942-49; free lance accompanist, New York, 1949-57; faculty, Dominican Coll.,
Houston, 1964, chairman, department of music,
1973-   .
WORKS: Opera: The pearl, 3 acts, based on
Steinbeck's novel; Orchestra: The Chinese nightingale, ballade for orch., based on Vachel
Lindsay's poem; chamber music; songs.
Department of Music, Dominican College
2401 East Holcombe, Houston, TX 77021

CRAWFORD, JOHN
b. Philadelphia, Pa., 19 Jan. 1931. Studied at
Yale Univ. with Paul Hindemith, Quincy Porter;
in Paris with Nadia Boulanger; at Harvard Univ.
with Walter Piston and Randall Thompson. He

(CRAWFORD, JOHN)
received a Fulbright grant, 1950-51; Boott Prize in choral composition, Harvard, 1957; annual ASCAP awards 1969-   . He was instructor, Amherst Coll., 1961-63; assistant professor, Wellesley Coll., 1963-70; associate professor, Univ. of California, Riverside, 1970-   .
WORKS: Opera: Don Cristobal and Rosita, chamber opera, 1970; Orchestra: Metracollage, 1973; Chamber music: 2 string quartets; Chorus: Magnificat, chorus and piano or string orch., 1956; Ash Wednesday, oratorio, 1960; Two Herrick settings, 1965.
924 23rd St., Santa Monica, CA 90403

*CRAWFORD, LOUISE
Canzonetta and Legend, violin and piano.

*CRAWFORD, ROBERT M.
b. Dawson, Yukon Terr., Canada, 27 July 1899; d. New York, N. Y., 12 Mar. 1961. Studied at Princeton Univ.; Fontainebleau Cons., France; Juilliard School. He taught at Juilliard School and at Univ. of Miami; was conductor of various opera and choral groups. He wrote several orchestral suites and many songs.

*CRAWFORD-SEEGER, RUTH PORTER
b. East Liverpool, Ohio, 3 July 1901; d. Chevy Chase, Md., 18 Nov. 1953. Studied with Adolf Weidig in Chicago; with Charles Seeger in New York. She received a Juilliard scholarship, 1927-29; a Guggenheim fellowship for study in Paris and Berlin, 1930. She held various teaching posts, then married Charles Seeger in 1931. A retrospective concert of her works was presented in New York, 19 Feb. 1975.
WORKS; Orchestra: Music for small orchestra; 3 songs on Sandburg texts, voice and orch., 1930-32, New York premiere, 24 Apr. 1974; Rissolty, rossolty, 10 winds, drums, and strings, 1941; 2 movements for chamber orch., Cambridge, Mass., 25 Feb. 1975; Chamber music: Diaphonic suite, solo flute or oboe or chamber orch., 1930; string quartet, 1931; violin sonata; Suite for wind quintet, 1952; Chorus: Canon; Chant, 1930; Piano: 9 preludes; Study in mixed accents.

CRESHEVSKY, NOAH
b. Rochester, N. Y., 31 Jan. 1945. Studied with Virgil Thomson, Nadia Boulanger, and Luciano Berio. He received a Nadia Boulanger scholarship, 1964; Juilliard fellowship, 1967. He was on the faculty, Juilliard School, 1968-70; assistant professor, Brooklyn Coll., CUNY, 1970-   ; part-time lecturer, Hunter Coll., CUNY, 1971-72.
WORKS: Chamber music: Vier Lieder, narrator, pianist, theatre props, 1966; Electronic: Circuit, 1970; Variations, 1970; Chaconne, 1973.
Ansonia Hotel
2109 Broadway, New York, NY 10023

CRESTON, PAUL
b. New York, N. Y., 10 Oct. 1906. Is entirely self-taught in harmony, orchestration, and composition. Although he began to compose at the age of 8, he did not choose music as his life work until he was 26. Since that time his prolific

(CRESTON, PAUL)
compositions have earned him such honors as Citation of Merit, Nat. Assoc. for American Composers and Conductors, 1941; Music Award, American Acad. of Arts and Letters, 1943; New York Music Critics' Circle award, for Symphony No. 1, 1943; first place, Paris Internat. Competition, also for Symphony No. 1, 1952; honorary member, Kappa Kappa Psi, Pi Kappa Lambda, and Phi Mu Alpha Sinfonia; Gold Medal, Nat. Arts Club; and many more, including many commissions. In addition to being composer, pianist, organist, and conductor, he has been teacher, guest composer, and lecturer at a score of colleges and universities and on the faculties at Univ. of Southern California, 1948; Swarthmore Coll., 1956; New York Coll. of Music, 1964-68; and composer-in-residence and professor, Central Washington State Coll., 1968-   . In 1960 he was American Specialist in Israel and Turkey for the U.S. State Department.
WORKS: Over 90 major works: 35 orchestral works (5 symphonies, 15 concertos, including concertos for marimba, trombone, saxophone, harp, accordion, as well as violin and piano); symphonic band works; chamber music for various instrumental groups; choral works, cantatas, an oratorio; songs; piano compositions; numerous scores for radio, television, and films. He is author of 2 textbooks: Principles of rhythm and Creative harmony.
P. O. Box 794, Ellensburg, WA 98926

*CREWS, LUCILE (MRS. LUCILE MARSH)
b. Pueblo, Col., 23 Aug. 1888. Studied at New England Cons., Redlands Univ.; American Cons.; with Nadia Boulanger in Paris; and in Berlin. She received a Pulitzer traveling fellowship, 1926; Calif. Fed. of Music Clubs prize for a 1-act opera; Festival of Allied Arts prize. Her works include the opera, Ariadne and Dionysus; a tone poem, chamber music, piano pieces, songs.

*CRISP, BARBARA
Concert trio in D; 3 pieces for viola and piano.

*CRIST, BAINBRIDGE
b. Lawrenceburg, Ind., 13 Feb. 1883; d. Barnstable, Mass., 7 Feb. 1969. Studied law at George Washington Univ., L. L. B. 1906; composition with Paul Juon in Berlin. He abandoned law after a few years and taught singing in Boston, 1915-21, and in Washington, D.C., 1922-23.
WORKS: Ballet: Le pied de la momie; Pregiwa's marriage; Orchestra: La morte amoureuse; American epic, 1920; The night remembered; Hymn to Nefertiti; Hindu rhapsody; Festival overture; many choral works, songs, and piano pieces. He was author of The setting of words to music, 1945.

CRITSER, WILLIAM
b. Columbus, Ohio, 9 July 1928. Attended Northwestern Univ.; South Dakota School of Mines and Tech.; studied composition with Nikolai Lopatnikoff and Robert Delaney. He was minister of music, Presbyterian Church, Beckley, W. Va., 1956-65; director, Beckley Choral Society,

CRITSER, WILLIAM

(CRITSER, WILLIAM)
1960-64; principal oboist, Charleston Symphony, Charleston, W. Va., 1957-62; private teacher in Pittsburgh, 1965-   .
WORKS: Chamber music: oboe sonata; Theme and variations, piano; saxophone quartet; Chorus: Psalm of praise, mixed chorus and organ; How long, O Lord, a cappella.
443 Royce Ave., Pittsburgh, PA 15216

CROLEY, RANDELL
b. Knoxville, Tenn., 23 Sep. 1946. Studied at The Juilliard School with Vincent Persichetti, Roger Sessions, Luciano Berio; Univ. of Louisville with Moritz von Bomhard; Accademia Musicale Chigiana, Siena, Italy, with Roman Vlad. He received the Outstanding String Composition award for his Thesis for string trio, 1963, at the 1966 Exposition of Contemporary Music, Cincinnati; and the 1969 Lado Prize in Composition, Juilliard School; annual ASCAP awards since 1968. He was music editor with Autograph Editions, New York, 1968-72; and with Joseph Boonin, Inc., 1973-   .
WORKS: Orchestra: Concerto for flute and metal orch., 1967; Cinque espressioni per orchestra piccola, 1969; Song of my youth, wind orchestra, 1968; Chamber music: Sinfonietta for brass quintet, 1966; Quattro espressioni, piano, 1968; Microespressioni I, wind quintet, 1969; Electronic tape: White on white, 1967; and many other works for small ensembles and solo instruments.
Suite 536
152 West 42nd St., New York, NY 10036

CROOKS, MACK
b. Knoxville, Tenn., 7 Feb. 1937. Studied with Robert Erickson and Sol Joseph at San Francisco Cons.; with Roger Nixon and Wayne Peterson at San Francisco State Coll., B. A., M. A.; with George Kyme, Joaquin Nin-Culmell at Univ. of California, Berkeley, Ph. D. 1969. He was research assistant, Univ. of California, 1966-68; clinician, Kodaly Inst., Stanford Univ., 1966; instructor, Univ. of California Extension, 1967-73; associate professor, Lone Mountain Coll., 1967-   .
WORKS: Chamber music: Emanations, for 8 instruments, 1965; Chorus: Kyrie, 1968; December carol, 1970; Psalm 91, a cappella, 1973; Piano: Tonatina, 1966; Movements for piano, 1966, revised 1971; Film: Film as art, electronic tape for film by Lynn Vardamin, 1966.
3394 Market St., San Francisco, CA 94114

CROOM, JOHN ROBERT
b. Jennings, La., 27 Apr. 1941. Studied at Louisiana State Univ. with Kenneth B. Klaus; McNeese State Univ. with Woodrow James. He was selected as chairman for the Louisiana Music Educators Assoc. annual composition contest, 1970-74. He has been assistant professor, Nicholls State Univ., 1970-   .
WORKS: He has written 12-tone, free 12-tone, chromatic, and quarter-tone works for brass, woodwinds, strings, piano, and chorus. Major works include: Chamber music: Pentagon for brass, quintet; Variations for a dozen clarinets;

(CROOM, JOHN ROBERT)
Five subconscious flights, for piano; Metamorphosis, for 2 pianos; Didactic material, for clarinet; Chorus: Mass in English.
503 Willow St., Thibodaux, LA 70301

CROSS, LOWELL
b. Kingsville, Tex., 24 June 1938. Studied with Mary Jeanne van Appledorn at Texas Technological Univ., B. A. in English, 1961, B. A. in Music, 1963; electronic music with Myron Schaeffer and Gustav Cimiaga, Univ. of Toronto, M. A. 1968. He received Woodrow Wilson and Province of Ontario graduate fellowships, 1964. He established the electronic music studio at Texas Technological Univ., 1961; was research associate, Univ. of Toronto, 1968; artistic director, Tape Music Center, Mills Coll., 1968-69; consultant, Experiments in Art and Technology, New York, 1969-70; guest consultant, Nat. Inst. of Design, Ahmedabad, India, Apr. 1970; and at Univ. of Iowa, audio engineer, School of Music, artist, Center for New Performing Arts, 1971-   , assistant professor of music, 1972-   .
WORKS: Electronic: Four random studies, 1961; 0.8 century, 1962; Decaphonics, 1963; Antiphonies, 1964; After long silence, 4-channel tape, Stirrer, soprano, 1964; Video I and Video II, tape, audio system, television, 1965; Video III, with David Tudor, phase-derived audio system, monochrome and color television; etc. He has written articles on electronic music and has designed circuits including the Stirrer, a 4-channel device for directing and mobilizing sounds in space; version #2 was built for CBS and Columbia Records, 1970.
1705 Glendale Road, Iowa City, IA 52240

*CROSS, RONALD
B. Fort Worth, Tex., 18 Feb. 1929. A musicologist, has written choral pieces and chamber music.

*CROSSMAN, ALLAN
Studied with Hugo Weisgall. Formerly on the faculty at Wheaton Coll., in 1974 he joined the staff of the School of Contemporary Music, Brookline, Mass.
WORKS: Chamber music: The least grain of remembered dust, trio, 1967; The wind sings, trio, 1968; Dances of the distant planet Earth, 1972; string quartet, Cambridge, Mass., 3 June 1974.
35 Regent St., Cambridge, MA 02140

CROTTY, MICHAEL
b. Putnam, Conn., 29 Apr. 1950. Studied with John Bavicchi, William Maloof, Herb Pomeroy, Phil Wilson, at Berklee Coll., B. M. 1972. He received a John Philip Sousa award in 1968. He was composer-in-residence, Woodstock Music and Arts Program, 1971, and United States Air Force Band, 1972-   .
WORKS: Six Psalms, 1968; Experiment in blues, 1967-69; My Lai, 1970; Unanswered questions, 1971-72; Dichotomy, 1972; Warm rain, 1972; Oasis, 1973; Multiple woodwind concerto, 1973.
3403 Eastern Ave., N.E., Washington, DC 20018

CROWLEY, ROBERT DENNIS

b. Great Falls, Mont., 12 Apr. 1921. Studied at Reed Coll. with Herbert Gladstone; Mills Coll. with Darius Milhaud; Univ. of California with Roger Sessions and Andrew Imbrie. He has received several commissions. He has been professor, Portland State Univ., 1958- .

WORKS: Orchestra: Aspects of otherness, chamber orch. with concertante winds and piano, 1958; Toccata for trumpet and orch., 1963; Band: Colluctation, 1969.

Music Department, Portland State Univ.
Portland, OR 97207

CRUMB, GEORGE

b. Charleston, W. Va., 24 Oct. 1929. Attended Mason Coll., Charleston; Univ. of Illinois, M. M. 1953; Univ. of Michigan, D. M. A. 1959; he studied with Ross Lee Finney in Michigan, and with Boris Blacher in Berlin. His awards include Fulbright fellowship, 1954; grants from Rockefeller Found., 1964, Koussevitzky Found., 1965, Guggenheim Found. 1967, 1973; Pulitzer Prize in Music, 1968; Coolidge Found. award, 1970; Nat. Inst. of Arts and Letters award, 1967; Internat. Rostrum of Composers, UNESCO, award, 1970; and Koussevitzky Internat. Recording Award, 1970; elected to Nat. Inst. of Arts and Letters, 1975. He was on the faculty, Univ. of Colorado, 1959-64; associate professor, then professor, Univ. of Pennsylvania, 1965- ; visiting professor, Harvard, 1968, Tanglewood, 1970.

WORKS: Orchestra: Variazioni, 1959; Echoes of time and the river, 1967 (Pulitzer, 1968); Chamber music: string quartet, 1954; sonatina for unaccompanied cello, 1955; 5 pieces for piano, 1962; Four nocturnes (Night music II), violin and piano, 1964; Eleven echoes of autumn, violin, alto flute, clarinet, piano, 1966; Night of the four moons, alto flute, banjo, electric cello, percussion, 1969; Black Angels: 13 images from the darkland, electric string quartet, 1970; Vox balaenae (Voice of the whale), amplified flute, cello, piano, the 3 players to wear black half-masks, commissioned by New York Camerata, New York, 10 Oct. 1971; Makrokosmos I, piano, 1973, II amplified piano, New York, 12 Nov. 1974; Voice: Night music I, soprano, celesta, piano, percussion, 1963; Madrigals, Book I, soprano, vibraphone, double bass, 1965; Madrigals, Book II, soprano, alto flute, percussion, 1965; Songs, drones and refrains of death, baritone, electric guitar, electric double bass, electric piano, percussion, text by Garcia Lorca, 1968; Madrigals, Book III, soprano, harp, percussion, 1969; Madrigals, Book IV, soprano, flute, harp, double bass, percussion, 1969; Ancient voices of children, soprano, boy soprano, 7 instruments, text of Garcia Lorca, 1970.

240 Kirk Lane, Media, PA 19063

CUBBAGE, JOHN

b. Tuscaloosa, Ala., 21 Sep. 1937. Studied at Washington Univ. with Robert Wykes and Paul Pisk; and at Univ. of Montana with Eugene Weigel. He has been assistant professor, Coll. of Great Falls, 1965-68 and 1970- .

(CUBBAGE, JOHN)

WORKS: Chamber music: Chorale and variations, woodwind trio, 1962; string quartet, 1965; Recitative, solo violin, 1969; violin sonata, 1968; string trio, 1969; Piano: Three structural studies, 1963; piano sonata, 1970; Three pieces for piano, 1969; Adagio for piano, 1970.

Box 821, R.R. 2 South, Great Falls, MT 59401

CUMBERWORTH, STARLING A.

b. Medina, Ohio, 25 July 1915. Studied with Herbert Elwell at Cleveland Inst. of Music, M. M., M. A. 1941; with H. L. Baumgartner and Quincy Porter, Yale Univ. M. A. 1948; with Bernard Rogers and Howard Hanson at Eastman School of Music, Ph. D. 1958. He received awards at Cleveland Inst., Yale Univ. and from the Cleveland Woman's Club. He has been a faculty member at Cleveland Institute of Music; Mississippi Southern Coll.; Cuyahoga Community Coll.; Cleveland Music School Settlement, 1959- .

WORKS: Home burial, concert opera, 1955; Chamber music: trio for violin, clarinet, piano; trio for violin, cello, piano; flute sonata; oboe sonata; violin sonata; 2 string quartets; Songs: Sleep, child; Three Chinese love lyrics, soprano; 2 Macabre whims, baritone.

1844 Alvason Road, East Cleveland, OH 44112

CUMMING, RICHARD

b. Shanghai, China, 9 June 1928, American parents. Attended San Francisco Cons.; Music Acad. of the West, Santa Barbara; Aspen Inst. of Music; and studied privately with Ernest Block, Arnold Schoenberg, and Roger Sessions. He won a Nat. Fed. of Music Clubs prize, 1954; annual ASCAP awards, 1961- ; Ford Found. grant, 1963; Wurlitzer Found. grant, 1964; Rhode Island State Council for the Arts award, 1973. He was instructor, San Francisco Cons., 1947-54; vocal accompanist, 1954-66; composer-in-residence, Milwaukee Repertory Theatre, 1965-66 season, Trinity Square Repertory Company, Providence, 1966- ; on the staff, Rhode Island Governor's School for Youth in the Arts, 1969, 1970, 1972.

WORKS: Theatre: The picnic, 2-act opera, 1964-74; Years of the locust, Edinburgh Festival, 1968; Feasting with panthers, NET network, Jan. 1974; Voice: Tzu-Yeh songs, 1953; The crowne, 7 songs for bass and orch., 1956; We happy few, 10 songs, 1963; Mass for solo voice, oboe, string quartet, 1965; over 300 songs; Piano: sonata, 1951; 24 preludes, 1966-68.

c/o ASCAP
1 Lincoln Plaza, New York, NY 10023

CUMMINS, RICHARD

b. Petersburg, Va., 30 Sep. 1936. Graduated from Curtis Inst. of Music with the artist's diploma, and from Westminster Choir Coll. with B. M. and M. M. degrees. He is an organ and harpsichord recitalist and has held organist-choirmaster posts in churches in Pennsylvania and New Jersey; in 1973 at Virginia Heights Baptist Church, Roanoke.

WORKS: Chamber music: Three love songs, text by Sara Teasdale, high voice and piano; Introduction and allegro, oboe trio; Passacaglia

CUMMINS, RICHARD

(CUMMINS, RICHARD)
for harp; Chorus: Rise heart, thy Lord is risen, treble voices with organ; A psalm of destiny, chorus and organ, text by Dag Hammarskjold; Organ: Four chorale preludes.
2331 Denniston Ave., S.W., Roanoke, VA 24015

*CUNDICK, ROBERT
Divertimento and sonatina for organ.

CUNNINGHAM, ARTHUR
b. Piermont, N. Y., 11 Nov. 1928. Graduated from Fisk Univ., B. A. 1951; Columbia Teachers' Coll., M. A. 1957; and attended Juilliard School, 1951-52. His teachers were Wallingford Riegger, Johnny Mehegan, Teddy Wilson, Peter Wilhousky, Margaret Hillis, Henry Brant, Norman Lloyd, Peter Mennin, John W. Work. A fund for his music education was set up in 1946 by Lucinda Ballard and others; he has received 5 ASCAP awards and many commissions. He was in the U.S. Army Special Services, 1953-55; toured as bass player in a trio; played double bass in Rockland County Symphony; was advisor to the Rockland County Playhouse, 1964.
WORKS: Theatre scores: The beauty part, 1963; Violetta, 1964; Ostrich feathers, 2-act musical for children, 1964; Louey, Louey, minirock opera, 1968; Shango, 1969; Harlem suite ballet, Fisk Univ., 21 Apr. 1971; Orchestra: Adagio, string orch. and oboe, 1954; Theatre piece for orchestra, 1966; Prometheus, bass voice and orch., 1966; Dialogue, piano and chamber orch., 1967; Concentrics, New York, 2 Feb. 1969; Dim du mim, oboe and orch., 1969 (for English horn and orch., 1971); Lullaby for a jazz baby, trumpet and orch., 1970; The Walton statement, double bass and orch., for Ortiz Walton, 1971; Romp, strings and woodwinds, 1971; Strut, bass clarinet and orch., 1971; Litany for the flower children, chorus, orch., rock, blues, and gospel, Stanford Univ., 4 Aug. 1972; The prince, bass-baritone and orch., Detroit, 3 Apr. 1973; Chamber music: Perimeters, flute, clarinet, vibraharp, double bass, 1965; Minakesh, oboe and piano, 1969; Trinities, cello and 2 double basses, 1969; Eclatette, solo cello, 1971; Covenant, cello and double bass, 1972; Chorus: The gingerbread man, 1955; He met her at the Dolphin, 1963; The garden of Phobos, Suffern, N. Y., 2 Mar. 1969; Lord look down, 1970; We gonna make it, 1970; Harlem suite choral, Canton, N. Y., 21 Mar. 1971; World goin down, soprano and chorus, 1972; Call his name, 1972; Songs: Song of songs, poem by Wilfred Owen, soprano and piano, 1951; Turning of the babies in the bed, poem by Paul L. Dunbar, baritone and piano, 1951; Prometheus, baritone and piano, 1965; Minakesh, contralto and piano, Washington, D.C., 15 Nov. 1970; Born a slave, voice and piano, 1972; more than 400 songs in jazz-rock style; Piano: Engrams, 1969.
4 North Pine St., Nyack, NY 10960

CUNNINGHAM, MICHAEL
b. Warren, Mich., 5 Aug. 1937. Studied with Ruth Wylie at Wayne State Univ.; with Ross Lee Finney and Leslie Bassett, Univ. of Michigan; and Bernhard Heiden at Indiana Univ. He won honorable mention, Sigma Alpha Iota Interamerican

(CUNNINGHAM, MICHAEL)
Music awards, 1971; 2nd prize, Pittsburgh Flute Club contest, 1971; annual ASCAP awards since 1970. He was on the music faculty, Wayne State Univ., 1967-69; Kansas Univ., spring, 1972; Univ. of Pacific, spring, 1973; Univ. of Wisconsin-Eau Claire, 1973-
WORKS: Opera: Figg and bean, on play by J. M. Morton, Eau Claire, Wis., 7 Mar. 1975; Orchestra: Counter currents, 1967; Free designs, 1972; Band: Suite montage, 1969; Chamber music: Eusebius, viola, cello, piano; Coffee-cake walk, violin and piano; Dark vista, harpsichord and bass; Chorus: Gnosis, women's voices, 1972; Piano: sonata, 1970.
Music Department, University of Wisconsin Eau Claire, WI 54701

*CUOMO, JAMES
Chamberpiece for bearded percussionist and tape; Dry Ralph, solo trombone; Song at year's end, flute and vibraphone; For Zabulon Pike and Henry, 3 oboes, bassoon, marimba, percussion, rebab or any melody instrument.

CURNOW, ROBERT H.
b. Easton, Pa., 1 Nov. 1941. Studied at West Chester State Coll., Pa., and Michigan State Univ. with H. Owen Reed, Johnny Richards, and Russell Garcia. He won first place, Nat. Jazz Composition Contest, 1967. He was director of instrumental music, Case Western Reserve Univ., 1967-73; and has been director of artists and music, Creative World Records, Los Angeles, 1973-   .
WORKS: Concert jazz: Passacaglia; Festival piece; and some 45 published jazz and concert jazz works.
918 17th St., Apt. 3, Santa Monica, CA 90403

CURRAN, ALVIN
b. Providence, R. I., 13 Dec. 1938. Studied with Arlan Coolidge and Ron Nelson, Brown Univ., B. A. 1960; with Elliott Carter, Mel Powell, Alan Forte, Yale Univ., M. M. 1963. He received the Ditson Award, 1963; BMI Prize, 1963; Ford Found. Young Artists in Residence Program, 1963-64 (West Berlin).
WORKS: Chamber music: First piano piece; Thursday afternoon, unaccompanied violin; Homemade, percussion; Second trio, piano, clarinet, violin, 1963; Improvisational music: Community sing, 1966; La lista del giorno, 1967; Rounds, 1968; Tape and instruments: Under the fig tree; Madonna and child; Songs and views from the magnetic garden; and Music for every occasion, a collection of 50 original monophonic pieces.
Via dell' Orso 28, Rome, 00186, Italy

*CURRAN, PEARL GILDERSLEEVE
b. Denver, Colo., 25 June 1875; d. New Rochelle, N. Y., 16 Apr. 1941. Studied at Denver Univ. She wrote Nocturne, women's chorus; The crucifixion for solo voice; many other choral works and songs.

CURRIE, RANDOLPH NEWELL
b. Atmore, Ala., 5 Apr. 1943. Attended Ohio State Univ., B. M., M. M., in organ, Ph. D. candidate in musicology; studied composition with

(CURRIE, RANDOLPH NEWELL)
Marshall Barnes. He won an award in an organ music contest sponsored by Ohio State Univ. He has been organist and choirmaster, Immaculate Conception Church, 1969-   ; and lecturer in music, Ohio State Univ., Newark campus.
WORKS: Chorus: Bretheren, we have met to worship, women's voices and keyboard; Bless the Lord, o my soul, with organ and clarinet; Organ: Passacaglia on L'homme arme; and various English masses and service music, organ and piano works.
2678 Indianola Ave., Columbus, OH 43202

*CURTIS, EDGAR
Concerto for organ and strings.
Department of Music, Union College
Schenectady, NY 12308

CURTIS-SMITH, CURTIS O. B.
b. Walla Walla, Wash., 9 Sep. 1941. Studied at Northwestern Univ. with Alan Stout; Univ. of Illinois with Kenneth Gaburo and Herbert Brun; at Tanglewood with Bruno Maderna. He held a fellowship for Tanglewood, and was awarded the Koussevitzky Prize at Tanglewood, 1972. for Comedie. He has been assistant professor, Western Michigan Univ., 1968-   .
WORKS: Chamber music: Till thousends thee. Lps.: A secular alleluia without..., for 6 sopranos, 2 trumpets, 4 percussion, celeste, and rubbed water glasses, 1969; Xanthie, for 9 instrumental groups, 1972; Canticum novum/Desideria, 10 voices, 6 instruments, percussion, 1971; Comedie, 2 sopranos and chamber orch., 1972; A song of the degrees, 2 pianos, one percussion, 1972-73; Five sonorous inventions, violin and piano, 1973; Piano: Ordres, 1973; Mixed media: Passant. Un. Nous passons. Deux. De notre somme passons, Trois., for 19 solo voices (6-4-4-4, and mezzo soprano narrator), flute, double bass, harp, piano, celeste, percussion, and electronic sounds, 1970; Fanaffair for Fanny, 9 trumpets in 3 unequal groups and 4-channel tape, 1971.
933 Austin St., Kalamazoo, MI 49008

*CUSENZA, FRANK J.
b. San Vito, Italy, 25 Dec. 1899; U.S. citizen 1923. Studied at Royal Cons., Palermo, Italy; Great Lakes Coll., M. A. From 1922 he taught at the Detroit Cons.; Univ. of Detroit; Detroit Inst. of Musical Art. His works include an opera, a symphony, an oratorio, piano pieces and songs.

*CUSHING, CHARLES C.
b. Oakland, Calif., 8 Dec. 1905. Studied at Univ. of California and with Nadia Boulanger in France, 1929-31. He received the George Ladd Prix de Paris for achievement in composition, 1929; Legion of Honor of the French Government, 1952. He joined the faculty, Univ. of California, Berkeley in 1931; is also violinist and violist; founded and conducted the Univ. of California Band; has conducted choral, orchestral operatic and theatrical groups.
WORKS: Orchestra: Cereus, poem for orch., 1960; Chamber music: 2 string quartets; 2 violin sonatas; clarinet sonata; Fantasy, woodwind

(CUSHING, CHARLES C.)
trio; Lyric suite, soprano, flute, viola; The Eclogues for winds.

CUSTER, ARTHUR
b. Manchester, Conn., 21 Apr. 1923. Attended Univ. of Hartford, 1940-42; Univ. of Connecticut, B. A. 1949; Univ. of Redlands, M. M. 1951; Univ. of Iowa, Ph. D. 1959. He studied composition with Timothy Cheney, Paul Hindemith, Paul Pisk, Philip Bezanson, and Nadia Boulanger (1961-62). He received an award of the Society for the Publication of American Music, 1962; 2 Univ. of Rhode Island grants for creative work; and commissions. His undergraduate study was interrupted in 1942-46 for service in the Navy as a fighter pilot. He joined the faculty at Kansas Wesleyan Univ., 1952-55, chairman of fine arts division, 1954-55; then at Univ. of Omaha, 1955-58; music supervisor, U.S. Air Force Dependent Schools in Spain, 1959-62; was music consultant to USIA in Madrid; assistant dean for fine arts, Univ. of Rhode Island, 1962-65; dean, Philadelphia Musical Acad., 1965-67; director, St. Louis Metropolitan Educational Center in the Arts, 1967-73; named composer-in-residence, Rhode Island State Council on the Arts, 1973-   .
WORKS: Orchestra: Passacaglia for small orchestra, 1957, Chicago, 14 Apr. 1963; Concert piece, 1959, Austin, Tex., 27 Apr. 1963; Symphony No. 1, 1961, Madrid, 28 Apr. 1962; Songs of the seasons, soprano and small orch., 1963, Philadelphia, 20 Mar. 1966; Found objects II (Rhapsodality brass), New York, 8 Nov. 1969; Doubles for violin and small orch., 1972; Chamber music: Rhapsody and allegro, cello and piano, 1957; Three canons, 2 trumpets and piano, 1958; Three pieces for brass, Lawrence, Kan., 6 Apr. 1959; sextet, woodwinds and piano, 1959. Madrid, 3 May 1969; Divertimento, bassoon and piano, 1963; Pastorale and hornpipe, violin, clarinet, cello, 1963; Cycle for nine instruments, Univ. of Mass., 11 Mar. 1964; Concertino for second violin and strings, New York, 14 Nov. 1964; woodwind quintet, 1964; Permutations, violin, clarinet, cello, 1967, St. Louis, 14 Jan. 1969; Concerto for brass quintet, 1968, Univ. of Rhode Island, 17 Apr. 1969; Stream music, 11 instruments, 1969; Parabolas, viola and piano, 1970; Chorus: Quodlibetnam, motet, 1966; Songs: Three songs of death, mezzo-soprano, 1958; Songs of the seasons, soprano, 1963; Cartagena songs, bass-baritone, oboe, horn, piano, 1964; Three love lyrics, tenor, flute, viola, harp, Philadelphia, 18 Feb. 1966; Comments on this world, contralto and string quartet, 1967; Piano: Four ideas for piano, Washington, 2 May 1965; Rhapsodality Brown, Philadelphia, 5 Jan. 1969; Mixed media: Found objects I, chorus and tape, 1968; Interface I, string quartet, 2 recording engineers, and tape, 1969; Interface II, trombone, percussion, 2 recording engineers, and tape, 1969; Found objects III, contrabass and tape, 1971; Found objects IV, cello and tape, 1972; Found objects VI, flute and tape, Yale Univ., 10 Nov. 1973; A little sight music, an entertainment for 6 players and tape, Providence, 5 Apr. 1973; Found object VII, piano and tape, New York, 4 Apr. 1974. He has also

CUSTER, ARTHUR

(CUSTER, ARTHUR)
written incidental music for a dramatization of Thornton Wilder's novel, The Ides of March, and music for a number of television productions and films. His essays and articles in both English and Spanish have appeared in music journals.
4365 Post Road, East Greenwich, RI 02818

CYR, GORDON CONRAD
b. Oakland, Calif. 5 Oct. 1925. Studied at Univ. of California, Berkeley, A. B. 1966, Ph. D. 1969, with Roger Sessions, Joaquin Nin-Culmell, Charles Cushing, and William Denney. He received honorable mention in the 1955 James D. Phelan awards. He was lecturer at Univ. of California, Berkeley, San Francisco State Coll., and Coll. of the Holy Names, 1970-71; and has been assistant professor Towson State Coll., 1971-   .
    WORKS: Chamber music: string quartet, 1969; Voice: Peter Quince at the clavier, baritone, 1954; Three Shakespeare songs, high voice and chamber orch., 1962; Lamentations for Jeremiah, 2 sopranos and string orch., 1964; Sinfonias and arias, soprano and 7 instruments, Baltimore, 18 Mar. 1973.
    110 Glen Argyle Road, Baltimore, MD 21212

*CYTRON, SAMUEL
Suite for unaccompanied violin.

CZAJKOWSKI, MICHAEL
b. Milwaukee, Wis., 7 June 1939. Studied with Leo Sowerby at American Cons., with Bernard Wagenaar and Vincent Persichetti, Juilliard School; Morton Subotnick, New York Univ.; and Darius Milhaud at Aspen School. He won Gretchaninoff awards in choral composition, 1965, 1966. He has been on the faculty at Juilliard School, 1966-   ; Aspen Music School, 1966-   ; New York Univ., School of Education, 1971-   ; and director, New York Univ. Composers Workshop, 1969-   .
    WORKS: Chamber music: string trio; woodwind quartet; Toccata, romance and sundance, piano; Chorus: Three Shaker songs; and many choral works: Electronic: A Sunday in Hohocus, oboe and electronic score; Serenade, concert band, rock groups, electronic score, lights, film; People the sky, electronic score.
    3111 Broadway, New York, NY 10027

*CZERWONKY, RICHARD RUDOLPH
b. Birnbaum, Germany, 23 May 1886; U.S. citizen 1915; d. Chicago, Ill., 16 Apr. 1949. Studied violin with Joseph Joachim, Royal School of Music and made his debut with the Berlin Philharmonic, 1906. In the U.S. he was violinist, conductor and teacher in Boston, Minneapolis, Chicago; conductor, Kenosha (Wis.) Symphony, 1940-49.
    WORKS: Orchestra: symphony; violin concerto; Carnival of life; Weltschmerz, symphonic poem; Episode, a rhapsody; also chamber music and works for violin, voice, and piano.

*DA COSTA, NOEL
b. Lagos, Nigeria, 1930; to U.S. 1941. Studied at Queens Coll. and Columbia Univ.; with Luigi Dallapiccola in Italy on a Fulbright fellowship.

(DA COSTA, NOEL)
He received a New York State Council on the Arts grant, 1974. He is assistant professor, Rutgers Univ., and conductor of the Triade Chorale.
    WORKS: In the circle, 4 electric guitars, brass, percussion, 1969; The confessional stone, soprano and 10 instruments, text by Owen Dodson; The last judgment, women's chorus, narrator, piano, percussion, text by James Weldon Johnson, 1970; Blues mix, contrabass and tape, New York, 20 Oct. 1971; Fanfare rhythms, New York premiere, 30 Apr. 1974.
    Rutgers, The State University
    New Brunswick, NJ 08903

*DAHL, INGOLF
b. of Swedish parents, Hamburg, Germany, 9 June 1912; U.S. citizen 1943; d. near Bern, Switz., 7 Aug. 1970. Studied at Cologne Cons., Zurich Cons., and Univ. of Zurich; also with Nadia Boulanger. His awards include 2 Guggenheim fellowships; 2 Huntington Hartford grants; Nat. Inst. of Arts and Letters award; Society for Publication of American Music award; Alice Ditson Found. award; and commissions. In 1938 he settled in Hollywood, Calif., as arranger for films and radio; joined the faculty, Univ. of Southern California, 1943; toured West Germany for the U.S. State Department, 1961-62; conducted the Ojai Festivals, 1964-65.
    WORKS: Orchestra: Symphony concertante, 2 clarinets and orch., 1953; The tower of St. Barbara, Louisville, 29 Jan. 1955; Aria sinfonica, 1965; Variations on a theme by C.P.E. Bach, string orch.; Wind ensemble: concerto for saxophone and wind orch., 1949; Sinfonietta for band, 1961; Chamber music: Allegro and arioso, woodwind quintet, 1942; Music for brass instruments, 1944; Concerto a tré, clarinet, violin, cello, 1946; duo for cello and piano, 1946; Divertimento, viola and piano, 1946; piano quartet, 1957; piano trio, 1962; Sonata da camera, clarinet and piano; Duettino concertante, flute and percussion, 1966; Serenade, woodwind quartet; brass quintet; Chorus: A noiseless, patient spider, women's voices; Piano: Sonata seria, 1953; Sonata pastorale, 1960; Quodlibet on American folk tunes.

*DALLAM, HELEN
b. Chicago, Ill., 4 Oct. Studied at American Cons., M. M., on scholarship. She received several prizes in contests sponsored by the Chicago News. She taught at American Cons.; Acad. of Allied Arts, New York; privately in Columbus, Ohio, and Buffalo, N. Y.
    WORKS: Chamber music: quartet for strings and piano; The earth in cycle, soprano, harp, string quartet; also violin pieces and songs.

DALLIN, LEON
b. Silver City, Utah, 26 Mar. 1918. Studied with Howard Hanson and Bernard Rogers at Eastman School of Music, B. M., M. M.; with Miklos Rozsa and Ernest Kanitz at Univ. of Southern California, Ph. D. He has been on the faculties at Colorado State Univ., 1946; Univ. of Southern California,

(DALLIN, LEON)
1946-48; Brigham Young Univ., 1948-55; California State Univ., Long Beach, 1955-
WORKS: Orchestra: Symphony in D; Film overture; Symphonic sketches; Band: Sierra overture; Chamber music: string quartet; Chorus: Songs of praise, alto and tenor soli, chorus, orchestra or band; Keyboard: Interlude, organ; Prelude to midnight; Concert rondo; Autumn vignette. He is author of several textbooks on music.
Music Department, California State University Long Beach, CA 90840

DAMESEK, ABBE
b. New York, N. Y., 25 May 1904. Studied composition with Vittorio Giannini, piano with Rosina Lhevinne. He was a theatre pianist, 1924-27; played in hotels and supper clubs, 1929-70; was accompanist to Arthur Tracy on radio.
WORKS: Chamber music: string quartet, played by the Roman Totenberg Quartet, WQXR, 1948; Piano: 3 novelty piano solos, 1927; Runaway fingers, 1928; Dark keys, 1930.
1625 Rugby Road, Schenectady, NY 12309

DANA, WALTER
Real name Wladyslaw Danilowski. b. Warsaw, Poland, 26 Apr. 1902; U.S. citizen 1949. Studied at Warsaw Cons. with Henryk Melcer, Stanislaw Kazuro, Piotr Rytel. He received the Gold Cross of Merit from Poland's president; Royal Pin from Queen Elena of Italy; was named to the Polka Music Hall of Fame in the U.S. He was founder and conductor of Chor Dana, which twice toured the U.S. before World War II. Escaping from Poland in 1939 he made his way to the U.S. via Italy and settled first in Detroit, where he organized an American Chor Dana. War and army service interrupted this work, but on discharge in 1945, he went to New York and established Dana Records, for which he was artist and repertoire director, 1946-66.
WORKS: Orchestra: Jazz symphony in c; Florida sketches, Miami, 15 Mar. 1970; The wailing wall, Miami, 22 Mar. 1971; Aria and interlude for strings; Emotions; Chorus: Ora pro nobis, choir and orch.; Piano: Israeli's victory dance.
1130 Stillwater Drive, Miami Beach, FL 33141

*DANBURG, RUSSELL L.
b. Miller, S. Dak., 2 Mar. 1909. Studied with Cyrus Daniel and LaVahn Maesch, Lawrence Univ., B. M. 1931; with Edward Royce, Howard Hanson, Bernard Rogers, Eastman School of Music, M. M. 1935; graduate work at Juilliard School, 1941. He was awarded a research grant, 1961; Humanities Council grant, 1969. He taught at Dakota Wesleyan Univ., 1931-37; Washington State Univ., 1937-48; Univ. of Florida, 1948-   .
WORKS: Chamber music: Poeme, horn and piano, 1956; Lament and fanfare, trumpet and piano, 1971.
Department of Music, University of Florida Gainesville, FL 32601

D'ANGELO, JAMES
b. Paterson, N. J., 17 Mar. 1939. Studied at Manhattan School of Music with Vittorio Giannini, Nicolas Flagello, and Ludmila Ulehla; Lenox School

(D'ANGELO, JAMES)
School of Jazz with Gunther Schuller; privately with Lester Trimble, Jan Gorbaty, William Russo; and Jean Catoire in Paris. He received a BMI scholarship award in 1960. He has been a faculty member, New York Coll. of Music, 1967-68; New York Univ. School of Education 1968-69; Bronx Community Coll., CUNY, 1970-   .
WORKS: Orchestra: Concertino for saxophone quartet and orch.; The festival of Attis and Cybele, symphonic poem; The sign of Jonas: In memoriam Thomas Merton, orch. and speaker; Chamber music: Toccata, solo percussionist; tuba sonata; An essay for brass quintet; Quietude, 4 muted trumpets and percussion; The three gunas, woodwind trio; movements for 2 trombones; incidental music to Richard of Bordeaux; Chorus: Lord, it could be paradise, mixed choir; Nirvana, women's choir; Songs: 10 songs on texts of e.e. cummings; 6 modal songs on Chinese verse; various songs on texts of Blake, Merton, Poe, Frost, and Rumi.
1614 York Ave., New York, NY 10028

DANIEL, CYRUS
b. Carpenter, Ill., 27 Feb. 1900. Studied composition with Arne Oldberg in Chicago and York Bowen in London; he also studied violin, piano, and organ. He was professor, Lawrence Univ., 1925-44; director of music, Vanderbilt Univ., 1944-68; and organist and choirmaster, First Presbyterian Church, Nashville, 1944-69.
WORKS: Nocturne, New Haven Symphony, 1937; Chorus: Remember now thy creator, men's choir; Festival cantata, soloists, chorus, organ or orch.; A Biblical trilogy, mixed chorus a cappella; many other choral works.
703 Southeast 9th St., Delray Beach, FL 33444

*DANIELS, MABEL WHEELER
b. Swampscott, Mass., 27 Nov. 1878; d. Cambridge, Mass., 10 Mar. 1971. Studied at Radcliffe Coll., B. A. magna cum laude 1900; with George W. Chadwick, New England Cons.; and with Ludwig Thuille in Munich. Her awards included a MacDowell fellowship, 1931; honorary M. A., Tufts Coll., 1933; D. M., Boston Univ., 1939; citation Radcliffe Coll., 1954; D. M. Wheaton Coll., 1957; D. M., New England Cons., 1958; awards from Nat. Fed. of Music Clubs, 1911; Nat. League of American Pen Women; Nat. Asso. of American Composers and Conductors, 1958. She was music director, Simmons Coll., 1913-18; member and advisor for many musical groups in the Boston area.
WORKS: Theatre: The court of hearts, operetta, 1900; Alice in Wonderland continued, operatic sketch, 1904; Orchestra: Suite for strings, 1910; The desolate city, with chorus, 1913; Peace with a sword, with chorus, 1917; Songs of elfland, with chorus, 1924; The holy star, with chorus, 1928; Exultate deo, with chorus, for 50th anniversary of Radcliffe Coll., 1929; Deep forest, 1931; Pirates' Island, 1934; Song of Joel, with chorus and soprano, 1940; Pastoral ode, flute and strings, 1940; Digression for strings, a ballet, 1947; A night in Bethlehem, 1954; Chamber music: 3 observations, woodwind trio, 1943;

DANIELS, MABEL WHEELER

(DANIELS, MABEL WHEELER)
Chorus: In springtime, choral cycle for women's voices, 1910; Eastern song, women's voices, piano, 2 violins; The voice of my beloved, women's voices, piano, 2 violins; The Christ child, a cappella; Salve, festa dies, a cappella; Through the dark the dreamers came; Dum Dianae vitrea, women's voices; Flower wagon, women's voices; A psalm of praise; Piper, play on!, 1960; also composed choruses for the dedication of the Radcliffe Graduate Center, 1966. She wrote a book on her student days in Germany, An American girl in Munich, 1905.

DANIELS, MELVIN L.
b. Cleburne, Tex., 11 Jan. 1931. Studied at North Texas State Univ. with Samuel Adler and Merrill Ellis. He twice won the Nat. School Orch. Assoc. Roth composition contest, 1968, 1970. He has been on the faculty, Abilene Christian Coll., 1959-   , and music department head 1964-   .
WORKS: Orchestra: Festique, 1970; Celebration suite, Abilene Philharmonic Orch., Nov. 1973; many band compositions and choral anthems.
401 E.N. 23rd, Abilene, TX 79601

*DANIELSON, JANET
Music for 3 percussionists.

DANKNER, STEPHEN
b. Brooklyn, N. Y., 5 Nov. 1944. Studied with Paul Creston and Vittorio Rieti, New York Coll. of Music, B. M. 1966; with Hugo Weisgall, Queens Coll., 1966-68; and with Roger Sessions and Vincent Persichetti, Juilliard School, Ph. D. 1969. He received a BMI student composer award, 1968, and the Elizabeth Sprague Coolidge chamber music award, 1971. He was teaching fellow, Juilliard School, 1970-71; assistant professor, Brooklyn Coll., 1971-73; assistant professor, Williams Coll., 1973-   .
WORKS: Orchestra: symphony, 1969; Chamber music: string quartet, 1968; Three pieces for bass clarinet and piano, 1971; many other chamber and vocal works.
21 Berkshire Drive, Williamstown, MA 02167

*DANKWORTH, JOHNNY
Piano concerto.

DAPOGNY, JAMES
b. Berwyn, Ill., 3 Sep. 1940. Studied with Robert Kelly, Hunter Johnson, and Benjamin Johnston at Univ. of Illinois. He is on the faculty, Univ. of Michigan, instructor, 1966-71, assistant professor, 1971-   .
WORKS: Variations for orchestra, 1967, Univ. of Colorado, Contemporary Festival, 1968; Chamber music: Six variations for clarinet and piano, 1968; and works in most forms. He is editor of The collected piano works of Ferdinand 'Jelly Roll' Morton, published by Smithsonian Institution Press.
617 Kuehnle Ave., Ann Arbor, MI 48103

DARCY, WARREN JAY
b. Buffalo, N. Y., 10 Dec. 1946. Studied with Richard Hoffmann and Walter Aschaffenburg at

(DARCY, WARREN JAY)
Oberlin Cons.; with Benjamin Johnston and Edwin London at Univ. of Illinois. He was lecturer, Univ. of Illinois, 1972-73; and has been assistant professor, Oberlin Cons., 1973-   .
WORKS: Theatre: Hecuba, 1-act melodrama, 1972; Orchestra: Variations, 1967; Chamber music: Grand sonata for violin and piano, 1966; 5 structures for 5 instruments, 1966; Improvisations I, violin, clarinet, piano, 1967; Episode for string quartet, 1968; Dichotomy, flute, horn, cello, piano, 1969; Expansions, violin and piano, 1970; Chorus: War cantata, 1971.
143 East College St., Oberlin, OH 44074

DARGAN, WILLIAM T.
b. Monroe, N. C., 14 Aug. 1948. Studied with T. J. Anderson, Morehouse Coll.; Lloyd Ulten, American Univ.; and with Charles Jones at Aspen School of Music. He won third prize in the Darius Milhaud competition, Aspen, 1973. He was instructor, Morehouse Coll., 1972-74.
WORKS: Chamber music: 3 movements for 7 winds, 1974; Lyric dance, flute, oboe, clarinet, bassoon, horn, harp, cello, percussion, 1973. His music is post-Webern, avant garde, with material derived from jazz and Afro-American folk sources.
3235 Drexel Lane, Atlanta, GA 30304

DARROW, STANLEY
b. Camden, N. J., 16 Mar. 1934. Studied with J. Bazant in Czechoslovakia and P. Hoch in Germany. He won the 1970 Musician of the Year award of the American Accordion Assoc. He makes regular concert tours of Europe and is director, Acme Accordion School, Westmont, N. J.
WORKS: Accordion: Spanish rhapsody; 3 emotions: Excitement, melancholy, happiness; Reflections, for ensemble of mixed instruments.
322 Haddon Ave., Westmont, NJ 08108

DARST, W. GLEN
b. Shelby County, Ill., 21 Apr. 1896. Studied trumpet at an early age with his father, piano at American Cons.; played clarinet in 149th Field Artillery Band in World War I; then studied organ and composition privately. He won first prize in the Texas Composers' Guild Contest, 1961, 1962, first prize, Broadman Anthem competition, 1961. He was active as organist and choirmaster 1927-58; at St. John's Episcopal Church, Ft. Worth, 1945-58.
WORKS: Numerous choral compositions including: Ride on! Ride on in majesty!, sung by the Bell Telephone Chorus in 1956 and 1958; Thee we adore, 1961; Praise the Lord, Alleluia, 1961; O Son of Man, 1962.
6808 Koldin Trail, Fort Worth, TX 76119

DARTER, THOMAS E., JR.
b. Livermore, Calif. 13 Feb. 1949. Studied with Robert Palmer and Karel Husa at Cornell Univ., B. A. summa cum laude, 1969, M. F. A. 1972; D. M. A. candidate in 1973. He received the Otto Stahl award at Cornell, 1971; 2 first prizes and the Devora Nadworney award, Nat. Fed. of Music Clubs, 1969, 1971. He has been instructor and

(DARTER, THOMAS E., JR.)
director, Contemporary Music Ensemble, Chicago
Musical Coll., Roosevelt Univ., 1972-   .
WORKS: Orchestra: Aphorisms, 1972-73; Chamber music: piano sonata, 1967-68; Sonata-
fantasia, cello and piano, 1968-69; sonatina,
solo trumpet, 1970; quartet for piano and strings,
1970-72, Chicago, 16 May 1973; Four aphorisms,
for piano, 1970; Dual and fried, ensemble, 1973;
Chorus: Psalm 90, a cappella, 1968; Songs:
Batter my heart, baritone, 1967.
1130 South Michigan Ave., #616
Chicago, IL 60605

DARZINS, VOLFGANGS
b. Riga, Latvia, 25 Sep. 1906; to U.S. 1950;
d. Seattle, Wash., 24 June 1962. Studied at the
Latvian State Cons., earning his master's degree
in composition and piano and winning a first
prize for his piano concerto. He became a music
critic on one of the Riga papers, and as pianist
went on several tours of northern Europe playing
his second piano concerto with the Riga Symphony.
He and his wife fled from Latvia, and after five
years in DP camps were able to reach the U.S. and
settled in Spokane as pianist, teacher and composer. In 1955 he received an award from the
Latvian Cultural Fund in Exile for his second
piano sonata, and in 1960 for his arrangements
of 200 Latvian folk songs.
WORKS: Piano: sonata in F, 1951-52; sonata
#2, 1955; sonatina in G, 1956; suite in A, 1956;
Triade de preludes, 1957; Trittico barbazo, 1958;
Preludes, 1960; 8 petite suites, 1960.

*DASCH, GEORGE
b. Cincinnati, Ohio, 14 May 1877; d. Chicago,
Ill., 12 Apr. 1955. Was violinist with the
Chicago Symphony for 25 years. He wrote orchestral pieces.

DASHOW, JAMES
b. Chicago, Ill., 7 Nov. 1944. Studied with
J. K. Randall, Earl Kim, Edward Cone, Milton
Babbitt at Princeton Univ.; Arthur Berger,
Seymour Shifrin, and Martin Boykan at Brandeis
Univ.; and with Petrassi, Accad. Naz. di Santa
Cecilia, Rome. He received a Presser Found. fellowship; 2 Wilson Found. grants; Fulbright grant
to Rome; Premio Nicola D'Atri and Premio Bonaventura Somma in Rome. He was founder in 1971 of The
Forum Players, an international group of performers and composers dedicated to the performance of
new music. He has been director of the Rome-
based group since 1971.
WORKS: Orchestra: Astrazioni Pomeridiane,
quasi-variazioni per orchestra, 1970-71; Chamber
music: Songs of despair, soprano and large chamber ensemble, 1968-69; Timespace extensions, flute,
piano, pitched percussion, 1969; Duo for violin
and piano, 1970; Ashberry setting, soprano, flute,
piano, 1971-72; Maximus, to himself, soprano,
flute, piano, 1973; Mixed media: BURST!, soprano
and electronic accompaniment, 1971; Schiaffini
music, trombone and electronic accompaniment,
1972.
Via della Luce 66, 00153, Roma, Italia

DAUGHS, EUGENE WILLIAM
b. Idaho, 11 Oct. 1927. Studied at California
State Univ., Los Angeles, M. A. 1966; with Karl

(DAUGHS, EUGENE WILLIAM)
Kohn at Claremont Graduate School; and with
Anthony Vazzana at Univ. of Southern California.
He has been music coordinator and department
chairman, Azusa School District, 1971-   .
WORKS: Chamber music: Abstraction, viola
and piano; Two songs for soprano.
1123 Alamosa Drive, Claremont, CA 91711

*DAVENPORT, LA NOUE
b. Texas, 26 Jan. 1922. Studied with Erich Katz,
New York Coll. of Music.
WORKS: Chamber music: 3 duets, 2 flutes or
2 oboes or 2 clarinets; Variations on The ravens,
3 recorders; A day in the park, children's suite
for 4 recorders; Carols for recorders.

DAVID, AVRAM
b. Boston, Mass., 30 June 1930. Studied at Boston
Univ., B. A. 1955, M. A. 1956, D. M. A. 1964; also
at New England Cons.; Tanglewood; Brandeis Summer Inst., 1960; and Darmstadt, Germany, 1961,
1966. His composition teachers were Francis Judd
Cooke, Roslyn Brogue Henning, Harold Shapero,
Karlheinz Stockhausen, Pierre Boulez. He received a BMI award, 1958; second prize, Royaumont Concours, 1965; Factorial 17, No. 1 selected
for St. Cecilia Library, Rome, 1965; fellowships
at Boston Univ., 1966-68; Brandeis, 1960; research
fellowship to study the relationship of graphic
arts to music, Carpenter Center for the Visual
Arts, Harvard Univ., 1965-66. He is active as
composer, teacher, writer.
WORKS: Orchestra: Introduction and allegro,
1958; ESRAJ, a symphony; Chamber music: 2 string
trios; 3 string quartets; 2 violin sonatas;
Densities for chamber orch.; Canonic sonata, 3
trumpets; Utterances, trumpet solo; Voices and
whirlwinds, The breath of God, guitar sonata;
Vision, solo tuba; Paeans for Carl Ruggles, 8
brass instruments; Hexagrams, flute solo; Saturn
I, bass drum solo; A duet with the heart, clarinet; Canon for 4 trumpets; Piano: 2 sonatas;
Book of fragments I; The expected moment; Hommage a Marcel Duchamp; Chorus: Intonements,
6-part choir.
249 Commonwealth Ave., Boston, MA 02116

DAVIDOVSKY, MARIO
b. Buenos Aires, 4 Mar. 1934; to U.S. 1960.
Studied in Argentina with G. Graetzer, Erwin
Leuchter, Teodoro Fuchs, Ernesto Epstein. His
awards include 2 Guggenheim fellowships, 1960-62;
2 Rockefeller grants, 1960, 1965; Nat. Inst. of
Arts and Letters award, 1964; Brandeis Univ.
Creative Arts award, 1965; Pulitzer Prize, 1971,
for Synchronisms #6 for piano and electronic
sounds; special citation in Koussevitzky Internat. Recording award, 1972, for Synchronisms #5.
He has been associate director, Electronic Music
Center, Columbia-Princeton Univ., 1964-   ; and
associate professor, City College, CUNY,
1969-   .
WORKS: Orchestra: Planos, 1961; Electronic:
3 Electronic studies, 1961, 1962, 1965; 6 Synchronisms for various instruments and electronic
sounds, 1963-70; Instrumental: Inflexions, 2
flutes, clarinet, trumpet, trombone, 4 percussionists, piano, strings, 1970.
490 West End Ave., New York, NY 10024

DAVIDSON, CHARLES

*DAVIDSON, CHARLES
b. Pittsburgh, Pa., 8 Sep. 1929. Studied at
Univ. of Pittsburgh, B. M.; Eastman School of
Music; Jewish Theological Seminary, M. S. M.;
and on scholarship at Brandeis Univ. He was
chaplain's assistant, U.S. Army in Korea,
1952-53; cantor, Wantagh Jewish Center,
1955-   .
    WORKS: Chorus: Chassidic Sabbath; Hymn to
the 4 freedoms; I never saw another butterfly,
New York, 13 Mar. 1973.
    Wantagh Jewish Center, Wantagh, NY 11793

*DAVIDSON, HAROLD GIBSON
b. Low Moor, Va., 20 Feb. 1893; d. Glendale,
Calif., 14 Dec. 1959. Wrote for piano and
percussion.

*DAVIDSON, LYLE
b. 1938. Studied with Francis Judd Cooke and
Daniel Pinkham, New England Cons., B. M., M. M.;
with Arthur Berger, Brandeis Univ. He is on the
faculty, New England Cons.
    WORKS: Chamber music: A certain gurgling
melodiousness, chamber orch. and double bass,
Boston, 12 May 1973; Chorus: Voices of the dark,
with tape and optional bass instruments.
    265 Putnam Ave., Cambridge, MA 02139

DAVIDSON, WALTER
b. Poland, 21 Sep. 1902; U.S. citizen 1927.
Studied composition with Boris Levenson in New
York and with Solomon Ancis at the Denver Coll.
of Music; also studied at Pope Pius School of
Sacred Music. He has been on the faculty, School
of Sacred Music, Hebrew Union Coll.-Jewish Inst.
of Religion, 1957-   ; and cantor, Temple Beth
Sineth, Flatbush.
    WORKS: Vocal: High Holy Day music, solo,
choir, and organ; Songs of Israel, solo, choir,
organ; Friday evening and Saturday morning services for 2 voices and organ; Praise ye the Lord,
choir and organ.
    111 East 21st St., Brooklyn, NY 11226

DAVIS, ALBERT OLIVER
b. Cleveland, Ohio, 9 Apr. 1920. Studied at
Western Reserve Univ. with Max Smith, Myron
Schaeffer; Cleveland Inst. of Music with Herbert
Elwell; Arizona State Univ. with Kenneth Wright,
Grant Fletcher, Clifford Barnes, Paul Yoder. He
received the Mu Rho Alpha award at Arizona State
Univ., and ASCAP awards, 1966-71. He has been
arranger for various bands including the NORAD
Band, 1960-64; on the faculty at public schools,
1947-59; and at Phoenix Coll., 1968-   .
    WORKS: Band: Desert star; Hollywood sere-
nade; Threebones; Three cardinals; Festival at
Tikal, From shire and sea; etc.
    1329 East Catalina Drive, Phoenix, AZ 85014

DAVIS, ALLAN GERALD
b. Watertown, N. Y., 29 Aug. 1922. Studied with
William Berwald and William Naylor at Syracuse
Univ., B. M. 1944, M. M. 1945; and with Herbert
Elwell at Eastman School of Music. He received
commissions for 2 operas. He has held many faculty positions including lecturer, Queens Coll.,
1954-55, 1958-62; Hunter Coll., 1961-67; Lehman

(DAVIS, ALLAN GERALD)
Coll., CUNY, 1968-   . He has also been editor
and author for musical journals and for program
notes for records.
    WORKS: Opera: The sailing of the Nancy
Belle, chamber opera, 1945; The ordeal of Osbert,
1-act, 1949; The departure, Univ. of Montevallo,
Ala., 24 Apr. 1975; 3 acts, 6 scenes; Band:
Home town suite; Italian festival suite, brass
choir and percussion; Chamber music: Folk-
sonatine, bassoon and piano; Chorus: The married years, a cappella; A psalm of praise, chorus, brass, percussion; A song for Daniel, chorus, brass, percussion and piano; Piano:
Stackalee dances for 2 pianos; Razorback reel;
Sonata Veneziana; Three nursery miniatures.
    210 Riverside Drive, New York, NY 10025

DAVIS, ALLEN H.
b. Riverdale, Md., 12 Dec. 1945. Studied at
California Inst. of the Arts, and privately with
Richard Fenno and Harold V. Johnson. In 1974 he
was studying with Lloyd Rogers at California
State Univ., Fullerton. He composed and arranged
for Stan Kenton's Neophonic Orch., 1965, and for
Kenton's road orch., 1970.
    WORKS: Orchestra: Lamentations, for neo-
phonic orch.; Recollection of hoedown, wind orch.;
Chamber music: string quartet; Ballet suite, for
strings and jazz quintet; Piano, for alto voice
and piano.
    508 North Citron, Anaheim, CA 92805

*DAVIS, HARVEY O.
b. Cresson, Pa., 1915. Studied at Westminster
Coll. (pa.), A. B. 1937; Univ. of Michigan,
M. A. 1949; at Tanglewood, 1954. He has been
head, music department, Transylvania Coll.,
1951-   . He has published On Jordan's stormy
banks for chorus.
    606 Judy Lane, Lexington, KY 40507

DAVIS, JAMES FRANKLIN
b. Princeton, N. J., 14 Nov. 1944. Studied composition with Karel Jirak, conducting with
Gerald Ruquet and Francois D'Albert at Chicago
Cons. Coll. He played trumpet in the Irving
Symphony Orch., 1966-67; was founder and director, Illinois Symphonette, 1968-71; and has been
lecturer and director of bands, Florida Inst. of
Technology, 1972-   .
    WORKS: Orchestra: violin concerto; con-
certo for 10 instruments and piano; Chamber
music: string quartet; woodwind quintet; Nocturne; Chorus: Crucifixion; Etiam pro nobis.
    1201 Riverside Drive, Indialantic, FL 32903

DAVIS, JEAN REYNOLDS (Mrs. Warren H., Jr.)
b. Cumberland, Md., 1 Nov. 1927. Studied with
Robert Elmore and William R. Smith at Univ. of
Pennsylvania, B. M. She received the Thornton
Oakley Medal; Benjamin Franklin Medal; Cultural
Olympics Award of Merit; ASCAP award. She was
editorial consultant for a New York publisher,
1960-65; piano teacher, 1945-64.
    WORKS: Opera: The mirror; The elevator;
Orchestra: Shenandoah holiday, ballet story for
young people; 2 symphonies; Chamber music: woodwind quintet; many published choral works, vocal
solos, and piano teaching materials.
    226 Righters Mill Road, Gladwyne, PA 19035

DAVIS, JOHN JEFFREY
b. Chicago, Ill., 15 Aug. 1944. Studied with
Deems Taylor; and with Don Gillis and Gordon
Goodwin at Univ. of South Carolina, where he is
a graduate assistant.
WORKS: Chamber music: Short elegy for
strings, 1959; Three liturgical dances on the
first psalm tone, wind ensemble, 1970; Sweet
around C, woodwind quintet, 1974; 2nd woodwind
quintet, 1974; Chorus: Te Deum, trumpet, choir,
strings, 1964; Festival mass for the feast of
St. John, piccolo, 2 organs, mallet percussion,
cantors and choir, 1966; Mass for Easter Even,
2 cantors, choir, and bell, 1967; Lament on the
death of Lorenzo de' Medici, a cappella choir,
1970; Mass for the resurrection of the faithful,
unison choir and organ, 1971; Silent night, violin harp, treble solo and choir, 1973; Songs:
Five songs after e. e. cummings, soprano and
chamber orch., 1960; Three songs after Garcia
Lorca, unaccompanied soprano, 1964; Andante from
Masks of April, poems by Hester G. Storms, mezzo-
soprano and small orch., 1968; Four songs after
Hermann Hesse, baritone and string orch., 1974;
Keyboard: Four chorale preludes, organ, 1965;
piano sonatina, 1968.
    Institute of Media Arts
    University of South Carolina
    Columbia, SC 29208

DAVIS, JOHN S.
b. Evanston, Ill., 1 Oct. 1935. Studied with
Robert McBride at Univ. of Arizona, B. M. 1959,
M. M. 1964, D. M. A. 1967. He received a composer award of the Southern Arizona Opera Group,
1967; and the Music Teachers Nat. Assoc. commission for his Middle Earth suite. He has been
associate professor, North Carolina Wesleyan
Coll., 1967-   .
    WORKS: Opera: The pardoner's tale, 1967;
How a fish swam in the air and a hare in the
water, 1971; The tale of the golden goose, musical comedy; Orchestra: 2 symphonies; Chorus:
Psalm 148, 1967; Psalm 57, 1970; Agnus Dei, 1971;
200 other choral works; 40 instrumental ensembles, piano solos and duets, organ preludes.
    Music Department
    North Carolina Wesleyan College
    Rocky Mount, NC 27801

DAVIS, KATHERINE K.
b. St. Joseph, Mo., 25 June 1892. Attended
Wellesley Coll.; studied with Stuart Mason and
Nadia Boulanger. She won the Billings Prize for
composition at Wellesley, 1914; hon. degree,
Stetson Univ.; ASCAP award, 1969. She taught at
Wellesley Coll., 1916-18; Concord Acad., 1921-22;
Shady Hill School, Philadelphia, 1923-30.
    WORKS: Orchestra: The burial of a queen,
symphonic poem; Chorus: Carol of the drum (The
little drummer boy); This is noel, cantata; Fanfare for Palm Sunday; Sing gloria; The tiger,
Blake text; The lamb, Blake text, women's voices;
Renew a right spirit within me, women's voices;
many other choral works, vocal solos, piano
works.
    12 Bow St., Concord, MA 01742

DAVIS, MARGARET MUNGER
b. Spencer, Iowa, 22 July 1908. Graduated from
Northwestern Univ., 1931, and studied at American Cons. and privately with August Maekelberghe
in Detroit. She was teacher, accompanist,
1931-47; organist, Trinity Episcopal Church,
Detroit, 1965-   .
    WORKS: Many published choral works and
sacred vocal solos.
    855 Commerce Road, Milford, MI 48042

*DAVIS, MARY
Columbine, 3-act opera, Boulder Civic Opera,
Colo., 12 Apr. 1974.

DAVIS, NATHAN
b. Kansas City, Kan., 15 Feb. 1937. Studied at
Univ. of Kansas; Wesleyan Univ., Ph. D. 1974;
and with Andre Hodeir at the Sorbonne, Paris.
He received the WAMO Distinguished Musician
award, and was selected by Ebony Magazine for
its success series of Who's Who in Black America.
He is vice president, Segue Records; director
and founder of jazz studies, Paris American Acad.;
director and founder, jazz studies, Univ. of
Pittsburgh.
    WORKS: Jazz orchestra: The united spirited,
jazz orch., string quartet, choir; Makatuka;
Rules of freedom; Happy girl; To Ursula with
love.
    5619 Kentucky Ave., Pittsburgh, PA 15219

DAVIS, WILLIAM DWIGHT
b. Natchitoches, La., 6 Apr. 1949. Studied with
John W. Pozdro and Allen I. McHose, Univ. of
Kansas, B. M. 1971, M. M. 1972. He was 6th U.S.
Army Staff Bands officer, 1972-74.
    WORKS: Orchestra: Symphony in two move-
ments, 1971, Univ. of Kansas, 1972; Chamber
music: bassoon sonata, 1969; woodwind quintet,
1970; Music for a chamber ensemble, 1970; Sonata
for brass quintet, 1971; Chorus: Acquainted
with the night, 1969; My God, why hast Thou for-
saken me?, 1970; Piano: Aria and toccata, 1969;
Two impressions for piano, 1971.
    380 Talbot Ave., Apt. 109
    Pacifica, CA 94044

*DAVISON, ARCHIBALD THOMPSON
b. Boston, Mass., 11 Oct. 1883; d. Brant Rock,
Mass., 6 Feb. 1961. Studied at Harvard Univ.,
B. A. 1906, M. A. 1907, Ph. D. 1908. He
taught at Harvard, 1912-54.
    WORKS: Theatre: The girl and the chauffer,
musical comedy, 1906; Orchestra: Hero and
Leander, overture; Tragic overture. He wrote
several books on church music and on music history and education.

DAVISON, JOHN H.
b. Istanbul, Turkey, 31 May 1930; U.S. citizen
1948. Studied with Alfred Swan, Haverford, Coll.,
B. A. 1951; with Walter Piston and Randall
Thompson, Harvard Univ., M. A. 1952; with Howard
Hanson, Bernard Rogers, Alan Hovhaness, Eastman
School of Music, Ph. D. 1959; with Robert Palmer
at Cornell Univ. He received a Woodrow Wilson
fellowship, 1951; Knight Prize, Harvard, 1952;
Paine fellowship, 1953, 1954; MacDowell fellowship, 1960; Penn. Fed. of Music Clubs prize,

DAVISON, JOHN H.

(DAVISON, JOHN H.)
1962; Ford Found.-MENC fellowship, 1964-65; and many commissions. He was teaching assistant, Eastman School of Music, 1958-59; on faculty, Haverford Coll., 1959-   , professor, 1970-   .

WORKS: Orchestra: Concertino for 10 winds, cello, bass viol, 1954, rev. 1957, Rochester, N. Y., 23 May 1958; symphony No. 1 for small orch., Eastman School, May 1958; symphony No. 2, Eastman School, Apr. 1959; concerto for trombone and chamber orch., 1959, Arlington, Va., 10 Feb. 1963; symphony No. 3 for winds, 1964, Rochester, N. Y., 13 Dec. 1968; symphony No. 4 for strings, 1969; concertino for 3 violas and strings, 1973; Chamber music: sonatina No. 1, violin and piano, 1950; horn sonata, 1954; suite for flute and piano, 1955; trombone sonata, 1958; woodwind quintet, Lawrence, Kan., 3 May 1965; Trio-fantasia, violin, cello, piano, 1962, Philadel-phia, 15 May 1963; sonatina No. 2, 1964, New York, 27 Nov. 1966; clarinet sonata, 1966, Philadelphia, 7 May 1967; suite for marimba and strings, Phila-delphia, 29 Nov. 1967; sextet for English horn, piano, strings, 1968, Springfield, Pa., 10 Oct. 1969; Serenade for cello and piano, 1969; Quin-tet for trombone and string quartet, 1970; Chorus: Te Deum, choir and orch., solo soprano and solo oboe, 1960, West Chester, Pa., 22 Nov. 1964; Triptych: 3 canticles for men's voices and small orch., 1960, Haverford Coll., 24 Feb. 1961; Hodie Christus natus est, 1965; Great service, 1972-73; Magnificat of the planets, women's voices, 1973; Three psalms, 1955-72; Songs: Hymns of paradox, medium-high voice, 1955-65, Boston, 29 Dec. 1966; many other works for small ensembles, chorus, and for piano and organ.
3 College Circle, Haverford, PA 19041

DAVISON, PETER
b. Los Angeles, Calif., 26 Oct. 1948. Studied with Aurelio de la Vega, California State Univ. at Northridge; and with Roger Reynolds at Univ. of California, San Diego. He won a composition award at Los Angeles Valley Junior Coll., 1970. He was teaching assistant in electronic music, California State Univ., Northridge, 1970-73; and at Univ. of California, San Diego, 1973-   .

WORKS: Orchestra: Polyphemus; Chamber music: Hekhalot, for 3 flutes, or oboe, English horn, bassoon, or 3 clarinets, or string trio; Elec-tronic: Transgressions, tape.
4450 Piute Place, San Diego, CA 92117

*DAVYE, JOHN JOSEPH
b. Milton, Mass., 19 Oct. 1929. Studied at Univ. of Miami, B. M. 1952; with Warren Benson, Ithaca Coll., M. M. 1965. He has been faculty member, Old Dominian Coll., 1966-   . His published works include Canonic fantasy for 2 flutes; A child is born to us for chorus of treble voices.
Music Department, Old Dominian College
Norfolk, VA 23508

DAWES, WILLIAM
b. Kansas City, Mo., 27 July 1942. Studied pri-vately with Louis Callabro for a short time in 1966 and is otherwise self-taught.

(DAWES, WILLIAM)
WORKS: Chamber music: Chorale for 4 celli; Film score: violin-cello duet; Electronic tape: Three geese, 1968; Bluejay, 1968; Eve, 1968; Throwaway, 1968; Electronic study No. 1, 1968; Invitation to a gunfight, 1969; Lil, 1970; Cry for me, 1970; Rosebud, 1970; Bad Henry, 1973. The sound synthesis equipment used for the elec-tronic compositions was designed by Beman G. Dawes and constructed by the composer.
433 Broome St., New York, NY 10013

*DAWSON, WILLIAM LEVI
b. Anniston, Ala., 23 Sep. 1897. Studied at Tuskegee Inst., A. B. 1921; American Cons., M. A. 1927. He played first trombone, Chicago Civic Orchestra, 1926-30; conducted the Tuskegee Inst. Choir, 1931-54.

WORKS: Orchestra: Negro folk symphony, 1932, revised 1952; Out in the fields, soprano and orch.

*DAY, RICHARD
Grief for orchestra.

DEAK, JON
b. Hammond, Ind., 27 Apr. 1943. Studied contra-bass at the Juilliard School, B. M. 1965; Univ. of Illinois, M. M. 1968; composition with Alcides Lanza in New York. He had a Fulbright fellowship, 1967 for research in Rome. He was instructor, Interlochen Arts Acad., 1965-67; solo bassist, Chicago Little Symphony, 1965-67; teaching assistant, Univ. of Illinois, 1968-69; member, New York Philharmonic, 1969-   , assis-tant principal bassist, 1972-   .

WORKS: Instrumental music and music using natural sounds, mostly live, sometimes reinforced by visuals, e.g. self-made sculpture. Solo bass: Color studies, 1969; Surrealist studies, 1970; Chamber ensembles: Landforms, 1971; The Great Plains, 1973; Iowa, 1974; Static study No. 2; A December evening in the Adirondacks, New York, 22 Mar. 1974; Antrim County, Michigan, and Young Giacometti, New York, 8 Feb. 1975; Split Rock, with dance.
509 West 110th St., New York, NY 10025

DEAN, TALMAGE WHITMAN
b. Russellville, Tenn., 29 Jan. 1915. Studied with E. Edwin Young, Hardin-Simmons Univ.; Bernard Rogers, Eastman School of Music; Ellis Kohs, Halsey Stevens, Univ. of Southern Califor-nia. He received a special award Nat. Conf. on Church Music, 1964; special award, William Jewell Coll., 1964; Piper Professor award, Hardin-Simmons Univ., 1969, 1970; second award, Texas Composers Guild contest, 1971. He taught aerial navigation for the Navy at Univ. of Texas, 1943-44; spent 1956-67 at Southwestern Baptist Seminary as professor and chairman of graduate studies; and has been instructor to professor, Hardin-Simmons Univ., 1941-   , administrative dean, School of Music, 1953-56, dean, 1967-   . He was also a church music director, 1940-56.

WORKS: Chorus: The raising of Lazarus, chorus, soloists, organ, 1959; Behold the glory of the lamb, oratorio for chorus, soloists, orch.,

(DEAN, TALMAGE WHITMAN)
1963, premiered by Louisville Symphony and 800-voice chorus, 1964; Pax nobis, cantata for chorus, children's chorus, baritone, orch., 1967; Proclaim the word, cantata for chorus and brass, 1967; four cantatas for multiple choirs and organ; many shorter choral works. He was author of papers contributed to the Nat. Church Music Festival Program, Hattiesberg, Miss., April 1973.
School of Music, Hardin-Simmons University
Abilene, TX 79601

DE BERADINIS, JOHN ARTHUR
b. Stamford, Conn., 21 May 1943. Studied with Arnold Franchetti and Edward Miller at Hartt Coll. of Music, B. M., M. M. He was a fellow at the MacDowell Colony. He has been instructor, Hartt Coll. of Music, 1968- .
WORKS: Chamber music : Dialogues, violin and percussion; Music for percussion and piano; Rhapsody for vibraphone and violin; Two sketches for flute and vibraphone; Four miniatures for flute and vibraphone; Interlude for oboe and vibraphone Contrasts for vibraphone.
362 Bloomfield Ave., West Hartford, CT 06117

*DEBRAS, LOUIS
Sequenza II, solo oboe.

DE BRUYN, RANDALL KEITH
b. Portland, Ore., 2 June 1947. Studied with Robert Stoltze, Lewis and Clark Coll.; and with Salvatore Martirano and Benjamin Johnston, Univ. of Illinois. He was teaching assistant, Univ. of Illinois, 1970-74.
WORKS: Theatre: Composition for music and theatre, a multi-media event; Chamber music: violin sonata; Three Fantasies, violin, oboe, bassoon, cello, piano; Chorus: Christmas cantata, with chamber ensemble; Easter cantata, with chamber ensemble; Songs: Three songs for soprano; Piano: Prelude in the Phrygian mode; Rondo brilliante; Variations on a tonal theme; sonata.
2133 South Burdick, Kalamazoo, MI 49001

*DECEVEE, ALICE
b. Harrisburg, Pa., 25 Feb. 1904. Studied at Harrisburg Cons.; with Ernest Hutcheson, Juilliard School; also with Harvey Gaul and Henry Hadley. She received Nat. Fed. of Music Clubs awards and commissions. She taught at Harrisburg Cons.
WORKS: Theatre: Love in a bottle, music drama; Coney Island, a ballet; Orchestra : Memorabilia; Piano: Boogie Woogie goes high hat; Holland Tunnel, 2 pianos; and many songs.
105 South St., Harrisburg, PA 17101

DEDRICK, ARTHUR
b. New York, 1 Aug. 1915. Graduated from State Univ. Coll., Fredonia, N. Y., 1937. He was trombonist and arranger with the Red Norvo and Vaughn Monroe bands and staff arranger, WBEN Radio, Buffalo; then taught in public schools, 1949-55; since 1955 has been president of Kendor Music, Inc.
WORKS: He has published over 200 compositions and arrangements for stage bands, school bands, and solos and ensembles.
McKinstry Road, Delevan, NY 14042

DEDRICK, CHRISTOPHER
b. New York, 12 Sep. 1947. Attended State Univ. Coll., Fredonia, N. Y.; and Manhattan School of Music, 1965-69. He received an ASCAP award, 1968. He is arranger for U.S. Air Force Band, Airmen of Note, and writer, arranger, and performer with The Free Design, a vocal group.
WORKS: Orchestra: Four love seasons, with chorus, premiered by Buffalo Philharmonic; Band: Twilight, with solo oboe; Awakening, with solo trombone; Chamber music: Inspiration, solo bass trombone, winds, cello; many solos for bass trombone.
c/o Kendor Music, Inc., Delevan, NY 14042

*DEDRICK, LYLE (RUSTY)
Concert jazz: Follow me, New York, 28 Mar. 1973. Nocturne for trombone; The modern art suite, 4 saxophones.
Manhattan School of Music
120 Claremont Ave., New York, NY 10027

DEE, RICHARD
b. Knoxville, Tenn., 13 June 1936. Studied with Higo Harada and Lou Harrison. He was accompanist for Modern Dancers, 1965-68; lecturer, San Jose State Univ., 1970-73.
WORKS: Theatre: Bacchae, incidental music; Antigone, incidental music; Orchestra: suite; concerto for flute and percussion; Chamber music: Praises for voices and instruments; suite for cheng (Chinese 16-string psaltery); Chorus: Four patrons of the palestra, chorus and gamelan.
35 North 11th, San Jose, CA 95044

DE FILIPPI, AMEDEO
b. Ariano, Italy, 20 Feb. 1900, to U.S. 1905. Studied composition with Rubin Goldmark, and received a four-year fellowship at the Juilliard School. His viola sonata won an award at Princeton, 1936; and his Concerto for Orchestra was entered in the Philharmonic-Symphony Society of New York, American Composers contest in 1936-37. It won the award, but was disqualified because the contest was open to native-born composers only. He was composer and arranger for films, theatre, and radio, 1924-30; with CBS, 1930-58.
WORKS: Theatre: The green cuckatoo, 1-act opera; Malvolio, 2-act opera; Robert E. Lee, incidental music; Orchestra: Suite; Concerto for orchestra; symphony; Twelfth Night overture; Medieval court dances; Five Arabian songs, voice and orch.; Five medieval Norman songs, voice and orch.; Two sonnets, voice and orch.; 4 pieces for string orch.; Chamber music: string quartet; piano quintet; viola sonata; suite for brass quartet; Chorus: Three poems by Thoreau, a cappella; Three poems by Whitman, men's voices and brass; Children of Adam, cantata; Piano: sonata; 6 sonatinas; Prelude, passacaglia, and toccata; Partita; Film scores: Blockade; Leatherneck; Jazz age; Housekeeper's daughter; Everything on ice.
4101 Wilkinson Ave.
North Hollywood, CA 91604

DE GASTYNE, SERGE

DE GASTYNE, SERGE
b. Paris, France, 27 July 1930; U.S. citizen
1957. Attended Univ. of Portland, B. A. 1950;
Univ. of Maryland, M. M. 1968, D. M. A. 1971;
and studied composition with Howard Hanson at
Eastman School of Music, 1952. He was composer-
in-residence, USAF Symphony Orchestra and Band,
1954-71; and has been head, music department,
Northern Virginia Community Coll., 1971-   .
     WORKS: Orchestra: 6 symphonies, #5 1970.
#6 1973, premiered by Air Force Symph. in Alex-
andria, Va.; Band: Prelude to a play; Chamber
music: Ballata, vibraharp solo; Toccata for
marimba; Perpetual motion, vibraharp; Preludes
#1-8, vibraharp; quartet for mallet percussion;
Abacus in trio, horn, bassoon, vibraharp, marimba,
1969; Four musical moments, trumpet and piano,
1969; bassoon sonata, 1969; Fantasia, for piano,
1970; string quartet, 1971; Songs: May my heart;
Three young maidens; Sweet spring; Two songs on
Tanka poems; Deux chansons francaises, 1968.
     8534 Forrester Blvd., Springfield, VA 22152

*DEIS, CARL
b. New York, N. Y., 7 Mar. 1883; d. New York, 24
July 1960. Was teacher and choral conductor,
1906-19; organist, 1919-33, music editor, E. C.
Schirmer, Inc., 1917-53. He wrote chamber music
and songs, many of which were published.

DE JONG, CONRAD
b. Hull, Iowa, 13 Jan. 1934. Studied at North
Texas State Univ., B. M. 1954; with Bernhard
Heiden at Indiana Univ., M. M. 1959; and with
Ton de Leeuw at the Amsterdam Cons., summer 1969.
He received ASCAP awards, 1970, 1971, 1972; and
a commission for Grab bag for tuba ensemble. He
has been associate professor, Univ. of Wisconsin-
River Falls, 1959-   .
     WORKS: Chamber music: Three studies, brass
septet, 1960; Music for two tubas, 1961; Suite
of Wisconsin folk music, brass trio, 1962; string
trio, 1964; Fun and games, for any woodwind,
brass, or string instrument and piano, 1966;
Three pieces, 3 trumpets and piano, 1968;
Aanraking (Contact), solo trombone, 1969; Hist
whist, voice, flute, viola, percussion, 1969;
Grab bag, tuba ensemble, 1970; Etenraku (The
upper cloud music) for carillon or piano, 1971;
Chorus: Four choruses after Langston Hughes,
women's voices, 1964; Peace maker, a cappella,
1966; Peace on Earth, unison chorus and organ,
1969; Mixed media: Elm Street Dance Company
capers, tape and dance, 1972; Quarter break bit,
an activity, 1972; Kaleidoscopic vision (with
flashbacks) for tape and synchronized swimmers,
1973.
     800 South Fork Drive, River Falls, WI 54022

*DELAMARTER, ERIC
b. Lansing, Mich., 18 Feb. 1880; d. Orlando, Fla.,
17 May 1953. Studied with Guilmant and Widor in
Paris; was organist, conductor, music critic, and
teacher, 1903 to retirement. He received the
Eastman publishing award and was elected to membership, Nat. Inst. of Arts and Letters. His
works include 3 ballets, 4 symphonies, 3 overtures, 2 organ concertos, organ pieces, songs.

*DELANEY, CHARLES
b. Winston-Salem, N. C., 21 May 1925. Studied
at Davidson Coll., B. S.; Univ. of Colorado,
M. M.; Cons. of Lausanne on a Huntington Hartford
grant. He has been faculty member, Univ. of
Illinois, 1953-   , professor 1972-   ; chairman of instrumental music and orchestra conductor,
North Carolina Governor's School, 1962-   .
His compositions include Serenade for woodwind
quintet.
     School of Music, University of Illinois
     Urbana, IL 61801

*DELANEY, ROBERT MILLS
b. Baltimore Md., 24 July 1903; d. Santa Barbara,
Calif., 21 Sep. 1956. Studied with Nadia
Boulanger and Arthur Honegger in Paris. His
awards include a Guggenheim fellowship, 1929;
Pulitzer prize for music to John Brown's body by
Stephen Vincent Benet, 1933.
     WORKS: Orchestra: John Brown's song, cho-
ral symphony, 1931; Night, chorus, string orch.,
piano, on Blake text, 1934; Western star, chorus
and orch., 1944; Chamber music: Suite for woodwind quintet; Chorus: My lady clear.

*DELANO, JACK
Sonatina for flute.

DELAVAN, MACON
b. San Antonio, Tex., 7 Sep. 1932. Studied with
Samuel Adler at North Texas State Univ.; with
Woodrow James at Univ. of Oklahoma. He was faculty member, East Texas Baptist Coll., 1962-64;
North Texas State Univ., 1964-66; and chairman,
music department, Grand Canyon Coll., 1966-   .
     WORKS: Opera: House by the stable, Christ-
mas opera, 1-act, Phoenix, 1971; Orchestra: Hill
country, tone poem, Dallas Symphony, 1963; Chamber music: brass quintet; Prodigal son, cantata
for baritone and string quartet; The Christ who
died for me, song.
     1540 North Flower Circle, Phoenix, AZ 85026

DEL BORGO, ELLIOT ANTHONY
b. Port Chester, N. Y., 27 Oct. 1938. Studied
with Vincent Persichetti at the Philadelphia
Cons. He received awards from the Univ. Awards
Committee and the Festival of the Arts, Potsdam,
N. Y. He taught in Philadelphia, 1960-66; and
has been associate professor, State Univ. Coll.,
Potsdam, 1966-   .
     WORKS: Orchestra: Symphonic ode; Variations
on a folk melody; A festival piece; Chorale and
fugue; Serial music for orchestra; Suite for
strings; Band: Symphonic essay; Chorale and
variant; Music for winds and percussion; Concerto
grosso for brass quintet; chamber music, songs,
and 2 etude books for piano: The tonality of
contemporary music, and The rhythm of contemporary music.
     RD #1, Potsdam, NY 13676

*DE LEONE, FRANCESCO B.
b. Ravenna, Ohio, 28 July 1887; d. Akron, Ohio,
10 Dec. 1948. Studied with Ernest Bloch. He
was opera conductor, 1927-35; founded the music
department, Univ. of Akron; head of piano

(DE LEONE, FRANCESCO B.)
department in his own school, 1934-48. His works include 2 operas, 2 operettas, 4 music dramas, an oratorio, orchestral pieces, numerous songs and piano pieces.

DELINGER, LAWRENCE ROSS
b. Hyannis, Neb., 11 Nov. 1937. Studied with Ernest Kanitz, Los Angeles, and with Edward Applebaum, Univ. of California, Santa Barbara. He was music director, Pacific Cons. of the Performing Arts, Santa Maria, 1968-73; professor, Allan Hancock Coll., Santa Maria, 1971-73; and in 1973 joined the staff, Univ. of California, Santa Barbara.
WORKS: Theatre: Photograph, opera on text of Gertrude Stein; Othello, incidental music commissioned by Oregon Shakespeare Festival, 1973; incidental music for some 15 productions; Orchestra: Chromoscape, 28 winds and percussion; Chamber music: Inflections, woodwind quartet and piano; Invention No. 1 for piano; Invention No.2, bassoon, cello, piano, and percussion; Monolog, unaccompanied cello; and Ray Bradbury's dark carnival, pop-rock songs to Bradbury stories from October country.
1000 West Oak, Lompoc, CA 93436

DELLA PERUTI, CARL
b. Plainfield, N. J., 1 Apr. 1947. Attended Ithaca Coll., B. F. A. 1969; and Cleveland Inst. of Music, M. M. 1971; studied with Donald Erb. He received a Kappa Gamma Psi prize, 1969; and won an award in the Catgut Acoustical Society competition for New String Music, 1973. He is a free-lance trombonist and instrumental instructor in the public schools, Piscataway, N. J.; also co-director of New Music Coalition, a group dedicated to performance of recent music.
WORKS: Chamber music: Four movements for winds and contrabass; brass quintet; Diversion for trombone and percussion; Autumn music, flute, clarinet, trombone, piano; Sections, Leftovers I, II, III, for clarinet, bass clarinet, trombone, piano; string quartet for new violins.
1316 Walnut St., South Plainfield, NJ 07080

DELLO JOIO, NORMAN
b. New York, N. Y., 24 Jan. 1913. Attended City Coll., CUNY; Inst. of Musical Art; Juilliard School; Yale Univ.; studied with Casimir Dello Joio, Gaston Dethier, composition with Paul Hindemith and Pietro Yon. His many honors include Elizabeth Sprague Coolidge award 1937; Town Hall Composition award, 1941; 2 Guggenheim fellowships, 1943, 1944; grant from Nat. Inst. of Arts and Letters, 1945; 2 New York Music Critics Circle awards, 1949, 1958; Pulitzer Prize, 1957; television Emmy Award, 1964; Lancaster Symphony Composer Award, 1967; 5 honorary degrees. He was on the faculty, Sarah Lawrence Coll., 1944-50; professor, Mannes Coll. of Music, 1956-72; acting dean, School of Fine and Applied Arts, Boston, Univ., 1972, dean, School of the Arts, 1974- .
He was cultural representative for the U.S. State Department to the USSR, Rumania, and Bulgaria.
WORKS: Opera: The triumph of St. Joan, 1950; The ruby, 1955; The trial at Rouen, 1956; Blood

(DELLO JOIO, NORMAN)
moon, 1961; Ballet: Prairie, 1942; Duke of Sacramento, 1942; On stage!, 1944; Wilderness stair, 1948; Orchestra: Sinfonietta, 1941; Magnificat, 1942; concerto for 2 pianos, 1942; To a lone sentry, 1943; Concert music, 1944; Western star, orch., narrator, soloists, 1944; harp concerto, 1944; Ricercari, piano and orch., 1946; Serenade, 1948; Variations, chaconne, and finale, 1947; New York Profiles, 1949; Concertante, clarinet and orch., 1949; Epigraph, 1951; Trimph of St. Joan suite, 1951; Meditations on Ecclesiastes, 1956; Air power, symphonic suite, 1957; Fantasy and variations, piano and orch., 1962; Antiphonal fantasy on a theme of Vincenzo Albrisi, organ, brass, strings, 1966; Choreography, string orch., 1972; Homage to Haydn, Boston Univ., 17 Apr. 1974; Chamber music: concertino for piano and chamber orch., 1939; concertino for flute and strings, 1940; concertino for harmonica and strings, 1943; sextet for 3 recorders and string trio, 1943; trio for flute, cello, piano, 1945; Variations and capriccio, violin and piano, 1948; Chorus: Vigil strange, 1942; Mystic trumpeter, cantata, 1943; A jubilant song, 1946; Madrigal, 1947; Psalm of David, with brass, percussion, and strings, 1950; Mass, choir, brass, organ, percussion, 1968; To St. Cecilia, choir and brass, 1968; Evocations, choir, piano, orch., 1970; Bright star, Light of the world, 1971; Psalm of peace, chorus, brass, organ, piano, 1971; Songs: Lamentation of Saul, baritone and orch., 1954; Songs of Abelard, band and optional voice, 1969; Piano: suite, 1941; Duo concertante, 2 pianos, 1943; 3 sonatas, 1942, 1943, 1947; Prelude: To a young musician, 1945; Prelude: To a young dancer, 1946; 2 Nocturnes, 1949.
41 Crafts Road, Chestnut Hill, MA 02167

*DELMAR, DEZSO
b. Timisoara, Hungary, 14 July 1891; to U.S. 1922. Studied with Bartok and Kodaly. His works include a symphony, 3 string quartets, string trio, violin sonata, choral works, songs.

DEL MONACO, ALFREDO
b. Caracas, Vzla., 29 Apr. 1938; to U.S. 1969. Studied with Primo Casale in Caracas and also earned a J. D. in law, 1961; studied with Mario Davidovsky and Vladimir Ussachevsky at Columbia Univ., D. M. A. 1974. He received the Venezuela Nat. Award in Music, 1968, and in the same year was founder and director of the Internat. Society for Contemporary Music.
WORKS: Electronic: Electronic study No.2, 1970; Dualismos, ensemble and electronic sounds, commissioned by Vth Inter-american Music Festival, Washington, 1971; Alternancias, ensemble and electronic sounds, 34th Internat. Music Festival, Venice, Biennale, 1971; Syntagma, trombone and electronic sounds, 1972; Tropicus, 1973.
622 West 114th St., New York, NY 10025

*DE LONE, PETER
Introduction and capriccio, brass and percussion.

DE LONE, RICHARD PIERCE

*DE LONE, RICHARD PIERCE
Wayne, Pa. Studied at Peabody Cons., B. M. 1953, M. M. 1954. He received a scholarship at Peabody, 1952; Maryland Fed. of Music Clubs prize, 1952; Gustav Klemm prize, 1953, 1954. One of his prize-winning compositions was Impromptu and romance, cello and piano. He is professor and chairman, School of Music, Indiana University.

DELP, RON
b. Tampa, Fla., 27 Sep. 1946. Studied with John Bavicchi and William Maloof, Berklee Coll. of Music. He has been instructor, Berklee Coll. of Music, 1971-   .
WORKS: Percussion: Scherzo; Modogenesis; Dreams; Quaternion; Phonetiks.
845 Boylston St., Boston, MA 02116

*DEL RIEGO, THERESA
Homing, vocal duet.

DEL TREDICI, DAVID
b. Cloverdale, Cal., 16 Mar. 1937. Studied with Seymour Shifrin and Arnold Elston, Univ. of California, Berkeley, B. A. 1959; with Earl Kim and Roger Sessions, Princeton Univ., M. F. A. 1964. He received the Woodrow Wilson award, 1960; Hertz award, 1962; Guggenheim fellowship, 1966; Fromm Found. commission, 1964; Koussevitzky Found. commission, 1966; Nat. Inst. of Arts and Letters award, 1968; Naumberg award, 1972; Brandeis award, 1973. He was assistant professor, Harvard Univ., 1966-71; creative associate, Buffalo Univ., 1972; teaching associate, Boston Univ., 1973-   .
WORKS: Chamber music: string quartet; string trio, 1959; Vocal; Songs to texts of James Joyce, soprano and piano, 1959; I hear an army, soprano and string quartet; Syzygy, soprano and chamber orch.; Night conjure-verse, soprano, mezzo-soprano, chamber ensemble, 1965; Pop-pourri, soprano, chorus, rock group, orch.; Alice, Return of Alice, Vintage Alice, three large works for soprano, folk group (mandolin, banjo, saxophones, accordion) and orch., based on Alice in Wonderland; Piano: Scherzo for 2 pianos; Fantasy pieces.
Bog Schoolhouse, Alexandria, NH 03222

*DEMAREST, CLIFFORD
b. Tenafly, N. J., 12 Aug. 1874; d. Tenafly, N. J., 13 May 1946. Wrote choral works, organ pieces and songs.

DE MARINIS, PAUL MICHAEL
b. Cleveland, Ohio, 6 Oct. 1948. Studied with Robert Ashley, Terry Riley, and Lars Gunnar Bodin at Mills Coll., M. A. 1973. He is technical assistant with Buchla and Associates, Berkeley.
WORKS: Electronic: P. L. L. Bach, live synthesizer, 1972; Morning music, 2 keyboards, 1972; In Sara, Mencken, Christ, and Beethoven there were men and women, tape in collaboration with Robert Ashley, 1973; The pygmy gamelan, concrete electronic circuitry, 1973; Duet, live electronics, 1974.
2807 Piedmont Ave., Berkeley, CA 94705

DEMMING, LANSON F.
b. Buffalo, N. Y., 25 Oct. 1902. Attended Eastman School of Music, B. M.; Univ. of Illinois, M. M. He was professor, Univ. of Illinois, 1930-45; Univ. of Houston, 1945-60; music director, radio station WILL, 1935-45; minister of music, St. Paul's Methodist Church, Houston, 1945-73; organist, Temple Beth Yeshurun, Houston, 1953-73.
WORKS: Many choral compositions including: The eternal gate; In Bethlehem of Judea; Oh, Crown Him, double chorus; seasonal introits and responses; A festival processional.
2217 Portsmouth, Houston, TX 77006

DENBOW, STEFANIA BJÖRNSON
b. Minneota, Minn., 28 Dec. 1916. Attended Univ. of Minnesota, B. A., M. A.; studied composition with Karl Ahrendt. She received a Mu Phi Epsilon award, 1973; and was finalist in Festival of Contemporary Music, Marshall Univ. She teaches piano and organ, has been church organist since 1949, and part-time at Christ Lutheran Church, Athens, 1950-   .
WORKS: Chamber music: string quintet; Chorus: Christ is risen, cantata for choir, soloists, chamber orch., 1972; Magnificat, choir, mezzo-soprano, chamber orch., Athens, Ohio, March 1974; Contemporary mass; Songs: Four songs of The Eremite Isle; By the Willows, song cycle; Keyboard: Three Hellenic stanzas, piano; Exaltatio, organ; Organ suite, chorale, chorale prelude, fugue, passacaglia.
61 Columbia Ave., Athens, OH 45701

DENNIS, ROBERT
b. St. Louis, Mo., 5 May 1933. Studied with Vincent Persichetti at The Juilliard School; with Tony Aubin at Paris Cons.; and with Boris Blacher at Tanglewood. He received Fulbright scholarships, 1956-57. He was a founding member of the composer-performer group, The Open Window (with Peter Schickele and Stanley Walden), 1968-71.
WORKS: Theater: scores for Oh! Calcutta; Bartholomew fair; Medicine show; Slaughterhouse play; Endicott and the Red Cross by Robert Lowell; Orchestra: Pennsylvania Station, from Three views from the open window; Klezmorim; Chamber music: Improvisations and variations for cello and piano, 1962-65.
885 West End Ave., New York, NY 10025

DENNISON, SAM
b. Geary, Okla., 27 Sep. 1926. Studied with Spencer Norton, Harrison Kerr, Univ. of Oklahoma; with Halsey Stevens, Univ. of Southern California. He received a Phi Mu Alpha award, 1949; Carolyn Alchin award, 1952. He was a private teacher and arranger, 1953-55; teacher, Louisville Acad. of Music, 1955-60; faculty, Inter-American Univ., Puerto Rico, 1960-64; music librarian in charge of American Music Collection, Free Library of Philadelphia, 1964-   . In Puerto Rico he worked with Roy Harris in preparing his scores for publication; in Philadelphia, he is also conductor and teacher, teaching music theory as a volunteer in the city's prison system.

(DENNISON, SAM)
WORKS: Opera: The last man on Earth, 1-act, 1952; Conrad Crispin's broom, 1-act, work in progress; Chamber music: Mother wears army boots, violin and piano, 1949; Quodlibet, flute, oboe, bassoon, 1953; Folksong medley, violin, horn, piano, 1957; brass sextet, 1963; suite for flute solo, 1968; Vocal: Jesu Christes milde moder, chorus, 1963; The faucon hath taken my mate away, chorus, 1963; The days of the week, song cycle for countertenor and harpsichord, 1953; Epithalamium, 1968; Piano: Thirteen pieces for Helen, 1948; Monologue of a water faucet, 1948; 3 sonatas, 1949, 1950, 1963; Film scores: Good speech for Gary, 1952; History of Delaware; Penn relays, 1968; radio and television scores.
4608 Wilbrock St., Philadelphia, PA 19136

*DENNY, WILLIAM
b. Seattle, Wash., 2 July 1910. Has written 2 symphonies, other orchestral works, chamber music, choral works, organ pieces. He is professor and chairman, music department, Univ. of California, Berkeley.

*DENSMORE, JOHN H.
b. Somerville, Mass., 9 Aug. 1880; d. Boston, Mass., 21 Sep. 1943. Studied at Harvard Univ., A. B. 1904; wrote operettas for the Hasty Pudding Club and choral works.

DE PUE, WALLACE EARL
b. Columbus, Ohio, 1 Oct. 1932. Studied at Capital Univ., B. M. 1956; Ohio State Univ., M. A. 1957; with H. Owen Reed at Michigan State Univ., Ph. D. 1965. He received Bowling Green State Univ. research grants, 1973, and a MacDowell fellowship, 1973. He taught in public schools, 1957-60; was music supervisor, Toledo Museum of Art, 1964-66; faculty, Bowling Green State Univ., 1966-
WORKS: Opera: Dr. Jekyll and Mr. Hyde, Bowling Green, Apr. 1974; Orchestra: concerto for percussion; Prelude and sarabande, string orch.; Chamber music: Sonata primitif, marimba and piano; Toccatina, 2 drums and piano; Vocal: Psalm 90, chorus and viola; Dedication, baritone and organ.
950 Fairview Ave., Bowling Green, OH 43402

DERBY, RICHARD
b. Indianapolis, Ind., 23 Jan. 1951. Studied with Peter Racine Fricker, Univ. of California, Santa Barbara, B. A. 1973, candidate for Ph. D. He has won 3 second prizes in Nat. Fed. of Music Clubs contests.
WORKS: Orchestra: Elegy, 1973; Chamber music: trio for violin, viola, piano, 1971; flute sonata, 1972; Variations for string quartet, 1972; Five short pieces, cello solo, 1973; Chorus: To everything there is a season, a cappella, 1969; Four sacred texts, a cappella, 1971; Magnificat, with orch., 1972; Mass, a cappella, 1972-73; Keyboard: piano sonata, 1970-71; Piano episodes, 1971; Piano preludes, 1972-73; organ sonata, 1973.
9121 Mediterranean Drive
Huntington Beach, CA 92646

*DES MARAIS, PAUL
b. Menominee, Mich., 23 June 1920. Studied with Walter Piston, Harvard Univ., B. A. 1949, M. A. 1953; also with Nadia Boulanger in Cambridge. He received the Lili Boulanger prize, 1948; Boott prize, 1949; John Knowles Paine traveling fellowship, 1949-51; Thorne Music Fund award, 1970-73, for the study of the sounds made by underwater animals. In 1974 he was studying plant responses to various stimuli and measuring the results with electronic equipment. He has been professor, Univ. of California, Los Angeles, 1960-   . His works include 2 piano sonatas; chamber music; choral pieces.
Department of Music, University of California
Los Angeles, CA 90024

DE SOMERY, GENE DAVID
b. Quincy, Calif., 3 Mar. 1948. Studied with Peter Racine Fricker, Thea Musgrave, Douglas M. Green, and Daniel Lentz, Univ. of California, Santa Barbara, B. A. 1970; with Donald Martino, New England Cons., M. M. 1973. He held scholarships for his study at the New England Cons.
WORKS: Orchestra: Chamber symphony, Boston, 14 Mar. 1973; Chamber music: Sounds for 12 winds and percussion, Boston, 12 May 1973; Three songs, voice and piano, Boston, 27 Mar. 1973.
284 Pepperwood Lane, Garberville, CA 95440

*DETT, ROBERT NATHANIEL
b. Drummondville, Quebec, Canada, 11 Oct. 1882; d. Battle Creek, Mich., 2 Oct. 1943. Studied at Oberlin Coll., B. M. 1908, D. M. 1926: Columbia Univ.; Harvard Univ.; Eastman School of Music, M. M.; Howard Univ., D. M. 1924; Univ. of Pennsylvania. He received the Bowdoin literary prize at Harvard, and the Harmon prize, 1927. He was church pianist, Niagara Falls, 1898-1903; director of music, Lane Coll., 1908-11, Lincoln Inst., 1911-13; Hampton Inst., 1913-35; Sam Houston Coll., 1935. The Hampton Inst. Choir, which he founded and directed for 22 years, toured Europe in 1929.
WORKS: Oratorios: The ordering of Moses, chorus and orch.; The chariot jubilee, tenor, chorus, and orch.; many other choral works; Piano suites: Magnolia; In the bottom; Tropic winter; Enchantment; Cinnamon grove; 8 Bible vignettes.

*DEUTSCH, ADOLPH
b. London, England, 20 Oct. 1897; U.S. citizen 1920. Studied at the Royal Acad. of Music, London; continued studies in composition and conducting in the U.S. In the 1920s he became a film score composer for Warner Brothers. His Scottish suite, commissioned by Paul Whiteman, was performed by the Philadelphia Orchestra and the New York Philharmonic. He founded the Screen Composers' Asso. and was its president, 1943-53.

*DEUTSCH, HERBERT A.
b. Baldwin, N. Y., 9 Feb. 1932. Studied with Elie Siegmeister at Hofstra Univ.; with Nicolas Flagello and Ludmila Ulehla, Manhattan School of Music. He has been director, Electronic Music

DEUTSCH, HERBERT A.

(DEUTSCH, HERBERT A.)
Studio, Hofstra Univ., 1970-   , and chairman, music department, 1973-   .
WORKS: Chamber music: Soliloquy, clarinet solo; Chorus: Mutima, chorus, percussion, flute; Mixed media: Sonorities, tape and orchestra; Moon ride, tape and band; Fantasia on Es Ist Genug, tape and wind ensemble; Jazz images, tape and piano.
19 Crossman Place, Huntington, NY 11743

DE VITO, ALBERT
b. Hartford, Conn., 17 Jan. 1919. Studied at New York Univ., B. S., M. A.; and Columbia Univ. He has received ASCAP awards, honorary D. M. A., Eastern Nebraska Christian Coll., 1974. He is a free-lance composer, teacher, editor, and author of magazine articles on piano technique and methods.
WORKS: Many choral works, piano solos, piano methods, organ arrangements, and popular songs.
361 Pin Oak Lane, Westbury, NY 11590

DE VOE, ROBERT ALAN
b. Elmira, N. Y., 9 July 1928. Was trained as a painter and sculptor at Temple Univ., Tyler Art School, M. F. A., and is self-taught in music. He taught humanities and art in a demonstration high school for Univ. of Connecticut, 1959-68; and has been assistant professor of humanities, Fairleigh Dickinson Univ., 1968-   .
WORKS: Electronic: Music of the spheres; Electronic Zen charts; Celestial pavan; Electronic meditations; Electronic visions.
32 Piermont Ave., Hillsdale, NJ 07642

DE VOTO, MARK BERNARD
b. Cambridge, Mass., 11 Jan. 1940. Studied at Longy School of Music, Harvard Univ., and Princeton Univ.; his principal teachers were Randall Thompson, Walter Piston, Roger Sessions, Earl Kim, Milton Babbitt. He received a BMI student composer award, 1961; Fromm Found. commission, 1968. He has been on the faculty, Reed Coll., 1964-68; Univ. of New Hampshire, 1968-   .
WORKS: Orchestra: Night songs and distant dances, 1962; piano concerto No. 2, 1965-66; piano concerto No. 3, The distinguished thing, 1968; Vocal: Planh, for 6 voices, flute, oboe, clarinet, trombone, and harp, 1961; Two songs, soprano, flute, viola, trombone, harp, 1961; Three songs of Edgar Allan Poe, soprano, concertina, guitar, harpsichord, and 8 flutes, 1967, revised 1970; Fever-dream vocalise, soprano, soprano, flute cello, piano, percussion, 1968.
Music Department, University of New Hampshire
Durham, NH 03824

*DEYO, FELIX
b. Poughkeepsie, N. Y., 21 Apr. 1888; d. Baldwin, N. Y., 21 June 1959. Wrote 3 symphonies, 2 piano sonatas, violin sonata, piano pieces, etc.

*DEYO, RUTH LYNDA
b. Poughkeepsie, N. Y., 20 Apr. 1884; d. Cairo, Egypt, 4 Mar. 1960. Studied composition with Edward MacDowell. She made her piano debut at age 9; later appeared in recitals with Kreisler

(DEYO, RUTH LYNDA)
and Casals, and was soloist with major orchestras in the U.S. and Europe. In 1925 she went to live in Egypt and turned full attention to composition. Her works include The diadem of stars, a full-length opera on Egyptian themes.

DE YOUNG, LYNDEN E.
b. Chicago, Ill., 6 Mar. 1923. Studied at Roosevelt Univ. and Northwestern Univ.; his principal teachers were Karel Jirak, M. Liede-Tedesco, Oswald Jones, Anthony Donato. He received the Thor Johnson award for a brass ensemble composition, 1951. He was instructor, Roosevelt Univ., 1951-59; associate professor, Northwestern Univ., 1971-74, chairman, department of theory and composition, 1968-   .
WORKS: Orchestra: Fugue; Theme and variations; Poem; Brass ensemble: Divertissement, 1951; 3 brass quintets, 1952-54; choral works and chamber music.
664 Pine Court, Lake Bluff, IL 60044

DIAMOND, ARLINE
b. New York, N. Y., 17 Jan. 1928. Studied with Bernard Rogers at Eastman School of Music; Univ. of Miami; Columbia Univ., M. A., and with Benjamin Boretz, Felix Greissle, Ralph Shapey, Bernard Wagenaar, privately. She teaches piano.
WORKS: Orchestra: symphony, performed by Miami Symphony; Chamber music: violin sonata; Composition, clarinet solo.
186 Birch Drive, New Hyde Park, NY 11040

DIAMOND, DAVID
b. Rochester, N. Y., 9 July 1915. Had his first formal training at Cleveland Inst. of Music, 1927-29; then entered Eastman School of Music, 1930-34, studying with Bernard Rogers; later in New York with Roger Sessions and in Paris with Nadia Boulanger. He held scholarships for all study; received Juilliard Publication award, 1937; 2 Guggenheim fellowships, 1938, 1941; Prix de Rome, 1942; Paderewski Prize, 1943; Nat. Acad. of Arts and Letters grant, 1944; 2 New York Music Critics Circle awards, 1947, 1948; Fulbright grant, 1951; Rheta Sosland Chamber Music prize, 1966; ASCAP-Stravinsky award, 1967; many commissions; and has been elected to the Nat. Inst. of Arts and Letters. He went to Europe in 1951 as a Fulbright professor and eventually settled in Florence, remaining in Italy until 1965 except for brief appointments at Univ. of Buffalo in 1961 and 1963. He joined the faculty at Manhattan School of Music in 1965, but since 1967 has devoted his time exclusively to composition.
WORKS: Orchestra: Aria and hymn; Sinfonietta, 1936; Psalm, 1936; Overture; violin concerto, 1937; Elegies, flute, English horn, strings, 1937; cello concerto, 1938; Elegy in memory of Maurice Ravel, brass, harp, percussion, or strings and percussion, 1938; Heroic piece, 1938; Concert piece, 1940; concerto for chamber orch., 1940; concerto for 2 pianos, 1941; 8 symphonies, 1941-61; Rounds for string orch., 1944; Romeo and Juliet, 1947; Timon of Athens, symphonic portrait after Shakespeare, 1949; The enormous room, 1949; piano concerto, 1949; Ceremonial

(DIAMOND, DAVID)
fanfare, brass ensemble; Ahavah, narrator and orch., 1954; Sinfonia concertante, 1956; The world of Paul Klee, 1957; Chamber music: Partita, oboe, bassoon, piano, 1935; concerto for string quartet, 1936; quintet, flute, string trio, piano, 1937; sonata for cello solo, 1938; 10 string quartets, 1940-   , No.10 premiere, New York, 4 Feb. 1974; violin sonata, unaccompanied, 1945; Chaconne, violin and piano, 1947; Introduction and dance, accordion; piano sonata, 1947; sonatina for accordion; Night music, string quartet and accordion; quintet, 4 woodwinds and horn; quintet, clarinet, 2 violas, 2 cellos, 1951; piano trio, 1951; Nonet, 3 violins, 3 violas, 3 cellos, 1962; Chorus: This sacred ground, baritone, mixed chorus, children's chorus, orch.; The martyr, men's voices and orch., or a cappella; To music--Chorale symphony, tenor, bass-baritone, chorus, orch.; Let us all take to singing, men's voices a cappella; All in green went my love riding, women's voices a cappella; The glory is fallen out of the sky, women's voices a cappella; Chorale, women's voices a cappella; Prayer for peace, mixed choir, a cappella; Three madrigals, mixed choir a cappella; and many songs.
249 Edgerton St., Rochester, NY 14607

DIAMOND, STUART SAMUEL
b. New York, N. Y., 15 Jan. 1950. Studied with John Davison at Haverford Coll., B. A. 1971, cum laude; with Meyer Kupferman and Edmund Haines, Sarah Lawrence Coll., M. F. A. 1973. He was Phi Beta Kappa member at Haverford Coll., and named Outstanding Young Composer-1973, by Nat. Found. for the Arts and Sciences. He is associate conductor, Bronx Philharmonic, 1971-   ; member of The Allegri Consort, 1973-   ; principal bassoonist, Mannes Orch.; director, Electronic Studio, Sarah Lawrence Coll., 1973-   .
WORKS: Orchestra: symphony in one movement; overture; Chamber music: quartet for winds and piano; piano sonata; string quartet; The dreams of Jez, clarinet and piano; Voice: Song of songs, cycle for voice and piano; Resurrection, cantata for chamber ensemble; Film scores: The zoo story; Winding down; High school horror; Electronic: The jester, tape; The adventures of Andrew in the land of Odibil, tape, flutes, narrator; Darling, poor darling, electronic theatre piece.
c/o Diamond and Golomb
99 Park Ave., New York, NY 10016

*DIBDEN, CHARLES
The waterman, opera.

*DI CHIERA, DAVID
Rumpelstiltskin, children's opera, Detroit, Jan. 1973.
Department of Music, Oakland University
Rochester, MI 48063

*DICK, MARCEL
b. Miskolcz, Hungary, 28 Aug. 1898; to U.S. 1934. Studied at Royal Acad. of Music, Budapest, degree and title of professor, 1917. He was violist, Detroit Symphony, 1934-35; Stradivarius Quartet,

(DICK, MARCEL)
1935-42; Cleveland Orchestra, 1943-49; professor and chairman of theory and composition, Cleveland Inst. of Music, 1948-   .
WORKS: Orchestra: symphony, 1950; Adagio and rondo; Capriccio, 1956; symphony for strings, 1964; Chamber music: 2 string quartets; piano trio; 4 elegies and an epilogue, solo cello, 1951; sonata for violin and cello, 1952; Essay for violin and piano, 1955; Suite for piano, 1959.
2608 Norfolk Drive
Cleveland Heights, OH 44106

*DICK, ROBERT
b. New Haven, Conn., 1950. Received a BMI award for Afterlight for solo flute, 1973.

DICKERSON, ROGER
b. New Orleans, La., 24 Aug. 1934. Studied at Dillard Univ., B. A. 1955, cum laude; with Bernhard Heiden, Indiana Univ., M. M. 1957; and with Karl Schiske and Alfred Uhl, Vienna Acad. of Music, 1959-62. His awards include scholarships for all study 1951-57; Dave Frank music award, 1955; Fulbright grants, 1959, 1960; John Hay Whitney fellowship, 1964; American Music Center award, 1972; B# music award, 1973. He served in the U.S. Army, 1957-59; was program associate in humanities, Inst. for Services to Education, Washington, D.C., 1970-73; free-lance musician and composer, 1962-
WORKS: Orchestra: Concert overture, 1957; A musical service for Louis, requiem for Louis Armstrong, commissioned, New Orleans Philharmonic, Mar. 1972, New York, 4 Feb. 1973; Band: Essay for band, 1958; Orpheus, New Orleans, 21 Jan. 1975; Chamber music: sonatina for piano, 1956; string quartet, 1956; Chorale prelude for organ, 1956; clarinet sonata, 1960; quintet for winds, 1961; Concert pieces for young string players, 1973; Songs: Music I Heard, 1956; The Negro speaks of rivers, 1961.
2855 Allen St., New Orleans, LA 70119

*DICKEY, MARK
b. Ludlow Center, Mass., 2 July 1885. Studied piano with Arthur Foote, organ with Albert Snow; won the H. W. Gray prize, American Guild of Organists, 1935. He was church organist at age 12; organist-choirmaster, First Universalist Church, Somerville, Mass.
WORKS: Opera: Little Red Riding Hood; Chamber music: Rhapsody, violin and piano, 1936; Allegro scherzando for string quartet; Chorus: Let not your heart be troubled, anthem, 1935; also songs and piano pieces.

*DICKINSON, CLARENCE
b. Lafayette, Ind., 7 May 1873; d. New York, N. Y., 2 Aug. 1969. Studied at Miami Univ., Ohio; Northwestern Univ., A. M. 1909, D. M. 1917; composition with Gabriel Pierné in Paris. He was organist at the Brick Presbyterian Church and Temple Beth-El, New York; professor, Union Theological Seminary, New York, 1912-45. He wrote an opera, a comic opera; Storm King for orchestra; choral works, organ pieces.

DI DOMENICA, ROBERT

DI DOMENICA, ROBERT
b. New York, N. Y., 4 Mar. 1927. Studied with
Wallingford Riegger and Josef Schmid in New York.
He held a Guggenheim fellowship, 1972-73. He has
been on the faculty, New England Cons.,
1969   , and associate dean, 1973-   .
WORKS: Opera: The balcony, 1973; Orchestra:
symphony, 1961, Baltimore, 1965; concerto for
violin and chamber orch., 1962, 20th Century Innovations, 1965; Chamber music: quintet for
clarinet and string quartet, 1965, Univ. of Illinois, 1971; flute sonata; saxophone sonata; woodwind quintet; Variations on a tonal theme,
unaccompanied flute.
17 Paul Revere Road, Needham, MA 02194

DIEBEL, WENDEL H.
b. Des Moines, Iowa, 20 Feb. 1914. Studied with
Bernard Wagenaar at Juilliard Graduate School.
He has received several commissions. He was
piano assistant to James Friskin and Ernest
Hutcheson, Chautauqua Summer Inst., 1940-48; and
was professor, Colorado State Univ., 1948-74.
WORKS: Orchestra: Concert piece for piano
and orch., 1938, CBS international broadcast;
piano concerto, 1940; Chamber music: Fantasy,
harp, flute, and string orch., 1964; Toccata,
solo harp, 1966; Two etudes, solo harp, 1968;
Ten bagatelles, brass quintet and harp, 1969;
Three American folk tunes, brass quartet and
harp, 1970; horn sonata, 1970; trio sonata for
flute, cello, and harp.
1314 West Mountain Ave.
Fort Collins, CO 80521

DIEMENTE, EDWARD
b. Cranston, R. I., 27 Feb. 1923. Attended Bos-
ton Univ.; studied with Isadore Freed at Hartt
Coll. of Music; and with Bernard Rogers, Eastman
School of Music. He has been professor, Hartt
Coll. of Music, 1949-   ; and music director
and organist, Cathedral of St. Joseph, Hartford,
Conn., 1961-   .
WORKS: Chamber music: string quartet, 1967;
Unvelopment, double bass solo and wind ensemble;
Celebration, wind ensemble; 2 wind quartets;
3-31-70, wind ensemble; 3 pieces for 2 clarinets;
trio, flute, trumpet, percussion; For miles and
miles, solo vibes; Response, saxophone and piano;
Designs, trumpet and trombone; Chorus: Magnifi-
cat, chorus, boys' choir, organ; 3 motets for
chorus; 2 pieces for mixed chorus; Piano:
clavier sonata; 4 waltzes; In a call of wind;
Organ: 2 preludes; Three versets on Pange lingua;
Mixed media: Something else, recorder and tape;
The eagles gather, organ, percussion and tape.
72 Montclair Drive, West Hartford, CT 06107

DIEMER, EMMA LOU
b. Kansas City, Mo., 24 Nov. 1927. Studied with
Richard Donovan and Paul Hindemith, Yale School
of Music, B. M. 1949, M. M. 1950; with Ernst
Toch, Roger Sessions, Tanglewood, 1954, 1955;
with Bernard Rogers, Howard Hanson, Eastman
School of Music, Ph. D. 1960. Her awards include
a Fulbright scholarship, 1952; Louisville Orch.
Student award, 1955; 2 Mu Phi Epsilon awards,
1955; Arthur Benjamin award, 1959; Ford Found.-
Nat. Music Council Young Composers Project grant,
1959-61; ASCAP-Nat. Fed. of Music Clubs award,

(DIEMER, EMMA LOU)
1969; ASCAP awards, 1962-   . She was composer-
in-residence, Arlington, Va., 1959-61; composer-
consultant, Arlington and Baltimore schools,
1964-65; assistant professor, Univ. of Maryland,
1965-70; assistant professor, Univ. of California,
Santa Barbara, 1971-73, associate professor,
1973-   .
WORKS: Orchestra: Festival overture; Symphonic antique; Rondo concertante; Pavane; Band:
The brass menagerie; suite; Chamber music: sextet for winds and piano; woodwind quintet; violin sonata; flute sonata; Toccata for flute
chorus; Toccata for marimba; Chorus: Fragments
from the Mass, women's voices; Three madrigals,
chorus and piano; Verses from the Rubaiyat;
Anniversary choruses, with orch.; The prophecy,
women's voices; Piano: Seven etudes; Sound pictures; Organ: Toccata; Fantasie; Fantasy on
'O Sacred Head.'
Department of Music, University of California
Santa Barbara, CA 93106

DIERCKS, JOHN
b. Montclair, N. J., 19 Apr. 1927. Studied with
Herbert Elwell at Oberlin Coll., B. M.; with
Bernard Rogers, Alan Hovhaness, Howard Hanson at
Eastman School of Music, M. M. Ph. D. He received a Southern Found. fellowship, 1958;
Danforth Found. grants, 1960, 1962; MacDowell
fellowship, 1963; Cooperative Program in the
Humanities award, 1965; ASCAP awards, 1968-72;
and many commissions. He was conductor, Blue
Ridge Chamber Music Players, 1961-62; music
critic, Roanoke Times, 1962-   ; chairman, music
department, Hollins Coll., 1962-72, professor,
1973-   .
WORKS: Chamber music: quintet for piano
and strings; suite, alto saxophone and piano;
oboe sonata; Fantasy for horn; Variations for
tuba; Figures on china; brass quartet; wind quintet; Mirror of brass, 7 instruments; horn quartet; Chorus: Ascribe ye greatness, festival
cantata for chorus, brass, percussion; A star
arises, cantata for mixed or women's chorus,
flute, percussion; Why do the nations rage,
Psalm 2, chorus, piano or organ.
Hollins College, VA 24020

DIETZ, NORMAN C.
b. Michigan, 12 Mar. 1919. Studied with H. Owen
Reed at Michigan State Univ. He is professor and
conductor of bands, Central Michigan Univ.
WORKS: Band: Prelude and scherzo; Brass
ensemble: Modern moods, sextet; Piece for 11
brass and percussion; trio for trumpet, horn,
trombone; Fantasy for percussion; Chorus: Book
of Job, baritone, chorus, and orch.
Central Michigan University
Mount Pleasant, MI 48858

*DI GIACOMO, FRANK
The beauty and the beast, 1-act opera, Syracuse,
N. Y., 24 May 1974.

DILL, WILLIAM L.
b. Chiselhurst, N. J., 27 Oct. 1913. Studied
with private instructors. He is conductor, Philadelphia Civic Concert Band.

(DILL, WILLIAM L.)
WORKS: Band: Champions of democracy, march; Synocracy, march; Modeerf, concert piece; Rhythmology, advanced method for drums.
749 South 19th St., Philadelphia, PA 19146

DILLER, SARALU C.
b. Ohio, 3 June 1930. Studied at Baldwin-Wallace Cons., B. M.; Univ. of Maryland, M. M.; Univ. of Colorado; and with Carlisle Floyd at Florida State Univ., 1969. She was staff accompanist, Univ. of Colorado, 1966-68; director-actor, Nomad Playhouse, Boulder, 1959-72; director, Vail Summer Theater, Vail, Colo., 1973; violinist, Akron Symphony Orch., Akron, Ohio, 1956-59.
WORKS: Theatre: A child is born, score for a play, 1962; Cave dwellers, score, 1963; Ding-an-sich, 3 players, 1 percussion, 1 tape, 3 voices, 1967; The little prince, child's folk opera, 1972; Chamber music: Three sketches, piano, 1966; Format: #1, #2, #3, for 6 players, 2 percussion, voice, 1970; The bad quartet, brass, 1970; Chorus: Ship of death, 2 poems, with orch., 1971; Songs: In that strange city, 1968; Lonely; The feast, 1968; Outside in, 1969.
1526 Sunset Blvd., Boulder, CO 80302

*DILLON, FANNIE CHARLES
b. Denver, Colo., 16 Mar. 1881; d. Altadena, Calif., 21 Feb. 1947. Studied at Claremont Coll.; in Berlin; and with Rubin Goldmark in New York. She taught at Pomona Coll. and in Los Angeles schools. She wrote orchestral works and many piano pieces.

DILLON, ROBERT M.
b. Downs, Kan., 29 Sep. 1922. Studied with Spencer Norton at Univ. of Oklahoma; with Halsey Stevens at Univ. of Southern California; with Cecil Effinger and Philip Batstone, Univ. of Colorado. He received first prize in the Harvey Gaul competition, 1950; and a commission from Oklahoma Music Teachers Assoc., 1971. He taught in public schools, Bethany, Okla., 1951-65; and has been associate professor, Central State Univ., Okla., 1966- .
WORKS: Band: Southwestern panorama; Quartz Mountain; The far country; Four winds; Distant hills; Small ensemble: brass quintet; March and chorale, brass quartet; Allegro festoso, 4 clarinets; High tide, brass quintet; Lament, bassoon and piano; Petite etude, flute and piano; Night shade, 4 saxophones; Scherzo, oboe and piano; many unpublished works for orchestra, band, and ensembles.
1300 East Drive, Edmond, OK 73034

DILSNER, LAWRENCE
b. New York, N. Y., 22 July . Studied at New York Univ., B. S., M. Ed.; with Charles Courboin and Nadia Boulanger in France; Philadelphia Musical Acad., D. M. He held a scholarship for study at Guilmant Organ School; received several prizes for teaching. He has been a teacher and church organist in the New York metropolitan area 1945- .

(DILSNER, LAWRENCE)
WORKS: Piano, organ, chorus, and flute compositions.
41 Branchport Ave., Long Branch, NJ 07740

DINERSTEIN, NORMAN
b. Mass., 18 Oct. 1937. Studied with Gardner Read at Boston Univ.; with Arnold Franchetti at Hartt Coll.; with Gunther Schuller, Aaron Copland, and Lukas Foss at Tanglewood; with Boris Blacher in Berlin; and with Roger Sessions, Milton Babbitt, and Edward T. Cone at Princeton. His honors include the Koussevitzky Prize; Sagalyn Orchestral award; Fulbright grants, 1964, 1969-70; Ford Contemporary Music Project fellowship, 1966-68; Univ. of Rhode Island Arts Council award; Di Tella award, Buenos Aires, 1970. He was teaching fellow, Hartt Coll., 1960-63; teaching assistant, Princeton Univ., 1965-66; faculty member, New England Cons., 1968-71; Fulbright lecturer in Buenos Aires, 1969-70; faculty, Hartt Coll., 1971- .
WORKS: Orchestra: Cassation; Serenade; Chamber music: Four settings for soprano and string quartet; Three miniatures, for strings; Chorus: Cinque laude; Answered question; Our father.
43 Thomas St., Rockville, CT 06066

DI PASQUALE, JAMES A.
b. Chicago, Ill., 7 Apr. 1941. Studied with Anthony Donato, James Hopkins, Alan Stout at Northwestern Univ.; with David Diamond, Nicolas Flagello, and Ludmila Ulehla at Manhattan School of Music; privately with Joseph Daley and Leon Stein. He won awards in the Collegiate Jazz Festival, 1961, 1962; and in the American Film Festival, 1965 for the score to The way back. He has been visiting lecturer-clinician, Univ. of Montana; music director, Winter Consort, 1965, 1969-70.
WORKS: Chamber music: saxophone sonata; Interplay, chamber ensemble; Showing great restraint, chamber ensemble; and many jazz works.
9031 Phyllis Ave., Los Angeles, CA 90069

DI PIETRO, ROCCO
b. Buffalo, N. Y., 15 Sep. 1949. Studied privately with Lukas Foss in Buffalo, and with Bruno Maderna at Tanglewood. He received an ASCAP fellowship to Tanglewood, 1971, and performance by Gunther Schuller of his composition Drafts. He was visiting artist, Stockbridge School, 1971-72-73; composer-in-residence, Earlham Coll., 1973; staff for Contemporary Sound Series, Recording Laboratories, 1973- .
WORKS: Orchestra: Chrysalis, 48 strings; Refractions; Chroma; Chamber music: 4 temperatures, 4 flutes; Two colors for Robert Bly; Electronic: Electrosignals, for massed tape cassettes.
605 Elmwood Ave., Apt. 7A, Buffalo, NY 14222

*DIRKSEN, RICHARD WAYNE
b. 1921. Studied at Peabody Cons.

DIRKSEN, RICHARD WAYNE

(DIRKSEN, RICHARD WAYNE)
WORKS: Chorus: <u>Chanticleer</u>; <u>I sing the</u>
<u>birth</u>; <u>Nowell we sing</u>; Organ: <u>Prelude on Urbs</u>
<u>beata</u>; <u>Hilariter</u>.
c/o National Cathedral, Washington, DC 20013

DITTENHAVER, SARAH LOUISE
b. Paulding, Ohio, 16 Dec. 1901; d. Asheville,
N. C., 4 Feb. 1973. Graduated from Oberlin Cons.
She taught in private and public schools for
many years, then settled in Asheville as teacher
and composer. She was made a Fellow, Internat.
Inst. of Arts and Letters, Switzerland, 1961;
her compositions have won awards from N. C. Fed.
of Music Clubs; Nat. League of American Pen Women; Delta Kappa Gamma Society Internat., 1963;
Nat. Guild of Piano Teachers, 1967.
WORKS: Chorus: <u>Alleluia, Jesus child</u>,
mixed chorus; <u>Light of the lonely pilgrim's</u>
<u>heart</u>, youth choir; <u>Trust in the Lord</u>, unison
choir; <u>Bless the Lord, O my soul</u>, mixed chorus;
Songs: <u>Hurdy-gurdy playing in the street</u>; <u>Lady</u>
<u>of the amber wheat</u>; <u>Passage</u>; <u>Once more, beloved</u>;
many piano teaching pieces.

*DLUGOSZEWSKI, LUCIA
b. Detroit, Mich., 16 June 1925. Studied at
Detroit Cons.; medical studies at Wayne State
Univ.; composition privately with Edgard Varese
in New York. She received the Tomkins literary
award for poetry, 1947; Nat. Inst. of Arts and
Letters award, 1966; BMI-Thorne fellowship, 1972;
more than 30 commissions. She has taught at New
School for Social Research and Found. for Modern
Dance; is music director and composer-in-
residence, Erick Hawkins Dance Company, New York;
has invented over 100 percussion instruments
including ladder harps, unsheltered rattles,
tangent rattles, closed rattles, consisting of
wood, glass, metal, plastic, paper; and the timbre piano in which bows of glass, felt, metal,
plastic, or wood are run across the strings while
the keyboard is also being used.
WORKS: Ballet: <u>Of love</u>, New York, Mar.
1971; Chamber music: <u>Space is a diamond</u>, trumpet solo, 1970; <u>Theater flight Nagiere</u>, for her
instruments, New York, 7 Mar. 1971; <u>Fire fragile</u>
<u>flight</u>, New York, 29 Apr. 1973; <u>Densities</u>, cham-
ber ensemble, New York, 5 May 1974; <u>Abyss and</u>
<u>caress</u>, concerto for trumpet and 17 instruments,
New York, 21 Mar. 1975; and nearly 100 other
vocal and instrumental works. She has also published a book of poetry, <u>A new folder</u>, 1967, and
studies on philosophical esthetics and modern
dance in various journals.
107 West 10th St., New York, NY 10011

*DOBBINS, WILLIAM
<u>Variations</u> for piano and percussion; <u>Fabric</u> for
for piano.

DOBRY, WALLACE B.
b. Baltimore, Md., 21 June 1933. Studied with
George Hurst, Spencer Huffman, Henry Cowell at
the Peabody Cons., B. M. 1956. He received a
3-year scholarship at Peabody, 1952; and twice
won the Thatcher Prize. He has been music director, St. John's Church, Chevy Chase, Md.,
1970-   ; lecturer, George Washington Univ.,
1972-   .

(DOBRY, WALLACE B.)
WORKS: Orchestra: <u>Scherzo</u>, Baltimore Symphony, 1951; Chamber music: woodwind quintet,
1968; <u>Divertimento</u> for string trio, 1972; Organ:
<u>Theme and variations</u>, 1961; <u>Toccata</u>, 1969.
4804 Wellington Drive, Chevy Chase, MD 20015

*DOCKSTADER, TOD
b. 1932. Writes electronic music: <u>8 elec-</u>
<u>tronic pieces</u>, 1960; <u>Traveling music</u>, 1960;
<u>Apocalypse</u>, 1961; <u>Luna Park</u>, 1961; <u>Drone</u>, 1962;
<u>Water music</u>, 1963; <u>Quatermass</u>, 1964.
96 Joralman, Brooklyn, NY 11201

DODGE, CHARLES
b. Ames, Iowa, 5 June 1942. Studied with Philip
Bezanson and Richard Hervig, Univ. of Iowa,
B. A. 1964; with Darius Milhaud, Aspen Music
School, 1961; with Gunther Schuller and Arthur
Berger, Tanglewood, 1964; with Jack Beeson,
Chou Wen-chung, Otto Luening, Vladimir
Ussachevsky at Columbia Univ., M. A. 1966. He
received BMI awards, 1963, 1964, 1966, 1967;
Bearns Prize, 1964, 1967; Sagalyn Award, 1964;
Koussevitzky Found. grant, 1969; Guggenheim fellowship, 1972; many commissions. He was instructor, Princeton Univ., 1969-70; instructor, Columbia Univ., 1967-69, assistant professor,
1970-   ; president, American Composers Alliance, 1971-73.
WORKS: Orchestra: <u>Rota</u>, 1966; Chamber
music: <u>Folia</u>, 7 instruments and percussion,
1963; Electronic: <u>Changes</u>, 1970; <u>Earth's mag-</u>
<u>netic field</u>, realization in computer sound;
<u>Extensions</u>, tape, New York, 23 Apr. 1973; <u>Speech</u>
<u>songs</u>, New York, 9 Feb. 1973.
39 Claremont Ave., New York, NY 10027

*DOENHOFF, ALBERT VON
b. Louisville, Ky., 16 Mar. 1880; d. New York,
3 Oct. 1940. Was a concert pianist and published many piano pieces.

*DOHERTY, ANTHONY
<u>A song of joy</u> for chorus.

*DOHNANYI, ERNST VON
Pressburg, Bratislava, 27 July 1877; to U.S.
1949; d. New York, 9 Feb. 1960. Graduated from
Royal Acad. of Music, Budapest, 1897; then
toured Europe and the U.S. as concert pianist.
He joined the faculty of Florida State Univ. in
1949. His works composed since 1949 include:
2nd violin concerto, San Antonio, 26 Jan. 1952;
concertino for harp and orch., 1952; <u>American</u>
<u>rhapsody</u> for orch., Athens, Ohio, 21 Feb. 1954;
<u>12 etudes</u> for piano, 1950.

*DOLIN, SAMUEL
Violin sonata.

DOLLARHIDE, THEODORE J.
b. Santa Rosa, Calif., 30 Aug. 1948. Studied
with Higo Harada at San Jose State Coll. on
scholarships and received university honors. He
also received the Eva Thompson Phillips award
and commissions.
WORKS: Orchestra: <u>A fantasy of ivory</u>
<u>thoughts and shallow whispers</u>; <u>Movements for</u>

(DOLLARHIDE, THEODORE J.)
orchestra; Band: Music for the food king; Daughter of the food king; Chamber music: Shadows, woodwind quintet; trumpet sonata.
421 South 11th St., San Jose, CA 95112

*DONAHUE, BERTHA TERRY
Make we joy, chorus; Laude delle creature a dio, cantata, premiere, New York, 29 Apr. 1973.
3005 Albemarle St., N. W.
Washington, DC 20016

*DONAHUE, ROBERT L.
b. 1931. Studied at Univ. of Wisconsin; with Ben Johnston, Univ. of Illinois; with Karel Husa and Robert Palmer, Cornell Univ., D. M. A. He is assistant professor, Spelman Coll.
WORKS: Chamber music: 5 canonic duets, flute and clarinet; 5 pieces for brass quartet; Little suite, brass trio.
626 Sherwood Road, Atlanta, GA 30324

DONALDSON, SADIE
b. New York, N. Y., 2 July 1909. Studied at Hunter Coll. and New School for Social Research. She received 2 prizes in hymn contests of the American Guild of Organists, 1970, 1972. She was a teacher, 1934-39.
WORKS: Operetta: Horse opera; Hymns: Thanksgiving hymn; Hallelujah! Christ was born; Have you not known?; many art songs and ballads.
810 El Olmo Court, S. E.
Rio Rancho, NM 87124

DONATO, ANTHONY
b. Prague, Neb., 8 Mar. 1909. Attended Eastman School of Music, B. M. 1931, M. M. 1937, Ph. D. 1947; studied composition with Howard Hanson, Bernard Rogers, Edward Royce, conducting with Eugene Goossens, violin with Gustave Tinlot. His many awards include Blue Network award, 1945; Society for Publication of American Music award, 1947; Composers Press Publication awards, 1946, 1953; Mendelssohn Glee Club award, 1950; Fulbright lecture grant for England, 1951-52; Piano Technical Information Service awards, 1955, 1961; Huntington Hartford fellowship, 1961; and many commissions. He was head, violin department, Drake Univ., 1931-37; Iowa State Teachers Coll., 1937-39; Univ. of Texas, 1939-46; professor of composition, Northwestern Univ., 1947-   , conductor of NU Chamber Orch., 1947-58.
WORKS: Opera: The walker through walls, 1964; Orchestra: Divertimento, 1939; 2 symphonies, 1944, 1945; Prairie schooner, overture, 1947; Suite for strings, 1948; The plains, 1953; Solitude in the city, with narrator, 1954; Episode, 1954; Sinfonietta No. 2, 1959; Serenade for small orch., 1961; Band: The lake shore, 1950; The hidden fortress, 1950; Cowboy reverie, 1955; Concert overture, 1958; Chamber music: 2 violin sonatas, 1938, 1949; 3 string quartets, 1941, 1947, 1951; Drag and run, clarinet, 2 violins, cello, 1946; Precipitations (Fog, snow, rain, hail), violin and piano, 1946; Pastorale and dance, 4 clarinets, 1947; Three pieces for 3 clarinets, 1947; Sonatine, 3 trumpets, 1949; horn sonata, 1950; quintet for winds, 1955; suite for brass, 1956; piano trio, 1959;

(DONATO, ANTHONY)
clarinet sonata, 1966; Three poems from Shelley, tenor and string quartet, 1971; Nonet, 3 trumpets, 3 trombones, 3 percussionists, 1972; Chorus: March of the hungry mountains, tenor solo, chorus, small orch., 1949; The sycophantic fox and the gullible raven, mixed chorus or men's voices and piano, 1950; Roll a rock down, men's voices and piano, 1950; The Last Supper, double chorus, baritone solo, 1952; Thou art my God, women's voices, 1953; How excellent is thy name, chorus and organ, 1956; The congo, chorus, soprano solo, full orch., 1957; Prelude and choral fantasy, men's voices, brass, timpani, organ, Make a joyful noise, children's choir, organ, brass, 1964; Blessed is the man, chorus, organ, brass quartet, 1970; Piano: African dominoes, 1948; Recreations, 1948; Three preludes, 1948; sonata, 1951; songs and teaching pieces. He is also author of Preparing music manuscript, 1963 and 1969.
School of Music, Northwestern University
Evanston, IL 60201

*DONOVAN, RICHARD FRANK
b. New Haven, Conn., 29 Nov. 1891; d. Middletown, Conn., 22 Aug. 1970. Studied at Inst. of Musical Art, New York; Yale Univ., B. M. 1922, honorary M. A. 1947. He received the Naumburg recording award, 1962. He taught at Smith Coll., 1923-28; Inst. of Musical Art, 1925-28; Yale Univ., 1928-60, professor, 1947, Battell professor emeritus, 1960-70; conductor, Bach Cantata Club, New Haven, 1933-44; New Haven Symphony, 1936-51; staff member, Middlebury Coll. Composers' Conference, 1946, 1947; director Yaddo Corporation and member of the Yaddo Festivals music committee.
WORKS: Orchestra: Design for radio, 1945; Passacaglia on Vermont folk tunes, 1949; symphony, 1956; New England chronicle; Chamber music: clarinet sonata; piano trio, 1937; sonata for flute and cello; Music for 6, 1961; Chorus: 5 Elizabethan lyrics, 1932-57; Mass; Organ: Antiphon and chorale, 1955. His sons have given his complete papers and music manuscripts to the Yale University Library.

DORAN, MATT H.
b. Covington, Ky., 1 Sep. 1921. Studied at Univ. of Southern California; composition teachers were Ernst Toch, Hanns Eisler, Ernest Kanitz, Gail Kubik, and Peter Jona Korn; studied orchestration with Lucien Caillet. He received a MacDowell fellowship and 2 Hartford fellowships. He has been professor, Mount St. Mary's Coll. 1956-   .
WORKS: 4 operas, including The committee, 1955; 2 symphonies; Chamber music: string quartet; sonatina, 2 flutes; sonatina, flute and cello; woodwind quintet; quartet for oboe, clarinet, bassoon, viola; clarinet sonata; trio for oboe, violin, viola; Poem for flute; Pastorale for organ; choral works, songs, piano pieces.
2614 Military Ave., Los Angeles, CA 90064

DORATI, ANTAL

*DORATI, ANTAL
    b. Budapest, Hungary, 9 Apr. 1906; U.S. citizen
1947. Studied at the Budapest Acad. of Music,
diploma, 1924; Univ. of Vienna; Macalester Coll.,
D. M. 1957. His awards in 1975 included the
Decca/London Records' gold record for his re-
cordings of the complete Haydn symphonies;
French Government's Cross of the Chevalier des
Arts et Lettres; and an honorary doctorate,
George Washington Univ. He was opera conductor
and ballet conductor in Europe, 1933-44; conductor, Dallas Symphony, 1945-49; Minneapolis
Symphony, 1949-60; chief conductor, BBC Symphony
Orchestra, London, 1962-70; conductor, Nat. Symphony Orchestra, D.C., 1970-75, music director,
1975-   ; senior conductor, Royal Philharmonic
Orchestra, London, 1975-   .
    WORKS: Ballet: Magdalena; Orchestra: 2
symphonies, 1957, 1960; 7 pieces for orch.;
cello concerto; Divertimento for small orch.;
3 American serenades for strings; Madrigal suite,
chorus and orch.; 2 enchantments of Li Tai Pe,
baritone and small orch.; The way of the cross,
cantata for chorus and orch., 1957; Chamber
music: string quartet; oboe quintet, 1926; 2
Hungarian peasant tunes, violin and piano, 1945;
string octet; Chorus: Missa brevis, with
percussion.
        c/o National Symphony Orchestra
        Washington, DC 20009

*DORIS, HUBERT
    Trio for flute, harp, cello, Wheaton Coll.,
Mass., Dec. 1954.
        Department of Music, Barnard College
        New York, NY 10027

*DORITY, BRYAN
    Duo for 2 violins.
        St. John's Abbey, Collegeville, MN 56321

DORSAM, PAUL
    b. New York, N. Y., 25 Jan. 1941. Studied at
New England Cons., B. M., M. M.; Boston Univ.,
D. M. A.; composition with Felix Wolfes, F. Judd
Cooke, Hugo Norden; trumpet with Roger Voisin,
Armanda Ghitalla, John Coffey. He received commissions from American Guild of Organists, 1969,
1970; Vermont Philharmonic Orch., 1967, 1970,
1971; Belmont Choral Society, 1973. He was on
the music faculty, State Coll., Lyndonville, Vt.,
1964-67; St. Michael's Coll., Winooski, Vt.,
1967-70; Berklee Coll. of Music, 1970-71; Virginia Commonwealth Univ., 1972-   .
    WORKS: Orchestra: Prelude, 1967; symphony
No.2, 1970; symphony No.4, 1971; Chamber music;
piano sonata; trumpet sonata; cello sonata;
Music for organ and trumpet, 1970; Chorus:
Music in honor of Bayside, Long Island; Gloria,
chorus, percussion, 2 trumpets; Mass, 1973;
Songs: Lost, Sandburg text; it may not always
be so, cummings text; The Barton River Falls,
Kinnell text.
        2162 East Tremont Court, Richmond, VA 23225

*DORSEY, JAMES ELNO
    b. San Antonio, Tex., 22 Nov. 1905. Was
awarded the Wanamaker prize in 1931 for his
composition, Sandals.

*DORTCH, EILEEN WIER
    Has published anthems and vocal solos and duets.
        242 South 9th St., Gadsden, AL 35901

DOUGHERTY, CELIUS
    b. Glenwood, Minn., 27 May 1902. Studied piano
and composition with Donald Ferguson, Univ. of
Minnesota; piano with Josef Lhevinne and composition with Rubin Goldmark at Juilliard School,
where he held scholarships in both piano and
composition. He has received many commissions
and was accompanist for many noted singers.
    WORKS: Opera: Many moons, 1-act, based on
Thurber text; Songs: Love in the dictionary,
text from Funk & Wagnalls; A minor bird, Frost;
Primavera, Amy Lowell; Song for autumn, Mary
Webb; Loveliest of trees, Housman; Listen! the
wind, Humbert Wolfe; Five sea chanties; seven
songs, e. e. cummings; Ballade of William
Sycamore; Portuguese sonnets.
        320 West 76th St., New York, NY 10023

DOUGLAS, SAMUEL OSLER
    b. Mansfield, La., 31 Mar. 1943. Studied with
Dinos Constantinides and Kenneth B. Klaus,
Louisiana State Univ., M. M. 1968, D. M. A.
1972. He has been assistant professor, Univ.
of South Carolina, 1973-   .
    WORKS: Opera: The devil's heir, 1-act,
Baton Rouge, July 1972, in concert form; Orchestra: Prelude and passacaglia, 1968; Sinfonia
ecclesiastica, chamber symphony for orch. and
chorus, 1970; Sonata, reader and orch., poem by
Leo Stanford, McNeese State Univ., Oct. 1972;
The night before Christmas, narrator and orch.,
Univ. of South Carolina, Dec. 1973; Chorus:
Bow down thine ear, anthem; Songs: Selected
definitions from the devil's dictionary, by
Ambroise Bierce, set of songs for soprano, clar-
inet, double bass, piano, Baton Rouge, June
1972; Piano: Twelve trifles, 1970; Film score:
Disciples of death, 1971.
        6506 Christie Road, Columbia, SC 29209

DOUGLAS, WILLIAM
    b. London, Ont., 7 Nov. 1944; to U.S. 1970.
Studied with Mel Powell, Yale Univ. He received
the Margaret M. Grant award, Tanglewood, 1969.
He was bassoonist, New Haven Symphony, 1966-69;
faculty member, California Inst. of the Arts,
1969-   .
    WORKS: Chamber music: Improvisation II,
flute and piano; Improvisation III, clarinet
and piano; Vajra, clarinet and piano; string
quartet, 1969; Celebration, piano solo.
        c/o California Institute of the Arts
        Valencia, CA 91355

DOWD, JOHN ANDREW
    b. Jacksonville, Fla., 19 Feb. 1932. Studied
with Stephen Park, Univ. of Tampa; Francis Judd
Cooke and Billy Jim Layton, New England Cons.
He was instructor, West Virginia Univ., 1966-68;

(DOWD, JOHN ANDREW)
Ohio Univ., 1968-69; and chairman of fine arts, Milligan Coll., 1963-66, 1969-
WORKS: Orchestra: Simulacra noctus, orch. and voices; Chorus: Why seek ye the living, anthem, a cappella, 1963; chamber music, orchestral works, piano pieces, a short opera, several choral compositions.
819 West Pine St., Johnson City, TN 37601

DOWNEY, JOHN
b. Chicago, Ill., 5 Oct. 1927. Studied at De Paul Univ., B. M. 1949; Chicago Musical Coll., M. M. 1951; Univ. of Paris, Ph. D. 1956; composition with Leon Stein, Vittorio Rieti, Arthur Honneger, Nadia Boulanger, Darius Milhaud. His awards include 2nd prize in composition, Paris Cons., 1956; 2 Fulbright grants; French Government fellowship and scholarship; 2 Copley awards; winner of Aspen contest; invited participant, Princeton Univ. seminars in new music techniques; Distinguished alumnus award, De Paul Univ. He was founder and chairman, Wisconsin Contemporary Music Forum, 1970-   ; professor, Univ. of Wisconsin, Milwaukee, 1970-   .
WORKS: Orchestra: Jingalodeon; Symphonic modules five; Chamber music: Eastlake Terrace, piano; Pyramids, piano; cello sonata; Agort, woodwind quintet; Voice: What if?, choir, brass ensemble, timpani; A dolphin, high voice and chamber ensemble.
4413 North Prospect Ave., Shorewood, WI 53211

DOWNS, LAMONT WAYNE
b. Warren, Ohio, 9 Mar. 1951. Studied with Samuel Adler and Warren Benson, Eastman School of Music. He received the Howard Hanson award for wind ensemble, 1970.
WORKS: Band: Sinfonia for wind band, 1969; Electric symphony for junior wind ensemble; RS-2, concert march, 1970; DDA40X, concert march; Song: A (more or less) brief diversion for tenor, trumpet, trombone, and percussion.
8482 Old Farm Trail, N.E., Warren, OH 44484

DRENNAN, DOROTHY E.
b. Hankinson, N. Dak., 21 Mar. 1929. Studied with Clifton Williams and Alfred Reed at Univ. of Miami. She received Sigma Alpha Iota awards, 1971, 1972, 1973. She has been instructor, Univ. of Miami, 1972-
WORKS: Chorus: Here is the rose (Dance thou here), concerto for trombone and modern chorus; The word, cantata for Pentecost; Seashores, Tagore text, chorus and wind quintet; Chamber music: Turn, quintet for widely separated performers, violin, clarinet, trombone, 2 percussionists.
7880 S.W. 12th St., Miami, FL 33144

*DRETKE, LEORA N.
Sing, alleluia, Christ is born.

DREW, JAMES
b. New York, N. Y., 9 Feb. 1929. Studied at New York School of Music; Tulane Univ.; Washington Univ.; and privately with Wallingford Riegger and Edgard Varese. He received a Rockefeller

(DREW, JAMES)
Found. grant, 1965; Northwestern Univ. research grant, 1966; Morse award, 1968-69; Guggenheim Fellowship, 1972; Fromm Found. grant, 1973; Tanglewood fellowship, 1973. He was composer-in-residence and faculty member, Northwestern Univ., 1965-67; Yale Univ., 1967-73; Louisiana State Univ., 1973-   .
WORKS: Ballet: Toward yellow, 1970; Orchestra: symphony, 1968; concerto for 2 pianos and strings, 1968; chamber symphony, 1966-68; October lights, 1969; violin concerto, 1969-70; synphony No.2, 1971; Metal concert, percussion ensemble, 1971; concerto for small percussion orch., 1973; West Indian lights, Tanglewood, 9 Aug. 1973; Lux incognitus, 1973; viola concerto, 1973; Epitaph for Stravinsky, 1973; Chamber music: Quinteto d'microtonos, brass quintet, Atlanta, Ga., 12 Feb. 1971; The maze maker for cello, 1970; Almost stationary, piano trio, 1971; Gothic lights, chamber ensemble, 1971. He is also author of numerous magazine articles in Spanish and English.
1078 Rodney Drive, Baton Rouge, LA 70808

DREWS, STEVE
b. Oshkosh, Wis., 29 May 1945. Studied at Lawrence Univ., B. M. 1965; with Darius Milhaud at Aspen, 1966; and with Robert Palmer and Karel Husa, Cornell Univ., 1967-69.
WORKS: Electronic: Ceres motion; Train; Almost two years; Before day; Grover Whalen: Next door; Ice; Bells; all performed by Mother Mallard's Portable Masterpiece Company.
2861 Elmira Road, Newfield, NY 14850

DRISCOLL, JOHN
b. Philadelphia, Pa., 3 Oct. 1947. Studied with Rudi Staffel in Rome, Italy, 1967-68, and with Jim Sterritt, 1969. He won a Ferullo Found. award for the composition Bad taste, 1972. He has been instructor, Philadelphia Coll. of Art, 1972-   ; and producer, In Between Sounds, 1971-   .
WORKS: Compositions for immobile or mobile objects with and without electronic modulation, performed usually as individual or group improvisations--to wit: 25 nymphomaniacs singing nebulous melodies to 50 lawn mowers, 1970; A tour around Cicero's bath, 1972; Under the putting green (series), 1973-   .
605 Silver Spring Ave.
Silver Spring, MD 20910

DROSSIN, JULIUS
b. Philadelphia, Pa., 17 May 1918. Studied with Harl McDonald at Univ. of Pennsylvania, B. M. 1938; with George Rochberg at the New School, 1946-48; with F. Karl Grossman at Western Reserve Univ., M. A. 1951, Ph. D. 1956. He held a scholarship at Univ. of Pennsylvania and has received commissions. He was assistant professor, Villa Maria Coll., 1951-58; assistant professor, Fenn Coll., 1956-   ; professor and department chairman, Cleveland State Univ., 1956-   . He was cellist with the Cleveland Orchestra, 1948-57; and choir director, Park Synagogue, 1957-65.

DROSSIN, JULIUS

(DROSSIN, JULIUS)
    WORKS: Orchestra: 4 symphonies; Rhapsody
for cello and orch.; Essay for orch; Chamber
music: 8 string quartets; Chorus: Kaddish,
soloists, chorus, orch.; Friday night service.
        3141 Somerset Drive
        Shaker Heights, OH 44122

DROSTE, DOREEN (Mrs. Gerard J.)
    b. Tacoma, Wash., 29 May 1907. Studied pri-
vately with George Tremblay; and with Henry
Leland Clarke at Univ. of California, Los
Angeles, M. A. She won first prize in a national
anthem contest, 1958.
    WORKS: Chorus: Hear my prayer, 1958; Six
pence in her shoe, women's voices; To drive the
cold winter away, a cappella; The ship of state;
The happy heart; The hymn of St. Columba; Ride
on in majesty; The song of wandering Aengus, a
cappella, 1973.
        2025 Kenilworth Ave., Los Angeles, CA 90039

*DRUCKMAN, JACOB
    b. Philadelphia, Pa., 1928. Studied with Peter
Mennin, Bernard Wagenaar, Vincent Persichetti,
Juilliard School, B. S., M. S. 1955; with Aaron
Copland at Tanglewood and in France on a Ful-
bright grant. His other awards include a
Guggenheim fellowship, 1956-57; Koussevitzky
Internat. recording award, special citation,
1970; Pulitzer prize, 1972; ASCAP award, 1972;
and commissions from Berkshire Music Center,
Tanglewood Alumni, Juilliard School, Chicago and
Albany Symphonies. He has held teachings posts
at Juilliard School; Bard Coll.; Yale Univ.; and
is associate professor, Brooklyn Coll.
    WORKS: Ballet: Performance, for Jose Limon;
Orchestra: concerto for violin and small orch.;
concerto for string orch.; Incenters, trumpet,
horn, trombone, orch., 1968, Minnesota Orchestra,
30 Nov. 1973; Windows, 1970, New York premiere,
16 Jan. 1975; Chamber music: 3 string quartets;
Dark upon the harp, voice, brass quintet and percussion, 1962; Animus I, 1966; Animus II, trombone and tape; Animus III, clarinet and tape;
Valentine for double bass, the player uses a
mallet, vocal sounds, and reads aloud the instructions, 1972; Chorus: 4 madrigals, with soprano
solo, 1968; Electronic: Synapse.
        780 Riverside Drive, Apt. 8C
        New York, NY 10032

*DUBENSKY, ARCADY
    b. Viatka, Russia, 15 Oct. 1890; to U.S. 1921;
d. Tenafly, N. J., 14 Oct. 1966. Studied violin
and conducting, Moscow Cons. He was first violinist, Moscow Imperial Opera Theatre Orch.,
1910-19; was violinist with the New York Symphony, then New York Philharmonic to retirement
in 1953. His compositions include 3 operas, a
comic opera, a symphony, concerto grosso, trombone concerto, suites, overtures, other orchestral works, a string quartet, and a fugue for
18 violins, his most frequently played
composition.

DUCKWORTH, WILLIAM
    b. Morganton, N. C., 13 Jan. 1943. Studied with
Ben Johnston, Thomas Fredrickson, Salvatore
Martirano, and Robert Kelly, Univ. of Illinois;
with Martin Mailman at East Carolina Univ. His
awards include 2 prizes, East Carolina Univ.
composition contest, 1964, 1965; 3 North Carolina Fed. of Music Clubs prizes, 1968, 1969;
grand prize, Cleveland Inst. of Music percussion
composition contest, 1968; finalist, Sigvald
Thompson Award, 1972; award, Competition for
New String Music, 1973. He was associate professor, Atlantic Christian Coll., 1966-73;
assistant professor, Bucknell Univ., 1973-   .
    WORKS: Band: Fragments, solo saxophone,
winds percussion, 1967; The Sleepy Hollow Elementary School Band, 20 to 60 instruments, 1968;
Chamber music: An unseen action, flute, prepared piano, 4 percussionists, 1966; Statements
and interludes, trombone and piano, 1967; Trans-
parent interludes, trumpet, horn, trombone,
1967; An imaginary death dance, oboe and guitar,
A ballad in time and space, saxophone and piano,
1968; The journey, solo percussion, 1968; Pitch
City, any four wind players, 1969; Time fields,
solo percussion, 1969; Reel music, 4 saxophones,
1970; Images, for new string instruments (soprano, mezzo, alto, tenor), Rutgers Univ., 14
Oct. 1973; Mixed media: Gambit, solo percussion
and tape, 1967.
        Music Dept., Bucknell University
        Lewisburg, PA 17837

DUESENBERRY, JOHN
    b. Boston, Mass., 10 Oct. 1950. Studied with
John Goodman, Joyce Mekeel, Allen Schindler,
Boston Univ., B. M. 1974; and at Boston School
Electronic Music, where he is on the faculty.
    WORKS: Chamber music: 3 miniatures, string
quartet, 1972; Movement for harp, violin, cello;
3 songs from A season in hell, 1973; electronic
pieces.
        Boston School of Electronic Music
        326 Dartmouth St., Boston, MA 02116

DUFFY, JOHN
    b. New York, N. Y., 23 June 1928. Studied at
New School for Social Research, Tanglewood,
Lenox School of Jazz; his teachers were Aaron
Copland, Luigi Dallapiccola, Salomon Rosowsky,
Ludwig Lenel. He received scholarships to
Tanglewood and Lenox School of Jazz; Berkshire
Bicentennial award; 7 ASCAP awards; Outstanding
Composer in Theatre award. He was music direc-
tor and composer, American Shakespeare Festival,
Stratford, Conn., 1965-69; composer, Tyron
Guthrie Theatre, Long Wharf Theatre, Univ. of
Michigan Theatre, 1970-73.
    WORKS: Theatre: Everyman absurd, music
drama; MacBird; Horseman pass by; incidental
music for Hamlet, King Lear, Romeo and Juliet,
Macbeth; Orchestra: Antiquity of freedom; Band:
Concerto for Stan Getz and concert band; songs
on texts of Joyce, Brecht, Rosenberg.
        120 West 70th St., New York, NY 10023

DUGGER, EDWIN
b. Poplar Bluff, Mo., 21 Mar. 1940. Studied with Richard Hoffmann at Oberlin Cons.; with Roger Sessions, Earl Kim, Milton Babbitt at Princeton Univ. He received Fromm commission, 1969; Koussevitzky Found. commission, 1973; Guggenheim fellowship, 1973. He was instructor, Oberlin Cons., 1967-69; assistant professor, Univ. of California, Berkeley, 1969-.
    WORKS: Chamber music: Structure for chamber orch.; Divisions of time, 4 winds, piano, 6 percussionists; Intermezzi, 12 performers; Mixed media: Music for synthesizer and 6 instruments; Abwesenheiten und Wiedersehen, 11 performers and 4-track tape; Adieu, wind and percussion ensemble and 4-track tape.
    268 Columbia Ave., Kensington, CA 94708

DUKE, JOHN WOODS
b. Cumberland, Md., 30 July 1899. Studied with Gustav Strube at Peabody Cons., 1915-58; later with Bernhard Wagenaar in New York; and in 1929-30 with Nadia Boulanger in Paris and Artur Schnabel in Berlin. He won the Peabody Alumni Assoc. award for distinguished service to music, 1969. He was professor and teacher of piano, Smith Coll., 1923-67; now professor emeritus.
    WORKS: Theatre: The cat that walked by itself, children's musical, 1944; Love among the ruins, faculty show, 1952; Captain Lovelock, 1-act chamber opera, 1953; The Yankee Pedlar, 1-act operetta, 1962; Orchestra: Carnival overture, 1940; concerto for piano and strings, 1938; Chamber music: suite for viola alone, 1933; string trio, 1937; Fantasy, violin and piano, 1936; Narrative, viola and piano, 1942; 2 string quartets, 1941, 1967; piano trio, 1943; Dialogue, cello and piano, 1943; Melody, cello and piano, 1946; Chorus: O sing unto the Lord a new song, women's voices and string orch. or organ, 1955; Magnificat, unison chorus and organ, 1961; Three river songs, texts from the Chinese, women's voices and piano, 1963; and 180 songs.
    82 Harrison Ave., Northampton, MA 01060

*DUKE, LEWIS BYRON
b. 1924. Violin sonata, Op. 21.

*DUKE, VERNON (DUKELSKY, VLADIMIR)
b. Russia, 10 Oct. 1903; to U.S. in 1920s; d. Santa Monica, Calif., 10 Jan. 1969. Studied at Kiev Cons. He adopted the name Vernon Duke as a pen name for his lighter compositions, then in 1955 dropped Dukelsky entirely.
    WORKS: Opera: Demoiselle Paysanne, 1928; Yvonne, operetta, 1926; Ballet: Zephyr and Flora, 1925; Public gardens, 1935; Le bal des blanchisseuses, 1946; Souvenir de Monte Carlo, 1956; Orchestra: 3 symphonies; violin concerto; cello concerto; piano concerto, 1924; Chamber music: 2 piano sonatas; violin sonata, 1949; Etude, violin and bassoon; many works for chamber groups, chorus, solo voice, piano; also many scores for musicals and films, and popular songs.

*DUMESNIL, EVANGELINE LEHMAN
Wrote a choral symphony, cantatas, piano pieces, songs.

*DUNBAR, RUDOLPH
b. British Guiana, 5 Apr. 1907; to U.S. 1919. Studied at Juilliard School and in Paris, Leipzig, and Vienna. His compositions include a ballet: Dance of the 21st century.

DUNCAN, JAMES L.
b. Clarksville, Mo., 14 June 1926. Studied with A. I. McHose and Anthony Donato at Eastman School of Music. He is professor and chairman, music department, Southern Colorado State Coll.
    WORKS: Orchestra: Psalm for Palm Sunday, a sketch for chamber orch.
    3101 Vail Ave., Pueblo, CO 81005

DUNCAN, JOHN
b. Lee County, Ala., 25 Nov. 1913. Earned his B. M. and M. M. degrees in composition at Temple Univ.; later studied with Philip James, Gustave Reese, and Curt Sachs at New York Univ. He received 2 commissions from Davis Shuman, and an opera commission from Xavier Univ., La. He was teacher, Samuel Huston Coll., 1936-37; free-lance arranger in Philadelphia, 1937-39; and at Alabama State Univ., bandmaster, 1939-46; registrar, 1950-63; chairman, music department, 1963-64; professor and composer-in-residence, 1965- ; received D. M. 1974.
    WORKS: Opera: Gideon and Eliza; The hellish banditi, 1974; Orchestra: trombone concerto; Chamber music: Divertimento for trombone and string quartet; Black bards, flute, cello, piano; Atavistic, string quartet (No.2); Chorus: Burial of Moses, a cantata.
    Alabama State University
    Montgomery, AL 36101

DUNFORD, BENJAMIN C.
b. Winston-Salem, N. C., 2 Sep. 1917. Attended Salem Coll., B. M.; Univ. of Texas, M. M.; Eastman School of Music, Ph. D., studying with Charles Vardell, Kent Kennan, Bernard Rogers, Herbert Elwell, Wayne Barlow, Howard Hanson. He won an award for the best short orchestral work, Annual Southwestern Symposium of American Music, Austin, Tex., 1956. He has been composer, conductor, arranger, lecturer, pianist, organist, choir director, 1935- ; was chairman, music department, Montreat Coll., N. C., 1955-59; professor, William Carey Coll., 1963- .
    WORKS: Opera: The twelve dancing princesses; Chorus: The promise, sacred cantata; Psalm 103, chorus, baritone solo, organ or brass and percussion; The unspeakable gift, a Christmas cantata; approximately 1000 works, choral and instrumental, commissioned and performed.
    1712 2nd Terrace, Hattiesburg, MS 39401

*DUNGAN, OLIVE
b. Pittsburgh, Pa., 19 July 1903. Studied at Pittsburgh Inst. of Musical Art; Univ. of Miami; Univ. of Alabama. She was the first recipient of the Chi Omega Bertha Foster award. She has been piano recitalist and teacher. Her works include many songs and Tropic night suite for piano.
    650 Northeast 68th St., Miami, FL 33138

DUNING, GEORGE

*DUNING, GEORGE
   b. Richmond, Inc., 25 Feb. 1908. Studied at
Cincinnati Cons.; Univ. of Cincinnati; and with
Castelnuovo-Tedesco.
   WORKS: Film scores: From here to eternity;
Miss Sadie Thompson; Salome; Picnic; The Eddie
Duchin story; Toys in the attic; many others;
numerous songs.
      211 South Beverly Drive
      Beverly Hills, CA 90212

DUNN, GARY
   b. Los Angeles, Calif., 10 Mar. 1950. Studied
with Nikhil Banerjee and Kani Dutta in Oakland,
Calif.; with Morton Feldman, Armand Russell, and
Neil McKay at Univ. of Hawaii; with Morgan Powell
at Univ. of Illinois.
   WORKS: Large ensembles: Sunness, 23 instruments including shakuhachi, vyuteki, hichiriki,
koto, bass koto, and biwa; Coming is going, percussion solo for 19 instruments; Sounding high-
koo, percussion ensemble of 4, 8, 12, or 16 players; Small ensembles: Ensemble I, II, III, solo
violin, duets, or trio; From the willow, percussion and cello; Wed, percussion and cello; Three
images of a dove's passing, violin and cello; To
the ant, piano solo; Asa gao no tsuru, 8
instruments.
      95-537 Wailoale, Mililani Town, HI 96789

*DUNN, JAMES PHILIP
   b. New York, N. Y., 10 Jan. 1884; d. Jersey City,
N. J., 24 July 1936. Studied at City Coll. of
New York; with Edward MacDowell and Cornelius
Rybner, Columbia Univ. He was a church organist
in New York and New Jersey.
   WORKS: Opera: The galleon; Orchestra: We,
tone poem; Overture on negro themes; Chamber
music: 2 string quartets; piano quintet; violin
sonata; Voice: The phanton drum, a cantata;
songs.

DUNN, REBECCA WELTY
   b. Guthrie, Okla., 23 Sep. 1890. Studied at
Washburn Coll., Southwestern Coll., and with
Otto Fischer, Friends Univ. She won a national
first prize for operetta Sunny, and a Kansas
Authors Club prize for Purple on the moon.
   WORKS: Chorus: Channels of thy grace,
Halleluiah rain; and other choral works and
songs.
      3121 MacVicar, #202, Topeka, KS 66611

DU PAGE, FLORENCE
   b. Vandergrift, Pa., 20 Sep. 1910. Studied with
Rubin Goldmark, Aurelio Giorni, and Tibor Serly.
She taught in private schools on Long Island,
N. Y., 1954-69.
   WORKS: Theatre: Trial universelle, chamber
opera; New world for Nellie, ballad opera;
Whither, sacred drama for chamber orch., solo
voices and chorus; Orchestra: Alice in Wonder-
land, ballet suite; The pond, Eastman American
Composers Festival; Lost valley, Chautauqua
Symph.; Chamber music: Rondo, trombone and
piano.
      3760 Harts Mill Lane, Atlanta, GA 30139

*DURE, ROBERT
   Trio for flute, clarinet and cello, was performed Composers' Conference, Bennington, Vt.,
1965.

DURHAM, LOWELL M.
   b. Boston, Mass., 4 Mar. 1917. Studied at Univ.
of Utah; with Philip Greeley Clapp and Addison
Alspach at Univ. of Iowa; and privately with
Leroy Robertson. He received commissions for
arrangements for the Tabernacle Choir, 1961-64;
from Beloit (Wis.) Symphony, 1969; Univ. of
Utah Theatre, 1964. He was assistant dean, Coll.
of Fine Arts, Univ. of Utah, 1948-53; dean,
1953-64; professor, 1946- . He is also chairman of the committee for the Univ. of Utah Festival of Contemporary Music.
   WORKS: Orchestra: Suite for string orch.,
1943; Prelude and scherzo for string orch.,
1944, Utah Symph., Feb. 1954; New England pastorale, strings, 1955; Variations for string
orch., Univ. of Utah Symph., Nov. 1960; Folk-
scape for orch., Beloit (Wis.) Symph., Oct.
1967; Chorus: This is my country, double chorus, 1961, performed by Tabernacle Choir in Jan.
1964 at President Johnson's inauguration; at
President Nixon's inauguration; Calm as a summer morn, chorus and orch., 1971; Choralise, a
cappella, 1972, commissioned and performed, Univ.
of Utah Chamber Choir, Apr. 1973.
      Music Dept., University of Utah
      Salt Lake City, UT 84111

DUSHKIN, DOROTHY
   b. Chicago, Ill., 26 July 1903. Studied with
Werner Josten at Smith Coll.; continued study
with Nadia Boulanger in Paris. She was awarded
honors in music at Smith Coll. and performances
of a choral and an orchestral work; received
prize for quintet in a Chicago competition. She
was co-founder and director with her husband of
the Winnetka (Ill.) Music School, 1931-52, and
of Kinhaven Music School, Weston, Vt.,
1952- .
   WORKS: Orchestra: concerto for orch.;
piano concerto; suite for strings; Chamber
music: 3 quintets for piano and woodwinds;
quintet for oboe and strings; quintet for flute
and strings; woodwind octet; sextet for woodwinds, piano, and horn; suite for 4 woodwinds
and 4 strings; 2 suites for percussion ensemble;
chorale for 2 brass antiphonal choirs; septet
for brass; sonata for 2 celli and piano; flute
sonata; Chorus: cantata for chorus and orch.
      Weston, VT 05161

DUTTON, FREDERIC M.
   b. San Jose, Calif., 26 Apr. 1928. Studied with
Raymound Kimbell, Wolfgang Fortner, Lukas Foss.
He has played with the Dave Brubeck Quartet,
Stan Kenton and Les Brown Big Bands, Chamber
Jazz Sextet, Southwest Radio Symphony Orchestra
and South Radio Entertainment Orchestra (Germany), and Los Angeles Philharmonic.
   WORKS: Orchestra: flute concerto; concerto for English horn and string orch.: Chamber music: Bits and pieces, march for brass
quartet; octet for trumpets; quintet for oboe,

(DUTTON, FREDERIC M.)
clarinet, viola, cello, bass; Rondymiths, solo trumpet.
19553 Gault St., Reseda, CA 91335

*DVORAK, ROBERT
Lament and repose, brass ensemble; Songs of deliverance, a cantata; West Point symphony for band.
2423 South Austin Blvd., Cicero, IL 60650

*DVORINE, SHURA
Graduated from Peabody Cons., 1943, and joined the Preparatory School piano faculty, 1971.
WORKS: Ballet: The lovers' concerto, 1967; The ballet school; Ballet #3, 1972; Ballet school II, 1973; Piano: Pensive nocturne, 1948. He was commissioned by the Union of Hebrew Congregations to write an experimental service which was performed in Chicago, Nov. 1962.
Peabody Conservatory
1 East Mt. Vernon Place, Baltimore, MD 21202

*DVORKIN, JUDITH
b. 1930. Maurice, a modern madrigal, 1955.
19 East 80th St., New York, NY 10021

DWORAK, PAUL EDWARD
b. Natrona, Pa., 25 Jan. 1951. Studied with Roland Leich and Leonardo Balada at Carnegie-Mellon Univ. He was consultant and instructor, Pittsburgh Center for the Musically Talented, 1971-73; and at Carnegie-Mellon Univ., instructor, Extension Department, 1972- , graduate fellow and instructor, 1973- .
WORKS: A serial/aleatoric quintet for strings and winds, 1972; Chromokinetics, a study in timbral contrasts and organization, for computer generated tape, 1973. Dworak believes this is the first original work composed and performed in Pittsburgh using the Stanford Univ. Score compiler.
15 Pine St., Natrona, PA 15065

*DYDO, (JOHN) STEPHEN
b. New York, N. Y., 1949. Received a BMI student composer award, 1972 for Solomon songs, soprano and chamber ensemble, and Mass, 6 instruments and chamber chorus. He is an associate editor, Contemporary Music Newsletter, New York Univ.
c/o Music Department, Columbia University
New York, NY 10027

*EAGLES, MONETA
Scherzino, Soliloquy, 2 sketches for clarinet.

EAKIN, CHARLES
b. Pittsburgh, Pa., 24 Feb. 1927. Studied with Vittorio Giannini at Manhattan School of Music; with Nikolai Lopatnikoff at Carnegie-Mellon Univ.; and with Paul Fetler at Univ. of Minnesota. He was assistant professor, Baylor Univ. 1960-64; associate professor, Univ. of Colorado, 1964- .
WORKS: Theatre: The box, 1-act opera; Being of sound mind, musical piece for theatre; Pasticcio, speaking chorus, 3 dancers, 3 actors; Orchestra: Dialogues for cello, percussion and

(EAKIN, CHARLES)
orchestra; Chamber music: Passacaglia for piano; Improvisation for harp and piano pizzicato; Mixed media: Tonight I am, soprano and tape.
350 South 41st, Boulder, CO 80302

*EAKIN, THOMAS
Pasticcio, opera, Univ. of Northern Iowa, Cedar Falls, 2 May 1974.

EAKIN, VERA O.
b. Emlenton, Pa., 6 Aug. 1890. Studied with Ernest Hutcheson at New England Cons.; at Juilliard School; and privately with Hugh Giles, organist. She has received many Nat. Fed. of Music Clubs awards, the most recent, 1973. She was staff pianist and coach, CBS, and organist in the greater New York area for over 30 years.
WORKS: Songs: Ay, gitanos; Flamenco gypsy moon; Wind and girl; To live and dream; Sand stars; Blind eyes; Christmas morn; The place prepared for thee; her concert songs were used by such well-known singers as Lawrence Tibbet, James Melton, Eileen Farrell, etc.
Fairfax Apts-803
4614 Fifth Ave., Pittsburgh, PA 15213

EARLS, PAUL
b. Springfield, Mo., 9 June 1934. Studied with Bernard Rogers and Howard Hanson at Eastman School of Music. He received a recording prize, Rochester Philharmonic, 1959; Guggenheim, Fulbright, MacDowell, and Yaddo fellowships; Huntington Hartford Found. and Mary Duke Biddle Found. grants. He has held faculty positions at Southwest Missouri State Coll.; Chabot Coll.; Univ. of Oregon; Duke Univ.; Massachusetts Inst. of Technology; Massachusetts Coll. of Art; Boston Univ.; artist-fellow, MIT Center for Advanced Visual Studies, 1969- .
WORKS: Orchestra: And on the seventh day, chamber orch., Rochester, Nov. 1959; A band of Solomon's dukes, Duke Univ., Apr. 1968; Chamber music: Nun danket fantasy, organ, Berkeley, Mar. 1963; Huguenot variations, organ, Berkeley, Mar. 1963; string quartet, New York, Nov. 1968; Five notables, violin solo, New York, Nov. 1968; Preparation, organ, Chapel Hill, June 1968; Coronach for K, K, K for piano, New York, Nov. 1968; Alpha/Numeric:E, aleatoric work for 3-7 players, any instruments, made from personal data of the performers, Conway, N. H., Nov. 1970; Chorus: Psalm 100, Penfield, N. Y., May 1961; The Lord's prayer, children's choir, organ or brass, Berkeley, Mar. 1963; Brevis Mass, bilingual setting for choir and instrumental octet, Penfield, N. Y., May 1967; Trine, soloists, choir, clarinet, Duke Univ., Mar. 1967; Alpha/Numeric I: Prologue and ten events, non-verbal choral piece with audience participation, Duke Univ., Apr. 1970; What's in a name, participatory audience piece, MIT, Feb. 1972; Tape and electronic: Divisions in twelve, 2 pianos and tape, New York, Oct. 1967; Trio/duo, tape, violin, piano, Boston, Oct. 1969; Analogue, on Moog synthesizer, Duke Univ., Apr. 1970; The Hindenberg, environmental work with collaboration of Maurice Wright and Edgar Williams, Duke Univ.,

EARLS, PAUL

(EARLS, PAUL)
Nov. 1969; Lincoln 'n love, environmental gallery work, Brandeis Univ., Feb. 1970; Monday music, Moog synthesizer, MIT, Nov. 1970; The love suicide at Schofield Barracks, music for Romulus Linney's play, New York, Mar.-Apr. 1971; Laser loop #1, deflection of laser beam by music, with Ted Kraynik, in permanent collection of Art and Science Museum, Tel Aviv, May 1971; Processional music, 8-channel variable-length academic march, Buchla and Moog with brass and percussion, MIT Commencement, June 1971; The lobbyist, real-time processing of speech into sustained amplitude-modulated pitches, Boston Univ., Jan. 1972; Joyce, 5 readers and tape, Boston Univ., Jan. 1972; Flame orchard I, II, III, music that modulates a field of flame, devised by Gyorgy Kepes with collaboration of William Walton and Mauricio Bueno for Bienal Coltejar, Medellin, Colombia (first prize awarded), MIT traveling exhibition, Apr.-June 1972; Dialogue: Music and..., a mixed media presentation, New York, 24 Feb. 1974
    55 Langdon St., Cambridge, MA 02138

EASTMAN, JULIUS
b. New York, N. Y., 27 Oct. 1940. Studied with Constant Vauclain at Curtis Inst. of Music. He has been professor, State Univ. of New York at Buffalo, 1971-
    WORKS: Orchestra: symphony, 1969; Chamber music: Trumpet, for any 7 soprano instruments, 1970, New York, 2 May 1973; Stay on it, for 2 singers and instruments, 1973; Wood in time, for 8 amplified metronomes, 1973; Chorus: Thruway, chorus and instruments, 1970; The moon's silent modulation, chorus, instruments, narrators, and 3 dancers, 1969.
    Music Dept., State University of New York
    Buffalo, NY 14214

EATON, JOHN C.
b. Bryn Mawr, Pa., 30 Mar. 1935. Studied with Roger Sessions, Milton Babbitt, Edward Cone at Princeton Univ., B. A., M. F. A. He received the Prix de Rome three times; 2 Guggenheim felloships; commissions from Fromm Found., Koussevitzky Found., and Public Broadcasting Corporation. He toured the U.S. in 1958 with his own jazz group, and in 1962 as co-leader of the American Jazz Ensemble. He has been associate professor, Indiana Univ., 1970-   .
    WORKS: Opera: Ma Barker, 1957; Heracles, 1970; The lion and Androcles, children's opera, Cincinnati, summer 1971; Myshkin, 1-hour television opera, based on Dostoyevsky's The idiot, 1970, (NET, Boston, 23 Apr. 1973); Orchestra: Overture for orch.; Adagio and allegro, flute, oboe, strings; Concert piece for Syn-Ket and and symphony orch., Tanglewood, 9 Aug. 1967; Chamber music: Piano variations, 1958; string quartet, 1959; Concert music for clarinet, 1961; Ajax; Microtonal fantasy, piano, 1965; Vibrations, wind ensemble, 1967; Song cycles: Holy sonnets of John Donne, soprano and orch., 1957; Songs for R. P. B., soprano and Syn-Ket, 1964; Thoughts on Rilke, soprano, Syn-Ket, 1967; Blind man's cry, soprano and ensemble of synthesizers,

(EATON, JOHN C.)
1968: Electronic: Concert piece for solo Syn-Ket, #1, 2, 3 (1966), 4 (Soliloquy, 1967); Duet, Syn-Ket and Moog, 1968; Mass, soprano, clarinet, synthesizer, tape, 1970; Electro-vibrations.
    828 South Woodlawn, Bloomington, IN 47401

*EBERHARD, DENNIS
Verse varied, string quartet; Paraphrases, woodwind quintet; Chamber music, 2 percussionists.

EDDLEMAN, DAVID
b. Winston-Salem, N. C., 20 Aug. 1936. Studied at Appalachian State Univ., B. S.; with Milton Cherry, Virginia Commonwealth Univ., M. M. 1963; with Gardner Read, Boston Univ., D. M. A. 1971. He received a composition award, Boston Univ., 1970. He was public school music teacher, 1963-68; instructor, Boston Univ., 1968-72; music editor, N. J. publishing firm, 1972-   .
    WORKS: Opera: The cure, 1965; Chamber music: brass quartet, 1971; Diversions, clarinet and piano, 1971; Latin woods; Two in three for Mimi; Chorus: Continuum, 1972; Sound and Fury, 1972; Infinitude, 1972; Autumn, 2-part chorus, recorder, and finger cymbal, 1974; Songs: Silent sea; End of summer; I'm gonna walk; I don't mind; A song with no key.
    12 James Court, Rockaway, NJ 07866

EDMONDSON, JOHN BALDWIN
b. Toledo, Ohio, 3 Feb. 1933. Studied with Russell Danburg, Univ. of Florida; with Kenneth Wright, Bernard Fitzgerald, Univ. of Kentucky. He was staff arranger, Univ. of Kentucky Band, 1963-70; band director, public schools, 1960-70; educational editor, Miami music publishing firm, 1970-   .
    WORKS: Band: Hymn and postlude; Pagentry overture; Song for winds; Winchester march; Fantasy on a fanfare.
    20501 N.W. 2nd Court, Miami, FL 33169

*EDMUNDS, JOHN
b. San Francisco, 10 June, 1913. Studied at Univ. of California, B. A.; with Rosario Scalero at Curtis Inst.; with Walter Piston, Harvard Univ., M. A.; Roy Harris at Cornell Univ.; and Otto Luening at Columbia Univ. His awards include the Bearns prize; Seidl traveling fellowship; Fulbright fellowship; Alice Ditson award; Italian Government grant. He was head of the American Collection, Music Division, New York Public Library, 1957-61; director, American Music Center, 1957-61.
    WORKS: Chorus: Clambake on the Potomac; Come sweet peace; Lord God of hosts; many more; and many songs. He is author of History of American music in pictures, co-author, Some 20th century American composers.
    68 Central Ave., Sausalito, CA 94965

*EDMUNDSON, GARTH
b. Pittsburgh, Pa., 11 Apr. 1895. Studied at Leipzig Cons.; with Harvey Gaul and Joseph Bonnet; and at Westminster Coll., D. M. He has been teacher and organist, Newcastle, Pa.

(EDMUNDSON, GARTH)
WORKS: Organ: 2 organ symphonies; 56 chorale preludes; In modum antiquum, suite; Toccata brilliante on All praise to thee; Epiphany; Gargoyles; 7 classic preludes; 7 contrapuntal preludes; 7 modern preludes; 7 polyphonic preludes; From heaven high, toccata.

*EDWARDS, ANDREW J. C.
Variations on a theme of homage to Henry Purcell, violin and piano, Boston, 24 Apr. 1973.

*EDWARDS, CLARA
b. Mankato, Minn., 18 Apr. 1887; d. New York, N. Y., 17 Jan. 1974. Studied at Mankato State Normal School; Cosmopolitan School of Music; and in Europe. She was a singer and pianist; wrote music for Tony Sarg's Marionettes and for animated films.
WORKS: Songs: By the bend of the river; Into the night; With the wind and the rain in your face; The fisher's widow; Stars of the night; Sing softly, et al.

EDWARDS, GEORGE
b. Boston, Mass., 11 May 1943. Studied with Richard Hoffmann at Oberlin Coll.; with Milton Babbitt and Earl Kim at Princeton Univ. He won the Koussevitzky Prize at Tanglewood, 1967; and the Prix de Rome for study in Italy, 1973-75. He has been on the faculty, New England Cons., 1968-   .
WORKS: Orchestra: Two pieces for orchestra, 1964; Monopoly, 1972; Chamber music: Two piano pieces; 2 Bagatelles, piano; Bits, 1966; string quartet, 1967; Double play, 2 pianos, 1970; The captive, soprano and 12 instruments, 1970; Three Hopkins songs, 1971; Kreuz und Quer, chamber group, 1971; Suspension bridge, cello solo, New York, 15 Apr. 1974.
409 Beacon St., Boston, MA 02115

EDWARDS, H. NEIL
b. Dalton, Ga., 12 Dec. 1931. Attended Univ. of Georgia and Florida State Univ., and studied with Charles Douglas and Everett Pittman. He taught in public schools, 1956-64; chairman, music department, Brewton Parker Coll., 1964-66; was acting chairman, music department, Georgia Southwestern Coll., 1967-69, and faculty, 1969-73.
WORKS: Band: Suite religioso, 1962; Pride of the red devils, 1964; Fanfare and chorale, 1965; March Opus 2, 1969; Chamber music: quartet for trumpets and trombones, 1963; Trombone-piano apogee, 1964; Chorus: Psalm 118, 1965; It is enough, 1965; Motet: In festo aposlotorum, 1965; Electronic: sound track for No exit by Sartre, tape, 1968; Reverbo ostinato, fugue for inexpensive oscillator and tape, 1970.
3661 North Decatur Road, N.E., Apt. E5
Decatur, GA 30033

*EDWARDS, JESSIE B.
Published choral works and vocal solos.

EDWARDS, LEO
b. Cincinnati, Ohio, 31 Jan. 1937. Studied with Scott Huston in Cincinnati; with Norman Dello

(EDWARDS, LEO)
Joio at Mannes Coll. of Music; and with Robert Starer at City Univ. of New York. He taught at Shumiatcher School of Music, 1968; has been instructor, Mannes Coll. of Music, 1968-; and assistant professor, Brooklyn Coll., CUNY, 1970-   .
WORKS: Orchestra: Fantasy overture, commissioned by Orchestral Soc. of Westchester, Lyndhurst, N. Y., 24 July 1971; Chamber music: string quartet, 1968, revised 1970; Etude for brass, Brooklyn, 25 Apr. 1972; Chorus: 150th Psalm, soprano, chorus, orch., commissioned by Triad Chorale, New York, 10 Dec. 1972.
3021 Ave. I, Brooklyn, NY 11210

*EDWARDS, RYAN
Has had songs performed in New York, 1971, and in Boston, 1975; flute work performed by Jean-Pierre Rampal, 1973. He was accompanist for all performances.

EFFINGER, CECIL
b. Colorado Springs, Colo., 22 July 1914. Studied with Nadia Boulanger in France; and with Boothroyd and Bernard Wagenaar in Colorado Springs. His awards include Presser scholarship in oboe, 1931; Stoval Prize, 1939; Naumburg Recording Award, 1959; Doctor of Music, Colorado Coll., 1959; Faculty fellowship, Univ. of Colorado, 1969; Governor's Award in Arts and Humanities, Aspen, Colo., 1971. He was mathematics instructor, Colorado Springs, 1936; music instructor, Colorado Coll., 1936-41, assistant professor, 1946-48; first oboist, Denver Symphony, 1937-41; music editor, Denver Post, 1946-48; and at Univ. of Colorado, associate professor, 1948-46, professor, 1956-   .
WORKS: Opera: Pandora's box, 1961; Cyrano de Bergerac, 1965; Orchestra: Little symphony, No.1, 1945, No.2, 1958; symphony for chorus and orch., 1952; symphony No.5, 1958; Trio concertante, trumpet, horn, trombone, and chamber orch., 1964; Capriccio, Denver, 3 Mar. 1975; Band: Prelude and fugue, 1942; Interlude on a blues tune, 1944; Silver plume, 1961; Let your mind wander over America, band, chorus, and strings, 1969; Chamber music: Melody, clarinet and piano, 1947; Rondino, horn and piano, 1949; Dialogue, clarinet and piano, 1957; Solitude, saxophone and piano, 1960; string quartet, No. 5, 1963; Fantasia agitato, clarinet and piano, 1972; Chorus: Fanfare on Army chow call, male chorus and brass, 1943; American men, male chorus and band, 1942; Sing we merrily unto God, chorus, organ, strings, soli, 1948; Time, Shelley text, a cappella, 1947; The St. Luke Christmas story, choir, soloists, organ, chamber orch., 1953; Shepherds in the field, 1955; Why was Cupid a boy, 1955; An American hymn, choir and brass, 1957; A prairie sunset, 1959; Set of three, chorus and brass, 1961; Behold thy brother man, 1962; Four pastorales, choir and oboe, 1962; Forget not my law, 1967; Spring rain, a cappella, 1970; The long dimension, choir and orch., 1970; Cantata for Easter, 1971; Paul of Tarsus, oratorio with organ and strings, 1968.
2620 Lafayette Drive, Boulder, CO 80303

EFREIN, LAURIE

*EFREIN, LAURIE
Attraction, unaccompanied flute.

EHLE, ROBERT C.
b. Lancaster, Pa., 7 Nov. 1939. Studied with
Louis Menneni, Bernard Rogers, Robert Sutton,
Wayne Barlow at Eastman School of Music; pri-
vately with William Russo; with Samuel Adler,
Merrill Ellis, and Martin Mailman at North
Texas State Univ. He was George Eastman fellow,
1961; and received a Dallas Symphony-Rockefeller
award, 1966. He was teaching assistant, North
Texas State Univ., 1965-70; instructor, Denver
Inst. of Technology, 1970-71; assistant professor, Univ. of Northern Colorado, 1971-   .
WORKS: Orchestra: Soundpiece, Dallas, 1966;
Electronic: Five pieces for electronically prepared instruments; Algorythms, soprano and electronically prepared instruments.
2107 26th Ave. Court, Greeley, CO 80631

*EHRENKREUTZ, STEVE
b. 1949. Studied with Edward Cohen, Brandeis
Univ.; wrote Recollections and reflections for
orch., Boston, 13 May 1973.

*EHRLICH, JESSE
b. 1920. 6 short pieces for 3 cellos.

*EICHHEIM, HENRY
b. Chicago, Ill., 3 Jan. 1870; d. Montecito,
Calif., 22 Aug. 1942. Graduated from Chicago
Musical Coll. with the violin prize. He was member, Boston Symphony Orchestra, 1890-1912; then
toured as soloist and conductor of his own works.
He made several trips to the Orient, collected
native instruments which he used in orchestral
compositions. He wrote many works for orchestra
and for chamber groups, all with oriental themes.

EILERS, JOYCE ELAINE
b. Mooreland, Okla., 28 July 1941. Studied at
Oklahoma City Univ., B. M. 1963; Univ. of Oregon,
M. M. She has taught in public schools since
1963; in Corvallis, Ore., 1972-   .
WORKS: Chorus: Tiny king; The gift; Born
today; A star shone bright; and many other published choral works.
2520 N.W. Highland Drive
Corvallis, OR 97330

EISENSTEIN, ALFRED
b. Brody, Poland, 14 Nov. 1899; U.S. citizen
1948. Studied piano in Vienna with Anton Trost
and is self-taught in composition. He received
ASCAP awards; and N. Y. State Audio Society
award, 1967.
WORKS: Orchestra: Adagio lamentoso, tone
poem; Impromptu, tone poem; Melodic reflections,
cello and orch.; Movements for strings: Petite
suite; Romance for violin and orch; Souvenir,
violin and orch.; Tango of love; Songs: The
fisherman; If you were mine; Life was beautiful;
Love's grief; Two castanets; Barcarolle; When I
look into your eyes; Elegy; all songs have orchestral accompaniment.
18900 N.E. 14th Ave.
North Miami Beach, FL 33162

*EISENSTEIN, JUDITH KAPLAN
The sacrifice of Isaac, Jewish liturgical drama,
New York, 19 Dec. 1972.

EISENSTEIN, STELLA PRICE
b. Glasgow, Mo., 16 Feb. 1886; d. Moberly, Mo.,
28 Mar. 1969. Studied violin and piano at the
Goetz Cons. Moberly, Mo., and at Cincinnati
Cons.; later studied composition with Felix
Borowski at Chicago Musical Coll., and organ
with Hans Feil in Kansas City. She was awarded
the associate degree in the American Guild of
Organists, 1928. She toured as violinist in
the Chataqua series with the Price Concert Company, which included her mother, Emma Price,
and sister, Lucile Price. After marriage, she
settled in Moberly as violin, piano, and organ
teacher. Her published works include Memories
of the South, for violin and piano, and many
anthems and organ works.

*EL-DABH, HALIM
b. Cairo, Egypt, 4 Mar. 1921; to U.S. 1950.
Graduated from Cairo Univ. with a degree in
agricultural engineering, but turned full attention to music in 1949. He received a Fulbright
fellowship for study in the U.S. at Brandeis
Univ., Univ. of New Mexico, with Francis Judd
Cooke, New England Cons., and with Irving Fine
and Aaron Copland at Tanglewood; has worked also
at the Columbia-Princeton Electronic Music Laboratory. He received a Guggenheim fellowship,
1959. He is professor, Kent State Univ.
WORKS: Ballet: Clytemnestra, dance epic
for Martha Graham, 1958; Ballet of lights, 1960;
Orchestra: 3 symphonies, 1951, 1952, 1955; concerto and Fantasia-Tahmeel for derabucca, or
timpani, and strings, 1954; Symphonic eclogue,
1956; Bacchanalia, 1958; Agamemnon and Furies
in Hades, ballet suites for orch., 1958; House
of Atreus, soprano, baritone, chorus, and orch.,
1958; Opera flies, based on the shootings at
Kent State Univ., 1969, Washington, D.C., 5 May
1971; Electronic: Leiyla and the poet, 1962;
Symphonies in sonic vibration; Spectrum #1.
Music Department, Kent State University
Kent, OH 44242

*ELKUS, ALBERT
b. Sacramento, Calif., 30 Apr. 1884; d. Oakland
Calif., 19 Feb. 1962. Studied at Univ. of
California, B. A., M. A.; piano with Harold
Bauer and Josef Lhevinne. He taught at San
Francisco Cons., Mills Coll., Univ. of Califor-
nia at Berkeley; was director, San Francisco
Cons., 1951-57.
WORKS: Orchestra: Impressions from a Greek
tragedy (received Juilliard award); concertino
on Lezione III of Ariosti, cello and string
orch.; Chamber music: Serenade for string quar-
tet; violin sonata; Chorus: I am the reaper;
Sir Patrick Spens.

ELKUS, JONATHAN
b. San Francisco, 8 Aug. 1931. Studied with
Charles Cushing at Univ. of California, Berkeley;
with Ernst Bacon and Leonard Ratner, Stanford

(ELKUS, JONATHAN)
Univ.; and with Darius Milhaud at Mills Coll. He was professor of music, Lehigh Univ., 1957-73.
WORKS: Operas: The mandarin; Medea; The outcasts of Poker Flat; Helen in Egypt; Tom Sawyer; Treasure Island; also chamber music, choruses, songs, and works for band.
8 Pearl St., Provincetown, MA 02657

*ELLINGTON, EDWARD KENNEDY (DUKE)
b. Washington, D.C., 29 Apr. 1899; d. New York, N.Y., 23 May 1974. Has been acclaimed as one of the most important, indeed, the greatest American composer. At the celebration of his 70th birthday at a White House gala in 1969, he was awarded the Presidential Medal of Freedom. The Swedish Acad. of Music elected him to membership in 1971; two African countries, Chad and Togo, have issued postage stamps bearing his picture; Yale Univ. in 1972 established the Duke Ellington Fellowship Fund "to preserve and perpetuate the Afro-American musical tradition;" in 1973 President Pompidou of France gave him the Legion of Honor; also in 1973 he was awarded an honorary doctorate at Columbia Univ. The young Edward took some piano lessons at age 7 and ended this formal training at about the time he acquired the nickname Duke at age 8. From then on he learned by listening and watching. He wrote his first piece, Soda fountain rag, when he was working as a soda jerk after school. By the time he was 20 he had his own small band, and in late 1927 took his expanded 10-piece band into the Cotton Club in Harlem. A nightly radio broadcast from the Cotton Club soon made the Ellington Band known throughout the country, and his unique style drew musicians of all schools to the Cotton Club. His first tour of Europe and Britain in 1933 established his reputation abroad as composer and band leader. In the thirties, the band made four feature-length movies, in 1943-50 gave annual Carnegie Hall recitals, and in 1963 toured the Mid East for the State Department. Through all this he maintained a steady pace of composing; his total number of works of varying length exceeds 6000.
WORKS: Theatre: Jump for joy, Los Angeles, 1941; Beggar's holiday, lyrics by John Latouche, adapted from John Gay's Beggar's opera, New York, 1947; Timon of Athens, stage background score; My people, pageant of black history, Chicago, 1963; The river, ballet, written for Alvin Ailey and American Ballet Theatre, 1970; Orchestra: Reminiscing in tempo, 1934; Diminuendo and crescendo, 1936; Black and tan fantasy; The mooche; Blue belles of Harlem, 1938; Creole love call; Mood indigo; East St. Louis toodle-oo; Black, brown and beige, 1943; New world a-comin, 1945; Deep South suite; Perfume suite (with William Strayhorn); Liberian suite, 1948; Togo bravo; Harlem, 1950; Night creatures, 1955; Such sweet thunder, Shakespearean suite (with Strayhorn), 1957; Suite Thursday, after Steinbeck's Sweet Thursday, 1960; Chorus: In the beginning, God..., concert of sacred music for orchestra, 3 choirs, soloists, dancer, performed at Grace Cathedral, San Francisco, 1965, repeated twice in 1965 at Fifth Avenue Presbyterian Church, New York;

(ELLINGTON, EDWARD KENNEDY)
Second sacred concert, Cathedral Church of St. John the Divine, New York, 1968; Third sacred concert, Westminster Abbey, London, 1973; Songs: Solitude, Sophisticated lady; In a sentimental mood; I let a song go out of my heart; I got it bad; Film scores (1956-71): Paris blues; Anatomy of a murder; Assault on a queen; Change of mind; Janus, a German film. The tune Duke Ellington used as a theme for many years and is probably most often associated with him, Take the A train, was not written by Ellington but by his long-time close associate and collaborator, William Strayhorn. Ellington's autobiography, Music is my mistress was published in 1973.

ELLIOT, WILLARD
Bassoon concerto; sextet for chamber ensemble.

*ELLIOT, WILLIAM F.
Between the war, lyric-theatre piece with music, actors, film, 1975 NEA grant.

*ELLIOTT, CLINTON
Pope Joan, 1-act musical comedy; The owl and the pussy cat, women's chorus.

ELLIOTT, MARJORIE REEVE (Mrs. Charles H.)
b. Syracuse, N. Y., 7 Aug. 1890. Studied with Adolph Frey at Syracuse Univ., B. M., honorary D. M. She received the Arents Pioneer Award, Syracuse Univ. 1973; Centennial Award, City of Syracuse, 1948; was 3 times guest of honor, Chicago Music Festival. She is composer, teacher, and head of her own studio.
WORKS: 400 published choral and piano works.
4085 High Bridge Ave., Oneida, NY 13421

ELLIOTT, TIMOTHY ALLEN
b. Chicago, Ill., 21 May 1946. Studied with Ruth Shaw Wylie and Harold Laudenslager at Wayne State Univ. He has been a teacher in public and private schools in Detroit and has been engaged in research on electronic music.
WORKS: Chamber music: piano cycle, 6 pieces for piano solo; string quartet; 5 ensembles, #1, woodwinds, brass, percussion; #2, brass, woodwinds, string bass; #3, percussion; #4, string quintet, clarinet, percussion; #5, 9 instruments, piano, percussion, and tape.
26405 Couzens, Madison Heights, MI 48071

*ELLIS, DON
b. Los Angeles, Calif., 25 July 1934. Studied with Gardner Read, Boston Univ.; with John Vincent, Univ. of California, Los Angeles. He played first trumpet with the National Symphony Orchestra, then with various jazz bands until forming his own group.
WORKS: Concert Jazz: Contrasts for 2 orchestras and trumpet, 1965; Improvisational suite #1.
c/o MJQ Music, Inc.
200 West 57th St., New York, NY 10019

ELLIS, MERRILL

*ELLIS, MERRILL
b. 1916. Studied with Roy Harris, Univ. of
Oklahoma, B. S.; and at Univ. of Mississippi,
M. M. He is associate professor and director
of the electronic laboratory, North Texas State
Univ. His works include Kaleidoscope for orchestra, synthesizer, and soprano; Mutations, a
multimedia piece for brass, tapes, projectors,
films, and dancer, 1971.
North Texas State University
Denton, TX 76203

ELLISTON, RONALD ROBERT
b. Colorado Springs, Colo., 20 Feb. 1935. Studied with Homer Keller at Univ. of Oregon. He has
been assistant professor, Adams State Coll.,
1970-   .
WORKS: Chamber music: suite for piano;
Conservations, flute, cello, piano; concerto
for trumpet, brass choir, percussion.
217 LaVeta Ave., Alamosa, CO 81101

*ELLSTEIN, ABRAHAM
b. New York, N. Y., 9 July 1907; d. New York,
22 Mar. 1963. Studied at Manhattan School of
Music; with Frederic Jacobi, Rubin Goldmark,
Albert Stoessel, Juilliard School. His awards
included an Ohio Univ. prize and a Ford Found.
commission. He was music director, WMGM, New
York; had his own program on WEVD, New York,
1951-63.
WORKS: Opera: The thief and the hangman,
1-act; The Golem; Theatre: Great to be alive,
stage score; operettas for the Yiddish theatre;
Orchestra: Negev, piano concerto; Ode to the
King of Kings, cantata for 2 soli and orch.; The
redemption, oratorio for narrator, 3 soli, orch.;
Ima, cantata; Chorus: Friday evening service;
Shabbat Menuchah; A Passover service; and songs.

ELMORE, ROBERT HALL
b. Ramaputnam, India, of American parents, 2
Jan. 1913. Studied organ and piano, Royal Acad.
of Music, London, licentiate degree, 1933; Royal
Coll. of Music, London, associate degree, 1933;
Univ. of Pennsylvania, B. M. 1937; teachers were
Harl McDonald and Pietro Yon. He received the
Nitsche Prize, 1934, 1935, 1936; Thornton Oakley
Medal, 1936; Mendelssohn Club award, 1938;
L. H. D., Moravian Coll., 1958; L. L. D. Alderson-
Broaddus Coll., 1958. He has held various church
posts as organist-music director since 1933; was
faculty member, Clark Cons., 1935-45; head, organ
department, Philadelphia Musical Acad., 1938-69;
vice chairman, music department, Univ. of Penn-
sylvania, 1969-   .
WORKS: Opera: It began at breakfast, 1-act,
first American opera on television; Orchestra:
Three colors, suite; Valley Forge-1777, tone
poem; Legend of Sleepy Hollow, suite; Narrative,
horn and orch.; Prelude to unrest, tone poem;
Chorus: Out of the depths, cantata, Philadelphia,
16 Apr. 1972; Psalm of redemption; Three psalms;
The incarnate word; The cross; The prodigal son;
Organ and brass: Meditation on Veni Emmanuel;
Fanfare for Easter; concerto for organ, brass,
percussion; Poem for carillonic bells and organ;

(ELMORE, ROBERT HALL)
2 pianos: Swing rhapsody; many anthems and
organ works.
130 Walnut Ave., Wayne, PA 19087

*ELSTON, ARNOLD
b. New York, 1907; d. on trip to Vienna, Austria,
summer 1971. Studied at Columbia Univ. and Harvard Univ., Ph. D.; with Anton Webern, 1933-35.
He taught at the Univ. of Oregon; then was professor, Univ. of California at Berkeley, 1956-71.
His works for various media include a string
quartet, 1961.

*ELWELL, HERBERT
b. Minneapolis, Minn., 10 May 1898. Studied at
Univ. of Minnesota; with Ernest Bloch in New
York; with Nadia Boulanger in Paris; and on fellowship at the American Acad. in Rome. He received the Paderewski prize, 1945; an honorary
doctorate, Western Reserve Univ., 1946; Ohioana
Library Asso. award, 1947. He taught at Cleveland Inst. of Music, 1928-45; joined faculty at
Oberlin Cons., 1945; was music critic, Cleveland
Plain Dealer, 1932-65.
WORKS: Orchestra: The happy hypocrite,
ballet suite, 1927; Introduction and allegro;
Ode for orchestra, 1950; The forever young,
voice and orch., 1954; Concert suite for violin
and orch., 1957; Chamber music: Blue symphony,
voice and string quartet; violin sonata; piano
sonata; 2 string quartets; Tarantella, piano;
Chorus: Lincoln: Requiem aeternum, baritone,
chorus, orch.; I was with him, tenor, male chorus, 2 pianos; and songs.
2371 Edgerton Road, Cleveland, OH 44108

EMIG, LOIS MEYER (Mrs. Jack)
b. Roseville, Ohio, 12 Oct. 1925. Studied at
Ohio State Univ., B. M. E., graduate work in
composition; Queens Coll. She was a public
school teacher, 1946-65; church organist,
1966-   ; private teacher, 1948-   .
WORKS: Cantatas: Beautiful savior; The
children's alleluia; Song of Bethlehem; many
anthems, secular choral works, and two piano
books.
82 Fletcher Ave., Valley Stream, NY 11580

ENCISO, FRANZ
b. Los Angeles, Calif., 12 July 1941. Studied
with Leonard Stein, California State Univ.,
B. M. 1965; with Michael Senturia, Univ. of California, Berkeley, M. A. 1969. He has been on
the music faculty, North Peralta Community Coll.,
1972-   .
WORKS: Chamber music: trio for flute,
clarinet, violin; improvisational compositions
for keyboard.
2643 Hillegass, Berkeley, CA 94704

END, JACK
b. Rochester, N. Y., 31 Oct. 1918. Studied with
Howard Hanson, Bernard Rogers, Burrill Phillips,
Rufus Arey at Eastman School of Music. He was
a faculty member, Eastman School of Music,
1940-50; music staff, WROC-TV, 1950-60; director

(END, JACK)
of radio and television, Univ. of Rochester, 1960-   .
     WORKS: Orchestra: Three American pastimes; Fantasy for orchestra; Overture; Song for sleepy children; Wind ensemble: Portrait by a wind ensemble; The rocks and the sea; Floorshow; Chamber music: string quartet; woodwind quintet; brass quintet; pieces for trombone choir, jazz band; Chorus: Snowfall.
     36 Potter Place, Fairport, NY 14450

ENDRES, OLIVE PHILOMENE
     b. Johnsberg, Wis., 23 Dec. 1898. Began piano at 4, organ with her father at 12; graduated in piano, Wisconsin School of Music; in composition with honors, American Cons., studying with Adolph Weidig and Leo Sowerby; summer study at Juilliard School. She has received several prizes in Wisconsin State Composer Contests. She taught at Wisconsin School of Music and at Milton Coll.; organist, St. James Church, Madison; private teacher.
     WORKS: String orchestra: Prelude and fugue, Theme and variations; Romanza (12-tone); Divergent moods (12-tone); Chamber music: violin sonata; Summer night, violin and piano; Poem, violin and piano; Cradle song, piano trio; Prelude for 2 trumpets, 2 trombones; Chorale and variations for 3 horns; Prelude for organ; Chorus: The canticle of Judith, mezzo-soprano and women's voices; Magnificat, soprano, mixed chorus, strings, trumpet; many other choral works, piano pieces.
     1827 Rowley Ave., Madison, WI 53705

ENENBACH, FREDRIC
     b. Des Moines, Iowa, 1 Dec. 1945. Studied with Anthony Donato and Alan Stout at Northwestern Univ.; with Bulent Arel and Mel Powell at Yale Univ. At Yale he won the Rene Chandler award, 1969. He was instructor, Wabash Coll., 1969-72, assistant professor, 1972-   .
     WORKS: Theatre: background score to Euripides' Bacchae, 1971; Orchestra: symphony, 1973; Chamber music: string quartet, 1968; Music for piano, 1968; Music for viola and percussion, 1968; from 'Chamber music' for voices, winds, percussion, 1969; Music for flute and percussion, 1972.
     105 Vernon Court, Crawfordsville, IN 47933

*ENGEL, CARL
     b. Paris, France, 21 July 1883; U.S. citizen; d. New York, 6 May 1944. Attended Strasbourg and Munich Univ.; studied composition with Ludwig Thuille in Munich. He was editor, Boston Music Company, 1909-21; chief, music division, Library of Congress, 1921-29; president, G. Schirmer, Inc., and editor, Musical Quarterly, 1929-37.
     WORKS: Chamber music: Triptych, violin and piano; Presque valse, piano; Never lonely child, piano; 5 perfumes, violin and piano; Songs: Chanson intimes; 3 epigrams; 3 sonnets; 5 songs to texts of Amy Lowell.

ENGEL, LEHMAN
     b. Jackson, Miss., 14 Sep. 1910. Attended Cincinnati Coll. Cons., Univ. of Cincinnati; studied with Rubin Goldmark, Juilliard School. His honors include the Society for Publication of American Music award, 1946; 2 Antoinette Perry conducting awards, 1950, 1953; Bellamann Found. award, 1964; 3 honorary doctorates, Bogulawski Coll., 1944, Univ. of Cincinnati, 1971, Millsaps Coll., 1971; special citations, Hartford Cons., 1971, Jackson, Miss., Chamber of Commerce, 1973. Since 1934, he has been conductor and producer on Broadway, for radio and television and films; has toured with musical shows; has been guest conductor of many major U.S. orchestras, and has been as well, author, lecturer, composer.
     WORKS: Opera: The soldier; Malady of love; Pierrot of the minute; Medea; Ballet: Transitions, 1938; The shoe bird, Jackson, Miss., 20 Apr. 1968; Theatre: incidental music for nearly 50 plays; Orchestra: The creation, narrator and orch., 1948; viola concerto; 2 symphonies; overture, 1961; Chamber music: Dialogue, violin and viola; The gates of paradise, piano; cello sonata, 1946; string quartet; piano sonata; Chorus; Now praise we famous men; Chinese nightingale, cantata, 1928; Rain; Film scores: Beyond Guagin; Boogie's bump; Honduras; Strategic attack; National defense; Berlin powder keg; 5 U.S. Navy films; The hedgerow story, for State Department. He was author of the following books: Planning and producing musical shows, 1957, revised 1966; Music for the classical tragedy; Renaissance to baroque, 7 vol; 2 books of folk songs; Poor wayfaring stranger; Words with music, 1927, received ASCAP Deems Taylor award, 1974; Getting started in the theatre, 1973; This bright day, an autobiography, 1956, revised 1974.
     350 East 54th St., New York, NY 10022

ENGLERT, EUGENE E.
     b. Cincinnati, Ohio, 15 Mar. 1931. Studied at Athenaeum of Ohio, B. M. 1952; Univ. of Cincinnati, M. M. 1956. He won an award for a choral composition, 1966. He has been church organist, 1949-   ; taught high school, 1961-69.
     WORKS: Chorus: Ye heavens, praise the Lord, 1966; I am the bread of life; The touch of a hand; Winds through the olive trees; Out of the depths; many other published anthems and masses.
     2113 Raeburn Drive, Cincinnati, OH 45223

*ENGLISH, GRANVILLE
     b. Louisville, Ky., 27 Jan. 1895; d. New York, 1 Sep. 1968. Studied with Felix Borowski, Chicago Musical Coll., B. M.; also with Charles Haubiel, Wallingford Riegger, Tibor Serly, and Nadia Boulanger. His awards include 3 New York Fed. of Music Clubs prizes; Mendelssohn Glee Club prize; Ford Found. grant for composer residency at Baylor Univ., 1961. He taught in Chicago, 1923-25; then privately in New York.
     WORKS: Opera: Wide, wide river, a folk opera; Orchestra: An island festival, ballet suite; Colonial portraits, suite for strings, Evening by the sea, tone poem; Ugly duckling, cantata for chorus and orch., 1924; Alabama

ENGLISH, GRANVILLE

(ENGLISH, GRANVILLE)
twilight; Ballet fantasy, 1937; Among the hills, scherzo for orch.; Mood tropicale, Baltimore, 5 Feb. 1955; Chorus: Robin in the rain, treble voices; Tropicana; Song of the caravan, 1937; Law, west of the Pecos, male voices; Promised land; Piano: Valse lyrique; Danse antique.

EPPERSON, JOHN
b. Harrisonburg, Va., 5 Sep. 1950. Attended North Carolina School of the Arts, B. M. in horn; Queens Coll., CUNY, and City Coll., CUNY, studying with Mario Davidovsky, Henry Weinberg, Hubert Howe, and Jacques-Louis Monod. He has played horn with the Winston-Salem Symphony and Greensboro Symphony; was lecturer, Queens Coll., co-leader, Mark V jazz quintet; free-lance composer and arranger, private teacher, 1973-   .
WORKS: Chamber music: Metallurgical report, for metal percussion orch., 5 players; In the shape of four pears, wind octet; Electronic: if i have been unfaithful it has been only with my friend, the sea, solo oboe and stereo tape recorder; Until the last syllable of recorded time, for 4 harps, 2 percussion, and electronic sound, commissioned by Patricia Pence, Salem Coll., for concert performance; commissioned by Creative Arts Ensemble as quadraphonic tape for modern dance.
5 St. Mark's Place, NY 10003

*EPPERT, CARL
b. Carbon, Ind., 5 Nov. 1882; d. Milwaukee, Wis., 1 Oct. 1961. Studied with Hugo Kaun and Arthur Nikisch in Germany. He received first prize in an NBC composition contest, 1932; first prize, Chicago Symphony Orchestra Jubilee contest, 1940; Juilliard award, 1941. He was founder and conductor, Terre Haute Symphony, 1903-07, and of the Milwaukee Civic Orchestra, 1921-25; then conductor, Milwaukee Symphony. He taught theory and composition, Wisconsin Cons., Wisconsin Coll. of Music, and Milwaukee Inst. of Music, 1922-28.
WORKS: Opera: Kaintuckee; Orchestra: 7 symphonies; City shadows, symphonic poem; Speed, symphonic poem; 2 symphonic impressions; Traffic, symphonic fantasy; Ballet of the vitamins; Image of America; and choral works.

EPSTEIN, ALVIN L.
b. Hartford, Conn., 5 Jan. 1926. Studied with Isadore Freed and Arnold Franchetti, Hartt Coll. of Music; with Aaron Copland at Tanglewood; with Cesar Bresgen and Rolf Liebermann, Mozarteum, Salzburg. He received a BMI award, 1952; Fulbright grant, 1953; honorable mention for the Harvey Gaul award, 1966 and the Delius award, 1972. He was assistant professor, Hartt Coll., 1948-70; composer-in-residence, Southern Methodist Univ., 1970-73; director of music, Temple Emanu-El, Dallas, 1970-73; director of music, Temple Sholom, Dallas, 1973-   .
WORKS: Theatre: Music for Oedipus, 1972; Orchestra: Music for orchestra; Collage; piano concerto; Chamber music: duo for oboe and piano; duo for violin and piano; string quartet; Four dialogues, flute, double bass, percussion, 1965; Chorus: Fancy.
4430 Shady Hill, Dallas, TX 75229

EPSTEIN, DAVID M.
b. New York, N. Y., 3 Oct. 1930. Studied at Antioch Coll., A. B.; with Francis Judd Cooke, Carl McKinley, Felix Wolfes at New England Cons., M. M. 1953; with Arthur Berger, Irving Fine at Brandeis Univ., M. F. A. 1954; and with Roger Sessions, Milton Babbitt, Edward T. Cone at Princeton Univ., Ph. D. 1968. He received Louisville Orch. award, 1953; BMI award; Fromm Found. award, 1958; Ford Found. recording grant; Arthur Shepherd award, 1964; Harvey Gaul award; and commissions from Eastman Wind Ensemble, Philadelphia String Quartet; Union of Hebrew Congregations; Boston Symphony Orch. He was music critic, Musical America, 1956-57; faculty member, Antioch Coll., 1957-62; music director, Educational Broadcasting Corp., Channel/WNDT, New York, 1962-64; professor, Massachusetts Inst. of Technology, 1965-   ; music director Harrisburg Symphony Orchestra, 1975-76.
WORKS: Orchestra: Movement for orch., 1953; symphony, 1958; Sonority variations, 1968; Vent-ures, symphonic wind ensemble; Chamber music: piano trio, 1953; piano variations, 1961; string trio, 1964; string quartet, 1971; Chorus: Sing to the Lord; Five scenes; Song cycles: Excerpts from a diary, 1953; The seasons, 1956; Four songs, soprano, solo horn, string orch.
54 Turning Mill Road, Lexington, MA 02173

EPSTEIN, PAUL
b. Boston, Mass., 23 Apr. 1938. Studied with Harold Shapero, Brandeis Univ., A. B. cum laude, 1959; with Seymour Shifrin, Univ. of California, Berkeley, M. A. 1964; privately with Luciano Berio, Milan, 1962-63, under a Fulbright grant. He was on the faculty and director, Electronic Music Studio, Tulane Univ., 1963-69; assistant professor, Temple Univ., 1969-   .
WORKS: Theatre: Makbeth, vocal music for version of The Performance Group, New York, 1969-70; Caligula, by Camus, incidental music, San Francisco, 1961; Chamber music: True and false unicorn, reader, clarinet, horn, viola, piano, 1960; Three songs, soprano and clarinet, 1960; Two autumn songs, soprano and 6 instruments, 1961; sextet for winds and strings, 1961; quartet, flute, clarinet, viola, cello, 1964; Concert for TPG: In memory of, Intersections 7: Prelude and jam, vocal work for 5 performers, 1971; Electronic: Tonegroups I and II, stereophonic tape, 1965; Intersections I, tape, 1967, III, 1968, VI, Moog synthesizer, 1970; Mixed media: Intersections IV, any number of performers, any media, 1969, version for conductor, 4 performers, Moog, and film, 1970; various electronic compositions for theater productions performed in New Orleans, 1967-68. He is author of magazine articles.
379 Heathcliffe Road
Huntingdon Valley, PA 19006

ERB, DONALD
b. Youngstown, Ohio, 17 Jan. 1927. Studied with Harold Miles and Kenneth Gaburo, Kent State Univ., B. S. 1950; with Marcel Dick, Cleveland Inst. of Music, M. M. 1953; with Bernhard Heiden, Indiana Univ., D. M. 1964. He has held grants

(ERB, DONALD)
from the Ford Found., 1962; Guggenheim Found., 1965; Nat. Endowment of the Arts, 1967; Rockefeller Found., 1967, 1968; and won the Cleveland Arts Prize, 1966. After service in the Navy he was trumpet player and arranger for dance bands. He joined the faculty, Cleveland Inst. of Music, 1953-61; was composer-in-residence, Bakersfield, Calif., school system, 1962-63, and with Dallas Symphony, 1968-69; faculty member, Case Inst. of Technology, 1965-67; and Kulas professor of music, Cleveland Inst. and Case Western Reserve Univ., 1966-

WORKS: Orchestra: Bakersfield pieces; chamber concerto; Symphony of overtures, 1965; concerto for solo percussionist and orch., 1966; Christmasmusic, 1967; The seventh trumpet, 1969; Klangfarbenfunk I for orch., rock band, and electronic sounds, 1970; New England prospect, narrator and orch., text from 8 American writers (including Julian Bond's I too hear America singing), Cincinnati May Festival, 17 May 1974; Band: Compendium; Concert piece, stage band, alto saxophone; The purple-roofed ethical suicide parlor, wind ensemble and tape; Spacemusic, 1963; Reticulation, with tape, 1965; Stargazing, with tape, 1966; Chamber music: Dialogue, violin and piano, 1958; string quartet, 1960; sonata for harpsichord and string quartet, 1962; Sonneries for brass choir; music for brass choir; quartet for 4 winds, string bass; Antipodes, string quartet and percussion quartet, 1963; Music for Mother Bear, alto flute; music for violin and piano; Hexagon, 5 winds, piano, 1963; Three pieces, brass quintet and piano; Dances pieces, violin, piano, trumpet, percussion; Four for percussion; VII miscellaneous, flute, string bass, 1964; Concertant, harpsichord and strings; Trio for two, alto flute/percussion, string bass; Phantasma, flute, oboe, string bass, harpsichord, 1965; Diversion for two (other than sex), trumpet, percussion, 1966; trio for violin, cello, electric guitar, 1966; Reconnaissance, violin, string bass, piano, percussion, electronics, 1967; And then, toward the end, trombone and 4 tracks pre-recorded trombone; In no strange land, tape, trombone, string bass, 1968; Basspiece, string bass, 4 tracks prerecorded string bass, 1969; Z Milosci do Warszawy, piano, clarinet, trombone, cello, electronic sounds; Chorus: Cummings cycle, with orch.; Fallout, with narrator, string quartet, piano; God love you now; Kyrie, with piano, percussion, electronic tape, 1967; Piano: Correlations; Summermusic, 1966; Multi-media: Fission, tape, soprano, piano, dancers, lighting, 1968; Souvenir, tape, instruments, lighting.
1681 Cumberland Road
Cleveland Heights, OH 44118

*ERB, JOHN LAWRENCE
b. Reading Pa., 5 Feb. 1877; d. Eugene, Ore., 17 Mar. 1950. Studied at the Metropolitan School of Music, New York. His academic posts included Wooster Cons., Ohio; School of Music, Univ. of Illinois; American Inst. of Applied Music, New York; and Connecticut Coll. for Women. He composed choral works, organ and piano pieces and songs.

*ERB, JOHN WARREN
b. Massillon, Ohio, 17 Apr. 1887; d. Pittsburgh, Pa., 2 July 1948. Studied with Siegfried Ochs, Xaver Scharwenka, and Felix Weingartner in Berlin; with Edgar Stillman Keley in the U.S. He was active as a choral conductor; was chairman, department of instrumental music, New York Univ., School of Education. He wrote choral pieces and works for instrumental ensembles.

ERICKSON, FRANK
b. Spokane, Wash., 1 Sep. 1923. Studied with Mario Castelnuovo-Tedesco privately, and with Halsey Stevens at Univ. of Southern California, B. M., M. M. He served in the Army Air Force in World War II, then was an arranger for dance bands; was lecturer, Univ. of California, Los Angeles; assistant professor, San Jose State Coll., 1959-61; guest conductor, colleges and universities; editor, music publishers.
WORKS: Band: 2 symphonies; concerto for saxophone; double concerto for trumpet and trombone; Rhythm of the winds; Arietta for winds; Balladair; Tamerlane; Chroma; and more than 100 published works for band.
7404 Crisp, Independence, MO 64051

ERICKSON, ROBERT
b. Marquette, Mich., 7 Mar. 1917. Studied with May Strong, Chicago Cons., 1937-38; privately with Wesley LaViolette in Chicago, 1938; with Ernst Krenek, Hamline Univ., B. A. cum laude 1943, M. A. 1947; and with Roger Sessions, 1950. His awards include scholarships, 1941-43; Drew prize, 1943; Ford Found. fellowship, 1951; Yaddo fellowships, 1952, 1953, 1965; Marion Bauer prize, 1957; Guggenheim fellowship, 1966; Univ. of California, Inst. for Creative Arts fellowship, 1968. He taught in San Francisco, 1952-66; professor, Univ. of California, San Diego, 1967- .
WORKS: Orchestra: Introduction and allegro, 1948; Fantasy, cello and orch., 1953; Variations for orch., 1957; Sirens and other flyers, 1965; Chamber music: piano sonata, 1948; 2 string quartets, 1950, 1956; piano trio, 1953; Divertimento, flute, clarinet and strings, 1953; duo for violin and piano, 1957; Chamber concerto for 17 players, 1960; Toccata, piano, 1962; Concerto for piano and 7 instruments, 1963; Piece for bells and toy pianos, 1965; Scapes, a contest for 2 groups, 1966; General speech, trombone, 1969; Electronic: Ricercar à 5, trombone and tape, 1966; Ricercar à 3, contrabass and tape, 1967; Birdlands, Tape, 1967; Cardenitas, singer, mime, 7 players and tape, 1968; Pacific sirens, instruments and tape, 1969.
1849 Crest Drive, Encinitas, CA 92024

ERNEST, DAVID JOHN
b. Chicago, Ill., 16 May 1929. Studied at Chicago Musical Coll.; with Robert Palmer and Robert Kelly at Univ. of Illinois; with Cecil Effinger at Univ. of Colorado; and with Roland Lamoriette at Paris Cons. His many scholarships and awards include a Fulbright grant and Danforth Found. award. He was faculty member, Univ. of Colorado, 1956-61; division chairman,

ERNEST, DAVID JOHN

(ERNEST, DAVID JOHN)
Glenville State Coll., 1961-63; professor and chairman, music department, St. Cloud State Coll., 1963- .
WORKS: Opera: Ten year thunder; Chamber music: sonatine for oboe and strings; numerous works for orchestra, band, and voice.
Crest Road, Route 5, St. Cloud, MN 56301

ERNEST, SR. M. See SCHWERDTFEGER, E. ANNE

ERNST, DAVID
b. Pittsburgh, Pa., 6 Sep. 1945. Studied with W. Thomas McKinley and Joseph W. Jenkins, Duquesne Univ.; with Robert Erickson at Univ. of California, San Diego; and with Robert Moevs at Rutgers Univ. He was assistant professor, San Diego State Univ., 1970-71; and instructor, York Coll., CUNY, 1972- .
WORKS: Piano: P-2 for 2 pianos; Multimedia: Exit, trumpet and tape; Four and more, percussion quartet and 2 tape recorders, Internat. Music Week, Utrecht, 1969; Excerpt for string bass and tape; Rounds, viola and tape. He is author of a book on electronic music, Musique concrete, Boston, 1973.
2198 Richmond Road, Staten Island, NY 10306

ESCOT, POZZI
b. Lima, Peru, 1 Oct. 1933; U.S. citizen. Studied composition with Andres Sas, Sas-Rosay Acad. of Music, Lima, 1949-53; with William Bergsma, Juilliard School, B. S. 1956, M. S. 1957; with Philipp Jarnach, Hamburg, 1957-58. Her many awards include scholarships at Juilliard; grants from the German Govt., Ford Found., MENC; 4 MacDowell fellowships; fellow, Radcliffe Inst., 1968-69; commissions by Organization of American States, Venezuelan Govt., Hartt Chamber Players; Lima 4th of July Prize 1955 for string quartet II; laureate composer of Peru, 1956. Her works have been performed in Germany, Spain, Venezuela, Peru, as well as in the U.S.; her lectures on contemporary music have been highly acclaimed by the composers who have been subjects for her analyses, and she was invited jointly by the U.S. State Department and the Ministry of Culture of Peru as advisor and lecturer, 1972. She was appointed to the faculty, New England Cons., 1964-72; professor Wheaton Coll., 1972- .
WORKS: Theatre: Metamorphosis, ballet, 5 dancers, chamber orch., 1951; Interra, overture for opera in progress, 1968; Orchestra: 3 symphonies, 1953, 1955, 1957; Sands...I, orch., chorus, solo alto, 1958; Sands...II, 1966; Chamber music: 3 string quartets, 1951, 1954, 1956; 3 movements, violin and piano, 1959; Three poems of Rilke, narrator and string quartet, 1959; Cristos, flute, contrabassoon, percussion, 3 violins, 1963; Visione, solo double bass, flute, alto saxophone, soprano, percussion, ghost speaker, Wesleyan Univ., 22 Nov. 1964; Chorus: Ainu, epilogue for opera in progress, for 4 groups of 5 voices, text by composer, 1969; Songs: Songs of my country, soprano and piano, 1954; Songs of wisdom, soprano, 1955; Credo, soprano and string quartet, 1958; Lamentos, soprano, chamber group, percussion, 1962; Piano:

(ESCOT, POZZI)
sonatina III, 1952; Differences I, 1960; Differences II, 1963; 13 preludes, 1968; Film score: Razapeti, film by Yugoslavian Nat. Television, 1973; Electronic: In memoriam, tape. She is co-author with her husband, Robert Cogan, of Sonic design: The nature of sound and music.
24 Avon Hill St., Cambridge, MA 02140

ESCOVADO, ROBIN
b. Dallas, Tex., 20 Aug. 1931. Studied with Charles Shatto in San Diego and with Mario Castelnuovo-Tedesco in Los Angeles. He is a computer programmer/analyst.
WORKS: Chorus: more than 200 compositions for a cappella chorus including 4 motets; 4 short masses; 2 hymns on poems of Christopher Smart; Psalm 131; What child is this?; etc.
12 Remsen St., Brooklyn, NY 11201

*ESPINOSA, FELIPE
Macias, opera, Puerto Rico Opera Festival, New York, Sep. 1971.

ESTABROOK, DEAN MONTE
b. San Jose, Calif., 7 June 1940. Studied with Wilson Coker at California State Univ., San Jose, M. A. He received the Eva Thompson Phillips award. He is choral director and teacher, Yuba City High School.
WORKS: Band: Corrente for band, 1969; Chamber music: Epigram, saxophone quartet; Chorus: To spring, chorus and bassoon.
678 Washington, #3, Yuba City, CA 95991

ESTES, CHARLES BYRON
b. Denver, Colo., 17 June 1946. Studied at Coll. of Idaho; and with Frank McCarty and Donal R. Michalsky at California State Univ. at Fullerton.
WORKS: Chamber music: A trio of inspirational songs, voice and piano, 1971; Trio resoluto, saxophone, cello, piano, 1972; Tilbury Town, soprano, baritone, 2 oboes, electric piano, tape, 1973; Chorus: Make a joyful noise, choir and jazz quartet, 1967; Psalm 13; Multi-media: The third memory, stereo tape and dancers.
1207 North Concord Ave., Fullerton, CA 92631

ETLER, ALVIN D.
b. Battle Creek, Iowa, 19 Feb. 1913; d. Florence, Mass., 13 June 1973. Studied with Arthur Shepherd at Case Western Reserve Univ.; and with Paul Hindemith at Yale Univ., M. B. 1944. He was Guggenheim fellow, 1940-41, 1963-64; recipient,4th award Concours Musique Internat. Reine Elisabeth de Belgique, 1953; first recipient, Yale Distinguished Alumnus Award, 1965; many commissions. He was oboist, Indianapolis Symphony, 1938-40; faculty member, Yale Univ., 1942-46; Cornell Univ., 1946-47; Univ. of Illinois, 1947-49; and professor, Smith Coll., 1949-73; visiting professor, Mount Holyoke Coll., 1952-53, 1959, 1960; Yale, 1965-66; artist-in-residence, Univ. of Wisconsin, summers, 1960, 1972.
WORKS: Orchestra: Dramatic overture, 1956; concerto in one movement, 1957; Elegy, 1959; concerto for woodwind quintet and orch., 1960; Triptych, 1961; concerto for clarinet and chamber ensemble, 1962; concerto for brass quintet,

(ETLER, ALVIN D.)

string orch., percussion, 1967; Convivialities, 1968; concerto for string quartet and orch., 1968; Chamber music: sonata for oboe, clarinet, viola, 1945; quartet for oboe, clarinet, viola, bassoon, 1949; music for 3 recorders, 1949; bassoon sonata, 1951; 2 clarinet sonatas, 1952, 1969; Introduction and allegro, oboe and piano, 1952; duo for oboe and viola, 1954; 2 woodwind quintets, 1955, 1957; concerto for violin and woodwind quintet, 1958; sonata for viola and harpsichord, 1959; sextet for winds and strings, 1959; 3 pieces for recorder trio, 1960; suite for flute, oboe, clarinet, 1960; Fragments, woodwind quartet, 1963; 2 string quartets, 1963, 1965; quintet for brass, 1963; Sonic sequence, brass quintet, 1967; XL plus 1, solo percussionist, 1970; concerto for cello with chamber group, 1970, New York, 2 Mar. 1971; Chorus: Peace be unto you, 1958; Under the cottonwood tree, 1960; Under stars, 1960; A Christmas lullaby, 1960; Ode to Pothos, 1960; Lord God, hear our prayer, 1961; Onomatopoesis, male chorus, winds, percussion, 1965; Piano: Prelude and toccata, 1950; sonatina, 1955. The Smith Coll. Department of Music and the New Valley Music Press have established The Alvin Etler Memorial Competition for a chamber music composition.

EUBANKS, CHARLES G.

b. Atlanta, Ga., 2 Nov. 1942. Studied with G. Winston Cassler at St. Olaf Coll.; with John MacIvor Perkins and Ralph Shapey, Univ. of Chicago.

WORKS: Theatre: Bang (he said) you're dead, musical play; incidental music to Williams' Summer and smoke; Orchestra: Othello, overture; Chorus: Vespers for Lent, choir, organ, congregation; numerous choral works for liturgical use.

315 Sterling Place, Brooklyn, NY 11238

EVANS, BILLY G.

b. Big Spring, Tex., 27 Oct. 1938. Studied with Samuel Adler at North Texas State Univ. He has been on the piano faculty, West Texas State Univ., 1961-   .

WORKS: Chamber music: concerto for piano and winds; piano sonata; quartet for piano, violin, clarinet, cello; Scherzo for trumpet, baritone horn, brass choir; Caprice, flute and piano; 5 variations on an old Englishe ayre, flute, clarinet, bassoon, piano.

2509 14th Ave., Canyon, TX 79015

*EVANS, GIL

A concert opera commissioned by New York Jazz Repertory Company and New York State Council grant for the American Bicentennial.

*EVANS, HUMPHREY III

b. Washington, D.C. Studied at Peabody Cons. and Yale Univ. He received BMI student awards, 1964, 1967; Gustav Klemm prize, 1965; Nat. Fed. of Music Clubs awards, 1965, 1969. His Happenings for orchestra was performed by the Redlands (Calif.) Symphony, Mar. 1966.

EVANS, SALLY HAZEN. See HAZEN, SARA

EVERETT, THOMAS GREGORY

b. Philadelphia, Pa., 4 Dec. 1944. Studied with George Andrix and Warren Benson, Ithaca Coll., B. S. 1966, M. S. 1969; with Robert Ceely, New England Cons., 1972. He has been director of bands, Harvard Univ., 1971-   ; on the staff, New England Cons., 1973-   ; faculty, Nat. Trombone Workshop, Nashville, 1972, 1973; and is associate editor, Composer Magazine and Brass World Magazine.

WORKS: Band: Feowertig nu; Chamber music: Vietnam 70 for tenor saxophone, string bass, bass trombone, 1970; duos for bass trombone and clarinet, 1970; trio for trumpet, horn, bass trombone.

15 Chester St., Apt. 2, Cambridge, MA 02140

EVETT, ROBERT

b. Loveland, Colo., 30 Nov. 1922; d. Takoma Park, Md., 4 Feb. 1975. Studied with Roy Harris, 1941-47; with Vincent Persichetti at Juilliard School, 1951-52. He has received many commissions including Pan American Union, Nat. Symphony Orch., Georgetown Univ., Composer's Forum for Catholic Worship, etc. He was chairman, music department, Washington Inst. of Contemporary Arts, 1947-50; book editor and music critic, The New Republic, 1952-68; editor, Arts and Letters section, Atlantic Monthly, 1968-69; contributing critic on books and music, Washington Star, 1961-75, book editor, 1970-75.

WORKS: Orchestra: 3 symphonies; concerto for orch.; piano concerto, 1957; 2 cello concerti; harpsichord concerto, 1961; Chamber music: harpsichord sonata, 1961; quintet for piano and strings; 7 piano sonatas; 2 violin sonatas; 2 movements and a fragment of a 3rd movement of an incomplete sonata for violin solo were performed at the Nat. Gallery, Washington, D.C., 18 May 1975; other chamber music and piano pieces; Chorus: The mask of Cain; liturgical pieces.

*EZELL, HELEN INGLE

b. Marshall, Okla., 18 May 1903. Studied at Juilliard School; with Otto Luening and Henry Cowell, Columbia Univ.; with Violet Archer and Spencer Norton, Univ. of Oklahoma. She has many published songs including I know that mind unfolds; and piano pieces.

*FAIRCHILD, BLAIR

b. Belmont, Mass., 23 June 1877; d. Paris, France, 23 Apr. 1933. Studied with John Knowles Paine and Walter Spalding, Harvard Univ.; piano with Guisseppe Buonamoci in Florence, Italy; later with Charles-Marie Widor in Paris. His service in the diplomatic corps and residence in Constantinople and Persia colored his subsequent compositions with eastern themes. After 1903 he lived in Paris.

WORKS: 3 ballets; 3 symphonic poems; Etude symphonique, viola and orch.; Rhapsody on Hebrew melodies, violin and orch.; many works for chamber ensembles, choruses; many songs; organ and piano pieces.

FAIRLIE, MARGARET

*FAIRLIE, MARGARET
Has composed for modern dance, orchestra, chamber groups, film, television and electronic music.
835 Taughannock Blvd., Ithaca, NY 14850

FAITH, RICHARD BRUCE
b. Evansville, Ind., 20 Mar. 1926. Studied with Max Wald in Chicago; with Bernhard Heiden, Indiana Univ.; with Robert McBride, Univ. of Arizona; and held a Fulbright fellowship for study in Italy. He received a Univ. of Arizona grant for composition of an opera. He was assistant professor, Morningside Coll., 1956-60; associate professor, Univ. of Arizona, 1961-   .
WORKS: Opera: Sleeping beauty, 2-act opera; Orchestra: piano concerto; concerto for 2 pianos; Chamber music: trio for violin, horn, piano; movements for horn; Piano: Fingerpaintings; Legende; The dark riders, toccata for piano; sonata.
1032 East Adelaide, Tucson, AZ 85719

FALARO, ANTHONY J.
b. Bridgeport, Conn., 12 Apr. 1938. Studied at Berklee Coll. of Music, 1961-63; with Avram David at Boston Cons., B. M. 1965, M. M. 1967. He was awarded 2nd prize in the Gaudeamus Found. competition, Netherlands, 1968. He was composer-in-residence, Long Island School System, N. Y., Feb.-June 1971.
WORKS: Orchestra: Cosmoi, for 56-part string orch., 1967, Rotterdam, 1968; Chamber music: The windhover, voice and 11 instruments, 1965; Spaces, 9 brass, 7 percussion instruments, 1966; suite for string quintet, commissioned by Mu Phi Epsilon, Cleveland, Aug. 1972; Refraction, chamber orch., 1972; Chorus: Irenicon, mass for voices, string orch., percussion, 1970.
66-05 110th St., Apt. 2A
Forest Hills, NY 11375

FARBERMAN, HAROLD
b. New York, N. Y., 2 Nov. 1929. Studied at Juilliard School and New England Cons. His awards include a commission for an opera by Juilliard American Opera Theatre, 1970; ASCAP award, 1972; $10,000 award, American Acad. of Arts and Letters, 1972. He played viola in the Boston Symphony Orchestra, 1951-63; was conductor, New Arts Orchestra, 1964-69; conductor, Oakland Symphony Orchestra, 1970-   .
WORKS: Opera: The losers, New York, 26 Mar. 1971; Orchestra: concerto for alto saxophone and string orch., 1965; Elegy, fanfare, and march, 1965; trumpet concerto; Reflected realities, violin concerto with orch. and tape, Oakland, Cal., 15 Jan. 1974; Band: Box; Chamber music: Variations, percussion and piano; Variations on a familiar theme, percussion ensemble; Progressions, flute and percussion, 1960; 3 states of mind for 6 musicians; Quintessence, woodwind quintet, 1963; Trio, violin, piano, percussion, 1963; Alea: a game of chance for 6 players; 5 images brass quintet, 1964; Songs: Evolution, soprano and percussion, 1954; Greek scene, 1957; Impressions, 1959; New York Times, Aug. 30, 1964, 4 songs for soprano, piano, percussion, 1964; film

(FARBERMAN, HAROLD)
score: The great American cowboy, full orchestra, jazz quartet, guitar, won an Oscar, Apr. 1974.
1726 Oakland Ave., Piedmont, CA 94611

FARMER, PETER RUSSELL
b. Boston, Mass., 14 Oct. 1941. Studied with Avram David, Boston Cons., 1964-69; with Karlheinz Stockhausen, summer 1968; and privately with Hugo Norden. He held a MacDowell Colony fellowship, 1973, and won the Brookline Library composition contest, 1973. He was music editor, Allyn & Bacon, Boston, 1969-71, and book designer, 1971-   .
WORKS: Chamber music: Three seascapes, string sextet; Ensemble, Darmstadt, Aug. 1968; Capriccio for flute and harpsichord, Brookline, Mass., 11 Aug. 1973; Sonata for 5 brass instruments, Tanglewood, 7 Aug. 1973.
93 Cheever St., Milton, MA 02187

FARRAND, NOEL
b. New York, N. Y., 26 Dec. 1928. Studied with Edward Royce and Wayne Barlow, Eastman School of Music, 1946; William Flanagan, Israel Citkowitz, New York, 1949; Manhattan School of Music, B. M. 1952; Aaron Copland, Lukas Foss, Seymour Lipkin, Jean Morel, Leonard Bernstein at Tanglewood. He received Tanglewood scholarships, 1951-54; MacDowell fellowship, 1953; Univ. of California grant, 1954; Huntington Hartford grant, 1964; Helene Wurlitzer Found. grant, 1973-74. He was on staff, New Edition Records, 1950-56; faculty member, Regis School, New York, 1957-61.
WORKS: Theatre: The pearl, dance drama in 2 acts, Los Angeles, 21-24 Apr. 1954; Orchestra: Epitaph for orchestra: Time's long ago, orch. with speaker, Tanglewood, 14 July 1953; 3 symphonies, 1955, 1964, 1973; Chamber music: string trio; A retrospection, cello and piano; duo for oboe and bassoon; Adagio assai, violin and piano; Vocalise, oboe, string quartet; Songs: Autumn is on the wind; When autumn severs the golden fruit; Herbsttag; Doria; Autumn is over the long leaves; Piano: 2 sonatas; 2 rhapsodies; At MacDowell's grave; sonatina; partita in 5 movements.
100 Sullivan St., Apt. 6-J
New York, NY 10012

*FARRELL, KENNETH L.
2 impressions for band.

FARREN, MARTIN
b. Lompoc, Calif., 10 July 1942. Studied with Stanworth Beckler, Mary Bowling, Univ. of the Pacific; with Robert Shallenberg and Richard Hervig, Univ. of Iowa. He was instructor, Arkansas Polytechnic Coll., 1969-70; Univ. of Iowa, 1971-72; California State Univ., Fresno, 1972-73; assistant professor, Massachusetts Inst. of Technology, 1973-   .
WORKS: Chamber music: flute sonata; bassoon sonata; Paean for spring, English handbells; other chamber works for instruments, vocal ensembles, voice and piano, percussion.
43 Locke St., Cambridge, MA 02140

*FARWELL, ARTHUR
b. St. Paul, Minn., 22 Apr. 1872; d. New York,
20 Jan. 1952. Graduated from Massachusetts Inst.
of Technology, 1893; studied organ in Boston and
Paris; composition with Humperdinck in Germany.
He received the first composers' fellowship
given by the Music and Art Asso. of Pasadena,
1921-25; first prize, Nat. Fed. of Music Clubs,
1931. He was on the staff of Musical America,
1909-15; held many teaching posts in New York
and California, and finally at Michigan State
Coll., 1927-39. There he established his own
music press, handling the whole job himself on
a lithographic hand press. Earlier, in 1901
he had set up the Wa Wan Press in Newton, Mass.
He wrote many works for orchestra, including The
gods of the mountains. Many of his compositions
for orchestra, chamber ensembles, vocal ensembles, and piano are based on American Indian
melodies and folksongs of the South and West.

FAST, WILLARD S.
b. Mountain Lake, Minn., 21 June 1922. Attended
Univ. of Michigan and Millikan Univ. He was choral director in Illinois and Michigan public
schools, 1949-56; at Alpena Community Coll.,
1956-61; and instructor, Charles Stewart Mott
Community Coll., 1961-
    WORKS: Chorus: Spring, 2-voice canon;
Bread and music, men's voices; Let me grow
lovely, growing old, women's voices; Our friendly
house; Autumn; The blessed night; When I was one-
and-twenty; Be not afraid; Alleluia to the Lord
of being, double chorus; many other choral works.
    5183 South Seymour Road
    Swartz Creek, MI 48473

FAULCONER, JAMES H.
b. Frederick, Okla., 19 Oct. 1945. Studied with
Normand Lockwood, Univ. of Denver; David Diamond,
Univ. of Colorado; Harrison Kerr, Spencer Norton,
Stanley Gibb, Univ. of Oklahoma. He has received
several commissions. He has been instructor,
Univ. of Oklahoma, 1972-
    WORKS: Large ensembles: Suite for brass
and percussion, 10 brass, 5 percussion; ...and
on this original chorale tune, trombone choir
and rhythm section; A theme for something, jazz
ensemble; Chorus: Let nothing disturb thee, a
cappella; Council of hell, multi-percussion solo
with chorus and piano; Keyboard: accordion
sonata.
    1719 Avondale, Norman, OK 73069

FAUST, GEORGE T.
b. New Brunswick, N. J., 6 June 1937. Studied
with Daniel Pinkham, New England Cons., B. M.
1963; privately with Paul Creston, 1965; with
Burrill Phillips, Bernard Rogers, Wayne Barlow,
Eastman School of Music, M. M. 1967, Ph. D. candidate 1973. He held scholarships at New England
Cons.; received 4 graduate awards at Eastman,
and Edward B. Benjamin Award, 1966. He taught
in private music schools, 1964-65; was graduate
assistant at Eastman, 1966-69; on faculty,
Hochstein Music School, Rochester, 1971-74.
    WORKS: Orchestra: Four muses; Adagio for
small orchestra; Revelation 6:1-11; Wind

(FAUST, GEORGE T.)
ensemble: Symphony for brass and percussion;
Piano: sonata; 2 preludes.
    29 University Ave., Rochester, NY 14605

*FAX, MARK
1911-1974. Was professor and chairman, School
of Music, Howard Univ. His published works for
chorus include Go tell it on the mountain; To an
unknown soldier; Whatsoever a man soweth; Till
victory is won; and vocal solos: Longing; May
Day song.

*FEASEL, RICHARD
Mystic overture for band, 1952; Poem for horn,
1956. He is associate professor, School of
Music, Stetson University, De Land, FL 32720

FELCIANO, RICHARD
b. Santa Rosa, Calif., 7 December 1930. Studied
with Darius Milhaud at Mills Coll. and at Paris
Cons.; privately with Luigi Dallapiccola in
Florence, Italy; and at Univ. of Iowa, Ph. D.
1969. He received grants from the French and
Italian governments; Wooley Found.; Copley
Found.; Guggenheim fellowship; 2 Ford Found.
fellowships; Nat. Endowment for the Arts fellowship; Fromm Found. commissions; American Acad.
of Arts and Letters award, 1974. He was chairman, department of Music, Lone Mountain Coll.,
1959-67; associate professor, Univ. of California, Berkeley, 1967-   ; composer-in-residence,
Nat. Center for Experiments in Television, San
Francisco, 1967-   .
    WORKS: Opera: Sir Gawain and the Green
Knight, chamber opera in 2 acts; Orchestra:
Expression for orchestra; Mutations for orchestra; Galactic rounds; Chamber music: Aubade,
string trio, harp, piano; Contractions, mobile
for wind quintet; Spectra, flute and double bass;
Evolutions, clarinet and piano; Gravities, piano
4-hands; Crasis, 6 instruments, percussion, tape;
Lamentations for Jani Christou, 9 instruments,
percussion, tape; Vineyards music, piano quintet
and tape; Noösphere I, alto flute and tape;
Soundspace for Mozart, flute, live electronics,
tape; Genesis 4: Sunbirth, tape; Meditation
music, 14-channels, 7 self-repeating stereo tapes;
Noösphere II, tape; Chorus: Pshelley's psalm,
Poem by Shelley Hischiet, a cappella, with hand
clapping, shouting and physical movement; Two
hymns to howl by, texts by Allen Ginsburg,
rounds for equal voices; The captives, chorus
and orch.; Out of sight (The ascension that nobody saw), chorus, organ, tape; A Christmas
madrigal, chorus, 7 winds, percussion, piano;
Three-in-one-in-three, 2 choruses, 1 or 2 organs,
tape; Organ: Ekàgrata, organ, 2 drummers, tape;
God of the expanding universe, organ and tape;
I make my own soul from all the elements of the
Earth, organ and tape; Litany, organ and tape;
Audio-visual: Sic transit, chorus, organ, tape,
and light sources; Signs, chorus, tape, and 1,
2, or 3 film strips; Linearity, television piece
for harp and live electronics; Trio for speaker,
screen and viewer, audience participation television; The municipal music box, 14 electronic
sound sources and 3 light sculptures, Boston
City Hall, 4 May 1972; Background music, a

FELCIANO, RICHARD

(FELCIANO, RICHARD)
theatre piece for solo harp, sympathetic piano, stereo tape, FM tuner, transistor radio.
1326 Masonic Ave., San Francisco, CA 94117

FELDMAN, HERBERT BYRON
b. New York, N. Y., 6 Oct. 1931. Studied at Juilliard School, 1948-52. He was instructor at Juilliard School, 1955-56; and at Henry Street Settlement Music School, 1956-58.
WORKS: Chamber music: string quartet, Hempstead, N. Y., 21 Apr. 1974; string trio; wind quintet; trio for oboe, viola, bassoon; duets for 2 violins; Vocal: Ecclesiastes, cantata for solo voice, chorus, orch.; Moon mad, song cycle for soprano and piano; Dark house, songs for soprano and string quartet.
108-21 69th Road, Forest Hills, NY 11375

FELDMAN, JOANN E.
b. New York, N. Y., 19 Oct. 1941. Studied with Hugo Weisgall at Queens Coll., CUNY; with Arnold Easton, Seymour Shifrin, and William Denny, Univ. of California, Berkeley. She received the Mechlis composition prize at Queens Coll., 1962; and a Univ. of Redlands orchestral composition prize, 1966. She was teaching assistant, Univ. of California, Berkeley, 1965-66; faculty member, California State Coll., Sonoma, 1966- , associate professor, 1972- .
WORKS: Orchestra: Antiphonies, 1965; Chamber music: woodwind quintet, 1966; variations for viola and piano, 1963; Chorus: The three peoples; Piano: variations, 1973.
7510 St. Helena Road, Santa Rosa, CA 95404

*FELDMAN, MORTON
b. New York, N. Y., 12 Jan. 1926. Studied composition with Wallingford Riegger and Stefan Wolpe, and was influenced by close association with Earle Brown, John Cage, David Tudor, and Christian Wolff in the early 1950s. He received a Nat. Inst.-American Acad. of Arts and Letters award, 1970; Koussevitzky Found. commission, 1975. He is professor, State Univ. of New York, Buffalo.
WORKS: Ballet: Ixion; Chamber music: Projections 1 and 2, flute, trumpet, violin, cello, 1951; Intersection I, 1951; Pieces for 4 pianos, 1957; Atlantis, chamber orch., 1959; Durations, I-V, 1960-61; The swallows of Salangan, chorus and 16 instruments; Last pieces, piano, 1962; Christian Wolff in Cambridge, 1963; Journey to the end of night, soprano and 4 wind instruments; De Kooning, piano trio, horn, percussion; 4 instruments, 1965; First principles, 1966-67; Chorus and instruments, 1967; Vertical thoughts 2, 1968; False relationships and the extended ending, 2 chamber groups, 1968; For string quartet and orchestra; The Straits of Magellan, 7 instruments; The viola in my life, viola and 6 instruments; Mme. Press died last night at 90; Rothko Chapel, viola, percussion and chorus, New York premiere, 28 Apr. 1974; King of Denmark, electronic; many other works for solo instruments and ensembles.
Department of Music
State University of New York
Buffalo, NY 14214

FELDSTEIN, SAUL
b. New York, N. Y., 9 July 1940. Studied at State Univ. Coll., Potsdam, N. Y., and at Columbia Univ. He has received 5 ASCAP awards. He was professor, State Univ. Coll. Potsdam, 1964-69; director of education, Alfred Publishing Co., 1969-70, vice president, 1970- .
WORKS: numerous published works for orchestra, concert band, stage band, chorus, and method books for all instruments.
75 Moss Lane, Jericho, NY 11753

FELICE, JOHN
b. St. Catherines, Ont., Canada, 5 June 1938. Studied with John Beckwith, John Weinzweig, Univ. of Toronto, B. M.; with Robert Cogan, New England Cons., M. M. He received a Sigma Alpha Iota composition prize, 1968; assistantships in the opera and theory departments, New England Cons., 1966-68. He was head, theory department, University Settlement House, Toronto, 1961-63; music director, Nat. Ballet School, 1963-65; at New England Cons., faculty, preparatory and extension departments, 1966- , theory departmen department, 1968- .
WORKS: Orchestra: Vision, 1973; Chamber music: Quartet 1968, horn, violin, flute, piano; Trio (1968), trumpet, flute, clarinet; Trio: October 1968, clarinet, horn, piano; Trio: David '69, 9 instruments; Trio: In nomine 1970, horn, piano; Trio: In nomine (1971), flute, clarinet, harpsichord; Trio: In nomine 1331 (1971), piano solo; Night spaces, harp, 1972; Triatro, piano, 1972; An American ceremony, solo clarinet, 1973; Triod, piano, 1973; Trio: Lirico 1969, cello and harpsichord; Trio: Lirico 1969, flute and harpsichord; Trio: Lirico 1969, viola and harpsichord; Trio: Espressivo 1969, 2 harpsichords; Trio: Sur la nom – Martha Foltz 1971, 1-manual harpsichord; Vision, string quartet; Museum piece, toy piano, string bass, speaker/singer, 1973. (Similar titles are different pieces, not different versions, composer says.)
50 Naples Road, Brookline, MA 02146

*FENINGER, MARIO
Pavan and sonatina III for piano, played by composer, Carnegie Hall, New York, 14 Apr. 1973.

FENNELLY, BRIAN
b. Kingston, N. Y., 14 Aug. 1937. Studied with Mel Powell, Donald Martino, Allen Forte, George Perle, and Gunther Schuller at Yale Univ., M. M. 1965, Ph. D. 1968. He received the Noss prize at Yale for a choral composition, 1965. He has been associate professor, New York Univ., 1968- ; editor, Contemporary Music Newsletter, 1969- .
WORKS: Chamber music: wind quintet, Tanglewood, 1967; Evanescences, instruments and tape, 1969; SUNYATA, 4-channel tape, New York, 1970, Internat. Soc. Contemporary Music Festival, Iceland, 1973; string quartet in 2 movements, 1971.
Dept. of Music, New York University
New York, NY 10003

FENNER, BURT L.
b. New York, N. Y., 12 Aug. 1929. Studied with Roy Travis, Peter Pindar Stearns, Mannes Coll. of Music., B. S. 1959; with Otto Luening and Jack Beeson, Columbia Univ., M. A. 1961. He was faculty member, Mannes Coll. of Music, 1961-70, assistant dean, 1966-69; associate professor, Pennsylvania State Univ., 1970-   .
WORKS: Orchestra: Chamber symphony; symphony no.2; Variations for string quartet and orch.; GIALD; untitled piece; Wind ensemble: Music for brass and timpani; Prelude for brass and tape; Chamber music: string quartet; wind quintet; brass quintet; many works for mixed ensembles; electronic music.
620 Elmwood St., State College, PA 16801

FENNIMORE, JOSEPH
b. New York, N. Y., 16 Apr. 1940. Studied at Eastman School of Music, B. M. 1962; Juilliard School, M. S. 1963. He received a Fulbright grant, Rockefeller grant, Hour of Music, Inc., grant. He is founder and director of Hear America First, a New York City band concert series since 1971 devoted to the music of American composers.
WORKS: Theatre: incidental music to Business of good government by John Arien, off Broadway production, 1972; Orchestra: piano concerto, 1962; Chorus: Cynic's song; Songs: Berlitz: Introduction to French, solo song cycle; 7 songs from Shakespeare, 1971; Piano: 3 piano sonatas, no.3 premiere, New York, 6 Mar. 1971; Bits and pieces, suite for young pianists.
463 West St., #350-D, New York, NY 10014

FERGUSON, EDWIN EARLE
b. Brocket, N. Dak., 4 Aug. 1910. Studied piano, voice, and theory at Drake Univ., but took his degrees, L. L. B., J. S. D., in law and was a lawyer for the Atomic Energy Commission, keeping music as an avocation. He has won several composition awards in local competitions. He was pianist and arranger, Radio Station WHO, Des Moines, 1929-35; director of music, United Methodist Church, Chevy Chase, Md., 1960-   .
WORKS: Theatre: The confrontations of Judas, sacred opera, 3 male voices, chorus, actors, organ; Sorely tried, musical play for actors, baritone, chorus, organ, tape recorder; Chamber music: Three idiomatic exercises, clarinet, violin, piano; Franky and Johnny revisited, piano quintet; Pastorale, string quartet; Chorus: The betrayal, passion oratorio; Coffee grows on white oak trees, male voices; The dark ocean; Upstream; Songs: What if a much of a which of a wind, 2 voices and string quartet; Four songs for voice and solo clarinet; Film score: background for film on volcanoes shown at Smithsonian Institution, D.C.; numerous sacred songs, art songs, and choral settings.
5821 Osceola Road, Bethesda, MD 20016

FERRAZANO (ZANO), ANTHONY JOSEPH
b. Worcester, Mass., 4 June 1937. Studied at New England Cons., 1954-56; Boston Cons., 1956-57; Boston Univ., 1958-63; Forest Cons., Sussex Univ., England, 1963; his principal

(FERRAZANO [ZANO], ANTHONY JOSEPH)
composition teachers were Rouben Gregorian, Hugo Norden, Walter Piston. He held a scholarship at New England Cons., was a teaching fellow, Boston Cons., and has received several commissions. He taught in public schools, 1956-57; was faculty member, New York School of Music, 1959; Worcester Polytechnic Inst., 1961; Schenectady Cons., 1966-67.
WORKS: Orchestra: 2 symphonies, 1959, 1960; The gathering place, 1959; symphonic suite, 1963; Atonement, 1968; Dispersion, 1969; Chamber music: 2 string quartets, 1956, 1967; jazz sonata for bass and piano, 1958; flute sonata, 1958; clarinet sonata, 1958; Hale recollections, flute, clarinet, piano, 1967; Preconception, double bass and piano, 1971; Chorus: Laudi Vergine Maria, 1959; The soul's season, 1967; Mass, 1967; He who comes from above, chorus and orch., 1970.
P. O. Box 195, Wilmington, MA 01887

*FERRIS, JOAN
6 songs for chorus on texts of James Joyce.

FERRIS, WILLIAM
b. Chicago, Ill., 26 Feb. 1937. Attended Loyola Univ. and De Paul Univ. and studied privately with Leo Sowerby. He received 2 awards, Chicago Chapter, Internat. Soc. for Contemporary Music, 1958, 1960; Leo Sowerby award, 1969; and a commission for an opera, Little moon of Alban. He was music director, Sacred Heart Cathedral, Rochester; professor of music, St. Bernard's Seminary; founder and conductor, William Ferris Chorale, 1960-   .
WORKS: Orchestra: Concert piece for organ and string orch., Boston, Nov. 1967; symphony, Rochester, Oct. 1968; Concert piece for organ and 5 brass instruments, Long Beach, Calif., June 1970; Bristol Hills, string orch., Rochester, Mar. 1970; Chamber music: trio for flute, bassoon, piano, 1957; Three short lyrics, tenor, flute, cello, 1958; A festival flourish, 2 trumpets and organ, 1966; Chorus: De profundis, chorus, soprano and tenor soli, orch., Fordham Univ., 22 Nov. 1964, composer conducting; The angelic salutation: Glory to God in the highest, chorus, organ, orch., Rochester, Nov. 1968; Out of Egypt, cantata for chorus, soli, organ, 1969; Songs: Sorrowful dreams, text by Millay mezzo soprano, piano, 1972; A clear midnight, text by Whitman, baritone and piano, 1973; many other songs, choral works, instrumental works.
75 East Harris Ave., La Grange, IL 60525

*FERRITTO, JOHN E.
b. Cleveland, Ohio, 1937. Graduated from Cleveland Inst. of Music; later studied piano with Ward Davenny and composition with Mel Powell at Yale Univ. He served as co-conductor, 7th Army Symphony Orchestra in Europe. He is now (1974) music director, Springfield (Ohio) Symphony Orchestra, and devotes his time to conducting, performing on piano, and composing. His works include Sogni for soprano and orch., and Oggi,

FERRITTO, JOHN E.

(FERRITTO, JOHN E.)
soprano, clarinet, and piano, 1969. He wrote
the texts for both pieces.
128 The Post Road, Apt. B
Springfield, OH 45503

FETLER, PAUL
b. Philadelphia, Pa., 17 Feb. 1920. Studied at
Northwestern Univ., Yale Univ., and Berlin Acad.
of music. He received 2 Guggenheim fellowships;
Alice M. Ditson award; Rockefeller commission;
Ford Found. grant; and others. He is professor,
Univ. of Minnesota.
WORKS: Orchestra: 4 symphonies; Contrasts
for orchestra; Chorus: 5 cantatas, more than 40
choral works; works for solo instruments, ensembles, films, theatre, and dance.
420 Mt. Curve Blvd., St. Paul, MN 55105

*FETTKE, TOM
Love is merely a madness, a cappella chorus.

*FICKENSCHER, ARTHUR
b. Aurora, Ill., 9 Mar. 1871; d. San Francisco,
Calif., 15 Apr. 1954. Studied at Munich Cons.
He toured the U.S. as accompanist; taught at
schools in San Francisco and Oakland, then privately in Berlin and New York; was head, music
department, Univ. of Virginia, 1920-41; returned
to San Francisco in 1947. He developed a system
of pure intonation and invented an instrument,
the polytone, on which the octave was divided
into 60 tones; published an article on the polytone and its possibilities (Musical Quarterly,
July 1941).
WORKS: Orchestra: Willowwave and wellowway,
1925; The day of judgment, 1927; Dies irae, chamber orch., 1927; Out of the Gay Nineties; Variations on a theme in medieval style, 1937; The
chamber blue, mimodrama for orch., soli, women's
chorus, dancers; The land east of the sun and
west of the moon, chorus and orch.; Chamber
music: piano quintet containing a second movement, From the 7th realm, 1920-29, salvaged by
memory from a work, Evolutionary quintet, which
was burned in the San Francisco fire of 1906;
Willow wood for soprano.

*FIELDING, JERRY
b. Pittsburgh, Pa., 17 June 1922. Attended
Carnegie Inst. of Technology. He has been
composer and arranger for films and the television show Hogan's heroes. His works
include City of Brass; Polynesian peace chant;
Paris magicque; The essence of calculated calm.
2201 Marvilla Drive, Hollywood, CA 90028

*FILAS, THOMAS J.
b. Chicago, Ill., 5 Mar. 1908. Attended Armour
Inst. of Technology. He played oboe, clarinet,
and saxophone in orchestras throughout the country and on Chicago radio stations. He received
the Paul Whiteman $1000 award for Concerto for
reed doubles, 1947. His other works include
Hushabye lullaby, tone poem; Lost River, rhapsody for oboe, harp, string orch.; Velocity,
clarinet; Campaign march; hymns and marches.
1921 South Central Park Ave.
Chicago, IL 60623

*FILLMORE, HENRY
b. Cincinnati, Ohio, 2 Dec. 1881; d. Miami, Fla.,
7 Dec. 1956. Attended Miami Inst. In 1916 he
organized the Henry Fillmore Concert Band. He
wrote many popular marches including Men of Ohio,
Men of Florida, Military escort march, et al.

FINCKEL, MICHAEL PHILIP
b. Bennington, Vt., 8 Oct. 1945. Studied with
Henry Brant and Louis Calabro, Bennington Coll.;
and cello with his father and with Jack Frazer
and George Neikrug, Oberlin Cons. He has taught
at Buxton School, Williamstown, Mass., 1972-73;
professor of cello and assistant in composition,
Bennington Coll., 1971-   ; principal cellist
and soloist, Vermont State Symphony, 1971-   .
WORKS: Orchestra: Tyco; cello concerto,
the orchestra includes bird calls, 2 TV sets,
2 radios; Chamber music: The red cow is dead,
cello quartet and voice; Mira, 2 flutes, clarinet, cello; Prelude to the green dream, cello
quartet, tape, 4 bass gongs, hurdy-gurdy, hammer
dulcimer, kazoo, voice and hambone artist, Music
in our time series, New York, 6 May 1973; Anti-
phonists, 12 celli; Chamber, 3 clarinets, 3
celli, piano; Grim trio, bass drum, vibraphone,
cello.
Bennington College, Bennington, VT 05201

*FINE, IRVING
b. Boston, Mass., 3 Dec. 1914; d. Boston, 23
Aug. 1962. Studied with Walter Piston, Edward
Burlingame Hill, Archibald T. Davison, Harvard
Univ., B. A. 1937, M. A. 1938; with Nadia
Boulanger in Cambridge, 1938, in Paris, 1939.
His awards included 2 Guggenheim grants; Fulbright grant; Wyman Found. grant; MacDowell fellowship; Nat. Inst. of Arts and Letters award;
Society for Publication of American Music award;
commissions from Ford Found.; Univ. of Illinois;
Louisville Orch.; Koussevitzky Found., Library
of Congress; Juilliard School; League of Composers. He was faculty member, Harvard Univ.,
1939-50; Berkshire Music Center, 1946-50;
professor and chairman, School of Creative
Arts, Brandeis Univ., 1950-62.
WORKS: Theatre: music for Alice in Wonderland, 1942; Orchestra: Toccata concertante,
1948; Serious song and lament, string orch.,
1955; Diversion, 1960; symphony #2, 1962; Chamber music: Fantasia, string trio; violin sonata,
1946; Partita for wind quintet, 1948; string
quartet, 1952; Romanza, wind quintet, 1961;
Voice: The choral New Yorker, cantata, 1944;
The hour glass, choral cycle, 1949; Mutability,
song cycle, 1952; piano works.

FINE, VIVIAN
b. Chicago, Ill., 28 Sep. 1913. Studied composition privately with Ruth Crawford-Seeger and
Roger Sessions. She has received the Dollard
award; Ford Found. award in the humanities; commissions from the Wooley Found. and Rothschild
Found. She taught at Juilliard School, 1948;
State Univ. Coll., Potsdam, N. Y., 1951; Connecticut Coll., School of Dance, 1963; Bennington Coll., 1964-   .

(FINE, VIVIAN)
  WORKS: Theatre: Opus 51, ballet for piano
and percussion, 1938; A guide to the life expec-
tancy of a rose, stage work, 1956; Alcestis,
ballet, 1960; Orchestra: Concertante for piano
and orch., 1944; concerto for piano, strings and
percussion, Finch Coll., New York, 15 Apr. 1973;
Chamber music: suite for oboe and piano, 1939;
Variations for harp; string quartet; quintet for
trumpet, harp, string trio; Chorus: Valedic-
tions, chorus and 10 instruments, 1959; Paean,
brass ensemble, chorus, speaker, 1969; Songs:
4 songs for contralto and strings; The Great
Wall of China, voice, flute, cello, piano, 1947;
The confession, 1963; The song of Persephone,
1964; Two Neruda poems, 1971; Missa brevis, 4
cellos and taped voice, 1972, Finch Coll., New
York, 15 Apr. 1973; Piano: Small sad sparrow;
Sinfonia and fugato, 1963; many other works in
all genres.
  R.D. 1, North Bennington, VT 05257

FINK, MICHAEL
  b. Long Beach, Calif., 15 Mar. 1939. Studied
guitar with Vicente Gomez at an early age; composition with Ernest Kanitz, Ingolf Dahl, Halsey
Stevens at Univ. of Southern California, B. M.
1960; with David Pinkham, New England Cons.,
M. M. 1962. He received the Alchin award for
full scholarship to Univ. of Southern California;
a 2-year scholarship and teaching fellowship at
New England Cons.; Tanglewood fellowship; 1961;
and a BMI award for further graduate study at
Columbia Univ. From age 13 he has composed and
worked professionally as guitarist.
  WORKS: Chamber music: Sonata da camera,
flute; Caprices for clarinet, 1961; Three lyric
pieces, piano, 1961; Chorus: From a very little
sphinx, women's voices, string quartet; Septem
angeli, cantata, chorus, piano 4-hands, 2 cellos,
2 contrabasses, timpani, percussion; Te deum,
tenor, chorus, piano, 1962; Jubilate deo, chorus
and brass quintet, 1971; Songs: What lips my
lips have kissed, soprano, Millay text, 1958;
Rain comes down, soprano, Millay text, 1963.
  17162 Erwin Lane, Huntington Beach, CA 92647

FINK, MYRON S.
  b. Chicago, Ill., 19 Apr. 1932. Studied with
Felix Borowski, 1942-48; with Mario Castelnuovo-
Tedesco in Los Angeles, 1948-50; with Bernard
Wagenaar at Juilliard School, 1951-52; Burrill
Phillips, Univ. of Illinois, 1952-55; and with
Robert Palmer at Cornell Univ., 1959-60. He
received a Woodrow Wilson Memorial fellowship;
Fulbright grant; City Univ. of New York, research
grant. He was on the faculty, Alma Coll.,
1958-61; Hunter Coll., 1966-   , associate
professor, 1973-   .
  WORKS: Opera: The boor; Susanna and the
elders; Jeremiah; Orchestra: piano concerto;
Chamber music: 2 string quartets; Vocal: 15
songs to poems of Witter Bynner; Piano: 12
etudes; Sinfonia; Triptych.
  10 Park Ave., Old Greenwich, CT 06870

FINK, ROBERT R.
  b. Belding, Mich., 31 Jan. 1933. Studied with
H. Owen Reed and James Niblock, Michigan State

(FINK, ROBERT R.)
  Univ., B. M. 1955, M. M. 1956; and with Mario
Castelnuovo-Tedesco. He was faculty member,
State Univ. Coll., Freedonia, N. Y., 1956-57;
Western Michigan Univ., 1957-   , professor
and chairman, department of Music, 1973-   .
  WORKS: Chamber music: Modal suite, brass
trio, 1959; Four modes for winds, woodwind quartet, 1967; Variations on a theme by Vivaldi,
woodwind quintet; Chorus: Seal lullaby; There
was once a puffin, 1967; Cantata on Psalm 48,
soprano, chorus, brass; Songs: Dialogue,
soprano, tenor, chamber orch.; Seven parables,
soprano and woodwind quintet.
  Department of Music
  Western Michigan University
  Kalamazoo, MI 49001

FINLEY, LORRAINE NOEL (Mrs. Theodore F. Fitch)
  b. Montreal, P. Q., 24 Dec. 1898; d. Greenwich,
Conn., 13 Feb. 1972; U.S. citizen. Attended
schools in Canada, Switzerland, Germany; studied
composition with Percy Goetschius and Rubin
Goldmark, Juilliard School; violin, piano, voice
with various teachers; graduate study at Columbia Univ. Her compositions won numerous awards
in national competitions. She traveled extensively in Europe, Near East, Africa, South
America, China, and Japan. From 1934 she worked
for publishing firms translating into English
lyrics of compositions of Bach, Beethoven,
Brahms, Faure, Debussy, et al. Her English
translation for Milhaud's Le pauvre matelot was
used for the Broadway premiere of that opera.
With her husband, she appeared in "Mr. and Mrs.
Composer" recitals.
  WORKS: Theatre: Persian miniatures, ballet;
Orchestra: Three theatre portraits, orchestral
suite; symphony; Chamber music: violin sonata;
clarinet sonata; Chorus: Trees of Jotham, cantata; numerous songs and instrumental pieces.

*FINN, WILLIAM J.
  b. Boston, Mass., 7 Sep. 1881; d. Bronxville,
N. Y., 20 Mar. 1961. Attended St. Charles Coll.,
Md.; Catholic Univ.; ordained 1906; Notre Dame
Univ., L. L. D. 1914. He was choirmaster and
choral conductor, Old St. Mary's, head, Paulist
Choristers, Chicago, 1904-18; Church of St. Paul
the Apostle, New York, 1918-46; returned to Old
St. Mary's, Chicago, 1947. He was author of
books on voice training and choral art.
  WORKS: Orchestra: Paschal suite; Chorus:
60 Christmas carols; Quintette of carols; A
rhythmic trilogy for Easter; Easter sermon of
the birds; Brother Ass and Saint Francis.

FINNEY, ROSS LEE
  b. Wells, Minn., 23 Dec. 1906. Studied with
Donald Ferguson, Univ. of Minnesota, 1924-25;
Carleton Coll., B. A. 1927, L. H. D.; with Nadia
Boulanger, 1927-28; Harvard Univ., 1928-29;
Alban Berg, 1931-32; Roger Sessions, 1935-36.
He received a Johnson fellowship, 1927; 2
Guggenheim fellowships, 1937, 1947; Pulitzer
fellowship, 1937; Connecticut Valley Prize, 1935;
Purple Heart and Certificate of Merit, 1945;
Boston Symphony award, 1955; Rockefeller grant,

FINNEY, ROSS LEE

(FINNEY, ROSS LEE)
1956; American Acad. of Arts and Letters award, 1956; Brandeis Gold Medal, 1967. He was faculty member, Smith Coll., 1929-48; served in Office of Strategic Services, 1943-45; professor and composer-in-residence, Univ. of Michigan, 1949-74.

WORKS: Orchestra: violin concerto, 1933, revised 1952; 4 symphonies, 1942, 1959, 1960, 1972, No.4 commissioned by Baltimore Symphony and performed, 9 May 1973; Hymn, fuguing and holiday, 1943; 2 piano concertos, 1948, 1968; Variations, 1957; percussion concerto, 1965; Symphony concertante, Kansas City, 28 Feb. 1968; Landscapes remembered, chamber orch., 1971; Spaces, 1971, Fargo, N. D., 26 Mar. 1972: Band: Summer in Valley City, Univ. of Michigan, 1 Apr. 1971; Chamber music: 3 violin sonatas, 1934, 1951, 1955; 8 string quartets, 1935-1960; 2 viola sonatas, 1937, 1953; 2 piano trios, 1938, 1954; duo for violin and piano, 1944; Fiddle-doodle-ad, violin and piano, 1945; cello sonata, 1950; 2 piano quintets, 1953, 1961; Elegy and march, solo trombone, 1954; Fantasy in two movements, solo violin, 1958; string quintet, 1958; 3 pieces for strings, winds, percussion, tape recorder, 1962; Divertimento, woodwind quintet, 1963; Divertissement, clarinet, violin, cello, piano, 1964; Three studies in fours, 4 percussionists, 1965; 2 acts for 3 players, clarinet, percussion, piano, 1970; Chorus: Pole Star for this year, chorus, soli, orch., 1939; Oh, Bury me not, 1940; When the curtains of night, 1940; Trail to Mexico, 1941; Pilgrim psalms, chorus, soli, organ, 1945; Words to be spoken, canon a 4, 1946; Spherical madrigals, 1947; Immortal autumn, chorus, tenor, 1952; Edge of shadow, chorus, 2 pianos, percussion, 1959; Still are new worlds, chorus, narrator, orch., 1962; Nun's priest's tale, chorus, soli, narrator, folk singer with electric guitar, orch., 1965; The martyr's elegy, chorus, tenor solo, orch., 1969; The remorseless rush of time, chorus and 13 instruments, River Falls, Wis., 23 Apr. 1970; Songs: Poems by Archibald MacLeish, 1935; Bleheris, tenor and orch., 1937; Three 17th century lyrics, 1938; Poor Richard, 7 songs, 1946; Three love songs, 1948; Chamber music, 36 songs, 1951; The express, 1955; Piano: 4 sonatas, 1933-45; Fantasy, 1939; Nostalgic waltzes, 1947; piano quartet, 1948; Variations on a theme by Alban Berg, 1952; Sonata quasi una fantasia, 1961; 32 piano games, 1968; 24 Inventions, 1970; Organ: Fantasy, 1958; 5 Organ fantasies, 1967.
2015 Geddes Ave., Ann Arbor, MI 48104

*FIORILLO, DANTE
b. New York, N. Y., 4 July 1905. Studied cello at the Greenwich House Music Settlement, but is largely self-taught in composition. He received a Guggenheim fellowship in 1935, renewed for 3 successive years; Pulitzer grant in 1939 "on the basis of 8 of 12 symphonies he had composed."

WORKS: Orchestra: 12 symphonies; music for chamber orchestra; concerto for harpsichord and strings; concerto for oboe, horn, strings and timpani; several partitas for orch.; concerti for various instruments; Chamber music: 11

(FIORILLO, DANTE)
string quartets; piano quintets and trios; instrumental sonatas; horn quintet; choruses and songs.

*FIRESTONE, IDABELLE (Mrs. Harvey S.)
b. Minnesota City, 10 Nov. 1874; d. Akron, Ohio, 9 July 1954. Wrote If I could tell thee, theme song of the Voice of Firestone, radio and television program. Other songs are: You are the song in my heart; Do you recall; Melody of love; Bluebirds.

FISCHER, EDITH STEINKRAUS
b. Portland, Ore., 9 Jan. 1922. Studied with Donald Ferguson, Univ. of Minnesota; with Bernard Wagenaar, Vittorio Giannini, Sergius Kagen, Juilliard School, voice with Florence Kimball. She was Rhode Island Woman Composer of the Year, 1969. She is adjunct professor of voice, Brown Univ. and Rhode Island Junior Coll.; soloist, Newman Congregational Church, Rumford, R. I.

WORKS: Chamber music: 5 string quartets; string duo; violin solos; woodwind ensemble works; and many anthems and songs.
33 Euclid Ave., Riverside, RI 02915

FISCHER, IRWIN
b. Iowa City, Iowa, 5 July 1903. Studied with Kathryn Williams, American Cons., M. M. summa cum laude 1930; with Nadia Boulanger, 1931; Zoltan Kodaly, 1936; Bruno Walter, Nicolai Malko, Bernhard Paumgartner, Mozarteum, Salzburg, 1937. He held a scholarship for study at Salzburg. He was organist, Chicago Symphony Orch., 1944-67; conductor, Gary Civic Symph., 1950-54, American Cons. Orch., 1945-57, Evanston Symph. Orch., 1953-58, West Suburban Symph., 1955-   ; faculty member, American Cons., 1930-   , associate director in 1973.

WORKS: Orchestra: Rhapsody on French folk tunes, 1934; piano concerto, 1936; Marco Polo, fantasy overture, 1937; Lament, cello and orch., 1939; Ariadne abandoned, 1941; Chorale fantasy, organ and orch.; Concerto giocoso, clarinet and orch.; Idyll, violin and orch.; Mountain tune trilogy; Sketches from childhood, 1946; symphony no. 1; short symphony; Hungarian set (The pearly bouquet), strings and celesta, 1948; Overture on an exuberant tone row; many choral works, piano and organ pieces, sacred songs.
219 Golf Terrace, Wilmette, IL 60091

*FISCHER, WILLIAM S.
b. Shelby, Miss., 5 Mar. 1935. Has studied at Xavier Univ.; Colorado Coll.; Univ. of Vienna; and Vienna Acad. of Music. His awards include a Fulbright grant; Rockefeller Found. grant; Stern Family Found. grant; German State Government award. He is owner of a record company.

WORKS: Orchestra: A quiet movement, 1966.

FISHER, ALFRED
b. Boston, Mass., 30 June 1942. Studied with David Burge, Univ. of Colorado; John Pozdro and Douglas Moore, Univ. of Kansas; with H. Owen Reed, Michigan State Univ. He held scholarships

(FISHER, ALFRED)
for study and in 1968 won first prize in a Michigan Music Teachers Assoc. contest. He was faculty member, Univ. of Western Ontario, 1969-72; Univ. of Saskatchewan, 1972; Acadia Univ. 1973-   .
WORKS: Chamber music: Five time prisms; Chorus: Lamentation canticle; My Lai canticle, with tape; Songs: Songs of the gentle night; Piano: 6 Aphorisms; electronic and improvisatory pieces.
R.R. #1, Port Williams
Kings County, Nova Scotia

*FISHER, DORIS
b. New York, N. Y., 2 May 1915. Studied at Juilliard School. She sang with the Eddie Duchin Orch., 1943; then formed her own group. She has composed scores for the films Gilda; Down to earth; Thrill of Brazil; and many popular songs.
17471 Hamilton Road, Detroit, MI 48203

FISHER, FRED
b. Chicago, Ill., 27 Aug. 1930. Studied with his father, Irwin Fischer; with Robert Delaney, Northwestern Univ., B. M. 1952; Eastman School of Music, M. M. 1953, D. M. A. 1963; with Nadia Boulanger in Paris, 1958, on a Fulbright grant. He was assistant/associate professor, Oklahoma State Univ., 1959-68; professor, North Texas State Univ., 1968-   .
WORKS: Piano: 3 sonatas, 1957; Variations on a happy tune, piano 4-hands, 1965; Cindy, 2 pianos, 1963; The commuter society, 2 pianos, 2 narrators, 1972.
1318 Ridgecrest Circle, Denton, TX 76201

FISHER, GLADYS W.
b. Klamath Falls, Ore., 16 May 1900. Studied at Mills Coll., A. B., B. M.; composition teachers were W. J. McCoy, Domenico Brescia, Darius Milhaud, Harvey Gaul, and Roland Leich. She won 10 awards in Pennsylvania Fed. of Music Clubs contests and a Mu Phi Epsilon prize. She was faculty member, Indiana, Pa., Normal School, 1921-24; assistant professor, Mills Coll., 1924-25; director of music, Presbyterian Church, Indiana, Pa., 1932-66.
WORKS: Chamber music: A hike in the woods, cello trio; Contrasts, cello trio; Chorus: Wake my heart; What child is this?; Music, I yield to thee; Songs: To us in Bethlehem; Piano: Three waltzes for duo piano; Caprice, piano solo.
620 School St., Indiana, PA 15701

FISHER, NORMAN Z.
b. Fessenden, N. Dak., 27 June 1920. Attended Lewis and Clark Coll., B. A. 1942; Reed Coll.; Univ. of Oregon; Union Theological Seminary, New York, M. S. M. 1946; his composition teachers were T. Tertius Noble and Harold Friedell. He has been church organist, 1946-   , Shreveport, La., 1950-   ; director, Shreveport Symphony Chorale, 1946-   ; faculty, Centenary Coll., 1955-70.
WORKS: Organ: Prelude on a French psalm tune; Toccata on a French psalm tune.
3708 Greenway Place, Shreveport, LA 71105

*FISHER, STEPHEN D.
b. Albany, N. Y., 27 May 1940. Studied with Billy Jin Layton and Daniel Pinkham, New England Cons. He received a BMI student composer award, 1960, and was on the BMI judging panel for the awards in 1972.
WORKS: Chamber music: Involution for piccolo, trumpet, and harpsichord, 1963; Music for 9 instruments, 1963; string quartet, 1964.
88-11 34th Ave., Apt. 6-C
Jackson Heights, NY 11372

FISHER, TRUMAN REX
b. Taft, Calif., 10 Nov. 1927. Attended Occidental Coll., M. A.; studied with Ernest Kanitz and Ingolf Dahl. He is assistant professor, Pasadena City Coll., Calif.
WORKS: Opera: Lysistrata, 2-act; The wasps, 2-act; Band: Harlequinade; Chamber music: piano trio; piano sonata; sonatina, flute and piano; Chorus: Lincoln, man of the people, chorus and orch.; Christmas, one B.C., chorus, organ, percussion; Magnificat, chorus, piano 4-hands, harp, percussion.
635 Valle Vista Drive
Sierra Madre, CA 91024

*FISHMAN, JACK
Bim! Bam! Bim!, children's opera, with and for children, Bicentennial project of New Theatre, Inc., N. J.

FISHMAN, MARIAN
b. Brooklyn, N. Y., 7 Dec. 1941. Studied privately with Wallingford Riegger; with Thomas Beversdorf at Indiana Univ., B. M.; with Donald Lybbert, Hunter Coll., M. A.; she is candidate for the D. M. in composition, Indiana Univ. She has been a fellow at the MacDowell Colony. She was instructor, Prairie View A&M Coll., 1967-68; associate instructor, Indiana Univ., 1971.
WORKS: Orchestra: Adagio for orchestra; Chamber music: Six studies in sonorities, 4 woodwinds; Glimpses, solo clarinet; Four miniatures, violin, viola 2 cellos; Three epigrams, flute and harp; Conceptions, solo bassoon; Interplay, violin and harp; Lines and figures, solo flute; Contrasting moods, trumpet and piano; 5 pieces for solo oboe or English horn; Vignettes, piano; Chorus: The hollow men, cantata for tenor, bass-baritone, chamber ensemble; Translations of the exile, male voices, chamber ensemble; Songs: Expressions of loneliness, voice and piano; Evocations, soprano, percussion piano.
102-55 67th Drive, Apt. 6D
Forest Hills, NY 11375

*FISSINGER, ALFRED J.
b. 1925. Suite for marimba, 1953.

FISSINGER, EDWIN R.
b. Chicago, Ill., 15 June 1920. Studied with Leo Sowerby and Stella Roberts at American Cons. He received the Kimball Award, 1951; Fine Arts Award, 1952; and numerous commissions. He was head, music department, Univ. of Illinois at Chicago Circle, 1964-67; chairman, music

FISSINGER, EDWIN R.

(FISSINGER, EDWIN R.)
department, North Dakota State Univ., 1967-   ;
and music editor, World Library Publications,
1965-71.
WORKS: Chorus: O make a joyful noise,
Psalm 66; Star that I see; many choral pieces.
57 15th Ave., North Fargo, ND 58102

FITCH, THEODORE F.
b. Rochester, N. Y., 17 Feb. 1900. Attended
Univ. of Rochester, A. B. 1922, M. A. 1927;
studied with Eugene Goosens, T. Yorke Trotter,
Selim Palmgren in Rochester; Constantin Schevdoff
in New York; Richard Terry in London. He received commissions for 2 cantatas. He was a
faculty member Univ. of North Carolina, 1922-24;
Univ. of Rochester, 1925-36; Univ. of Minnesota,
1952; director, Brooklyn Music School Settlement,
1936-58; with his wife, Lorraine Noel Finley,
appeared in "Mr. and Mrs. Composer" recitals.
WORKS: Orchestra: Terra nova, tone poem;
Divertimento for chamber orch.; Blue oxen; piano
concerto; Mariposa suite; Tuesday's tabloid; Four
New England fancies; Chamber music: Sestina,
clarinet and strings; cello sonata; string quartet; Triptych for strings; Chorus: High tide of
the year, cantata; Anne Rutledge, cantata;
General Booth enters heaven, cantata; Canticle
of a questing soul, 8-part chorus and orch.;
many songs, anthems, and other choral works.
25 West Elm St., Greenwich, CT 06830

FITCH, MRS. THEODORE F. See FINLEY, LORRAINE NOEL

*FITELBERG, JERZY
b. Warsaw, Poland, 20 May 1903; to U.S. 1940;
d. New York, N. Y., 25 Apr. 1951. Studied with
his father, then at the Hochschule für Music,
Berlin. He received the Elizabeth Sprague
Coolidge award in 1936 for a string quartet.
WORKS: Orchestra: 3 suites, 1926-30; concerto for string orch., 1928; 2 violin concertos,
1932, 1937; The golden horn, string orch.; 1942;
Nocturne, 1946; Chamber music: 5 string quartets; wind octet; sonata for 2 violins and 2
pianos; sonatina for 2 violins; many songs.

FITT, ROBERT J.
b. Philadelphia, Pa., 3 July 1945. Studied at
Temple Univ. and Trenton State Coll., M. A. He
has been band director and percussion instructor,
Centennial School District, Warminster, Pa.,
1968-   ; band director, Delaware Valley Coll.,
1970-   .
WORKS: Percussion ensemble: Mallets in
wonderland; Shades of Latin.
105 Earl Lane, Hatboro, PA 19040

*FITZ, RICHARD
Chamber sonata for percussion; duet for 2 snare
drums.
311 West 95th St., New York, NY 10025

FITZGERALD, R. BERNARD
b. Martinsville, Ill., 11 Apr. 1911. Studied at
Oberlin Coll., B. M. 1932; Jordan Cons., M. M.
1935. His faculty positions have included
Jordan Cons., 1933-35; Univ. of Idaho, 1938-40;

(FITZGERALD, R. BERNARD)
professor and band director, Univ. of Texas,
1940-56; Univ. of Kentucky, 1956-   , head
department of music, 1957-63, professor,
1965-   ; director, Ford Found. Contemporary
Music Project, administered by MENC, 1963-65
(on leave from Univ. of Kentucky).
WORKS: Trumpet and piano: Introduction
and fantasy, 1933; concerto, 1935; Modern suite
(Call, Legende, Frolic), 1936; Rondo capriccio,
1937; Brass ensemble: Scherzino, 4 trumpets,
1936; Prelude, 4 trumpets, 1936; Andante
cantabile, 2 trumpets, horn, trombone, 1936;
Tarantella, 2 trumpets, horn, trombone, 1936;
2 Brass fanfares, 1950; Dixieland fanfares, 1951;
Fanfares for brass and organ, 1973; Suite for
brass choir, 1973; Chorus: The sky is up above
the roof, 1937; Music at night, 1938; The horseman, male voices, 1938; Fratres in unum, male
voices, 1947; Now sing we noel, 1961; She walks
in beauty, a cappella, 1968; Stanzas for music,
a cappella, 1968; Songs: Triptych, soprano, chamber ensemble, Univ. of Kentucky, 14 Feb. 1969.
Department of Music, University of Kentucky
Lexington, KY 40506

FITZRANDOLPH, CHARLES I.
b. Nile, N. Y., 3 Dec. 1921. Studied with
Bernhardt Westlund, Milton Coll.; with Cecil
Effinger, Univ. of Colorado. He has taught in
public schools, Wisconsin, 1947-53; Pueblo,
Colo., 1956-57; Denver, 1960-63; Boulder,
1963-71.
WORKS: Chorus: Parting gifts, 8-part chorus, text by Elinor Wylie, 1968; With music
strong I come, 8-part chorus, text by Whitman,
1969; Boulder Valley, a school district song,
text by composer, 1971.
700 36th St., Boulder, CO 80302

FLAGELLO, NICOLAS
b. New York, N. Y., 15 Mar. 1928. Studied piano
with Adele Marcus, violin, viola, cello, oboe
with various teachers, conducting with Dmitri
Mitropoulos; Manhattan School of Music, B. M.,
M. M. 1950; St. Cecilia Acad., Rome, doctorate
1956; composition with Vittorio Giannini and
Ildebrando Pizzetti. He received a Fulbright
grant, 1955; first prize in creativity, St.
Cecilia Acad., 1956; annual ASCAP awards,
1960-   ; New York Critics' Circle award, 1961;
Citation, Vatican's Order of Peter and Paul for
opera, The judgment of St. Francis; City of
Salerno Gold Medal, 1968; and many commissions.
He has been a faculty member, Manhattan School
of Music, 1950-   ; head, composition department, Curtis Inst., 1964-65; coordinator with
V. Giannini, North Carolina School of Performing
Arts, 1964, and present consultant; piano recit-
alist and accompanist; violinist, violist, and
oboist in symphonic and operatic orchestras;
conductor, Chicago Lyric Opera, 1960-61; New
York State Theatre, 1968; assistant to Antonino
Votto, La Scala, 1960, etc.
WORKS: Opera: Mirra, 3-act, 1953; The wig,
1-act, 1953; Rip Van Winkle, children's operetta,
1957; The sisters, 1-act, 1958; The judgment of
St. Francis, 1-act, 1959; The piper of Hamelin,

(FLAGELLO, NICOLAS)
children's opera to composer's libretto, 1970; Orchestra: Beowulf, tone poem, 1949; 3 piano concertos, 1950, 1955, 1962; Suite for Amber, 1951; Symphonic aria, 1951; overture, 1952; flute concerto, 1953; Theme, variations, and fugue, 1955; violin concerto, 1956; Missa sinfonica, 1957; concerto for string orch., 1959; Capriccio, cello and orch., 1961; Concertino for piano, brass and timpani, 1963; Lautrec, ballet suite, 1965; Symphony for orchestra, 1967; Serenade for small orch., 1968; Symphony of winds, 1970; Chamber music: Episode and chorale for 11 brass instruments, 1944; Lyra for brass sextet, 1945; Divertimento, piano and percussion, 1960; harp sonata, 1961; Burlesca, flute and guitar, 1961; violin sonata, 1963; Introduction and allegro, accordion, 1964; Suite for harp, violin, viola, cello, 1965; Electra, piano and percussion, 1966; Declamation, violin and piano, 1967; Two pieces (Marionettes), harp solo, 1968; Chorus: Pentaptych, with orch., 1953; Tristis est anima mea, with piano or orch., 1959; Virtue, a cappella, 1961; Tu es sacerdos, with organ, 1963; The star, a cappella, 1964; The arrow and the song, Laughing song for youthful chorus, 1966; Te deum for mankind, with orch., New York, 7 May 1969; Passion for Martin Luther King, Jr., solo, chorus, orch., 1968, Washington, 19 Feb. 1974; Songs: Three songs for soprano, piano or orch., 1949; The lamb, soprano and piano, 1953; The land cycle, bass-baritone and small orch., 1954; Song after Petrarca, tenor and orch., 1956; L'infinito, bass, piano or orch., 1956; The rainy day, low voice, piano, 1958; Dante's farewell, soprano and orch., 1962; Contemplations, soprano and orch., 1963; Island in the moon, soprano and orch., 1964; Piano: Etude, 1945; Three dances, 1945; Episode, 1957; Prelude, ostinato, and fugue, 1960; sonata, 1962; Petite pastels, Notturno, 1969.
120 Montgomery Circle
New Rochelle, NY 10804

FLANAGAN, THOMAS J., JR.
b. New Haven, Conn., 30 Nov. 1927. Attended Columbia Univ., B. A.; New England Cons., B. M., M. M.; City Coll. of New York; Cornell; studied with Jack Beeson, Carl McKinley, Normand Lockwood, Robert Palmer. He has been a faculty member, St. John's Univ., Jamaica, N. Y., 1963- , professor and director, music division, in 1973.
WORKS: Vocal: Psalm 130, chorus; Four songs of unknown poets, women's voices; Melody lost, baritone; Summer song for me, soprano.
845 West End Ave., Apt. 8C
New York, NY 10025

*FLANAGAN, WILLIAM
b. Detroit, Mich., 14 Aug. 1923; d. New York, N. Y., 31 Aug. 1969. Studied with Burrill Phillips and Bernard Rogers, Eastman School of Music; with Arthur Berger, Aaron Copland, and Arthur Honegger at Tanglewood; with David Diamond in New York. He was a reviewer for the New York Herald Tribune, 1957-60.

(FLANAGAN, WILLIAM)
WORKS: Theatre: Bartleby, 1-act opera, 1952-57; music for Albee's The sandbox, 1961, and The ballad of the Sad Cafe, 1963; Orchestra: Divertimento for classical orchestra, 1948; A concert ode, 1951; A concert overture; Notations, 1960; Narrative for orchestra; Chamber music: Divertimento, string quartet, 1947; Chaconne, violin and piano, 1948; Passacaglia, piano, 1947; piano sonata, 1950; Chorus: Chapter from Ecclesiastes, chorus and string quintet; Billy in the darbies; Songs: Song for a winter child, 1950; The weeping Pleiades, 1953; The lady of tearful regret, soprano, baritone, chamber orch., 1958; Another August, soprano, piano, and orch., 1967; Goodbye my fancy, soprano, flute and guitar; many songs.

*FLEMING, SHARI BEATRICE
b. St. Johnsbury, Vt. Graduated from Peabody Cons., 1958. She received the Gustav Klemm prize, 1957, 1958. She has been faculty member, Univ. of Vermont, 1970- . Her Break forth into joy for chorus was performed in Brookline, Mass., Feb. 1963.
University of Vermont, Burlington, VT 05401

FLETCHER, GRANT
b. Hartsburg, Ill., 25 Oct. 1913. Attended Wesleyan Univ., B. M.; Univ. of Michigan, M. M.; Eastman School of Music, Ph. D.; studied with Healy Willan, Ernst Krenek, Howard Hanson. His many honors include 38 compostion awards, 14 ASCAP awards, and 18 commissions. He was conductor, Akron Symphony, 1945-48; Chicago Musical Coll. Symphonies, 1949-52; Chicago Symphonietta, 1951-56; and has been professor, Arizona State Univ., 1956- .
WORKS: Theatre: The carrion crow, opera, 1944; Lomatawi, ballet pantomime, 1957; The sack of Calabasas, opera, 1966; incidental music, Two gentlemen of Verona, 1969; incidental music, Blood wedding, 1970; Cinco de Mayo, ballet, 1973; Orchestra: A rhapsody of dances, chamber orch., 1935; Rhapsody for flute and strings, 1935; Nocturne, 1935; Sailors' songs and dances, 1941; Musicke for christening, string orch., 1944; A song for warriors, 1944; An American overture, 1945; Panels from a theatre wall, 1949; 2 symphonies, 1950, 1970; The pocket encyclopedia of orchestral instruments, 1953; 2 piano concertos, 1953, 1966; Sumare-Wintare, chamber orch., 1956; Concerto grosso, chamber orch., 1956; Dictionary of orchestra, 1959; Seven cities of Cibola, 1961; Glyphs, 1968; Diversion for strings, 1971; Band: Diaphony, 1968; Concerto for winds, 1969; Multiple concerto for five solo winds, 1970; Dyad, 1970; Chamber music: Caprice Argentine, violin, piano, 1934; Tower music, brass choir, 1957; clarinet sonata, 1959; Uroboros, percussion ensemble, 1961; Dances from the Southwest, strings, 1966; Who is Sylvia?, baritone, flute, oboe, bassoon, guitar, 1969; Octocelli, 8 solo cellos, 1971; Son, cello and piano, 1972; TR-IO, flute, guitar, piano, 1972; Chorus: The time for making songs has come, text by Hagedorn, 1937; A noel, composer's text, 8-part chorus, 1941; The crisis, with orch., 1945; Song of America, with band,

FLETCHER, GRANT

(FLETCHER, GRANT)
1955; Chorale, carol and finale, with band
1968; Fife tune, text by Manifold, male voices,
1972; The dark hills, text by Robinson, 1972;
Piano: 2 books of nocturnes, 1935; Four American
dance pieces, 1944; Diversion No.1, 1949, No. 2,
1946; Openend triptych, 1963; Chromixolyd, 1967;
Izquierdas (5 pieces for left hand alone), 1967;
Folkdance from Lorca, 1970; Organ: Dodecachordon,
1967; 2 pieces for organ pedals alone, 1968;
Carillon: Passacaglia and Two song preludes,
1954; Film scores: Magic, flute, oboe, bassoon,
1953; The fourth opinion, oboe, violin, viola,
piano, 1958; Arcosantos, on architectures of
Paolo Solari, 1970; many other choruses, songs,
piano pieces.
    1626 East Williams St., Tempe, AZ 85281

FLOYD, CARLISLE
    b. Latta, So. Car., 11 June 1926. Studied at
Converse Coll. and with Ernst Bacon at Syracuse
Univ., B. M., M. M.; piano with Sidney Foster and
Rudolf Firkusny. He received the New York Music
Critics' Circle award, 1956; Guggenheim fellow-
ship, 1957; Citation of Merit, Nat. Assoc. of
Authors, Conductors, Composers, 1957; Ten Out-
standing Young Men in the U.S., Junior Chamber
of Commerce, 1959; annual ASCAP awards,
1963-   ; commissions from Ford Found., Brown
Univ., Santa Fe Opera. He has been professor,
Florida State Univ., 1947-   .
    WORKS: Theatre: Slow dusk, 1-act musical
play, 1949; Fugitives, 3-act music drama, 1951;
Lost Eden, ballet, 2 pianos, 1952; Susannah, 2-
act music drama, 1954; Wuthering Heights, opera,
1958; The passion of Jonathan Wade, opera, 1962;
The sojourner and Mollie Sinclair, opera, 1963;
Markheim, opera, 1966; Of mice and men, opera,
1969; Orchestra: In celebration, overture;
Flower and hawk, Jacksonville, May 1973; Songs:
Pilgrimage, 3-song cycle for baritone and orch.,
1955; Mystery, 5 songs of motherhood, soprano and
orch., 1960.
    806 Middlebrook Circle
    Tallahassee, FL 32303

FLYNN, GEORGE W.
    b. Miles City, Mont., 21 Jan. 1937. Attended
Columbia Univ., B. S. 1964, M. A. 1966, D. M. A.
1972. He taught at Columbia Univ., 1966-73; at
Lehman Coll., CCNY, 1973-   .
    WORKS: Chamber music: Duo for violin and
piano; wind quintet; Wound, piano solo.
    33 Tower Place, Mount Vernon, NY 10552

FLYNT, HENRY ALLEN, III
    b. Greensboro, N. C., 19 Jan. 1940. A Ph. D.
candidate in economics, New School for Social
Research, is chiefly self-taught in music. In
1961 he was an avant garde composer of the post-
Cage era. In 1962 he repudiated all European
"classical" and "modern" music and began to devote his attention to ethnic music, concentrating
on two systems that originated in his native
region: blues and country music. He began to
compose fully notated avant garde music within
the country music "mode," assimilating the
electronic capabilities and open forms of the

(FLYNT, HENRY ALLEN, III)
avant garde to ethnic hillbilly music. He feels
he is unique, and can claim to be the only person with the right to call himself a composer of
contemporary American music in the fullest and
most literal sense. Speaking of the esthetic
values of his system Flynt says they are: "first
the whangy, peckerwood values of the South and
its music, with some attention to the blues;
second, the weird narcissistic child values, the
intricate self-reflections of the creep personality. The goal is to bring listeners to a state
of exaltation."
    WORKS: Hoedown/Stock car race; Three demos
for apple; Cowboy corroboree; all performed at
The Kitchen, New York, 26 Feb. 1972; Cool cat
twang; Improvisation in A; Double spindizzy; all
performed at Virginia Commonwealth Univ., 18 Apr.
1974.
    349 West Broadway, New York, NY 10013

*FOCH, DIRK
    b. Batavia, Java, 18 June 1886; to U.S. 1928.
Studied in Holland and in Germany. He was orchestral conductor in Sweden and Holland, then
in New York. His compositions include a musical
pageant, a work for narrator and orchestra,
piano pieces, songs.

FOLEY, DANIEL
    b. Toronto, Canada, 24 Apr. 1952; to U.S. 1959.
Studied at Florida Junior Coll.; with Thomas
Cousins and Emme Lou Diemer, Northern Virginia
Music Center; with Louis Mennini and Robert Ward,
North Carolina School of the Arts. He has received 3 BMI student composer awards and 5
Vittorio Giannini Memorial awards. He was private instructor in music theory and history,
1973-74.
    WORKS: Theatre: Mysterium, ballet in 7
acts; Orchestra: Glasperlenspiel; Chamber concerto for small orchestra; Chamber music:
Three songs after Hermann Hesse, baritone and
string quartet; Menagerie, piano; Chorus: Stabat
mater, women's voices and 6 winds.
    Box 271-A, North Carolina School of the Arts
    Winston-Salem, NC 27107

*FOLEY, DAVID
    b. 1945. 4 pieces for Saturday afternoon,
orch.
    School of Music, Ball State University
    Muncie, IN 47306

FOMINAYA, ELOY
    b. New York, N. Y., 10 June 1925. Studied with
James Ming, Lawrence Coll.; Violet Archer, North
Texas State Univ.; H. Owen Reed, Michigan State
Univ. He was associate professor, Northeast
Louisiana State Coll., 1953-66; professor and
chairman, Fine Arts department, Augusta Coll.,
1966-   . He composes for orchestra, band,
and chamber ensembles.
    Augusta College, Augusta, GA 30904

FONTRIER, GABRIEL
    b. Bucharest, Rumania, 21 Nov. 1918, American
father. Studied with Karol Rathaus at Queens

(FONTRIER, GABRIEL)
Coll., B. A. 1942; Otto Luening and Paul H. Lang, Columbia Univ., M. A. He held a Ford Found. faculty fellowship, 1953-54. He has been professor, Queens Coll., CUNY, 1947-   ; music editor, Long Island Press, 1947-61, music critic, 1964-   .
WORKS: Chamber music: string quartet, 1948; wind quintet, New York, Nov. 1973; violin sonata, 1973; Chorus: 3 choruses on texts of Hilaire Belloc, a cappella; 3 choruses on humorous texts, a cappella; Three new directions in music; Songs: 3 American songs for high voice and orch. or piano; Piano: Little piano suite; Lullaby; sonata for 2 pianos, Boston, 1965.
28 Chaffee Ave., Albertson, NY 11507

*FOOTE, GEORGE
b. Cannes, France, 19 Feb. 1886, American parents; d. Boston, Mass., 25 Mar. 1956. Studied with Edward Burlingame Hill at Harvard Univ.; with Friedrich Koch in Berlin. He taught at Harvard Univ., 1921-23; was president, South End Music School, Boston, to 1943.
WORKS: Orchestra: Variations on a pious theme; In praise of winter; Chorus: 98th psalm; also chamber music.

FORCUCCI, SAMUEL L.
b. Granville, N. Y., 8 July 1922. Studied with Charles O'Neill, Potsdam State Univ.; Ernst Bacon, Syracuse Univ.; Thomas Canning, Eastman School of Music. He taught in Boonville, N. Y., 1947-50; has been professor, State Univ. Coll., Cortland, N. Y., 1951-   .
WORKS: Chorus: Child of wonder, cantata; Eucharistic prayer, oratorio, mixed chorus, soloists, brass and percussion; works for orchestra and band.
17 Stevenson St., Cortland, NY 13045

FORMAN, JOANNE
b. Chicago, Ill., 26 June 1934. Studied privately with Carolyn Trojanowski in Los Angeles. She was resident composer, San Francisco Marionette Theater, 1959; founder-director, The Loft Children's Theater, 1959, Berke-Children's Theater, 1968, The Migrant Theater, 1966-   ; and resident composer, The Mime Experiment Co., 1972-   .
WORKS: Theatre: incidental music for Noah, The innocents, The scarecrow, Twelfth night, Dark of the moon, The miser, Three sisters; musicals for children, Hansel and Gretel, Petticoat pirate, The dancing princess, Mime show, Beauty and the beast; My heart lies south, operetta; chamber music and songs.
P.O. Box 4058, Albuquerque, NM 87106

FORNUTO, DONATO D.
b. New York, N. Y., 12 Sep. 1931. Studied with Mark Brunswick at City Coll. of New York; privately with Josef Schmid. He taught in public schools, 1954-67; at Columbia Univ. Teachers Coll., 1965-74; and was associate professor, William Paterson Coll., 1965-74.
WORKS: Band: concerto for piano and concert band; Chamber music: 3 pieces for clarinet and piano; suite for alto saxophone and piano;

(FORNUTO, DONATO D.)
Chorus: The lamb; The tiger; Songs: Songs of innocence and experience.
26 Duncan St., Waldwick, NJ 07463

*FORREST, HAMILTON
b. Chicago, Ill., 8 Jan. 1901. Studied with Adolf Weidig in Chicago. He received the Bispham medal of the American Opera Society of Chicago in 1925.
WORKS: Opera: Yzdra, 1925; Camille, Chicago, 10 Dec. 1930, with Mary Garden singing Camille; also ballets and chamber music.

FORST, RUDOLF
b. New York, N. Y., 20 Oct. 1900; d. Valhalla, N. Y., 19 Dec. 1973. Studied with Daniel Gregory Mason, Columbia Univ. He won the 1936 NBC Music Guild award for a string quartet; honorable mention in the 1973 competition of the Catgut Acoustical Society. He has been a violin teacher and musical director of a radio station.
WORKS: Orchestra: Fragment poetique; Symphonia brevis; Symphonic rhapsody on Ozark folk melodies; Aubade Mexicaine, 1938; Chamber music: Symphonietta for strings; Music for 10 instruments; Sonata da camera; Divertimento for chamber orch., 1938; Introduction and allegro, string quartet of new instruments (mezzo, alto, tenor, baritone), Douglass Coll., 14 Oct. 1973.

FORTE, JAMES
b. Boston, Mass., 19 Sep. 1936. Studied at Brandeis Univ., Lowell State Coll., Longy School of Music, and Boston Univ. He has received many commissions. He has been director of music, Robbins Library Concert Series, 1973-   .
WORKS: Chamber music: Sinfonia for strings, first movement, Boston, 7 May 1972; string quartet no. 3, 1973; duo for violin and piano, Boston, 28 Apr. 1974; Chorus: The holy child, chorus, soprano solo, orch., Boston, 18 Dec. 1968; Homeland, chorus, soprano, orch., Boston, 16 Dec. 1970; Piano: 3 sonatas, no. 2, Boston, 31 Mar. 1971; no. 3, Boston, 23 May 1974; other choral works, songs, piano solos, etc.
37 Cleveland St., Arlington, MA 02174

FORTNER, JACK
b. Grand Rapids, Mich., 2 July 1935. Studied with Ross Lee Finney and Leslie Bassett at Univ. of Michigan; Hall Overton, New York; N. Castigliono in Italy. He won a Found. Royaumont award, 1966; Rome Prize fellowship, 1967; Eastern Washington State Coll. award, 1972. He was lecturer, Univ. of Michigan, 1965-70; associate professor, California State Univ., Fresno, 1971-   ; artistic director, Merced, Calif., Symphony, 1971-   .
WORKS: Orchestra: Quadri, 1968; June dawns, July moons, August evenings, Eastern Washington State Coll., 13 Nov. 1973; Chamber music: Burleske, 2 chamber orch., Ann Arbor, 1965; Spring, voice and 9 instruments, 1966; string quartet, Rome, 1968; Cantilene, flute and piano; Nocturne, electronic tape; Mixed media: De plus en plus, clarinet, piano, tape, films, slides, lights, 1972.
1460 East Vartikian, Fresno, CA 93710

FOSS, LUKAS

FOSS, LUKAS
b. Berlin, Germany, 15 Aug. 1922; U.S. citizen
1942. Studied piano with Lazare Levy, flute
with Louis Moyse in Paris; coming to the U.S.
in 1937, studied at Curtis Inst. of Music. His
teachers include Isabelle Vengerova, piano;
Noel Gallon, Rosario Scalero, Paul Hindemith,
compostion; Fritz Reiner, Serge Koussevitzky,
conducting. He spent several summers at Tanglewood and took special courses at Yale. He received 9 composition awards, including a
Guggenheim, 2 New York Music Critics' Circle
awards, Prix de Rome; ASCAP awards; 3 honorary
doctorates; membership, Nat. Inst. of Arts and
Letters, Board of Directors, Naumburg Found.,
Koussevitzky Found., and Perspectives of New
Music. He was professor, Univ. of California,
Los Angeles, 1951-62; founder and director, Cen-
ter for Creative and Performing Arts, Buffalo
Univ., 1963- ; music director, conductor,
Buffalo Phil. Orch., 1962-70; visiting professor,
Harvard Univ., 1969-70; conductor, Brooklyn
Philharmonia, 1971-75; music advisor, conductor,
Jerusalem Symph. Orch., 1972- ; composer-in-
residence, Cincinnati Coll.-Cons., from Sep.
1975. He has been guest conductor of major sym-
phony orchestras in the U.S., Europe, Israel,
South America, Japan, and Canada.
 WORKS: Opera: The jumping frog of Calaveras
County, 1949; Griffelkin, 1955; Introductions and
goodbyes, 1959; Ballet: The heart remembers,
1944; Within these walls, 1944; The gift of the
Magi, 1955; Orchestra: music for The tempest,
1940; 2 symphonic pieces, 1940; Allegro concertante, 1941; Dance sketch, 1941; clarinet concerto, 1942 (later arranged as piano concerto No.
1); Ode, 1944, revised 1958; symphony, 1944;
Ricordare, 1948; oboe concerto, 1948; piano concerto no. 2, 1949; Symphony of chorales, 1958;
Elytres, 1964; Discrepancy, 24 winds, 1966; cello
concerto, 1967; Phorion, orch., electric organ,
harpsichord, guitar, 1967; Baroque variations,
1967; Geod, with optional voices, 1969; Orpheus,
viola, cello or guitar, and orch., New York, 18
May 1974; Fanfare, 1973; Chamber music: 4 preludes, flute, clarinet, bassoon, 1940; duo, cello
and piano, 1941; Paradigm, percussion, 1943; Composer's holiday, violin and piano, 1946; string
quartet, 1947; Capriccio, cello and piano, 1948;
Time cycle, soprano, clarinet, cello, piano, percussion, 1960; Echoi, clarinet, cello, piano,
percussion, 1963; Ni bruit, ni vitesse, 2 pianos,
2 percussion, inside piano, 1972; Cave of the
winds, wind quintet, 1972; MAP, a musical game
for an entire evening, any 4 musicians can play,
New York, 2 May 1973; Chorus: Melodrama and dramatic song of Michael Angelo, 1940; We sing, children's cantata, 1941; The prairie, with soloists
and orch., 1944; Tell this blood, 1945; Behold!
I build an house, 1950; Adon Olom, with organ,
1951; Parable of death, tenor, narrator, orch.,
1952; Psalms, with orch., 1956; Fragments of
Archilochos, chorus, speakers, soloists, chamber
ensemble, 1965; 3 airs for Frank O'Hara's Angel,
soprano, female chorus, instruments, 1972; Songs:
Drei Goethe Lieder, 1938; Song of anguish, voice
and piano or orch., 1945; The song of songs,
voice and orch., 1946; Where the bee sucks, 1951;

(FOSS, LUKAS)
 Time cycle, voice and orch., 1960; Piano: Four
2-voice inventions, 1938; Grotesque dance, 1938;
sonatine, 1939; Set of 3 pieces for 2 pianos,
1940; Passacaglia, 1941; Fantasy rondo, 1946;
Scherzo ricercato, 1953; Etudes for organ, 1967.
 4 East 95th St., New York, NY 10028

FOSTER, DOROTHY
b. Melrose, Mass., 17 Sep. 1930. Studied with
Hugo Norden and Gardner Read, Boston Univ., B. M.
with Henry Cowell, Peabody Cons.; and with Donal
Michalsky, California State Coll. at Fullerton,
M. A. She won first place in the Mu Phi Epsilon
internat. composition contest, 1971; and Music
Teachers Assoc. of California contest, 1971.
She is a private teacher of piano, organ, and
composition.
 WORKS: Chamber music: flute quintet; Vocal:
Moses, oratorio; What's for dinner?, song cycle,
soprano and piano; Fair Mary, soprano and cello;
4 Christmas songs, unison junior choir; Piano:
suite.
 18002 Yorba Linda Blvd.
 Yorba Linda, CA 92686

*FOSTER, DUDLEY
b. 1935. Piece in free form for organ, 1961.
 Department of Music
 California State University
 Los Angeles, CA 90032

*FOSTER, FAY
b. Leavenworth, Kan., 8 Nov. 1886; d. Bayport,
N. Y., 17 Apr. 1960. Studied composition with
Salomon Jadassohn in Germany. She won the Internat. Waltz Competition prize of 2000 marks,
Berlin, 1910; 1st prize, American Composers'
contest, New York, 1913; Etude prize; Nat. Fed.
of Music Clubs prize. She toured the U.S. as
concert pianist; taught in Illinois and Rydall,
Pa., then settled in New York. Her compositions
include 2 operas on Chinese themes; 3 operettas;
Songs: My journey's end, The Americans come!,
The place where I worship, and many others;
piano pieces.

FOSTER, ROBERT E.
b. Raymondville, Tex., 21 Jan. 1939. Studied
with J. Clifton Williams and Kent Kennan, Univ.
of Texas, Austin, M. M. He was assistant director of bands, Univ. of Florida, 1964-71; director of bands, Univ. of Kansas, 1971- .
 WORKS: Band: Blues rock; The dude; Folk
rock; The pony express; Rock a la Bach; etc.;
Chamber music: Scherzetto for trumpet and piano.
 School of Fine Arts, University of Kansas
 Lawrence, KS 66044

FOSTER, WILL J.
b. Brookfield, Mo., 10 Feb. 1890; d. Fort Worth,
Tex., 14 Feb. 1960. Studied piano and organ in
Fort Worth. Except during service in both World
Wars he held organist posts from 1912; his last
position was at Arlington Heights Methodist
Church, Ft. Worth, 1946-60. In 1959 he was
ordained minister of music in the Methodist
Church.

(FOSTER, WILL J.)
WORKS: Chorus: <u>Fear not, I am with thee</u>, 1941; <u>Father, forgive them</u>, 1943; <u>And with His stripes</u>, 1950; <u>Have mercy on me</u>, 1953; <u>Hear my prayer</u>, 1953; <u>Thy will be done</u>, 1955.

FOWLER, MARJE
b. New Haven, Conn., 8 Jan. 1917. Studied with Morris Ruger, California State Univ. at Long Beach, A. B.; David Ward-Steinman, California State Univ., San Diego, M. A.; violin with Hugo Kortschak, Yale Univ., and Vera Barstow in Los Angeles. She received the Sigma Alpha Iota Alumni Chapter, San Diego, composers award, 1967, 1973. She was violinist, Stockton Symphony Orch., 1951-60; youth choir director, 1953-70; instructor, Grossmont Coll., 1970-71.
WORKS: Orchestra: <u>Introduction and fantasia</u>; Chorus: Sacred service for 3 choirs, organ, liturgist; <u>All praise to Thee</u>, a cappella; Songs: <u>Deux ballades sombres</u> de Francois Villon, tenor, viola, piano, 1967; <u>Cante jondo</u>, setting of <u>Romance de la luna, luna</u>, Garcia Lorca, mezzo soprano, percussion harpsichord, 1973; Organ: <u>Elegie</u>; <u>Introduction and fantasia</u>.
13348 Community Road, Poway, CA 92064

*FOX, CHARLES
b. New York, N. Y., 1940. Studied with Nadia Boulanger in Paris, 1959-61. He received an Emmy for his music contributions to ABC's <u>Love American style</u>.
WORKS: Film scores: <u>The incident</u>, 1967; <u>Goodbye Columbus</u>; <u>Pufnstuf</u>; <u>Making it</u>; <u>First class</u> (electronic); <u>Star-spangled girl</u>; <u>In the path of history</u>, documentary; Television: <u>Love American style</u>; <u>Bugaboo</u>; theme for the <u>Tonight show</u>.
c/o Broadcast Music, Inc.
40 West 57th St., New York, NY 10019

*FOX, FELIX
b. Breslau, Germany, 25 May 1876; to U.S. 1897; d. Boston, Mass., 24 Mar. 1947. Studied at the Leipzig Cons.; piano with Isidor Phillip in Paris. On coming to the U.S. he was co-founder of a music school in Boston; after his partner's death it was called the Felix Fox School of Piano Playing. He wrote piano pieces and songs.

FOX, FRED
b. Detroit, Mich., 17 Jan. 1931. Studied with Bernhard Heiden, Indiana Univ.; Ross Lee Finney, Univ. of Michigan; Ruth Wylie, Wayne State Univ. He held a fellowship, Dallas Composers Conf., 1960; Ford Found.-Nat. Music Council grant, 1963. Faculty posts include Franklin Coll., 1959-61; Sam Houston State Coll., 1961-62; California State Univ. at Hayward, 1964-   .
WORKS: Orchestra: violin concerto, 1971; <u>Ternion</u>, oboe and orch., 1972; Chamber music: many compositions for solo instruments and ensemble groups including <u>Quantic I</u>, woodwind quintet, 1969; Variations for piano trio, 1970; <u>Ad rem</u>, solo guitar, 1970; <u>Matrix</u>, cello, strings, percussion, 1972; <u>Variables 1</u>, violin and piano, 1972; <u>Variables 2</u>, solo flute, 1973; <u>Variables</u>

(FOX, FRED)
<u>3</u>, 6 instruments, 1973; <u>Variables 4</u>, solo clarinet, 1973; Chorus: <u>Jubilate Deo</u>, chorus and orch.; <u>The descent</u>, text by W. C. Williams, chorus, piano, percussion, 1969; <u>A stone, a leaf, an unfound door</u>, text by Wolf, soprano, clarinet, percussion, chorus; many other works for chorus.
Department of Music
California State University
Hayward, CA 94544

FOX, OSCAR J.
b. Burnet County, Tex., 11 Oct. 1879; d. Charlottesville, Va., 13 July 1961. Studied with Karl Attenhofer, Zurich, Switzerland, 1896-99; and with Percy Goetschius in New York. He was organist and director of choirs, glee clubs, and University Choral Society, Univ. of Texas, 1925-28. He was also recitalist and radio performer.
WORKS: Songs: <u>Hills of home</u>; <u>My heart is a silent violin</u>; <u>Rain in the river</u>, <u>Petal drift</u>, etc.

FRABIZIO, WILLIAM V.
b. Stockton, N. J., 10 Oct. 1929. Studied at Trenton Cons.; Rutgers Univ.; and with Clifford Taylor, Temple Univ. He received the Beaver Coll. Lindback award for distinguished teaching, 1972-73; Outstanding Educators of America award, 1973. He taught in private schools 1957-63; Temple Univ., 1965-68; New England Cons., 1968-69; and Beaver Coll., chairman, music department, 1970-   . He is also associate editor for a New York publishing company.
WORKS: Orchestra: 3 symphonies; <u>Statement for trumpet and 18 players</u>; Band: <u>Symphonic paraphrase</u>; <u>Synesthesia</u>; tuba concerto; <u>Prelude</u>; Chamber music: string quartet; <u>Comments among four players</u>, piano 4-hands, cello, percussion; saxophone quintet; trio for flute, clarinet, bassoon; trio for trumpet, horn, trombone; brass quintet; woodwind quintet; <u>Psalm 150</u>, string quartet and voice; <u>Dialogues</u>, trombone and string quartet; Chorus: <u>Octet for voices</u>; <u>Credo Americana</u>, solo voice, chorus, band; more than 70 compositions and 200 arrangements for jazz orch.
P. O. Box 111, Stockton, NJ 08559

FRACKENPOHL, ARTHUR
b. Irvington, N. J., 23 Apr. 1924. Studied with Bernard Rogers at Eastman School of Music, B. A., M. A.; with Darius Milhaud at Tanglewood; with Nadia Boulanger at Fontainebleau; McGill Univ. D. M. He won first prize in composition at Fontainebleau, 1950; received Ford Found. grant, 1959-60; university research fellowships at Potsdam. He has been faculty member, State Univ. Coll., Potsdam, N. Y., 1949-   .
WORKS: Opera: <u>Domestic relations</u>, chamber opera in 1 act; Band: <u>Academic processional march</u>; <u>Allegro giocoso</u>; <u>On the go</u>; <u>Cantilena</u>; <u>Chorale episode</u>; <u>Rondo marziale</u>; <u>Seaway valley</u>; Chamber music: string quartet, 1971; concertino for tuba and strings; brass quartet; 2 brass quintets; <u>Breviates for brasses</u>; Chorus: <u>The</u>

FRACKENPOHL, ARTHUR

(FRACKENPOHL, ARTHUR)
natural superiority of men, women's voices and orch.; Te Deum, chorus and orch.; Gloria, chorus and orch.; Hogamus, higamus, double fugue for speaking chorus and percussion; 7 essays on women, Ogden Nash text, men's voices; Songs: Recent rulings, song cycle; many compositions for chorus and chamber groups.
    Crane School of Music
    State University College, Potsdam, NY 13676

*FRAENKEL, WOLFGANG
b. Berlin, Germany, 10 Oct. 1897; to U.S. 1947. Studied in Berlin at the Klindworth-Scharwenka Cons. He received 1st prize, Internat. Competition, City of Milan, for his Symphonic aphorism, 1965; He was a judge in Berlin until the Nazi regime put him in a concentration camp, 1933-39. He then lived in Shanghai and Nanking, making his way in 1947 to Los Angeles, where he worked as music copyist in film studios. His compositions include an opera, flute concerto, many chamber music pieces, songs.

FRANCESCHINI, ROMULUS
b. Brooklyn, N. Y., 5 Jan. 1929. Studied with Vincent Persichetti at Philadelphia Cons.; privately with Stefan Wolpe and Morton Feldman in New York. He has received several commissions and composed score for award-winning film, Effects, by John Gati. He was partner, EMP Electronic Music Productions, 1969-71; director, Electronic Music Division, Magna Sound Recording Co., 1971-   ; and was co-leader of an orchestra in New York, 1970-72.
    WORKS: Orchestra: 5 paintings for orchestra; Sinfonia for strings, percussion, piano, celeste, 1970; Band: Prelude and celebration; De profundis, 1969; Chamber music: Metamusic 1: In memoriam, Edgard Varese, 8 players, 1966; Après Josquin, alto and 6 players; Chorus: Geography of this time, text by Archibald MacLeish; Missa brevis, chorus, congregation, and organ, 1972; Songs: Blake cycle, 1964; On the nature of solidity, text by Joseph Tonda, 1965; Piano: Polar, 2 pianos, 1967; Piano journal, 1951-73; Electronic: Metamusic 2, 4 instrumental groups, magnetic tape and ring modulators, 1970; Echelon mix, 1971; Interactions, for 4 synthesizers, 1971.
    434 West Ellet St., Philadelphia, PA 19119

FRANCHETTI, ARNOLD
b. Lucca, Italy, 18 Aug. 1906; U.S. citizen 1950. Studied with his father Alberto, director of the Florence Cons., and graduated from Univ. of Florence as physics major; studied with Richard Strauss in Germany. He received the Lehman composition award at the Mozarteum, Salzburg; Fromm Found. grant, 1950; Nat. Inst. of Arts and Letters grant, 1958; Koussevitzky Found. grant through Library of Congress, 1961; Guggenheim grant, 1961; Columbia Univ. Ditson award, 1964; and many commissions. Before coming to the U.S. he taught in Italy, Austria, and Sweden; joined the faculty, Hartt Coll. of Music, 1948, professor and chairman, composition and theory, 1960-73.

(FRANCHETTI, ARNOLD)
    WORKS: Opera: 8 operas including Notturno in La, commissioned in 1966 by the Cesare Barbieri Center for Italian Studies, Trinity Coll., Hartford; Chamber music: Three Italian masques, piano, brass quintet, percussion, 1953; Concertino, solo violin and chamber ensemble, 1965; Piece for man alone, oboe and strings, New York, 16 Jan. 1971; Doppio quartet, double quartet for brass and woodwinds, Hartford, 1972; Do, re, mi, do, re, mi, bemolle, piano, New York, 4 Dec. 1973; 4 piano sonatas; numerous orchestral works, chamber pieces, songs, and a film score for Life of Dante Alighieri, commissioned by the Trinity Coll. Center for Italian Studies, 1968.
    Lyme, CT 06371

*FRANCO, CLARE J.
Studied with Vincent Persichetti and Luciano Berio, Juilliard School, M. S.; also with Darius Milhaud, Leonard Stein, Stefan Wolpe, Karlheinz Stockhausen. She was awarded the Fromm prize in composition, 1963-64. In 1969 she was a doctoral candidate at the Univ. of Illinois. She has published Piano fantasia and The wind sprang up at four o'clock for mezzo soprano. Within, for 10 instruments, 1975; was premiered in Los Angeles, 17 Feb. 1975.

FRANCO, JOHAN
b. Zaandam, Netherlands, 12 July 1908; U.S. citizen 1942. Studied chiefly with Willem Pijper in Amsterdam. In 1972 he received a Virginia Music Teachers Association commission to compose Diptych for flute and electronic tape, performed at the VMTA convention, Charlottesville, Nov. 1972.
    WORKS: Theatre: music for Romans by St. Paul, The Book of Job, The pilgrim's progress, Electra, The tempest; Orchestra: 5 symphonies; concerti for violin, cello, piano, percussion, guitar; Chamber music: sonatas for piano, violin, viola, cello, saxophone, guitar; Chorus: As the prophets foretold, cantata for soloists, chorus, brass, and carillon, 1955; Song cycles: Songs of the spirit; Twelve works; Sayings of the word; many other works for voice and instruments, and 100 works for carillon.
    403 Lake Drive, Virginia Beach, VA 23451

FRANK, ANDREW
b. Los Angeles, Calif., 25 Nov. 1946. Studied with Jacob Druckman at Bard Coll.; with George Crumb and George Rochberg, Univ. of Pennsylvania. He received BMI student composer awards, 1969, 1970; Los Angeles French Horn Club award, 1972. He has been assistant professor, Univ. of California at Davis, 1972-   .
    WORKS: Orchestra: Eucalyptus; Nepenthe; Chamber music: string quartet; Dreams of reason, viola, bassoon, percussion, piano; Night music III, guitar; Amaranth, string orch.; Fantasy for 6 horns, 1972; Alto rhapsody, solo alto saxophone; A rebours, solo contrabass; many other chamber works and songs.
    635 Adams St., Davis, CA 95616

FRANK, JEAN FORWARD (Mrs. Thomas W.)
b. Pittsburgh, Pa., 13 Aug. 1927. Studied with
Louis P. Coyner and Russell Wichmann at Chatman
Coll.; privately with Roland Leich and Joseph
Wilcox Jenkins.
WORKS: Operetta: Time of our lives; Princess of a thousand moons; Chamber music: Scat-
terpunctus, string orch.; Chorus: The Christmas
story; Into the woods my master went; If God be
for us; So answereth my soul; Piano: Afternoon
street noise; Contemplation; Melodic mood;
Chimera; Thoughts before dawn; sonata, etc.
Box 234C Ridge Drive, Mars, PA 16046

*FRANK, MARCEL GUSTAVE
b. Vienna, Austria, 3 Dec. 1909; U.S. citizen
1942. Studied with Joseph Marx, Florent Schmitt,
Felix Weingartner, Vienna Acad. of Music. He
received the Grand Prix at Geneva for Homage to
Claude Debussy for chorus and orchestra. He was
conductor and pianist, Vienna State Opera; accompanist to many noted singers; opera conductor in Pittsburgh and Dallas. His works include
4 ballets; 3 symphonies; piano concerto; Arkansas traveler variations; Heather hills for band;
Pas de deux, ballet for band; Conversation piece,
4 saxophones; Passacaglia for organ.

FRANK, ROBERT E.
b. Los Angeles, Calif., 27 Nov. 1943. Studied
with Charles Cushing and Richard Hoffmann, Univ.
of California, Berkeley; with Robert Palmer and
Karel Husa, Cornell Univ., D. M. A. He has been
assistant professor, State Univ. of New York,
Plattsburgh, 1973-   .
WORKS: Orchestra: symphony; Chamber music:
movement for flute and piano, 1969; string quartet; Chorus: Drop down, ye heavens, a cappella
motet for 8 voices; in Just-spring, 8 voices,
flute, piano, percussion; Organ: 3 preludes.
Department of Music, State Univ. of New York
Plattsburgh, NY 12901

FRATTURO, LOUIS M.
b. Stamford, Conn., 19 Apr. 1928. Studied with
Paul Creston, Manhattan School of Music, B. M.,
M. M. E. He was orchestrator and conductor for
C. B. DeMille's award-winning film, Ten commandments. He taught in public schools, 1958-67; was
jazz band director, Los Angeles Pierce Coll.,
1967-72; has played with Glenn Miller, Ray
McKinley, and Mundell Lowe.
WORKS: Jazz: Gospel swing; Jubilee; Nightmare; also educational works: Learn to play
jazz solos, etc.
1829 Post Road, Darien, CT 06820

FRAZEUR, THEODORE C.
b. Omaha, Neb., 20 Apr. 1929. Studied with
Louis Mennini, Bernard Rogers, Wayne Barlow,
Eastman School of Music. He was guest composer,
First Internat. Tuba Symposium, Indiana Univ.
He was percussionist, Rochester Philharmonic,
1949-52, 1954-56; Erie Philharmonic, 1957-69;
professor, State Univ. of New York, Fredonia,
1956-   .
WORKS: Ballet: Four beauties; Uhuru, 7
percussionists; Orchestra: Allegro giocoso;

(FRAZEUR, THEODORE C.)
Poem for strings; Chiastic for string orch.;
Poets in a landscape, percussion ensemble,
piano, harp, mixed chorus, soloists, narrator;
Chamber music: Divertimento, trombone and
wind ensemble; Frieze, tenor saxophone and percussion; suite for viola and percussion; The
quiet place, marimba and piano; Rondo, marimba
and piano; Film score: Spotlight on Fredonia.
3 Westerly Drive, Fredonia, NY 14063

FREDRICKSON, THOMAS
b. Kane, Pa., 5 Sep. 1928. Studied with Tilden
Wells, Ohio Wesleyan Univ.; Burrill Phillips,
Univ. of Illinois. He has received ASCAP
awards. He has been a faculty member, Univ. of
Illinois, 1952-   , and director, School of
Music, 1970-   .
WORKS: Chamber music: Allegro, cello and
piano; string quartet; duo for violin and cello;
piano variations; music for double bass alone;
music for 5 instruments; trio for flute, vibraphone, double bass; brass quintet; Wind music 1;
Sinfonia concertante, Illinois variations;
Chorus: Silence; various jazz compositions and
orchestral works.
1814 Robert Drive, Champaign, IL 61820

*FREED, ARNOLD
b. New York, N. Y., 29 Sep. 1926. Studied with
Mark Brunswick, City Coll. of New York; Philip
James at New York Univ.; Vittorio Giannini,
Juilliard School; and with Luigi Dallapiccolo
in Italy on a Fulbright grant, 1952-54.
WORKS: Orchestra: Alleluia; Chamber music:
violin sonata; piano sonata; Chorus: Gloria;
4 seasonal madrigals; From out of a wood;
Heaven-haven; 3 shepherd carols; Lord, lord,
lord, jazz-rock, with electric organ, bass
guitar, drums; Songs: Acquainted with the
night.
c/o Boosey & Hawkes
30 West 57th St., New York, NY 10019

*FREED, ISADORE
b. Brest-Litovsk, Russia, 26 Mar. 1900; to U.S.
as a child; d. Rockville Center, N. Y., 10 Nov.
1960. Studied at Univ. of Pensylvania, B. M.
1918; with Ernest Bloch and Vincent d'Indy in
Paris. He received the Soc. for Publication of
American Music Award, 1943. He was faculty
member, Curtis Inst.; Fine Arts School, Temple
Univ.; visiting professor, Julius Hartt Found.,
Hartford, Conn.; organist-choirmaster, Keneseth
Israel Temple, Philadelphia.
WORKS: Opera: Homo sum, 1930; The princess
and the vagabond; Ballet: Vibrations, 1928;
Orchestra: Jeux de timbres, 1933; 2 symphonies;
Applachian sketches, 1946; Festival overture,
1946; Rhapsody, trombone and orch.; violin concerto; cello concerto, 1952; concertino for English horn and chamber orch., 1953; Chamber music:
3 string quartets, 1931, 1932, 1937; trio for
flute, violin, harp, 1940; Triptych, string trio
and piano, 1943; Passacaglia, cello and piano,
1947; woodwind quintet, 1949; oboe sonatina;
Rhapsody, clarinet, strings, piano; piano sonata;

FREED, ISADORE

(FREED, ISADORE)
violin sonata; Suite for viola; Suite for harp;
also choral works, songs.

*FREEDMAN, ISRAEL
b. Brooklyn, N. Y., 1910. Studied violin with
Ondricek, composition with Rimsky-Korsakov; held
a scholarship at the New England Cons., 1934.
His works for orchestra included a symphony;
Hiawatha, a tone poem; Adagio for strings; also
songs.

FREEDMAN, ROBERT M.
b. Mt. Vernon, N. Y., 23 Jan. 1934. After an excellent basic training in public school has been
self-taught in music through score analysis and
listening to all kinds of music. He was faculty
member, Berklee Coll. of Music, 1956-59.
WORKS: Orchestra: trumpet concerto; Chamber
music: string quartet; Journeys of Odysseus,
jazz suite for chamber orch.; Beautiful music,
popular song, sung by Lena Horne.
4 Greenwood Lane, Westport, CT 06880

FREEMAN, EDWIN ARMISTEAD
b. Spartanburg, S. C., 2 May 1928. Studied with
Kenneth Klaus at Louisiana State Univ.; with Jack
Beeson and Otto Luening, Columbia Univ.; conducting with Pierre Monteux, Hancock, Me. He won a
BMI student composer award, 1955. He was director of the high school and chairman, arts program,
Dalton School, New York, 1965-69; assistant professor, Clemson Univ., 1969-   .
WORKS: Orchestra: Fantasy on a ground; Chamber music: string quartet, 1954; Chorus: Dr.
Donne preaches on death, oratorio.
148 Folger St., Clemson, SC 29631

*FREITAG, DOROTHEA
b. Baltimore. Studied with Howard Rutledge
Thatcher, Peabody Cons., grad. 1932; also with
Nadia Boulanger, Mario-Castelnuovo-Tedesco,
Bohuslav Martinu. She received an ASCAP award
for her ballet, Storyville, 1967; Peabody Alumni
award, 1968. She composes and arranges for Broadway shows and television programs. Among the
shows she has contributed to are Mame, Fiddler on
the roof, Golden boy.
333 East 30th St., New York, NY 10016

FREMDER, ALFRED
b. Sioux City, Iowa, 14 Mar. 1920. Attended Con-
cordia Seminary, St. Louis, B. A. 1942; Univ. of
Minnesota, M. A. 1955; North Texas State Univ.,
Ph. D. 1970; studied with Liborius Semmann, Donald
Ferguson, Paul Fetler, James Aliferis, Earl
George, Martin Mailman, William P. Latham. He
received the Nora Seeley Nichols award, 1964,
1967; Prescott award, 1966; Prescott prize, 1966.
He was piano recitalist throughout the U.S.,
1940-50; faculty member, Bethany Coll., 1945-56;
Arizona State Univ., 1966-68; teaching fellow,
North Texas State Univ., 1968-70; professor,
Texas Wesleyan Coll., 1970-   , composer-in-
residence, 1971-   .
WORKS: Orchestra: piano concerto, 1970,
Oslo, 27 Aug. 1973; Chamber music: wind quintet,
1969; Chorus: O ye shepherds, a cappella motet,
1953; Surely He hath borne our griefs, 1954; The

(FREMDER, ALFRED)
Passion according to St. Mark, chorus, orch.,
narrator, Phoenix, 17 May 1964; Songs of Solomon,
a cappella, Phoenix, 12 Apr. 1964; The tabernacle
of God, 1968; That great city, with strings, percussion, 1969; A song of time, 1971; Piano:
Intrada, intermezzo, and capriccio, St. Paul,
27 Apr. 1953; Landi variations, 2 pianos, Denton,
Tex., 28 Mar. 1969; Left hand complements for
piano, Ft. Worth, 2 May 1971; Trinity chorales,
2 pianos, Ft. Worth, 27 Feb. 1972.
Texas Wesleyan College, Ft. Worth, TX 76105

FREUND, DONALD WAYNE
b. Pittsburgh, Pa., 15 Nov. 1947. Studied with
Joseph Wilcox Jenkins, Duquesne Univ., B. M. 1969;
with Darius Milhaud and Charles Jones, Aspen
School; with Wayne Barlow, Samuel Adler, and
Warren Benson, Eastman School of Music, M. M.
1970, D. M. A. 1972. He received a composition
award at Aspen, 1968; Hanson Prize, Eastman
School, 1970. He is associate professor, Memphis
State Univ., 1972-   .
WORKS: Orchestra: Adagio for orchestra,
1966; piano concerto, 1970; Canzone, 1971; The
waste land, wind ensemble, 1972; Chamber music:
2 string quartets, 1965, 1966; trio, flute, oboe,
clarinet, 1966; 3 bagatelles, viola and piano;
Passion and resurrection, 3 speakers and 10 players, 1969; Pas de deux, clarinet and bassoon,
1969; 4 pieces for horn quartet, 1969; Romanza,
brass sextet, 1970; trio for violin, trombone,
piano, 1971; Intermezzo, solo horn, 1971; Elegy
for Simonas Kudirka, 6 instruments, 1972; choral
works, songs, piano pieces, and electronic music.
4472 Edenshire Ave., Memphis, TN 38117

FRICKER, PETER RACINE
b. London, England, 5 Sep. 1920; to U.S. 1964.
Studied at the Royal Coll. of Music. After serving in the Royal Air Force, 1940-46, he resumed
composition studies in London with Matyas Seiber.
His awards include the Order of Merit, Federal
Republic of Germany; Freedom of the City of London; honorary doctorate, Leeds Univ.; honorary
membership, Royal Acad. of Music, London. He was
director of music, Morley Coll., London, 1952-64;
at the same time, professor of composition, Royal
Coll. of Music; he joined the faculty, Univ. of
California, Santa Barbara, 1964-   , chairman,
music department, 1970-   .
WORKS: Orchestra: Rondo scherzoso, 1948; 4
symphonies, 1949, 1951, 1960, 1966; Prelude, elegy, and finale, 1949; violin concerto, 1950;
concertante no. 1, English horn and strings, 1950;
concertante no. 2, 3 pianos, strings, timpani,
1951; viola concerto, 1953; piano concerto, 1954;
Dance scene, 1954; Rapsodia concertante (violin
concerto no.2), 1964; Litany, double string orch.,
1955; Comedy overture, 1958; Toccata, piano and
orch., 1959; O longs désirs, 5 songs, soprano and
orch., 1963; 4 songs, soprano and orch., 1965;
Three scenes, 1966; 7 counterpoints, 1967; concertante no. 4, flute, oboe, violin, strings, 1968;
Nocturne, chamber orch., 1971; Introitus, chamber
orch., 1972; Chamber music: wind quintet, 1947;
2 string quartets, 1947, 1953; violin sonata,
1950; Aubade, alto saxophone and piano, 1951;
Pastorale, 3 flutes, 1954; horn sonata, 1955;

(FRICKER, PETER RACINE)
trio, 2 clarinets, bassoon, 1956; suite for recorders, 1956; cello sonata, 1956; octet, winds and strings, 1958; Serenade no.1, 6 instruments, 1959; Serenade no.2, flute, oboe, piano, 1959; 4 dialogues, oboe and piano, 1965; Fantasy, viola and piano, 1966; 5 canons, 2 flutes, 2 oboes, 1966; Refrains, solo oboe, 1968; Serenade no.3, saxophone quartet, 1969; 3 arguments, cello and bassoon, 1969; Sarabande, In memoriam Igor Stravinsky, solo cello, 1971; A bourree for Sir Arthur Bliss, solo cello, 1971; The groves of Dodona, 6 flutes, 1973; Chorus: The vision of judgment, oratorio, 1958; Commissary report, male voices, 1965; Threefold amen, chorus and instruments, 1966; Ave maris stella, male voices and piano, 1967; Magnificat, soprano, alto, tenor, chorus, orch., 1968; 7 little songs, 1972; 4 songs, soprano and piano, Gryphius text, 1965; The day and the spirits, soprano and harp, 1967; Cantilena and cabaletta, solo soprano, 1968; Some superior nonsense, tenor, flute, oboe, cello, harpsichord, 1968; The roofs, coloratura soprano and percussion, 1970; Ich will mein Seele tauchen, baritone and piano, 1970; many works for piano, organ; 2 pieces for carillon, 1969, 1970; Paseo for guitar, 1970; film scores, radio plays and operas, etc.

Department of Music, University of California
Santa Barbara, CA 93106

*FRIEDELL, HAROLD W.
Elegy, violin, harp, organ; Verses for the Nunc dimittis, for organ.

FRIEDMAN, KEN
b. New London, Conn., 19 Sep. 1939. Attended California Western Univ., Shimer Coll., San Francisco State Coll., B. A., M. A.; in 1967 studied theory and composition with Richard Maxfield, collaborated with Maxfield, 1967-68. In addition to avant-garde music his activities have extended to art and poetry. He has presented many one-man art shows and group shows from San Diego to Berkeley on the West Coast, in New York, Boston, Buenos Aires, and throughout Europe. He was founder and director of the Fluxus group, 1966-   ; editor, Fluxus West publications including Fluxus/Underground Press Syndicate, 1966-   ; editor and contributor to other similar publications. In 1967 he taught Literature of Surrealism and the Avant Garde in the English Dept., and Expanded Arts in the Radio-Television-Film Dept., San Francisco State Coll.; was music director, Karen Ahlberg dance group, 1967; artist-in-residence, Unitarian-Universalist Church, Ventura, 1969; faculty, Free Univ. of Berkeley, 1970-   ; general manager, Something Else Press, 1971; guest editor, SOURCE Magazine, 1971-74; chairman, The Expanded Ear, music conference, Bay Area, 1973; has lectured extensively on art, poetry, surrealism. Nicolas Slonimsky (in Baker's Biog. Dict.) calls Friedman's works "verbal exhortations to existentalist actions," and gives cogent examples. Such being the case, it might be more prudent to attend a performance of the O.K. Joe sonata rather than of Skulls like eggshells, 1968.

(FRIEDMAN, KEN)
WORKS: Audio-visual: Two bells or one?, Dog walking swiftly, Let's talk turkey, a Thanksgiving concert for John Cage, 1972; The Imus are out walking logarythms, 1973; In silence it is finished, 1974.
6361 Elmhurst Drive, San Diego, CA 92120

*FRIEDMAN, RICHARD
b. New York, N. Y., 6 Jan. 1944. Was trained in electronics and science. He worked with Morton Subotnick at the Intermedia Electronic Music Studio, New York Univ., 1966-68; since that time has done experimental work in the KPFA radio station in Berkeley, Calif.
WORKS: Electronic: Lumia mix, 1967; Crescent, 1967; To the star messenger, 1968; Alchemical manuscript, 1968; Multimedia: Outside/Inside, uses closed-circuit television, sculptures, light beams, etc.

FRIGON, CHRIS D.
b. Barre, Vt., 26 July 1949. Studied with John Goodman, Hugo Norden, Gardner Read at Boston Univ., B. M., cum laude, 1971. He placed first in the composition contest of the American Accordion Musicological Society, 1972.
WORKS: Chamber music: 3 miniatures for string quartet, 1970; Keyboard: Adagio, piano, 1969; Spectra, piano 4-hands and accessories, 1971; Knozonos, piano 4-hands, 1972; 4 preludes, free bass accordion, 1972; Chorus: Antithesis, chorus, soloists, cello, piano, 1971.
150 Brown St., Waltham, MA 02154

*FRIML, RUDOLF
b. Prague, Czech., 7 Dec. 1879; U.S. citizen 1925; d. Los Angeles, Calif., 12 Nov. 1972. Studied at Prague Cons. and with Anton Dvorak. He toured Europe as accompanist to violinist Jan Kubelik and came to the U.S. with him in 1906. He remained in New York as pianist and composer, playing his own piano concerto with the New York Symphony in 1906. He began composing operettas in 1912, when he replaced Victor Herbert as composer of The firefly. He went to Hollywood in 1934 and composed for films.
WORKS: Operettas: The firefly, 1912; High jinks, 1913; Katinka, 1915; You're in love, 1916; Gloriana, 1918; Tumble in, 1919; Sometime, 1919; Rose Marie, 1924; Vagabond king, 1925; No foolin'; The wild rose; The 3 musketeers; also many songs, piano pieces.

FRINK, GEORGE M. D.
b. Ft. Pierce, Fla., 16 Sep. 1931. Studied with T. W. Dean and David L. Conley, Southwestern Baptist Theological Seminary. He was minister of music, Warner Robbins, Ga., 1967-69; Marion Baptist Church, Marion, S. C., 1969-73.
WORKS: Theatre: Peter, musical drama; Really free, folk-rock musical; and sacred anthems.
P. O. Box 22492, Ft. Worth, TX 76122

*FRISKIN, JAMES
b. Glasgow, Scotland, 3 Mar. 1886; to U.S. 1914; d. New York, N. Y., 16 Mar. 1967. Attended

FRISKIN, JAMES

(FRISKIN, JAMES)
Royal Coll. of Music, London. On coming to the
U.S. he taught at Juilliard Graduate School;
also gave recitals in New York. His compositions include a piano quintet and a violin so-
sonata.

FRISKIN, REBECCA CLARKE. See CLARKE, REBECCA

FROCK, GEORGE
b. Danville, Ill., 16 July 1938. Studied percussion with his father, with Roy Knapp; with
Jack McKenzie at Univ. of Illinois; composition
with John Pozdro. He was on the faculty, Univ.
of Kansas, 1960-63; Memphis State Univ., 1963-66;
Univ. of Texas, Austin, 1966-   .
    WORKS: Percussion: Variations for flute
and percussion; Concertino for marimba and
piano; Fanfare for double trio; 3 Asiatic dances;
Concert etude.
        Department of Music, University of Texas
    Austin, TX 78712

FROHBEITER, ANN W.
b. Evansville, Ind., 27 Sep. 1942. Studied
organ, Indiana Univ., B. M.; Southern Methodist
Univ., M. M.; and choral arranging with Lloyd
Pfautsch. She was organist in Dallas, 1964-66;
Temple Emanuel, Houston, 1967-   ; and associate organist, St. Luke's United Methodist
Church, Houston, 1967   .
    WORKS: Anthem for chorus, trumpet, organ,
on hymn tune Blow ye the trumpet, blow, 1972.
        11127 Sagepark Lane, Houston, TX 77034

FROHMADER, JEROLD C.
b. Seattle, Wash., 3 Dec. 1938. Studied with
George F. McKay, Central Washington State Coll.,
B. A. 1960; with William Billingsley, Univ. of
Idaho, M. M. 1965; with Clifford Taylor and
George Rochberg, Temple Univ., Ph. D. candidate.
He taught in public schools in Washington,
1960-65; assistant professor, Glassboro State
Coll., 1965-   .
    WORKS: Wind ensemble: Symphonia for winds,
33 players; Chamber music: sextet, 1969; Contrasts, saxophone quartet; Zeitgeist for prepared piano; Electronic: Gestures I, brass trio
and tape; Yardbird's skull, for tape; Watergate,
solo performer and tape; Sequence, dancers and
tape.
        Glassboro State College, Glassboro, NJ 08028

FROMM, HERBERT
b. Kitzingen, Germany, 23 Feb. 1905; U.S. citizen 1944. Studied at the Munich Acad. of Music
and with Paul Hindemith at Tanglewood, 1941,
1942. He received the Ernest Bloch award, 1945;
honorary doctorate, Lesley Coll., 1969. He was
organist and music director, Temple Beth Zion,
Buffalo, 1937-41; and at Temple Israel, Boston,
1941-72.
    WORKS: Chamber music: violin sonata; string
quartet; Chorus: 6 Shakespeare songs, a cappella; 8 cantatas for chorus, solo, and orch.,
including Song of Miriam, 1945; Psalm cantata;
chamber cantata; The stranger, 1957; Transience,

(FROMM, HERBERT)
tenor, choir, 7 instruments; Memorial cantata,
Brookline, 23 Mar. 1973; Song cycle: The crim-
son sap, 1954; Keyboard: Let all mortal flesh
keep silent, partita for organ, 1940; Fantasy
for piano; many liturgical works.
        94 Addington Road, Brookline, MA 02146

FRUMKER, LINDA
b. Geneva, Ohio, 11 Dec. 1940. Studied piano
with Arthur Loesser, horn with Martin Morris,
composition with Marcel Dick, Cleveland Inst. of
Music, B. M., M. M. She received the Ernest
Bloch composition award 3 times; cash award at
1962 Aspen Music Festival; and commissions. She
taught at Cleveland Inst. of Music, 1964-67; at
Cleveland Supplementary Education Center,
1967-   .
    WORKS: Orchestra: symphony, 1964; WCLV
anniversary overture, 1973; Chamber music:
Music for friends, string quartet; wind quintet;
Four for Fred, clarinet quartet; 2 string quartets; Songs: 3 songs of love, 1960; Four Aspen
songs, 1962; octet for soprano and 7 instruments,
1962; Like Noah's dove, soprano and ensemble
1972; Angell songs, 1973.
        1661 Cumberland Road
    Cleveland Heights, OH 44118

*FRYSINGER, J. FRANK
b. Hanover, Pa., 7 Apr. 1878; d. York, Pa., 4
Dec. 1954. Studied organ with F. W. Wolff in
Baltimore; with Edgar Stillman Kelley in New
York. He was organist in York, Pa., 1909-11,
1922-53. He wrote some 200 organ works; also
piano pieces and songs.

FRYXELL, REGINA HOLMEN
b. Morganville, Kan., 24 Nov. 1899. Studied at
Augustana Coll., Rock Island, Ill., B. A., M. B.,
1922, Litt. B. 1961; with Wallingford Riegger
and A. Madeley Richardson, Juilliard School,
organ diploma, 1927; in Europe, 1948, 1971-72;
privately with Leo Sowerby; and many summer
courses. She has been church organist, 1922-   ;
private organ and piano teacher, 1922-   ;
taught at various times at Augustana Coll., Juilliard School, Knox Coll., and Black Hawk Coll.
    WORKS: Many published anthems and other
liturgical works; unpublished manuscripts include works for various chamber ensembles and
choral groups.
        1331 42nd Ave., Rock Island, IL 61201

*FUCHS, CHARLES EMILIO
b. Cluj, Hungary, 27 June 1907. Studied with
Zoltan Kodaly in Budapest. He taught in Vienna,
Paris, and Berlin; wrote a film score in Berlin,
another in Buenos Aires. Among his other works
are 4 symphonies; 3 rhapsodies; piano trios;
trio for clarinet, viola, harp; etc.

FUCHS, LILLIAN
b. New York, N. Y., 18 Nov. Studied violin
with Louis Svecenski and Franz Kneisel and
composition with Percy Goetschius, Inst. of
Musical Art, New York. On graduation she received the Morris Loeb Memorial Prize and the

(FUCHS, LILLIAN)
Silver Medal. She is a faculty member, Manhattan School of Music and has taught at Juilliard School and at Aspen, Colo. She is concert violist, chamber player, and has performed in recitals with her brother, Joseph Fuchs, in the U.S. and abroad.
WORKS: Chamber music: 15 characteristic studies, viola solo; 16 fantasie etudes, viola solo; Sonata pastorale, viola solo; Jota, violin and piano; 2 pieces in olden style, violin and piano; arrangements from Paganini and Mozart.
186 Pinehurst Ave., New York, NY 10033

FUCHS, PETER PAUL
b. Vienna, Austria, 30 Oct. 1916; U.S. citizen 1943. Studied conducting with Felix Weingartner and Josef Krips at the Vienna State Acad.; composition privately with Karl Weigl and Eugene Zador, piano with Leonie Gombrich and Robert Goldsand. He received a Ford Found. grant for study of contemporary opera production, 1954-55; honorary doctorate, Combs Coll., 1959. He was on the music staff, Metropolitan Opera, 1940-50; San Francisco, 1946, 1950, 1954; Cincinnati Opera; Berkshire Music Center; head of opera and symphony, Louisiana State Univ., 1950-   ; music director, Baton Rouge Symphony, 1960-   ; Beaumont (Tex.) Civic Opera, 1962-   .
WORKS: Opera: Serenade at noon, Baton Rouge, 1965; Orchestra: violin concertino; Chamber music: 3 string quartets; piano sonata; wind quintet; songs.
6776 Menlo Dr., Baton Rouge, LA 70808

FUERSTNER, CARL
b. Strasbourg, France, 16 June 1912; U.S. citizen 1945. Studied with Walter Braunfels, Philipp Jarnach, Ernst Gernot Klussmann, Hochschule für Musik, Cologne, Germany. He was director, opera department, Eastman School of Music, 1945-50; resident pianist, 1957-61; head of composition department, Brigham Young Univ., 1955-61; principal coach and conductor, Opera Theater, Indiana Univ., 1961-   .
WORKS: Orchestra: Symphorama; cello concerto; quintuple concerto, 5 instruments and strings; Band: Overture; Allegro ritmico; Metamorphoses on a chorale, brass choir; Chamber music: Allegro for 4 violins; Divertimento, string quartet; violin sonata; piano sonata; clarinet sonata; bass clarinet or cello sonata; The rat and the dinosaur, trumpet and tuba; Nocturne and dance, flute and piano; Little dance suite, piano; Configurations, saxophone and piano; Chorus: Hymn for a cappella choir; many songs.
2518 East 7th St., Bloomington, IN 47401

*FULEIHAN, ANIS
b. Kyrenia, Cyprus, 2 Apr. 1900; to U.S. 1915; d. Stanford, Calif., 11 Oct. 1970. Studied piano with Alberto Jonas in New York. He held a Guggenheim fellowship, 1939; Fulbright research fellowship, 1952. He toured the U.S. and the Near East, 1919-25; lived in Cairo to 1928; on staff, G. Schirmer, Inc., 1932-39; professor,

(FULEIHAN, ANIS)
Indiana Univ., 1947-52; director, Beirut Cons., 1953-60; went to Tunis for U.S. State Department, 1962-63.
WORKS: Opera: Vasco, 1960; Orchestra: Mediterranean suite, 1922; Preface to a child's storybook, 1932; 2 symphonies, 1936, 1966; piano concerto with string orch., 1937; 2 piano concertos, 1938, 1963; Fantasy, viola and orch., 1938; 2 violin concertos, 1938, 1965; Symphony concertante, string quartet and orch., 1939; concerto for 2 pianos, 1940; Epithalamium, piano and strings, 1940; Invocation to Isis, 1940; Theremin concerto, 1945; 3 Cyprus serenades, 1946; Rhapsody, cello and strings, 1946; The pyramids of Giza, 1952; Duo concertante, violin, viola and orch., 1958; Toccata, piano and orch., 1960; Islands suite, 1961; cello concerto, 1963; viola concerto, 1963; Chamber music: 5 string quartets; horn quintet; clarinet quintet; 11 piano sonatas; violin sonata; cello sonata; viola sonata; and choral pieces, songs.

FULKERSON, JAMES
b. Streator, Ill., 2 July 1945. Studied with Will Ogdon and Abram Plum, Illinois Wesleyan Univ.; with Ben Johnston, Salvatore Martirano, Kenneth Gaburo, Lejaren Hiller and Herbert Brün, Univ. of Illinois. He held a fellowship, Center for Creative and Performing Arts, Buffalo, 1969-72; composition grant for residence in Berlin, 1973-74; commissions, Brooklyn Acad. of Music; RIAS Radio, Berlin. He was on the staff, Center for New Music, Buffalo, 1969-72; free lance composer and trombonist, New York, 1972-73.
WORKS: Orchestra: Globs, 1968; Something about mobiles, 1969; Planes, pts., 1969; Behind closed doors, 1971; Patterns X, 1972; guitar concerto, 1972; trombone concerto, 1973; Chamber music: 2 woodwind quintets, 1965, 1966; Quartet for dancers, bassoon, piano, violin, trombone, 1967; string quartet, 1968; Patterns III, solo tuba, 1969; Chord, any instruments or voices, 1972; Coordinative systems, no. 2, string quartet, 1972, no. 4, chamber ensemble, 1973, no. 5. 4 contrabasses, 1973; Mixed media: 6 studies for light, sounds, and dancers, 1967; Now II, sound modulators, amplified clavichord, trombone, trumpet, 1969; Mobiles and loops, 4 percussion and tape, 1969; Empty whiskers, voice and tape, 1972; What is performance, solo trombone, tape, slides, films, 1973; many other works for various small ensembles and multi media.
Dartington College of Arts
Totnes, Devonshire, England

*FULLER, DONALD SANBORN
b. Washington, D.C., 1 July 1919. Attended Yale Univ.; studied composition with Aaron Copland, Darius Milhaud, Bernard Wagenaar.
WORKS: Orchestra: symphony; Chamber music: trio for clarinet, cello, piano; sonatina, oboe, clarinet, piano; sonata for 2 pianos; piano sonatina; other piano pieces, songs.

FULLER, JEANNE WEAVER

FULLER, JEANNE WEAVER
b. Regina, Sask., Canada, 23 Oct. 1917; to U.S.
1923. Studied at Pomona Coll., B. A. 1937; California State Univ., M. A. 1964; with Halsey
Stevens, Univ. of Southern California. She has
been part-time instructor, El Camino Coll.,
1965-   ; and also a private teacher.
WORKS: Chamber music: Fugue for woodwinds;
Chorus: Three motets; Exsultate justi; Maggy
and milly and molly and may, women's voices;
Now (more near ourselves then we); The praise of
Christmas; Songs: At the window, Sandburg text,
When young hearts break, Heine text; Piano:
Dorian rondo; sonata; Jeux aux douze tons, piano
4-hands.
7025 Hedgewood Drive
Rancho Palos Verdes, CA 90274

FULLER, RAMON C.
b. Murray, Utah, 27 July 1930. Studied with
Leon Dallin and Carl Fuerstner, Brigham Young
Univ.; with Kenneth Gaburo, Ben Johnston,
Lejaren Hiller, Univ. of Illinois. He was instructor, Univ. of Maryland, 1963; creative associate, Center for Performing Arts, Buffalo,
1965-67; assistant professor, State Univ. of New
York at Buffalo, 1967-   .
WORKS: Wind ensemble: 2 pieces for 9 brasses, 1969; Chamber music: 3 short pieces for
piano, 1971; string quartet, Buffalo, 22 May
1973; Electronic: Music for 2-channel tape and
2 percussionists, 1964; 3 improvisations for
tape, 1972.
327 Windermere Blvd.
Eggertsville, NY 14226

FUNK, ERIC
b. Deer Lodge, Mont., 28 Sep. 1949. Studied with
Tomas Svoboda, Sandor Veress, Portland State Univ.,
B. A.; with Krzysztof Penderecki at Yale Univ.;
Univ. of Oregon, doctoral candidate, 1973, under
a Ruth Lorraine Close fellowship.
WORKS: Orchestra: Trimorphism, orch.,
piano, string quartet, 1972; 2 preludes for orch.
and percussion, 1972; The prophet, 1973; Chamber
music: Meditations, string quartet and guitar;
Triste, string quartet; Images, chamber orch.;
Nocturne for piano, 1972; Chorus: 2 movements
for choir, percussion, and piano, 1972; Abyss, 1972.
Rt. 1, Box 544, Beaverton, OR 97005

FURMAN, JAMES
b. Louisville, Ky., 23 Jan. 1937. Studied with
George Perle, Claude Almand, Moritz Bomhard,
Univ. of Louisville, B. M. E. 1958, M. M. 1965;
with Arthur Berger, Irving Fine, Harold Shapero,
Brandeis Univ., 1962-64. He received the
Omicron Delta Kappa award, 1958; Louisville Philharmonic Society's Young Artists' award, 1953;
Brandeis Univ. fellowship, 1962-64; first place,
Brookline Library composition contest, 1964;
Awards of Merit, Nat. Fed. of Music Clubs,
1965-66, 1967. He was choral director for the
BBC documentary film on the life of Charles Ives;
recording director for avant garde music, Desto
Records; musical director, arranger-pianist of
world-touring army show, Rolling along of 1961;

(FURMAN, JAMES)
voice and piano recitalist, New York Town Hall
debut, May 1967; assistant professor, Western
Connecticut State Coll., 1965-   .
WORKS: Chamber music: Variants, violin,
cello, prepared piano, 1964; Chorus: I have a
dream, symphonic oratorio; Ave Maria, motet;
Four little foxes, choral cycle; Let us break
bread together, spiritual; Salve Regina, motet;
The quiet life, chorus, 4 soloists, a cappella;
Go tell it on the mountain, chorus soloists,
brass, percussion, piano, electric bass; Some
glorious day, with piano or organ; This train;
The threefold birth, chorus, boys' voices,
organ.
512 South 22nd St., Louisville, KY 40201

FUSSELL, CHARLES C.
b. Winston-Salem, N. C., 14 Feb. 1938. Studied
with Bernard Rogers, Eastman School of Music,
B. M. 1960, M. M. 1964, conducting certificate
1962. He received Fulbright grant, 1962-63;
Ford Found. grant, 1964-65; and commissions.
He taught at North Carolina Governor's School,
summers, 1964-66, Smith Coll., 1970; assistant
professor, Univ. of Massachusetts, 1966-   .
WORKS: Theatre: Julian, drama in 5 scenes
after Flaubert, for soli, chorus, orch.; Orchestra: symphony in one movement; symphony no. 2,
soprano and orch.; Chamber music: Poems for
chamber orch. and voices, after Hart Crane;
Voyages, soprano and tenor soli, women's choir,
oboe or clarinet.
Music Department
University of Massachusetts
Amherst, MA 01002

GABER, HARLEY
b. Chicago, Ill., 5 June 1943. Studied with
Darius Milhaud at Aspen, 1961; with Kenneth
Gaburo and Lejaren Hiller, Univ. of Illinois,
1961-63; in Rome, 1963-64; and with William
Sydeman, Mannes Coll. of Music, 1964-67. He
received BMI student awards, 1965, 1968; was
creative associate, Center for Creative and Performing Arts, Buffalo, 1967; held fellowship,
Bennington Conference, 1968. He has been general manager, Composers' Forum, New York,
1972-   ; music director, Hudson Valley New
Music Ensemble, 1972-   .
WORKS: Chamber music: 5 pieces for piano,
Aspen, 1961; quartet for violin, oboe, clarinet,
trumpet, 1961; 4 pieces for string quartet,
1961; Fantasy, solo flute, 1962; Scambio, flute,
piano, 1963; Omaggio a Feldman, 1965; string
quartet, 1966; Ludus primus, 2 flutes vibraphone, 1966; Chimyaku, solo alto flute, 1968;
Kata, solo violin, 1969; Koku, solo flute,
1970; Three ideas for a film, piano, string
orch., 1970; Narrow road to the deep north,
graphic music for percussion, 1971; October
piece, piano, vibraphone, gongs, 1972; Sovereign
of the centre, 4 violins, 1972; so-shi-sai-rai-
i, tenor recorder, pre-recorded gong, 1972;
Michi, solo violin, 1972; Voice: Voce I, female
voice, harp, 1964; Voce II, female voice, alto
flute, percussion, 1965; Voce III, 2 female
voices, flute, viola, percussion.
853 7th Ave. New York, NY 10019

GABURO, KENNETH
b. Somerville, N. J., 5 July 1926. Studied with Bernard Rogers, Eastman School of Music, B. M., M. M.; Goffreda Petrassi, Cons. de Santa Cecilia, Rome; with Burrill Phillips, Univ. of Illinois, D. M. A. He received awards from Eastman Alumni Assoc., 1954; Sigma Alpha Iota, 1954; George Gershwin Memorial, 1954; Fulbright grant, 1954; Sagalyn Orch. award, 1956; Yaddo fellowship, 1960; UNESCO, 1962; Univ. of Illinois, 1967; Guggenheim grant, 1967; Thorne Found. 1968; Univ. of California grants, 1968, 1970; Kunstler program, 1971; and many commissions. He was a faculty member, Kent State Univ., 1949-50; McNeese State Coll., 1950-54; Univ. of Illinois, 1955-68; professor, Univ. of California, San Diego, 1968- .
WORKS: Theatre: The snow queen, 3-act opera, 1952; Music for tiger rag, musical play, 1956; Bodies, an opera for actors, text by composer, 1957; Trilogy of 1-act operas, The widow, The hermit, The dog-king, librettos by composer, 1959; The hydrogen jukebox, electronic score, 1963; Lingua I-IV, a massive 6-hour theatre composed between 1965-70, and consisting, Gaburo says, "of diverse explorations of the acoustical, physiological, and structural properties of language in a musical context;" other linguistic theatre pieces; Orchestra: 3 interludes for string orch., 1949; piano concertante, 1949; On a quiet theme, 1950; Elegy, 1954; Antiphony I, 3 string groups tape, 1957; viola concerto, 1959; Shapes and sounds, 1960; Chamber music: 4 Inventions, clarinet and piano, 1954; Music for 5 instruments, piano and winds, 1954; Ideas and transformations, no. 1-3, string duos, 1954; string quartet, 1 movement, 1956; Line studies, flute, clarinet, viola, trombone, 1957; Antiphony IV (Poised), piccolo, trombone, double bass, electronics, 1966; Inside, quartet for 1 double bass player, 1969; Mouthpiece, sextet for solo trumpet player, slides, 1970; Antiphony VI, (Cogito), string quartet, slides, tape, 1971; Chorus: Snow and the willow, 1949; Alas!, cycle for children's voices, 1949; 3 dedications to Lorca, Arid land, Surprise, The cry, 1953; 4 Latin motets, 1957; Antiphony II, chorus with electronic sounds, 1962; Antiphony III (Pearl White moments), 16 soloists, electronic sounds, 1962; Psalm, 1965; Never₁ and Never₂, male voices, 1966; Circumcision, 3 groups of male voices, 1966; Carissima, women's voices, 1968; December 8, male voices; Songs: The night is still, 1950; Stray birds, cycle for high voice, 1959; Two, mezzo-soprano, alto flute, double bass, 1962; Electronic: The wasting of Lucrecetzia, 1964; Fat Millie's lament, 1964; Lemon drops, 1965; For Harry, 1965; The flow of (i), 1965; Piano: Two shorts and a long, 1949; Antiphony V, solo piano, tape, slides, 1971.
Department of Music
University of California at San Diego
La Jolla, CA 92038

*GADBOIS, CHARLES E.
b. 1905. People's mass.

GAIDELIS, JULIUS
b. Lithuania, 5 Apr. 1909; U.S. citizen, 1956. Studied at Lithuania State Cons.; with Francis Judd Cooke, Carl McKinley, New England Cons., M. M. He has been a private music teacher, 1951- ; conductor, Boston Lithuanian Mixed Choir and Lithuanian Male Choir, 1952- ; organist and choirmaster, St. Casimir Church, Brockton, 1969- .
WORKS: Opera: Dana; Orchestra: 6 symphonies; Chamber music: 2 violin sonatas; quintet; string quartets; etc.; Chorus: Freedom fighters, cantata.
31 Sunflower Road, Holbrook, MA 02343

*GALAJIKIAN, FLORENCE GRANDLAND
b. Maywood, Ill., 29 July 1900. Studied with Albert Noelte, Northwestern School of Music, B. M. 1918; at Chicago Musical Coll.; and with Rubin Goldmark. She received an NBC Orchestra award and performance of her Symphonic intermezzo, 1932. Her other works include Tragic overture, 1936; Transitions, ballet suite, 1937; choral works; songs.
217 North 3rd Ave., Maywood, IL 60153

GALLAGHER, CHRISTOPHER S.
b. Ashland, Ky., 10 June 1940. Studied with Bernhard Heiden and Juan Orrego-Salas, Indiana Univ., M. M. He was assistant professor, Frostburg State Coll., 1966-70; assistant professor and theory chairman, Morehead State Univ., 1970- .
WORKS: Orchestra: Variations, 1973; Chamber music: Impressions of summer, alto saxophone and piano; 4 pieces for clarinet and cello, 1971; trio for flute, cello, piano; Music for brass, quartet; Music for cello, 1972; quartet for saxophones, 1973; 3 fragments, contralto, flute, 3 clarinets, 1973.
Hill 'n' Dale Estates, Morehead, KY 40351

GALLAGHER, JACK
b. Forest Hills, N. Y., 27 June 1947. Studied with Elie Siegmeister, Hofstra Univ., B. A. cum laude 1969; with Robert Palmer and Burrill Phillips, Cornell Univ.
WORKS: Chamber music: Theme and variations, woodwind quintet, 1971; piano sonata, 1973; Theme and variations, cello and piano, 1973.
Music Department, Cornell University
Ithaca, NY 14850

*GALLA-RINI, ANTHONY
b. Manchester, Conn., 18 Jan. 1904. Studied with his father, a bandmaster, and learned to play accordion, cornet, mandolin, piano, oboe, horn, contrabassoon, euphonium, sarrusaphone, and several other instruments. He invented several mechanical improvements for the accordion. His compositions include an accordion concerto which he played with the Oklahoma City Orchestra, 15 Nov. 1941.

GALLOWAY, MICHAEL
b. Memphis, Tenn., 16 July 1946. Studied with Jane Soderstrom, Southwestern at Memphis, B. M. 1968; and with Marshall Barnes, Ohio State Univ.,

GALLOWAY, MICHAEL

(GALLOWAY, MICHAEL)
M. M. 1970. He won the Ohio concerto competition, 1969, and the Centennial composition contest, 1970; received a Garrigues Found. scholarship at Southwestern. He has been instructor and head of piano department, Mississippi Valley State Coll., 1971- .
WORKS: Ballet: Cassandra; Chorus: Missa brevis; The descent of the dove; Songs: Love is a deep and a dark and a lonely; numerous songs and song cycles, piano works, and chamber works, and pop songs.
4096 Barron Ave., Memphis, TN 38111

GAMBINO, JAMES JOHN
b. Summit, N. J., 15 June 1919. Attended Ithaca Coll., B. S.; Univ. of Texas, Austin, M. M. He is founder and director of the Permian Basin Chamber Music Society.
WORKS: Orchestra: Movie theme; Chorus: Jubilate Deo; Surely the Lord is in this place; Word seven; This moment is my life; Time for prayer.
1210 West Missouri, Midland, TX 79701

*GAMER, CARLTON
Ragas for piano.
Colorado College
Colorado Springs, CO 80903

GANGWARE, EDGAR B. JR.
b. Sandusky, Ohio, 17 May 1921. Studied with Helen Grace Williams, Wittenberg Univ.; with Anthony Donato, Northwestern Univ., D. M. 1952. He won honorable mention in a Thor Johnson Brass Choir contest, 1949. He was instructor, Boston Univ., 1949-50; professor, Bemidji State Coll., 1952-66; professor, Northeastern Illinois Univ., 1966- .
WORKS: Orchestra: piano concerto; Wind ensemble: Concerto miniature for timpani and brass choir; brass quintet; Prelude and allegro for brass choir; Chamber music: string quartet.
1225 Candlewood Hill Road
Northbrook, IL 60062

GANICK, PETER
b. Boston, Mass., 14 Dec. 1946. Studied with Jacob Druckman, Bard Coll.; Gardner Read, Boston Univ.; Martin Boykan, Seymour Shifrin, Brandeis Univ.; privately with John Huggler.
WORKS: Chamber music: Octet, 4 clarinets and string quartet, 1971; Cavafy sonata, 1971; piano trio no. 2, 1968; Islands, for Maharishi Mahesh Yogi, 2 pianos; string quartet, 1973.
331 Harvard St., Cambridge, MA 02139

*GANZ, RUDOLPH
b. Zurich, Switz., 24 Feb. 1877; to U.S. 1900; d. Chicago, Ill., 2 Aug. 1972. Studied composition with Charles Blanchet in Lausanne and with Heinrich Urban in Berlin. His many honors included honorary doctorates from De Paul Univ., Cincinnati Cons., Grinnell Coll., Univ. of Rochester; Northwestern Univ. centennial award; appointment as officer, French Legion of Honor. He made his debut as pianist with the Berlin Philharmonic Orchestra in 1899; was head, piano department, Chicago Musical Coll., 1900-05;

(GANZ, RUDOLPH)
toured U.S., Europe, as concert pianist, 1912-21; conductor, St. Louis Symphony, 1921-27; Young People's Concerts of New York Philharmonic and San Francisco Orchestra, 1938-49; director, Chicago Musical Coll., 1929-54.
WORKS: Orchestra: Symphony in E, Berlin, 1900; Animal pictures, suite; Konzertstück, piano and orch.; piano concerto; Piano: Variations on a theme by Brahms; choral works; some 200 songs. He was author of Rudolph Ganz evaluates modern piano music, New York, 1968.

GARDNER, MILDRED ALVINE
b. Quincy, Ill., 12 Oct. 1899. Studied with Edgar Stillman Kelley, Cincinnati Cons., graduating with honors in piano and composition; with Marion Bauer in New York, piano with Sigismund Stojowski. She received a 2-year graduate fellowship at Cincinnati Cons.; 4 Yaddo fellowships; 2 Penn. Fed. of Music Clubs awards; Nat. Fed of Music Clubs award. She was artist accompanist and coach, Cincinnati and New York, 1920-33; taught in Pittsburgh privately, 1935-39, at Fillion Studios, 1940-68; on faculty, Carlow Coll., 1969- ; organized and conducted composers' forums, 1939-42.
WORKS: Chamber music: sonata for 2 pianos; string quartet; woodwind quartet; Songs: September separation, song cycle; The daisies; Madonna. Her compositions were performed frequently in New York and Pittsburgh.
223 Underwood Ave., Greensburg, PA 15601

*GARDNER, SAMUEL
b. Elizabethgrad, Russia, 25 Aug. 1891; to U.S. as a child. Studied violin with Felix Winternitz and Franz Kneisel; composition with Percy Goetschius at Juilliard School; with Charles Loeffler in Boston. His awards include a Pulitzer scholarship, 1918; Loeb prize; and an honorary D. M., New York Coll. of Music. He was a member of the Kneisel String Quartet, 1914-15; Chicago Symphony, 1915-16; Elshuco Trio, 1916-17; faculty, Juilliard School.
WORKS: Orchestra: Country moods, string orch.; Broadway, tone poem; violin concerto; New Russia, tone poem; Chamber music: Hebraic fantasia for clarinet quintet; piano quintet, 1925; string quartet; Prelude and fugue, string quartet; Essays, solo violin; From the canebrake, violin and piano; Jazzetto, violin and piano; From the Rockies, violin and piano. He was author of School of violin study based on harmonic thinking; and Violin method, 2 vol.

GARFIELD, BERNARD H.
b. Brooklyn, N. Y., 27 May 1924. Studied with Otto Luening and Henry Cowell, Columbia Univ.; with Marion Bauer, New York Univ.; privately with Hugo Kauder. He was director, New York Woodwind Quintet, 1946-57; oboe and bassoon teacher, Yale School of Music, 1956-57; solo bassoonist, Philadelphia Orchestra, 1957- ; faculty, Temple Univ., 1957- .
WORKS: Orchestra: Concert overture; Chamber music: quartet for bassoon, violin, viola,

(GARFIELD, BERNARD H.)
cello; piano sonata; Soliloquy, bassoon and
piano; 2 pieces for bassoon and piano; 6 songs
for soprano and piano.
871 Wayside Lane, Haddonfield, NJ 08033

GARLICK, ANTONY
b. Sheffield, Yorks., England, 9 Dec. 1927; U.S.
citizen 1969. Studied at Royal Coll. of Music,
London, 1947-49; Acad. Musicale Chigiana, Siena,
Italy, diploma, 1952; Cons. di St. Cecilia, Rome,
M. M. 1954; Univ. of Toronto, M. M. 1958; studied organ with William Harris and Fernando
Germani. He held positions as assistant organist 1941-64; joined faculty Wayne State Coll.,
1960; associate professor, 1964-   .
WORKS: Orchestra: Canto, symphonic poem;
Band: Canticle; Festival overture; Sinfonietta
for brass choir; Chamber music: Sonata da
chiesa, oboe and organ; violin sonata; clarinet
sonata; 2 string quartets; woodwind quartet;
Rhapsody for alto saxophone and piano; 5 study
patterns for alto saxophone and piano; duo for
flute and viola; 4 episodes, brass quintet;
Essay and Suite, brass quartet; Colloquy, bass
clarinet and piano; Piece for eight, clarinets;
2 trios for 3 clarinets; Concert piece, clarinet
and piano; choral works and organ pieces.
602 Main St., Wayne, NB 68787

*GARNER, ERROLL
b. Pittsburgh, Pa., 15 June 1921. Is entirely
self-taught on piano, drums and bass. He was
the first jazz artist to be presented by Sol
Hurok; has made many concert tours in the U.S.
and Europe.
WORKS: Film scores: A new kind of love;
many popular songs including Misty and Play,
play, play.

GARRIGUENC, PIERRE
b. Narbonne, France, 20 Aug. 1921; U.S. citizen
1955. Studied theory and violin with his father
and began composing at age 13, later attended
the conservatory and studied composition privately. Since coming to the U.S. in 1948 he has
studied with Karel Husa, Warren Benson, and
Samuel Adler. From 1948 to 1962 he was staff
composer at various times for Columbia, American, and National Broadcasting Companies.
WORKS: Orchestra: Partita, 6 movements;
Reflections for brass ensemble, piano, celesta,
percussion; II Genesis, for 2 narrators, brass,
percussion, strings; Wind ensemble: Synthesis
for 13 winds; Chorus: Dreamland, narrator, chorus, and orch.; 3 poems; Piano: Preludio e toccata; 3 pieces for piano; Polychromes I, vol 1
and 2, no. 1-43; Polychoromes II, vol. 3 and 4,
no. 44-84.
P. O. Box 8, Wolcott, NY 14590

GARRIGUENC, RENE
b. Vesoul, France, 18 Oct. 1908; U.S. citizen
1966. Studied composition with Charles Koechlin,
orchestration with Roger Desormiere in Paris.
He came to the U.S. in 1941, and was staff composer for the Columbia Broadcasting Company,
Hollywood, 1943-65.

(GARRIGUENC, RENE)
WORKS: Orchestra: violin concerto; Preambule and scherzo; 5 pieces for orch.; Prelude
and fugue; Chamber music: violin sonata; 7
piano pieces; 2 pieces for string quartet; art
songs; Television scores: Twilight zone; Perry
Mason; Gunsmoke; etc. He is also author of a
textbook, Serial procedures and fundamentals,
1974.
3324 North Knoll Drive, Hollywood, CA 90068

GARTLER, ROBERT
b. Los Angeles, Calif., 15 Feb. 1933. Studied
with Klaus Pringsheim in California and in
Tokyo; piano with Egon Petri. He was conductor
of the Renaissance Octet, 1964-68.
WORKS: Opera: The outcasts of Poker Flat
in progress; Songs: Two statements from Jones
Bar outpost; The boy waits, cycle for baritone,
English horn, piano.
Box 1267, Berkeley, CA 94701

GARWOOD, MARGARET
b. New Jersey, 22 Mar. 1927. Studied composition with Miriam Gideon, orchestration with
Romeo Cascarino. She received a Whiteside Found.
grant, 1965-68; Nat. Endowment for the Arts
grant, 1973. She taught piano at Philadelphia
Musical Acad., 1953-69; Settlement Music School,
1960-69; was pianist and composer, Young Audiences, Inc., 1965-70.
WORKS: Opera: The Trojan women, 1-act,
Philadelphia, 22 Oct. 1967; The nightingale and
the rose, 1-act, Philadelphia, 21 Oct. 1973;
Ballet: Aesop's fables; Song cycles: The
cliff's edge, soprano; Spring songs, soprano;
Love songs, soprano.
R. D. 1, East Greenville, PA 18041

*GARZA, EDWARD
The blue angel, 1-act opera, Univ. of Arizona,
Tucson, 13 Apr. 1973.

*GASSMANN, REMI
b. 1908. Music to the ballet, electronic,
1961.

*GATES, CRAWFORD
b. San Francisco, Calif., 29 Dec. 1921. Studied at Coll. of the Pacific; Columbia Univ.;
San Jose State Coll., B. A.; with Leroy
Robertson, Brigham Young Univ., M. A.; with
Howard Hanson and Bernard Rogers, Univ. of Rochester, Ph. D.; privately with Ernst Toch. He
conducted choral and orchestral groups, 1941-64;
was on faculty Brigham Univ., 1948, chairman,
music department, 1960-71; professor, Beloit
Coll., 1972-   .
WORKS: Theatre: Promised valley, musical
play; Sand in their shoes, musical play; Orchestra: piano concerto; Chorus: Hora breve; The
new Zion.
Beloit College, Beloit, WI 53511

*GATES, EVERETT
Quartet for saxophones.
Eastman School of Music
Rochester, NY 14604

GATES, GEORGE

GATES, GEORGE
b. Kankakee, Ill., 21 May 1920. Was with the Dallas Symphony Orchestra 5 years; taught in public schools 16 years; was percussion instructor, Southern Methodist Univ. 3 years.
WORKS: Band: Sol y sombra, concert march; Mosaico de Mexico, 3 movement suite; 2 Russian songs; 2 Mexican songs of Chiapas; La contessa, concert march.
5553 Harvest Hill Road, #1127
Dallas, Tx 75221

GATES, KEITH
b. Lake Charles, La., 29 Sep. 1949. Studied with Louis Mennini, North Carolina School of the Arts, 1966-69; with Roman Vlad, Italy, summer 1967; with Hugo Weisgall, Juilliard School, 1969-71. His chamber opera received honorable mention, BMI student competition, 1968.
WORKS: Opera: Migle and the bugs, chamber opera, 1967; Orchestra: violin concerto, 1968; Chamber music: piano sonata, 1967; string quartet, 1968.
916 Audubon, Lake Charles, LA 70601

GATLIN, HELEN STANLEY, see: STANLEY, HELEN

GAUGER, THOMAS
b. Wheaton, Ill., 20 Dec. 1935. Studied with Kenneth Gaburo, Univ. of Illinois; percussion with Paul Price and Jack McKenzie. He was principal percussionist, Oklahoma City Symphony, 1959-62; percussionist, Boston Symphony Orch., 1963-   .
WORKS: Percussion: Gainsborough, quintet; solos and duets for drums and mallet instruments.
23 Auburn St., Brookline, MA 02146

*GAUL, HARVEY BARTLETT
b. New York, N. Y., 11 Apr. 1881; d. Pittsburgh, Pa., 1 Dec. 1945. Studied with George Le Jeune and Dudley Buck in New York; with Alfred Gaul and Philip Armes in London; at Schola Cantorum and with Vincent d'Indy in Paris. His awards included an honorary D. M., Univ. of Pittsburgh; Chicago Madrigal Club prize; Tuesday Music Club prize; Mendelssohn Club prize; honorary membership, Pennsylvania Fed. of Music Clubs, which established the Harvey Gaul scholarship. He held various conducting and academic posts in Pittsburgh; was music critic, Pittsburgh Post-Gazette.
WORKS: Operettas: Pinnochio; Storybook; Alice in Wonderland; Chamber music: Thanksgiving, organ, strings, timpani; Chorus: A spring ditty; Water lilies; For the numberless unknown heroes; Thou art the night wind; The carol of the White Russian children; Johnny Appleseed; I hear America singing; many songs.

GAUDLIN, ROBERT
b. Vernon, Tex., 30 Oct. 1931. Studied with Violet Archer at North Texas State Univ.; with Bernard Rogers and Alan Hovhaness at Eastman School of Music, Ph. D. 1959. He received first prize in the BMI awards, 1952; Benjamin Award, 1956; first prize, Berkshire string quartet award, 1964. He was theory chairman, William

(GAUDLIN, ROBERT)
Carey Coll., 1958-63; assistant to associate professor, Eastman School of Music, 1963-70, chairman of theory department, 1970-   .
WORKS: Orchestra: Scenes from Hamlet, 1968; Chamber music: wind quintet, 1952; Diverse dances, 1956; Partita for string quartet, 1964; Collage for 6 instruments, Cambridge, 8 May 1973; Chorus: Sanctus, 1971.
379 Wellington Ave., Rochester, NY 14619

GEBUHR, ANN K.
b. Des Moines, Iowa, 7 May 1945. Attended Indiana Univ., M. M. 1969. She received a commission for the South Dakota Music Teachers Assoc., 1973. She was teaching associate, Indiana Univ., 1967-69; assistant professor, Northern State Coll., 1969-   .
WORKS: Chorus: Advent carol, women's voices; Te Deum, chorus, soloists, brass, tympani; Bidding prayer, with organ; SAI symphony, women's voices and instrumental trio; Songs: 2 sacred songs for soprano; Psalm 103, soprano; Cycle of duets for soprano and piano on Tennyson poems, 1973.
1305 South 3rd, Aberdeen, SD 57401

GEHRENBECK, DAVID MAULSBY
b. St. Paul, Minn., 30 June 1931. Studied at Macalester Coll., B. A. 1953; with Searle Wright and Seth Bingham, Union Theological Seminary, New York, S.M.M. 1957, S.M.D. 1971. He held church positions 1957-71, director of music Broadway Presbyterian Church, New York, 1966-71; was on faculty, Union Theological Seminary, 1965-71; assistant professor, Illinois Wesleyan Univ., 1971-   .
WORKS: Organ: Prelude on Venite adoremus, 1962.
1405 Maplewood Drive, Normal, IL 61761

GEHRING, PHILIP
b. Carlisle, Pa., 27 Nov. 1925. Studied with Herbert Elwell, Oberlin Cons.; with Ernst Bacon, Syracuse Univ.; organ with Andre Marchal in Paris. He won second prize, 1966, first prize, 1970, American Guild of Organists national improvisation contest. He was organist in Kannapolis, N. C., 1950-52; faculty member, Davidson Coll., N. C., 1952-58; Valparaiso Univ., 1958-   .
WORKS: Chorus: Shenandoah, male voices, 1960; Draw nigh and take the body of the Lord, mixed chorus, 1966; Art thou weary, unison, 1970; Organ: 6 hymn-tune preludes, 1966; 4 pieces for the church, 1969; 2 folk-hymn preludes, 1972, etc.
M.R. 35, Box 283, Valparaiso, IN 46383

GEISSLER, FREDRICK DIETZMANN
b. Bethesda, Md., 7 Mar. 1946. Studied with Walter B. Ross, M. Donald MacInnis, David H. Davis, Univ. of Virginia; with Robert M. Palmer, Karel Husa, Burrill Phillips, Cornell Univ. He received the Arnold Salop award, Southeastern Composers' League, 1967. He was teaching assistant, Cornell Univ., 1971-72, also assistant band director, 1972-74.

(GEISSLER, FREDRICK DIETZMANN)
WORKS: Orchestra: Concerto for woodwind quintet and orch.; Band: Variations on a modern American trumpet tune, trumpet solo and band; Chamber music: concertino for piano and 10 solo instruments; triple brass trio; Christmas Eve sketch, flute, clarinet, bassoon, and tape, 1967.
154 Indian Creek Road, Ithaca, NY 14850

GELLER, IAN
b. Chicago, Ill., 18 Mar. 1943. Studied with Karel B. Jirak, Robert Lombardo, Ramon Zupko, Roosevelt Univ.; with Stella Roberts, American Cons.; Stanley Wolfe and Vincent Persichetti, Juilliard School. He received a grant from the Illinois Arts Council to compose a ballet, 1973; scholarship in voice at Juilliard, 1966. He was music director, Temple Israel, Long Beach, Calif., 1971-72; conductor, American Jewish Choral Society, Los Angeles, 1971-72; cantor, Am Shalom, Chicago, 1972- ; assistant professor, Northeastern Illinois Univ., 1972-
WORKS: Ballet: Time, string quartet, baritone, quartet of dancers, and solo dancer, 1973; Orchestra: Poem; Aria and variation; From one who stays, voice and orch.; Chamber music: string quartet; woodwind quartet; violin sonata; piano trio; choral works; songs; instrumental pieces.
2715 Oak St., Highland Park, IL 60035

GELT, ANDREW LLOYD
b. Albuquerque, N. Mex., 2 Feb. 1951. Studied with George Lynn, William Wood, Univ. of New Mexico, B. M. cum laude 1973; clarinet with Stanley Drucker, Mitchell Lurie, William E. Rhoads. He played clarinet, Albuquerque Symphony; candidate for master's degree, Univ. of Southern California, 1974.
WORKS: Band: To the war; Chamber music: Concerto-quintet for 5 clarinets; Lamento, string orch.; Massivo triole no. 1, organ, violin, clarinet; Massivo triole no. 2, organ, bassoon, oboe; Divertissement for organ; Saedes, organ; Night vice, organ.
10919 Fairbanks, N.E.
Albuquerque, NM 87112

GENA, PETER
b. Buffalo, N. Y., 27 Apr. 1947. Studied with Ramon Fuller, William Kothe, Lejaren Hiller, Morton Feldman, State Univ. of New York, Buffalo, B. M. 1969. He received a grant to attend Internat. Music Inst., Darmstadt, Germany, 1972, and taught a course in computer music; Nat. Science Found. grant for research in computer music, 1973-74. He has been teaching assistant, State Univ. of New York, Buffalo, 1969- ; director, Electronic Music Studio, Brock Univ., Ont., 1971- .
WORKS: Orchestra: Syzygy, 1967; Schoenberg in Italy, Buffalo, 11 Oct. 1973; Chamber music: o thou to whom the music white spring, soprano, flute, viola, guitar, 1968; Upon arriving in the city by the bay, piano, 1970; Homage to G. K. Zipf, 8 instruments, 1971; Scherzo, wind quintet, 1973; Chorus: The egg and the machine, 1967; a clown's smirk in the skull of a baboon, with

(GENA, PETER)
tenor solo, instruments, percussion, 1967; Aleutian lullabies, 1972; Mixed media: quartet for violin, marimba, 2-channel tape, 1969; Scenes from Paterson, piano, narrator, tape, 1969; Anthem, 2 b-flat winds, percussion, tape, 1970; Electronic: Wedding music, tape, 1970; Untitled 1971, film soundtrack, 1971; Egerya, computer synthesized sound, New York, 6 Apr. 1972.
120 Meyer Road, Apt. 104
Buffalo, NY 14226

*GENET, MARIANNE
God save the people, chorus.

GENTEMANN, SISTER MARY ELAINE
b. Fredericksburg, Tex., 4 Oct. 1909. Studied at Our Lady of the Lake Coll., B. M.; with Rudolph Reuter, Leo Sowerby, American Cons.; with Otto Luening, Columbia Univ. Her many awards include honorary membership, Sigma Alpha Iota, 1958; elected Composer of the Year, Texas Music Teachers Assoc., 1963, 1968; 2 awards, Nat. Catholic Music Educators Assoc., 1966, 1968. She has been professor, Our Lady of the Lake Coll., 1929- .
WORKS: Numerous masses, anthems, other liturgical works, secular choral compositions, piano pieces.
Our Lady of the Lake College
411 Southwest 24th
San Antonio, TX 78285

GEORGE, EARL
b. Milwaukee, Wis., 1 May 1924. Studied with Howard Hanson and Bernard Rogers, Eastman School of Music, B. M., M. M., Ph. D.; with Bohuslav Martinu at Tanglewood and in New York. His awards include George Gershwin Memorial Prize; Nat. Fed. of Music Clubs awards; Millikan Univ. choral prize; Guggenheim fellowship; ASCAP awards. He was teaching assistant, Eastman School, 1946-47, 1956-57; instructor, Univ. of Minnesota, 1948-56; Fulbright lecturer, Univ. of Oslo, 1955; professor, Syracuse Univ., 1959- .
WORKS: Orchestra: Introduction and allegro; violin concerto; piano concerto; concerto for string orch.; Introduction, variations and finale; A Thanksgiving overture; Declamations, wind ensemble; Chamber music: string quartet; Chorus: Missa brevis, chorus and orch.; Abraham Lincoln walks at midnight, chorus and orch.; Voyages, soprano, chorus, 13 instruments; many other choral works, songs, piano pieces, chamber music works, film scores.
21 Sewickley Drive, Jamesville, NY 13078

GEORGE, LILA GENE
b. Sioux City, Iowa, 25 Sep. 1918. Studied with Otto Luening and Vladimir Ussachevsky, Columbia Univ.; with Nadia Boulanger, Fontainebleau, France. She received the Oklahoma Sigma Alpha Iota Alumnae award, 1969.
WORKS: Chamber music: trio for horn, violin, piano, 1969; violin sonata; Quintad, suite for violin and cello; Introduction and dance.

GEORGE, LILA GENE

(GEORGE, LILA GENE)
solo flute; Jeux d'esprit, piano; L'etang, piano;
Chorus: A merry-go-round for Christmas; For
winter's rains and ruins are over.
2301 Reva Drive, Houston, TX 77019

*GEORGE, THOM RITTER
Received the Sigvald Thompson composition award
of the Fargo-Moorhead Symphony for 1975. He was
instructor, Cumberland Coll. in 1972; later was
named conductor and composer-in-residence for
Quincy, Ill. His published compositions include
Hymn and toccata and Proclamations, both for
band.

GERRISH, JOHN O.
b. New York State, 1 Sep. 1910. Attended State
Univ. Coll., Potsdam, and Syracuse Univ., studying composition with George Mulfinger. He taught
at State Univ. Coll., Potsdam, 1935-45; Newark
State Coll., 1945-   ; and Caldwell Coll.,
1954-66.
WORKS: Chorus: The falcon, women's voices;
A virgin most pure, women's voices; recorder
music, piano pieces.
114 North Essex Ave., Orange, NJ 07050

GERSCHEFSKI, EDWIN
b. Meriden, Conn., 10 June 1909. Studied at
Yale Univ., B. M. 1931; Matthay Pianoforte
School, London; piano with Artur Schnabel, Italy;
composition with Joseph Schillinger, New York.
His many awards include the first Charles Ditson
fellowship, 1931; 2 Yaddo fellowships, 1936,
1937; League of Composers' radio commission,
1937; first prize, Band Music Competition, N. Y.
World's Fair, 1939; Carnegie grant, 1947; Gold
Medal, Arnold Bax Society, 1963; citation for
"distinguished service to the art and profession
of music," Alumni Assoc., Yale Univ., 1968. He
taught piano at private schools in New York City,
1933-40; was professor, Converse Coll., 1940-59;
chairman, music department, Univ. of New Mexico,
1959-60; head, music department, Univ. of
Georgia, 1960-   .
WORKS: Orchestra: Classic symphony;
Fanfare, fugato, and finale, 1937; Saugatuck
suite, 1938; Celebration, rhapsody for violin
and orch.; Toccata and fugue; Band: Guadalcanal
fantasy; Streamline; Music for a stately occasion; Chamber music: 100 variations for unaccompanied violin; 8 variations for string
quartet; piano trio; Rhapsody for piano trio;
piano quintet; Workout, 2 violins, 2 violas;
The mountain, cello solo; Chorus: Half Moon Mountain, women's voices, baritone solo, orch.; 6
songs on poems by Carl Sandburg, women's voices;
And thou shall love the Lord; The Lord's Contro-
versy, cantata for men's voices, tenor solo,
orch.; The salutation of the dawn, chorus and
orch.; The Lord's Prayer, a cappella; A man on
the cross, chorus, contralto, organ; The 100th
Psalm; Border raid, an Irish yarn; Songs: On
his blindness, Milton text, soprano; Lai, Mary
Branard text, soprano; and piano pieces. He is
also author of many articles in music journals.
Department of Music, University of Georgia
Athens, GA 30601

*GERSHWIN, GEORGE
b. Brooklyn, N. Y., 26 Sep. 1898; d. Hollywood,
Calif., 12 July 1937. Studied with Edward
Kilenyi, Rubin Goldmark, and Joseph Schilinger,
but was drawn to jazz and popular music and at
15 became a song plugger for a music publisher.
Later he studied with Henry Cowell and
Wallingford Riegger. He received the first
Pulitzer given for a musical for Of thee I sing,
1931; was one of the first 10 inductees into the
Entertainment Hall of Fame, 23 Apr. 1974.
WORKS: Opera: Porgy and Bess, 1935; Musicals: La, la, Lucille, 1919; George White's
Scandals, 1920, 1921, 1922, 1923, 1924; Our Nell,
1922; Sweet little devil, 1923; Primrose, 1924;
Lady be good, 1924; Song of the flame, 1925; Tip
toes, 1925; Oh Kay, 1926; Funny face, 1927; Treasure girl, 1928; Strike up the band, 1929; Show
girl, 1929; Girl crazy, 1930; Of thee I sing,
1931; Pardon my English, 1932; Let 'em eat cake,
1933; Orchestra: Rhapsody in blue, 1924; Concerto in F, 1925; An American in Paris, 1928;
Second rhapsody, 1931; Cuban overture, 1932;
many songs including his first tremendous success, Swanee, written at age 19; Piano: 5 preludes, 3 of which were orchestrated by Arnold
Schoenberg; Film scores: Delicious; A damsel in
distress; Shall we dance; The shocking Miss
Pilgrim; The Goldwyn follies (completed by
Vernon Duke). Biographies: Merle Armitage, ed.,
George Gershwin, New York, 1938; David Ewen, A
journey to greatness: The life and music of
George Gershwin, New York, 1956.

GERSTER, ROBERT
b. Chicago, Ill., 13 Oct. 1945. Studied with
Marshall Barnes, Ohio State Univ.; with William
Bergsma and William O. Smith, Univ. of Washington. He received the Nat. Inst. of Arts and
Letters Charles E. Ives scholarship, 1973. He
was teaching assistant, Univ. of Washington,
1968, 1971-73.
WORKS: Orchestra: Synchromy, 1972; Chamber
music: Music for brass and percussion, brass
quartet, 6 percussionists, 1971; Mobiles, 11
players, 1971; Bird in the spirit, solo flute,
1972; Mixed media: Chance dance game, 12 players in 6 locations, dancers, video tape projection, 1973.
5319 24th N.E., #201, Seattle, WA 98105

GERTZ, IRVING
b. Providence, R. I., 19 May 1915. Studied with
Wassili Leps in Providence; with Ernst Toch and
Mario Castelnuovo-Tedesco in Los Angeles. He
was composer-music director, Columbia Pictures,
1946-48; National Broadcasting Company, 1949-51;
Universal Studios, 1952-59; Twentieth Century
Fox, 1960-69.
WORKS: Chorus: I hear America singing; O
captain! My captain!; For you, o democracy; Song
of the Exposition; Beat! beat! drums; Pioneers!
O pioneers!; all on Walt Whitman texts; Buffalo
Bill, poem by Carl Sandburg.
351 Veterans Ave., Los Angeles, CA 90024

GESENSWAY, LOUIS
b. Dvinsk, Latvia, 19 Feb. 1906; U.S. citizen
1942. Studied violin with Luigi von Kunits,
Toronto Cons.; with Lea Luboschutz, Reginald
Owen Morris, and Tibor Serly, Curtis Inst.,
1926-29; with Zoltan Kodaly, Budapest Academy,
Hungary, 1930-31. He received the Philadelphia
Orchestra's Kuhn award, 1945; several commissions.
He was first violinist, Philadelphia Orchestra,
1926-71; and was co-founder of the Toronto Symphony. His works have been performed by some of
the major orchestras of the U.S. and by the
Helsinki Symphony.
    WORKS: Opera: The great Boffo and his talk-
ing dog, 1-act comic opera for children, 1953;
Orchestra: 5 Russian pieces, 1936; suite for
strings and percussion, 1939; concerto for 13
brass instruments, 1942; flute concerto, 1944;
Suite on Jewish themes, 1948; Four Squares of
Philadelphia, tone poem, 1951; Double portrait,
1952; Let the night be dark for all of me, 1953;
Ode to peace, tone poem, 1959; March, 1963;
Revery, strings, 1964; Commemoration symphony,
1968; A Pennsylvania overture, 1972; cello concerto, 1973; Chamber music: piano sonata, 1937;
2 string quartets, 1938, 1954; Fantasy for organ,
1941; duo, violin and viola, 1941, revised 1967;
quartet for English horn, flute, violin, cello,
1942; 8 miniatures for flute, percussion, timpani, 1949; sonata for solo bassoon, c. 1950;
Aria, cello and piano, 1950; quartet for clarinet, violin, viola, cello, c. 1951; duo for
clarinet and flute, 1952; 12 rounds, 4 percussion
instruments, 1955; quartet for oboe, bassoon,
violin, viola, 1956; quartet for timpani, percussion, violin, cello, 1957; duo for oboe and
guitar, 1959; duo for viola and bassoon, 1960;
Interlude for harmonium, 1961; Wedding march,
harmonium or organ, 1967; Dance suite for harp,
1968; Divertimento, flute, 2 violins, viola,
1969; Divertimento, wind quintet, 1969; duo for
violin and cello, 1970; duo for 2 celli, 1970;
2 silhouettes, flute and piano, 1971; many arrangements of his own orchestral works for small
ensembles, and of classical works for orchestra
or chamber ensembles.
    433 East Sedgwick St., Philadelphia, PA 19106

GESSLER, CAROLINE
b. Indiana, Pa., 7 Mar. 1908. Studied at Indiana
Univ. of Pennsylvania; Fillion Studios, Pittsburgh; and privately with Harvey Gaul in Pittsburgh. She won 3 first prizes in Pennsylvania
Fed. of Music Clubs contests. She taught in public schools, 1929-70; Fillion Studios, 1944-49;
private teacher, 1970-   .
    WORKS: Chamber music: Creation for strings,
3 movements; Chorus: Give ear to my prayer; God
is our hope; Bless the Lord, O my soul; I wait
alone beside the sea; A psalm of trust; O let
the nations be glad; Psalm of the harvest; Songs
of praise.
    606 Wayne Ave., Indiana, PA 15701

*GETTEL, WILLIAM D.
I taste a liquor never brewed, chorus.

*GHENT, EMMANUEL
b. Montreal, P. Q., 15 May 1925. Studied music
and psychoanalysis at McGill Univ.; then became
a psychiatrist and composer in New York City.
He received an ASCAP award, 1973.
    WORKS: Chamber music: Movement for wind
quintet, 1944; Natasha and Pygmalion and Galatea,
flute duos, 1944; Lament for string quartet,
1958; woodwind quartet, 1960; Entelechy, viola
and piano; 2 duos for flute and clarinet, 1963;
Dance movement, trumpet and string quartet,
1963; Trialty I and II, violin, trumpet, bassoon,
1964; brass quintet, 1965; Helices, electronic
tape and 2 players.
    131 Prince St., New York, NY 10012

GHIGLIERI, SYLVIA M.
b. Stockton, Calif., 13 Mar. 1933. Studied at
Dominican Coll., San Rafael, B. M. 1954; with
Stanworth Beckler, Univ. of the Pacific, M. M.
1961; piano with Egon Petri; Gyorgy Sandor;
Robert and Jean Casadesus in France. She won
first prize, 1959, honorable mention 1963, in
Mu Phi Epsilon composition contests. She has
been associate professor, California State Coll.,
Stanislaus, 1961-   .
    WORKS: Chorus: Psalm 56, chorus and orch.,
1963; Piano: 3 Irish pieces, 1959; sonata.
    4 East Alder St., Stockton, CA 95204

*GIANNINI, VITTORIO
b. Philadelphia, Pa., 19 Oct. 1903; d. New York,
N. Y., 28 Nov. 1966. (Brother of Dusolina
Giannini, soprano) Studied on scholarship at
the Milan Cons.; with Rubin Goldmark at Juilliard
School; American Acad. in Rome, 1931-35. His
many awards included honorary doctorates from
New York Coll. of Music, 1939, Curtis Inst.,
1957, Cincinnati Cons. of Music, 1961; commissions from New York World's Fair for a symphony,
1939; American and Canadian Governments for an
educational film score, 1956; Moravian Church
for a choral work, 1957; fellow, Internat. Inst.
of Arts and Letters. He was faculty member,
Juilliard School, 1939-66; Manhattan School of
Music, 1941-66; Curtis Inst. of Music, 1956-66;
first director, North Carolina School of the
Arts.
    WORKS: Opera: Lucedia, 1934; Flora, 1937;
The scarlet letter, 1938; Beauty and the beast,
1938; Blennerhasset, 1939; The taming of the
shrew, 1952; The harvest, 1961; Rehearsal call,
1962; The servant of 2 masters, performed New
York, 1967; Orchestra: Prelude and fugue for
strings, 1926; Concerto grosso for strings, 1931;
Suite, 1931; 4 symphonies, 1935, 1939, 1950,
1960; Triptych, 1937; organ concerto, 1937; concerto for 2 pianos, 1940; trumpet concerto, 1949;
Frescobaldiana, 1949; Canticle for Christmas,
with chorus, 1950; Divertimento #2, 1961; Chamber music: piano quintet, 1931; woodwind quintet, 1933; piano trio, 1933; 2 violin sonatas,
1926, 1945; piano sonata; many choral works and
songs.

*GIANNINI, WALTER
Modal variations for piano; piano sonatina.

GIBB, ROBERT W.

*GIBB, ROBERT W.
b. Dedham, Mass., 2 May 1893; d. Dedham, Mass., 15 May 1964. Studied with Frederick S. Converse, New England Cons.; at Boston Univ. and Harvard Univ. His works include Oriental suite for orchestra, and 3 overtures: Youth, Carnival, Festival.

GIBB, STANLEY GARTH
b. Chicago, Ill., 22 June 1940. Studied with Herbert Bielawa, Wayne Peterson, Merril Bradshaw, and Merrill Ellis. He was on the faculty, Oklahoma Univ., 1971-72; instructor and head, electronic music laboratory, North Texas State Univ., 1972-   .
WORKS: Wind ensemble: Localization, 12 trombones, 1971; Mixed media: Parity, trombone and tape, 1972; Overture to the second coming, tape and 16-voice choir, 1971; Electronic: Sonic flight, commissioned by North Texas Modern Dance Troupe, 1972; Monolithes, commissioned by Dena Madole, 1973.
1023 Aileen, Denton, TX 76201

GIBBS, GEOFFREY DAVID
b. Copiague, N. Y., 29 Mar. 1940. Studied privately with Elie Siegmeister, and with Bernard Rogers, Howard Hanson, and Wayne Barlow at Eastman School of Music. He held 2 summer fellowships at Univ. of Rhode Island, 1970, 1972. He was instructor, Univ. of Rhode Island, 1965-69, assistant professor, 1969-   .
WORKS: Orchestra: Icon: Igor Stravinsky, Delius Festival, Jacksonville, Fla., 1972; symphony no. 2, Kingston, R. I., 7 May 1973; Chamber music: Pastorale, cello or bassoon and piano; Chorus: Praise ye the Lord, 1970; Symposium, oratorio, 1970; The bond of peace, cantata, 1973.
Box 291, West Kingston, RI 02892

*GIBBS, MICHAEL
Concert jazz: Melanie; 6 improvisatory sketches.

*GIBSON, ARCHER
b. Baltimore, Md., 5 Dec. 1875; d. Lake Mahopac, N. Y., 15 July 1952. Wrote an opera, Yzdra; 2 cantatas, Emancipation and A song to music; and organ pieces.

GIBSON, DAVID
b. Albany, N. Y., 20 Sep. 1943. Studied with Stanley Wolfe at Juilliard School; with Jacob Druckman at Yale Univ. He received the Harriet Fox Gibbs award at Yale. He was cellist with the U.S. Army String Quartet, 1967-70; composer-cellist, Center for the Creative and Performing Arts, State Univ. of New York, Buffalo, 1972-   .
WORKS: Chamber music: 13 ways of looking at a blackbird, voice and instruments; Embellishments #2, string quartet; Lion's head, amplified bass; Shadows, 3 percussionists; 3 fragments, cello and piano; Fragment #4, 3 trumpets, clarinet, vibraphone, bass; Fragment #5, viola or vibraphone; Mixed media: Embellishments #1, string quartet and tape.
59 Anderson Place, Buffalo, NY 14222

GIBSON, JON C.
b. Los Angeles, Calif., 11 Mar. 1940. Studied at San Francisco State Univ., B. A. 1964; and with Larry Austin and Richard Swift, Univ. of California at Davis. He is a teacher and performer in New York with activities centering around the avant garde group in music.
WORKS: Electronic: Visitations: An environmental soundscape; Vocal tape delay, 1968; 30's, 1970; Multiples, 1972; Melody, 1973; and "continuous textural music dealing with varying degrees of structure and improvisation."
17 Thompson St., New York, NY 10013

GIBSON, MICHAEL P.
b. Columbus, Ohio, 10 Aug. 1948. Studied with Alan Stout, Lyndon DeYoung, James Hopkins at Northwestern Univ.; also studied trombone and conducting. He received a John Philip Sousa band award. He was trombonist in the Norad Band, 1971-73; Air Force Acad. Band, 1973-75; conductor and musical director, Colorado Springs Chamber Music Society, 1971-   .
WORKS: Chamber music: Effectuoso, trombone and piano; A dialectical quintessence, 4 winds and percussion; A dulcet ebullience, brass quintet.
622 West Kiowa St.
Colorado Springs, CO 80905

GIDEON, MIRIAM
b. Greeley, Colo., 23 Oct. 1906. Attended Boston Univ., B. A.; Columbia Univ., M. A.; Jewish Theological Seminary, D. S. M.; studied piano with Hans Barth and Felix Fox. She received the Bloch prize for a choral work, 1948; Nat. Fed. of Music Clubs and ASCAP award for contribution to symphonic music, 1969; commission from The Temple, Cleveland, 1969; elected to Nat. Inst. of Arts and Letters, 1975. She was instructor, Brooklyn Coll., 1944-54; professor, Jewish Theological Seminary, 1955-   ; professor, City Univ. of New York, 1971-   .
WORKS: Theatre: Fortunato, opera, 1958; The adorable mouse, French folk tale for narrator and chamber orch., 1960; Orchestra: Lyric piece, string quartet, 1941; Symphonia brevis, 1953; Chamber music: Lyric piece, string quartet, 1941; The hound of heaven, voice, oboe, string quartet, 1946; viola sonata, 1948; Fantasy on a Javanese motive, cello and piano, 1948; Divertimento, woodwind quartet, 1948; Air, violin and piano, 1950; Sonnets from Shakespeare, voice, trumpet, string quartet, 1950; Sonnets from Fatal interview, Millay, voice, string trio, 1952; 3 Biblical masks, violin and piano, 1960; cello sonata, 1961; The condemned playground, soprano, tenor, 2 winds, string quartet, 1963; Rhymes from the hill, voice, clarinet, cello, marimba, 1968; The seasons of time, voice, flute, cello, piano, celesta, 1969; suite for clarinet and piano, 1972; Chorus: Slow, slow, fresh fount, madrigal, Ben Johnson text, 1941; How goodly are Thy tents, women's voices, 1947; Adon Olom, chorus, oboe, trumpet, strings, 1954; The habitable Earth, cantata, 1965; Spiritual madrigals, male voices, viola, cello, bassoon, 1965; Sacred service, 1971; Songs: Epitaphs from Robert Burns, 1952; Mixco, Asturias text, 1957; To music, Herrick, 1957;

(GIDEON, MIRIAM)
Songs of voyage, 1969; Piano: Canzona, 1945; 6 cuckoos in search of a composer, 1953; Of shadows numberless, suite, 1966; 7 suites; sonatina for 2 pianos; suite for 4 hands.
410 Central Park West, New York, NY 10025

*GILBERT, DAVID
b. Pennsylvania, 1936. Studied at Eastman School of Music; was assistant conductor, New York Philharmonic, 1970; co-conductor, American Ballet Theatre, 1971.
WORKS: Chamber music: Poem VI, alto flute, 1966; Centering I, chamber ensemble, 1969; Centering II, chamber ensemble, 1970; Poem VII, oboe, 1970; Voice: 2 unaccompanied songs for soprano, 1965.
535 West 110th St., New York, NY 10025

*GILBERT, HARRY M.
b. Paducah, Ky., 1879. Studied at Cincinnati Coll. of Music and in Berlin. He taught in Dallas for a few years then toured as soloist and accompanist with David Bispham and other noted singers; was organist for 33 years, Fifth Avenue Presbyterian Church, New York City.
WORKS: Chorus: A vision of music, cantata for men's voices and orch.; Fantasie on Swedish folk songs, male chorus; The great eternal Christmas, 2 soli, chorus, piano trio, organ; Scotch fantasie, soprano solo with male chorus.

*GILBERT, LOUIS WOLFE
b. Odessa, Russia, 31 Aug. 1886; to U.S. 1887; d. Beverly Hills, Calif., 12 July 1970. Sang in vaudeville and night clubs at 14; toured as entertainer with John L. Sullivan, the prize fighter. He went to Hollywood in 1929 and wrote for films. He wrote extremely popular songs including Waitin' for the Robert E. Lee, 1912; Ramona, 1927; Peanut vendor; Down yonder; Lucky Lindy, 1927; and some 245 others.

GILBERT, PIA
b. Germany, 1 June 1921; U.S. citizen 1944. Studied at New York Coll. of Music; has been composer-in-residence and professor, Univ. of California, Los Angeles, 1947-
WORKS: Theatre: music for plays, The deputy; The devils, Murderous angels; ballets, Metamorphoses; Game of gods; and many others.
11400 Berwick St., Los Angeles, CA 90049

GILBERT, STEVEN E.
b. New York, N. Y., 20 Apr. 1943. Studied with Robert Starer, Brooklyn Coll., B. A. 1964, M. M. 1967; with Gunther Schuller and Mel Powell, Yale Univ., M. Phil., Ph. D. 1970; with Darius Milhaud and Charles Jones at Aspen, Colo;; and with Yannis Xenakis at Tanglewood. He won 3 BMI student composer awards, 1964, 1966, 1967. He has been assistant professor, California State Univ., Fresno, 1970-   .
WORKS: Orchestra: symphony, 1964-65; Chamber music: string quartet, 1963; Mosaics, trumpet, cello, 2 percussionists, 1966.
4220-B North College Ave., Fresno, CA 93704

*GILBERTÉ, HALLETT
b. Winthrop, Me., 14 Mar. 1872; d. New York, N. Y., 5 Jan. 1946. Studied composition with Ethelbert Nevin in Boston. He wrote about 250 songs including Spanish serenade; In reverie; Song of the canoe; Ah, Love but a day; Spring serenade; Moonlight and starlight; etc.

*GILBERTSON, VIRGINIA
b. Memphis, Tenn., 2 Dec. 1914. Studied at DeShago Coll. of Music, B. M.; Memphis State Univ.; Winthrop Coll. She is a piano teacher and accompanist. Her works include One bronze feather, a stage show for the New Jersey tercentenary; shows for summer stock theatre; songs.

*GILL, MILTON
Toccata for organ.

GILLAM, RUSSELL C.
b. Mount Union, Pa., 11 July 1909. Studied with Donald Hardisty, Univ. of Arizona; John Boda and Irvin Cooper, Florida State Univ.; John Barnes Chance, Univ. of Kentucky; Glen Morgan, Lycoming Coll. He won 2nd prize for a choral composition, Pennsylvania Fed. of Music Clubs. He taught in public schools, 1927-48; Lock Haven State Coll., 1948-71; organist and choir director, Great Island Presbyterian Church, 1950-   .
WORKS: Chamber music: Rondino, horn and piano, 1972; Larghetto, oboe and piano, 1973; Chorus: Mass in English; White lilacs, women's voices; Suffer the little children, 1955; God is everywhere, unison choir, 1972.
426 West Main St., Lock Haven, PA 17745

GILLESPIE, DONALD
b. Pittsburgh, Pa., 11 Oct. 1942. Studied with Roger McDuffie, Converse Coll. He won a Pi Kappa Lambda award, 1966. He taught in public schools, 1968-69; was assistant professor, Morningside Coll., 1969-   ; choir director, Methodist Church, Sioux City, 1969-   .
WORKS: Chorus: Tis winter now; Service music for worship; 2 motets; 6 carols; Songs: 3 songs on e e cummings texts; Keyboard: 4 organ chorale preludes; 6 young moments for piano; Fugue for piano; 3 piano sonatas.
3301 Laurel Ave., Sioux City, IA 51106

*GILLETTE, JAMES ROBERT
b. Roseboom, N. Y., 30 May 1886. Studied at Syracuse Univ. He held faculty posts at Wesleyan Coll. and at Carleton Coll., where he established the Carleton Symphonic Band in 1923 and the Gillette Chamber Orchestra in 1937; later was organist, Lake Forrest, Ill.
WORKS: Orchestra: Cabins, an American rhapsody; Band: Pagan symphony; 7 symphonettes; many choral works, songs and about 40 organ pieces.

GILLIAM, ROGER WAYNE
b. Rangely, Colo., 22 Nov. 1948. Studied with William Schroeder, Del Mar Coll.; with Alvin Epstein, Southern Methodist Univ.
WORKS: Band: Quotient '69; Wind ensemble: Variations on 8 notes, brass quintet.
63 Hiltbrand Road, #4-I, Bristol, CT 06010

GILLIS, DON

(GILLIS, DON)
b. Cameron, Mo., 17 June 1912. Studied with Keith Mixon, Texas Christian Univ., A. B., B. M. 1936; with Roy Will and Floyd Graham, North Texas State Univ. His awards include an honorary doctorate, Texas Christian Univ., honorary membership, Phi Mu Alpha Sinfonia; Christopher Award; and many commissions. He taught at Texas Christian Univ. and Southwestern Baptist Seminary School, 1935-42; was on production staff, WBAP, Ft. Worth; joined production staff, NBC, New York, 1944-45; script writer, commentator; guest orchestra and band conductor throughout U.S.; chairman, music department, Southern Methodist Univ., 1967-68; chairman, arts department, Dallas Baptist Coll., 1968-72; composer-in-residence and director, Inst. of Media Arts, Univ. of South Carolina, 1973- .

WORKS: Opera: The Park Avenue kids; Pep rally; The gift of the Magi, 1-act; The libretto, The world premiere, 1-act; The legend of Star Valley Junction; The Nazarene; Behold the man; Ballet: Shindig, a ballet of the old west; Orchestra: 12 symphonies, including no. 5 1/2 and A short, short symphony; 5 suites, The panhandle; Portrait of frontier town; Atlanta: 5 choreographic impression of a southern town; Twinkletoes; 4 scenes from yesterday; 4 symphonic poems, Tulsa-A symphonic portrait in oil; The Alamo; To an unknown soldier; Amarillo-A symphonic celebration; 9 works with narrator, The man who invented music; Alice in Orchestralia; Thomas Wolfe, American; Toscanini: A portrait of a century; Ceremony of allegiance; The night before Christmas; The raven; His name was John; The answer; other, January February March; Short overture to an unwritten opera; Bing bang bong; Paul Bunyon--A portrait of a legend; Overture: Season's greetings; Intermission--ten minutes; 2 piano concertos; Chamber music: piano quintet; 3 woodwind quintets; Sinfonia for brass; Streamliner, brass choir; 2 trumpet sonatinas; trumpet quartet; piano trio; 5 string quartets; bassoon quartet; pieces for string orch.; pieces for various solo instruments; Chorus: This is our America, solo and chorus; So they may also learn, narrator, chorus, band; 7 golden texts, narrator, chorus, band or orch.; Doubting Thomas; Hymn and prayer for peace; The coming of the king, narrator, chorus, orch.; The yellow dog September; How long?; Serving only Thee; The dilemna; Multimedia: Let us pray, dramatic essay for chorus, orch., narrator, soloists, pre-recorded tape, slides, motion pictures; many pieces for band and for solo instruments with band. He is author of magazine articles, lyrics and librettos for several of his operas, and a humorous book, The unfinished symphony conductor.
900 Gregg St., Apt. 1-A, Columbia, SC 29201

GILMORE, BERNARD
b. Oakland, Calif., 19 Nov. 1937. Studied with John Vincent, Boris Kremenliev, Lukas Foss, Univ. of California, Los Angeles; with Josef Tal in Jerusalem; Stanford Univ., D. M. A. (conducting) 1966. He was Eastern Division winner, Coll. Band Directors Nat. Assoc., composition contest, 1965; recipient 2 Oregon State Univ. Found. grants. He played horn, Boston Pops Tour Orch., 1957; Los

(GILMORE, BERNARD)
Angeles Philharmonic, 1956-61; instructor, Cornell Univ., 1961-64; associate professor, orchestra director, Oregon State Univ., 1966- ; principal horn, assistant conductor, Haifa Symphony Orch., Israel, 1972-73.
WORKS: Orchestra: symphonic movement; Band: 5 folk songs, soprano and band; Chamber music: Music for 6 horns; Dover Beach, soprano, clarinet, string trio; duo for flute and viola; 3 poems of love, chamber chorus, chamber orch.; 5 pieces for piano; Scarlatti doesn't live here anymore, piano and harpsichord.
Department of Music, Oregon State University
Corvallis, OR 97331

GINN, JIM
b. Bozeman, Mont., 27 Oct. 1935. Studied with William Jones, Linfield Coll.
WORKS: Piano: piano concerto; preludes, bagatelles, etc.
41-020 Alaihi, Waimanalo, HI 96795

*GINSBURG, GERALD
b. Nebraska. Studied with Roy Harris. A recital of his songs was presented at Carnegie Recital Hall, New York, 13 Feb. 1974. He has also had a work performed at a concert of the Nat. Asso. of American Composers and Conductors, New York, 11 Mar. 1973.

*GIORNI, AURELIO
b. Perugia, Italy, 15 Sep. 1895; to U.S. 1915; d. Pittsfield, Mass., 23 Sep. 1938. Studied at the St. Cecilia Cons. in Rome; with Humperdinck in Berlin. He taught at Smith Coll.; Philadelphia Cons.; Hartford School of Music; and in New York.
WORKS: Orchestra: Orlando furioso, symphonic poem, 1926; Sinfonia concertante, 1931; symphony, 1937; many chamber works and songs.

*GIRON, ARSENIO
b. Renteria, Spain, 15 Dec. 1932. Studied with Joseph Wood and Herbert Elwell, Oberlin Cons., B. M. 1956; with Charles Hamm, Tulane Univ., M. A. 1962. He received a Ford Found. grant, 1962-63. He was assistant professor, Lindenwood Coll., 1965-68; associate professor, Univ. of Western Ontario, 1968- .
WORKS: Chamber music: quartet for flute, clarinet, viola, piano; Vias, flute, clarinet, cello, piano, percussion; Disparities and differences, brass quintet; sextet for woodwinds and trumpet.
Department of Music
University of Western Ontario
London, Ontario, Canada

*GIUFFRE, JAMES
b. Dallas, Tex., 26 Apr. 1921. Studied at North Texas State Univ., B. M. 1942; at Univ. of Southern California, 1946. He has played with Jimmy Dorsey, Buddy Rich, Woody Herman, and others; was faculty member, Lenox School of Jazz, 1957; instructor, School of Education, New York Univ., 1972- .

(GIUFFRE, JAMES)
WORKS: Orchestra: Fugue, 1953; Mobiles,
clarinet and strings; Piece, clarinet and
strings; Composition for trio and string orch.,
1961; Threshold, vibraphone, piano, double bass,
drums, chamber orch.; viola concerto; Hex, 1965;
Concert jazz: 4 brothers; Fine; Fun; Suspensions;
Passage to the veil; Affinity; Quest; Motion-
eterne; The quiet blues, New York, 12 Feb. 1971;
Chamber music: clarinet quintet; The pharaoh,
brass ensemble.
School of Education, New York University
New York, NY 10003

*GLANVILLE-HICKS, PEGGY
b. Melbourne, Australia, 29 Dec. 1912; U.S. citizen 1948. Studied with Ralph Vaughan Williams,
Royal Coll. of Music, London, 1932-36; with Egon
Wellesz in Vienna; and with Nadia Boulanger in
Paris. Her many honors include American Acad.
of Arts and Letters award, 1953; Guggenheim fellowships, 1956-58; Rockefeller travel grant,
1960; Fulbright research grant, 1961; many commissions. She was music critic, New York Herald-
Tribune, 1948-58; director, Composers Forum,
producer, Donnell Library Concerts, 1950-60.
WORKS: Opera: Caedmon; The transposed heads,
1953; The glittering gate, 1959; Nausicaa, 1961;
Sappho, 1963; Ballet: Masque of the wild man,
1958; Orchestra: Letters from Morocco, tenor and
chamber orch., 1953; Concerto romantico, viola
and orch., 1957; Chamber music: string quartet;
Concertino da camera, 1945; harp sonata, 1950;
sonata for piano and percussion, 1951; Etruscan
concerto, piano and orch., 1956; Prelude for a
pensive pupil, piano, 1963.
c/o American Composers Alliance
170 West 74th St., New York, NY 10023

GLARUM, L. STANLEY
b. Portland, Ore., 19 Apr. 1908. Studied with
Dent Mowrey, Portland; with F. Melius
Christiansen, St. Olaf Coll.; George F. McKay,
Univ. of Washington, M. A. He has received
ASCAP awards; Danforth fellowship; honorary
music doctorate, Whitworth Coll., 1969. He has
been professor, Lewis and Clark Coll., 1947-
WORKS: More than 200 published choral
compositions.
6843 S.W. Raleighwood Way
Portland, OR 97225

GLASER, VICTORIA M.
b. Amherst, Mass., 11 Sep. 1918. Studied with
Walter Piston, Tillman Merrit, Archibald T.
Davison, Nadia Boulanger, Harvard Univ., B. A.,
M. A.; with Frederick Tillotson, Margaret
Macdonald, Longy School, Boston; and flute with
George Laurent. She won a prize in the Brookline
Library Composers' Forum; honorable mention,
Gedok Competition, Mannheim, Germany, 1961. She
taught at Dana Hall School, 1944-59; chairman of
theory, Preparatory Division, New England Cons.,
1959-   .
WORKS: Orchestra: Birthday fugue, Boston
Pops, 1962; Music for orchestra, 1964; Chamber
music: suite for harpsichord; sonatina for
flute and violin; Chorus: Homeric hymn, women's

(GLASER, VICTORIA M.)
voices; An idle song, women's voices; 3 suburban carols, Boston, Dec. 1972; La musique,
Cambridge, May 1973.
37 Hawthorn St., Cambridge, MA 02138

*GLASOW, GLENN
Rakka, violin and electronic sounds.
Department of Music
California State College
Hayward, CA 94542

*GLASS, PAUL EUGENE
b. Los Angeles, Calif., 19 Nov. 1934. Studied
with Ingolf Dahl, Univ. of Southern California,
B. M.; with Goffredo Petrassi in Rome; Roger
Sessions at Princeton Univ.; and with Witold
Lutoslawski in Warsaw. He received a Fulbright
grant for study in Rome; a fellowship at Princeton; an Inst. of Internat. Education grant for
Poland.
WORKS: Ballet: Eschatos; Orchestra: symphony; cello concerto; Chamber music: clarinet
quintet; Music for brass and percussion; trio
for flute, cello, piano; 3 pieces for violin and
piano; woodwind trio; Film scores: The abduc-
tors; Fear no more; Lady in a cage; Interregnum,
and others.

GLASS, PHILIP
b. Baltimore, Md., 31 Jan. 1937. Studied at
Univ. of Chicago, B. A. 1956; with Vincent
Persichetti and William Bergsma, Juilliard
School, M. M. 1962; and with Nadia Boulanger in
France, 1964-65. He received a Fulbright grant
for study in France; Ford Found. grant, 1962-64.
On returning to the U.S. in 1967, he settled in
New York and, jettisoning all previous concep-
tional compositions, developed a new system of
composing based on amplified ensembles of keyboard instruments, winds, and voice; his aim is
to achieve music that will be perceived as a
pure medium of sound freed of dramatic structure.
WORKS: Music in similar motion, 1969; Music
in fifths, 1969; Music with changing parts, 1970;
Music in 12 parts, 1973, premiere of total piece
(6pm to 12 m, 1½ hour for dinner) New York, 1
June 1974.
231 2nd Ave., New York, NY 10003

GLASSER, ALBERT
b. Chicago, Ill., 25 Jan. 1916. Studied with
Arne Oldberg, Univ. of Southern California on a
scholarship from the Alchin Chair Found., 1934.
He won the California Composers contest, 1937;
Southern California contest, 1945. He was orchestrator for MGM Studios, 1943-47; composer,
orchestrator, and conductor for 155 motion picture scores; 450 television shows; 500 radio
shows; conductor, Gershwin Night, Hollywood Bowl,
1947; etc.
WORKS: Orchestra: 2 symphonic etudes; violin concerto; string bass concerto; Pied piper
of Hamelin, tone poem; The raven, tone poem;
symphonic variations on Jolly good fellow; Chamber music: string quartet; piano quintet; Flute
rhapsody; viola sonata; sextet for flute, piano,
string quartet; songs.
11812 Bellagio Road, Los Angeles, CA 90049

GLAZOR, STUART

*GLAZOR, STUART
Orchestra: Structures; Soundprint; Chamber music: 5 pieces for trumpet, horn, piano; 3 movements for string quartet.
Valley City State College
Valley City, ND 58072

GLEN, IRMA
b. Chicago, Ill., 3 Aug.   . Studied with John Palmer and Adolf Weidig, American Cons.; Univ. of Southern California; Inst. of Religious Science, Los Angeles. She was theatre and radio organist in Chicago, then staff organist NBC, Chicago; moved to Los Angeles in 1946 as free-lance organist and composer for radio and television; became minister of music, Beverly Hills Church of Religious Science, and churches in Arcadia, Palm Springs, and La Jolla, Calif.
WORKS: Organ: A bridge to higher consciousness, 11 inspirational compositions; Music-prayer therapy, 12 pieces; Music, ecology and you, 6 pieces; Christmas miracles now!, 5 pieces; many hymns.
7860 Monument Drive, Grants Pass, OR 97526

*GLICK, HENRIETTA
Paris, 1927, symphonic suite, performed at the Eastman School Festival of American Music, Apr. 1931.

*GLICKMAN, EUGENE C.
Divertimento for brass and percussion.
Nassau Community College
Garden City, NY 11530

GLICKMAN, SYLVIA
b. New York, N. Y., 8 Nov. 1932. Attended Juilliard School and Royal Acad. of Music, London, studying with Beveridge Webster, Harold Craxton, Manuel Frankel. She received the Morris Loeb prize in performance at Juilliard; Edward Hecht composition prize at Royal Acad. of Music. She taught at New England Cons. 1956-58; Rubin Acad. of Music, Israel, 1967-68; summer director, Haverford Chamber Music Center, 1967-   , pianist-in-residence and director of chamber music, Haverford Coll., 1969-   , lecturer, 1973-   .
WORKS: Chamber music: Small suite, cello and piano; piece for clarinet and piano; Early dance movements for piano; Chorus: The hollow men, chorus, soprano, and piano.
1210 West Wynnewood Rd.
Wynnewood, PA 19096

GLOVINSKY, BEN
b. St. Louis, Mo., 28 Oct. 1942. Studied with Robert Wykes, Harold Blumenfield, Washington Univ.; with Humphrey Searle, Stanford Univ.; Bernhard Heiden, Indiana Univ. His Sinfonietta was chosen to represent Western Division, Coll. Band Directors Nat. Assoc. Convention, 1969. He has been associate professor, Sacramento State Univ., 1965-   ; principal oboe, Sacramento Symphony Orch., 1966-   .
WORKS: Orchestra: Variation-fantasy on a pioneer theme, commissioned by Sacramento Symph.; Band: Sinfonietta for winds, brass, percussion, 1969; Ceremonial music; Chamber music: Music

(GLOVINSKY, BEN)
for bass clarinet and piano; Romanza, wind quintet; oboe sonatina; Vocal: 4 songs on poems of Robert Herrick.
489 Fairgrounds Drive, Sacramento, CA 95817

GNAZZO, ANTHONY J.
b. New Britain, Conn., 21 Apr. 1936. Attended Univ. of Hartford, B. A. in math. 1963; Brandeis Univ., M. F. A. 1965, Ph. D. 1970. He served in the U.S. Navy, 1957-61; was research associate, Univ. of Toronto, 1965-66; computer scientist, IBM Corporation, 1966-67; director, Tape Music Center, Mills Coll., 1967-69; technician, California State Univ., Hayward, 1969-71; assistant professor, York Univ., 1971-72; lecturer, Univ. of California, Davis, 1972-73; electronic music consultant, Univ. of California, Berkeley, 1969-73.
WORKS: Chamber music: Music for piano III, 1971; 5-part invention, mixed voices, 1972; Multimedia: Space and motion no. 1-4, dancers and tape, 1965-66; Theatre pieces no. I-XXVI, film, tape, slides, actors, dancers, narrators, voices, etc., 1967-71; Prime sources no. 1-19, tape and solo voice, 1971-73; music for cello and tape, 1972; Stereo radio 5: about talking, tape, 1972; Compound skill fracture, actor, tape, film, 1973.
3005 Dana St., Berkeley, CA 94705

*GODOWSKY, LEOPOLD
b. Vilnius, Poland, 13 Feb. 1870; U.S. citizen 1921; d. New York, N. Y., 21 Nov. 1938. Began composing and giving piano concerts at age 9, and made tours to the U.S. and Canada, 1884-86. He returned to Europe, becoming a pupil and protege of Saint-Saens. In 1890 he was back in the U.S. as faculty member at the New York Coll. of Music; taught in Philadelphia, 1894-95; then became head of the piano department, Chicago Cons., 1895-1900. From 1900 to 1914 he taught and played in Europe, then returned again to the U.S. He edited many piano works, made arrangements of works by Brahms, Johan Strauss, and Weber, and composed 53 studies on Chopin Etudes. His works are noted for extreme difficulty and for expanding piano technique to amazing limits.
WORKS: Piano: Miniatures, 46 pieces for piano 4-hands, pupil and teacher, 1918; Triakontameron, 30 pieces, including Alt Wien, 1920; Java suite, 12 pieces; 6 waltz poems for left hand alone; Prelude and fugue, left hand alone; Passacaglia; Renaissance, 23 pieces; Walzermasken, 24 pieces; piano sonata.

GODWIN, JOSCELYN
b. Kelmscott, England, 16 Jan. 1945; to U.S. 1966. Studied with Philip Radcliffe and Alan Ridout, Cambridge Univ.; Robert Palmer and Karel Husa, Cornell Univ. Her string trio won the Abyngdon Prize at Cambridge Univ., 1966. She taught at Cleveland State Univ., 1969-71; has been assistant professor, Colgate Univ., 1971-   .
WORKS: Orchestra: Epiphanies, 1967-68; Chamber music: flute sonata; piano sonata, 1968; Chorus: Epistle to Harmodius, 1966; Carmina amoris, women's voices and 2 instrumental groups, 1967; many other instrumental works.
R.D. #1, Earlville, NY 13332

*GOEB, ROGER
b. Cherokee, Iowa, 9 Oct. 1914. Studied agriculture along with violin, viols, horn and trumpet, Univ. of Wisconsin, B. S. 1936; composition with Nadia Boulanger in Paris; at Cleveland Inst. of Music, M. M. 1942; State Univ. of Iowa, Ph. D. 1945; also with Otto Luening. He received 2 Guggenheim fellowships, 1950, 1952; American Acad. of Arts and Letters award, 1953. He has taught at Stanford Univ.; Univ. of Oklahoma; State Univ. of Iowa; Bard Coll.; and at Juilliard School, 1947-50. He was executive secretary, American Composers Alliance for a number of years, then secretary-treasurer, Composers Recordings, Inc.
WORKS: Orchestra: 4 symphonies, 1945, 1946, 1952, 1954; Fantasy, oboe and strings, 1947; 5 American dances, 1952; viola concerto, 1953; concerto #2 for orch., 1956; concertino, trombone and strings; Chamber music: sonata for solo viola, 1942; piano sonata, 1942; concerto for 2 sopranos and chamber orch., 1942; 2 string quartets, 1942, 1948; string trio, 1945; suite for 4 clarinets, 1946; suite for woodwind trio, 1946; Lyric piece, trumpet and piano, 1947; Prairie song, woodwind quintet, 1948; brass septet, 1949; quintet for trombone and string quartet, 1950; woodwind quintet, 1956.
Composers Recordings, Inc.
170 West 74th St., New York, NY 10023

*GOEHR, RUDOLPH
Pastorales for orch., New York, 18 Apr. 1974.

GOEMANNE, NOEL
b. Poperinge, Belgium, 10 Dec. 1926; U.S. citizen 1959. Graduated from the Lemmens Inst. of Belgium with the Laureate diploma, later studied at the Royal Cons. in Liege. His teachers included Marinus DeJong, Staf Nees, Jules Van Nuffel, and Flor Peeters. Before coming to the U.S. in 1952, he was organist in Rochefort and piano recitalist on Belgian radio. He has held organ posts in Texas and Michigan since 1952; St. Monica's in Dallas, 1968-72; Christ the King Church, Dallas, 1972-   ; and has been on the faculty, Tarrant County Junior Coll. Ft. Worth.
WORKS: Chorus: This is the day, with organ, flute, trumpet, percussion, Ft. Worth, May, 1973; A musical instrument, text by Elizabeth Browning; Rondo for children, text by composer; Daffodils, Wordsworth text, women's voices; Ode to St. Cecilia, chorus, winds, timpani, organ, Dryden text, Ft. Worth, 3 June 1973; Organ: Fantasia; Festival voluntary; March; Rhapsody; Victorious song; Marche solennelle; Solemn overture, with brass and timpani; Triptych, Manila, P.I., Oct. 1971; many Latin masses, English masses, anthems, hymns, organ works.
3523 Woodleigh Dr., Dallas TX 75229

GOETSCHIUS, MARJORIE
b. Raymond, N. H., 23 Sep. 1915. Attended Georgian Court Coll.; Tufts Univ.; studied composition with Percy Goetschius (grandfather) and Bernard Wagenaar, Juilliard School, and Joseph Schillinger; piano with James Friskin, voice with Maria Stefany. She has been piano soloist, singer, and cellist, author of scripts for network programs.

(GOETSCHIUS, MARJORIE)
WORKS: Chamber music: Theme and variations, piano; piano suite; The magic of Christmas, 12 songs for solo voice; Lament, violin and piano; Tango del ensueno, violin and piano; Poetique, piano; Reminiscence, soprano; piano sonata; Valse burlesque, violin; etc.; background music for CBS Theatre.
300 Broadway, #18, Dobbs Ferry, NY 10522

GOLD, ERNEST
b. Vienna, Austria, 13 July 1921; U.S. citizen 1946. Studied piano at the Vienna State Acad; on coming to the U.S. in 1938 studied composition with Otto Cesano in New York, later with George Antheil in Hollywood; studied conducting with Leon Barzin in New York. While working as a song writer for BMI he wrote two hits, Practice makes perfect and Accidentally on purpose. In 1946 he went to Hollywood and began writing for motion pictures. After a brief return to New York in 1954, he settled in Hollywood, dividing his time among composing, conducting, lecturing, musical theatre, and the creation of educational music. His awards include Carl Fischer award for string quartet, 1956; Laurel award, 1958; Foreign Press Assoc. award, 1959; Downbeat award, 1959; Academy Award nominations, 1959, 1963, 1969; Academy Award, 1961; commission, Musical Arts Society of La Jolla.
WORKS: Theatre: Song of the bells, pageant, Santa Barbara Bowl, Fiesta Week, 1956; Maria, pageant, Barbara Bowl, Fiesta Week, 1957; I'm Solomon, musical, New York, 1968; Orchestra: Pan American symphony; piano concerto, 1946; Symphony for 5 instruments; Boston Pops march; Band: Introduction and fugue; Gavotte and march; Chamber music: string quartet, 1956; Songs of love and parting; piano sonata, won Steinway award; flute sonatina, 1964; 3 miniatures for piano; Film scores: The true story of the Civil War, 1956; The defiant ones, 1958; The young Philadelphians, 1959; On the beach; 1959; Inherit the wind, 1960; Exodus, 1960; The last sunset, 1961; Judgment at Nuremberg, 1961; Pressure point, 1962; A child is waiting, 1963; It's a mad, mad, mad, mad world, 1963; Ship of fools, 1965; The secret of Santa Vittoria, 1969; music for 3 experimental pictures: Architecture of Frank Lloyd Wright; The picnic; The assignation. He has published articles in many music journals.
8021 Ocean Terrace, Hollywood, CA 90046

GOLD, MORTON
b. New York, N. Y., 6 Oct. 1933. Studied with Hugo Norden and Gardner Read, Boston Univ.; Walter Piston, Harvard Univ.; conducting with Hugo Ross, Lorna Cooke de Varon at Tanglewood, 1954, 1955, 1958; with Pierre Monteux, Hancock, Me., 1956, 1957, 1958; was guest conductor of own works at Boston Pops, 1954, 1959. He has taught at various schools in New England; was organist and choir director, Temple Emanuel, Providence; faculty, Nasson Coll., 1964-   , associate professor, 1969-   ; conductor, Amherst Summer Music Center, 1969-   .
WORKS: Orchestra: Rhapsody, 1954; A dedication overture, 1959; piano concerto, 1960;

GOLD, MORTON

(GOLD, MORTON)
Elegy for strings, 1967; Chamber music: Psalm, viola and piano, 1965; string trio, 1967; Recitative, solo cello, 1968; string quartet, 1970; 5 songs without words, violin and piano, 1970; Toccata, piano, 1971; Remembrances, wind quintet, 1971; Chorus: Sabbath Eve sacred service, 1966; Psalm 119, 1966; Psalm 98, double chorus, organ, brass, percussion, 1969; Prayer of Micah, 1971; A song at eventide, with orch., 1971; Prayer of Solomon, 1973; Haggadah, oratorio for tenor solo, chorus, Orch., organ, Syracuse, N. Y., March 1974.
16 Bradeen St., Springvale, ME 04083

GOLDBERG, STEPHEN EDWARD
b. Albany, N. Y., 20 Aug. 1952. Studied with Burt Fenner, Mannes Coll. of Music; Morris Lawner, High School of Music and Art; Leo Kraft, Hugo Weisgall, Queens Coll., CUNY. He won 3rd prize in a Sigma Alpha Iota contest.
WORKS: Theatre: Follie di Baseball, 1-act opera, 1973; Piano: The death of Moses, 1971; Terpsichore, 1972; Variations on a short theme, 1972.
33-27 91st St., Jackson Heights, NY 11372

GOLDBERG, WILLIAM B.
b. New York, N. Y., 24 Jan. 1917. Studied piano with Lonny Epstein at Juilliard School; composition with Jacob Weinberg, New York Coll. of Music. He was awarded a $500 commission and prize by Georgia State Univ. for music for brass, 1971. He is a private music teacher.
WORKS: Wind ensemble: Tenebrae, 7 brass, 2 voices, organ, percussion, 1971; Works and days, brass quintet, voice, tape, commissioned by New York Brass Quintet, 1972; Antiphonies, 3 brass quintets and organ, 1973; Piano: Prelude and toccata, 1950; 3 piano sonatas; 3 sonatinas.
11 Fifth Ave., Northport, NY 11768

*GOLDE, WALTER
b. Brooklyn, N. Y., 4 Jan. 1887; d. Chapel Hill, N. C., 4 Sep. 1963. Studied at Columbia Univ.; Dartmouth Coll., B. A. 1910; and the Vienna Cons. He was head of the voice department, Columbia Univ., 1944-48; head, Inst. of Opera, Univ. of North Carolina, 1953. He wrote many songs and piano pieces.

*GOLDENBERG, WILLIAM LEON
b. Brooklyn, N. Y., 10 Feb. 1936. Studied at Columbia Univ., B. A.; privately with Hall Overton. He was arranger and composer for Broadway shows; music director and composer, Kukla, Fran and Ollie on television; later film composer.
WORKS: Chamber music: brass quintet; woodwind quintet; string quartet.
3688 Wrightwood Dr., Studio City, CA 91604

*GOLDMAN, EDWIN FRANKO
b. Louisville, Ky., 1 Jan. 1878; d. New York, N. Y., 21 Feb. 1956. Studied with Antonin Dvorak at the Nat. Cons., New York. A master bandsman and composer for the band, he received 2 honorary doctorates and more than 100 medals and citations from governments and organizations all over the world. He played solo cornet with the Metropolitan Opera orchestra, 1895-1905; taught cornet

(GOLDMAN, EDWIN FRANKO)
and trumpet, 1905-1918; organized his own band in 1911 and began the Goldman Band Concerts in 1918. He wrote more than 100 marches; other works for band; solos and methods for band instruments; and songs.
WORKS: Marches: On the mall, 1924; Emblem of freedom; On parade, etc. He was also author of an autobiography, Facing the music.

GOLDMAN, RICHARD FRANKO
b. New York, N. Y., 7 Dec. 1910; son of Edwin Franko Goldman. Studied with Pietro Floridia, Wallingford Riegger, Ralph Leopold, Clarence Adler in New York. His awards include Alice M. Ditson award, 1961; Kappa Kappa Psi award, 1971; honorary citizen, New Orleans; honorary doctorates, Lehigh Univ., Univ. of Maryland, Mannes Coll. of Music. He has been conductor, The Goldman Band, 1956- ; faculty member, Juilliard School, 1946-60; visiting professor or lecturer, Princeton, Columbia, New York Univ.; president Peabody Inst., 1968- .
WORKS: Opera: Athalia, commissioned by Little Orch. Society; The mandarin; Orchestra: The Lee Rigg; Band: A sentimental journey, 1941; A curtain raiser and country dance; Hymn for brass choir; many marches including The foundation; Chamber music: 3 clarinet duets, 1944; duo for tubas, 1948; piano sonatina; violin sonata, 1952; Divertimento, flute and piano; 2 monochromes, solo flute; Le bobino, 2 pianos. He is author of the books: The band's music, 1938; The concert band, 1946; Harmony of western music, 1965.
Peabody Institute, Baltimore, MD 21202

*GOLDMARK, RUBIN
B. New York, N. Y., 15 Aug. 1872; d. New York, 6 Mar. 1936. Studied at City Coll. of New York and with Johann Nepomuk Fuchs, Vienna Cons.; with Antonin Dvorak, Nat. Cons., New York. He received the Paderewski chamber music prize, 1909. He taught at the Coll. Cons., Colorado Springs, 1895-1901; privately in New York, 1902-24; then was head of the composition department, Juilliard School, 1924-36.
WORKS: Orchestra: Hiawatha, overture, 1900; Samson, symphonic poem, 1914; Gettysburg requiem, 1919; A negro rhapsody, 1923; The call of the plains, 1925; Chamber music: piano quartet, 1909; piano trio; songs.

*GOLDSMITH, JERRY
His score for Planet of the apes was selected by the Australian Ballet Company for use in the ballet, Othello, performed Melbourne, 7 June 1971; his score for Patton was a multiple Oscar winner, 1971; score for NBC's The red pony received an Emmy award, 1973.

GOLDSMITH, OWEN L.
b. Borger, Tex., 8 Oct. 1932. Studied with Wendell Otey and William Ward, San Francisco State Univ., A. B. magna cum laude 1959, M. A. 1965. He taught at Livermore High School, Cal., 1960-69; Clayton Valley High School, Concord, Cal., 1969- .

(GOLDSMITH, OWEN L.)
WORKS: Orchestra: Festival overture; music for Our Town; Chorus: The weather's criminal, cycle for women's voices; Cleavings, cycle for mixed voices; Alleluia; Interlude; Tears; many vocal solos.
3967 Stanford Way, Livermore, CA 94550

GOLDSTEIN, MALCOLM
b. Brooklyn, N. Y., 27 Mar. 1936. Studied with Otto Luening at Columbia Univ. He has been instructor, Columbia Univ., 1961-65; New School for Social Research, 1963-65, 1967-69; New England Cons., 1965-67; Dickinson Coll., 1969-71; Goddard Coll., 1972- ; and is also a free-lance violinist.
WORKS: Chamber music: upon the string, within the bow....breathing; frog pond at dusk; Emanations, violin and cello; Majority-1964; Sirens for Edgard Varese; Still point, for brass quintet; Paradoxes; Vocal: Illuminations from fantastic gardens; death: act or fact of dying; Yosha's morning song; Tape collages: Cantos; Sheep meadow; Images of Cheng Hsieh; State of the nation; Ludlow blues; It seemed to me....
Sheffield, VT 05866

GOLDSTEIN, WILLIAM
b. Newark, N. J., 25 Feb. 1942. Studied with Vittorio Giannini, Nicolas Flagello, Ludmila Ulehla at Manhattan School of Music; Trenton State Coll.; 2 years in the BMI Musical Theatre Workshop, under Lehman Engel. He was composer and arranger, U.S. Army Band and Chorus, Washington, 1966-69; staff composer Columbia Music, 1969-70; free lance in recordings, commercials, film, and theatre.
WORKS: Theatre: Dimensions of peacocks, 1961, and Human being, 1961, incidental music; Dancing, dancing good-by, musical, 1963; A bullet for Billy the Kid, short folk opera, 1964; A total sweet success, musical, 1965; The peddler, 1-act opera, 1966; Mr. Tambo, Mr. Bones, 12 songs, incidental music, 1969; Orchestra: Whole tone fantasy, 1960; Historical suite, 1962; Excursion, ballet, 1965; trumpet concerto, 1972; Band: Symphonic movement, 1966; Colloquy, trombone and band, 1967; Chamber music: Modes for three, 2 violins and cello, 1962; Quietude, harp, 2 violins, cello, 1963; Gigue, 1963; Two moods, 1964; woodwind quintet, 1964; Fugue for 10 instruments, 1964; Fusion, 7 winds, percussion, 1971; Vocal: I sit and look out, male chorus, 1968; Rejoice, song cycle, tenor and orch., 1973; Piano: Suite for April, 1962; Scherzo, 1963; Sea chanty, 1963; sonata, 1964; Film scores: Stoolie, 1972; theme for NET's The advocates, 1972; etc.
315 West 86th St., New York, NY 10024

GOLSON, FLORENCE (Mrs. W. W. Bateman)
b. Fort Deposit, Ala., 4 Dec. 1891. Attended Tenn. School for the Blind; Huntingdon Coll.; graduated, Cincinnati Cons.; studied privately in New York with Edgar Stillman Kelley, Roy Harris, Frederick Jacobi; voice with Walter Golde; attended American Cons. She held a scholarship at Cincinnati Cons.; won an award for

(GOLSON, FLORENCE)
a cantata; her portrait was chosen to hang in the Alabama Museum of Archives and History as Alabama's first musician. She was church soloist and recitalist, 1919-42; choral director, 1923-48; maintained private voice studio, College Park, Ga., 1924-36, Montgomery, Ala., 1943-67.
WORKS: Chamber music: Solitude, violin and piano; The banjo, violin and piano; Moods, for piano; Chorus: Night, women's voices; A spring symphony, cantata for women's voices with soprano solo; Songs: The bird with a broken wing; A message; Rest; Little boy blue; A kiss from Columbine.
311 Government St., Wetumpka, AL 36092

GONZALEZ, LUIS JORGE
b. San Juan, Argentina, 22 Jan. 1936; to U.S. 1971. Studied at Nat. Univ. of Cuyo, Argentina; with Earle Brown and Robert Hall Lewis, Peabody Inst. He has received honorable mention, Viotti Internat. Competition, 1971; 3rd prize, Annapolis Fine Arts Competition, 1972, 1973; 2nd prize, Phi Mu Alpha Sinfonia, 1973. He was staff member, Teatro Argentina, 1969; professor, State Univ. of San Juan, 1965-71; piano instructor, Peabody Inst., Preparatory Div., 1972- .
WORKS: Chamber music: Ague larre, piano and chamber orch.; Voces I, 3 pieces for clarinet and piano; At the beginning was the word, organ; Motables, vibraphone and harpsichord; Metaphores, trio; Exorcisms, viola and string orch.; Voces II, chamber ensemble; Hypallages, chamber ensemble, New York, Dec. 1973.
3401 North Charles St., Apt. 410
Baltimore, MD 21218

*GONZALEZ, MANUEL B.
Nela, 3-act opera, Puerto Rico Opera Company, Hostos Coll., Bronx, N. Y., May 1974.

GOODE, DANIEL
b. New York, N. Y., 24 Jan. 1936. Studied at Oberlin Coll.; with Henry Cowell, Jack Beeson, Otto Luening, Columbia Univ.; with Kenneth Gaburo, Robert Erickson, and Pauline Oliveros, Univ. of California, La Jolla. He received the Anton Seidl fellowship for composition, Columbia Univ.; 2 grants, Rutgers Research Council; and commissions. He was instructor, Univ. of North Dakota, 1963-64; Univ. of Minnesota, 1964-67; music director, Walker Art Center, Minneapolis, 1967-68; research assistant, Univ. of California, 1968-70; assistant professor, Livingston Coll., Rutgers Univ., 1971- .
WORKS: Chamber music: Inner motions, 14 instruments, 1969-73; Orbits, 2 instrumentalists and 6 moving bodies, 1970; Circular thoughts, clarinet solo, 1973; 4 paths, piano, 1973; Tape: Worm, 1970; Barn gongs, 1972.
458 West 20th St., New York, NY 10011

GOODE, JACK C.
b. Marlin, Tex., 20 Jan. 1921. Attended Baylor Univ., B. M. 1942, M. M. 1947; American Cons. of Tulsa; Berlin Hochschule, 1957; studied with Leo Sowerby, Bela Rozsa, Ernst Pepping, Stella Roberts, and organ with Joseph Ahrens. His

GOODE, JACK C.

(GOODE, JACK C.)
   awards include 2 first prizes, Phi Mu Alpha; and
commissions. He was instructor, Northwestern
Univ., 1949-50; professor, Wheaton Coll., Ill.,
1950-66; private instructor, organ, church music,
composition, 1954-
      WORKS: Orchestra: Trilogy; Wheels of au-
tumn, chorus and orch.; Pity me not, chorus and
orch.; Sketch; Band: Burlesque march; Rondino,
alto saxophone and band, Paris, 2 Feb. 1966;
Chamber music: Sonatina, clarinet and piano,
Chicago, 29 Oct. 1963; 2 string quartets, no. 1,
Tulsa, 30 Mar. 1949; Petite suite, 4 saxophones;
Sonata from Joel, trumpet and organ, Evanston,
Ill., 22 June 1961; brass quintet, 1968; 5 fiddle
fancies; Songs: The silence of the night; A song
cycle, for soprano, Tulsa, 8 May 1948; 3 songs of
love and despair, baritone, Chicago, 15 June 1970;
Pastorale for an August night, Organ point, 3
for Ruth, baritone, Chicago, 16 Mar. 1971; Organ:
Sonata, Albany, N. Y., 1958; Fancy for the trumpet stop, New York, 28 July 1959; Aria, Chicago,
13 Oct. 1961; Magnificat, Ghent, 12 July 1926;
3 tableaux, Michigan State Univ., 5 Oct. 1969;
many works for organ, piano, chorus.
      2742 Helen Dr., Glenview, IL 60025

*GOODENOUGH, FORREST
   b. South Bend, Ind., 1918. Studied at Butler
Univ.; DePauw Univ.; and Eastman School of Music.
He received grants from the Woodstock Found. for
the Arts, 1948, 1949; performance award, Austin
Symphony Orchestra. He has been faculty member,
Texas School for the Blind at Austin.
      WORKS: Orchestra: Chorale fantasy; Elegy,
1960.

*GOODMAN, AL
   b. Nitropol, Russia, 12 Aug. 1890; to U.S. 1895;
d. New York, N. Y., 10 Jan. 1972. Studied on
scholarship at the Peabody Cons. He was conductor for Broadway shows, 1920-40, then for
radio and television.
      WORKS: Musicals: Linger longer Lettie;
Cinderella on Broadway; The whirl of New York;
The lady in ermine; The passing show of 1922;
Artists and models of 1925; Gay Paree; and many
songs.

*GOODMAN, ALFRED
   b. Berlin, Germany, 1 Mar. 1920; to U.S. 1940.
Studied with Henry Cowell and Otto Luening,
Columbia Univ., B. S. 1952, M. A. 1953. He was
in the U.S. Army in World War II; in 1946 was an
arranger for dance bands. He returned to Germany
in 1960. His works include a 1-act opera, The
audition, 1954; 2 symphonies; choral pieces and
chamber music.

*GOODMAN, JOHN
   Studied at Northeastern Univ., B. A.; Yale Univ.,
M. M.; Boston Univ., D. M. A. He received the
Woods-Chandler prize in composition. He has
held faculty posts at the New England Cons. and
Emmanuel Coll.; has been assistant professor,
Boston Univ., 1969-
      WORKS: Orchestra: Songs of parting, on
Chinese verses, for soprano, tenor and orch.,

(GOODMAN, JOHN)
   1963; Chamber music: string quartet in one
movement, 1964; piano sonata, 1965.
      School of the Arts
      Boston University, Boston, MA 02215

GOODMAN, JOSEPH M.
   b. New York, N. Y., 28 Nov. 1918. Attended
Johns Hopkins Univ., B. A. 1938; Harvard Univ.,
M. A. 1948; studied with Richard Donovan, Paul
Hindemith, Walter Piston; and Gian Francesco
Malipiero on a Fulbright grant for study in
Italy. He has taught at City Univ. of New York,
1952-   , professor Queens Coll., 1973-   ;
lecturer, School of Sacred Music, Union Theological Seminary, 1956-   , head, composition
department, 1959-   .
      WORKS: Chamber music: trio, flute, violin,
piano; wind quintet, 1954; 5 bagatelles, flute,
clarinet, bassoon; Music for 2 flutes; Chorus
a cappella: 4 motets; 3 motets for benediction;
Laudate Dominum; Crucem Tuam; Adoremus te,
Criste; Trinity of blessed light; A king en-
throned on high; Before the ending of the day;
How beautiful the queen of night; Song in the
wood; Green brooms; 3 Christmas alleluias; Behold the handmaid of the Lord; Lyrics from the
Spanish; Love came down at Christmas, chorus and
organ; Organ: Fantasia on the hymn tune Windsor;
Fantasy, 1968; 3 preludes on Gregorian melodies;
Fantasia on Panis angelicus; concerto for organ
and orch.; concertante for organ and 8 chamber
players.
      100 Sunnyside Ave.
      Pleasantville, NY 10570

*GOODMAN, SAUL
   b. Brooklyn, N. Y., 17 July.   Is on the faculty
Juilliard School.
      WORKS: Percussion: Ballad for dance;
Canon; Dance patterns; Introduction and allegro;
Off we go; Timpiana.

*GOODRICH, (JOHN) WALLACE
   b. Newton, Mass., 27 May 1871; d. Boston, Mass.,
6 June 1952. Studied with Henry Dunham and
George W. Chadwick, New England Cons.; with
Rheinberger in Munich and Widor in Paris. He
taught at the New England Cons., was dean,
1907-31, director, 1931-42; organist, Trinity
Church, 1902-09; with the Boston Symphony Orchestra, 1897-1907. He founded the Choral Arts
Society in 1902; was conductor at various times
of the St. Cecilia Society, Boston Opera Company,
Worcester County Choral Assoc. He wrote choral
works.

GOODSMITH, RUTH B.
   b. Chicago, Ill., 27 Sep. 1892. Studied with
Arne Oldberg and Carl Beecher, Northwestern Univ.
B. M. 1922; with Andre Bloch, Fontainebleau,
1927; Alfred Rossi, Milan, 1930; Adolf Weidig
and Leo Sowerby, American Cons., M. M. 1939.
She won first prize, Mu Phi Epsilon contest,
1954; 3rd place, Nat. Fed. of Music Clubs, 1967.
She was on the faculty, Stephens Coll., 1920-58;
visiting professor, Univ. of Redlands, 1952-53.

(GOODSMITH, RUTH B.)
WORKS: Opera: Lolita, chamber opera, 1953; Orchestra: God's rider, orch. and chorus; And in the Hanging Gardens, orch. and chorus; Chamber music: Lullaby, piano or harp; piano pieces.
2235 Florencita Dr., Montrose, CA 91020

GOODWIN, GORDON
b. Cape Girardeau, Mo., 22 Jan. 1941. Studied with Hunter Johnson, J. Clifton Williams, Lothar Klein, and Anthony Donato, Univ. of Texas, D. M. A. 1969. He was faculty member, Univ. of Texas, 1967-73; Univ. of South Carolina, 1973- .
WORKS: Orchestra: Codes for orchestra; Band: Casts; Large ensembles: Voyages, percussion; Forks, brass choir; Chamber music: sonata for bass trombone and piano; Concerns, woodwind quartet and trombone.
Department of Music
University of South Carolina
Columbia, SC 29208

GOOSEN, FREDERIC
b. St. Cloud, Minn., 30 July 1927. Attended Univ. of Minnesota and Longy School of Music; studied with Donald Ferguson, Arthur Shepherd, James Aliferis; piano with William Lindsay. He was faculty member, Univ. of Minnesota, 1953-54; Berea Coll., 1955-58; Univ. of Alabama, 1958- .
WORKS: Orchestra: Litanies; Stanzas and refrains; Dance measures; Hae: In memoriam Thomas Mann; Chamber music: Equali, 4 trombones; Clausulae, violin and piano; Temple music, violin and piano; Chorus: Hodie.
3124 4th Court East, Tuscaloosa, AL 35401

*GORDELL, EVAN
A lonely sailor's life, men's chorus.

*GORDON, LOUIS B.
Man and machine for band.
Fairleigh-Dickinson University
Madison, NJ 07940

GORDON, PETER LAURENCE
b. New York, N. Y., 20 June 1951. Studied with Kenneth Gaburo, Roger Reynolds, electronics with Lew Prince, Univ. of California, San Diego, B. A. 1972; with Robert Ashley, Terry Riley, Mills Coll., M. F. A. 1974. He has received the Alice Q. McPherson Memorial prize, 1968; Gogglestead award, 1971; Univ. of California fellowship, 1972-73.
WORKS: Chamber music: Fur cruiser, quartet, 1969; Wind-finger songs, 6 flutes, 3 keyboards, 1971; Vertices, sextet, 1971-72; Les enfants terribles, string trio, 1972; Electronic: Hi F, tape, 1969; Machomusic 1, live electronics and 6 saxophones, 1973; Monodies and monologues, electronic and spoken voice, 1973.
46 Belvedere St., San Francisco, CA 94117

*GORDON, PHILIP
b. Newark, N. J., 14 Dec. 1894. Studied at Columbia Univ., B. A., M. A., Ph. D. He has been professor, Chicago Musical Coll.; Seton

(GORDON, PHILIP)
Hall Univ.; visiting professor, Westminster Choir Coll.; Princeton Univ.; has conducted the Newark Civic Symphony and the Bach Cantata Society.
WORKS: Orchestra: Northern saga; Exotic dance, string orch.; 2 moods; Little baroque suite; 3 preludes for strings; Band: American frontier; Colonial diary; New England chronicle; Olympia; Prairie saga; Robert Burns overture; etc.; also chamber pieces and choral works.

GORE, RICHARD T.
b. Takoma Park, Md., 25 June 1908. Studied piano and organ in New York; attended Columbia Univ., B. A. 1933, M. A. 1938; Univ. of Rochester, Ph. D. 1956. He became a fellow, American Guild of Organists, 1935; held Victor Baier fellowship, Columbia Univ., 1936; won anthem contest of The Composers' Press, 1945. He was assistant professor, Mt. Holyoke Coll., 1928-29; assistant professor and university organist, Cornell Univ., 1939-45; professor, Coll. of Wooster, 1945, department chairman, 1945-72.
WORKS: Many church choral and organ works including Let God arise, anthem; Psalm diptych (Psalms 50 and 150), chorus and organ.
1628 Cleveland Road, Wooster, OH 44691

GORELLI, OLGA
b. Bologna, Italy, 14 June 1920; U.S. citizen 1945. Studied with Gian Carlo Menotti and Rosario Scalero at Curtis Inst.; with Quincy Porter and Paul Hindemith at Yale Univ., Werner Josten and Alvin Etler, Smith Coll.; and with Darius Milhaud at Tanglewood, Mill Coll., and Aspen, Colo. She received the Fatman Prize at Smith Coll., 1949, 1950. She was teaching fellow, Smith Coll., 1948-50; instructor, Hollins Coll., 1950-54; faculty member, Trenton State Coll., 1954-57.
WORKS: Opera: Dona Petra; Between the shadow and the dream; Chorus: Mass in English; many other choral works, songs, 2 dance dramas, incidental music, orchestral works, and chamber music.
Scotch Road, Pennington, NJ 08534

*GORIN, IGOR
b. Grodek, Ukraine, 26 Oct. 1908; U.S. citizen 1939. Studied with Victor Fuchs, Vienna Cons.; Brigham Univ. D. M. 1956. He made his debut as a singer at Hollywood Bowl, 1939. He is professor of voice, Univ. of Arizona.
WORKS: Songs: Lament; The jumping jack; Caucasian song; Lullaby; Safe by de Lawd; Remembered mornings; Within my dreams.
Department of Music, University of Arizona
Tucson, AZ 85721

GOTTLIEB, JACK
b. New Rochelle, N. Y., 12 Oct. 1930. Studied first with Robert Strassberg; then with Karol Rathaus, Queens Coll.; New York Univ., B. A. cum laude 1953; with Irving Fine, Brandeis Univ., M. F. A. 1955; with Aaron Copland and Boris Blacher at Tanglewood; with Burrill Phillips and Robert Palmer, Univ. of Illinois, 1955-58,

GOTTLIEB, JACK

(GOTTLIEB, JACK)
D. M. A. 1964. He received the Nadworney Memorial award, Nat. Fed. of Music Clubs, 1957; first prize, NFMC choral works contest, 1957; Ohio Univ. opera competition, 1957; Brown Univ. choral contest, 1960; Ford Found. grant for New York City Center Opera Workshop, 1959; various Yaddo and MacDowell fellowships, 1962-67, 1971; annual ASCAP awards, 1963-   ; citation, Park Avenue Synagogue, New York, "for outstanding contribution to liturgical music." He was assistant to Leonard Bernstein, 1958-66; free-lance conductor and composer, 1966-70; music director, Congregation Temple Israel, St. Louis, 1970-73; faculty member and composer-in-residence, School of Sacred Music, Hebrew Union Coll., New York, 1973-   .
WORKS: Opera: Tea party (Sonata allegro), movement 1 of A symphony of operas (4 1-act operas), 1955; Public dance (Variations) movement 2, 1964; Orchestra: Pieces of seven, Jacksonville, 23 Oct. 1962; Articles of faith, orch. and memorable voices, Detroit, 14 Apr. 1966; Chamber music: Horton hatches the egg, text by Dr. Seuss, narrator and chamber orch., Queens Coll., 6 Jan. 1952; clarinet quartet, 1952; Pastorale and dance, violin and piano, 1953; string quartet, Brandeis Univ., 25 Apr. 1955; piano sonata, New York, 9 Feb. 1963; Twilight crane (Yuzuru), woodwind quintet, New York, 24 Mar. 1962; The silent flickers, 12 diversions for piano, 4-hands, 1968; Chorus: Sunday morning in Manhattan, text by composer, a cappella, 1952; Kids' calls, 1957; Didn't my lord deliver Daniel; with soloists and piano, 1957; In memory of...., cantata, choir, solo, organ, New York, 18 Mar. 1960; Love songs for Sabbath, cantor, choir, organ, percussion, female readers and dancers, New York, 7 May 1965; Shout for joy, Psalms 95, 84, 81, New York, 19 Jan. 1969; The song of songs, which is Solomon's, soloists, women's chorus, chamber orch., work in progress for a setting of the entire Biblical text, excerpts performed 22 Nov. 1969; Verses from Psalm 118, choir and organ, St. Louis, 6 June 1973; Songs: Hoofprints, 3 songs for soprano, 1954; revised 1963; Two blues, female voice and clarinet, 1954, revised 1963; Mama's cooking, words by composer, 1961; Downtown blues for uptown halls, voice, clarinet and piano, 1967; Songs of loneliness, cycle for baritone and piano, Washington, 7 Mar. 1964; Haiku souvenirs, 5 songs on poems of Leonard Bernstein, Elmont, N. Y., 22 Nov. 1969. He is author of many magazine articles.
150 West 79th St., Apt. 2E
New York, NY 10024

GOTTLIEB, JAY
b. Brooklyn, N. Y., 23 Oct. 1948. Studied with Stepan Wolpe, Chatham Square Music School, 1960-64; with Louise Talma and Ruth Anderson, Hunter Coll., 1966-70; with Nadia Boulanger, France, summers, 1967-71; with Lukas Foss, Earl Kim, Harold Shapero, Leon Kirchner, Arthur Berger, Harvard Univ., 1970-   , M. M. 1972. He received Lincoln Center award, 1966; High School of Performing Arts award, 1966; Heintz

(GOTTLIEB, JAY)
scholarship, Hunter Coll. 1966; full scholarship for study with Nadia Boulanger, first prize in composition, Fontainebleau, 1969; Woodrow Wilson fellowship, 1970; Phi Beta Kappa, 1970. He has been teaching fellow and resident tutor in music, Harvard Univ., 1971-   ; rehearsal pianist, Boston Symphony Orchestra, Oct. 1973-   .
WORKS: Orchestra: Essay for orchestra, 1969; Bagatelle, 1971-72; Chamber music: Slow movement for piano trio, 1969; June Wyatt songs, 1969-70; Synchronisms, 2 percussionists and tape, 1970; violin sonata, 1970-71; Piano: sonata, 1964-67; suite of 6 pieces, 1968-69; suite for piano, 4-hands, 1968, revised 1970.
64 Linnaean St., Cambridge, MA 02138

GOULD, ELIZABETH
b. Toledo, Ohio, 8 May 1904. Attended Oberlin Coll. and Cons. and Univ. of Michigan, studied piano with Artur Schnabel and Guy Maier. She won 6 first prizes and 2 special citations in Mu Phi Epsilon contests, 1952-69; Arthur Shepherd award, 1969; Delta Omicron first prize, 1965; award for string quartet, Mannheim, Germany, 1961. She is a private teacher and composer.
WORKS: Comic opera: Ray and the gospel singer, 1966; Orchestra: piano concerto, 1953; Declaration for peace, chorus and orch., 1955; concertino, clarinet, trumpet, strings, 1958; concerto for trumpet and strings, 1959; Escapade, 1960; Chamber music: violin sonata, 1950; Prologue to "Men are naive," piano, flute, violin, narrator, 1955; cello sonata, 1959; string quartet, 1960; viola sonata, 1962; 6 affinities, brass quintet, 1962; Disciplines, oboe, clarinet, bassoon, 1963; music for viola, 1964; piano trio, 1964; suite for woodwind, brass, percussion, 1965; flute quartet, 1968; Fantasie and fugue, bassoon and piano, 1968; Vocal: Madrigal cycle, chorus, 1964; Personal and private, song cycle for soprano and flute, 1968; Halleluia, choir, organ, timpani, 1964; Piano: Toccata, 1950; 2 sonatas, 1957, 1961; sonatina, 1962; Effects, piano 4-hands, 1968; Scintillations, ballet for 2 pianos, 1969.
3137 Kenwood Blvd., Toledo, OH 43606

GOULD, MORTON
b. Richmond Hill, N. Y., 10 Dec. 1913. Studied with Abby Whiteside and Vincent Jones, Inst. of Musical Art, New York. His awards include the Nat. Acad. of Recording Arts and Sciences Grammy for recording of Ives Symphony #1, 1966; Nat. Assoc. of American Composers and Conductors Gold medal; many commissions, including commissions for a piano concerto, violin concerto, and a ballet on Audubon for Balanchine, all for the 1976 Bicentennial. He was on the staff of Radio City Music Hall and later of NBC; conducted his own program on radio for many years, and has been guest conductor of most major U.S. orchestras. His first composition, Just six, was published at age 6.
WORKS: Theatre: Billion dollar baby, musical, 1945; Fall River legend, ballet suite, 1948;

(GOULD, MORTON)

Arms and the girl, musical, 1950; Fiesta, ballet, 1957; Orchestra: Chorale and fugue in jazz, 2 pianos and orch., 1932; 3 American symphonettes, 1933, 1935, 1937; piano concerto, 1937; violin concerto, 1938; Foster gallery, 1940; Spirituals for orch., 1941; Cowboy rhapsody, 1942; Lincoln legend, 1942; Interplay, piano and orch., 1943; viola concerto, 1944; Family album; concerto for orch.; Minstrel show, 1946; Philharmonic waltzes, 1947; 4 symphonies, 1943, 1944, 1947, 1952; Dance variations, 2 pianos and orch.; Showpiece, 1954; Inventions, 4 pianos and orch.; Declaration, chorus, orch., 2 speakers, 1956; Jekyll and Hyde variations; Dialogues, piano and string orch., 1958; World War I: Sarajevo suite, Wilson suite, Verdun suite, 1964-65; Venice--Audiograph for double orch. and brass choirs, 1966; Columbia, 1967; Soundings, 1969; Vivaldi gallery, divided orch. and string quartet; Band: Ballad for band, New York, 21 June 1946; Battle hymn of the Republic, 1951; symphony #4, West Point, 1952; Hillbilly; Rumbolero; Tap dance concerto, 1952; Santa Fé saga, 1956; St. Lawrence suite; Jericho; Derivations, clarinet and jazz band, 1957; Marches; Formations, 1964; World War I: Revolutionary prelude, 1964-65; Chamber music: 3 piano sonatas, 1930, 1933, 1936; Prelude and toccata for piano; Pavane, piano; Harvest, harp, vibraphone, strings; Rag-blues-rag, piano, c. 1963; suite for tuba and 3 horns, 1971; Film scores: Delightfully dangerous; Cinerama holiday; Windjammer, 1957.

c/o Chappell and Co.
609 Fifth Ave., New York, NY 10017

GOWER, ALBERT E., JR.

b. Weed, Calif., 4 June 1935. Studied with James Adair, California State Univ., Sacramento; with George F. McKay, Univ. of Oregon; Samuel Adler and William Latham, North Texas State Univ. He received Fine Arts award in music, California State Univ., 1956; $100 award, Mississippi Educational Television contest. He has been associate professor, Univ. of Southern Mississippi, 1966-   .

WORKS: Orchestra: symphony #1; Band: Excursion; Chamber music: 3 short pieces for baritone horn and piano; string quartet; tuba sonata; trumpet sonata; 3 improvisations for brass trio; Adagio and allegro, woodwind quintet; Chorus: 3 motets, a cappella.

817 Hillendale Drive, Hattiesburg, MS 39401

GRADY, J. W.

b. Louisville, Ky., 19 Apr. 1943. Studied with Kenneth Wright, Univ. of Kentucky; with John Verrall, George F. McKay, William O. Smith, James Beale, Kenneth Benshoof, Gerald Kechley, Univ. of Washington. He was co-winner, Cleveland Inst. percussion composition contest, 1968; received 2nd prize, Phi Mu Alpha contest, 1968. He taught in public schools, Federal Way, Wash., 1969-71; was composer-in-residence, Washington State Public Schools, 1971-72.

WORKS: Chamber music: Timbre stream, percussion, alto piccolo, flute; concerto for 2 trumpets, strings, percussion; Mixed media;

(GRADY, J. W.)

Echoi, symphonic band and tape; Earthlight suite, strings and tape; Mother Goose revisited, chorus and tape.

7314 Eastside Drive, N.E., Tacoma, WA 98422

*GRAEFFE, A. DIDIER

Polyglot sequence, voice and piano, 1957; Scherzo for 4 timpani and percussion.

GRAF, WILLIAM

b. Brooklyn, N. Y., 21 Dec. 1946. Studied with Gregg Smith, Billy Jim Layton, David Lewin, Isaac Nemiroff, State Univ. of New York at Stonybrook; at Ithaca Coll.; and with Claudio Spies at Harvard Univ. He has been on the faculty, State Univ. of New York, Fredonia, 1971-   ; member of the Gregg Smith Singers and choral director, 1967-   .

WORKS: Incidental music: Teahouse of the August moon; You can't take it with you; The absence of a cello; It's never too late; The imaginary invalid; Romanoff and Juliet; Luv; Rhinoceros; The doll's house; Chorus: Ode on solitude; Rondo for voices, 16-part chorus, 1970; 6 contrasts, with 3 winds and piano, 1970; Walk in love as Christ loved us, 1970; O mistress mine, 1970; Missa brevis, solo quartet and 16-part chorus, 1971; Concert piece 1972, at least 30 voices; Joy train, stage piece for soloists, chorus, piano, electric piano and bass, percussion, 1972; Songs: Contentment, baritone, 1967; 3 songs on Millay texts; 2 songs on Hesse texts, 1971; piano pieces.

13 Leon Place, Fredonia, NY 14063

GRAGSON, WESLEY

b. Greenville, Ky., 3 May 1923. Attended Western Kentucky State Univ.; studied with Weldon Hart at West Virginia Univ.; with Herbert Elwell and Bernard Rogers, Eastman School of Music. He received an award for a band piece, 1963. He is associate professor, Elizabeth City State Univ., N. C.

WORKS: Orchestra: John Henry suite; Piece for orchestra; Band: Folk suite; Chamber music: Suite for harp and percussion.

1806 Sanford Drive, Elizabeth City, NC 27909

GRAHAM, ROBERT

b. El Dorado, Kan., 5 Sep. 1912. Studied with Edward Royce, Bernard Rogers, Wayne Barlow, Howard Hanson, and Herbert Elwell at Eastman School of Music, B. M.; with Paul Pisk at Univ. of Redlands, M. M. He received the Hubert award for composition, Univ. of Redlands, 1951; his manuscripts, recordings, etc. are being preserved in El Dorado, Kan. He was organist and music director, Tokyo, 1951-54; music therapist, 1954-57; church organist, California and Arizona, 1954-61; Hawaii, 1961-   .

WORKS: Orchestra: harpsichord concerto; Kansas suite; Oilwells; Chorus: Obookiah, oratorio; Come Lord Jesus, oratorio; many cantatas, more than 200 published anthems; piano and organ pieces.

Box 586, Waianae, HI 96792

GRAHN, ULF

GRAHN, ULF
b. Solna, Sweden, 17 Jan. 1942; to U.S. 1972.
Studied composition with Hans Eklund in Stockholm, 1962-66; at Royal Acad. of Music, 1967-71;
Catholic Univ., M. M. 1973. He held scholarships at the Royal Acad., 1967, 1969, 1970, and
from the Swedish Government, 1971, 1973; graduate fellowships at Catholic Univ., 1972-74; won
first prize in organ composition, Stockholm,
1973. He has been teaching, Catholic Univ.,
1972-   .
    WORKS: Orchestra: Concerto for orchestra;
Chamber music: This reminds me of...., 4 winds
and percussion; Soundscape, flute, English horn,
bass clarinet, percussion, Washington, 28 Oct.
1973; Electronic: Peer Gynt's farewell to Norway, Albany, Apr. 1973; music for The tempest,
Washington, Dec. 1973; Mixed media: Pace, flute
and tape, Washington, 15 July 1973; The wind of
dawn, orch. and tape; Music for 2 ballets, Washington, 21 Jan. 1974.
    900 Quincy St., N.E., Washington, DC 20017

*GRAINGER, PERCY ALDRIDGE
b. Melbourne, Australia, 8 July 1882; U.S. citi-
zen 1918; d. White Plains, N. Y., 20 Feb. 1961.
Studied piano with Louis Pabst in Melbourne,
James Kwast in Frankfurt, Germany; and with
Ferruccio Busoni in Berlin. He began concert
appearances in England in 1900; made tours to
South Africa and Australia; American debut in
New York, 1915. He served in the U.S. Army in
World War I, in the army band and as instructor
in the army music school; taught at Chicago
Musical Coll., summers, 1919-31; was chairman,
music department, New York Univ., 1932-33.
    WORKS: Orchestra: Irish tunes from County
Derry, 1909; Mock morris, 1911; Molly on the
shore, 1913; Shepherd's hey, 1913; Colonial song,
1913; In a nutshell, 1916; English dance, with
organ, 1925; To a Nordic princess, 1928, written
for his wedding at Hollywood Bowl to Ella Viola
Ström; Ye banks and braes of Bonnie Doon, 1932;
Harvest hymn, 1933; Danish folk song suite, 1937;
many works for chorus and orch., chorus and band,
a cappella chorus; Chamber music: Handel in the
Strand, 1913; My Robin is to the greenwood gone,
octet; Walking tune, woodwind quintet; Green
bushes, 1921; many songs and piano pieces.

GRANDJANY, MARCEL
b. Paris, France, 3 Sep. 1891; U.S. citizen 1945;
d. New York, N. Y., 24 Feb. 1975. Studied harp
on scholarship at Nat. Cons., Paris, winning the
Premier Prix at age 13. He made his Paris debut
at 17 and continued to give recitals until World
War I, when he served in the French Army. He
then resumed his career as harpist and also
taught at the Fontainebleau Summer School,
1921-36. He came to the U.S. in 1936 and was
appointed head of the harp department at
Juilliard School, 1938, and at Cons. de Musique,
Quebec, 1938-58; also taught at Manhattan School
of Music, 1956-66.
    WORKS: Orchestra: Poeme, harp, horn, orch.;
Aria in classic style, harp and strings or organ;
Harp: Children's hour suite; Colorado trail;
Divertissement; Rhapsody.

*GRANT, ALLAN
b. Newcastle-on-Tyne, England, 2 July 1892; to
U.S. 1897; d. Chicago, Ill. Studied at Balatka
Music Coll., Chicago; with Percy Goetschius and
Franklin Robinson, Inst. of Musical Art, New
York. Paderewski invited him at age 4 to give a
recital in Cardiff, Wales, He was concert pian-
ist and soloist with many major orchestras.
    WORKS: Orchestra: symphony; piano concerto;
Southland, written for and performed at New York
World's Fair, 1939; Piano: Gramercy Square; In
a Chinese tearoom; educational suites - Arabian
nights, Paul Bunyan, Jungle book, Paul Revere,
Marco Polo; and songs.

*GRANT, BRUCE
The women of Troy, opera, Indiana Univ., 12 Apr.
1973.

GRANT, DONALD P.
b. Chicago, Ill., 4 Sep. 1932. Attended Azusa
Pacific Coll., B. A.; Claremont, M. A.; Univ. of
Southern California, Ed. D. He was chairman,
Division of Fine Arts, Azusa Pacific Coll.,
1962-71; dean of instruction, 1971-   .
    WORKS: Chorus: Were you there, Easter can-
tata; Go tell it on the mountain, Christmas cantata; many anthems.
    Azusa Pacific College
    Hwy 66 at Citrus Ave., Azusa, CA 91702

GRANT, W. PARKS
b. Cleveland, Ohio, 4 Jan. 1910. Studied with
Harold G. Davidson, Capital Univ., B. M. 1932;
at Ohio State Univ., M. A. 1933; with A. I.
McHose, Herbert Elwell, Bernard Rogers, Wayne
Barlow, Eastman School of Music, Ph. D. 1948.
He held fellowships at Yaddo, 1949, Huntington
Hartford Found., 1959, 1963; received Mississippi Educational Television award, 1969;
prizes from Penn. Fed. of Music Clubs, Texas
Fed. of Music Clubs, Louisiana Fed. of Music
Clubs, Texas Manuscript Society. His faculty
positions include Ohio public schools, 1934-37,
1943-44; Tarleton State Coll., 1937-43; Louisiana State Univ., 1944-47; Temple Univ., 1947-51;
professor, Univ. of Mississippi, 1953-   .
    WORKS: Orchestra: 3 symphonies; The masque
of the red death, symphonic poem; 6 overtures;
Character sketches, suite; horn concerto; clarinet concerto; double-bass concerto; Scherzo
for flute and orch.; Autumn woodland poem,
string orch.; instrumental motet, strings; 3
suites for strings; Chamber music: 3 Night
poems, string quartet; 2 string quartets; Poem,
string quintet; The dream of the ballet master,
piano quintet; Prelude and canonic piece, flute
and clarinet; Soliloquy and jubilation, wind
quintet; 3 brass quartets; brass quintet; brass
sextet; brass septet; Prelude and dance, 11
brass instruments; Poem, horn or cello and organ;
Essay, horn or cello and organ; Concert duo,
tuba and piano; Percussion concert piece; Varied
obstinacy, saxophone and tape; Chorus: Friendship and freedom, a cappella; Prayer for Philadelphia, a cappella; Lines from the Magnificat,
a cappella; The cry of the persecuted, a cappella; There is a Santa Claus; A Pennsylvania

(GRANT, W. PARKS)

Dutch tale; Trains; Piano: 2 sonatas; Miniatures; Mood-pair; The world of shadows; The world of muse; The world of fantasy; songs, organ pieces. He has prepared corrected editions of 4 Mahler symphonies; is the author of 2 textbooks and of many articles in music journals.

    1720 Garfield St., Oxford, MS 38655

GRANTHAM, DONALD

b. Duncan, Okla., 9 Nov. 1947. Studied with Spencer Norton, Univ. of Oklahoma; with Ramiro Cortes and Robert Linn, Univ. of Southern California; Nadia Boulanger in Fontainebleau. He received first prize, Nat. Fed. of Music Clubs contests, 1964-66; McHugh composition prize, 1972. He has been teaching assistant, Univ. of Southern California, 1970- .

    WORKS: Orchestra: Variations, 1970; The war prayer, Mark Twain text, baritone and orch., 1973; Chamber music: brass quintet, 1971; piano trio, 1972; chamber concerto, harpsichord and strings, 1973; Film score: The world of Patty Sommers, 1970.

    3105 Cedar, Austin, TX 78705

*GRANT-SCHAEFER, GEORGE ALFRED

b. Williamstown, Ont., 4 July 1872; to U.S. 1896; d. Chicago, Ill., 11 May 1939. Studied in Montreal, Chicago, and London. He was organist in Chicago, 1896-1908; on faculty, Northwestern Univ., 1908-20. He wrote school operettas, piano pieces, songs.

*GRASSE, EDWIN

b. New York, N. Y., 13 Aug. 1884; d. New York, 8 Apr. 1954. Blind violinist, studied with Carl Hauser in New York; with César Thomson in Brussels at age 12; then at the Cons., winning first prize in 1900 and Prix de Capacité in 1901. He made his debut in Berlin in 1902, in New York, 1903; toured the U.S. and Europe. His compositions include American fantasy for violin and orch.; a violin sonata; violin pieces; 3 piano trios; organ pieces.

GRAUER, VICTOR A.

b. Poughkeepsie, N. Y., 11 Oct. 1937. Studied with Franklin Morris, Ernst Bacon, Syracuse Univ.; with Darius Milhaud at Aspen; with Leo Smit, Lejaren Hiller at Univ. of Buffalo; with Henri Pousser and Karlheinz Stockhausen in Cologne. He has been assistant professor, Univ. of Pittsburgh, 1970- .

    WORKS: Orchestra: Mt. Fuji in fine weather; North, percussion ensemble; Vocal: Book of the year 3000; Ezekiel I, chorus; Piano: But for the rain; White River; The liberation; Tape: Inferno; Pipes.

    5731 Centre Ave., Pittsburgh, PA 15219

GRAVES, WILLIAM LESTER, JR.

b. Terry, Miss., 26 Aug. 1915. Studied at Northwest Missouri State Coll., B. S. Ed.; with Francis J. Pyle, Drake Univ., M. M. Ed.; and with Cecil Effinger, Univ. of Colorado, Ed. D. He received 7 grants, Mississippi State Coll.

(GRAVES, WILLIAM LESTER, JR.)

for Women, 1965-72. He is professor at Mississippi State Coll. for Women.

    WORKS: Orchestra: Prelude and fugue, 1965, Two moods, 1969; Chamber music: Passacaglia and fugue for strings, 1963; 3 woodwind quintets, 1965, 1966, 1967; woodwind quartet, 1966; woodwind suite, 1969; Chorus: Hear us, O Lord, from heaven thy dwelling place, 1964; Unto to thee do we cry, women's voices, 1969; Psalm 150, 1972; Peace I leave with you, 1972; other choral works.

    P.O. Box 2363, Columbus, MS 39701

*GRAY, JUDITH

Studied with Stefan Grove, Peabody Cons. Her piano piece, Convocation #3 was performed on WBAL-TV, Baltimore, 26 Mar. 1967.

GRAYSON, RICHARD

b. Brooklyn, N. Y., 25 Mar. 1941. Studied with John Vincent, Leonard Stein, Roy Travis, Robert Trotter, Univ. of California, Los Angeles; with Easley Blackwood and John Perkins, Univ. of Chicago; Henri Pousseur, Karlheinz Stockhausen, Luciano Berio, Earle Brown in Brussels. He received a Fulbright grant and an Atwater-Kent composition prize. He was teaching associate, Univ. of California, Los Angeles, 1967-68; assistant professor, Occidental Coll., 1969- .

    WORKS: Orchestra: Symphonic inventions on a medieval lied; 3 pieces for orch.; Chamber music: 5 pieces for string quintet; 5 pieces for string quartet; Aurore, chamber ensemble; music for string trio and woodwind quartet; Happy and melancholy; Music for Arachne; Choralis; 3 songs; Meadow music, piano; Electronic: Rain; Homage to J.S. Bach; Ostinato.

    11671 Weddington St.
    North Hollywood, CA 91601

*GREEN, BERNARD

b. New York, N. Y., 14 Sep. 1908; d. Westport, Conn., 8 Aug. 1975. Was composer and conductor for films, television, and records.

    WORKS: Orchestra: symphony; Waltz etudes; The magnolia tree; Chamber music: Idyll, clarinet solo with 4 clarinets; Film scores: 30 years of fun; All the way home.

GREEN, GEORGE

b. Mt. Kisco, N. Y., 23 Aug. 1930. Studied with Boris Koutzen and Bernard Rogers, Eastman School of Music, B. M., M. M.; with Aaron Copland at Tanglewood; with Robert Palmer at Cornell Univ., D. M. A. He received a composition award, Cummington School of the Arts, 1963. His faculty positions include Univ. of Kansas, 1954-58; Ohio State Univ., 1958-59; Univ. of Vermont, 1962-63; Cornell Univ., 1966-71; professor and chairman, music department, Skidmore Coll., 1971- .

    WORKS: Band: Perihelion, 1973; Chamber music: string quartet, 1963; Prologue and fugue, violin and cello; Fantasies concertantes, violin and cello; violin sonata; 3 pieces for violin and piano; Triptych, trumpet solo; suite for solo trombone; woodwind quintet.

    Sunny Lane, Ballston Spa, NY 12020

GREEN, JOHN

*GREEN, JOHN
b. New York, N. Y., 10 Oct. 1908. Studied with
Walter R. Spalding, Harvard Univ., B. A. in eco-
nomics 1928. His awards include citations from
Nat. Fed. of Music Clubs and City and County of
Los Angeles; 3 Academy awards for conducting.
He went to Hollywood in late 1930s, became arranger for Guy Lombardo; song writer, conductor
for Paramount Studios; accompanist for Gertrude
Lawrence, Ethel Merman, James Melton; led his
own orch., etc.
    WORKS: Musicals: Mr. Whittington (London);
Here goes the bride; Orchestra: Night club; 6
impressions, piano and orch.; Merry wives of
Windsor, overture; Music for Elizabeth, piano
and orch.; Songs: Body and soul, 1931; I cover
the waterfront, Film scores: Something in the
wind; Raintree County; Empire, television film.
    903 North Bedford Drive
    Beverly Hills, CA 90210

*GREEN, RAY
b. Cavendish, Mo., 13 Sep. 1907. Studied with
Ernest Bloch, San Francisco Cons.; with Albert
Elkus, Univ. of California, Berkeley. His awards
include Carnegie Found. grant; George Ladd Prix
de Paris, 1935-37; Ford Found. grant, 1957-62;
and commissions. He was supervisor, Fed. Chorus,
San Francisco, then of Northern California Federal Music Project 1939-41; served in several
capacities as music instructor and supervisor in the
armed forces and Veterans Service, 1943-48; executive secretary, American Music Center, 1948.
    WORKS: Theatre: ballets and incidental
music to plays; Orchestra: symphony, 1945-53;
Sunday sing symphony, 1946; Rhapsody, harp and
orch., 1950; Country dance symphony; Band: Folk
song fantasies, with solo trumpet; Kentucky mountain running set; Chamber music: 3 inventories
for Casey Jones, percussion and piano, 1936;
Dance energies, solo flute; Holiday for 4, viola,
clarinet, bassoon, piano; 4 conversations, 4
clarinets; Dance sonata, 2 pianos, 1950; Duo concertante, violin and piano, 1950; 5 epigrammatic
portraits, string quartet, 1954; Concertante,
viola and piano, 1955; many works for chorus and
many songs.

GREEN, ROBERT LEE
b. Big Sandy, Mont., 13 June 1927. Studied at
Univ. of Southern California, B. M. E.; Univ. of
Montana, M. M. E.; privately with Roy Harris in
Los Angeles. He has been director, instrumental
music, Covina High School, 1963- ; director
of bands, Whittier Coll., 1964-68; conductor,
West Covina Symphony Orch., 1971-73; conductor,
American Youth Symphony Orchestra, European tour,
1973.
    WORKS: Orchestra: Polka-promenade and pro-
cession; Great are the myths, chorus and orch.;
Band: AYSB march; Chamber music: Encore, string
quartet; Capriccio, piano.
    3261 Armel Drive, Covina, CA 91723

GREGORIAN, ROUBEN
b. Tiflis, Russia; U.S. citizen. Studied at
Armenian Central Coll., Tabriz, Iran; Tehran
Cons., Iran; with Arthur Honneger, Forestier,

(GREGORIAN, ROUBEN)
and Fournier, in Paris. He was violin instructor, Tehran Cons., 1946-51, director, 1948-51;
conductor, Tehran Symphony, 1948-51; faculty
member, Boston Cons., 1952- ; founder and
first violinist, Komitas String Quartet,
1955- ; director, Komitas Choral Society,
1955- ; conductor, Portland, Maine Symphony,
1959-62; guest conductor annually, Boston Pops,
1952- .
    WORKS: Orchestra: Iranian suite; Tatragoms
bride, symphonic poem; Nairy symphonic suite;
Hega fantasie; symphony no.1; horn concerto,
Boston Pops, 1974; Chamber music: string quartets; Scherzo, piano; pieces for violin and
piano; Chorus: Easter cantata, chorus and orch.;
Iranian folk songs; other choral and solo songs.
    617 Betts Road, Belmont, MA 02178

*GRESHAM, ANN
Baroque lament, 4 saxophones.

GRESSEL, JOEL
b. Cleveland, Ohio, 23 Mar. 1943. Studied with
Martin Boykan, Arthur Berger, Harold Shapero,
Brandeis Univ.; with Milton Babbitt, Edward T.
Cone, J. K. Randall, Earl Kim, Princeton Univ.
He was treasurer and member Board of Directors,
League of Composers-Internat. Soc. for Contemporary music, U.S. Section, 1973-75.
    WORKS: Chamber music: Klavierstück, for 7
instruments, 1967; Notes for solo flute, 1969;
piece for unaccompanied cello, 1970; piece for
piano, 1969-71; Computer synthesized: Pvibes:
3 canons, 1971-72; Exercycles, 1972.
    945 West End Ave., #8B, New York, NY 10025

*GRIEB, HERBERT
b. Syracuse, N. Y., 17 Sep. 1898; d. Birmingham,
Ala. Studied at Syracuse Univ. He was organist
at radio station WAPI, 1930-34; music director,
WBRC, 1944-50; music director, Episcopal Church
of the Advent, 1926- , and Temple Eman-El,
1939- , both in Birmingham, Ala.
    WORKS: Chorus: A carol service for children;
An Easter carol service; Magnificat; Hail the day.

*GRIFFES, CHARLES TOMLINSON
b. Elmira, N. Y., 17 Sep. 1884; d. New York,
N. Y., 8 Apr. 1920. Studied with Engelbert
Humperdinck in Berlin, 1903-07. He taught at
Hackley School for Boys, Tarrytown, N. Y.,
1908-20.
    WORKS: Theatre: The Kairn of Koridwen,
dance drama, woodwinds, harp, celesta, piano,
1916; Sho-jo, pantomimic drama, 4 woodwinds, 4
strings, harp, percussion, 1917; Orchestra:
Pleasure dome of Kubla Khan, 1912-16; The white
peacock, 1917, also for piano; Poem for flute
and orch., 1918; Chamber music: 2 sketches on
Indian themes, string quartet, 1922; Piano: 3
tone pictures: The lake at evening, The vale of
dreams, The night wind, 1915; fantasy pieces:
Barcarolle, Notturno, Scherzo, 1915; Roman
sketches: The white peacock, Nightfall, The
fountain of Acqua Paola, Clouds, 1916; a sonata;
many choral works and songs.

174

*GRIFFIS, ELLIOT
b. Boston, Mass., 28 Jan. 1893; d. Los Angeles, Calif., 8 June 1967. Studied with Horatio Parker, Yale Univ.; with Stuart Mason and George W. Chadwick, New England Cons.; at New York Coll. of Music, D. M. He received Juilliard and Pulitzer scholarships. He taught in several schools in the U.S.; privately in Paris and Vienna; then was head of the theory department, Progressive Series Teachers Coll.
WORKS: Opera: Port of pleasure, 1-act; Orchestra: Paul Bunyan - Colossus, symphonic poem, 1926-34; symphony, 1931; Fantastic pursuit, for strings, 1941; A Persian fable; Yon Green Mountain suite; Montevallo, concerto grosso for piano, organ, strings; Sunlight and shadow, soprano, narrator and orch.; Chamber music: Suite for trio; violin sonata; The Aztec flute, 1946; Elegy, violin and piano; piano sonata; woodwind quartet; Letters from a Maine farm, piano; Playa laguna - arabesque, piano; and songs.

*GRIFFITH, PETER
b. Ann Arbor, Mich., 1943. Studied with Ross Lee Finney, Univ. of Michigan, M. A. 1970; was the first guitarist to be admitted to the School of Music. His One string quartet was one of four selected for recording in the first annual Composers String Quartet Composition Contest, sponsored by the New England Cons. and the Composers String Quartet, 1970.

*GRIFFITH, ROBERT B.
b. Washington, D.C., 1914. Studied at Univ. of Kentucky, B. S. 1937, M. A. in music education 1954. He taught in Louisville schools, 1937-61; has been associate professor and head, department of Music education, Univ. of Louisville, 1961-   ; horn player, Louisville Orchestra. 1949-   .
WORKS: Band: Defiance march; Courier-Journal march; 2 hymns; 2 more hymns; Britannica march; many unpublished works.
1837 Roanoke Ave., Louisville, KY 40205

GRIGSBY, BEVERLY PINSKY
b. Chicago, Ill., 11 Jan. 1928. Attended San Fernando Valley State Coll., B. A. 1961, M. A. 1963; Univ. of Southern California, candidate for D. M. A. 1973; studied with Ernst Krenek, Gerald Strang, Aurelio de la Vega, Robert Linn and Ingolf Dahl. She taught privately and in various schools, 1948-63; has been on faculty, California State Univ., Northridge, 1963-   , assistant professor 1967-   ; has conducted research in electronic music in her own studio using the Buchla Synthesizer, 1966-   .
WORKS: Chamber music: Sonnet XI, voice and piano, Los Angeles, May 1949; Dialogues, tenor and guitar, Los Angeles, Nov. 1973; Electronic: The awakening, Los Angeles, Mar. 1963; Ayamonn the terrible, film score, 1964; Mixed media: Preludes, poems of T. S. Eliot, voice and electronics, Los Angeles, Jan. 1968; Fragments from Augustine, the saint, dramatic cantata for tenor, oboe, harp, percussion, multi-media, Los Angeles, Apr. 1972.
17639 Osborne St., Northridge, CA 91324

*GRILLER, ARNOLD
b. 1937. Symphony for 8 celli and piano.

GRIMES, DOREEN
b. Weatherford, Tex., 1 Feb. 1932. Studied with Jack Frederick Kilpatrick, Southern Methodist Univ., B. M., M. M.; with Samuel Adler and George Morey, North Texas State Univ., Ph. D. 1966. She was director of her own music school, 1950-62; chairman of theory, Eastern New Mexico Univ., Portales, 1962-71; music coordinator, Angelo State Univ., 1971-   .
WORKS: Opera: Drugstore panorama, 1-act; Chamber music: Americana, chamber orch.; Vocal: The canyon, chorus; It satisfies my longing, solo; Piano: A day in the country; Prelude and allegro, 2 pianos.
3202 Lindenwood, San Angelo, TX 76901

*GRIMM, CARL HUGO
b. Zanesville, Ohio, 31 Oct. 1890. Was organist in Cincinnati and taught at Cincinnati Cons., 1907-31.
WORKS: Orchestra: Erotic poem; trumpet concerto; An American overture; Byzantine suite; Montana, symphonic sketch; and organ pieces.

*GRISELLE, THOMAS
b. Sandusky, Ohio, 10 Jan. 1891; d. Hollywood, Calif., 27 Dec. 1955. Studied at Cincinnati Coll. of Music; with Nadia Boulanger and Arnold Schoenberg in Europe. He won the Victor Records prize of $10,000 for 2 American sketches, 1928. He was accompanist for Norah Bayes, Alice Nielsen, Clarence Whitehill; taught at Muskingum Coll.; settled in Hollywood in 1939.
WORKS: Piano: A keyboard symphony, for 6 pianos; Tutti frutti; Czerny pilots a flying saucer; Songs: The cuckoo clock.

*GROFÉ, FERDINAND RUDOLPH VON (FERDE)
b. New York, 27 Mar. 1892; d. Santa Monica, 3 Apr. 1972. Studied with Pietro Floridia in New York; at St. Vincent's Coll.; received honorary doctorates, Illinois Wesleyan Univ., Western State Coll. of Colorado. He was violist in the Los Angeles Symphony, 1909-19; pianist and arranger, Paul Whiteman's Band, 1919-33; orchestrated Gershwin's Rhapsody in blue, 1924; conducted his own works in Hollywood Bowl, Lewisohn Stadium, Robin Hood Dell, etc.; appeared with his wife in 2-piano concerts.
WORKS: Orchestra: Grand Canyon suite, 1931; Broadway at night; Symphony in steel, 1937, used 4 pairs of shoes, 2 brooms, locomotive bell, pneumatic drill, compressed air tank, commissioned by president of American Rolling Mills Company; Tabloid; Death Valley suite; Mississippi suite; Mark Twain suite; Hollywood suite; Milk, paid for by a dairy; Wheels, paid for by an automobile company; 3 shades of blue; New England suite; Metropolis; Aviation suite; World's Fair suite, 1964; Film scores: King of jazz; Time out of mind; The return of Jesse James; Minstrel man.

GROLNIC, SIDNEY

GROLNIC, SIDNEY
b. Philadelphia, Pa., 15 Mar. 1946. Studied
privately with Harold Boatrite and Temple Painter.
WORKS: Orchestra: Overture for violin and
string orch.; Chamber music: Introduction and
allegro, violin and piano; Theme and variations,
oboe solo; suite for oboe and bassoon; Capriccio,
violin and piano; Chorus: Psalm 130; Alleluia;
Kyrie eleison.
411 South 18th St., Philadelphia, PA 19146

GRONQUIST, ROBERT
b. Illinois, 15 Oct. 1938. Studied at Univ. of
Illinois; Univ. d'Aix-en-Provence; Univ. of California, Berkeley. He received a Rockefeller
grant and a fellowship at Aspen. He has been
faculty member, Smith Coll.; Trinity Coll.; and
is assistant professor and director of musical
activities, Simmons Coll.
WORKS: Chorus: This endris night; Quittez
pasteurs; Mixed media: Revelation, with assis-
tance from Robert Morris, electronics by Morton
Subotnick, 1972; The Lord Zouches maske, in collaboration with Arawana Campbell, Paul Earls,
Larry Johnson, 1973.
Simmons College, Boston, MA 02115

*GROOM, LESTER H.
Gothic fanfare, organ; Processional march on
St. Dunstan's, organ.
School of Music, Seattle Pacific College
Seattle, WA 98119

*GROSS, CHARLES
b. Boston, Mass., 13 May 1934. Studied at Harvard Univ., B. A.; New England Cons.; with Darius
Milhaud at Mills Coll. on a scholarship. He was
arranger for the West Point Band for 3 years;
writes for industrials, cartoons, films.
WORKS: Theatre: music for The blacks; The
firebugs; Band: An American folk suite; Songs
of the sea; Black-eyed Susie; Irish suite; Film
score: Robert Frost - A lover's quarrel with the
world, documentary.

GROSS, ROBERT A.
b. Colorado Springs, Colo., 23 Mar. 1914. Studied with Bernard Wagenaar, Juilliard School,
1932; at Colorado Coll., A. B. 1940, Mus. D.
1967. He was assistant professor, Colorado Coll.,
1937-43, associate professor, 1943-46; professor,
chairman, music department, Occidental Coll.,
1949-   .
WORKS: Opera: The bald soprano, chamber
opera; Chamber music: 5 string quartets; violin
sonata; sonatina, viola solo; Epode, solo cello,
1955; octet, strings, woodwinds, piano; 3-4-2,
violin and cello.
2989 Alta Laguna Blvd.
Laguna Beach, CA 92651

*GROSSMAN, NORMAN
Studied with Peter Mennin at Juilliard School,
B. S., M. S.; with Aaron Copland, at Tanglewood;
in Italy on a Fulbright fellowship; then with
Vincent Persichetti. He held a teaching fellowship at Juilliard, taught at Peabody Cons.
1960-70; Juilliard School, 1972-   .
245 East 21st St., New York, NY 10010

*GROSVENOR, RALPH L.
b. Grosvenor's Corners, N. Y., 5 Dec. 1893.
Studied with Huntington Woodman in New York;
composition with Ernest Bloch. After military
service in World War I, he remained in France
for further study on the organ. He has been
pianist, organist, choral director, singer,
accompanist, and teacher in the New York area.
He wrote many sacred and secular songs.

GRUBER, ALBION
b. Savannah, Ga., 27 Oct. 1931. Studied at Univ.
of Alabama; with Samuel Adler and Wayne Barlow,
Eastman School of Music. He received a Music
Teachers Nat. Assoc. award, 1962; NDEA Title IV
fellowship, Eastman School, 1966-69; graduate
teaching assistantship, Eastman, 1968-69. He
was director, WUOA-FM, Univ. of Alabama, 1955-57;
faculty member, Savannah Country Day School,
1957-64; associate professor, Nazareth Coll.,
1964-   .
WORKS: Orchestra: Charade; Trichotomy;
Chamber music: Woodforms, flute, clarinet, violin, viola; trio for violin, clarinet, piano;
Carriwitchet, woodwind ensemble; woodwind quintet; Chorus: Mass for the people.
4245 East Ave., Rochester, NY 14610

*GRUEN, JOHN
b. 1927. Song cycles for soprano; Pomes
Penyeach, for soprano.

*GRUENBERG, LOUIS
b. Brest-Litovsk, Poland, 3 Aug. 1883; to U.S.
1885; d. Los Angeles, Calif., 9 June 1964. Studied piano in New York and at Vienna Cons.; composition with Ferrucio Busoni in Berlin. His
many awards included the Flagler prize; Heifetz
commission; Coolidge medal; David Bispham medal;
Juilliard award, RCA Victor prize, 1930; membership in the Nat. Inst. of Arts and Letters. He
toured Europe and the U.S. as pianist, 1912-19;
was chairman, composition department, Chicago
Musical Coll. several years; then lived in Santa
Monica, Calif.
WORKS: Opera: The witch of Brocken, 1912;
The bride of the gods, 1913; The man who married
a dumb wife, 1921; Jack and the beanstalk, 1930;
Queen Helena, 1936; Green mansions, radio opera,
1937; The miracle of Flanders, mystery play,
1950; Orchestra: 5 symphonies, 1919-48; 2 piano
concertos; The hill of dreams, 1919; Vagabondia,
1920; Jazz suite, 1928; The enchanted isle, 1929;
9 moods, 1929; Music for an imaginary ballet, 2
suites, 1929, 1944; Serenade to a beauteous lady,
1935; violin concerto, Heifetz soloist, Philadelphia, 1 Dec. 1944; Chamber music: 2 violin sonatas, 1912, 1919; Suite, violin and piano, 1914;
Indiscretions, string quartet, 1922; 4 whimsical-
ities, string quartet, 1923; cello sonatina,
1925; Jazzettes, violin and piano, 1926; 2 piano
quintets, 1929, 1937; Diversions, string quartet,
1930; 2 string quartets, 1937, 1938; Songs:
Daniel Jazz, tenor and chamber ensemble, 1924;
Creation, baritone and chamber ensemble, 1925;
Animals and insects, voice and piano; 4 contrasting songs; Piano: Jazzberries; Polychromatics,
1924; Jazz masks; 6 jazz epigrams; 3 jazz dances.

176

GRUNDMAN, CLARE EWING
b. Cleveland, Ohio, 11 May 1913. Studied at
Ohio State Univ., B. S. 1934, M. A. 1940; composition with Paul Hindemith at Tanglewood, 1941.
He taught in public schools in Kentucky, 1935-37;
at Ohio State Univ., 1937-41; has been arranger
and composer for radio, television, and Broadway
shows, 1945-   .
WORKS: Band: 3 American folk rhapsodies;
Burlesque; Little English suite; Holiday; Interval town; Music for a carnival; A medieval story;
Western dance; Japanese rhapsody; Festive piece;
Welsh rhapsody; Two sketches; Fantasy on American
sailing songs; Three sketches for winds; and
others.
RFD 2, Box 346, South Salem, NY 10590

*GRUNN, JOHN HOMER
b. West Salem, Wis., 5 May 1880; d. Los Angeles,
Calif., 6 June 1944. Studied piano in Chicago
and Berlin; taught piano in Chicago, Phoenix,
and Los Angeles.
WORKS: Operettas: The Mars diamond; The
golden pheasant; The isle of cuckoos; In a woman's reign; Ballets: Xochitl; The flower goddess; Orchestra: Hopi Indian dance; Zuni Indian
suite; Songs: Peyote drinking song; From desert
and pueblo.

*GUALILLO, NICHOLAS
The phantom princess, trilogy of 1-act operas
commissioned by Inter-City Opera Fund of Syracuse
and New York for American Bicentennial 1976.

GUDAUSKAS, GIEDRA
b. Kaunas, Lith., 10 July 1923; U.S. citizen
1952. Studied voice and piano, Kaunas State
Cons.; composition with Karel Jirak, Roosevelt
Univ., B. M. 1952; film scoring and jazz improvisation at Univ. of California, Los Angeles,
1961-63. She was modern dance accompanist in
Lithuania and Germany, 1940-44, in Chicago,
1946-49, in Los Angeles, 1963-65; teaches privately and is a free-lance composer.
WORKS: Chamber music: Lithuanian suite, 2
cellos and piano, 1967; Impressions on 3 proverbs,
piano and percussion, 1969; Lithuanian suite,
xylophone, electric guitar, piano, 1969; Variations for piano; Rondo, piano; Songs: The swal-
low; Little girl and the hope clover; Love dream;
The journey; I'm alone; Requiem for my friends;
The world of God, etc.
1030 Gretna Green Way, Los Angeles, CA 90049

GUDEHUS, DONALD H.
b. Jersey City, N. J., 13 Sep. 1939. Studied
piano, guitar, clarinet; composition with John
Vincent, Douglas Leady, Paul Chihara at Univ. of
California, Los Angeles.
WORKS: Piano: suite of dances in various
styles; Film score: Water in the wilderness,
educational film; solo instrumental works and
electronic music.
5115 West 134th Place, Hawthorne, CA 90250

*GUDENIAN, HAIG
b. Caeserea, Asia Minor, 19 May 1886; to U.S.
1918. Studied violin with Cesar Thomson in

(GUDENIAN, HAIG)
Brussels; violin with Otakar Sevcik, composition
with Viteslav Novak in Prague, where he also
began his lifelong study of folk tunes. In 1918
he married the concert pianist, Katherine Lowe
and toured the U.S. and England.
WORKS: Orchestra: O. W.; H. H.; Nostalgia;
Mulawiah II; In memoriam; Requiem; Over the
graves forward; many folksongs, dances, and
works for drums accompanied by western
instruments.

GUENTHER, RALPH R.
b. Concordia, Mo., 24 Nov. 1914. Attended Central Methodist Coll., A. B.; Univ. of Rochester,
M. A.; studied with Bernard Rogers, Edward Royce,
Anthony Donato, Burrill Phillips, Eastman School
of Music, Ph. D. He has been professor, Texas
Christian Univ., 1948-   ; principal flutist,
Fort Worth Opera Orch., 1949-   , Fort Worth
Symphony, 1956-   .
WORKS: Chamber music: Variations for oboe
and strings; Eclogue for strings; Chorus: Celebration, oratorio, commissioned by Texas Christian Univ. for its centennial, premiere, 9 Nov.
1973.
4604 Barwick Drive, Fort Worth, TX 76132

GUINALDO, NORBERTO
b. Buenos Aires, Arg., 2 Mar. 1937; U.S. citizen
1970. Studied at La Plata Univ., and with
Alberto Ginastero at Santa Maria de los Buenos
Aires Univ.; Univ. of California at Riverside,
M. M.; organ improvisation with Jean Langlais
and Jean Guillou in Paris. He won the J.
Fischer and Bro. Centennial competition prize,
1964; Southwestern Youth Music Festival prize,
1966; 2 prizes in the Organ Historical Society competition, 1966, 1967; American Guild of Organists contest, 1970. He was assistant organist,
Basilica del Santisimo Sacramento, Buenos Aires,
1954-59; has been concert organist and church
and temple organist in the U.S., 1959-   .
WORKS: Organ: Toccata and fugue, 1964;
Prelude and fugue, 1966; Passacaglia, 1966;
Suite for an old tracker organ, 1967; Laudes
tonales, organ and brass quintet, 1970; 3 litanies; 5 Spanish carols; Prelude for the passion
of the Lord; Partita on: In memory of the crucified; Fantasia and fugue; Ricercare; Dialogues,
organ, brass quartet, timpani; other organ works;
Chamber music: string trio; string quartet.
11247 Crewe St., Norwalk, CA 90650

GUION, DAVID WENDELL
b. Ballinger, Tex., 15 Dec. 1892. Attended Polytechnic Coll.; studied with Leopold Godowsky,
Royal Cons., Vienna; at Howard Payne Coll., D. M.
He was named distinguished alumnus, Texas
Wesleyan Coll., 1973; a Guion museum is to be
built at Baylor Univ. He taught piano at Chicago
Musical Coll., 1925-27, but has been mainly performer and composer; faculty, Baylor Univ. in
1973.
WORKS: Ballet: Western ballet; Shingandi,
primitive African ballet; Orchestra: Texas suite;
Prairie suite; Sheep and goat walkin to the pasture; Southern nights; Alley tunes; Suite for

GUION, DAVID WENDELL

(GUION, DAVID WENDELL)
orch.; many choral pieces and songs including
Home on the range, Carry me home to the lone prairie; and arrangements of American folk songs.
5526 Monticello Ave., Dallas, TX 75206

*GULESIAN, GRACE WARNER
b. Lawrence, Mass., 16 May   . Attended Radcliffe Coll.; studied piano with Agide Jacchia;
composition with Karl Weigl and Frederick
Converse.
WORKS: Operettas: A honeymoon in 2000;
Princess Marina; Dick Whittington and his cat;
Cape Cod Ann; Ballets: Ballet of Bacchus; Ballet
of Nubi; songs and piano pieces.
85 Commonwealth Ave.
Chestnut Hill, MA 02167

GUNTHER SPRECHER, WILLIAM
b. Saarbrucken, Germany, 20 Jan. 1924; U.S. citizen 1955. Studied piano, theory and conducting
in Germany and with Paul Ben Haim in Israel;
piano in New York with Isabelle Vengerova. He
was a member of the First Piano Quartet, which
toured the U.S. and Europe; music director Radio
Station WEVD; founder and director, Bronx Philharmonic Orch., 1969-   ; founder and director,
Mini Opera Theatre, 1971-   .
WORKS: Orchestra: Jerusalem concerto for
piano and orch., 1967; Vocal: The Yinglish song
book; Great is thy faith, Biblical cantata; Si
j'fais ca, song; 3 ghetto songs; Ghetto factort
76, cantata; Piano: Variations on a theme by
Paganini; piano sonata; Theme and variations;
First love, tango.
2235 Cruger Ave., Bronx, NY 10467

*GUSIKOFF, MICHEL
b. New York, 15 May 1895. Studied with Franz
Kneisel and Percy Goetschius at Juilliard School.
He was concertmaster with the Philadelphia Orchestra, New York Symphony Orchestra, NBC Orchestra; associate conductor, Pittsburgh Symphony
Orchestra.
WORKS: Orchestra: American concerto, violin
and orch., commissioned by Paul Whiteman; Fantasy,
viola and orch.; Variations on Oh, Susannah,
string orch.; and Gershwin paraphrases for violin
and piano.

GUSTAFSON, DWIGHT LEONARD
b. Seattle, Wash., 20 Apr. 1930. Studied with
Carlisle Floyd and John Boda, Florida State Univ.
He held a university graduate fellowship; and won
prizes in the Erskine Coll. anthem contest,
Broadman Press anthem contest, Charleston Choral
Society contest. He has been dean, School of
Fine Arts, Bob Jones Univ., 1954-   .
WORKS: Theatre: The hunted, 1-act opera;
The jailer, 1-act opera; music scores for
Antigone and Henry IV: Chorus: Three prophecies,
oratorio for chorus and orch.; numerous short
choral works; music scores for 6 educational and
religious films.
111 Stadium View Dr., Greenville, SC 29614

GUTCHE, GENE
b. Berlin, Germany, 3 July 1907; to U.S. 1925.
Studied with Donald Ferguson, Univ. of Minnesota,
M. A. 1950; at Iowa State Univ., Ph. D. 1953.
His many honors include 4 creative music scholar-
ships, Univ. of Minnesota, 1947-50; Univ. of
Minnesota Centennial prize, 1958; Albuquerque
Nat. composition prize, 1961; Oscar Espla Inter-
nat. composition prize, 1962; 2 Premio Citta di
Trieste, 1969, 1971; Louis Moreau Gottschalk
Gold Medal, 1970; 3 Guggenheim fellowships, 1963,
1964, 1965; commissions from: St. Paul Philhar-
monic, 1962; St. Paul Arts and Sciences, 1965;
Univ. of Minnesota Regents, 1966; Fargo-Moorhead
Symphony, 1967; Detroit Symphony, 1969; National
Symphony, 1976.
WORKS: Orchestra: 6 symphonies; Rondo
capriccioso, uses microtones (3 woodwinds at
A-425); piano concerto; Holofernes, Luria award
1959; Judith prologue, uses microtones and
speaking voice; Concertino for orch.; Timpani
concertante; Bongo divertimento, 1962; violin
concerto; Genghis Khan; Raquel; Rites in
Tenochtitlan; Hsiang Fei; Gemini, uses microtones and piano 4-hands, 1965; Aesop Fables
suite, 1966-67; Epimetheus USA, 1969; Chamber
music: 4 string quartets; 3 piano sonatas;
choral works.
c/o Galaxy Music Corporation
2121 Broadway, New York, NY 10023

HA, JAE EUN
b. Seoul, Korea, 16 Sep. 1937; to U.S. 1965.
Studied with David Van Vactor, Univ. of
Tennessee; and with Donald Erb, Cleveland Inst.
of Music. He was a teaching fellow at Cleveland
Inst.; and has been associate professor,
Mississippi Valley State Coll., 1973-   .
WORKS: Orchestra: Theme and variations;
2 symphonies, no. 2 premier, Cleveland, 22 Jan.
1974; 2 pieces for wind and percussion; Chamber
music: 3 studies for percussion; tuba quartet;
sonata for clarinet and string quartet; Sanjo
for solo flute; trio for trumpet, percussion,
cello, New York, May 1974.
203 West Jefferson St.
Greenwood, MS 38930

HABAN, SISTER M. TERESINE
b. Columbus, Ohio, 15 Jan. 1914. Studied with
Bernard Dieter, Coll. of St. Francis, Ill.; with
Wayne Barlow, Eastman School of Music. She has
been professor, Coll. of St. Francis, 1958-   ;
chairman of music department, 1959-70.
WORKS: Theatre: musical score for The Bells
of St. Francis, 1965; Chamber music: Sonata-
allegro, trumpet and piano, 1970; Piece for
chamber orch., 1970; Chorus: Mass in honor of St.
Ambrose, 1959; Hymn of praise, women's voices
and organ, 1965; miscellaneous hymns, antiphons,
psalms; Keyboard: Prelude, 1966.
500 Wilcox St., Joliet, IL 60435

*HABER, LOUIS
b. 1915. Parade, blues and allegro, flute,
violin, piano; violin sonata; violin sonatina;
suite for violin solo; trio, flute, violin,
piano; 6 miniatures, flute and violin.

*HACKETT, CHARLES F.
  Dona Rosita, 3-act opera, Ithaca Opera Assoc.,
  6 Apr. 1973.

HADDAD, DON
  b. Marietta, Ohio, 11 Jan. 1935. Studied with
  Ernst Von Dohnanyi and Karl Ahrendt, Ohio Univ.
  He received annual ASCAP awards, 1967-72. He has
  held faculty positions at West Texas State Univ.,
  1958-61; Amarillo Coll., 1961-63; Interlochen
  Arts Acad., 1963-66; Colorado State Univ.,
  1966-70; Shenandoah Cons., 1970-73; Univ. of
  Kentucky, 1973-   .
    WORKS: Orchestra: horn concerto; Band:
  Adagio and allegro, with solo horn; Air and
  adagio, woodwind quintet and band; Grand processional; Introduction and dance; Libyani; Scherzo;
  Valley Forge fantasy; Allegro giocoso, horn and
  band, 4 symphonic sketches; Wind ensemble: Blues
  au vent, woodwind quintet; Contrapunctus and
  quartal piece, 4 horns; Encore 1812, woodwind
  quintet; Fugue, brass choir; etc.; pieces for
  solo winds and piano.
    School of Music, University of Kentucky
    Lexington, KY 40506

*HADDEN, FRANCES ROOTS
  b. Hankow, China, 24 Aug. 1910, daughter of the
  Episcopal Bishop of Hankow. Attended Mt. Holyoke
  Coll., B. A.; received an Otto Kahn scholarship
  for music study. She taught in China, 1932-34;
  toured as pianist in the U.S., Europe, and Far
  East, 1934-40; then with her husband, Richard
  Hadden as duo-pianist. On the invitation of
  Premier Chou En Lai, they returned to China in
  1972 to present the first performance of her Lu-
  Shan suite for 2 pianos.
    WORKS: Theatre: music for A stateman's
  dream; The good road, a revue; The hurricane;
  Jotham Valley, a musical; The crowning experience,
  musical play; Turning of the tide, Asian musical;
  and many songs.

*HADLEY, HENRY
  b. Somerville, Mass., 20 Dec. 1871; d. New York,
  N. Y., 6 Sep. 1937. Studied with Stephen Emery
  and George W. Chadwick, New England Cons.; with
  Eusebius Mandyczewski in Vienna. His many honors
  included Paderewski prize, 1901; New England
  Cons., prize, 1901; Nat. Fed. of Music Clubs
  $1000 prize, 1909; William Hinshaw prize, 1917;
  honorary doctorate, Tufts Coll., 1925; election
  to the Nat. Inst. of Arts and Letters and American Acad. of Arts and Letters; French Government
  Order of Merit. He was music director, St. Paul's
  School, Garden City, N. Y., 1895-1902; conducted
  in Germany, 1905-09; Seattle Symphony, 1909-11;
  San Francisco Symphony, 1911-15; was associate
  conductor, New York Philharmonic, 1915-22; conducted in Europe and Buenos Aires; Manhattan
  Symphony, 1929-32; opening of Berkshire Music
  Festival, 1933. He founded the Nat. Asso. of
  American Composers and Conductors, 1932.
    WORKS: Opera: Nancy Brown, comic opera;
  Safie, 1909; Azora, daughter of Montezuma, 1917;
  Merlin and Vivien; Bianca; Cleopatra's night; A
  night in old Paris, 1925; The atonement of Pan,
  a festival play; incidental music to plays;

(HADLEY, HENRY)
  Orchestra: 5 symphonies, 1897-1934; 8 overtures;
  Salome, symphonic poem, 1909; Lucifer, symphonic
  poem, 1913; 4 suites; piano concerto; The culprit
  Fay, 1909; ballet suites; Chamber music: 2
  piano quintets; 2 string quartets; 2 piano trios;
  violin sonata; many choral works, songs; Film
  score: When a man loves.

*HAGEMAN, RICHARD
  b. Leeuwarden, Holland, 9 July 1882; U.S. citizen 1915; d. Beverly Hills, Calif., 6 Mar. 1966.
  Studied at Brussels Cons. and Royal Cons. of
  Amsterdam. He received the David Bispham medal,
  1931. He was conductor, Royal Opera House,
  Amsterdam, 1899-1903; came to the U.S. as accompanist for Yvette Guilbert, 1906; conducted
  Metropolitan Opera House, New York, 1908-26; was
  guest conductor of many orchestras; taught at Curtis
  Inst. and Chicago Musical Coll.; went to Hollywood, 1938, conducted Hollywood Bowl Orchestra
  for 6 seasons.
    WORKS: Opera: Caponsacchi, 1931; Orchestra:
  The crucible, soli, chorus and orch.; I hear
  America calling, baritone and orch.; Overture in
  a nutshell; Suite for strings; Songs: Do not go
  my love; At the well; The night has a thousand
  eyes; Charity; many others; Film scores: Stage
  coach; The long voyage home; The Shanghai gesture, If I were a king; Mourning becomes Electra;
  She wore a yellow ribbon.

*HAGEMANN, PHILLIP
  The musical menagerie for chorus on Ogden Nash
  text.

HAGER, REV. CARL
  b. Plymouth, Ind., 15 Oct. 1911. Studied with
  Leon Stein and Alexander Tcherepnin, DePaul
  Univ. He was chairman, department of music,
  Univ. of Notre Dame, 1955-71, professor,
  1969-   .
    WORKS: Band: sonatine; Chorus: And time
  shall be no longer, cantata; Mass in English;
  and organ compositions.
    University of Notre Dame
    Notre Dame, IN 46556

HAGGH, RAYMOND HERBERT
  b. Chicago, Ill., 4 Sep. 1920. Studied with
  Robert Delaney, Northwestern Univ., B. M., M. M.;
  with Randall Thompson, Harvard Univ.; and with
  Bernhard Heiden, Indiana Univ., Ph. D. He was on
  the faculty, Memphis State Univ., 1950-60; Univ.
  of Nebraska, 1960-   , professor and associate
  dean, Coll. of Arts and Sciences in 1973.
    WORKS: orchestral works, chorus and orch.,
  chorus, chamber music, all written and performed
  before 1965.
    1725 South 52nd St., Lincoln, NB 68501

*HAHN, CARL
  b. Indianapolis, Ind., 23 Oct. 1879; d.
  Cincinnati, Ohio, 13 May 1929. Studied with Otto
  Singer, Cincinnati Coll. of Music; played cello
  in Theodore Thomas Orchestra; conducted San
  Antonio Orchestra, 1900-11, New York Arion Asso.,
  1914-20, and other groups. He wrote choral
  works and songs.

HAHN, SANDRA LEA

HAHN, SANDRA LEA
b. Spokane, Wash., 5 Jan. 1940. Studied with William Brandt, Washington State Univ.; with Robert Crane, Univ. of Wisconsin. She won an award in the Wisconsin State Music Teachers composition contest for a cello sonata. She was pianist, Milwaukee Symphony Orch., 1966-67; instructor of piano, Univ. of Idaho, 1970-   .
WORKS: Theatre: music for The cave dwellers, commissioned by Washington State Univ. Speech and Drama Department; Chamber music: Variations, flute and piano; Scherzo, piano; harp sonatina; Toccata, piano; cello sonata; piano trio; Fantasy, piano; quartet for flute, clarinet, bassoon, piano; 5 miniatures, flute and piano; Sonorities, flute, harpsichord, percussion.
719 East Mabelle, Moscow, ID 83843

*HAIEFF, ALEXEI
b. Blagoveshchensk, Russia, 25 Aug. 1914; to U.S. 1931. With Rubin Goldmark and Frederick Jacobi, Juilliard School; with Nadia Boulanger in Paris, 1938-39; at American Acad. in Rome. His awards include a Fulbright grant, 1942; American Acad. in Rome medal, 1942; Lili Boulanger prize, 1943; Guggenheim fellowships, 1946, 1949; fellow, American Acad. in Rome, 1947-48, composer-in-residence, 1952-53, 1958-59; New York Music Critics Circle award, 1952; UNESCO internat. recording award, 1958. He was professor, Univ. of Buffalo, 1962-68; composer-in-residence, Univ. of Utah, 1968-71.
WORKS: Ballet: Divertimento, 1944; The Princess Zondilda and her entourage, 1946; Beauty and the beast, 1947; Ballet in E, 1955; Orchestra: 3 symphonies, 1942, 1957, 1961; violin concerto, 1948; piano concerto, 1950; Eclogue, harp and strings, 1963; Eloge, chamber orch., 1967; Caligula, baritone and orch., New York, 5 Nov. 1971; Chamber music: sonatina for string quartet, 1937; Bagatelles, oboe and bassoon, 1939-55; Serenade, woodwind trio and piano, 1942; sonata for 2 pianos, 1945; Eclogue, cello and piano, 1947; string quartet, 1953; La nouvelle Heloise, harp and strings, 1953; piano sonata, 1955; cello sonata, 1965; songs and piano pieces.
c/o Chappell & Co., Inc.
609 5th Ave., New York, NY 10017

HAIGH, MORRIS
b. San Diego, Calif., 26 Jan. 1932. Studied with Carl Parrish, Halsey Stevens, Pomona Coll., B.M. 1953; with Bernard Rogers, Samuel Adler, Wayne Barlow, Eastman School of Music, M. A. 1954, Ph. D. 1973. His awards include a Woodrow Wilson fellowship for study at Eastman, 1953; awards from Los Angeles Horn Club and Los Angeles Chapter, American Guild of Organists, 1962; Howard Hanson prize for winds, 1972; Howard Hanson prize for an orchestral work, 1973. Following discharge from military service in 1956, he was computer programer and systems analyst until 1970, when he decided to resume studies in music at the Eastman School and devote full time to music.
WORKS: Orchestra: Music for orchestra, 1963; Night song: Scene for orchestra, 1964; 2 studies for string orch., 1971; Concerto for wind quintet

(HAIGH, MORRIS)
and orch., 1973; Wind ensemble: Music for winds, quintet, 1970; Symphonic variations, 1972; Pantomines, brass and percussion, Atlanta, Mar. 1973; Chamber music: Serenade, flute and piano,; Fantasia, horns and organ, 1962; string quartet, 1968; Piano: 24 preludes, 1966.
259 Barrington St., Rochester, NY 14607

*HAILSTORK, ADOLPHUS C. III
b. Rochester, N. Y., 17 Apr. 1941. Piano: Capriccio for a departed brother; Spartacus speaks; Rhapsody.
Dana School of Music
Youngstown State University
Youngstown, OH 44503

HAIMO, ETHAN T.
b. St. Louis, Mo., 22 Mar. 1950. Studied with Ralph Shapey and Roger Sessions at Univ. of Chicago; with J. K. Randall and Paul Lansky at Princeton Univ. He received the Olga Menn prize and the Binyon prize at Univ. of Chicago: Fromm scholarship to Composers Conference, Bennington, Vt., 1971.
WORKS: Chamber music: Scene from Macbeth, soprano and 10 chamber players; string quartet; Variations for piano; Chorus: Absalom, my son.
901 Lawrence Apts.
West Drive, Princeton, NJ 08540

HAINES, EDMUND
b. Ottumwa, Iowa, 15 Dec. 1914; d. Bronx, N. Y., 5 July 1974. Attended Univ. of Missouri, Kansas City; Eastman School of Music, Ph. D. 1941; studied with Aaron Copland, Roy Harris, Howard Hanson, and Bernard Rogers. He received a Pulitzer award, 1941; Ford Found. commission, 1958; 2 Guggenheim fellowships, 1957, 1958; 2 Fulbright grants, 1966, 1967; Miami Univ. Sesquicentennial commission, 1959. He was faculty member, Univ. of Michigan, 1941-47; Sarah Lawrence Coll., 1948-74.
WORKS: Orchestra: symphony, Pulitzer award, 1941; Concertino for 7 soloists and orch., 1959; Rondino and variations; Informal overture; 3 dances; Chamber music: 4 string quartets; 2 piano sonatas; sonata for brass quintet; Toccata for brass ensemble; Vocal: Dialogue from the Book of Job, in memoriam November 22, 1963, women's chorus; Four loves, soprano and 7 instruments, 1972; Organ: Snow dance; Promenade, air and toccata, AGO award; Mixed media: Soliloquy, dialogue, and bacchanale, trio and electronic tape, 1971.

*HAINES, EDWARD BENJAMIN
American sonata, unaccompanied cello, New York premiere, Carnegie Recital Hall, 22 May 1973.

HAIR, NORMAN J.
b. Covington County, Ala., 2 May 1931. Studied organ and church music with Betty L. Lumby, Univ. of Montevallo. He won first place in the Birmingham Art Festival competition, 1958. He has been chairman, Division of Fine Arts, Gulf Coast Community Coll., 1960-   .

(HAIR, NORMAN J.)
WORKS: Chorus: <u>Prayer</u>, 1958; <u>Alleluia,
Amen</u>.
Gulf Coast Community College
Panama City, FL 32401

HAIRSTON, JESTER
b. N. Carolina, 9 July 1901. Studied at Tufts
Univ., B. A. 1929, and at Juilliard School. He
has received honorary doctorates from Univ. of
Massachusetts, Tufts Univ., and Univ. of the
Pacific. He was assistant conductor of the Hall
Johnson Choir for 15 years; conducted choirs for
radio and Broadway shows; in 1943 formed his own
choir; has arranged, composed, and conducted
background scores for films. He has made 3
choral conducting trips to Africa, 2 to Europe,
and one to Mexico, as goodwill tours for the
State Department.
WORKS: Chorus: <u>Mary's little boy chile</u>,
calypso for chorus; <u>Elijah rock</u>; <u>Poor man Lazrus</u>;
<u>Amen</u>; numerous arrangements; Film score: <u>Lilies
of the field</u>, 1963.
5047 Valley Ridge Ave.
Los Angeles, CA 90043

HAKIM, TALIB RASUL. <u>See</u> CHAMBERS, STEPHEN A.

HALDEMAN, LYNN E.
b. Portland Ore., 1 Apr. 1935. Studied with
Robert Crowley at Portland State Univ., B. S.
1958, with Homer Keller, Univ. of Oregon, M. S.
1963. His musical was selected for performance
in the 1973 Contemporary Series, Catawba Coll.,
Salisbury, N. C. He was public school music
educator in Oregon, 1960-72.
WORKS: Musical comedy: <u>How to be a successful educator without really...</u>, 2 acts, Catawba
Coll., 2-5 May 1973.
P. O. Box 175, Cloverdale, OR 97112

HALEN, WALTER J.
b. Hamilton, Ohio, 17 Mar. 1930. Studied with
Karl Ahrendt, Ohio Univ.; with Anthony Donato,
Northwestern Univ.; and with Mark Walker, Ohio
State Univ. He taught in Ohio public schools,
1955-61; was assistant professor, Drury Coll.,
1962-67; associate professor, Central Missouri
State Univ., 1967-   .
WORKS: Orchestra: <u>Sinfonia sonore</u>, 1957;
Chamber music: violin sonata, 1956; string
quartet, 1960; Suite for violin and viola, 1961;
<u>Prelude and dance</u>, violin and piano; woodwind
quartet, 1961; <u>Meditation</u>, oboe, prepared piano,
and percussion, 1972.
1100 Tyler, Warrensburg, MO 64093

*HALL, ARTHUR E.
<u>Toccata</u> for organ.
Rice University, Houston, TX 77001

HALL, CHARLES J.
b. Houston, Tex., 17 Nov. 1925. Studied at
Andrews Univ., B. A. 1952; Univ. of New Mexico,
M. M. 1960; and Michigan State Univ., Ph. D. 1970;
his teachers included H. Owen Reed, Paul Harder,
Charles Garland. He received the 1970 Sigvald
Thompson award for <u>5 microscopics for orchestra</u>,

(HALL, CHARLES J.)
He is host of WAUS <u>Adventures in music</u> and <u>Hall's
musical years</u> on educational radio; founder and
editor of a music press; assistant professor,
Andrews Univ.
WORKS: Orchestra: <u>City in the sea</u>, narrator, soprano, chorus, and orch.; <u>5 microscopics
for orchestra</u>, 1970; <u>Recitative for orchestra</u>,
1971; <u>Ulalume</u>, text after Poe, narrator, soprano,
orch., Houston, 8 Feb. 1972; Chamber music: <u>Pe-
tite suite</u>, flute, clarinet, bassoon; 5 short
pieces for piano.
Route 1, Box 397B, Berrien Springs, MI 49103

*HALL, FRANCES
<u>Go to the well</u>, solo voice.

*HALL, JAMES
b. Buffalo, N. Y., 1930. Is a guitarist; has
played and recorded with many noted jazz groups;
at The Guitar, New York, 1972; has published
<u>Pieces for guitar and strings</u>.

*HALL, REGINALD
b. Laurel, Md., 23 Jan. 1926. Studied at Pea-
body Cons.; with Ross Lee Finney, Univ. of Mich-
igan; and with Halsey Stevens in Los Angeles.
He is an engineer who composes as an avocation.
His <u>Elegy</u> for orchestra won the George Gershwin
Memorial award, 1955; was performed by the New
York Philharmonic, 21 Apr. 1956.

*HALL, RICHARD
<u>Etudes</u> for piano; <u>5 epigrams</u>, cello and piano;
<u>Suite</u>, violin and viola.

HALLOCK, PETER R.
b. Kent, Wash., 19 Nov. 1924. Studied with
George Frederick McKay at Univ. of Washington.
He received a Guggenheim fellowship, 1974. He
has been organist and choirmaster, St. Mark's
Cathedral, Seattle, 1951-   .
WORKS: Choral and service music for the
church.
1245 10th East, Seattle, WA 98102

HALLORAN, DON
b. Houston, Tex., 9 Jan. 1933. Studied with
James Ming, Lawrence Coll.; with Nicolas Flagello,
Manhattan School of Music; with William P. Latham
and Merrill Ellis, North Texas State Univ. He
taught in New York public schools, 1961-70; was
graduate teaching fellow, North Texas State Univ.,
1970-73.
WORKS: Band: <u>Essay</u>, 1970; Chamber music:
clarinet trio, 1965; <u>Anna Livia Plurabelle</u>, contralto and chamber ensemble, 1971; <u>Saxophrenic</u>,
alto saxophone, percussion, piano, 1972; Chorus:
<u>Moon soliloquy</u>, Lorca text, 1972; <u>Psalm 117</u>, 1972;
Mixed media: brass quintet with tape, 1972;
<u>Chant and rant</u>, trombone and tape, Nashville,
1973 Trombone Clinic.
Route 5, Lot 8, Acorn Ranch
Denton, TX 76201

HALLSTROM, HENRY
b. Sweden, 12 July 1906; U.S. citizen c. 1920.
Earned an A. B., Univ. of California; M. A.,

HALLSTROM, HENRY

(HALLSTROM, HENRY)
Columbia Univ., Ph. D., Univ. of Rochester; studied with Randall Thompson, Univ. of Virginia; Howard Hanson, Eastman School of Music. He received several Ford Found. Humanities awards and an American Guild of Organists composition award. He has been faculty member, Randolph-Macon Woman's Coll., 1939- .
WORKS: Opera: Blood on the moon; Orchestra: symphony; Chorus: God came like the dawn; Midsummer night's dream, women's voices; Organ: Easter festival; 3 pieces on familiar hymn tunes; numerous published choral and organ compositions; Film score: The Oresteia.
70 Columbia Ave., Lynchburg, VA 24503

HALPERN, STELLA
b. Austria, 18 May 1923; U.S. citizen, 1949. Studied composition with Leo Kraft in New York. She was lecturer, Queens Coll., 1968-71; instructor, Queensborough Coll., 1971- .
WORKS: Chamber music: 3 brevities, percussion, trumpet, clarinet, piano; Music for 11 players; Movement for 5 players; Caprice, clarinet, trumpet, piano, temple blocks; Pentagram, cello, horn, clarinet, blocks.
31-49 29th St., Astoria, NY 11106

*HAMILL, PAUL
Aria da chiesa for organ.

*HAMILTON, IAIN
b. Glasgow, Scotland, 6 June 1922; to U.S. 1961. First studied to be an engineer; studied composition with William Alwyn, Royal Acad. of Music, London. He was composer-in-residence at Tanglewood, 1962; professor, Duke Univ., 1962-71; professor, City Univ. of New York, 1971- .
WORKS: Opera: Agamemnon, 1967-69; The royal hunt of the sun, 1967-69; The Cataline conspiracy, to his own text, commissioned by the Scottish Opera Company and performed, Stirling, Scotland, 1974; Ballet: Clerk Saunders, 1951; Orchestra: 2 symphonies, 1949, 1951; clarinet concerto, 1951; concerto for jazz trumpet and orch., 1958; Sinfonia for 2 orch., 1959; Ecossaisse, 1959; piano concerto, 1960; revised 1967; Circus, 2 trumpets and orch., 1969; Voyage, horn and orch., 1970; Alastor, 1970; Chamber music: clarinet quintet, 1949; string quartets, 1950, 1965; Nocturne, clarinet and piano, 1951; viola sonata, 1951; cello sonata, 1951; sextet for flute, 2 clarinets, piano trio, 1962; Variants for 10 instruments, 1963; Sonata notturna, horn and piano, 1965; Sonata for 5, wind quintet, 1966; Chorus: Epitaph for this world and time, 3 choirs, 3 organs, and conductor, text from Revelations, 1970; and piano pieces.
40 Park Ave., New York, NY 10016

*HAMILTON, TOM
b. 1946. Studied composition with John W. Downey, Univ. of Wisconsin. His Dialogue for flute and alto saxophone received top award in the woodwind category, Wisconsin Composers Contest, 1968.
621 Westwood Drive, Clayton, MO 63105

*HAMM, CHARLES E.
b. 1925. Round, for unspecified chamber ensemble; anyone lived in a pretty how town, for medium voice, e.e. cummings text; Canto, voice and chamber ensemble, 1963. In September 1976 he will become professor at Dartmouth Coll.
School of Music, University of Illinois Urbana, IL 61801

*HAMMOND, DON
b. 1917. Quintet for brass.
139 Alpine Drive, Closter, NJ 07624

*HAMMOND, MICHAEL
Montage and variations on the name of Bach, New York, 20 Nov. 1971.

*HAMMOND, RICHARD
b. Kent, England, 26 Apr. 1896; to U.S. at an early age. Studied at Yale Univ.; and with Nadia Boulanger and Mortimer Wilson.
WORKS: Ballet: Fiesta; Orchestra: 6 Chinese fairy tales, 1921; Voyage to the east, voice and orch., 1926; West Indian dances, 1930; Chamber music: 2 piano suites, oboe sonata; choruses and songs.

*HAMMOND, SAM
Symphony for band.

*HAMMOND, TERRENCE
The friend, 2-act opera, Interstate Opera Assoc., Lincoln Center, New York, 16 Sep. 1972.

*HAMMOND, WILLIAM G.
b. Melville, N. Y., 7 Aug. 1874; d. New York, N. Y., 22 Dec. 1945. Was organist, Dutch Reformed Church, Brooklyn, N. Y., 1914-45. He wrote many songs.

HAMPTON, GEORGE CALVIN
b. Kittanning, Pa., 31 Dec. 1938. Studied with Joseph Wood and Richard Hoffman at Oberlin Cons.; at Mozarteum in Salzburg; organ with Arthur Poister at Syracuse Univ. He taught at Salem Coll., Winston-Salem, N. C., 1960-61; at Choate School, 1969-70; was organist, St. Peter's Church, Cazenovia, N. Y., 1961-62; organist and choirmaster, Calvary Episcopal Church, New York, 1963- .
WORKS: Chorus: 3 hymn tunes, 1969; Easter alleluia, 1972; Lord, speak to me, 1972; This is the day, 1972; Keyboard: Prisms, piano, 1963; Triple play, 2 pianos, 1967; Ondes Martenot, 2 pianos, 1967; Mixed media: Catch-up, 2 pianos and tape, 1967; God plays hide and seek, organ with Moog synthesizer, 1971; The road to Leprechaunia, organ, Moog synthesizer, soprano, 1973.
61 Gramercy Park, New York, NY 10010

HAMVAS, LEWIS
b. Budapest, Hungary, 10 Nov. 1919; U.S. citizen 1935. Studied composition with Lehman Engel, Leo Weiner, Bernard Wagenaar, Vincent Persichetti at Juilliard School; piano with Josef Raieff. He received the Morris Loeb prize at Juilliard and commissions from the Music Teachers Nat.

(HAMVAS, LEWIS)
Asso., South Dakota Music Teachers Asso., and the South Dakota All State Chorus and Orch. He was instructor and composer for dance, Bard Coll., 1952-54; professor of piano, Yankton Coll., 1954- .
WORKS: Chamber music: oboe sonata; violin sonata; cello sonata, piano sonata; Introduction and dance, clarinet, violin, piano, cello; Explorations, piano; Chorus: On the plain of Chelyabinsk, chorus and 4 instruments; I have a dream, chorus and orch.; music for dance, theatre, etc.
Conservatory of Music, Yankton College
Yankton, SD 57078

HANCOCK, EUGENE WILSON
b. St. Louis, Mo., 17 Feb. 1929. Attended Univ. of Detroit, B. M.; Univ. of Michigan, M. M.; School of Sacred Music, Union Theological Seminary, S. M. D.; studied composition with Robert Hernried, Seth Bingham, Joseph Goodman; organ with Robert Baker, Alec Wyton, Marcel Dupre. He was organist and choirmaster in Detroit, 1953-63; assistant organist, Cathedral of St. John the Divine, New York, 1963-66; minister of music, New Calvary Baptist Church, Detroit, 1967-70; St. Paul St. Andrew Methodist Church, New York, 1973- ; assistant professor, Manhattan Community Coll., CUNY, 1970- .
WORKS: Chorus: A Palm Sunday anthem, choir and unison children's choir, 1971; Come here, Lord, 1973; Collection of 13 spirituals for unison and 2-parts; Organ: An organ book of spirituals, 1973.
257 Central Park West, 10C
New York, NY 10024

HANCOCK, GERRE
b. Lubbock, Tex., 21 Feb. 1934. Studied with Kent Kennan, Univ. of Texas; with Nadia Boulanger in Paris; with Searle Wright, Union Theological Seminary, New York; studied organ with E. W. Doty, Robert Baker, and Jean Langlais. He was assistant organist, St. Bartholomew's Church, New York, 1960-62; organist and choirmaster, Christ Church, Cincinnati, 1962-71; faculty, Univ. of Cincinnati, 1965-71; faculty, Juilliard School, 1971- ; organist and choirmaster, St. Thomas Church, New York, 1971- .
WORKS: Chorus: In thanksgiving; Out of the deep; Kindle the gift of God; A song to the lamb; The plumb line and the city, cantata for choir, organ, and orch.; Organ: Improvisation; Air; Fantasy on divinum mysterium.
Saint Thomas Church
1 West 53rd St., New York, NY 10019

*HANDY, WILLIAM CHRISTOPHER
b. Florence, Ala., 16 Nov. 1873; d. New York, N. Y., 28 Mar. 1958. Graduated from Teachers' Agricultural and Mechanical Coll., Huntsville, 1892, then was a school teacher and also worked in the iron mill. He taught at the A&M Coll., 1900-02; organized a quartet and played cornet with it at the Chicago World's Fair, 1893; organized an orchestra and toured the South after

(HANDY, WILLIAM CHRISTOPHER)
1902. He published an autobiography, Father of the blues, New York, 1941.
WORKS: Orchestra: Blue destiny; Opportunity, setting of poem by Walter Malone; setting of Lincoln's Gettysburg address; Jazz: Memphis blues; St.Louis blues; Yellow dog blues; Beale Street blues; Joe Turner blues; Hesitating blues; East St. Louis blues; Atlanta blues; Harlem blues; etc.

HANKIN, JEFFREY D.
b. Boston, Mass., 14 Nov. 1949. Studied with Easley Blackwood and W. Thomas McKinley at Univ. of Chicago, 1967-71; with Arthur Berger, Seymour Shifrin, and Harold Shapero at Brandeis Univ., 1971-73.
WORKS: Orchestra: Tacit II, winds and percussion, 1970; Fantasy for orchestra, 1971; The parliament of fowls - a suite for dance, 1973; Chamber music: 3 lyrics for piano, 1971-72; And here I am, soprano and 14 players, 1972.
6007 Park Heights Ave.
Baltimore, MD 21215

HANLON, KENNETH M.
b. Baltimore, Md., 16 May 1941. Studied with Ramiro Cortes, Univ. of Southern California; and with Louis Cheslock, Peabody Cons. He was trombone and tuba instructor, Peabody Preparatory School, 1961-68, brass ensemble conductor, 1965-68; assistant professor, Univ. of Nevada, Las Vegas, 1970- .
WORKS: Chamber music: Contemplations, clarinet and piano; Suite for doubles, woodwind soloist and jazz ensemble, premiere by Ralph Gair and Stan Kenton Neophonic Orch., July 1970; Mourning sound, baritone and piano, Las Vegas, Apr. 1971.
4912 San Sebastian, Las Vegas, NV 89114

HANNA, JAMES B.
b. Siloam Springs, Ark., 15 Oct. 1922. Attended Northwestern Univ., B. M. 1948, M. M. 1949; studied with Robert Delaney and Bernhard Heiden, Indiana Univ. He won the Louisiana Fed. of Music Clubs contest, 1954, 1956, 1958, 1964; received grant from Louisiana Council of Music and Performing Arts, 1968 for Symphony no.2. He joined the faculty of Univ. of Southwestern Louisiana in 1949, associate professor of theory and composition and also violist.
WORKS: Orchestra: 3 symphonies, 1948, 1956, 1965; Prelude for orch., 1960; Little concerto for orch., 1961; Band: Essay, 1956; Sinfonia, 1963; Chamber music: duo for violin and viola, 1955; Elegy, chamber orch., 1957; 3 string quartets, 1949, 1951, 1960; violin sonata, 1948; Song of the redwood tree, narrator, 6 brass, timpani, 1954; woodwind trio, 1957; Fugue and chorale, 4 percussionists, 1961; sonatina, viola and piano, 1969; Fantasy, cello and piano, 1970; Vocal: Sobbing of the bells, chorus, 1952; War: cycle of 5 songs, Whitman text, high voice and piano, 1954; Night, cycle of 3 songs, Whitman text, tenor, viola, piano, 1967.
Box 118, University of Southwestern Louisiana
Lafayette, LA 70501

HANNAHS, ROGER C.

*HANNAHS, ROGER C.
Cantata for the nativity, chorus.
White St., Saratoga Springs, NY 12866

HANNAY, ROGER DURHAM
b. Plattsburg, N. Y., 22 Sep. 1930. Studied with
Franklin Morris, Syracuse Univ.; Hugo Norden,
Boston Univ.; Howard Hanson, Eastman School of
Music; and with Lukas Foss at Tanglewood. He
held scholarships for all study except Eastman
School. He was associate professor, Concordia
Coll., Moorhead, Minn., 1958-66; Univ. of North
Carolina, Chapel Hill, 1966-   .
WORKS: Orchestra: Sonorous image; Listen;
Chamber music: Marshall's medium message, percussion and speaker; Fantome, viola, clarinet,
piano; Fragmentation, chamber ensemble; Chorus:
Carol; Christmastide; 3 Fantasias; Requiem, chorus and orch.; Sayings for our time, chorus and
orch.; Mixed media: Elegy, viola and tape; Episodic refraction, piano and tape; Live and in
color!, multi-media; Tuonelan Joutsen, English
horn and tape; Squeeze me, chamber ensemble and
tape.
609 Morgan Creek Road, Chapel Hill, NC 27515

HANSEN, THEODORE (TED)
b. Denver, Colo., 5 Feb. 1935. Studied with
Cecil Effinger, Univ. of Colorado; with Ronald
Lo Presti, Arizona State Univ., M. M.; with
Robert McBride, Univ. of Arizona. He has been
assistant professor, Arizona State Univ.,
1966-   .
WORKS: Orchestra: 3 movements for orchestra; Coloration in brass; Toccata for winds;
Chamber music: Configurations, trumpet and piano;
4 sketches for piano; string quartet; Contrasts,
woodwind quintet; Nocturne, clarinet and piano;
Suite for viola and piano; Chorus: The meaning
of life.
5102 North 32nd Place, Phoenix, AZ 85018

*HANSON, HOWARD
b. Wahoo, Neb., 28 Oct. 1896. Studied at Univ.
of Nebraska; with Percy Goetschius, Inst. of
Musical Art, New York; with Arne Oldberg, Northwestern Univ. His honors include the Prix de
Rome; fellow American Acad. in Rome, 1921-24;
member Nat. Inst. of Arts and Letters, 1935;
Pulitzer prize, 1944; Ditson award, 1945; George
Foster Peabody award, 1946; Huntington Hartford
Found., grant, 1959; 16 honorary D. M.'s, 4
L. L. D.'s, 2 Litt. D.'s, 2 L. H. D.'s. He was
instructor, Coll. of the Pacific, 1916, dean,
1919-21; director, Eastman School of Music,
1924-64; in 1925 instituted at Eastman the series
of American music concerts; has conducted programs of American music in Europe as well as with
major orchestras in the U.S.; has been president
of many national musical organizations.
WORKS: Opera: Merry Mount, 1933, Metropolitan Opera, New York, 10 Feb. 1934; Ballet:
California forest play, 1920; Orchestra: Symphonic prelude, 1916; Legend, 1917; Rhapsody,
1919; 5 symphonic poems, 1920-26; 6 symphonies,
1923, 1930, 1938, 1944, 1955, 1967; Serenade,
flute, strings, harp, orch., 1945; Elegy in memory of Serge Koussevitzky, 1956; Mosaics, 1957;

(HANSON, HOWARD)
4 psalms for baritone and orch.; Chamber music:
2 piano quintets, 1916, 1917; string quartet,
1923; Fantasia on a theme of youth, piano and
strings, 1950; Pastorale, oboe and piano; Chorus:
The lament of Beowulf, 1926; Heroic elegy, with
orch., 1927; 3 songs from Drum taps by Whitman,
with baritone solo and orch., 1935; Hymn for the
pioneers, male voices, 1938; The cherubic hymn,
1949; How excellent thy name, 1952; The song of
democracy, with soli and orch., 1957; Song of
human rights, cantata, 1963; The mystic trumpeter, with narrator and orch.; Streams in the
desert, with orch.; Psalms 121 and 150, with
orch.
362 Oakdale Drive, Rochester, NY 14604

*HARADA, HIGO
b. 1927. Sketch for piano.
Department of Music
California State University
San Jose, CA 95114

HARBISON, JOHN
b. Orange, N. J., 20 Dec. 1938. Studied at Harvard Univ., B. A. 1960; with Roger Sessions and
Earl Kim, Princeton Univ., M. F. A. 1963. His
awards include Brandeis Creative Arts citation,
1971; American Acad. of Arts and Letters prize,
1972; Fromm Found. commission, 1973; Koussevitzky
Found. commission, 1973; Nat. Endowment for the
Arts commission, 1973. He was Rockefeller
composer-in-residence, Reed Coll., 1968-69;
associate professor, Massachusetts Inst. of
Technology, 1969-   ; music director, Cantata
Singers, 1969-73.
WORKS: Theatre: Winter's tale, opera in 2
acts, 1973-   ; incidental music to Merchant
of Venice, Boston, 16 Mar. 1974; Orchestra:
Sinfonia, violin and double orch., 1963; violin
concerto, 1967; Chamber music: Confinement,
chamber ensemble, 1965; Serenade for 6 players,
1968; Parody-fantasia, piano, 1968; piano trio,
1969; Bermuda triangle, jazz ensemble, 1970; Die
Kurze, solo violin, New York, 15 Oct. 1971; 6
dumb shows, chamber ensemble, excerpts for Winter's tale, Cambridge, Mass., 8 Oct. 1974; Chorus: Music when soft voices die, Shelley text;
5 songs of experience, Blake text, 4 soli, chorus, string quartet, percussion, Cambridge, Mass.,
28 Feb. 1973; Songs: Elegiac songs, Dickinson
text, soprano and chamber ensemble, New York,
12 Jan. 1975.
563 Franklin St., Cambridge, MA 02139

HARDER, PAUL
b. Indianapolis, Ind., 10 Mar. 1923. Studied at
Butler Univ., B. M. 1944; Eastman School of
Music, M. M. 1945; with Nadia Boulanger, France,
1948; Royal Acad. of Music, Copenhagen, 1951-52;
with Philip Bezanson, Univ. of Iowa, Ph. D. 1959.
He was faculty member, Michigan State Univ.,
1945-73; dean of Arts and Humanities, California
State Coll., Stanislaus Turlock, 1973-   . He
was also member, Rochester Philharmonic Orch.,
1944-45; Lansing Symphony, 1945-55.
WORKS: Orchestra: Serenade; Sinfonietta,
Univ. of Redlands, 4 Apr. 1959; Overture, Ohio

(HARDER, PAUL)
State Univ., 23 Mar. 1962; A wisp of time, string
orch., East Lansing, Mich., 22 Aug. 1964; The
pleasant truth, Michigan State Univ., 20 Nov.
1972; Band: Refractions; Contention; Mosaic,
Icons; Chamber music: brass quintet; 3 woodwind
quintets; 2 string trios; sextet, woodwind quintet and piano; clarinet sonata; oboe sonata;
Serenade, soprano, clarinet, horn, strings;
Serenade, tenor, clarinet, bassoon, strings;
string quartet; Chorus: Let God arise; The swal-
low; also scores for radio and stage productions.
He is author of several books on music technique
and theory and Bridge to 20th-century music,
Boston, 1973.
California State College
Stanislaus Turlock, CA 95380

HARDIE, GARY
b. Coral Gables, Fla., 20 Apr. 1948. Studied
with Iain Hamilton, Duke Univ.; and with Mel
Powell, California Inst. of the Arts, M. F. A.
1973. He received a BMI Student Composer award,
1972 for For five/four, a requiem to Kent State.
He was instructor, Virginia Commonwealth Univ.,
1973-74.
WORKS: Chamber music: Protusions, alto
flute, cello, piano, 1970; Skin deep, piano,
1970; Yellow with connection, flute, clarinet,
violin, cello, trombone, harp, 1971; For five/
four, a requiem to Kent State, 16 solo voices,
1972.
4872 Warwick Road, Richmond, VA 23224

HARDIN, BURTON ERVIN
b. Lincoln, Neb., 21 Aug. 1936. Studied with
Samuel Scott, Violet Archer, and Charles Hoag,
Univ. of Oklahoma; with Joshua Missal, Univ. of
Wichita. He won a Sigma Alpha Iota award, 1967.
He was faculty member, Univ. of South Carolina,
1964-67; Eastern Illinois Univ., 1968-   .
WORKS: Band: Horn quartet with band; Regal
festival music, brass choir; Chamber music:
woodwind quintet, 1967; Chorus: a cantata.
1120 Arthur Ave., Charleston, IL 61920

HARDIN, LOUIS T. (MOONDOG)
b. Marysville, Kan., 26 May 1916. After losing
his sight at age 13, studied violin, viola, piano,
organ, and harmony at Iowa School for the Blind.
He then taught himself by studying books in
braille and listening. Hardin considers himself
a tonalist and contrapuntalist, but has developed
a new stringed instrument, the hüs, and a new
drum, the trimba.
WORKS: Opera: Die Ershaffung der Weld;
Orchestra: Theme; Stamping ground; Minisym #1;
Lament I; Witch of Endor; 6 symphoniques for orchestra; Vocal: Madrigals, Books I-XII; Moondog's Mother Goose Book; and Art of Canon, Books
I and II.
Candor, NY 13743

*HARKNESS, REBEKAH
b. St. Louis, Mo., 17 Apr. 1915. Studied with
Fred Werle, Mannes Coll. of Music; with Nadia
Boulanger in Paris; Dalcroze School, Geneva;
orchestration with Lee Hoiby. She has received

(HARKNESS, REBEKAH)
honorary doctorates from Franklin Pierce Coll.,
1968; Lycoming Coll., 1970. She established the
Rebekah Harkness Found. ballet workshop at Watch
Hill, R. I., and Harkness House, New York; is
owner and director, Harkness Ballet Company.
WORKS: Ballet: Journey to love, 1958; Orchestra: Safari, tone poem, 1955; Mediterranean
suite, 1957; Musical chairs, 1958; Barcelona
suite, 1958; Gift to the Magi, 1959; Letters to
Japan, 1961; Macumba, a suite, 1965; Elements,
1965.
4 East 75th St., New York, NY 10021

HARLAN, CHARLES LEROY
b. Lewiston, Ida., 4 Dec. 1920; d. Seaside,
Calif., 14 Feb. 1972. Studied with Joseph Brye,
Univ. of Idaho; with Roger Sessions, Univ. of
California, Berkeley; and at Colorado State Coll.,
Ed. D. 1961. He taught in California public
schools from 1957, at Monterey, 1970-72.
WORKS: Orchestra: Arioso; Psalm 98, chorus
and orch., 1961; Chamber music: Trio for brass,
trumpet, horn, trombone; Fantasy for alto
saxophone.

*HARLINE, LEIGH
b. Salt Lake City, Utah, 26 Mar. 1907; d. Long
Beach, Calif., 10 Dec. 1969. Studied at Univ.
of Utah. He was on the Walt Disney staff, 1932;
became free-lance composer and orchestrator for
film studios, 1941.
WORKS: Film scores: Pride of the Yankees;
Johnny come lately; 7 faces of Dr. Lao; Strange
bedfellow; also wrote Civic Center suite for
orchestra.

*HARLING, WILLIAM FRANKE
b. London, England, 18 Jan. 1887; to U.S. 1888;
d. Sierra Madre, Calif., 22 Nov. 1958. Studied
at Grace Church Choir School, New York; Royal
Acad. of Music, London; with Theophile Ysaye in
Brussels. He was organist and choirmaster in
Brussels, 1907-08; at U.S. Military Acad., West
Point, 1909-10. He received the Bispham opera
medal, 1925.
WORKS: Opera: A light from St. Agnes, 1-
act, 1925; Deep River, 1926; Alda; Theatre:
music for the plays Paris bound; Machinal; Out-
ward bound; In love with love; The outsider;
Orchestra: Jazz concerto; Venetian fantasy; 3
elegiac poems, cello and orch.; Monte Casino,
tone poem; Before the dawn; At the tomb of the
unknown soldier, tone poem; My captain, my captain; Band: West Point forever, official march;
Film scores: Stagecoach; Penny serenade; So red
the rose; Man with wings; The scarlet empress.

*HARLOS, STEVEN
Sonatina for flute and piano.

*HARMAN, CARTER
b. Brooklyn, N. Y., 14 June 1918. Studied with
Roger Sessions, Princeton Univ., 1936-40; at
Columbia Univ., 1945-48. He was a pilot in the
Army Air Corps, 1942-45; music critic, New York
Times, 1947-52; music editor, Time magazine,

HARMAN, CARTER

(HARMAN, CARTER)
1952-72; executive vice president, Composers Recordings, Inc., 1972-   .
WORKS: Voice: A hymn to the Virgin, vocal quintet, 1956.

HARMON, JOHN C.
b. Oshkosh, Wis., 25 Oct. 1935. Studied with Clyde Duncan, Lawrence Univ.; with Henri Pousseur and Livingston Gearhart, Univ. of Buffalo. He has been a professional jazz musician since 1960, and director of jazz studies, Lawrence Univ., 1971-   .
WORKS: Jazz ensemble: Montage for orchestra and jazz trio; An unfair argument with life, ballet for jazz trio; Gates and beginnings; Bottoms up; Kurtains; There's a world out there waitin'; Another lonely spring.
2885 Oakwood Lane, Oshkosh, WI 54901

*HARMON, ROBERT
Passacalle, 3 trumpets; Suite no.1, 5 clarinets.
10949 Fruitland Drive, Studio City, CA 91604

HARMONIC, PHIL (KENNETH WERNER)
b. Newton, Mass., 10 June 1949. Has been director, The Radio Music City Hall Symphony Orchestra, 1967-   ; Chicken Band, 1972-   ; Phil Harmonic and the Nu-Tones, 1973-   .
WORKS: Duke of Windsor, mixed media opera for solo performer; High fidelity, live electronic music; Stars over San Francisco, repetitive musical metaphor; Keyboard Acc., piano; Fugitive from culture, personal entertainment; Win a dream date with Phil, intimate cultural event contest; Gertrude Stein in North America 1974, for collaborating readers, musicians, engineers.
1940 Channing Way, Berkeley, CA 94704

*HARNICK, SHELDON
Frustration, 1-act mime opera, a spoof on Debussy's Pelleas and Melisande, for 2 women and piano trio.

HARRER, JAMES P.
b. La Porte, Ind., 24 Apr. 1946. Studied with Donald H. White, DePauw Univ.; with William Billingsley, Univ. of Idaho. He received a Nat. Fed. of Music Clubs award in composition, 1970. He was teaching assistant, Univ. of Idaho; instructor, Hollins Coll., Va.
WORKS: Wind ensemble: Free rondo for 32 winds and percussion; Meliorism, 32 winds and 24 solo voices; Chamber music: string quartet, 1970; Phoresy, solo flute; Phoresy, trumpet and piano; Phoresy, solo oboe; Locomotive sandwich, nocturne for piano; Music for a great American painting, chamber winds, and tape; other symphonic works and chamber music.
235 Norcrest Place, Holland, MI 49423

HARRINGTON, AMBER ROOBENIAN (Mrs. W. Clark)
b. Boston, Mass., 13 May 1905. Studied organ at New England Cons., 1924-25; Eastman School of Music, 1926-27. She was church organist near Boston, 1921-24, New York, 1928-31; motion picture organist, Brooklyn, 1928-31.

(HARRINGTON, AMBER ROOBENIAN)
WORKS: Orchestra: Desert solitude, 1939; Caucasian dance song, strings, 1939; Reverie, 1957; Chorus: In an old English garden, 1936; The tryst, 1948; Vigil, 1949; Two red roses across the moon, 1949; The willow tree, 1955; Samarkand, 1956; Songs: My love, 1966; In memoriam, 1967.
Station Road, Brookfield, CT 06804

HARRINGTON, W. CLARK
b. Worcester, Mass., 28 June 1905. Attended Dartmouth Coll. and New England Cons.; studied with Vittorio Giannini in New York. He received the Endicott Prize at the New England Cons., 1929, for 3 songs. He was on the staff, Columbia Broadcasting System, 1930-59.
WORKS: Orchestra: Alas, that spring should vanish with the rose, voice, piano, and orch., 1929; Faun call, tone poem; numerous songs, piano pieces, choruses and works for strings.
Station Road, Brookfield, CT 06804

*HARRIS, ALBERT
Theme and variations for 8 horns; sonatina for guitar.
5622 Allott Ave., Van Nuys, CA 91401

HARRIS, ARTHUR
b. Philadelphia, Pa., 3 Apr. 1927. Studied with Paul Hindemith at Yale Univ. He is a free-lance composer, arranger, and conductor.
WORKS: Ballet: Bintel brief; Orchestra: March of the Mandarins; Chamber music: piano sonata; 4 pieces for 3 instruments; Theme and variations, 4 horns; 4 moods and finale, brass quintet; sundry compositions and arrangements.
R.D. 1, Box 310, Mt. Bethel, PA 18343

HARRIS, DONALD
b. St. Paul, Minn., 7 Apr. 1931. Studied with Ross Lee Finney, Univ. of Michigan, B. M. 1952, M. M. 1954; also with Paul Wilkinson in St. Paul; Max Deutsch, Nadia Boulanger, in France; with Boris Blacher, Lukas Foss, Andre Jolivet at Tanglewood. He has received Fulbright and Guggenheim fellowships; Prince Rainier of Monaco Composition prize; Louisville Orchestra award; Rockefeller and Chapelbrook Found. grants in aid; Nat. Endowment for the Arts grant of $4500, 1973; commission, French Nat. Radio, 1973. He was music consultant to the American Cultural Center, USIS, 1965-67; assistant to President for academic affairs, New England Cons., 1967-71, vice president, 1971-73, vice president for administrative affairs, 1974-   .
WORKS: Orchestra: Symphony in 2 movements, 1961; Chamber music: piano sonata, 1956; Fantasy, violin and piano, 1957; string quartet, 1965; Ludus for 10 instruments, 1966; Ludus II, flute, clarinet, violin, cello, piano, Cambridge, 8 May 1973.
New England Conservatory
290 Huntington Ave., Boston, MA 02115

HARRIS, ETHEL RAMOS (Mrs. Chester E.)
b. Newport, R. I., 18 Aug. 1908. Studied with Charles Dennee and Warren Storey Smith, New

(HARRIS, ETHEL RAMOS)
England Cons.; with Nikolai Lopatnikoff, Carnegie-Mellon Univ.; Isidor Philipp in New York; Aaron Copland at Tanglewood. She studied with Harvey Gaul on a scholarship, and also received a scholarship to Israel from American Christian Palestine Committee; Delta Sigma Theta award, 1959, 1973; Nat. Asso. of Negro Women Outstanding Musician award, 1971; Martin Luther King, Jr. award, 1972. She was Sophisticated Lady on Radio Station KDKA; pianist, Nat. Negro Opera Company; concert pianist, lecturer, composer.

WORKS: Chorus: Stan' steady; I've been in the storm so long; There'll be a jubilee; When I reach the other side; many other choral works and arrangements, songs, and piano pieces.
2840 Leechburg Road
New Kensington, PA 15068

HARRIS, FLOYD OLIN
b. Wichita, Kan., 30 Nov. 1913. Studied at McPherson, Coll., Univ. of Northern Colorado, Univ. of Nebraska, Univ. of Denver. He has taught in public schools in Kansas and Colorado; Englewood, Colo., 1962- .
WORKS: Sacred and secular choral works; instrumental solos and ensemble pieces, songs.
3032 South Ivan Way, Denver, CO 80227

HARRIS, HOWARD C., JR.
b. New Orleans, La., 18 June 1940. Graduated from Southern Univ., 1963; studied with Kenneth Klaus, Louisiana State Univ., M. M. 1969; with William S. Fischer in New York; and with William P. Latham, North Texas State Univ. He was public school band director, 1963-69; band director, Southern Univ., 1969-70; instructor, Delaware State Coll., 1970-71; assistant professor and composer-in-residence, Texas Southern Univ., 1972- .
WORKS: Orchestra: Folk psalm, 1973; Band: Phonosynthesis; A drum movement, winds and percussion; Jazz ensemble: Passion is; Black roots, 1972.
1406 Richmond Ave., #325, Houston, TX 77006

HARRIS, ROBERT A.
b. Detroit, Mich., 9 Jan. 1938. Studied with Ruth Wylie, Wayne State Univ., B. S. 1960, M. A. 1962; Bernard Rogers, Eastman School of Music, 1963-66; with H. Owen Reed, Michigan State Univ., Ph. D. 1971. He has received commissions from 2 churches and 2 from Wayne State Univ. He taught in Detroit public schools, 1960-64; was assistant professor, Wayne State Univ., 1964-70; associate professor, Michigan State Univ., 1970- ; and has held various church and choral conducting posts, 1959- .
WORKS: Theatre: Incidental music to Caligula by Camus, 1970; Orchestra: Concert piece for horn and orch., 1964; Concert piece for bassoon and orch., 1965; Contrasts, 4 winds and strings, 1966; Adagio, string orch., 1966; Moods for Orch., 1969; Chamber music: Fantasia, solo flute, 1958; Sonatine, 2 violins, 1960; 5 bagatelles, 3 woodwinds, 1963; string quartet, 1960-68; Psalms, soprano, horn and piano, 1968; Chorus: 3

(HARRIS, ROBERT A.)
children's prayers, women's voices, a cappella, 1959; O perfect love, motet, a cappella, 1960; For the beauty of the Earth, 1963; Benedictus, women's voices, 1968; Requiem: A canticle of immortality, 2 soloists, chamber choir, chorus, orch., 1970-71; many other choruses, songs.
Department of Music
Michigan State University
East Lansing, MI 48824

HARRIS, ROGER W.
Evansville, Ind., 20 May 1940. Studied with Grant Fletcher, Arizona State Univ.; with Halsey Stevens, Robert Linn, Ingolf Dahl, Univ. of Southern California, M. M. 1965. He has won an Arizona State Univ. composition contest and a Phi Mu Alpha contest. He taught at Arizona State Univ., 1966-67; Mesa Community Coll., 1967- .
WORKS: Band: Kroma III; Chamber music: 2 brass quintets; Kroma II, trumpet and 4 percussion; Women go to heaven and men go to hell, trombone, piano, percussion; Silent things, clarinet, horn, piano, percussion; Caliban in apartment 112, tenor voice, alto saxophone, piano, percussion.
1111 South San Jose, #145, Mesa, AZ 85202

*HARRIS, ROY ELLSWORTH
b. Lincoln County, Okla., 12 Feb. 1898. Attended Univ. of California, 1919-20; studied composition with Arthur Farwell, Henry Schoenfeld, and Nadia Boulanger, Modest Altschuler, Arthur Bliss, Rosario Scalero. His honors include Guggenheim fellowships, 1928, 1929, 1930; creative fellowship, Pasadena Music and Art Asso., 1930-33; 1st honors Committee for Appreciation of American Music, for Folksong symphony, 1940; Certificate of honor, Nat. Asso. for American Composers and Conductors, 1940; Elizabeth Sprague Coolidge medal, 1942; membership, Nat. Inst. of Arts and Letters, 1942; honorary doctorates, Rutgers Univ., 1941, Univ. of Redlands, 1946; Letter of distinction award, American Music Center, 1973. He taught at Westminster Choir School, 1934-38; was composer-in-residence, Cornell Univ., 1941-42, Colorado Coll., 1942-48, Utah State Agricultural Coll., 1948-49, Peabody Coll. for Teachers, 1949-51, Cumberland Summer Festivals, 1951; taught at Pennsylvania Coll. for Women, 1951-56; Univ. of Southern Illinois, 1956-57; Indiana Univ., 1957-60; Inter-American Univ., Puerto Rico, 1960-61; Univ. of California, Los Angeles, 1961-73; composer-in-residence, California State Univ. at Los Angeles, 1973, commissioned by the university to write a symphony for the U.S. bicentennial in 1976.
WORKS: Ballet: Western landscape, 1940; From this earth, 1941; What so proudly we hail, 1942; Orchestra: American portraits, 1929; Toccata, 1931; 14 symphonies, 1933-1975; When Johnny comes marching home, overture, 1934; Prelude and fugue for strings, 1935; Farewell to pioneers, 1935; Time suite, 1937; Evening piece, 1940; Ode to truth, 1940; Acceleration, 1941; Radio piece; accordion concerto, 1946; 2-piano concerto, 1946; Quest, 1947; Elegy and paean,

HARRIS, ROY ELLSWORTH

(HARRIS, ROY ELLSWORTH)
viola and orch., 1948; Kentucky spring, 1949;
Cumberland concerto, 1951; Abraham Lincoln walks
at midnight, soprano, piano and orch., 1953;
piano concerto, 1953; Ode to consonance, 1957;
Fantasy, piano and orch., 1954; Elegy and dance,
1958; Give me the splendid silent sun, baritone
and orch., 1961; Canticle to the sun, soprano
and chamber orch., 1961; Epilogue to Profiles in
courage: J.F.K., 1964; Horn of plenty, 1964;
Rhythm and spaces, string orch., 1965; Band:
Cimarron, overture, 1940; Take the sun and keep
the stars, 1944; Fruit of gold, 1949; Dark devo-
tion, 1950; Chamber music: Impressions of a
rainy day, string quartet, 1926; concerto for
clarinet and string quartet, 1927; string quartet, 1930; Fantasy, piano and woodwind quintet,
1932; Chorale for strings, 1932; 3 variations
on a theme, string quartet, 1933; 4 minutes and
20 seconds, flute and string quartet, 1934; piano
trio, 1934; piano quintet, 1936; string quartet,
1939; Soliloquy and dance, viola and piano, 1939;
string quintet, 1940; violin sonata, 1941; 4
charming little pieces, violin and piano, 1942;
many works for chorus and solo voice; piano and
organ pieces; Film score: One tenth of a nation.
    California State University
    Los Angeles, CA 91803

HARRIS, RUSSELL G.
    b. Graymont, Ill., 3 Aug. 1914. Studied with
Ernst Krenek, Darius Milhaud, Ernst Toch, Egon
Wellesz. He won first prize for Fugue with cho-
rale for organ, Clarke Cons. composition contest,
1935. He was faculty member at Baylor Univ.,
Upper Iowa Univ., Hamline Univ. 1935-48; at
Hamline Univ., chairman, music department,
1948-71, professor, 1948-   .
    WORKS: Chamber music: string quartet, 1951;
3 movements for chamber orch., 1969; Chorus:
Tarye no lenger; It was beginning winter, 1961;
The moon is hiding, 1961; 3 songs, 1941; 5 piano
pieces, 1951.
    1615 Lafond Ave., St. Paul MN 55104

HARRISON, CHARLES SCOTT
    b. Seattle, Wash., 27 Feb. 1950. Studied with
James Hanna, Univ. of Southwestern Louisiana.
    WORKS: Theatre: Artist of the beautiful,
musical comedy based on Nathaniel Hawthorne,
1973; Orchestra: symphony, 5 orchestral miniatures; Chamber music: string quartet; sonata
breve, string bass; organ preludes; piano sonata,
1972; Electronic: Time changes, music for modern
dance.
    1111 Eagle Drive, Apt. 24, Denton, TX 76201

HARRISON, LOU
    b. Portland, Ore., 14 May 1917. Attended San
Francisco State Coll., 1934-35; studied privately with Henry Cowell and Arnold Schoenberg.
His awards include American Acad. of Arts and
Letters grant, 1947; Guggenheim fellowships,
1952, 1954; 20th Century Masterpiece award, Rome,
1954; Fromm Found. award, 1955; Louisville Orch.
commission, 1961; Rockefeller fellowship for
study in Asian music, 1961; senior scholar, East-
West Center, Univ. of Hawaii, 1963; Phebe Ketchum

(HARRISON, LOU)
Thorne fellowship, 1966; panel member, World
Music Council and UNESCO Conf., 1968; membership,
Nat. Inst. of Arts and Letters, 1973. He taught
at Mills Coll., 1937-40; Univ. of California,
Los Angeles, 1942; Reed Coll., 1950; Black Mt.
Coll., 1951; San Jose State Coll., 1968-   .
Moving to New York in 1943 he wrote for several
publications, composed for dance groups, and
conducted often, including the first performance
of any Charles Ives symphony, the 3rd, 5 Apr.
1947. After a decade in New York he has lived
chiefly in California, lecturing, developing his
interest in oriental music and microtones, in-
venting the instruments to play them, and exper-
imenting with unorthodox sonorities--from automobile brake drums, lengths of pipe, et al.--has
organized and performed in concerts of Chinese
music; written plays, poetry, liner notes for
Ives' records, and a pamphlet on Carl Ruggles.
Harrison reads and speaks Esperanto fluently,
has given Esperanto titles to some of his compositions and even wrote an essay on chlorophyl in
Esperanto and set it for 8 baritones and
orchestra.
    WORKS: Jeptha's daughter, a theatre kit;
Rapunzel; Young Caesar, puppet opera; Ballet:
Almanac of the seasons; Changing world; Green
mansions; Io and Promethus; Johnny Appleseed;
The marriage at the Eiffel Tower; Labyrinth;
Solstice; Praises for hummingbirds and hawks;
Something to please everybody; Western dance;
incidental music to several plays; Orchestra:
Alleluia; The only jealousy of Emer; Simfony I,
from Simfonies in free style; suite for violin,
piano, orch.; 3 suites for strings; Symphony on
G; Percussion: Canticles No.1 and 2; Koncherto
por la violono kun perkuta orkestro; flute concerto; Double music (with John Cage); Fugue;
Song of Queztecoatl; Chamber music: Air for
flute; At the tomb of Charles Ives; Concerto in
slendro for violin; Motet for the Day of Ascension; 7 Pastorales; suite for cello and harp;
suite for string quartet; string trio; Chorus:
A joyous procession and a solemn procession;
Mass; 4 Strict songs; Songs: Alma redemptoris
mater; Fragment from Calamus; Piano: 6 cembalo
sonatas; Little suite; 3 sonatas; Praises for
Michael The Archangel; Prelude and sarabande;
suite.
    7163 Viewpoint Road, Aptos, CA 95003

*HART, FREDERIC PATTON
    b. Aberdeen, Wash., 5 Sep. 1898. Studied at
American Cons.; also with Rubin Goldmark, Ernest
Hutcheson and Nadia Boulanger. He taught at the
Diller-Quaile School and at Sarah Lawrence Coll.
    WORKS: Opera: The wheel of fortune, 1934;
The romance of Robot, 1-act, 1937; also chamber
music, piano pieces, songs.
    c/o American Composers Alliance
    2121 Broadway, New York, NY 10023

*HART, WELDON
    b. Place-Bear Spring, Tenn., 19 Sep. 1911; d.
East Lansing, Mich., 20 Nov. 1957. Studied at
Univ. of Michigan; with Howard Hanson and
Bernard Rogers, Eastman School of Music, Ph. D.

(HART, WELDON)
1946. He was chairman, music department, Western Kentucky State Coll., 1946-49; director,
School of Music, West Virginia Univ., 1949-57;
chairman, music department, Michigan State Univ.,
1957. He wrote orchestral works and chamber
music.

HART, WILLIAM SEBASTIAN
b. Baltimore, Md., 30 Oct. 1920. Graduated cum
laude, Peabody Cons.; attended Johns Hopkins
Univ., B. A., Ph. D. He has received honorary
doctorates from Allen Univ., Mt. St. Mary's Coll.,
and Univ. of Texas. He was percussion teacher,
Peabody Cons., 1939-62; special instructor of
instrumental music, Baltimore public schools,
1939-52; lecturer, Morgan State Coll., 1962-65;
musical director, Gettysburg Symphony Orch.,
1958-   .
    WORKS: Chamber music: sonatina for 2 flutes;
concert piece for timpani duet.
    1800 Cromwell Bridge Road
    Baltimore, MD 21234

HARTKE, STEPHEN PAUL
b. Orange, N. J., 6 July 1952. Studied with
Laurence Widdoes in New York; with Leonardo
Balada, United Nations Internat. School; with
James Drew, Yale Univ. He received New York
State School Music Asso. composition award, 1969;
BMI awards, 1970, 1972; William DeVane award,
Yale Univ., 1973.
    WORKS: Chamber music: The bull transcended,
string orch., 1970; Alysoun, cantata for con-
tralto and 8 instruments, 1971; The hunting of
the snark, chamber oratorio on text by Lewis
Carroll, baritone solo, chorus, chamber orch.,
Yale Univ., May 1972; Passion, poison, and pet-
rifaction, chamber symphony, New York, Mar. 1973.
    c/o Saunders, 530 East 23rd St., Apt. 8F
    New York, NY 10010

HARTLEY, GERALD
b. Spokane, Wash., 18 Sep. 1921. Studied with
George Frederick McKay and John Verrall, Univ.
of Washington. He was instructor, Gonzaga Univ.,
1855-60, 1968-70; choral director, Lewis and
Clark High School, Spokane, 1953-   .
    WORKS: Orchestra: Sonatine for piano and
orch.; Band: Plymouth Town--Sea chantey rhapsody;
A fuguing tune; Concerto grosso for winds and
percussion; Chamber music: Sketches for strings;
Divertissement for woodwind quintet; Chorus:
Four 19th century lyrics, choral suite; The
builders, chorus and orch.
    East 1011 Overbluff Road, Spokane, WA 99203

HARTLEY, WALTER S.
b. Washington, D.C., 21 Feb. 1927. Studied with
Bernard Rogers and Howard Hanson, Eastman School
of Music, B. M. 1950, M. M. 1951, Ph. D. 1953.
He received a Koussevitzky Found. commission,
1954; Conn Brass Music award, 1964; State Univ.
of New York research grants, 1970-71; ASCAP
awards annually since 1962. He was instructor,
Nat. Music Camp, 1956-64; professor, Davis and
Elkins Coll., 1958-69; associate professor,
State Univ. Coll., Fredonia, N. Y., 1969-   .

(HARTLEY, WALTER S.)
    WORKS: Orchestra: Variations for orch.,
1973; Band: Concerto for 23 winds, 1957;
Sinfonia no.3 for brass choir, 1963; Sinfonia
no.4 for wind ensemble, 1965; Concerto for alto
saxophone and band, 1966; Canticles for voices
and wind ensemble, 1970-71; Chamber music:
Sonata concertante for trombone and piano, 1958;
duo for saxophone and piano, 1964; tuba sonata,
1967; piano sonata, 1968; numerous works for
various instrumental ensembles and chorus.
    50 Maple Ave., Fredonia, NY 14063

*HARTMANN, ARTHUR MARTINUS
b. Mate Szalka, Hungary, 23 July 1881; U.S. citizen; d. New York, N. Y., 30 Mar. 1956. Studied
with Charles Martin Loeffler. He toured the
U.S. and Europe as solo violinist with symphony
orchestras and with the Hartmann String Quartet.
    WORKS: Orchestra: Suite in ancient style;
Caprice; Impressions from the Balkans; Chorus:
Oh weep for those that wept, chorus and orch.;
The prayer of Moses.

*HARTMEYER, JOHN
Negev, tone poem for brass.

HARTWAY, JAMES JOHN
b. Detroit, Mich., 24 Apr. 1944. Studied with
Ruth Shaw Wylie, Wayne State Univ., B. A. 1966,
M. M. 1969; with H. Owen Reed, Michigan State
Univ., Ph. D. 1972. He received graduate assistantships, scholarships, and Hinman fellowship; 2nd place, Phi Mu Alpha composition
contest. He was instructor, Lansing Community
Coll., 1970; instructor, head of theory and composition, Wayne State Univ., 1971-   .
    WORKS: Orchestra: Dialogue, piano and orch.;
Coleus, with guitar and piano; 7 ways of looking
at a blackbird, with soprano and prepared piano;
Band: 2 Rube Goldbergs; Jazz band: Tomorrow's
dream; Judgement of Solomon; Impressions of
childhood; 5-4-3; Chamber music: wind octet; 3
ways of looking at a blackbird, soprano, prepared piano, 3 percussion, flute; Anagogia,
piano; Piece for quartet and Mirror image, for
improvisation ensemble; Chorus: Sequence, with
percussion and siren; Multi-media: 6 nocturnal
explorations, flute, clarinet, double bass,
piano, percussion, 2 dancers, narrator, lights
and slides, New York, 22 Feb. 1974; other multimedia works.
    20524 Shady Lane, St. Clair Shores, MI 48080

HARTWEG, JERRY
b. Ann Arbor, Mich., 23 June 1939. Studied at
Univ. of Michigan and Univ. of Illinois. He was
elected to Pi Kappa Lambda at Univ. of Michigan.
He has been instructor of percussion, Interlochen
Center for the Arts, 1968-   .
    WORKS: Percussion: solo for snare drum.
    P. O. Box 164, Interlochen, MI 49643

HARTZELL, LAWRENCE WILLIAM
b. Mt. Pleasant, N. Y., 1 July 1942. Studied at
Baldwin-Wallace Coll., B. M.; with John Pozdro,
Edward Mattila, and Douglas Moore, Univ. of
Kansas, M. M., Ph. D. He has received several

HARTZELL, LAWRENCE WILLIAM

(HARTZELL, LAWRENCE WILLIAM)
commissions for compositions. He taught at Univ. of Kansas, 1965-67; was assistant professor, Univ. of Wisconsin-Eau Claire, 1968-73; assistant professor, Baldwin-Wallace Coll., 1973-   .
WORKS: Wind ensemble: Introduction and allegro for brass and percussion, 1969; Toccata concertata, organ and brass choir, 1970; Thunder Bay, symphony for band, 1971-73; Chamber music: horn sonata, 1964; piano sonata, 1966; quintet for trumpet and strings, 1970-71; Jefferson variations, saxophone and percussion, 1972; 4 places, clarinet alone, 1973; Electronic: Conversation, bass trombone and tape, 1971; Discourse, jazz ensemble and tape, 1972.
Baldwin-Wallace College, Berea, OH 44017

*HARVEY, RUSSELL
Sonata for band.
American Conservatory of Music
Chicago, IL 60605

HASKINS, ROBERT JAMES
b. Denver, Colo., 27 Dec. 1937. Attended Univ. of Denver, 1956-59; Wittenberg Univ., B. M. 1961, M. A. 1962; and is completing work toward a D. M. A. at Univ. of Cincinnati; studied with William Walters, Waldo Williamson, and Paul Cooper. He received first prize, Nat. Fed. of Music Clubs, 1962; Nat. Endowment for the Arts grant to compose 3 1-act operas, 1974. He has been musical director, Springfield Civic Opera Company, 1961-63, 1974-   ; conductor, Wilmington Chamber Orch., 1963-   ; chorusmaster, Dayton Opera Company, 1974-   ; associate professor, Wilmington Coll., 1963-   , chairman, Fine Arts Division and Music Department, 1971-   .
WORKS: Opera: Benjamin, 1960; Mr. Godfry, 1961; Cassandra Southwick, 1963; The prisoners, 1964; The cask of amontilado, 1968; Young Goodman Brown, 1971 (librettist for the last 4 was Allen John Koppenhaver); Orchestra: 4 symphonies, #1 in 1 movement; #2 for chorus, soli, and orch.; #3 And man created God in his own image, text by Koppenhaver; #4 Sinfonia requiem, soprano, baritone, orch., text by Koppenhaver; songs, theatre music, chamber music.
729 North South St., Wilmington, OH 45177

*HASLAM, HERBERT
b. Philadelphia, Pa., 23 Apr. 1928. Studied at Temple Univ.; Juilliard School, B. S., M. S. He has taught at Bronx House Music School; The Barker School; was founder and co-director, Composers Circle, New York; composer-in-residence, Riverdale Country Schools; executive associate, Riverdale School of Music.
WORKS: Orchestra: Special starlight, with chorus, narrator, Sandburg text; Chamber music: Antimasque, brass quartet; Haiku set, viola and cello.

*HASSELL, JON
b. Memphis, Tenn., 22 Mar. 1937. Studied with Bernard Rogers, Eastman School of Music, B. M. 1969, M. M. 1970; with Karlheinz Stockhausen and Henri Pousser in Cologne, 1965-67. He was composer-in-residence, Center for Creative and

(HASSELL, JON)
Performing Arts, Buffalo, N. Y., 1967-69. In Elemental warnings, a part of his experimental work Landscape series, he uses results achieved by burying electronic oscillators in the ground and floating them on balloons.
463 West St., New York, NY 10014

HASSELL, MICHAEL RICHARD
b. Omaha, Neb., 4 Jan. 1951. Studied with Hans Janowitz in Central America; piano with Margaret Chaloff, composition with William Maloof, John Bavvichi, Gregg Smith, John La Porta, conducting with Jeronimas Kacinskas, in Boston. He has been on the faculty, Berklee Coll. of Music, 1971-   ; was conductor, Chorus pro Terra in Panama, guest conductor of choruses in Boston area.
WORKS: Orchestra: Trois femme fatales, suite; Chamber music: piano sonata, no.2, 1972; Chorus: On the elements, a cycle, Boston, 25 Apr. 1974; Missa brevis, chorus, brass, percussion, 1973; Ode: Intimations of immortality, 1973.
400 Commonwealth Ave., #325
Boston, MA 02215

*HASTINGS, ROSS
b. Los Angeles, Calif., 26 Feb. 1915. Was organist-choirmaster, San Diego, 1948-53; music coordinator, Hollywood Bowl.
WORKS: Orchestra: Sinfonia brevis; sonatine; Sketch for orchestra; Chorus: Festival prayer; My heart changes key; O God, our help in ages past.

HATTON, GAYLEN
b. Red Mountain, Calif., 4 Oct. 1928. Studied with Leon Dallin, Crawford Gates, and Leroy Robertson. He received the Intermountain Concert Society award, 1957; Rosenblatt award, 1958; Nat. Endowment for the Arts grant, 1970. He was instructor, Univ. of Utah, 1957-63; professor, California State Univ., Sacramento, 1963-   ; teacher-administrator, Sun Valley Music Camp, 1963-72; performer Utah Symphony and Sacramento Symphony.
WORKS: Ballet: Seasonal episode; Toxcatl ballet; Odette baby, jazz ballet on 2nd act of Swan Lake; Opus psychedelia, electronic ballet; Orchestra: Music for orchestra; Jeu-parti; Band: Divertimento; Music for band; Chamber music: 3 string quartets; trio for oboe, viola, cello; Music for tape and horn.
7720 Dar Du Lane, Sacramento, CA 95823

HAUBIEL, CHARLES TROWBRIDGE
b. Delta, Ohio, 30 Jan. 1892. Studied with Rudolph Ganz in Berlin, 1909-13; Rosario Scalero at Mannes Coll. of Music, 1919-25; with Josef and Rosina Lhevinne in New York, 1928-31. His many awards include the first prize in America in the Internat. Schubert Centennial contest, 1928; Swift Symphonic award; New York Philharmonic Symphony contest, 1938; Martha Kinney Cooper, Ohioana Library Asso. citation, 1953; Harvey Gaul Memorial prize; Nat. Fed. of Music Clubs Awards of Merit, 1963, 1965; honorary

(HAUBIEL, CHARLES TROWBRIDGE)
doctorate, Southwestern Cons. He made his debut as recitalist in 1909, then in 1913 toured the U.S. as associate artist with Jaroslav Kocian, violinist. He was faculty member, Kingfisher Coll. and Inst. of Musical Art, Oklahoma City, 1913-17; served as bandmaster, U.S. Army, 1917-19; was on faculty at Juilliard School, 1921-29; professor, New York Univ., 1922-47. He founded The Composers press in 1935.

WORKS: Opera: Brigands preferred, comic opera, 1925; The witch's curse, fairy opera; Sunday costs 5 pesos, Mexican folk opera, 1950; Berta, Mexican folk opera; Orchestra: Mars ascending, 1923; Of human destiny (formerly called Karma) 1928; Portraits, 1935; Suite passecaille, 1935; symphony, 1937; Vox cathedralis, 1937; The plane beyond, 1938; Solari, 1938; Passacaglia triptych; Pioneers; Portals, high voice and orch.; Miniatures, 1938; Metamorphoses; Vision of St. Joan, chorus and orch., 1941; Serenade, lyric cantata for chorus and orch.; Gothic variations, violin and orch., 1943; 1865 A.D.; The cosmic Christ, high voice and orch.; Both grave and gay, 1944; American rhapsody; Chamber music: piano trio, 1932; 5 moods, string quartet and woodwind quintet; Gay dances, piano trio, 1932; Echi classici, string quartet, 1936; string trio, 1943; cello sonata, 1944; violin sonata; Nuances, violin and piano, 1947; Cryptics, cello and piano; numerous other instrumental works, choral works, and piano pieces.
4941 Ambrose Ave., Los Angeles, CA 90027

HAUFRECHT, HERBERT
b. New York, N. Y., 3 Nov. 1909. Studied with Quincy Porter and Herbert Elwell, Cleveland Inst. of Music; with Rubin Goldmark at Juilliard Graduate School on a fellowship in composition. He was resettlement administrator, Special Skills Division, W. Va., 1936-37; staff composer and arranger, Federal Theatre, 1938-39; editor and arranger for various music publishers, 1945-   ; music director, Young Audiences, Inc., 1961-68.

WORKS: Opera: Boney Quillen, comic opera in 1 act; Orchestra: Suite for string orch., 1934; Overture for an American mural, 1939; The story of Ferdinand, narrator and orch., 1939; 3 fantastic sketches, 1941; Square set for string orch., 1941; Band: Walkin' the road, 1944; Prelude to a tragedy; symphony for brass and timpani, 1956; Chamber music: brass quintet; A woodland serenade, woodwind quintet, 1955; Etudes in blues, piano, 1951; Chorus: Poor Richard's almanack, cycle of 6 songs; 6 songs by Charles Ives in choral settings.
245 Bennett Ave., New York, NY 10040

HAUGLAND, A. OSCAR
b. Emmons, Minn., 28 Jan. 1922. Studied with Robert Delaney, Northwestern Univ.; Howard Hanson, Bernard Rogers, Herbert Elwell, Eastman School of Music. He has received 3 dean's grants, Northern Illinois Univ., for composition. He was faculty member, West Virginia Univ., 1949-52, 1954-60; professor, Northern Illinois Univ., 1960-   .

(HAUGLAND, A. OSCAR)
WORKS: Theatre: incidental music to Peer Gynt by Ibsen, 1965; Orchestra: 3 psalms; concertino for horn and strings; Chamber music: Little suite, woodwind quintet; string quartet; Chorus: From the universe, choral cycle; many solo and ensemble works for instruments, vocal solos and choral works.
756 South 3rd St., DeKalb, IL 60115

*HAUSSERMANN, JOHN
b. Manila, P. I., 21 Aug. 1909. Studied at Cincinnati Cons.; with Paul Le Flem in Paris.
WORKS: Orchestra: 3 symphonies, 1941, 1944, 1949; concerto for voice and orch., 1942; Chamber music: quintet for harpsichord and woodwind quartet; 2 string quartets; Suite rustique, flute, cello, piano; organ works, piano pieces, songs.

*HAYDON, GLEN
b. Inman, Kan., 9 Dec. 1896; d. Chapel Hill, N. C., 8 May 1966. Studied at Univ. of California, B. A. 1918, M. A. 1921; with Eugene Cools, Vienna Univ., Ph. D. 1932. He was musicologist as well as composer; held various teaching posts in the Berkeley (Calif.) schools, 1920-25; was chairman, music department, Univ. of California, Berkeley, 1929-31; professor and chairman, music department, Univ. of North Carolina, from 1934; in 1947 was appointed Louis C. Elson lecturer at the Library of Congress, Washington, D.C.
WORKS: Ballet: The druid's weed, 1929; Theatre: incidental music for Aristophanes' Lysistrata, 1936; Chorus: Mass, a cappella, 1930. He was author of many musicological works.

*HAYES, ISAAC
b. near Memphis, Tenn., 20 Aug. 1942. Is an exceedingly popular soul singer and organist. The theme from his film score Shaft won a BMI Oscar; the score was nominated for the best score category; received a Grammy award, 1972, Golden Globe award, and the Nat. Asso. for the Advancement of Colored People Image award. He also wrote the film score for The man.

HAYES, JOSEPH
b. Marietta, Ohio, 5 Dec. 1920. Studied at Boston Cons., 1940-41; with Warren Storey Smith, New England Cons., 1946-49; with Gardner Read, Boston Univ., 1949-50, 1955. He has received citations and commissions. He was faculty member, Claflin Coll., 1952-53; Jarvis Christian Coll., 1953-56; instructor in flute, saxophone, composition, Detroit Community Coll., 1963-   , composer-in-residence, 1973-
WORKS: Orchestra: Sunday 3:00 p.m., a symphony scored for woodwind quintet, saxophone quintet, brass sextet, piano, percussion and strings; Music for viewing, orch., singing and speaking chorus, and dancers, in 5 parts, performed as a set or singly: Curtain call, Councils of war, On contemplating a flower, Sleep, Retrospect; Band: Chorale; Chamber music: Recitative and air, horn and piano; Hornotations No.1, horn and strings; quintet for clarinet,

HAYES, JOSEPH

(HAYES, JOSEPH)
bassoon, violin, cello, piano; Fanfare and
ricercare, brass quartet; Quartet miniature,
strings; Episodes, woodwind quintet; 2 soliloquies, solo cello; Praeludium for organ; Chorus: Lord's prayer, a cappella; Lullaby; Song
of the colours, a cappella; Time capsules,
double women's chorus and woodwind quintet;
many vocal solos and piano pieces.
17160 Kentucky, Detroit, MI 48221

*HAYES, WILLIAM
Sonata in D for organ.

HAYMAN, RICHARD PERRY
b. Albuquerque, N. Mex., 29 July 1951. Studied
with Vladimir Ussachevsky, Columbia Univ.; and
with Philip Corner, Gordon Mumma, and Sari
Dienes. He has been organmeister, Space for
Innovative Development, New York, 1972-   .
WORKS: I am a toupee, for flashlight and
bell, performed Columbia Univ. Commencement,
1973; Prelude, electronic work and Carry for
organ, performed with multigravitational dance,
New York, 1973; Don't mean a thing if it ain't
got that swing, chorus, Chocorua Music Festival,
N. H., 1973.
326 Spring St., New York, NY 10013

HAYS, DORIS ERNESTINE
b. Memphis, Tenn., 6 Aug. 1941. Studied with
Harold Cadek, Univ. of Chattanooga; with Richard
Hervig, Univ. of Iowa; Friedrich Wuhrer in
Munich; Paul Badura-Skoda, Univ. of Wisconsin.
She won a performance award, Wisconsin State Composition contest, 1968; first prize, 1971
Internat. Competition for Interpreters of Contemporary Music, Rotterdam; received fellowships, Bavarian Ministry of Culture, and Univ.
of Wisconsin. She was on the faculty, Univ. of
Wisconsin, 1967-68; Cornell Coll., Iowa, 1969;
special consultant in contemporary music to an
educational music publisher, 1972-73.
WORKS: Chamber music: Scheveningen Beach,
5 flutes; Help compose, pianist and audience;
Mixed media: Pamp (ceremony in high places) for
amplified piano, bird calls and tape; If for 2
pianos and tape. She is author of Sound symbol
structures, an introduction to new keyboard
notation.
241 West 97th St., Penthouse 2
New York, NY 10025

HAYS, ROBERT D.
b. Boise, Idaho, 31 Jan. 1923. Studied with
Arnold Elston and Francis McKay, Univ. of Oregon;
Bernhard Heiden, Indiana Univ., D. M. 1967. He
received a Mississippi Educational Television
award, 1969. He was director of bands, Univ. of
Southern Mississippi, 1956-61, director, Electronic Studio, 1965-69; with a private audio
firm, Los Angeles, 1969-73; professor, Central
Michigan Univ., 1973-   .
WORKS: Orchestra: To the memory of the
author, chorus, orch., and narrator; symphony
1965; Band: Dramatic fanfares, 1961; Design for
band, 1963; Chamber music: string quartet, 1965;
Music for 7, 1969; cello sonata, 1973; Music for

(HAYS, ROBERT D.)
winds, woodwind quintet, 1973; Mixed media:
Oracle of Apollo, for tape, band, electronic
synthesizer, 1967; Chronograms I, tape, tuba,
electric guitar, clarinet, piano, and mixer,
1973.
622 South Franklin, Mt. Pleasant, MI 48858

*HAYTON, LEONARD GEORGE (LENNIE)
b. New York, N. Y., 13 Feb. 1908; d. Palm
Springs, Calif., 24 Apr. 1971. Played piano in
many noted jazz bands; was music director, MGM
Studios, 1940-53; with 20th Century Fox Film
Corporation, after 1953.
WORKS: Jazz ensemble: Flying fingers; Mood
Hollywood, Midnight mood; Film scores: On the
town, 1949; The Harvey girls; Singing in the
rain; Star.

*HAYWARD, LOU
Concert vocalize, 3 soli, chorus, piano.

*HAYWARD, MAE SHEPARD
Composed 3 piano trios, other chamber works,
piano pieces, and songs which were performed in
Boston, 1936-37.

HAZELMAN, HERBERT R.
b. Topton, N. C., 13 Oct. 1913. Studied with
Lamar Stringfield, Univ. of North Carolina. He
was oboist, North Carolina Symphony, 1930-35;
bandmaster, Greensboro High School, 1936-   .
WORKS: Orchestra: Pastoral passacaglia,
commissioned work; Band: A short ballet for
awkward dancers; Dance variations on an obscure
theme; Prelude and fugue; Gallic galop; Dance
for three.
3206 Madison Ave., Greensboro, NC 27403

HAZEN, SARA (Sally Hazen Evans)
b. Sarasota, Fla., 14 July 1935. Studied with
John Carter, Rollins Coll.; attended Duke Univ.,
A. B. 1957; studied with Roland Leich and
Leonardo Balada, Carnegie-Mellon Univ., 1972-73;
piano with Ferguson Webster.
WORKS: Chamber music: City serenade, saxophone quartet, 1972; Delta suite, brass instruments, 1973; Chorus: Christ is born, 1964;
Alleluia, we live in thee, 1967; Piano: Festival, 1964; Fantasy, 1972; Omega alpha variations,
Carnegie-Mellon Univ., 13 Dec. 1973.
11 Ellsworth Terrace, Pittsburgh, PA 15213

HAZZARD, PETER PEABODY
b. Poughkeepsie, N. Y., 31 Jan. 1949. Attended
Boston Univ., 1966-68; studied with John Bavicchi
and William Maloof, Berklee Coll. of Music, B. M.
1971. He has been guitarist, pianist, composer-
arranger for his own groups and others' since
age 16; instructor, Berklee Coll. of Music,
1971-   .
WORKS: Orchestra: Harwichport interlude,
1971; Merlin, cantata for solo bass, chorus and
orch., text by Barbara Hazzard, 1971; Band:
Mentor, brass choir and percussion, 1971;
Canzona and overture, Boston, 5 Dec. 1972; Chamber music: string quartet, 1971; clarinet quartet, 1971; contrabass sonata, 1971; woodwind

(HAZZARD, PETER PEABODY)
sextet, 1971; suite for English horn, 1972; Chorus: A praise book, text by Nancy Willard, chorus, brass, percussion, 1971; Massage, 3 solo voices, winds, percussion, no text, Boston, 25 Mar. 1971; Mass no.1, choir, woodwind quintet, brass quintet, percussion, 1972; Venite, exultemus Domino, choir, 5 winds, cello, timpani, 1973.
Fairview Ave., Scituate, MA 02066

HEATH, JAMES E. (JIMMY)
b. Philadelphia, Pa., 25 Oct. 1926. Studied at Theodore Presser School, Philadelphia, and with Rudolf Schramm in New York. He received the Jazz Festival award, Harstad, Norway; Jazz at Home Club award, Philadelphia; Creative Arts Public Service composers grant, New York. He has been saxophonist with Howard McGhee, Dizzy Gillespie, Miles Davis, Art Farmer; instructor for Jazzmobile and private teacher, 1968-   ; has presented jazz lecture concerts in New York City schools and colleges.
WORKS: Jazz: Jazz themes with improvisations for saxophone; Gemini; Gingerbread boy; A time and a place; One for Juan; Big P; The gap sealer; Love and understanding.
112-19 34th Ave., Corona, NY 11368

HEBBLE, ROBERT CHRISTIAN
b. Orange, N. J., 14 Feb. 1934. Studied with Quincy Porter, Yale Univ., B. M. 1952; Nadia Boulanger in Paris, 1955-56; Vittorio Giannini and Roger Sessions at Juilliard School, M. S. 1966. He was assistant organist, Riverside Church, New York, 1950-63; department head, Red Bank Catholic High School, N. J., 1957-   ; on music faculty, Stevens Inst. of Technology, 1969-   .
WORKS: Chorus: Celebration of unity, a mass; Praise to the Lord, the Almighty; And rejoice; My spirit longeth for thee; and organ pieces and arrangements.
19 Grandview Ave., West Orange, NJ 07052

HEDWALL, PAUL D.
b. Hartford, Conn., 18 Apr. 1939. Studied with Malloy Miller, Hugo Norden, Gardner Read, Boston Univ.; with Vittorio Giannini, Manhattan School of Music; with Ingolf Dahl, Halsey Stevens, Univ. of Southern California. He received first prize in Brookline, Mass. Library Asso. contest, 1961, for sonata for piano 4-hands; first prize, Music Society of Santa Barbara, 1968, for song cycle, Sky and clouds. He has been assistant professor, Univ. of Alabama, 1969-   , chairman of composition and theory, 1971-   .
WORKS: Orchestra: Symphony--Psalm 148, for chorus, orch., and soloists, 1972; Chamber music: flute sonata, 1965; Teleologiae, trumpet, trombone, piano, commissioned by Alchin Fund, 1972; 5 x 5 = 5 = 1, woodwind quintet, Univ. of Alabama grant, 1973.
9 Hickory Hill, Tuscaloosa, AL 35401

*HEFTI, NEAL
b. Hastings, Neb., 29 Oct. 1922. Was trumpeter in dance orchestras, 1941-51; staff conductor at

(HEFTI, NEAL)
ABC for the Arthur Godfrey show and the Kate Smith show; then played his own orchestra.
WORKS: Orchestra: Wheels of freedom, written for the Nat. Auto show, 1960; Film scores: Sex and the single girl; How to murder your wife; Synanon; Harlow; Boeing, Boeing; Lord love a duck; and many songs.
c/o Cimino Publ., Inc., Mapel Ave., Westbury, NY 11590

*HEGEDUS, ARPAD
Memory of John Fitzgerald Kennedy, orchestra, Columbus, Ohio, 19 May 1971.
College Conservatory of Music
Cincinnati, OH 45221

HEGENBART, ALEX F.
b. Amsterdam, Neth., 2 Aug. 1922; U.S. citizen 1955. Studied with Arend Koole in Amsterdam. He was minister of music, Hickory, N. C., 1958-60; Oakhurst Baptist Church, Charlotte, N. C., 1960-72; First Baptist Church, Belmont, N. C., 1972-   .
WORKS: Theatre: Hurt doesn't always, a jazz musical; Chorus: Hear ye!, Christmas cantata; Simeon's prayer; Behold what love; Meditation; Behold a stranger; Psalm of life; I am the door; Follow me; Going to Bethlehem.
Rt. 1, Box 120-M-2, Belmont, NC 28012

HEIDEN, BERNHARD
b. Frankfurt, Germany, 24 Aug. 1910; U.S. citizen 1941. Studied with Paul Hindemith in Berlin; with Donald Grout, Cornell Univ., M. A. 1946. He received the Mendelssohn prize, 1953; Fine Arts composition award, 1951; Guggenheim fellowship, 1966. He has been professor and chairman of composition, Indiana Univ., Bloomington, 1946-   .
WORKS: Opera: The darkened city, Bloomington, 23 Feb. 1963; Orchestra: Euphorion, 1949; concerto for small orch., 1949; 2 symphonies, 1938, 1954; Memorial, 1955; concerto for piano, violin, cello, and orch., 1956; Variations for orch., 1960; Envoy, 1963; concertino for string orch., 1967; horn concerto, 1969; Partita for orch., 1970; Chamber music: alto saxophone sonata, 1937; horn sonata, 1939; Sinfonia, woodwind quintet, 1949; quintet for horn and string quartet, 1952; violin sonata, 1954; clarinet sonata, 1955; piano trio, 1956; cello sonata, 1958; flute sonatina, 1958; viola sonata, 1959; Siena, cello and piano, 1961; woodwind quintet, 1965, brass quintet, 1967; Inventions, 2 celli, 1967; Intrada, woodwind quintet and alto saxophone, 1970; 5 canons for horns, 1971; Chorus: Two songs of spring, 1947; Divine poems, 1949; In memoriam, 1964; Piano: sonata 4 hands, 1946; sonata, 1952.
915 East University, Bloomington, IN 47401

*HEIFETZ, VLADIMIR
b. Russia, 28 Mar. 1893; to U.S. 1921; d.   . Studied at St. Petersburg Cons. He was accompanist to Feodor Chaliapin on his Russian tour; conducted in Pittsburgh, Pa.; conducted Heifetz

HEIFETZ, VLADIMIR

(HEIFETZ, VLADIMIR)
Singers in U.S. and Israel; was accompanist and arranger for radio, television, and films.
WORKS: Opera: Pharaoh; Le mizele maizele, children's opera; Chorus: The golem, oratorio; Cantatas: Yiddishe legende; President Roosevelt's message; Ani Yehudi; Lebern mire; Piano: Biblical suite; Film scores: Potemkin; Green fields.

*HEILMAN, WILLIAM CLIFFORD
b. Williamsport, Pa., 27 Dec. 1877; d. Williamsport, 20 Dec. 1946. Studied at Harvard, B. A. 1900; with Joseph Rheinberger and Charles Widor in Europe. He taught at Harvard, 1905-30. His compositions include a symphonic poem, chamber music, choral works, piano pieces.

HEILNER, IRWIN
b. New York, N. Y., 14 May 1908. Studied with Rubin Goldmark and Roger Sessions, Juilliard School; with Nadia Boulanger in Paris; attended Teachers Coll., Columbia Univ., B. S., M. A. He won honorable mention for Suite for harp and orch., Northern California Harpists' Asso., 1950. He is music librarian, Passaic (N. J.) Public Library; since 1970 has written music and record reviews for Jewish Currents.
WORKS: Orchestra: Suite for orch.; Songs: The tide rises; The traveler; Chinese songs, 1947; Piano: Boogie woogie rhapsody.
101 Dawson Ave., Clifton, NJ 07012

HEIM, NORMAN MICHAEL
b. Chicago, Ill., 30 Sep. 1929. Attended Univ. of Evansville, B. M. E., and Eastman School of Music, M. M., D. M. A., majoring in clarinet and is primarily self-taught as a composer. He received Lilly Found. grants, 1959, 1960; Univ. of Maryland grants, 1965, 1968, 1974; and sabbaticals granted for research, writing and composing. He was instructor, Central Missouri Coll., 1952-53; assistant professor, Univ. of Evansville, 1953-60; professor, Univ. of Maryland, 1960-   .
WORKS: Band: Sea prelude; Chamber music: Suite for 2 clarinets; sonata for clarinet solo; 5 songs of nature, for tenor, clarinet and piano; Elegiac poem, clarinet and piano; Chorus: Lord, give us strength; Have faith in the Lord; A prayer.
7402 Wells Blvd., Hyattsville, MD 20783

*HEINEMAN, JOHN
Views, 3 clarinets, basset horn, vibraphone.

HEINKE, JAMES
b. Cedar Rapids, Iowa, 20 Aug. 1945. Studied with Richard Hoffmann at Oberlin Coll.; with Arthur Berger and Seymour Shifrin at Brandeis Univ.; and computer-generated sound with John Chowning and Leland Smith, Stanford Univ. He received a German-American Exchange fellowship, 1970; Rome Prize fellowship, 1970-72.
WORKS: Orchestra: Canto; Chamber music: Skandha, violin and piano; Quartet, piano 4-hands, violin, cello, percussionist; Eden Road, piccolo, flute, bass flute, cello, piano 4-hands.
980 Altschul Ave., Menlo Park, CA 94025

HEINRICH, ADEL
b. Cleveland, Ohio, 20 July 1926. Studied at Flora Stone Mather Coll., B. A. magna cum laude; Union Theological Seminary, M. S. M.; in 1973, doctoral candidate, Univ. of Wisconsin. She received the Clemens Award in music, 2 scholarships; and 1969 Award of Merit, Nat. Fed. of Music Clubs. She was church organist, 1954-64; served as guest organist with Chicago Symphony Chorus under Margaret Hillis; has given numerous organ recitals; assistant professor, Colby Coll., 1964-   .
WORKS: Chorus: A carol is born, women's voices, flute, piano, and drama; Alleluia-alleluia, choric dance for women's choir, mixed chorus, modern dance choir, piano and violin, 1969; Organ: 4 Choral paraphrases on hymns of praise.
Colby College, Waterville, ME 04901

*HEISINGER, BRENT
Essay; Fantasia; Soliloquy; all for band.

HEISS, JOHN C.
b. New York, N. Y., 23 Oct. 1938. Attended Lehigh Univ., B. A.; Columbia Univ.; Princeton Univ., M. F. A.; Aspen School; principal teachers were Otto Luening, Milton Babbitt, Edward T. Cone, Earl Kim, Darius Milhaud. He received the Bowdoin Coll. composition prize, 1971, for Quartet; Fromm Found. commission, 1973; American Acad. of Arts and Letters award, 1973; Nat. Endowment for the Arts grant, 1974. His faculty appointments include Columbia Univ., 1963-65; New England Cons., 1967-   ; he is principal flute, Boston Musica Viva.
WORKS: Orchestra: 4 short pieces, 1962; Movements for orch., 1968; Chamber music: Suite for flute alone, 1962; flute sonatina, 1962; 5 pieces for flute and cello, 1963; Sketches, woodwind quintet, 1966; Movements for 3 flutes, 1966, 1969; Music for solo oboe, 1970; quartet for flute, clarinet, cello, piano, 1971; Inventions, contours, and colors, for 11 instruments, 1973; Songs of nature, soprano and chamber ensemble, Cambridge, Mass., 8 Oct. 1974; also choral works, songs, piano pieces.
60 The Fenway, Boston, MA 02115

*HELBIG, OTTO H.
b. New Haven, Conn., 28 Oct. 1914. Studied with Richard Donovan, David Stanley Smith, Hugo Kortschalk, at Yale Univ.; at Columbia Univ., M. A., Ed. D. He has been violinist in symphony orchestras; conducted Trenton State Orch.; professor, Trenton State Coll., 1949-   .
WORKS: Band: Introduction and tango; Prelude and beguine; Short piece.
Music Department, Trenton State College
Trenton, NJ 08625

HELD, WILBUR C.
b. Des Plaines, Ill., 20 Aug. 1914. Studied with John Palmer, American Cons.; with Normand Lockwood and Wallingford Riegger, Union Theological Seminary, S. M. D. He has been professor, Ohio State Univ., 1946-   ; organist Trinity Episcopal Church, Columbus, 1949-   .

(HELD, WILBUR C.)
WORKS: Chorus: 6 calls to worship, 1953; God of a universe; Jesus, name of wondrous love; Advent service; Organ: Partita on O sons and daughters; 6 carol settings; Processional on The King's majesty; many other choral and organ works.
221 Oakland Park Ave., Columbus, OH 43214

*HELFER, WALTER
b. Lawrence, Mass., 30 Sep. 1896; d. New Rochelle, N. Y., 16 Apr. 1959. Studied at Harvard Univ., B. A.; Columbia Univ., M. A.; with Ottorino Respighi in Rome, 1925-28. His awards included the New England Cons. Endicott prize; Paderewski prize, 1939; fellowship, American Acad. in Rome. He was faculty member, Hunter Coll., 1929-50, chairman, music department, 1938-50.
WORKS: Orchestra: In modo giocoso; Water idyll; Fantasie on children's tunes, 1953; Symphony on Canadian airs, 1937; A midsummer night's dream, overture, 1939; concertino for piano and chamber orch., 1947; Chamber music: Elegiac sonata, piano, 1931; string quartet; string trio; Nocturne for piano; Soliloquy, cello and piano, 1947; Appassionata, violin and piano; choral works.

*HELFMAN, MAX
b. Radzin, Poland, 25 May 1901; to U.S. 1909; d. Dallas, Tex., 9 Aug. 1963. Studied at Mannes Coll. of Music, 1919-23; with Rosario Scalero and Fritz Reiner, Curtis Inst., 1929-32. He was choral conductor of groups in Newark, New York, and Los Angeles; on faculty, Hebrew Union Coll., 1949-52; music director, Hillel Found., Los Angeles, 1954-58; Washington, D.C. Hebrew Congregation, 1959-62. His compositions included New Hagadah, cantata for narrator, chorus, and orch., 1949; and Jewish liturgical works.

*HELLER, ALFRED
2 Heine songs for medium voice.

*HELLER, HANS EWALD
b. Vienna, Austria, 17 Apr. 1894; to U.S. 1938; d. New York, N. Y., 1 Oct. 1966. Wrote 3 light operas produced in Europe. Other works include Carnival in New Orleans, overture, 1940; Ode to our women, cantata, 1942; 2 string quartets; suite for clarinet; many songs.

*HELLER, JAMES G.
b. New Orleans, La., 4 Jan. 1892. Studied at Tulane Univ., B. A. 1912; Univ. of Cincinnati, M. A. 1914; Hebrew Union Coll., Rabbi 1916; Cincinnati Cons., D. M. 1934. He wrote program notes for the Cincinnati Symphony; taught at Cincinnati Cons. He wrote Elegy and pastorale, voice and string orch., 1934; string quartet; violin sonata; Jewish liturgical works.

HELLER, JOHN H., JR.
b. Philadelphia, Pa., 22 Feb. 1945. Studied with Joseph Castaldo, Michael White, Andrew Rudin, Philadelphia Musical Acad.; with Clifford Taylor and Robert Morgan, Temple Univ. He received a Creative Accomplishment award, Philadelphia Musical Acad., 1966. He taught in public

(HELLER, JOHN H., JR.)
schools, 1968-69; was instructor, Philadelphia Community Coll., 1969-70; Temple Univ. 1970-72; Trenton State Coll., 1973-   .
WORKS: Orchestra: Symphony-concerto, bass clarinet and orch. 1966; Chamber music: brass quintet, 1963; Projective variations, chamber ensemble, 1964; string quartet, 1965; Rückblick, 3 pieces for trombone and percussion, 1969; Variations on a theme by Stravinsky, 1969-70.
4801 Penn St., Apt. D-3
Philadelphia, PA 19124

*HELLERMANN, WILLIAM
b. Milwaukee, Wis., 1939. Studied at Univ. of Wisconsin; Columbia Univ.; and on a Prix de Rome at the American Acad. in Rome, 1972-73. He is on the music faculty at Columbia Univ.
WORKS: Orchestra: Time and again, 1969; Chamber music: 4 pieces for guitar; Distances and spaces, guitar, 1972; On the edge of a node, guitar, violin, cello, all prepared with paper clips, 1974; Electronic: Ek-stasis I, tape, 1968; Passages 13 - The fire, trumpet and tape, 1970-71.
90 Morningside Drive, New York, NY 10027

*HELM, EVERETT
b. Minneapolis, Minn., 17 July 1913. Studied at Harvard Univ., B. A. 1935; with Riccardo Malipiero and Ralph Vaughan Williams in Europe. He held a John Knowles Paine traveling fellowship for European study. He was music officer, U.S. Army in Germany, 1948-50.
WORKS: Opera: The siege of Tottenburg, 1956; Ballet: Le roy fait battre tambour, 1956; Theatre: Adam and Eve, an adaption of a 12th century mystery play, 1951; 500 Dragon-Thalers, musical comedy, 1956; Orchestra: concerto for string orch., 1950; 2 piano concertos, 1954, 1956; Cambridge suite; 3 gospel hymns; Chamber music: woodwind quartet; string quartet; 2 piano sonatas; flute sonata; violin sonata; Sinfonia da camera; concerto for 5 solo instruments and chamber orch.; woodwind quintet; choral works; songs; piano pieces. He is author of Composer, performer, public: A study in communications, 1970.

HELPS, ROBERT
b. Passaic, N. J., 23 Sep. 1928. Studied piano with Abby Whiteside, composition with Roger Sessions at The Juilliard School; also attended Columbia Univ. and Univ. of California at Berkeley. He received the Hertz award, 1951; Fromm Found. award, 1956, commission, 1960; Naumburg Found. award, 1958; Guggenheim grant, 1964-65; Ingram-Merrill grant, 1966; 3 Thorne Music Fund commissions; Friends of 4-Hand Music commission, 1967; Ford Found. commission, 1972. He has taught piano at Stanford Univ., San Francisco Cons., Univ. of California at Berkeley, New England Cons.; Princeton Univ., 1963-67, 1971-72, 1973-   ; Manhattan School of Music, 1971-72, 1973-   . He was artist-in-residence, Univ. of California at Davis, spring 1973.
WORKS: Orchestra: Symphony n.1, 1955; 2 piano concertos, 1968, 1972; Chamber music:

HELPS, ROBERT

(HELPS, ROBERT)
string quartet, 1951; piano trio, 1957; Serenade, in 3 parts: 1) Fantasy for violin and piano, 2) Nocturne for string quartet, 3) Postlude for horn, piano and violin, 1964; Songs: 2 songs for soprano and piano, 1950; The running sun, soprano and piano, text by James Purdy, New York, 13 Nov. 1972; Piano: Fantasy, 1952; 3 etudes, 1956; Image, 1958; Recollections, 1959; Portrait, 1960; Solo, 1961; Saccade, 4-hands, San Francisco, June 1968; Quartet for piano solo, 1970; 3 Hommages, New York, 6 Nov. 1972; 3 Nocturnes, New York, 19 Mar. 1973.
156 Montague St., Brooklyn, NY 11201

HEMMER, EUGENE
b. Cincinnati, Ohio, 23 Mar. 1929. Studied with Felix Labunski, Cincinnati Coll. of Music. His honors include ASCAP awards; honorary membership, Liberal Society of Composers of Tokyo; twice named composer of the year, Ohioana Library Asso.; 3 MacDowell fellowships; 3 Huntington Hartford fellowships; 2 Dumler prizes in composition. He is head, music department, Marymount Coll., Palos Verdes, and part-time instructor, El Camino Coll.
WORKS: Compositions are basically tonal and in all forms: orchestra, opera, chamber music, choral works, songs, and piano pieces. Many are published.
25212 Narbonne Ave., Lomita, CA 90717

*HENDERSON, ALVA
Medea, opera on Robinson Jeffers' play, San Diego, 29 Nov. 1972; The last of the Mohicans, commissioned by Wilmington (Del.) Opera Society for the American Bicentennial 1976; The tempest and The unforgiven, operas in preparation.

HENDERSON, KENNETH
b. Richmond, Va., 28 June 1928. Is band director in the public schools of Chesterfield County, Va.
WORKS: Band: The lancers; Trade winds; and some 100 published compositions and arrangements for orchestra, band, various ensembles and choir.
1308 Buford Road, Richmond, VA 23235

*HENDERSON, RAY
b. Buffalo, N. Y., 1 Dec. 1896; d. Greenwich, Conn., 31 Dec. 1970. Studied at Univ. of Southern California; later privately with Benjamin Britten. He was church organist and Jazz pianist in Buffalo; then went to New York, where he was song-plugger, staff arranger and composer for a music publishing firm.
WORKS: Songs: Georgette, 1922; You're the cream in my coffee; Alabamy bound, 1925; Hold everything; Three cheers; Sonny boy, 1928; Button up your overcoat, 1928; Keep your sunny side up, 1929; The best things in life are free, 1927, this was also the title of his film biography made in 1966.

HENDERSON, ROSAMON (Mrs. Stanley P.)
b. Shellman, Ga., 13 July 1894. Studied at Andrew Coll. and Wesleyan Coll. She won awards for choral works in contests of the Nat. League

(HENDERSON, ROSAMON)
of American Pen Women and the Alabama Writers Conclave.
WORKS: Chorus: Sing praises to God; The Lord's day; Wave on Old Glory; Think on these things; and others.
4142 Crescent Road, Birmingham, AL 35222

*HENDL, WALTER
b. West New York, N. J., 12 Jan. 1917. Studied with Fritz Reiner at Curtis Inst. and at Tanglewood. He taught at Sarah Lawrence Coll., 1931-41; was associate conductor, New York Philharmonic, 1945-49; conductor, Dallas Symphony Orchestra, 1949-58; associate conductor, Chicago Symphony Orchestra, 1958-64; director, Eastman School of Music, 1964-72; music director, Chautauqua Festival, 1952-   .
WORKS: Theatre: music for Dark of the moon, 1945; Chorus: A village where they ring no bells; women's voices; Loneliness, women's voices.
c/o Chautauqua Institution
Chautauqua, NY 14722

*HENDRIKS, FRANCIS MILTON
b. New York, N. Y., 28 Nov. 1883; d.   . Studied with Leopold Godowsky and Hugo Kaun; Denver Coll. of Music, M. A. He gave piano recitals in Europe then taught at Scott School of Music, Wolcott Cons., Denver Coll. of Music. He wrote a piano concerto, piano sonata, and many piano pieces.

HENINGER, ROBERT E.
b. Utah, 18 Oct. 1924. Studied with Ingolf Dahl and Richard Donovan, Univ. of Southern California; with Nadia Boulanger in Paris. He received an award from Composers Forum. He is professor and chairman, music department, San Diego Mesa Coll.
WORKS: Orchestra: Passacaglia; Variations on He's gone away; Variations and dance; Band: Variations; Chamber music: string quartet; Little suite, flute and piano; Chaconne, piano; Chorus: 3 songs on Shakespearean texts; Psalm 148; and songs.
3510 Charles St., San Diego, CA 92106

HENN, RICHARD
b. Santa Monica, Calif., 31 Oct. 1946. Studied with Matt Doran, Mt. St. Mary's Coll.; with Harold Budd and Mel Powell, California Inst. of the Arts.
WORKS: Percussion: Symphony for multi-percussion; Intro and extro duction; In Egypt; Chamber music: Reverie for harp; Prelude for harp; Prelude, inventions 1 and 2, postlude, for horn and tuba.
938 1/2 Milwood Ave., Venice, CA 90291

HENNAGIN, MICHAEL
b. The Dalles, Ore., 27 Sep. 1936. Studied with Leonard Stein, Los Angeles City Coll., 1957-59; with Darius Milhaud at Aspen, Colo.; Curtis Inst. of Music, B. M. 1963; with Aaron Copland at Tanglewood, 1963; electronic music, Southern Illinois Univ., 1968. He received scholarships

(HENNAGIN, MICHAEL)
for study at Aspen, Curtis Inst., and Tanglewood; Fromm Found. award, 1961; Ford Found-MENC grant, 1965-66; ASCAP awards, 1967-70; and commissions. He taught in public schools, 1963-66; was faculty member, Kansas State Teachers Coll., 1966-72; associate professor, Univ. of Oklahoma, 1972-   .
WORKS: Ballet: The barren song; The plumed serpent; Theatre: incidental music to The world of my America; Becket; The skin of our teeth; Antigonae; Christmas carol; Band: Jubilee; Chorus: 5 children's songs; Go 'way from my window; Hosanna; The house on the hill; La cucaracha; Psalm 23; Under the greenwood tree; The unknown; Waillie, waillie; Walking on the green grass; Mixed media: The unknown, chorus, piano, flute, percussion, trumpets, tape and slides; The family of man, chorus, percussion, piano, film, tape, slides; also chamber music songs, orchestral works, film scores, radio and television scores.
1022 Walnut Rd., Norman, OK 73069

HENNING, ERVIN ARTHUR
b. Marion, S. Dak., 22 Nov. 1910. Studied at New England Cons., B. M. 1946, with honors and special honors in contemporary music; organ with Carl McKinley and E. Power Biggs. Awards include a prize in Brookline Library Music Asso. contest, 1971; purchase of manuscript of Fantasia for violin and harpsichord by Harvard Univ. for the Houghton Library rare manuscript collection, 1962; scholarship at New England Cons.; many commissions. He was church organist-music director in Chicago and Boston; 1942-50; held various teaching posts in New England, 1949-58; was composer and music coordinator for a Boston theatre company, 1963-70.
WORKS: Ballet: Time after time, flute, clarinet, cello, piano, 1967; Theatre: incidental music to Pinter's The dwarfs, 1966; The breasts of Tiresias, 1967; Chamber music: Badinage, woodwind quartet; quintet for flute, horn, string trio, 1946; Partita for string quartet, 1948; Suite for viola concertante, 2 violins, cello, 1950; violin sonata; Divertimento for bassoon solo, 1950; trio for clarinet, viola, piano, 1959; Fantasia, violin and harpsichord, 1962; Chorus: And death shall have no dominion, Dylan Thomas text, chorus and 6 brass instruments, 1953; By the rivers of Babylon, women's voices; Piano: sonata, 1959; 2 toccatas; and works for harpsichord, organ, and recorder.
1130 Massachusetts Ave.
Cambridge, MA 02138

HENNING, ROSLYN BROGUE. See BROGUE, ROSLYN

*HENRY, HAROLD
b. Neodesha, Kan., 20 Mar. 1884; Orangeburg, N. Y., 15 Oct. 1956. Studied with Carl Preyer, Univ. of Kansas; with Leopold Godowsky in Berlin; with Moritz Moszkowski in Paris. He made his piano debut in the U.S. in 1906 in Chicago; taught privately in New York. He wrote piano pieces and songs.

HENRY, JOSEPH
b. Toledo, Ohio, 12 Oct. 1930. Studied with Wayne Barlow and Bernard Rogers, Eastman School of Music, B. M., M. M., A. M. D. 1965. He received 2 Fulbright grants for study in Vienna, 1957, 1958. He was visiting professor, Univ. of Rochester, 1961, Lawrence Univ., 1962; music director, Utica Symphony, 1962-66; associate professor and orchestra conductor, State Univ. Coll., Oswego, 1967-   .
WORKS: Orchestra: Suite for orch., 1953; Chromophon, premier by Buffalo Philharmonic, composer conducting, 1970; Chamber music: Music for horn, piano, and string quartet, 1952; Integrals, violin and harpsichord, 1972.
Blythe Rd., Hannibal, NY 13074

HENRY, OTTO W.
b. Reno, Nev., 8 May 1933. Studied with Gardner Read and Hugo Norde, Boston Univ. He was chairman, music department, Washington and Jefferson Coll., 1961-65; associate director, electronic music studio, Tulane Univ., 1965-68; assistant professor and director, electronic music studio, East Carolina Univ., 1968-   .
WORKS: Chamber music: Passacaglia, bass trombone and piano, 1959; Omnibus 1, for unspecified number of players, 1971; Percussion: Liberty bell, 10 percussionists and tape, 1970; Omnibus 2, for unspecified unpitched percussion, 1971; Do not pass go, 3 timpani, 2 players, 1971; The sons of Martha, soprano and 4 percussionists, 1972.
School of Music, East Carolina University
Greenville, NC 27834

*HENSEL, RICHARD
b. Chicago, Ill., 1926. Studied with Burrill Phillips and Gordon Binkerd, Univ. of Illinois, D. M. A.; also with Leo Sowerby, Goffredo Petrassi, and Milton Babbitt. He is professor, Eastern Kentucky Univ.
WORKS: Chamber music: string quartet; piano sonata; Chorus: 3 songs on poems of Edward Arlington Robinson.
Department of Music
Eastern Kentucky University
Richmond, KY 40475

HERDER, RONALD
b. Philadelphia, Pa., 21 Dec. 1930. Studied with Constant Vauclain, Univ. of Pennsylvania, B. F. A. 1952; with Eugene Hill, Miami Univ., Ohio, MA 1954; with Nadia Boulanger, Fontainebleau, 1957. He received the Ravel Prize in composition, 1957; Concorso Internazionale Prize, Italy, for Dany: recitative and symphonic dance, 1962, and Movements for orchestra, 1963; and many commissions. He has been a free lance composer and arranger, 1957-59; instructor, Brooklyn Coll., 1959-60; associate editor, Associated Music Publishers, 1960-65, editor-in-chief, 1965-   ; guest lecturer, Columbia Univ., 1971; member of jury for BMI Student Composer Awards, 1963, 1969, 1971; author of educational publications on music.
WORKS: Ballet: At the hawk's well, chamber ensemble, 1953; Requiem for Jimmy Dean, jazz

HERDER, RONALD

(HERDER, RONALD)
ballet; Band: Saëta (Rites and ceremonies), 1967-71; Chamber music: Concerto for 2 pianos alone, 1950; The death of children, voice and piano, 1950; string quartet, 1952; 2 songs for tenor and 2 violas, 1956; L'Infinito, chamber cantata for voice and brass ensemble, 1957; Chorus: The Job elegies, 1964; From the 23rd Psalm, 1967; Mixed media: Requiem II/Games of power, 1969; Requiem III/Birds at Golgotha, pre-recorded ensembles, tape, and band.
    230 Mt. Vernon Place, Apt. 14N
    Newark, NJ 07106

HERFURTH, C. PAUL
    b. Cambridge, Mass., 7 Oct. 1893. Studied with Gustave Strube, Felix Winternitz, Paul Poulson at New England Cons., graduated 1916. He is an honorary life member of the New Jersey Music Educators Asso. He was public school director of music, Ashville, N. C., 1919-22, and East Orange, N. J., 1922-55.
    WORKS: More than 50 compositions for school bands and orchestras; and A tune a day, a series of 32 method books for all instruments.
    1216 Allaire Rd.
    Spring Lake Heights, NJ 07762

*HERLINGER, JAN:
    Ormand's Bar, 4 voices, 5 instruments.
    Music Department, University of Chicago
    Chicago, IL 60637

*HERMAN, JERRY
    b. New York, N. Y., 10 July 1933. Studied drama at Univ. of Miami, B. A. He has written both words and music for most of his musical comedies. Hello, Dolly!, which had the second longest run for a musical in Broadway history (topped by Fiddler on the roof) received a Tony award and the New York Drama Critics' Circle award, 1964. His other shows are: Parade, 1960; Milk and honey, 1961; Mame, 1966.

HERMAN, THOMAS
    b. Alexandria, Va., 3 June 1947. Studied with Samuel Adler, Eastman School of Music, B. M.; privately with Peter Maxwell Davies in London; with Arthur Berger, Brandeis Univ.
    WORKS: Theatre: Crystallization of the equivocal and Death's door, both music-theatre works in what the composer calls a merged-medium genre. He has also written for orchestra and chamber ensembles.
    9 Eustis St., Apt. 2-L
    Cambridge, MA 02140

*HERNRIED, ROBERT
    b. Vienna, Austria, 22 Sep. 1883; to U.S. 1933; d. Detroit, Mich., 3 Sep. 1951. Studied at Univ. of Vienna; conducted at theatres and taught at various schools. In the U.S. he taught in New York, Iowa, North Dakota, Indiana, and finally at Detroit Inst. of Musical Art, 1946-51. He composed an opera, orchestral pieces, many choral works. He also published musicological works.

*HERRMANN, BERNARD
    b. New York, N. Y., 29 Jan. 1911; d. Los Angeles, Calif., 24 Dec. 1975. Studied with Philip James at New York Univ.; with Albert Stoessel and Bernard Wagenaar at Juilliard School. He was radio conductor for the CBS Symphony; then turned to film composing.
    WORKS: Opera: Wuthering Heights, 1950; Orchestra: The city of brass, 1934; Sinfonietta for strings, 1935; Currier and Ives suite, 1935; Fiddle concerto, 1940; symphony, 1942; For the fallen, 1943; Chamber music: Aubade, 14 instruments, 1933; string quartet; Chorus: Moby Dick, cantata, with orch., 1940; Johnny Appleseed, cantata, 1940; Film scores: Citizen Kane, 1940; The devil and Daniel Webster, 1941; Anna and the King of Siam, 1947; Jane Eyre; North by northwest; Psycho; Vertigo.

*HERSTEIN, PETER
    Wall fantasy, wind ensemble.

HERVIG, RICHARD B.
    b. Story City, Iowa, 24 Nov. 1917. Studied with Philip Greeley Clapp, Univ. of Iowa. He was instructor, Luther Coll., 1942; associate professor, Long Beach State Coll., 1952-55; professor, Univ. of Iowa, 1955- . director, Center for New Music, 1966- .
    WORKS: Orchestra: 2 symphonies; Chamber music: string quartet; Introduction and allegro, piano and woodwind quintet; 2 clarinet sonatas; Antiphon, 13 instruments; Chorus: Ubi sunt?, motet; Quid est musica?, antiphon.
    1822 Rochester Ave., Iowa City, IA 52240

HEUSSENSTAMM, GEORGE
    b. Los Angeles, Calif., 24 July 1926. Attended Los Angeles City Coll. and Los Angeles State Coll.; studied privately with Leonard Stein. He won awards in the Rochester Religious Arts Festival competition, 1965; First Internat. Tuba Ensemble composition competition, 1969; and 8th Annual Symposium of Contemporary Music for Brass, 1971. He was formerly music critic Pasadena Star News; has been manager, Coleman Chamber Music Assoc., 1971- .
    WORKS: Orchestra: Chamber symphony; Scherzo; 17 impressions from the Japanese; Wind ensembles: Museum piece, double brass choir, 4 percussion; Tournament, 4 brass sextets, 4 percussion, 1971; Labyrinth, 4 brass quintets, nominated for Pulitzer Prize; Score, 4 saxophone quartets, 4 percussion; Chamber music: trio, clarinet, violin, cello; Chorale partita, organ; string trio; Die Jugend, solo clarinet; string quartet; 7 etudes, woodwind trio; Callichoreo, woodwind quartet; Mini-variations, flute, oboe, string trio, nominated for Pulitzer Prize; Das Dreieck, woodwind quintet, string trio, percussion ; Canonograph #1, woodwind trio; Canonograph #2, string trio; Ambages, flute and clarinet; Tubafour, tuba quartet; Tetralogue, 4 clarinets, percussion; Tre celli, 3 cellos; Set for double reeds; Texture variations 1972, flute, violin,

(HEUSSENSTAMM, GEORGE)
cello, harpsichord; Trio philharmonia, piano trio; Fluxus, violin and cello; also choruses and mixed media.
5013 Lowell Ave., La Crescenta, CA 91214

HEWITT, HARRY DONALD
b. Detroit, Mich., 4 Mar. 1921. Makes what seems to be a valid claim to be one of the most prolific composers in the history of American music. His some 3000 compositions include 20 symphonies among several hundred orchestral works, 20 string quartets in hundreds of pieces of chamber music, several operas, and songs and keyboard works. Among his more recent works are - Opera: Pierre, c. 1954-64; Orchestra: Night without neon, A star a tree a man, The wheel, The mad clockmaker, Seven, tone poems of the 1950s; Songs: Poems of Po-Chu-1, cycle of 35 songs; Animal anguish, to composer's text; Piano: A Tolkien tapestry; Lantern songs; Meadow year, 1964.
345 South 19th St., Philadelphia, PA 19103

*HEYMANN, WERNER RICHARD
b. Konigsberg, Germany, 14 Feb. 1896. Studied with Paul Juon in Berlin; composed orchestral works and chamber music. On coming to the U.S. he settled in Hollywood as a film composer.

HIBBARD, WILLIAM
b. Newton, Mass., 8 Aug. 1939. Studied with Francis Judd Cooke, New England Cons., B. M. 1961; M. M. 1963; with Richard B. Hervig, Univ. of Iowa, Ph. D. 1967. He received a BMI composer award, 1960; Chadwick Medal, New England Cons., 1961; Beebe Found. grant, 1963; Sutherland Dows graduate study award, Univ. of Iowa, 1964-66; Tanglewood fellowship, 1965; Philip Greeley Clapp award, Univ. of Iowa, 1967; Old Gold summer research fellowship, 1969; and commissions. He has been faculty member, Univ. of Iowa, 1966- , associate professor, School of Music, music director, Center for New Music, and Director, Center for New Performing Arts, 1969- .
WORKS: Orchestra: Reliefs, 1962; Chamber music: Trio for violin, clarinet, guitar, 1959; Variations, brass nomet, 1960; 4 pieces, chamber ensemble, 1962; Gestures, flute, double bass, percussion, 1963; Portraits, flute and piano, 1963; string trio, 1964; Fantasy, organ, trumpet, trombone, percussion, 1965; Intersections I and II, woodwind quintet, piano, 2 percussionists, 1966; Stabiles, 13 players, 1969; Variations, cello solo, 1970; string quartet, 1971; trio for bass clarinet, bass trombone, harp, 1973; Songs: The dream lady, alto voice and chamber ensemble, 1958; Super flumina Babylonis, 6 solo singers, string sextet, 1968; Reflexa, soprano and 5 players.
725 East College St., Iowa City, IA 52240

*HIER, ETHEL GLENN
b. Cincinnati, Ohio, 25 June 1889; d. New York, N. Y., 14 Jan. 1971. Studied at Cincinnati Cons., B. M. 1911; composition with Edgar Stillman Kelley, Percy Goetschius, and Ernest Bloch. She received honorary degrees from Inst. of Musical Art, New York, 1917; Cincinnati Cons., 1922; was

(HIER, ETHEL GLENN)
a private teacher in Cincinnati and New York.
WORKS: Orchestra: Asolo bells, 1939; Mountain preacher, chorus and orch., 1941; Carolina suite; Scherzo; Chamber music: Sextet suite, flute, oboe, string trio, piano, 1925; 3 quintets for flute, viola, cello, harp, and voice; 1936; string quartet; Rhapsody, violin and piano, 1940; Joy of spring, violin and piano; piano works.

HIGGINS, RICHARD CARTER (DICK)
b. Cambridge, England, 15 Mar. 1938; U.S. parents. Attended Yale Univ., Columbia Univ., Manhattan School of Printing; studied with John Cage and Henry Cowell in New York, 1958-60. He has been active in Happenings, 1958- ; in Fluxus, 1961- ; founded Something Else Press, 1964; developed and named concept of intermedia, 1965; taught at California Inst. of the Arts, 1970-71; writing and publishing, 1972- .
WORKS: Opera: The peaceable kingdom, speaking performers and bells, 1961; Lavender blue, 1963; Electronic and multimedia: A loud symphony, tape, 1958; 5 electronic constellations, 1959; symphony #3 1/2 (length 50 seconds), 1959; Theater music, collage, 1959; Mechanical music #1 and #2, 1959; Big constellation, 1960; In the context of shoes, happening for tape recorder, microphones, vacuumcleaners, drills, ribbons, motion pictures, slide projectors, gardener's shears, piano, "antidancers," and other performers, 1960; In memoriam, 164-part canon, 1960; Requiem for Wagner, the criminal mayor, 1961; For the dead, 1965; Automatic processions, uses random transportation and lumbering equipment, 1966-67; The thousand symphonies, composed by shooting machine gun bullets through music manuscript paper, 1968.
P. O. Box 26, West Glover, VT 05875

*HIJMAN, JULIUS
b. Almelo, Neth., 25 Jan. 1901; to U.S. 1939; d. Philadelphia, Pa. Taught at Houston Cons., 1940-42; Kansas City Cons. 1945-49; from 1949 at Philadelphia Musical Acad. He composed chiefly chamber music: 4 string quartets, many sonatas for various instruments, etc.

*HILL, EDWARD BURLINGAME
b. Cambridge, Mass., 9 Sep. 1872; d. Francestown, N. H., 9 July 1960. Studied with John Knowles Paine at Harvard Univ., B. A. summa cum laude 1894; with George W. Chadwick, New England Cons.; piano with B. J. Lang and Arthur Whiting. His honors included membership in the Nat. Inst. of Arts and Letters; American Acad. of Arts and Letters; Chevalier Legion of Honor. From 1908 he was on the faculty at Harvard Univ., James E. Ditson professor, 1937-40. After retirement in 1940 he lived chiefly in New Hampshire.
WORKS: Theatre: Jack Frost in midsummer, pantomine with orch., 1908; Pan and the star, pantomine with orch., 1914; Orchestra: The parting of Lancelot and Guinevere, symphonic poem, 1915; 2 Stevensoniana suites, 1917, 1923; The fall of the House of Usher, symphonic poem, 1920; Waltzes, 1922; Scherzo, 2 pianos and orch., 1924;

HILL, EDWARD BURLINGAME

(HILL, EDWARD BURLINGAME)
Lilacs, symphonic poem, 1927; 3 symphonies, 1928; 1931, 1937; An ode, 1930; piano concertino, 1932; Sinfonietta for strings, 1936; violin concerto, 1938; concertino for string orch., 1940; Music for English horn and orch., 1945; Prelude for orchestra, 1953; Chamber music: sonatas for various instruments; string quartet; sextet for woodwinds and piano; clarinet quintet; etc.; many vocal works.

HILL, JACKSON
b. Birmingham, Ala., 23 May 1941. Studied with Iain Hamilton, Univ. of North Carolina, Chapel Hill, A. B. 1963, M. A. 1966, Ph. D. 1970. He received Nat. Fed. of Music Clubs and Fed. of Women's Clubs awards, 1957, 1959; Plymouth, Mass. Philharmonic Prize, 1965; Greensboro, N. C., Symphony award, 1966; East Carolina Univ. award, 1966; commission from Pennsylvania Council on the Arts and was selected for support in the Pennsylvania Composers Project, 1973. He taught at Duke Univ., 1965-68; has been assistant professor, Bucknell Univ., 1968-   .
    WORKS: Orchestra: Variations for orchestra, 1964; Mosaics, 1965, Philadelphia, 22 June 1974; Paganini set, 1973; Chamber music: 4 studies for violin and piano, 1964; Synchronie for 6 or 7 players; 4 studies for trumpet and piano, 1968; Chorus: Agnus Dei, 1971; Magnificat and Nunc dimittis, 1972; The new age, a festival ode, chorus and band, 1973; Songs: Death cycle, soprano and string quartet, 1964; 6 mystical songs, 1973; Organ: 3 mysteries, 1973.
    Department of Music, Bucknell University
    Lewisburg, PA 17837

HILLE, WALDEMAR
b. St. Elmo, Minn., 5 Mar. 1908. Attended Elmhurst Coll., B. A. 1929; American Cons., B. M. 1934, M. M. E. 1936; Columbia Univ.; Univ. of Southern California; studied composition with W. Riegger in New York. He received the Celia Buck award for his oratorio, Denmark Vesey, 1960. He was dean of music, Elmhurst Coll., 1932-40; music editor, New York, 1943-47; music director, Eden Theological Seminary, 1949-52; music director, First Unitarian Church, Los Angeles, 1952-   .
    WORKS: Chorus: Monticello, cantata, text by Kramer; Denmark Vesey, oratorio for chorus, soloists, orch.; Song of the Warsaw ghetto, 1968; Moses, oratorio; Strange funeral; To those in power; 4 songs for peace and Peace cantata, 1972, many songs.
    926 South Westmoreland Ave.
    Los Angeles, CA 90006

HILLER, LEJAREN
b. New York, N. Y., 23 Feb. 1924. Attended Princeton Univ., B. A. 1944, M. A. 1946, Ph. D. 1947, studying with Milton Babbitt, 1941-45; Univ. of Illinois, M. M. 1958. He was an associate member, Center for Advanced Study, Univ. of Illinois, 1966-67; and senior Fulbright lecturer in music to Poland, 1973-74. He was a chemist with E.I. du Pont de Nemours, 1947-52, then joined the chemistry department, Univ. of

(HILLER, LEJAREN)
Illinois, 1953-58; became professor of music and director, Experimental Music Studio, Univ. of Illinois, 1958-68; then Slee professor of music and co-director, Center of the Creative and Performing Arts, State Univ. of New York, Buffalo, 1968-   .
    WORKS: Theatre music: A dream play, Strindberg, 1957; The birds, Aristophanes, 1958; The man with the oboe, Smalley, 1962; Spoon River anthology, 1962; Orchestra: piano concerto, 1949; Suite for small orch., 1951; 2 symphonies, 1953, 1960; Chamber music: piano trio, 1947; 6 string quartets, 1949, 1951, 1953, 1957 (Illiac suite), 1961 (in quarter tones), 1972 (premier, New York, 24 Jan. 1973); 3 violin sonatas, 1949, 1955, 1970; 5 Appalachian ballads, voice and guitar, 1958; Divertimento, chamber ensemble, 1959; Piano: 6 sonatas, 1946-48, 1947-53, 1949, 1950, 1961, 1972 (Rage over the lost Beethoven, text by Parman); 7 artifacts, 1948-73; Fantasy for 3 pianos, 1951; 12-tone variations, 1954; 2 theater pieces, 1956; Scherzo, 1958; A cenotaph, 2 pianos, 1971; Film score: Time of the heathen, 1961; Electronic: music for Blue is the antecedent of it, Leckel, 1959; 7 studies for 2-channel tape, 1963; Mixed media: Cuthbert bound, chamber music for 4 actors and tape, 1960; Amplification, tape and theater band, 1962; Computer cantata, soprano, tape, and chamber ensemble (co-composer, Robert Baker), 1963; Machine music, piano, percussion, tape, 1964; A triptych for Hieronymus, for actors, acrobats, projections, tape, and antiphonal instrumental groups, 1966; suite for 2 pianos and tape, 1966; An avalanche for pitchman, prima donna, player piano, percussionist, and prerecorded playback, text by Parman, 1968; HPSCHD, for 1-7 harpsichords and 1-51 tapes, (co-composor, John Cage), 1968; Algorithms I, versions 1-4, for 9 instruments and tape, 1968; Computer music, percussion and tape (co-composer, G. Allan O'Connor), 1968; 3 rituals for percussion and lights, 1969; Algorithms II, versions 1-4, 9 instruments and tape (co-composer, Ravi Kumra), 1972.
    Department of Music
    State University of New York
    Buffalo, NY 14214

HILLERT, RICHARD
b. Granton, Wisc. 14 Mar. 1923. Studied at Concordia Coll., Ill.; with Robert Delaney and Anthony Donato, Northwestern Univ.; with Goffredo Petrassi at Tanglewood. He won first prize, Internat. Society of Contemporary Music, Chicago Chapter, 1961, for a piano sonata. He taught in St. Louis, 1951-53; Wassau, Wis., 1953-59; has been professor, Concordia Coll.; River Forest, Ill., 1959.
    WORKS: Orchestra: Symphony in 3 movements, 1955; Variations for orch., 1968; Chamber music: violin sonata, 1953; flute sonata, 1954; 3 Christmas carols for brass, 1962; Alternations no. 1, for 7 instruments, 1966; Alternations no. 2, for flute and piano, 1967; Divertimento, for 5 instruments, 1967; Chorus: Chorale cantata: May God bestow on us His grace, choir and brass, 1966; The Christmas story according to St. Luke, choir, flute, oboe, strings, organ, 1967; Passion

(HILLERT, RICHARD)
according to St. Mark, choir, soloists, vibraphone, 1973; numerous shorter choral works and
organ pieces.
1620 Clay Court, Melrose Park, IL 60160

HILSE, WALTER
b. New York, N. Y., 16 July 1941. Studied with
Vincent Persichetti at Juilliard School; with
Jack Beeson, Otto Luening, Chou Wen-chung at
Columbia Univ.; with Nadia Boulanger in Paris.
He received the Joseph H. Bearns prize, 1966.
He has been faculty member, Columbia Univ.,
1967-   , assistant professor, 1972-   ;
organist-choirmaster, St. Luke's Lutheran Church,
New York, 1969-
    WORKS: Chamber music: 6 songs from The song
of Solomon, tenor and woodwind quintet, 1966;
The 23rd Psalm, unaccompanied solo voice; Magnificat, 2 solo female voices and organ; Prelude,
oboe, viola, organ; Piano: sonata; suite; works
for chorus.
432 West 22nd St., New York, NY 10011

HILTY, EVERETT JAY
b. New York, N. Y., 2 Apr. 1910. Studied at
Univ. of Miami; with Hunter Johnson, Univ. of
Michigan, M. B. 1934; with Mark Wessel, Univ. of
Colorado, M. M. 1939; with Seth Bingham, Normand
Lockwood, Union Theological Seminary; organ with
various teachers. He received an award from the
Diocese of Bethlehem for a hymn tune, Sing out;
2 faculty fellowships, Univ. of Colorado; outstanding teacher awards, 1964-65. He was church
organist, 1928-68; dean, Denver Coll. of Music,
1935-37; faculty, Univ. of Colorado, 1940-   ,
professor and director, division of organ and
church music, 1951-   .
    WORKS: Organ: Pedal study on Ein feste
Burg; Fanfare, toccata and chorale on Aurelia;
many anthems and organ pieces.
2241 Fourth St., Boulder, CO 80302

*HINDEMITH, PAUL
b. Hanau, Germany, 16 Nov. 1895; U.S. citizen
1946; d. Frankfurt, Germany, 28 Dec. 1963.
Studied with Arnold Mendelssohn and Bernhard
Sekles in Frankfurt. His honors included membership in the Nat. Inst. of Arts and Letters,
1947; appointment as Charles Eliot Norton professor at Harvard Univ., 1950-51; the Sibelius
award of $35,000, 1954. He was concertmaster,
Frankfurt Opera, 1915-23; formed the Amar-
Hindemith String Quartet, in which he played
viola, in 1921 and toured with it for several
years; in 1927 was appointed professor at the
Berlin Hochschule fur Musik. By 1935 he had
come in conflict with the Nazi regime and accepted an invitation of the Turkish Government
to teach in Ankara. In 1939 he came to the U.S.
and in 1940 joined the faculty at Yale Univ.,
where he became Battell professor in 1947. He
revisited Germany in 1949, conducting his own
works with the Berlin Philharmonic, and in 1953
went to Switzerland and settled in Zurich as
professor at the University. His large volume
of works includes 9 operas, 4 ballets, a

(HINDEMITH, PAUL)
pantomime; Orchestra: 2 symphonies; 9 concertos;
2 sinfoniettas; The 4 temperaments; Symphonic
metamorphosis; Symphonic dances; Der Schwan-
endreher, viola and orch.; Trauermusik, viola
and orch.; Konzertmusik, brass and strings; Chamber music: 7 string quartets; numerous sonatas
for all instruments, with and without piano;
quintets, trios; many works for voice; choral
works, piano pieces.

*HIVELY, WELLS
b. San Joaquin Valley, Calif., 1902; d. Palm
Beach, Fla., 1969. Studied at Paris Cons.;
Royal Cons. of Brussels; Mannes Coll. of Music;
Juilliard School. In the 1920s he alternated
studies in Paris with playing organ in silent-
film movie houses; played at Grauman's Chinese
Theatre in Hollywood in 1928; With the advent
of talking pictures he moved to New York; composed and directed for Ruth St. Denis, composed
music plays for NBC, accompanied singers; later
lived in Florida, teaching, composing, and playing the organ in church.
    WORKS: Orchestra: Tres himnos; Summer hol-
iday (Rive gauche), 1944; Icarus, 1961.

*HOAG, CHARLES
Symphonic movement for orch.
    Department of Music
    University of Kansas, Lawrence, KS 66044

HODKINSON, SYDNEY P.
b. Winnepeg, Manitoba, 17 Jan. 1934; to U.S.
1953. Studied with Bernard Rogers at Eastman
School of Music, B. M., M. M.; with Leslie
Bassett, George B. Wilson, Ross Lee Finney,
Univ. of Michigan, D. M. A.; with Elliott Carter,
Roger Sessions, Milton Babbitt at Princeton
Univ.; and with Niccolo Castiglioni. Major composition awards include those from the Internat.
Jeunesses Musicales, Prix de Composition Prince
Pierre de Monaco, Danforth Found., Canada Council, American Acad. of Arts and Letters, and the
Contemporary Music Project-Ford Found. Clarinetist and conductor, he has conducted chamber
music and orchestral concerts throughout the U.S.
and Canada. He taught at the Univ. of Virginia,
1958-63; Ohio Univ., 1963-68; Univ. of Michigan,
1968-72; was composer-in-residence, Minneapolis,
1970-71; faculty member and conductor of Musica
Nova Ensemble, Eastman School of Music,
1973-   .
    WORKS: Orchestra: Caricatures, 5 paintings
for orch., 1966; Fresco, a mural for orch., 1968;
Drawings, Set no. 7 and Set no. 8, string orch.,
1970; Stabile, for youth orch., 1971; Chamber
music: Stanzas, piano trio, 1959; Drawings, Set
no. 1, percussion quartet, 1960, Set. no. 3,
clarinet and drums, 1961, Set. no. 4, percussion
trio, 1961; Structures, percussion ensemble,
1962; Mosaics, brass quintet, 1965; Armistice,
for dancers and musicians, 1966; Imagined quarter, percussion quartet, 1967; Valence, chamber
orch., 1970, New York premiere, 23 Feb. 1974;
One man's meat, for solo recorded double bass,

HODKINSON, SYDNEY P.

(HODKINSON, SYDNEY P.)
1971; Multi media: <u>Vox populous</u>, with Lee Devin, commissioned by St. Paul Chamber Orch. and Minnesota Opera, premiere, St. Paul, Dec. 1973.
18 Timber Lane, Fairport, NY 14450

HOFFMAN, ALLEN
b. Newark, N. J., 12 Apr. 1942. Studied with Arnold Franchetti, Hartt Coll. He has received awards from the Nat. Found. on the Arts and the Humanities, 1966; Nat. Society of Arts and Letters, 1968; Sigma Alpha Iota, 1971; and MacDowell fellowships, 1968-72. He has been on the adjunct faculty, Hartt Coll., 1967- , and Hartford Cons., 1971- .
WORKS: Chamber music: Duo for saxophone and narrator; Chorus: <u>Madrigals</u>, a cappella; <u>Mass...for the passing of all shining things</u>, a cappella choir and baritone solo; chamber music and orchestral works, songs.
716 Farmington Ave., West Hartford, CT 06117

HOFFMAN, THEODORE B.
b. Palo Alto, Calif., 18 Oct. 1925. Studied with Darius Milhaud at Mills Coll.; with Burrill Phillips, Univ. of Illinois. He received an award at Mills Coll., 1951; Heller Fund scholarship, 1952; Southeastern Band Directors award, 1965. He has been music director, WILL-TV (Univ. of Illinois) and WBGH-TV (Boston); chairman music department, Gavilan Coll., 1950-62; professor, Univ. of South Florida, 1962- .
WORKS: Orchestra: <u>Suite from The Tempest</u>; a teaching symphony; Chorus: <u>9 Japanese haiku</u>; <u>2 contemporary madrigals</u>; Piano: <u>Variations on We shall overcome</u>; also chamber music, theatre scores, wind ensemble pieces, songs, etc.
Humanities Program, Univ. of South Florida
Tampa, FL 33620

HOFFMANN, JAMES A.
b. Manchester, N. H., 2 Oct. 1929. Studied with Carl McKinley and Francis Judd Cooke, New England Cons., B. M. with highest honors; with Quincy Porter and Normand Lockwood, Yale Univ., B. M., M. M.; with Boris Blacher in Berlin; and with Burrill Phillips at Univ. of Illinois, D. M. A. He received the Chadwick Medal at the New England Cons.; John Day Jackson prize and Woods-Chandler prize at Yale Univ. He was instructor, Oberlin Coll., 1959-62; assistant professor, San Jose State Coll., 1963-64; faculty member, New England Cons., 1964- , chairman, undergraduate theoretical studies, 1969- .
WORKS: Chamber music: <u>Diversion</u>, 2 oboes, 1964; <u>Crystals</u>, string trio, 1967; <u>Vortices</u>, violin, flute, oboe, trumpet, percussion, marimba, mandolin, 1968; <u>Sound circuits</u>, for 3 violins, or 3 violas, or 3 cellos, or 3 basses, 1968; <u>Jupiter's maze</u>, woodwind quintet, Boston, 12 May 1973; <u>Follow the leader</u>, for any number of soprano instruments, 1973; <u>Four to go</u>, 2 pianos, 8-hands, 1973; <u>Volleys</u>, for drums, 1973.
11 Ferndale Road, Natick, MA 01760

HOFFMANN, NEWTON
b. Chicago, Ill., 16 July 1921. Studied with Nadia Boulanger, Longy School of Music; Bernard Rogers, Herbert Elwell, and Howard Hanson,

(HOFFMANN, NEWTON)
Eastman School of Music, M. M., D. M. A. He taught at Shenandoah Cons., 1946-48; Univ. of Bridgeport, 1949-51; Hartwick Coll., 1952-53; in public schools, 1954-62; at Ball State Univ., 1962- , associate professor, 1969- .
WORKS: Orchestra: symphony; overture; <u>Pastoral</u>; Chamber music: string trio; Movement for piano, clarinet and violin.
620 North McKinley, Muncie, IN 47303

HOFFMANN, PEGGY (Mrs. Arnold E.)
b. Delaware, Ohio, 25 Aug. 1910. Studied with Edward G. Mead, Miami Univ. Ohio; with Cecil Smith, Univ. of Chicago; and with Elmer Ende, Univ. of Akron. She has been church organist since graduation from school; in Raleigh, N. C., 1950-66; Cary, N. C., 1967-73.
WORKS: Chorus: <u>God's son is born</u>, Christmas cantata; <u>The cross shines forth</u>, Easter cantata; many anthems, chorales, organ pieces, etc.
1013 Gardner St., Raleigh, NC 27607

HOFFMANN, RICHARD
b. Vienna, Austria, 20 Apr. 1925; U.S. citizen 1963. Emigrated to New Zealand in 1935, studied at Auckland Univ. Coll; came to the U.S. in 1947 and studied with Arnold Schoenberg in Los Angeles. He received Huntington Hartford fellowships, Guggenheim fellowship; Nat. Inst. of Arts and Letters award; and a Fromm Found. commission. He was lecturer, Univ. of California, Los Angeles, 1950-52; faculty member, Oberlin Coll. Cons., 1954- ; visiting associate professor, Univ. of California, Berkeley, 1965-66; visiting professor, Harvard Univ., summer 1970.
WORKS: Orchestra: <u>Fantasy and fugue, in memoriam A. Schoenberg</u>, 1951; <u>2 orchestra pieces</u>, 1952, 1961; piano concerto, 1954; cello concerto, 1959; Chamber music: 2 string quartets, 1947, 1950; trio for piano, violin, bass clarinet, 1948; quartet, piano and strings, 1950; 2 string trios, 1963, 1971; <u>Decadanse</u>, 10 players.
11 Shiperd Circle
Oberlin, OH 44074

HOFFRICHTER, BERTHA CHAITKIN (Mrs. Maurice J.)
b. Pittsburgh, Pa., 8 Dec. 1915. Attended Carnegie-Mellon Univ., B. A., M. A.; and studied privately with Joseph Jenkins. She received the Martin Leisser award, Pittsburgh Art Society, for a piano sonata; Penn. Fed. of Music Clubs award for Song cycle to texts of James Joyce; Composers Division prize for a piano trio; was elected president, Tuesday Musical Club of Pittsburgh, 1973-74.
WORKS: Chamber music: violin sonata; sonata for 2 pianos; Chorus: <u>The 23rd psalm</u>, soprano and chorus; <u>The 24th psalm</u>, a cappella; also piano suites, 2-piano suites, songs, and choral works.
5412 Northumberland St.
Pittsburgh, PA 15217

*HOFMANN, JOSEPH
b. Podgorze, near Krakow, Poland, 20 Jan. 1876; U.S. citizen 1926; d. Los Angeles, Calif., 16

(HOFMANN, JOSEPH)
Feb. 1957. A noted pianist, at age 10 played the Beethoven Concerto No. 1 with the Berlin Philharmonic, Hans von Bulow conducting; repeated the performance at the Metropolitan Opera House, New York, playing also works by Chopin and some of his own compositions. He later studied piano with Moszkowski and Rubenstein, composition with Urban, then resumed his career as a concert pianist. As a composer he sometimes used the pen-name of Michael Dvorsky. His works were chiefly for piano, including several piano concertos, Chromaticon for piano and orch., many piano pieces; and some orchestral works.

HOGENSON, ROBERT CHARLES
b. Kirksville, Mo., 22 Nov. 1936. Studied with Leon Karel, Northeast Missouri State Univ.; Helen Gunderson, Louisiana State Univ.; and with H. Owen Reed, Michigan State Univ., Ph. D. He was faculty member, Southwest Texas State Univ., 1962-68; associate professor, Univ. of Delaware, 1968- .
WORKS: for band, instrumental solos, voice, and piano.
Department of Music
University of Delaware
Newark, DE 19711

HOGG, MERLE E.
b. Lincoln, Kan., 25 Aug. 1922. Studied with Philip Greeley Clapp, Univ. of Iowa, Ph. D.; with Nadia Boulanger, Fontainebleau, France, 1960. He received 2nd prize Thor Johnson Brass Composition contest, 1953. He taught at Eastern New Mexico Univ., 1953-62; has been professor, San Diego State Univ., 1962- ; member, San Diego Symphony Orch., 1964- .
WORKS: Orchestra: Concerto for brass, 1953; trombone concerto; Band: Suite for band; Chamber music: Invention for brass quintet; sonatina, tuba and piano; sonata for brass choir; 3 short pieces for brass trio; Toccata for brass quartet; Variations for brass trio; Variations for bassoon and piano; jazz compositions and songs.
Department of Music
San Diego State University
San Diego, CA 92115

HOHMANN, WALTER H.
b. Holstead, Kan., 27 Oct. 1892; d. North Newton, Kan., 9 Mar. 1971. Studied with Edgar Brazelton, Chicago Musical Coll. He received honorary doctorates from Bethel Coll., 1947, and Chicago Musical Coll., 1947. He taught at Freeman Junior Coll., S. Dak., 1921-23; was chairman, music department, Bethel Coll., 1923-62; was co-editor, Mennonite Hymnary, published 1940, and on the joint committee for its revision in 1969.
WORKS: Chorus: Wind in the pines; Po' good Jesus; O power of love; and others. He was author of Outlines of hymnology, Bethel Coll. Press.

HOIBY, LEE
b. Madison, Wis., 17 Feb. 1926. Studied at Univ. of Wisconsin, B. M. 1947; piano with Egon Petri

(HOIBY, LEE)
at Mills Coll., M. A. 1952; and composition with Gian Carlo Menotti at Curtis Inst. of Music. He received a Fulbright fellowship, 1952; Nat. Inst. of Arts and Letters award, 1957; Guggenheim fellowship, 1958; ASCAP award for score of Summer and smoke, 1972.
WORKS: Opera: The witch, 1956; The scarf, 1958; Beatrice, 1959; Natalia Petrovna, 1964; Summer and smoke, 1971; Ballet: After Eden; Landscape; Hearts meadows and flags; Theatre: incidental music to The Duchess of Malfi; She stoops to conquer; The octoroon; Androcles and the lion; Under milkwood; Tartuffe; Orchestra: Noctambulation, 1952; piano concerto, 1958; Chamber music: violin sonata, 1952; Study in design, string orch., 1953; Diversions, 4 pieces for woodwind quintet, 1954; Pastoral dances, flute; Chorus: Hymn of the Nativity; Ascension; Inherit the kingdom; Let this mind be in you; Songs of the fool, 1956; Songs: Go, and catch a falling star; An immortality; The tides of sleep, low voice with orch.; Piano: Capriccio on 5 notes; Toccata, 1950; 5 preludes, 1952.
Box 111, North Salem, NY 10560

*HOKANSON, DOROTHY CADZOW
b. Edmonton, Alta., 9 Aug. 1916. Studied at Univ. of Washington; with Frederick Jacobi and Bernard Wagenaar at Juilliard School, 1942-45. Her works include Northwestern sketches, a suite for orch., 1945; a string quartet; Golden dawn, vocal solo.
2636 11th Ave. East, Seattle, WA 98102

*HOKANSON, MARGRETHE
b. Duluth, Minn., 19 Dec. 1893. Studied at American Cons.; composition with Arthur Andersen. She won a Nat. Fed. of Music Clubs prize for an orchestral work; was associate professor, Allegheny Coll., 1944-54.
WORKS: Chorus: O praise him; Songs: In the primeval forest; Nordic song; Ring dans; Song without words; A summer idyl; Come, close the curtain of your eyes; Organ: A nordic reverie.

HOLBROOK, GERALD W.
b. York, Neb., 29 Oct. 1946. Studied voice and viola, Univ. of Nebraska; piano at Univ. of Michigan, Royal Coll. of Music, London, and Boston Cons. He has held various positions as church organist, music director, and vocalist; was violist with Lincoln, Neb. and Plymouth, Mich., symphony orchestras; private teacher of voice and piano.
WORKS: Theatre: The 8th deadly sin, musical play, 1975; Voice: 4 masses for unison voices, 1969-71; Magnificat, unison voices, 1969; Litany for the enthronement of an abbot, unison voices and cantor, 1969; Kyrie, mixed chorus, 1969; Alleluia, chorus, 1970; an oratorio for solo voices, chorus and orch., 1970; As the deer yearns for running streams, chorus, 1971; Questions, solo voice and piano, 1975.
c/o First Parish Church
330 First Parish Road
Scituate, MA 02066

HOLDEN, DAVID JUSTIN

HOLDEN, DAVID JUSTIN
b. White Plains, N. Y., 16 Dec. 1911. Studied
with Walter Piston and Aaron Copland, Harvard
Univ.; with Bernard Wagenaar, Juilliard School.
He received the Knight Prize at Harvard; NBC
Music Guild award; Cleveland Orchestra 25th Anniversary award; Society for Publication of American Music grant. He was instructor, Boston
Cons., 1938-43; faculty member, Mt. Holyoke Coll.,
1943-   , professor, 1963-   ; music critic
and editor, Chautauquan Daily, 1949-68; faculty,
Chautauqua Summer School of Music, 1950-64; Syracuse Univ. Summer School, 1965-68.
        WORKS: Orchestra: Symphony; choral sym-
phony; Toccata for orch.; Chamber music: Music
for piano and strings; 2 string quartets; Chorus:
Christmas cantata on Appalachian carols; Keyboard: Improvisation on We three kings, organ;
Passacaglia, piano.
        61 Silver St., South Hadley, MA 01075

HOLDRIDGE, LEE
b. Haiti, 3 Mar. 1944, U.S. parents. Studied
with Henry Lasker in Boston. He received Circle
of Friends of Music award, Arenzano, Italy, 1972.
He has been a free-lance composer-conductor-
arranger for records, films, and television,
1962-   .
        WORKS: Ballet: Trinity, 1970; Ballet fan-
tasy no. 2, strings and harp, 1972; Theatre:
incidental music for Another part of the forest,
Hellman, 1972; Orchestra: Scenes of summer; The
other world music, violin and string orch., 1973;
Chamber music: Fantasy sonata, cello and piano,
New York, May 1971; concerto for bass trombone
and instrumental ensemble, New York, Apr. 1971;
concertino for cello and strings, New York, June
1973; Songs: The conscientious objector, Millay
text, soprano and piano or orch.; Ocean's poem,
cycle for soprano, New York, Apr. 1972; Antigone,
soprano, 1973.
        3605 Valley Meadow Road
        Sherman Oaks, CA 91403

HOLLANDER, LORIN
b. Queens, N. Y., 19 July 1944. Studied with
Eduard Steuermann and Vittorio Giannini at
Juilliard School. He is a concert pianist,
        WORKS: Piano: Up against the wall; Lul-
laby.
        Stockton Springs, ME 04981

HOLLIDAY, KENT ALFRED
b. St. Paul, Minn., 9 Mar. 1940. Studied with
Paul Fetler and Dominick Argento, Univ. of Minnesota; electronic music with Pietro Grossi,
Florence, Italy; with Jon Appleton, Dartmouth
Coll. He was associate professor, Southern
Colorado State Coll., 1965-72; associate professor, Colorado State Univ., 1972-   .
        WORKS: Orchestra: Poems into darkness,
cantata for chorus and orch.; symphony; Symphonia brevis; The longest road, tenor and wind
ensemble; Chamber music: Toccata for piano; And
four are one, flute and violin; Fanfare, brass
sextet.
        608 Tulane Drive, Ft. Collins, CO 80521

*HOLLINGSWORTH, STANLEY
b. Berkeley, Calif., 27 Aug. 1924. Studied at
San Jose State Coll.; with Darius Milhaud at
Mills Coll.; with Gian Carlo Menotti at Curtis
Inst.; and at the American Acad. in Rome,
1955-56.
        WORKS: Opera: The mother; La Grande
Bretèche, television opera, 1957; Chamber music:
oboe sonata; quintet for harp and woodwinds;
Chorus: Dumbarton Oaks mass, with string orch.;
Stabat mater, with orch., 1957.
        1530 38th St., Sacramento, CA 95816

HOLLISTER, DAVID M.
b. New York, N. Y., 1 May 1929. Studied with
Wallingford Riegger, Metropolitan Music School,
1952; Henry Brant, Juilliard School, 1954-55;
Darius Milhaud, Aspen School, 1958; Richard
Hervig, Univ. of Iowa, 1964-67; and with
Wlodzimierz Kotonski in Warsaw, 1967-68. He
received fellowships from MacDowell Colony, 1961;
Huntington Hartford Found., 1964; Howard Found.,
1967-68; Yaddo, 1973; Villa Montalvo, 1973; and
the Zelosky grant, Kosciuszko Found., 1967. He
was composer-musician, New York, 1952-64; assistant professor, Louisiana State Univ., 1968-70;
assistant professor, York Coll., CUNY, 1970-
and adjunct professor, Bronx Community Coll.,
1973-   .
        WORKS: Ballet: Tablet; Rebus; Jazz adver-
sary; A time for parting; Orchestra: Concertino
for strings; Serenade for orchestra; Syncretisms;
Essay for winds and strings; Chamber music:
Partita for 6 instruments; woodwind trio; string
quartet; clarinet quintet; Vocal: Songs of
death; Winter madrigals; My holy mountain; Piano:
Variations on Moscow nights; Toccata.
        10 East 16th St., New York, NY 10003

*HOLMAN, WILLIS
b. Olive, Calif., 1927. Has played tenor saxophone with jazz orchestras; was arranger for
Stan Kenton and Woody Herman. His compositions
include Trilogy, written for the Los Angeles
Neophonic Orch., 1965; and Festival prologue,
for wind symphony.

HOLMES, MARKWOOD
b. Lexington, Neb., 18 Aug. 1899. Studied with
David Van Vactor, Kansas City; Otto Luening, New
York; Charles Koechlin in Paris; Darius Milhaud
and Charles Jones, Santa Barbara; Bela Rozsa,
Tulsa Univ., M. M. He was co-winner of the
Ernest Bloch award 1949, and received many first
prizes in Kansas Music Teachers Asso. contests.
His faculty positions include Kansas City Cons.,
1919-25, 1930-36; Kansas State Coll., 1947-69;
positions as violinist in Vaudelle String Quartet, Paris, 1927-28; Kansas City Philharmonic
Orch., 1933-38, 1944-46; Tulsa Philharmonic,
1961-73.
        WORKS: Opera: Telemachus; Orchestra:
Passacaglia and fugue; Sinfonia; Symphonic episode, solo cello and piano with orch.; Agnus Dei,
4 soloists, chorus, and orch.; Chamber music:
Street scenes, violin, clarinet, piano; cello
sonata; Prelude, elegy and fugue, piano quintet;

(HOLMES, MARKWOOD)
Concerto grosso, 6 instruments and string orch.; March-fantasy, viola and piano; Vocal: Island, song cycle; By the greatness, women's choir; 3 songs on Chinese love poems, voice, viola, piano.
2602 Omaha, Pittsburg, KS 66762

HOLMES, PAUL
b. Abilene, Tex., 20 Jan. 1923. Studied at Hardin Simmons Univ., B. M.; and Univ. of Texas, M. M. He received the Texas Composers Award of Houston Symphony, 1957; and commissions from Univ. of Tennessee at Martin, Tennessee Tech. Univ., Phi Mu Alpha Sinfonia, and Society for Commissioning New Music. He is associate professor and head, theory and composition, Lamar Univ.
WORKS: Orchestra: 3 archaic dances; Fable for orchestra, 1957; Band: Prince Consort, concert march; Concertino for 3 solo tubas and band, 1972; Chamber music: Suite for brass; Lento for tuba; Serenade for horn; trumpet sonata; clarinet suite; 6 little pieces, flute and piano; tuba quartet, 1971; brass quintet, 1972; Chorus: Hymn and alleluia; And nature shall be healed, cantata for choir, brass, percussion, 1970; Songs: Song cycle for soprano on poems of Gini Carter; Amazing grace, medium voice.
1879 Cartwright, Beaumont, TX 77701

*HOMANS, PETER
b. 1951. Studied with Robert Stewart, Washington and Lee Univ.; with Donald Martino, New England Cons.
WORKS: Voice: Cantata on texts of Wallace Stevens and Ezra Pound, 1973; Lumori, 1973; 3 Italian songs, 1974.

HOOPER, WILLIAM L.
b. Sedalia, Mo., 16 Sep. 1931. Studied at William Jewell Coll., B. A. 1953; with Philip Bezanson, Univ. of Iowa, M. A. 1956; Philip Slates, George Peabody Coll., Ph. D. 1966; and with Humphrey Searle, Royal Coll. of Music, London, 1969-70. He received the Jesse Jones scholarship, Peabody Coll.; won honorable mention 1972, first place 1973, Delius Composition competition; won Louisiana State Univ. composition contest; a Scholastic Achievement Award in Music has been named in his honor, William Jewell Coll. He has been Baptist pastor, public school teacher; professor, Southwest Baptist Coll., 1956-60; minister of music, First Baptist Church, Old Hickory, Tenn., 1960-62; baritone soloist in church, opera, oratorio, 1962-66; professor and chairman of theory, New Orleans Baptist Theological Seminary, 1966-
WORKS: Cantatas: His saving grace proclaim; Jubilee; A litany of praise; Organ: Praeludium.
4131 Seminary Place, New Orleans, LA 70126

*HOPKINS, HARRY PATTERSON
b. Baltimore, Md., 25 May 1873; d. Baltimore, 21 Sep. 1954. Graduated from Peabody Cons., 1896; studied with Antonin Dvorak in Bohemia. From 1899 he was organist and teacher in Baltimore.
WORKS: Orchestra: a symphony; Spring journey, chorus and orch.; Chamber music: piano

(HOPKINS, HARRY PATTERSON)
trio; 2 piano quintets; string quartet; piano sextet; Organ: Exaltation; Heavenly glory; also a comic opera, anthems and other choral works.

HOPKINS, JAMES FREDERICK
b. Pasadena, Calif., 8 Apr. 1939. Studied with Ernest Kanitz and Halsey Stevens, Univ. of Southern California; with Quincy Porter, Yale Univ.; with Edward T. Cone, Princeton Univ. He was a Woodrow Wilson fellow, 1960-62. Faculty posts include instructor, Northwestern Univ., 1962-66, assistant professor, 1968-71; associate professor, Univ. of Southern California, 1971-   .
WORKS: Orchestra: Phantasms; Variations for orchestra; Band: 2 symphonies; Chamber music: Diferencias, piano trio; Fantasia, 8 cellos and 2 basses; Theatrikomelos, chamber orch.; Chorus: Hymn of progress; Jubilate Deo, Psalm 150, choir, organ, 2 trumpets, percussion; Missa Regina Coeli, with organ and harp.
2859 Westbrook Ave., Los Angeles, CA 90046

HOPSON, HAL
b. Coryell County, Tex., 12 June 1933. Studied at Baylor Univ.; with Helmut Schiller, Erlangen Univ., Germany; with Lloyd Pfautsch, Southern Methodist Univ. He held a Royalty-Edwards scholarship at Baylor Univ. His posts as organist-choirmaster include Baltimore, MD., 1962-65; Ashland, Ky., 1965-69; Vine Street Christian Church, Nashville, 1969-   .
WORKS: Chorus: Canticle of praise, choir, organ, 3 trumpets; A psalm of praise, choir and organ; more than 40 published choral compositions.
c/o Vine Street Christian Church
Nashville, TN 37205

*HORACEK, LEO
The tell-tale heart, 1-act opera, Opera Theatre of West Virginia, Morgantown, 7 Aug. 1968.

*HORN, PAUL
b. New York, N. Y., 17 Mar. 1930. Studied at Oberlin Cons., B. M.; on scholarship at Manhattan School of Music, M. M. He played flute with Chico Hamilton, then formed his own group in 1959. He wrote the film score Clutch cargo; many songs.

HORTON, KENNETH JOHN
b. Long Beach, Calif., 29 Oct. 1950. Studied with Stanley Lunetta. He has been percussionist, Sacramento Symphony Orch., 1965-   ; timpanist, Reno Philharmonic Orch., 1973-   .
WORKS: Opus T, 1968; St. Francis, 1969; Light song, 1970; September toad ritual, joint work with Lunetta and others, 1971; AMRA/ARMA, 1970-   (Horton says most major works now require performance before completion).
6925 Chevy Chase Way, Sacramento, CA 95823

HORTON, LEWIS HENRY
b. Youngstown, Ohio, 8 Nov. 1898. Studied at Oberlin Cons., B. A. 1923; Ohio State Univ., M. A. 1938. He was public school teacher, 1926-30; head of music department, Morehead

HORTON, LEWIS HENRY

(HORTON, LEWIS HENRY)
State Coll., 1930-42; faculty member, Univ. of Kentucky, 1942-46; Transylvania Univ., 1946-51, composer-in-residence, 1951-   . He was also music critic on the Lexington, Ky., Herald and the Sunday Herald Leader.
WORKS: Chorus: The white pilgrim, folk cantata, 1940; An Appalachian nativity, folk cantata, 1955; An Appalachian Easter, 1959; Mother Goose suite; Ancient of days; Weep you no more sad fountains; A cappella primer; A cappella frontiers.
338 Kilmore Court, Lexington, KY 40508

*HORVIT, MICHAEL
b. New York, N. Y., 22 June 1932. Studied with Quincy Porter, Yale Univ., B. M. 1955, M. M. 1956; with Gardner Read,, Boston Univ., D. M. A. 1959; also with Walter Piston, 1957, Aaron Copland, 1959, Lukas Foss, 1961. His honors include a BMI award, 1959; College Band Directors Nat. Asso. new music contest award, 1961; Rockefeller grant, 1968; Univ. of Houston research grants, 1968, 1974; Nat. Endowment on the Arts grant, 1974. He was associate professor, Southern Connecticut Coll., 1959-66; professor, Univ. of Houston, 1966-
WORKS: Opera: Homo, 1 act, Houston, 21 Nov. 1968; Orchestra: Toccatina; Wind ensemble: Antique suite, antiphonal brass choir; Chamber music: Little suite, woodwind trio; The crystal cave, harpsichord sonata; Chorus: Lullaby on text of James Agee; Electronic: Antiphon, saxophone and tape; Antiphon II, clarinet and tape; 2 songs for choir and tape.
School of Music, University of Houston
Houston, TX 77004

HORWOOD, MICHAEL S.
b. Buffalo, N. Y., 24 May 1947. Studied with Ramon Fuller, Leo Smit, William C. Kothe, and Lejaren Hiller, State Univ. of New York at Buffalo, B. A., M. A. He taught high school in Buffalo, 1969-71; has been instructor, Humber Coll. of Applied Arts and Technology, Ont., 1972-   .
WORKS: Theatre: incidental music, Dog in the manger, Lope de Vega, 1972; Tantrums, Hrant Alianak, 1972; Chamber music: 6 pieces for piano, 1967; Timpanic suite for 2 timpanists, 1967; Piece percussionique for 3 percussionists, 1967; Microduet No. 1, oboe and bass drum, 1967; Microduet no. 3, tuba and almglocken, 1968; New York State Thruway, clarinet and piano, 1969; Electronic tape: Motility; Monday afternoon, 1966; Mixed media: For the Class of '71; 4 settings of poems of Robert Creeley, narrator, tape, chamber ensemble, Buffalo, Apr. 1968.
2981 Islington Ave. North
Weston, Ontario, Canada

HOSKINS, WILLIAM BARNES
b. St. Lucie, Fla., 26 Oct. 1917. Studied with Normand Lockwood, Oberlin Coll., 1936-40; with Nadia Boulanger, Wisconsin, 1941; with Otto Luening, Columbia Univ. 1947. His works have received many performances, and he was awarded a commission by the Florida State Music Teachers

(HOSKINS, WILLIAM BARNES)
Assoc., 1970. His faculty positions have included instructor, West Virginia Univ., 1940-42; director, composition and theory, Jacksonville Coll. of Music, 1948-54, president, 1954-58; dean, Jacksonville Univ. Coll. of Music, 1958-61; composer-in-residence, Jacksonville Univ., 1961-   , director, electronic music, 1968-   .
WORKS: Orchestra: Israfel, chorus and orch.; Ballad of the trumpet boy; Concert overture; The lost lands, cycle for mezzo soprano and string orch.; Requiem for the 6 million, chorus, soloists, brass and percussion ensemble, piano, organ; Chamber music: string quartet; Variations on a random theme, piano; sonata for brass quartet; Suite Balinesque, for western gamelan; Electronic: Galactic fantasy, Moog synthesizer; Mixed media: Dialogs I and II for chorus, soloists, synthesizer/tape, 1970.
5454 Arlington Road, Jacksonville, FL 32211

HOSMER, JAMES B.
b. Johnstown, Pa., 27 May 1911. Studied composition with Bernard Wagenaar and Howard Murphy, flute with Kincaid, Barrere and M. Moyse. He was flutist with the Indianapolis Symphony, 1937-42; Metropolitan Opera, 1946-   .
WORKS: Orchestra: From the mail box, a suite, 1953; Chamber music: Fugue for woodwind quintet, 1938; Rhapsody for flute and strings, 1957; 4 flute duos, 1961; 7/4 serenade, flute, oboe, bassoon, harpsichord, 1965.
49 Seaview Ave., New Rochelle, NY 10801

*HOSMER, LUCIUS
b. South Acton, Mass., 14 Aug. 1870; d. Jefferson, N. H., 9 May 1935. Studied with George W. Chadwick, New England Cons.; was church organist and conducted theatre orchestras.
WORKS: Opera: The rose of the Alhambra, 1905; The walking delegate, comic opera, revised as The Koreans; Orchestra: Chinese wedding procession; Southern rhapsody; Northern rhapsody; Ethiopian rhapsody; On tiptoe; and songs.

*HOUSMAN, ROSALIE
b. San Francisco, Calif., 25 June, 1888; d. New York, N. Y., 28 Oct. 1949. Studied with Arthur Foote in Boston; with Ernest Bloch in New York. She wrote Color sequence for soprano and small orch.; choruses, songs.

HOVEY, SERGE
b. New York, N. Y., 10 Mar. 1920. Studied piano with Richard Buhlig, composition with Arnold Schoenberg and Hanns Eisler. His film scores have received many awards including 3 CINE Gold eagles; Sholem Aleichem suite received 2nd place, Koussevitzky Found. competition, 1958. He has been orchestrator, accompanist, music director for Brecht's Galileo, 1948, composer for various film studios, 1951-   .
WORKS: Opera: Dreams in spades, 1-act, Philadelphia, Dec. 1949; Ballet: Fable, Philadelphia, Jan. 1949; Theatre: The world of Sholem Aleichem, music for the play, 1953; Tevya and his daughters, 1957; Orchestra: Sholem Aleichem suite, soloists, chorus, orch.,

(HOVEY, SERGE)

Cincinnati, 21 Feb. 1958; Robert Burns rhapsody, soloists, chorus, orch., 1958; African ballet suite, 1960; Weekend - U.S.A., 1961; A little New York music, 1961; symphony, 1967; Freedom variations, 1969; Chamber music: The fiddle, narrator and chamber ensemble, 1948; A ballad of August Bondi, narrator, vocalists, chamber ensemble, 1956; Intermezzo, piano and strings, 1961; 4 Afro-American variations, clarinet, piano duet, percussion, 1965; Film scores: The magic hat, 1952; Hangman, 1964; Storm of strangers, 1969; Denmark 43, 1970-71; Gulliver in Automobilia, 1974; also many songs and The Robert Burns Song Book, 4-volumes, 1968-73.

512 Abramar Ave.
Pacific Palisades, CA 90272

HOVHANNES, ALAN

b. Somerville, Mass., 8 Mar. 1911. Began piano study early with Adelaide Proctor and Heinrich Gebhard; studied composition with Frederick Converse, New England Cons. His many honors include a Tanglewood scholarship, 1942; 3 honorary doctorates; Guggenheim fellowships; Nat. Inst. of Arts and Letters award; many commissions. He taught privately in Boston; was on faculty, Boston Cons., 1948-51; then moved to New York, where he composed prolifically, including scores for radio and television; began his first world tour in 1959, achieving remarkable success in India and Japan.

WORKS: Orchestra: 24 symphonies, 1939-1973; 3 Armenian rhapsodies; Lousadzak, Op. 48, concerto for piano and string orch., 1945; Is there survival?, ballet suite, Op. 59; Zartik partim, Op. 77; Artik, concerto for horn and strings, Op. 78; Janabar, violin, trumpet, strings, Op. 81; Arevakal, concerto for orch., Op. 88; concerto for violin and string orch., Op. 89a; Concerto no. 7 for orch., Op. 116, 1953; Concerto no. 8, Op. 117; Meditation on Orpheus, Op. 155, 1958; Meditation on Zeami, Op. 207, 1964; Floating world, Op. 209; Fantasy on Japanese wood prints, Op. 211, 1965; Fra Angelico, Op. 220, 1967; Requiem and resurrection, Op. 224; Mountains and rivers without end, Op. 225; Shambala, Op. 228; And God created great whales, Op. 229, 1970; Firdausi, New York, 12 May 1973; Manjun symphony, Lubbock, Tex., Jan. 1974; Band: Suite for band, Op. 15; 3 journeys to a holy mountain, Op. 223, 1968; Chamber music: 4 string quartets, Op. 8, 147, 208, 208 #2; 2 piano quintets, Op. 9 and 109; violin sonata, Op. 11; suite for oboe and bassoon, Op. 23; Divertimento, wind quartet, Op. 61; 2 fantasies for brass choir, Op. 70; Upon enchanted ground, flute, cello, harp, tamtam, Op. 90, 1951; Khaldis, piano, 4 trumpets, percussion, Op. 91; 2 quartets for flute, oboe, cello, piano, Op. 97 and 112; suite for violin, piano, percussion, Op. 99; Hanna, 2 clarinets, 2 pianos, Op. 101; sextet, violin and 5 percussion, Op. 108; flute sonata, Op. 118, 1954; duet for violin and harpsichord, Op. 122, 1954; The flowering peach, chamber ensemble, Op. 125; harp sonata, Op. 127, 1957; Tower music, Op. 129; sonata for 2 oboes and organ, Op. 130; The world beneath the sea, Op. 133, #1 and 2; October

(HOVHANESS, ALAN)

mountain, percussion sextet, Op. 135; wind quintet, Op. 159; sextet for alto recorder, string quartet, harpsichord, Op. 164; Koke no niwa, chamber ensemble, Op. 181; Yakamochi, cello, Op. 193; sonata for trumpet and organ, Op. 200; Nagooran, cello, timpani, 4 percussion, Op. 237; Island of the mysterious bells, 4 harps, Op. 244; The garden of Adonis, flute and harp, Op. 245; Chorus: 30th ode of Solomon, baritone, chorus, chamber ensemble, Op. 76; Transfiguration, tenor, chorus a cappella, Op. 82; I will lift up mine eyes, Op. 93; Make a joyful noise, Op. 105; Anabasis, narrator, 2 soli, chorus, orch., Op. 141; Ad lyram, 4 soli, double chorus, orch., Op. 143, 1956; Magnificat, 4 soli, chorus, orch., Op. 157, 1959; Look toward the sea, baritone, chorus, trombone, organ, Op. 158; Fuji, female chorus, chamber ensemble, Op. 182; Symphony no. 12, chorus, orch., ad lib tape of sounds of mountain waterfall, Op. 188; In the beginning was the word, 2 soli, chorus, orch., Op. 206; Adoration, women's or men's chorus and orch., Op. 221; Praise the Lord with psaltery, chorus and orch., Op. 222; Lady of light, 2 soli, chorus, orch., Op. 227; Songs: Angelic song, soprano, tenor, horn, strings, Op. 19; Avak, the healer, soprano, trumpet, strings, Op. 65; Canticle, soprano and ensemble, Op. 115; Saturn, soprano, clarinet, piano, Op. 243; The flute player of the Armenian mountains, 5 songs for low voice and piano, Op. 239; 4 songs for low voice and piano, Op. 242; many more works in all categories.

100 West Olympic Place, Apt. 304
Seattle, WA 98119

HOWARD, BERTRAND E.

b. Houston, Tex., 27 Sep. 1937. Studied with Kent Kennan, Univ. of Texas, Austin; with John Verrall, Donald Keats, William O. Smith, Univ. of Washington, D. M. A. He received a commission from the Music Teachers Nat. Asso. and Arkansas State Music Teachers Asso., 1972. He has been faculty member, Univ. of Arkansas, 1965-   , associate professor, 1973-   .

WORKS: Orchestra: Metacrylic three, 1972; Chamber music: sextet for winds and strings, 1970; Soliloquy, piano; Trinomicron for inner piano, 1973; Chorus, Rain; Green fox; Songs: Where is the nightingale, 1963; Windon, 1968; A sea cycle, soprano and inner piano, 1971; Mixed media: Bardos, chamber group, tape, lights, film, dancer, 1972; uv ajeD, 1973; Hydrohms, trombone, prepared tape, tape loop, 1971.

Department of Music
University of Arkansas
Fayetteville, AR 72701

HOWARD, DEAN CLINTON

b. Cleveland, Ohio, 17 Nov. 1918. Studied at Baldwin-Wallace Coll., B. M. E.; with Edmund Haines at Univ. of Michigan, M. M.; and at Indiana Univ. He received the first award, Nat. Composers Congress, 1944; first award, Iowa Composers' Contest, 1948; Putnam Award for excellence in teaching, 1961-62; local and national

HOWARD, DEAN CLINTON

(HOWARD, DEAN CLINTON)
prizes for watercolor paintings. He was professor, Buena Vista Coll., 1946-48; professor, Bradley Univ., 1948-   ; first clarinetist, Peoria Symphony, 1969-   .
WORKS: Orchestra: <u>Divertimento</u>, 1960; <u>An Illinois symphony</u>, 1967; <u>Perspectives</u>, 1972; Band: <u>Holiday parade</u>, 1959; <u>Sea drift</u>, 1962; <u>Salute to freedom</u>, 1962; <u>Triumph of youth</u>, 1965; <u>Proud heritage</u>, 1972; Chamber music: clarinet sonata, 1962, sonatina, 1965; violin sonata, 1963; cello sonata, 1964; piano sonata; Chorus: <u>The road to song</u>, 1958; <u>Whistle your blues away</u>, 1958; <u>Listen to my heart</u>, 1958; <u>Come bless the Lord</u>, 1961; <u>Most glorious God</u>, 1964; <u>O sacred banquet</u>, 1966; <u>Our fathers' faith we hold</u>, 1972.
School of Music, Bradley University
Peoria, IL 61606

HOWARD, GEORGE S.
b. Reamstown, Pa., 24 Feb. 1903. Attended Ohio Wesleyan Univ., A. B.; New York Univ., M. A.; Chicago Cons., B. M., M. M., D. M. His awards include Legion of Merit with Oak leaf Cluster; Commendation Medal with 5 Oak leaf Clusters; citation by Nat. Asso. of American Composers and Conductors; Gold record, Nippon Columbia Co., Tokyo. He taught in public schools, 1930-36; private school, 1936-38; Pennsylvania State Teachers Coll., Mansfield, 1938-40; director of bands, orchestra, and chorus, Pennsylvania State Univ., 1940-42; chief of music and conductor, U.S. Air Force Symphony Orchestra and Band, 1943-63; director of band and music program, Metropolitan Police Dept., Washington, D.C., 1963-73.
WORKS: Band: <u>The Red Feather</u>; <u>American doughboy</u>; <u>A niece of Uncle Sam</u>; <u>My Missouri</u>; <u>General Spaatz March</u>; <u>Central Canada Exhibition March</u>; <u>Washington Star March</u>; <u>Alfalfa Club March</u>; 8 published songs; numerous unpublished works.
Air Force Village, 4917 Ravenswood Drive
San Antonio, TX 78227

*HOWARD, JOHN TASKER
b. Brooklyn, N. Y., 30 Nov. 1890; d. West Orange, N. J., 20 Nov. 1964. Studied at Williams Coll., 1910-13; honorary M. A. 1937; composition with Howard Brockway and Mortimer Wilson. He held many posts as music editor; was curator, American Music Collection, New York Public Library, 1940-64; author of many books on American music and musicians.
WORKS: Orchestra: <u>Fantasy on a choral theme</u>, piano and orch.; <u>Foster sinfonietta</u>; <u>March of the grenadiers</u>; <u>Mosses from an old manse</u>; Chamber music: <u>Foster sonatina</u>, violin and piano; <u>From Foster Hall</u>, string quartet; many choral works, songs, piano pieces.

HOWE, HUBERT S., JR.
b. Portland, Ore., 21 Dec. 1942. Studied with Milton Babbitt, J. K. Randall, and Godfrey Winham, Princeton Univ., M. M. 1967. He has been on the faculty, Queens Coll., CUNY, 1967-   , associate professor and director of electronic music studio, 1972-   ; associate editor, Perspectives of new music.

(HOWE, HUBERT S., JR.)
WORKS: Electronic: <u>Computer variations</u>, 1967-68; <u>Kaleidoscope</u>, 1969; <u>Interchanges</u>, 1970-71; <u>Macro-structure</u>, 1971; <u>Freeze</u>, 1972; <u>3 studies in timbre</u>, 1970-73.
309 West 104th St., Apt. 34
New York, NY 10025

*HOWE, MARY
b. Richmond, Va., 4 Apr. 1882; d. Washington, D.C., 14 Sep. 1964. Studied in Paris with Nadia Boulanger; with Gustav Strube, Peabody Cons. diploma in composition, 1922. A full program of her works was performed by the National Symphony Orchestra, Washington, D.C., 21 Dec. 1952; by the Howard Univ. Choir and soloists, Town Hall, New York, 24 Feb. 1953; she received an honorary doctorate from George Washington Univ., 1961.
WORKS: Orchestra: <u>Dirge</u>, 1931; <u>Polka and waltz</u>; <u>Cards</u>; <u>Mists</u>; <u>Castellano</u>, 2 pianos and orch., 1935; <u>Spring pastorale</u>, 1936; <u>Stars</u>, 1937; <u>Sand</u>, 1938; <u>Rock</u>, symphonic poem; <u>Potomac suite</u>, 1940; <u>Agreeable overture</u>, 1949; <u>Axiom</u>; <u>American piece</u>; Chamber music: violin sonata, 1922; suite for piano quintet, 1923; <u>Elegy</u> for organ; Chorus; <u>Chain gang song</u>, 1925; <u>Great land of mine</u>; <u>Prophecy, 1792</u>, male chorus, 1943; 7 volumes of songs published in 1960.

HOWELL, HUDSON DAVIS
b. West Frankfort, Ill., 11 July 1919. Studied with Bela Rozsa and Strom Bull, Baylor Univ.; with Thomas Richner, Harry Wilson, and Howard Murphy, Columbia Univ. He was minister of music and organist, Hapeville, Ga., 1952-56.
WORKS: Church music for organ and chorus.
2515 North Camino de Oeste
Tucson, AZ 85705

*HOWLAND, WILLIAM LEGRAND
b. Asbury Park, N. J., 1873; d. Long Island, N. Y., 26 July 1915. Studied with Philip Scharwenka in Poland. His works include 2 operas, <u>Sarrona</u>, 1903, and <u>Nita</u>; 2 oratorios, <u>The resurrection</u> and <u>Ecce homo</u>; and choral works.

HOY, BONNEE
b. Jenkintown, Pa., 27 Aug. 1936. Studied with Roy Harris and Joseph Castaldo, Philadelphia Musical Acad.; with Nadia Boulanger at Fontainebleau; and at Temple Univ. She was on the music faculty, St. Basil's Acad., 1962-64; Settlement Music School, 1966-72; music consultant, WUHY-FM, 1973.
WORKS: Ballet: <u>Pinocchio</u>, 1958; Orchestra: violin concerto, 1963; Chamber music: <u>The hourglass suite</u>, soprano, tenor, chamber ensemble, 1966; piano trio, 1968; <u>The freeman celebration songs and dances</u>, soprano, flute, cello, piano, 1971; string quartet, 1972; piano quintet, 1973; Chorus: <u>3 sacred motets</u>, a cappella, 1963; <u>Quartet and gloria</u>, a cappella, 1968; <u>The spring of Earth's rebirth</u>, oratorio, for chorus, 2 solo choruses, 4 soloists, orch., 1971; <u>Threnody</u>, with recorder, cello, and drums, 1973; Piano: <u>Preludes</u>, 1969; <u>Storybook suite for children</u>, 1970; 2 sonatas, 1970, 1971; <u>Excursions</u>, vol. 1, 1973.
7744 Albright Ave., Elkins Park, PA 19117

HSU, WEN-YING
b. Shanghai, China, 2 May 1909; U.S. citizen 1972. Studied with Philip Slates, George Peabody Coll.; with Carl McKinley and Francis Judd Cooke, New England Cons.; John Vincent, Univ. of California, Los Angeles; with Harold Owen, Ingolf Dahl, and Frederick Lesemann, Univ. of Southern California. Her awards include first prize, Manuscript Club of Los Angeles, 1969, 1971; Parade of American Music, 1969; Nat. Music Week, 1971; Nat. Fed of Music Clubs, 1973; Nat. League of American Pen Women, 1974. She was professor of music, Nat. Inst. of Fine Arts, Taiwan, 1958-59, 1960-63; and Coll. of Chinese Culture, Taiwan, 1971-72.
    WORKS: Band: March of Chinese cadets, 1966; Chamber music: piano trio, 1955; Theme and variations, flute, clarinet, bassoon, 1964; violin suite, 1966; Percussions east and west, 14 players, 1966; Songs of Sung, 1967; Sonorities of Chinese percussions, 1971; Tune of 3 plum blossoms, 6 percussionists, 1971; Piano: Fantasia for 2 pianos, 1955; sonata, 1958; Scenes in a Chinese village, 1958; piano suite, 1967; Perpetual momentum, 1973.
        114 South New Hampshire Ave., #105
        Los Angeles, CA 90004

*HUBBELL, FRANK ALLEN
b. Denver, Colo., 9 May 1907; d. Calif. Studied at Univ. of Southern California; conducting with Albert Coates and Vladimir Bakaleinikov. He organized the Los Angeles Symphonette in 1946 and was its conductor; also was guest conductor of orchestras in Burbank, San Diego, Bakersfield, and Santa Monica.
    WORKS: Orchestra: California Eldorado suite; Passacaglia and scherzo; Theme and variations; also composed for the Hollywood Bowl music spectaculars: The California story, 1950, 1956-58; The Oregon story, 1959; The Kansas story, 1961.

*HUBBELL, RAYMOND
b. Urbana, Ohio, 1 June 1870; d. Miami, Fla., 13 Dec. 1954. Studied music in Chicago; led his own dance orchestra; was staff composer for a Chicago publishing company. He was one of the 9 founders of ASCAP and its director, 1914-41.
    WORKS: Musicals: The runaways; Fantana; Mexicana; Ziegfeld Follies, 1911-1914; The big show; Good times; Yours truly; et al; Songs: Poor Butterfly; Chu Chin Chow; and many others.

HUBER, CALVIN RAYMOND
b. Buffalo, N. Y., 12 July 1925. Studied with Hilmar Luckhardt, Univ. of Wisconsin, B. A., M. A.; with Curt Sachs, Gustave Reece, New York Univ.; with William S. Newman, Univ. of North Carolina, Chapel Hill, Ph. D. He was associate professor, Carson-Newman Coll., 1951-56, 1959-62; assistant director of bands, Univ. of North Carolina, 1956-59; associate professor and chairman, music department, Wake Forest Univ., 1962- .
    WORKS: Band: Bossa nova holiday; The pusillanimous pussycat; Fanfare for a ceremony; Baubolero; Chamber music: Elegy for 5 flutes; Invention for 2 dissimilar instruments and percussion.
        2080 Royall Drive, Winston-Salem, NC 27106

HUDSON, JOSEPH A.
b. Cleveland, Ohio, 17 Apr. 1952. Studied with Mario Davidovsky, City Coll. of New York. He received scholarships to the Vermont Composers Conference, 1971, 1973.
    WORKS: Chamber music: 5 inventions, flute and guitar, 1971; 3 short movements, 1971; Electronic: Transfixations, electronic sounds and ensemble, 1973.
        1831 Empire Road, Wickliffe, OH 44092

HUDSON, RICHARD A.
b. Alma, Mich., 19 Mar. 1924. Studied at Oberlin Cons., 1946-49; Syracuse Univ., 1950-51; and Univ. of California, Los Angeles, 1959-67. He has taught organ and music theory, Converse Coll., 1949-50; Oberlin Cons., 1953-55; and has been associate professor and music librarian, Univ. of California, Los Angeles, 1967- . He is chiefly a musicologist, with many published articles in music journals.
    WORKS: Organ: Trios for organ, Vol.1, 1971, Vol.2, 1972.
        16160 Magnolia Blvd., Encino, CA 91316

HUFF, JAY A.
b. Lubbock, Tex., 16 Jan. 1926. Studied at Univ. of Colorado, B. M. 1948, M. M. 1951; Northwestern Univ., Ph. D. 1965. He was assistant professor, Northern State Coll., 1952-54; Stephen F. Austin Coll., 1954-59; violinist, San Antonio Symphony, 1959-60, Minneapolis Symphony, 1960-61; faculty member, Millikin Univ., 1963-65; Ohio State Univ., 1966- .
    WORKS: Chamber music: Fugue for 2 violins.
        School of Music, Ohio State University
        Columbus, OH 43210

*HUFFMAN, W(ALTER) SPENCER
Graduated from Peabody Cons., 1947; joined the Peabody faculty in 1949.
    WORKS: Orchestra: piano concerto, Nat. Gallery Orchestra, Washington, D.C., 24 Mar. 1946; 7 symphonies, 1951-55; cello concerto, New York, 3 May 1951; violin concerto, 1953; March, chorale and variations, 1957; harpsichord concerto, 1959; Band: symphony, 1953; Chamber music: string quartet no.6, 1950; violin sonata, New York, 24 Sep. 1951; piano quintet, 1957; piano sonata no.9, 1959; Chorus: Magnificat, 1958.
        5811 Falls Road, Baltimore, MD 21209

HUGGLER, JOHN
b. Rochester, N. Y., 30 Aug. 1928. Studied composition with Dante Fiorello in New York but is chiefly self taught. He received Guggenheim fellowships, 1962, 1969; Horblit award, Boston Symphony, 1967; Fromm Found. commission, 1973; and was composer-in-residence with the Boston Symphony Orchestra, 1964-65. He has been associate professor, Univ. of Massachusetts, Boston, 1965- ; and taught at Massachusetts Inst. of Technology, 1965, Brandeis Univ., 1967, Harvard Univ. 1974.
    WORKS: Orchestra: Concerti for horn, trumpet, flute, viola, violin, saxophone; Elegy; Divertimento, viola and orch.; Variations for

HUGGLER, JOHN

(HUGGLER, JOHN)
orch.; Sculptures, song cycle for soprano and
orch.; symphony for 13 instruments, 1971; Ecce
homo, 1959, premiere, Boston, 12 May 1973; Band:
Celebration, 1966; Chamber music: 3 brass quintets; 3 string quintets; 10 string quartets.
189 Rawson Road, Brookline, MA 02146

*HUGHES, E. KENT
Studied at Univ. of Texas, D. M. A. 1966. He has
published Allegro assai, string orch. and percus-
sion, and Second chance, flute and oboe.
Department of Music, Midwestern University
Wichita Falls, TX 76308

*HUGHES, FRANK C.
d. Fort Worth, Tex. Benediction, chorus.

HUGHES, HOWARD, S. M.
b. Baltimore, Md., 28 June 1930. Studied piano,
organ, and choral conducting with private instructors, He was glee club director, 1951-71, organist, 1951-73.
WORKS: Numerous liturgical compositions for
the church service.
Marianist Provincial House
4301 Roland Ave., Baltimore, MD 21210

*HUGHES, MARK
d. Jackson, Miss. Divertimento for trumpet,
horn, trombone; horn sonata.

HUGHES, SISTER MARTINA
b. Hibbing, Minn., 2 Sep. 1902. Studied with
Ralph Doty and Louise Cuyler, Univ. of Michigan;
with Bernard Rogers, Eastman School of Music.
She received the Minnesota Composers award, 1941
for The highwayman. She was head of the music
department, Coll. of St. Scholastica, 1935-54.
WORKS: Orchestra: The highwayman, chorus
and orch., 1941; April 1943; Invocation, 1947;
Revelation, 1964; Chamber music: Occasional
music, strings; Polytonal Puck, flute, clarinet,
piano; Chorus: Stars, women's voices; Rejoice
unto God, women's voices; Piano: Diko, written
for Gina Bachauer; many other choral and instrumental works; several masses and small works for
the church service.
St. Scholastica Priory, Duluth, MN 55811

*HUGHES, ROBERT
Has studied with Lou Harrison, Luigi Dallapiccola,
Leon Kirchner, and Robert Ashley. He has held
teaching posts at San Francisco Cons., Mills Coll.,
and Cabrillo Coll.; is contrabassoonist, Oakland
Symphony; has conducted Oakland Symphony, San
Francisco Ballet, Cabrillo Music Festival, West-
ern Opera Festival, and others.
WORKS: Ballet: Kama Sutra, for 12 players;
Landscapes; Cones, 19 instruments and tape; Or-
chestra: Radiances; Edge; Cadences, with tape;
Chamber music: Anagnorisis, trombone and percussion; Sonitude, flute and cello; Quadroquartet,
4 flutes, 4 horns, 4 double basses, 4 electronic
tracks; Chorus: Missa corporis, on poems by
James Broughton, with tape; Amo ergo sum, Ezra

(HUGHES, ROBERT)
Pound text, 2 choruses, instruments and tape,
Hayward, Calif., 8 June 1975; and 15 film scores.
c/o Oakland Symphony Association
Latham Square Bldg., Oakland, CA 94612

*HUGO, JOHN ADAM
b. Bridgeport, Conn., 5 Jan. 1873; d. Bridgeport,
29 Dec. 1945. Studied at Stuttgart Cons.,
1888-1897; then gave piano recitals in Germany,
England, and Italy to 1899.
WORKS: Opera: The temple dancer; The hero
of Byzanz; The sun god; Orchestra: symphony; 2
piano concertos; Chamber music: piano trio; violin pieces; cello pieces; piano pieces; songs.

*HUHN, BRUNO
b. London, England, 1 Aug. 1871; to U.S. 1891;
d. New York, N. Y., 13 May 1950. Studied piano
in London and New York; toured as concert pianist, then was active in New York as pianist,
accompanist, and choral conductor.
WORKS: Chorus: Christ trimphant, cantata;
Praise Jehovah, cantata; Songs: Seafarers,
Invictus; Destiny; The divan, a cycle; Love's
triumph, a cycle.

*HULL, ANNE
Ancient ballad, piano ensemble.
96 Grove St., New York, NY 10014

HUMEL, GERALD
b. Cleveland, Ohio, 7 Nov. 1931. Studied with
Herbert Elwell and Walter Aschaffenburg, Oberlin
Cons.; Elie Siegmeister, Hofstra Univ.; Herbert
Howells, Royal Coll. of Music, London; Ross Lee
Finney and Roberto Gerhard, Univ. of Michigan;
with Boris Blacher and Josef Rufer in Berlin.
He received Univ. of Michigan fellowship, 1958;
BMI award, 1959; Fulbright grant, 1960-62; Ber-
lin Senate Stipend, 1962; Nat. Inst. of Arts and
Letters award, 1965; Arthur Shepherd prize, 1964;
Guggenheim grant, 1966; German Critics prize for
music, 1968; Berlin Arts prize for music, 1973.
He is a free-lance composer.
WORKS: Opera: The proposal, 1950; The tri-
angle, 1955; Jochim Wessels, 1960-62; Ballet:
Devil's dice, 1957; Erste Liebe, 1966; Herodias,
1967; Die Folterungen der Beatrice Cenci, 1971;
Lilith, 1972; Orchestra: flute concerto, 1961;
Flashes, 1968; Temno, 1969; Nitra, 1968-70;
Amplitüden, 1973.
1 Berlin 19, Fredericiastrasse 15
West Germany

HUMPHREYS, HENRY S.
b. Vienna, Austria, 27 Nov. 1909, father was U.S.
citizen. Studied with Sudney C. Durst, Cincinnati Coll. of Music. He won first prize in the
Harvey Gaul Internat. Composition contest, 1971,
for Montserrat for oboe and strings. He was instructor, Cincinnati Coll. of Music, 1946-50;
organist and choirmaster, Church of the Advent,
1946-   ; music editor and critic, Cincinnati
papers, 1950-70; composer-in-residence, Coll. of
Mount St. Joseph, 1970-   .
WORKS: Opera: Mayerling, 3 acts, 1958;
Joan of Arc at Reims, 1 act, 1968; Ballet:

(HUMPHREYS, HENRY S.)
Prometeo de los Andes, cantata-ballet, 1970;
Orchestra: The waste land, narrator and orch.,
1957; Danubiana, 1960; and songs and arias.
5661 Delhi Road, Cincinnati, OH 54238

HUNDLEY, RICHARD
b. Cincinnati, Ohio, 1 Sep. 1931. Attended
Cincinnati Coll. Cons. and studied privately
with Israel Citkowitz and William Flanagan in
New York. He received 3 MacDowell fellowships;
ASCAP awards, 1963-72; commissions from Metro-
politan Opera Studio and from concert singers.
He is accompanist, coach, organist, choirmaster,
teacher, as well as composer.
    WORKS: Opera: Wedding finger, play by
James Purdy; Chorus: Vocal quartets to poems of
James Purdy, Portland, Me., 27 July 1971; The sea
is swimming tonight, cantata; Songs: Softly the
summer; Maiden snow; For your delight; Postcard
from Spain; The astronomers; God of the sheep,
Chicago, 28 Nov. 1965; Three Richards and Wings,
New York, 11 July 1972.
    28 Grove St., New York, NY 10014

HUNKINS, ARTHUR B.
b. New York, N. Y., 12 Apr. 1937. Studied first
with his mother, Eusebia Simpson Hunkins; later
with Karl Ahrendt, Ohio Univ.; Nadia Boulanger
in Paris; and Ross Lee Finney, Univ. of Michigan,
D. M. A. He won 3 Nat. Fed. of Music Clubs Young
Composer awards; BMI Student Composer award;
Joseph Bearns composition prize, Columbia Univ.;
and a Brown Univ. choral competition. He was
lecturer, Southern Illinois Univ., 1962-63;
assistant professor, North Texas State Univ.,
1963-65; associate professor, Univ. of North
Carolina at Greensboro, 1965-   , and director,
electronic music, 1965-   .
    WORKS: Orchestra: 5 pieces for orch.; Te
Deum, tenor, baritone, male chorus, orch.; Chamber music: Suite for violin and cello; Chorus:
Gloria; Libera nos; Ave Maria; Mass for male
voices and organ; Songs: 5 short songs of gladness; Keyboard: Ecce quam bonum, organ; Fantasy,
piano; Electronic: Pairs, 2-channel tape; 3
untitled songs of Emily Dickinson for mezzo
soprano and tape.
    2521 Cezanne Drive, Greensboro, NC 27407

HUNKINS, EUSEBIA SIMPSON
b. Troy, Ohio, 20 June 1902. Studied with James
Friskin, Rubin Goldmark, and Albert Stoessel at
Juilliard School; later studied with Darius
Milhaud, Ernest Hutcheson, Ernst von Dohnanyi;
attended classes at Aspen, Chautauqua, Tanglewood, and Salzburg. She taught at Cornell Coll.
and at Barnard School for Boys; was project director, Musical World of Ohio Broadcasts, 1972-74;
and was appointed by the Nat. Opera Asso. to com-
pile material for a series of broadcasts of American operas in 1976.
    WORKS: Opera: Smoky Mountain, 1954; Won-
drous love, choral drama, 1955; Mice in council,
1956; Reluctant hero, 1956; Spirit owl, 1956;
Maniian, 1956; Young Lincoln, 1958; Young Lincoln
II, 1960; Child of promise, choral dance opera,
1964; What have you done to my mountain?, musical

(HUNKINS, EUSEBIA SIMPSON)
play, 1973; Ballet: 4-H on parade, 1973; Chamber music: violin sonata; Wisps of smoke, flute,
mezzo soprano, piano, 1973; Dance suite for woodwind quintet, 1973; Chorus: Shall I marry, 1961;
Americana, festive chorus with orch., 1966;
Appalachian mass, 1971.
    12 North College St., Athens, OH 45701

HUNT, JERRY E.
b. Waco, Tex., 30 Nov. 1943. Attended North
Texas State Univ.; is self-taught in composition.
He has been on the faculty, Southern Methodist
Univ., 1967-   ; technical consultant, Audio-
Visual Studio Ensemble, 1967-   .
    WORKS: Electronic: Helix; Transhelix;
Sequential helix; Hakamand plane: discontinuous
mode, 1969; Hakamand plane: parallel regenera-
tive, 1969; Infrasolo; Autotransform glissando;
Sur Dr. John Dee.
    5815 Swiss Ave., Dallas TX 75214

HUNT, MICHAEL F.
b. New Castle, Ind., 28 Nov. 1945. Studied with
Robert Wykes, Paul Pisk, Robert Baker, John
Perkins at Washington Univ.; with Manus Sasonkin
and Graham Hollobon, St. Louis Inst. of Music.
He received a Nat. Defense Education Act Title
IV fellowship, 1970-73. He was assistant director, Washington Univ. Wind Ensemble, 1971-72;
instructor, Washington Univ., 1973-74; director,
instrumental music, Clayton Acad. of Music,
1973-74.
    WORKS: Orchestra: Asymptopia I and II,
1972; Chamber music: 3 Contemporary interval
studies: Melancholy, mischievous, mysterious,
piano, 1969; Unresolved dialogue for unaccompanied cello, 1973; Multi-media: The sound of
algae, 1972.
    444 South Hanley Road, St. Louis MO 63105

HUNT, THOMAS W.
b. Mammoth Spring, Ark., 28 Sep. 1929. Studied
at Juilliard School, Ouachita Baptist Univ.,
North Texas State Univ., and Memphis Coll. of
Music. He received a Gooch Found. scholarship
and a Hibberd-Pi Kappa Lambda award for musical
research. He was faculty member, Oklahoma Coll.
for Women, 1961-63; associate professor, Southwestern Baptist Theological Seminary, 1963-   ;
guest faculty, Spanish Baptist Seminary, Barcelona, 1969-70; organist, 1962-   , Rosen Heights
Baptist Church, Ft. Worth, 1972-73.
    WORKS: Gentle guide, children's anthem, 1961;
A canticle of God's love, 1973; Keyboard: Voluntary on Old Hundredth, piano or organ, 1963;
Salvationist, piano prelude, 1974.
    Box 22000, Southwestern Baptist Seminary
    Fort Worth, TX 76122

*HUNTER, RALPH
More nursery rhymes for chorus and piano.
    Department of Music, Hunter College
    New York, NY 10021

HURD, INGRAHAM
b. Niskayuna, N. Y., 16 May 1952. Studied with
Richard T. Gore, Brian Dykstra, and Ruth Still,
Coll. of Wooster, B. M. 1974.

HURD, INGRAHAM

(HURD, INGRAHAM)
WORKS: Chamber music: Vision quest (hanbleceya) for soprano and chamber orch.; Keyboard: Variants I-III, piano; suite for carillon; 3 sonatas for carillon; Idyll for Hiems for carillon; works for solo voice, chorus, organ, recorders.
Old Mill Road, Gates Mills, OH 44040

*HURST, GEORGE
Sinfonia, a 4-movement symphony.

HUSA, KAREL
b. Prague, Czech., 7 Aug. 1921; U.S. citizen 1959. Studied composition and conducting at the Prague Cons. and Prague Acad., diplomas, summa cum laude, 1946; also studied with Arthur Honneger and Nadia Boulanger in Paris, conducting with E. Bigot. His awards include French Government scholarship, 1946-51; Prague Acad. of Fine Arts prize, 1948; Lili Boulanger prize, Boston, 1950; Bilthoven Contemporary Festival award, 1951; Guggenheim fellowship, 1964; Pulitzer Prize, 1969, for his 3rd string quartet; many commissions. He has been a member of the faculty, Cornell Univ., 1954-   , professor, 1961-   , director of the Univ. Orchestra; conductor, Ithaca Chamber Orchestra, 1954-   ; guest conductor of many orchestras in Europe and the U.S.
WORKS: Orchestra: Divertimento for string orch., 1948; Concertino for piano and orch., 1949; Musique d'amateurs, 1953; Portrait for string orch., 1953; Symphony no.1, 1953; 4 little pieces for strings, 1955; Fantasies for orch., 1956; Poem for viola and chamber orch., 1959; Mosaiques, 1961; Serenade for woodwind quintet, string orch., xylophone and harp, 1963; Concerto for brass quintet and strings, 1965; Music for Prague, 1968; 2 sonnets from Michelangelo, 1972; Band: Divertimento for brass and percussion, 1959; Concerto for alto saxophone and band, 1967; Apotheosis of this Earth, 1970; Concerto for percussion and wind ensemble, 1970-71; Chamber music: 3 string quartets, 1948, 1953, 1968; Evocations of Slovakia, clarinet, viola, cello, 1951; Poem for viola and piano, 1959; Elegie et rondeau, saxophone and piano, 1961; Serenade, woodwind quintet and piano, 1963; 2 preludes, flute, clarinet, bassoon, 1966; Divertimento, brass quintet, 1968; Studies for percussion, 1968; violin sonata, New York, 31 Mar. 1974; Chorus: Festive ode for chorus and orch., 1965; Apotheosis of this Earth, New York, 14 Apr. 1973, composer conducting the Cornell Univ. chorus and orch.; Piano: sonatina, 1943; sonata, 1949; 8 Czech duets for piano 4-hands, 1955; Elegie, 1957.
Department of Music, Cornell University
Ithaca, NY 14850

*HUSTED, BENJAMIN
Fugue for strings; Snowstorm, for chorus.

*HUSTON, JOHN
Meditation on 7 last words and Psalm prelude, for organ.

HUSTON, SCOTT
b. Tacoma, Wash., 10 Oct. 1916. Studied with Howard Hanson and Bernard Rogers, Eastman School of Music, B. M. 1941, M. M. 1942, Ph. D. 1952. His awards include Danforth Found. grant; Olympiad of the Arts award; Major Armstrong FM-Radio award; BMI awards; Eastman graduate school fellowship; MacDowell Colony fellowship; many commissions. He was associate professor, Coll. Cons. of Music, Univ. of Cincinnati, 1952-67, professor, 1967-   .
WORKS: Orchestra: 4 Phantasms, symphony #3; symphony #4 for strings; Wind ensemble: Quintessences, brass quintet; Suite for our times, brass sextet; Sounds at night, brass choir; Intensity #1, wind ensemble; Chamber music: Venus and Mercury, violin sonata; Idioms, violin, clarinet, horn; A game of circles, clarinet, piano or celeste; Phenomena, baroque quartet; Life styles, piano trio; 3 cameras, solo flute; 4 scenes for 2 trumpets; Suite of 3 for harp; Suite for solo timpanist; Voice: Song of Deborah, cantata; I walked by night last moon; Keyboard: Penta-Tholoi, piano; Diorama, organ.
2626 Knight Ave., Cincinnati, OH 45212

*HUTCHESON, ERNEST
b. Melbourne, Australia, 20 July 1871; to U.S. 1900; d. New York, N. Y., 9 Feb. 1951. Studied with Carl Reinecke, Leipzig Cons., grad. 1890. He was head of piano department, Peabody Cons., 1900-12; dean, Juilliard School, 1924-37, president, 1937-   .
WORKS: Orchestra: piano concerto, 1898; Merlin and Vivien, symphonic poem, 1899; a symphony; 2-piano concerto; violin concerto.

HUTCHESON, JERE T.
b. Marietta, Ga., 16 Sep. 1938. Studied with Helen Gunderson, Louisiana State Univ.; with H. Owen Reed, Michigan State Univ., Ph. D. 1966; with Ernst Krenek and Gunther Schuller, Tanglewood. He won first and second places, Nat. Fed. of Music Clubs young composers contest, 1963; and has received annual ASCAP awards. He has been faculty member, Michigan State Univ., 1965-   , associate professor, 1973-   .
WORKS: Orchestra: Transitions; Band: Sensations, for band and audience; Passacaglia; Wind Ensemble: Designs for 14, brass and percussion; About, brass ensemble; Chamber music: Wonder music, violin and piano; Rondo brillante, clarinet, violin, piano; 3 things for Dr. Seuss, harp and percussion; Night gallery, 4 trombones; Construction set, oboe and piano; bassoon sonata; 3 pictures of Satan, trumpet and organ; Chorus: Eldorado, chorus and brass; Sabronorbas, chorus and percussion; God, 4 antiphonal choruses, tambourine, piano; Lament.
6064 Abbott Road, East Lansing, MI 48823

HUTCHESON, THOMAS
b. El Paso, Tex., 18 Aug. 1942. Studied with Richard Henderson, Univ. of Texas, El Paso; Anthony Donato, Northwestern Univ.; with John Boda and Carlisle Floyd, Florida State Univ., D. M. He has been assistant professor, Middle Tennessee State Univ., 1972-   .

(HUTCHESON, THOMAS)
WORKS: Wind ensemble: Fanfares for band; The tightrope walker march; Roller skate, jazz ensemble; Macarena, jazz ensemble; Dimensions, 12 horns; Requiem, 4 horns; Chamber music: Concertino, horn and piano; Mnemonix, string trio and alto saxophone; Coeval suite, woodwind quintet; Voice: Come, follow me; Rise, Whispering wind; 2 songs, with cello and harpsichord; Multimedia: Theme and variations, horn and 4-channel tape; Synvironment, mixed media doctoral dissertation; Cinecology, 4 slide projectors, 4 movie projectors, 4-channel electronic sound, Atlanta, Aug. 1972.
1802 Susan Drive, Murfreesboro, TN 37130

HUTCHINS, FARLEY KENNAN
b. Neenah, Wis., 12 Jan. 1921. Studied with T. Tertius Noble, Harold Friedell, Normand Lockwood, School of Sacred Music, Union Theological Seminary, New York, 1950. He was professor, Mississippi Southern Coll., 1946-50; Baldwin Wallace Cons., 1950-57; Univ. of Akron, 1957-   ; and is an active church musician, recitalist, and music journalist.
WORKS: Orchestra: Set of American folk songs; November 22, 1963; concerto for harpsichord and chamber orch.; Band: Suite; trumpet concerto; Fantasia, organ and brass choir; Chamber music: 3 songs for low voice and piano; Suite for flute and piano; Concert piece, tuba and piano; 6 Medieval songs for baritone and 4 instruments; sonata for horn and organ; Passacaglia, trumpet and organ; Chorus: 6 choruses on Biblical texts; Thou art the rock, soli, chorus, orch.; David, soli, chorus, orch.; Forest green, choir, organ, brass; piano and organ pieces; incidental music.
691 Dorchester Road, Akron, OH 44320

HUTCHINS, GUY STARR
b. Spartanburg, S. C., 12 Mar. 1905. Attended Wofford Coll., Clemson Univ., B. S. 1928; and Curtis Inst. of Music; also studied clarinet, oboe, bassoon, horn, and piano. He conducted various orchestras, 1932-48; was solo clarinetist, North Carolina Symphony, 1943; staff assistant for bands, Syracuse Univ., 1960-67; Univ. of South Carolina, 1973-   .
WORKS: Band: Florentine march, 1932; Valse caprice, 1934; The spirit of Transylvania, 1954.
102 Kirkwood Lane, Camden, SC 29020

HUTCHISON, WARNER
b. Denver, Colo., 15 Dec. 1930. Studied with George Morey, Samuel Adler, Merrill Ellis, William Latham, North Texas State Univ., M. M. 1956, Ph. D. 1971; with Wayne Barlow and Kent Kennan, Eastman School of Music; with Roy Harris, Indiana Univ. His awards include Texas Music Society prize, 1954; graduate scholarship, North Texas State Univ., 1964; Ford Found.-MENC Contemporary Music Project professor, 1967-68; nomination of hornpiece 1 for Pulitzer Prize, 1971; award from Southwest Region College Band Directors Nat. Asso., 1971; MacDowell fellowship, 1973. Faculty appointments have been Houghton Coll., 1956-58; Union Univ., 1959-66; associate

(HUTCHISON, WARNER)
professor and director, Electronic Music Laboratory, New Mexico State Univ., 1967-
WORKS: Orchestra: Prairie sketch, 1956; Prologue, 1959; Band: Dirge and hosanna, 1969; Chamber music: woodwind quintet, 1955; Chrysalis, 5 flutes, 1971; Mini-suite, brass trio, 1972; Chorus: Psalm 135, 1964; I shall have music, double choir, 1972; Keyboard: Suite no.1, Mountain climbing, piano, 1954; Hymntune suite, organ, 1968; Suite a-la-mode, piano, 1972; Electronic and mixed media: hornpiece 1, horn and tape, Lincoln Center, May 1971; The sacrilege of Alan Kent, baritone, orch., tape, 1971; Antigone, incidental music, tape, 1972; Homage to Jackson Pollock, narrator, percussion, slides, 1973; Monday music, piano and synthesizer, MacDowell Colony, June 1973.
Box 3174, University Park Branch
Las Cruces, NM 88003

*HYDE, GEORGE
Suite for 4 trombones.
5214 Palm Drive, La Canada, CA 91011

HYLA, LEON
b. Niagara Falls, N. Y., 31 Aug. 1952. Studied with Bernhard Heiden, Indiana Univ.; with Malcolm Peyton and John Heiss, New England Cons.
WORKS: Chamber music: White man on snowshoes, vol.1, for alto or tenor saxophone, flute, violin, cello, 1972-73; concerto for piano and chamber orch., Boston, 22 Apr. 1974.
3 Symphony Road, Boston, MA 02115

HYTREK, SISTER THEOPHANE
b. Stuart, Neb., 28 Feb. 1915. Studied at Alverno Coll.; Wisconsin Cons.; with Leon Stein, De Paul Univ.; with A. Irvine McHose, Wayne Barlow, Bernard Rogers, Eastman School of Music. She received awards from Nat. Asso. of Coll. Wind and Percussion Instructors, 1959; Wisconsin Fed. of Music Clubs, 1962; American Guild of Organists, Milwaukee Chapter, award 1967, commission 1969. She has been on the faculty, Alverno Coll., 1941-   , chairperson, music department, 1956-68, professor, 1968-74.
WORKS: Orchestra: The hound of heaven, tone poem, also in 2-piano version; Chamber music: violin sonata, 1962; chamber concerto; Prelude for oboe and piano, 1959; Organ: Postlude-partita on the Old One Hundredth, 1967; also masses, hymns, motets, psalms.
3401 South 39th St., Milwaukee, WI 53215

IANNACCONE, ANTHONY J.
b. Brooklyn, N. Y., 14 Oct. 1943. Studied with Vittorio Giannini and David Diamond, Manhattan School of Music; with Warren Benson and Samuel Adler, Eastman School of Music. He received the Howard Hanson award, 1970; NDEA fellowship, 1968-71; Michigan Music Teachers Asso.-Music Teachers Nat. Asso. commission, 1972. He has been assistant professor, Eastern Michigan Univ. 1971-   .
WORKS: Orchestra: Lysistrata, concert overture, 1970; 2 symphonies; Chamber music: string quartet; Anamorphoses, brass trio and

IANNACCONE, ANTHONY J.

(IANNACCONE, ANTHONY J.)
percussion; 3 mythical sketches, brass quartet; Remembrance, viola or alto saxophone; Partita, piano; Songs on immortality; Chorus: The Prince of Peace, cantata, soloists, chorus, wind ensemble; Solomon's canticle, a cappella.
1503 West Cross St., Ypsilanti, MI 48197

*ICHYANAGI, TOSHI
Extended voices, for voices with Moog synthesizer and Buchla electronic modular system.

IHRKE, WALTER R.
b. Milwaukee, Wis., 21 May 1908. Studied with Adolph Brune, Wisconsin Cons.; Healey Willan Univ. of Michigan; and Howard Hanson, Eastman School of Music. He won first place in a Coll. Band Directors Asso., Eastern Div., contest, 1952. He was faculty member, Mission House Coll., 1932-38; Stephens Coll., 1938-43; professor, George Peabody Coll., 1943-49; professor, Univ. of Connecticut, 1949-   , department head, 1949-65.
WORKS: Ballet: Pavane, 3 acts; Orchestra: violin concerto; Band: Pageantry; Ode and scherzo; Chorus: An answer of peace, cantata; That continent, cantata.
88 Storrs Height Road, Storrs, CT 06268

·*IMBRIE, ANDREW WELSH
b. New York, N. Y., 6 Apr. 1921. Studied with Roger Sessions, Princeton Univ., B. A. 1942; with Sessions, Univ. of California, Berkeley, M. A. 1947; with Nadia Boulanger; at American Acad. in Rome, 1947-49, 1953-54. His awards include the New York Music Critics' Circle award, 1944; Alice Ditson fellowship, 1946; Prix de Rome, 1947; Nat. Inst. of Arts and Letters grant, 1950; 2 Guggenheim grants, 1953, 1960; Boston Symphony Orchestra merit award, 1955; Naumberg recording award, 1960. He has been faculty member, Univ. of California, Berkeley, 1947-   , professor, 1960-   .
WORKS: Opera: 3 against Christmas, 1964; Orchestra: Ballad, 1947; 2 violin concertos, 1953, 1957; Legend, 1959; 3 symphonies; piano concerto, Music at the Vineyards, Saratoga, Calif., 4 Aug. 1973; Chamber music: 3 string quartets; piano trio, 1946; piano sonata, 1947; Divertimento for 6 instruments, 1948; Serenade, flute, viola, piano, 1952; Impromptu, violin and piano, New York, 10 Nov. 1971; Dandelion wine, 6 instruments; Chorus: On the beach at night, with string orch., 1948.
2625 Rose St., Berkeley, CA 94708

IMLAY, TIMOTHY JOHN
b. San Francisco, Calif., 15 May 1951. Studied with William Johnson in Berkeley; with Billy Jim Layton, David Lewin, Bulent Arel at State Univ. of New York, Stony Brook. He received the Kaltenborn award, 1970.
WORKS: Orchestra: Triptych, chamber orch., Oakland, 23 May 1969; Mosaics, 1970; Chamber music: Just desserts, tenor and chamber ensemble, Stony Brook, 16 Apr. 1972; Needles, harpsichord, 1972-73; 5 duos for English horn and bass clarinet, 1973-74.
250 Curry Lane, Sausalito, CA 94965

*INCH, HERBERT REYNOLDS
b. Missoula, Mont., 25 Nov. 1904. Studied at Montana State Univ.; with Howard Hanson, Eastman School of Music, B. M. 1925, M. M. 1928; B. A. 1931. He held an American Acad. in Rome fellowship, 1931; received the Ernest Bloch award; Univ. of Rochester traveling fellowship, 1934; honorary Ph. D., Montana State Univ.
WORKS: Variations on a modal theme, 1927; 3 pieces for small orch., 1930; symphony, 1932; Serenade, 1939; piano concerto, 1940; Answers to a questionnaire, 1942; Northwest overture, 1943; violin concerto, 1946; Chamber music: piano quintet, 1930; Mediterranean sketches, string quartet, 1933; Divertimento for brass, 1934; string quartet, 1936; cello sonata, 1941; 3 conversations, string quartet, 1944; Chorus: Return to Zion, women's voices, 1945.

*INGALLS, ALBERT M.
Song of peace for orch.

*ISAACS, GREGORY
The death of Tintagiles, 2-act opera, Simpson Coll., Indianola, Iowa, 4 May 1973.

ISAACSON, MICHAEL NEIL
b. Brooklyn, N. Y., 22 Apr. 1946. Studied at Hunter Coll., B. S.; with Robert Starer, Brooklyn Coll., M. A.; with Samuel Adler and Warren Benson, Eastman School of Music, Ph. D.; conducting with Ralph Hunter, Robert Hickok, Robert DeCormier. He received scholarships at Eastman School; Schubert grant for a musical theatre work. He is theory instructor and conductor, Festival Chorus, State Univ. of New York, Fredonia.
WORKS: Chamber music: Assumed identities, viola and percussion; Chorus: Meditations of my heart, Friday Evening service; Avodat Ammamit, folk service; The sound of joy, wedding service; A message from within, choral protest; In praise of our percussionist, commissioned by DeCormier Singers.
State University College, Fredonia, NY 14063

ISRAEL, BRIAN M.
b. New York, N. Y., 5 Feb. 1951. Studied with Ulysses Kay, Lehman Coll., CUNY, B. A. 1971; with Robert Palmer and Burrill Phillips, Cornell Univ., M. F. A. 1974, candidate for D. M. A. He received BMI student composer awards, 1966, 1968; Cornell fellowship, 1971-72. He has been teaching assistant, Cornell Univ., 1972-   .
WORKS: Band: Symphony #1, Cornell, Apr. 1974; Chamber music: clarinet sonata, 1969; sonata in 2 movements, cello and percussion, 1969; 6 views of the Caspian Sea, violin solo, 1971; Canonic variations, string quartet, 1971; trio for recorders, 1971; Pastoral, oboe, strings, piano, 1971; Divertimento, brass quintet, 1971; oboe sonata, 1972; woodwind quartet, 1972; piano quintet, 1973; Chorus: Madrigal on nudity, 1970; Ladies' voices, 10-minute chamber opera, 1970; Komical khoral kanons, women's voices, 1973; Keyboard: Prayer and fantasia for carillon, 1970; Night variations, piano, 1973; Electronic:

(ISRAEL, BRIAN M.)
Satires, 1971; Dance variations, trumpet and tape, 1973; and songs.
5775 Mosholu Ave., Bronx, NY 10471

ISRAEL, MCKELLAR
b. Union, S. C., 4 Apr. 1931. Studied with Donald Packard, Southern Baptist Theological Seminary; with Martin Mailman, East Carolina Univ.; with Nadia Boulanger, Fontainebleau, 1961. He was choral director, public schools, and private teacher, 1964-68; instructor, Sandhills Community Coll., 1968- ; organist-choirmaster, 1968- .
WORKS: Chorus: Hear my cry, anthem, 1955; Keyboard: Chorale preludes for organ; Passacaglia for piano, 1964.
425 Dogwood Lane, Southern Pines, NC 28387

ISRAELS, CHARLES HENRY
b. New York, N. Y., 10 Aug. 1936. Studied with Harold Shapero and Irving Fine, Brandeis Univ.; John Lewis and George Russell, Lenox School of Jazz; with Gunther Schuller and Bruno Maderno at Tanglewood; privately with Hall Overton. He held a Crofts fellowship at Tanglewood. He played bass with Bill Evans, 1961-65; then played and recorded with his own group; has been assistant professor, Brooklyn Coll., CUNY, 1973- ; director, Nat. Jazz Ensemble, 1973- .
WORKS: Jazz Ensemble: Young person's guide to the jazz orchestra; Lyric suite for flugelhorn and jazz ensemble; Extract 1; Environments; Pacemaker, brass quintet; Chamber music: Songs for soprano and string quartet.
463 West St., New York, NY 10014

IVERS, PETER
b. Chicago, Ill., 20 Sep. 1946. Attended Harvard Univ., B. A. 1968; studied with Gilbert Moses, Robert Pozar, and Buell Neidlinger. He was composer-in-residence with El Monte Art Ensemble, Los Angeles, 1971-72.
WORKS: Ballet: Air, dance by Lindsay Crouse, 1969; Brain slave, 30-minute ballet for contemporary ensemble and synthesizer, 1969; Theatre music: The Bacchae, 1968; Jesus: A passion play for Americans, 1969; Job: An American mystery, 1969; As you like it, 1971; Small ensemble: Opus animus, oboe and blues band, New York, Jan. 1970; Knight of the Blue Communion, rock and roll for oboe, bassoon, harmonica, and voice, 1969; Make me, blues textures for suffering avant-gardists, 1973; Chorus: Ash Wednesday service, chamber ensemble, girls' choir, percussion, 1970; Film scores: Desire is the fire, 1967; Devil's bargain, 1970; In pursuit of treasure, 1971; Saturday, 1971; Love song of Charles Faboman, 1972; Yesterday's shore, 1972; Frontier's end, 1973.
8591 Crescent Drive, Hollywood, CA 90046

*IVES, CHARLES EDWARD
b. Danbury, Conn., 20 Oct. 1874; d. New York, N. Y., 19 May 1954. Studied first with his father, George E. Ives, a Civil War bandmaster; then with Horatio Parker, Yale Univ., B. A. 1898. Now hailed as the pioneer of atonality and the greatest innovator of contemporary music, he

(IVES, CHARLES EDWARD)
nevertheless received his first award, the Pulitzer prize for his 3rd symphony, in 1947, more than 3 decades after its composition; the Henry Hadley medal of the Nat. Asso. for American Composers and Conductors in 1948. Recognition of his genius has continued since the awards. He was organist at 13 at the Danbury Congregational Church; organist-choirmaster in churches in New Haven, Bloomfield, N. J. and New York City, 1893-1902; entered an insurance company as a clerk in 1898 and by 1916 was senior partner of Ives & Myrick, one of the largest insurance firms of its kind in the U.S.; retired in 1930. Most of his works were written before 1916.
WORKS: Orchestra: 4 symphonies; 3 suites; Browning overture; Central Park in the dark; Holidays symphony: Washington's birthday, Decoration Day, 4th of July, Thanksgiving or Forefathers' Day; 3 places in New England; Band: Holiday quickstep, 1888; Chamber music: 4 violin sonatas; 2 string quartets; 2 piano sonatas; 11 volumes of chamber music; Chorus: The celestial country; 3 Harvest home chorales; General Booth's entrance into heaven, with brass band; many psalm settings and other choral works; some 200 songs; many piano pieces including the 3-page sonata; Some southpaw pitching; The Abolitionist riots; 3 quarter-tone piano pieces; et al.

IVEY, JEAN EICHELBERGER
b. Washington, D.C., 3 July 1923. Attended Trinity Coll., Washington, A. B. magna cum laude; Peabody Cons., M. M. in piano; Eastman School of Music, M. M. in composition; Univ. of Toronto, D. M. in composition. She has received commissions from Margaret Lauer, 1969; Collegium Musicum, Univ. of North Dakota, 1972; New York Music Teachers Asso. and Music Teachers Nat. Asso.; and a Rockefeller Fund grant, 1973; ASCAP awards, 1972, 1973. Founder and director of the electronic music studio and faculty member Peabody Cons., 1969- , she has toured as a concert pianist in Germany, Austria and the U.S., and in Mexico under the auspices of the U.S. Embassy.
WORKS: Orchestra: Overture; Dinsmoor suite, Univ. of Alabama, Apr. 1964; Ode for orch., 1965; Forms in motion, symphony in 3 movements, 1972; Tribute: Martin Luther King, baritone and orch., 1969, Baltimore, 3 Mar. 1973; Chamber music: piano sonata, 1958; suite for cello and piano, 1960; sonatina, clarinet solo; Ode, violin and piano; Song of Pan, flute and piano; 6 Inventions for 2 violins, 1964; Electronic: Montage IV, film score, 1962; The exception and the rule, film score; Enter 3 witches, 1964; Pinball, 1965; Cortege for Charles Kent, 1969; Mixed media: Terminus, mezzo soprano and tape, Baltimore, 21 Feb. 1971; 3 songs of night, soprano, 5 instruments, tape, 1971; Aldebaran, viola and tape, New York, 12 Jan. 1973; Hera, Hung from the sky, mezzo soprano, winds, percussion, piano, tape, Univ. of North Dakota, 12 Apr. 1973; Skaniadaryo piano and tape, 1973.
83-33 Austin St., Kew Gardens, NY 11415

JABLONSKY, STEPHEN

JABLONSKY, STEPHEN
b. New York, N. Y., 5 Dec. 1941. Studied with Mark Brunswick and Paul Turok, City Coll. of New York; with Pierre Boulez and Leon Kirchner, Harvard Univ. He was lecturer, City Coll. of New York, 1968-74.

WORKS: Orchestra: Passacaglia; Band: Minimarch; Chamber music: Gestures for string quartet; 3 pieces for clarinet; Jabberwocky, soprano and septet; Ancient lyric tune, for bassoon and wind sextet; Mechanisms, wind trio; Chorus: Sim shalom, baritone, chorus, organ.

740 West End Ave., New York, NY 10025

JACKSON, DAVID L.
b. Abilene, Tex., 29 Dec. 1944. Studied with John Nagosky, Univ. of South Florida, M. M. 1968; trumpet with John Haynie, North Texas State Univ. He played first trumpet with the St. Petersburg Symphony, 1967-68; 3rd trumpet, Tampa Philharmonic, 1967-68; instructor, Cameron State Coll., 1971-73.

WORKS: Chamber music: Chamber suite, flute, clarinet, 2 violins, cello, percussion; 3 Appalachian folk songs, brass quintet.

P.O. Box 72, Denton, TX 76201

JACKSON, DUKE W., JR.
b. Clearwater, Fla., 15 Aug. 1946. Studied with John Boda, Carlisle Floyd, Harold Schiffman at Florida State Univ. He was assistant professor, Georgia Southwestern Coll., 1970-73.

WORKS: Orchestra: Concerto for 2 pianos and harpsichord and chamber orch.; Chamber music: 3 movements for 2 pianos; 5 Serious songs from the Chinese, soprano and piano; Theme and variations, harpsichord, flute, and cello.

104F Country Club Apts., Americus, GA 31709

JACKSON, HANLEY
b. Bryan, Tex., 7 June 1939. Studied with Aurelio de la Vega and Ronald Stein, California State Univ., Northridge; with Gerald Strang, California State Univ., Long Beach. He received the Cecilia Buck award, 1964; Nat. Fed. of Music Clubs award, 1965; Southwest Music Festival award, 1967; Esther Tow Newman award, 1969. He was instructor, California State Univ., Long Beach, 1967-68; assistant professor, Kansas State Univ., 1968-   .

WORKS: Orchestra: Cassandra's dance; Tangents II, orch. and tape; Band: Tangents III, with tape; Chamber music: Tangents IV, piano and tape; string quartet, 1964; Chorus: A child's ghetto, chorus and tape; Requiem, soloists, chorus, orch.; Maat, cantata for chorus and percussion ensemble.

Department of Music, Kansas State University
Manhattan, KS 66506

*JACKSON, MILTON
b. Detroit, Mich., 1932. Was co-founder with John Lewis of the Modern Jazz Quartet, 1952; plays piano, guitar and vibraharp and sings.

WORKS: Concert jazz: Ralph's new blues; Jazz theme with improvisations, for vibraharp.

*JACOBI, FREDERICK
b. San Francisco, Calif., 4 May 1891; d. New York, 24 Oct. 1952. Studied composition with Rubin Goldmark and Ernest Bloch in New York; with Paul Juon in Berlin. He received the David Bispham medal, 1944; 2 awards, Society for Publication of American Music; was director, Internat. Society for Contemporary Music. He was assistant conductor, Metropolitan Opera, 1913-17; saxophonist in army bands, 1917-18; taught at the Master School of United Arts, New York, 1927; Juilliard School, 1936-50; lecturer at Univ. of California, Mills Coll., Julius Hart Memorial Found.

WORKS: Opera: The prodigal son, 1944; Orchestra: The pied piper, 1915; California suite, 1917; The eve of St. Agnes, 1919; 2 symphonies, 1922, 1948; Indian dances, 1928; cello concerto, 1932; 3 psalms, cello and orch., 1933; piano concerto, 1936; violin concerto, 1939; Night piece, flute and orch., 1942; Ode for orchestra, 1942; concertino, piano and strings, 1946; 2 pieces in Sabbath mood, 1946; Chamber music: Nocturne, string quartet, 1918; 3 preludes, violin and piano, 1921; 3 string quartets, 1924, 1933, 1945; Scherzo, woodwind quintet, 1936; Hagiographa, 3 Biblical narratives for string quartet and piano, 1938; Fantasy, viola and piano, 1941; Ballade, violin and piano, 1942; Meditation, trombone and piano, 1947; also choral works, piano pieces.

JACOBY, HUGH WILLIAM
b. Coalinga, Calif., 25 Jan. 1935. Attended California State Univ., Los Angeles, B. A.; California State Univ., Chico, M. A.; Washington Univ., D. M. E.; principal teachers were Ingolf Dahl, Wesley LaViolette, Louis Palange. He taught in public schools in Temple City and Paradise, Calif., 1956-68; was acting head of music department, Shasta Coll., 1968-69; director of bands, Laboratory Schools, Illinois State Univ., 1969-72; director of bands, Washington Univ., 1972-73.

WORKS: Jazz band: Be my valentine, with voice, 1958; Sunrise to sunset, 1959; What to do, 1959; What ya gonna do?, with voice, 1959; A lover like thee, 1960; The freeway, 1960; Outside looking in, 1961; 7 days till spring, with voice, 1961; Special no.1, 1969; Jazz suite no.2, 1970.

Department of Music, Washington University
St. Louis, MO 63130

*JAFFE, GERARD G.
b. Germany, 22 Jan. 1925. Studied with William Bergsma and Vincent Persichetti, Juilliard School, B. S. 1948, M. S. 1949. He was on the staff, Wesleyan Univ., 1953-66; Incarnate Word Coll., 1974-   . His published works include Centone buffo concertante, trombone and piano; Short suite for strings.

Incarnate Word College
San Antonio, TX 78209

JAGER, ROBERT
b. Binghamton, N. Y., 25 Aug. 1939. Attended Wheaton Coll., Ill., and Univ. of Michigan; is

(JAGER, ROBERT)
self-taught in composition. His awards include
Ostwald award, American Bandmasters Asso., 1964,
1968, 1972; Roth award, Nat. School Orch. Asso.,
1964, 1966; ASCAP awards, 1967-   ; Distinguished Service to Music Medal, Kappa Kappa Psi,
1973; Tennessee Composer of Year, 1973. He was
assistant professor, Old Dominion Univ., 1968-71;
associate professor and composer-in-residence,
Tennessee Technological Univ., 1971-   .
    WORKS: Orchestra: Concerto for jazz band
and orch.; The war prayer; Band: Symphony;
Diamond variations; Quincunx; 3rd suite; Variations on a theme of Robert Schumann; Chorale and
toccata; A child's garden of verses, soprano and
wind ensemble; Sinfonietta; Suite from Edvard
Munch.
    Music Department, Tennessee Tech University
Cookeville, TN 38501

JAKUBENAS, VLADAS
    b. Birzai, Lith., 15 May 1904; U.S. citizen 1956.
Studied with Joseph Wihtols in Riga and with
Franz Schreker in Berlin; was granted the "free
artist" degree in composition in Riga. He won
second prize for a piano piece, Chicago Chapter,
Internat. Society for Contemporary Music, 1962.
He was associate professor, Nat. Cons. in Kaunas,
1932-44; private teacher, vocal coach, organist,
and conductor in Chicago, 1952-70; music critic,
Lithuanian daily newspaper, 1949-   .
    WORKS: Orchestra: Forest festival suite,
1954; Intermezzo rustico, string orch.; Chorus:
Mano pasaulis (My world), chorus, soloists, orch.,
New York, 1959; De profundis, chorus and orch.;
Piano: From the fairyland; Legend; many other
piano pieces and songs.
    6506 South Artesian Ave.
Chicago, IL 60629

JAMBOR, AGI
    b. Budapest, Hungary, 4 Feb. 1909; U.S. citizen
1954. Studied composition with Zoltan Kokaly
and Leo Weiner, Budapest Royal Cons. She won
the Brahaus prize, Berlin, 1928, and the Philharmonic Orch. prize, Internat. Chopin competition, Warsaw, 1937, both for piano performance.
She has been professor, Bryn Mawr Coll.,
1958-   .
    WORKS: Piano: sonata; preludes; Psalmus
humanus, piano accompaniment to words of Albert
Szent-Gyorgyi.
    103 Pine Tree Rd., Radnor, PA 19087

JAMES, DOROTHY
    b. Chicago, Ill., 1 Dec. 1901. Studied with
Adolf Weidig, American Cons., M. M.: Howard
Hanson, Eastman School of Music; Ernst Krenek,
Univ. of Michigan; and with Healey Willan in
Toronto. Her awards include 3 first prizes, Mu
Phi Epsilon contests; first prize, Choral Clinic,
Milliken Univ.; Michigan Composers Club contest;
Adolf Weidig Gold Medal; 4 MacDowell fellowships;
honorary doctorate, Eastern Michigan Univ., 1971.
She taught at Eastern Michigan Univ., 1927-68,
and is now professor emeritus.
    WORKS: Opera: Paolo and Francesca; Orches-
tra: Symphonic fragments, Rochester, 24 Mar.

(JAMES, DOROTHY)
1932; Elegy for the lately dead; Suite for
chamber orch.; Chamber music: Recitative and
aria, viola, 2 violins, 2 cellos, 1943; Chorus:
Paul Bunyan, chorus and orch., 1938; Niobe,
1941; The jumblies, chorus and orch.; The
golden year, with orch.; Mutability, women's
voices, clarinet, flute, piano; Songs: 4
lacquer prints, soprano; Organ: Dedication;
numerous choral works, organ and piano pieces,
songs, chamber music. Many of her works were
commissioned and several were performed on WNYC
broadcasts of Festivals of American Music.
    516 Fairview Circle, Ypsilanti, MI 48197

*JAMES, PHILIP
    b. Jersey City, N. J., 17 May 1890. Studied with
Rubin Goldmark and Rosario Scalero in New York.
His many awards include the Homiletic Review
prize for a hymn, 1927; NBC $5000 first prize
for the orchestral suite, WGZBX; $500 first prize
prize, Women's Symphony Orchestra, New York,
1938; election to Nat. Inst. of Arts and Letters,
1933; New York Philharmonic award; Juilliard
publication award. He was bandmaster, AEF
General Headquarters Band in World War I; conductor, Winthrop Ames Theatrical Productions,
1915-16; Victor Herbert Opera Company, 1919-22;
New Jersey Symphony Orchestra, 1922-29; Brooklyn
Orchestral Society, 1927-30; Bamberger Little
Symphony (WOR), 1929-36; guest conductor, New
York Philharmonic and Philadelphia Orchestra;
taught at New York Univ., 1922-33, was chairman,
music department, 1933-55.
    WORKS: Theatre: Judith, ballet, 1927; music
for Arms for Venus, 1937; Orchestra: 3 Bret
Harte overtures, 1926, 1933, 1935; Sea symphony,
1928; Song of the night, 1931; 2 suites for
strings, 1933, 1946; Gwalia, Welsh rhapsody,
1939; 2 symphonies, 1943, 1949; Chaumont, symphonic poem, 1948; Chamber music: string quartet, 1924; suite for woodwind quintet, 1934;
piano quartet, 1938; Chorus: Stabat mater
speciosa, with orch., 1921, revised 1930;
General William Booth enters into heaven, tenor
male chorus and orch., 1932; many other choral
works; organ pieces.

*JAMES, THOMAS
    Slow movement for strings and wind quintet.
    506 West 113th St., Apt. 4A
    New York, NY 10025

JAMES, WOODROW
    b. Biloxi, Miss., 3 Jan. 1936. Studied with
Arthur Kreutz, Univ. of Mississippi; Helen
Gunderson, Louisiana State Univ.; with H. Owen
Reed and Paul Harder, Michigan State Univ., Ph.
D. 1966. He received cash awards, Louisiana
Fed. of Music Clubs contests, 1961, 1967, 1968.
He was assistant professor, Florence State Coll.,
1964-65; McNeese State Coll., 1965-68; Univ. of
Oklahoma, 1968-71; California State Univ.,
Northridge, 1972-73; California State Polytech-
nic Univ., Pomona, 1973-   .
    WORKS: Orchestra: 2 symphonic movements;
Band: Elegy for trumpet and band; Jazz en-
semble: Crawfish; Chamber music: brass quartet;

JAMES, WOODROW

(JAMES, WOODROW)
Scherzo, trumpet, trombone, piano; 3 songs on
poems of Dylan Thomas, soprano and piano.
    1620 Amar Rd., Apt. E
    West Covina, CA 91791

JANNERY, ARTHUR A.
    b. Millbury, Mass., 24 Mar. 1932. Studied with
Hugo Norden, Gardner Read, Malloy Miller, Robert
Wykes, Ulysses Kay, Boston Univ., B. M., M. M.;
with Paul Pisk, Washington Univ. He received a
scholarship at Washington Univ.; awards from
Fairfax Symphony, 1971; Internat. Delius Competition, 1971; Nat. School Orch. Asso., Roth
competition, 1972; and commissions. He was instructor, Salem Coll., W. Va., 1967-69; assistant
professor, Radford Coll., 1969-   .
    WORKS: Orchestra: Sinfonietta, chamber
orch.; Sharon, an overture, 1971; Wind ensemble:
Appalachian structures, brass and percussion ensemble, 1971; Libera me, Domine, brass quintet;
4 movements for 4 trumpets, 1973; Chamber music:
Big balloons, soprano, piano, harpsichord, 2
flutes, 1971; Chorus: Crucifixus--Resurrexit,
women's voices and brass, 1971.
    1010 Sutton St., Radford, VA 24141

*JANSSEN, WERNER
    b. New York, N. Y., 1 June 1899. Studied with
Frederick Converse in Boston; graduated from
Dartmouth Coll. His awards include the Prix de
Rome for study at the American Acad. in Rome,
1930; honorary Ph. D., Dartmouth Coll.; Finnish
Order of the White Rose, First Class, 1954. He
began to compose operettas and special musical
numbers for Broadway shows in the 1920s; conducted symphony orchestras in Europe; made U.S.
debut as conductor with the New York Philharmonic
in 1934; conducted Baltimore Symphony Orchestra,
1937-39; organized Janssen Symphony in Los
Angeles, 1940; conducted orchestras throughout
the U.S.
    WORKS: Orchestra: New Year's Eve in New
York, symphonic poem, 1929; Louisiana suite, 1930;
Foster suite, 1937; Chamber music: Obsequies of
a saxophone, 6 wind instruments and snare drum,
1929; 2 string quartets; Kaleidoscope for string
quartet; also film and television scores.

*JARECKI, TADEUSZ
    b. Lwow, Poland, 31 Dec. 1888; to U.S. 1913; d.
New York, N. Y., 29 Apr. 1955. Studied with
Sergei Taneyev, Moscow Cons., graduating in 1913.
He received the Elizabeth Sprague Coolidge prize
in 1918 for a string quartet. He conducted in
Europe, 1932-48; then returned to New York.
    WORKS: Orchestra: Chimère, symphonic poem,
1926; La foule, suite, 1928; Sinfonia breve, 1932;
Chamber music: 3 string quartets; songs.

JARRETT, JACK MARIUS
    b. Asheville, N. C., 17 Mar. 1934. Studied at
Univ. of Florida; with Bernard Rogers, Eastman
School of Music; Boris Blacher in Berlin; with
Bernard Heiden, Indiana Univ., D. M. He received
the Edward Benjamin award, 1957; Fulbright grant,
1961; Ford Found. composer-in-residence award
(Oshkosh public schools), 1965-67. He was

(JARRETT, JACK MARIUS)
instructor, Dickinson Coll., 1958-61; choral
conductor, Univ. of Richmond, 1962-64; assistant
professor, Univ. of North Carolina, and visiting
professor, North Carolina School of the Arts,
1972-   .
    WORKS: Opera: Cyrano de Bergerac, Greens-
boro, N. C., 1972; Orchestra: Serenade for
string orch., 1957; Choral symphony on American
poems, chorus and orch. or band; Band: Holiday
for horns, 4 horns and band; numerous short
choral works.
    University of North Carolina
    Greensboro, NC 27412

JARRETT, KEITH
    b. Allentown, Pa. 8 May 1945. Studied with
Eleanor Sokoloff, Curtin Inst.; at Berklee Coll.
of Music. He received a Guggenheim fellowship,
1972.
    WORKS: Chamber music: Metamorphosis, flute
solo and strings; In the cave - In the light,
strings, percussion, piano; Crystal moment;
Fughata for harpsichord; string quartet; brass
quintet; A pagan hymn, piano; Jazz ensemble:
Lalene; Expectations; The mourning of a star;
Fort Yawuh; Still life, still life; Treasure Island; My lady, my child; Ritooria.
    P. O. Box 85, Oxford, NJ 07863

JEFFERS, RONALD H.
    b. Springfield, Ill., 25 Mar. 1943. Studied with
George Wilson, Ross Lee Finney, Leslie Bassett,
Univ. of Michigan, B. M. 1966, M. A. 1968; with
Roger Reynolds, Pauline Oliveros, Robert Erickson,
Univ. of California, San Diego. He received an
award, Ohio State Univ. choral competition;
commission, Huntington, N. Y., High School. His
faculty posts include Occidental Coll., 1969-70;
Univ. of California, San Diego, 1970-72; Univ.
of Wisconsin, Eau Claire, 1972-73; State Univ.
of New York, Stony Brook, 1973-74; Oregon State
Univ., 1974-   .
    WORKS: Wind ensemble: In memoriam, 7 trum-
pets, 4 oboes, 2 flutes, piano, percussion, 1973;
Chorus: Dawn, double chorus, 1965; Mass confu-
sion, men's voices, 1966; In time of war, with
instruments, 1967; Now conscience wakes, with
soloists, handbells, orch., 1968; Missa concrete,
triple chorus, 1969, rev. 1973; Tota pulcra es,
4 voices, cello, clarinet, 2 narrators, 1974;
Songs: Prayer of St. Francis, a cappella, 1964;
Multimedia: Time passes, female vocalist, 4-
channel tape, gongs, bells, dancer, 1974.
    234 Northwest 30th, Corvallis, OR 97330

JEFFERSON, MICHAEL GRAHAM
    b. Philadelphia, Pa., 18 Apr. 1927. Attended
Temple Univ., A. B. 1952; studied with Joseph
Castaldo, Philadelphia Musical Acad.; Romeo
Cascarino, Combs Coll. of Music.; with Matthew
Colucci, New School of Music, Philadelphia. He
received an award from Community Children's
Theatre, Kansas City. He has been pianist,
arranger, orchestrator, 1956-   ; conductor for
Judimar School and John Hines Dance Co.; lecturer,
Philadelphia public schools, 1969-71; music di-
rector, Youth Workshop, Germantown Presbyterian

(JEFFERSON, MICHAEL GRAHAM)
Church, 1970-   ; wrote articles for Black History Journal, 1973.
WORKS: Ballet scores for piano, cello, clarinet, flute; Circus, 1959; Cinderella, 1960; The black doll, 1961; Theatre: music for Servant of two masters, 1965; Pecos Bill, children's musical, 1968; Treasure Island, musical, 1968; Chorus: De profundis, with organ, 1972.
8626 Temple Rd., Philadelphia, PA 19150

*JENKINS, EDWARD WALKER
b. Worcester, Mass. Studied with Frederick Converse and George W. Chadwick, New England Cons., graduated in 1926; with Nadia Boulanger in France, 1929; received 4 Endicott prizes in composition, 1925-29. He taught at the Perkins Inst. for the Blind, 1933; then at the New England Cons.
WORKS: Chamber music: 2 violin sonatas; Winter idyll and Summer idyll, strings and piano; woodwind trio; songs.

JENKINS, JOSEPH WILLCOX
b. Philadelphia, Pa., 15 Feb., 1928. Studied with Vincent Persichetti, Philadelphia Cons.; with Thomas Canning, Bernard Rogers, Howard Hanson, Eastman School of Music, B. M., M. M.: with Ralph Vaughan Williams in England. He received ASCAP awards, 1965-73; Otswald award, American Bandmasters Asso., 1961; Ford Found. grant for composer-in-residence, Evanston, Ill., schools, 1960-61. He was affiliated with the U.S. Army Band and Chorus, 1951-53, 1956-59; editor, music publishing firm, 1961-62; on faculty, Duquesne Univ., 1962-   .
WORKS: Orchestra: 2 symphonies; Sinfonia de la frontera, commissioned for New Mexico bicentennial celebration; Band: American overture; Charles County; Cuernavaca; Cumberland Gap; 2 sinfonias; Chamber music: string quartet; many secular and religious choral works.
412 South Linden Ave., Pittsburgh, PA 15208

JENKS, ALDEN FERRISS
b. Harbor Beach, Mich., 10 Aug. 1940. Attended Yale Univ., B. A. 1962; Univ. of California, Berkeley, M. A. 1968; studied with Karlheinz Stockhausen, Univ. of California, Davis, 1966-67; with David Tudor, Mills Coll., 1968; and with Ben Weber in New York, Darius Milhaud at Aspen. He was an officer of Composers' Forum, 1964-67; co-director and founder of Deus ex Machina, a live-electronic performance, 1968-70; director of electronic music, San Francisco Cons., 1973-   .
WORKS: Orchestra: Expedition, 1964; Chamber music: Quasar, brass and percussion, 1966; Almost untitled, chamber orch., 1968; Chorus: The exterminator, double chorus, speaking, shouting, laughing, singing, etc., 1968; Electronic tape: Chez elle, 1968; At its, 1968; Lapis, 1968; Namo, 1971; Space, 1972; Bardo I and II, 1971-72; Seeing in the dark, with or without male actor-singer, 1972; Multi-media: Q.E.D., amplified autoharp, amplified spoken material, metal wastebasket, "concrete" poem shown through a slide projector, 1969 (Full description of this and the following items are available upon request to

(JENKS, ALDEN FERRISS)
the composer.); Emissions, 1969; Overtone, 1969; Temporary music I and II, 1970; KPFA 2/9/70; The magic pillow show, 1970; Videom, 1971; Videom II, 1973; also music for plays and experimental films.
1201 Ortega St., San Francisco, CA 94122

*JENNI, DONALD
Cucumber music, chamber ensemble, 1969.
Center for New Music, University of Iowa
Iowa City, IA 52240

JENSEN, ERIC CHRISTIAN
b. Fargo, N. D., 14 Apr. 1943. Studied with Richmond Browne and Yehudi Wyner, Yale Univ.; with Richard Hervig, Univ. of Iowa, M. M. He was associate in performance, Center for New Music, Univ. of Iowa, 1967-70; assistant professor, Grinnell Coll., 1970-   .
WORKS: Theatre: Music for King Lear; Mixed media: Ikons, for oscilloscopes and recorded electronic sounds; Avidya, cello, electronics, 4-channel tape; Sound textures, for 4 improvising performers and tape.
Department of Music, Grinnell College
Grinnell, IA 50112

JENSEN, JAMES A.
b. Dayton, Ohio, 29 Dec. 1944. Studied with Donald Key and Markwood Holmes, Kansas State Coll.; John Boda and Carlisle Flyod, Florida State Univ. He was conductor, Birmingham Youth Symphony Orch., 1969; instructor, Samford Univ., 1968-   .
WORKS: Orchestra: symphony, 1968; Orpheus variations, chamber orch., 1970; Chamber music: 3 pieces for solo clarinet, 1968; 3 movements for brass quartet, 1969; viola sonata, 1972; woodwind quintet, 1972; Voice: 5 songs for tenor and piano, 1968; In memorium: Dr. Martin Luther King, Jr. for soprano and 7 instruments, 1969; 4 songs for soprano and piano, 1971; Primogenitur, cycle for soprano and chamber orch., 1973.
2515 15th Avenue South
Birmingham, AL 35205

*JEPSON, HARRY BENJAMIN
b. New Haven, Conn., 16 Aug. 1870; d. Noank, Conn., 23 Aug., 1952. Studied with Horatio Parker at Yale Univ.; joined the Yale faculty in 1899, was professor and organist, 1906-50. He published works for organ and voice.

JEPSON, WARNER
b. Sioux City, Iowa, 24 Mar. 1930. Studied with Robert Erickson, Oberlin Cons., B. M. He was dance accompanist for several groups in San Francisco, 1953-63; faculty member, San Francisco Cons., 1965-68; composer-in-residence, Nat. Center for Experiments in Television, 1972-   .
WORKS: Dance: The branch, 1961; Totentanz, electronic and concrete tape, 1967; The awakening, electronic tape, 1968; Peace, flute and tape, 1970; NRA, collage of dance music and radio from 1930-40, 1972; Theatre music: Rites of women, songs and tape, 1960; San Francisco's burning, ballad opera with 60 songs, 1962;

JEPSON, WARNER

(JEPSON, WARNER)
Brouhaha, review, 1963; Saddle the unicorn, play
with songs, 1964; The devil's disciple, 1969;
Alice in Wonderland, 1969; The world we live in,
1969; Blood knot, 1970; The relapse, 1971; Chamber music: Excursion, woodwind trio, 1965; Rough
ground, brass, piano, percussion, 1966; Joy journey, tape, 1967; Accumulation, 4 tympany, 8 tom-
toms, 1967; Peace, flute and tape, 1969;
Film scores: The bed, 1968; Ascent, KQED documentary, 1970; Luminous procuress, 1971; electronic music for many museum and gallery shows
and for videotapes at KQED: Vidio synthesis,
Irving Bridge, Light forms, Floating man, all
1972; Environments: Dome 2, audio-visual-sensual
environment installed in Art and Garden Center,
Berkeley, 1973.
512 Diamond St., San Francisco, CA 94114

*JERGENSON, DALE
The vision, for mixed chorus of speaking voices
and 7 soloists.
15035 Wyandotte, Van Nuys, CA 91408

JESSYE, EVA
b. Coffeyville, Kan., 20 Jan. 1895. Attended
Western Coll., Kan.; Wilberforce Univ., M. A.:
Allen Univ., D. M.: studied with Percy
Goetschius in New York, and with Will Marion
Cook. She received awards from the U.S. Treasury;
Nat. Negro Musicians; St. Louis Trailblazers;
Council of Negro Women Musicians Arts Committee;
Detroit Freedom Citat.; Martin Luther King Found.;
Centennial Medal Afro-Methodist Episcopal Church;
and the City of Ann Arbor, Mich., made 19 Jan.
1974 Eva Jessye Day in recognition of the Afro-
American Music Collection she gave to the Univ.
of Michigan. In 1926 she organized the Eva
Jessye Choir and conducted it in concerts throughout the U.S., Europe, and the Middle East; was
musical director for MGM film Hallelujah, 1929;
conducted the choir for Virgil Thomsno's Four
Saints in three acts, 1934; was choral director
for all Broadway performances and European tours
of Porgy and Bess, 1935-58; appeared in many
films, was television writer, director; American
consultant, BBC, London; head, music department,
Morgan State Coll.; composer-in-residence, Maryland State Coll.
WORKS: Theatre: Chronicle of Job, drama
with music, 1955; Chorus: My spirituals (16),
1926; Paradise lost and regained, oratorio,
Milton text, 2 narrators, chorus, organ (1936),
Washington, 11 July 1972.
Miller Manor, Ann Arbor, MI 48103

*JIRAK, KAREL BOLESLAV
b. Prague, Czech., 28 Jan., 1891; to U.S. 1947;
d. Chicago, Ill., 30 Jan. 1972. Was a conductor
in Germany and Czechoslovakia; professor, Prague
Cons., 1920-30; music director, Czechoslovak
Radio, 1930-45; from 1948, professor, Roosevelt
Coll., Chicago. His many compositions include
an opera; 5 symphonies; 7 string quartets, #7
performed in Chicago, 17 Jan. 1961; woodwind trio,
1956; sonatas for many instruments; 8 song cycles
with orch.

JOCHSBERGER, TZIPORA H.
b. Germany, 27 Dec. 1920; U.S. citizen 1956.
Studied at Acad. of Music, Jerusalem, Israel;
and with Hugo Weisgall at Jewish Theological
Seminary of America, D. S. M. She was a director,
Rubin Acad., Jerusalem, 1947-50; founder and
director, Hebrew Arts School for Music and Dance,
1952- ; assistant professor, Seminary Coll.
of Jewish Music, 1960- .
WORKS: Chamber music: Melodies of Israel,
duets and trios for recorders and other melody
instruments; 5 duets for 2 oboes; Holiday suite,
flute and clarinet; Chorus: Bekol Zimrah, collection of Jewish choral music; 4 madrigals to
Hebrew poems of Radel; From the beginning, choir
and orch.; Psalms for young people; Songs: 4
songs for voice and piano; 2 songs for voice,
violin and flute; Piano: Contrasts; Melodies of
my people.
5 West 86th St., New York, NY 10024

*JOHANNESEN, GRANT
b. Salt Lake City, Utah, 30 July 1921. Studied
piano with Robert Casadesus at Princeton Univ.,
1941-46; with Egon Petri at Cornell Univ. He
launched his long career as concert pianist in
New York in 1944; was appointed consultant and
advisor, Cleveland Inst. of Music, 1973-74,
director, 1975- . He has published Improvisation on a Mormon hymn for piano.

*JOHANSEN, GUNNAR
b. Copenhagen, Denmark, 21 Jan. 1907; to U.S.
1929. Studied with Egon Petri and others in
Berlin; toured Europe as concert pianist,
1924-29; spent first years in the U.S. in California until appointed artist-in-residence and
professor at Univ. of Wisconsin, 1939- .
WORKS: Orchestra: 2 piano concertos, 1930,
1970; Piano: 31 sonatas, 1941-51; and 246 improvised sonatas recorded on tape, 1952-70.
Department of Music, University of Wisconsin
Madison, WI 53706

JOHNS, DONALD
b. Chicago, Ill., 9 June 1926. Studied with
Frank B. Cookson and Wallingford Riegger, Northwestern Univ., B. M. 1951, M. M. 1952, Ph. D.
1960; with Karl Schiske, Vienna Acad. of Music,
diploma in composition 1956. He held a Fulbright
scholarship, 1952-54; was associate, Creative
Arts Inst., Univ. of California, 1966-67. He
has been professor, Univ. of California, Riverside, 1957- .
WORKS: Chamber music: Concerto piccolo for
flute, clarinet, strings and tympani, Chorus:
Magnificat, soprano, chorus, organ; Organ: Organ
mass; Partita on a passion chorale; 3 chorale
preludes; 3 meditations; Triptych on Aberystwyth.
270 Goins Court, Riverside, CA 92507

*JOHNS, LOUIS EDGAR
b. 1886. Medieval suite for strings.

*JOHNSON, ALFRED
Midwinter carol, chorus.

JOHNSON, CHRISTOPHER. See YAVELOW, CHRISTOPHER
JOHNSON

220

JOHNSON, CLYDE E.
b. Fennimore, Wis., 16 Feb. 1930. Studied with
Philip Bezanson, Univ. of Iowa, M. A., Ph. D.
He received a Fulbright grant, 1957; and 2 commissions. He has been professor, Univ. of Minnesota, Morris, 1961- .
    WORKS: Band: Intermezzo, 1963; Etudes, 1967;
Chamber music: 2 clarinet sonatas, 1956, c1961;
Toccata for piano, 1957; Iowa flowering, song
cycle for contralto and piano, 1960.
    408 West 5th St., Morris, MN 56267

JOHNSON, DAVID N.
b. San Antonio, Tex., 28 June 1922. Studied with
Rosario Scalero, Curtis Inst. of Music; with
Ernst Bacon, Syracuse Univ. He was chairman,
music department, St. Olaf Coll., 1965-67; professor, Syracuse Univ., 1967-69; professor,
Arizona State Univ., 1969- ; organist and
music director, Trinity Cathedral, Phoenix,
1970- .
    WORKS: Chorus: Joseph, cantata; Gloria Deo,
Books I and II; Organ: Beautiful saviour; Deck
thyself, my soul, with gladness; Fugue a la gigue;
Of the Father's love begotten; 3 trumpet tunes;
4 organ books; organ method books and many works
for organ; Multi-media: Light.
    5105 South La Rosa Dr., Tempe, AZ 85282

JOHNSON, GORDON A.
b. Wautoma, Wis., 10 Aug. 1924. Studied at Milwaukee State Teachers Coll., B. S., 1948; Eastman School of Music, M. M. 1954; with H. Owen
Reed, Michigan State Univ., Ph. D. 1963. He
taught at East Carolina Univ., 1959-63; and Univ.
of South Florida, 1963- .
    WORKS: Chorus: 3 Japanese songs, 1970;
Power to rise, 1971; many choral works and art
songs.
    11325 Carrollwood Dr., Tampa, FL 33618

JOHNSON, HALL
b. Athens, Ga., 12 Mar. 1888; d. New York, N. Y.,
30 Apr. 1970. Studied at Univ. of Atlanta and
Univ. of Southern California; with Percy
Goetschius in New York. His awards included an
honorary D. M., Philadelphia Musical Acad.; citation by the City of New York. He formed the Hall
Johnson Choir in 1925, performed on radio and in
concert; Negro Chorus of Los Angeles in 1936;
toured Germany and Austria in 1951 under auspices
of the State Department.
    WORKS: Theatre: Fi-yer, operetta; Run little
chillun, play with music; Chorus: Ride on King
Jesus; The crucifixion; Son of man, cantata.

JOHNSON, HAROLD VICTOR
b. Omaha, Neb., 16 May 1918. Attended Univ. of
California, Los Angeles; studied with Wesley La
Violette, Fritz Zweig, Eric Zeisl, Arthur Lange.
He has been faculty member, American Operatic
Laboratory; Jarman Cons.; Southern California
Cons.; member of music department, MCA-TV.
    WORKS: Opera: Judas, 4 acts; Orchestra:
3 symphonies; Chamber music: 4 string quartets;
Chorus: 2 oratorios; Requiem mass; many songs.
    305 North Oakland Dr.
    Beverly Hills, CA 90210

*JOHNSON, HARRIETT
    Pet of the Met, opera.

*JOHNSON, HENRY
    The mountain, 2-act folk opera, Univ. of Arizona,
Tucson, 12 Dec. 1967.

*JOHNSON, HORACE
b. Waltham, Mass., 5 Oct. 1893; d. Tucson, Ariz.,
30 May 1964. Studied with John Patton Marshall
and Bainbridge Crist in Boston; at Tufts Coll.;
and in Italy, Germany and France. He was managing editor of the Musical Courier; head of Fed.
WPA Music Project, 1939.
    WORKS: Orchestra: Imagery, 1925; Astarte,
1935; Streets of Florence, 1936; In the American
manner; and songs.

JOHNSON, HUNTER
b. Benson, N. C., 14 Apr. 1906. Attended Univ.
of North Carolina; studied with Bernard Rogers,
Eastman School of Music, B. M. 1929; also studied
with Alfredo Casella. He received the Rome Prize,
1933; Guggenheim fellowships, 1941, 1954; Nat.
Inst. of Arts and Letters award, 1958; honorary
doctorate, Univ. of North Carolina. He taught
at Univ. of Michigan, 1929-33; Univ. of Manitoba,
1944-47; Cornell Univ., 1948-53; Univ. of
Illinois, 1958-65; and Univ. of Texas, 1966-71.
    WORKS: Ballet: Letter to the world, 1940;
Deaths and entrances; Orchestra: symphony, 1931;
Concerto for piano and chamber orch.; North
State; Past the evening sun; Chamber music: For
an unknown soldier, flute and strings; piano
sonata.
    Benson, NC 27504

*JOHNSON, JAMES LOUIS (J. J.)
b. Indianapolis, Ind., 1924. Has written concert
jazz: Perceptions, solo trumpet, contrabass and
drum with winds, 2 horns, timpani; Poem for brass;
Turnpike; El camino real; Sketch for trombone;
Scenario, trombone and orch.; Rondo, vibraphone,
piano, contrabass, drum and chamber orch.

*JOHNSON, JOHN ROSAMOND
b. Jacksonville, Fla., 11 Aug. 1873; d. New York,
N. Y., 11 Nov. 1954. Studied with Charles Dennee,
George Whiting, and David Bispham, New England
Cons.; received an honorary M. A., Atlanta Univ.
He was public school music supervisor in Jacksonville; toured in vaudeville in U.S. and Europe,
1896-98; appeared in Porgy and Bess, Mamba's
daughters, Cabin in the sky.
    WORKS: Ballet: African drum dance; Musicals:
Humpty Dumpty; Shoo-fly regiment; The red moon;
Mr. Load of Kole; Songs: Lift every voice and
sing (called the Negro national anthem); many
songs for revues.

JOHNSON, LOCKREM
b. Davenport, Iowa, 15 Mar. 1924. Studied with
George Frederick McKay, Univ. of Washington. He
received first prize in piano and in chamber
music, Nat. Fed. of Music Clubs, both 1959;
Guggenheim fellowship, 1951; MacDowell fellowships, 1956, 1965; various commissions. He was
faculty member, Univ. of Washington, 1947-49;

JOHNSON, LOCKREM

(JOHNSON, LOCKREM)
pianist, Seattle Symphony, 1948-51; music publishing executive, New York, 1951-62; director,
music department, Cornish School, Seattle,
1962-69; private teacher and music publisher,
1969-   .
WORKS: Opera: A letter to Emily, chamber
opera; Ballet: She; Theatre: music for King
Lear; Orchestra: symphony; Chamber music: 6
piano sonatas; 3 violin sonatas; 2 cello sonatas;
Impromptu, piano; guitar sonata; 2 piano sonatinas; 24 piano preludes; 7 guitar preludes.
18456 40th Place Northeast, Seattle, WA 98155

JOHNSON, MERRITT
b. Dunkirk, Ohio, 29 Oct. 1902. Attended
Oberlin Cons., B. M., M. M.; studied composition
with Leo Sowerby and Darius Milhaud; piano with
Josef Lhevinne and Egon Petri. He received com-
missions from the South Dakota Music Teachers
Asso. He taught piano and organ, Univ. of North
Dakota, 1935-43; Northern State Coll., 1934-73.
WORKS: Orchestra: Concert overture; Band:
Divertimento; Chamber music: piano sonata; many
pieces for piano, organ, anthems, songs, etc.
Melody Lane, Aberdeen, SD 57401

JOHNSON, ROGER
b. San Mateo, Calif., 12 Nov. 1941. Studied with
George McKay, John Verrall, Univ. of Washington;
with Mel Powell, Bulent Arel, Yale Univ.; and
with Chou Wen-chung and Otto Luening, Columbia
Univ. He received a Woodrow Wilson fellowship,
1963; BMI prize, 1966; Los Angeles Horn Club
first prize, 1972. He was instructor, Lincoln
Univ., Pa., 1966-67; Upsala Coll., 1967-71; associate professor, Ramapo Coll., N. J., 1971-   .
WORKS: Chamber music: Suite for 6 horns,
1959; 4 pieces for horn and piano, 1962; trio for
clarinet, horn, harpsichord, 1965; quartet #1,
1968; 5 songs, 1967; Trio da camera; woodwind
quintet; Ritual music, 6 horns; Inventions, flute
and viola; 5 miniatures, violin and piano; Summer songs, soprano and guitar; Chorus: Love
is...; Circle of Maradit, ritual drama.
336 Canal St., New York, NY 10013

JOHNSON, ROY HENRY
b. Moline, Ill., 25 Feb. 1933. Studied with
Louis Mennini, Wayne Barlow, Bernard Rogers,
Eastman School of Music; with John Boda, Florida
State Univ. He was instructor, Bethany Coll.,
1956-58; on faculty, Florida State Univ.,
1960-   , associate professor, 1972-   .
WORKS: Orchestra: Canzona liturgica, 1955;
piano concerto, 1960; Chamber music: piano sonata, 1960; Serenade, solo flute, 1963; 3 pieces
for marimba, 1968; Variations for 2 pianos, 1972;
Fantasy, trombone and piano, 1973; Chorus, Missa
brevis, a cappella, 1961.
School of Music, Florida State University
Tallahassee, FL 32306

JOHNSON, TOM
b. Greeley, Colo., 18 Nov. 1939. Studied with
Elliott Carter, Alvin Etler, Yehudi Wyner at
Yale Univ.; privately with Morton Feldman. He
was assistant editor, Musical America Magazine,

(JOHNSON, TOM)
1962-63; worked frequently as accompanist for
dance classes; music critic for Village Voice,
1971-   .
WORKS: Opera: The four note opera (D,E,A,B),
5 singers and pianist; Piano: An hour for piano,
1971; Septapede, 1973; also orchestral works,
chamber music, theatre pieces.
39 Bedford St., New York, NY 10014

JOHNSTON, BEN
b. Macon, Ga., 15 Mar. 1926. Attended Coll. of
William and Mary, B. A. 1949; Cincinnati Cons.,
M. M. 1950; Mills Coll., M. A. 1952; studied with
Darius Milhaud, Harry Partch, John Cage, Burrill
Phillips. He received a Guggenheim fellowship,
1959; Nat. Found. for the Arts and Humanities
grant; continuing research grants, Univ. of Illinois; and numerous commissions. He has been faculty member, School of Music, Univ. of Illinois,
1951-   , part time, Division of Dance, 1951-59.
WORKS: Chamber opera: Gertrude, or Would
she be pleased to receive it?, 1965; Carmilla,
1970; Ballet: St. Joan, for Sybil Shearer, piano,
1955; Gambit for dancers and orch., for Merce
Cunningham, concert version entitled Ludes for
12 instruments, 1959; Theatre: music for The
wooden bird, with Harry Partch, 1951; Fire, 1952;
The zodiac of Memphis Street (Trapdoors of the
Moon), 1954, revised 1958; Tango for The taming
of the shrew, 1961; Museum piece, sound track
for Smithsonian Inst. film, 1968-69; Auto mobile,
sound environment for automobile exhibit, Smithsonian Inst., 1968-69; Orchestra: Passacaglia
and epilogue, from St. Joan, 1955-60; Quintet
for groups, 1966; Band: Concerto for brass and
percussion, 1951; Jazz band: Ivesberg revisited,
1960; Newcastle troppo, 1960; Chamber music:
Dirge, percussion ensemble, 1952; septet, wind
quintet, cello and bass, 1956-58; 9 variations
for string quartet, 1959; cello sonata, 1960;
Knocking piece, 2 percussionists and grand piano,
1962; duo for flute and string bass, 1963; Lament,
3 winds, 3 strings, 1966; One man, solo trombone
and percussion, 1967; 4 string quartets, 1959,
1964, 1973, 1973, No.4, Fine Arts Quartet, New
York, 21 Apr. 1974; Chorus: Night, cantata, 1955;
Of vanity, with 2 percussion, 1964; Prayer, boys'
choir, 1966; CI-Git Satie, double chorus, bass
voice, drums, 1967; Rose, 1971; Mass, with 8
trombones, rhythm section, 1972; Piano: Sonata
for microtonal piano grindlemusic, 1965; other
piano pieces and some do-it-yourself pieces.
1003 West Church St., Champaign, IL 61820

JOHNSTON, DONALD O.
b. Tracy, Minn., 6 Feb. 1929. Attended Macalester Coll.; Indiana Univ.; studied with Philip
Warner and Robert Delaney, Northwestern Univ.;
with Bernard Rogers and Howard Hanson, Eastman
School of Music. He was band and orchestra director, Coll. of Idaho, 1954-55; director of instrumental music, Ripon Coll., 1955-58; professor,
Univ. of Montana, 1960-   .
WORKS: Orchestra: 4 symphonies; Band: Prelude for band; Ritual for band; Essay for trumpet and band; Chorus: Sing to the Lord; Praise
the Lord; Be glad and sing for joy; Missa brevis;

(JOHNSTON, DONALD O.)
Song of praise; The eyes of the Lord are upon the righteous; many unpublished works for orchestra, band, chorus and chamber ensembles.
91 Arrowhead Drive, Missoula, MT 59801

*JOHNSTON, JACK
Bunker Hill fantasy, orch.; Pastorale and fugue, string orch.; Games for band; Sweet was the song the virgin sang, chorus.
Department of Music, Ashland College
Ashland, OH 44805

*JOKL, GEORG
b. Vienna, Austria, 31 July 1896; to U.S. 1938; d. New York, N. Y., 29 July 1954. Brother of Otto Jokl, wrote a symphony, symphonic poem, Burletta piccola for winds, 1952.

*JOKL, OTTO
b. Vienna, Austria, 18 Jan. 1891; to U.S. 1940; d. New York, N. Y., 13 Nov. 1963. Studied with Alban Berg, 1926-30. His works include Suite for orchestra; a sinfonietta; 2 string quartets; piano sonatina.

JOLLEY, FLORENCE
b. Kingsburg, Calif., 11 July 1917. Attended Univ. of the Pacific; Wheaton Coll., Ill.; Eastman School of Music; Univ. of Southern California, M. M.; Univ. of California, Los Angeles. She has received yearly ASCAP awards. She was on the music faculty, Pierce Coll., 1962-65; and associate professor, Los Angeles City Coll., 1965-   .
WORKS: Chamber music: Recollections, oboe and piano, with visual of Hilo, Hawaii, 1971; Little suite for piano; Journey thru' a rock, organ and tape; Chorus: Gloria in excelsis; Christmas time; Holy Lord God of hosts; All people that on Earth do dwell; The light has come, with brass choir and organ, Los Angeles, 31 Mar. 1971.
1122 Tenth St., Santa Monica, CA 90403

JONES, CHARLES
b. Tamworth, Ont., 21 June 1910; to U.S. 1928. Studied with Bernard Wagenaar at Juilliard School. He then began teaching at Mills Coll. and also began a long association with Darius Milhaud. Other teaching posts have included the Seminar in American Studies, Salzburg; Bryanston Summer School, England; Music Acad. of the West, Santa Barbara; Aspen Music School, 1951-   ; Juilliard School, 1954-   ; chairman of composition, Mannes Coll. of Music, 1973-   .
WORKS: Ballet: Down with drink, 1943; Orchestra: Suite for small orch., 1937; Suite for strings, 1937; 4 symphonies, 1939, 1957, 1962, 1965; Cassation, 1948; Little symphony for the New Year, 1953; Concerto for 4 violins and orch., 1963; Allegory, 1970; Chamber music: 6 string quartets, 1936, 1944, 1951, 1954, 1961, 1970; Threnody, solo viola, 1947; Lyric waltz suite, woodwind quartet, 1948; Epiphany, speaker and 4 instruments, 1952; violin sonata, 1958; The seasons, cantata for soprano, baritone, speaker, 6 instruments, 1959; sonata for oboe and

(JONES, CHARLES)
harpsichord, 1965; I am a mynstral, tenor, violin, harpsichord, piano, percussion, 1967; string trio, 1968; Masque, speaker and 12 instruments, 1968; Anima, cycle for voice, piano and viola, 1968; Serenade, flute, violin, cello, harpsichord, 1973; Chorus: On the morning of Christ's nativity, 5-part chorus, 1953; Piers the plowman, tenor, chorus and orch., 1963; Piano: 2 sonatas; and other works.
311 East 58th St., New York, NY 10022

*JONES, CHARLES ("BIG")
b. 1931. Symphony #6.

*JONES, COLLIER
Studied at Yale Univ. His works include 4 movements for 5 brasses, 1957; Suite for brass and piano; sonatina for 2 trumpets.

JONES, DONALD R.
b. Rochester, N. Y., 3 May 1922. Studied with Wayne Barlow, Bernard Rogers at Eastman School of Music. He has been assistant librarian and librarian, Ensemble Library, Eastman School, 1960-   .
WORKS: Band: Rhapsody for percussion and band; Chamber music: Allegro, horn and piano; Chorus: This is the prophet; Lord's prayer.
143 Croydon Road, Rochester, NY 14610

*JONES, GEORGE SYKES
In a strange land, Psalm 137, for chorus.

JONES, GEORGE THADDEUS
b. Asheville, N. C., 6 Nov. 1917. Studied with Jan Philip Schinhan, Univ. of North Carolina; with Bernard Rogers and Howard Hanson, Eastman School of Music; and privately with Nicolas Nabokov and Nadia Boulanger. His awards include a Fulbright grant, 1953; Benjamin award, 1962; State Dept. Cultural Exchange, 1967-68. He has been professor, Catholic Univ., 1950-   .
WORKS: 2 operas; 2 symphonies; numerous chamber and choral compositions.
School of Music, Catholic University
Washington, DC 20017

JONES, SISTER IDA, O.S.U.
b. Louisville, Ky., 9 Aug. 1898. Studied at Ursuline Coll.; with George Leighton and Carl Hugo Grimm, Cincinnati Cons.; also studied piano, organ, and harp. She won a Composers' Press publication award, 1961. She taught in church schools, 1922-34; Ursuline Coll., 1934-40, chairman of music department, 1940-66; staff member, Ursuline School of Music, 1968-   .
WORKS: Chamber music: The immortal, soprano and piano, 1958; Scherzo, flute, clarinet, bassoon, 1961; Chorus: Supplication, women's voices, 1958; Hodie Christus natus est, women's voices, a cappella, 1959; Mass in honor of Our Lady, 1968; Mass in honor of the Prince of Peace, 1970; The magnificat, 1971; The benedictus, 1971; Ave Maria, 1972; Mass for the Christ Child, 1972.
Ursuline School of Music
3105 Lexington Road, Louisville, KY 40206

JONES, JEFFREY

JONES, JEFFREY
b. Los Angeles, Calif., 11 May 1944. Studied with Dorrance Stalvey, Immaculate Coll., B. M.: with Goffredo Petrassi, St. Cecilia Acad., Rome, diploma; with Seymour Shifrin, Arthur Berger, Martin Boykan, Harold Shapero, Brandeis Univ., M. F. A.; with Franco Donatoni, Acad. Chigiana, diploma. His awards include the Celia Buck grant; Fulbright-Hays grant to Italy, 1967, 1968; D'Atrio and Bonaventura Somma prizes; St. Cecilia Acad., 1969; first grand prize, Fest. Internat. du Son, Radio-Television Francaise, 1970; BMI award to young composers, 1970; Rome Prize, 1972-74. He taught guitar, 1962-67; was instructor, Brandeis Univ., 1969-72; composer-in-residence, Marlboro Festival, 1970.

WORKS: Theatre: Orythia, ballet opera in 5 tableaux; music for Von Hofmanstahl's Everyman, 1966; music for television series Insight, 1966, Orchestra: 2 movements for orch., 1965; Chamber music: 13 ways of looking at a blackbird, soprano, alto, baritone, 7 instruments, 1966; Variance for 7 players, 1970; Rideau d'amethystes, harp, guitar, cello, 1970; Modi movendi su temi di Arcangelo Corelli, 7 players, 1970; Expressions, solo guitar, 1971; Ambiance, soprano and 18 players, 1972; Pieces mouventes, piano.
5159 Highland View, Eagle Rock, CA 90041

*JONES, QUINCY DELIGHT, JR.
b. Chicago, Ill., 14 Mar. 1933. Studied at Seattle Univ.; Berklee Coll. of Music; Boston Cons.; and with Nadia Boulanger and Olivier Messiaen. He held a scholarship at Berklee Coll.; 3 film scores were nominated for Academy awards, 1971. He has been trumpeter and arranger with Lionel Hampton, 1950-53; with Dizzy Gillespie on State Dept. tour to Near East, Middle East, South America, 1956; arranger for many singers; led own band in European tour, 1960; music director, Mercury Records, 1961, vice president, 1964; chairman, Inst. of Black American Music, 1970-   .

WORKS: Film scores: The boy in the tree, Sweden; Mirage, 1965; The pawnbroker, 1965; The slender thread, 1965; Jigsaw, 1966; In the heat of the night, 1967; In cold blood, 1967; The deadly affair, 1967; The getaway, 1967; Enter laughing, 1967; The counterfeit killer, 1968; The split, 1968; A dandy in aspic, 1968; For the love of joy, 1968; The hell with heroes, 1968; The last of the mobile hotshots, 1969; The Italian job, 1969; Bob and Carol and Ted and Alice, 1969; Cactus flower, 1969; The lost man, 1969; John and Mary, 1969; McKenna's gold, 1969; The out-of-towners, 1970; They call me Mr. Tibbs, 1970; Honkey, 1971; The Anderson tapes, 1971; Brother John, 1971; Dollars, 1971; Come back Charleston blue, 1972; The new centurions, 1972; The hot rock, 1972; theme for TV's Ironsides; also many songs and jazz works.
2670 Deep Canyon Drive
Beverly Hills, CA 90210

JONES, RALPH III
b. Philadelphia, Pa., 9 July 1951. Studied with Julius Eastman and Morton Feldman, State Univ. of New York, Buffalo; with Jacob Druckman at

(JONES, RALPH III)
Tanglewood. He held an ASCAP fellowship at Tanglewood, 1972.
WORKS: Chamber music: Made in 1860, musique, concrète, 1971; Epitaph/mobile for David, guitar, percussion, tape, 1972; Saturday afternoon/5 o'clock, 5 flutes, 1973; Chorus: Night journey, large chorus, 3 percussionists, tape, 1972.
2803 Main St., Apt. #3
Buffalo, NY 14214

JONES, ROBERT W.
b. Oak Park, Ill., 16 Dec. 1932. Attended Univ. of Redlands, B. M., M. M.; studied with Wayne Bohrnstedt, but is largely self-taught in composition. He has received awards from Chicago Club of Women organists, 1955; Nat. Asso. of Coll. Wind and Percussion Instructors, 1958; Episcopal Diocese, Albany, N. Y., 1968; Episcopal Diocese, Southwestern Virginia, 1968; Premio Valle D'Aosta, Italy, 1969; Ford Found. resident composer grants, 1965, 1969; MacDowell fellowship, 1973; and many commissions. He was resident composer, West Hartford, Conn., public schools, 1965-69; and Schoolcraft Coll. District, Livonia, Mich., 1969-   .

WORKS: Theatre: music for The governess, 1962; Murder in the Cathedral, 1964; Orchestra: The juggler, choreographic essay, 1959; Serenade, strings, 1968; A song for strings, 1968; Fiddlers three, 3 solo violins and orch., 1971; Concertino for string orch., 1971; Band: How the mighty are fallen (In memoriam MLK and RFK), 1967; Odds on (Etude in 5/8), 1968; Tower sonata I, brass septet, 1968; Declamation and dance, trombone and band, 1969; Toccata concertante, 1969; Elmwood, chorale for band, 1971; Chamber music: trombone sonatina, 1960; sonata for cello quartet, 1968; Penillion pen rhaw, flute, clarinet, bass, vibraphone, tape, 1968; clarinet sonatina, 1970; Three by three, brass trio, 1971; On the way to freedom, soprano, piano, organ, harpsichord, percussion, 1972; Chorus: Columbiad, male chorus, audience, string quartet, organ, 1966; I am the door, speakers, chorus, soloists, organ, 1967; An orison for our time, chorus and band, 1968; O, Come quickly, madrigal, 1968; Missa media, on the collapse of advertising communication, chorus, soprano solo, speakers, and up to 15 Renaissance instruments, 1970; Days of thy youth, 1971; Revelations, speakers, 2 choirs, brass, percussion, 2 organs, tape, 1971; many published choral works and organ pieces. He is also the author of magazine articles on music.
624 Church St., Plymouth, MI 48170

JONES, ROGER PARKS
b. Coral Gables, Fla., 7 Aug. 1944. Studied with Frederick Ashe, Alfred Reed, and Clifton Williams at Univ. of Miami. He has been composer-in-residence at Kansas State Teachers Coll., 1971-   .

WORKS: Band: Symphony for band; Symphonic variations; The faces of Janus, band and chorus; Wind ensemble: 21 distinctive duets for tubas.
605 East 11th St., Emporia, KS 66801

JONES, SAMUEL
b. Inverness, Miss., 2 June 1935. Studied with
Virginia Hoogenakker, Belhaven Coll.; Charles
Watson, Millsaps Coll.; with Wayne Barlow,
Bernard Rogers, and Howard Hanson, Eastman School
of Music. His honors include the Tribbett award;
Woodrow Wilson fellowship; commissions from American Symphony Orch. League, Shenandoah County Bicentennial Committee, and Utica Symphony. He was
director of instrumental music, Alma Coll.,
1960-62; music director, Saginaw Symphony,
1962-65; composer-in-residence and founder and
director, Coll. Summer Cons., Delta Coll.,
1963-65; assistant conductor, 1965-68, associate
cond., 1968-69; resident cond., 1969-70; conductor, Rochester Philharmonic Orchestra, 1970-73;
associate director, American Symphony Orchestra
League Conductor Study Inst., 1968-   ; director,
Shepherd School of Music, Rice Univ., 1973-   .
    WORKS: Orchestra: Elegy, for strings; Fes-
tival fanfare; Fugue and finale on a theme of Dan
Emmett; In retrospect; Let us now praise famous
men; Meditation and scherzo; Overture for a City;
symphony no. 1; Chamber music: piano sonata no.
2; sonata for unaccompanied viola.
    P. O. Box 1892, Houston, TX 77001

JONES, WENDAL S.
b. Erie, Colo., 7 Aug. 1932. Studied with Philip
Bezanson, Univ. of Iowa, Ph. D. He won first prize,
Nat. Asso. Coll. Wind and Percussion Instructors competition. He was associate professor, Univ. of
Arizona, 1961-67; professor and department chairman, Eastern Washington State Coll., 1967-   .
    WORKS: Orchestra: Overture; The kid's new
bag; Chamber music: 3 fantasies for horn and
piano; woodwind quintet.
    Eastern Washington State College
    Cheney, WA 99004

JORDAHL, ROBERT A.
b. Ottumwa, Iowa, 19 Sep. 1926. Studied with
Kent Kennan, Univ. of Texas, Austin; with Wayne
Barlow, Eastman School of Music, D. M. A. He
received commissions from Alaska Centennial
Committee and Anchorage Arch-Diocese. He was
assistant professor, Keuka Coll., 1962-65; Associate professor, Alaska Methodist Univ.,
1965-68; associate professor, McNeese State Univ.,
1968-   .
    WORKS: Ballet: The prospector, 1967; Cham-
ber music: Lyric serenade, oboe and piano;
Diptych, bassoon and piano; Chorus: The temple,
cantata for soloists, chorus, brass, organ; Mass
for the Holy Family; 3 Prayer anthems, children's
choir and organ; Where shall my wondering soul
begin?; Sweet hymns and songs, a cappella anthem;
Organ: Festive prelude on O for a thousand
tongues.
    4706 Ponderosa Rd., Lake Charles, LA 70601

JORDAN, ALICE (Mrs. Frank B.)
b. Davenport, Iowa, 31 Dec. 1916. Studied with
Francis J. Pyle, Drake Univ., B. M. E. She received the Alumni Distinguished Service award,
Drake Univ., 1970; first place, Composers Press
contest, 1959; Contemporary Music award,
Choristers Guild, 1959.

(JORDAN, ALICE)
    WORKS: Chorus: The beatitudes; God who
touchest Earth with beauty; Prayer is the soul's
sincere desire; Late have I loved thee; Only a
manger; All things are thine; many more published choral works.
    4106 Ovid Ave., Des Moines, IA 50310

JORDAN, PAUL
b. New York, N. Y., 12 Mar. 1939. Studied with
Emil Platen, Bonn, Germany; Harvard Coll.;
Columbia Univ.; with Kurt Hessenberg, State High
school for Music, Frankfurt, Germany, degree in
sacred music; with Mel Powell, Yale Univ., M. M.;
privately with Tui St. George Tucker in New York;
and private study in piano, organ, oboe, recorder, conducting. He has been director of
music, United Church on the Green, New Haven,
1964-   ; assistant professor, State Univ. of
New York, Binghamton, 1973-   ; has made frequent tours as organist in Europe and the U.S.
    WORKS: Chamber music: sonata for alto re-
corder and oboe, 1957; Fantasia on the Passion
Chorale, flute, bass clarinet, and cello, 1960;
O, piece for 21 solo instruments, 1972; trio for
oboe, viola, piano, 1973; Chorus: Why hidest
thou thy face?, boy sopranos, male voices, 3
winds, organ, timpani, 1973; Organ: Chorale
prelude, 1962; To Martin Luther King, April 5,
1968; Cry to a lost spirit, 1970, version for
trumpet and 5 woodwinds, 1972; Vater unser, 1971.
    27 Eld St., New Haven, CT 06511

JORDAN, ROLAND
b. Galveston, Tex., 15 Sep. 1938. Studied with
Kent Kennan, Clifton Williams, Univ. of Texas,
Austin; with Merrills Lewis and David Reck, Univ.
of Houston; with George Rochberg, Univ. of Pennsylvania; and Robert Wykes, Washington Univ. He
received a Brittenham Found. grant, 1961; commissions from Univ. of Houston Band, 1963; Delaware State Music Teachers Asso., 1964; Bennington
fellowship, 1971. He taught at Wilmington Music
School (Del.), 1961-66; was assistant professor,
Auburn Univ., Auburn, Ala., 1966-68; instructor,
Washington Univ., 1970-   .
    WORKS: Orchestra: 3 minor statements; What
we did on our summer vacation, 1971; Wind ensemble: Interpolations, with tape, 1963; Tangents I; Chamber music: 3 spacial studies, 4
winds, piano, percussion; First construction,
percussion; 3 movements for solo trombone; Four/
1964; piano pieces; Songs and games, woodwind
trio; Tangents II, clarinet, viola, cello, piano,
tape, 1971; Chorus: Time's space (Encounters),
with tape; Mixed media: Projected images.
    1055 Jackson, University City
    St. Louis, MO 63130

JOSEPH, DON VERNE
b. Elk City, Okla., 8 June 1926. Studied with
Charles Hoag, Frank Hughes, J. Thomas Matthews,
Univ. of Oklahoma; with Everett Gates, Oklahoma
City Univ. He has been staff arranger-composer
for Univ. of Missouri and Tampa Univ.; composer-
arranger for Orange Bowl shows (4), Sugar Bowl
(2), Pro Bowl (2), Sun Bowl and Bluebonnet Bowl;
and received commissions. His faculty posts

JOSEPH, DON VERNE

(JOSEPH, DON VERNE)
include Cameron State Coll.; Jefferson City Jr. Coll.; associate professor, Drury Coll.; dean, Stan Kenton Summer Jazz Orchestra-in-Residence Workshops, 1970-   .
WORKS: Orchestra: symphony, Suite of American Indian dances; Band: symphony; Dissertation; Chamber music: string quartet, brass quartet; and many other chamber works; Jazz ensemble: Suite for trumpet; Jazz waltz-Shish-ka-Bach; Blues; Sunday go-to-meetin' time. He is author of articles in music journals and has been jazz editor, School Musician Magazine, since 1963.
Drury College, Springfield, MO 65807

JOSEPH, WARREN
b. Ossining, N. Y., 8 Feb. 1924. Studied at State Univ. of New York at Potsdam, B. S., M. S.; with Charles O'Neill, Hugo Norden, and Julius Herford, Boston Univ., Ph. D. He was head, music department, Univ. of Southern Mississippi, 1959-61; director of choral activities, Bowling Green State Univ., 1961-63; head, music department, Eastern Michigan Univ., 1963-65; professor, Southern Illinois Univ. at Edwardsville, 1965-   , assistant vice president, Academic Affairs, 1969-   .
WORKS: Theatre: Who's the boss, musical comedy; Chorus: Benedictus es; Psalm 100; Magnificat.
1605 Biscay Drive, Godfrey, IL 62035

*JOSEPHS, WILFRED
Mortales, opera commissioned for the Cincinnati May Festival, 23 May 1970.

*JOSTEN, WERNER
b. Elberfeld, Germany, 12 June 1885; to U.S. 1920; d. New York, N. Y., 6 Feb. 1963. Studied in Munich and Paris. He received an honorary D. M. from Colby Coll.; Juilliard publication awards. On coming to the U.S. he was accompanist to singers in New York; was professor, Smith Coll., 1923-49; conducted joint Amherst-Smith orchestra; directed Northhampton opera festival; was guest conductor at Lewisohn Stadium, New York.
WORKS: Ballet: Balouata, 1931; Joseph and his brethren, 1932, produced at Juilliard School, 1936; Orchestra: Concerto sacro I-II, string orch. and piano, 1925; Jungle, 1929; Endymion suite, 1933; symphony in F, 1936; Canzona seria, 1940; Chamber music: string quartet, 1934; violin sonata, 1936; piano sonata, 1937; cello sonata, 1938; violin sonatina, 1939; woodwind trio, 1941; string trio, 1942; trio for flute, cello, piano, 1943; horn sonata, 1944; also choral works, works for voice and orch., songs.

JULIAN, JOSEPH
b. Los Angeles, Calif., 22 Jan. 1948. Studied at Univ. of California, Los Angeles; and with Robert Erickson, Kenneth Gaburo, Roger Reynolds, Univ. of California, San Diego. He received a composition award from California State Univ., Northridge. He was on the staff, Experimental Coll. of California State Univ., Northridge, 1970-71; Univ. of Hartford, summer 1972; Palomar Coll., 1972-73; Univ. of California, San Diego, 1973-74.
WORKS: Chamber music: Variations, flute and guitar; Piece for string orchestra: Revelations I, II, III, for chamber ensemble; Mixed media:

(JULIAN, JOSEPH)
Synthesis, orch., chorus, and live electronics; Wave, flute, percussion, contrabass, and tape; Akasha, contrabass and tape; Windows and clouds, percussion and tape; Between: 8 poems for instruments, dancers, film projection, and tape.
7874 Caminito Huerta, San Diego, CA 92122

*KABAKOV, JOEL
Studied with Roger Sessions, Univ. of California, Berkeley, B. A.; with Aurelio de la Vega, State Univ. of California, Northridge, M. A.; with Leon Kirchner, Seymour Shifrin, and Earl Kim, Harvard Univ., Ph. D. candidate 1973. He is on the faculty, Boston Cons.
WORKS: Ballet: Por el viento, premier, Boston Symphony Orchestra, 1973.
16 Grove St., Belmont, MA 02178

KACINSKAS, JERONIMAS
b. Vidukle, Lith., 17 Apr. 1907; U.S. citizen 1954. Studied with Stasys Simkus, Juozas Zilevicius, State Cons., Klaipeda; with Alois Haba, Jaroslav Kricka, Pavel Dedecek, State Cons. Prague, Czech. He was conductor City Orchestra and Opera, Klaipeda, 1932-38; State Radio Orchestra, Kaunas, Vilnius, 1938-41; conductor, State Opera and Philharmonic, Vilnius, 1941-44; was guest conductor with many European orchestras; faculty member, Berklee Coll. of Music, 1967-   .
WORKS: Opera: Black ships; Orchestra: Mystery of redemption; Symphonic fantasy No. 2; Concerto for flute and strings; Band: Transcendental expressions; Chamber music: septet; woodwind quintet; saxophone quartet; Chorus: Mass in honorem Innaculati Cordis B. V. M.
16 Thomas Park, South Boston, MA 02127

KADERAVEK, MILAN
b. Oak Park, Ill., 5 Aug. 1924. Studied with Leo Sowerby, American Cons., B. M., M. M.; with Gordon Binkerd, Univ. of Illinois, Urbana, D. M. A. He received a Tamiment Inst. award of $1000 and performance of string quartet, no. 1 by the Curtis String Quartet, 1956; Albuquerque award of $250 and performance of Sinfonietta, 1960. He was instructor, Rizzo School of Music, Chicago, 1950-53; Central Coll., Fayette Mo., 1953-54; assistant professor, Drake Univ., 1954-60; instructor, Univ. of Illinois, Urbana, 1960-65; associate professor and head, music department, Univ. of Illinois, Chicago Circle, 1965-72; professor and chairman, theory, composition and musicology, Drake Univ., 1972-   .
WORKS: Orchestra: Sinfonietta, 1960; Music for orchestra; Chamber music: string quartet, no. 1, 1956; cello sonata; Introduction and allegro, saxophone quartet; 3 short pieces for piano; several published choral works.
5617 Waterbury Circle, Des Moines, IA 50312

*KAGEN, SERGIUS
b. St. Petersburg, Russia, 22 Aug. 1909; to U.S. 1925; d. New York, 1 Mar. 1964. Graduated from Juilliard School, 1930; was later appointed to the faculty. His works include an opera, piano pieces songs.

KAHLE, DENNIS E.
b. Pittsburgh, Pa.; 30 May 1944. Studied with Joseph Wilcox Jenkins, Duquesne Univ.; with Frank McCarty, Victor Graner, Univ. of Pittsburgh. He was graduate assistant at Duquesne; teaching fellow, Univ. of Pittsburgh; then held Andrew Mellon predoctoral fellowship. He was a percussion extra, Pittsburgh Symphony Orch., 1963-68; creative associate, State Univ. of New York, Buffalo, 1972-   ; and percussion extra, Buffalo Philharmonic, 1972-   .
    WORKS: Orchestra: Emergences flux #1; Chamber music: The third beat of nothing, instrumental quartet; Film scores: She-man; The outdoorsman; Mixed media: Nothing profound.
    183 Norwood Ave., Buffalo, NY 14222

*KAHMAN, CHESLEY
Studied at the Peabody Cons. His works include a song cycle for soprano; New York impressions for piano.

*KAHN, ERICH ITOR
b. Rimbach, Germany, 23 July 1905; to U.S. 1941; d. New York, N. Y., 5 Mar. 1956. Studied in Frankfurt; toured as accompanist to Pablo Casals, 1938-39; with Benar Heifetz and Alexander Schneider organized the Albeneri Trio in New York.
    WORKS: Orchestra: Symphonies bretonnes, 1955; Chamber music: Suite for violin and piano, 1939; string quartet, 1953; 4 Nocturnes for voice and piano, 1954; Actus tragicus, for 10 instruments, 1955; Piano: 8 inventions, 1937; Ciaconna dei tempi di guerra, 1943; 5 short piano pieces, 1955.

KALMANOFF, MARTIN
b. Brooklyn, N. Y., 24 May 1920. Studied with Walter Piston at Harvard Univ., B. A., M. A. He was winner of the Robert Merrill contest for best 1-act opera; has been head of Operation Opera since 1950.
    WORKS: Opera (3-act): The insect comedy, based on Capek play; Empty bottle; Godiva; (1-act): The bald prima donna; The victory at Masada; King David and David King; Brandy is my true love's name; The delinquents; Fit for a king; Opera, opera; Photograph-1920, libretto by Gertrude Stein; A quiet game of cribble; Video-mania; Noah and the stowaway; The great stone face; The audition, 10 to 30 minutes, called the first aleatory opera; Musicals: No bed of roses; This week, East Lynne; Green mansions; Maestro; The mating machine; The fourposter; 8 children's musicals including Young Tom Edison; Legends three, a biblical rock musical; Chorus: George Washington comes to dinner; Benjamin Franklin's prayer; Moo!; To music; Song of peace; Under the wide and starry sky; Sermon on the mount; Khadish for a warring world; 23rd Psalm. Kalmanoff wrote many of his opera librettos.
    392 Central Park West, New York, NY 10025

KAM, DENNIS
b. Honolulu, Hawaii, 8 May 1942. Studied with Cesar Bresgan, Mozarteum, Salzburg, 1962-63; with Joseph Wood, Oberlin Coll. Cons., B. M. 1964; Yoshiro Irino in Tokyo, 1965; with Ernst Krenek and Armand Russell, Univ. of Hawaii, M. F. A. 1966; and with Salvatore Martirano, Univ. of

(KAM, DENNIS)
Illinois, D. M. A. 1974. He received a Ford Found.-MENC grant for professional-in-residence, 1970; BMI student composer awards, 1963, 1976; Phi Mu Alpha Sinfinia composition award; professional award, East-West Center, Univ. of Hawaii, 1966; Creative and Performing Arts fellowship, Univ. of Illinois, 1966-68. He taught at Univ. of Illinois, 1968-70; was composer-in-residence, Honolulu and State of Hawaii, 1970-72; director, New Music Ensemble, 1971-72.
    WORKS: Orchestra: Sections, chamber orch., 1963; Interplay, chamber orch. and 2 ensembles, 1966; Blue maroon I, 1969; Ditto varianti, 1973; Band: Gagaku impressions, 1971; Scatter four, 1972; Chamber music: trombone sonata, 1962; woodwind quintet, 1962; Ensemble II, voice, violin, clarinet, piano, tom-toms, 1965; string quartet, 1966; Rendezvous II, bass trombone and piano, 1967; Go, for trombone, clarinet, cello, 1971; Ad hoc, 7 winds, strings, piano, percussion, 1971; Strata-spheres, for 8 flutes, or 3 double basses, or 4 sopranos and piano, or 2 pianos 8-hands, or any combination of the above, 1972; Re-actions, piano, 3 trombones, and timpani, 1972; A very valentine, Gertrude Stein text, 1972; Scatter five, 3 winds, vibraphone, piano, 1972; Chorus: Alleluia, for first Sunday after Easter, 1969; Two moves and the slow scat, 1972; Most of the time, 1972.
    2153 Aupuni St., Honolulu, HI 96817

KAMIEN, ANNA
b. New York, N. Y., 29 Jan. 1912. Studied at Ecole Normale de Musique, Paris; was a choral conductor, 1944-72.
    WORKS: Opera: Ruth; Orchestra: Chinese odes, suite for chorus and orch.; Chamber music: violin sonatina; string quartet; piano quintet; Chinese odes, flute, oboe, 2 violins, viola, piano; Voice: Memories, solo voice and piano.
    185 West End Ave., New York, NY 10023

KAMIN, FRANZ
b. Milwaukee, Wis., 25 May 1931. Studied with Charles Hoag and Leonard Klein, Oklahoma Univ.; with Roque Cordero, Iannis Xenakis, Bernhard Heiden, Indiana Univ., B. M. 1968. He is a private teacher of piano, composition, analysis, creative writing; founder and coordinator of FIASCO at Bloomington, Ind. and on the board of FIASCO, New York.
    WORKS: Chamber music: Buffalo Bill's, soprano and piano, 1962; Patchen triptych, narrators, vocal soloists, chamber groups totaling 20 performers, 1964; Screw piece, soprano, baritone, chamber ensemble, 1967; Aleatoric Systemic Reactory Bulletin #1 (ASRB #1), bass and soprano narrators, violin, cello, piano, slide whistle, conch, household utensils, trash, 1967; Chorus: Kyrie, men's voices a cappella, 1966; Multimedia: ASRB #5 (minute opera: The latter days of Janet Quubyn), soprano, 2 dancers, instruments on stage, in the audience, and in the balcony, timing device, fully mapped sculptural layout on stage, 1971; Witness, ballet for 3 dancers, 2 children, timer, piano, violin, contrabass, flute, oboe, trumpet, trombone, 1972.
    19 Leonard St., New York, NY 10013

KANE, IRVING

*KANE, IRVING
    Fourth stream, for symphonic band.

KANITZ, ERNEST
    b. Vienna, Austria, 19 Apr. 1894; U.S. citizen
    1944. Studied privately with Richard Neuberger,
    1912-14; Franz Schreker, 1914-20. His awards in-
    clude a Marion Bauer performance award for Sonata
    breve, 1952; annual ASCAP awards, 1963-73. He
    was professor, New Vienna Cons., 1922-38; assis-
    tant professor and glee club conductor, Winthrop
    Coll., 1938-41; professor, head, music department,
    orchestra director, Erskine Coll., 1941-44; pro-
    fessor, Univ. of Southern California, 1945 to
    retirement in 1959, guest professor, 1960-61;
    professor, Marymount Coll., Palos Verdes, 1961-64.
        WORKS: Opera: Kumana, 1953; Royal auction,
    1958; Room No. 12, 1958; The lucky dollar, 1959;
    Perpetual, commissioned by After Dinner Opera
    Company of New York, premiered at Lancaster,
    Calif., Spring Festival, 1961; Orchestra: Motion
    picture, 3 phantasies; Concerto grosso, Vienna
    Internat. Festival, 1947; Concert piece for trum-
    pet and orch., 1951; Intermezzo concertante, alto
    saxophone and wind orch., 1953; Concerto for cham-
    ber orch., 1957; bassoon concerto, San Francisco,
    8 Apr. 1964; Sinfonia seria, St. Louis, 17 Oct.
    1964; symphony no. 2, 1965; Sinfonia concertante,
    solo violin and cello and orch.; Chamber music:
    sonata for violin and cello, 1947; suite for
    violin and piano; Divertimento, viola and cello,
    1949; duo for violin and viola; Notturno, flute,
    violin, viola, 1950; violin sonata no. 2; string
    quartet; string trio, 1951; Sonata breve, violin,
    cello, piano, 1952; Sonata Californiana, alto
    saxophone and piano, 1952; Quintettino, 4 winds
    and piano; sonata for cello alone, 1956; sona-
    tina, viola and piano, 1958; Concertino for 5
    players, clarinet, string trio, piano; Suite for
    brass quintet, 1960; bassoon sonata; Little Con-
    certo for unaccompanied saxophone, Chicago, 15
    Dec. 1970; Sinfonietta da camera, violin, 2 saxo-
    phones, piano and celesta, percussion, Los Ange-
    les, 10 Mar. 1973; Chorus: Cantata 1961, with 2
    pianos, 1961; Visions at twilight, women's voices
    in unison, flute, string quintet, piano, Los
    Angeles, Apr. 1964.
        6206 Murietta Ave., Van Nuys, CA 91401

*KANNER, JEROME HERBERT
    b. New York, N. Y., 17 Nov. 1903. Made his debut
    as a violinist in New York at age 8; later stu-
    died with Franz Kneisel, Paul Stoeving, Leopold
    Auer, composition with Edward Kilenyi; attended
    Columbia Univ., B. A., B. S.; New York School of
    Music and Art; Paris Coll. of Music, M. A.; Lon-
    don Lyceum, M. M. summa cum laude. His awards
    include Prix de Rome; Gold Medal of Rome; Pur-
    cell award; honorary doctorates from Berne Inst.,
    Kenyon Coll., and Boston Coll. He was concert-
    master, NBC Symphony and Victor Recording Orch.;
    made concert tours of the U.S. and Europe for 10
    years; then devoted his time to composing for
    radio and films and to activities in music pub-
    lishing and recording.
        WORKS: Orchestra: 2 symphonies; The Rubai-
    yat, symphonic poem; Homage to Debussy; Tribute
    to Kreisler; Chamber music: string quartet;
    Minute at the spinet; choral works and songs.

*KANTOR, JOSEPH
    Dialogue for flute and piano; Serenade woodwind
    quartet.

KANWISCHER, ALFRED OSWALD
    b. Rochester, N. Y., 29 Nov. 1932. Studied with
    James Niblock and H. Owen Reed, Michigan State
    Univ.; with Darkus Milhaud, Mills Coll. and
    Aspen, Colo.; piano with Egon Petri, Oakland,
    Calif., and Bela Nagy, Boston Univ., D. M. A. He
    held scholarships at Heidelberg Univ., Kansas
    Univ., Michigan State and Boston Univ., and at
    Aspen. He won Young Artists Auditions, San Fran-
    cisco, and made his debut as pianist with the
    San Francisco Symphony. He taught piano at Bos-
    ton Univ., 1965-72; has toured the U.S. and Eur-
    ope as solo pianist and as duo pianist with his
    wife, Heidi; artistic director, John Ringling
    Towers Festival Concerts, 1973-   .
        WORKS: Orchestra: 3 pieces for orch.; Cham-
    ber music: 3 pieces for woodwind quintet; Piano:
    2 1-movement sonatas; Duet for one performer;
    5 impressions; Episodes for 4 hands; Suite in 4
    movements, piano 4-hands; 3 pieces for 2 pianos;
    Piece for 2 pianists and percussion; also songs.
        748 Dream Island Rd., Sarasota, FL 33577

*KAPER, BRONISLAW
    b. Warsaw, Poland, 5 Feb. 1902; to U.S. in 1930s.
    Studied at the Univ. and Cons. of Warsaw. On
    coming to the U.S. settled in Hollywood as film
    composer.
        WORKS: Film scores: San Francisco; Gas-
    light; Our vines have tender grapes; The stranger;
    Mrs. Parkington; Lili; Green mansions; Butter-
    field 8; Mutiny on the Bounty; The brothers
    Karamazov; A day at the races; many songs.
        616 North Bedford Dr.
        Beverly Hills, CA 90210

*KAPLAN, ELLIOT
    Collaborated with Easley Blackwood and Frank
    Lewin on the score for Gulliver, an opera con-
    ceived by Opera Today, Inc., and presented by
    the Minnesota Opera Company on 22 Feb. 1975.

KAPLAN, ROBERT BARNETT
    b. Brookline, Mass., 26 July 1924. Studied
    piano with Myron Whitney, Charles Dennee, Lucy
    Dean, New England Cons., privately with Jules
    Wolffers; and held a scholarship in composition
    with Willson Osborne, Settlement Music School,
    Philadelphia. He was music director, Salon of
    Allied Arts, 1948-52; private teacher of piano
    and composition, 1938-   ; piano recitalist
    in concert and on radio.
        WORKS: Chamber music: Tempo di ballo,
    piano, 1939; 5 Luna seas, cello and piano, 1951;
    piano sonatina, 1954; piano sonata, 1955;
    Andante con variazioni, piano 4-hands, 1969;
    Trio concertante, piano trio, 1972; Notturno for
    flute, 1973; Duo da camera, viola and piano,
    1974.
        196 Old Ocean St., Marshfield, MA 02050

KARCHIN, LOUIS S.
    b. Philadelphia, Pa., 9 Aug. 1951. Studied with
    Joseph Castaldo, Philadelphia Musical Acad.;

(KARCHIN, LOUIS S.)
with Samuel Adler and Joseph Schwantner, Eastman School of Music, B. M. 1972; with Gunther Schuller and Bruno Maderna, Tanglewood; Earl Kim, Harvard Univ. He received the Koussevitzky Prize (in a tie), 1971; Nat. Fed. of Music Clubs composition prize, 1972; Columbia Univ. Bearns prize, 1972; Bernard Rogers award, 1972; McCurdy composition award, 1973.
WORKS: Chamber music: <u>Pentamorphos</u>, piano and tape; trio for flute, cello, piano; <u>Fantasy I</u>, violin or viola; <u>Fantasy II</u>, piano. Chorus: <u>May the words of my mouth</u>, a cappella.
96 Prescott St., Cambridge, MA 02138

*KARLIN, FREDERICK JAMES
b. Chicago, Ill., 16 June 1936. Studied at Amherst Coll.; privately with John Becker, William Russo, Rayburn Wright, Tibor Serly; has composed and arranged for Benny Goodman, Harry James, and others,
WORKS: Chamber music: string quartet; <u>Music for percussion trio</u>; <u>Re: Percussion</u>.
406 Adelaide Drive, Santa Monica, CA 90406

KARLINS, M. WILLIAM
b. New York, N. Y., 25 Feb. 1932. Studied with Vittorio Giannini, Manhattan School of Music, B. M., M. M.; with Philip Bezanson and Richard Hervig, Univ. of Iowa, Ph. D.; privately with Frederick Piket, Stefan Wolpe, Gunther Schuller. He was awarded scholarships to Bennington Conference, 1959, 1961; Princeton Seminar, 1960; and a Composers Forum program, 1963. He was graduate assistant, Univ. of Iowa, 1963-65; assistant professor, Western Illinois Univ., 1965-67; associate professor, Northwestern Univ., 1967-   .
WORKS: Orchestra: <u>Concert music</u> No.1, for orch., 1959, No.II, chorus and orch., 1960, No. III, winds, piano, percussion, 1964, No.IV, for orch., 1964, No.5, for orch., Chicago, 20 Dec. 1973; Wind ensemble: <u>Lamentations-In memoriam</u>, winds percussion, organ, speaker, 1968; <u>Passacaglia and rounds</u> for band, 1970; <u>Reflux</u>, concerto for double bass and winds, 1972; Chamber music: 2 concerti grossi, 1959, 1961; 3 piano sonatas, 1959, 1962, 1965; string quartet, 1960; trio for flute, violin, cello, 1960; <u>Outgrowths-variations</u>, piano, 1961; <u>Fantasy and passacaglia</u>, flute, viola, bassoon, double bass, 1961; <u>Little piece</u>, 4 double basses, 1962; <u>4 Inventions and a fugue</u>, bassoon, piano, female voice (opt.), 1962; <u>Birthday music</u>, No.1, 1962, No.2, 1963; string trio, 1963; <u>Variations</u>, clarinet and string trio, 1963; <u>Obiter dictum</u>, organ, 1964; <u>Variations on Obiter dictum</u> for cello, piano, percussion, 1965; <u>Music for oboe, bass clarinet</u>, piano, 1966; <u>Music for cello alone</u>, No.1, 1966, No.2, 1967; <u>Variations and outgrowths</u>, bassoon and piano, 1967; saxophone quartet, 1967; <u>Music for English horn and piano</u>, 1968; <u>Music for tenor saxophone and piano</u>, 1969; <u>Graphic mobile</u> for any 3 or multiple of 3 instruments, 1969; woodwind quintet, 1970; and songs.
1809 Sunnyside Circle, Northbrook, IL 60062

*KARRICK, CECIL
b. Irvine, Ky., 1919. Studied at Eastern State Coll., B. S. 1939; with Gordon Kinney and Kenneth Wright, Univ. of Kentucky, M. A. 1951; at Louisiana State Univ.; Western State Coll.; with Felix Labunski, Cincinnati Coll. of Music. He was arranger for Air Force bands, 1942-46; band director, Bowling Green High School, 1957-   .
WORKS: Orchestra: <u>Laurel land</u>, 1949; <u>Pastorale</u>, 1951; 2 symphonies, 1956, 1957; <u>Piece for orchestra</u>, 1961; Band: <u>Shake, shake, shake</u>, 1953; 2 hymns, 1955; <u>Hoskins parade march</u>, 1959; <u>Bradley band day</u>, 1962; other works for band and for small wind ensembles.
Bowling Green High School
Bowling Green, KY 42101

KARVONEN, PAUL E.
b. Mass, Mich., 6 Oct. 1917. Studied at Suomi Coll., with Donald Ferguson, Univ. of Minnesota; Quincy Porter, Univ. of Michigan; Philip Greeley Clapp and Philip Bezanson, Univ. of Iowa. He received an award, Broadman Anthem competition, 1964; College Band Directors Nat. Asso., 1966. He was assistant professor, Univ. of North Dakota, 1945-48; Gustavus Adolphus Coll., 1948-52; music director, Lutheran Church of North Tanganyika, 1953-57; associate professor, Sul Ross State Coll., 1960-62; Carthage Coll., 1962-64; professor, Mankato State Coll., 1964-   .
WORKS: Orchestra: <u>Prairie festival overture</u>; <u>Concert overture</u>; <u>Cripple Creek</u>, string orch.; Band: <u>Catalan Christmas suite</u>; <u>Allegro, adagio and finale</u>; Chamber music: string quartet; <u>The little black boy</u>, soprano, clarinet, string quartet; Chorus: <u>The temple of holiness</u>; <u>Rejoice, all ye believers</u>; <u>Light of the anxious heart</u>; <u>Father, I sing thy wondrous grace</u>; <u>On that holy Christmas night</u>; Organ: <u>Wonder, love, and praise</u>, 16 organ pieces.
307 Floral, Mankato, MN 56001

*KASSERN, TADEUZ ZYGFRIED
b. Lwow, Poland, 19 Mar. 1904; to U.S. 1948; d. New York, 2 May 1957. Was cultural attache at the Polish Consulate, New York, 1948. He defected from the Polish Government and applied for U.S. citizenship. It was denied, but he remained in the U.S.
WORKS: Opera: <u>The anointed</u>, 1951; <u>Sun-up</u>, 1952; Orchestra: concertino for flute, string orch., xylophone, celesta, 1948; <u>Teen-age concerto</u>, piano and orch., 1956; choral works, chamber music, piano pieces, songs.

KASSLER, MICHAEL
b. New York, N. Y., 8 Apr. 1941. Studied with Henry Cowell, Peabody Cons.; Gian-Carlo Menotti, Bohuslav Martinu, Vittorio Giannini, Curtis Inst. of Music; Charles Jones and Darius Milhaud, Aspen School; Irving Fine, Aaron Copland, Tanglewood; Walter Piston, Harvard Univ.; Roger Sessions and Milton Babbitt, Princeton Univ. He received BMI student composer awards, 1956, 1957, 1958; Bohemian Club prize in composition; grants from American Philosophical Society and American

KASSLER, MICHAEL

(KASSLER, MICHAEL)
Council of Learned Societies for research in
theoretical and historical musicology. He has
been lecturer, American Society of University
Composers, Tanglewood, 1967, and at universities
in U.S. and Europe; author of articles in music
journals; contributor to Grove's Dictionary; and
is professionally employed as data processing
consultant.
WORKS: Chamber music: 4 string quartets;
Duo for violins; Passacaglia for piano; 2 violin
sonatas; Vocal: Sea poems, chorus, oboe, trumpet, string quartet, contrabass; Songs of the
Civil War, soprano and orchestra.
1330 Massachusetts Ave., N.W.
Washington, DC 20005

*KASTLE, LEONARD
b. New York, N. Y., 11 Feb. 1929. Studied with
Rosario Scalero and Gian Carlo Menotti at Curtis
Inst., graduated 1950; also piano with Isabelle
Vengerova, conducting with Carl Bamberger.
WORKS: Opera: The swing, NBC television
network, 11 June 1956; Deseret, NBC network, 1
Jan. 1961; Pariaha, Deerfield Found. commission;
The pariahs, an opera on early whaling in the U.S.,
commissioned by Seattle Opera Asso. for 1976;
Chorus: Whale songs from Moby Dick, received
Barter prize; Whispers of heavenly death, 1956;
Piano: sonata, 1950.

KATWIJK, PAUL VAN
b. Rotterdam, Holland, 7 Dec. 1885; U.S. citizen
1921. Studied at Royal Cons., The Hague; with
William Klatte in Berlin; piano with Leopold
Godowsky in Vienna. He received the Sigma Alpha
Iota Service to Music award, 1959; Texas Fed. of
Music Clubs award; DAR Medal; Concert Gebeouw
Orchestra, Amsterdam, Certificate of Merit, 1961;
named Texas Music Teacher of the Year, 1962. He
taught at Christian Coll., Mo., 1912-13; Columbia
School of Music, Chicago, 1913-14; Drake Univ.,
1914-18; was dean, School of Music, Southern
Methodist Univ. 1918, retired 1955. He conducted
the Dallas Civic Opera 1922-25; Dallas Symphony
Orch., 1925-37; also the Kosloff Ballet at Hollywood Bowl and in Dallas.
WORKS: Orchestra: Hollandia suite; symphonies; Songs: Row gently here; Hey, the dusty
miller, My only love; Heart, be still and listen;
Piano: Barcarolle, Kermesse; many manuscripts
for piano, voice, and orchestra.
4610 Wildwood Road, Dallas, TX 75209

*KATZ, ERICH
b. Posen, Germany, 31 July 1900; U.S. citizen
1949; d. Santa Barbara, Calif., 30 July 1973.
Studied in Berlin and at Freiburg Univ., Ph. D.;
won the internat. composition prize, Zurich, 1937.
He was professor, New York Coll. of Music,
1945-59; then taught privately in Santa Barbara;
was music director, American Recorder Society.
WORKS: Chamber music: Toy concerto, 3 recorders, keyboard instrument, percussion; 6
inventions, piano; 6 cantus firmus settings, 3
recorders, voice ad lib.; The eternal day, mezzo
soprano and recorders; Toccata for 4 recorders;
other works, mostly for recorders.

*KATZ, FREDERICK
b. Brooklyn, N. Y., 25 Feb. 1919. Was music
director for 7th Army Headquarters, for Lena
Horne, and others; on staff of Decca Records;
composed for films and television; cellist with
Chico Hamilton Quintet, 1955-56.
WORKS: Orchestra: cello concerto, 1961;
Chamber music: viola sonata; Adagio, string
quartet; Lord Randall, quintet; Blues for
Piatigorsky, cello and piano; violin and cello
duet; Chorus: Madrigal, choir and cello; songs.

KAUDER, HUGO
b. Tobitschau, Moravia, 9 June 1888; U.S. citizen
1944; d. New York, N. Y., 22 July 1972. Studied
violin at an early age, but was entirely self-
taught in composition. He received the Prize of
the City of Vienna for Symphony No.1, 1928;
Fromm Found. award, 1953. He wrote a book on
harmony and one on counterpoint, and essays on
musical events from 1920 to 1950.
WORKS: Theatre: In search of a dream,
music for a Chinese drama; Orchestra: 5 symphonies; 3 shorter works; 9 concerti; Chamber
music: quartet for oboe, clarinet, horn, bassoon, 1949; 19 string quartets; trio for violin,
horn and piano, 1954; English horn sonata, 1970;
numerous works for various small ensembles and
solo instruments; choruses; songs.

*KAUER, GUNTHER (GENE)
Quartet for horns.
11621 Montana Ave., Los Angeles, CA 90049

*KAUFMANN, WALTER
b. Carlsbad, Czech., 1 Apr. 1907; to U.S. 1957.
Studied in Berlin and at Univ. of Prague; was
director, Bombay Radio, 1935-46; taught at Halifax (N.S.) Cons., 1947-48; conducted Winnipeg
Symphony, 1948-57; professor, Indiana Univ.
1957-   .
WORKS: Opera: 4 operas, 1934-52; Orchestra:
5 symphonies, 1930-40; Madras Express, fantasy
for orch.; piano concerto, 1950; Rubaiyat, voice
and orch., 1952; Wind ensemble: Passacaglia and
capriccio, brass ensemble; Chamber music: 2
piano trios; 2 string trios; 7 string quartets;
wind quintet; piano pieces; songs.
School of Music, Indiana University
Bloomington, IN 47401

*KAVANAUGH, PATRICK
Jack and the beanstalk, Hartke Theatre, Washington, D.C., 29 Nov. 1974.

KAVASCH, DEBORAH
b. Washington, D.C., 15 July 1949. Studied with
Wallace E. DePue, Burton Beerman, Donald M.
Wilson, Bowling Green State Univ.; with Roger
Reynolds, Univ. of California, San Diego. She
received the Religious Arts award, 1969; first
prize, Ohio Music Teachers Asso. contest, 1971;
first prize, Ohio Fed. of Music Clubs contest,
1972. She was lecturer, Bowling Green State
Univ., summer 1973.
WORKS: Opera: Legends, chamber opera;
Chamber music: Abraxas, cello and piano; Gestures, chamber ensemble, 1972; Chorus: Kyrie

(KAVASCH, DEBORAH)

eleison, women's voices, 1969; I will lift up mine eyes; Songs; The philosopher, song cycle, 1971.

   6802 Beadnell, #26, San Diego, CA 92117

*KAY, HERSHY

b. Philadelphia, Pa., 17 Nov. 1919. Studied at Curtis Inst. He has been arranger and orchestrator for the Balanchine Ballet Company and for many Broadway musicals.

   WORKS: Opera: Good Soldier Schweik, a completion of Robert Kurka's unfinished opera, 1959; Ballet: Thief who loved a ghost, 1950; Cakewalk, 1951; Western symphony, 1954; Concert, an arrangement from Chopin, 1956; Stars and stripes, 1958; L'Inconnue, 1965; Orchestra: Mother Goose suite; Let's go to the fair; Theatre set; Concerto for 2; Band: Deck the halls, a merry fugue; Variations on Joy to the world.

   205 West 57th St., New York, NY 10019

KAY, ULYSSES

b. Tucson, Ariz., 7 Jan. 1917; nephew of Joseph "King" Oliver. Learned to play piano, violin, and saxophone at home; then attended Univ. of Arizona, B. M. E. 1938; studied with Bernard Rogers and Howard Hanson, Eastman School of Music, M. A.; with Paul Hindemith at Yale Univ. and Tanglewood; and with Otto Luening at Columbia Univ. His many awards include a Ditson fellowship at Columbia; Julius Rosenwald fellowship; Prix de Rome, 1949, 1951; Fulbright grant, 1950; Nat. Inst. of Arts and Letters grant; BMI prize; Gershwin Memorial Prize; ABC prize; Guggenheim fellowship, 1964; honorary doctorates, Lincoln Coll., 1963; Bucknell Univ., 1963; and numerous commissions. He served in a Navy band in World War II, playing saxophone, flute, piccolo, and piano, as well as arranging and composing. In 1965 he toured in the USSR as member of the first group of composers sent on a State Dept. cultural exchange mission. Other such missions have taken him to England, France, Italy, and Yugoslavia. He has been music consultant, Broadcast Music, Inc., 1953- ; visiting professor, Boston Univ. and Univ. of California, Los Angeles; professor, Lehman Coll., CUNY, 1968- .

   WORKS: Opera: The boor, 1-act, 1955; The juggler of Our Lady, 1956, New Orleans, 23 Feb. 1962; Orchestra: A short overture, 1947; Aulos, flute and chamber orch., Bloomington, Ind., 21 Feb. 1971; Concerto for orchestra, 1948; Fantasy variations, Portland, Me., 19 Nov. 1963; Markings, dedicated to Dag Hammarskjold, Detroit, 18 Aug. 1966; Overture: Of new horizons, 1944; Portrait suite; Presidential suite; Reverie and rondo; Serenade for orchestra, 1954; Sinfonia in E, 1950; Suite for orchestra; Suite for ballet, Danse Calinda, 1941; Suite for film, The quiet one, 1948; Symphony, New York premier, 29 Mar. 1974; Trigon; Umbrian scene, 1964; Ancient saga, piano and strings; Brief elegy, oboe and strings; Pieta, English horn and strings; 6 dances, 1954; Suite for strings, 1949; Band: Concert sketches; Forever free; Short suite; Solemn prelude; Chamber music: brass quartet, 1952; 3 string quartets, 1953, 1956, 1961; Partita in A, violin and piano;

(KAY, ULYSSES)

Serenade no. 2, 4 horns; Suite for flute and oboe; Triptych on texts of Blake, soprano, piano trio, 1955; Trumpet fanfares, 4 trumpets; 5 Portraits, violin and piano, Washington, D.C., 22 Feb. 1974; Chorus: Choral triptych, cantata for chorus and strings, 1962; Inscriptions from Whitman, with orch., 1964; Phoebus arise, soprano, baritone, chorus and orch., 1959; Song of Jeremiah, bass-baritone, chorus, orch., 1954; Stephen Crane set, 4 pieces for chorus and 13 players; A Lincoln letter, bass solo, chorus a cappella; How stands the glass around?, 1954; What's in a name?, 1954; many other choral works; Piano: sonata, 1940; 10 Essays; 2 Short pieces for piano 4-hands; 4 Inventions.

   143 Belmont St., Englewood, NJ 07681

*KAYDEN, MILDRED

b. New York, N. Y. Studied at Juilliard School; Vassar Coll., B. A.; Radcliffe Coll., M. A.; with Ernst Krenek and Walter Piston; taught at Vassar, 1946-50, 1951-52; had radio program on WEVD, 1956-63.

   WORKS: Theatre: music for The seed and the dream; The riddle of Sheba; Mardi gras; The last word; Chamber music: piano sonata; Theme and variations, piano; string quartet; woodwind trio; Chorus: The valley of dry bones, chamber cantata; Green gown; Songs: The call of the prophet, tenor and organ; Psalm 121, soprano and organ; Film scores: The pumpkin coach; The procession; Leaven for the cities; Television score: Strangers in the land.

   33 Broadway, Irvington-on-Hudson, NY 10533

KAYLIN, SAMUEL

b. Russia, c. 1890. Received an honorary doctor of music degree from the London Inst. for Applied Research, 1972. He became music director for Hollywood motion pictures in 1916; was with Warner Bros. Pictures, 1929-31, and 20th Century-Fox Film Corp. thereafter until retirement. He wrote scores for more than 50 films in the 1930s including Ever since Eve; Steamboat round the bend; Little Miss Nobody; the Charlie Chan series; and the Jeeves series.

   422 South Western Ave., #210
   Los Angeles, CA 90020

KAZZE, LOUIS

b. Russia, 18 July 1896. Studied with Randall Thompson in New York; with Ernest Bloch in Philadelphia; and with Herbert Elwell, Eastman School of Music. He received a Pennsylvania Fed. of Music Clubs award in composition. He taught in public schools in Philadelphia then founded his own piano school.

   WORKS: Orchestra: Panar, ballet suite; Chamber music: Variations for flute and piano; Lights and shadows, violin and piano; 3 songs to texts by Poe; Piano: Panar suite; Suite in C; Passacaglia and fugue.

   21 Allendale Rd., Philadelphia, PA 19151

KEATS, DONALD

b. New York, N. Y., 27 May 1929. Studied with Quincy Porter and Paul Hindemith, Yale Univ.,

KEATS, DONALD

(KEATS, DONALD)
B. M. 1949; with Otto Luening, Douglas Moore, Henry Cowell, Columbia Univ., M. A. 1953; with Philipp Jarnach, Hamburg, Germany, 1954-56; with Paul Fetler, Dominick Argento, Univ. of Minnesota, Ph. D. His awards include the Yale Univ. Kellogg prize, 1948, Jackson prize 1949, teaching fellowship, 1948-49; Fulbright grants 1954, 1955; Danforth Found. grant, 1959, 1961; Lilly Found. grant, 1960; Guggenheim fellowships, 1964, 1972; annual ASCAP awards 1964-73; Rockefeller Found. performance grants, 1965, 1966; Ford Found.- Antioch Humanities awards for recording, 1970, publication, 1972. He was instructor, U.S. Navy School of Music, 1953-54; post music director, Fort Dix, U.S. Army, 1956-57; professor, Antioch Coll., 1957-   , chairman, music department, 1967-71; visiting professor, Univ. of Washington, 1969-70.
WORKS: Ballet: The new work, 1967; Orchestra: Symphony no. 1, 1959; Elegiac symphony, Kansas City, Apr. 1964; Concert piece, 1968; Chamber music: Divertimento, winds and strings, 1949; string trio, 1949; 2 string quartets, 1956, 1965; Polarities I and II, violin and piano, 1968, 1970; Chorus: The hollow men, 1955; The naming of cats, 1961; A drinking song; anyone lived in a pretty how town, 1970; Songs: A love triptych, 1970; Piano: Variations, 1956; sonata, 1960.
Meredith Rd., Yellow Springs, OH   45387

KECHLEY, DAVID STEVENSON
b. Seattle, Wash., 16 Mar. 1947. Studied cello with Pietro Grossi, Florence, Italy; composition with Paul Tufts, William Bergsma, Robert Suderberg, Niccolo Castiglioni, Univ. of Washington, B. M. 1969; Istvan Anhalt and Paul Peterson, McGill Univ. He received 2 Louis Brechemin scholarships, Univ. of Washington, 1965, 1967; Rockefeller Found. performance grant, 1967. He was on the graduate faculty, McGill Univ., 1970; music specialist, City of Seattle, Department of Parks and Recreation, 1972-   ; teaching assistant, Univ. of Washington, 1973-   .
WORKS: Orchestra: 2nd composition for large orchestra, 1967; Band: Concerto for band; Chamber music: string quartet; sonata for flute and harp; violin sonata; cello sonata; string trio; Variations, 7 players; trio for piano, cello and flute; Music for the dance.
8052 Meridian Ave. North
Seattle, WA   98103

KECHLEY, GERALD
b. Seattle, Wash., 18 Mar. 1919. Studied with George F. McKay, Univ. of Washington, B. A., M. A.; and with Aaron Copland in New York. He received Guggenheim fellowships, 1949, 1951; commissions from Seattle Symphony, George Gershwin Memorial Found., Univ. of Portland. He was director of music, Centralia Junior Coll., Wash., 1953; professor, Univ. of Washington, 1954-   .
WORKS: Operas: The golden lion; The beckoning fair one; Robin Goodfellow; Orchestra: symphony; Daedalus and the minotaur; Band: Antiphony for winds; Suite for concert band; Suite for brass and percussion; Chamber music, piano trio; Chorus:

(KECHLEY, GERALD)
Drop, slow tears; For men yet unborn; Cantata for St. Cecilia's Day; Psalm 150; Pleasure it is; In the lonely midnight; Thank we now the Lord of heaven; Maker of all the Earth; Psalm 121; We are thy servants, O Lord; Sing no sad songs; Song: I sing of a maiden, voice and piano.
School of Music, University of Washington
Seattle, WA   98115

*KEENE, CHRISTOPHER
b. Berkeley, Calif., 21 Dec. 1946. Studied at Univ. of California, Berkeley. He formed his own opera company at age 18 and produced Benjamin Britten's Rape of Lucretia; was assistant conductor, San Francisco Opera at 18; conducted New York City Opera at 23; has also conducted the Santa Fe Opera, and at the Spoleta Festivals, 1968, 1969, 1971; then was on the conducting staff, New York City Opera Company and musical director, American Ballet Company; in 1975 he was named music director, Syracuse Symphony. His compositions include the ballet, The consort, 1970.
Syracuse Symphony Orchestra
113 East Onandaga St., Syracuse, NY   13202

KEESE, KEN
b. Stone Mountain, Ga., 24 Mar. 1914. Attended Univ. of Tennessee at Chattanooga. He was named composer of the year by Chattanooga Music Teachers Asso., 1971. He has been staff pianist for radio stations WGST and WAT1, Atlanta, Ga., and WESC, Greenville, S. C.
WORKS: Chorus: O Lord, how excellent is thy name; Sing unto the Lord a new song; Father, teach me how to pray; Let all mortal flesh; Christmas Eve; Only three; Once to every man and nation.
1001 Tremont St., Chattanooga, TN   37405

KEEZER, RONALD
b. Eau Claire, Wis., 4 June, 1940. Is a faculty member, Univ. of Wisconsin.
WORKS: Orchestra: Composition for percussion and orch.; Eloszo; Wind ensemble· 4 brass structures; Percussion: For 3 percussionists; For 4 percussionists; Fantasy on raga; 3 movements for percussion; Film music; Impetus; Chamber music: Transformations, piano trio; string quartet; Punical muse, 7 instruments and percussion; Introspections, 5 players, narrator, percussion; Composition for Dominic Spara; Chorus: The man whose rage was rose, cycle for chorus and percussion; The Lord is in his holy temple; Doth not wisdom cry.
1711 State St., Eau Claire, WI   57401

KEISER, LAUREN KEITH
b. Portland, Ore., 13 June 1945. Studied privately with Elie Siegmeister and Ann Chanee; with Harold Gilmore, Plainfield, Vt. He was president of a publishing company, 1970-72; composer-in-residence, Sam Ash Music Stores, 1972-   .
WORKS: Opera: Goose Hollow, 2-act opera for electronic instruments and amplified voices;

(KEISER, LAUREN KEITH)
Chamber music: The music of Erich Zann, string
quartet; Temporal synthesis, piano.
41 Riggs Place, Locust Valley, NY 11560

KELDERMANS, RAYMOND ALBERT
b. Mechelen, Belgium, 17 Apr. 1911; U.S. citizen
1965. Studied with Flor Peeters, Marinus de
Jong, and Staf Nees at Lemmens Inst., Malines,
M. A. 1932; graduated with great distinction from
Royal Carillon School, Mechelen; also studied in
Berlin, 1939. He received a City of Mechelen
prize for a carillon composition, Barock suite,
1964; and Leon Henry prize, Mechelen, 1966. He
has been Park District carillonneur, Thomas Rees
Memorial Carillon, Springfield, Ill., 1960-   ;
organist-choirmaster, Blessed Sacrament Church,
1960-73; instructor, Springfield Coll.,
1958-   .
WORKS: Orchestra: Symphony; Pastorale;
Feast; Tyliana; Til Uilenspiegel suite; chamber
orch.; Chamber music: bassoon sonatina; trumpet
sonata; quintet for woodwinds; Chorus: The Lord
is my shepherd, choir and chamber orch.; Vachel
Lindsay suite; Organ: Magnificat; Suite for
organ; Carillon: Toccata; sonatina.
1625 Holmes Ave., Springfield, IL 62704

*KELLER, HOMER
b. 1915. Studied with Howard Hanson and
Bernard Rogers, Eastman School of Music, B. M.,
M. M.; with Arthur Honegger in Paris.
WORKS: Orchestra: 3 symphonies, 1940, 1950,
1956; Serenade for clarinet and strings; Chamber
music: brass quartet; 5 pieces for clarinet and
bassoon; Fantasy and fugue for organ.
School of Music, University of Oregon
Eugene, OR 97403

*KELLER, WALTER
b. Chicago, Ill., 23 Feb. 1873; d. Chicago, 7
July 1940. Studied at American Cons. and at
Leipzig Cons. He was teacher and organist in
Chicago. His works include a comic opera;
Synchronous prelude and fugue for orch.; works
for organ, chorus, and solo voice.

KELLIS, LEO ALAN
b. Los Angeles, Calif., 17 Aug. 1927. Studied
privately with Julius Gold in Hollywood.
WORKS: Piano: Variations on a theme of
Rachmaninoff; 15 preludes; sonata; 3 capriccios;
Variations on a theme of Balakirev; Fantasy;
Rhapsody Arevelian; 11 etudes on an original
theme; 3 impromptus; Hello from the zoo, a suite;
Rhapsody on a children's tune; 2 concert etudes.
771 Norumbega Dr., Monrovia, CA 91016

KELLY, ROBERT
b. Clarksburg, W. Va., 26 Sep. 1916. Studied
privately with Matthew Lundquist; with Rosario
Scalero, Curtis Inst. of Music, B. M.; with
Herbert Elwell at Eastman School of Music, M. M.
He was guest composer, American Symph. Orch.
League, Monterey, Calif., 1957, and at New York
Composers Forum, 1958; received commissions from
Univ. of Illinois, 1962, 1964; Nat. Endowment
for the Arts and the Champaign-Urbana Symphony,

(KELLY, ROBERT)
1967. He has been professor, Univ. of Illinois,
1946-   .
WORKS: Opera: Tod's gal, 1-act folk opera,
1951, Virginia City, Va., 8 Jan. 1971; The white
gods, 3-acts, Urbana, Ill., 3 July 1966; Ballet:
Paiyatuma; Orchestra: Adironack suite, 1941;
An American diptych, Austin, Tex., 26 Apr. 1963;
Colloquy for chamber orch., Chicago, 17 Apr.
1965; Concerto for violin, cello and orch.,
Urbana, Ill., 8 Mar. 1961; Emancipation symphony
(symph. no. 3), Washington, D.C., 5 Feb. 1963;
A miniature symphony (symph. no. 1), Austin, Tex.,
15 Oct. 1950; Symphony no. 2, 1958; violin concerto, Urbana, 18 Oct. 1968; Band: Chorale and
fugue, 1951; Concerto for winds and percussion;
Fluctuations, organ, brass ensemble, percussion;
Chamber music: Diacoustics, piano and percussion;
Expressions, violin and cello or viola; A free
fugue on 2 themes, 2 violins and piano; Introduction and dialogue, horn, cello, piano; Passacaglia and fugue, wind quintet; quintet for
clarinet and strings, 1956; sonata for 2 violins;
viola sonata, 1950; violin sonata, 1952; trombone sonata, 1952; sonata for oboe and harp, 1955;
cello sonata, 1958; 2 string quartets, 1944, 1952;
Suite for solo cello; Theme and variations, violin, viola, piano; Toccata for marimba and percussion, 1959; Triptych for cello and piano, 1962;
Variant, piano trio; Chorus: The word of God,
cantata for soprano, baritone, chorus, brass quartet, strings; Songs: Patterns, cantata for soprano and orch., Amy Lowell text; Song cycle,
soprano and piano, Millay text; The buck in the
snow, contralto and piano, Millay text.
School of Music, University of Illinois
Urbana, IL 61801

*KEMMER, GEORGE
b. New York, N. Y., 11 Oct. 1890. Was organist-
choirmaster, Grace Church, Orange, N. J.,
1911-23; at St. George's Episcopal Church, New
York, 1923-55. He wrote choral works, organ
pieces, songs.

KEMNER, GERALD
b. Kansas City, Mo., 28 Sep. 1932. Studied with
Quincy Porter, Yale Univ.; with Howard Hanson,
Eastman School of Music, D. M. A. He taught at
Augustana Coll., Sioux Falls, S. D., 1962-66;
has been associate professor, Cons. of Music,
Univ. of Missouri, Kansas City, 1966-   .
WORKS: Chorus: Ezekiel, with electronic
sounds; Organ: Variations on the Easter sequence;
First light and the quiet voice.
Conservatory of Music, University of Missouri
Kansas City, MO 64111

*KENDALL, GARY
Epithalamium, flute solo.

KENDRICK, VIRGINIA (Mrs. W. Dudley Kendrick)
b. Minneapolis, Minn., 8 Apr. 1910. Studied at
Univ. of Minnesota. She was pianist with a
ballet company, 1960-73; organ music consultant
with a publishing firm, 1970-73; organist, First
Church of Christ Scientist, Excelsior, 1965-73.

KENDRICK, VIRGINIA

(KENDRICK, VIRGINIA)
WORKS: Choral works and songs including
White sky, women's voices; Before the world was,
solo voice, 1973.
Route 7, Box 70, Excelsior, MN 55331

KENNAN, KENT WHEELER
b. Milwaukee, Wis., 18 Apr. 1913. Studied with
Hunter Johnson, Univ. of Michigan, 1930-32; with
Howard Hanson and Bernard Rogers, Eastman School
of Music, B. M. 1934, M. M. 1936; with Ildebrando
Pizzetti, Acad. of Saint Cecilia, Rome. He won
the Prix de Rome, 1936. His faculty posts have
been Kent State Univ., 1939-40; Univ. of Texas,
1940-42, 1946-47, 1949- ; Ohio State Univ.,
1947-49.
WORKS: Orchestra: Il campo dei fiori, trumpet and orch., 1937; Nocturne, viola and orch.,
1937; symphony, 1938; Dance divertimento, 1938;
Promenade, 1938; Andante, oboe and orch., 1939;
Concertino, piano and orch., 1946; revised for
piano and wind ensemble, 1963; Chamber music:
Night soliloquy, flute, strings, piano, 1936;
Sea sonata, violin and piano, 1939; Scherzo, aria,
fugato, oboe and piano, 1948; trumpet sonata,
1956; Chorus: The unknown warrior speaks, male
voices a cappella, 1944; Blessed are they that
mourn, chorus and orch.; Piano; 3 preludes, 1939;
sonatina, 1945; 2 preludes, 1951. He is author
of 2 books: The technique of orchestration, 1952,
revised 1970; Counterpoint, 1959, revised 1972.
Music Department, University of Texas
Austin, TX 78712

*KENNEDY, JOHN BRODBIN
b. 1934. Symphonic fantasy for orch; Gloria,
trumpet and organ; Rise, my soul, and stretch thy
wings, chorus and organ; Alleluia fanfare, chorus
and brass; other choral works and songs.

KENNELL, RICHARD PAUL
b. Dansville, N. Y., 17 Apr. 1949. Studied with
M. William Karlins and Stephen Syverud, Northwestern Univ. He won a prize in the First Internat. Contest of Electronic Music, Bourges, France,
1973. He was graduate assistant, electronic music
studio, Northwestern Univ., 1972-73; assistant
music director, Rolling Meadows High School,
1973-74.
WORKS: Chamber music: Quartet for winds,
1972; solo for clarinet and electronic reverbera-
tion unit, 1972; Wiesenhuttenplatz 29, electronic
tape, 1972; Metamorphose, tape, 1972; Elestroax
II, alto saxophone and tape, 1972; Fantasia and
fugue, for tape, Bourges, France, 20 Oct. 1973.
1914 Sherman Ave., Evanston IL 60201

*KENT, CHARLES STANTON
b. Minneapolis, Minn., 20 Jan. 1914. Studied at
Univ. of Louisville, B. M. 1936; Juilliard School,
1933-35; Eastman School of Music, M. M. 1938,
Ph. D. 1951. He was faculty member, Oberlin Coll.,
1938-41; Western Reserve Univ., 1941-42; New
England Cons., 1945-48; Univ. of Mississippi,
1951-56; Indiana Univ., 1956-61; Peabody Cons.,
1961-62, acting director, 1962-63, director,
1963-68; visiting professor and acting chairman,
music department, Univ. of Miami, 1968- .

(KENT, CHARLES STANTON)
WORKS: Opera: A room in time, 1954; a
number of string quartets; songs.

KENT, RICHARD LAYTON
b. Harris, Mo., 23 Jan. 1916. Studied with Francis J. Pyle, Drake Univ.; Francis Judd Cooke and
Carl McKinley, New England Cons.; with Hugo
Norden, Boston Univ.; and musicology at Harvard
Univ. He taught in public school, Larrabee, Iowa,
1940-42; has been music director and professor,
State Coll. at Fitchburg, Mass., 1947- ;
founder and director, Wachusett Chorale,
1963- .
WORKS: Chorus: Time; Bright star; May the
road rise; 23rd Psalm; 3 spring songs; How sweet
the moonlight sleeps; When icicles hang; Reasons
for singing; Come fill the cup; In the bleak midwinter; Concord hymn; more than 50 more published
choral works and organ pieces; many manuscript
works for orchestra, chamber groups, etc.
1171 Main St., Leominster, MA 01453

*KENTON, STANLEY NEWCOMB (STAN)
b. Wichita, Kan., 19 Feb. 1912. Began composing
at 16; was pianist in dance orchestras and night
clubs; organized own orchestra in 1941 and has
performed widely with it; has conducted workshops
for teen-age musicians.
WORKS: Concert jazz: Artistry in rhythm;
Eager beaver; Intermission riff; Southern scandal;
Concerto for doghouse; Concerto to end all concertos; Painted rhythm; et al.

*KEPNER, FRED
b. Waynesboro, Pa., 26 Sep. 1921. Studied at
Catawba Coll.; Juilliard School; Manhattan School
of Music. He was in the Army Air Force in World
War II; chief arranger, USAF Band, Washington,
1947-50; led USAF dance orch., Airmen of Note;
assistant to chief of bands and music, USAF,
1955- ; leader, Headquarters Command Band,
Washington.
WORKS: Band: Cuban fantasy; Latin lament;
The clown, suite; Forward for peace; A medieval
tournament; Merry-go-round polka; 2nd Street overture; Fiesta finale.
7804 Oxon Hill Rd., King's Grant
Oxon Hill, MD 20021

*KERN, JEROME DAVID
b. New York, N. Y., 27 Jan. 1885; d. New York,
11 Nov. 1945. Studied at New York Coll. of Music
and privately in Berlin. He began his composing
career in London writing numbers for musical shows;
was staff writer for T. B. Harms, 1904; wrote
scores for the Princess Theatre, New York, 1915-18;
then his great hits began to appear on Broadway.
WORKS: Musicals: Rock-a-bye baby, 1918;
Sally, 1920; Stepping stones, 1923; Sunny, 1925;
Show boat, 1927; Sweet Adeline, 1929; The cat and
the fiddle, 1931; Music in the air, 1932; Roberta,
1933; Very warm for May, 1939; Film scores: Men
of the sky, 1930; I dream too much, 1935; Swing
time, 1936; High, wide and handsome, 1937; When
you're in love, 1937; The joy of living, 1938; One
night in the tropics, 1940; You were never lovelier,
1944; Cover girl, 1944; Can't help singing, 1944.

*KERNOCHAN, MARSHALL RUTGERS
b. New York, N. Y., 14 Dec. 1880; d. Edgartown, Mass., 9 June 1955. Studied with Hermann Wetzler and Ivan Knorr; with Percy Goetschius, Juilliard School. He was music editor of The outlook; then president, Galaxy Music Corporation, New York.
WORKS: Voice: The foolish virgin, cantata; The sleep of summer, women's chorus and orch.; Out of the rolling ocean, baritone and orch.; numerous songs.

KERR, HARRISON
b. Cleveland, Ohio, 13 Oct. 1897. Studied with James Hotchkiss Rogers in Cleveland; with Nadia Boulanger in Paris, 1921. He received a Huntington Hartford Found. fellowship; and commissions from Bennington School of the Dance, 1938; Edizioni Musicali Berben, 1971; Chorus of Damascus (Md.) High School, 1971. He was director of music, Greenbrier Coll., W. Va., 1927-28; Chase School, Brooklyn, N. Y., 1928-35; editor of Trend, bi-monthly magazine of the arts, 1932-35; secretary, American Composers Alliance, 1937-51; executive secretary, American Music Center, 1940-47; with Civil Affairs Division, Dept of the Army, 1946-49; dean, Coll. of Fine Arts, Univ. of Oklahoma, 1949-64, professor and composer-in-residence, 1960-68, emeritus professor, 1968-   .
WORKS: Theatre: Dance sonata, dancers, 2 pianos, percussion, Bennington, Vt., 5 Aug. 1938; The tower of Kel, 4-act opera, 1958-60; Orchestra: Symphony no. 1, 1929, Rochester, N. Y., 24 Oct. 1945; symphony no. 2, 1945, Oklahoma City, 23 Feb. 1951; symphony no. 3, 1954, Norman, Okla., 19 Nov. 1971; Notations on a sensitized plate, voice and chamber orch., New York, 24 June 1936; Dance suite, Rochester, N. Y., 27 Oct. 1942; violin concerto, 1951, New York, 12 Dec. 1954; Variations on a ground bass, 1966; Sinfonietta, Norman, Okla., 25 Apr. 1968; Movement for string orch., Saratoga Springs, N. Y., 16 Sep. 1937; Chamber music: string quartet, Paris, France, 5 Mar. 1936; string quartet, no. 2, New York, 13 Dec. 1937; trio, clarinet, cello, piano, New York, 24 June 1936; Study for cello alone, 1937; piano trio, New York, 21 Dec. 1938; Suite for flute and piano, Philadelphia, 22 Nov. 1942; Overture, arioso, and finale, cello and piano, Norman, Okla., 27 Apr. 1952; sonata for violin solo, New York, 5 Feb. 1955; violin sonata, 1956; Variations on a theme from The tower of Bel, guitar, 1971; Chorus: Wink of eternity, chorus and orch., New York, 15 Dec. 1937; In cabin'd ships at sea, Damascus, Md., 30 Apr. 1972; Piano: Poem, 1926; sonata no. 1, 1929, New York, 30 July 1933; sonata no. 2, 1943, New York, 28 Jan. 1947; 4 preludes, 1943; Frontier day, 1956; and many songs.
1014 Louisiana St., Norman, OK 73069

*KERR, THOMAS H., JR.
b. Baltimore, Md. Holds 3 degrees from Eastman School of Music. He received the Rosenwald fellowship in composition; first prize, Composers and Authors of America contest, 1944. His Anguished America, Easter, 1968 was performed at

(KERR, THOMAS H., JR.)
the Martin Luther King, Jr., Memorial, National Cathedral, Washinton, D.C., on 30 Mar. 1969, and simultaneously in cathedrals in Germany, Holland, France and Denmark. His Prayer for the soul of Martin Luther King, Jr. was featured on a Washington Oratorio Society program, 17 May 1975.
School of Music, Howard University
Washington, DC 20001

*KESNAR, MAURITS
b. Amsterdam, Neth., 8 July 1900; d. Carbondale, Ill., 22 Feb. 1957. Studied at Amsterdam Cons.; Berlin Hochschule fur Musik; Univ. of Iowa, M. A., Ph. D. He was violin soloist in Europe and U.S.; then chairman, music department, Southern Illinois Univ.
WORKS: Orchestra: symphony; sinfonietta; Poem; Sundown; Chamber music: string quartet; Chorus: Mass in E flat.

KESSLER, MINUETTA
U.S. citizen, 1940. Studied piano with John Williams in Canada; with Ernest Hutcheson at Juilliard School, teacher's and artist diplomas; piano with Ania Dorfman and Mieczyslaw Munz, composition with Ivan Langstroth in New York. She received 2 composition prizes from Composers, Authors, and Publishers Asso. of Canada, 1945, 1946; and Brookline (Mass.) Library Music Asso. composition award.
WORKS: Theatre: Kiddy City, children's operetta; Memories of Tevye, ballet on Jewish themes; Orchestra: Alberta concerto, piano and orch.; New York suite, piano and orch., also for piano solo; Chamber music: cello sonata; violin sonata; piano trio; Ballet sonatina, piano; Etude brilliante (Hora), piano; Chorus: Sacrifice of the innocents, cantata for chorus, organ, brass, percussion; Peace and brotherhood through music, cantata; Victory hora, with piano; Hear my prayer, with organ; Confirmation prayer, for solo voice.
30 Hurley St., Belmont, MA 02178

KESSNER, DANIEL AARON
b. Los Angeles, Calif., 3 June 1946. Studied with Henri Lazarof, Univ. of California, Los Angeles, A. B., M. A., Ph. D. He received first prize in Atwater Kent competitions, 1969, 1970, 1971; first prize, Music Society of Santa Barbara competition, 1970; BMI awards, 1970, 1971; Queen Marie-Jose composition prize, Geneva, 1972. He was instructor, California State Univ., Northridge, 1970-72, assistant professor, 1972-   .
WORKS: Orchestra: Strata, 1971; Mobile, 1973; Chamber music: Ensembles, violin, clarinet, harp, 1968; Equali I, 4 flutes and 4 string instruments, 1968-69; sonatina for solo harp, 1969; Equali II, piano, celesta, 3 percussionists, 1970; Interactions, flute, cello, piano, electronic tape, 1971; Chamber concerto, recorder, high voice, and oboe soli, with string quartet, piano, percussion, 1972; Nebulae: Equali III, string trio, 2 guitars, harpsichord, 1972; Intercurrence for harp and tape, 1972.
2730 Armacost Ave., Los Angeles, CA 90064

KETTERING, EUNICE LEA

KETTERING, EUNICE LEA
b. Savannah, Ohio, 4 Apr. 1906. Studied at
Oberlin Cons., B. M.; School of Sacred Music,
Union Theological Seminary, M. S. M.; with Bela
Bartok in Austria; privately with Edwin J.
Stringham, Normand Lockwood, and Felix Labunski.
She won first award, Nat. Fed. of Music Clubs
contest for choral-orchestral work, Johnny Apple-
seed; 3 awards, Nat. League of American Pen Wo-
men, 1972. She was instructor, Madison Coll.,
1929-1932; professor and composer-in-residence,
Ashland Coll., 1935-58.
WORKS: Chorus: A-shining far in the east;
Bells of Sunday; Christmas sermon; Factory win-
dows are always broken; God of the dew; I hear
America singing; The lamb; The mysterious cat;
Psalm 86, Silence, Valley Forge; many other choral works and piano and organ pieces.
2121 1/2 Coal Ave., S.E.
Albuquerque, NM 87106

KEVAN, G. ALEX
b. England, 28 Jan. 1908, U.S. citizen 1951.
Studied organ in England and with George Coutts,
Regina Coll. of Music, Regina, Sask. He has received commissions for several anthems. He held
organist and choirmaster posts in Saskatchewan
and Alberta before appointment at St. John the
Divine Church, Houston, where he is also chairman, music department, St. John's School. He
has published many anthems and piano pieces.
3435 Westheimer, #511, Houston, TX 77027

KEYES, NELSON
b. Tulsa, Okla., 26 Aug. 1928. Studied with
Kent Kennan and Wilbur Ogdon, Univ. of Texas;
with Ingolf Dahl and Halsey Stevens, Univ. of
Southern California. He received a Huntington
Hartford Found. award, 1951; USC Friends of Music
prize, 1957; Ford Found., Young Composers' Project appointment in Louisville, Ky., 1961-65.
He was instructor, Long Beach City Coll.,
1955-59; assistant professor, Univ. of Southern
California, 1960-61; associate professor, Kansas
State Teachers Coll., Emporia, 1965-69; associate professor, Univ. of Louisville, 1969-   .
WORKS: Orchestra: Music for Monday evenings, 1959; Abysses, bridges, chasms; Band:
Bandances; Hardinsburg joys, brass quintet; Chorus: Give you a lantern; All is safe; also 2
ballets, musical plays, vocal solos.
2338 Strathmoor Blvd., Louisville, KY 40205

KHAN, ALI AKBAR
b. Shibpur, Bengal, 14 Apr. 1922; to U.S. 1965.
Studied with his father, Allauddin Khan, master
of more than 200 instruments who died in 1972 at
age 110. Ali Akbar Khan received 4 awards from
Jodhpur State, Rajistan; President's award and
Padmabhooshan from Govt. of India; and awards
for film scores. He was music director, All
India Radio, Lucknow, 1946-48; court musician,
State of Jodhpur, 1948-54; music director, Bombay Film Industries, 1954-55; president, Ali
Akbar Coll. of Music, Calcutta, 1956-   ; faculty, McGill Univ., 1959-61; head, music department, American Society for Eastern Arts, 1965-67;

(KHAN, ALI AKBAR)
president, Ali Akbar Coll. of Music, Marin
County, Calif., 1967-   .
WORKS: Film scores: Mornings of creation;
The prophet; and numerous new ragas.
18 Napa Ave., Fairfax, CA 94930

KIBBE, MICHAEL
b. San Diego, Calif., 26 June 1945. Studied
with David Ward-Steinman, San Diego State Univ.;
Warner Hutchinson, New Mexico State Univ.; with
Aurelio de la Vega and Frank Campo, California
State Univ. at Northridge. He was first oboe,
Norad Command Band, 1966-69; 2nd oboe, El Paso
Symphony, 1969-70; part-time instructor, California State Univ., Northridge, 1973-   .
WORKS: Chamber music: Concert music, oboe
and strings; trio for 3 horns; wind quintet;
Night music, alto recorder, celeste, string trio;
Chroasis, harp, flute, cello, English horn; 3
modal pieces for recorders and strings; Serenade,
14 winds; quintet for oboe and strings; Chorus:
3 settings from Omar Khayyam, chorus, oboe,
guitar.
7124 Orion, Van Nuys, CA 91406

*KIES, CHRISTOPHER
Variations for piano, Boston, 2 Feb. 1975.
5407 Surrey St., Chevy Chase, MD 20015

KIHLKEN, HENRY
b. Sandusky, Ohio, 25 Sep. 1939. Studied at
Oberlin Cons., 1958-59. He received the Capital
Univ. composition award for 1967. He was organist in Port Clinton, Ohio, 1960-65; assistant
organist, St. Paul Lutheran Church and Old First
Presbyterian Church, Sandusky, 1973-   .
WORKS: Chorus: O saving victim, a cappella;
Lute book lullaby, with harp; Grand choeur; O
living bread, with soprano and alto solos; The
crucifixion, with brass quartet and organ; That
Easter Day with joy was bright; Organ: Prelude
on Palestrina's Adoramus te.
5216 East Harbor Road
Port Clinton, OH 43452

*KILENYI, EDWARD, SR.
b. Bekes, Hungary, 25 Jan. 1884; U.S. citizen
1915; d. Tallahassee, Fla., 15 Aug. 1968. Studied at the Hungarian State Coll., B. A.; with
Pietro Mascagni, Nat. Music School, Rome;
Cologne Cons.; Columbia Univ., M. A., Ph. D. He
was music director in film theatres in New York;
then music director and supervisor in film studios in Hollywood for 30 years. His works include a string quartet and a string quintet.

*KILPATRICK, JACK FREDERICK
Now deceased, taught at Southern Methodist Univ.
in the 1960s. His works include Festival piece
for orch.

KIM, BYONG-KON
b. Taegu, Korea, 28 May 1929; U.S. citizen 1973.
Studied with Bernhard Heiden, Indiana Univ.,
M. M., D. M. He received a John Edward fellowship, Indiana Univ., 1965; research grant, American Council of Learned Societies, 1970. He was

(KIM, BYONG-KON)
director of theory, Villa Maria Coll., Buffalo,
N. Y., 1966-68; program head, Northeastern Region, Contemporary Music Project, 1967-68; assistant professor, California State Univ., Los
Angeles, 1968-   .
    WORKS: Orchestra: Nak-Dong-Kang, symphonic
poem; Concertino for percussion; a symphony;
Chamber music: violin sonata; oboe sonata;
string quartet; 4 short pieces for piano.
    30458 Via Victoria
    Rancho Palos Verdes, CA 90274

KIM, EARL
    b. Dinuba, Calif., 6 Jan. 1920. Studied with
Roger Sessions, Univ. of California, Berkeley,
M. A. 1952; and also with Arnold Schoenberg.
His awards include the Prix de Paris; grants
from Guggenheim Found., Nat. Inst. of Arts and
Letters, Fromm Found., Koussevitzky Found.; and
the Brandeis Creative Arts Medal, 1971. He was
associate professor, Princeton Univ., 1952-67;
professor, Harvard Univ., 1967-   .
    WORKS: Orchestra: Dialogues, piano and
orch., 1959; Chamber music: violin sonata;
cello sonata; Songs: The road, cycle for baritone; Letters found near a suicide, cycle for
soprano; Piano: 2 bagatelles, 1948, 1950; Multimedia: Exercises en route, soprano, chamber ensemble, dancers, actors, film, text by Samuel
Beckett; Earthlight, muted violin, soprano,
piano, and lights, Cambridge, Mass., 19 May 1973.
    Music Department, Harvard University
    Cambridge, MA 02138

KIMBELL, MICHAEL ALEXANDER
    b. Glen Cove, N. Y., 15 Mar. 1946. Studied with John
Davison, Haverford Coll., B. A. 1967; with Robert
Palmer and Karel Husa, Cornell Univ., Ph. D. 1971. He
has been instructor, Johnson State Coll.,
1971-73, assistant professor, 1973-   .
    WORKS: Orchestra: Wanderers Sturmlied,
chorus, baritone, orch., 1971; Pastorale, for
small orch.; Chamber music: string quartet;
woodwind quintet; Passacaglia, woodwind quintet;
5 dialogues for 2 clarinets; Songs: 3 sonnets
from the Portuguese; 3 Lieder.
    P.O. Box 141, Johnson, VT 05656

KIMMEL, WALTER S.
    b. New York, N. Y., 22 Jan. 1941. Studied with
Herbert R. Inch and Donald Lybbert, Hunter Coll.,
B. A., M. A.; with Vladimir Ussachevsky and Mario
Davidovsky, Columbia-Princeton Electronic Music
Center. He has received awards from Class of
1895, Hunter Coll., 1962; 2nd Dartmouth Coll.
competition for electronic music, 1969; Oregon
Coll. of Education, Kinetic Theatre competition,
1971; Cannes Internat. Film Festival, silver
medal with Dale Amundson, 1971; and commissions.
He was lecturer, Hunter Coll., 1965-68; director,
electronic music, assistant professor, Moorhead
State Coll., 1968-72; assistant professor,
Sangamon State Univ., 1972-   .
    WORKS: Chamber music: Kireji, alto voice
and 10 players, 1965; Dialogues, brass quartet,
1966; 5 Haiku settings, soprano, flute, violin,
cello, 1966; Film scores: Steps toward art,

(KIMMEL, WALTER S.)
1969; Variegations on a theme of Chopin, film
score to Dots, 1970; General Motors enters into
heaven, score to Onus I, 1971; A just and last-
ing piece, score to A majority of 1, 1971 (all
films by Dale Amundson); Electronic: Electronic
piece #1, 1967; Cronaca, 1967; Hide and seek,
1968; The painting, 1968; Bacchanalysis, 1971;
8 minimal pieces, 1971; The Dickens, What?, 1971;
Multimedia: Trilogue for pianist and 2 loudspeakers, 1969; A generation of piece, or
Warsore concerto for trombone, radios, and
president, 1971.
    104 Outer Park Drive, Springfield, IL 62704

KING, ALVIN
    b. Orrville, Ohio, 24 Aug. 1917. Studied with
Cecil Effinger and George Crumb, Univ. of Colorado, D. M. A.; with Arthur Honneger in Paris;
and with Paul Hindemith at Yale Univ. He received a Charles S. McClesky commission, Univ.
of Texas; and a Woolley fellowship for study in
France. His faculty posts include Univ. of Arkansas,
1956-59; chairman, Fine Arts, Midland Coll., 1959-63;
Mesa Coll. and conductor, Civic Symphony, 1964-67;
professor, Macalester Coll., 1967-   .
    WORKS: Orchestra: Variations for orch.;
Sketch for orch.; Fantasy on a hymn tune, chorus
and orch.; Daniel, baritone and tenor soloists,
narrator, orch.; Chamber music: string quintet;
Periodic variations, string quartet; trio for
violin, viola, piano; suite for 4 recorders;
piano sonata; sextet for 2 tubas, 4 parts pre-
recorded; 4-hand intervals for piano; Chorus:
Psalm 47, with 8 brasses; Psalm 67; My shepherd;
Psalm 117; Psalm 93, with drum; Song of Solomon,
double chorus and 8 brasses; Joseph, an oratorio;
Psalm 131, with brass.
    722 East 5th St., St. Paul, MN 55106

KING, JEFFREY
    b. Ft. Wayne, Ind., 27 June 1942. Studied with
Jon Polifrone, Indiana State Univ.; with
Carlisle Floyd, Florida State Univ. He won 2nd
place, Nat. Fed. of Music Clubs contest, 1968;
first place, Brown Univ. choral contest, 1971;
first place, Tennessee Technological Univ. contest, 1973. He has been associate professor,
Athens Coll., 1966-   ; on sabbatical leave in
1973 for doctoral work at Ball State Univ.
    WORKS: Band: Excursion; Manifesto; Cham-
ber music: Facets, string orch.; violin sonata;
Chorus: Dialogue; a wind has blown the rain
away; what if a much of a which of a wind; i
thank you God.
    106 Tyrone Drive, Muncie, IN 47304

KING, KARL L.
    b. Paintersville, Ohio, 21 Feb. 1891; d. Fort
Dodge, Iowa, 31 Mar. 1971. Published his first
march at 17 and began playing professionally.
By 1914 he was bandmaster of the Sells-Floto
Buffalo Bill combined circuses; from 1920 to
1970 was director of the Fort Dodge Municipal Band.
Hundreds of his marches are published.

KING, ROBERT DAVIS
    b. North Easton, Mass., 27 Nov. 1913. Studied
with Walter Piston, Edward Burlingame Hill, and

KING, ROBERT DAVIS

(KING, ROBERT DAVIS)

Nadia Boulanger, Harvard Univ.; with Fritz Mahler at Juilliard School. He received a fellowship to the MacDowell Colony. He was music supervisor, public schools, 1941-42; assistant professor, Boston Univ., 1946-50; public school music supervisor, 1950-55; music publisher and baritone horn player with Boston Brass Quartet, 1955-   .

WORKS: Wind ensemble: Prelude and fugue for 7 brass; Prelude and fugue for brass quartet and organ; French suite for trumpet and baritone horn; 7 conversation pieces for brass choir.

7 Canton St., North Easton, MA 02356

KINGMAN, DANIEL C.

b. Los Angeles, Calif., 16 Aug. 1924. Studied with Bernard Rogers, Eastman School of Music; with H. Owen Reed, Michigan State Univ., Ph. D. 1964. He received a Huntington Hartford fellowship. He has been professor, California State Univ., Sacramento, 1956-   .

WORKS: Opera: The indian summer of Dry Valley Johnson, 1965; Orchestra: symphony in 1 movement, 1965; 5 Earthscapes with birds, soprano and orch., 1973; Chamber music: quintet for winds; 4 miniatures for brass quartet; Canonic etudes for brass, 1973.

600 Shangri Lane, Sacramento, CA 95825

KINGSFORD, CHARLES

b. Brooklyn, N. Y., 16 Aug. 1907. Studied with Rubin Goldmark, Juilliard School, 1925-29; piano with Harold Trigg, Rosina Lhevinne, Edith Ricci. He held fellowships for study at Juilliard. He was music director, Ft. Washington Synagogue, New York, 1938-44, at Mt. Vernon, N. Y., 1944-50; on faculty, American Theatre Wing, 1946-57; music therapist, Veterans Admin. Hospital, East Orange, N. J., 1953-72.

WORKS: Orchestra: We'll answer Stalingrad, chorus and orch., New York, Dec. 1943; And already the minutes, voice and chamber orch., Saratoga Spa, N. Y., 27 Sep. 1937; Songs: Alas, that spring should vanish with the rose; The ballad of John Henry; Eros; Rivets; Wallpaper; and many other songs.

150 West 57th St., New York, NY 10019

KINGSLEY, GERSHON

b. Germany, 28 Oct. 1928; U.S. citizen 1950. Studied at Jerusalem Cons., Los Angeles Cons., Columbia Univ., and Los Angeles State Coll. He has received award for radio and television commercials, 1968; International Broadcasting award, 1968; Emmy awards, 1968, 1969; CINE award, 1970; Lion d'Or, Venice Film Festival, 1970; ASCAP award, 1972. He was a faculty member, New School of Social Research, 1969-70.

WORKS: Orchestra: Concerto Moogo; Confrontations; several works for orchestra and synthesizer; Chorus: Sabbath for today, 1971; What is man, 1971; Bronze cactus, 1972.

150 West 55th St., New York, NY 10010

KINNEY, GORDON J.

b. Rochester, N. Y., 10 Apr. 1905. Studied with Edward Royce, Eastman School of Music, B. M. 1930; Univ. of South Dakota, M. M. 1941; with

(KINNEY, GORDON J.)

Ernst von Dohnanyi, Florida State Univ., Ph. D. 1962. He received an award, Nat. Composers Competition, 1942. His faculty positions include Morningside Coll., 1937-41; Ohio Univ., 1941-45; Univ. of Kentucky, 1948-74.

WORKS: Orchestra: Piece for orchestra with piano, 1935; symphony, 1951; Concert piece, horn and chamber orch., Lexington, Ky., 29 Nov. 1973; Chamber music: string quartets, 1942, 1953; cello sonata, 1942; Fantasy, horn and piano, 1952; Suite for tuba solo, 1968; Ricercar, tuba solo, 1968.

149 Rosemont Garden, Lexington, KY 40503

*KINSCELLA, HAZEL GERTRUDE

b. Nora Springs, Iowa, 27 Apr. 1895; d. Seattle, Wash., 15 July 1960. Studied at Univ. of Nebraska, B. M., B. F. A., B. A.; Columbia Univ., M. A.; with Rossetter Gleason Cole and Howard Brockway; received an honorary doctorate, Univ. of Washington. She was professor, Univ. of Nebraska, later at the Univ. of Washington; author of books on piano pedagogy.

WORKS: Chamber music: Indian sketches, string quartet; Chorus: A child is born, cantata; Psalm 150; Our prayer; My days have been so wondrous free.

*KINYON, JOHN

b. Elmira, N. Y., 23 May 1918. Studied at Eastman School of Music, B. M.; Ithaca Coll., M. S. He taught in public schools for 20 years; then assistant professor, Univ. of Miami.

WORKS: Band: Ballad for Bambi; Carnival for clarinets; Carnival for flutes; Carnival for trumpets; Carnival for trombones.

1638 Northeast 7th Place
Fort Lauderdale, FL 33310

*KIRCHNER, LEON

b. Brooklyn, N. Y., 24 Jan. 1919. Studied at Univ. of California, A. B. 1940. His awards include the Prix de Rome, 1940; Guggenheim fellowship, 1948-50; New York Music Critics' Circle award, 1950, 1960; Naumburg award, 1954; American Acad. of Arts and Letters award; membership in the Nat. Inst. of Arts and Letters. He was faculty member, Mills Coll., 1952-61, professor, 1954-61; professor, Harvard Univ., 1961-   ; visiting professor, Univ. of California at Los Angeles, 1970.

WORKS: Orchestra: Sinfonia, 1951; piano concerto, 1952-53; Toccata, strings, winds, percussion, 1955; concerto for violin, cello, 10 winds, percussion, 1960; Chamber music: duo for violin and piano, 1947; piano sonata, 1948; piano suite, 1949; 2 string quartets, 1949, 1958; Sonata concertante, 1952; piano trio, 1954; quartet #3, strings and tape; Voice: Daun, chorus, on text by Garcia Lorca, 1943; Lily, soprano and chamber ensemble, Cambridge, Mass., 23 Apr. 1973.

8 Hilliard St., Cambridge, MA 02138

KIRK, THERON

b. Alamo, Tex., 28 Sep. 1919. Studied with Bernard Rogers, Eastman School of Music; with

(KIRK, THERON)
Karel Jirak at Roosevelt Univ.; Bernice Hensler, Baylor Univ. He received several ASCAP awards; commissions from Kansas State Centennial, West Virginia Creative Arts Festival, San Antonio Symphony; Benjamin award; Knox-Galesburg award. His latest faculty post is professor, San Antonio Coll., 1965-   .
WORKS: Theatre: The Lib: 393 b.c., 1-act comic opera; Orchestra: 2 symphonies; Intrada; Concerto for orchestra; Vignettes; An orchestra primer; Band: Aylesford variations; Smoky Mountain suite; Chorus: cantatas with orch. and more than 600 published choral works.
3430 Fallen Leaf Lane, San Antonio, TX 78230

KISS, JANOS
Hungary, 21 Mar. 1920; U.S. citizen 1973. Attended Bela Bartok Cons., Franz Liszt Acad., and People's Educational Inst. in Budapest; Western Reserve Univ., Cleveland. He has received commissions from Western Reserve Acad., Mimura Harp Ensemble of Japan, New York Harp Ensemble, Vienna Symphony Trombone Quartet; and is honorary member of Zoltan Kodaly Acad., Chicago. He has been on the faculty, Cleveland Music School Settlement, 1964- ; Western Reserve Acad., 1967-72, composer-in-residence, 1971-72; St. Edward High School, Lakewood, 1968-   , composer-in-residence, 1970-   .
WORKS: Orchestra: piano concerto; string bass concerto, Budapest, 8 June 1970; violin concerto; flute concerto; Symphonic poem, 1971; Interlude 40, organ and orch., 1972; trombone concerto, Berea, Ohio, 27 May 1972; Andante, piano and orch.; Wind ensemble: Te deum, brass ensemble, 1970; Processional and recessional, brass quartet and organ, Cleveland, 20 Aug. 1972; Ceremonial march, 3 trumpets and organ; quintet for violin and 4 trombones, Bregenz, Austria, 15 Aug. 1973; Chamber music: Spring--at last!, harp ensemble, 1970; harp and woodwind quintet; trio for harp, flute, viola, 1970; Fantasy for flute, Cleveland, 24 Oct. 1971; Osiris, nonet, 1972; The mystery of spring, string quartet and harp; On the wing, flute and guitar; Adagio, viola and piano.
229 Bradley Road, Bay Village, OH 44140

KLAUS, KENNETH BLANCHARD
b. Earlville, Iowa, 11 Nov. 1923. Studied with Philip Greeley Clapp, Univ. of Iowa, Ph. D. 1950. He received awards from Nat. Fed. of Music Clubs. He has been faculty member, Louisiana State Univ., 1950, professor, 1963-   ; alumni professor, 1966-   ; principal viola, 1950, associate conductor, 1967-   , Baton Rouge Symphony.
WORKS: Theatre: Tennis anyone?, operatic farce, 1957; Moira, monodramatic opera; music for Death of a salesman, Baton Rouge, 24 Feb. 1954; On our way, a pageant, 1940; Always Acadia, pageant, 1955; Louisiana's Koasati, film score, 1955; Orchestra: 3 symphonies; Antonyms, Baton Rouge, 19 Mar. 1959; Adagio, bassoon and orch.; The Alamo by night; violin concerto; Concerto brevis, flute and strings, 1950; cello concerto; percussion concerto; Fugato concertanto; Markings, 1970; Chamber music: 4 string quartets,

(KLAUS, KENNETH BLANCHARD)
1947, 1951, 1957, 1963; 2 violin sonatas; woodwind sextet; cello sonata; suite for cello and piano; horn sonata; oboe sonata; Music for 4 trombones; woodwind quintet; 2 sonatas for violin solo; 3 aleatory matrices; also songs, piano and organ pieces. He is also lecturer, panelist, author of articles in music journals, and of a book: The romantic period in music, Boston, 1970.
823 Kenilworth Parkway
Baton Rouge, LA 70808

KLAUSMEYER, PETER BALLARD
b. Cincinnati, Ohio, 28 Nov. 1942. Studied with T. Scott Huston, Univ. of Cincinnati; Leslie Bassett, Ross Lee Finney, George Cacioppo, George Balch Wilson, Univ. of Michigan. He tied for first place, 2nd Internat. Competition for Electronic Music, Dartmouth Arts Council; won honorable mention, 6th Internat. Composition Contest, Societa Italiana Musica Contemporanea, 1972. He became instructor, Meredith Coll., 1973-   .
WORKS: Orchestra: ...partial fulfillment..., D. M. A. thesis, Ann Arbor, Mich., 15 Nov. 1972; Electronic: Cambrian Sea; Teddy-bears' picnic, 1972.
313-J Hastings Place, Raleigh, NC 27511

*KLAUSS, KENNETH
Studied with Ernst Toch, Univ. of Southern California. His works include a sonata for harpsichord and timpani; sonata for solo trumpet; sonata for solo tuba.

KLAUSS, NOAH
b. Lebanon, Pa., 14 Oct. 1901. Studied at Harrisburg Cons.; at Elizabethtown Coll.; violin with Max Pollikoff and Ottakar Cadek. He has taught violin for 50 years; at Elizabethtown Coll., 1958-61; assistant director, Harrisburg Symphony, 1948-   ; founder and director, Harrisburg Youth Symphony Orchestra, 1949-   .
WORKS: Wind ensemble: Jakarta, solo horn and clarinet choir; Night song, saxophone choir; Prelude, 6 clarinets; Chamber music: Evangeline, harp and organ.
219 North Mount Joy St.
Elizabethtown, PA 17022

KLEEN, LESLIE
b. Minden, Neb., 27 Nov. 1942. Studied with Normand Lockwood, Univ. of Denver; Robert Palmer and Karel Husa, Cornell Univ.; with Lejaren Hiller and Morton Feldman, State Univ. of New York at Buffalo. He was instructor, State Univ. of New York, Buffalo, 1971-74.
WORKS: Orchestra: Conserere for 2 orchestras; Chamber music: Air, for male voice, 2 flutes, 2 clarinets, percussion; 2 Walt Whitman songs; string trio; Electronic: 4 movements by computer; O progress, electronic tape.
9445 Main St., Clarence, NY 14031

KLEIMAN, STEPHEN ROBERT
b. Brooklyn, N. Y., 18 Aug. 1943. Studied with Peter Pindar Stearns, Mannes Coll. of Music;

KLEIMAN, STEPHEN ROBERT

(KLEIMAN, STEPHEN ROBERT)
with Ross Lee Finney, Leslie Bassett, George Cacioppo, George Wilson, Univ. of Michigan. He received the Sigvald Thompson award, Fargo-Moorhead Symphony, 1973; Fulbright-Hays grant for study in France with Max Deutsch, 1973. He taught at Sacred Heart Acad., New York, 1968-69; Brooklyn Acad., of Music, 1969-70; was teaching fellow, Univ. of Michigan, 1971-73.
    WORKS: Orchestra: Concerto for orchestra, 1971, Fargo-Moorhead Symphony, 24 Jan. 1974; Chamber music: 6 short pieces for string quartet, 1948; Suite for guitar; 6 Haiku, voice and piano, 1970; Patterns, piano, 1970; Sanctuary, flute, bassoon, string quintet, percussion, 1971; Festivity, flute, viola, harp, 1972; 4 graphic duets, 2 instruments or groups of instruments, 1972; Sweet, bassoon, marimba, piano, and 3 voices, 1972; 31 Connallystrasse (in memoriam) for clarinet, violin, cello, horn, piano, 1972; Fairytale, 2 flutes and tape, 1973; Quattre a battre, 4 conductors and audience, 1973; Chorus: So shy, shy, shy, 1972; Carnival, with brass and organ, 1972.

KLEIN, JOHN M.
    b. Rahns, Pa., 21 Feb. 1915. Studied with H. Alexander Matthews, Philadelphia Music Acad.; at the Mozarteum, Salzburg; with Nadia Boulanger, Marcel Dupre in Paris; Paul Hindemith in Leipzig and at Tanglewood. He was free-lance composer and arranger for major networks and film studios, New York and Hollywood, 1944-57; and musical director and carilloneur, Schulmerich Carillons, Sellersville, Pa., 1957-   .
    WORKS: 450 published works for orchestra, symphonic band, brass ensemble, percussion ensemble, hand bells, carillon, chorus, solo voice, piano, organ, other solo instruments. He is also author of a 2-volume work: The first four centuries of music, 1350-1750; and The art of playing the modern carillon.
    Rahns, PA 19426

KLEIN, LEONARD
    b. Clarkdale, Ariz., 19 Feb. 1929. Studied with Darius Milhaud, Mills Coll.; with Jean Rivier in Paris; and with Philip Bezanson, Univ. of Iowa. He won 2 Copley awards and 2 first prizes at Aspen, Colo. He has been on the faculties of Univ. of Oklahoma, 1961-63; Indiana Univ., 1963-65; Mills Coll., 1965-71; Stockton State Coll., 1971-   .
    WORKS: Orchestra: Concerto for piano, winds, and percussion; Chamber music: Concertpiece for cello; duo for violin and piano; Chorus: Psalm XLVII, women's voices, soloists, organ, and ring modulator; Piano: sonata for 2 pianos; Fantasies, piano solo.
    Stockton State Coll., Pomona, NJ 08240

KLEIN, LOTHAR
    b. Hannover, Germany, 27 Jan. 1932; U.S. citizen 1945. Studied at Univ. of Minnesota, Ph. D.; with Boris Blacher in Berlin. He was Fulbright fellow, 1958-60; Fulbright visiting professor, Hochschule fuer Musik, Berlin, guest lecturer for 150th anniversary of the Hochschule; received

(KLEIN, LOTHAR)
    Rockefeller New Music Project awards, 1946, 1965, 1967; and has been a MacDowell Colony fellow. He was assistant professor, Univ. of Texas, 1962-70; director, Inter-American Symposium, Univ. of Texas, 1964-68; associate professor, Univ. of Toronto, 1970-   .
    WORKS: Orchestra: 2 symphonies, 1955, 1959; Concerto for 4 winds and orch., 1958; Appassionata for orch., 1959; Symmetries, I-IV, 1959-64; Trio concertante, solo strings and orch., 1964; Charivari, music for an imaginary comedy; Musique a go-go; Janizary music; Symfonia concertante; Epitaphs for orch.; Chamber music: Suite for contrabass solo; trio sonata, clarinet, cello, piano, with jazz set of drums; Chorus: A little book of hours; 3 laments; Epigrams of Sappho, cantata for actress, 3 soloists, percussion.
    c/o ASCAP
    1 Lincoln Plaza, New York, NY 10022

*KLEIN, PHILIP G.
    Lullaby, chorus on Agee text.
    127 East Lafayette Ave., Syracuse, NY 13205

KLEINSINGER, GEORGE
    b. San Bernardino, Calif., 13 Feb. 1914. Studied with Marion Bauer and Philip James, New York Univ.; with Frederick Jacobi and Bernard Wagenaar, Juilliard School. He held a graduate fellowship in composition at Juilliard; received Emmy nomination for filmscore, Greece: The Golden Age, 1963; Oscar nomination for film, Tubby the tuba. He was guest lecturer, Brooklyn Coll., 1956, 1957.
    WORKS: Theatre: Life in the diary of a secretary (Nat. New Theatre prize); Shinbone Alley, Broadway musical based on archie and mehitabel, 1954; Orchestra: symphony, 1942; Fantasy, violin and orch.; Victory against heaven; Scherzo; Westward Ho!; Western rhapsody; Pantomime; Joie de vivre; cello concerto, 1946; Street corner concerto, clarinet and orch., 1947; Orchestra with narrator, for children: Tubby the tuba, 1942; Story of Celeste; Johnny the stranger; Pan the piper; Peewee the piccolo; Band: Symphony of winds, with narrator; Chamber music: clarinet quintet; sonatina for flute, cello, piano; string quartet; Design for woodwinds; Vocal: I hear America singing, baritone and orch.; Farewell to a hero; Brooklyn baseball cantata; many other compositions in all genres including film scores.
    222 West 23rd St., New York, NY 10011

KLEMENT, JEROME
    b. Chicago, Ill., 19 Mar. 1922. Studied with Hans Rosenwald, Bernard Brindell, Chicago Musical Coll. of Roosevelt Univ., American Operatic Laboratory. He was cantor, Beth Hillel, Wilmette, Ill., 1959-64; Temple Emanu-el, Ft. Lauderdale, 1965-   .
    WORKS: Vocal (Jewish liturgy): Li Lekach Tov; Eili, Eili; Vohauta; Ma Tovu.
    4760 N.E. 18th Terrace
    Ft. Lauderdale, FL 33308

*KLEMM, GUSTAV
b. Baltimore, Md., 6 Feb. 1897; d. Baltimore, 5 Sep. 1947. Studied with Gustave Strube, Peabody Cons.; held scholarship in cello with Bart Wirtz. His other awards included an Etude prize and the Chicago Singing Teachers Guild award. He was an army bandmaster in World War I; conductor, City Park Band, Baltimore, 1922-25; music critic, Baltimore Sun, 1920-32; radio program director, 1925-38; head, preparatory department, Peabody Cons., 1944-47. He composed several hundred songs and many film scores.

*KLENNER, JOHN
b. Germany, 24 Feb. 1890; d. New York, N. Y., 13 Aug. 1955. Fantasia, viola and orch.; Variations, string orch.; squares and rounds on My old brown fiddle, string orch.; popular songs.

KLETZSCH, CHARLES
b. Milwaukee, Wis., 4 Apr. 1926. Studied with Walter Piston at Harvard Univ. He has been composer-in-residence, Dunster House, Harvard Univ., 1958-   .
WORKS: Instrumental and vocal chamber music performed at Harvard Univ., liturgical music performed at St. Paul's Church, Cambridge.
Dunster House Library, Cambridge, MA 02138

KLIMISCH, SISTER MARY JANE
b. Utica, S. D., 22 Aug. 1920. Studied with Sister Florence Therese, St. Mary-of-the-Woods Coll.; at American Cons.; with John B. Egan, St. Joseph's Coll., Rensselaer, Ind.; and with Robert Wykes, Washington Univ., Ph. D. She was faculty member, Mt. Marty High School, 1943-50; chairman, music department and creative arts division, Mt. Marty Coll., 1950-68, professor, 1970-   .
WORKS: Chorus: Mass to honor Joan of Arc; Nativity antiphon; Glory hymn book (a collaboration); and numerous unpublished liturgical works.
Mount Marty College, Yankton, SD 57078

KLIMKO, RONALD JAMES
b. Lena, Wis., 13 Dec. 1936. Studied with Irwin Sonenfield, Milton Coll., B. A. 1959; with Hilmar Luckhardt and Robert Crane, Univ. of Wisconsin, Ph. D. 1968. He received a Leaman Stringer award, 1959; Wisconsin composer contest awards, 1962-65; graduate fellowship, Univ. of Wisconsin, 1966. He was faculty member, Moorhead State Coll., 1966-67; Indiana State Univ., 1967-68; associate professor, Univ. of Idaho, 1968-   .
WORKS: Ballet: The highway, 1965; Orchestra: The hollow men, chorus and orch., 1963; Edgewood overture, 1964; Introduction, pastorale, and ricercare, 1965; Echoes, chorus, orch., and electronic sounds, 1967; Chamber music: A child's garden of weeds, woodwind quintet, 1964; Canonic variations, chamber orch., 1964; woodwind quintet, 1965; Contours, cello and piano, 1967; violin sonata, 1968.
210 North Grant St., Moscow, ID 83843

KLOTZ, LEDRA. See DRETKE, LEORA N.

KLUCEVSEK, GUY
b. New York, N. Y., 26 Feb. 1947. Studied with Robert Bernat, Indiana Univ. of Pennsylvania; Gerald Shapiro, Univ. of Pittsburgh; Morton Subotnik, California Inst. of the Arts. He is a free-lance composer-accordionist.
WORKS: Accordion: Phantasmagoria; Amplifaccordion; Ave Maria misty; Coruscation; Aeolian variations; 3 A.M.; Cassandra, a duet; Unspecified instruments: Rain piece; Piano: Toronto:(seventh); Cadence; Electronic: Happenings; Fawos; Serenity; Resolution; Spheres, ensemble with tape.
98 Lincoln Ave., Clementon, NJ 08021

KNIGHT, MORRIS
b. Charleston, S. C., 25 Dec. 1933. Studied at Univ. of Georgia and Ball State Univ. He received commissions from the Organization of American States for the 5th Inter-American Music Festival, 1970, and Music Teachers Nat. Asso., 1972; annual ASCAP awards, 1967-73; Ford publication and recording award, 1972; MacDowell award, 1970. He was radio announcer in Athens, Ga., 1956-62, in San Francisco, 1962; assistant professor, Ball State Univ., 1963-   .
WORKS: Chamber music: Introduction and allegro, trumpet; Cassation, trumpet, horn, trombone; Selfish giant suite, flute, clarinet, bassoon, trombone; 6 brass quartets; alto saxophone sonata, 1964; Instances, woodwind quintet, 1965; saxophone quartet, Muncie, Ind., 18 Feb. 1969; 4 brass quintets, 1972; Chorus: Miracles, settings of 26 poems by children for chorus and chamber orch., 1968; Electronic: Refractions, clarinet and tape, 1962; Origin of prophecy, 1964; Luminescences, 1967; After Guernica, 1969; Entity one - Music for the global village, for 20 tape recorders and 40 speakers arranged along the walls of the performance area; the piece was taken on a nationwide tour in 1973. Knight is also co-author of Aural comprehension in music, 1972.
2424 Petty Road, Muncie, IN 47304

KNOX, CHARLES
b. Atlanta, Ga., 19 Apr. 1929. Studied with Bernhard Heiden, Indiana Univ. He received first prize, Georgia Fed. of Music Clubs, 1955; commissions from Symposium of Contemporary Music for Brass, 1965, Georgia Music Educators Asso., 1967, 1968, 1969. He was principal trombonist, Atlanta Symphony Orch., 1948-51; associate professor, Mississippi Coll., 1955-65; professor, Georgia State Univ., 1965-   .
WORKS: Wind ensemble: Symphony for brass and percussion, 1965; solo for trumpet with brass trio; solo for tuba with brass trio; Chorus: Sing we to our God above; Festival Procession; Psalm of praise.
Georgia State University
33 Gilmer St., S.E., Atlanta, GA 30303

*KNUDSON, PAUL
The actress or Doll in the pink dress, commissioned by Montclair State Coll., N. J., for American Bicentennial 1976.

KOBLITZ, DAVID
b. Cleveland, Ohio, 5 Oct. 1948. Studied with
George Crumb, Univ. of Pennsylvania, B. A.;
Ross Lee Finney, Leslie Bassett, George Cacioppo,
Univ. of Michigan; and with Donald Martino at
Tanglewood. He received BMI student composer
awards, 1970, 1971, 1973.
    WORKS: Orchestra: Trism, 1971; Gris-gris;
Chamber music: Oxolotyl, 2 contrabasses, 1970;
Nomos, solo contrabass; Lobo, chamber ensemble,
1971; Levitation boogie, chamber ensemble; Rigor
vitus, chamber ensemble; Electronic: Ceremony
of shrugs, tape; Dwellers of the threshold.
    70 Mt. Pleasant Court, Somerville, MA 02145

KOCH, FREDERICK
b. Cleveland, Ohio, 4 Apr. 1924. Studied with
Herbert Elwell, Cleveland Inst. of Music, B. M.
1949; Arthur Shepherd, Western Reserve Univ.,
M. A. 1950; with Henry Cowell and Bernard Rogers,
Eastman School of Music, D. M. A. 1969; piano
with Beryl Rubinstein and Leonard Shure. He has
held 2 MacDowell fellowships, 1971, 1972; received commissions from National Gallery Orch.;
Elie Apper, Brussels Cons.; Ohio Arts Council;
won Homer B. Hatch award; Composers Press composition award; was participant in 1st Ohio Composers Symposium, Columbus, 1971; grants from
National Found. on the Arts; American Music
Center. He was founder and director of a private music school, 1952-   , affiliated with
Cleveland Music School Settlement, 1971-   ; on
faculty Baldwin Wallace Cons., 1964-66; lecturer,
Cuyahoga Community Coll., 1969.
    WORKS: Opera: Invasion, 1974; Orchestra:
Short symphony; Concertino, saxophone and orch.
or band; Symphonic suite, voice and orch.;
Dance overture; River journey; Chamber music:
3 string quartets; string quintet; Trio of
praise, voice, viola, piano; Sound particles,
piano, percussion, and reciter; 3 dance episodes,
saxophone and tape; Microcosms, percussion quartet, electronic sounds, film; Veltin fantasy,
oboe and strings; Monadnock cadenzas and variations, 8 instruments and tape; 3 pictures, violin and piano; choral works, songs, piano pieces.
    2249 Valleyview Drive, Rocky River, OH 44116

*KOCH, JOHN
b. 1928. Elegy for string orch.; many published duets and trios for recorders; 7 songs on
texts of Ezra Pound, Edward Lear, Walter de la
Mare, et al.

KOELLING, ELOISE
b. Centralia, Ill., 3 Mar. 1908. Studied at
Northwestern Univ. and with Bernard Dieter,
Chicago Cons. Coll. She received 3 Univ. of
Wisconsin grants; 14 first prizes, Wisconsin
Composers contests; Padro Pas award, Olivet Coll.;
Delta Omicron Sorority commission; performance
at Fed. of Women Convention and 2 works at
Internat. Society for Contemporary Music, Chi-
cago. She was professor, Univ. of Wisconsin,
Milwaukee, 1949-68.
    WORKS: Orchestra: a symphony; 2 piano con-
certos; Chamber music: 4 string quartets; 5
woodwind ensembles; Improvisation for timpani;

(KOELLING, ELOISE)
Chorus: As long as my Saviour reigns; Naomi's
lament, women's voices and woodwinds; Democratic
thinking in 18th, 19th, 20th centuries; number
of anthems and works for women's voices; numerous songs.
    P.O. Box 131, Palmyra, WI 53156

KOHN, KARL
b. Vienna, Austria, 1 Aug. 1926; U.S. citizen
1945. Attended New York Coll. of Music;
studied with Walter Piston, Irving Fine, Randall
Thompson, Harvard Univ., B. A. 1950, M. A. 1954.
He was Fulbright research fellow, Helsinki,
1954-55; Guggenheim fellow and grantee of Howard
Found., 1961-62; Ford Found. sabbatical fellow,
1968-69; recipient of Mellon Found. grant. 1973.
He has been faculty member, Pomona Coll.,
1950-   , Thatcher professor and composer-in-
residence in 1973.
    WORKS: Orchestra: Sinfonia concertante,
piano and orch., Claremont, Calif., 23 Mar. 1952;
Castles and kings, suite for children, Claremont,
22 Mar. 1959; 3 scenes, 1960, Los Angeles, 5 May
1965; Concerto mutabile, piano and orch., San
Francisco, 18 Mar. 1963; Interludes, 1964; Episodes, piano and orch., 1966, Oakland, 19 Apr.
1968; Intermezzo, piano and strings, 1969;
Esdras - anthems and interludes, flute and piano
solo, chorus, and orch., 1970; Centone, Claremont, 27 July 1973; Wind ensemble: Fanfare for
brass and percussion, Tanglewood, 31 July 1952;
Motet for 8 horns, Los Angeles, 23 Feb. 1954;
horn quartet, 1957; Chamber music: Concert
Music for 12 winds, Claremont, 17 Feb. 1957;
Adagio and allegro, brass quartet and piano,
Tanglewood, 18 July 1957; 3 pieces, flute and
piano, 1958; Divertimento, woodwind quartet,
1959; Capriccios, chamber ensemble, Los Angeles,
5 Nov. 1962; Serenade, wind quintet and piano,
1962; Little suite, wind quintet, 1963; Kaleidoscope, string quartet, New York, 3 Dec. 1965;
Introductions and parodies, 3 winds, string
quartet, piano, 1967, Pasadena, 15 Nov. 1970;
Rhapsodies, marimba, vibraphone, percussion,
1968, Los Angeles, 6 Oct. 1969; Impromptus for
8 winds, 1969; Reflections, clarinet and piano,
1970; Variations, horn and piano, 1971; Souvenirs, violin and piano, 1971; Encounters III,
violin and piano, 1971; trio for violin, horn,
piano, Claremont, 12 July 1972; Encounters IV,
oboe and piano, 1972; Chorus: Winter song, 1952;
The red cockatoo, 1953, Cambridge, Mass., 15
Mar. 1955; A Latin fable, Cambridge, 15 Apr.
1955; 3 descantes from Ecclesiastes, 1957; 3
Goliard songs, men's voices a cappella, 1958;
Sensus spei, double chorus and winds, 1961,
Santa Barbara, 6 Feb. 1963; Madrigal, 1966; Only
the hopeful, 1972; many songs; Piano: 5 pieces,
1955, Brandeis Univ., 15 Apr. 1958; Rhapsody,
New York, 21 Nov. 1960; 5 bagatelles, Hilversum,
Holland, 12 Feb. 1961; Partita, 1963; Recrea-
tions, piano 4-hands, 1968; Second rhapsody,
Los Angeles, 15 Nov. 1971; Organ: Prelude and
fantasia, 1968.
    674 West 10th St., Claremont, CA 91711

KOHS, ELLIS B.
   b. Chicago, Ill., 12 May 1916. Studied with Carl
   Bricken, Univ. of Chicago, M. A. 1938; with
   Bernard Wagenaar at Juilliard School; with Walter
   Piston, Harvard Univ.; also musicology with Willi
   Apel and Hugo Leichtentritt. His awards include
   BMI publication award; Columbia Univ. Ditson a-
   ward; fellowships at MacDowell and Wurlitzer
   Found.; commissions from Pierre Monteux, Ferenc
   Molnar, Ludwig Altman, Fromm Found., Univ. of
   Illinois, and others. After serving as Air
   Force band leader in World War II, he taught at
   Wesleyan Univ., 1946-48; Coll. of the Pacific,
   1948-50; Univ. of Southern California, 1950-   .
      WORKS: Opera: Amerika, based on Kafka,
   1969; Rhinoceros, based on Ionescu, 1974; Theatre:
   music for Macbeth, 1974; Orchestra: Concerto for
   orchestra, 1942; Passacaglia for organ and
   strings, 1946; Legend for oboe and strings; cello
   concerto, 1947; Psalm XXV, chorus and orch., 1947;
   4 orchestral songs, voice and orch.; 2 symphonies,
   1950, 1956; Lord of the ascendant, concert narrative in 3 acts for 8 solo dancers, 7 solo
   voices, chorus, orch., 1956; Band: Life with
   Uncle (Sam); Chamber music: Night watch, flute,
   horn, timpany, 1943; 2 string quartets, 1942,
   1948; sonatina, bassoon and piano, 1944; brass
   trio; sonatine for violin and piano, 1948; Chamber concerto for viola and string nonet, 1949;
   clarinet sonata, 1951; Studies in variation
   (Part I: woodwind quintet, Part II: piano quartet, Part III: piano sonata, Part IV: sonata
   for unaccompanied violin) 1962; snare drum sonata, 1966; suite for cello and piano, 1970;
   Chorus: The automatic pistol, men's voices a
   cappella, 1943; 3 Greek choruses, women's voices
   a cappella; 3 Medieval Latin student songs;
   Psalm XXIII, double chorus, 4 soloists; 1957-58;
   3 songs from the Navajo; Piano: Etude in memory
   of Bartok, 1946; Piano variations; sonata no. 1;
   Toccata, 1948; Fantasy on la, sol, fa, re, mi,
   1949; Ten 2-voice inventions, 1950; Variations on
   L'homme armé; and songs and organ pieces. He has
   published the textbook Music theory, 1961; a second book, Musical form, is scheduled for publication in 1974-75.
      School of Music
      University of Southern California
      Los Angeles, CA 90007

KOK, JAN
   b. Wormerveer, Neth., 23 Aug. 1921; U.S. citizen
   1945. Studied with George F. McKay, Univ. of
   Washington; Arnold Elston, Univ. of Oregon; and
   with Walter Piston, Harvard Univ. He received a
   performance award, Composers Congress, Akron,
   Ohio, 1944. He taught in public schools, 1945-46,
   1951; has been instructor to professor, Univ. of
   Maine at Presque Isle, 1951-   .
      WORKS: Vocal: Round about, 34 original
   canons and rounds; also choral music, chamber,
   and piano pieces.
      10 Pleasant St., Presque Isle, ME 04769

*KOLAR, VICTOR
   b. Budapest, Hungary, 12 Feb. 1888; to U.S. 1900;
   d. Detroit, Mich., 16 June 1957. Graduated from

(KOLAR, VICTOR)
   Prague Cons.; was violinist in the New York Symphony, 1907-19; associate conductor, Detroit Symphony, 1920-41.
      WORKS: Orchestra: Hiawatha, 1908; A fairy
   tale, symphonic poem, 1912; Americana, symphonic
   suite, 1914; symphony, 1916; Slovakian rhapsody,
   1922; also marches, violin pieces, songs.

KOLB, BARBARA
   b. Hartford, Conn., 10 Feb. 1939. Studied with
   Arnold Franchetti, Hartt Coll. of Music, 1957-64;
   with Lukas Foss and Gunther Schuller at Tanglewood,
   1960, 1964, 1968. She received a Fulbright
   scholarship for Vienna, 1966-67; fellowships at
   Tanglewood and MacDowell Colony; Prix de Rome,
   1969-71; Guggenheim fellowship, 1972; grant from
   New York State Council on the Arts, 1973; Inst.
   of Arts and Letters award, 1973; commissions
   from Fromm Found., 1970, Koussevitzky Found.,
   1971, Univ. of Wisconsin, Milwaukee, 1972,
   Phillips and Remzulli, 1972, New York Harp Ensemble, 1972. She was clarinetist with the Hartford Symphony Orchestra, 1960-65; assistant
   professor, Brooklyn Coll., 1973-75; Wellesley
   Coll., 1975-   .
      WORKS: Chamber music: Chansons bas, so-
   prano and chamber ensemble, 1966; 3 place settings, narrator and chamber ensemble; Figments,
   flute and piano, 1967; Trobar clus, clarinet and
   chamber ensemble; Rebuttal, 2 clarinets; Toccata,
   harpsichord and tape; Soundings, 13 instruments
   and tape, 1971; double woodwind quintet; Solitaire, piano and vibraphone, 1971; Frailties,
   tenor, 4-channel tape and orch., Univ. of Wisconsin, May 1973.
      41 West 72nd St., New York, NY 10023

KOMAIKO, WILLIAM
   b. Chicago, Ill., 23 Jan. 1947. Studied with
   Robert Lombardo, Donald Erb, Raymond Wilding-
   White, Roosevelt Univ.; with Roger Sessions,
   Vincent Persichetti, Elliot Carter, Juilliard
   School, B. M. 1970, M. S. 1973, candidate for
   D. M. A. 1975; also piano with Rudolph Ganz and
   Robert Helps. His awards include 4-year scholarship, Roosevelt Univ.; Rudolph Ganz prize in
   piano, 1967; 3 grants, Fine Arts Found., 1967-69;
   Juilliard scholarship, 1970; Gershwin Memorial
   prize, 1972; 3 graduate fellowships, Juilliard,
   1972-74; Rogers and Hammerstein scholarship,
   1973. He is a faculty member at Juilliard School;
   co-founder and pianist with Notes from Underground, a performing ensemble for new music.
      WORKS: Theatre: The metamorphosis, staged
   mime piece based on Kafka's story; Chamber music:
   Improvisations, string quartet; Dialogues,
   string trio and bassoon; 3 pieces for woodwind
   trio; woodwind quintet; 2 narratives, voice and
   percussion; Rondo, clarinet and piano; Song cycle
   on Heine poems; string trio; string quartet no.
   2; Form in 2 parts, viola and piano; Mandala,
   solo violin; Umbra-penumbra, chamber ensemble,
   New York, 14 Oct. 1974.
      2647 Broadway, Apt. 5-S
      New York, NY 10025

KONDOROSSY, LESLIE

KONDOROSSY, LESLIE
b. Bratislava, Czech., 25 June 1915; U.S. citizen 1957. Studied at Liszt Acad. of Music, Budapest, and at Western Reserve Univ. He received the Certificate of Merit for Creative Art, City of Cleveland, 1958, 1959-60; Decoration Medal, Hungarian World Fed., Budapest, 1968; and jointly with his wife, Elizabeth Kondorossy, his lyricist and librettist, the Martha Holden Jennings Found. award, 1970. He held various positions as cantor, violinist, and conductor in Hungary and Germany, 1932-51; settled in Cleveland 1951; founder, later president, American New Opera Theater Society, 1953; teacher, Cleveland Cultural Arts Bureau, 1954-71; conducted Opera of the Air, WSRS, 1955-56; representative abroad for WCLV Fine Arts Station, 1966-70; private teacher and choral director.
    WORKS: Opera: The pumpkin, 1-act, Cleveland, 14 May 1954, (all performance sites are Cleveland unless noted otherwise); The voice, 1-act, 14 May 1954; The midnight duel, 1-act, 20 Mar. 1955; Two imposters, 1-act, 21 Oct. 1956; Unexpected visitor, 1-act, 21 Oct. 1956; The headsman, 1955; The fox, 1956; The string quartet, 1956; Mystic fortress, 1957; Alms from the beggar, 1957; The Baksheesh, 1960-64; Nathan the wise, 1961-64; Poorest suitor, children's opera-oratorio, 24 May 1967; Shizuka's dance, children's opera-oratorio, 29 Apr. 1969; Ruth and Naomi, church opera, 1969; Kalamona and the 4 winds, opera-oratorio, 12 Sep. 1971; Ballet: King Solomon, 1952; La danse macabre, 1965; Orchestra: Apotheosis, chorus and orch., 1956; trombone concerto, 19 May 1961; trumpet concerto, 18 Mar. 1962; cimbalom concerto, 1970; harpsichord concerto, 1972; Music for orchestra, 1973; Chamber music: string quartet, 9 Dec. 1960; 3 sketches for chamber orch., 1959; Concertino for chamber orch., 1961; Music for percussion, 1963; Chorus: Kossuth cantata, 16 Mar. 1952; Lament of the Lord, 17 May 1952; New dreams for old, cantata, 29 Nov. 1961; Son of Jesse, oratorio, 4 June 1967; Jazz mass, soloists, chorus, jazz band, 1968; Ode to the loyalty of first, cantata, 19 Sep. 1971; many other chamber works, piano pieces, and songs.
    14443 East Carroll Blvd.
    University Heights, OH 44118

*KONDRACKI, MICHEL
b. Poltava, Ukraine, 4 Oct. 1902; to U.S. 1948. Studied at the Warsaw Cons.; with Paul Dukas in Paris; also with Szymanowski. He was music critic in Warsaw, 1933-39; left Poland and lived in Brazil, 1940-48. He has composed an opera, a ballet, a symphony; Brazilian dances for orch.; choral works.

KONOWITZ, BERTRAM D.
b. Bronx, N. Y., 22 Feb. 1931. Studied with Karol Rathaus, Leo Kraft, Sol Berkowitz, Normand Lockwood. He received the Raymond Burrows award, Columbia Univ.; ASCAP awards, 1971-73; Nat. Endowment for the Arts grant, 1972. He has been associate professor, Manhattanville Coll., 1969- ; adjunct professor, Teachers Coll., Columbia Univ.; on summer faculty, Univ. of Wisconsin-Milwaukee and others.

(KONOWITZ, BERTRAM D.)
    WORKS: Vocal: Speak your pieace (sic), chorus, New York, 4 Apr. 1973; Zodiac; The last word; Growing up free; Cantus firmus; Piano: Jazz waltz; Raga rock; Time changes; Surf swing; Poundin' the beat; Blue note boogie; Choo choo stomp; Jazz spooks; Lazy daze. He specializes in vocal and piano improvisation and rock improvisation. He has published The complete rock piano method and Jazz for piano.
    12 Hemlock Dr., Syosset, NY 11791

KOPP, CHARLES MICHAEL
b. Athens, Ga., 9 Jan. 1951. Attended Univ. of Southern California; studied composition with his father, Frederick Kopp. In 1973 he was in the Dragonfire Band, Ft. Bragg.
    WORKS: Orchestra: Wave, a suite; Chorus: Pacem nobis donate; many songs.
    1833 Los Robles, San Marino, CA 91108

KOPP, FREDERICK
b. Hamilton, Ill., 21 Mar. 1914. Attended Carthage Coll., A. B.; Univ. of Iowa, A. M.; Eastman School of Music, Ph. D.; studied privately with Pierre Monteux, Gustav Strube, Louis Hasselmanns. He received scholarships at Carthage Coll. and Univ. of Iowa; Phi Mu Alpha award. He was conductor, Baton Rouge Civic Symphony, 1947-48; taught at Southeastern Louisiana State Univ., 1940-41; New York State Univ. Teachers Coll.-Fredonia, 1948-49; Univ. of Georgia, 1950-52; California State Univ. at Los Angeles, 1959-62; composer, arranger, conductor for motion pictures, 1962- .
    WORKS: Theatre: Pepito, children's musical; That woman's gotta hang!, musical melodrama; Orchestra: 2 symphonies; Trilogy; Deep forest; Wind ensemble: Terror suite, brass, woodwinds, piano, percussion; And the Earth shook, winds, piano, percussion; Chamber music: October '55, clarinet and string quartet; woodwind quintet; Portrait of a woman, flute and piano; Passacaglia, string quartet; Passacaglia, woodwind quintet; Shenandoah summer, clarinet, piano, and strings; Chorus: The denial of St. Peter, oratorio; Dance mass, chorus and orch.; Songs of David, cantata; We thank thee, Lord, motet; songs, organ and piano pieces, film scores.
    1833 Los Robles, San Marino, CA 91108

KORN, PETER JONA
b. Berlin, Germany, 30 Mar. 1922; U.S. citizen 1944. Studied with Edmund Rubbra in London; Stefan Wolpe in Jerusalem; with Arnold Schoenberg Ernst Toch, and Hanns Eisler in Los Angeles. He received the Frank Huntington Beebe Fund award, 1956, 1957; Huntington Hartford Found. fellowships, 1956, 1957, 1961; City of Munich Music award, 1968; Univ. of Maryland Fine Arts award, 1971. He taught at Trappsches Kons., Munich, 1960-61; was visiting lecturer, Univ. of California, Los Angeles, spring semesters, 1964, 1965; director, Richard Strauss Kons., Munich, 1967- .
    WORKS: Opera: Heidi, 1961-63; Orchestra: 3 symphonies, 1946, 1952, 1956; Tom Paine overture, 1950; Rhapsody, oboe and strings, 1952;

(KORN, PETER JONA)

Concertino for horn and strings, Ojai, Calif., Festival, 1953; In medias res, overture, 1953; Variations on a tune from The beggar's opera, Louisville, 1 Oct. 1955; saxophone concerto, 1956; Exorcism of a Liszt fragment, Pittsburgh, 5 Feb. 1971; Chamber music: Prelude and scherzo, brass quintet; cello sonata, 1949; 2 string quartets, 1950, 1963; Passacaglia and Fugue for 8 horns, 1952; horn sonata, 1953; Quintettino, 3 woodwinds, cello, piano, 1964; quintet for winds.
Mozartring 10, D-8011 Baldham, West Germany

KORNGOLD, ERICH WOLFGANG

b. Brno, Austria, 29 May 1897; d. Hollywood, Calif., 29 Nov. 1957; U.S. citizen 1943. Studied with Alexander von Zemlinsky, Hermann Graedener, and Robert Fuchs in Vienna. He was a child prodigy both in piano and in composition, writing a piano trio that was published when he was 12. He received the title of professor from the president of Austria; Art Prize, City of Vienna, 1924; Academy awards for best original scores: Anthony Adverse, 1936, The adventures of Robin Hood, 1938, The sea wolf, 1941. He came to the U.S. in 1934 and settled in Hollywood as a film composer.

WORKS: Theatre: Die Kathrin, opera, 1939; The silent serenade, comedy with music, 1946; Orchestra: violin concerto, 1945; cello concerto, 1946; Symphonic serenade for strings, 1947; Symphony in F#, 1951; Theme and variations, 1953; Straussiana, 1953; Chamber music: string quartet no. 3, 1945; Chorus: Prayer, tenor, chorus, and orch., 1942; Psalm, solo, chorus, orch., 1941; Songs: Songs of the clown, 1940; 4 Shakespeare songs, 1940; Tomorrow, 1942; 5 songs for middle voice, 1947; Sonnet to Vienna, 1952; Film scores: 18 original scores, 1934-47, including The prince and the pauper; The private life of Elizabeth and Essex; King's Row; Juarez; Of human bondage; etc.

KORTE, KARL

b. Ossining, N. Y., 25 Aug. 1928. Studied with Peter Mennin, William Bergsma, Vincent Persichetti, Juilliard School; and with Otto Luening and Aaron Copland. His awards include a Fulbright grant to Italy; 2 Guggenheim fellowships; Ford Found. Young Composers Project grant; Belgian Government Prize for 1969 Queen Elizabeth Competition; Harpur Found. grant; State Univ. of New York Research Found. grant; and special grants from the Alice Ditson Fund. He was composer-in-residence, Oklahoma City and Albuquerque schools; professor, State Univ. of New York, Binghamton, 1964-71; professor, Univ. of Texas at Austin, 1971- .

WORKS: Orchestra: Concertato on a choral theme, 1955; For a young audience, 1959; Symphony no. 2, 1961; Southwest, a dance overture, 1963; Symphony no. 3, 1968; Band: Nocturne and march, 1962; Prairie song, trumpet and band, 1963; Ceremonial prelude and passacaglia, 1962; Gestures, electric brass, percussion, piano and band, 1970; I think you would have understood, stage band, solo trumpet, 2-channel tape, 1971; Chamber music: 2 string quartets, 1948, 1965; Fantasy, violin and piano, 1959; quintet, oboe and strings, 1960;

(KORTE, KARL)

Matrix, woodwind quintet, piano, percussion, saxophone, 1968; Facets, saxophone quartet, 1969; Dialogue, saxophone, tape, 1969; Introductions, brass quintet, 1963; Diablerie, woodwind quintet, 1964; Remembrances, flute and tape, 1971; Chorus: 4 Blake songs, women's voices and piano, 1961; Mass for youth, with orch. or keyboard, 1963; Aspects of love, 7 songs on various texts, 1965; May the Sun bless us, 4 settings of texts of Tagore, male voices, brass, percussion, 1968; Psalm XIII, chorus and tape, 1970; anthems, carols, songs for solo voice, piano pieces.
Department of Music, University of Texas
Austin, TX 78712

*KOSAKOFF, REUVEN

b. New Haven, Conn., 8 Jan. 1898. Studied at Yale Univ.; with Ernest Hutcheson and Carl Friedberg, Juilliard School; with Artur Schnabel in Berlin. He received many commissions for compositions; gave piano concerts in the U.S. and Europe; was organist, Genesis Hebrew Center, Tuckahoe, N. Y.

WORKS: Opera: The cabalists, 1-act; Orchestra: piano concerto, 1941; Jack and the beanstalk, narrator and orch., 1944; Chamber music: violin sonata; clarinet sonata; woodwind quartet; Chorus: Song of songs; Message of peace; Ruth and Naomi; Creation; and Sabbath services.

KOSTECK, GREGORY

b. Plainfield, N. J., 2 Sep. 1937. Studied at Univ. of Maryland, B. M.; with Leslie Bassett and Ross Lee Finney, Univ. of Michigan, M. M., D. M. A.; privately with Ton de Leeuw in Amsterdam. His many awards include Woodrow Wilson Nat. fellowship; 3 Horace Rackham fellowships; Univ. of Michigan Distinguished Scholar; Fulbright grant; Ford-MENC grant; Nat. Asso. of American Composers and Conductors grant; first prizes, Spoleto Festival, 1965; Ohio State Univ., 1967; Penn. Society of Arts and Letters, 1967; World Library Publ., 1967; 2 Sigvald Thompson awards, 1968, 1972; 2 silver medals, Competition of Queen Elizabeth of Belgium, 1969; first prizes, American Guild of Organists, 1969; San Jose State Coll., 1970; Internat. Delius Award, 1971; Concours pour Quatuor a Cordes, Liege, Belgium, 1973; and many commissions. He was composer-in-residence, Norwalk Conn., schools, 1964-65; chairman, music department, Washington and Jefferson Coll., 1965-66; composer-in-residence, East Carolina Univ., 1966-73; Appalachian State Univ., 1973- .

WORKS: Opera: Vengeance is mine, 1964; Maurya, 1966; Orchestra: Capriccio, piano and orch., 1958; 4 pieces for cello, winds, harp, percussion, 1962; Slow piece, 1964; Rhapsody, cello and orch., 1964; Variations, viola and orch., 1965; 3 lyric pieces, 1966; Concert fantasy, violin, piano, orch., 1967; Strophes, 1968; Nightingales and the moon, 1969; Clouds, strings and percussion, 1969; symphony, 1971; saxophone concerto, 1973; Band: Elegy, 1964; Requiem for trombone and band, 1967; Concert music for band, 1967; Adonai roee, Psalm 32 for alto and wind orch., 1973; Chamber music: Bagatelles, string

KOSTECK, GREGORY

(KOSTECK, GREGORY)
trio, 1960; 2 piano sonatas, 1961, 1964; Fantasy for cello, 1963; Sonatine, violin and piano, 1964; Variations, clarinet and piano, 1964; string trio, 1966; piano trio, 1966; Serenade, flute and trumpet, 1967; string quartets no. 3, 1969, no. 4, 1971; Music for piano duo, 1969; Summer music, wind trio, 1969; Eclogue, cello and piano, 1972; violin sonata no. 4, 1972; Cantilena for piano, 1973; Chorus: Canons and refrains, women's voices, 4 clarinets, 1965; A Christmas lullabye, 1965; Love poems from youth, 1967; Oratio Jeremiae Prophaetae, 1969; Cantata 1973, male voices and brass; also songs, organ pieces, music for brass.
Department of Music
Appalachian State University
Boone, NC   28607

KOTIK, PETR
b. Prague, Czech., 27 Jan. 1942; to U.S. 1969. Studied composition with Jan Rychlik in Prague; with Hanns Jelinek and Karl Schiske, Vienna Music Acad., 1963-66. He was founder and director of Musica Viva Pragensis, 1961-64, and of Quax Ensemble 1966-69; creative associate, State Univ. of New York at Buffalo, 1969-   ; founder and director, SEM Ensemble, 1970-   ; artistic director, Chocorua activities sponsored by New Music in New Hampshire.
WORKS: Chamber music: Aley, variable number of instruments, 1970-71; How empty is my wilderness, variable instruments, 1971; There is singularly nothing, variable instruments and voices, 1971-   .
567 Forest Ave., Buffalo, NY   14222

*KOUGELL, ARKADIE
b. Simferopol, Russia, 25 Dec. 1897; to U.S. 1952. Studied at St. Petersburg Cons. and Vienna Cons. He has received many awards for excellence in piano playing and teaching, and the California Harp Asso. award in composition. He was founder and director, Inst. of American Music, Univ. of Beirut; has held academic posts in Tel Aviv, Paris, and New York; has given piano recitals in the U.S., Europe, Russia, and the Middle East.
WORKS: Orchestra: Impressions of Damascus, 1930; piano concerto, 1930; Bedouin dance for 60 cellos, 1932; piano concerto for the left hand, 1934; Rapsodie tartare, 1947; cello concerto, 1950; trombone concertino, 1956; Ballade, soprano and orch.; Chamber music: 2 string quartets; 3 piano sonatas; violin sonata; 2 cello sonatas; Poeme, harp and cello; Danse Hebraique, cello and piano; Suite ancienne, viola and piano.

*KOUNTZ, RICHARD
b. Pittsburgh, Pa., 8 July 1896; d. New York, N. Y., 14 Oct. 1950. Was executive in a New York music publishing company, 1927-32. He wrote songs: The sleigh; Cossack love song; By love alone; etc.; organ pieces and choral works.

*KOUSSEVITZKY, SERGE
b. Vyshniy Volochek, Russia, 26 July 1874; U.S. citizen 1941; d. Boston, Mass., 4 June 1951. Studied double bass, Moscow Philharmonic Music

(KOUSSEVITZKY, SERGE)
School, graduating in 1894; became leading bass player in the Moscow Imperial Orchestra; gave solo recitals on the bass throughout Europe; organized a symphony orchestra and toured Russia with it, 1910-17, making 3 trips down the Volga River on a chartered vessel; was guest conductor in London; instituted the Concerts Koussevitzky in Paris, 1921; in 1924 was invited to head the Boston Symphony Orchestra. During his 25 years with the Boston Symphony he established the Berkshire Music Center and the Berkshire Music School at Lenox, Mass.
WORKS: Orchestra: concerto for double bass, 1905; Passacaglia on a Russian theme; Double bass and piano: Humoresque; Valse miniature; Chanson triste; etc.

*KOUTZEN, BORIS
b. Uman, Russia, 1 Apr. 1901; U.S. citizen 1929; d. Mount Kisco, N. Y., 10 Dec. 1966. Studied with Reinhold Gliere, Moscow State Cons.; graduated 1922; Philadelphia Cons., D. M. 1940. His honors include a Society for Publication of American Music award, 1944; Juilliard publication award, 1944. He was faculty member, Philadelphia Cons., 1924-44; professor, Vassar Coll., 1944-66.
WORKS: Opera: The fatal oath, 1-act, 1954; You never know, 1-act comic opera, 1960; Orchestra: Solitude, symphonic poem, 1927; Symphonic movement, violin and orch., 1929; Valley Forge, symphonic poem, 1931; concerto for 5 solo instruments and strings, 1934; symphony, 1939; Concert piece, cello and string orch., 1940; From the American folklore, 1943; violin concerto, 1946; Sinfonietta, 1947; An invocation, women's chorus and orch., 1948; viola concerto, 1949; Morning music, flute and strings, 1950; Divertimento, 1955; concertino for piano and strings, 1957; Elegiac rhapsody, 1961; Fanfare, prayer and march, 1961; Band: Rhapsody, 1959, Chamber music: 2 violin sonatas, 1929, 1951; piano sonatina, 1931; 3 string quartets, 1932, 1936, 1944; trio, flute, cello, harp, 1933; Enigma, piano, 1938; duo concertante, 1944; sonatina for 2 pianos, 1944; Sonnet for organ, 1946; piano trio, 1948; sonata for violin and cello, 1952; Eidolus, piano, 1953; Landscape and dances, woodwind quintet, 1953; Poem, violin solo and string quartet, 1963; Pastorale and dance, violin and piano, 1964; Chorus: Words of cheer to Zion, 1962.

KOZAK, EDWARD JOHN
b. Chicago, Ill., 17 Nov. 1925. Studied at Centenary Coll.; and with Robert Krause, Northwestern State Univ. He was soloist and arranger for Xavier Cugat, 1949-50; music director and arranger, Shreveport Summer Theatre, 1957-60; clinician for drum companies, 1972-73; lecturer, Centenary Coll., 1959-   .
WORKS: Orchestra: marimba concerto; Wind ensemble: Variation on a chant for percussion and winds; Circus suite, brass sextet; Suite for woodwinds in 12-tone technique; Swingatina, clarinet sextet; Chamber music: Etude for marimba; Theme and variation, piano; Toot suite, Rudiments rococo-Swingin'fifer, duets for snaredrum and flute; also anthems and songs.
3729 Greenway Pl., Shreveport, LA   71105

*KOZINSKI, DAVID
b. Wilmington, Del., 29 July 1917. Studied at Univ. of Delaware; West Chester State Coll., B. S.; with A. Constant Vauclain, Univ. of Pennsylvania, M. S.; Army Music School, Ft. Myer, Va. He has taught privately and in public schools; has conducted opera, orchestra, choral groups; has been music critic for the Evening Journal.
WORKS: Chamber music: Suite for strings; Project percussion, percussion ensemble; Songs: Wonder! Wonder!; Glory to God in heaven; Old Polish carols.

*KRAEHENBUEHL, DAVID
b. 1932. Concerto for piano 4-hands, Wisconsin festival, La Cross, summer 1975; Diptych, violin and piano; Variations for 2, piano or any combination of 2; Variations, 3 clarinets and bass clarinet; Elegy and Nocturne for piano; City scene, chorus; 4 Christmas choruses.
School for New Music, Princeton, NJ 08540

KRAFT, LEO
b. New York, N. Y., 24 July 1922. Studied with Karol Rathaus at Queens Coll.; Randall Thompson, Princeton Univ.; and with Nadia Boulanger in Paris. He received a Fulbright fellowship, 1954; annual ASCAP awards, 1961-   . He has been on the faculty, Queens Coll., CUNY, 1947-   , professor in 1973.
WORKS: Orchestra: Concerto no. 3, cello, winds, percussion; Band: Toccata for band, 1970; Chamber music: Two's company, 2 clarinets, 1957; Partita no. 3, wind quintet, 1969; 5 pieces for clarinet and piano, 1969; Fantasy, flute and piano, 1971; Dualities, 2 trumpets, 1971; Short suite, flute, clarinet, bassoon; Trios and interludes, flute, viola, piano; Spring in the harbor, chamber cycle for soprano, flute, cello, piano; Dialogues, flute and tape; Chorus: Festival song, 1951; Let me laugh, 1954; Thanksgiving, 1958; A proverb of Solomon, with orch., 1958; When Israel came forth, 1963; I waited patiently, Psalm 40, male choir, 1964; A new song, male choir, 1966; Piano: Allegro giocoso, 1947; Partita no. 1, 1969; Statements and commentaries; Short sonata no. 1, harpsichord, 1972; Piano piece 1971; New York, 4 Apr. 1974.
9 Dunster Rd., Great Neck, NY 11021

KRAFT, WILLIAM
b. Chicago, Ill., 6 Sep. 1923. Studied with Otto Luening, Vladimir Ussachevsky, Henry Cowell, Paul Henry Lang, Columbia Univ., B. S. 1951, M. A. 1954; and at Cambridge Univ., England. He received Anton Deidl fellowships, 1952, 1953; Huntington Hartford fellowship, 1964; Guggenheim fellowships, 1967, 1972; Ford Found. commission, 1972; Rockefeller Found. grant for Italy, summer 1973; 8 Pulitzer nominations; and many commissions. He has been principal timpanist and principal percussionist, Los Angeles Philharmonic Orchestra, 1955-   , was assistant conductor, 1969-72; founder and music director, Los Angeles Percussion Ensemble and Chamber Players, 1956; music director, Young Musicians Found., 1970-72; faculty member, Univ. of Southern California, 1961-64; California Inst. of the Arts, 1973-   .

(KRAFT, WILLIAM)
WORKS: A simple introduction to the orchestra, 1958; 3 Miniatures for percussion and orch., 1958; Variations on a folksong, 1959; Symphony for strings and percussion, New York, 21 Aug. 1961; Concerto grosso, 1961, San Diego, 22 Mar. 1963; Derivations, 1964; Concerto for 4 percussion soloists and orchestra, 1964, Los Angeles, 10 Mar. 1966; Contextures: Riots decade 60, Los Angeles, 4 Apr. 1968; Configurations: concerto for 4 percussion soloists and jazz orch., 1968; Games: Collage No. 1, Pasadena, 21 Nov. 1969; piano concerto, Los Angeles, 21 Nov. 1973; Chamber music: Theme and variations, percussion quartet, 1956; Nonet for brass and percussion, Los Angeles, 13 Oct. 1958; Suite for percussion, 1958; French suite, solo percussion, 1962; 6 pieces for string trio, 1963; Silent boughs, song cycle for soprano, Millay text, Stockholm, 15 Nov. 1963; Double trio, piano, prepared piano, amplified guitar, tuba, 2 percussion, Los Angeles, 31 Oct. 1966; Momentum for 8 percussionists, 1966; Encounters II, unaccompanied tuba, 1966; Triangles: A concerto for percussion and 10 instruments, 1968, Los Angeles, 8 Dec. 1969; Fanfare 1969; 8 trumpets; Mobiles, 10 instruments, Berkeley, 18 Oct. 1970; Encounters III: Duel for trumpet and percussion, Santa Monica, 21 Jan. 1972; Cadenze, 5 winds, 2 strings, San Francisco, 10 Apr. 1972; Encounters IV: Duel for trombone and percussion, 1972; Requiescat: Let the bells mourn for us we are remiss, electric piano, Ojai, Calif., 31 May 1975.
4823 Ben Ave., North Hollywood, CA 91607

*KRAMER, A. WALTER
b. New York, N. Y., 23 Sep. 1890; d. New York, 8 Apr. 1969. Studied violin with Carl Hauser and Richard Arnold; graduated from City Coll. of New York, 1910. He was on the staff of Musical America, 1910-22, editor-in-chief, 1929-36; managing director and vice president, Galaxy Music Corporation, 1936-56; was a co-founder of the Society for the Publication of American Music.
WORKS: Orchestra: Symphonic rhapsody, violin and orch., 1912; Elizabethan suite; 2 symphonic sketches; In Normandy, choral cycle with orch., 1925; Chamber music: Eklog, cello and piano; Chant negre, violin and piano; Interlude for a drama, wordless voice, oboe, cello, piano; Chorus: The lady of Ceret; The hour of prayer; songs, piano pieces.

KRAMER, GREGORY PAUL
b. Los Angeles, Calif., 14 Oct. 1952. Attended Univ. of California, Santa Cruz, and California Inst. of the Arts, B. F. A. 1972; principal influences have been William Douglas, Gordon Mumma, David Tudor, Keith Jarrett. He composed music for film Nothing, which received first prizes in Educational Film category, Atlanta Film Festival and San Francisco Film Festival; received Golden Cloud award, Aspen Live Electronic Music Festival; first prize, WANT Festival, San Francisco, 1971. He is president of Electron Farm, 1972-   ; leader of The New Choir, Venice, Calif., 1973-   .

KRAMER, GREGORY PAUL

(KRAMER, GREGORY PAUL)
WORKS: Electronic: Vessels; Absence; Role; Poseidon; Clubhouse; Greenhouse; Nothing; Song for the new prince; Precipitation III--Weeds; etc.
2810 Grand Canal, Venice, CA 90291

KRAMER, JONATHAN D.
b. Hartford, Conn., 7 Dec. 1942. Studied Hartt Coll. of Music; Harvard Univ., A. B. magna cum laude 1965; Univ. of California at Berkeley, M. A., Ph. D. 1969; Stanford Univ., Cummington Community of the Arts; Bennington Composers Conference, 1970; principal teachers were Karlheinz Stockhausen, Roger Sessions, Leon Kirchner, Andrew Imbrie, Seymour Shifrin, Jean-Claude Eloy, Richard Felciano, Billy Jim Layton, Arnold Franchetti. His awards include Hartt Junior award, 1960; David McCord Prize in creative arts, Harvard, 1965; NDEA Title IV 3-year humanities fellowship, 1967; DeLorenzo award, Berkeley, 2nd prize 1968, first prize 1969; Ohio Music Teachers Asso. award and commission, 1971. He was program annotator, San Francisco Symphony, 1967-70; lecturer, Univ. of California, Berkeley, 1969-70; assistant professor, Oberlin Cons., 1970-71; assistant professor, Yale Univ., 1971- .
WORKS: Orchestra: Requiem for the innocent, Berkeley, 10-23 May 1970; Band: Variations, Berkeley, 28 May 1969; Chamber music: 3 pieces, clarinet alone, 1966; septet, 1968; One for five in seven, mostly, woodwind quintet, 1971; An imaginary dance, tape, 1972; Piano: Music for piano, 4 parts, 1966-72; Multimedia: Prayer, choir, broken piano, etc., tape and projections, 1969; Blue music, actor, tape, lights, 1972; Higher education, for teacher with office, 1971; You, too, can be a composer, music theory class with teacher, 1971; Irrealities, 2 dancers, tape, projections, lights, 1973.
Department of Music, Yale University
New Haven, CT 06520

KRAPF, GERHARD
b. Meissenheim, Germany, 12 Dec. 1924; U.S. citizen 1959. Earned a diploma at the Staatliche Hochschule fur Musik, 1950; studied with Paul Pisk and Leslie Spelman, Univ. of Redlands, M. M. 1951. He was music supervisor, Synod of the Evangelical Church, Baden, 1951-53; director of music, Starr Commonwealth for Boys, Albion, Mich., 1953-54; on faculty, Northwest Missouri State Coll., 1954-58; head of organ and theory, Univ. of Wyoming, 1958-61; associate professor, head of organ department, Univ. of Iowa, 1961-68, professor, 1968-   ; also organist-choirmaster, various churches, 1953-66.
WORKS: Numerous organ works and choral compositions for all vocal combinations and with varying accompaniments.
1209 East Davenport St.
Iowa City, IA 51240

KRAUSE, ROBERT JAMES
b. Milwaukee, Wisc., 1 July 1943. Studied with Frederic Ashe, Alfred Reed, J. Clifton Williams, Univ. of Miami, B. M., M. M. He has been faculty

(KRAUSE, ROBERT JAMES)
member, Eastern New Mexico Univ., 1967-68; Northwestern State Univ., 1968-73; West Texas State Univ., 1973-
WORKS: Theatre: Music for The winter's tale; Chamber music: woodwind quintet; Impetuoso, bassoon and piano; Cantilena, English horn and piano; Petits variations, piano; Chorus: Psalm 121, chorus and English horn.
Department of Music,
West Texas State University
Canyon, TX 79015

KREIGER, ARTHUR V.
b. New Haven, Conn., 8 May 1945. Studied with Charles Whittenberg, Hale Smith, Walter Ihrke, Univ. of Connecticut; with Vladimir Ussachevsky, Chou Wen-chung, Mario Davidovsky, Columbia Univ. He was graduate assistant, Univ. of Connecticut, 1968-69; teaching assistant. Columbia Univ., 1972-74.
WORKS: Chamber music: 2 woodwind quintets; Short pieces for piano; Composition for electronic tape; Short computer piece; also pieces for mixed chamber groups, and songs.
70 Morningside Drive, Apt. 33
New York, NY 10027

KREISLER, ALEXANDER VON
b. St. Petersburg, Russia, 21 Sep. 1894; d. Austin, Tex., 21 Aug. 1969; U.S. citizen 1939. Earned a masters in law at St. Petersburg Univ.; then studied with Alexander Glazunov and Nicolas Tcherepnin at the St. Petersburg Cons. He was conductor, Riga Symphony, Latvia, 1920-29; conductor of Columbia radio orchestra that originated coast to coast radio broadcasts; was faculty member, Cincinnati Cons., 1930-1939; composer for March of Time radio network program, 1939-44; professor and conductor of orchestra, Univ. of Texas at Austin, 1945-69.
WORKS: Some 80 published works for string orchestra, string ensembles, brass and woodwind solos and ensembles.

*KREISLER, FRITZ
b. Vienna, Austria, 2 Feb. 1875; U.S. citizen 1943; d. New York, 29 Jan. 1962. Entered the Vienna Cons. at 7, studied with Auber and Hellmesberger, winning the Gold Medal at 10; with Massart and Delibes, Paris Cons., graduated at 12, taking the Grand Prix. He toured the U.S. with Moriz Rosenthal, pianist, 1888-89; then studied medicine in Vienna, painting in Paris and Rome; served in Austrian Army. He resumed violin playing in 1899, making brilliant return debuts in Europe and the U.S.
WORKS: Theatre: The marriage knot, comic opera, 1919; Apple blossoms, operetta, 1919; Sissy, operetta, 1933; Orchestra: violin concerto; Chamber music: string quartet; Violin and piano: Caprice Viennois; Tambourin Chinois; Recitativo and scherzo; Schoen Rosmarin; Liebesfreud; Liebeslied; Chanson Louis XIII and Pavane; La Precieuse; Sicilienne and rigaudon; Praeludium and allegro; Aubade Provencale; The old refrain; and songs.

KREISS, HULDA E.
b. Strasbourg, France, 15 Dec. 1924; U.S. citizen 1933. Studied at San Diego State Coll., B. A. 1946; U.S. Internat. Univ., M. A. 1968; studied harp with Carlos Salzedo and others. She has received many awards for poetry, for teaching, for community service in many ways; and a set of States of the Union Commemorative Medals for her book, Reaching the exceptional child through music. She was harpist with the San Diego Youth Symphony, 1948-52, and with the San Diego County Symphony for 9 years; teacher in San Diego public schools, 1946- .
WORKS: Chamber music: Moonlight reverie, harp and voice; Dream love, harp and cello; Chorale, piano and voice; Fantasie, piano; Beth's lullaby, piano and voice; many transcriptions for harp.
4706 East Mountain View Drive
San Diego, CA 92116

KREMENLIEV, BORIS
b. Razlog, Bulgaria, 23 May 1911; U.S. citizen 1944. Studied with Wesley La Violette, De Paul Univ., B. M., M. M.; with Howard Hanson, Eastman School of Music, Ph D.; privately with Roy Harris; conducting with Modest Altschuller. He has received annual ASCAP awards, 1968-73; Creative Arts Inst. grant to write opera; American Philosophical Society--Ford Found. grant for research in Bulgarian and Slavic folk music. He has been professor, Univ. of California, Los Angeles, 1945- .
WORKS: Opera: The bridge; Orchestra: Symphonic variations, 1937; Prelude and poem, chorus, soloists, orch., 1937; Song symphony, contralto and orch., 1941; Bulgarian rhapsody, 1952; Crucifixion, suite from a film score, 1952; Elegy, 1968; Study for orchestra; Chamber music: 2 string quartets; flute sonatina; horn sonata; 2 piano quintets; quartet for oboe and string trio; woodwind trio; saxophone quartet; double bass sonata; 5 miniatures for piano; Chorus: They are slaves, from cantata Once to every man and nation; Grapes, women's voices and string quartet; Song for parting, women's voices, string orch., English horn; also works for radio, television, the stage, and films. He is author of the book, Bulgarian-Macedonian folk music, and articles in music journals.
10507 Troon Ave., Los Angeles, CA 90064

*KREMMER, RUDOLPH
3 fantasies for organ.

KRENEK, ERNST
b. Vienna, Austria, 23 Aug. 1900; U.S. citizen 1945. Studied with Franz Schreker in Vienna and Berlin. His many awards include prizes from City of Vienna, Republic of Austria, State of Nordrhein-Westfalen, Cities of Hamburg and Braunschweig; Great Cross of Merit from Republic of Austria, German Federal Republic; membership, Nat. Inst. of Arts and Letters; honorary membership, Academies of Music in Vienna, Graz, Salzburg, Stuttgart, Hamburg Opera House; honorary citizen of Minnesota; honorary doctorates in music, Univ. of New Mexico, Hamline Univ.,

(KRENEK, ERNST)
Chapman Coll. He was professor, Vassar Coll., 1939-41; professor, dean of Fine Arts, Hamline Univ., 1942-47; guest lecturer, Univ. of Michigan, Univ. of Wisconsin, Univ. of New Mexico, Chicago Musical Coll., Brandeis Univ., Univ. of Hawaii, Peabody Inst., Tanglewood, Univ. of California, San Diego, all at various times, 1939-73.
WORKS: Opera: Jonny spielt auf, 1927, an international success, was brought to the Metropolitan Opera House, New York, 19 Jan. 1929; What price confidence?, 1946; Dark waters, 1951; The bell tower; The life of Orestes, 1930, U.S. premiere, Portland, Ore., 20 Nov. 1974; Pallas Athene weeps, 1955; Ausgerechnet und verspielt, 1961; The magic mirror; The golden ram, 1963; Sardakai, 1969; Orchestra: 4 piano concertos; 2 violin concertos; cello concerto; Symphonic elegy, 1946; harp concerto, 1952; Medea, contralto and orch., 1952; concerto for 2 pianos, 1953; 11 transparencies, 1955; Horizon circled; Perspectives; 6 profiles; Fivefold enfoldment; Quaestio temporis; Chamber music: organ sonata, 1941; piano sonata no.3, 1943, no.4, 1948, no.5, 1950; viola sonata, 1948; violin sonata; sonata for violin solo, 1948; harp sonata, 1955; Monologue, clarinet solo, 1956; Pentagram for winds, 1957; Sechs vermessene, piano, 1958; New music for guitar, New York, 22 May 1973; Chorus: Lamentations of Jeremiah, 1941; 6 motets; Songs: Sestina, voice and 10 instruments, 1958; Electronic: Spiritus intelligentiae sanctus, with voices; Tape and doubles, with 2 pianos; Organastro, with organ; Quintina, with voice and instruments; Aulokithara, oboe, harp, tape, U.S. premiere, Baltimore, 4 Feb. 1973 (a version of Kitharaulos, commissioned by Swiss oboist Heinz Holliger and given its world premiere at the 1972 Olympic Games in Munich).
623 Chino Canyon Road
Palm Springs, CA 92262

KRENEK, MRS. ERNST. See NORDENSTROM, GLADYS

KRESKY, JEFFREY JAY
b. Passaic, N. J., 14 May 1948. Studied with Otto Luening, Charles Wuorinen, Harvey Sollberger, Columbia Univ.; Milton Babbitt, J. K. Randall, Peter Westergaard, Princeton Univ. He received a BMI student composer award, 1969; Tanglewood fellowship, 1969; ASCAP awards, 1971-73. He was instructor, Mannes Coll. of Music, 1972-73; assistant professor, William Paterson Coll., 1973-74.
WORKS: Chamber music: clarinet sonata; Variations for piano and ensemble; Puppets, chamber ballet; In nomine, flute solo, Chorus: Cantatas I and II; other vocal and instrumental chamber works.
175 Union Ave., Rutherford, NJ 07070

KRETER, LEO
b. Rochester, Minn., 29 Aug. 1933. Studied with Henry Woodward, Carleton Coll.; with Robert Palmer and Karel Husa, Cornell Univ., D. M. A. He received a George Baker scholarship at Carleton Coll., graduate fellowship at Cornell

KRETER, LEO

(KRETER, LEO)
Univ. He was assistant professor, Wichita State Univ., 1960-65; associate professor, California State Coll., San Bernardino, 1965-68; professor and chairman, department of music, California State Univ., Fullerton, 1968- .
WORKS: Orchestra: a symphony; Overture for orchestra; Wind Ensemble: Polarities I and II; Vortex for brass and percussion; Chamber music: Melisma, strings and harp; various small ensemble works; Chorus: Alleluia; Gloria in excelsis Deo; Sound a trumpet; Show us thy ways, O Lord.
219 Nata, Newport Beach, CA 92660

KREUTZ, ARTHUR
b. La Crosse, Wis., 25 July 1906. Attended Univ. of Wisconsin, B. S., B. M.; Columbia Univ., M. A.; studied with Roy Harris and Cecil Burleigh; Royal Cons., Ghent, Belgium, diploma in violin; American Acad. in Rome. His awards include Premier Prix, Royal Cons., 1933; Prix de Rome, 1940; Publication award, Nat. Asso. American Composers and Conductors, 1941; Guggenheim fellowship, 1944-46; BMI-ACA award, 1945; many commissions. He has held faculty posts at Univ. of Texas, 1942-44; Rhode Island State Coll.; Columbia Univ.; Univ. of Mississippi, 1952- .
WORKS: Opera: Acres of sky, ballad opera, Fayetteville, Ark., 16 Nov. 1950; The university greys, Univ. of Mississippi, 15 Mar. 1954; Sourwood Mountain, Roanoke, Va., 4 Apr. 1958; Verbena, after Faulkner; Ballet: Litany of Washington Street, from Land be bright, for Martha Graham; Theatre: music for E equals MC^2; Wanhope Building; Galarie vivante; Orchestra: 2 symphonies, 1940, 1946; Symphonic jam session; American Dances; Paul Bunyan; Symphonic sketch; Scenes from Hamlet; March; The university greys, overture; Winter of the blue snow; 2 violin concertos; piano concerto; Dance concerto for clarinet and orch.; Dixieland concerto for clarinet, trumpet, trombone; Concertino for oboe, horn, and strings; Variations on a pop tune, piano and orch.; Mosquito serenade, string orch.; Hoedown, string orch. and piano; New England folksing, chorus and orch.; Gettysburg, 1863, chorus and orch.; Band: Jazz prelude; Jazz fugue; Jamboree; Concertino, violin and band; Chamber music: Quartet Venuti, string quartet; Jazzonata no.1 and no.2, violin and piano; Variations, violin and piano; 3 Shakespeare songs, soprano and chamber orch.; 4 Robert Burns songs, soprano and chamber orch.; Study in jazz, piano; Toccata, violin and piano.
Route #6, Oxford, MS 38655

KREUTZ, ROBERT EDWARD
b. La Crosse, Wis., 21 Mar. 1922. Studied Leo Sowerby, American Cons.; Arnold Schoenberg, Univ. of California, Los Angeles; and Normand Lockwood, Univ. of Denver. His honors include choral premiers before MENC, 1964, 1969; American Guild of Organists, 1972; American Choral Directors Asso., 1973. He has been a private teacher, 1950- ; director, St. Bernadette Choir, Lakewood, Colo., 1958- .
WORKS: Chamber music: trio for 2 marimbas and piano; Gargoyle for 3 trumpets; Parable for

(KREUTZ, ROBERT EDWARD)
organ; Portraits of the West, piano suite; Chorus: 7 Latin masses; 4 English masses; Laudate Dominum; Sing a new song; Who loves the rain; This is the day; 3 sea songs; 14 Psalms and alleluias; many anthems and works for the church service.
1909 Zinnia St., Golden, CO 80401

*KRIENS, CHRISTIAAN B.
b. Amsterdam, Neth., 29 Apr. 1881; to U.S. 1906; d. West Hartford, Conn., 17 Dec. 1934. Studied at the Hague Cons.; made debut with his father's orchestra in Amsterdam, playing the Emperor Concerto and a violin concerto and conducting his own 2nd symphony. He came to the U.S. as conductor of the French Opera Company in New Orleans; was teacher and conductor in New York, 1907-29; then music director of radio station WTIC, Hartford, Conn. He wrote orchestral works and chamber music.

KRIESBERG, MATTHIAS
b. New York, N. Y., 21 Mar. 1953. Studied with Isaac Nemiroff, State Univ. of New York at Stony Brook; with Harvey Sollberger and Charles Wuorinen, Columbia Univ., B. A. He received a BMI award, 1971; Ditson Fund composing grant, 1973.
WORKS: Chamber music: Scalene, string trio, 1971; 2 untitled pieces for piano, 1972; Esja, concerto for piano and 7 instruments, New York, 25 Mar. 1974.
300 Riverside Drive, New York, NY 10025

KROEGER, KARL
b. Louisville, Ky., 13 Apr. 1932. Studied with Claude Almand and George Perle, Univ. of Louisville; with Gordon Binkerd, Univ. of Illinois; Brown Univ., Ph. D. in musicology. He received the Ostwald Award, American Bandmasters Asso., 1971; Ford Found. grant, 1964-67; other awards in composition. He was curator, Americana Collection, New York Public Library, 1962-64; composer-in-residence, Eugene, Ore., public schools, 1964-67; assistant professor, Ohio Univ., 1967-68; assistant professor, Moorhead State Coll., 1971-72; director, Moravian Music Found., 1972- .
WORKS: Orchestra: 2 suites; Sinfonietta for string orch.; Band: Divertimento; Variations on a hymn by William Billings; Declaration, trumpet and band; Wind ensemble: 2 brass quintets; 3 brass sextets; Chamber music: Sonata breve, trumpet, horn, trombone; Toccata, clarinet, trombone percussion; 2 string quartets; Toccata for percussion; a number of choral works, songs, piano pieces.
Moravian Music Foundation
Winston-Salem, NC 27108

*KROLL, WILLIAM
b. New York, N. Y., 30 Jan. 1901. Studied in Berlin and at Inst. of Musical Art, New York, graduated 1922. He was first violinist of the Coolidge String Quartet, 1935-45; organized the Kroll Quartet, 1945; has been faculty member,

(KROLL, WILLIAM)
Mannes School of Music, Peabody Cons., Cleveland
Inst. of Music, Queens Coll., CUNY.
WORKS: Chamber music: 4 bagatelles for
string quartet; 4 characteristic pieces, string
quartet; pieces for solo violin, solo piano.
Department of Music, Queens College, CUNY
Flushing, NY 11367

*KRUGER, LILLY CANFIELD
b. Portage, Ohio, 13 Apr. 1892; d. 1969. Studied at Univ. of Toledo, B. A., B. Ed.; was a
public school teacher. She wrote settings of
Psalm 1; Psalm 128; He lives; Christmas pastorale; and piano pieces.

*KRUL, ELI
b. Pabianice, Poland, 1 Jan. 1926; to U.S. 1950.
Studied at Hochschule fur Musik, Munich, 1945-49.
His works include a string quartet, 1958; O come,
let us sing, chorus and organ, 1960; Alleluia,
a cappella chorus, 1962.

KUBIK, GAIL
b. South Coffeyville, Okla., 5 Sep. 1914. Studied with Edward Royce and Bernard Rogers, Eastman School of Music, B. M. with distinction 1934;
with Leo Sowerby, American Cons., M. M. cum laude
1935; with Walter Piston and Nadia Boulanger at
Harvard Univ., 1937-38. His awards include an
honorary doctorate, Monmouth Coll.; Guggenheim
fellowship, 1948; American Prix de Rome; Chicago
Symphony Golden Jubilee award, 1941, for Scherzo
for orch.; Heifetz prize for 2nd violin concerto,
1943; Pulitzer prize for Symphony concertante,
1952; Academy award and British Film Inst. award
for score to Gerald McBoing Boing, 1950; Edinburgh Film Festival award for Transatlantic, 1952.
He has held faculty posts at Monmouth Coll.,
1934-36; Dakota Wesleyan Univ., 1936-37; Columbia
Teachers Coll., 1938-40; was staff composer, NBC,
1940-41; music director, Office of War Information, Bureau of Motion Pictures, 1942-43;
composer-conductor, film, radio, USAAF 1943-46;
guest conductor, lecturer, visiting professor,
etc., 1946-   ; professor and composer-in-
residence, Scripps Coll., 1970-
WORKS: Theatre: Mirror for the sky, folk
opera, 1946; Boston baked beans, 1-act operatic
farce, 1950; Frankie and Johnny, ballet for dance
band and folk singer, 1946; music for They walk
alone, 1941; Orchestra: American caprice, piano
and chamber orch., 1936; 2 violin concertos, 1938,
1943; Scherzo for orch., 1941; Paratroops, 1941;
Whoopee-ti-yi-yo, on cowboy themes, 1941; Camptown races, 1946; Erie Canal, 1947; 3 symphonies,
1949, 1955, 1956; Symphony concertante, trumpet,
viola, piano, orch., 1952; Bachata, 1956; A festival opening, 1957; Scenes for orch., 1963;
Band: Stewball variations, 1941; Fanfare and
march, 1946; Overture, 1946; Chamber music:
Trivialities, flute, horn, string quartet, 1934;
piano trio, 1934; Puck, a Christmas score, speakers, strings and winds, 1940; suite for 3 recorders, 1941; Bennie the beaver, children's tale for
narrator, percussion soloist and chamber orch.;
violin sonatina, 1944; Toccata for organ and
strings, 1946; Little suite, flute, 2 clarinets,

(KUBIK, GAIL)
1947; 2 Divertimentos, 1959; clarinet sonatina,
1959; piano sonata; piano sonatina; Celebrations
and epilogue, piano; Divertimento, piano trio,
1971; 5 theatrical sketches, piano trio, Scripps
Coll., 14 Jan. 1973; Chorus: Variations on a
13th century troubadour song, 1935; Soon one
morning, American folksong; Oh dear, what can
the matter be, choral scherzo; In praise of
Johnny Appleseed, 1938; Profiles, 1948; Litany
and prayer, men's voices, 1945; A record of our
time, narrator, chorus, soloists, orch., 1970;
Film scores: The world at war, 1942; The Memphis
Belle, 1943; Gerald McBoing Boing, 1950; 2 gals
and a guy, 1951; Transatlantic, 1952; The desperate hours, 1955; Down to Earth, 1959.
Music Department, Scripps College
Claremont, CA 91711

KUDO, E. TAKEO
b. Honolulu, Hawaii, 10 June 1942. Studied with
Armand Russell, Univ. of Hawaii; Bernhard Heiden,
Indiana Univ.; and with Manoah Leide-Tedesco at
Colorado Springs. He was composer-arranger for
Air Force bands at the USAF Academy and in Washington, D.C., 1968-74.
WORKS: Band: Variants on a popular tune,
Seattle, Jan. 1968; Partials, trumpet and wind
ensemble, 1970; Chamber music: woodwind quartet;
brass quartet; Fragments of once upon a time,
flute, piano, cello, percussion, 1972.
1977 Halekoa Drive, Honolulu, HI 96821

*KUNC, BOZIDAR
b. Zagreb, Croatia, 18 July 1903; to U.S. 1950;
d. Detroit, Mich., 1 Apr. 1964. Studied at
Zagreb Music Acad.
WORKS: Orchestra: piano concerto, 1934; 2
violin sonatas, 1950, 1954; symphonies; 3 episodes, piano and string orch., 1956; Chamber
music: string quartet; piano trio; piano quartet; songs and piano pieces.

*KUPFERMAN, MEYER
b. New York, N. Y., 3 July 1926. Studied at the
High School of Music and Art; and at Queens Coll.,
CUNY, where he received the first La Guardia
award. He has been professor, Sarah Lawrence
Coll., 1951-   .
WORKS: Opera: In a garden, 1949; Dr.
Faustus lights the lights; The curious fern,
1957; Voices in a mirror, 1957; Draagenfut girl,
1958; Orchestra: 6 symphonies; Divertimento,
1948; chamber symphony, 1950; Variations for
orchestra, 1959; Libretto for orch.; Ostinato
burlesca, 1954; Jazz: Tunnel of love for jazz
combo; concerto for cello and jazz band; concerto for cello, tape, and orch., Westchester,
N. Y., Dec. 1975; Chamber music: 5 string quartets; Cycle of infinities 1-8, for various instruments; 4 pieces for cello and piano; 3
ideas, trumpet, 1967; Winds of the highest tower,
New York, 3 Mar. 1973; sonata for 2 cellos; Curtain raiser, flute, clarinet, bassoon, piano,
New York, 2 May 1973; Angel footprints, violin
and tape, New York, 6 May 1973; Piano: Fantasy
sonata; Little sonata, 1948; Variations 1948;
Sonata on jazz elements, 1958; Film scores:

KUPFERMAN, MEYER

(KUPFERMAN, MEYER)
Blast of silence; Black like me; Hallejuah the hills; Cool wind; High arctic; Goldstein.
Department of Music, Sarah Lawrence College
Bronxville, NY 10708

*KURKA, ROBERT
b. Cicero, Ill., 22 Dec. 1921; d. New York, N. Y., 12 Dec. 1957. Studied with Otto Luening and Darius Milhaud. He held Guggenheim fellowships, 1951, 1952.
WORKS: Opera: The good soldier Schweik, New York, 23 Apr. 1958; Orchestra: 2 symphonies; violin concerto; Serenade, chamber orch.; concerto for 2 pianos, string orch., and trumpet; concerto for marimba and orch.; Ballad for horn and strings; Chamber music: 5 string quartets; piano trio; 4 violin sonatas; also choral works and piano pieces.

KURTZ, ARTHUR DIGBY
b. Chicago, Ill., 7 May 1929. Attended St. Louis Inst. of Music, M. M.; studied with Nadia Boulanger in Paris; further studies at the Sorbonne. He received the Nadia Boulanger award, in 1956 for a piano sonata performed at Univ. of Southern Illinois, Carbondale. He is a private teacher.
WORKS: Orchestra: Prelude; Serenade, 1958; symphony, 1969; piano concerto, 1972; Wind ensemble: Variations for brass and percussion, 1969; Chamber music: oboe sonata; 2 piano sonatas, 1956, 1970; 2 violin sonatas, 1964, 1969; 2 string quartets, 1963, 1969; flute sonata, 1964; wind octet, 1965; 3 concert pieces for trumpet and piano, 1968; Fantasy for clarinet and piano, 1970; sonatina for unaccompanied flute, 1970; Isaiah, spoken voice, saxophone, piano, percussion, 1971; 2 choral works, songs; piano pieces.
685 Oakwood Ave., Webster Groves, MO 63119

*KURTZ, EDWARD FRAMPTON
b. New Castle, Pa., 31 July 1881. Studied at Pittsburgh Cons.; with Philip Greeley Clapp, Univ. of Iowa, M. A.; at Detroit Cons., B. M.; with Edgar Stillman Kelley, Cincinnati Cons., M. M.; also with Percy Goetschius and violin with Eugene Ysaye. He was faculty member at Franklin Coll., Westminster Coll., Geneva Coll., Univ. of Kansas, and from 1940 chairman, music department, Iowa State Teachers Coll.
WORKS: Orchestra: 3 symphonies; The daemon lover, symphonic poem; La charmante, 1914; Parthenope, violin and orch., 1922; Chamber music: string quartet; From the west, suite for string quartet, 1928; suite for organ; violin pieces; songs.

KURTZ, EUGENE ALLEN
b. Atlanta, Ga., 27 Dec. 1923. Studied with Bernard Rogers, Eastman School of Music, 1946-49; with Darius Milhaud at Tanglewood, 1948, and in Paris, 1949-50; Arthur Honneger, Paris, 1952; privately with Max Deutsch in Paris, 1953-57; also audited classes with Olivier Messiaen. He received commissions from WUOM, Univ. of Michigan, 1958; American Cultural Center, Paris, 1966; French Ministry of Cultural Affairs, 1970;

(KURTZ, EUGENE ALLEN)
Univ. of Nevada, 1973; ORTF (French Nat. Radio), 1973. He has been visiting lecturer, Univ. of Michigan, 1967-68, 1970-71, 1973-74; lives in Paris the rest of the year.
WORKS: Orchestra: Symphony for string orch.; The solitary walker; Ca..., diagramme pour orchestre, Strasbourg Radio Symph. Orch., Dec. 1972; 3 songs from Medea, soprano and orch., (also for voice and piano); Concert nocturne, from film score; Suite Parisienne, from film score; Chamber music: Chamber symphony for the 4th of July, WUOM, Univ. of Michigan, 1958; Conversations for 12 players, French Nat. Radio, May 1966; The last contrabass in Las Vegas, 1 man, 1 woman, and 1 contrabass, Univ. of Nevada, Feb. 1974; Sonata (quasi un' opera), solo violin; Improvisations for solo contrabass; Piano: 4 movements for piano; La capricorne; Motivations, Books I and II; Animations: Resonances and Rag.
36 Avenue Jean Moulin, 75014 Paris, France

KURTZ, S. JAMES
b. Newark, N. J., 8 Feb. 1934. Studied with Philip James and Simeon Bellison (clarinet), New York Univ.; at Univ. of Iowa, Ph. D. He won an award in a Marion Bauer contest. He taught at Mannes Coll. of Music and was free lance clarinetist in New York; on faculty, Madison Coll., 1965- .
WORKS: Chamber music: Suite for 3 clarinets; 3 impressions for 2 clarinets; Fantasy for unaccompanied clarinet; Notturno for clarinet or flute and piano; works for voice, piano, strings, winds.
Music Department, Madison College
Harrisonburg, VA 22801

KYNASTON, TRENT P.
b. Tucson, Ariz., 7 Dec. 1946. Studied with Robert McBride, Wendal Jones, and Henry Johnson, Univ. of Arizona. He has been assistant professor, Western Michigan Univ., 1973- .
WORKS: Orchestra: symphony, 1969; Band: Underture for band, 1967; Mind expansion, tape and wind ensemble, 1970; Chamber music: Dance suite, saxophone, 1966; Sonata duet, saxophone and clarinet, 1967; Dawn and jubilation, saxophone and piano, 1973; Chorus: Corinthians 13, choir and 13 brass, 1970; The man who was summoned, choir, guitar, horn, string orch., 2 pianos, 1970.
816 Boswell Lane, Kalamazoo, MI 49007

KYR, ROBERT HARRY
b. Cleveland, Ohio, 20 Apr. 1952. Studied with Alejandro Planchart and Robert Morris at Yale Univ. He received 2 fellowships and a Scholar of the House award at Yale.
WORKS: Chamber music: Chronicles, 10 instruments, 1972; Canticles I: Music to hear, 12 instruments, 1973; The fall of the rebel angel, 21 instruments, 1973; Multimedia: Voyage: Dream play for instruments, chamber orch., tape and film, 1974.
22289 Blossom Drive, Rocky River, OH 44116

*LABACH, PARKER
b. Lexington, Ky., 1918. Studied with Lewis
Henry Horton, Univ. of Kentucky, A. B. 1942,
M. A. 1947; with Merrill Lewis, Syracuse Univ.,
Ph. D. 1960. He has taught at Georgia State
Coll. for Women; Syracuse Univ.; and in 1964 was
assistant professor of education, Kent State Univ.
    WORKS: Chamber music: April 1950, flute and
piano; February 1951, cello and piano; woodwind
quintet; also band marches; choral works; songs;
piano pieces.

LABAR, DANIEL
b. Berwyn, Ill., 6 May 1944. Studied with Stella
Roberts, American Cons. He received an award for
an anthem, 1968, and a commission to write a work
for the Texas Boys' Choir, Fort Worth, 1969. He
has been instructor, American Cons., 1970-   .
    WORKS: Orchestra: Textures, fantasy for
orch., 1974; Chamber music: string quartet,
1971; Chorus: De profundis, 1968; Nativity
suite, boys' choir, narrator, organ, 1969; A song
of war, a song of peace, 1972; Ode to mankinde,
chamber choir, 1974; Songs: Stopping by woods,
tenor, 1967; Grass, tenor and piano, 1972; 3
songs from Sandburg for baritone, clarinet and
cello, 1974.
    3506 North Greenview Ave., Chicago, IL 60657

LABOUNTY, EDWIN MURRAY
b. Garretson, S. D., 19 Feb. 1927. Studied with
Bernhard Heiden, Indiana Univ., B. M. 1949, M. M.
1953, D. M. 1962. He was music supervisor, North
Country School, Lake Placid, N. Y., 1954-59;
assistant to associate professor, Memphis State
Univ., 1962-68; associate professor, Western
Washington State Coll., 1968-   .
    WORKS: Orchestra: 3 pieces for orchestra,
1960; Excursus, piano and orch., 1962; Excursus
no.2, 1972; Chamber music: sonata for 2 celli
and piano, 1952; horn sonata, 1953; cello sonata,
1959; wind quintet, 1960; Voice: Songs of recollection, a cycle, 1952; Fatal interview, song
cycle, 1952; Sea afternoon, choir, harp, oboe,
cello, glockenspiel, 1961; Piano: sonatina, 1951;
sonata, 1954-73; Concert piece, 4 pianos with
percussion, 1958; Blue and blue green, 2 pianos,
1960-73; Electronic: incidental music for Now
is the time for all good men, tape, 1973.
    433 16th St., Bellingham, WA 98225

LABUNSKI, FELIX
b. Ksawerynow, Poland, 27 Dec. 1892; U.S. citizen
1941. Studied with Lucien Marczewski and Witold
Maliszewski in Warsaw; with Nadia Boulanger and
Paul Dukas in Paris. His honors include Mac-
Dowell fellowship, 1941; Huntington Hartford
Found. fellowship, 1951; honorary doctorate,
Chicago Musical Coll., 1951; Alfred Jurzykowski
Found. award, 1969; Nat. Endowment of the Arts
fellowship, 1973-74. He was faculty member,
Marymount Coll., Tarrytown, N. Y., 1940-41; fac-
ulty, Coll. Cons., Univ. of Cincinnati, 1945-64,
professor emeritus, 1964-   .
    WORKS: Ballet: God's man, 1937; Orchestra:
In memoriam for Ignace Paderewski, 1941; Suite
for string orch., 1941; Variations for orch.,
1951; Elegy, 1954; Symphony in B, 1954; Xaveriana,

(LABUNSKI, FELIX)
fantasy for 2 pianos and orch., 1956; Nocturne,
1957; Images of youth, 1958; Symphonic dialogues,
1960; Canto di aspirazione, 1963; Polish rennaissance suite, 1967; Salut a Paris, ballet suite,
1968; Music for piano and orchestra, 1968;
Primavera, 1973; Wind ensemble: Intrada festiva,
brass choir, 1968; Chamber music: Divertimento,
4 woodwinds, 1956; Diptych (Pastorale and danse),
oboe and piano, 1958; string quartet no.2, 1962;
Chorus: There is no death, chorus and orch.,
1950; Images of youth, children's chorus, 2 soli,
orch., 1956; Ave Maria, motet a cappella, 1957;
Mass for treble voices and organ, 1957; 2 madrigals, a cappella, 1960; Songs: Vocalise for
soprano, no.1 1941, no.2 1950; Song without
words, soprano and strings, 1946; Piano:
Threnody, 1941; piano sonata no.2, 1955; 2
Kujawiaks, 1959; organ pieces.
    2324 Park Ave., Cincinnati, OH 45206

*LABUNSKI, WIKTOR
b. St. Petersburg, Russia, 14 Apr. 1895; to U.S.
1928; d. Lenexa, Kans., 26 Jan. 1974. Brother
of Felix Labunski, studied at the St. Petersburg
Cons. He made his debut as pianist in New York
in 1928; toured the U.S.; was professor and
director, Coll. of Music, Memphis, Tenn.,
1931-37; Kansas City Cons., 1937-63; professor
and artist-in-residence, Univ. of Missouri at
Kansas City from 1963.
    WORKS: Orchestra: symphony, 1936; piano
concerto, 1937; Variations, piano and orch.;
2-piano concerto, 1951; piano pieces.

*LADERMAN, EZRA
b. New York, N. Y., 29 June 1924. Studied at
Brooklyn Coll., B. A.; with Otto Luening, Stefan
Wolpe, and Douglas Moore, Columbia Univ., M. A.
His awards have included 3 Guggenheim grants;
Prix de Rome; Ford Found. commission. He is
professor, State Univ. of New York at Binghamton.
    WORKS: Opera: Jacob and the Indians, 1957;
Sarah, 1958; Goodby to the clown, 1960; The hunting of the snark, 1961; Shadows among us;
Galileo Galilei, opera oratorio, 1967; Orchestra:
2 symphonies; Concerto for orchestra; violin
concerto; Triptych, flute, oboe, strings; Magic
prison, 2 narrators and orch., 1967; Double
helix, flute, oboe, and strings; Celestial
bodies, flute and strings; Stanzas, chamber orch.;
Chamber music: Nonet, winds and piano; Theme,
variations and finale, string quartet and wind
quartet, 1957; 3 piano sonatas; flute sonata;
3 string quartets; duo for violin and piano;
piano trio; A single voice, oboe and string quartet; 2 duos for violin and cello; clarinet
sonata; Celestial bodies, flute and string quartet, Milwaukee, 23 June 1975; Portraits, violin
solo; Serenade, clarinet solo; Elegy for viola,
New York, 17 Feb. 1974; Chorus: The eagle
stirred, oratorio; And David wept, cantata, 1971;
Thrive upon the rock, New York, 9 May 1973; Song
cycles: Songs for Eve, MacLeish text; From the
Psalms; Songs from Michelangelo, New York, 18
Mar. 1973; Film score: The Eleanor Roosevelt

LADERMAN, EZRA

(LADERMAN, EZRA)
story (received an Oscar); Image of love; Grand Canyon.
Music Department
State University of New York
Binghamton, NY 13901

LADIGIN, DONALD R.
b. San Francisco, Calif., 14 July 1939. Studied with Alan Chaplin and Virko Baley, California Inst. of the Arts. He won a first prize in composition, Young Artists of Tomorrow contest, Los Angeles. He has been teaching privately and in Los Angeles institutions, 1966-   .
WORKS: Piano: Variations, Las Vegas, Apr. 1971.
11743 1/2 Goshen Ave., Los Angeles, CA 90049

LAFFERTY, DONALD
b. Buffalo, N. Y., 8 Sep. 1942. Studied with Robert Mols and Allen Sapp, State Univ. of New York, Buffalo; with Arthur Berger and Harold Shapero, Brandeis Univ.; with Malcolm Peyton, New England Cons., piano with Irma Wolpe. He was instructor, Clark Univ., 1968-69; New England Cons., 1970-   .
WORKS: Piano: Grace period, Boston, Oct. 1972.
61 Salem St., Reading, MA 01867

*LA FORGE, FRANK
b. Rockford, Ill., 22 Oct. 1877; d. New York, N. Y., 5 May 1953. Studied piano with Harrison Wild and Leschetizky; received an hon. D. M. from the Detroit Found. Music School. He was accompanist to Marcella Sembrich, Lily Pons, and Schumann-Heink; voice teacher in New York, 1920-53. He composed songs and piano pieces.

*LA GASSEY, HOMER
Sea portrait and Sequoia, both for band.

*LAHMER, REUEL
b. Maple, Ont., Canada, 27 Mar. 1912. Studied at Stetson Univ.; Westminster Choir Coll., B. M.; Columbia Univ.; with Roy Harris, Cornell Univ. He has received many commissions. He was minister of music Grace Church, Montclair, N. J., 1934-39; instructor, Cornell Univ., 1941-42; U.S. Army, World War II; composer-in-residence, Carroll Coll., 1946-48; chairman of theory and composition, Colorado Coll., 1948-51; organist-choirmaster, Pittsburgh, Pa., 1951-62; lectured in Europe and Mexico for the USIA; was in residence at the American Coll. in Switzerland at Leysin, 1973.
WORKS: Chorus: A song of our own; Spring cantata; Suite on Methodist hymns; Sing the sweet land; Civil War suite; Ye sons and daughters of the king; Hear Lord; also songs and organ works.

*LAIRD, BRUCE
The partisans, Wilmington Opera Society, Del., Feb. 1969.

*LAMB, HUBERT WELDON
b. Walpole, N. H., 29 June 1900. Studied at Harvard Univ., B. A. 1930; received the John

(LAMB, HUBERT WELDON)
Knowles Paine traveling fellowship, 1930, 1931; Guggenheim fellowship, 1948; honorary D. M., New England Cons., 1963. He was faculty member, Longy School of Music, 1934-35; on faculty Wellesley Coll., 1935-   , professor, 1957-   .
WORKS: Orchestra: Capriccio for string orch., 1946; Chamber music: Concerto da camera, harpsichord and chamber ensemble, 1943; string trio, 1946; The Intervale variations, violin and piano, 1950; Rondo serio, cello and piano, 1951; A solemn air, horn and piano, 1951; Capriccio and fugue, clarinet and piano, 1963; Chorus: Remember now thy creator, 1940; The end of the world, women's voices, 1941; Hymn of the cherubim, 1943; 6 scenes from the Protevangelion, women's voices and small orch., 1949; Pastorale, women's voices and 9 instruments.
Department of Music, Wellesley College
Wellesley, MA 02181

LAMB, JOHN DAVID
b. Portland, Ore., 11 Mar. 1935. Studied at Univ. of Washington and with Volfgangs Darzins, 1956-60. He received a Ford Contemporary Music grant, 1964-65; and a Rockefeller performance award. He has been a teacher in the Seattle public schools, 1960-   .
WORKS: Theatre: King Midas, a play for dancers, speaking chorus, recorders, Orff instruments; Orchestra: horn concerto; Scherzo and chaconne, flute and strings; Diptych; Cloud Cuckoo Land, saxophone concerto; Comoedia, suite; Band: Night music, saxophone and chamber band; Serenade; Chorus: The song of Solomon, chorus, soloists, orch.; Short mass; An entertainment, female voices, piano and horn; Rhymes, female voices, recorders, drums; The monotony song, chorus and clarinet; many songs and works for chamber ensembles.
1907 East Blaine, Seattle, WA 98112

LAMB, MARVIN LEE
b. Jacksonville, Tex., 12 July 1946. Studied with John Butler and Newton Strandberg, Houston State Univ., B. M.; William P. Latham, Martin Mailman, Merrill Ellis, North Texas State Univ., M. M.; with Herbert Brun and Paul Zonn, Univ. of Illinois. He received a scholarship at North Texas State Univ.; commissions from NTSU Saxophone Quartet; Philip Brink, trombonist; Atlantic Christian Coll. Chorus. He was brass instructor, Weatherford, Tex., 1969-71; graduate assistant, Univ. of Illinois, 1972-73; instructor, Atlantic Christian Coll., 1973-   .
WORKS: Orchestra: Movements for trumpet, string orch., percussion; Band: Quiet statement for band; Chamber music: In memoriam Benjy, saxophone quartet; Prairie suite, brass quintet; The professor march and rag, Phonemes, spoken choir; 3 moments for piano and tape; woodwind quintet, 1973; Multimedia: This banana is for you, 2 dancers and solo trumpet; Intonazione, tapes, lights, sculpture.
704 North Rountree, Wilson, NC 27893

*LAMBERT, CECILY

Acrobats, Rhumba rhythm, Sonata-fantasy, all for
violin and piano.
76 Lexham Gardens, Kensington W8, England

*LAMBORD, BENJAMIN
b. Portland, Me., 10 June 1879; d. Lake Hopatcong,
N. J., 6 June 1915. Studied with Edward
MacDowell and Cornelius Rybner, Columbia Univ.;
with Paul Vidal in Paris. He was organist-
choirmaster and teacher in New York.
WORKS: Orchestra: Introduction and variation on an English dance theme; Clytie, soprano
and orch.; Verses from Omar Khayyam, chorus and
orch.; piano pieces; songs.

LAMBRO, PHILLIP
b. Wellesley Hills, Mass., 2 Sep. 1935. Studied
with Donald Pond and Gyorgy Sandor, Music Acad.
of the West. Together with Shimon Ben-Bassat,
Israeli-American structural designer, he has
developed plans for the concert hall of the
future: circular in design, with hydraulically
controlled stages which can be raised or lowered,
natural and amplified acoustics, and equipped
with multi-channel audio and visual recording
devices.
WORKS: Orchestra: Miraflores, string orch.;
2 pictures for solo percussionist and orch.; 4
songs, soprano and orch.; Structures, string orch.;
Wind ensemble: Parallelograms, flute quartet
and jazz ensemble; Music for wind, brass and
percussion; Fanfare and tower music for brass
quintet; Chamber music: Dance barbaro, percussion; Toccata for piano; Toccata for guitar;
Obelisk, oboe and percussion; Night pieces for
piano; Biospheres for 6 percussionists; Film
scores: Energy on the move (documentary); The
invisible magician; And now Miguel; Celebration.
1888 Century Park East, Suite 10
Century Park, CA 90067

LAMM, ROBERT CARSON
b. New Albany, Ind., 9 Apr. 1922. Studied with
Warren Babb, Univ. of Louisville; Arthur Olaf
Andersen, Univ. of Arizona; and Bernhard Heiden,
Indiana Univ. He was assistant professor, Hart-
wick Coll., 1948-52; teaching fellow, Indiana
Univ., 1952-53; chairman, music department, Park
Coll., 1953-56; instructor, Univ. of Arizona,
1956-59; director, Center for the Humanities,
Arizona State Univ., 1959-
WORKS: Band: Saturday in the park; Chamber
music: Tramway, trombone and piano; piano sonata;
violin sonata.
630 Wesleyan Drive, Tempe, AZ 85282

LA MONTAINE, JOHN
b. Oak Park, Ill., 17 Mar. 1920. Studied with
Stella Roberts and Rudolph Ganz in Chicago;
Bernard Rogers and Howard Hanson, Eastman School
of Music, B. M.; with Bernard Wagenaar at
Juilliard; and with Nadia Boulanger. His awards
include a scholarship at Eastman; Ford Found.
commission, 1958; 2 Guggenheim fellowships, 1959,
1960; Pulitzer Prize, 1959, for a piano concerto;
Rheta Sosland Chamber Music competition prize,
1960; commission for the inaugural concert, 1961;

(LA MONTAINE, JOHN)
composer-in-residence, American Acad. in Rome,
1962; commission for work for dedication of
Filene organ at Kennedy Center, 1973; Eastman
School Distinguished Alumni award. He played
celeste and piano with the NBC Symphony under
Arturo Toscanini, 1950-54; was visiting professor, Eastman School of Music, 1964-65.
WORKS: Opera: Spreading the news, 1-act;
Novellis, novellis, Christmas pageant, Washington Cathedral, 24 Dec. 1961; The shephardes playe,
2nd part of the Christmas pageant trilogy, Washington Cathedral, 24 Dec. 1967; Erode the Great,
3rd part, Washington, 30 Dec. 1969; Orchestra:
Songs of the Rose of Sharon, soprano and orch.;
piano concerto, Washington, 25 Nov. 1958; Canons
for orch.; Ode for oboe and orch.; 5 sonnets for
orch.; Jubilant overture; symphony; Fragments
from the Songs of songs, soprano and orch.; From
sea to shining sea, Washington 20 Jan. 1961;
Birds of Paradise, piano and orch.; Te Deum,
chorus, wind orch., percussion; Mass of nature,
chorus, narrator and orch.; Incantation for jazz
band; Wilderness journal, symphony for bass-
baritone, organ, and orch., Washington, Nov.
1972; Chamber music: cello sonata; string quartet; sonata for flute solo; woodwind quartet;
sonata for piano 4-hands; Scherzo, 4 trombones;
Conversations, clarinet and piano, Atlantic City,
N. J., Apr. 1973; many choral works, songs, piano
pieces.
c/o Paul Sifler
3947 Fredonia Drive, Hollywood, CA 90028

*LANDAU, SIEGFRIED
b. Berlin, Germany, 4 Sep. 1921; to U.S. 1940.
Studied in Berlin; at Trinity Coll., London;
conducting with Pierre Monteux in the U.S. He
organized the Brooklyn Philharmonia in 1954,
was conductor to 1970; conductor, Music for Westchester Symphony, 1962-   ; music director and
conductor, Chattanooga Opera Asso., 1959-   .
WORKS: Opera: The sons of Aaron; Ballet:
The golem, 1946; The dybbuk; Orchestra: Longing
for Jerusalem, soprano and orch.; Chamber music:
Chassidic suite, viola and piano; also Friday
evening services.
c/o Westchester Symphony, Box 35
Gedney Station, White Plains, NY 10605

LANDAU, VICTOR
b. Brooklyn, N. Y., 18 June 1916. Studied with
Charles Haubiel and Philip James, New York Univ.
He received the Talbott prize, Westminster Choir
School, 1938. He was instructor, Brooklyn Coll.,
1946-50; professor, State Univ. Coll., New Paltz,
N. Y., 1950-   .
WORKS: Band: Variations on a Russian theme;
Chamber music: Adagio for strings; Scherzo, vio-
lin and piano; 3 James Joyce songs; Chorus: The
laughters; Eli, eli.
5 Lincoln Place, New Paltz, NY 12561

LANDRY, RICHARD MILES
b. Cecilia, La., 16 Nov. 1938. Studied with
John Gilfry, Southwestern Louisiana Univ.; and
with Arthur Lora. Since 1968 he has been associated with Philip Glass in performance.

LANDRY, RICHARD MILES

(LANDRY, RICHARD MILES)
WORKS: Electronic: avant garde works performed at the Dance Gallery, New York.
10 Chatham Square, New York, NY 10038

LANDY, H. LEIGH
b. Bronxville, N. Y., 23 Nov. 1951. Studied with Jack Beeson, Charles Dodge, Vladimir Ussachevsky, and Charles Wuorinen, Columbia Univ.; and with Bulent Arel and Alfredo Del Monaco. He was graduate assistant, Columbia Univ., 1973-74.
WORKS: Theatre: cummings again, Absurdist Theatre piece for 7 actors-singers, 1973; Chamber music: Flute study, no.1, 1972; Opus 1, flute, horn, piano, 1973; Electronic: Computer study no.1, 1971; Ambiguité, musique concrète tape, 1973; Nixon phase (out) 1, computer piece, 1973.
622 West 114th St., Apt. 42
New York, NY 10025

*LANE, EASTWOOD
b. Brewerton, N. Y., 22 May 1879; d. Central Square, N. Y., 22 Jan. 1951. Studied at Syracuse Univ. He was assistant director of the Wanamaker Concerts for 23 years.
WORKS: Ballet: Boston fancy; Abelard and Eloise; A caravan from China comes; Orchestra: Sea burial, tone poem; Persimmon pucker (orchestrated by Ferde Grofe); Piano suites: Adirondack sketches; 4th of July; Sleepy Hollow; Sold down the river; 3 American sketches.

LANE, LEWIS
b. Freehold, N. J., 3 Aug. 1903. Studied with Rubin Goldmark, New York Coll. of Music; with Thomas Tapper and Henry Krehbiel, Inst. of Musical Art, New York. He was music librarian, NBC, 1928-31; founder and director of NBC's Division for Musical Research, 1931-51; archivist, Leschetizky Asso., 1938-48.
WORKS: Piano: Prelude in C; Fragments after Lucretius; 2 character sketches; Green Mountain sketches; and songs.
1091 Boylston St., Boston, MA 02215

LANE, RICHARD B.
b. Paterson, N. J., 11 Dec. 1933. Studied with Bernard Rogers, Louis Mennini, and Wayne Barlow, Eastman School of Music, B. M. 1955, M. M. 1956. He received the Eastman School publication and recording award, 1956; 2 Ford Found. grants, 1959, 1960. He has been a private teacher of piano and composition and an accompanist, 1961- .
WORKS: Orchestra: 4 songs, mezzo-soprano and orch.; String song and passacaglia, string orch.; Chamber music: Suite for saxophone and piano; flute sonata; Chorus: Hymn to the night; Cradle song.
173 Lexington Ave., Paterson, NJ 07502

LANERI, ROBERTO
b. Arzignano, Italy, 25 Mar. 1945; to U.S. 1968. Studied privately with William O. Smith; with Lejaren Hiller, State Univ. of New York at Buffalo; with Keith Humble and Edwin London, Univ. of California, San Diego. He was clarinetist

(LANERI, ROBERTO)
and composer, Center for the Creative and performing Arts, Buffalo, 1970-72; member of SEM Ensemble, 1970-72; teaching assistant, Univ. of California, San Diego, 1973- .
WORKS: Ballet: Black Ivory suite, large ensemble of instruments and voices, commissioned by Company of Man Dance Company, Buffalo, 26 Feb. 1972; Chamber music: Finis, soprano and piano, 1969; Changes for 5 players, with speaker, Montreal, 16 Mar. 1969; Sleep soft smiling, soprano, chamber ensemble and tape, 1969; The night brings a rabbit, clarinet and percussion, 1970; Dies irae, soprano and chamber ensemble, 1971; Summer music, horn and piano, 1971; Esorcismi #1, clarinet, trombone, viola, percussion, voice, 1972; August visitors, soprano, tenor, cello, harpsichord, 1973; Electronic: Entropic islands, amplified clarinet and 2 tapes, 1970; L'arte del violino, amplified violin, 2 pianos, 2 percussionists, violinist, speaker or tape, and girls, 1970.
Music Department, University of California
P.O. Box 109, La Jolla, CA 92037

*LANG, EDITH
East Indian lullaby, vocal solo; Lord, who through these 40 days, vocal duet; Meditation, organ prelude.

LANGERT, JULES
b. New York, N. Y., 25 Mar. 1932. Studied at Queens Coll.; and with Andrew Imbrie, Univ. of California at Berkeley. He received a Fulbright scholarship; Hertz scholarship; and a California Cello Club award. He was lecturer, San Francisco State Univ., 1965-70; instructor, Dominican Coll. of San Rafael, 1971-74.
WORKS: Opera: Sea change, 4 singers and chamber ensemble; Orchestra: Fantasy, for small orch.; Chamber music: Duo for cello and piano; quartet, flute, clarinet, cello, and piano; 3 capriccios, piano; 2 sets of songs for voice and piano.
6504 Raymond St., Oakland, CA 94609

*LANGSTROTH, IVAN SHED
b. Alameda, Calif., 16 Oct. 1887; d. New York, 18 Apr. 1971. Studied in San Francisco; with Paul Juon, Engelbert Humperdinck, and Josef Lhevinne in Berlin; remained in Europe as opera coach, organist, concert pianist, teacher to 1935. He was chairman of composition, Chatham Square Music School, New York, 1940-43; lecturer, City Coll. of New York, 1942-45; lecturer, Brooklyn Coll., 1943-45; thereafter, a private teacher in New York.
WORKS: Orchestra: piano concerto; Aria, soprano and orch.; Chamber music: string quartet; piano sonatina; Chorus: Cradle song; Butterfly; a cappella mass; Organ: Toccata and double fugue; Fantasia and fugue; Theme and variations; Introduction and fugue.

*LANIER, GARY
Ye that stand in the house of the Lord, chorus.

*LANSKY, PAUL
    Modal fantasy, piano, 1970.
        Department of Music, Princeton University
        Princeton, NJ 08540

LAPIN, LAWRENCE
    b. New York, N. Y., 24 Nov. 1935. Studied with
    J. Clifton Williams, Alfred Reed, Frederick Ashe,
    Univ. of Miami, B. M., M. M. He has been assis-
    tant professor, Univ. of Miami, 1968-   .
        WORKS: Band: Tubarondo, tuba and wind en-
    semble, 1965; 6 pieces for jazz band, 1971;
    Nothin' fancy, stage band, 1970; Chamber music:
    violin sonata, 1964; Mazurka, piano, 1965; duet
    for flute and clarinet, 1965.
        10465 Southwest 96 Terrace, Miami, FL 33101

LA PORTA, JOHN DANIEL
    b. Philadelphia, Pa., 13 Apr. 1920. Studied with
    Nicolas Flagello, Alexei Haieff, and Ernst Toch,
    Manhattan School of Music, M. M. He received
    annual ASCAP awards, 1969-73. He was faculty
    member, Manhattan School of Music, 1951-58;
    supervisor of instrumental performance, Berklee
    Coll. of Music, 1962-   ; member of Berklee
    Faculty Saxophone Quartet.
        WORKS: Band: Mid-century event, 1961; Theme
    and variations on the blues, a 40-minute work for
    jazz octet; Chamber music: Trio, 1955; Spanish
    rhapsody, saxophone quartet; numerous composi-
    tions for small ensembles and many jazz works.
        34 Maple St., South Hamilton, MA 01982

LA PORTA, LOUIS F.
    b. Chicago, Ill., 23 Sep. 1944. Attended St.
    Ambrose Coll.; studied with Bernard Dieter,
    Arnold Allenius, Chicago Cons.; with Alfred Uhl,
    Friedrich Cerha, Hans Swarowsky, Vienna Acad. of
    Music; and at Univ. of Vienna. He received the
    Kodaly composition prize, 1970; Outstanding
    Young Men of America award, 1972. He was high
    school music director, Northfield, Ill., 1967-68;
    chairman, theory and composition, Chicago Cons.
    Coll., 1970-   ; conductor, Chicago Opera
    Players, 1972-   .
        WORKS: Orchestra: Symphony in 1 movement;
    violin concerto; Chamber music: violin sonata,
    1967; string quartet, 1970; Concertpiece, cello
    and piano; Recitative, solo viola; sonata for
    unaccompanied cello; string trio; sonata for 4
    percussionists; Piano: sonatina; Variations;
    Fantasy; also choral works, songs, and song
    cycles.
        11421 South Western Ave., Chicago, IL 60643

*LA PRADE, ERNEST
    b. Memphis, Tenn., 20 Dec. 1889; d. Sherman,
    Conn., 20 Apr. 1969. Studied at Cincinnati Coll.
    of Music; with Cesar Thomson, Royal Cons. in
    Brussels; with Joseph Jongen in London. He
    taught at Cincinnati Coll. of Music; was violin-
    ist in the Cincinnati Symphony, 1909-12; Belgian
    and Holbrook Quartets, London, 1914-17; New York
    Symphony, 1919-28; staff member, NBC, 1929-   ,
    supervisor of music research from 1950. He wrote
    Xantha, a comic opera, 1917; and songs. He was
    author of books and articles on music criticism.

LARGENT, EDWARD J., JR.
    b. Waukegan, Ill., 8 Feb. 1936. Studied with
    Marshall Barnes, Mark Walker, Ohio State Univ.;
    with Salvatore Martirano and Thomas Frederickson,
    Univ. of Illinois. He received 2nd prize, Phi
    Mu Alpha contest, Ohio State Univ., 1963, 1966.
    He was instructor, Western Kentucky Univ.,
    1966-70; assistant professor, Youngstown State
    Univ., 1970-   .
        WORKS: Band: Symphony for brass, Ohio
    State Univ., Jan. 1966; Chamber music: trio,
    violin, horn, piano, 1967; sextet for winds,
    1969; Song for soprano, flute and piano, 1969;
    horn sonata, 1970; Chorus: Cantata for Easter,
    1966; Electronic: Experimental tapes - #2
    Sirens, 1973.
        161 Melbourne Ave., Youngstown, OH 44505

LARKIN, JOHN
    b. Cincinnati, Ohio, 24 Mar. 1927. Studied with
    Felix Labunski, Cincinnati Coll. of Music, B. M.,
    M. M.; with Paul Cooper, Univ. of Cincinnati,
    D. M.; with Ben Weber in New York. He received
    the Dumler award, Cincinnati Composers, 1952;
    Huntington Hartford fellowships, 1954, 1956,
    1958; Yaddo fellowship, 1957. He was instructor,
    Immaculate Heart Coll., Los Angeles, 1959-64;
    instructor, Univ. of Cincinnati, 1965-71; head
    of music theory, Newark, N. J., Boys Choir
    School, 1971-   .
        WORKS: Orchestra: symphonic movement;
    Chorus: Mass in praise of the Trinity, 1960;
    The Beatitudes, 1962; The witnesses, cantata for
    soloists, chorus, orch.; Piano: sonata no.4,
    1971.
        221 West 14th St., Apt. LL
        New York, NY 10011

LARSEN, LIBBY
    b. Wilmington, Del., 24 Dec. 1950. Studied with
    Paul Fetler, Dominick Argento, Eric Stokes,
    Univ. of Minnesota, B. A. 1971, M. A. 1974. She
    won first place in a Minnesota Fed. of Music
    Clubs contest; a commission, First Unitarian
    Society of Minneapolis. She has been teaching
    assistant, Univ. of Minneapolis, 1973-   .
        WORKS: Theatre: Psyche and the pskyscraper,
    short opera; Some pig, opera, 1973; The art of
    love, tenor, soprano, harp, oboe, percussion,
    dancers; Chamber music: Argyle sketches, guitar;
    Istar fantasia, guitar; Theme and deviations for
    harp; Chorus: Lacrimosa Christe, soli, chorus,
    orch.
        3345 Southeast University Ave.
        Minneapolis, MN 55414

LARSEN, WILLIAM
    b. Sioux Falls, S. D., 28 Mar. 1951. Studied
    with Sister Jane Klimisch, Mt. Marty Coll.,
    B. A.; with Milan Kaderavek, Drake Univ. He has
    been high school band and chorus director,
    Oldham, S. D., 1973-   .
        WORKS: Chamber music: Thus fourth, 12-tone
    piece for 5 instruments; Torna-Do, for 12 instru-
    ments; 12-tone piece for 12 instruments; 2 move-
    ments for piano; Chorus: Sheer levity, with
    percussion and strings; Had I seen the sun,
    women's voices, piano, 2 flutes, electric bass.
        R.R.1, Oldham, SD 57051

LASZLO, ALEXANDER

*LASZLO, ALEXANDER
b. Budapest, Hungary, 22 Nov. 1895; U.S. citizen 1944; d. Invented the Colorlight machine to coordinate music and color; was music professor, Inst. of Design, Chicago, 1938; then was film orchestrator in Hollywood, 1944-48; music director for NBC Radio.
WORKS: Orchestra: Mechanized forces; Structural music; Hollywood concerto, piano and orch.; The ghost train of Marshall Pass, piano and orch.; 4D-122, piano and orch.; Mana Hawaii, piano and orch.; Pacific triptych; This world--tomorrow, chorus and orch.; Piano: News of the day; Hungarian dance suite; Fantasy of colors.

LATEEF, YUSEF
b. Chattanooga, Tenn., 9 Oct. 1920. Studied at Wayne State Univ.; with Charles Mills, George Dufalo, Teal School of Music; Manhattan School of Music, B. A., M. A. He has received 2 Playboy Magazine awards; Music Achievement Award for outstanding contribution to African-American music; and was first American to win the Downbeat award for oboe. He plays flute, oboe, argol (an Indian reed flute) shanai, tenor, and alto saxophone, bassoon, and rabat. He has toured the U.S. with several bands; at Wayne State Univ., organized the Yusef Lateef Quintet; is associate professor, Borough of Manhattan Community Coll. His works have been performed by several major orchestras.
WORKS: Lateef calls his music "autophysiopsychic," and in this idiom has written and recorded many compositions for various combinations of instruments including: A flat, G flat and C; Eastern sounds; Other sounds; Cry--tender; Fabric of jazz; Into something; 1984; Golden flute; Jazz round the world; Psychicemotus; Down in Atlanta; In the evening; Constructs, New York, 4 Feb. 1973.
201 Cross St., #15J, Fort Lee, NJ 07042

LATHAM, WILLIAM PETERS
b. Shreveport, La., 4 Jan. 1917. Studied at Univ. of Cincinnati, B. S.; with Eugene Goosens, Cincinnati Cons., B. M., M. M.; with Herbert Elwell and Howard Hanson, Eastman School of Music, Ph. D. He won first prize, Phi Mu Alpha contest; citation, Texas Fed. of Music Clubs, 1967. He was professor, Univ. of Northern Iowa, 1946-65; professor, North Texas State Univ., 1965- , director of graduate studies in music, 1969- .
WORKS: Orchestra: The lady of Shalott, Cincinnati, 7 Mar. 1941; Fantasy concerto, flute and strings, 1941; Fantasy for violin and orch., 1946; And thou America, Rochester, 18 Oct. 1948; Symphony No. 1, 1950; Suite for trumpet and string orch., Rochester, 4 May 1951; Symphony no. 2, 1953, Fish Creek, Wis., 20 Aug. 1955; American youth performs, Fort Worth, 1 Aug. 1969; Band: Brighton Beach, 1954; Proud heritage, 1955; Court festival, 1957; Suite for trumpet and band, 1958; Concerto grosso, 2 saxophones and band, Chicago, 16 Dec. 1960; Escapades, 1965; Dodecaphonic set, 1966; saxophone concertino, 1968; Fantasy, trumpet and band, 1969; Prayers in space, 1971; Chamber music:

(LATHAM, WILLIAM PETERS)
flute sonatina, 1937; 5 sketches for string quartet, 1938; 3 string trios, 1938-39; 3 string quartets, 1938-40, #3, Cincinnati, 14 Nov. 1940; oboe sonata, 1947; violin sonata, 1949; 5 atonal studies for clarinet, 1966; Sisyphus 1971, saxophone and piano; S.B.F., solo flute, 1973; Chorus: Peace, chorus and orch., 1943, Univ. of Minnesota, 23 May 1948; Prayer after world war, 1945; Prophecy of peace, chorus and orch., 1952; The shrine, 1953; Psalms 130 and 148, with band, 1954; Music for 7 poems, chorus, soli, orch., 1958; Blind with rainbows, chorus, soli, orch., 1962; Songs of a day Rome was not built in, male choir, a cappella, 1966; The music makers, band, chorus, rock group, and guru, 1972; Songs: River to the sea, baritone and orch., Cincinnati, 11 Dec. 1942; The ascension of Jesus, baritone, oboe and organ, 1952; Scatter the petals, tenor, harp, alto flute, viola, 1968; Piano: A modern trilogy, 2 pianos, composed for Cincinnati Dance Guild and performed 2 Apr. 1941; sonatina, 1949, Washington, D.C., 19 Oct. 1953.
1815 Southridge Dr., Denton, TX 76201

LATHROP, GAYLE POSSELT
b. Chicago, Ill., 7 Feb. 1942. Studied with Thomas Beversdorf and Bernhard Heiden, Indiana Univ.; Leon Wagner, California State Univ. at Humboldt; flute with Pellerite, Houdeshel, Johnson and Peck. She was director of music, public schools, Hoopa, Calif., 1968-70; guitar instructor, California State Univ. at Humboldt, 1972, and at Coll. of the Redwoods, 1973- .
WORKS: Band: Tish tang; The party; State of the Union, 1968; Chamber music: Triskelion, chamber orch.; Piece 4-5, quintet; flute sonatina; Joamerdap, flute trio; Preludes for guitar; Black, soprano and piano.
Box 503, Hoopa, CA 95546

LATIMER, JAMES H.
b. Tulsa, Okla., 27 June 1934. Studied percussion at Indiana Univ., B. M. 1956; Boston Univ., M. M. 1964; at Tanglewood, 1963. He received a John Hay Whitney fellowship, 1962; Harvard Univ. scholarship, summer 1968; Univ. of Wisconsin graduate research award, summer 1973. He was instructor and assistant band director, Florida A&M Univ., 1957-62; percussion instructor and free-lance artist in New England, 1964-68; associate professor and head of percussion department, Univ. of Wisconsin, Madison, 1969- ; director, Wisconsin Youth Symphony Percussion Ensemble, 1969- ; music director and conductor, Wisconsin Youth Symphony Orchestras, 1972- .
WORKS: Orchestra: MEH, 1959; Band: Movement, 1957; March of deceit, 1959; Chorus: Spiritual, chorus with 5 timpani, 1958; Epic of Man, with percussion and brass choir, 1959; Piermont, (N.H.) 1964; Voice: Andante for timpani, 2 or 4 timpani, solo voice or flute, 1959; Psalm 139, solo bass with piano, 1965; Percussion: Variations on the Westminster Clock theme, 4 unaccompanied timpani, 1955; Exercise for percussion orch., 1956; FAMU march cadences 11 and 12, 1957; Reminiscing, 1957; Blood on the moon, 1958;

(LATIMER, JAMES H.)
Music for a kool Kristmas, 1960; Unsleeping city, 1962; Assignment prison, 1964; Coquette, 1967; Woman in red, 1968; Motif for percussion, 1969.
3922 Hillcrest Dr., Madison, WI 53705

LATIOLAIS, JAYNE
b. Natchitoches, La., 20 Oct. 1928. Studied with Helen Gunderson, Louisiana State Univ.; Ross Lee Finney, Univ. of Michigan; Eastman School of Music; and with Marshall Barnes, Ohio State Univ. Her clarinet sonata won the Nat. Fed. of Music Clubs contest, 1973; compositions have been featured on Musical World of Ohio broadcasts, 1973, 1974. She was guest lecturer, Ohio State Univ., 1970-71; part-time faculty member, Denison Univ., 1973-74.
WORKS: Orchestra: Passacaglia; Chamber music: piano suite; clarinet sonata; Movement for cello and violin; piano quartet; Introduction, passacaglia and fugue, 2 pianos; Lithuanian suite, violin and piano; Voice: Trilogy for a cappella choir; Songs from the Chinese.
677 West Broadway, Apt. C
Granville, OH 43023

LAUFER, BEATRICE
b. New York, N. Y., 27 Apr. 1923. Studied with Roger Sessions, Marion Bauer, Vittorio Giannini, Juilliard School, 1944. Her first symphony was performed in Germany and Japan in 1948 under the auspice of the State Department. She received commissions from the American Asso. of the United Nations for Song of the fountain to dedicate the UN Freedom Fountain, performed by the Interracial Chorus of 250 voices, 1952; from the Performing Arts Concerts, 1961; State of Connecticut 1973, for a choral work for the 1976 Bicentennial year.
WORKS: Opera: Ile, 1-act, on O'Neill's The long voyage home, premiered by Royal Opera Company, Sweden, 1958; Orchestra: 2 symphonies, 1947, 1961; Dance festival, 1946; Frolic; Concerto for flute, oboe, trumpet and strings, 1962; Prelude and fugue, 1964; Cry, orchestral prelude, 1966; Chamber music: Lyric, string trio, 1966; Chorus: Under the pines; Spring thunder, 1949; Song of the fountain, 1952; He who knows not; Everyone sang; Do you fear the wind; Percussion; And Thomas Jefferson said..., for 2 choruses, narrator, orch., in progress; Song: Soldier's prayer.
P. O. Box 544, Lenox Hill Station
New York, NY 10021

LAURIDSEN, MORTEN JOHANNES
b. Colfax, Wash., 27 Feb. 1943. Studied with Halsey Stevens, Ingolf Dahl, Robert Linn, and Harold Owen, Univ. of Southern California. He received a Stark fellowship; Alchin composition fellowship. He has been on the faculty, Univ. of Southern California, 1967-   .
WORKS: Orchestra: Variations for orchestra; Chamber music: trumpet sonata; A winter come, song cycle; brass sextet; 3 songs from Backyard Universe; piano variations; Chorus: Praise ye the Lord; Te Deum, chorus and orch.; many other choral and chamber works.
4072 Oakwood Ave., Los Angeles, CA 90004

LA VIOLETTE, WESLEY
b. St. James, Minn., 4 Jan. 1894. Attended Northwestern Univ. and Chicago Musical Coll., D. M. 1925. His awards include the David Bispham Medal, American Opera Society, Chicago, 1930; nomination of his book, The crown of wisdom, 1949, for the Nobel prize in literature, 1960; the Wisdom Award of Honor and election to the Wisdom Hall of Fame, Los Angeles, 1970; and commissions. Two chamber works were taken on tour by the NBC Chamber Orch., under Rudolph Ganz, 1931-33; other works have been played by major orchestras. He was dean and head of theory and composition, Chicago Musical Coll., 1923-33; educational director, De Paul Univ. School of Music, 1933-40; then settled in Los Angeles for private teaching, writing, lecturing, and composing.
WORKS: Theatre: Shylock, 3-act opera, 1927; Schubertiana, Chicago Opera Ballet, 1935; The enlightened one, 3-act opera on life of Buddha, 1955; Orchestra: Requiem, 1925; Penetrella, string orch. in 18 parts, 1928; Osiris, Egyptian legend, 1929; 2 violin concertos, 1929, 1939; Festival ode, 1930; Ode to an immortal, 1934; 3 symphonies, 1936, 1940, 1942; Chorale, 1936; Collegiana rhapsody, 1936; Prelude and aria, 1937; Concert piece, piano and orch., 1937; concerto for string quartet and orch., 1939; San Francisco overture, 1939; Commemoration ode, 1939; The song of the angels, choral symphony, 1952; Chamber music: 3 string quartets, 1926, 1932, 1936; piano quintet, 1927; Scherzo, chamber orch., 1931; sonata for 2 violins, 1931, revised 1951; 5 songs for soprano and string quartet, 1931; Nocturne, chamber orch., 1933; 2 violin sonatas, 1934, 1937; octet, woodwinds and strings, 1935; Evocation, violin and piano, 1936; 3 pieces for string quartet, 1937; woodwind sextet, 1939; Filigree quartet, 4 flutes, 1940; Masquerade, woodwind quartet, 1940; Rhapsody for cello, 1940; flute sonata, 1941; Dedication, clarinet and piano, 1941; Incantation, clarinet and piano, 1941; Song of freedom, cello and piano, 1941; Charade, flute quartet, 1941; Queen of night, trumpet and piano, 1941; quintet, flute and strings, 1943; Largo lyrico, string quartet, 1943; Serenade, flute and string quartet, 1945; Suite for chamber orch., 1947; Suite for flute alone, 1963; Suite for clarinet alone, 1963; Chorus: The broken vine, 1921; Anima mundi, with orch., 1932; The garden, 1950; The road to Calvary, with narrator and orch., 1952; Delphic psalm, with brass ensemble, 1964; also pieces for band, piano, organ. His published books are: Music and its makers, 1937; The Bhagavad Gita, 1944, revised 1955; The creative light, 1946; The crown of wisdom.
12090 Pastoral Rd., Rancho Bernardo, CA 92100

LAWERGREN, BO
b. Sweden, 4 Jan. 1937; to U.S. 1967. Earned a Ph. D. in nuclear physics at Australian Nat. Univ., 1963; studied composition with Friedrich Mehler in Sweden, 1951-55; with Chou Wen-chung, Columbia Univ., 1967-68. He held 2 fellowships, Bennington Conference; 3 MacDowell fellowships. He has been associate professor of physics, Hunter Coll., 1970-   .

LAWERGREN, BO

(LAWERGREN, BO)
WORKS: Chamber opera: Captain Cook,
1968-69; Deep tongue, 1973-74; Chamber music:
Marche Funèbre, trombone, piano, and metronomes;
Two step, trumpet, marimba/vibraphone; Ensembles,
13 instruments; 7 one-minute pieces for piano.
404 West 116th St., New York, NY 10027

LAWNER, MORRIS
b. New York, N. Y., 8 Apr. 1910. Studied at Inst.
of Musical Art; New York Univ.; and at Univ. of
Wisconsin. His Rhythmic overture won an award
for performance by the New York Philharmonic
Orch., 1949. He taught in New York City high
schools, 1940-50; and has taught theory and
composition, High School of Music and Art,
1950- .
WORKS: Orchestra: Rhythmic overture, 1949;
Chamber music: Latin dance, clarinet and piano;
Cocktail hour, piano; Suite for woodwinds; also
2 works for band.
820 West End Ave., New York, NY 10025

LAYTON, BILLY JIM
b. Corsicana, Tex., 14 Nov. 1924. Studied with
Carl McKinley, Francis Judd Cooke, New England
Cons.; with Quincy Porter, Yale Univ.; and with
Walter Piston, Harvard Univ., Ph. D. His awards
include Rome Prize; Hertz Traveling fellowship,
Univ. of California; Nat. Inst. of Arts and Letters grant; Brandeis Univ. Creative Arts award;
Guggenheim fellowship; Thorne Music Fund grant.
He was faculty member, New England Cons.,
1959-50; Harvard Univ., 1960-66; professor,
State Univ. of New York at Stony Brook,
1966- , chairman of music department, 1966-72.
WORKS: Orchestra: An American portrait,
symphonic overture; Dance fantasy; Chamber music:
5 studies for violin and piano; string quartet,
1956; 3 studies for piano; Divertimento, for
chamber orch.; Chorus: 3 Dylan Thomas poems,
chorus and brass sextet.
4 Johns Rd., Setauket, NY 11733

LAYZER, ARTHUR
b. Cleveland, Ohio, 21 Sep. 1927. Is self-taught
in music. He has been associate professor of
physics, Stevens Inst. of Technology, 1963- ;
resident visitor in computer music, Bell Laboratories, Murray Hill, N. J., 1969- .
WORKS: Chamber music: woodwind quintet,
1966; Inner and outer forms for 7 players, brass,
saxophones, percussion, 1967; Computer-synthesized music: Piece for 6 voices, 1970; Morning
elevator, animated poetry for computer-generated
film and music sound track, 1971.
161 West 75th St., New York, NY 10023

*LAZAROF, HENRI
b. Sofia, Bulgaria, 12 Apr. 1932; to U.S. 1957.
Studied at Sofia Acad. of Music; with Paul Ben-
Haim in Jerusalem; Goffredo Petrassi, Ste. Cecilia
Acad., Rome, 1955-57; Harold Shapero, Brandeis Univ., M. F. A. 1959. He held a fellowship
for study at Brandeis; received first prize,
Internat. Competition of Monaco, 1962; La Scala
award, City of Milan, 1966; Koussevitzky Internat.

(LAZAROF, HENRI)
Recording award, 1969. He has been associate
professor, Univ. of California, Los Angeles,
1965- .
WORKS: Orchestra: piano concerto, 1957;
Piccola serenata, 1959; viola concerto, 1961;
concerto for piano and 20 instruments, 1963;
Odes, 1963; Tempi concertati, violin, viola,
and chamber orch., 1964; Structures sonores,
1965; cello concerto, 1968, American premiere,
Los Angeles, 6 May 1971; Omaggio, chamber concerto, 1968; Textures, piano and orch., 1970;
Ricercar, viola, piano, orch.; Variations for
orch.; Chamber music: 2 string quartets, 1956,
1963; string trio, 1957; sonata for violin a-
lone, 1958; Concertino da camera, woodwind quintet, 1959; Inventions, viola and piano, 1962;
Asymptotes, flute and vibraphone, 1963; Quan-
tetti, 4 pianos, 1964; Rhapsody, violin and
piano, 1966; Espaces, 10 instruments, 1966; Divertimenti for 5 players, 1969; Continuum,
string trio, Los Angeles, 10 Nov. 1970; Cadence
II, viola and tape; Cadence III, violin and percussion, 1970; Partita, brass quintet and tape,
1971; duo for cello and piano, Baltimore, 27
Jan. 1974.
718 North Maple Dr.,
Beverly Hills, CA 90210

*LEACH, ROWLAND
b. Haverhill, Mass., 26 Apr. 1885. Studied violin and composition, New England Cons.; Yale
Univ., B. M. 1910. He taught in Rockford, Ill.,
1910-13; Calgary, Alberta, 1913-14; Chicago,
1914-28; De Pauw Univ., 1928-33; Univ. of Redlands, 1933-47. He wrote orchestral works, violin pieces, songs (Welcome, day of the Lord).

LEAHY, MARY WELDON
b. St. Louis, Mo., 20 Aug. 1926. Studied at
North Texas State Univ.; privately with Carl
Eppert and Normand Lockwood; with Gordon Jacob
in England. She won first prize in a Wisconsin
State contest for a song and a string quartet,
1949.
WORKS: Orchestra: Suite for strings;
Modern dance rhapsody, string orch.; Symphony in
1 movement, strings and percussion; many works
for chamber ensembles, solo instruments, chorus,
and solo voice.
703 Alexander Hamilton Dr.
San Antonio, TX 78228

LEBOW, LEONARD STANLEY
b. Chicago, Ill., 25 Feb. 1929. Studied with
Karel Jirak and Hans Tischler, Chicago Musical
Coll.; at Northwestern Univ.; M. M.; also
studied trumpet, piano, and arranging. He was a
finalist in the Chicago Internat. Society for
Contemporary Music contest, 1962; received an
ASCAP award, 1973. He was trumpet player and
arranger, Hotel Sahara, Las Vegas, 1952-54;
teacher, Chicago and Cook County public schools,
1964- ; free-lance trumpet and bass player,
composer, and arranger, 1954- .
WORKS: Band: Pastorale and tarantella;
Festival parade; Ride the Matterhorn; Wind ensemble: Suite for brass, 1956; Popular suite,

(LEBOW, LEONARD STANLEY)
brass quintet; Second suite, brass quintet; Allegro energico, brass quintet; all composed for and performed by Chicago Symphony Brass Ensemble; Descriptive scenes, saxophone quartet.
4411 Stern Ave., Sherman Oaks, CA 91403

*LEDERHOUSE, BRUCE
Celebration, mass with a rock beat; Praise and jubilee, contemporary mass; Rejoice, mass in country-folk style (all with Draesel).

LEE, DAI-KEONG
b. Honolulu, Hawaii, 2 Sep. 1915. Studied at Univ. of Hawaii; with Roger Sessions, Princeton Univ.; with Frederick Jacobi, Juilliard School, 1938-41; with Aaron Copland at Tanglewood, 1941; Columbia Univ., M. A. 1951. He held fellowships for Juilliard and Tanglewood; Guggenheim fellowships, 1945, 1951; received commissions for Inst. of Musical Art, 1940; Albert Metz, 1946; League of Composers, 1947.
WORKS: Opera: Poet's dilemma, 1-act, 1940; Open the gates, 1951; Phineas and the nightingale, 1952; Ballet: Children's caprice, 1948; Waltzing Matilda, 1951; Theatre: Teahouse of the August moon, background score; Orchestra: Valse pensieroso, 1936; Hawaiian festival overture, 1940; Introduction and allegro, 1941; Golden Gate overture, 1941; Pacific Prayer, 1943; Overture in C, 1945; 2 symphonies, 1946, 1952; violin concerto, 1947; Concerto grosso, string orch., 1952; 2 Knickerbocker tales, 1957; Suite for orch., 1958; Polynesian suite, 1959; The golden lotus, 1961; The gold of their bodies, 1963; Chamber music: string quartet, 1947; piano sonatina, 1947; Introduction and allegro, cello and piano, 1947; Incantation and dance, violin and piano; Chorus: Mele ololi, with soli and orch., 1960; Canticle of the Pacific, with orch., 1968; Film score: Letter from Australia, 1945.
245 West 104th St., New York, NY 10025

LEE, EU-GENE
b. Seoul, Korea, 29 Aug. 1942; to U.S. 1967. Studied with Ruth S. Wylie, Wayne State Univ., B. M. 1969; Chou Wen-chung, Charles Wuorinen, Harvey Sollberger, Vladimir Ussachevsky and Jacques-Louis Monod, Columbia Univ., M. A. 1973, candidate for D. M. A. He held a Crofts fellowship at Tanglewood, 1972; received Rapoport prize, Columbia Univ., 1973; scholarships at Wayne State Univ., 1966-69. He has been a teaching fellow at Columbia Univ., 1972-   .
WORKS: Chamber music: 2 movements for solo violin, 1970; Duet for violin and clarinet, 1970; Duet for viola and vibraphone, 1970; Empty infinity, string quartet, 1970; woodwind quintet, 1971; Moo-sahng (Transcience) for the victims of My-Lai, 1971; Yuh-Woon, wind septet and percussion, 1972; Chamber symphony for 18 players, 1973; Lyric for solo flute, 1973.
8131 Baxter Ave., Elmhurst, NY 11373

LEE, JOHN
b. England, 29 Apr. 1908; U.S. citizen 1955. Is a licentiate, Royal Acad. of Music and Trinity Coll. of Music, London; a fellow of the Royal

(LEE, JOHN)
Coll. of Organists, London; and a member, Royal Society of Teachers. He has been organist-choirmaster, St. Vincents Church, Los Angeles, 1949-   ; is lecturer, organ recitalist, and private organ teacher.
WORKS: Chorus: over 80 published choral works, masses, anthems, liturgical settings; organ works.
22 Chester Place, Los Angeles, CA 90007

LEE, NOEL
b. Nanking, China, American parents, 25 Dec. 1924. Studied with Walter Piaton, Irving Fine, Harvard Univ., B. A. cum laude 1948; Miklos Schwalb, New England Cons., artist's diploma, 1948; with Nadia Boulanger in Paris. He received Prix Lili Boulanger, 1953; prize in Young Composers contest, Louisville Orch., 1954; Nat. Inst. of Arts and Letters award, 1959; Arthur Shepherd composition prize, 1961. He has been visiting professor in piano, Cornell Univ., 1967 and 1972.
WORKS: Orchestra: Fievres, ballet, 1950; Capriccio, 1952; 4 rhapsodies, 1952; Paraboles, tenor solo, chorus, orch., 1954; Overture and litanies, string orch., 1954; Profile, 1958; Variations for orchestra, 1960; 4 ballades, soprano and orch.; Dichroismes, with piano and violin; Diversions, chamber orch.; Band: Errances; Chamber music: Sonata mostly in minor, solo violin; Pavane; 3 preludes, 2 harps; Quintette, winds and piano, 1952; Variations, harpsichord, flute, violin, cello, 1953; string trio, 1953; string quartet, 1956; Dialogues, violin and piano, 1958; Commentaries on a theme by Copland, trumpet, clarinet, piano; Convergences, flute and harpsichord; Fantaisie, 2 pianos; Song cycles: The song of songs; 5 songs on poems of Lorca, 1955; 3 Intimate songs; Sonnets of summer and sorrow; Seis canciones amarillas; 4 Chants sur Baudelaire; and many piano works.
4 Villa Laugier, Paris 75017, France

LEE, NORMAN
b. Chicago, Ill., 18 Nov. 1895. Studied with Arne Oldberg and Carl Beecher, Northwestern Univ.
WORKS: Songs: The river; Nocturne; Piano: Fantasia; Temple song; 2 sonatas; Variations; The Eunice caprice.
360 Forest Ave., Palo Alto, CA 94301

LEE, T. CHARLES
b. Madison, Minn., 22 Oct. 1914. Studied at Oberlin Coll.; with Clarence Dickinson, Union Theological Seminary; with Nadia Boulanger in Fontainebleau; and with Charles Kennedy Scott in London. He was conductor of the Worcester (Mass.) Music Festival, 1949-61; Oratorio Society of New York, 1959-73; organist-choirmaster, Brick Presbyterian Church, New York, 1959-   ; assistant professor, Lehman Coll., CUNY, 1968-   .
WORKS: Chorus: Psalm III; Farewell, voyager, with soli, organ and piano; A requiem, commissioned by Kings Coll., Briarcliff Manor, N. Y., 1968.
115 East 92nd St., New York, NY 10028

LEE, WILLIAM F. III
    b. Galveston, Tex., 20 Feb. 1929. Studied at
North Texas State Univ., B. M. 1949, M. S. 1950;
Univ. of Texas, M. M. 1956, Ph. D. 1956; Eastman
School of Music, 1962; and with Nadia Boulanger
in France, 1965. His honors include UM grant in
humanities, 1965; honorary doctorate, Cons. Nac.
de Musica, Lima, Peru, 1968, annual ASCAP awards,
1968-73; Wisdom Award of Honor, Wisdom Hall of
Fame, 1970; and many commissions. He taught in
public schools, 1951-55; was assistant to the
dean of Fine Arts, Univ. of Texas, 1955-56; professor and director, music department, Sam Houston State Univ., 1956-64; professor and dean,
School of Music, Univ. of Miami, 1964-   .
    WORKS: Orchestra: Concerto grosso, brass
quintet and orch.; Earth genesis, string orch.;
Band: Alamjohoba; Introduction and fugue; Time
after time; Brass choir: Suite for brass; 4
sketches for brass; Fanfare for Ralph, quintet;
Piece for brass, quintet; Mosaics, quintet; Reg-
imentation, quintet; Chamber music: Nocturne,
flute and piano; Soliloquy, horn and piano; Mini-
suite, trumpet and piano; 3 reflections, alto
saxophone and piano; Interlude, guitar; Tone
poem, oboe, violin, viola, 2 celli; 2 woodwind
quintets; and piano pieces.
    90 Edgewater Drive, #824
    Coral Gables, FL 33133

LEEDY, DOUGLAS H.
    b. Portland, Ore., 3 Mar. 1938. Studied with
Karl Kohn, Pomona Coll., B. A. 1959; with Lukas
Foss at Tanglewood; with Andrew Imbrie, Seymour
Shifrin, William Denny, Univ. of California,
Berkeley, M. A. 1962. He received a Fromm Found.
commission, Tanglewood, 1966; and other commissions. He was lecturer and head, electronic
music studio, Univ. of California, Los Angeles,
1967-70; professor of electronic music and associate, Estudio de Fonologia del Centro Simon
Bolivar, Caracas, Venez., 1972; visiting assistant professor, Reed Coll., 1973-74.
    WORKS: Theatre: Decay, theatre piece with
tape, 1965; Teddybears picnic, theater work for
dancers and electronics; Wind ensemble: Anti-
fonia, brass, 1965; Usable music I for instruments with very small holes, 1966; Usable music
II in Bflat, 1966; Chamber music: Quaderno
Rossiniano, chamber ensemble; 88 is great, piano
18-hands, 1968; Igor Stravinsky in memoriam,
guitar, 1971; Chorus: Dulces exuviae, Virgil;
Gloria, with soprano, strings, flutes, harpsichord, 1970; Psalm 24, chorus, 6 soprano soli,
orch.; I am the rose of Sharon, small chorus and
instruments; Electronic: The electric zodiac,
1969; Entropical paradise: 6 sonic environments,
1970.
    8517 Southeast 19th Ave.
    Portland, OR 97202

LEES, BENJAMIN
    b. Harbin, China, 8 Jan. 1924; U.S. citizen 1931.
Studied with Halsey Stevens, Ingolf Dahl, Ernest
Kanitz, Univ. of Southern California; and with
George Antheil. His honors include Fromm Found.
award, 1953; 2 Guggenheim fellowships, 1954,
1955; Fulbright grant, 1956; Copley Found. award;

(LEES, BENJAMIN)
    Sir Arnold Bax Medal; UNESCO award; ASCAP award,
1972. He studied and traveled in Europe to 1962.
Since returning to the U.S. he has taught on the
faculties of Peabody Cons.; Queens Coll., CUNY:
and Manhattan School of Music.
    WORKS: Theatre: The oracle, 1-act music
drama, libretto by composer, 1955; The gilded
cage, 1971; Orchestra: 2 piano concertos, 1955,
1966; Divertimento burlesca, 1957; 3 symphonies,
1953, 1958, 1969; violin concerto, 1958; Concertante breve, 1959; Concerto for orchestra,
1959; Interlude, 1960; Prologue, capriccio and
epilogue, 1961; Visions of poets, cantata for 2
soli, chorus, and orch., 1961; oboe concerto,
1963; Concerto for string quartet and orch.,
1964; Spectrum, 1964; Concerto for chamber orchestra, 1966; Silhouettes, 1967; Medea of
Corinth, 4 solo voices, wind quintet, and timpani, 1970; The trumpet of the swan, text by
E. B. White, narrator and orch., 1972; Etudes,
piano and orch., Houston, Tex., 28 Oct. 1974;
Chamber music: 2 string quartets, 1952, 1955;
horn sonata, 1952; 2 violin sonatas, 1953, 1972;
3 variables, 4 winds and piano, 1955; Fanfare
for a centennial, brass and percussion, 1966;
duo, flute and clarinet, 1969; Study no. 1, cello
solo, 1970; Piano: sonata for 2 pianos, 1951;
Fantasia, 1954; Sonata breve, 1956; 6 ornamental
etudes, 1957; Kaleidoscopes, 1958; Epigrams,
1960; 3 preludes, 1962; sonata no. 4, 1963;
Odyssey, 1970; Songs: 6 songs of the night,
soprano and piano, 1952; 3 songs for contralto,
1959; Cyprian songs, baritone and piano, 1960.
    c/o Boosey & Hawkes, 30 West 57th St.
    New York, NY 10019

LEESON, CECIL
    b. Cando, N. D., 16 Dec. 1902. Studied at Dana
Musical Inst., B. M. 1925; with Max Wald and
John J. Becker at Chicago Musical Coll., M. M.
1947, D. F. A. 1955. He was named Fellow in the
Art of Music, 1933; awarded a scholarship, 1941;
honorary membership, Kappa Kappa Psi, 1952; World
Saxophone Congress award, 1970; commissioned by
Univ. of Illinois Band Department to compose a
saxophone concerto, 1950. Except for service in
the Navy, 1942-45, he has been teaching and performing on the saxophone since 1924; faculty
member, Ball State Univ., 1961-   ; and has dedicated his career to making the saxophone a
recognized concert instrument. In addition to
his own compositions, he has played works written
especially for him by such composers as
Weinberger, Creston, Moritz, Sherman, Knight,
and Van Vactor. He has also written extensively
on the history of the saxophone.
    WORKS: Saxophone: 4 concertos, 1947, 1949,
1950, 1957; 3 sonatas, 1953, 1966, 1973; various
smaller pieces.
    14 Brenda Lane, R. R. 7
    Muncie, IN 47302

LEFEVER, MAXINE LANE
    b. Elmhurst, Ill., 30 May 1931. Studied with
John Noonan, Illinois Wesleyan Univ.; Western
State Coll., Colo.; Purdue Univ. Awards include
honorary membership in the United States Navy

(LEFEVER, MAXINE LANE)
Band. Positions with the Nat. Band Asso, have been executive secretary-treasurer, 1968- , editor, NBA Journal and NBA Directory, 1968- .
WORKS: Percussion ensemble: De Chelly, quintet; Desert; Dolores; Durango; Summit; and others.
Purdue University Bands
West Lafayette, IN 47907

*LEFTWICH, VERNON
b. London, England, 19 June 1881. Studied at the Guildhall School of Music, London. On coming to the U.S. he settled in Los Angeles as composer and arranger for films.
WORKS: Orchestra: Cremation of care, symphonic poem, 1929; Sunken ships, tone poem, 1939; cello concerto, 1941; What the moon saw, suite; 7 ages of man, baritone and orch., 1942; The lion and the mouse; Reverie, string orch.; Chamber music: Musical forum, 9 instruments; string quartet; string quintet; piano quartet; cello sonata; brass quintets; also choruses; songs; piano pieces; marches.

*LEGINSKA, ETHEL
b. Hull, England, 13 Apr. 1886; d. Los Angeles, Calif., 26 Feb. 1970. Studied piano in Frankfurt and with Leschetizky in Vienna; composition with Rubin Goldmark and Ernest Bloch in the U.S. She made her debut in London, then toured Europe; her American debut took place in New York on 20 Jan. 1913. She took up conducting and organized the Boston Philharmonia Orch. and the Boston Women's Symphony Orch.; also conducted the Chicago Women's Symphony. From 1939 she was pianist and piano teacher in Los Angeles. Her compositions include 2 operas, orchestral works, and chamber music.

LEHR, MANGHAM DAVID
b. Greenwood, Miss., 1 June 1928. Studied with Bernhard Heiden and Carl Van Buskirk, Indiana Univ., B. M. E. 1956; with Bruce Benward, Univ. of Wisconsin, M. M. 1966; Michigan State Univ., candidate for Ph. D. He was assistant professor, Purdue Univ., 1958-70; instructor, Michigan State Univ., 1972-74.
WORKS: Orchestra: Overture, 1957; Chorus: Palm Sunday cantata, tenor, bass, chorus, organ, 1956; Poem and alleluia for the Christ Child, a cappella, 1958; In excelsis gloria, 1966; Organ: 6 modal chorale preludes on hymn tunes, 1963; Concerto for organ, strings and brass, 1966; Chorale partita on Veni Emmanuel.
910 Abbott Road, Apt. 102
East Lansing, MI 48823

*LEHRMAN, LEONARD
Karla and Notes from a lady at a dinner party, 1-act operas on Malamud stories, Ithaca, N. Y., 3 Aug. 1974.

LEIBIG, BRUCE
b. Lebanon, Pa., 29 Dec. 1946. Studied with Merrill Ellis and William Latham, North Texas State Univ.; with Robert Erickson and Kenneth Gaburo, Univ. of California at San Diego. He

(LEIBIG, BRUCE)
received an award from the Texas Manuscript Society for 2 songs, 1968. He was a fellow, Project for Music Experiment, Univ. of California, San Diego, 1973.
WORKS: Chamber music: 2 songs for soprano and piano, 1968; Encahc, woodwind quintet, 1968; Sounds I for 2 pianos, 1969; Pex-mix, tape, 1969; Multimedia: Parlour piece, for instructor and bodies, 1972; Probe, for 3 cue-groups, 3 movers, tape, controller, electronics, and audience, 1972.
4167 Hamilton, San Diego, CA 92014

LEICH, ROLAND
b. Evansville, Ind., 6 Mar. 1911. Studied with Felix Borowski and Leo Sowerby in Chicago; with Rosario Scalero at Curtis Inst., 1929-33; with Anton Webern in Vienna, 1933-34; and with Bernard Rogers, Eastman School of Music, M. M. 1942. He received the Bearns Award, 1933, 1937; Lauber award, 1933; Pennsylvania Fed. of Music Clubs awards, 1953, 1956. He was instructor, Dartmouth Coll., 1935-41; has been on faculty, Carnegie-Mellon Univ., 1946- , professor, 1972- ; associate conductor, Mendelssohn Choir of Pittsburgh, 1951-68.
WORKS: Orchestra: Concert piece for oboe and strings, 1952; Rondo for orch., 1953; Prelude and fugue, 1955; The town of Pittsburgh, chorus and orch., 1958; Chamber music: 5 A. E. Housman songs, 1933; string quartet, 1937; 47 settings of Emily Dickinson poems; and choral pieces.
105 Bevington Road, Pittsburgh, PA 15221

*LEICHTENTRITT, HUGO
b. Pleschen, Poland, 1 Jan. 1874; d. Cambridge, Mass., 13 Nov. 1951. Studied with John Knowles Paine, Harvard Univ., 1891-94; returned to the U.S. to join the Harvard faculty, 1934. He was noted chiefly as a music scholar and author of books on music criticism, but was also a composer.
WORKS: Orchestra: a symphony; Symphonic variations on a Siamese dance; violin concerto; cello concerto; piano concerto; many works for chamber groups; song cycles, cantatas; also a comic opera and a music drama.

*LEICHTLING, ALAN
b. Brooklyn, N. Y., 1947. Studied at the New York High School of Music and Art; with Vincent Persichetti and Roger Sessions, Juilliard School, B. S., M. S., D. M. A. 1971; with Darius Milhaud and Charles Jones, Aspen School, 1966. His awards include the McCollin prize of the Musical Fund Society of Philadelphia. He was assistant professor, Drew Univ., 1971-72; faculty member, William Paterson Coll., 1972- .
WORKS: Opera: The white butterfly; The tempest; Orchestra: 2 symphonies; concerto for chamber orch., 1966; Chamber music: 4 string quartets; 3 wind quintets; Fantasy piece, bass clarinet solo; Bagatelles, brass quintet, 1969; Voice: 3 songs of Emily Dickinson, baritone and cello, 1967; Psalm 37, mezzo soprano and chamber ensemble; 2 proverbs, mezzo soprano and clarinet

LEICHTLING, ALAN

(LEICHTLING, ALAN)
trio; 11 songs from A Shropshire lad, tenor and chamber ensemble, 1969; Canticle I, high voice; Trial and death of Socrates, tenor, harp, flute, clarinet; Moon songs in January, Shelley text, women's chorus and chamber orch., 1974.
878 West End Ave., New York, NY 10025

*LEIDZEN, ERIK
b. Stockholm, Sweden, 25 Mar. 1894; to U.S. 1915; d. New York, N. Y., 20 Dec. 1962. Studied at the Royal Cons., Stockholm. He taught at various schools including the Univ. of Michigan summer school and the Nat. Music Camp at Interlochen; was guest conductor and arranger for the Goldman Band.
WORKS: Band: Irish symphony; Swedish rhapsody; Storm King overture; Symphony in the sky; The happy warrior; works for brass quartet.

*LEKBERG, SVEN
b. 1899. Has written works for chorus: Lord of the earth and sky, cantata; Block city; Envoy; In quiet night; The lamplighter; Fragrant the prayer; The love messengers; Rain song; So wondrous sweet and fair; and songs.
Department of Music, Simpson College Indianola, IA 50125

*LEMONT, CEDRIC WILMOT
b. Frederickton, N. B., 15 Dec. 1879; U.S. citizen 1933; d. New York, N. Y., 27 Apr. 1954. Studied at Univ. of New Brunswick; Faelton Piano School; New England Cons.; Capitol Coll., M. M.; taught piano and theory in schools and privately. His compositions for chorus, solo voice, and piano number in the hundreds.

LENEL, LUDWIG
b. Strasbourg, France, 20 May 1914; U.S. citizen 1955. Was an artist pupil of Albert Schweitzer, 1932; holds diplomas from Hochschule fur Musik, Cologne and Basel Cons.; studied at Oberlin Cons., M. M. 1940. He has held faculty posts at Oberlin Cons. Monticello Coll., Westminster Coll., Pa., Elmhurst Coll., New School for Social Research, and professor, Muhlenberg Coll., 1952-   ; is also lecturer, organ recitalist, and choral conductor.
WORKS: Opera: Young Goodman Brown, 1-act, 1962; The boss, 1-act folktale opera, 1964; Orchestra: Partita for orchestra, 1972; Band: 2 pieces for band, 1957; Concertino for woodwinds, brass and percussion, 1965; Chamber music: 2 brass quintets, 1960, 1967; Music for organ, brass and timpani, 1968; 5 pieces for violin and viola with taped percussion, 1973; many choral works, organ and piano pieces, and songs.
R.D. 1, Box 185, Orefield, PA 18069

*LENTZ, DANIEL
Pastime and ABM, both for chamber ensemble.
67 La Vuelta Drive, Santa Barbara, CA 93107

LEON, GARBY
b. Manhattan, N. Y., 14 May 1947. Studied at Marlboro Coll., B. A.; with Leon Kirchner and

(LEON, GARBY)
Earl Kim, John MacIvor Perkins, and Harold Shapero, Harvard Univ. M. A. He received the Knight prize, 1973.
WORKS: Chamber music: string quartet, 1971; A reading of poems, for speaker, string sextet, electric piano, piano and percussion, 1972; Death's bright angel (and the choir invisible), soprano, flute, cello, piano and percussion, 1973.
18 Buena Vista Park, Cambridge, MA 02140

LEONARD, GRACE (Mrs. Lloyd L.)
b. Dallas, Tex., 13 Jan. 1909. Studied with Francis Buebendorf, Univ. of Missouri, Kansas city. She held a scholarship for piano study; received 3rd place award, Otto Preminger competition. She was piano teacher and accompanist, Dallas, 1928-48.
WORKS: Chorus: Thanks be to thee; Invincible we stand; Songs: So oft I invoked thee; From fairest creatures; Spring and fall; Jenny kissed me; Piano: Israel le Chaim Preminger award; other choral works, piano pieces, etc.
11131 East 84th Terrace, Raytown, MO 64138

*LEPLIN, EMANUEL
b. San Francisco, Calif., 3 Oct. 1917; d. Martinez, Calif., 2 Dec. 1972. Studied violin with Georges Enesco, composition with Roger Sessions and Darius Milhaud, conducting with Pierre Monteux. He won the Prix de Rome in composition while a student at Univ. of California at Berkeley. Stricken with polio in 1954 when a violinist with the San Francisco Symphony, he taught himself to paint with a brush held in his teeth and continued to compose.
WORKS: Orchestra: Galaxy, 2 cellos and orch., 1942; Cosmos, violin and orch., 1944; 2 symphonic poems; a symphony, 1962; also chamber music and piano pieces.

*LEPS, WASSILI
b. St. Petersburg, Russia, 12 May 1870; to U.S. 1894; d. Toronto, Ont., 22 Dec. 1943. Studied at Dresden Cons.; became choirmaster at the Dresden Opera Company. In the U.S. he taught at Philadelphia Musical Acad. and was conductor, Philadelphia Opera Society, 1894-1923; organized the Providence Symphony Orchestra in 1932 and was conductor until retirement in 1941. His compositions include an opera, a cantata, and orchestral pieces.

*LERDAHL, FRED
b. Madison, Wis., 1943. Studied at Lawrence Univ.; with Milton Babbitt, Edward T. Cone, and Earl Kim, Princeton Univ.; with Wolfgang Fortner in Germany, 1969-70. His awards include the Koussevitzky prize at Tanglewood, 1966; fellowships at Marlboro Festival, 1967, 1968; Fulbright grant for study in Germany, 1969; Nat. Inst. of Arts and Letters award, 1971; Fromm Found. commissions, 1972, 1974. He taught at Univ. of California, Berkeley, 1970-71; has been assistant professor, Harvard Univ., 1972-   .

LEVEY, JOSEPH A.

(LERDAHL, FRED)
WORKS: Orchestra: Wake, voice and orch.; Chromorhythmos, 1972, was to have been performed at Tanglewood, but Bruno Maderna, conductor, declared it impossible to play; has been revised and rechristened Color-rhythm; Aftermath, 3 voices and chamber orch., to own text, Cambridge, Mass., 19 May 1973; Chords, Tanglewood, 8 Aug. 1974.

38 Fells Road, Winchester, MA 01890

*LESEMANN, FREDERICK
b. Los Angeles, Calif., 12 Oct. 1936. Studied at Oberlin Cons., B. M. 1958; Univ. of Southern California, M. M. 1961, D. M. A. 1972; received the Helen S. Anstead award, 1961; USC School of Music Alumni Asso. award, 1972. He was manager, Ojai Festival, 1963-66; teaching assistant, Univ. of Southern California, 1964-66, lecturer, 1961-71, assistant professor, 1971- . His works include a symphony in 3 movements, performed, Buffalo, N. Y., Apr. 1973; and a sonata for clarinet and percussion, 1972.

6337 B South Bright Ave.
Whittier, CA 90601

*LESSARD, JOHN AYRES
b. San Francisco, Calif., 3 July 1920. Studied with Nadia Boulanger in Paris. He received a Guggenheim grant, 1946; Nat. Inst. of Arts and Letters award, 1952. He is professor, State Univ. of New York at Stonybrook.
WORKS: Orchestra: violin concerto, 1941; Box Hill overture, 1946; Cantilena, oboe and strings; concerto for wind instruments; concerto for woodwind trio and strings, 1952; Sinfonia concertante; Chamber music: quintet for flute, clarinet and string trio, 1943; 2 piano sonatas, 1944, 1945; 3 movements, violin and piano, 1952; wind octet, 1954; cello sonata, 1954; Toccata for harpsichord, 1955; Quodlibets, 2 trumpets and a trombone; Perpetual motion, piano; Partita, wind quintet; Songs: Mother Goose, 6 songs, 1953; Fragment from the Cantos of Ezra Pound, baritone and 9 instruments.

Department of Music
State University of New York
Stonybrook, NY 11790

*LESSNER, GEORGE
b. Budapest, Hungary, 15 Dec. 1904; U.S. citizen 1926. Studied with Bela Bartok, Zoltan Kodaly, and Ernst von Dohnanyi, Budapest Royal Acad. of Music. In the U.S. he scored films; was composer and arranger for the radio programs Prudential Hour, Texaco Star Theatre, Great Moments of Music; composer and conductor for the television series Bobo and his traveling troup. His works include scores for the stage play, Sleepy Hollow, and the television play, The rose and the nightingale; 8 symphonies; many songs.

LESTER, JAMES T.
b. Detroit, Mich., 31 Aug. 1933. Studied at Alma Coll.; with Gregory Stone, Los Angeles Cons., B. M.; at Univ. of Southern California; and privately with Mario Castelnuovo-Tedesco. He was instructor, Brentwood Acad., 1965-69, and held other positions while establishing a music engraving business.

(LESTER, JAMES T.)
WORKS: Theatre: Puss and boots, children's musical; Casey at the bat, children's musical; Orchestra: Dance alla marcia; The farmer and the cat, clarinet and bassoon solos with orch.; Chamber music: Tango de concert, woodwind quintet; Romance exotique, oboe and piano; Serenade to a plucked ostrich, piano; Chorus: The mountain and the squirrel, a fable by Ralph Waldo Emerson.

345 South Citrus Ave.
Los Angeles, CA 90036

*LESTER, THOMAS WILLIAM
b. Leicester, England, 17 Sep. 1889; to U.S. 1902; d. Berian Springs, Mich., 4 Dec. 1956. Studied with Wilhelm Middelschulte; was organist and music critic in Chicago. His compositions included 8 cantatas, songs, piano works, organ pieces.

*LEVANT, OSCAR
b. Pittsburgh, Pa., 27 Dec. 1906; d. Beverly Hills, Calif., 14 Aug. 1972. Studied composition with Arnold Schoenberg and Joseph Schillinger; piano with Sigismund Stojowski. He was concert pianist and jazz pianist; gave many concerts of Gershwin's music; was music expert on Information Please radio program, 1938; appeared in films as actor; played his own piano concerto with the NBC Symphony, 17 Feb. 1942.
WORKS: Orchestra: Nocturne, 1936; piano concerto, 1942; Chamber music: piano sonata, 1931; 2 string quartets; piano pieces; also film scores. He was author of 3 books: The unimportance of being Oscar; A smattering of ignorance; Memoirs of an amnesiac.

*LEVENSON, BORIS
b. Ackerman, Bessarabia, 10 Mar. 1884; U.S. citizen 1927; d. New York, N. Y., 11 Mar. 1947. Studied with Glazunov and Rimsky-Korsakov, St. Petersburg Cons., graduating in 1907; was conductor in St. Petersburg and Moscow, 1907-12; toured as conductor.
WORKS: Opera: Woman on the window; Orchestra: symphony, 1903; Palestine suite, 1927; Night in Bagdad, tone poem, 1938; Stalingrad overture; Volga, tone poem; Chamber music: Hebrew suite, 8 instruments; 2 string quartets; Poem, violin and piano; Chorus: David and Abraham, oratorio.

LEVEY, JOSEPH A.
b. Clarksburg, W. Va., 9 May 1925. Studied with Weldon Hart, West Virginia Univ.; with Anthony Donato, Northwestern Univ.; and Philip Bezanson, Iowa State Univ. He received a commission from American Dance in Repertory; Ohio State Univ., College of the Arts grant. He has been assistant professor, Madison Coll., 1962-63; Radford Coll., 1963-65; Ohio State Univ., Columbus, 1965- .
WORKS: Ballet: Timepiece; Wind Ensemble: Mosaic for brass choir; Chamber music: string quartet.

3266 Leighton Road, Columbus, OH 43221

LEVEY, LAUREN
b. New York, N. Y., 20 June 1947. Studied with
Joel Spiegelman and Meyer Kupferman, Sarah
Lawrence Coll.; with Jacob Druckman, Bulent Arel,
K. Penderecki, Mario Davidovsky, Yale Univ. She
has been associate, piano faculty, Sarah Lawrence
Coll., 1971-   ; assistant professor and acting
director, Bregman Electronic Music Studio,
Dartmouth Coll., 1973-   .
WORKS: Chamber music: Dissolves, chamber
group, 1973; Chorus: A womb (with a view) of
one's own, women's voices, 1974; Electronic:
Study for tape, 1973; and now a message from our
sponsor especially for you ladies, tape, 1974.
7 Valley Road, Hanover, NH 03755

LEVIN, GREGORY
b. Washington, D.C., 8 Mar. 1943. Studied with
Leon Kirchner and Billy Jim Layton, Harvard Univ.,
B. A. cum laude 1967; with Arthur Berger and
Seymour Shifrin, Brandeis Univ., M. F. A. 1969;
and with Luciano Berio and Pierre Boulez. His
more than 30 commissions and awards include
Woodrow Wilson fellowship, 1967-68; Brandeis fellowship, 1968-70; Harvard scholarship, 1961-67;
and grants from New York State Council of the
Arts, 1970, Syracuse Symphony, 1971, Nat. Council
on the Arts. He was assistant professor, Syracuse Univ., 1970-72; conductor, Syracuse New Music
Ensemble, 1970-72; conductor, Syracuse Symphony
Orchestra, 1971; assistant professor, Univ. of
Rhode Island, 1972-73; faculty, Univ. of Calgary,
1973-   .
WORKS: Theatre: Crazy Horse, opera to own
libretto, 1957; The election of Andrew Jackson,
play with music, 1958; Sunrise, play with music,
1958; Buffalo, opera, 1959; A minuet, opera,
1959; incidental music for: Rosmerholm, 1961,
Playboy of the Western World, 1962, Midsummer
night's dream, 1962, Twelfth night, 1962; Rebel
and empire, opera, libretto by composer's father,
Dan Levin, 1970; Son of Judah, opera trilogy,
libretto by Dan Levin, 1970-   ; Chamber music:
Suite for flute, oboe, piano, 1963; piano sonata,
1965; Suite for chamber orchestra, 1966; improvisation on levin #1, 1966, #2, 1967; sonata for
flute and harp, 1971; Illuminations, piano,
soprano, saxophone, 1971; 5 Picasso portraits,
brass quintet, 1972; Infinities, soprano, violin,
percussion, piano, 1973; Raga, trumpet and organ,
Calgary, Alberta, 5 Oct. 1973; Two short, one
long, piano, 1974; Multimedia: The white goddess,
tape, audio and visual feedback, film, string
bass, voice and piano, Northampton, Mass., Nov.
1972; Black-Point cut-off, film, string bass,
piano and tape, 1973; Feedback, color television,
piano, tape, Boston, May 1973; Neap tide, film
and tape, 1973. He is also poet, painter, actor,
and dramatist.
Department of Music, University of Calgary
Alberta, Canada T2N 1N4

LEVINE, BRUCE
b. New York, N. Y., 24 Jan. 1950. Studied with
Ursula Mamlock, New York Univ., B. S. 1972, M. A.
1974. He held scholarships for Tanglewood, 1966,
Presser Found., 1969-70; and the Lado award for
instrument study. He has been a public school

(LEVINE, BRUCE)
teacher, Long Beach, N. Y., 1972-   ; free lance
oboist, English horn player and conductor.
WORKS: Theatre: music for A Thurber carnival, piano, 1970; Band: An English round
dance, 1969-72; Chamber music: Poem, flute solo,
1968; Introduction and allegro, flute, violin
and piano, 1968; Duet, alto flute and English
horn, 1969; wind quintet, 1970; Monologue I,
English horn, 1971; Introspection, oboe solo,
1971; Colours, oboe and piano, 1972; Design for
2 or more instruments, 1972; Traces, for clarinet solo, 1972; Syncrons, oboe, clarinet, viola,
tuba and electronic sound, 1973; Serenade, flute
and piano, 1973; 3 pieces for acoustic guitar,
1973; also choral works, songs, and piano pieces.
135 Clinton St., Hempstead, NY 11550

LEVINE, JEFFREY L.
b. New York, N. Y., 15 Sep. 1942. Studied at
Brown Univ., B. A.; with Mel Powell at Yale
Univ., M. M.; with Gunther Schuller and Franco
Donatoni. He received a Fromm Found. commission
at Tanglewood, 1967; Fulbright grant, 1968. He
was lecturer, Rutgers Univ., 1965-68; lecturer,
Univ. of California at Berkeley, 1972-74.
WORKS: Orchestra: piano concerto, 1971;
Chamber music: Form, 2 pianos; Cadenza, piano
solo; Parentheses, any number of stringed instruments; harpsichord quartet; Chamber setting #2;
clarinet sextet.
2822 Garber St., Berkeley, CA 94704

LEVINSON, GERALD
b. Mineola, N. Y., 22 June 1951. Studied with
George Crumb, Richard Wernick, and George
Rochberg, Univ. of Pennsylvania; with Bruno
Maderna at Tanglewood; and with Ralph Shapey,
Univ. of Chicago. He received BMI student composer awards, 1969, 1970, 1973; Univ. of Penn-
sylvania music prize, 1972; Univ. of Chicago
humanities fellowship, 1972-74; Georges Lurcy
Found. fellowship for study in France, 1974-75.
WORKS: Orchestra: Suono oscuro, 1969;
Chamber music: quintet for piano and strings,
1971; Winds of light (images and echoes), violin
and piano, 1973; Odyssey, solo flute, 1973;
Skrzybka, violin solo, 1973; piano pieces,
1968-72; Vocal: In wind, soprano and instruments,
1970; In dark, soprano, chamber ensemble, 1972;
Job, baritone, string quartet, choir, and organ,
1972.
182 Wilton Road, Westport, CT 06880

LEVITCH, LEON
b. Belgrade, Yugo., 9 July 1927; U.S. citizen
1951. Studied at Los Angeles State Coll., B. A.;
and at Univ. of California, Los Angeles, M. A.
1971; his teachers were Erich Zeisl, Mario
Castelnuovo-Tedesco, Darius Milhaud, and Roy
Harris. He received 2nd prize, Atwater Kent
award, 1968; Young Musicians Award, Los Angeles
Jewish Community Center, 1952. He has been staff
technician and concert tuner, Univ. of California,
Music Department, 1969-   , and instructor of
piano tuning and technology, Extension Division
1970-   .

(LEVITCH, LEON)
WORKS: Orchestra: Symphony; <u>Fantasy</u> for oboe and strings; Suite for flute, string orch, and harp; flute sonata; viola sonata; violin sonata; solo violin sonata; trio for flute, clarinet or viola, piano; quartet for flute, viola, cello, piano; string quartet; quintet for strings and flute; piano sonata; <u>Little suite</u>, piano; Chorus: <u>Plants and humans</u>, cantata for soprano and tenor soli, chorus, chamber orch., text by composer.
13107 Kelowna St., Pacoima, CA 91331

*LEVITT, RODNEY CHARLES
b. Portland, Ore., 1929. Played trombone with Dizzy Gillespie and others; has had his own band since 1960.
WORKS: Concert jazz: <u>Breathin' easy</u>; <u>El general</u>; <u>The lost soul</u>; <u>Safari</u>; <u>Speedway</u>; <u>Cathedral city</u>; <u>Circle 5</u>; <u>M'lord is at Olympia House</u>; <u>Onion chicken</u>; <u>Woodman of the world</u>.

*LEVITZKI, MISCHA
b. Kremenchug, Russia, 25 May 1898; to U.S. 1906; d. Avon, N. J., 2 Jan. 1941. Studied with Sigismund Stojowski at Juilliard School; with Ernst von Dohnanyi at the Berlin Hochschule fur Musik; was twice awarded the Mendelssohn piano prize; made his debut at 15 in Berlin; at 16 in New York; toured as pianist in the U.S., Europe, and the Orient. He composed many piano pieces.

*LEVY, BURT
b. Brooklyn, N. Y., 5 Aug. 1936. Studied at Univ. of Oregon and Temple Univ.; with George Rochberg and Salvatore Martirano; has taught at Univ. of Illinois and Univ. of Wisconsin. His <u>Orbs</u> for flute had its New York premiere on 5 Feb. 1973.

*LEVY, EDWARD I.
b. Brooklyn, N. Y., 2 May 1929. Attended City Coll. of New York, B. A. 1957; Princeton Univ., M. F. A. 1960; Columbia Univ. Teachers Coll., Ed. D. 1967; studied with Ralph Shapey, Milton Babbitt, Stefan Wolpe. He received the Frederick Jacoby Memorial award; Tremaine scholarship; 2 fellowships at Princeton; Heft scholarship at Columbia. He was linguistic researcher, Univ. of Pennsylvania, 1960-61; assistant professor, C. W. Post Coll., Long Island Univ., 1961-67; assistant professor, Yeshiva Univ., 1966-   .
WORKS: Chamber music: 2 songs on texts by Garcia-Lorca, 1951; clarinet sonata, 1955; piano suite 1956; string quartet, 1959; oboe sonata 1959; string trio, 1959; <u>Lento</u> for 9 instruments, 1959; trio for clarinet, violin and piano, 1961; <u>3 Images</u> for soprano and piano, 1961; quintet for flute, alto saxophone, vibraphone, viola, and bass, 1967.
838 West End Ave., New York, NY 10025

*LEVY, ELLIS
b. Indianapolis, Ind., 23 Oct. 1887. Studied violin with Eugene Ysaye and Cesar Thamson in Brussels. He was assistant concertmaster, St. Louis Symphony, 1910-36. He composed works for orchestra, for violin and piano, and for piano solo.

*LEVY, ERNST
b. Basel, Switz., 18 Nov. 1895; to U.S. 1939. Taught at New England Cons., 1941-45; Bennington Coll., 1946-51; Chicago Univ., 1951-54; was professor of piano at Massachusetts Inst. of Technology from 1954 to retirement. His works include 14 symphonies (no. 14 performed in Basel, 20 Jan. 1964); cello concerto; other orchestral works.
La Mirclaz, Chemin de Toulous
Morges (Vaud), Switzerland

LEVY, FRANK
b. Paris, France, 15 Oct. 1930; U.S. citizen 1955. Came to the U.S. with his father, Ernst Levy, in 1939, began studying cello and in 1941 composition with Hugo Kauder. He attended the High School of Music and Art, 1944-48; was a scholarship student under Leonard Rose at Juilliard School, B. S. 1951; studied musicology at Univ. of Chicago, M. A. 1954; cello with Janos Starker. He played cello with the St. Louis Symphony, 1951-52; principal cellist, Radio City Music Hall, 1960-   ; has taught privately and at Brooklyn Coll. and the New School.
WORKS: Orchestra: Concerto for oboe, horn, bassoon, timpani and string orch., 1958; concerto for bassoon and strings, 1960; <u>Dialogue</u>, tuba, harp, timpani, string orch., 1964; symphony no. 1 for small orch., 1968; symphony no. 2, brass and percussion, New York, Feb. 1972, nominated for Pulitzer Prize, 1973; Chamber music: <u>Variations on a Swiss folksong</u>, 1949; string quartet, 1951; sextet for winds and strings, 1955; Suite for solo cello, 1959; <u>Fantasy</u>, brass quintet and timpani, 1959; <u>Ricercar</u>, 4 celli, 1959; Suite for horn and piano, 1960; Concert piece, brass quartet, 1961; quintet for flute and strings, 1961; wind trio, 1962; bassoon sonata, 1963; <u>Fanfare</u>, brass quintet, 1965; clarinet sonata, 1967; violin duo, 1967; duo for flugelhorn and bass trumpet; violin sonata; 2 pieces for harpsichord; <u>Adagio and rondo</u>, 3 clarinets; Voice: <u>This is my letter to the world</u>, a cappella chorus, Dickinson text, 1957; <u>Specks of light</u>, song cycle for voice, flute, horn, string trio.
19 Virginia St., Tenafly, NJ 07670

*LEVY, HENIOT
b. Warsaw, Poland, 19 July 1879; to U.S. 1900; d. Chicago, 16 June, 1946. Studied with Max Bruch; taught piano at American Cons. in Chicago. His works include a piano concerto; <u>Variations</u> for orch.; many works for chamber ensembles.

*LEVY, MARVIN DAVID
b. Passaic, N. J., 2 Aug. 1932. Studied with Philip James at New York Univ.; with Otto Luening at Columbia Univ. His awards include the Prix de Rome; Guggenheim fellowship; grants from Ford Found., Damrosch Found., Huntington Hartford Found.; many commissions.
WORKS: Opera: <u>Sotoba Komachi</u>, 1957; <u>The tower</u>, 1957; <u>Escorial</u>, 1958; <u>Mourning becomes Electra</u>, Metropolitan Opera, 17 Mar. 1967; Orchestra: <u>Caramoor festival overture</u>, 1959; symphony, 1960; <u>Kyros</u>, dance poem; piano

LEVY, MARVIN DAVID

(LEVY, MARVIN DAVID)
concerto, 1970; Trialogue, 1972; In memoriam
W. H. Auden, New York, 25 Feb. 1974; Chamber
music: string quartet, 1955; Rhapsody, violin,
clarinet and harp, 1956; Chassidic suite, horn
and piano, 1956; Chorus: For the time being,
Christmas oratorio, 1959; Alice in Wonderland;
During wind and rain; Masada, oratorio, commissioned by National Symphony for Israel's 25th
anniversary, premiere, Washington, D.C., 30 Oct.
1973.
c/o Boosey and Hawkes
30 West 57th St., New York, NY 10019

*LEWIN, DAVID
Classical variations on a theme by Schoenberg,
cello and piano.
Department of Music
State University of New York
Stony Brook, NY 11790

LEWIN, FRANK
b. Breslau, Germany, 27 Mar. 1925; U.S. citizen
1946. Studied at New York Cons.; with Felix Deyo
and Wallingford Riegger, Brooklyn Cons.; with
Roy Harris, Utah State Agricultural Coll.;
Richard Donovan and Paul Hindemith, Yale Univ.
He received a Certificate of Merit at Yale. He
has been lecturer, Yale Univ., 1971-   .
WORKS: Theatre: Gulliver, opera using film
and recorded sound in interaction with live
actors and orch., in collaboration with 2 other
composers, 1972; incidental music for 14 plays,
1953-71; Orchestra: harmonica concerto; Evocation, symphonic poem, Princeton Univ., 27 Mar.
1961; viola concerto, Norfolk, Conn., 15 July
1965; Chorus: Psalm 148; Psalm 137, with orch.;
Behold, how good, Psalms 132 and 133, Princeton,
10 Dec. 1961; Music for the White House, cantata
on early American songs, composed at the request
of Mrs. Lyndon B. Johnson, composer conducted,
The White House, 14 Dec. 1965; Mass for the dead,
performed at memorial service for Robert F.
Kennedy, Princeton Univ., 27 May 1969; Songs:
Innocence and experience, cycle on Blake poems,
soprano and chamber orch., New Haven, Conn., 15
Feb. 1961; Film scores: Nine miles to noon,
1963; Harry, 1970; The angel Levine, 1970; and
more than 20 documentary films.
113 Magnolia Lane, Princeton, NJ 08540

*LEWIS, H. MERRILLS
b. Meriden, Conn., 1908. Studied with David
Stanley Smith and Richard Donovan, Yale Univ.;
with Rubin Goldmark at Juilliard School. He has
taught at Furman Univ. and Univ. of Houston; was
minister of music, First Christian Church, Houston. His compositions include a symphony, 1936,
3 serenades for orchestra, 1937; and Lake song,
women's voices, 1936.

LEWIS, JAMES
b. Mattoon, Ill., 13 Nov. 1938. Studied with
Samuel Adler, North Texas State Univ., Gordon
Binkerd, Univ. of Illinois; Charles Eakin, Univ.
of Colorado. He received first prize, Nat. Jazz
Composition contest, 1969; Nat. Endowment for
the Arts grant for jazz composition, 1973. He

(LEWIS, JAMES)
was instructor, Xavier Univ., 1965-67; Stephen F.
Austin State Coll., 1967-68; assistant professor,
Univ. of South Dakota, 1968-71; Univ. of South
Florida, 1971-   .
WORKS: Wind ensemble: Song from somewhere,
jazz band, 1969; Jazz sextet, 1972; Synergy for
brass and percussion, 1973; Chamber music: 4
personalities, violin, trumpet, flute, trombone,
1961; Music for flute and piano, 1970; Voice: 4
songs on texts by Ezra Pound, 1962; Epilogue,
voices and instruments, 1970.
5412 Riverhills Drive
Temple Terrace, FL 33617

*LEWIS, JOHN
b. La Grange, Ill., 3 May 1920. Studied at
Manhattan School of Music, B. M., M. M. He
served in the U.S. Army, 1942-45; co-founder in
1952 and pianist, Modern Jazz Quartet; president,
MJQ Music, Inc.; executive director, Lenox School
of Jazz.; music director, Orchestra USA.
WORKS: Ballet: Original sin, 1961; Concert
jazz: 6 vocalizes for vocal quartets with varying accompaniments; The Milanese story; The comedy, piano and brass ensemble; Fanfare I and II,
brass ensemble; The golden striker, piano and
brass ensemble; 3 little feelings, brass; Bel
(belkis); Django; Django (arranged by G.
Schuller); Sundance; Exposure; Little David's
fugue; Milano; N.Y. 19; Polchinella; 2 degrees
east, 2 degrees west; Animal dance; Jazz ostinato;
In memoriam; Sketch for double string quartet;
Jazz themes with improvisation, piano; Film
scores: No sun in Venice, 1958; Odds against
tomorrow, 1959; The Milanese story, 1962.
c/o MJQ Music, Inc.
200 West 57th St., New York, NY 10019

*LEWIS, JOHN LEO
b. Chicago, Ill., 11 May 1911. Studied at De
Paul Univ., B. A., M. A.; with Leo Sowerby,
American Cons. He received the Harvey Gaul
award and several prizes for choral works. From
1950 he was organist at Trinity Episcopal Church,
Aurora, Ill. He composed many organ works and
choral pieces.

LEWIS, KERRY G.
b. Santa Rosa, Calif., 6 Dec. 1948. Studied
with Lou Harrison, San Jose State Univ.
WORKS: Chamber music: Variations, woodwind
quintet, 1973; Chorus: Impressions of spring,
chorus, wind septet, and piano, 1973; Songs: 5
songs on poems of e.e. cummings, 1970; Hesperides,
cycle for voice and piano, 1972
565 Saratoga Ave., #6
Santa Clara, CA 95050

*LEWIS, LEON
b. Kansas City, Mo., 30 Mar. 1890; d. California,
5 Oct. 1961. Studied with Theodor Leschetizky
and Hermann Graedener at Vienna Cons.; toured
Europe, the U.S., and Canada as concert pianist;
then taught at Chicago Cons.
WORKS: Orchestra: Jessica - A portrait,
piano and orch.; Israeli suite; cello concerto;
Nocturne and moonspirits; Chamber music: cello

(LEWIS, LEON)
sonata; Quartetto Americano; Wind and the willow, piano trio; Chorus: God's image, baritone solo, chorus and orch.; songs.

LEWIS, MALCOLM
b. Cuba, N. Y., 14 Nov. 1925. Studied at Ithaca Coll., Juilliard School; New York Univ.; with Robert Palmer, Cornell Univ.; also studied art at various schools. He was a private teacher in Billings, Mont., 1955-61; art teacher, public schools, Bozeman, Mont., 1961-62; assistant professor of music, Ithaca Coll., 1962-   .
    WORKS: Orchestra: clarinet concerto; Concert piece for horn, strings and percussion; Suite for string orch.; Band: Elegy for a hollow man, saxophone and band; Phrygios; Wind ensemble: Movement for brass quintet and piano; 2 contrasting studies for 8 horns; Chamber music: Suite for 2 pianos; 2 piano trios; saxophone quartet; woodwind quartet; Reverie, saxophone solo; piano pieces.
    309 Farm St., Ithaca, NY 14850

LEWIS, PETER TOD
b. Charlottesville, Va., 6 Nov. 1932. Studied with Roger Chapman, Irving Eisley, Univ. of California at Santa Barbara; Lukas Foss, John Vincent, Univ. of California, Los Angeles; Arthur Berger, Irving Fine, Brandeis Univ.; and Wolfgang Fortner at Tanglewood. He received a Crofts scholarship, Tanglewood, 1960; Wechsler commission, 1960; Huntington Hartford Found. grant, 1960; MacDowell fellowship, 1961-62. He was instructor, Philadelphia Musical Acad., 1965-68; composer-in-residence, Southern Illinois Univ., Edwardsville, and Metropolitan Educational Center in the Arts, 1968-69; associate professor and director, electronic music studio, Univ. of Iowa, 1969-   .
    WORKS: Orchestra: Evolution, 1961; Chamber music: Capriccio concertato, 2 pianos, 1960, revised 1962; string quartet, #1, 1960; piano trio, 1960; 3 epigrams for chamber ensemble, 1961; Contrasts, wind quintet, 1962; Lament for Mrs. Bridge, chamber orch., 1963; Sestina, 11 winds, 1963; septet, woodwind trio, string trio, piano, 1963; ...and bells...and time, a dialogue for violin and piano, 1967; Signs and circuits, string quartet, #2, with tape, 1969; Manestar, chamber orch. and tape, 1970; Innerkip, piano and tape, 1972; Chorus: When I was born, with tenor and soprano soli, 1956; 3 insignificant tragedies, 1962; The cherry tree carol with soprano solo and harp, 1962; We stood on the wall, 1965; 3 for jazz choir, 1968; also songs, piano pieces, electronic works.
    510 Grant St., Iowa City, IA 52240

LEWIS, ROBERT HALL
b. Portland, Ore., 22 Apr. 1926. Studied with Bernard Rogers, Howard Hanson, Eastman School of Music, B. M. with distinction; with Nadia Boulanger in Paris; Karl Schiske, Hans Erich Apostel, in Vienna; also studied at Princeton Univ., and Univ. of Rochester, Ph. D. His many honors include the Posciuszko Found. Chopin Award in composition, 1951; Fulbright scholarship,

(LEWIS, ROBERT HALL)
1955-57; Graduation prize in composition, Vienna Acad., 1957; LADO prize, 1961; Guggenheim fellowship, 1966; Walter Hinrichsen award for composers, Columbia Univ., 1972; annual ASCAP awards, 1969-   ; several of his scores were selected for presentation to members of the Peking Orchestra by members of the Philadelphia Orchestra on the trip to Peking in September 1973. He has been professor, Goucher Coll., 1957-   ; Johns Hopkins Univ., 1969-   ; faculty member, Peabody Cons., 1958-62, 1964-66, 1972-   ; music director, Baltimore Chamber Music Society.
    WORKS: Orchestra: Acquainted with the night, with soprano solo, 1951; Prelude and finale for small orch., 1959; symphony #1, 1964; Designs for orch., 1964; 3 pieces for orch., 1966; Concerto for chamber orch., 1967, revised 1972; symphony #2, commissioned by Baltimore Symphony, performed in Baltimore, 6 Oct. 1971; Intermezzi, 1973; Chamber music: 2 string quartets, 1956, 1962; 5 songs for soprano, winds and piano, 1957; 5 movements for piano, 1960; Toccata for solo violin and percussion; Music for 12 players, 1965; trio for violin, clarinet, piano, 1966; brass quintet, 1966; Divertimento for 6 instruments, 1969; Tangents for double brass quartet, 1968; sonata for solo violin, 1968; Inflections I, contrabass solo, 1969; Inflections II, piano solo, 1970; Serenades for piano, 1970; Monophony I-IX for various solo instruments, 1966-72; Combinazioni, clarinet, violin, cello, piano, 1973; Fantasiemusik, cello and piano, New York, 3 Dec. 1973; Nuances, violin and piano, Baltimore, 7 Apr. 1975; Chorus: Due madrigali, with percussion, Baltimore, 21 Nov. 1972.
    328 Broadmoor Road, Baltimore, MD 21212

*LICHTER, CHARLES
b. Philadelphia, Pa., 15 Jan. 1910. Studied at Juilliard School; was staff violinist, conductor, and music consultant at CBS, 1936-   ; music coordinator, Bell Telephone Hour. His works for orchestra include Romantic suite and Vermont summer.

LIEBERMAN, FREDRIC
b. New York, N. Y., 1 Mar. 1940. Studied with Thomas Canning, Louis Mennini, John LaMontaine, Wayne Barlow, Eastman School of Music. He has been assistant professor, Brown Univ., 1968-   .
    WORKS: Chamber music: piano suite; piano sonatina; 2 short string quartets; Leaves of brass, brass quartet; Ternary systems; Card music for John Cage; Chorus: By the waters of Babylon.
    Music Department, Brown University
    Providence, RI 02912

LIEBERMAN, GLENN
b. New York, N. Y., 29 May 1947. Studied with Charles Wuorinen, Ludmila Ulehla, Howard Rovics, Manhattan School of Music.
    WORKS: Orchestra: T for orchestra; Piece for chamber orch. and tape; Chamber music: woodwind and string quintet; trio for flute, clarinet

LIEBERMAN, GLENN

(LIEBERMAN, GLENN)
and cello; piano suite; clarinet and bass clarinet duos; violin sonata.
1440 Ocean Parkway, Brooklyn, NY 11730

*LIEBERSON, GODDARD
b. Hanley, Staffordshire, England, 5 Apr. 1911; to U.S. 1915. Studied with George Frederick McKay, Univ. of Washington; with Bernard Rogers, Eastman School of Music; received honorary doctorates from Temple Univ. and Cleveland Inst. of Music. He was on the staff, Masterworks Department, Columbia Records, 1939-56; president, Columbia Records, 1956-66; senior vice president, Columbia Broadcasting System, 1971-73; president, CBS Records Group, 1973- ; president Record Industry Asso. of America, 1964-71.
WORKS: Theatre: music for Alice in Wonderland, 1936; Yellow poodle, ballet, 1937; Orchestra: 5 modern painters, suite, 1929; 2 Chassidic dances, 1929; Tango, piano and orch., 1936; Homage to Handel, string orch., 1937; symphony, 1937; Chamber music: Suite for 20 instruments, 1928; Sonata for quintet, oboe, bassoon, piano trio, 1934; string quartet, 1938; Chorus: 3 Chinese poems; songs to texts of Ezra Pound, James Joyce, et al.; Piano: Complaints of the young, 1932; 9 melodies, 1933; Piano pieces for advanced children or retarded adults, 1965. He is author of music criticism and articles in music journals; and a novel, 3 in bedroom C.
Columbia Records, Inc.
51 West 52nd St., New York, NY 10019

LIEBERSON, PETER
b. New York, N. Y., 25 Oct. 1946. Studied at New York Univ., B. A. 1970; with Charles Wuorinen and Harvey Sollberger, Columbia Univ., M. A. 1973; informally with Milton Babbitt. He received the Rapoport prize, 1972; Charles Ives scholarship, Nat. Inst. of Arts and Letters, 1973. He was production engineer, WNCN-FM, New York, 1969-71; musical assistant to Leonard Bernstein, 1972-73.
WORKS: Orchestra: cello concerto, New York, 15 Apr. 1974; Chamber music: Variations for solo flute, 1971; Mottetti (di Eugenio Montale), soprano, alto, clarinet, bass clarinet, harp and piano, 1971-72; Concerto for 4 groups of instruments, Tanglewood, 1973.
106 East 31st St., New York, NY 10016

*LIEBLING, LEONARD
b. New York, N. Y., 7 Feb. 1874; d. New York, 28 Oct. 1945. Studied at City Coll. of New York; piano with Leopold Godowsky; with Franz Kullack in Berlin. He was staff member, Musical Courier, 1902-11, editor-in-chief, 1911; music critic, New York American, 1923-37. He composed chamber music, piano pieces, songs.

*LIEURANCE, THURLOW
b. Oskaloosa, Iowa, 21 Mar. 1878; d. Boulder, Colo., 9 Oct. 1963. Studied at Cincinnati Coll. of Music, D. M.; and in Fontainebleau, France, on scholarship. He received an award from the American Scientific Research Society for his study of American Indian music. He was bandmaster in

(LIEURANCE, THURLOW)
the Spanish-American War; toured in concerts with his wife, a singer, 1918-27; was professor, Univ. of Nebraska, 1927-40; dean of fine arts, Univ. of Wichita, 1940-47.
WORKS: Orchestra: Colonial Exposition sketches; Prairie sketches; Water moon maiden; Chamber music: Fantasia, violin and piano; Songs: By the waters of the Minnetonka; Hail, Wichita; many other songs on Indian themes.

LIFCHITZ, MAX
b. Mexico City, 11 Nov. 1948; to U.S. 1966. Studied with Luciano Berio, Juilliard School, B. M. 1970, M. A. 1971; with Leon Kirchner and Arthur Berger, Harvard Univ., candidate for Ph. D.; with Bruno Maderna at Tanglewood; Darius Milhaud at Aspen School. His awards include 2 Darius Milhaud awards, 1967, 1968; Richard Rogers scholarship, 1968; C. D. Jackson prize, 1972; the following fellowships: Irving Berlin, 1969, 1970; Juilliard School, 1968-70; Leonard Bernstein for Tanglewood, 1972; Harvard Univ., 1971-74; Ford Found., 1974; Michigan Univ. Society of Fellows, 1974-77. He was pianist with the Juilliard Ensemble, 1968-73; music director and conductor, Beaux Arts Opera Co., New York, and Vineyard Players, Martha's Vineyard, 1970-71; chairman of composition and theory, School for Contemporary Music, Boston, 1973-74.
WORKS: Chamber music: Duo, violin and cello, 1966; Fibers, chamber wind ensemble, Aspen Music Festival, Aug. 1967; Solo, realization of a score by Sylvano Bussotti, 1967; Pieza, 3 pianos, Aspen, Aug. 1968; Tiempos, chamber ensemble, New York, 29 Nov. 1970; Consorte, viola and viola d'amore, commissioned by Karen Phillips and Walter Trampler, Honolulu, July 1970; Mosaicos, chamber ensemble, Honolulu, July 1971; Globos, chamber ensemble, Honolulu, July 1971; Elegia, voice and piano, New York, 3 Oct. 1971; Fantasia, piano trio, New York, 20 Feb. 1972; Canto - in memoriam Igor Stravinsky, 1972; Roberta, chamber orch., St. Paul, Min., 14 Oct. 1972; Kaddish, cantor, choir and brass ensemble, New York, 9 Mar. 1973; Bluebells, dramatic musical, Boston, 26 Mar. 1973.
153 Walden St., Cambridge, MA 02140

LINCOLN, ROBERT DIX
b. Woodstock, Ohio, 3 Dec. 1924. Studied with Carl Hugo Grimm, Univ. of Cincinnati, B. M. 1949, M. M. 1950; with Nadia Boulanger in Paris, 1952, 1954-55. He held a French Government fellowship, 1954; Fulbright award, 1954. He was associate professor, East Tennessee State Univ., 1950-57; professor, Douglass Coll., 1957- ; graduate school, Rutgers Univ., 1960- .
WORKS: Theatre: incidental music for The Trojan women; Chamber music: trio for viola, cello, doublebass; sonatina for strings; Variations with a theme for 2 pianos; Arioso, string orch., Etude for 2 pianos; Chorus: Mass for women's voices and orch.; Alleluia, women's voices and instruments.
251 Lawrence Ave., Highland Park, NJ 08904

LINDENFELD, HARRIS NELSON
    b. Benton Harbor, Mich., 15 May 1945. Studied
with Walter Ross and Donald MacInnis, Univ. of
Virginia, B. A. 1969, M. A. 1971; with Burrill
Phillips, Karel Husa, Robert Palmer, Cornell
Univ., candidate for D. M. A. He received the
Philip Slates award, Southeastern Composers
League, 1971; University Union Fine Arts Award,
Univ. of Virginia, 1972.
    WORKS: Orchestra: piano concerto, 1972;
Band: Symphonia for concert band, 1971; Direc-
tions for wind ensemble, 1973; Chamber music:
Tritogenea, brass quintet, 1970; Inflation, for
3 tubas, 1972; 3 songs on poems by Roethke, 1973.
    154 1/2 Indian Creek Road, Ithaca, NY 14850

LINDH, JODY WAYNE
    b. Lindsborg, Kan., 25 Feb. 1944. Studied at
Bethany Coll., Lindsborg, Kan.; with Lloyd
Pfautsch and Carlton R. Young, Southern Methodist
Univ.; with Michael Schneider in Cologne, Germany,
under a Fulbright-Hays grant, 1968-69. He has
been music director-organist, University Park
Methodist Church, Dallas, 1969-   ; lecturer,
Southern Methodist Univ., 1972-   .
    WORKS: Chorus: If thou but suffer God to
guide thee, 1971; At the Lord's table, hymn
accompaniment, 1972; Psalm 47, 1973.
    6411 Kenwood Ave., Dallas, TX 75214

LINN, ROBERT
    b. San Francisco, Calif., 11 Aug. 1925. Studied
with Halsey Stevens, Univ. of Southern California,
M. M.; also with Darius Milhaud and Roger
Sessions. His honors include awards from Phi
Mu Alpha, 1950; Nat. Fed. of Music Clubs, 1951;
Calif. Fed. of Music Clubs, 1952; Louisville
Orchestra, 1955; Los Angeles Chamber Symphony,
1956; grants from the MacDowell Assoc., 1963;
Huntington Hartford Found., 1964; Alchin Found.,
1969; and many commissions. He has been on the
faculty, Univ. of Southern California, 1956-   ;
professor and chairman of theory in 1973.
    WORKS: Orchestra: Overture, 1952; Symphony
in 1 movement, 1956, revised 1961; The hexameron,
orchestration reconstructed from Liszt's piano
version of 1837, Los Angeles, Feb. 1963; Sinfonia
for string orch., 1967; Concertino for oboe, horn,
percussion and string orch., Pasadena, Mar. 1973;
Band: 4 pieces, 1954; March of the Olympians,
commissioned for and performed at the Winter
Olympics, 1960; Concerto grosso, trumpet, horn,
trombone and band, 1961; Elevations, 1964;
Propagula, 1970; Chamber music: clarinet sonata,
1949; 5 pieces, flute and clarinet, 1950; string
trio, 1950; string quartet, 1951, New York, Mar.
1953; saxophone quartet, 1953; Adagio and allegro, chamber orch., 1956; horn quartet, 1957; duo
for clarinet and cello, 1959; Prelude and dance,
saxophone quartet, 1960; Suite for viola and
cello, 1962; brass quintet, New York, Oct. 1963;
woodwind quintet, 1963; Dithyramb for 8 celli,
1965; Concertino, violin and wind octet, 1965;
Ayre and ground, solo cello, 1968; duo for cello
and piano, 1971; Fanfares for 3 clarinets, 1972;
Chorus: 3 madrigals, 1951; An anthem of wisdom,
chorus and orch., Los Angeles, 23 Oct. 1958; 3
German folksongs, male voices, 1959; Pied Piper

(LINN, ROBERT)
    of Hamelin, narrator, tenor, chorus, orch., 1968;
Keyboard: 2 piano sonatas, 1955, 1964;
Toccatina, organ, 1973; Film score: The story
tellers of the Canterbury tales, 1952.
    3275 De Witt Drive, Los Angeles, CA 90068

LINTHICUM, DAVID H.
    b. Baltimore, Md., 7 May 1941. Studied at West-
ern Maryland Coll., with Earle Brown, Peabody
Cons., B. M. 1964; with Howard Brucker, Catholic
Univ., M. M. 1969; Ben Johnston and Morgan
Powell, Univ. of Illinois, D. M. A. 1972. He
received the Marie K. Thatcher award, Peabody
Cons., 1963; 2 fellowships, Univ. of Illinois,
1970, 1971. He was instructor, Westminster
Choir Coll., 1969-70; assistant professor, Lone
Mountain Coll., 1972-73.
    WORKS: Orchestra: Serie, 1969; Tropos,
cello, string orch., percussion and brass, 1972;
Chamber music: Pour la flute seule, 1969; wood-
wind quintet, 1969; string quartet, 1969; Contingencies, alto flute and chamber orch., 1971;
A quatre, flute, harpsichord, cello, percussion,
1972; Ave Maria, male quartet, 1973; Requiem
mass, 1973.
    224 Warren Ave., Baltimore, MD 21230

LIPSCOMB, HELEN
    b. Georgetown, Ky., 20 Apr. 1921; d. Lexington,
Ky., 4 Jan. 1974. Studied at Univ. of Kentucky,
B. A. 1941, M. A. 1945; with Robert L. Sanders,
Indiana Univ., 1944; and with Nadia Boulanger,
Longy School, Cambridge, Mass. She won an award
in the song division, Phu Mu Alpha competition.
She taught piano and composition at Univ. of
Kentucky for 5 years, and privately more than 27
years.
    WORKS: Chamber music: Design, clarinet and
string quartet; 3 clarinet trios; Variations,
woodwind quintet; 3 solos for clarinet and piano;
Two by two, violin and cello; Nocturne and waltz
for strings; Chorus: The ballad of William
Sycamore, baritone, male chorus, piano; many
anthems; Keyboard: piano sonata; Passacaglia
and toccata, organ; piano pieces. She also
composed for the Modern Dance Group, Univ. of
Kentucky.

*LIPSKY, ALEXANDER
    Lilac time, voice, 1935.

LISSAUER, FREDRIC DAVID
    b. Cleveland, Ohio, 26 Jan. 1945. Studied with
Marcel Dick and Donald Erb, Cleveland Inst. of
Music. His works include Variations for piano,
performed at a Bennington Composers' Conference.

*LISSAUER, ROBERT
    b. New York, N. Y., 1 May 1917. Studied with
Bernard Wagenaar at Juilliard School; Schillinger
System at New York Univ. He wrote scores for
Army shows; taught at New York Univ.; Eastern
Cons.; Newark Cons., 1948-52; in music publishing
from 1940.
    WORKS: Orchestra: Sinfonietta; 2 preludes
for concertina and orch.; Chamber music: string
quartet; woodwind quintet; also popular songs.

271

LIST, GARRETT

*LIST, GARRETT
Your own self, 3 voices, winds, 2 pianos, percussion, and bass.
197 East 4th St., New York, NY 10009

LISTER, RODNEY
b. Ft. Payne, Ala., 31 May 1951. Studied with Malcolm Peyton and Donald Martino, New England Cons., B. M. with honors 1973; at Tanglewood, 1973, on fellowship.
WORKS: Chamber music: Music for a while, flute, oboe, piano, 1971; Nuns fret not, soprano and 7 instruments, 1971-73; The bell doth tolle, bass, oboe, viola, trombone, vibraphone, 1973; Agreeably of love, soprano and piano, 1973; My world and welcome to it, contrabass, 1973.
Bell Road, Route 3, Antioch, TN 37013

LIVINGSTON, DAVID
b. Corbin, Ky., 10 Jan. 1925. Studied with Weldon Hart and Roy Harris, Western Kentucky Univ.; Kenneth Wright, Univ. of Kentucky; and with Marshall Barnes, Ohio State Univ., D. M. A. His string quartet won a Phi Mu Alpha award. He was public school music supervisor, Frankfort, Ky., 1952-63; associate professor, Western Kentucky Univ., 1965- .
WORKS: Wind ensemble: Adagio, 4 trombones; How firm a foundation; Pastorale for winds; Prelude and fugue; Mirage; Symphony #1; Killarney holiday; Clarinada; Saxville.
2325 Bellevue Drive, Bowling Green, KY 42101

LLOYD, ALAN
b. Baltimore, Md., 10 Jan. 1943. Studied with Donald Keats, Antioch Coll. He is music director, Byrd Hoffman Found., New York.
WORKS: Keyboard: The druid's harp; Virelai; Christmas music; The ostrich entrance; The cat up the tree in the terrible wind; The recluse.
c/o Byrd Hoffman Foundation
147 Spring St., New York, NY 10012

LLOYD, CAROLINE PARKHURST
b. Uniontown, Ala., 12 Apr. 1924. Studied with John D. Robb, Univ. of New Mexico, B. M.; with Bernard Rogers, Eastman School of Music; with Donata Fornuto, Arpad Szabo, and Charles Wuorinen, Columbia Univ., 1973. She received Sigma Alpha Iota scholarship, 1944, and honors work in composition, Univ. of New Mexico, 1944. She was a private piano teacher, 1946-73; musical activities director, Centro Venezolano Americano, Caracas, 1955-68; organist and choral director.
WORKS: Opera: Dona Barbara, given 8 performances to commemorate the 400th anniversary of Caracas and to reopen the newly renovated Teatro Municipal in 1967; Songs: 3 songs of the Bolivar countries, 1965; 3 songs on poems of Garcia Lorca, 1966; 2 songs on poems of Jose Ramon Medina, 1968; other works for solo voice, chorus, keyboard, string quartet.
c/o General Electric Co., J. Lomonaco
159 Madison Ave., New York, NY 10016

LLOYD, GERALD J.
b. Lebanon, Ohio, 6 Sep. 1938. Studied with Scott Huston, Jeno Takacs, Cincinnati Coll. Cons.;

(LLOYD, GERALD J.)
Bernard Rogers, Eastman School of Music; and with Everett Hafner, Electronic Music Studios, Amherst. He received a commission from Kalamazoo Symphony Orchestra, 1970; 2 Rockefeller Found. performance awards. He was faculty member, Western Michigan Univ., 1966-69; head, music division, School of Performing Arts, San Diego, 1969-71; assistant dean, Coll. of Fine Arts, Drake Univ., 1971- .
WORKS: Orchestra: Associations I; concertino for piano and orch.; Chamber music: L'evenement, trumpet and piano; 3 sketches, tuba and piano.
1302 30th St., Des Moines, IA 50311

LLOYD, NORMAN
b. Pottsville, Pa., 8 Nov. 1909. Studied with Vincent Jones, New York Univ., B. S., M. A.; and privately with Aaron Copland. He has received ASCAP awards, 1962- ; many commissions; honorary doctorates, Philadelphia Cons., 1963; New England Cons., 1965; Peabody Cons., 1973. He was on the faculty, New York Univ., 1936-45; Sarah Lawrence Coll., 1936-46; Juilliard School, 1946-63, director of education, 1946-49; dean, Oberlin Coll. Cons., 1963-65, director of arts and humanities, Rockefeller Found., 1965-73.
WORKS: Ballet: Panorama, for Martha Graham; Lament, for Doris Humphrey; La Malinche, for Jose Limon; Band: A Walt Whitman overture; Chamber music: 3 pieces for violin and piano; Episodes, piano; piano sonata; 3 scenes from memory, piano; Voice: Song for summer's end; Restless land, choral ballet; Nocturne for voices. His published books include: The fireside book of folksongs; The golden encyclopedia of music; Keyboard improvisation, 1973.
Richmond Hill Road, Greenwich, CT 06830

LOBINGIER, CHRISTOPHER CRUMAY
b. Danville, Pa., 5 Feb. 1944. Studied with Carlos Surinach, Carnegie Inst. of Technology, 1966-67; with Nikolai Lopatnikoff, Carnegie-Mellon Univ., 1967-68; Nadia Boulanger, Paris, 1968-69; Robert Hall Lewis, Peabody Cons., 1973-74.
WORKS: Orchestra: Epitaph, 1967; Chamber music: Qui n'est pas né, cello and piano, 1968; trio for clarinet, trombone, piano, 1968; 2 pieces for piano trio, 1970; string quartet, 1973; Keyboard: Rondo à "camp", piano, 1966; piano sonata, 1967; Nuptial colors, organ, 1969; 5 gallactic dances, piano, 1974; and songs.
Apt. 3R, 2814 St. Paul St.
Baltimore, MD 21218

LOCKLAIR, DAN
b. Charlotte, N. C., 7 Aug. 1949. Studied with David Richey, Davidson Coll.; Joan Groom and Donna Robertson, Mars Hill Coll.; with Joseph Goodman in New York. He received the Crisp award, 1971; first prize in a D.C. national contest, American Guild of Organists, 1972. He was organ instructor, Hartwick Coll., 1973; organist-choirmaster, First Presbyterian Church, Binghamton, 1973.

(LOCKLAIR, DAN)
    WORKS: Wind ensemble: Modal suite for
brass; Chorus: All my heart this night rejoices;
Prayer of supplication and thanksgiving; In
praise of Easter, cantata for 4 soli, chorus,
organ and brass; other works for orchestra, band,
solo instruments, etc.
    139 Matthews St., Apt. 2
    Binghamton, NY 13905

LOCKSHIN, FLORENCE LEVIN
    b. Columbus, Ohio, 24 Mar. 1910. Studied with
Morris Wilson, Ohio State Univ., B. A. 1931; with
Alvin D. Etler, Smith Coll., M. A. 1953. She was
selected composer-performer to represent Ohio,
Nat. Fed. of Music Clubs, 1951; honorary life
member, American Fed. of Musicians, 1951. She
was a private piano teacher and performer,
1924-45; member of a 4-piano team, 1945-55.
    WORKS: Orchestra: The cycle, ballet; Aural;
Song form; Paean, Mexican folksong; Annie
Bradley's tune, negro folksong; Scavarr, American
Indian; Introduction, lament, and protest; Chorus:
Do not go gentle into that good night, male
voices and instruments; other choral works, piano
pieces, chamber music.
    Baker Hill, Northampton, MA 01060

LOCKWOOD, LARRY PAUL
    b. Duluth, Minn., 18 June 1943. Studied with
James Beale, Univ. of Washington; Nicolas
Flagello, Ludmila Ulehla, David Diamond, Mario
Davidovsky, Manhattan School of Music, M. M.
1967; Burrill Phillips, Robert Palmer, Cornell
Univ., D. M. A. 1973. He received a John James
Blackmore scholarship, 1972. He was instructor,
Ithaca Community Music School, 1970-71; teaching
assistant, Cornell Univ., 1970-73; cataloguer
and reference librarian, Manhattan School of
Music Library, 1973-
    WORKS: Orchestra: Divertimento, 1967; sym-
phony, 1969; Band: Suite for band, 1973; Chamber music: woodwind octet, 1967; sonata for 2
violins and cello; Trio variations, flute, clarinet, violin; trio for amplified piano, electric
harpsichord, percussion; Ricercar, flute and
piano; Voice: 4 Psalms, soli, chorus, orch.;
6 song sets; Piano: 3 sonatas; sonata for 2
pianos.
    255 East 18th St., Brooklyn, NY 11226

LOCKWOOD, NORMAND
    b. New York, N. Y., 19 Mar. 1906. Studied at
Univ. of Michigan; with Ottorino Respighi in
Rome, and with Nadia Boulanger in Paris. His
many awards include a fellowship, American Acad.
in Rome, 1929-32; Swift prize, 1934; World's
Fair prize, 1939; Elizabeth Sprague Coolidge
award, 1941; 2 Guggenheim fellowships, 1943,
1944; Alice M. Ditson award, 1944; Nat. Inst. of
Arts and Letters award; Ernest Bloch award; Soc.
for the Publication of American Music award, 1947;
Colorado Governor's award in the arts and humanities; and many commissions. He held faculty posts at Oberlin Coll., 1932-45; Columbia
Univ., 1945-48; Union Theological Seminary,
1945-50; Westminster Choir Coll., 1948-50; Yale
Univ. 1950-53; Trinity Univ., Tex., 1953-55;

(LOCKWOOD, NORMAND)
    Univ. of Wyoming, 1955-57; Univ. of Oregon,
1957-59; Univ. of Hawaii, 1960-61; composer-in-
residence, Univ. of Denver, 1961-   , associate
professor, 1968-   .
    WORKS: Opera: The scarecrow; Early dawn;
Wizards of Balizar; The hanging judge; Requiem
for a rich young man, 1-act; Land of promise,
staged oratorio; Theatre: music for 16 plays;
Orchestra: oboe concerto; piano concerto; Symphonic sequences; Chamber music: quintet, clarinet and strings; flute sonata; Fun piece, wind
quintet; 8 pieces for 2 trumpets; 6 string quartets; 6 serenades for string quartet; Sonata-
fantasia, accordion; sonata for 3 cellos; piano
quintet; trio for flute, viola and harp; Chorus:
Inscriptions from the catacombs, 1935; Out of the
cradle endlessly rocking, 1938; Choreographic
cantata; I will give thanks with all my heart;
Carol fantasy, with orch. or band; Ballad of the
North and South; The closing doxology, with band;
Prairie, with orch.; The birth of Moses, women's
voices, flute, piano; Light out of darkness, with
baritone and orch.; Children of God, with soloists and orch.; O, Come let us sing, with flute,
oboe, string quartet; Give me the splendid silent
sun, with orch.; Magnificat, with soprano and
orch.; Sing unto the Lord a new song, 1952; Dirge
for 2 veterans; Drum taps, with orch.; Fragments
from Sappho, women's voices; Keyboard: Fantasy,
piano, organ sonata; sonata for 2 pianos; Fantasy on Jesus, my joy, organ; concerto for
organ and brasses; Stopping on a walk to rest,
organ; Fugue-sonata, piano; Lyric arabesque,
piano.
    c/o American Composers Alliance
    170 West 74th St., New York, NY 10023

LOEB, DAVID J.
    b. New York, N. Y., 11 May 1939. Studied with
Peter Pindar Stearns, Mannes Coll. of Music;
Quincy Porter, Francis Judd Cooke, Yehudi Wyner,
Yale Univ.; Otto Luening, Columbia Univ.; Aaron
Copland, Wolfgang Fortner and Witold Lutoslawski
at Tanglewood. He received the Bohuslav Martinu
award, 1961; Viola da Gamba Society award, Lon-
don, 1966; citation and honorarium, Chinese
Classical Music Asso., Taipei, 1971; annual
ASCAP awards, 1965-   . He was faculty member,
Mannes Coll. of Music, 1964-   ; Brooklyn Coll.,
CUNY, 1971-73; Curtis Inst. of Music, 1973-
    WORKS: Orchestra: concerto for oboe and
string orch.; Siddhartha; The wreck of the Hope;
Chamber music: 4 songs for baritone and viola;
quintet for clarinet, 2 violas, 2 cellos; 5
string quartets, no.4, New York, 14 Nov. 1974;
3 sonatas for violin and viola; string octet;
Prelude and 2 scherzi, bassoon solo; 3 Hiroshima
songs; 4 preludes for violin solo; 3 sonatas for
viola solo; 2 violin sonatas; 3 piano sonatas;
The Opium War through Chinese eyes, soprano and
chamber orch.; Romanza, violin and wind ensemble;
Partita da camera, chamber orch.; Fantasia and
allemande, guitar; also some 50 compositions for
Japanese instruments with scores in Western and
Japanese notation; 15 compositions for Chinese
instruments with scores in Western and Chinese

LOEB, DAVID J.

(LOEB, DAVID J.)
notation; 35 works for renaissance and baroque
instruments.
233 West 99th St., New York, NY 10025

*LOESSER, FRANK
b. New York, N. Y., 29 June 1910; d. New York,
28 July 1969. Studied at City Coll. of New York,
where he wrote songs for college shows. His
awards for musicals include Academy award, 1949;
Tony award, 1951; New York Drama Critics' Circle
award for libretto to Most happy fella, 1957;
Grammy award, 1962; Pulitzer prize, 1962. He was
newspaper reporter, pianist, singer; wrote Army
shows in World War II.
WORKS: Musicals: Where's Charlie?, 1948;
Guys and dolls, 1950; The most happy fella, to
own libretto, 1956; How to succeed in business
without really trying, 1961. Film scores: College swing; Destry rides again; Kiss the boys
goodbye; 7 days leave; Thank your lucky stars;
Happy-go-lucky.

*LOEWE, FREDERICK
b. Vienna, Austria, 10 June 1904; to U.S. 1924.
Studied piano with Ferruccio Busoni and d'Albert,
composition with Reznicek in Berlin; then came to
New York. He received Tony awards, 1947, 1957;
Academy award for the film score, Gigi, 1958.
WORKS: Musicals: Salute to spring, 1937;
Great lady, 1938; What's up?, 1943; The day
before spring, 1945; Brigadoon, 1947; Paint your
wagon, 1951; My fair lady, 1956; Camelot, 1960;
many songs.
Palm Springs, CA 92262

*LOGAN, FREDERICK KNIGHT
b. Oskaloosa, Iowa, 15 Oct. 1871; d. Oskaloosa,
11 June 1928. Is best known for composing the
Missouri waltz, c.1916. After many years of
success as a musical director and coach, he
returned to Oskaloosa to spend time composing.
His song, Iowa, proud Iowa, was adopted by the
Iowa Fed. of Women's Clubs.

LOGAN, ROBERT
b. Beatrice, Neb., 14 Feb. 1926. Studied with
Francis Pyle, Drake Univ., B. M. E., M. M. E. He
was finalist in the Leblanc composition contest,
Chicago, 1963. He taught in public schools,
1953-55; has been music director, Clear Lake Jr.
Coll., 1955-   .
WORKS: Band: El chaco; Joi; Dimension, overture; Have horn will travel, solo with band;
Presto chango, solo with band; Sugar and spice,
solo with band.
519 North Shore Drive, Clear Lake, IA 50428

*LOGAN, WENDELL
b. Thompson, Ga., 1940. Studied at Southern
Illinois Univ., M. A. 1964; State Univ. of Iowa,
Ph. D. He has taught at Ball State Univ.; Flor-
ida A&M Coll.; is professor, Oberlin Coll.-Cons.
Songs of our time for chorus and instrumental
ensemble has been recorded.
Oberlin College Conservatory
Oberlin, OH 44074

*LOJEWSKI, HARRY VICTOR
b. Detroit, Mich., 23 Dec. 1917. Studied with
Homer Grunn. He was pianist in dance orchestras;
rehearsal pianist in film studios; since 1954,
music supervisor, MGM feature and television
films; choirmaster, Our Lady of Lourdes Church,
Northridge, Calif. His compositions include
Americana mass for chorus, organ, and guitar.

*LOMBARDO, MARIO
b. Elizabeth, N. J., 30 May 1931. Studied at
Seton Hall Univ., B. A., M. A.; Columbia Univ.;
and privately. He was staff member, Shapiro-
Bernstein, 1963; assistant professor of literature and music, Seton Hall Univ. to 1964.
WORKS: Orchestra: Near nostalgia; Blue
interlude, piano and orch.; Remembrance of things
past, tone poem; Euphony in jazz; Roxanne; Variations in a mod mood, Cincinnati Symphony, 14
June 1972; also songs.

LOMBARDO, ROBERT
b. Hartford, Conn., 5 Mar. 1932. Studied with
Arnold Franchetti, Hartt Coll.; Philip Bezanson,
Univ. of Iowa; with Boris Blacher, Berlin; Aaron
Copland and Goffredo Petrassi at Tanglewood; and
with Guido Turchi in Rome. His awards include
the Koussevitzky prize at Tanglewood; 2 Nat. Fed.
of Music Clubs awards; 2 BMI awards; Sigma Alpha
Iota award; 2 Ford Found. grants for public
school composer-in-residence; Guggenheim fellowship; Roosevelt Univ. research grant; commissions
from Fromm Found., Koussevitzky Found., Chicago
Musical Coll., Fine Arts Quartet. He has been
composer-in-residence, Chicago Musical Coll.,
Roosevelt Univ., 1964-   .
WORKS: Opera: Sorrows of a supersoul, chamber opera; Orchestra: Threnody for strings;
Aphorisms; Band: In my craft or sullen art,
Dylan Thomas text, narrator and band; Chamber
music: Dialogues of lovers, chamber ensemble;
Largo for string quartet; Nocturne, contrabass
solo, 1966; Duels and duets; Fourplay; Aria and
fragments; Yes!; Laude, fuga et cavatina, piano;
3 Fantasy variations, no.1 cello solo, no.2 harpsichord solo, no.3 violin solo; Voice: As the
hart panteth, chorus; A song for Morpheus,
soprano.
1040 West Wellington, Chicago, IL 60657

LONDON, EDWIN
b. Philadelphia, Pa., 16 Mar. 1929. Studied at
Oberlin Coll., B. M. 1952; with Philip Greeley
Clapp and Philip Bezanson, Univ. of Iowa, Ph. D.;
and with Luigi Dallapiccola and Darius Milhaud.
He received awards from Guggenheim Found.; Univ.
of Illinois, Center for Advanced Study; Nat.
Endowment for the Arts. He was conductor and
professor, Smith Coll., 1960-68; professor, Univ.
of Illinois, 1968-   ; visiting professor, Univ.
of California, San Diego, 1972-73.
WORKS: Opera: Tala obtusities; Santa Claus;
Orchestra: Pressure points, alto saxophone and
orch.; Portraits of 3 American ladies, voice and
orch.; overture to The imaginary invalid; Wind
ensemble: Symphonic movements for band;
Lsinsame Blumen, brass choir, Chamber music:
brass quintet; trio for flute, clarinet, piano;

(LONDON, EDWIN)
Song and dance for flute; woodwind quintet; viola
sonatina; Chorus: Bells, Poe text, narrator,
singers and percussion; Dream thing on Biblical
episodes; 3 settings of the 23rd Psalm; 5 haiku;
4 proverbs; A Washington miscellany; Enter madmen;
Polonius platitudes; Songs: The bear's song,
tenor voice; Electronic: Geistliche Musik, 3
choruses, 3 instrumental groups, and tape; Point
of view, tape; Hoopla!, tape; Carnivore of Uranus,
trombone, electronic costume and tape.
910 West Hill St., Champaign, IL 61820

LONG, NEWELL H.
b. Markle, Ind., 12 Feb. 1905. Studied with
Winifred Merrill and Robert Sanders, Indiana
Univ. He received first prize in a competition,
Illinois Wesleyan Univ., 1945; Huntington Hartford Found. fellowships, 1961, 1965. He taught
in public schools, 1925-27, 1932-34; trombonist
and arranger, 1928-29, band-orchestra director,
Central Michigan Univ., 1929-31; music faculty,
Indiana Univ., 1935-
    WORKS: Band: Concertino for woodwind quin-
tet and band; Art show, a suite; symphony;
Christmas rhapsody; Twas the night before Christmas, with narrator; Symphonic variations; American rhapsody; Red Rock rhapsody; Descantation;
Lincoln lyric overture; works for instrumental
solos or ensembles.
1304 East University, Bloomington, IN 47401

*LONG, PAGE C.
Lenten elegy on Passion chorale, for organ.

*LONGAS, FEDERICO
b. Barcelona, Spain, 18 Aug. 1895. Studied with
Granados. He was accompanist for Tito Schipa and
toured with him in Europe, the U.S., and South
America; eventually settled in New York. He
wrote piano pieces and many songs.

*LOOMIS, CLARENCE
b. Sioux Falls, S. D., 13 Dec. 1888; d. Aptos,
Calif., 3 Jan. 1965. Studied at Dakota Wesleyan
Univ., B. M.; with Adolf Weidig, American Cons.,
M. A., D. M.; with Leopold Godowsky in Vienna.
He received the Kimball Gold Medal in piano;
Weidig Gold Medal in composition, Lilly Found.
grant. He taught at American Cons., 1914; Chicago
Musical Coll., 1929; Jordan Cons., 1930-36; Highland Univ., 1945-55; Jamestown Coll., 1955-56;
then taught privately in Aptos, Calif.
    WORKS: Opera: A night in Avignon; Castle of
gold; Yolanda of Cyprus; David; The fall of the
house of Usher; The white cloud, 1935; Revival,
1945; The captive woman, 1953; Ballet: The flap-
per and the quarterback; Oak Street Beach; Theatre: music to King Lear; Susanna don't you cry,
musical extravaganza, 1939; Orchestra: Gaelic
suite for strings, 1953; Fantasy, piano and orch.,
1954; Macbeth, 1954; The Passion play, chorus
and orch.; Chamber music: 2 string quartets,
1953, 1963; Chorus: Erin, choral cycle; Song of
the white earth, 1956.

LOOS, ARMIN
b. Darmstadt, Germany, 20 Feb. 1904; U.S. citizen 1937; d. 23 Mar. 1971. Studied harmony and
counterpoint with Paul Buttner in Dresden;
attended Universities of Dresden, Berlin, and
Geneva. In 1928 he came to the U.S. to complete
training for his father's banking business. He
did not return to Germany, but remained in New
York and taught himself composition and the 12-
tone system, successfully enough to win second
prize in a competition in which the first prize
went to William Schuman and the third prize to
David Diamond. The depression shattered his
hopes of earning a living in music and in 1940
he entered a family business in New Britain,
Conn., and continued to compose in his spare
time. Very few of his compositions were heard
in his lifetime, but his work is now highly
acclaimed by those participating in its
performance.
    WORKS: Orchestra: Ciaccona for orch., 1932;
Overture, 1932; Symphony - in memorium Ferruccio
Busoni, New Britain, Conn., 17 Mar. 1974; Symphony - View, approach, goodbye; Missa spiritorum;
Symphony in canon form, 1941; Pastorale and perpetuum mobile, 1941; Psalm 120, chorus and orch.,
1963; Percepts, 1969; Aquarius '70, New Britain,
16 Apr. 1972; Chamber music: 4 string quartets,
1933-65, no.4, Cambridge, Mass., 31 Mar. 1974;
string quintet; Idea in search of configuration,
piano trio, 1930-60; 2 pieces for horn and piano,
1963, Hartford, Conn., 3 Feb. 1974; Piano and
wind quartet, Hartford, Conn., 3 Feb. 1974; woodwind quintet #4, Boston, Mass., 15 Sep. 1974;
wind quintet; violin sonata, 1968, New Britain,
Conn., 4 Feb. 1973; stidy piece for horn, cello,
and piano, 1969; violin sonata #2, New Britain,
Conn., 10 Feb. 1974; Chorus: Elegy for 5 voices,
2nd prize, Fed. Music Project, 1938, performance
and recording through support of Conn. Commission on the Arts, 26 May 1972; Psalm 120, a
cappella; Songs: Triumph; Lebewohl; O Fair;
Piano: Barcarolle d' Hercule a Mooreux, 1929;
5 preludes, 1946; 3 sonatas, 1964, 1966, 1967;
Fantasia, 1967; suite, 1967; 4 klavierstucke,
1967.

LOPATNIKOFF, NIKOLAI
b. Reval, Estonia, 16 Mar. 1903; U.S. citizen
1944. Studied at Petrograd Cons., Helsingfors
Cons., and with Ernst Toch in Berlin. After
graduating from Karlsruhe Technological Coll. as
a civil engineer, he decided to devote full time
to music. He came to New York in 1939. His
many awards in the U.S. include 2 Guggenheim fellowships; Nat. Inst. of Arts and Letters grant;
first prize, Cleveland Orchestra competition,
1943; commissions from Koussevitzky Found.,
Pittsburgh Bicentennial Asso., 1958, Pittsburgh
Plate Glass Company, 1960, American Wind Symphony; election to membership, Nat. Inst. of
Arts and Letters, 1963; ASCAP awards, 1972-74.
He was head of theory and composition, Hartt
Coll. of Music, and at Westchester Cons., professor of composition, Carnegie-Mellon Univ.,
1945-68.
    WORKS: Opera: Danton; Orchestra: 4 sym-
phonies, 1929-72; Opus sinfonicum, 1941;

LOPATNIKOFF, NIKOLAI

(LOPATNIKOFF, NIKOLAI)
sinfonietta, 1942; 2 piano concertos; violin concerto; Concertino for orchestra, 1945; 2 Russian nocturnes, 1945; concerto for 2 pianos; Variazioni concertanti, 1958; Music for orchestra, Louisville, 14 Jan. 1959; Festival overture, Detroit, Oct. 1960; Concerto for wind orchestra, 1963; Chamber music: 3 string quartets; 2 violin sonatas; cello sonata; duo for viola and cello; Variations and epilogue, cello and piano, 1946.
5448 Bartlett St., Pittsburgh, PA 15217

LO PRESTI, RONALD
b. Williamstown, Mass., 28 Oct. 1933. Studied with Louis Mennini and Bernard Rogers, Eastman School of Music. He has received awards from Phi Mu Alpha, 1954, 1970; special Koussevitzky award, 1955; Eastman School for Sketch for percussion, 1956; Coll. Band Directors Nat. Asso., 1957; Syracuse Univ. Festival, 1960; Carl Fischer, 1961; Arizona State Univ. faculty grants, 1967, 1968, 1970; annual ASCAP awards, 1963-73. He was instructor, Texas Techonological Univ., 1959-60; Ford Found. composer-in-residence, Winfield, Kan., 1960-62; assistant professor, Indiana (Pa.) State Coll., 1962-64; associate professor, composer-in-residence, Arizona State Univ., 1964- .
WORKS: Opera: 4 1-act operas; Orchestra: 2 symphonies; The masks, 1956; Kansas overture, 1963; Nocturne, viola and string orch., 1965; Wind ensemble: suite for 8 horns; 1959; suite for 4 horns, 1960; suite for 5 trumpets, 1962; Miniature, brass quartet, 1964; March for winds and drums, 1969; Pageant overture, band, 1963; Elegy for a young American, band, 1967; Chamber music: duo for 2 horns, 1966; trombone trio, 1968; Rondo for timpani and piano, 1972; Chorus: Tribute, with orch., 1961; Meditation, 1964; Alleluia, Christus natus est, 1965; Bell song, 1965; The Earth; Flowers; Rain, 1969; Night, 1972; many works for school ensembles.
200 East Geneva Drive, Tempe, AZ 85281

*LORA, ANTONIO
b. Italy, 1899; to U.S. in early youth; d. 1965. Studied composition with Rubin Goldmark and Eduardo Trucco, piano with Alberto Jonas; with Philip James and Albert Stoessel, New York Univ., 1925-27; at Juilliard School on a fellowship, 1927-31. He made his debut as pianist in New York in 1924; taught at Juilliard School, 1931-36; then made extensive concert tours in Europe; later joined the faculty at Ohio State Univ.
WORKS: Theatre: Launcelot and Elaine, 3-act opera based on Tennyson's Idylls of the King, commissioned by the Cologne State Opera; The legend of Sleepy Hollow, light opera; an operetta for children; a ballet; Orchestra: 2 symphonies; piano concerto, 1948; many chamber works and instrumental pieces; some 50 songs.

LORENZ, ELLEN JANE (Mrs. James B. Porter)
b. Dayton Ohio, 3 May 1907. Studied at Wellesley Coll., B. A.; with Boulanger in Paris; Donald Keats, Antioch Coll. Her awards include Billings prize, Wellesley Coll.; Society of Women in

(LORENZ, ELLEN JANE)
Liberal Professions award, Paris; 2 Mu Phi Epsilon awards; 4 Chapel Choir awards; Sigma Alpha Iota award; and award from American Guild of English Handbell Ringers, Area II. She was editor, Lorenz Publishing Company, 1932-68; director, Dayton Madrigal Singers, 1945-67; choirmaster in various churches, 1932-
WORKS: Theatre: Up on Old Smoky, operetta; Orchestra: Appalachian suite; 5 fairy tales; overture; Chamber music: Japanese suite for flute; 4 short movements for viola; string quartet; 5 microstudies, piano; 4 elegies, string quartet; Chorus: The silver hind, madrigal; Paul Bunyan, cantata; Carols of Christmas, cantata; Stand in awe; Beauty shop quartet; Handbells: A festive ring; many other works for orchestra, chorus, chamber groups, organ, piano. She is also author of textbooks such as The learning choir, and Handbell ringing in church.
324 Oak Forest Drive, Dayton, OH 45419

*LOTH, LOUIS LESLIE
b. Richmond, Va., 28 Oct. 1888; d. Studied piano and composition in Berlin; gave concerts in Germany, then returned to the U.S. and lived in New York as teacher and composer. His more than 500 compositions included 2 symphonies, 2 piano concertos, symphonic poems; numerous piano pieces.

*LOUGHBOROUGH, WILLIAM
For the Big Horn, electronic, 1957. He collaborated with Harry Partch at the Sausalito Electronic Studio, 1951-56.

*LOURIE, ARTHUR VINCENT
b. St. Petersburg, Russia, 14 May 1892; U.S. citizen 1947; d. Princeton, N. J., 13 Oct. 1966. Studied at St. Petersburg Cons., 1909-16. He was a writer on music and political topics for Voice of America, 1947-66. His later compositions include The Blackamoor of Peter the Great, an opera, 1961; Concerto da camera, solo violin and string orch., 1947; The mime, solo clarinet, 1956; Sibylla dicitur, cantata for women's voices and instruments.

*LOVE, LORETTA
The stone princess, musical play on a fairy tale by Karl Bratton, Phoenix, 29 Apr. 1974.

LOVELACE, AUSTIN C.
b. Rutherfordton, N. C., 26 Mar. 1919. Studied at High Point Coll., A. B. 1939, D. M. 1963; at Union Theological Seminary, New York, M. S. M. 1941, D. S. M. 1950. His faculty positions have been at Univ. of Nebraska; Queens Coll., Charlotte, N. C.; Garrett Theological Seminary; Union Theological Seminary; Temple Buell Coll.; he has been organist-choirmaster at various churches; in 1973 at Lovers Lane Methodist Church, Dallas.
WORKS: More than 300 compositions for the church service. He is author of several books on church music and of articles in church music journals.
10428 Hedgeway Drive, Dallas, TX 75229

LOVELL, WILLIAM JAMES
b. Brooklyn, N.Y., 26 Oct. 1939. Studied with
Bain Murray and Julius Drossin, Cleveland State
Univ., B. M. magna cum laude 1973. He was faculty member, Cleveland Music School Settlement,
1971-73; teaching assistant, Cleveland State
Univ., 1973-74.
WORKS: Theatre: music for Lorca's Yerma,
1972; Band: Overture for band, 1971, Cleveland
3 Feb. 1974; Chamber music: Arabesque for reeds,
suite for 5 winds and percussion, 1970; string
quartet, 1972; Chorus: Because I could not stop
for death, with cello, 1971; Elegy, with Chamber
orch., 1972.
7118 Classen Ave., Cleveland, OH 44105

LOVETT, GEORGE
b. Chicago, Ill., 29 July 1932. Studied at
Cleveland Inst. of Music and privately in New
York.
WORKS: Orchestra: Conflict and consecra-
tion; Greatest City in the world, symphonic
suite on New York; Stevenson: A call to greatness; Opus 10: Viewpoint, overture; Note of
triumph: 1970, overture; Chamber music: Dramatic excursions, violin and piano; 2 string
quartets.
325 West 45th St., Apt. 905
New York, NY 10036

*LOWENBERG, KENNETH
The liturgy of the Lord's supper, chorus and
organ.

LOWENS, IRVING
b. New York, N.Y., 19 Aug. 1916. Studied with
Edwin John Stringham, Columbia Univ., B. S. 1939;
Univ. of Maryland, M. S. 1957; also with Howard A.
Murphy and Quinto Maganini. He has been music
critic, Washington Evening Star, 1953-60, chief
critic 1961- ; reference librarian for sound
recordings, Library of Congress, 1959-61, assistant head, reference section, music division,
1961-66.
WORKS: Orchestra: Variations on a Peruvian
theme; clarinet concertino; Fantasy for string
orch., string quartet, and flute; Chamber music:
The miller o'Fyfe, flute and piano: Chorus:
Laudate, women's voices; Sing, my tongue, the
Saviour's glory; Songs: Come away death; Love
is a sickness; Peasants; The rune of hospitality;
Old Christmas returned; many choral arrangements
of works by early American composers.
503 Heron House, Reston, VA 22090

LOWMAN, KENNETH E. W.
b. Walla Walla, Wash., 13 June 1916. Studied
with Dorothy James, Eastern Michigan Univ.; and
with Franklyn Marks in Los Angeles. He has been
a free lance composer for motion pictures and
television.
WORKS: Theatre: Chinese nightingale, children's musical; The magic fish, children's musical; music for Finnegan's Wake, woodwind trio;
Orchestra: Sea god and sandpiper, solo cello and
oboe with orch.; Suite for strings; Chamber music:
Los Angeles sketches, oboe, clarinet, viola, bassoon; 10 etudes for bassoon; 3 pieces for oboe

(LOWMAN, KENNETH E. W.)
and cello; trio for violin, viola, bassoon; Postcard suite, woodwind trio; Baroque and roll,
piano and 3 woodwinds; sonata for 2 oboes; woodwind quintet; horn trio; Concert piece for harp;
The nobleman, narrator, 3 winds, 2 strings; Treasure of the Tamarack, narrator, 3 winds, 2
strings; Frog pond symphony, narrator and quintet;
Variations for a mime, 3 winds, 2 strings; duos
for violin, clarinet, or oboe with bassoon.
P. O. Box 4261, Burbank, CA 91503

LOY, D. GARETH
b. Los Angeles, Calif., 20 June 1945. Studied
with Peter Sacco, Henry Onderdonk, Herbert
Bielawa, George Burt, San Francisco State Univ.
He held the Carla Roed scholarship for composition, 1970-73. He was director, New Arts Forum,
1970-72; acting director, electronic music laboratory, San Francisco State Univ., 1973.
WORKS: Chamber music: duet for violin and
cello, 1972-74; Musique concréte: Tetraque,
1972; 10A, 1972; Electronic: Suggestions, percussion and tape, 1973; Towards the garden, solo
synthesizer, 1973; Responsive reading #99, vocal
quartet and synthesizer, 1974.
27A Delmar St., San Francisco, CA 94117

LU, YEN
b. Nanking, China, 7 Sep. 1930; to U.S. 1963.
Studied with William Sydeman, Mannes Coll. of
Music; and with Mario Davidovsky, City Coll.,
CUNY. She has been editor with a music publisher, 1971- .
WORKS: Orchestra: Music for orchestra I,
1969, II, 1970; Chamber music: Piece for 7
players, 1967; quartet for flute, bass trombone,
piano, percussion, 1968; quartet for clarinet,
tuba, 2 percussionists, 1970; violin sonata,
1972; Some days I toss in bed, mezzo soprano and
chamber ensemble, 1973.
335 East 94th St., Apt. 28
New York, NY 10028

LUBIN, ERNEST
b. New York, N.Y., 2 May 1916. Studied with
Nadia Boulanger, summer 1932 in Fontainebleau;
Columbia Univ., B. S., M. S.; with Roger
Sessions, Manhattan School of Music; with Ernest
Bloch and Darius Milhaud. He held a scholarship
at Manhattan School; received the Bearns prize
at Columbia, 1938; annual ASCAP awards for a
number of years. He was music critic, New York
Times, 1945, 1949-50; has taught at High School
of Performing Arts, New York, 1959- .
WORKS: Opera: The pardoner's tale, 1-act;
Orchestra: Variations on a pastoral theme;
Band: Wayfaring stranger; Chamber music: 2
string quartets; trombone sonata; violin sonata;
many choral works, songs, piano pieces.
336 Fort Washington Ave., New York, NY 10033

*LUBOFF, NORMAN
b. Chicago, Ill., 14 May 1917. Studied at Chicago Univ.; Central Coll., B. A.; with Leo
Sowerby, American Cons. He taught at Central
Coll.; was arranger and coach for radio shows
in Chicago; from 1948 on staff of Warner

LUBOFF, NORMAN

(LUBOFF, NORMAN)
Brothers in Hollywood. His works include African mass for chorus and tuned drums; popular songs.

LUCAS, THEODORE D.
b. San Diego, Calif., 22 Jan. 1941. Studied with David Ward-Steinman, San Diego State Univ.; Gordon Binkerd and Thomas Frederickson, Univ. of Illinois, Ph. D.; and with Nadia Boulanger in Paris. He was faculty member, Univ. of Missouri, St. Louis, 1967-69; assistant professor, Beloit Coll., 1969-   .
WORKS: Chamber music: sextet for horns; Aberrations No.VII, piano; Chorus: America-God love it; Electronic: Trialog, flute, harpsichord and tape; Meta-music, flute and tape, New York, 3 Mar. 1973.
647 College St., Beloit, WI 53511

LUCIER, ALVIN
b. Nashua, N. H., 14 May 1931. Studied with David Kraehenbuhl, Howard Boatwright, Quincy Porter, Yale Univ.; Arthur Berger, Harold Shapero, and Irving Fine at Brandeis Univ.; with Lukas Foss at Tanglewood; with Boris Porena in Rome. His awards include a Fulbright scholarship for study in Rome, 1960-62; commissions from Merce Cunningham Dance Company; Gentle Fire Ensemble, Great Britain; New Music Ensemble, Providence, R. I.; Radio Bremen, 1972; Viola Farber Dance Company. He was director, Brandeis Univ. Choral Union, 1962-70; director, electronic and computer music facility, Wesleyan Univ., 1970-   ; music director, Viola Farber Dance Company, 1973-   .
He was co-founder with Robert Ashley, David Behrman, and Gordon Mumma of the Sonic Arts Union, a group for the composition and performance of electronic theatre music.
WORKS: Theatre: music for The water of Babylon, 1965; Fire! by John Roc; King Henry V, 1969; Chamber music: Action music for piano, 1962; Song for soprano, 1962; Electronic: Music for solo performer, enormously amplified brainwaves used to resonate percussion instruments, 1965; North American time capsule, voices and Sylvania vocoder, 1967; Vespers, acoustic orientation by means of echolocation, 1967; Chambers, sounds from moving resonant objects, 1968; The only talking machine of its kind in the world, for stutterer and tape delay system, 1969; Hartford memory space, environmental mimicry for orchestra, 1970; I am sitting in a room, voice and tape, 1970; Quasimodo, the great lover, long distance sound transmission, 1970; The Duke of York, alteration of vocal identities, 1971; Gentle Fire, 1971; The queen of the south, for players, responsive surfaces, strewn material, closed-circuit television monitoring system, 1972; Room simulation 1, The bird of Bremen flies through the houses of the burghers, a computer-controlled environment, 1972. He is author of the book, Chambers, interviews on music and environment.
7 Miles Ave., Middletown, CT 06457

*LUCKE, KATHARINE E.
b. Baltimore, Md., 22 Mar. 1875; d. Baltimore, 21 May 1962. Studied at Peabody Cons., diploma

(LUCKE, KATHARINE E.)
1904; joined the Peabody faculty in 1919. Her compositions included Family portrait, performed by the U.S. Marine Symphony Orchestra, Washington, D.C., 1950; a piano trio; numerous published choral works and songs. Her highly successful Keyboard harmony for piano was followed in 1959 by Keyboard harmony for organ.

LUCKMAN, PHYLLIS
b. New York, N. Y., 13 Sep. 1927. Studied at Hunter Coll., B. A. 1947; with Fred Fox, California State Coll. at Hayward; with Darius Milhaud, Mills Coll., M. A. 1973. She was professional cellist, 1959-69; private cello teacher, 1956-   .
WORKS: Orchestra: Symphony for massed cellos; Chamber music: Fantasia for 2 flutes; 5 puzzles, solo clarinet; Hart Crane/Proem, solo percussionist; Spirals, harpsichord; Songs from underground, tape and string quartet; Templates, 8 to 13 performers.
668 Fairmont Ave., Oakland, CA 94611

LUEDEKE, RAYMOND
b. Bronx, N. Y., 11 Nov. 1944. Studied with George T. Jones, Catholic Univ.; and with George Crumb at Dartmouth Coll. He received a Fulbright grant to study in Vienna, 1966-67. He has been faculty member, Univ. of Wisconsin, Stevens Point, 1971-   .
WORKS: Orchestra: Chamber symphony; Band: Paterson; Chamber music: Krishna, tuba and percussion; Pictures from Breughel, woodwind quintet; Wonderland duets, narrator and 2 tubas; 15 inventions, 2 clarinets; 5 pieces for flute, cello and harp.
1708 Strongs Ave., Stevens Point, WI 54481

LUENING, OTTO
b. Milwaukee, Wis., 15 June 1900. Studied at Royal Acad. of Munich, 1915-17; with Volkmar Andreae, Zurich Municipal Cons., 1917-20; and privately with Philipp Jarnach and Ferruccio Busoni. His honors include 3 Guggenheim fellowship, 1930, 1931, 1974; founder and chairman, American Music Center, 1940-60; Nat. Inst. of Arts and Letters grant, 1946, election to membership 1947, vice president 1953; composer-in-residence, American Acad. in Rome, 1958, 1961, 1965; honorary doctorate, Wesleyan Univ., 1963; Laurel Leaf, American Composers Alliance, for distinguished achievement in fostering and encouraging American music; Thorne Music Fund $1000 award and citation, 1972; membership on many boards and committees including USIA Music Advisory Committee, UNESCO, 1953-   . He was active as flute recitalist and conductor in Munich and Zurich, 1915-20; co-founder of American Grand Opera Company, Chicago, conducted first all-American opera performance, 1922; director opera department, Eastman School of Music, and conductor, Rochester American Opera Company, 1925-28; associate professor, Univ. of Arizona, 1932-34; chairman, music department, Bennington Coll., 1934-44; Barnard Coll., 1944-47; on faculty, Columbia Univ., 1949-68, professor emeritus,

(LUENING, OTTO)
1968-   ; faculty, Columbia School of the Arts,
1968-   ; co-director, Columbia-Princeton Electronic Music Center, 1959-   .
    WORKS: Opera: Evangeline, 1932-47, awarded
the David Bispham Medal, 1933; Orchestra: First
music for orchestra, 1924; 2 symphonic fantasias,
1924, 1939-49; Fantasia, 1925; Serenade, 3 horns
and string orch., 1927; 2 symphonic interludes,
1935; flute concertino, 1937; Pilgrims' hymn,
1947; Prelude for chamber orch., 1947; Legend,
oboe and string orch., 1951; Kentucky concerto,
1951; Music for orchestra, 1952; Wisconsin suite,
1955; Serenade, flute and strings, 1957; Lyric
scene, flute and strings, 1958, Johnson, Vt.,
23 Aug. 1972; Song, poem and dance, flute and
strings, 1958; Short symphony, chamber orch.,
1969; Sonority forms for orch., 1973; Chamber
music: sextet, 1918; 2 string quartets, 1919,
1928; trio, flute, violin, soprano, 1924; The
soundless song, soprano, string quartet, flute,
clarinet, piano, 1924; Fantasia, clarinet and
piano, 1936; flute sonata, 1937; suite for cello
and piano, 1946; Nocturnes, oboe and piano, 1951;
bassoon sonata, 1952; trio, violin, flute, piano,
1952; trombone sonata, 1953; sonata for solo bass,
1958; sonata for viola solo; sonata for cello
solo; 3 sonatas for violin solo, #3 premiered,
New York, 7 Mar. 1971; 5 suites for flute solo;
8 tone poems for 2 violas, Albany, N. Y., 27 Jan.
1972; Introduction and allegro, trumpet and
piano, New York, 13 Mar. 1972; Electronic: Fantasy in space, Low speed, Invention, all tape
alone, 1952; Theatre piece #2, tape, voice, brass,
percussion, narrator, 1956; Synthesis, tape and
orch., 1960; Gargoyles, violin and tape, 1961;
Sonority canon, 4 solo flutes with 33 flutes on
tape, 1962; Moonflight, tape, 1967; Fugue, chorale, fantasy, organ with electronic doubles,
1973; No Jerusalem but this, excerpts performed,
Johnson, Vt., 30 Aug. 1972; also a number of
pieces in collaboration with Ernst Bacon, Halim
El Dabh, and Vladimir Ussachevsky.
    460 Riverside Drive, New York, NY 10027

*LUKE, RAY E.
    b. 1928. Is professor, Oklahoma City Univ.
His works include 2 symphonies; bassoon concerto;
Prelude and march for band.
    6017 Glencover Place, Oklahoma City, OK 73132

LUND, JOHN-PETER
    b. Norwalk, Conn., 15 July 1948. Studied with
Lawrence Moss and Donald Martino, Yale Univ.;
with Bulent Arel, State Univ. of New York, Stony
Brook, where he is a part-time lecturer.
    WORKS: Chamber music: Soliloquy, unaccom-
panied clarinet; Tiamat, 2 pianos, 6 players;
Coupling, flute and tuba.
    29 Chestnut Stump Road, Northport, NY 11768

LUNDBORG, CHARLES ERIK
    b. Helena, Mont., 31 Jan. 1948. Studied with
Eugene Weigel, Univ. of Montana; with Charles
Wuorinen, New England Cons.; with Jack Beeson,
Harvey Sollberger and Wuorinen, Columbia Univ.
He received a Charles Ives scholarship, Nat. Fed.

(LUNDBORG, CHARLES ERIK)
    of Music Clubs. He teaches in the Newark Com-
munity Center of the Arts, 1973.
    WORKS: Orchestra: piano concerto, The
sleeping giant; Chamber music: sextet, 1971;
trio.
    403 West 115th St., Apt. 41
    New York, NY 10025

LUNDE, IVAR, JR.
    b. Tonsberg, Norway, 15 Jan. 1944; to U.S. 1966.
Studied at Oslo Cons., M. A.; with Lardrot,
Klepac, Melles and Scherchen, Salzburg Mozarteum;
with Axelsson, Univ. of Lund, Sweden. He was
solo oboist, Den Norske Opera, 1964-66; oboe and
saxophone instructor, Univ. of Maryland, 1966-68;
assistant professor of oboe and theory, Univ. of
Wisconsin, Eau Claire, 1968-   .
    WORKS: Orchestra: Metamorphoses (also
transcribed for band); Aiga; Nordic suite; Chamber music: Theme and variations, oboe and harpsichord; sonatine for violin and piano; horn
sonatine; Image, oboe, bassoon, percussion;
suite for woodwind quintet; Drawings, woodwind
trio; Four for nine, soprano, baritone, chamber
ensemble; 3 short pieces for solo oboe; oboe
sonatine; 6 Norwegian poems for soprano and piano;
suite for brass quintet; Chorus: Psalm 43;
Nocturne, chamber choir, narrator, 2 tape recorders, oboe, clarinet, percussion, 1973; Keyboard: Sonatina classique, piano; Toccata and
fugue, harpsichord; piano sonata #2.
    3443 Riley St., Eau Claire, WI 54701

*LUNDE, LAWSON
    b. 1935. Studied with Robert Delaney, North-
western Univ., B. A. 1957; with Vittorio Rieti
on scholarship. He was a Quiz Kid on radio for
8 years; piano soloist with the Chicago Symphony
at 14. His works include a sonata for saxophone
duo, Muncie, Ind., 8 May 1967; alto saxophone
sonata.

*LUNDQUIST, CHRISTIE
    Music for 2 clarinets and percussion, Fullerton,
Calif., 3 May 1969.
    1323 Norwood St., Anaheim, CA 92805

LUNETTA, STANLEY GEORGE
    b. Sacramento, Calif., 5 June 1937. Studied at
Sacramento State Coll., B. A.; with Larry Austin,
David Tudor, Karlheinz Stockhausen, and John
Cage, Univ. of California, M. A. He has been
composer/performer and percussion instructor,
1953-   ; editor of Source magazine, 1971-   .
    WORKS: Mostly multi-media: Quartet '65; A
piece for bandoneon and strings, 1966; PFFT, percussion trio, 1965; Zupfgeige Rinne, 1966; piano
music, 1966; Many things for orchestra, 1966;
PanJorGin, 1966; The word, 1966; Free music,
1967; The wringer, 1967; Funkart, 1967; Ta-ta,
1967; Hulk, 1967; I am definitely not running
for vice president, 1968; Spider-song, 1968;
Mr. Machine, 1969; The unseen force, 1972; A day
in the life of the Muzak machine, 1972.
    2101 22nd St., Sacramento, CA 95818

LUSE, ROBERT

*LUSE, ROBERT
b. Baltimore, Md. Studied with Stefans Grove at Peabody Cons. His Concerto grosso for guitar duo and his guitar quintet were performed in the Westinghouse World of the guitar, May 1969.

LUTHER, WARREN PHILLIPS
b. Chicago, Ill., 13 May 1939. Studied with Paul Bellam, Wittenberg Univ.; Carlos Surinach, Yale Univ.; Nadia Boulanger in Paris; Mario Davidovsky, Manhattan School of Music; Scott Huston, Cincinnati Coll. Cons. In addition to being composer/conductor, he plays viola, viola da gamba, piano, percussion, koto, horn and double bass. He has been a teacher in public schools and at Edward Williams Coll., N. J. He was founder of the Great Proletarian Cultural Locomotive Gamelan Society, a percussion ensemble devoted to playing newly commissioned works.
WORKS: Orchestra: Suite of autumn dances, strings, 1960; 3 pieces for small orch., 1961; viola concerto, 1962; Sinfonietta, 1968; double-bass concerto, 1970; Chamber music: 2 suites from The imperial river, chamber ensemble, 1970-72; Prelude and toccata, winds and percussion, 1971; The tropical helmsman, trombone, koto, percussion sextet, 1971; Theme with variations, chamber ensemble, 1971; The Tierra del Fuegan, musical joke for woodwind trio and basso continuo, 1974; Voice: 3 songs of e. e. cummings, soprano, 1960; 5 songs for soprano on composer's texts, 1961; 3 Haiku songs for soprano, 1961.
2427 Clifton Ave., Cincinnati, OH 45219

*LUTI, VINCENT F.
Mixed quintet, flute, clarinet, viola, cello, piano.

LUTYENS, SALLY SPEARE
b. Syracuse, N. Y., 31 Oct. 1927. Studied with Paul Poepple, Bennington Coll.; composition at Univ. of Southern California. She was a fellow, Bennington Composers Conference, 1968; has received commissions. She is head, music department, Cambridge School, Weston, Mass.
WORKS: Chamber music: Midsummer night's dream, prepared piano, 2 flutes, 2 cellos, 1969; A parody, flute, soprano, violin, piano; Encore, piano; Antigone, electronic tape, 1970; Dance technique demonstration, piano, flute, percussion, 1971, 1972; Journeys, piano and percussion, 1973; Alice is; Byzantine omlette; The birds, 1973; piano trio, 1973; recorder trio, 1973.
49 Wellesley St., Weston, MA 02193

LYBBERT, DONALD
b. Cresco, Iowa, 19 Feb. 1923. Studied at Univ. of Iowa, B. M. 1946; with Elliott Carter and Otto Luening, Columbia Univ. M. A. 1950; and with Nadia Boulanger at Fontainebleau, France. He received the Hunter Coll. Shuster award, 1963; faculty research grant, City Univ. of New York, 1970. He was instructor in brass ensemble, Juilliard School, 1947-48; professor, Hunter Coll., 1954- .
WORKS: Opera: Monica, 1952; The scarlet letter, 1965; Chamber music: Introduction and toccata, brass and piano, 1955; wind trio, 1957;

(LYBBERT, DONALD)
chamber sonata, horn, viola and piano, 1958; Sonorities for 11 instruments, 1960; Sonata brevis, piano, 1962; Praeludium, brass and percussion, 1962; Lines for the fallen, soprano and 2 pianos at the quarter tone, 1967; From harmonium, song cycle for high voice; Chorus: Austro terris influente, 3 motets; Zap, an oratorio.
R.R. 2, Box 465, Pound Ridge, NY 10576

*LYNN, GEORGE
b. Edwardsville, Pa., 5 Oct. 1915. Studied with Roy Harris, Westminster Choir Coll., B. M.; Princeton Univ., M. A.; received an honorary L. L. D., Harding Coll., Rockefeller grant. He was on the staff, Westminster Choir Coll. to 1950; visiting lecturer, Univ. of Colorado Iliff Theological Seminary, 1950-52; conducted Lynn Singers, 1956; guest conductor of various orchestras; lecturer at colleges and churches.
WORKS: Orchestra: 2 symphonies; Gettysburg address, baritone, chorus, orch.; Greek folksong rhapsody, contralto, chorus, orch.; Lincoln symphony, chorus and orch.; piano concerto; concert overture; Chamber music: 3 string quartets; 2 piano sonatas; organ trio sonata; piano quintet, organ pieces; Chorus: 3 sacred symphonies; And yet have believed, cantata; and songs.
2890 Joyce, Golden, CO 80401

MABRY, JOHN
b. Spartanburg, S. C., 9 Feb. 1926. Attended Stetson Univ.; and Columbia Univ. He was director, Spartanburg High School Chorus, 1951-72, coordinator of music Spartanburg City Schools, 1972- ; organist and choirmaster, Calvary Baptist Church, 1950- ; music director, Flat Rock Summer Playhouse, 1961-65.
WORKS: Theatre: music for Pied Piper of Hamelin; Chorus: Make way for Christ; Jesus our Lord; How tedious and tasteless the hour; Rejoice all ye nations; And peace shall reign again; Sounds of today; Higher ground; and others.
153 Victoria Road, Spartanburg, SC 29301

McAFEE, CARLTON FRED, JR.
b. Gadsden, Ala., 5 Jan. 1938. Studied at Campbell Coll., B. A.; with David Van Vactor, Univ. of Tennessee; Iain Hamilton, Duke Univ.; Roger Hannay, Univ. of North Carolina, M. M.; and with Richard Hervig, Univ. of Iowa, Ph. D. He has been assistant professor, Univ. of North Carolina at Wilmington, 1971- .
WORKS: Chamber music: Diaphonia for 12 strings; Abscissa for 4 female voices and 2 percussionists; Electronic: Box for alto recorder and 4-channel tape; Preamble: Foreplay, 4 cellos, 4 trombones, and electronics.
Box 866, Wrightsville Beach, NC 28480

McAFEE, DON
b. Roanoke, Va., 3 June 1935. Studied at Lynchburg Coll., B. A. 1956; Union Theological Seminary, M. S. M. 1958; with Nadia Boulanger in Fontainebleau, France; and with Robert Baker and Elaine Brown. He was a church music director, White Plains, 1958-65; editor, manager, and

(McAFEE, DON)
president of music publishing companies, 1965-71;
president, McAfee Music Corporation, 1971-   .
WORKS: Theatre: Great Scot!, off-Broadway
musical; Chorus: A choric psalm, speaking chorus and percussion; Corinthians on love; Graffiti;
The morning Times, a madrigal for tomorrow morning's breakfast; I will lift up mine eyes; and
some 200 other published choral works.
180 West End Ave., New York, NY 10023

McANANEY, HAROLD
b. Dublin, Ireland, 28 Oct. 1948; to U.S. 1967.
Studied at School of the Museum of Fine Arts,
Boston; privately with Tibor Pusztai, Oliver
Knussen, and Lawrence Scripp. He has held fellowships from Ford Found.; Louis Comfort Tiffany;
and Boston Museum of Fine Arts. He was composer-
in-residence, Movement Laboratory, Boston Center
for the Arts, 1970-73; founder of The Annex Players, a contemporary performance group, 1972-   .
WORKS: Chamber music: Braille music, 1970;
Card piece, 1971; Sentientevents, 1973;
Myxomycete, commissioned by Carpenter Centre for
the Visual Arts, Harvard Univ., 1973.
P. O. Box 605, Stinson Beach, CA 94970

McBETH, WILLIAM FRANCIS
b. Ropesville, Tex., 9 Mar. 1933. Studied with
Macon Sumerlin, Hardin-Simmins Univ.; with Kent
Kennan, Univ. of Texas; Howard Hanson and
Bernard Rogers, Eastman School of Music, Ph. D.
His awards include Presley award, Hardin-Simmins
Univ., 1954; College Band Directors Nat. Asso.
award, 1961; Howard Hanson prize, Eastman School,
1963; annual ASCAP awards, 1965-72; and many
commissions. He has been professor, Ouachita
Univ., 1957-   ; and conductor, Little Rock
Symphony, 1969-   .
WORKS: Orchestra: 4 symphonies; Suite on a
Biblical event; Overture; Quanah; Pastorale and
allegro; Allegro agitato; Pastorale for wood-
winds and strings; Band: Divertimento; Orfadh;
Cavata; Reflections past; Chant and jubilo; Nar-
rative; Mosaic; Joyant narrative; Battaglia;
Cantique and Faranade; Masque; Drammatico; Diver-
gents; Seventh seal; Big sounds for young bands;
Chamber music: 4 frescos for 5 brass; Canticle
for 11 winds and percussion; Chorus: Gloria;
And Isaiah prophesied; Billy in the Darbies;
Voice: Young thought; Lamentation and gloria of
David; The snow leopard; Piano: Scherzo; 5 projections; 3 pieces.
1811 Sylvia Road, Arkadelphia, AR 71923

MacBRIDE, DAVID HUSTON
b. Oakland, Calif., 3 Oct. 1951. Studied with
Andrew Imbrie and Richard Felciano, Univ. of
California, Berkeley; with Edward Miller and
Edward Diemente, Hartt Coll. of Music. He received a City of Berkeley Creative Achievement
award, 1969; Hartt Coll. composition award,
1971-72; Isadore Freed scholarship, 1970-73. He
has been accompanist, Hartford Ballet Company,
1972-   ; was music director, Aetna Players,
1973.
WORKS: Chamber music: Illegal tender,
bassoon and prepared piano; string quartet;

(MacBRIDE, DAVID HUSTON)
Once removed, string orch.; Chamber field, 4
unspecified instruments; Total recall, organ;
Envelop, solo percussion.
711 Main St., Newington, CT 06111

McBRIDE, ROBERT GUYN
b. Tucson, Ariz., 20 Feb. 1911. Studied with
Otto Luening, Univ. of Arizona, B. M. 1933,
M. M. 1935. He received a Guggenheim fellowship,
1937; American Acad. of Arts and Letters award,
1942; Composers Press award, 1943. He played
clarinet and saxophone in movie and dance bands;
was oboist, Tucson Symphony; faculty member
Bennington Coll., 1935-46; free-lance composer
and performer, New York, 1946-57; professor,
Univ. of Arizona, 1957-   .
WORKS: Orchestra: Bop pizzicato; Broken
ukelele; Prelude to a tragedy, 1935; Fugato on
a well-known theme, 1935; Concerto for doubles;
Mexican rhapsody, 1935; Workout for chamber
orchestra, 1936; Stringitis; Swing stuff, 1936;
Show piece, 1937; music to Turandot, 1941; Punch
and the Judy, 1941; Strawberry jam, 1942; Harlem
square dance; Ill-tempered; Popover, clarinet
and orch., 1943; Stuff in G, 1943; Jazz symphony,
ballet music; Variations on an unknown theme;
Bop sophisticate, 1947; March of the be-bops,
1948; Jingle-jangle; Pumpkin eater's little
fugue, 1952; Variety day, violin concerto, 1954;
Fantasy on a Mexican Christmas carol, 1955; Pioneer spiritual, 1956; Panorama of Mexico, 1960;
Band: Hollywood suite; Sherlock Holmes suite,
1945; Lonely landscape; Sideshow; Technicolor;
Chamber music: Aria and toccata, violin and
piano; piano quintet, 1933; Prelude, violin and
piano; Depression sonata, violin and piano, 1934;
5 winds blowing, woodwind quintet; Bells, horn
and piano, 1935; Fugue, oboe and 2 clarinets,
1935; Fugata no. 2 on a well-known theme, oboe
and 2 clarinets, 1935; In the groove, flute and
piano; Prelude and fugue, string quartet, 1936;
oboe quintet, 1947; Hot-shot divertimento, oboe
and clarinet, 1938; Swing stuff, clarinet and
piano, 1938; Wise apple five, clarinet quintet,
1940; Cuatro milpas por en quinteto, Mexico folk
tune, 1941; Jam session, woodwind quintet, 1941;
Stuff, violin and piano, 1942; Rudiments of
rug-cutting, piano trio or oboe, bassoon, piano;
Boogie, saxophone and piano, 1943; Popover,
clarinet and piano, 1945; Wise apple, clarinet
and piano, 1945; Workout, oboe and piano; The
world is ours, clarinet and piano; String four-
some, string quartet, 1947; Chorus: Hot stuff
(we hope), men's voices, clarinet and piano;
Sir Patrick Spence, men's voices; also songs
and piano pieces.
3236 East Waverly, Tucson, AZ 85716

McCARTY, FRANK L.
b. Pomona, Calif., 10 Nov. 1941. Studied with
David Ward-Steinman, San Diego State Coll.;
with David Raksin, Ingolf Dahl, Univ. of Southern California, M. M.; with Robert Erickson,
Kenneth Gaburo, Pauline Oliveros, Univ. of California, San Diego. His awards included Screen
Composers Guild fellowship, 1964; Univ. of California Regents fellowship, 1969; composition

McCARTY, FRANK L.

(McCARTY, FRANK L.)
awards from Phi Mu Alpha, 1962; Musical Merit of San Diego, 1962, 1963; Nat. Fed. of Music Clubs, 1963, 1965, 1966; Richmond Professional Inst. 1965; BMI 1966. He was assistant professor, California State Univ., Fullerton, 1966-71; Univ. of Pittsburgh, 1971-   .
WORKS: Chamber music: 5 pieces for flute and piano, 1965; Music for trombone and piano, 1966; Woodwind quintet, 1965; Clocks, percussion ensemble; Color etudes, solo tuba; 5 situations for 4 saxophones; Electronic: Tam-Tammany I-II, tape and lights; Suite - The Bacchae, tape.
549 South Braddock, Pittsburgh, PA 15221

McCARTY, MARY HELEN. See SNOW, MARY McCARTY

McCARTY, PATRICK
b. Zanesville, Ohio, 23 Jan. 1928. Studied with A. Oscar Haugland and Weldon Hart, West Virginia Univ.; Bernard Rogers, Alan Hovhaness, Howard Hanson, Eastman School of Music, Ph. D. He was faculty member, East Carolina Coll., 1954-56; Newark State Coll., 1957-60; professor, Loyola Univ., New Orleans, 1961-   .
WORKS: Orchestra: At a solemn music, soprano and orch.; Band: Ballata; Chorus: Benedictus, chorus and winds; other works for orchestra, band, and chamber groups.
1620 Haring Road, Metairie, LA 70001

McCLAIN, FLOYD A.
b. Alva, Okla., 30 Apr. 1917. Studied with Francis Judd Cooke, Carl McKinley, Leland Proctor, New England Cons.; and with Leo Sowerby, American Cons. He won 2nd place for a harp duet in a Harvey Gaul contest; has received commissions from South Dakota Music Teachers Asso., 1970, 1973; and South Dakota State Activities Asso. He has been professor, Yankton Coll., 1951-   .
WORKS: Theatre: The princess and the frog, 1-act musical; Dakota Dakota Dakota, full-length musical, 1961; Hangin', setting of the story of the murderer of Wild Bill Hickok; Arrow of love, based on novel by Manfred; also orchestral works, chamber music, and songs.
604 East 15th St., Yankton, SD 57078

McCLANAHAN, DAVID RUSSELL
b. Middletown, Ohio, 29 Oct. 1948. Studied with Scott Huston and Paul M. Palombo, Cincinnati Coll. Cons. He was winner in electronic music division, Ohio Fed. of Music Clubs contest, 1973. He was graduate assistant then assistant to the director, electronic music studio, Cincinnati Col. Cons., 1971-   ; music producer, WGUC Radio, 1970-   .
WORKS: Electronic: Linear landscapes, tape, 1971; Okto-echoi, tape, 1972; Modulations, I-IV, piano, synthesizer, and tape, 1972; Echoi I, trumpet and tape, 1972; Echoi II, piano and tape, 1973.
145 West McMillan St., Apt. 325
Cincinnati, OH 45219

McCLEARY, MILLARD A.
Autumn Blue Ridge, orch., York, Pa., 16 Jan. 1947.

*McCLELLAN, JOHN JASPER
b. Payson, Utah, 20 Apr. 1874; d. Salt Lake City, Utah, 2 Aug. 1925. Was appointed organist of the Mormon Tabernacle, Salt Lake City, 1900; organized the Salt Lake City Symphony in 1905, was its conductor to 1910. His compositions include Ode to irrigation for orch.; anthems and organ pieces.

*McCLELLAN, RANDALL
Arioso, oboe and piano; 3 motets, flute and 3 clarinets.
235 West St., Amherst, MA 01002

*MacCOLL, HUGH F.
1885-1953. Suite for violin and piano; Jamaica sketches and 2 Keats songs, medium voice; Noel sketches, organ.

*McCOLLIN, FRANCES
b. Philadelphia, Pa., 24 Oct. 1892; d. there, 26 Feb. 1960. Studied at Inst. for the Blind; Bryn Mawr Coll.; privately with William Gilchrist and H. Alexander Matthews. Her many awards include Chicago Madrigal Club prize; Clemson award; Nat. Fed. of Music Clubs prizes; Mendelssohn Club prize; Dayton Westminster Choir prize; Harvey Gaul prize; Capital Univ. prize; Sigma Alpha Iota prize. She was lecturer and choral conductor as well as composer.
WORKS: Chorus: Welcome, happy morning; The nights o' spring; What care; The singing leaves, cantata; Spring is heaven; Christmas bells; songs and organ pieces.

*McCULLOH, BYRON
Symphony concertante for timpani and orch., Pittsburgh Symphony Orchestra, 21 Dec. 1973.
Department of Music
Carnegie-Mellon University
Pittsburgh, PA 15213

McDANIEL, WILLIAM J.
b. Jellico, Tenn., 4 Mar. 1918. Studied with Weldon Hart and John Vincent, Western Kentucky Univ., B. M.; Walter Ihrke and Arnold Salop, George Peabody Coll., M. M.; with Philip Slates and Normand Lockwood, Univ. of Denver. He was chairman of theory, Wayland Baptist Coll., 1948-50; chairman, music department, Missouri Baptist Coll., 1951-52; and at Southern Baptist Coll., 1953-   .
WORKS: Opera: The green tint, chamber opera in 1 act, Eureka Springs, 18 July 1974; Waterhole, chamber opera; Ballet: The legend of petit Jean, Little Rock, 1965; Orchestra: symphonic movement; Chamber music: woodwind trio; woodwind quintet; Chorus: Whilst o'er the fields of Greece, spoken choral with percussion; A song from Solomon; Alleluia, Amen; Psalm 96; 'Tis the glory of my time; Songs: How do I love thee; Psalm IV; cycle from Aesop's Fables; settings from the Rubaiyat for baritone and women's voices.
221 Southeast 2nd St.
Walnut Ridge, AR 72476

*MacDERMID, JAMES G.
  b. Utica, Ont., 10 June 1875; U.S. citizen 1906;
  d. Brooklyn, N. Y., 16 Aug. 1960. Studied in
  London, Ont., and in Chicago; toured as piano
  soloist and accompanist to his wife, a soprano;
  wrote many sacred and secular songs: My love is
  like a red, red rose; Psalm 91; Behold what manner of love; etc.

*MacDERMOTT, GALT
  b. 1928. Hair, rock opera, 1968; Mass in F,
  1971.

McDERMOTT, VINCENT
  b. Atlantic City, N. J., 5 Sep. 1933. Studied
  with Andre Vauclain, George Rochberg, Karl-Heinz
  Stockhausen, Univ. of Pennsylvania; with Darius
  Milhaud at Aspen, Colo. He has been faculty member, Wisconsin Coll. Cons., 1967-   .
    WORKS: Chamber music: Three for five,
  flute, saxophone, vibraphone, piano, tabla;
  Komal usha-rudra nisha, flute, guitar, sitar,
  double bass; Electronic: He who ascends by
  ecstasy into contemplation of sublime things
  sleeps and sees a dream, piano and tape; Thou,
  restless ungathered, cantata for soprano, clarinet and tape.
    2804 East Linwood Ave., Milwaukee, WI 53211

MacDONALD, CATHERINE
  b. New York, N. Y., 22 Oct. 1940. Studied with
  Meyer Kupferman and Ezra Laderman, Sarah Lawrence
  Coll.; Jacob Druckman and Vittorio Giannini,
  Juilliard School; and with Jack Beeson, Otto
  Luening, Chou Wen-chung, Columbia Univ. She was
  assistant conductor, Interracial Chorale,
  1963-65; conductor, New York Fellowship Chorus,
  1964-65; composition and conducting teacher, The
  New Lincoln School, 1964-70.
    WORKS: Theatre: scores for Twelfth night;
  Enemies; Siamese connections; A streetcar named
  desire; Chorus: Madrigals, women's voices.
    Langdon R.F.D., Alstead, NH 03602

*McDONALD, HARL
  b. Boulder, Colo., 27 July 1899; d. Princeton,
  N. J., 30 Mar. 1955. Studied at Univ. of Southern California, B. M.; Univ. of Redlands, D. M.;
  was vocal accompanist and piano soloist, 1923-24;
  director, music department, Univ. of Pennsylvania,
  1926-46; manager, Philadelphia Orchestra, 1939-55.
    WORKS: Orchestra: 4 symphonies; 2-piano
  concerto; violin concerto; From childhood suite;
  Song of free nations, soprano and orch.; Dirge
  for 2 veterans, women's chorus and orch.; 2
  Nocturnes; Arkansas traveler; 3 Hebrew poems;
  Chamber music: 2 piano trios; quartet on Negro
  themes; Fantasy for string quartet; Chorus: God
  give us men, cantata; many other works.

*MacDONALD, JAMES F.
  b. Alameda, Calif. Studied with Frank Erickson
  and Stanley Hollingsworth, San Jose State Coll.,
  M. A.; has published Psalm 13, chorus and organ.

McDONELL, A. EUGENE
  b. Wausau, Wis., 6 Oct. 1915. Studied at Milwaukee State Teachers Coll., B. S. 1939; with Hilmar

(McDONELL, A. EUGENE)
  Luckhardt, Univ. of Wisconsin, M. S. 1950.
  Except for 1942-46, when he served in the U.S.
  Air Force, he taught in public schools, 1939-64;
  has been associated with the Univ. of Wisconsin
  Center System, 1964-   ; associate professor,
  Baraboo/Sauk County Center, 1972-
    WORKS: Chamber music: Invasion, percussion
  ensemble; piece for woodwinds; 2 choral works.
    6237 Charing Cross Lane, Middleton, WI 53562

*MacDOUGALL, ROBERT
  Studied with Stefans Grové at Peabody Cons.; his
  compositions include Requiem for orch.; and
  Anacoluthon: A confluence, for 4 winds, 3 cellos
  and double bass, New York premiere, 12 Jan. 1975.
    1676 Winder St., San Diego, CA 92103

*McDOWELL, JOHN HERBERT
  b. Washington, D.C., 21 Dec. 1926. Studied at
  Colgate Univ., B. A. 1948; with Jack Beeson,
  Roger Goeb, Otto Luening, Columbia Univ., M. A.
  1957; held a Guggenheim fellowship, 1962.
    WORKS: Modern dance: Insects and heroes,
  1961; From sea to shining sea, an homage to Ives,
  1965; Dark psalters, 1968; Orchestra: Four
  sixes and a nine, 1959; Accumulation, 35 flutes,
  strings, percussion, 1964; Chamber music: Sonia-
  piece (with Ezra Sims), quarter tones for flute
  and tape, Cambridge, Mass., 13 Mar. 1970;
  Tumescent lingam, for oboe, New York, 16 Jan.
  1971; Chorus: Goods news from heaven, cantata,
  1957; and some 400 more works.
    220 East 14th St., New York, NY 10003

*McELHERAN, BROCK
  Here comes the avantgarde, chorus of any type
  voices, narrator, piano, to own text.

MACERO, TEO
  b. Glens Falls, N. Y., 30 Oct. 1925. Studied
  saxophone at Juilliard School, M. S. 1953; composition privately with Henry Brant. He received a BMI student composers award for Areas
  while at Juilliard; 2 Guggenheim grants, 1957,
  1958; commissions from Kansas City Symphony,
  Univ. of Buffalo, and New York Philharmonic
  Orchestra. He was a bandsman, U.S. Navy,
  1944-47; artists and repertoire producer, Columbia Records, 1956-   ; and has appeared as saxophonist with famous jazzmen such as Charles
  Mingus and Thelonius Monk.
    WORKS: Orchestra: Torsion in space, Kansas
  City, Mo., 4 Feb. 1961; Paths, Buffalo, N. Y.;
  Fusions, New York, 11 Jan. 1958; Chamber music:
  One and three quarters, flute, violin, cello,
  trombone, tuba, 2 pianos; Canzona #1, 4 saxophones
  and a trumpet; also many jazz works, over 100
  ballets, documentary film scores, television
  scores, and television themes.
    200 East 71st St., New York, NY 10021

*MacFARLANE, WILLIAM CHARLES
  b. London, England, 2 Oct. 1870; to U.S. 1874;
  d. North Conway, N. H., 12 May 1945. Studied
  organ with his father and with Samuel P. Warren
  in New York. He was church organist in New York,
  1898-1912; municipal organist, Portland Me.,
  1912-19.

MacFARLANE, WILLIAM CHARLES

(MacFARLANE, WILLIAM CHARLES)
WORKS: Operettas: Little almond eyes, 1916;
Sword and scissors, 1918; Chorus: The message of
the cross, cantata; many anthems; Organ: Medita-
tion; Cradle song; Spring song; Scotch fantasy;
Reverie; etc.

*MacFEELEY, P.
They nobly dar'd, opera on American Revolutionary
theme, 1967, revised version to be presented by
New England Regional Opera, Boston, 1976.

McFEETERS, RAYMOND
b. Rushville, Ill., 11 Dec. 1899. Studied piano
with Carl Friedberg, composition with A. Madeley
Richardson, Juilliard School. He received the
Kimball award, Chicago Council of Teachers of
Singing, for a song, 1940. He has been a church
organist in Pasadena and Hollywood since 1920.
WORKS: His compositions are chiefly sacred
and secular art songs and works for piano, violin, and cello.
7169 Sunset Blvd., Hollywood, CA 90046

McGEE, WILLIAM JAMES
b. Great Falls, Mont., 8 June 1936. Studied
with Bernhard Heiden and Thomas Beversdorf,
Indiana Univ. He has been assistant professor,
Southern Mississippi Coll., 1966-   .
WORKS: Orchestra: Miniature for orchestra;
Chamber music: Variations for woodwind trio;
Rhapsody, violin and piano; Lamentation, trumpet
and piano; Hyfrydol, 3 instruments and piano;
3 pieces for cello solo; Chorus: Jesus was a
baby, double chorus, flute, piano, percussion;
I know a little ditty, men's voices; Piano: 2
philosophical observations; Dance-toccata for
the esoterists; Varium et mutabile; Organ: A
joyful procession (Homage to Beethoven); Variations and finale on Olivet; Carol-variations on
Nous voici dans la ville.
Box 333, Collegedale, TN 37315

*McGRATH, JOSEPH J.
b. Oswego, N. Y., 1889; d. Syracuse, N. Y., 1968.
Graduated from Syracuse Univ., 1926; was organist at Cathedral of the Immaculate Conception,
Syracuse; taught at Syracuse Univ. His works
include a symphony; 3 string quartets; many duo
sonatas; 6 brevities for brass quartet; 36
masses; 100 works for organ.

*McHOSE, ALLEN IRVINE
b. Lancaster, Pa., 14 May 1902. Studied at
Franklin and Marshall Coll., B. S. 1923; Eastman
School of Music, B. M. 1927, M. M. 1929; Oklahoma
City Univ., D. M. 1945. He was faculty member, Eastman School of Music, 1930-62, then associate director. His compositions include a
violin sonata, 1929; oboe concerto, 1932.
P.O. Box 247, Naples, NY 14512

McHUGH, CHARLES R.
b. Minneapolis, Minn., 5 Aug. 1940. Studied
with Dominick Argento and Paul Fetler, Univ. of
Minnesota, Ph. D. He won first prize in a contest, Univ. of Minnesota, 1968. He was instructor, Univ. of Minnesota, 1965-70; community

(McHUGH, CHARLES R.)
faculty, Minnesota Metropolitan State Coll. in
1973; co-editor, Synthesis, electronic music
magazine, 1970-71.
WORKS: Orchestra: Symphony no.1, 1965,
2nd movement performed by Minnesota Orchestra,
31 May 1973; symphony no.2, 1968; Divertimento,
small orch., 1968; Chamber music: quintet for
winds, strings, and piano, 1967; Electronic:
Fall music, a collage for 11 players and sound
track, 1971; Requiem, for 12 players and 2 sound
tracks, 1972.
1012 8th St., S.E., Minneapolis, MN 55414

*McHUGH, JIMMY
b. Boston, Mass., 10 July 1894; d. Beverly Hills,
Calif., 22 May 1969. Attended Holy Cross Coll.
His awards included honorary doctorates in music
from Harvard Univ., Georgetown Univ., Holy Cross
Coll.; Presidential Certificate of Merit for
work on war bonds in World War II; American
Legion, Court of Honor award. He was rehearsal
pianist for the Boston Opera Company to 1921,
then lived in New York, where composed for
shows, in Hollywood from 1930 composing for
films. The best known of his shows were Cotton
Club Revues (7 years) and Blackbirds of 1928;
and of his songs: I can't give you anything
but love, baby, 1928; On the sunny side of the
street, 1928; Cuban love song; South American
way, 1929; Comin' in on a wing and a prayer,
1943.

McILWRAITH, ISA ROBERTA
b. Paterson, N. J., 17 May 1909. Studied at
Barnard Coll., B. A.; with Philip James, Daniel
Gregory Mason, Douglas Moore, Columbia Univ.,
M. A.; with Seth Bingham, Union Theological Seminary; with Albert Stoessel, Juilliard School.
Her awards include Phi Beta Kappa; fellowships
at Columbia Univ. and Juilliard School; Associate American Guild of Organists. She was
organist in Brooklyn and New York, 1932-38;
assistant professor, Mt. Holyoke Coll., 1937-38;
associate professor, Univ. of Tennessee at
Chattanooga, 1938-   .
WORKS: Chorus: Appalachian Christmas carol;
Christ our passover; Christians all rejoice;
Hosanna to the son of David; Organ: Triptych
for organ; Adagio and fughetta; Fugue in a;
many unpublished choral and organ works.
105 Druid Drive, Signal Mountain, TN 37377

MacINNIS, DONALD
b. New York, N. Y., 4 Apr. 1923. Studied with
Milton Babbitt, Edward Cone, Bohuslav Martinu,
Roger Sessions, and Randall Thompson at Princeton Univ. He received the Princeton prize in
composition, 1949; 4 faculty fellowships for
humanities research, Univ. of Virginia, 1965,
1970, 1972, 1973; composition fellowship, Univ.
of North Carolina, 1967-68; composer-in-residence,
Atlanta Symphony, 1968-69; first prize, Bowdoin
Coll. national competition, 1973. He has been
faculty member, Univ. of Virginia, 1950-   ;
associate professor and director, electronic
music studio.

(MacINNIS, DONALD)
WORKS: Orchestra: Dialogues, 1960; Intersections for tape recorder and orch.; Wind ensemble: Variations for brass and percussion, 1964; Collide-a-scope, 12 brass instruments and stereo tape, 1971; Chamber music: Toccata for piano and 2-channel tape, 1971; Variations for cello and 2-channel tape, 1971, Bowdoin Coll., 9 Apr. 1973.
316 Kent Road, Charlottesville, VA 22903

McINTOSH, LADD
b. Akron, Ohio, 14 July 1941. Studied with Marshall Barnes, Ohio State Univ., B. M. 1966, M. M. 1970. He has won 5 awards in composition at collegiate and intercollegiate jazz festivals, 1965-68; many awards as leader of college bands; many commissions. He has arranged for night club acts and played in show bands; was woodwind instructor, Ohio State Univ., Ohio State Univ. 1967-68, 1970; assistant professor, Univ. of Utah, 1970-72; assistant professor, Westminster Coll., Salt Lake City, 1972-   .
WORKS: Opera: Today is a good day to die, rock opera, Salt Lake City, 20 Mar. 1972; Band: Reflections, 1965; Ascendancy, 1970; Wind ensemble: saxophone quartet, 1965; Viking suite, brass choir and percussion, 1967; Concert pieces for doublers, 1970; Jazz: A suite for jazz orch., 1965; 5 fantasies for 2 jazz orch., horns, tuba, percussion, 1966; Variations on a rock tune, 1967; The avenging angel and Ichabod Crane, 1972; The fallen warrior, 1972; Munich, Sept. 5, 1972; Groupies, 1973; Chamber music: Echoes from an ancient past, strings and improvised saxophone solo, 1969; many other concert works for jazz orchestra.
4444 Wallace Lane, Salt Lake City, UT 84117

*McINTOSH, THOMAS S.
b. Baltimore, Md., 6 Feb. 1927. Studied at Peabody Cons.; Juilliard School, graduated 1958; played trombone in the U.S. Army Band and with many jazz bands. He has written the song, Something old, something new; and the film score, The learning tree.

*McKAY, DAVID
I thank you god, chorus on e.e. cummings text.

McKAY, GEORGE FREDERICK
b. Harrington, Wash., 11 June 1899; d. Stateline, Nev., 4 Oct. 1970. Studied with Selim Palmgren and Christian Sinding, Eastman School of Music, B. M. 1923, the first graduate in composition. His awards include a national prize for symphony no.1, performed by Rochester Philharmonic; Harvey Gaul prize; first prize, Northern California Harpists Asso., 1960; and many commissions.
WORKS: Orchestra: 4 sinfoniettas, 1925-42; violin concerto, 1940; To a liberator, symphonic poem, 1940; Chamber music: woodwind quintet, 1937; 5 pieces for 4 clarinets; Lyric poem, 4 flutes; 4 string quartets; trombone sonata, 1956; Sonatina espressiva, brass quintet; Suite for harp and flute, 1960; Machine age poetry, instrumental duo suite; Andante mistico, 8 celli and piano; American street scenes, saxophone

(McKAY, GEORGE FREDERICK)
quartet and piano; Sonatina-ballade, clarinet and strings; many chamber works and choral compositions.

*MacKAY, HARPER
b. Boston, Mass., 13 Oct. Studied at Harvard Univ., B. A.; with Halsey Stevens, Univ. of Southern California, M. A., Ph. D. He was assistant music director, Los Angeles Civic Light Opera Company, 1960; arranger for films and television.
WORKS: Orchestra: overture; symphony; Chamber music: clarinet sonatina; 6 minutes for 6 pieces, woodwind trio and string trio; Film scores: Deadwood; Guest shot (television).
3405 Adina Drive, Hollywood, CA 90028

McKAY, NEIL
b. Ashcroft, B. C., Canada, 16 June 1924; U.S. citizen, 1962. Studied with John Weinzweig, Toronto Cons.; at Univ. of Western Ontario, B. A. 1953; with Wayne Barlow, Bernard Rogers, Howard Hanson, Eastman School of Music, Ph. D. 1956. He received the Ottawa Symphony first prize for Canadian composers, 1955; Benjamin prize for quiet music, 1956; MacDowell fellowships, 1961, 1963; Duluth Symphony commission, 1965. He was professor, Univ. of Wisconsin at Superior, 1957-65; professor, Univ. of Hawaii, 1965-   .
WORKS: Opera: Ring around harlequin; Planting a pear tree; Orchestra: symphony no.1; Dance overture; Fantasy on a quiet theme; Structure; Band: Evocations; Gamelan gong; Chamber music: string quartet; horn sonata; violin sonata; Triologue; Worlds, solo koto; Chorus: A dream within a dream; Folksong fantasy; Legends of Maui; Songs: Lazy man's song, baritone and piano; 3 songs on poems of Po Chu-i, soprano, guitar, recorder, percussion.
3310 Keahi St., Honolulu, HI 96822

McKENNEY, W. THOMAS
b. Falmouth, Ky., 24 June 1938. Studied with Scott Huston, Cincinnati Coll.-Cons.; with Bernard Rogers, Eastman School of Music, Ph. D. He received the Martin G. Dumler award, 1963; Music Teachers Nat. Asso. composer of the year award, 1971. He has been faculty member, Univ. of Missouri, Columbia, 1967-   , associate professor, 1971-   .
WORKS: Orchestra: clarinet concertino; Chamber music: 3 miniatures for piano; Dialogue, woodwind quartet; Electronic: The lake, tape.
1224 Jake Lane, Columbia, MO 65201

McKENZIE, JACK H.
b. Springfield, Mo., 11 Nov. 1930. Studied at Univ. of Illinois. He has been instructor to professor, Univ. of Illinois, dean, College of Fine Arts, in 1973.
WORKS: Percussion: Introduction and allegro; 3 dances; Nonet; Rites; Suite for sideman and handclappers; Paths I and II; Pastorale, flute and percussion; Song, trombone and percussion.
27 Sherwin Circle, R.R. 3, Urbana, IL 61801

McKENZIE, WALLACE

McKENZIE, WALLACE
    b. Alexandria, La., 16 June 1928. Studied with
    Philip Greeley Clapp, Univ. of Iowa; with
    George S. Morey, North Texas State Univ.;
    Kenneth B. Klaus, Louisiana State Univ. He
    taught at New Orleans Baptist Theological Sem-
    inary, 1955-64; Wayland Baptist Coll., 1964-68;
    and has been associate professor, Louisiana
    State Univ., 1968- .
        WORKS: Orchestra: Tagelied; Chamber music:
    Sonatina for clarinet, viola, cello, 1954; trum-
    pet sonata, 1957; Introduction and allegro for
    brass, 1958; Sounds for November, clarinet,
    piano, percussion; 3 danses anachronistiques,
    for recorders, cornemuse, viola da gamba, natural
    trumpet, 1973; Chorus: The palm branches, can-
    tata, with soloists and orch., 1960; Old chants,
    with band, 1966; Electronic: music for 2 clar-
    inets and tape; music for violin and tape, 1972;
    music for harp and tape, 1974; and organ pieces.
        School of Music, Louisiana State University
        Baton Rouge, LA 70803

*McKINLEY, CARL
    b. Yarmouth, Me., 9 Oct. 1895; d. Boston, Mass.,
    24 July 1966. Studied at Knox Coll.; with
    Edward Burlingame Hill, Harvard Univ.; with
    Rubin Goldmark and with Nadia Boulanger. Among
    his awards were the Boott prize, 1916; Naumburg
    award, 1917; Flagler prize, 1921; 2 Guggenheim
    fellowships, 1927, 1928. From 1929 he was on
    the faculty, New England Cons.
        WORKS: Orchestra: Indian summer idyll,
    1917; The blue flower, 1921; Masquerade, an
    American rhapsody, 1926; Chorale, variations and
    fugue, 1941; Caribbean holiday, 1948; Chamber
    music: string quartet, 1941; cello sonata, 1953;
    Chorus: The kid, cantata, 1955.

McKINLEY, WILLIAM THOMAS
    b. 9 Dec. 1939. Studied with Nikolai Lopatnikoff,
    Frederick Dorian, Carnegie-Mellon Univ., B. F. A.;
    with Mel Powell, Yehudi Wyner, Lawrence Moss,
    Yale Univ., M. A. and M. F. A.; with Gunther
    Schuller at Tanglewood. He received a BMI award,
    1963; commissions from Fromm Found., 1968, 1970;
    Chicago Symphony, 1971; and Univ. of Wisconsin,
    Univ. of Illinois, Paul Zukofsky, Lowell Creitz.
    He was assistant professor, Univ. of Chicago,
    1969-73; composer-in-residence, New England Cons.,
    1973-   .
        WORKS: Orchestra: Circular forms for grand
    orchestra; triple concerto, jazz trio and orch.;
    Chamber music: trio for 2 violins and cello;
    Quadruplum, large ensemble; Paintings, chamber
    ensemble; Interludes, oboe and piano; Stops II
    and III for woodwinds; Portfolio, solo cello; 6
    songs for voice and piano.
        43 Linnea Lane, Reading, MA 01867

*McKINNEY, HOWARD D.
    b. Pine Beach, N. Y., 29 May 1890. Studied at
    Rutgers Univ.; Columbia Univ., D. M. He was
    organist and music director, Rutgers Univ.,
    1917-22; faculty member to 1963, then professor
    emeritus; editor, J. Fischer & Bros.
        WORKS: Songs: The bagpipe man; 4 crumbs
    from peacock pie; The 3 Maries; A mystery for
    Christmas.

*McKINNEY, MATHILDE
    Studied at Oberlin Cons. and at Juilliard School;
    piano with Lee Pattison and Josef and Rosina
    Lhevinne. She has taught at Wooster Coll., Ohio;
    Douglass Coll.; privately in Pittsburgh, Okla-
    homa, New York, and Princeton; in 1962 was asso-
    ciate professor, Westminster Choir Coll.; gave
    premiere performance of Edward T. Cone's piano
    concerto at Princeton in 1962.
        WORKS: Orchestra: Elegy for string orch.,
    1953, revised 1958; Chamber music: violin
    sonata; string quartet; trio for violin, viola,
    piano; 7 modes, 2 alto recorders; Chorus:
    Christmas cantata, choruses and brass, 1957;
    The wise men, girls' voices, 1957; Organ:
    Fantasy toccata; and piano pieces.
        206 Linden Lane, Princeton, NJ 08540

*McKUEN, ROD
    b. Oakland, Calif., 29 Apr. 1933. Studied at
    San Francisco State Coll.; served in the army
    in the Korean war; has been roving minstrel,
    balladeer, poet and composer; for which he has
    received 11 ASCAP awards.
        WORKS: Orchestra: a symphony; 2 piano con-
    certos; Something beyond; The sea; Structures
    in Jazz; and many popular songs.
        Stanyan, Box 2783, Hollywood, CA 90028

*McLAIN, MARGARET STARR
    b. Chicago, Ill. Studied with Frederick
    Converse and George W. Chadwick, New England
    Cons., and at Trinity Coll., London. She re-
    ceived 2 Endicott prizes in composition at the
    Cons.; was a member of the MacDowell Colony from
    1924. She was faculty member, Boston Univ.,
    from 1928, associate professor, 1949-70, emer-
    itus professor, 1970-   . Her works include
    an overture, 1937; violin sonata; string quin-
    tet; choral works; and songs.

McLAUGHLIN, MARIAN (Mrs. T. R. Ostrom)
    b. Evanston, Ill., 26 Nov. 1923. Studied at
    Northwestern Univ., B. M. E.; with Francis Judd
    Cooke and Carl McKinley, New England Cons.,
    M. M.; and with Walter Piston. She won
    prizes in Northern Virginia American Guild of
    Organists competition; Friday Morning Music
    Club, Washington, D.C. She was instructor,
    Univ. of Evansville, Ind., 1944-46; graduate
    teaching fellow, New England Cons., 1947-48.
        WORKS: Chamber music: 3 fantasies for
    organ; Divertimento for viola and cello; Noc-
    turne and scherzo, solo flute; Chorus: Autumn
    fires, women's choir; Lullaby to a seafarer's
    son, women's voices; many published choral works
    and unpublished compositions for orchestra and
    chamber groups.
        70 North Hopkins Row
        Aberdeen Proving Grounds, MD 21005

*McLEAN, BARTON
    Rondo for band.
        58412 Locust Road, South Bend, IN 46614

MacLEAN, JOHN T.
    b. Jersey City, N. J., 12 Apr. 1933. Studied
    with Dika Newlin at Drew Univ.; Henry Cowell at
    Columbia Univ.; John Boda, Ernst von Dohnanyi,

(MacLEAN, JOHN T.)

Florida State Univ.; Bernhard Heiden, Indiana Univ.; and with Barry Schrader, California Inst. of the Arts. He was winner of Composers Symposium, Brevard Music Center, 1964. He taught in public schools, Jacksonville, Fla., 1961-63; North Carolina Wesleyan Coll., 1966-67; assistant to associate professor, West Georgia Coll., 1967-74; summer instructor, Brevard Music Center, 1964-66, 1968-69.

WORKS: Orchestra: Portrait for oboe and strings; Symphonic dance; Symphony, In memoriam; Chamber music: Suite for 7 wind instruments; Meditation, viola and piano; Portrait, flute, bassoon and strings; 5 movements for 4 household instruments; violin sonata; Canto, string trio; 3 abstractions on human behavior and conditions, string quartet.

West Georgia College, Carrollton, GA 30117

McLEAN, PRISCILLA

b. Fitchburg, Mass., 27 May 1942. Studied with Richard Kent, Fitchburg State Coll.; with Hugo Norden, Boston Univ.; Thomas Beversdorf and Bernhard Heiden, Indiana Univ. She has been lecturer, Indiana Univ., 1971-   .

WORKS: Chamber music: Lighting me as a match, tenor, violin, horn, piano, percussion, 1968; Interplanes, 2 pianos, 1970; Spectra II, prepared piano and percussion, 1972; Electronic: Spectra I, percussion, prepared piano, synthesizer, 1971; Messages, chorus, soloists, electronic auto harp, percussion, recorders, piano, 1973; Night images, synthesizers, 1973.

58412 Locust Road, South Bend IN 46614

*McLIN, LENA

Free at last: a tribute to Martin Luther King, Jr., cantata for chorus.

McMAHAN, ROBERT YOUNG

b. Washington, D.C., 12 July 1944. Studied with Stefan Grove, Robert Hall Lewis, and Jean Ivey, Peabody Cons., B. M., M. M.: and accordion with Louis Coppola. He won the Marie K. Thatcher award at Peabody, 1972; first place, Annapolis Fine Arts composition contest, 1972; and several awards as accordionist. He has been piano instructor, Baltimore County schools, 1968-   ; Samuel Ready School, Baltimore, 1969-70; instructor, Preparatory Department, Peabody Cons., 1972; organist and choirmaster, Stone Chapel Methodist Church, Pikesville, Md., 1972-   .

WORKS: Chamber music: 2 pieces, flute, clarinet, bassoon, and accordion, 1968; 3 movements for 2 winds, guitar, viola, celeste, accordion; Portrait of a Virgo, piano, 1971; Electronic: Whispers of heavenly death, soprano, chamber ensemble, and tape, 1971; Cantata for double chorus, guitar ensemble, accordion, and tape.

28 Wengate Road, Owings Mills, MD 21117

McMILLAN, ANN

b. New York, N. Y., 23 Mar. 1923. Attended Bennington Coll., B. A.; studied with Otto Luening and Edgard Varese; horn with Joseph Singer; was student assistant to Varese, 1953-55.

(McMILLAN, ANN)

Her awards include Tanglewood fellowship, 1948; Fulbright grant, 1955-57; MacDowell fellowships, 1970, 1973; Creative Arts Public Service grant, 1972; Guggenheim fellowship, 1972-73; and many commissions. She was music editor for recording companies, 1949-55; program director, French Broadcasting in North America (RTF/NYC), 1958-64; director, orchestra library, Carl Fischer, 1964-   ; music director, WBAI-FM, 1965-68; manager, Green Mountain Art Gallery, New York, 1968-69; free-lance composer, lecturer, and writer, 1969-   .

WORKS: Electronic: Gong song, tape, 1969; Carefours, tape, 1971; Theater I, music for Home or future soap by Megan Terry, 1971; music for Choose a spot on the floor, play by Schidman and Terry, Omaha, Neb., June 1972; Animal I, Munich, Germany, Mar. 1972; Piece for live saxophone and tape, 1972; Glass reflections, chamber orch., with solo parts for glass percussion, tape, harpsichord, viola, 1973; Sound-silence-song, from film score Black & white, 1972; Turn of the year, film score, 1973.

273 West 10th St., New York, NY 10014

McMULLEN, PATRICK T.

b. Saginaw, Mich., 11 Mar. 1939. Studied with Philip Bezanson, Univ. of Iowa. He taught in public schools, 1962-67; was graduate assistant, Univ. of Iowa, 1967-70; assistant professor, Eureka Coll., 1970-72; and assistant professor, State Univ. Coll., Fredonia, N. Y., 1972-   .

WORKS: Orchestra: Prelude and allegro, string orch., 1968; Band: Bring a torch, Jeanette, Isabella, 1967; March miniature, 1968; 3 sketches, 1973; Chamber music: 3 movements for 2 trumpets, 1966; Chorus: Sanctus, with brass quintet, 1966.

State University College, Fredonia, NY 14063

McNEIL, JAN PFISCHNER

b. Pittsburgh, Pa., 20 Mar. 1945. Studied with David Diamond, David Burge, Univ. of Colorado; with Ben Johnston and Salvatore Martirano, Univ. of Illinois. She has received Mu Phi Epsilon awards, 1967, 1969 (2), 1970, 1971; MacDowell fellowship, 1970; commission, Fischer Found., Iowa State Univ., 1971; appointment as guest composer, Baldwin-Wallace Coll. contemporary festival, 1972; Nat. Endowment for the Arts, South Dakota Council on the Arts grants, 1971, 1972. She was professor, Univ. of South Dakota, 1972-73; graduate assistant, Univ. of Illinois, 1973-   ; assistant director, Fine Arts Center, Clinton, Ill., 1973-   .

WORKS: Theatre: music to Jimmy Shine, 1971; music for Passion in the library, 1973; Chamber music: Epithets I and II, woodwind quintet, 1967; 1969; Snow gifts, large ensemble and tenor solo, 1969; In soundless grasses, 1972; Wind song, 1972; Aureate Earth, tenor, prepared piano, percussion, 1972; Multi-media: Asphodel, 1972.

66 Holiday Drive, Clinton, IL 61727

McNUTT, RONALD JAN

b. Salina, Kan., 4 Oct. 1936. Attended Idaho State Univ., B. A. 1958; studied with Howard

McNUTT, RONALD JAN

(McNUTT, RONALD JAN)
Akers, Herbert Bird, Paul Creston, Robert Paniero, Central Washington State Coll., M. M. 1965. He received the David Herts Memorial award, 1955. Except for a year on the nightclub circuit, 1962-63, he has taught in public schools since 1958, including an international school in Mangla, West Pakistan, 1965-67.
WORKS: Orchestra: Song for strings, 1966; End of a summer day, string orch., 1973; Band: Grand Trunk Road, 1967; R. J.'s Harem, stage band, 1968; India, B. C., 1970; Chamber music: Kern's patter, trio, 1962; Quatren for reflection, woodwind quintet, 1963; sonata for solo horn, 1964; Nocturne for 6 horns, 1964; Prayers, horn solo, 1971; Chorus: Thy kingdom come, with brass and woodwinds, 1965; Be not afraid, 1966; Life leads the thoughtful man, 1967; If anybody cares, 1969.
7526 Sunnycrest Rd., Seattle, WA 98118

*McPHEE, COLIN
b. Montreal, Canada, 15 Mar. 1901; U.S. citizen after 1939; d. Los Angeles, Calif., 7 Jan. 1964. Studied with Gustav Strube, Peabody Cons., graduated 1921; piano with Arthur Friedheim in Toronto, with Paul Le Flem and Isidor Philipp in Paris. His awards included Guggenheim, Huntington Hartford, and Bollingen Found. fellowships; Nat. Inst. of Arts and Letters grant; commissions from the Koussevitzky Found., Louisville Orchestra, and Broadcast Music, Inc. He lived in New York, 1926-30; then in Bali, 1931-39, studying the native music and instruments; taught at Univ. of California, Los Angeles, 1958-64.
WORKS: Orchestra: piano concerto, 1924; concerto for piano and wind octet, 1928; Tabuh-Tabuhan, 2 pianos and orch., 1936; Transitions; symphony #2, 1958; Nocturne, 1958; Pastorale; 4 Iriquois dances; Chamber music: sonatina for 2 flutes, clarinet, trumpet, piano; Chorus: Sea chanty suite, male chorus, 2 pianos, drums; Piano: Inventions and kinesis; Balinese ceremonial music, a set for 2 pianos; Film scores: HO2; Mechanical principles. He was also author of a scholarly work, Music in Bali, 1964; and 2 novels, A house in Bali, 1946, and A club of small men, 1948.

*McPHERSON, FRANCES MARIE
b. Tarkio, Mo., 1912. Studied at Lindenwood Coll., B. M. 1934; Michigan State Univ., M. M. 1942; piano privately with John Thompson in Kansas City; piano and composition in Barcelona. She composed music for the Little Theatre, St. Joseph, Mo., for 5 years; taught at Tarkio Coll.; Florida State Univ.; was associate professor, Eastern Kentucky State Coll., 1944 to retirement.
WORKS: Opera: The snow queen; Chamber music: violin sonata; Chorus: A man named John, cantata; Psalm 150; My Kentucky, with bass soloist; also songs and piano pieces.

*McPHERSON, RICHARD CECIL
b. Norfolk, Va., 6 Nov. 1883; d. 1 Aug. 1944. Was composer and publisher; founded own publishing company. His compositions included 2 operas and The camel walk.

*McWHOOD, LEONARD BEECHER
b. Brooklyn, N. Y., 5 Dec. 1870; d. Hanover, N. H., 4 Dec. 1939. Studied with Edward MacDowell, Columbia Univ., B. A. 1893; was graduate assistant to MacDowell to 1898; taught at various schools; from 1918 was professor at Dartmouth Coll. His compositions include a light opera; 3 cantatas; instrumental pieces; songs.

MACY, CARLETON
b. New York, N. Y., 10 Sep. 1944. Studied with Donal Michalsky, California State Univ., Fullerton; with Robert Suderburg, Univ. of Washington. He was instructor of winds, Ethiopian Nat. School of Music, 1968-69; taught in public schools, Pomona, Calif., 1969-71.
WORKS: Wind ensemble: Chamber symphony, winds and percussion; Chamber music: Concert duo, bassoon and cello; Recorder set, 2 alto recorders; Christmas trio, flute, oboe, horn; 2 atmospheres, sextet for winds and strings; 4 pieces for piano; Chorus: Song serenade, with brass quartet, received outstanding composition award, California State Univ., 1971.
15115 Manor Way, Alderwood Manor, WA 98036

*MADDEN, EDWARD J.
Has published music for band: Symphonic variations on a theme by Purcell; Fantasia on a folk theme; Rock movement for band.
40 Parker St., Westwood, MA 02090

*MADER, CLARENCE
1904-1971. The fifth mystery, cantata for narrator, chorus, organ; Dialogue for organ; Concerto for organ; 2 monograms, organ; Prelude, tune, and a masquerade, piano.

*MADSEN, FLORENCE J.
Spirit of spring, women's voices; many published choral works, unpublished string and vocal works.

*MAEKELBERGHE, AUGUST
b. Oostende, Belgium, 15 Jan. 1909. Studied at Oostende Acad. of Music; Royal Cons., Ghent; Notre Dame Coll.; Detroit Inst. of Music and Art, M. M. He has been organ recitalist and choral conductor; was professor of organ, Wayne State Univ.
WORKS: Orchestra: Scherzo impromptu, Detroit Symphony, Feb. 1946; Elegy for string orch.; Chorus: Christ is risen; A Christmas suite, with string orch. and harp; Communion in D; Organ: Elegy; Toccata and prelude; Toccata, melody in blue, and fugue.

*MAESCH, LA VAHN
b. Appleton, Wis., 15 Oct. 1904. Studied at Lawrence Univ., B. M. 1926; Univ. of Wisconsin; Univ. of Michigan; with Marcel Dupre in Paris, 1929-31; at Eastman School of Music, M. M., 1939. He received a distinguished service citation, Univ. of Wisconsin; distinguished alumnus award, Lawrence Univ. He has been organ recitalist, choirmaster, lecturer; director, Lawrence Univ. Cons., 1954-

(MAESCH, LA VAHN)
WORKS: Orchestra: Christmas suite, 1938; Children's suite, 1938; symphony, 1941; Chorus: Waking time, a cappella; Prayer after triumph; also works for solo voice and organ.

*MAGANINI, QUINTO
b. Fairfield, Calif., 30 Nov. 1897; d. Greenwich, Conn., 10 Mar. 1974. Studied at Univ. of California; flute with Georges Barrere in New York; composition with Nadia Boulanger in France. His awards included the Pulitzer scholarship, 1927; Guggenheim fellowship, 1928; David Bispham prize. He played flute in the San Francisco Symphony, 1917; was discovered by Walter Damrosch in Sousa's Band in 1918 and brought to New York; played in the New York Symphony orchestra, 1919-28; organized and conducted his own Chamber Symphony; was conductor, Norwalk (Conn.) Symphony, 1939; taught at Columbia Univ.; was president, American Schools of Music and Art, Fontainebleau, France; also president, Kingsbury Machine Works and Edition Musicus, Inc.
WORKS: Opera: The argonauts, 1927; Tennessee's partner, 1942; Orchestra: Tuolumne, rhapsody for trumpet and orch., 1924; South wind, a fantasy, 1930; Sylvan symphony, 1932; Concerto for strings, 1934; Napoleon, a portrait, 1935; An ornithological suite; Chorus: The cathedral at Sens, with cello and orch.

MAGEAU, SISTER MARY MAGDALEN
b. Milwaukee, Wisc., 4 Sep. 1934. Studied with Leon Stein, De Paul Univ., B. M.; with Ross Lee Finney and Leslie Bassett, Univ. of Michigan, M. M.; with George Crumb at Tanglewood, 1970. She held a fellowship at Tanglewood; won 2nd prize, Gottschalk Internat. Competition, 1970; received a commission, Univ. of Minnesota Concert Band. She was assistant professor, Scholastica Coll., 1969-73; part time instructor, Univ. of Wisconsin, Superior, 1971-72; guest lecturer, Kelvin Grove Coll., Brisbane, Univ. of Tasmania, Hobart, and Univ. of South Australia, Adelaide, 1974-76.
WORKS: Orchestra: Variegations, Gottschalk award; Montage, performed by Minnesota Orchestra, Duluth Symphony, Des Moines Symphony, Band; Celebration music; Chamber music: 3 movements for unaccompanied cello, Internat. Festival of the Arts, Honolulu, 1968; Chorus: A new lacrimae; Keyboard: Forecasts for piano; 3 pieces for organ.
Scholastica College, Kenwood Ave.
Duluth, MN 55811

MAGINNIS, WILLIAM RICHARD
b. Yreka, Calif., 15 Nov. 1938. Studied with Roger Nixon and Alexander Post, San Francisco State Coll. He was instructor, San Francisco State Coll., tape music center, 1964-67; Mills Coll., tape music center, 1967-68; independent technician and instructor, 1968-   .
WORKS: Chamber music: 3 pieces for piano, 1961; Music for string quartet, 1961; Winter voices, cyclic epigrams, 1963; Extension #1, 1964; Ambiet, 1972; Electronic: Mindways for

(MAGINNIS, WILLIAM RICHARD)
rock and roll band and tape, 1967; Genuine imitation plastic whirlpool, 1967; etc.
71 Whitney St., San Francisco, CA 94101

MAIBEN, WILLIAM
b. Salt Lake City, Utah, 15 June 1953. Studied with Vladimir Ussachevsky, Univ. of Utah, B. M. 1972; with David Richey at Sun Valley; with Richard Hoffmann, Oberlin Cons. He won first place, Utah State Fair composition contest, 1972, 1973; first place, Nat. Fed. Music Clubs contest, 1972; and Composers Guild contest, 1973.
WORKS: Orchestra: concerto for viola and string orch., 1970; Chamber music: string quartet, 1971; 4 pieces for viola and piano, 1971; Music for H.F.A.C., concerto for 14 instruments, 1972; Variations, piano and tape, 1972; From the 5 hills, violin and viola, 1972; Serenade, flute, violin, viola, harpsichord, 1972; The White Knight's song, 3 voices and 9 instruments.
2774 Wardway, Salt Lake City, UT 84117

MAILMAN, MARTIN
b. New York, N. Y., 30 June 1932. Studied with Louis Mennini, Wayne Barlow, Bernard Rogers, Howard Hanson, Eastman School of Music, B. M., 1954; M. M. 1955, Ph. D. 1960. His awards include a scholarship at Eastman School; Edward Benjamin award, 1955; first prize, Birmingham Arts Festival, 1966; 2 first prizes, Williamette Univ., 1966; first prize Walla Walla Symphony, 1967; annual ASCAP awards; and many commissions. He taught in the U.S. Naval School of Music, 1955-57; was composer-in-residence, Young Composers Project, Jacksonville, Fla., 1959-61; professor and composer-in-residence, East Carolina Coll., 1961-66; North Texas State Univ., 1966-   ; guest conductor and lecturer.
WORKS: Theatre: The hunted, 1-act opera, 1959; music for Moby Dick, 1965; Orchestra: Dance in 2 moods, 1952; Autumn landscape, 1954; Jubilate, 1955; Elegy, 1955; Cantiones, 1957; Prelude and fugue, 1959; Partita for strings, 1960; Gateway City overture, 1960; Suite in 3 movements, 1961; Prelude and fugue no. 2, 1963; sinfonietta, 1964; symphony no. 1, 1969; Generations 2 for 3 string orch. and percussion, 1969; Band: Partita, 1958; Commencement march, 1960; 4 miniatures, 1960; Geometrics 1-4, 1961, 1962, 1965, 1968; Alarums, 1962; Concertino for trumpet and band, 1963; Liturgical music, 1964; 4 variations in search of a theme, narrator and band, 1965; Associations no. 1, 1969; In memoriam Frankie Newton, 1970; Requiem, requiem, 1972; Shouts, hymns, and praises, 1972; Chamber music: Burlesque, trumpet and piano, 1951; string quartet, 1962; 4 diversions, percussion ensemble, 1966; Partita no. 4, 9 players, 1967; Chorus: Holy, holy, holy, 1957; Christmas music, with orch., 1959; Alleluia, with band, 1960; 3 madrigals, 1960; Genesis resurrected, with narrator and orch., 1961; Hosanna, 1961; Leaves of grass, with narrator and band, 1963; To everything there is a season, 1963; The rise and fall, choral fable, 1966; Shakespearean serenade, 1968; Songs: West wind, soprano and piano, 1956; 4 songs for soprano, 1962; Piano: Petite partita,

MAILMAN, MARTIN

(MAILMAN, MARTIN)
1961; Variations on a short theme, 1966; Martha's Vineyard, 1969.
School of Music, North Texas State University
Denton, TX 76203

MAIS, CHESTER L.
b. Philadelphia, Pa., 16 June 1936. Studied with Hugo Weisgall and Robert Sanders, City Univ. of New York; with Robert Palmer at Cornell Univ.; Samuel Adler and Wayne Barlow, Eastman School of Music. He held graduate assistantships at Brooklyn Coll., Cornell Univ., and Eastman School. He was lecturer, Brooklyn Coll., 1966-68; instructor, St. Francis Coll., Brooklyn, 1968-69.
WORKS: Wind ensemble: brass quintet, 1971; Lament for trombone choir, 1973; Fantasy on warm-up exercises, trombone choir, 1973; Chamber music: Fantasy on a phrase of Schoenberg, piano, 1970; woodwind quintet, 1970; string quartet no. 2; Establishment piece, violin, viola, 4 winds, 1973; Grey piece no. 1, for tuba, viola, English horn, 1973.
2685 Danby Rd., Willseyville, NY 13864

*MAITLAND, ROLLO FRANCIS
b. Williamsport, Pa., 10 Dec. 1884; d. Philadelphia, Pa., 7 Apr. 1953. Studied in Philadelphia; was church organist, music critic, and teacher there. He published works for organ.

*MALKIN, JOSEPH
b. Near Odessa, Russia, 24 Sep. 1879; to U.S. c. 1913; d. New York, N. Y., 1 Sep. 1969. Studied in Odessa and at Paris Cons. He was first cellist, Berlin Philharmonic, 1902-08; then toured Europe and North America with the Brussels Quartet; was first cellist, Boston Symphony, 1914-19; Chicago Symphony, 1919-22; formed Malkin Trio with his brothers, Jacques and Manfred; established Malkin Cons. in Boston, 1933-43; was cellist with New York Philharmonic, 1944-49. He wrote cellos works and studies.

*MALKO, NIKOLAY ANDREYEVICH
b. Brailov, Russia, 4 May 1883; U.S. citizen 1946; d. Sydney, Australia, 23 June 1961. Studied at St. Petersburg Univ. and with Rimsky-Korsakov, Liadov, Glazunov, and Tcherepnin at the Cons. He was conductor in St. Petersburg and Copenhagen; came to the U.S., was lecturer, De Paul Univ., Chicago, 1940-54; returned to conducting with the Yorkshire Symphony Orchestra, England, 1954-55; Sydney Symphony Orchestra, Australia, 1956-61. His compositions include a clarinet concerto, 1952.

*MALOOF, WILLIAM
Studied at Boston Univ., B. M.; received first prize, Indiana State Univ./Indianapolis Symphony 6th Annual Music Festival composition contest. His works include The centurion, suite for orch., 1972; From auguries of innocence, choir and chamber orch., Boston, 12 Dec. 1973.
Berklee College of Music
1140 Boylston St., Boston, MA 02215

*MALOTTE, ALBERT HAY
b. Philadelphia, Pa., 19 May 1895; d. Los Angeles, Calif., 16 Nov. 1964. Studied organ in Philadelphia; was concert organist in the U.S. and Europe; established a school for theatre organists in Los Angeles, 1927; was music director for Walt Disney Studios for several years.
WORKS: Ballet: Little Red Riding Hood; Carnival of Venice; Theatre: Lolama, musical play; Musicals: Fanfare; The big tree; Limbo; Chorus: Psalm 91; Voice of the prophet; Songs: The Lord's prayer; Psalm 23; Song of the open road; Film scores: Dr. Cyclops; Enchanted forest; Ferdinand the bull; some of Disney's Silly symphonies.

*MALTBY, RICHARD E.
b. Chicago, Ill., 26 June 1914. Studied at Northwestern Univ.; played trumpet with dance bands and with staff orchestra, WBBM, Chicago; went to New York in 1945.
WORKS: Band: Threnody, requiem for John F. Kennedy, with narrator; Trumpet nocturne; Blues essay, with solo horn; Jazz waltz; Hail to the fleet; 6 flats unfurnished, 1942; Esprit de corps; Manhattan discotheque; Fugue in 5 flats; Ballad, clarinet and band; Ballad for brass, contrabass, guitar, percussion.

MAMLOK, URSULA
b. Berlin, Germany, 2 Feb. 1928; U.S. citizen 1945. Studied with George Szell, Mannes Coll. of Music; with Roger Sessions, Ralph Shapey, and Stefan Wolpe, privately in New York; Manhattan School of Music, M. M. She has recieved awards from Nat. Fed. of Music Clubs; Nat. School Orchestra Asso.; and a grant from City Univ. of New York Research Found., 1972-73. She has been faculty member, New York Univ., 1968-   ; Manhattan School of Music, 1968-71; assistant professor, Kingsborough Coll., CUNY, 1971-   .
WORKS: Chamber music: Variations for solo flute, 1961; Stray birds, soprano, flute, and cello, 1963; 5 capriccios for oboe and piano; Variations and interludes for 4 percussionists; Haiku settings, soprano and flute.
315 East 86th St., New York, NY 10028

*MANA-ZUCCA (AUGUSTA ZUCKERMANN)
b. New York, N. Y., 25 Dec. 1887. Studied piano with Alexander Lambert in New York; with Busoni and Godowsky in Berlin; composition with Hermann Spielter in London; voice with Von zur Muhlen in London and Paris. She made her piano debut at age 8, playing a Beethoven concerto with the New York Symphony; then toured Europe. Her debut as a soprano was in Lehar's Count of Luxembourg in 1914. She appeared in other operettas, 1914-16; gave recitals, including her own works on the programs. Since 1940 she has been composer, pianist and teacher in Miami, Fla.
WORKS: Opera: Hypatia; The queue of Ki-Lu; Ballet: The wedding of the butterfly; Orchestra: piano concerto, 1919; Cuban dance; Frolic for strings; Fugato humoresque; Havana nights; violin concerto, 1955; Chamber music: violin sonata; cello sonata; piano trio; Walla-Kye, saxophone and piano; violin pieces; piano pieces,

(MANNA-ZUCCA)
including My musical calendar, a collection of
365 pieces in 12 books; Songs: I love life; The
brown bear; Nichevo; There's joy in my heart;
Time and time again; Honey lamb.

MANCINI, HENRY
b. Cleveland, Ohio, 16 Apr. 1924. Studied at
Carnegie Inst. and the Juilliard School; privately with Ernst Krenek, Mario Castelnuovo-
Tedesco, and Alfred Sendrey. His first award
was won at age 13, when he was first flutist in
the Pennsylvania All State Band. Awards for his
film and television scores include 20 Grammys,
3 Oscars, and many nominations. He was staff
composer, Universal-International Studios,
1952-57; then turned to television scores with
Peter Gunn in 1958 and Mr. Lucky in 1960.
WORKS: Film scores: High time; The great
impostor; Mr. Hobbs takes a vacation; Bachelor
in paradise; Breakfast at Tiffany's; Hatari; Experiment in terror; Days of wine and roses; Charade; The pink panther; Soldier in the rain;
Dear heart; Shot in the dark; Moment to moment;
The great race; Arabesque; Two for the road;
Wait until dark; Gunn; The party; Me, Natalie;
Gaily, gaily; The Molly Maguires; Sunflower;
Darling Lili; The Hawaiians; The night visitor.
6290 Sunset Boulevard
Hollywood, CA 90028

*MANDEL, JOHN
b. New York, N. Y., 23 Nov. 1925. Studied at
Manhattan School of Music; with Stefan Wolpe at
Juilliard; played trumpet the Joe Venuti and
Billie Rogers; trombone with Jimmy Dorsey, Buddy
Rich, Count Basie; was arranger for many bands.
He received a Grammy award, 1965 for The shadow
of your smile from The sandpiper, which won an
Academy award, 1965. Other film scores: Cold
day in the park; Harper; You're never too young;
The Russians are coming; The Americanization of
Emily; Markham (television).

MANDELBAUM, JOEL
b. New York, N. Y., 12 Oct. 1932. Studied with
Angela Diller, Diller-Quaile School; Walter Pis-
ton, Harvard Univ.; Irving Fine, Harold Shapero,
Brandeis Univ.; Bernhard Heiden, Indiana Univ.;
with Luigi Dallapiccola and Aaron Copland at
Tanglewood. He has been associate professor,
Queens Coll., CUNY, 1961-   .
WORKS: Opera: The man in the man-made moon,
1-act, 1956; The dybbuk, 4-acts, 1972; Orchestra:
Sinfonia concertante, oboe, horn, violin, cello,
and small orch., 1962; trumpet concerto, 1971;
Chamber music: woodwind quintet, 1957; string
quartet, 1958; microtonal quartet for 3 horns
and trombone; 10 Yeats settings for vocal quartet and instruments, 1965; Songs: cycles to
poems of Millay, 1958, J. Berman, 1971, Roethke,
1973; Experimental works: 9 studies in 19-tone
temperament. 1961; 10 studies in Euler genera
for 31-tone organ.
3949 46th St., Long Island City, NY 11104

MANERI, JOSEPH
b. New York, N. Y., 9 Feb. 1927. Studied for
11 years with Joseph Schmid, pupil of Alban

(MANERI, JOSEPH)
Berg; was trained in jazz and music of the Middle East as clarinetist, saxophonist, and pianist. He taught theory, Brooklyn Cons., 1964-65;
New England Cons., 1970-   ; teaches composition privately.
WORKS: Orchestra: piano concerto, commissioned by Eric Leinsdorf; Chamber music: string
quartet; trio; Woodwind, brass, and percussion,
1968; Ephphatha, quartet for piano, clarinet,
trombone, tuba; piano pieces.
334 East Main St., Marlborough, MA 01752

MANGINI, MARINO ANTHONY
b. Endicott, N. Y., 5 Feb. 1950. Studied with
James Willey and David Maslanka, State Univ.
Coll., Geneseo, N. Y., 1969-71. His string quartet, No. 1 won an award in a competition sponsored by the Catgut Acoustical Society and New
Jersey Council on the Arts, 1973. He has been
manager, Bristol Valley Playhouse, Naples, N. Y.,
1973-   .
WORKS: Chamber music: octet for woodwinds
and strings, 1971; string quartet, Douglas
Coll., 14 Oct. 1973; other chamber works in
progress.
162 South Main St., Naples, NY 14512

MANN, JAMES
b. Fort Worth, Tex., 27 Nov. 1942. Studied with
Ben Johnston, Thomas Frederickson, and Morgan
Powell, Univ. of Illinois; with Arthur Berger,
Brandeis Univ. He has been instructor, New
England Cons., 1973-   .
WORKS: Jazz ensemble: Rani Ban, 1970; Chamber music: Short piece, flute, clarinet, horn,
violin, cello, 1969; 2 songs, soprano, flute,
viola, bass clarinet, text by composer, 1970;
Realizations, 14 instruments, 1971; Kaleidophone,
7 instruments, Boston, Mass., 13 May 1973.
143 Fairview Ave., Belmont, MA 02178

*MANN, ROBERT
Tales, vocal trio.

*MANNES, LEOPOLD DAMROSCH
b. New York, N. Y., 26 Dec. 1899; d. Martha's
Vineyard, Mass., 11 Aug. 1964. Son of David
Mannes and Clara Damrosch Mannes, studied at the
David Mannes School of Music; with Rosario
Scalero and Percy Goetschius, Inst. of Musical
Art, New York; received Pulitzer award, 1925;
Guggenheim fellowship, 1926. He taught at the
Inst. of Musical Art and at the Mannes School,
succeeding his father as director. For a time
he worked at Eastern Kodak Co., Rochester, and
was co-inventor with Leopold Godowsky (son of
the pianist) of the Kodacolor photographic
process.
WORKS: Theatre: music to The tempest,
1930; Orchestra: a suite, 1926; Chamber music:
suite for 2 pianos, 1924; string quartet, 1928;
songs.

*MANNEY, CHARLES FONTEYN
b. Brooklyn, N. Y., 8 Feb. 1872; d. New York,
N. Y., 31 Oct. 1951. Studied at Brooklyn Polytechnic Inst.; with William Arms Fisher in New

MANNEY, CHARLES FONTEYN

(MANNEY, CHARLES FONTEYN)
York; with J. Wallace Goodrich and Percy Goetschius in Boston. He was editor for a Boston music publisher, 1898-1930; choral conductor for the MacDowell Club.
 WORKS: Cantatas: The resurrection; The manger throne; Songs: O captain, my captain; A Shropshire lad; also an opera.

*MANNING, KATHLEEN LOCKHART
 b. Hollywood, Calif., 24 Oct. 1890; d. Los Angeles, Calif., 20 Mar. 1951. Studied piano in Los Angeles; composition with Moritz Moszkowski in Paris. She made concert tours in England and France, 1909-14; sang with the Hammerstein Opera Company in London, 1911-12.
 WORKS: Opera: Mr. Wu; For the soul of Rafael; Songs: Sketches of Paris; Sketches of London; Sketches of New York; Songs of Egypt; Autumn leaves; Waterlily; The lamplighter; The street fair; In the Luxembourg Gardens, from Sketches of Paris, has been published for women's choir; also piano pieces.

MANNO, ROBERT
 b. Bryn Mawr, Pa., 27 July 1944. Studied with Romeo Cascarino, Combs Coll. of Music, 1964-65; with Ludmila Ulehla, Manhattan School of Music, B. M. 1968; with Vladimir Padwa, New York Univ., M. A., 1974. He received the Ernest Bloch award for a choral piece, 1971; New York Univ. scholarship; fellowship, Composers Conference, Johnson, Vt., 1973. He was jazz pianist, 1962-65; freelance baritone soloist and choral and opera singer, 1967-   ; private teacher of voice and theory.
 WORKS: Chamber music: 4 short pieces, clarinet and piano, 1966; Dirge and blues, tuba quartet, 1969; Fern Hill, baritone, wind quartet, string quintet, 1970-72; Birdsongs for soprano and violin, 1972; 5 thematic etudes, string quartet, 1973; Landscapes, voice, wind quintet and double bass, 1973; Chorus: This is the garden, 1969; God's grandeur, 1971; several songs and piano pieces.
 463 West St., Apt. C320
 New York, NY 10014

MANSFIELD, KENNETH ZOELLIN, JR.
 b. King City, Calif., 21 Aug. 1932. Studied with Randall Thompson and Walter Piston, Harvard Univ.; organ with Andre Marchel in Paris and Edward Mueller in Basel. He received a John Knowles Paine fellowship for European study, 1956; and a commission, San Francisco Chapter, American Guild of Organists for a work for 2 organs. He was organist in San Francisco, 1964-66, in Lafayette, Calif., 1968-   ; associate professor, Univ. of California, Hayward, 1966-   .
 WORKS: Chorus: The image, Christmas introit, with brass quartet and organ; Christ whose glory fills the sky; Collect for Advent IV; Magnificat and Nunc dimittis; Organ: Variations on a ground; Variations on Forest green; Elegy for a young child; sonata for flute and organ; Sinfonia for Easter morning, with string quartet; 6 movements for 2 organs.
 Music Department, University of California
 Hayward, CA 94542

*MANSON, EDDY LAWRENCE
 b. New York, N. Y., 9 May 1919. Studied with Vittorio Giannini, Adolf Schmid at Juilliard School; privately with Howard Brockway and Rudolf Schramm; and at New York Univ. He has been harmonica soloist in Town Hall and Carnegie Hall in New York.
 WORKS: Orchestra: symphony; Chorale fantasy on a theme by Bach; Wind ensemble: Fugue for woodwinds; Trilogy for woodwinds; Ballad for brass; Chamber music: Research, string quartet; Provocation, bass and piano; Film scores: The little fugitive; Lovers and lollipops; Johnny Jupiter; Supermarket; US 1 - American profile; The River Nile; Polaris submarine; American spectacle (television).

MANTON, ROBERT WILLIAM
 b. Dorchester, Mass., 9 Nov. 1894; d. Durham, N. H., 24 Dec. 1967. Studied with Archibald T. Davison and Edward Burlingame Hill, Harvard Univ.; privately with Harris S. Shaw in Boston; and with d'Indy in Paris; at MacDowell Colony; with Ralph Vaughan Williams, London, 1953. He was awarded an honorary doctorate, Univ. of New Hampshire, 1967. He served in the U.S. Marine Corps, 1918-19; taught privately in Boston, 1919-23; then was appointed head and organized the music department, Univ. of New Hampshire, retired 1964 as professor; organist, Community Church, Durham, and Christ Church, Exeter.
 WORKS: Orchestra: New England sketches; Wuthering Heights Fantasy; November woods; piano concerto; New England rhapsody; Dance rhapsody; Jeanie; Chamber music: 2 violin sonatas; 2 pieces for cello and piano; Chorus: The Saracens, The day grows old, male voices, 1925; Sea marge, male voices, 1926; Wanderer's song, 1926; 2 songs from the Spanish Main, male voices, 1928; Route step (France, 1918), male voices; The cycling seasons; This is the month; Piano: Improvisation, 1916; Marine sketches, 1924; New Hampshire idyls, 1926; North County pieces; 2 sonatas, Fire of spring; Scherzo; and many songs.

MANZ, PAUL
 b. Cleveland, Ohio, 10 May 1919. Studied at American Cons.; with Albert Riemenschneider, Baldwin Wallace Coll.; Arthur B. Jennings, Univ. of Minnesota; Flor Peeters in Belgium; Helmut Walcha in Germany. He received a Fulbright grant; J. Callaert prize; Firmin Swinnen award; honorary doctorate, Concordia Coll., Seward, Neb.; St. Cecelia medal, Boystown, Neb. He has held faculty posts at Winnebago Acad.; Univ. of Minnesota; Macalester Coll.; Concordia Coll., St. Paul, Minn.
 WORKS: Chorus: Let us ever walk with Jesus, 1954; Psalm 130, 1955; On my heart imprint thine image, 1956; Preserve me, O Lord, 1958; I caused thy grief, 1956; On Christmas Eve, 1960; Sing to the Lord a new song; Organ: 40 choral improvisations; other liturgical works for chorus and organ.
 7204 Schey Dr., Edina, MN 55435

MARALDO, WILLIAM
 b. Cheyenne, Wyo., 28 Mar. 1938. Studied at Univ of Colorado; Paris Cons.; master classes

(MARALDO, WILLIAM)
with Lukas Foss; privately with George Crumb.
He was assistant director, Centre de Musique,
Paris, 1963-64; co-director, Center for Contem-
porary Music, Mills Coll., 1968-   ; president,
Tantra Research Inst., Oakland, 1972-   .
WORKS: Electronic: Sound of breath; Song
of the vallies; Night music; Journey into night;
Textures; Film score: Transmutations.
2970 Burdeck Drive, Oakland, CA 94602

*MARCELLI, NINO
b. Santiago, Chile, 21 Jan. 1890; to U.S. 1918;
d. San Diego, Calif., 16 Aug. 1967. Studied at
Nat. Cons. of Chile and Univ. of Chile; was honorary member of the faculty of fine arts, Univ.
of Chile. He was conductor, American Headquarters Band in France, 1918-20; cellist, San Francisco Symphony, 1920; director of instrumental
music, San Diego schools, 1921 to retirement;
founded San Diego Symphony, 1927, conductor to
1937; guest conductor, Hollywood Bowl, Los Angeles Philharmonic, San Francisco Symphony, and
others; guest lecturer in western colleges.
WORKS: Light opera: Carmelita; Orchestra:
Suite Araucana; symphony; suite for strings; Ode
to a hero; March processional; 2 Christmas processionals; Songs: Solitude; Deep in the forest; Song of the Andes; Song of thanks; Harp of
sunset.

MARCUS, ADABELLE GROSS
b. Chicago, Ill., 8 July 1929. Studied with
Samuel Lieberson and Alexander Tcherepnin, De
Paul Univ.; with Leo Sowerby, American Cons.;
with Karel B. Jirak, Roosevelt Univ.; and piano
with Robert Goldsand, New York. She won an ap-
pearance as piano soloist with the Dayton Philharmonic; and performances of her compositions
by the Internat. Society for Contemporary Music.
She has been a concert pianist, 1939-   ; vocal
coach, 1942-49; piano teacher, 1959-   .
WORKS: Opera: Snow, chamber opera on Frost
text; Orchestra: 2 fantasias; piano concertino;
violin concerto; Symphony of the spheres; Chamber music: string quartet; Nocturne, flute and
piano; violin sonata; Song for flute; Chorus:
God, whom shall I compare to thee, with brass;
Setting to seasons, with chamber orch.; Songs:
cycles on Robert Frost and Dylan Thomas texts;
4 preludes on playthings to the wind, Sandburg
text; Piano: A day in New York City; A child's
day, suite; Youth in orbit; sonata.
9374 Landings Lane, Des Plaines, IL 60016

*MARCUS, WADE
A Moorish sonata, violin and piano, New York,
24 Feb. 1974.

*MAREK, ROBERT
Trio for trumpet, horn, trombone.
Department of Music
University of South Dakota
Vermillion, SD 57069

MARGOLIS, JEROME N.
b. Philadelphia, Pa., 30 Oct. 1941. Studied with
Vincent Persichetti, Philadelphia Cons.; with

(MARGOLIS, JEROME N.)
Joseph Castaldo, Philadelphia Musical Acad. He
was instructor, Philadelphia Settlement School,
1964-65; music director, Performing Arts, Bennett Coll., 1967-70; chairman, music department,
Harvard School, Van Nuys, Calif., 1970-   .
WORKS: Orchestra: A symphony; Chamber
music: woodwind trio; brass quartet; string
quartet; Gebrauchsmusik for dance, for solo
percussionist; also theatre music, electronic
and mixed media works, ballet music, piano
pieces, choral works.
5158 Balboa Blvd., Encino, CA 91316

*MARGOSHES, STEVEN
Concerto for violin and rock band, New York
premiere, 2 Apr. 1974.

MARKAITIS, BRUNO
b. Lithuania, 7 July 1922; U.S. citizen 1958.
Studied in Rome and London; with Alexander
Tcherepnin and Bernard Dieter in Chicago. He
has won prizes in Lithuanian-American composition contests, and is an honorary member of the
Kodaly Acad. and Inst.
WORKS: Orchestra: piano concerto, 1968;
concertino #2 for piano and orch., 1969; Wind
ensemble: concertino #1, piano, winds and percussion, 1968; concertino #3, organ, winds and
percussion, 1971; Chamber music: 2 violin sonatas, 1960, 1972; string quartet, 1961; Mirage,
piano, 1962; 3 dances for piano, 1973; Chorus:
The night of sorrow, cantata, 1958; Bells of
Vilnius, symphonic cantata, 1965; Christmas poem,
choral suite, 1966; Community mass, 1967; 100
suns, symphonic multi-media oratorio, 1970, commissioned by Loyola Univ. of Chicago for its
centennial.
739 22nd St., Santa Monica, CA 90402

MARKS, FRANKLYN
b. Cleveland, Ohio, 31 May 1911. Studied at
Dartmouth Coll., B. A. 1932; privately with
Joseph Schiller, 1937-41. He was elected to
Phi Beta Kappa; received an Emmy nomination,
1961. He was staff arranger, NBC, 1937-42; free-
lance arranger, 1942-55; composer-music director,
Walt Disney Studios, 1955-   .
WORKS: Theatre: The bridge, ballet; Orchestra: West Virginia, Jazz ensemble: Trajectories; The new world; Chamber music: Night and
the sea, guitar; Dialogue, guitar; Film scores:
Legend of the boy and the eagle; Charlie, the
lonesome cougar; and many songs.
3825 Ventura Canyon Ave.
Sherman Oaks, CA 91403

*MARKS, JAMES
Introduction and passacaglia for brass; Music
for brass and timpani.
Department of Music
Sam Houston State University
Huntsville, TX 77340

*MARSH, CHARLES HOWARD
b. Magnolia, Iowa, 8 Apr. 1885; d. San Diego,
Calif., 12 Apr. 1956. Studied with Walter Hall
and A. J. Goodrich in New York; with Widor,

MARSH, CHARLES HOWARD

(MARSH, CHARLES HOWARD)
Lipert, and Philipp in France. He held various posts as organist and teacher in Indiana, Florida, and California.
WORKS: Chorus: Benedictus es domine; Jubilate deo; Christus natus est; In this place will I give peace; Organ: Scherzo; 4 color prints; Legend triste; Beside still waters.

MARSH, MILTON R. W.
b. Bermuda, 29 Sep. 1945. Studied at Berklee Coll. of Music, B. M.; with Jaki Byard and Robert Ceely, New England Cons., M. M. He was on the faculty, State Univ. of New York, Oneonta, 1972-73; assistant professor and director of jazz studies program, State Univ. of New York, Buffalo, 1973- .
WORKS: Chamber music: Monism, for string quartet, spoken texts, jazz ensemble, Boston, May 1971; Poems for saxophone quartet; Psychic impulses; Ode to Nzinga; Elementals; Study in retrospect.
Department of Music
State University of New York
Buffalo, NY 14214

MARSHALL, INGRAM D.
b. Mt. Vernon, N. Y., 10 May 1942. Studied at Lake Forest Coll.; with Vladimir Ussachevsky and Ilhan Mimaroglu, Columbia Univ.; New York Univ.; with Morton Subotnick, James Tenney, Ki Wasitodipuro, California Inst. of the Arts; and with Bulent Arel, California School of the Arts, 1971- . He has been instructor, California School of the Arts, 1971- .
WORKS: Chamber music: Ricebowlthundersock, percussion and piano, 1973; Electronic: The East is red, setting of Chinese folksong, 1972; Gambuh, continuous music, Balinese flute and electronics, 1972-73; Cortés, text-sound piece, poem and voice, tape, 1973; Weather report, text-sound piece made from the voice of a Danish weatherwoman, Berkeley, Calif., 20 June 1974.
California Institute of the Arts
Valencia, CA 91355

*MARSHALL, JACK
1921-1973. The goldrush suite, 4 saxophones or woodwind ensemble.

MARSHALL, JAMES T.
b. Seattle, Wash., 12 Oct. 1941. Studied with George McKay and John Verrall, Univ. of Washington; with Paul Cooper and Scott Huston, Univ. of Cincinnati; and privately with George Rochberg. He was instructor, Drake Univ., 1966-68; and Montclair State Coll., 1968-71.
WORKS: Chamber music: string quartet, 1966; Songs for Jeanne, tenor, cello, piano, 1972; Suite in 5 movements, 3 winds, 2 strings, harpsichord, 1972; Elevation of imagery, violin and piano, 1973; Multisone, 3 winds, cello, piano, 1973; Petite lyrique, bassoon and piano, 1973.
1978 Kentucky Ave., #9
Cincinnati, OH 45223

MARSHALL, JANE M.
b. Dallas, Tex., 5 Dec. 1924. Studied piano, organ, voice, and conducting at Southern

(MARSHALL, JANE M.)
Methodist Univ. She won an American Guild of Organists prize for an anthem, 1957. She was faculty member, Southern Methodist Univ., 1948-50, 1968-73; and has held various positions as church organist.
WORKS: Chorus: Awake, my heart, 1957; God's own people; Blessed is the morn; He comes to us; Praise the Lord; and many other choral works.
4077 Northaven Road, Dallas, TX 75229

*MARSHALL, JOHN PATTON
b. Rockport, Mass., 9 Jan. 1877; d. Boston, Mass., 17 Jan. 1941. Studied with B. J. Lang, Edward MacDowell, George W. Chadwick, and Homer A. Norris; was professor at Boston Univ., 1903-41; composed songs and piano pieces.

*MARSHALL, YALE
Oedipus and the Sphinx, 2-part opera, Center Opera Company, Minneapolis, 29 Nov. 1969.

*MARTEL, TOM
Hard job being God, rock opera, New York, 14 May 1972.

MARTH, HELEN JUN
b. Alton, Ill., 24 May 1903. Studied organ and composition with C. Albert Scholin, St. Louis. She toured the Chautauqua circuit as accompanist and drama coach; has directed children's choirs and children's radio programs; worked in Little Theatre.
WORKS: Chorus: The triumph of Christ, cantata; Sing O ye heavens, cantata; many anthems.
526 George St., Alton, IL 62002

*MARTIN, DAVID L.
b. 1926. Suite for euphonium and small orch.

MARTIN, GILBERT M.
b. Southbridge, Mass., 6 Jan. 1941. Studied with James Waters and Warren Martin, Westminster Choir Coll. He is music director, Presbyterian Church, Dayton, and United Methodist Church, Kettering, Ohio.
WORKS: Organ: 2 preludes on American hymn tunes; Intercession; also works in musical theatre, ballet, chamber music, and numerous published anthems and other choral works.
3745 East Patterson Road, Dayton, OH 45430

*MARTIN, HUGH
b. Birmingham, Ala., 11 Aug. 1914. Studied at Birmingham Southern Coll.
WORKS: Theatre: Best foot forward, 1941; Look, Ma, I'm dancin', 1948; Make a wish, 1951; Love from Judy; High spirits; Film scores: Meet me in St. Louis, 1944; Athena; The girl most likely; Grandma Moses suite; Hans Brinker (television); and many songs: Buckle down Winsocki; Pass the peace pipe; et al.

MARTIN, PAUL A.
b. Philadelphia, Pa., 12 Dec. 1939. Studied with Clifford Taylor, Temple Univ., D. M. A. He has been associate professor, Edinboro State Coll., 1968- .

(MARTIN, PAUL A.)
WORKS: Chamber music: Symphony #1 for chamber orch.; Movements for flute and piano; Chorus: How the now disappeared, chorus and percussion.
R.D. #1, Edinboro, PA 15412

MARTIN, ROBERT EDWARD
b. Hagerstown Md., 22 July 1952. Studied with Stefan Grove, Richard Rodney Bennett, Jean Ivey, Robert Hall Lewis, Peabody Cons., B. M. 1974; with Jon Appleton, John E. Rogers, Hubert Howe, Jr., Electronic Music Inst., Univ. of New Hampshire and Dartmouth Coll., summer 1972. He held scholarships at Peabody Cons., 1970-74; received Marie K. Thatcher prize, 1971; James Sykes prize for electronic music, 1972; Gustav Klemm award, 1972; Otto Ortman award, 1973; Phi Mu Alpha Sinfonia award, 1973.
WORKS: Orchestra: Graduation march, 1970; Save the turtles, 1973; Chamber music: Fugue, woodwind quartet, 1971; 2 ancient pieces, piano, 1972; suite for unaccompanied cello; Chanson, tenor, viola, percussion, 1973; Couplet, 4 trombones, 1973; Antique forms of lost friends, flute and viola, 1973; Septet, flute and strings; Flute piece, solo flute; duet for oboe and cello; Electronic: Before the change, tape, 1972; Birthday song, piano and tape, 1972; Schmaug, tape, 1972, The black rock, tape, 1972.
44 McKee Ave., Hagerstown, MD 21740

MARTIN, VERNON
b. Guthrie, Okla., 15 Dec. 1929. Studied with Harrison Kerr, Univ. of Oklahoma, B. A.; with Henry Cowell, Columbia Univ.; and with Merrill Ellis, North Texas State Univ. He received commissions from Staten Island Symphony, 1961, Frank Marzan, tuba player; and ASCAP awards, 1968-72. He was music librarian, Columbia Univ., 1962-64; New York Public Library, 1964-66; North Texas State Univ., 1966-70; and has been director of library services, Morningside Coll., 1970- .
WORKS: Opera: Ladies voices, text by Gertrude Stein; Orchestra: Orchestra piece with birds; Man with a hoe, 1961; concerto for tuba and strings; Chamber music: Liber contrapunctum, woodwind quartet; Beginning, middle and end, violin and piano; Songs: Pasternack; Casals; Electronic: Didactic piece and nondance; Simultaneity; Contingencies.
4610 Glenn, Sioux City, IA 51106

MARTINO, DONALD JAMES
b. Plainfield, N. J., 16 May 1931. Studied with Ernst Bacon, Syracuse Univ., B. M. 1952; with Roger Sessions, Milton Babbitt, Princeton Univ., M. F. A. 1954; with Luigi Dallapiccola, Florence, Italy, on a Fulbright grant, 1954-56. He received 2 BMI awards, 1953, 1954; Pacifica Found. award, 1961; Brandeis Creative Arts citation, 1963; W. Ingles Morse grant, 1965; Nat. Inst. of Arts and Letters award, 1967; 2 Guggenheim grants, 1967, 1973; Nat. Endowment for the Arts grant, 1974; Pulitzer prize, 1974, for Notturno; and many commissions. He was faculty member, Princeton Univ., 1958-59; Yale Univ., 1959-69; chairman of composition New England Cons., 1969- ; visiting lecturer, Harvard Univ., 1971; and

(MARTINO, DONALD JAMES)
composer-in-residence, Berkshire Music Center, 4 summers.
WORKS: Orchestra: piano concerto, commissioned by New Haven Symphony 1965; Mosaic for grand orchestra, commissioned by Univ. of Chicago; cello concerto, 1970; Chamber music: Quodlibets, flute solo, 1954; Set for clarinet, 1954; Trio, violin, clarinet, piano, 1959; B,a,b,b,it,t, for clarinet; Strata, bass clarinet solo; Cinque frammenti, oboe and string bass, 1961; Fantasy variations for violin, 1962; Concerto for wind quintet, 1964; Parisonatina al' dodecafonia, cello solo; Notturno, chamber orch., New York, 15 May 1973; Chorus: any one lived in a pretty how town, with piano 4-hands; Portraits, chorus and orch.; Paradiso choruses, 14 soloists, chorus, orch., and 8-track tape, Boston, 7 May 1975; Piano: Piano fantasy; Pianississimo.
11 Pembroke St., Newton, MA 02158

*MARTINU, BOHUSLAV
b. Policka, Bohemia, 8 Dec. 1890; to U.S. 1941; d. Liestal, Switzerland, 28 Aug. 1959. Studied at the Prague Cons.; was violinist in the Czech Philharmonic Orch.; in 1923 went to Paris and studied with Albert Roussel, remaining there to 1940 when he went to Portugal and thence to the U.S. His voluminous works include 13 operas; 10 ballets; 6 symphonies; cello concerto; piano concerto; double concerto; concerto grosso; concerto for 2 pianos; violin concerto; concerto for orchestra; Rhapsody concerto, viola and orch.; many other works for orchestra; numerous compositions for chamber ensembles; 2 oratorios; piano pieces.

*MARTIRANO, SALVATORE
b. Yonkers, N. Y., 12 Jan. 1927. Studied at Oberlin Cons., B. M. 1951; with Bernard Rogers, Eastman School of Music, M. M. 1952; with Luigi Dallapiccola, Cherubini Cons., Florence, Italy, 1952-54; American Acad. in Rome, 1956-59. He received a Guggenheim fellowship, 1960; American Acad. of Arts and Letters award, 1960. He has been associate professor, Univ. of Illinois, 1968- ; introduced a new instrument, the Mar-Vil construction, in New York in March 1971.
WORKS: Opera: The magic stones, chamber opera, 1952; Orchestra: Prelude, 1950; Contrasto, 1954; Chamber music: wind sextet, 1949; Variations, flute and piano, 1950; string quartet, 1951; Cocktail music, piano, 1962; octet, 1963; Selections, alto flute, bass clarinet, viola, cello, 1970; Chorus: O, O, O, O, That Shakespeherian rag, vocal and instrumental chamber ensemble, 1959; Songs: Chansons innocentes, soprano, 1957; Multimedia: Underworld, 4 actors, percussion, 2 double basses, tenor saxohphone, tape, 1965; Ballad, amplified nightclub singer and instruments, 1966; L's GA, politico with gasmask, helium bomb, 3 16-mm movie projectors, tape, 1968; Action analysis, for 12 people, Bunny and controller, 1968.
Department of Music, University of Illinois Urbana, IL 61801

MASLANKA, DAVID HENRY

MASLANKA, DAVID HENRY
b. New Bedford, Mass., 30 Aug. 1943. Studied
with Joseph Wood, Oberlin Coll. Cons.; with Cesar
Bresgen, Mozarteum, Salzburg; and with H. Owen
Reed, Michigan State Univ., M. M. 1968, Ph. D.
1971. He has been assistant professor, State
Univ. Coll., Geneseo, N. Y., 1970- .
WORKS: Orchestra: Shibui symphony; Chamber
music: trio for violin, clarinet, piano; duo,
flute and piano; trio, viola, clarinet, piano;
Chorus: The nameless fear or: The unanswered
question put yet another way, chorus, instruments and percussion.
27 Wadsworth St., Geneseo, NY 14454

*MASON, DANIEL GREGORY
b. Brookline, Mass., 20 Nov. 1873; d. Greenwich,
Conn., 4 Dec. 1953. Was grandson of hymnwriter
Lowell Mason, nephew of pianist William Mason,
and son of Henry Mason, co-founder of Mason &
Hamlin piano company. He studied with John
Knowles Paine, Harvard Univ., B. A. 1895; with
Percy Goetschius and George W. Chadwick in Boston; with Vincent d'Indy in Paris. He joined
the faculty of Columbia Univ. in 1910, became
MacDowell professor in 1929, was chairman of the
music department to 1940; retired in 1942.
WORKS: Orchestra: 3 symphonies, 1915, 1930,
1937; Scherzo caprice, small orch., 1917; Russians, baritone and orch., 1918; Prelude and
fugue, piano and orch., 1921; Chanticleer, festival overture, 1928; Suite after English folksongs, 1934; Chamber music: piano quartet, 1912;
Pastorale, violin, clarinet and piano, 1913;
clarinet sonata, 1915; violin sonata; string
quartet on Negro themes, 1919; 3 pieces for flute,
harp, and string quartet, 1922; Intermezzo,
string quartet; Variations on a theme of John
Powell, string quartet, 1926; Divertimento,
woodwind quintet, 1927; Fanny Blair, folksong
fantasy for string quartet, 1929; Sentimental
sketches, piano trio, 1935; Chorus: Long, long
night; Twilight song; Ode to big business; Songs
of the countryside; Piano: Color contrasts;
Country pictures; Divertimento, 4-hands; Prelude
and fugue, 4-hands; Organ: A joyous prelude.
He was author of many books and articles on
musical subjects.

*MASON, F. STUART
b. Weymouth, Mass., 1883; d. Boston, Mass., 1929.
Taught piano at the New England Cons. He published 2 pieces for English horn and piano.

MASON, LUCAS
b. Beloit, Wis., 28 July 1931. Studied with
Cecil Burleigh, Hilmer Luckhardt, Robert Crane,
and Rudolph Kolisch, Univ. of Wisconsin. He was
on the staff of the Alwin Nikolais Dance Theatre,
1959-60; Noble Path Mime Theatre, 1963-68; Children of One, 1968-73; director, Composers' Circle,
1970-74.
WORKS: Opera: Requiem, 1-act; Orchestra:
3 symphonic works; Chamber music: 13 sonatas;
15 works for chamber ensembles; 40 songs; 4 film
scores; 4 off-Broadway shows, etc.
234 West 13th St., New York, NY 10011

MASON, THOM DAVID
b. Welch, W. Va., 10 Oct. 1941. Studied with
Milton Rush, Univ. of Wisconsin; Leon Stein,
De Paul Univ., with Anthony Donata and Alan
Stout, Northwestern Univ., D. M. He received
awards from Down Beat Hall of Fame, 1960;
Arthur J. Schmidt, 1964; W. T. Faricy, 1968; and
was Ford Found. musician-in-residence, Dallas/
Ft. Worth, 1972. He was assistant professor,
Eastern Michigan Univ., 1968-71; Queens Coll.,
1971-72; Southern Methodist Univ., 1973- .
WORKS: Opera: From Brave New World, chamber opera; Chamber music: 4 pieces for mixed
octet; Piece in search of a title, woodwind quartet; Thoughts, solo flute; Canzone de sonar,
saxophone; Chorus: Psalm 23; Electronic: Message, women's chorus, tape and slides; Nice trip,
tape; One afternoon while on my way back from
Philadelphia, tape; November '72, tape and synthesizer; Synthesis, tape and jazz saxophonist.
609 Northill, Richardson, TX 75080

MASONER, E. L. (BETTY)
b. Bemidji, Minn., 22 May 1927. Studied with
Edgar B. Gangware, Bemidji State Coll., B. S.
1948. She taught in public schools, 1948-72;
visiting instructor in percussion, Bemidji
State Coll., 1973.
WORKS: Percussion: Cymbal solo no.1, with
piano; Trio for percussion ensemble.
911 Dewey Ave., Bemidji, MN 56601

MATHEW, DAVID
b. Rochelle, Ill., 18 Dec. 1945. Studied with
Paul Steg and A. Oscar Haugland, Northern Illinois Univ.; with Merrill Ellis, North Texas
State Univ., D. M. A. 1973. He was teaching
fellow, North Texas State Univ., 1971-73; assistant professor and director, electronic music
center, Georgia Southern Coll., 1973- .
WORKS: Orchestra: AT70; 6 for 27; Chamber
music: Brass trio I; Cimaras, piano; Moods II,
piano; S.S.'s song, clarinet; Electronic: Reflections on October '68; Tinker toys; Multimedia: Intermedia piece, chamber orch. and
tape; Private mirrors, tape with dancer and
lights; Ease, tape with dancer.
Camaro Court, Bel-Air Estates
Statesboro, GA 30458

MATHEWS, M. V.
b. Nebraska, 13 Nov. 1926. Aside from early
piano lessons as a child, is self-taught in
music. He received the Sarnoff Medal, Inst. of
Electrical and Electronics Engineers, 1973, and
is on the staff, Acoustical and Behavioral Research Center, Bell Laboratories, N. J.
WORKS: Electronic: Numerology; Masquerades,
1963; Slider, 1965; Swansong, 1966; The second
law; May carol.
81 Oakwood Drive, Murray Hill, NJ 07974

MATSON, SIGFRED C.
b. Chicago, Ill., 17 Feb. 1917. Studied with
Leo Sowerby in Chicago; with Howard Hanson,
Eastman School of Music. He has received 8 com-
position grants from Mississippi State Coll. for
Women. He was instructor, Sioux Falls Coll.,

296

(MATSON, SIGFRED C.)
1939-41; Ohio Wesleyan Univ.; 1941-44; head,
music department, Monmouth Coll., 1948-49; head,
music department, Mississippi State Coll. for
Women, 1949-   .
    WORKS: Choral works and piano pieces.
    Mississippi State College for Women
    Columbus, MS 39701

*MATTFELD, JULIUS
b. New York, N. Y., 8 Aug. 1893; d. New York,
31 July 1968. Was chiefly music librarian, musi-
cographer, and organist; was author of books on
music history. His compositions included a ballet, Virgins of the Sun, 1922.

*MATTHEWS, H. ALEXANDER
b. Cheltenham, England, 26 Mar. 1879; U.S. citizen 1923. Studied organ with his father; received honorary doctorates of music from
Muhlenberg Coll. and Univ. of Pennsylvania, 1925.
He was organist-choirmaster in Philadelphia
churches, 1916-54; chairman of theory, Clarke
Cons., 1934-54; on retirement lived in Madison,
Conn.
    WORKS: Opera: Play the game; Hades, Inc.,
comic opera; Cantatas: The story of Christmas;
The triumph of the cross; The city of God; The
conversion; The life everlasting; The eternal
light; also introits and graduals of the church
Year.

MATTHEWS, HOLON
b. Oregon, Ill., 17 July 1904. Studied with
Sidney Durst and Edgar Stillman Kelly, Cincinnati,
Cons., B. M., M. M.; privately with Eugene
Goosens; with Howard Hanson and Bernard Rogers,
Eastman School of Music, Ph. D. He held scholarships for all study. He taught piano at Cincinnati Cons., Eastman School, Wilson Coll., and
was professor of music, Western Michigan Univ.,
1948-73.
    WORKS: Orchestra: 4 symphonies; tone poems
and suites; also chamber music, choral works,
and many songs.
    4708 Greenacres Drive, Kalamazoo, MI 49009

*MATTHEWS, JOHN SEBASTIAN
b. Cheltenham, England, 11 Dec. 1870; to U.S.
1900; d. Pawtucket, R. I., 23 July 1934. Brother
of H. Alexander Matthews, was also organist and
teacher in Philadelphia. He wrote anthems, organ
pieces, and songs.

MATTHEWS, JUSTUS
b. Peoria, Ill., 13 Jan. 1945. Studied with
Aurelio de la Vega, California State Univ. at
Northridge; with Lejaren Hiller, State Univ. of
New York at Buffalo. He received first prize in
composition at CSU Northridge, 1965; fellowships
at SUNY at Buffalo, 1968, 1969, 1970, summer 1971;
summer fellowship, CSU Long Beach, 1973. He
taught woodwinds privately, 1963-68; was teaching
assistant, State Univ. of New York, Buffalo,
1968-71; assistant professor, California State
Univ. at Long Beach, 1971-   .
    WORKS: Theatre: Artaud's Le jet de sang,
drama with music, 1968-70; Chamber music: Duet,

(MATTHEWS, JUSTUS)
flute and clarinet, 1963; 6 songs, soprano, baritone, chamber group, 1965; 4 miniatures, string
quartet, 1966; 3 Greek songs, soprano alone,
1966; 4 miniatures, guitar, cello, double bass,
1969; Hdoryut, for 16 solo instruments, 1971;
Chorus: One poem of A. A. Voznesenskii, 5-part
chorus a cappella, 1966; 7 pieces for choir and
orch., 1966; The argument, Blake text, 16-part
chorus a cappella, 1971; Announcement, 10-part
chorus, 1971; Electronic: Arabrabnamragus, tape,
1971; MUS15/1-35/S.EED, 35 compositions computed
and recorded in Stockholm, 1973.
    245 Harvard Lane, Seal Beach, CA 90740

MATTHEWS, THOMAS
b. Utica, N. Y., 1 April 1915. Studied with
Norman Coke-Jephcott in New York. His awards
include Pi Kappa Lambda, and a special award
from the Oklahoma Diocese. He was professor of
organ, Northwestern Univ.; music director, Sea-
bury Western Seminary; professor of organ, Univ.
of Tulsa, 1960-   ; organist and choirmaster
at various churches, 1946-   .
    WORKS: Anthems and liturgical works for
chorus and organ.
    1625 East 31st Place, Tulsa, OK 74104

MATTHEWS, WALTER E.
b. New Jersey, 17 Dec. 1917. Studied at Trenton
State Coll., B. S.; Teachers Coll., Columbia
Univ., M. A. 1948; and at New York Univ. He was
public school music supervisor, 1944-60; district
music director, West Hempstead, N. Y., 1959-70;
church music director, 1951-64.
    WORKS: Chorus: He led the way; When Jesus
was born; Jesus lies sleeping; O come and mourn.
    Lawton Rd., Eastham, MA 02642

*MATTHEWS, WILLIAM
b. Iowa City, Iowa, 1950. Letters from home,
antiphonal music for 11 players, won a BMI
award, 1973.

MATTILA, EDWARD CHARLES
b. Duluth, Minn., 30 Nov. 1927. Studied with
Halsey Stevens, Univ. of Southern California;
with Carl McKinley, New England Cons.; and Paul
Fetler, Univ. of Minnesota. He was instructor,
Concordia Coll., St. Paul, 1958-62; assistant
professor, Bishop Coll., 1962-64; associate professor, Univ. of Kansas, 1964-   .
    WORKS: Orchestra: Symphony no. 1; Parti-
tions for string orch.; Chorus: On teaching,
chorus, soloists, and orch.; 13 ways of looking
at a blackbird, reciter, chorus and chamber ensemble; Piano: 6 arrays; Electronic: Arp piece
for synthesizer.
    School of Fine Arts, University of Kansas
    Lawrence, KS 66044

MAULDIN, MICHAEL
b. Port Arthur, Tex., 14 June 1947. Studied
with Evan Tonsing, Amarillo Coll.; Max Ellsberry
and James Rivers, Washburn Univ.; William Wood,
Univ. of New Mexico. He won a Sigma Alpha Iota
contest with a woodwind quintet, Topeka, 1969.
He was graduate assistant in piano, Univ. of New

MAULDIN, MICHAEL

(MAULDIN, MICHAEL)
Mexico, 1972-73; director of Mauldin School of Music, 1972-   .
WORKS: Orchestra: Variations on a Huron carol, small orch., 1973; Tombeau for strings and timpani, Albuquerque Youth Symphony, 18 Oct. 1973; Chamber music: Etude in Phrygian mode, woodwind quintet, 1969; clarinet sonata, 3 studies of children; Wedding song, clarinet and organ; Wedding march, organ; 4 modal piano pieces.
12713 Summer Ave., N.E.
Albuquerque, NM 87112

MAURY, LOWNDES
b. Butte, Mont., 7 July 1911. Studied at Univ. of Montana, B. A. 1931; Chicago Musical Coll.; with Arnold Schoenberg on scholarship in Boston, 1934; later with Wesley LaViolette. His Sabbath Eve service won a contest of the Valley Jewish Community Center, North Hollywood. He has been film composer and pianist in film, radio, and television studios; was visiting professor, Montana State Univ., 1967, 1968.
WORKS: Orchestra: Passacaglia, string orch., 1959; Summer of green, rhapsody for flute and strings, 1964; Chamber music: Song without words, viola and piano; Lament, 3 pieces for solo flute; Reflection, flute and piano; Changes, 7 flutes; violin sonata, In memory of the Korean War dead, 1952; Night life, cello and piano, 1956; Springtime digressions, piano, flute, string quartet, 1961; Speculations, piano and string trio, 1964; Scene de ballet, piccolo and string quartet, 1965; 5 Rilke songs, mezzo and string quartet; The imprisoned cellist, suite for cello; Chorus: Proud music of the storm, Whitman text, soloists, chorus, orch., 1953; Man is my song, cantata, 1963; Concerto for English words, brass, and percussion, text by Cardona-Hine, solo quartet, 13 brass, 4 percussionists.
4279 Farmdale Ave.
North Hollywood, CA 91604

MAVES, DAVID W.
b. Salem, Ore., 3 Apr. 1937. Studied with Homer Keller, Univ. of Oregon; with Ross Lee Finney, Leslie Bassett and George Wilson, Univ. of Michigan. He received the John H. Reid choral prize, 1961, 1970; Ford Found. composer-in-residence grant, for Raleigh, N. C., 1964-66; College Band Directors Nat. Asso. award, 1965; Rockefeller performance grants, 1968, 1969; and commissions. He was chairman, music department, Shaw Univ., 1966-68; teaching fellow, Univ. of Michigan, 1962, 1968-71; assistant professor, Duke Univ., 1972-   .
WORKS: Orchestra: Symphony, 1970; Overture to an opera; Band: 5 moments from a spring day, 1966; Toccata, 1966; March with sleighbells, 1967; The wanderer recalls his homeland, 1970; Chamber music: Fantasy, cello and percussion, 1964; Duet for diverse instruments, clarinet and flute, 1970; Fugue for percussion, 1970; Homage to Lorca, violin and piano; violin sonata no. 2; Retrieval, chamber ensemble, 1971; piano sonata; string quartet; Variations, wind quintet; Chorus: God's grandeur, with orch., 1970; The storm is over, with orch., 1970; Psalm 134, 1970; Iubilate,

(MAVES, DAVID W.)
1970; The legend of Befana, cantata, 1970; Songs: 3 songs of affirmation, soprano; The siren, tenor and piano, New York, 6 Apr. 1974.
Route 1, Box 260-E
Hillsborough, NC 27278

*MAXFIELD, RICHARD
b. Seattle, Wash., 2 Feb. 1927; d. Los Angeles, Calif., 27 June 1969. Studied with Roger Sessions, Univ. of California, Berkeley; with Milton Babbitt, Princeton Univ.; and with Ernst Krenek and Luigi Dallapiccola. He taught at the New School for Social Research, New York, and at San Francisco State Coll.
WORKS: Electronic: Night music, 1960; Amazing grace, 1960; Pastoral symphony, 1960; Piano concerto for David Tudor, 1961; Bacchanale, 1963.

MAXSON, WILLIAM LYNN
b. Frankfort, Ind., 12 Nov. 1930. Studied with William Pelz, Jordan Coll. of Music; with Thomas Beversdorf and Bernhard Heiden, Indiana Univ., D. M. He was instructor, Lycoming Coll., 1955-58; professor, Eastern Washington State Coll., 1959-   .
WORKS: Chorus: Prayer and alleluia; Piano: sonatas, a sonatina; 12 preludes; also elementary harp solos.
Route 2, Box 18A, Cheney, WA 99004

*MAXWELL, EVERETT
Jubilant brass, band; Wall of brass, band; Voice in the wilderness, 3 unaccompanied flute solos; Idylls of 4 goblins, 4 bassoons; woodwind trio.
Music Department, Lubbock Christian College
Lubbock, TX 79407

MAXWELL, JACQUELINE PERKINSON
b. Denver, Col., 16 Sep. 1932. Studied with George Kuhlman in Brazil; with Walter Keller, Univ. of New Mexico; with Max di Julio and George Lynn, Loretto Heights Coll.
WORKS: Orchestra: Humoreske; Band: Chipmunks; Chamber music: Jubilo, piano and 2 flutes; Chorus: Psalm 98; Piano: Autumn suite, 2 pianos; 4 frustrations, piano solo.
7720 Westview Drive, Lakewood, CO 80215

MAY, WALTER B.
b. Springfield, Mo., 28 Sep. 1931. Studied with Relly Raffman, Southwest Missouri State Univ., B. S., B. S. E., 1951; with Darius Milhaud and Georges Dandelot, Paris Cons., 2nd medal in harmony, 1952; Univ. of Toronto, D. M. 1966. He received Fulbright grants, 1951, 1952; Nat. Fed. of Music Clubs award, 1962; Wisconsin Composers choral music award, 1964, 1965; Wisconsin Fed. of Music Clubs award, 1966; American Guild of Organists award, 1967. He was faculty member, Wisconsin State Univ., Eau Claire, 1955-67; department chairman, State Univ. of New York at Cortland, 1967-69; professor, Eisenhower Coll., 1969-   .
WORKS: Orchestra: 2 symphonies, no. 2 premiered, Rochester, 1973; Chamber music: 3 string quartets; Chorus: Job, oratorio; The last days;

(MAY, WALTER B.)
Cantate Domino; Song of songs, cantata; Service of Holy Communion.
17 Homestead Drive, Fairport, NY 14450

MAYER, LUTZ
b. Hamburg, Germany, 14 Dec. 1934; U.S. citizen 1946. Studied with Gordon Binkerd and Robert Kelly, Univ. of Illinois. He received first and second prizes, Texas Manuscript Society composition contest, 1963; 2 summer research fellowships, State Univ. of New York, 1964, 1966. He was assistant professor, Texas Wesleyan Coll., 1960-63; assistant to associate professor, State Univ. of New York at Cortland, 1963-   ; conductor, Ithaca Opera Asso., 1974.
    WORKS: Opera: Refuge, Cortland, N. Y., 1965; The paranoid parakeet, Cortland, 1968; Theatre: music for The boy with a cart, 1962; Chorus: The raven days; Psalm 23; also works for orchestra, chamber groups, voice, etc.
    Box 71, Little York, NY 13087

MAYER, WILLIAM
b. New York, N. Y., 18 Nov. 1925. Attended Yale Univ. and Mannes Coll. of Music; studied with Roger Sessions, Felix Salzer, and Otto Luening, conducting with Izler Solomon. He received a Guggenheim fellowship, 1966; 2 Ford Found. grants; Rockefeller grant; and ASCAP awards for 12 years. He taught at Boston Univ., 1965; was special writer for the U.S. Information Agency, 1965-67.
    WORKS: Opera: One Christmas long ago, 1-act, 1962; Brief candle, drama in 3 acts and 6 minutes, 1964; Ballet: The snow queen, 1963; Orchestra: The greatest sound around (The animal contest), baritone and orch., 1954; Hello world, singing narrator and orch., 1956; Andante for strings, 1956; Concert piece for trumpet and strings, 1957; Overture for an American, 1958; 2 pastels, 1961; Octagon, piano and orch., 1971; Chamber music: 2 movements for string quartet, 1952; Essay for brass and winds, 1954; Celebration trio, flute, clarinet, piano, 1956; Three for three, 2 percussion, piano; Messages, flute, string trio, piano; Country fair, brass trio, 1957; brass quintet, 1964; Miniatures, soprano and 7 players, text by Dorothy Parker, 1968; Khartoum, soprano and 4 players, 1968; Back talk, 15 players and animated page turner, 1970; News items, soprano and 7 players, 1972; Chorus: Festive alleluia, 1963; Letters home, soloists, chorus, and orch., 1968; The eve of St. Agnes, soloists, chorus, and orch., 1969; Lines on light, women's voices, 1971; Make a joyful noise, chorus and orch., New York, 17 May 1974; Spring and yes forever, cantata for soloists, triple chorus and orch., New York, 16 May 1975; Piano: Angles, 1956; sonata, 1959; Toccata, New York, 7 Oct. 1972; A most important train; Distant times, distant places; Subway in the sunlight; Claremont lights; and many songs.
    735 Ladd Rd., Bronx, NY 10471

*MAYS, WALTER A.
Funeral music for Jan Pollock, orch.
    Division of Music, Wichita State University
    Wichita, KS 67208

*MEAD, ANDREW
violin sonata.

MEAD, EDWARD G.
b. Reading, Mass., 26 June 1892. Attended Harvard Univ., B. A.; Yale Univ., B. M.; studied privately with Seth Bingham, Bainbridge Crist, Henry Cowell, and Ernst Krenek; with Harold Darke, Royal Coll., of Music, London; with Nadia Boulanger, Fontainebleau Cons., where he also received certificates in organ teaching and playing. He is a fellow of the American Guild of Organists; co-recipient with Mrs. Mead of Ohioana Library Asso. music citation, 1971. He was on the faculty, Denison Univ., 1925-27; organist and choir director, Cornell Univ., 1927-28; faculty member, Miami Univ., Ohio, 1929-60; composer-in-residence, 1957-60.
    WORKS: Over 100 published choral, organ, and piano compositions.
    2380 Madison Rd., Cincinnati, OH 45208

*MEAD, GEORGE
b. New York, N. Y., 21 May 1902. Studied at Columbia Univ., M. A. 1925; honorary D. M. He has been organist-choirmaster in Brooklyn and New York; was music director, Hofstra Coll., 1936-40.
    WORKS: Opera: The broker's opera, 1-act; Chorus: Benedictus es Domine; The Lord by wisdom hath founded the Earth; Lo. the winter is past; The voices of the wise; Once to every man and nation; Organ: Fantasy; Tidings of great joy.

*MEANS, CLAUDE
b. Cincinnati, Ohio, 1912. Studied with David McKay Williams in New York; was organist-choirmaster, Christ Church, Greenwich, Conn., 1934-72.
    WORKS: Chorus: Lord of all power and might; O come and mourn; The king rides forth; Seabury (hymn tune); Organ: Chorale prelude on Sawley.

MECHEM, KIRKE
b. Wichita, Kan., 16 Aug. 1925. Studied at Stanford Univ.; with Walter Piston and Randall Thompson, Harvard Univ.; and 3 years in Vienna. His honors include the Boott prize at Harvard; the triennial American music award for vocal music from Sigma Alpha Iota; and selection of his Psalm 100 as one of 3 works to represent American music at the United Nations 20th anniversary. He has taught at Stanford Univ. and San Francisco State Univ.; until 1972 was composer-in-residence, Lone Mountain Coll., San Francisco; full-time composer, lecturer, and conductor, 1972-
    WORKS: Orchestra: 2 symphonies; Haydn's return; The jayhawk, overture; Chamber music: suite for 2 violins; woodwind trio; piano trio; Divertimento, flute and string trio; string quartet; Whims, 15 vignettes for brass; 5 duets, violin and piano; piano suite; piano sonata; Chorus: Singing is so good a thing, tenor or soprano solo, orator, 13 players; The king's contest, comic cantata, with soloists and orch.; Speech to a crowd, MacLeish text, with baritone and orch.; Canon law for newlyweds, a cappella rounds and canons; Zorabel, chamber cantata, with wind quintet, string quintet, piano; Professor Nontroppo's

MECHEM, KIRKE

(MECHEM, KIRKE)
music dictionary, a cappella; many more choral
works, songs, piano pieces.
49 Marcela Ave., San Francisco, CA 94116

*MEHEGAN, JOHN
Jazz preludes for piano.

MEISTER, SCOTT R.
b. Elyria, Ohio, 19 Mar. 1950. Studied with Jack
Johnston, Ashland Coll.; with Clifton Williams,
Alfred Reed and Charles Campbell, Univ. of Miami,
He was on the faculty, Division of Musical Arts,
Univ. of Miami, 1972-74, graduate assistant,
1973-74.
WORKS: Percussion: Pagan place, 4 players;
Eerie interlude, 3 players; Introduction and fan-
tasy, 6 players; 7 short pieces for solo vibra-
phone; Gypsy festival, duet; Mallet with piano,
12 arrangements.
1228 Walsh Avenue, Apt. 26E
Coral Gables, FL 33146

MEKEEL, JOYCE
b. New Haven, Conn., 6 July 1931. Studied at
Longy School of Music, 1952-55; with Nadia
Boulanger in Paris, 1955-57; with David
Kraehenbuehl, Yale Univ., B. M. 1959, M. M. 1960;
with Earl Kim, 1960-62; candidate for master's
degree in applied anthropology, Boston Univ.,
1975. Her awards include a private grant for
study in France; full scholarship at Yale Univ.,
1957-60; fellowships at MacDowell Colony, 1963,
1964, 1974, Yaddo, 1974; Ingram-Merrill grant,
1964; Inter-American Music award, 1965; Radcliffe
Inst. grant, 1968-70; research grant in anthropology, Boston Univ., 1971; Nat. Endowment for
the Arts grant, 1975; and commissions. She taught
at the New England Cons., 1964-70; has been assistant professor, Boston Univ., 1970-   ; was composer for the Ina Hahn Dance Company, 1967-69;
composer and co-director, The Ensemble, 1969-71;
has also presented one-man shows of her sculpture
and participated in sculpture exhibits.
WORKS: Dance: Pleasure of merely circulating;
Duet for dancer and percussion; There were 2 of
them; Jaywalk, solo viola and dancer; Chains for
7 chains and 5 dancers, 1969; Feast, ceremony for
tape and dancers, New York, Nov. 1970; Theatre:
music for Androcles and the lion, 1961; Macbeth,
1962; Merchant of Venice, 1962; Knight of the
burning pestle, 1962; Yes is for a very young man,
1963; Fuente ovejuna, 1963; Othello, 1964; Richard
III, 1964; Moveable feast, with Paul Earls and
Lyle Davidson, 1973; Chamber music: String
figures disentangled by a flute, Boston, Apr.
1969; Shape of silence, solo flute, Boston, Sep.
1970; Spindrift, string quartet, Boston, Feb.
1971; Embouchures II, brass sextet, 1972; Corri-
dors of dream, mezzo-soprano and chamber ensemble,
1972; Homages, brass quintet, Boston, Feb. 1974;
Planh, solo violin, 1975; Serena, speaker, voice,
and prepared piano, Tanglewood, Aug. 1975; Chorus:
White silence, a cappella; Waterwalk, Boston, Apr.
1970; Toward the source; chorus and orch., Concord, Mass. Apr. 1975; Songs: Phrases, 1961;
Dark rime, 1966; also piano pieces.
320 Marlborough St., Boston, MA 02116

MELBY, JOHN B.
b. Whitehall, Wis., 3 Oct. 1941. Studied at
Curtis Inst. of Music, B. M.; with Henry Weinberg
and George Crumb, Univ. of Pennsylvania, M.A.;
with Peter Westergaard, Milton Babbitt, and
J. K. Randall, Princeton Univ., M. F. A., Ph. D.
His awards include a Princeton fellowship; NDEA
fellowship. He was associate professor, West
Chester State Coll., 1971-73; assistant professor,
Univ. of Illinois, 1973-   .
WORKS: Chamber music: 2 Norwegian songs;
piano sonata no. 2; Electronic: 91 plus 5,
brass quintet and computer; Forandrer for digital
computer.
511 South Chicago Ave.
Champaign, IL 61820

MELOY, ELIZABETH
b. Hoopeston, Ill., 7 Aug. 1904. Studied with
Carl Beecher and Albert Noelte, Northwestern
Univ.; Bernard Rogers, Eastman School of Music;
Nadia Boulanger in France; with Darius Milhaud
and Leo Sowerby in Colorado. She received a cash
award, Indiana Composers Guild, for Dance suite
for orch. She taught in public school, 1927-29;
Taylor Univ., 1929-32; Ball State Univ., 1933-69,
retiring as associate professor of theory and
organ.
WORKS: Orchestra: Overture; Dance suite;
Chamber music: piano trio; string quartet;
viola sonatina; sonatina for violin and viola;
trio for flute, oboe, cello; Chorus: Heaven and
earth and sea and air; This is my father's world;
many anthems, songs, organ preludes, piano pieces.
222 South Hutchinson, Muncie, IN 47303

*MENASCE, JACQUES DE
b. Bad Ischl, Austria, 19 Aug. 1905; to U.S.
1941; d. Gstaad, Switzerland, 28 Jan. 1960.
Studied with Alban Berg in Vienna; gave piano
recitals in Europe.
WORKS: Ballet: Status quo, 1947; Orchestra:
2 piano concertos, 1935, 1941; Divertimento,
piano and strings, 1940; Le chemin d'écume,
soprano and orch., 1942; Chamber music: viola
sonata, 1949; violin sonata, 1955; Piano: sonatine #2, 1942; Fingerprints, 1943; Romantic suite,
1950; Instantanés, 6 children's pieces, 1956-59.

MENEELY, SARAH SUDERLEY
b. Albany, N. Y., 18 Feb. 1945. Studied with
Robert Hall Lewis, Goucher Coll.; with Stefan
Grove and Earle Brown, Peabody Cons.; and with
Robert Morris, Yale Univ. She received an award
for Homegrown for piano, 1973.
WORKS: Chamber music: Narcissus monologue,
chamber orch. and tenor, 1968; 5 systems, Time,
and Buzz, 3 pieces using resonating bells, tubu-
lar chimes, kalimba, piano, voice, guitar, and
xylophone; Chorus: Everywoman: A morality tale,
oratorio for 6-18 voices, 3 female soloists, 15
toy instruments, 1971-73.
111 Fairy Dell Road, Clinton, CT 06413

MENNIN, PETER
b. Erie, Pa., 17 May 1923. Attended Oberlin Coll.,
1940-42; studied at Eastman School of Music, B. M.
M. M., Ph. D. 1947. He was recipient of the

(MENNIN, PETER)
first Gershwin Memorial prize; Bearns prize;
American Acad. of Arts and Letters award; 2
Guggenheim awards; Naumburg Found. recording
award; Gold Medal of Nat. Arts Club; Columbia
Records chamber music award; Univ. of Rochester
centennial citation; honorary doctorates from
Univ. of Chicago, Oberlin Coll., Univ. of Wisconsin, Univ. of Heidelburg, Temple Univ., Peabody Cons.; and many commissions. He served in
the U.S. Air Force, 1942-44; was member of the
composition faculty, Juilliard School, 1947-48;
director of Peabody Inst., 1958-62; president
of The Juilliard School, 1962- . He is member of the Nat. Inst. of Arts and Letters.

WORKS: Orchestra: 8 symphonies, 1942-73,
no.8 premiered, New York Philharmonic, 29 Nov.
1973; sinfonia, chamber orch.; Fantasia, string
orch., 1947; violin concerto, 1950; Concertato
for orchestra, 1952; cello concerto, 1956; piano
concerto, 1958; Canto for orchestra; flute concertino, with strings and percussion; Sinfonia
for orchestra, St. Paul-Minneapolis, 21-22 Jan.
1971; Band: Canzona, 1951; Chamber music: violin sonata; 2 string quartets; Canto and toccata,
piano, 1950; Divertimento and partita, piano;
Chorus: The Christmas story, cantata; 4 choruses based on Chinese texts; Cantate de virtute,
chorus, orch., children's chorus, soloists, and
narrator, Cincinnati, May 1969; many other compositions in all categories.
The Juilliard School, Lincoln Center Plaza
New York, NY 10023

*MENNINI, LOUIS
b. Erie, Pa., 18 Nov. 1920. Studied at Oberlin
Coll., 1939-42; with Bernard Rogers and Howard
Hanson, Eastman School of Music, B. M. 1947,
M. M. 1949, Ph. D. His awards include Nat. Inst.
of Arts and Letters grant, 1949; 2 Koussevitsky
Found. awards; commissions from Mary Duke Biddle
Found., and Erie Sesquicentennial Committee. He
served in the Army Air Force, 1942-45; was assistant professor, Univ. of Texas, 1948-49; on faculty, Eastman School, 1949-71.

WORKS: Opera: The well, 1951; The rope,
1955; Ballet: Allegro energico, 1948; Orchestra:
2 symphonies; Andante and allegro, 1946; Andante
and allegro energico, 1947; Arioso for strings,
1948; Canzona, chamber orch., 1950; Overtura
breve, 1952; Chamber music: violin sonata, 1947;
cello sonatina, 1952; Chorus: Tenebrae, a cappella; Proper of the mass, 1953.
Piazza da Mino 36
50014 Fiesole (Firenze), Italy

*MENOTTI, GIAN CARLO
b. Cadegliano, Italy, 7 July 1911; to U.S. 1928;
has kept Italian citizenship. Studied with
Rosario Scalero, Curtis Inst., graduated 1933,
honorary B. M. 1945. His other awards include
the Lauber composition prize, 1931; New York
Drama Critics Circle award, 1954; Pulitzer prize,
1955; Elizabeth Sprague Coolidge commission,
1955; Brussels Internat. Exposition commission,
1957; honorary membership, Nat. Inst. and Nat.
Acad. of Arts and Letters. He joined the faculty
at Curtis Inst. in 1941; has written the

(MENOTTI, GIAN CARLO)
librettos for all his own operas and for Samuel
Barber's Vanessa and A hand of bridge; also a
play, The leper, 1970.
WORKS: Opera: Amelia goes to the ball,
1937; The old maid and the thief, 1939; The
silent god, 1942; The medium, 1946; The telephone, 1947; The consul, 1950; Amahl and the
night visitors, 1951; The saint of Bleeker
Street, 1954; Maria Golovin, 1958; Labyrinth,
1963; The last savage, 1963; Martin's lie, 1964;
Help, help, the globolinks, children's opera,
1968; The most important man in the world, New
York City Opera Company, 7 Mar. 1971; Ballet:
Sebastian, 1944; Errand into the maze, 1947; The
unicorn, the gorgon, and the manticore, 1956;
Dramatic oratorio: Death of the Bishop of
Brindisi, 1963; Orchestra: piano concerto, 1945;
Apocalypse, 1951; Pastorale, piano and strings;
violin concerto; 1952; triple concerto in 3
movements, 1970; Chamber music: Variations on
a theme of Schumann, piano, 1931; Trio for a
house-warming party, flute, cello, piano, 1936;
suite for 2 cellos and piano, New York premiere,
20 May 1973.

*MERRILL, BOB
b. Atlantic City, N. J., 17 May 1921. Studied
acting with Richard Bennett. He served in the
Cavalry and Special Services, 1940-42; was
director, Columbia Pictures, then casting director, CBS-TV and television producer.
WORKS: Musicals: New girl in town, 1957;
Take me along, 1959; Carnival, 1961; Funny girl,
1964; Songs: If I knew you were comin' I'd've
baked a cake; Doggie in the window; Sparrow in
the treetop; and many others; Film score: The
wonderful world of the Brothers Grimm.

MERRILL, LINDSEY
b. Kentucky, 10 Jan. 1925. Studied with Claude
Almand, Univ. of Louisville; at Yale Univ.; with
Henry Cowell and Bernard Rogers, Eastman School
of Music; and with Mario Davidovsky and Vladimir
Ussachevsky, Columbia Univ. His faculty posi-
tions include Queens Coll., 1950-53; Smith Coll.,
1953-56; Univ. of Nebraska, 1956-57; Bucknell
Univ., 1957-67; professor and director, School
of Music, Kent State Univ., 1967- , director,
Blossom Festival School, 1967- .
WORKS: Chamber music: duo for 2 violins;
Ratio 4:5:6 for string quartet; Charles Ives
New England suite, tenor and piano.
335 Overlook Drive, Kent, OH 44240

MERRIMAN, MARGARITA
b. Barcelona, Spain, 29 Nov. 1927 of American
parents. Studied with Herbert Elwell, Alan
Hovhaness, Bernard Rogers, Eastman School of
Music. She was director of music, Shenandoah
Valley Acad., 1948-51; assistant professor,
Andrews Univ., 1951-56; and professor, Atlantic
Union Coll., 1959- .
WORKS: Orchestra: a symphony; Chamber
music: cello sonata; Expectation, voice and
piano; Chorus: The millenium, oratorio.
Box 704, South Lancaster, MA 01561

*MERRIMAN, THOMAS
Theme and variations, brass ensemble.

*MERRITT, CHARLES
Variations on Gott des Himmels, organ.

MESANG, THEODORE L. (TED)
b. Eau Claire Wis., 7 Dec. 1901. Attended
Northland Coll.; Univ. of Wisconsin, B. M.; Univ.
of Minnesota, M. Ed. He was band instructor in
Ashland, Wis., then at Oregon State Univ. from
1949.
    WORKS: Band: Symbol of glory; Carnival;
Oregon Trail; Men of Wisconsin; Westward go!;
and some 200-300 more published band pieces.
    1418 N.W. 11th St., Corvallis, OR 97330

MEYEROWITZ, JAN
b. Breslau, Germany, 23 Apr. 1913; U.S. citizen
1950. Studied with Walther Gmeindl and
Alexander V. Zemlinsky in Berlin; with Ottorino
Respighi and Alfredo Casella in Rome. He
received 2 Guggenheims, 1956, 1958. He has been
faculty member, City Univ. of New York,
1954-   ; taught at Tanglewood, 1948-51, 1960.
    WORKS: Opera: The barrier, Langston Hughes
text, 1950; Emily Dickinson, text by Dorothy
Gardner, 1951; Esther, Hughes text, 1957; Port
town, Hughes text, 1960; Godfather Death, 1961;
Orchestra: Symphony Midrash Esther, 1955; flute
concerto, 1962; oboe concerto, 1963; 6 pieces
for orchestra, 1967; Sinfonia brevissima, 1968;
7 pieces, 1974; Chorus: The 5 foolish virgins,
1954; The glory round his head, 1955; Missa
Rachel Plorans, 1957; Friday Evening service,
1962; The rabbis, 1965; chamber music, songs,
etc.
    27 Morningside Ave., Cresskill, NJ 07626

MEYERS, EMERSON
b. Washington, D.C., 27 Oct. 1910. Studied with
Howard Thatcher and Gustave Strube, Peabody Cons.
He received Nat. Fed. of Music Clubs award, 1943;
Fulbright grants, 1955, 1967 for Belgium; Peabody Distinguished Alumnus award, 1970; Kindler
Found. commission, 1974. He was head, piano
department, Catholic Sisters Coll., 1943-48;
associate professor, American Univ., 1948-51;
professor, Catholic Univ., 1951-   , director
electronic music laboratory, 1961-   ; director
of professional music, Nat. Capitol Sesquicentennial Commission, 1950-51.
    WORKS: Opera: Dolcedo, for television;
Orchestra: piano concertino; Symphony for small
orchestra; Chamber music: viola sonata; clarinet
quintet; 8 portraits, viola and piano; An aspect
of aleatory, violin and piano; Piano: Alarna
variations for 2 pianos; sonata; Electronic:
Rhythmus; Chez dentiste; Excitement; Moonflight
sound pictures; Episodes, piano duet and tape;
In memoriam, soprano and tape; In the mind's eye,
soprano, cello trombone, tape.
    3006 29th Ave., Hyattsville, MD 20782

*MEYERS, NICHOLAS
Mother Ann, opera-musical based on Shaker com-
munity life, 1974 NEA grant for American
Bicentennial.

MEYERS, ROBERT G.
b. Buffalo, N. Y., 29 Mar. 1932. Studied with
Ned Rorem and David Diamond, Univ. of Buffalo,
B. A. 1961; with Mel Powell and Quincy Porter,
Yale Univ., M. M. 1964. He held scholarships at
Univ. of Buffalo, 1960-61, at Yale Univ.,
1961-64; received St. John's Univ. Shell grant,
1967, 1968; commission, 1969. He was head,
music department, St. David's School, New York,
1965-67; assistant professor, St. John's Univ.,
1967-72; assistant professor, Hofstra Univ.,
1971-72; Dowling Coll., 1972.
    WORKS: Orchestra: Metachromatikos, string
orch., 1967; East to Setauket, 1969; Chamber
music: string quartet, 1969; Prelude for percussion trio, 1972; Chorus: Cremation of Sam
McGee, cantata for children's chorus, orch., and
narrator, 1965. Meyers has published extended
articles on Technical bases of electronic music;
also has a degree and years of experience in
mechanical engineering.
    1 Laura Lane, Setauket, NY 11733

*MICHAEL, DAVID MORITZ
Partita VI, 2 clarinets, 2 horns, 2 bassoons.

MICHAELIDES, PETER S.
b. Athens, Greece, 20 May 1930; to U.S. 1937.
Studied with Joseph Wood, Oberlin Coll.; with
Halsey Stevens, Univ. of Southern California,
D. M. A. He was on the faculty, Univ. of California, Santa Barbara, 1962-64; Lewis and Clark
Coll., 1964-65; and associate professor, Univ.
of Northern Iowa, 1965-
    WORKS: Forces II, 1970; Chamber music:
Perspectives 1967, song cycle for soprano, 1967;
Forces I, chamber wind and percussion ensemble,
1969; Forces IV, chamber orch., 1972; Chorus:
Lamentations, double chorus, double band, vocal
soloists, speaking chorus; Forces III, Psalm 130,
72-voice choir, a cappella; Magnification of the
nativity, 2 Eastern Orthodox hymns for Christmas;
other liturgical settings.
    2927 Minnetonka Drive, Cedar Falls, IA 50613

*MICHALOVE, PETER
Lauda, solo clarinet.

MICHALSKY, DONAL
b. Pasadena, Calif., 13 July 1928. Studied with
Ingolf Dahl, Univ. of Southern California, B. M.
1952, M. M. 1957, D. M. A. 1965; with Wolfgang
Fortner in Germany, 1958. His honors include
BMI award, 1958; Friends of Music award, 1958;
Fulbright scholarship, 1958; Sabbatical leave,
1967; annual ASCAP awards, 1967-72; Creative
leave grant, 1970. He was associate professor,
California State Coll., Fullerton, 1960-70, professor, 1970-   ; co-director and instructor,
Ford Found.-MENC Contemporary Music Project,
1966-67.
    WORKS: Opera: Der Arme Heinrich, in pro-
gress; Orchestra: Wheel of time, choral symphony, 1967; Sinfonia concertante, clarinet,
piano, orch., Idyllwild, Calif., Aug. 1969;
Elegy concerto of Ingolf Dahl, completed by
Michalsky, Los Angeles, Nov. 1971; Band: concertino, trombone and band, 1953; Little symphony

(MICHALSKY, DONAL)
for band, 1959; Fantasia sopra My funny valentine, brass ensemble, 1963; Fanfare after 17th century dances, 1965; concertino for 19 winds, 1965; Chamber music: duo for viola and piano, 1950; quintet, brass and piano, 1952; Divertimento, 3 clarinets, 1952; 6 pieces for chamber orch., 1956; Partita, oboe d'amore and strings, 1958; cello sonata, 1958; Morning music, chamber ensemble, 1959; Variations on Sweet Betsy from Pike, violin solo, 1961; Trio concertino, flute, oboe, horn, 1962; Fantasia alla marcia, brass quintet, 1963; Allegretto, clarinet and strings, 1964; Fantasia a due, horn and bass trombone, 1968; 4 short pieces for accordion, 1968; sonatina, flute and clarinet, 1968; Cantata memoriam, soprano and 12 instruments, 1971; Partita piccola, flute and piano, 1972; 3 times 4, saxophone quartet, 1973; Duo concertato, violin and viola, 1973; Chorus: Missa brevis, 1952; revised 1962; Fantasia on poems of Lorca, chorus and bass clarinet, 1957; Fanfare for a joyous occasion, women's voices, piano, percussion, 1959; Piano: 6 pieces, 1952; sonata for 2 pianos, 1958; Fantasies for the clavichord, 1961; Sonata concertante, 1961; Fantasy, 1969; Song suite, 1971; Happy birthday, Frank Campo, piano 4-hands, 1972.
116 East Oceanfront, Balboa, CA 92661

*MIDDENDORF, JOHN WILLIAM II
b. Baltimore, Md., 22 Sep. 1924. Attended Harvard Univ., B. A. 1947; Holy Cross Coll., B. Naval Sci. 1945; New York Univ., M. B. A. 1954. He was an investment banker and has written a book on banking; was ambassador to the Netherlands, 1969-73; was under secretary of the navy, 1973-74, secretary, 1974-   ; also paints on canvas, china, and stained glass windows. His compositions include 6 symphonies, one of which was broadcast nationwide in Holland during his term as ambassador; many marches, 5 of them were played at the Old Marine Barracks ceremonial parade, Dec. 1974.
McLean, VA 22101

*MIDDLETON, E. ARTHUR
Cold moon, jazz piano, 1971.

*MIDDLETON, JEAN B.
Symphony in C, 1942, revised 1962.

MIDDLETON, ROBERT
b. Diamond, Ohio, 18 Nov. 1920. Studied with Beveridge Webster, New England Cons., 1941-42; with Nadia Boulanger, Longy School of Music, 1941-42, later in Paris; at Harvard Coll., B. A. 1948, M. A. 1954; Tanglewood, Opera Department, 1946, 1947. He received scholarships at Harvard, 1939-41; John Knowles Paine fellowship, 1948-50; Guggenheim fellowship, 1965. He was instructor, Harvard Univ., 1950-53; faculty member, Vassar Coll., 1953-   , professor, 1966-   .
WORKS: Opera: Life goes to a party, 1-act, Tanglewood, 13 Aug. 1948; The nightingale is guilty, 1-act, Boston, 5 Mar. 1954; Command performance, 4-act opera-concerto, Poughkeepsie, N. Y., 11 Nov. 1961; Orchestra: Andante, 1948; violin concerto, 1949; Concerto di quattro duetti

(MIDDLETON, ROBERT)
solo winds and string orch., Poughkeepsie, 17 Mar. 1963; Variations, piano and orch., 1965; Sinfonia filofonica, Poughkeepsie, 4 May 1969; Gardens 1 2 3 4 5, 1972; Chamber music: 3 violin sonatas, 1941, 1948; string quartet, 1950; Ritratta della notte, flute and piano, 1966; Approximations, viola and piano, 1967; piano trio, 1970; Chorus: Why east wind chills, 1954; Winter wakens all my care, 1956; The Lord to me a shepherd is, 1956; O! O! O!, December, X and M, 3 Christmas carols for women's voices, 1963; De natura sirenis, De natura noctuae, women's voices, 1968; also songs and piano works. He is author of 2 books and many articles in music journals.
33 Sunrise Lane, Poughkeepsie, NY 12603

MIKHASHOFF (MAC KAY), YVAR-EMILIAN
b. Troy, N. Y., 8 Mar. 1944. Studied at Eastman School of Music, 1959-61; Juilliard School, 1961-62; with Elmer Schoettle, Univ. of Houston, B. M. 1967, M. M. 1968; with Nadia Boulanger in Paris, 1968-69; with Hunter Johnson, Kent Kennan, and Karl Korte, Univ. of Texas, D. M. A. 1973. He received scholarships for study at Eastman and Juilliard; Fulbright grant, 1968; Nansen Fund grant, 1968; 2 grants to annotate the Ives Concord Sonata, 1973; and commissions. He was a professional dancer, 1962-65; founded the Cambiata Soloists, a chamber ensemble; and was composer and recitalist in Houston and Austin; was appointed to the piano faculty, State Univ. of New York at Buffalo, 1973-   .
WORKS: Orchestra: piano concerto, Dallas, Apr. 1967; Chamber music: Dances for Davia, flute and piano, 1967; Sir Gawain and the Green Knight, narrator, soprano, 5 instruments, percussion, Houston, Apr. 1970; Four figures of a drowned maiden, narrator, soprano, 7 instruments, 1972; The pipes of Colchis, clarinet and piano, 1973; A little of the bandit's soul, violin and piano, 1973; several songs for soprano with varying instrumental accompaniment; several song cycles to French, German, Italian, and Spanish texts.
81 Heath St., Buffalo, NY 14214

MIKULAK, MARCIA LEE
b. Winston-Salem, N. C., 9 Oct. 1948. Studied piano at San Francisco Cons., B. M. 1969; graduate work at Mills Coll. She has received awards for piano performance. She is a concert pianist and has prepared works of Dane Rudhyar under his supervision.
WORKS: Piece for dance, free improvisation for prepared piano, voice, percussion, and tape.
1718 Channing Way, Berkeley, CA 94703

MILANO, ROBERT
b. Brooklyn, N. Y., 4 May 1936. Studied with Nicolas Flagello and Vittorio Giannini, Manhattan School of Music, B. M. 1960; and at City Coll. of New York, M. M. 1967. He taught at the U.S. Naval School of Music, 1960-61; in public schools, 1963-66; was adjunct lecturer, Queensborough Community Coll., 1967-70; adjunct lecturer, New York Community Coll., 1969-   ;

MILANO, ROBERT

(MILANO, ROBERT)
instructor, Adelphi Univ., 1967-   ; church organist and choirmaster, 1960-   .
WORKS: Opera: Flight into Egypt, chancel opera, Pittsburgh, 29 Aug. 1967; Rejoice and be glad, Christmas opera, 1969; Orchestra: Essay no.4 for string orch., 1961; Concierto pequeño, piano and string orch., 1973; Escenas Boringueñas, no.2, 1973; Chamber music: Toccata, piano; 4 arabesques, solo clarinet; Otto canzone e toccata, for 7 brass, 1966; Chorus: Kyrie eleison, 1962; Magnificat and Nunc dimittis, 1968; Easter sequence, 1971; Escenas Boringueñas, chorus and orch., San Juan, P. R., Apr. 1974; anthems, canticles and hymns. He is author of articles in music journals.
715 East 32 St., Apt. 4-H
Brooklyn, NY 11210

MILBURN, ELLSWORTH
b. Greensburg, Pa., 6 Feb. 1938. Studied with Scott Huston and Paul Cooper, Cincinnati Coll.-Cons.; Henri Lazarof, Univ. of California, Los Angeles; and with Darius Milhaud at Mills Coll. His awards include Elizabeth Mills Crothers prize and fellowship; Paul Henry Merritt prize; Morse fellowship; Univ. of Cincinnati research fellowship; and commissions. He was music director, Committee Theater, San Francisco, 1963-68; assistant professor, Univ. of Cincinnati Coll.-Cons., 1970-   ; director, Music '71-'74, a contemporary music series.
WORKS: Opera: Gesualdo, 1972-73; Orchestra: Voussoirs, 1970, Columbus, Ohio, Apr. 1972; Chamber music: 5 inventions for 2 flutes, 1965; concerto for piano and chamber orch., Mills Coll., May 1967; string trio, 1968; Soli, for 5 players, 10 instruments, 1968; string quintet, 1969; Soli II, for 2 players, flutes and double bass, 1970; Soli III, clarinet, cello, and piano, 1971; Soli IV, 4 instruments, 1972; violin sonata, 1972; Lament, for harp, 1972; Chorus: Massacre of the innocents, Auden text, San Francisco, Dec. 1965; Songs: 2 love songs, Millay texts, soprano, 1970; Spiritus Mundi, soprano and instruments, 1974.
341 Shiloh St., Cincinnati, OH 45220

*MILDENBERG, ALBERT
b. Brooklyn, N. Y., 13 Jan. 1878; d. Raleigh, N. C., 3 July 1918. Studied with Bruno Oscar Klein in New York; with Giovanni Sgambati in Rome; and with Jules Massenet in Paris. He was dean, music department, Meredith Coll. in Raleigh; wrote light operas, orchestral suites, and songs.

MILES, HAROLD
b. Knox, Pa., 5 Feb. 1908. Studied at Columbia Univ., Juilliard School, and in Paris. He received a MacDowell fellowship and honorary membership in the Cleveland Composers Guild. He was faculty member, Western Reserve Univ., 1931-36; professor Kent State Univ., 1960-64.
WORKS: Orchestra: piano concerto, 1946; Chamber music: piano sonata, 1933; Chorus: Memorial cantata, 1942; Song cycle: Amerasia, 1969.
Box 111, Mantua, OH 44255

MILKEY, EDWARD T.
b. Turners Falls, Mass., 2 July 1908. Studied at New York Univ., School of Education, B. S., M. A. He is a member of Phi Mu Alpha Sinfonia and Kappa Phi Kappa. He was public school music supervisor, 1930-45; educational representative for New York music publishing firms, 1946-61; taught in public schools, Parsippany, N. J., 1961-73.
WORKS: Orchestra: Suite for string orch., String section suite; Chorus: Christmas is coming; also songs.
De Camp Drive, R.D. #1, Boonton, NJ 07005

*MILLER, CHARLES
b. Russia, 1 Jan. 1899; to U.S. 1901. Studied with Hans Letz, Franz Kneisel, and Percy Goetschius at the Juilliard School; also with Leopold Auer, Carl Flesch, and Alfredo Casella. He conducted orchestras in Paris and Budapest; joined the Philadelphia Orchestra as violinist in 1941.
WORKS: Orchestra: symphony; Appalachian Mountains, a rhapsody; West Indies suite; Chamber music: Cubanaise for violin; string quartet; Chorus: New Orleans street crier.

MILLER, DOUGLAS, JR.
b. New York, N. Y., 14 Jan. 1951. Has studied in Bologna, Italy, and in New York. He received the Daniel Alpern Memorial medal, 1969. He was organist and choirmaster, 1970-71; remedial instructor, Bronx Community Coll., 1972-74.
WORKS: Chamber music: Prelude in g, flute and piano, 1971; Chorus: Hymn without words, 1970; Praise, 1973.
234 West 111th St., New York, NY 10026

MILLER, EDWARD J.
b. Miami, Fla., 4 Aug. 1930. Studied with Isadore Freed and Arnold Franchetti, Hartt Coll. of Music; with Carlos Chavez and Boris Blacher at Tanglewood, 1955, 1958; with Blacher and Josef Rufer, Berlin, 1956-58. He received Fulbright grants, 1956-58; Koussevitzky prize, 1955; Wechsler commission, 1958; Guggenheim fellowship for Rome, 1967; Library of Congress commission, 1968; E. C. Schirmer Handel and Haydn Society award, 1971. He taught at Hartt Coll., 1959-71; at Oberlin Coll.-Cons., 1971-   .
WORKS: Orchestra: Reflections - At the Bronx Zoo; Orchestral changes; Anti-heroic amalgam; Orchestral fantasies; Chamber music: 6 canons, recorder, harpsichord, viola da gamba; Song, recorder or flute solo; 3 trios for recorders; 5 short pieces for piano; The folly stone, brass quintet; percussion quintet; Study for bass harmonics and marimba, contrabass and percussion; La mi la sol - Isaac and interpolations, wind ensemble and 3 soloists; Fantasy concerto, alto saxophone and 16 winds; Around, 5 or any greater odd number of players; Electronic: Piece for clarinet and tape; Multimedia: The 7 last days, chorus, percussion, 2 tapes, 16-mm film; Quartet-variations, any 4 players and slides; The young god, a vaudeville, for actors, dancers, chorus, 2 flutes, saxophones, guitar, bass, percussion, and tape.
250 North Professor St., Oberlin, OH 44074

MILLER, FREDERICK
b. Lima, Ohio, 12 Dec. 1930. Attended Northwestern Univ. and Univ. of Iowa. He was faculty member, Univ. of Arkansas, 1958-64; assistant band director, Northwestern Univ., 1964-70, associate dean, 1970-   .
WORKS: Band: Procession and interlude, concert band; Willie's rock, marching band.
1322 Greenwood Ave., Wilmette, IL 60091

MILLER, HARVEY
b. Salisbury, N. C., 13 Apr. 1934. Studied with Juan Orrego-Salas, Bernhard Heiden, Roque Cordero, Yannis Xenakis, Indiana Univ.; with Wilton Mason, Univ. of North Carolina. He received Nat. Endowment for the Arts grant for study of computer composition. He has been associate professor, Brevard Coll., 1960-   .
WORKS: Orchestra: 3 pieces for orchestra; Chamber music: string trio; concertino, harpsichord and chamber ensemble; 3 Sandburg songs, voice, clarinet, horn, violin, harp; trio, piano, clarinet, cello; Concertare, organ and brass; Extensions, brass, percussion, and tape; Chorus: Litany for modern man; 5 mountain scenes, a cappella; The road, with baritone solo, brass, percussion; Songs: Evening song; The night wanderer; Piano: sonata; sonatina.
Brevard College, Brevard, NC 28712

*MILLER, JACQUES
b. Russia, 4 Aug. 1900. Has composed piano pieces: Fantasie; Impromptu elegante; Scherzo miniature; Impromptu in E-flat minor.

MILLER, JESSE PAUL
b. New York, N. Y., 3 Oct. 1935. Studied privately with Joseph Maneri, Josef Schmid, Norman Coke-Jephcott. He is an associate, American Guild of Organists, and has been church organist since 1954, in 1973 at St. Paul's Episcopal Church, Great Neck, N. Y. Here he has installed a Buchla synthesizer and launched a pilot program on 18 Nov. 1973 with The sum of its parts, a multimedia piece. He is also artistic director of The Final Mix Arts Center, Long Island.
WORKS: Chamber music: Settignano, 5 winds; string quartet; 5 pieces for piano; Electronic: The time predicted, an opera; Music for ascension; Multimedia: The nativity of Christ.
145 West 71st St., New York, NY 10023

*MILLER, JOAN
Tower of Babel, cantata, 1966.
2907 Normanstone Lane, N. W.
Washington, DC 20013

MILLER, LEWIS M.
b. Brooklyn, N. Y., 4 Sep. 1933. Studied with Karol Rathaus, Queens Coll.; with Vittorio Giannini, Manhattan School of Music; with Samuel Adler, North Texas State Univ., Ph. D. He received Ford Found. grants in the resident composer program, 1961, 1962. He was chairman, Fine Arts Division, Texarkana Coll., 1965-66; associate professor, Fort Hays Kansas State Coll., 1966-   .

(MILLER, LEWIS M.)
WORKS: Opera: The imaginary invalid, Hays, Kan., 1970; Orchestra: King Henry V, overture; Band: Variations on a sea chantey; Chorus: January thaw; The faucet, male voices; To the moon; River run.
208 East 32nd St., Hays, KS 67601

MILLER, MALLOY
b. Duenweg, Mo., 6 May 1918. Attended Univ. of Denver, A. B.; Boston Univ., M. M. E., D. M. A.; studied privately with Roy Harris and Nicholas Slonimsky. He was violinist, Denver Symphony and Central City Opera, 1936-40; public school music teacher, 1940-42, 1946-53; instructor USAF Statistical School, Harvard Graduate School, 1942-45; violinist, Pueblo Symphony and Colorado Springs Symphony, 1946-53; teaching fellow, Boston Univ., 1954-56, faculty, 1956-   , professor and associate dean, School of Fine and Applied Arts, 1968-   .
WORKS: Theatre: music for Richard III, 1967; The Trojan women, 1971; Orchestra: Variations for orchestra, 1949; Suite for orchestra; Tyuonyi, orchestral sketch; Western overture; concertino, oboe and chamber orch.; Ngoma, timpani and orch.; Band: Ode for band; Chamber music: Prelude for percussion, 1956; Poem, violin and piano; Pastorale, alto flute and organ; 2 rituals for percussion.
9 Fair Oak Road, Dedham, MA 02026

*MILLER, MICHAEL R.
b. Lisbon, Portugal, 24 July 1932. Studied at New York Univ., B. A.; Eastman School of Music, M. A. He was organist-choirmaster, St. Joseph's Church, New York, 1959-64; conductor, Washington Square Orchestra and Chorus, 1962-   .
WORKS: Opera: A sunny morning; Chorus: A spear of summer; Haiku set, 5 madrigals; Mass for peace.

*MILLER, NEWTON
The flying machine, 1-act opera, Univ. of Redlands, 23 Jan. 1969.

MILLER, THOMAS A.
b. Malden, Mass., 28 June 1941. Studied with Joshua Missal, Wichita State Univ.; with Francis X. Buebendorf, Jr., Univ. of Missouri, Kansas City, D. M. A. The film, Signs of the times, for which he wrote the electronic sound track, won an Excellence in Film award, Ohio State Univ. competition, 1971. He was composer-in-residence, Kentucky Educational Television Authority, Lexington, 1971; faculty member, Eastern Kentucky Univ., 1969-71; Wichita State Univ., 1968-69, 1971-   .
WORKS: Chorus: Alleluia, amen; The trumpeters and singers were as one, with trumpets and organ; A new song; A cuckoo flew out of the wood, with percussion and handbells; Sing, all ye people; Fairest Lord Jesus; Make a joyful noise; The frozen December; Eia, Susanni; Organ: Meditation.
1036 Shadyway, Wichita, KS 67203

MILLIGAN, HAROLD VINCENT

*MILLIGAN, HAROLD VINCENT
b. Astoria, Ore., 31 Dec. 1888; d. New York, N. Y., 12 Apr. 1951. Studied with T. Tertius Noble and Arthur E. Johnstone; was organist in Portland, Ore., and from 1907 in New York. He composed operettas, songs, works for organ; published 4 collections of early American folksongs, a biography of Stephen Foster, 2 books on opera.

MILLS, CHARLES
b. Asheville, N. C., 8 Jan. 1914. Studied with Max Garfield, Greenwich Music School, New York; privately with Aaron Copland, Roger Sessions, Roy Harris. His awards include Columbia Univ. band prize, 1948; Guggenheim fellowship, 1952; Roth String Quartet award; Church of the Ascension prize; grand prize, Venice Film Festival for incidental score of On the Bowery. He is a full-time composer of concert music and film and television background scores.
WORKS: Orchestra: Concertino for oboe and strings; piano concerto, 1948; Crazy Horse symphony, Cincinnati, 28 Nov. 1958; Prelude and fugue; Prologue and dithyramb, New York, 8 Mar. 1955; Serenade for winds and strings; 3 symphonies; Toccata; Chamber music: Chamber concerto for 10 instruments; Concerto sereno for woodwind octet; The brass piano, brass sextet; brass quintet; Paul Bunyan jump, jazz quintet; 5 string quartets; piano trio; 3 violin sonatas; 2 sonatas for solo violin; oboe sonata, English horn sonata; Sonata fantasia, clarinet solo; 3 recorder sonatas; sonata for flute solo; Serenade for flute, horn, piano; Little suite for flute and piano; sonatine, flute and string quartet; Suite for 2 flutes, soli; Breezy Point pipings, 2 recorders; 4 stanzas for violin solo; sonatine, violin and piano; The centaur and the phoenix, jazz ensemble, 1960; Summer song, jazz ensemble, 1960; choral works, songs, 2 piano sonatas.
P. O. Box 1186, New York, NY 10019

MILLS, EDGAR
b. Poland, 15 June 1915; U.S. citizen 1939. Studied with Victor Fuchs, Walter Klein, Vienna Cons., B. S.; Rutgers Univ., M. M.; New York Univ., Ph. D. He received the New York Univ. Founders Day award, 1965. He has been cantor, Oheb Shalom Congregation, South Orange, N. J., 1953-   ; assistant professor, Seton Hall Univ., 1968-70, associate professor, 1970-   .
WORKS: Vocal: Chassidic Sabbath Eve service; Chassidic Sabbath Morning service; supplementary songs.
84 Williamson Ave., Hillside, NJ 07205

MIMAROGLU, ILHAN
b. Istanbul, Turkey, 11 Mar. 1926; to U.S. 1959. Studied with Vladimir Ussachevsky and Stefan Wolpe, Columbia Univ.; privately with Edgard Varese. He received a Rockefeller fellowship, 1955; Guggenheim fellowship, 1971. He was teaching and technical assistant, Columbia-Princeton Electronic Music Center, 1964-67; faculty member, Teachers Coll., Columbia Univ., 1970-71; staff producer and engineer, Atlantic Records, 1969-   ; founder and director, Finnadar Records, 1972-   .

(MIMAROGLY, ILHAN)
WORKS: Piano: Pieces sentimentales, 1957; Electronic: Le tombeau d'Edgar Poe, voice and tape; 1964; Intermezzo, voice and tape, 1964; Bowery bum, voice and tape, 1964; Anacolutha, 1964; Agony, 1965; Preludes, 1965-67; Piano music for performer and composer, 1967; Wings of the delirious demon; White cockatoo, 1966; Interlude II, 1971; Provocations, 1971; Hyberboles, 1972; music for Dubuffet's Coucou Bazar, 1973; Music plus one, violin solo and tape, 1970; Sing me a song of Songmy for jazz quintet, reciters, chorus, string orch., synthesized and processed sounds, Hammond organ, 1971.
435 West 119th St., New York, NY 10027

MING, JAMES W.
b. Brownwood, Tex., 21 May 1918. Studied with Bernard Rogers and Howard Hanson, Eastman School of Music, B. M., M. M.; also with Darius Milhaud and Nadia Boulanger. His faculty positions include DePauw Univ., 1942-44; Chapman professor, Lawrence Univ., 1944-   ; visiting professor, Cornell Univ., 1955-56.
WORKS: Orchestra: Music for a film; Suite for chamber orchestra; Chorus: Missa brevis, with brass; 3 poems of Archibald MacLeish; Piano: sonatina; 3 pieces for piano.
Lawrence University, Appleton, WI 54911

*MINGUS, CHARLES
b. Nogales, Ariz., 22 Apr. 1922. Played double bass with Charles Parker, Stan Getz, Art Tatum, and others, then formed his own band in New York.
WORKS: Ballet: The Mingus dances, New York, Oct. 1971; Jazz: Pithecantropus erectus; Meditations on integration, 1964.

MIRANTE, THOMAS
b. Utica, N. Y., 11 Oct. 1931. Studied at State Univ. Coll. at Potsdam, B. S. 1954; Ithaca Coll., M. S. 1955; and privately with Earl George and David Diamond. He was musician, U.S. Army, 1955-56; public school music teacher, 1957 and 1960-   .
WORKS: Orchestra: a symphony; viola concerto; Night scene; Chamber music: string quartet; Portrait for strings; Prelude and march, alto saxophone and piano; Andante and allegro, trumpet and piano; Chorus: I AM; The house on the hill; Silent snow; Piano: sonata; A musical journey; 8 recital solos; 8 recital encores.
208 North Main St., Canastota, NY 13032

*MISHELL, KATHRYN LEE
b. Los Angeles, Calif., 5 June 1940. Studied with John Pozdro, Univ. of Kansas, B. M. 1963; with Ingolf Dahl, Univ. of Southern California, 1963-64; was opera coach, Oberlin Coll., 1964-67, lecturer, 1969-70; private piano teacher, 1964-72. She has published duo for trumpet and piano, 1971.
1406 Ridgecrest Drive, Austin, TX 78746

MISSAL, JOSHUA M.
b. Hartford, Conn., 12 Apr. 1915. Studied with Howard Hanson, Bernard Rogers, Eastman School of Music, B. M., M. M.; and with Roy Harris. He was violist, Rochester Symphony, 1934-40, Wichita

(MISSAL, JOSHUA M.)
Symphony, 1952-70, and with various string quartets; conductor, Albuquerque Philharmonic, 1940-42, Mississippi Southern Civic Orch., 1950-52, guest conductor of many orchestras; faculty member, Univ. of New Mexico, 1946-50; Southern Mississippi Univ., 1950-52; professor and chairman, theory and composition, Wichita State Univ., 1952-70.

WORKS: Orchestra: In memoriam; 3 American portraits; 3 miniatures, string orch.; Band: Overture for band; Concertante, for 5 solo percussion and band; Wind ensemble: Fanfare, chorale, and procession, brass choir; Gloria in excelsis deo, brass choir and chorus; Jericho suite, brass choir and percussion; Rondo caprice, flute sextet; Percussion: Hoedown; 2 miniatures; 2 impressions; Barbaric dance.

30 B2 Lakeshore Drive, Farmington, CT 06032

MISTERLY, EUGENE
b. Los Angeles, Calif., 25 Sep. 1926. Studied at Univ. of Southern California and Occidental Coll.; privately with Mary Carr Moore and Mario Castelnuovo-Tedesco in Los Angeles. He was awarded 2 Celia Buck grants by the Nat. Asso. of American Composers and Conductors, 1962, 1964, for his operas. He has been a private teacher of piano, orchestration, composition, and theory, 1947-   .

WORKS: Opera: Bettina, in 3 acts, 1962; Henry V, 3 acts, 1964; Orchestra: Balinaise, symphonic poem, Los Angeles, May 1974; Cantatas: Testimony, soprano and orch.; The cask of Amontillado, tenor and chamber orch.; The telltale heart, baritone, string quartet, piano.

1363 Brampton Road, Los Angeles, CA 90041

*MITCHELL, LYNDOL
1923-1964. Kentucky Mountain portraits: Cindy, Ballad, Shivaree, for orch.; River suite for band; When Johnny comes marching home, chorus, piano and drums.

MITCHELL, REX
b. Pittsburgh, Pa., 28 Sep. 1929. Attended Muskingum Coll., B. S.; Kent State Univ., M. E.; Pennsylvania State Univ., doctoral candidate in music education. He was public school music teacher, 1953-66; associate professor, Clarion State Coll., 1966-   .

WORKS: Band: Introduction and fantasia; Panorama for band; The silver cornets; Caprice for band; Song for the young; In a day or two; Concert miniature; Shindig!, jazz band.

Box 1051, Oil City, PA 16301

*MITSUOKA, I.
2 movements for trombone and piano.

*MITTLER, FRANZ
b. Vienna, Austria, 14 Apr. 1893; to U.S. 1939. Settled in New York; has written an opera, a piano trio, and the piano suites: Manhattan suite; Suite in 3/4 time; Newreel suite; Boogie-woogie; Waltz in blue; One-finger polka.

MIZELLE, DARY JOHN
b. Stillwater, Okla., 14 June 1940. Studied at Sacramento State Coll., B. A. 1965; with Larry Austin, Jerome Rosen, Karlheinz Stockhausen, Richard Swift, and David Tudor, Univ. of California at Davis, M. A. 1967; Univ. of California, San Diego, doctoral program, 1970-73. He received a commission for an electronic mass from St. Pius X Seminary, 1967; California State graduate fellowship, 1972; Rockefeller Found. research fellowship, 1972. He was associate instructor, Sacramento State Coll., 1963-64; associate editor, SOURCE Magazine, 1966-70; associate in music, Univ. of California, Davis, 1967-68; electronics technician, 1968-70; technical writer, U.S. Nat. Bank, 1970-73; teaching assistant, Univ. of California, San Diego, 1970-73; faculty member, Univ. of South Florida, 1973-   .

WORKS: Theatre: music for Ghelderode's Red magic; Brecht's The elephant calf; Shakespeare's Measure for measure; Chamber music: 5 pieces for violin and horn, 1964; Piece for solo violin, 1966; Green and red, quartet for 9 instruments, 1966; Piano opus, 1966; The vast beat game, chamber orch., 1971; Electronic: Straight ahead, 5 instruments and tape, 1966; Tangential energy, 1967; Wave forms, 1967; Radial energy, instruments and tape, 1967; Mass for voices and electronics, Westminster, Calif., Feb. 1968; Mrdangam, 1972; Helix II and Mandala, New York, 3 Nov. 1973; Multimedia: Light sculpture, electronics and mobile sculpture, 1967; Tiger! Tiger! for electronics, players, projections, actors, lights and tape, Davis, Calif., Apr. 1967; Photo oscillations, electronic ensemble and laser light, 1968; Art and technology concert, electronic ensemble and laser light, 1969.

11103 27th St., Tampa, FL 33612

MOE, DANIEL
b. Minot, N. D., 2 Nov. 1926. Studied with Paul J. Christiansen, Concordia Coll., Moorhead, Minn.; with Russell Harris, Hamline Univ.; George F. McKay and John Verrall, Univ. of Washington; Darius Milhaud, Aspen School; Karl F. Müller, Hannover, Germany; and with Philip Bezanson, Univ. of Iowa. He was awarded first prize, Seattle Centennial Composition contest; Danforth Found. grant; numerous commissions for choral works. He was director of choral music, Univ. of Denver, 1953-59; Univ. of Iowa, 1961-72; and has been professor of choral conducting, Oberlin Coll. Cons., 1972-   .

WORKS: Chorus: Exhortation from Proverbs, with brass sextet; Cantata of peace, with trumpet, narrator, organ; Psalm concertato, with brass quartet and string bass; Te Deum, with wind ensemble; Worship for today, with congregation and organ; Prelude and hodie; Hosanna to the son of David; The greatest of these is love, solo voice and piano.

35 North Cedar St., Oberlin, OH 44074

MOEVS, ROBERT
b. La Crosse, Wis., 2 Dec. 1920. Studied with Walter Piston at Harvard Univ., A. B. 1952, M. A. 1952; with Nadia Boulanger in Paris,

MOEVS, ROBERT

(MOEVS, ROBERT)
1946-51. He was fellow, American Acad. in Rome, 1952-55; Guggenheim fellow at Harvard, 1955-63. His commissions include Wisconsin Bicentennial Committee, 1973. He was assistant professor, Harvard Univ., 1955-63; associate professor, 1964-68, professor, Rutgers Univ., 1968-   .
WORKS: Orchestra: Variations for orch., 1952; 3 symphonic pieces, 1955; Attis, chorus and orch., 1958; concerto for piano, percussion, and orch., 1960; Et occidentem illustra, chorus and orch., 1964; Main-travelled road, Milwaukee, Wisc., 9 Feb. 1974; Chamber music: piano sonata, 1950; string quartet, 1957; sonata for violin solo; Variations for viola and cello, 1961; Musica da camera, chamber ensemble, 1965; Piece for synket, 1967; Musica da camera II; Chorus: Cantata sacra, 1952; Itaque ut, chorus and chamber orch., 1961; Et nunc reges, women's voices; Brief mass, 1968.
Blackwell's Mills, Belle Mead, NJ 08502

*MOKREJS, JOHN
b. Cedar Rapids, Iowa, 10 Feb. 1875; d. Cedar Rapids, 22 Nov. 1968. Studied with Leopold Godowsky and Adolf Weidig, American Cons.; was piano teacher in New York and Los Angeles; returned to Cedar Rapids in 1966. He wrote an opera, an operetta, chamber works, songs, piano pieces.

MOLINEUX, ALLEN WALTER
b. Upper Darby, Pa., 6 May 1950. Studied with Donald H. White, DePauw Univ., B. M. 1972; with Warren Benson and Joseph Schwantner, Eastman School of Music, M. M. 1974.
WORKS: Orchestra: Concertato; Wind ensemble: Solitary mood; Chamber music: A brief diversion, trumpet, trombone, and piano; Manipulation, solo trombone; trumpet sonata in 2 movements; Encounter, brass quintet; Psalm 13, mezzo soprano and piano; A little book of serial etudes for bassoon.
68 Sunshine Rd., Upper Darby, PA 19082

*MOLLICONE, HENRY
Assistant conductor, New York City Opera, was commissioned by the Nat. Opera Inst. to compose an opera based on David Guerdon's play, La buanderie (The laundry) with libretto by Howard Richardson. He has published 5 poems of love, Emily Dickinson text, for women's voices.
111 West 70th St., New York, NY 10025

MONACO, RICHARD A.
b. Richmond Hill, N. Y., 10 Jan. 1930. Studied with Hunter Johnson and Robert Palmer, Cornell Univ.; with Roberto Gerhard at Tanglewood. He has received Cornell Friends of Music award; ASCAP awards, 1970-73; Nat. Endowment for the Arts-Columbia Symphony commission. He was public school teacher, 1957-59; professor, Western Coll., 1959-   ; visiting associate professor, Cornell Univ., 1968-69; conductor, Oxford Chamber Orchestra, 1963-69.
WORKS: Chamber music: piano quintet; 3 miniatures for woodwind quintet; A company of creatures, soprano and chamber ensemble; trombone

(MONACO, RICHARD A.)
sonata; Chorus: Blessed be the Lord, cantata; The magnificat, soprano, tenor, chorus and orch.; The prophecy, cantata for women's voices, flute, horn, piano; An Easter carol, women's voices; 4 songs for literary naysayers.
131 West Collins St., Oxford, OH 45056

*MONHARDT, MAURICE
Studied at Peabody Cons. and Juilliard School. His works include The trumpet shall sound for orch.; and a suite for flute and piano; both performed at Cedar Rapids, Iowa, 14 Nov. 1960.
Music Department, Luther College Decorah, IA 52101

MONK, MEREDITH
b. Lima, Peru, 20 Nov. 1944; U.S. citizen 1945. Studied with Meyer Kupferman, Paul Ukena, Bessie Schoenberg, Sarah Lawrence Coll. She was recipient of the Obie award special citation, 1972; Guggenheim fellowship, 1972; appointment to board of directors, Center for New Music. She was director, The House, a performing group in Nat. Endowment for the Arts touring program, 1969-73; teaching fellow, Goddard Coll.; lecturer, New York Univ., 1970-72.
WORKS: Voice: Juice: a theatre cantata, 85 voices and mouth harps, violin, percussion; Raw recital, solo voice and organ; Key: an album of invisible theatre, solo voice and organ; Vessel: an opera epic, voice, organ, dulcimer; Our lady of late, voice and glass harmonica; Education of the girlchild, non-verbal opera, solo voice and piano, New York, 8 Nov. 1973.
228 West Broadway, New York, NY 10013

*MONK, THELONIOUS
b. Rocky Mount, N. C., 10 Oct. 1918. Played piano in New York bands; developed the style called bebop; appeared at Philharmonic Hall and Carnegie Hall, New York, in the 1960s; made tours of Japan and Europe.
WORKS: Jazz ensemble: Misterioso; Evidence; 4 in one; Off minor; Blue Monk; Crepuscle with Nelly; Epistrophy; Variations on Jerome Kern's Smoke gets in your eyes.

*MONOD, JACQUES-LOUIS
b. Paris, France, 1927; to U.S. 1950. Studied in Paris with Olivier Messiaen and Rene Leibowitz; at Juilliard School; Columbia Univ.; Berlin Cons. He has held faculty posts at the New England Cons., Princeton Univ., Harvard Univ., Columbia Univ., and Queens Coll., New York; has conducted premieres of works by Berg, Schoenberg, Webern, Babbitt, and Elliott Carter, mostly in New York. His Chamber aria for soprano and orch. was given its premiere in Boston, 11 May 1973.
395 Riverside Drive, New York, NY 10025

MONROE, JAMES FRANK
b. Rienzi, Miss., 28 Nov. 1908. Studied piano at Cincinnati Cons. and Baylor Univ., B. M.; composition with Stella Roberts and Leo Sowerby, American Cons., M. M. cum laude; musicology, Univ. of North Carolina, M. A., Ph. D. He was instructor, Southwest Missouri State Teachers

(MONROE, JAMES FRANK)
Coll., 1944-45; Friends Univ., 1945-46; professor, Northeast Louisiana Univ., 1946-74.
WORKS: Chamber music: Piece for woodwinds, percussion and solo horn; Suite for horn and piano; Suite for trumpet and piano; Voice: Motet, chorus; 2 miniatures, solo voice and piano; Piano: 3 fugues; sonatina; Fantasia; Passacaglia for organ.
Route 5, Box 358, Monroe, LA 71201

MONTGOMERY, MERLE
b. Davidson, Okla., 15 May 1904. Studied at Univ. of Oklahoma, B. F. A. 1924; Eastman School of Music, M. M. 1937, Ph. D. 1948; privately with Nadia Boulanger and Isidor Philipp in Paris, 1929-31; Fontainebleau School, diploma, 1936. She received Univ. of Rochester alumni citation; Mu Phi Epsilon citation 1967; Woman of the Year award in music, Theta Sigma Phi, Oklahoma City, 1972. She was faculty member, Univ. of Oklahoma, 1931-33; Southwestern Inst. 1934-38; assistant state supervisor Oklahoma WPA Music Project, 1938-41; supervisor, 1941-43; teacher, Eastman School, 1943-45; lecturer, Schillinger System, 1945-47; consultant, Oxford Music Ed., 1957-67; staff, Carl Fischer, 1947-55, 1968-72; president, Nat. Fed. of Music Clubs, 1972- .
WORKS: Chorus: Leisure; Madrigal, a cappella; many published pieces for piano, songs for children; unpublished works for orchestra, voice, and chorus. She is author of Music theory papers, I-IV, many articles in music journals.
222 East 80th St., New York, NY 10021

MOORE, CARMAN L.
b. Lorain, Ohio, 8 Oct. 1936. Studied at Ohio State Univ., B. M.; Juilliard School, M. M.; privately with Hall Overton, 1958-62; Vincent Persichetti, 1965; Luciano Berio, 1966. He received grants from Creative Arts Service Public Program, 1970; New York State Council on the Arts, 1971, 1972, 1974. He was assistant professor, Yale Univ., 1969-71; Brooklyn Coll., 1972-74; music critic and columnist, Village Voice, 1965- .
WORKS: Orchestra: Catwalk, ballet for orch. and tape; Gospel fuse, gospel quartet and orch.; Wildfires and field songs, commissioned by New York Philharmonic and New York State Council on the Arts, New York, 23 Jan. 1975; Chamber music: Drum major, to Martin Luther King, brass, percussion, and tape; Memories, ballet for bells and mixed instruments.
65 West 90th St., New York, NY 10024

MOORE, CHARLES
b. Vinita, Okla., 23 May 1938. Studied with Bela Rozsa, Tulsa Univ.; with Philip Bezanson and Richard Hervig, Univ. of Iowa. He won a Phi Mu Alpha contest, 1965, with a woodwind quintet. He was faculty member, Minot State Coll., 1965-67; Concordia Coll., Moorhead, Minn., 1968-74.
WORKS: Orchestra: Concertpiece; Chamber

(MOORE, CHARLES)
music: woodwind quintet; brass quintet, 1963; clarinet sonata; Cassation, wind sextet.
Box 44, Christine, ND 58015

MOORE, DAVID A.
b. Stillwater, Okla., 23 Feb. 1948. Studied with Daniel Lentz, Douglass Green, Peter Racine Fricker, and Edward Applebaum, Univ. of California, Santa Barbara, B. A., M. A.
WORKS: Opera: Jephtha, 2 acts, libretto by composer, 1973; Chamber music: string quartet, 1970; 3 Haiku, baritone, recorders, percussion, 1972; 3 songs on diverse texts, flute, clarinet, soprano, 1972; trio, violin, viols, piano, 1972; Chorus: Requiem cantata, with 5 instruments, percussion, piano, 1968; Passion cantata, small ensemble and tape, 1970; Songs of the Shulamites, women's voices, piano, harp, 1970.
4028 Patterson Ave., Oakland, CA 94619

MOORE, DONALD I.
b. Farnhamville, Iowa, 11 Apr. 1910. Studied at Carleton Coll., Colorado State Coll. of Education, and Univ. of Michigan; composition with James Robert Gillette, F. L. Lawrence, and Erik Leidzen. He was professor and director of bands, Baylor Univ., 1948-69, professor emeritus, 1969- .
WORKS: Orchestra: Burlesca; Oratory for horn, with orch.; Band: Domino variations; Bright and breezy; Tau Beta Sigma; Saul of Tarsus; Affirmation: Alleluia; Triumvirate, with trombone trio; The greatness of America, with chorus; Psalm 23, with chorus; numerous concert pieces and marches for band.
School of Music, Baylor University
Waco, TX 76703

*MOORE, DOUGLAS STUART
b. Cutchogue, N. Y., 10 Aug. 1893; d. Greensport, N. Y., 25 July 1969. Studied with Horatio Parker and David Stanley Smith, Yale Univ., B. A. 1915, B. M. 1917; with Vincent d'Indy and Nadia Boulanger in Paris, 1919-21. His many awards included honorary music doctorates, Cleveland Inst. of Music, 1924, Cincinnati Cons., 1946, Univ. of Rochester, 1947, Yale Univ. 1955; Pulitzer scholarship, 1925; Guggenheim fellowship, 1934; membership, Nat. Inst. of Arts and Letters, 1946, president, 1959-62; Pulitzer Prize, 1951; New York Music Critics' Circle awards, 1946, 1955; Huntington Hartford Found. award, 1960; honorary LHD, Columbia Univ., 1963. He served in the U.S. Navy, 1917-18; joined the faculty at Columbia Univ., 1926, was executive director, music department, 1940-62.
WORKS: Opera: The headless horseman, 1936; The devil and Daniel Webster, 1939; White wings, 1948; The emperor's new clothes, 1948; Giants in the Earth, 1950; Ballad of Baby Doe, 1955; Gallantry, a soap opera, 1957; The wings of the dove, 1961; Carry Nation, 1965; Orchestra: Pageant of P. T. Barnum, 1926; Moby Dick, 1928; A symphony of autumn, 1928; Overture on an American theme, 1930; Village music, 1941; In memoriam, 1944; symphony in A, 1945; Farm journal, chamber orch., 1948; Cotillion suite, string

MOORE, DOUGLAS STUART

(MOORE, DOUGLAS STUART)
orch., 1952; Down East suite, with violin solo;
Band: The people's choice; Chamber music: Violin
sonata, 1929; string quartet, 1933; quintet for
woodwinds and horn, 1942; clarinet quintet, 1946;
piano trio, 1953; Chorus: Dedication; The Green-
field Christmas tree, with orch.; The mysterious
cat, women's voices; Perhaps to dream, women's
voices; Simon Legree, male chorus; Songs: Come
away death; Dear dark head; Not this alone; Old
song; 3 sonnets of John Donne; Under the greenwood tree; Adam was my grandfather; also piano
pieces. He was author of Listening to music,
1932; and From madrigal to modern music, 1942.

*MOORE, EARL VINCENT
b. Lansing, Mich., 27 Sep. 1890. Studied at
Univ. of Michigan, B. A. 1912, M. A. 1915; and
in Europe; joined the faculty at Univ. of Michigan in 1913. His compositions include 2 children's cantatas, The voyage of Arion and The
bird man; choral works and organ pieces.

*MOORE, MARY CARTER
b. Memphis, Tenn., 6 Aug. 1873; d. Ingleside,
Calif., 11 Jan. 1957. Studied music privately;
received an honorary D. M., Chapman Coll.; 3
awards, Nat. League of American Pen Women;
David Bispham medal, 1930. She was a concert
and choir singer; taught at Chapman Coll.; was
professor, California Christian Coll.
WORKS: Opera: The oracle, operetta in
which she sang the leading role, 1894; Narcissa,
1912, conducted by the composer in San Francisco
in 1922; David Rizzio; Los rubios; The shaft of
Ku'Pish Ta Ya; Orchestra: piano concerto; My
dream; Chamber music: piano trio; piano quintet.

MOORE, MAURINE RICKS
b. Vermillion, Kan., 1 Nov. 1908. Studied with
Carl Preyer, Univ. of Kansas, B. A. 1937; and
with Elmer Schoettle; piano at Dingley-Matthews
School and with E. Robert Schmitz. She taught
piano, Renquist School, 1929-32; Denver Coll. of
Music, 1936; in her own studio, 1937-57; American Coll. of Musicians, 1963-73.
WORKS: Piano: Romantic reverie; Rhapsodic
melody; My prayer; Rhapsody on war and peace;
2 piano suites.
1330 East Nevada Drive, Tucson, AZ 85706

MOORE, ROBERT STEELE
b. Marshall, Tex., 22 Aug. 1941. Studied at
Centenary Coll., Sam Houston State Coll., and
Univ. of Iowa. His awards include Philip Greeley
Clapp award; Rockefeller Found. grant; Nat. Endowment for the Humanities fellowship; Sutherland
Dows chair in composition, Univ. of Iowa. He was
visiting lecturer, Univ. of Indiana, 1969; assistant professor and co-director, Program in Technology and Music, Oberlin Coll., 1969-73; research guest, Massachusetts Inst. of Technology,
1973-74.
WORKS: Orchestra: Homomorphisms; Blues
peoples for actor, soprano, chorus, orch., percussion ensemble, jazz quintet; Chamber music:
Blood wedding, soprano and 11 instruments; Electronic: Negentropy/entropy, quadraphonic tape;

(MOORE, ROBERT STEELE)
Phantasms, clarinet, trombone, cello, percussion,
real-time synthesizer; Hexagrams, for multiple
keyboards (one performer) and computer-generated
tape.
250 North Professor St., Oberlin, OH 44074

MOORE, THOMAS
b. Fairfield, Ala., 24 Jan. 1933. Studied with
Dika Newlin, Drew Univ.; with Jack Beeson and
Otto Luening, Columbia Univ. He was faculty
member, Mississippi State Coll. for Women,
1961-63; Middle Tennessee State Coll., 1963-64;
C. W. Post Coll., 1964-70; violinist, Kansas
City Philharmonic, 1970-71; Indianapolis Symphony
Orchestra, 1971-73; Florida Symphony Orchestra,
1973-   .
WORKS: Orchestra: Fantasy for violin and
orch.; A quality of spring, piano and orch.;
Chamber music: Piping songs, solo flute; Metamorphosis over the symphony of Webern, for piano
duet; other chamber music and songs.
2224 Indian Hill Rd., Lynchburg, VA 24503

MOOREFIELD, ARTHUR A.
b. Denver, Colo., 11 Dec. 1928. Studied with
William S. Naylor, Cincinnati Cons.; at New York
Univ., M. A.; Univ. of California, Ph. D. in
musicology. He was lecturer, Cincinnati Cons.,
1949-50; Univ. of California, Los Angeles,
1959-61; associate professor, California Lutheran
Coll., 1961-73; associate professor, California
State Coll., San Bernardino, 1973-   .
WORKS: Orchestra: Sarabande and gigue,
1966; Alamoth: symphonic introit on Psalm 46,
chorus and orch., 1967. He has edited the complete works of Johannes Galliculus for the Inst.
of Mediaeval Music.
Music Department, California State College
San Bernardino, CA 92407

*MOPPER, IRVING
b. Savannah, Ga., 1 Dec. 1914. Studied composition with Julius Herford and Olivier Messiaen;
received a Nat. Fed. of Music Clubs award for an
opera, 1955.
WORKS: Opera: The door, 1955; George;
Nero's mother; Orchestra: Patterns, piano and
orch.; clarinet concerto; Nero's daughter, 1961;
Chamber music: 3 piano sonatinas; clarinet sonatina; piano suite; Passacaglia and fugue, piano;
Chorus: The mountain of God; Resourceful Mary;
The frog; Love story; The lemon-colored dodo;
Cantatas: The wondrous works of God; The creation; The hand loved best of all; songs.

MORAN, ROBERT LEONARD
b. Denver, Colo., 8 Jan. 1937. Attended San
Francisco State Coll.; with Hans Erich Apostel
in Vienna, 1958; with Darius Milhaud and
Luciano Berio, Mills Coll., M. A. 1963; and with
Roman Haubenstock-Ramati in Vienna. He has re-
ceived commissions from Young Chamber Orchestra,
Oakland, Calif., Lehigh Univ.; San Francisco
Symphony Orchestra Asso. He has conducted
weekly radio shows on KQED-FM and KPFA; was fac-
ulty member and associate director of the New
Music Ensemble, San Francisco Cons., 1966-72.

(MORAN, ROBERT LEONARD)
A painter as well as composer, he uses the visual arts in conjunction with his musical compositions.
WORKS: Orchestra: Interiors, for orch., chamber orch., or percussion ensemble, 2nd Annual Festival of the Avant Garde, New York, 1964; Silver and the circle of messages, San Francisco, 24 Apr. 1970; Emblems of passage, San Francisco, 7 Aug. 1974; Chamber music: 4 visions, flute, harp, and string quartet, Osaka Festival, Japan, Oct. 1964; Elegant journey with stopping points of interest, for any instrumental ensemble, 1967; L'apres-midi du Dracoula, for any sound-producing instruments, 1966; For organ-1967, organ with 1-3 players, Berkeley, Aug. 1967; Divertissement no. 3, A lunch bag opera, for many walking full-size brown paper bags and sound-producing instruments, BBC-TV, 31 Oct. 1971; Multi-media: Jewel-encrusted butterfly wing explosions, orch., television, electronics, films, etc., MENC Convention, Seattle, Mar. 1968; 39 minutes for 39 autos, for 39 amplified auto horns, auto lights, Moog synthesizer (3 players), 30 skyscrapers, 2 radio stations (stereo), one television station, dancers, theatre groups, spotlights, airplanes, etc., San Francisco, 29 Aug. 1969; Hallelujah, for 20 marching bands, 40 church choirs, organs and carillons, rock groups, gospel group, and the entire city Bethlehem, Pa., premiered Bethlehem, 23 Apr. 1971.
031 Southwest Caruthers, Apt. D
Portland, OR 97207

MORAWECK, LUCIEN
b. Belfort, France, 24 May 1901; U.S. citizen 1941; d. San Diego, Calif., 20 Oct. 1973. Studied piano with Alfred Cortot, composition with Georges Caussade, Paris Cons. His score for Man in the iron mask was nominated for an Academy award, 1940. He was affiliated with Columbia Broadcasting System in New York and Hollywood from 1935 to retirement in 1963.
WORKS: Chamber music: World in turmoil, viola and piano; string quartet; brass quintet; many works for piano solo, piano 4-hands, 2 pianos, other chamber works; Film scores: Return of Monte Cristo; Radio shows: Suspense; Chesterfield hour; Television: Playhouse 90; Gunsmoke; Have gun, will travel; Twilight zone; Perry Mason; and others.

MORGAN, ERNIE
b. Sentinel, Okla., 14 June 1945. Studied with Fred Fox, California State Coll at Hayward; with Robert Ashley, Mills Coll.; with Roger Reynolds, Univ. of California, San Diego.
WORKS: Chamber music: piano sonata, 1969; Essence, sopranos, strings, and radios, 1969; Chorus: Beginning II, 1970; Electronic: Summit, saxophone and tape, 1970; Allelujah, tape, 1970; Plato's pup, an eternal electronic piece, 1971; Unit-E, toccata for organ and electronic instruments, 1972; Cottonballs and sodapop make sorry snowcones, string bass and tape, 1972; Willie wants a monkey, tape, 1972; Beginning to be from was 4 sea and ever shall, tape, 1973; Mono-melodies, tape, 1973; Richard Martin, electronic film score, 1972.
285 Juniper, Carlsbad, CA 92008

*MORGAN, HAYDN
b. Van West Co., Ohio, 25 Mar. 1898. Studied at Wooster Coll.; Cornell Univ.; New York Univ., B. S. M., M. A. He taught in public schools; from 1941 was chairman, music department, Eastern Michigan Univ.; visiting instructor at several colleges. His compositions include a cantata, Lament and alleluia, and many sacred songs.

*MORGAN, HENRY
Never weather-beaten soil, chorus and orch.

MORGAN, ROBERT
b. Houston, Tex., 31 July 1941. Studied with Samuel Adler, North Texas State Univ., B. M. 1963, M. M. 1965; with Gordon Binkerd, Thomas Fredrickson, Morgan Powell, Univ. of Illinois, candidate for D. M. A. 1973. He received first place, Phi Mu Alpha contest, 1960; first place, Ohio State Univ. contest, 1967; research grant, Sam Houston State Univ., 1968; first place, Texas Composers Guild contest, 1969; Nat. Endowment for the Arts grant, 1972; ASCAP awards, 1972, 1973; and several commissions. He was part-time instructor, North Texas State Univ., 1963-65; instructor, Sam Houston State Univ., 1965-70; instructor, Univ. of Illinois, 1970-72; and assistant professor, Sam Houston State Univ., 1972-   .
WORKS: Orchestra: Sinfonietta, Dallas, Apr. 1965; Band: Variations on a chorale theme, 1969; Introduction, allegro, and dirge, brass and percussion, 1966; Jazz band: Anadge, 1964; Collection, 1968; Requiescat in pace/Elegia, 1968; Market square, 1968; Threshold, 1971; Chamber music: woodwind trio, 1963; sonatine, flute and piano, 1964; 4 statements on a row by Webern, 5 winds, viola, cello, marimba/celeste, 1965; Poems, flute and guitar, 1967; Chorus: Take no thought, with brass and organ, 1964; Film score: More than a state of mind, flute, horn, strings, rhythm section, KPRC-TV, Houston, Apr. 1969.
335 Park Hill, Huntsville, TX 77340

MORGAN, ROBERT P.
b. Nashville, Tenn., 28 July 1934. Studied with Roger Sessions and Edward T. Cone, Princeton Univ.; with Andrew Imbrie, Univ. of California, Berkeley. He was recipient of a German Government grant 1960-62. He taught at Univ. of Houston, 1963-67; has been associate professor, Temple Univ., 1967-   .
WORKS: Orchestra: a symphony; Momentum; Chamber music: Convergence, chamber orch.; woodwind quartet; Interplay, for flute, oboe, and bass.
2203 1/2 St. James, Philadelphia, PA 19103

*MORGENSTERN, SAM
My apple tree, song for high voice.

MORITZ, EDVARD
b. Hamburg, Germany, 23 June 1891; U.S. citizen 1943; d. New York, N. Y., 30 Sep. 1974. Studied violin with Carl Flesch, piano with Ferruccio Busoni, conducting with Arthur Nikisch,

MORITZ, EDVARD

(MORITZ, EDVARD)
composition with Paul Juon, all in Berlin. He has been a conductor throughout Europe and in the U.S.

WORKS: Opera: Circe, 3 acts; Orchestra: 3 symphonies; Burleske; Nachtmusik; Gitanjali, baritone and orch.; Kammersymphonie; Concerto for winds, brass, and percussion; Concerto grosso; concertos for violin, piano, 2 violins, saxophone, viola, cello, violin and cello; Der Klingende Garten, baritone and orch.; Italian overture; American overture; Scherzo for strings; Divertimento for winds, brass, harp, percussion; Chamber music: 5 string quartets; 3 piano trios; 3 saxophone sonatas; trio for flute, violin, viola; 2 wind quintets; quintet for saxophone and string quartet; piano quintet; violin sonata; viola sonata; cello sonata; flute sonata; sonata for violin and viola; sonata for violin and cello; sonata for 2 violins; piano sonatas; many works for piano and more than 200 songs.

*MOROSS, JEROME
b. Brooklyn, N. Y., 1 Aug. 1913. Studied at New York Univ., B. S. Mus. Ed. 1932, and at Juilliard School. He has received 2 Guggenheim fellowships.
WORKS: Opera: Gentlemen, be seated, 1955; Ballet: Paul Bunyan, 1934; American pattern, 1937; Frankie and Johnny, 1938; Guns and castanets, 1939; Susannah and the elders, 1940; Willie the weeper, 1945; The eccentricities of Davy Crockett, 1945; Robin Hood revisited, 1946; Theatre: Parade, a revue, 1935; Blood wedding, music to Garcia-Lorca's drama; Ballet ballads, 1948; The golden apple, 1950; Orchestra: Paeans, 1931; Biguine, 1934; Tall story for orchestra, 1938; symphony, 1942; The last judgment; Chamber music: sonatina for 6 clarinets; sonatina for brass quintet; Film scores: Hans Christian Andersen, ballet; The big country, 1958; Seven wonders of the world; The war lord; Wagon train, television; The Cardinal, 1963.
610 West End Ave., New York, NY 10017

MORRILL, DEXTER G.
b. North Adams, Mass., 17 June 1938. Studied with William Skelton, Colgate Univ.; with Leonard Ratner, Stanford Univ.; Robert Palmer, Cornell Univ. He received a Ford Found. grant, Young Composers Project, 1962-64. He was resident composer, Flint Hills Project, Emporia, Kans, 1966; instructor, St. John's Univ., 1966-68; associate professor, Colgate Univ., 1969-   , chairman, music department, 1971-   .
WORKS: Orchestra: Concerto for trumpet and strings, 1966; symphony, 1971; Band: Divertimento, 1964; Chamber music: 3 pieces for solo clarinet, 1964; 3 lyric pieces for violin, New York, Oct. 1969; Chorus: No, chorus and tape, 1973.
20 Montgomery St., Hamilton, NY 13346

*MORRIS, FRANKLIN E.
b. Phoenixville, Pa., 1920. Earned a Ph. D. in organic chemistry at Massachusetts Inst. of Technology; then studied composition with Walter Piston at Harvard Univ.; with Paul Hindemith at

(MORRIS, FRANKLIN E.)
Yale Univ., M. M. 1951. He has been professor, Syracuse Univ., 1946-   . His compositions include The postponement, an opera; a symphony; concerto for 7 instruments, piano, percussion, and tape; string quartet; 5 esoteric pieces, suite for piano, 1941, revised as a woodwind quintet.
School of Music, Syracuse University
Syracuse, NY 13210

*MORRIS, HAROLD
b. San Antonio, Tex., 17 Mar. 1890; d. New York, N. Y., 6 May 1964. Studied at Univ. of Texas, B. A.; Cincinnati Cons., M. M., D. M.; also with Rosario Scalero. His awards included Nat. Fed. of Music Clubs award; 2 Texas Composers awards; Philadelphia Music Guild award; Society for Publication of American Music award; Fellowship of American Composers award; Nat. Asso. of American Composers and Conductors awards; 13 MacDowell Colony fellowships; life fellowship, Internat. Inst. of Arts and Letters, Switzerland. He held faculty posts at Juilliard School, 1922-39; Columbia Univ., 1939-46; was director, Internat. Society for Contemporary Music, 1936-40.
WORKS: Orchestra: Poem, after Tagore's Gitanjali, 1918; Dum-a-lum, variations on a spiritual, 1925; piano concerto, 1931; 3 symphonies, 1934-47; Passacaglia and fugue, 1939; suite for chamber orch.; violin concerto; Heroic overture, 1943; many chamber works.

MORRIS, ROBERT DANIEL
b. Cheltenham, England, 19 Oct. 1943, of American parents. Studied with John LaMontaine, Eastman School of Music, B. M. with distinction 1965; with Ross Lee Finney, Leslie Bassett, Eugene Kurtz, Univ. of Michigan, M. M. 1966, D. M. A. 1969; with Gunther Schuller at Tanglewood; and with Nicollo Castiglione. He received a BMI student composer award, 1969; Crofts fellowship at Tanglewood, 1967. He was teaching fellow, Univ. of Michigan, 1967-68; instructor, Univ. of Hawaii, 1968-69; assistant professor, Yale Univ., 1969-   , director, electronic music studio, 1971-   , coordinator composition department, 1973-   .
WORKS: Orchestra: Syzygy, 1966; Continua, 1969; Jazz: Versus, for double bass, jazz ensemble, other instruments, and 5 alto voices; Chorus: Wireless, double chorus and 2 prepared pianos, 1968; Reservoir, a cappella; Piano: Drift off; Tusk; Night vapors; Cairn, 1967-69; Head, 1970; Electronic: Entelechy, voice, cello, electronically modified piano, 1969; On, 1969; Phases, 2 pianos and photo-cell-mixers, 1970; Lissajous, stereo tape and oscilloscope, 1971; Rapport, tape, synthesizer, and tape-delay system, 1971-72.
56 Brownell St., New Haven, CT 06511

*MORRIS, STEPHEN M.
b. Hartford, Conn., 18 Oct. 1944. Studied with Leon Kirchner and Randall Thompson, Harvard Univ.; with Luciano Berio in Rome; with Boris Blacher in Berlin.

312

(MORRIS, STEPHEN M.)
WORKS: Orchestra: <u>7 pieces for orchestra</u>,
1967; Wind ensemble: <u>7 fanfares for 7 trumpets</u>,
1973.
Box 469, Grove Beach, Westbrook, CT 06498

*MORRISSEY, JOHN J.
b. New York, N. Y., 9 Nov. 1906. Studied at
Columbia Univ., B. A., M. A.; taught at Columbia
Univ. Teachers Coll.; served in U.S. Army in
World War II; then head, music department, Tulane
Univ.
WORKS: Band: <u>Bayou beguine</u>; <u>Dance fantasy</u>;
<u>Divertissement</u>; <u>Ghost town</u>; <u>Medieval fresco</u>;
<u>Caribbean fantasy</u>; <u>French Quarter suite</u>; <u>Music
for a ceremony</u>; <u>Viva Mexico!</u>, a symphonic suite;
<u>Display piece</u>; and many others.

MORROW, CHARLES
b. Newark, N. J., 9 Feb. 1942. Attended Columbia
Coll., B. A. 1961; studied with William Sydeman,
Mannes Coll. of Music, composition diploma 1965.
His awards include internat. prize, Union of
American Hebrew Congregations, 1965; resident
composer, UAHC Internat. Art Project with Paul
Ben-Haim, 1966; American Film Festival award,
1967; U.S. Film Board Golden Eagle award, 1968;
Creative Arts Public Service grant to study, collect, and make a piece from the language used by
farmers with their animals, 1973; many commissions. He writes for films, television and radio
commercials; formed own company 1970, with synthesizer, 1971; formed New Wilderness Preservation
Band and New Wilderness Found., 1973; arranged <u>An
evening with the two Charlies: Ives and Morrow</u>,
Lincoln Center, New York, 25 Jan. 1973.
WORKS: Orchestra: <u>And thou shalt love</u>,
tenor and orch., 1965; <u>Groovin'/Do you feel it</u>,
rock group and orch., Garden State Arts Center,
11 July 1968; Wind ensemble: <u>The birth of the
wargod</u>, New York, 8 June 1973; Songs: <u>The bless-
ingway</u>, voice and pipes, New York, 8 June 1973;
<u>66 songs for a Blackfoot bundle</u>, 120-minute piece
using authentic Blackfoot Indian rituals, 1973;
Film scores: <u>The language they speak</u>, 1967; <u>40
north, 67 west</u>, 1968; <u>La guerre</u>, 1969; <u>Moonwalk I</u>,
documentary, 1970; educational sound tracks for
The Center for the Humanities, Inc., 1972; <u>Film</u>,
1973; <u>Man, the symbolmaker</u>, 1973; Time-Life America series, 1973; Multi-media: <u>Near the wall</u>,
protest piece, 1967; <u>Poland 1931</u>, in collaboration with Jerome Rothenberg, 1970.
R. D. 1, Callicoon, NY 12723

MORTON, LAWRENCE
b. New York, N. Y., 4 Oct. 1942. Studied with
Donald Lybbert and Ruth Anderson, Hunter Coll.,
B. A., M. A. He received the Hunter Coll. Class
of 1895 prize, 1966; BMI Student award, 1966. He
was faculty member, Neighborhood Music School,
New York, 1966- ; teacher, public schools,
1966-68, 1972-73; adjunct lecturer, Hunter Coll.,
1970-73; staff member, Columbia Records, 1973.
WORKS: Opera: <u>Women</u>, 1-act; Orchestra:
<u>Mettā</u>, chorus and orch., Buddhist texts; Chamber
music: wind octet; woodwind quintet; Voice:
Songs on texts of Cummings and Stephen Crane.
1960 Williamsbridge Road, New York, NY 10461

MORYL, RICHARD
b. Newark, N. J., 23 Feb. 1929. Studied at
Columbia Univ.; with Arthur Berger, Brandeis
Univ.; and with Boris Blacher in Berlin. He
received Fulbright, Tanglewood, and Bennington
fellowships; grants from Ford Found., Rockefeller
Found., Kellogg Found., Connecticut Commission on
the Arts, Nat. Endowment for the Arts, American
Music Center; numerous commissions and composition awards. He was professor, Smith Coll.,
1971; assistant professor and chairman, music
department, Western Connecticut State Coll.,
1972- .
WORKS: Chamber music: <u>Modules</u>, flute, bass,
soprano, 1969; <u>Improvisations</u>, chamber ensemble;
<u>Salvos</u>; <u>Chroma</u>, chamber ensemble, 1972; <u>Sound-
ings</u>, brass quintet; <u>Corners</u>, trumpet ensemble,
New York, 6 May 1973; Chorus: <u>Illuminations</u>,
for soprano, voices, 8 string basses, chamber
ensemble; <u>Choralis</u>; <u>Contacts</u>; <u>Multiples</u>; <u>Fluo-
rescents</u>; <u>De morte cantoris</u>, New York, 11 Mar.
1974.
Shirley Court, Brookfield, CT 06804

MOSCOVITZ, HOWARD SAMUEL
b. Jacksonville, Fla., 29 Apr. 1946. Studied
with William Hoskins, Jacksonville Univ., B. M.;
with Leland C. Smith, Stanford Univ.; Samuel
Dolan, Royal Cons.; and with Robert Ashley, Mills
Coll., M. F. A. He received the E. Mills Crother
composition award, 1972. He has been director,
Electronic Music Associates, 1972- ; music
director, Berkeley Dance Theater and Gymnasium,
1972- .
WORKS: Electronic: <u>Lament for Josh</u>, tape,
1971; <u>Grid pattern #2</u>, tape, 1971; <u>Thin aire</u>,
tape, 1971; <u>March of the Alameda County sheriffs</u>,
tape, 1972; <u>Double standard</u>, tape and chamber
orch., KPFA-FM, Berkeley, June 1971; <u>Barriers</u>,
tape, live electronics, flute, cello, bass, 1972;
several commercial film scores.
3400 Wyman St., Oakland, CA 94619

MOSCOVITZ, JULIANNE
b. Oakland, Calif., 18 Jan. 1951. Studied with
William Hoskins, Jacksonville Univ.; privately
with John Fahey, at California State Univ. at
Hayward, B. A. 1972. She was faculty guitarist,
Ericksen School of Music, Berkeley, 1972-73;
assistant music director, Berkeley Dance Theater
and Gymnasium, 1972-73.
WORKS: Chamber music: <u>Once there was a
worm</u>, voice and guitar, 1967; <u>Guitar suite in
colors</u>, 1968; <u>Tuesday afternoon in October</u>, solo
guitar, 1972; Film score: <u>Atlanta, an international city</u>, 1973.
3400 Wyman St., Oakland, CA 94619

*MOSKO, STEPHEN
b. Denver, Colo., 1948. <u>Lovely mansions</u>, chamber
ensemble, received BMI student composer award,
1972; <u>Night of the long knives</u>, soprano and chamber ensemble, BMI award, 1973.

MOSS, LAWRENCE
b. Los Angeles, Calif., 18 Nov. 1927. Studied
at Univ. of California, Los Angeles, B. A. 1949;
Eastman School of Music, M. A. 1950; with Leon

MOSS, LAWRENCE

(MOSS, LAWRENCE)
Kirchner, Univ. of Southern California, Ph. D. 1957. He received a Fulbright grant, 1953; 2 Guggenheim fellowships, 1958, 1968; Morse fellowship at Yale, 1964. He was instructor, Mills Coll., 1956-58; assistant to associate professor, Yale Univ., 1959-68; professor, Univ. of Maryland, 1969- .
  WORKS: Opera: The brute, comic opera; Orchestra: Paths; Ariel, soprano and orch., 1969; Chamber music: violin sonata, 1959; Elegy, 2 violins and viola, 1969; Timepiece, violin, piano, percussion; Patterns, flute, clarinet, viola, piano; Windows, flute, clarinet, contrabass; Remembrances, chamber ensemble; Music for 5, brass quintet; Exchanges, ensemble; Auditions, woodwind quintet and tape, 1971; Evocation and song, saxophone and tape, 1972; Piano: Fantasy, 1952; 4 scenes for piano; Omaggio, piano 4-hands.
    220 Mowbray Road, Silver Spring, MD 20904

*MOSS, MICHAEL
Free energy, lyrical improvisation, New York, 31 Mar. 1973.

*MOSSMAN, TED
b. Chicago, Ill., 6 Apr. 1914. Studied with Rudolph Ganz, Chicago Musical Coll.; with Howard Hanson, Eastman School of Music, B. M.; Univ. of Illinois; Juilliard School. He made his debut as pianist with the Rochester Philharmonic.
  WORKS: Ballet: Salomé; Theatre: Abraham Lincoln, music drama; Orchestra: Chicago, Illinois, overture; Lotus blue, tone poem; Central Park romance; piano concerto; New York concerto; Chorus: Let freedom ring; Piano: 3 children's dances; also popular songs.

MOTT, DAVID HOWARD
b. Hinsdale, Ill., 1 July 1945. Studied with John Bavicchi and William Maloof, Berklee Coll. of music; with James Drew and Robert Morris, Yale Univ. At Yale he received the Bradley-Keefer Memorial award twice, Julia Silliman Memorial award; commissions from Massachusetts Inst. of Technology Band; Connecticut Music Teachers Asso.; Hope Coll.; and others.
  WORKS: Band: Form for band; Sound cycle, solo saxophone and wind ensemble; Jazz band: Hathu thingala; Moon trilogy; Chamber music: Elements I, Air:wind, 3 microphoned flutes and 2 percussionists; Elements II, Earth:mountains and expanses, brass quintet; Night flowers, double bass and alto flute.
    228 Huntington St., New Haven, CT 06511

*MOURANT, WALTER
b. Chicago, 1910. Studied with Bernard Rogers and Howard Hanson, Eastman School of Music; with Bernard Wagenaar at Juilliard School on a fellowship. Before entering on formal music study at Eastman in 1931 he was pianist and arranger for stage shows, radio, and dance bands.
  WORKS: Orchestra: setting of the Preamble to the Constitution, chorus and orch.; 3 dances for orchestra; 3 acts of Punch and Judy suites; clarinet concertino; In the valley of the Moon,

(MOURANT, WALTER)
string orch., 1955; Air and scherzo, string orch., 1955; Sleepy Hollow, 1955; Harper's Ferry, W. Va., aria for orchestra, 1960; several concert jazz pieces; themes for the Westinghouse Hour, March of Time, et al.

MOWERY, CARL DONALD JR.
b. Shamokin, Pa., 26 July 1941. Studied with Normand Lockwood, Univ. of Denver; with Charles Hoag and Spencer Norton, Univ. of Oklahoma. He received the NDEA Title IV fellowship, Univ. of Oklahoma. He taught at Shenandoah Cons., 1969-70; has been assistant professor, Murray State Univ., 1970- .
  WORKS: Chamber music: 3 moments for flute and string orch., 1966; 2 tuba sonatas, 1969; trio for 3 tubas, 1971; 4 songs from Troilus and Cressida by Chaucer, counter tenor and lute, 1972.
    Box 2815, University Station
    Murray, KY 42071

MOY, WILLIAM C. C.
b. Fiji Islands, 15 Feb. 1923; U.S. citizen 1960. Studied with George Frederick McKay, Univ. of Washington, B. A., M. A.; with Otto Luening, Felix Greissle, and Alan Hovhaness in New York; at Eastman School of Music, summers, 1957, 1958. He has been a music typographer, 1953- .
  WORKS: Compositions for chamber orchestra, chorus, percussion ensemble, piano, performed at Eastman School and at Composers Forum in New York.
    40-38 205th St., Bayside, NY 11361

MOYER, J. HAROLD
b. Newton, Kan., 6 May 1927. Studied with Roy Harris, George Peabody Coll.; with Philip Bezanson, Univ. of Iowa, Ph. D. He was named 1971 Kansas Composer of the Year by Kansas Fed. Music Clubs; has received many commissions. He has been chairman, music department, Bethel Coll., 1960- ; vice chairman, Mennonite Hymnal Revision Committee, 1968-69; board member, Harvey County Arts Council, 1971- .
  WORKS: Orchestra: symphony; Job, chorus and orch.; Chorus: Let us sing unto the Lord; Thou grace divine; Hymns and harmonizations for the Mennonite Hymnal; Organ: 9 preludes.
    Bethel College, North Newton, KA 67117

MUCZYNSKI, ROBERT
b. Chicago, Ill., 19 Mar. 1929. Studied with Alexander Tcherepnin, DePaul Univ., M. M. 1952. His honors include ASCAP awards; 2 Ford Found. grants, 1959, 1961; Internat. Society for Contemporary Music award, Chicago, 1961; Concours Internat. prize, Nice, France, 1961; commissions from Fromm Found., Louisville Orchestra, Chicago Little Symphony, National Symphony, and Linton String Trio. He has been associate professor, Univ. of Arizona, 1965- .
  WORKS: Orchestra: symphony, 1953; piano concerto, 1954; Galena, a town, 1958; Dovetail overture, 1959; Great unfenced; Yankee painter suite; Charade; Dance movements; Symphonic

314

(MUCZYNSKI, ROBERT)
dialogues; Chamber music: flute sonata; cello sonata; alto saxophone sonata; Fantasy trio, clarinet, cello, piano; trumpet trio, 1959; string trio; piano trio; Allegro deciso, brass sextet and timpani; Movements, wind quintet; Fragments, flute, clarinet, bassoon; Gallery suite, solo cello; 5 impromptus, solo tuba; 3 designs for 3 timpani, 1960; Statements for percussion, 1961; 3 preludes, solo flute, 1962; Voyage, suite for brass trio, 1970; Chorus: I never saw a moor; Alleluia; Piano: 2 sonatas; 6 preludes, 1954; Suite, 1960; Toccata, 1961; sonatina; A summer journal; Diversions; Fables; Film scores: for documentary films.

Route 8, Box 381-B, Tucson, AZ 85710

MUELLER, CARL F.
b. Sheboygan, Wis., 12 Aug. 1892. Studied piano, organ, voice, conducting, theory at Elmhurst Coll., honorary doctorate 1946. He was named fellow, Westminster Choir Coll.; associate, American Guild of Organists, 1933. He was organist and choirmaster in churches in Milwaukee, Wis., Montclair, N. J., and Red Bank, N. J., 1915-71; head of choral department, Montclair State Coll., 1928-53.

WORKS: Over 500 published works for piano, organ, voice, and sacred and secular choral works.

580 A Lake Point Drive, Lakewood, NJ 08701

MUELLER, FREDERICK A.
b. Berlin, Germany, 3 Mar. 1921; U.S. citizen 1943. Studied with Hans Sachsse, Munich, Germany; with Bernard Rogers, Eastman School of Music, M. M.; and with Ernst von Dohnanyi, Florida State Univ., D. M. He received the Texas Manuscript Society award, 1957; a commission from Music Teachers Nat. Asso.-Kentucky Music Teachers Asso., 1968; numerous commissions for ensemble and solo compositions. He was director of music, Spring Hill Coll., 1960-67; associate professor, Morehead State Univ., 1967- .

WORKS: Orchestra: euphonium concerto; Chamber music: Tuba variations on a theme of Samuel Barber; Dance suite for solo alto saxophone and danseuse; also bassoon pedagogy publications.

Music Department, Morehead State University
Morehead, KY 40351

MULFINGER, GEORGE (LEONIDAS)
b. Chicago, Ill., 25 Mar. 1900. Studied piano in Cleveland, Chicago and Vienna. He taught in Gunn School of Music, Chicago, 1926-28; was professor and chairman, piano department, Syracuse Univ., 1928-68.

WORKS: Orchestra: Symphonic variations for piano and orch.; Overture to an imaginary opera; Chamber music: piano quintet; Elegy, cello and piano; Piano: Childhood memories; Serenata, nocturne and scherzo; Octave prelude; Poéme and prelude; Suite for piano.

213 Hurlburt Ave., Syracuse, NY 13224

MULLINS, HUGH
b. Danville, Ill., 25 June 1922. Studied with Ernest Kanitz, Univ. of Southern California; with Bohuslav Martinu, Nicolai Lopatnikoff, Aaron

(MULLINS, HUGH)
Copland, at Tanglewood; with Bernard Wagenaar, Juilliard School. He received the C. J. Bond award of $2500 and 4 years at Univ. of Southern California. He was instructor in voice and French, James Millikin Univ., 1945-47; professor of music, California State Univ., Los Angeles, 1950- .

WORKS: Opera: The scarlet letter; The stone of heaven; Orchestra: cello concerto; flute concerto, with chamber orch.; The crown of Christ, John Donne text, chorus and orch.; Chamber music: 5 parables for violin and piano; quintet for clarinet and strings; duets, flute and clarinet; 12 songs for cello and soprano; Chorus: Follow your saints; Noel; Homebody ballads, male voices and 2 pianos.

1322 Walnut Ave., West Covina, CA 91790

MUMMA, GORDON
b. Framingham, Mass., 30 Mar. 1935. Studied horn and piano, Univ. of Michigan. He became interested in electronic music while still in school; was a co-founder of the Cooperative Studio for Electric Music, Ann Arbor, 1958-66; co-director of the ONCE Festival and ONCE Group, 1960-66; research associate in acoustics and seismics, Inst. of Science and Technology, Ann Arbor, 1962-63; composer and performing musician, Merce Cunningham Dance Company, 1966- , and with the Sonic Arts Union, 1966- ; visiting lecturer at Brandeis Univ., 1966-67; State Univ. Coll. of New York at Buffalo, 1968; Univ. of Illinois, 1969-70; Univ. of California, Santa Cruz, 1973-74; summers at other institutions; has made many concert tours alone and with groups in Europe, Mexico, South America, and Japan. He is author of numerous articles on electronic music and its uses.

WORKS: Instrumental: Suite for piano, 1959; A quarter of fourpiece, 4 instruments, 1960-62; Gestures II, 2 pianos, 1962; Very small size mograph 1962, any number of pianos and performers; Medium size mograph 1962, piano with any number of performers; Large size mograph 1963, piano solo; Electronic: Vectors, 1959; Densities, 1959; Sinfonia for 12 instruments and magnetic tape, 1958-60; Mirrors, 1960; Meanwhile, a twopiece, percussion and tape, 1961; Untitled mobile, 4-channel tape, 1962; Love in Truro, 1963; The analog computer, 1963; Megaton for William Burroughs, for 10 electronic, acoustical and communications channels, 1963; Temps for space theatre, 1963; Music for the Venezia Space Theatre, 1964; Sequences from galleries, 1964; Le Corbusier, orch., organ, tape, cybersonic concertante, 1965; Second horn, for horn and cybersonic console (an electronic device worn on the player's body, is activated by certain horn sounds, plays duets with the horn, and provides its own improvisational flights), 1965; Horn, 1965, same as above; Mesa, for cybersonic bandoneon, 1965; Diastasis, as in beer, 2 cybersonic guitars, 1967; Hornpipe, cybersonic horn, 1967; Swarmer, violin, concertina, saw, and cybersonic modification, 1968; Calm death on Phu Quoc: Defense intelligence makes an adjustment, tape, 1969; Conspiracy 8, for digital computer with up to 8 performers, 1970; Telepos, dancers

MUMMA, GORDON

(MUMMA, GORDON)
with telemetry belts and accelerators, 1971; Phe-
nomenon unarticulated, frequency-modulated ultra-
sonic oscillators, 1972; Ambivex, for surrogate
myoelectrical telemetering system with pairs of
performing appendages, 1972; Cybersonic canti-
levers, with public participation, 1973; also
film scores.
Artservices, 463 West St.
New York, NY 10014

MUMMERT, KENNETH J.
b. Waukegan, Ill., 26 Oct. 1939. Studied with
Donal Michalsky, California State Univ. at
Fullerton, B. M.
WORKS: Chamber music: Suite for 6 instru-
ments; Impressions of Victorian poets, song cycle
for soprano and piano; Wind dance, for trumpet,
clarinet, horn, bass clarinet, and percussion;
Sonata Espagnol for piano.
P. O. Box 6112, Anaheim, CA 92806

MUNGER, MILLICENT CHRISTNER
b. Rosamond, Ill., 15 Sep. 1905. Studied theory
at Milliken Univ. and Northwestern Univ.; piano
and organ in Chicago and New York. She won an
award for an anthem, Congregational Church,
Spencer, Iowa, 1959. She taught piano in private
music schools, 1926-35; was organist and choir
director, Spencer, Iowa, 1935-69, in Tucson,
Ariz., 1969-73.
WORKS: Chorus: Processional anthem, provides separate descants for each Sunday School
class using same hymn as accompaniment, the congregation joins in singing the hymn and all
classes sing their descant at the same time; organ
and piano works, songs, etc.
3435 East 5th St., Tucson, AZ 85716

MUNGER, SHIRLEY
b. Everett, Wash. Studied with George F. McKay
and John Verrall, Univ. of Washington, B. A.,
M. A.; with Halsey Stevens and Ingolf Dahl, Univ.
of Southern California, D. M. A.; piano at Cons.
Nat., Paris. She received 2 BMI grants for composition for television, Univ. of Southern California; Phi Beta Kappa. She was faculty member,
Univ. of California, Santa Barbara, 1954-60; Univ.
of Minnesota at Duluth, 1963-68; West Chester
State Coll., 1968-   .
WORKS: Band: American tribute; also compositions for organ, piano, voice, and instrumental
groups.
519 Sharpless St., West Chester, PA 19380

*MURPHY, LYLE
b. Salt Lake City, Utah, 19 Aug. 1908. Wrote
many works for saxophone ensemble: Notturno;
Prelude and canon; Rondino; Warm winds; etc.; and
Film scores: The Tony Fontane story; God's
country.

MURRAY, BAIN
b. Evanston, Ill., 26 Dec. 1926. Studied with
Herbert Elwell, Oberlin Coll., A. B. 1951; with
Randall Thompson and Walter Piston, Harvard Univ.,
A. M. 1952; with Nadia Boulanger in Paris; further
study in Belgium. He received the Arthur Knight

(MURRAY, BAIN)
prize and Francis Boott prize at Harvard;
Brookline Music Library Asso. prize; Cleveland
Fine Arts prize; Fulbright grant, 1953-54; 2
research awards, Cleveland State Univ.; Distinguished Service Medal, Union of Polish Composers.
He was teaching assistant, Harvard Univ.,
1954-55; instructor, Oberlin Coll., 1955-60;
assistant professor to full professor, Cleveland
State Univ., 1960-   .
WORKS: Ballet: Peter Pan, 1952; Orchestra:
Ballad, 1950; Chamber music: 2 string quartets,
1950, 1953; woodwind quintet; Epitaph for
strings; Chorus: Hopi flute song; Safe in their
alabaster chambers, with English horn and cello,
1962; On the divide, with 4 woodwinds; Winds of
truth; Ode to peace; Songs: The pasture, Frost
text; Now close the windows; Teasdale song cycle;
many other songs, choral works, chamber pieces.
1331 Cleveland Heights Blvd.
Cleveland Heights, OH 44121

MURRAY, DON
b. Louisville, Ky., 22 July 1925. Studied with
Claude Almand, Univ. of Louisville; was associated with Roy Harris at Pittsburgh Internat.
Festival of Contemporary Music, 1952. He received 3 ASCAP awards; and the Giovanni Martini
award at Bellarmine Coll. He is instructor,
Bellarmine Coll., and staff pianist, WAVE-TV,
Louisville, Ky.
WORKS: Orchestra: Seeds of contemplation,
chorus and orch., on text of Thomas Merton;
Chamber music: Concert piece for piano, bass,
and percussion; compositions in all forms with a
preference for jazz in the larger orchestral
forms.
530 Brentwood Ave., Louisville, KY 40215

MURRAY, JAMES ORVAL
b. Kannapolis, N. C., 2 May 1929. Studied at
Mars Hill Coll. and Baylor Univ. He has been
minister of music in churches in North Carolina,
Georgia, and Virginia, 1951-62; at First Baptist
Church, Greer, S. C., 1962-   .
WORKS: Chorus: Trust in the Lord, 1958; I
sought the Lord, 1966.
P. O. Box 415, Greer, SC 29651

*MURRAY, JEREMIAH
Marriage proposal, 1-act opera, Public Opera
Theatre Company, New York, 1 Feb. 1973; The
beauty and the beast, 1-act opera, Public Opera
Theatre Company, New York, 8 May 1974.

*MURRAY, LYN
b. London, England, 6 Dec. 1909; U.S. citizen
1929. Studied at Juilliard School and with
Joseph Schillinger. He was staff arranger, WCAU,
Philadelphia, 1931-34; composer, conductor,
arranger, CBS, 1934-47.
WORKS: Opera: Esther; Ballet: Camptown;
Orchestra: Leapfrog overture; Variations on a
children's tune, string orch.; Band: Collage,
clarinet and band; Chorus: The miracle, Christmas oratorio; Liberation, cantata; Sleep now on
thy natal day; Film scores: The prowler;

(MURRAY, LYN)
Cinderella; The bridges of Toko-Ri; To catch a thief; Period of adjustment; Son of Paleface; Wives and lovers; Promise her anything.
1919 Outpost Drive, Los Angeles, CA 90068

*MURTAUGH, JOHN
b. Minneapolis, Minn., 30 Oct. 1927. Gemini space project, film score.

MUSGRAVE, THEA
b. Near Edinburgh, Scotland, 27 May 1928; to U.S. 1972. Studied at Edinburgh Univ.; with Nadia Boulanger in Paris; and with Aaron Copland at Tanglewood, 1958. Her awards include the Lili Boulanger Memorial prize and the Koussevitzky award. She was visiting professor, Univ. of California, Santa Barbara, 1970.
WORKS: (For her large catalog of compositions composed before 1970 see Baker and Groves. Works composed in the U.S. are listed below.) Opera: The voice of Ariadne, chamber opera, 1971-73; Orchestra: horn concerto, 1971; viola concerto, premiere with Scottish Nat. Orch. conducted by composer with her husband, Peter Marks playing solo viola, London, Aug. 1973, American premiere, Pasadena, 26 Apr. 1975; Chamber music: Elegy, viola and cello, 1970; Impromptu no. 2, flute, oboe, and clarinet, 1970; Primavera, soprano and flute, 1971; Chorus: Carol for unaccompanied choir, 1973.
c/o J. W. Chester, Ltd., Eagle Court
London EC1M 5QD England

*MUSSER, CLARE
Prelude and 4 etudes for marimba.
c/o Ludwig Industries, 1728 North Damon Ave.
Chicago, IL 60647

MUSSER, PHILIP D.
b. Angola, Ind., 22 July 1943. Studied with Salvatore Martirano and Ben Johnston, Univ. of Illinois. He received a Ford Found. grant to study multi-track recording techniques in electronic music at Mills Coll. He was research assistant, Experimental Music Studio, Univ. of Illinois, 1970-72; lecturer, Univ. of Illinois, 1972-73.
WORKS: Electronic: (tape alone) Yaxkin, 1968; Sleep, 1970; Pomegranate, 1970; Ovarb, 1971; 4th of July, 1971; Soma, 1972; (tape and dance) Aeyrie, 1971; Cherokee, 1972; 9 doors, 1973; (tape and instruments) Life winds, tape and clarinet, Paul Zonn, co-composer, 1973; Patterns, tape and percussion, 1974; Multi-media: Monoliths, tape, film, visuals, and live electronics, 1971.
1003 South Douglas, Urbana, IL 61801

MUSTILLO, LINA
b. Newport, R. I., 13 Oct. 1905. Studied with Hugo Norden in Boston; with Arthur Custer, Univ. of Rhode Island. She was organist and choir director in Attleboro, Mass., 1930-35; director of her own music school, 1935-60.
WORKS: Songs: Trilogy, 3-song cycle for soprano and piano; Piano: Etude intervalle; Triphon; A thought; Passacaglia; and others.
5 Hornet Road, Warwick, RI 02886

MUTCHLER, RALPH D.
b. Northwood, N. D., 20 Nov. 1929. North Dakota State Univ.; with Frank Cookson and John F. Paynter, Northwestern Univ.; and with Dale Dykens, Univ. of Northern Colorado, Ed. D. He has been instructor, Olympic Coll., 1960-   , chairman, music department, 1972-73.
WORKS: Band: An American suite for band; Concerto grosso for jazz combo and symphonic band; Wiggy, stage band; numerous works for concert, marching, and stage band.
Department of Music, Olympic College
Bremerton, WA 98310

MYEROV, JOSEPH
b. Philadelphia, Pa., 21 Jan. 1928. Attended Temple Univ., B. S. 1949; studied piano at Juilliard School. He was choirmaster in Philadelphia, 1948-54; organist-director, Beth Sholom, Elkins Park, Pa., 1954-73; teacher public schools, 1950-73.
WORKS: Theatre: music for 5th season, a play about the garment industry; Chorus: 3 Friday Evening services, 1970, 1971, 1972; Songs: Who knows better than Israel; A new song, 1973; and many secular songs.
7007 Calvert St., Philadelphia, PA 19149

MYERS, ROBERT
b. Fredericksburg, Va., 20 Aug. 1941. Studied with Sydney Hodkinson, Univ. of Virginia; with John LaMontaine and Bernard Rogers, Eastman School of Music; and Nadia Boulanger in Paris. His awards include Walter Damrosch Memorial scholarship, 1967; Fulbright grants, 1965, 1966; Contemporary Music Project grants, 1967-1968. He was composer-in-residence, Midland Public Schools, Mich., 1967-69; assistant professor and chairman, music department, Saginaw Valley Coll., 1969-   .
WORKS: Chamber music: Movements, soprano saxophone and chamber orch., 1967; Fantasy duos, alto saxophone and percussion, 1968; Sonores V, trombone and piano; chansons innocentes, e. e. cummings text, treble voices and percussion ensemble, 1969; Reprise, alto saxophone and piano, 1969; in more recent years he has been working in jazz and multi-media techniques.
910 West Park Drive, Midland, MI 48640

MYERS, THELDON
b. Illinois, 4 Feb. 1927. Studied at Northern Illinois Univ., B. S.; with Arthur Bryon, Fresno State Coll., M. A.; with Nadia Boulanger in Paris; with Sandor Veress and Stefan Grove, Peabody Cons., D. M. A. He has held teaching positions in Illinois and California; professor, Towson State Coll., 1972-   .
WORKS: Orchestra: Concertino for orch.; Configuration; Chorale and fantasy; Chamber music: clarinet sonata; alto saxophone sonatine; Introduction and allegro, flute, clarinet and piano; string quartet; Theme and variations for piano; 3 studies for piano.
1205 Wakeford Circle, Baltimore, MD 21239

MYOVER, MAX L.
    b. Independence, Kan., 6 July 1924. Studied with
Albert Noelte and Anthony Donata, Northwestern
Univ. He was associate professor, Dakota
Wesleyan Univ., 1948-52.
    WORKS: Theatre: He's gone away, music drama,
chorus and orch.; Orchestra: Symphonetta; piano
concerto in one movement; The death of Dr.
Faustus, baritone and orch.; Vocalise for soprano
and strings; Suite for woodwind sextet; string
quartet; Declaration, baritone and chamber orch.;
Chorus: Lil' boy name David; Arise, my love; A
prayer; The garden hymn; Today is Sunday today;
Sleep; A leaf; Film scores: Together; The touch
of the craftsman; The door; America the beautiful;
Magic carpet 'round the world.
    1340 Arlington Drive, Florissant, MO 63033

*MYROW, FREDRIC
    b. Brooklyn, N. Y., 16 July 1939. Studied with
Ingolf Dahl, Univ. of Southern California, B. M.
1961; with Goffredo Petrassi, St. Cecilia Acad.,
Rome, 1962-64; with Darius Milhaud at Tanglewood,
1965. His many awards include a Rockefeller
grant, 1961; BMI awards, 1961, 1963, 1964;
Fulbright and Italian Government grants, 1961-63;
ASCAP award, 1964; Fromm Found. grant, 1965;
MacDowell fellowship, 1965; Brandeis Univ. award;
special citation, Koussevitzky Internat. Recording award, 1970. He was concert pianist of the
U.S. Information Service in Italy, 1964; pianist
for Evenings for New Music, New York, 1965; faculty member, State Univ. of New York, Buffalo,
1965-66.
    WORKS: Orchestra: Symphonic variations,
1960; Chamber symphony, 1963; Music for orchestra,
1965; Songs: 4 songs in spring, 1959; At twilight, 1960; Songs from the Japanese, 1965; Piano:
Theme and variations; 6 preludes in 6 styles;
Triple fugue for 2 pianos.
    12971 Galewood St., Studio City, CA 91604

*MYROW, JOSEF
    b. Russia, 28 Feb. 1910; to U.S. 1912. Studied
at Univ. of Pennsylvania; Philadelphia Cons. He
was piano soloist with symphony orchestras; program and music director, Philadelphia radio stations.
    WORKS: Film scores: 3 little girls in blue;
If I'm lucky; Mother wore tights; Wabash Avenue;
I love Melvin; The girl next door; The French
line; Bundle of joy; and popular songs; Autumn
nocturne, jazz piano, was performed in New York,
17 Oct. 1971.

*NABOKOV, NICOLAS
    b. Lubcha, Novogrudok, Russia, 17 Apr. 1903; U.S.
citizen 1939. Studied with Vladimir Rebikov in
Yalta; at the Stuttgart Cons.; with Ferruccio
Busoni in Berlin; at the Sorbonne, Paris, 1926.
He received the Commander's Cross, German Order
of Merit, Fed. Republic of Germany, for his work
in organizing the Berlin Festival, 1964-68, and
as advisor on international cultural affairs. He
taught at Wells Coll., 1936-41; Peabody Cons.,
1947-52; has been secretary-general, Congress for
Cultural Freedom, 1952-   ; organized Paris
Festival of 20th century music, 1952; Teheran
Festival, 1969.

(NABOKOV, NICOLAS)
    WORKS: Opera: The holy devil, 1958, revised
and produced as The death of Rasputin, Cologne,
Germany, Nov. 1959; Love's labour lost, text
from Shakespeare by W. H. Auden and Chester
Kallmann, Brussels, 7 Feb. 1973; Ballet: Ode or
Meditation at night, 1928; Union Pacific, 1934;
Theatre: music to Samson agonistes, 1938;
Orchestra: Symphonie lyrique, 1930; piano concerto, 1932; Sinfonia Biblica, 1941; The return
of Pushkin, elegy for voice and orch., 1947;
flute concerto, 1948; Vita nuova, soprano, tenor,
orch., 1950; Les hommages, cello concerto, 1953;
Symboli chrestiani, baritone and orch., 1956; A
prayer, symphony, 1967; Chamber music: 2 piano
sonatas, 1926, 1940; Collectioneur d'echoes,
soprano, bass, percussion, 1933; string quartet,
1937; bassoon sonata, 1941; Chorus: Job, oratorio, 1933.

NAGEL, ROBERT E.
    b. Freeland, Pa., 29 Sep. 1924. Studied with
William Bergsma, Peter Mennin, and Vincent
Persichetti at Juilliard School; with Aaron
Copland at Tanglewood. He was awarded a
Fulbright fellowship to France, 1950. He has
been director, New York Brass Quintet, 1954-   ;
president, Mentor Music, Inc., 1959-   ; associate professor, Yale Univ., 1956-   ; associate
professor, Rutgers Univ., 1966-   ; instructor,
Hartt Coll. of Music, 1968-   .
    WORKS: Orchestra: concerto for trumpet and
strings, 1951; Chamber music: 2 brass trios;
Divertimento for 10 winds; Suite for brass quartet and piano; Trumpets of Spain; Trumpets on
parade; Trumpet processional; Chorus: Triptych;
also Speed studies for trumpet; Rhythmic studies
for trumpet.
    Broadview Drive, Brookfield, CT 06804

*NAGINSKI, CHARLES
    b. Cairo, Egypt, 29 May 1909; to U.S. at an early
age; d. by drowning, Lenox, Mass., 4 Aug. 1940.
Studied with Rubin Goldmark, Juilliard School,
1928-33; and at American Acad. in Rome.
    WORKS: Orchestra: Suite for orch., 1931; 2
symphonies, 1935, 1937; Orchestral poem, 1936; 3
movements for chamber orch., 1937; sinfonietta,
1937; The minotaur, ballet for orch., 1938; Nocturne and pantomime, 1938; 5 pieces from a children's suite, 1940; Movement for strings;
Chamber music: 2 string quartets; songs.

*NAGY, FREDERICK
    b. Marmarossziget, Hungary; 18 Jan. 1894; to U.S.
1951; d. Chicago, Ill. Attended Budapest Univ.;
Debrecen Univ., L. L. D.; Budapest Acad. of
Music; also studied music privately. He practiced law, 1925-41; was district judge, 1941-45;
interpreter for U.S. Occupation Forces, Austria,
1945-51. He composed Serenade for string orch.;
Pledge of allegiance and Thanksgiving hymn of the
refugees for chorus.

NAGY-FARKAS, PETER
    b. B. Topolya, now Yugoslavia, of Hungarian
parents, 3 Feb. 1933; U.S. citizen 1967. Studied
in Subotica; at Music Acad. of Belgrade,
Yugoslavia; Schola Cantorum, Paris; with John

(NAGY-FARKAS, PETER)
Verrall, Univ. of Washington; Leroy Ostransky, Univ. of Puget Sound, M. M.; with Wayne Barlow and Samuel Adler, Eastman School of Music, Ph. D. He was visiting lecturer, Lewis and Clark Coll., 1963-65; assistant professor, Univ. of Montevallo, 1968-71; assistant professor, Westfield State Coll., 1973.
WORKS: Ballet: The uprising; Orchestra: violin concerto; Phoenix, symphonic poem; Concerto for 3 clarinets, double string orch. and percussion; Band: Variations on a theme by Thomas Campian; Chamber music: Springtime, baritone, piano, string quartet; Nocturne, trumpet and piano; Shadows, violin, trumpet, vibraphone, harp; Suite for clarinet and bassoon; E pluribus unum, 4 clarinets; Meditation, woodwind quintet; Chorus: Psalm XIII, a cappella; Adon Olom, choir and brass; Psalm 146; Piano: Toccata for 2 pianos; Variations on a theme by Paul Hindemith, 2 pianos; Electronic: Son et lumière, music for a slide show.
Moss Hill Road, Russell, MA 01071

NAJERA, EDMUND
b. Arizona, 1936. Studied at Univ. of California at Los Angeles and Berkeley.
WORKS: Opera: Scarlet letter; Freeway opera; Carlotta; Secundum Lucam, opera-oratorio setting of 2nd chapter of Luke, in Latin and English; Chorus: Exultate Deo; Ad flumina Babylonis; In dulci jubilo; Via dolorosa (choral stations of the cross); Plaudite; Psalms XII, CXIX, for "multidimensional" chorus; Requiems I and II; Fleurs du mal; The nightingale; How lonely is the night, men's voices; song cycles; Piano: sonata for 2 pianos.
1919 Graham Ave., Redondo Beach, CA 90278

NANCARROW, CONLON
b. Texarkana, Ark., 27 Oct. 1912. Studied at Cincinnati Cons.; with Nicolas Slonimsky and Walter Piston in Boston. He played trumpet in jazz orchestras; then fought in the Spanish Civil War; since 1940 has lived in Mexico City. To assure accuracy in the performance of his composition he composes only on player-piano rolls. Some of his studies for player piano have been recorded.

NEAL, CHARLES TAYLOR
b. Boulder, Colo., 4 July 1946. Studied with Rodney Ash, Western State Coll.; and with Paul Royer, South Dakota State Univ. He held a division scholarship at Western State Coll., 1967-68. He was first bassoonist, Rapid City Symphony, 1962-64, Black Hills Chamber Orchestra, 1967, 1968; 2nd oboist, Rapid City Symphony, 1969; public school music director, Philip, S. D., 1968-71; first bassoonist, NORAD Band, 1972-73, USAF Academy Band, 1973-   .
WORKS: Orchestra: Rhapsody in d; Band: 2 symphonies; Suite for band; also chamber works and piano pieces.
265 East Willamette, #26
Colorado Springs, CO 80909

*NEAR, GERALD R. A.
Was formerly on the faculty of Carleton Coll. His published works for chorus include Drop, drop, slow tears; He who would valiant be; Lord, keep us steadfast in thy word; Come, thou long-expected Jesus; and for organ: A triptych of fugues; Passacaglia; Preludes on 4 hymn tunes; Postlude on St. Dunstan's; etc.
307 5th Ave., S.W., Rochester, MN 55901

NEIKRUG, MARC
b. New York, N. Y., 24 Sep. 1946. Studied with Giselher Klebe in Germany; with Gunther Schuller at Tanglewood; he received a fellowship for Tanglewood Music Festival, 1972; was composer-in-residence, Marlboro Music Festival, 1972; was awarded $2500 to compose a violin concerto, Nat. Endowment for the Arts, 1974.
WORKS: Orchestra: viola concerto; clarinet concerto; piano concerto; Chamber music: cello sonata, 1971; sonata for cello solo; suite for cello and piano; violin sonata; piano sonata, 1972; 2 string quartets; quartet for flute, violin, viola, cello; Arianna's suite, flute and piano, New York, 3 Dec. 1973.
365 West End Ave., New York, NY 10024

*NELHYBEL, VACLAV
b. Polanka, Czech., 24 Sep. 1919; to U.S. 1957. Studied composition and conducting at Prague Cons.; musicology at Univ. of Prague and in Fribourg, Switz. He was composer and conductor for Prague Radio while still a student; with Swiss Nat. Radio, 1948-50; music director of Radio Free Europe in Munich, 1950-57.
WORKS: Opera: A legend, 1954; Ballet: Fetes de feux, 1942; In the shadow of a lime tree, 1946; The cock and the hangman, 1946; Orchestra: Ballade, 1946; Etude symphonique, 1949; 3 modes, 1952; 2 movements for chamber orch.; piano concertino; Numismata; Sinfonia concertante, 1960; viola concerto, 1962; Passacaglia, 1965; Houston concerto, 1967; Band: Chorale for brass and percussion; Impromptu, saxophone and winds; Adagio and allegro; Slavic march; Chamber music: 2 string quartets; 3 woodwind quintets; 3 organa for 4 bassoons, 1948; quartet for horns, 1957; 2 brass quintets, 1961, 1965; 9 clarinet trios, Quintetto concertante, 1965; 103 short, short pieces for piano.
Hattertown, CT 06810

NELSON, DOROTHEA BRANDT, see: BRANDT, DOROTHEA

NELSON, LARRY
b. Broken Bow, Neb., 27 Jan. 1944. Studied with Normand Lockwood, Univ. of Denver; Will Bottje, Southern Illinois Univ.; and with H. Owen Reed, Michigan State Univ. He received a MacDowell fellowship; was one of 4 winners in Philadelphia Orchestra Society contest, 1974. He was director, electronic music studio, Michigan State Univ., 1970-71, organizer-director, New Musical Art Ensemble, 1969-71; assistant professor, West Chester State Coll., 1971-   , director, experimental music studio, 1971-   , organizer-director, New Music Ensemble, 1972-   .

NELSON, LARRY

(NELSON, LARRY)
WORKS: Orchestra: Variations for orch.,
1973; Chamber music: Watch, for 12 instruments,
1970; Duo, cello and piano, 1972; Electronic:
Flute thing, flute and 2 tape decks, 1970; Things
that go wump in the night, tape, 1970; Music for
clarinet and tape, 1973; Multi-media: Conse-
quences: of ......, for performers, tapes,
slides, lights, 1973.
306 South High St., West Chester, PA 19380

NELSON, NORMAN J.
b. Alexandria, La., 2 Oct. 1943. Studied with
Hunter Johnson, Kent Kennan, and Clifton Williams,
Univ. of Texas at El Paso and at Austin, D. M. A.
He is assistant professor, West Texas State Univ.
WORKS: Orchestra: A thicket of sticks, com-
missioned by the Amarillo Symphony Orchestra;
Concepts of time in textures; Band: Ensembles of
wind and percussion instruments; Chamber music:
Stasis::13, flute choir; 5 adjacent, euphonium
quintet; Phrase studies, woodwind trio.
1502 Creekmere, Canyon, TX 79015

*NELSON, OLIVER E.
b. St. Louis, Mo., 4 June 1932. Studied at
Washington Univ.; with Elliott Carter in New York;
with George Tremblay in Los Angeles. He received
a citation as alumnus of Washington Univ. in
1971.
WORKS: Orchestra: Patterns, 1965; Berlin
dialogues, 4 movements: Confrontation, Neutral
zone, Swinging Berlin, Over the wall, Berlin Jazz
Days, 1970; The Kennedy dream; Wind ensemble:
Divertimento for 10 woodwinds, 1962; A study in
5/4, 1966; concerto for xylophone, marimba,
vibraphone and wind symphony, 1967; Jazz: Soundpiece for jazz orch., 1964; Jazzhattan suite,
1967; Film scores: Death of a gunfighter, 1969;
Skullduggery, 1970; Zigzag, 1970.
4326 Enoro Drive, Los Angeles, CA 90008

*NELSON, PAUL
b. Phoenix, Ariz., 26 Jan. 1929. Studied at
Phoenix Coll.; Arizona State Coll.; Columbia
Univ., B. S.; with Walter Piston and Randall
Thompson, Harvard Univ., M. A.; Univ. of Vienna;
American Acad. in Rome; also with Paul Creston,
Lukas Foss, and Paul Hindemith. His awards
include 3 Damrosch fellowships; 1st prize, Tucson
Festival of the Arts; 1st prize, Friends of
Harvey Gaul contest; Francis Boott prize; com-
mission from Contemporary Music Society, Houston.
He was an arranger for dance orchestras; played
first trumpet, Phoenix Symphony and Monterey
County Symphony; was instructor, Army Band train-
ing unit, 1950-51; staff composer and arranger,
U.S. Military Acad., West Point, 1951-53; instructor, Univ. of Louisville, 1955-56; assistant to
associate professor, Brown Univ., 1964- .
WORKS: Orchestra: Theme and passacaglia;
Narrative; sinfonietta; Idyll, horn and strings;
Trio for strings; Chamber music: Divertimento
for clarinet; Chorus: Easter cantata; Christmas
cantata; For theirs is the kingdom; 2 madrigals
on old English airs; The creation, with narrator,

(NELSON, PAUL)
piano, and percussion; In Bethlehem, that noble
place; Thy will be done; How happy the lover;
A lullaby; In memoriam.
Department of Music, Brown University
Providence, RI 02912

*NELSON, RON
b. Joliet, Ill., 14 Dec. 1929. Studied with
Howard Hanson and Bernard Rogers, Eastman School
of Music, B. M., M. M., D. M. A.; with Arthur
Honegger and Tony Aubin, Ecole Normale, Paris,
on a Fulbright fellowship. He received a $2000
grant, Nat. Educ. Asso., 1973. He is organist-
choirmaster, Central Baptist Church, Providence; chairman, music department, Brown Univ.
WORKS: Opera: The birthday of the infanta;
Orchestra: Savannah River holiday, overture;
Overture for late comers; Sarabande, for
Katharine in April; 5 pieces for orchestra, after
paintings by Andrew Wyeth; Band: Guide to the
elements of music; Elegy; Mayflower overture;
Rocky Point holiday; Meditation on the syllable
OM; Alleluia, July 20, 1969; Trilogy: JFK-MLK-
RFK; Chorus: The Christmas story, cantata; What
is man?, oratorio; God, bring thy sword; Fanfare
for a festival; Triumphal te deum; Sleep, little
one; Behold man, male choir; Autumn night and
Vocalise, women's voices; Prayer of the Emperor
of China on the altar of heaven, Dec. 21, 1539;
Thy truth is great; Chorale fanfare for
Christmas.
Department of Music, Brown University
Providence, RI 02912

NELSON, RONALD A.
b. Rockford, Ill., 29 Apr. 1927. Studied with
Olaf Christiansen and F. Melius Christiansen,
St. Olaf Coll.; with Cecil Burleigh and Robert
Crane, Univ. of Wisconsin. He was public school
music teacher, 1949-52; church music director,
Rockford, Ill., 1949-55; Westwood Lutheran
Church, Minneapolis, 1955- ; has been guest
lecturer, Luther Seminary, St. Paul, 1970, 1971,
1973.
WORKS: Chorus: How far is it to Bethlehem?;
And who is my neighbor?; The passion according to
St. Mark; and many anthems.
1457 Utah Ave. South, Minneapolis, MN 55426

NEMIROFF, ISAAC
b. Newport, Ky., 16 Feb. 1912. Studied with
Carl Hugo Grimm, Cincinnati Cons.; and with
Stefan Wolpe in New York. He received 2 awards
from the State Univ. of New York Research Found.;
commissions from Collegium Musicum of New York
and Greenwich House Music School. He was director, Contemporary Music School, New York,
1948-52; head of theory department, Greenwich
House Music School, 1954-61; professor, State
Univ. of New York at Stony Brook, 1959- .
WORKS: Chamber music: concerto for oboe and
strings; concertino, flute, violin, oboe,
strings; 2 string quartets; 2 violin sonatas;
Chamber work for piano and 10 instruments; solo
cantata for voice, flute, and strings; 3 pieces

(NEMIROFF, ISAAC)
for solo clarinet; Variations, flute, oboe, cello; Perspectives, woodwind trio; 4 treble suite, woodwinds; Atomyriades, solo oboe.
57 Boulevard, Greenlawn, NY 11740

*NERO, PAUL
b. Hamburg, Germany, 29 Apr. 1917; U.S. citizen 1929; d. Hollywood, Calif., 21 May 1958. Studied violin at Curtis Inst. He played violin, Pittsburgh Symphony; served in U.S. Navy in World War II; was soloist, Chamber Music Society of Lower Basin Street; on faculty, Juilliard School; Los Angeles Cons. His works included Concerto for hot fiddle; Prelude and allegro for oboe and strings; 7 etudes for violin.

*NERO, PETER BERNARD
b. Brooklyn, N. Y., 22 May 1934. Studied at Juilliard School and Brooklyn Coll.; played piano with Paul Whiteman's orchestra, in night clubs, etc. He performed the piano solo in his own Fantasy and improvisation with the Boston Pops Orchestra.

NESTICO, SAMUEL L.
b. Pittsburgh, Pa., 6 Feb. 1924. Studied at Duquesne Univ., B. S. 1950; and with George Thaddeus Jones, Catholic Univ. He was staff trombonist and arranger, WCAE, Pittsburgh, 1946-51; public school band director, 1950-51; staff arranger, USAF Band, Washington, D.C., and leader of Airmen of Note, 1951-66; chief arranger, U.S. Marine Band, 1966-71; arranger and orchestrator for recordings, movies, and television, 1951-   ; instructor, Los Angeles Pierce Coll., 1972-   .
WORKS: Band: Horizons west; The Greenbriars of Wexley; Chamber music: A study in contrasts, 4 saxophones or 6 clarinets.
18873 Killoch Way, Northridge, CA 91324

NEUHAUS, MAX
b. Texas, 9 Aug. 1939. Studied at Manhattan School of Music, B. M. 1961, M. M. 1962. He received a Nat. Endowment for the Arts fellowship, 1973. He toured the U.S. as percussionist with the Contemporary Chamber Ensemble under Pierre Boulez, 1962-63, and with Karlheinz Stockhausen, 1963-64; gave solo recitals in Carnegie Recital Hall, 1964, 1965, 1968, and in major European cities and the Spoleto Festival, Italy, 1965-66; was resident visitor, Bell Telephone Laboratories, Murray Hill, N. J., 1968-69; has mounted musical happenings called "Music for non-concert hall situations" all across the country in such places as Consolidated Edison Power Station, New York; Hudson Tubes, 9th Street Station; Cornell Coll.; WBAI-FM, New York; CURT-FM, Toronto; California Inst. of the Arts; Univ. of California at San Diego; Univ. of South Florida; Rochester Inst. of Technology, etc., etc.
WORKS: Music for non-concert hall situations: Listen, 1966-69; Public supply, 1966-70; Bi-product, 1966-67; American Can, 1966-67; Drive-in-music, 1967-68; Telephone access, 1968; Water whistle, 1971-73; Walkthrough, 1973. Water whistle, e.g., uses 8-10 water driven whistles which produce pleasant little reedy sounds that

(NEUHAUS, MAX)
are audible only to those submerged in the swimming pool in which they are installed.
210 Fifth Ave., New York, NY 10010

*NEUMANN, ALFRED
The rites of man, music drama, Silver Spring, Md., 18 May 1969; An opera for Christmas, 1-act.

NEUMANN, RICHARD
b. Vienna, Austria, 21 Jan. 1914; U.S. citizen 1942. Studied with Fidelio Finke and George Szell, Prague Cons.; music education at Vienna Acad. of Music, M. A. 1937; and at Columbia Univ., 1946-47. He received commissions from the Anna Sokolow Dance Group, 1941; Temple Israel, New York City, 1959. He was music director, Educational Alliance, New York, 1949-52; Hillcrest Jewish Center, 1953-63; music consultant, B'nai Brith Youth Org., 1964-   ; music director, Board of Jewish Education, 1972-   .
WORKS: Orchestra: oboe concerto, 1950; timpani concerto, 1972; Chorus: How goodly are thy tents; Torah service; Cuando El Rey Nimrod; Scalerica de oro; Los bilbilicos; Noches; Film scores: 8 film scores for United Nations Screen Magazine, Film Section, 1949.
3931 47th St., Long Island City, NY 11104

*NEVIN, ARTHUR FINLEY
b. Edgeworth, Pa., 27 Apr. 1871; d. Sewickley, Pa., 10 July 1943. Younger brother of Ethelbert Nevin, studied with Percy Goetschius, New England Cons.; with Humperdinck and Klindworth in Berlin; received an honorary D. M., Univ. of Pittsburgh, 1935. In 1903-04 he spent time in Montana studying Indian music; was professor, Univ. of Kansas, 1915-20; director, Memphis municipal music department and conductor, Memphis Orchestra, 1920-22.
WORKS: Opera: Poia, 1910; Daughter of the forest, 1918; Orchestra: piano concerto; Hindu dance; Lorna Doone suite; Love dreams suite; Chamber music: piano trio; string quartet; Voice: The Djinns, cantata; Roland, cantata; other choruses, songs, piano pieces.

*NEVIN, GORDON BALCH
b. Easton, Pa., 19 May 1892; d. New Wilmington, Pa., 15 Nov. 1943. Studied organ with John Frederick Wolle; received an honorary D. M., Westminster Coll. He was organist and teacher in Pennsylvania and Ohio; taught at Hiram Coll., 1915-17; was professor of organ and composition, Westminster Coll., 1932-43.
WORKS: Operetta: Following Foster's footsteps; Chorus: Behold the Christ, cantata; Organ: Sonata tripartite; Pageant triumphale; Tragedy of a tin soldier, a suite; Rural sketches; City sketches; In memoriam; 16 postludes. He was also author of books on organ playing.

NEWBURY, KENT A.
b. Chicago, Ill., 25 Nov. 1925. Studied with Bernhard Heiden, Indiana Univ., B. M., M. M.; with Leo Sowerby, American Cons. He was public school and church choral director in Chicago area, 1951-64, in Phoenix, 1965-   .

NEWBURY, KENT A.

(NEWBURY, KENT A.)
WORKS: Theatre: We owe it all to Edgar J., musical comedy; Band: Painting in parallels; Declamations for brass; Chorus: Duty, honor, country, with narrator and 2 pianos; Rise, O buried lord, with organ and brass; numerous published anthems and choral works.
6833 East Double Tree Road
Scottsdale, AZ 85253

NEWELL, JOHN
b. Charlotte, N. C., 4 May 1949. Studied with Iain Hamilton, Duke Univ.; with Mel Powell, California Inst. of the Arts.
WORKS: Theatre: Music for Crazy Jane, a collaboration; Chamber music: Image, song, vision, piano, flute, clarinet, cello; The aardvark looming, harp and tape.
22416 Fifth St., Newhall, CA 91321

NEWELL, ROBERT M.
b. Blandinsville, Ill., 18 May 1940. Studied with Salvatore Martirano and Kenneth Gaburo, Univ. of Illinois, M. M.; with Lukas Foss at Tanglewood; and with Olivier Messiaen, Paris Cons. He received a Fromm Found. commission at Tanglewood, 1965; Fulbright grant, 1965; and was winner of a Denver Symphony competition, 1969. He has been faculty member, Univ. of Illinois, 1968-74; music consultant, Maharishi Univ., 1973-74.
WORKS: Orchestra: Edifice in memoriam, Denver Symphony, 1969; Chamber music: Spirals, percussion and 2 singers.
MIU, 6689 Colegio Ave., Goleta, CA 93017

*NEWLIN, DIKA
b. Portland, Ore., 22 Nov. 1923. Studied at Michigan State Univ., B. A. 1939; Univ. of California at Los Angeles, M. A. 1941; Columbia Univ., Ph. D. 1945; privately with Roger Sessions and Arnold Schoenberg in California. Her awards include a Fulbright fellowship in Vienna, 1951-52; Mahler medal, Bruckner Society, 1957; Sigma Alpha Iota award; Silver mdeal, French Minister of Foreign Affairs; Honorary L. H. D., Upsala Coll., 1964. She taught at Western Maryland Coll., 1945-49; Syracuse Univ., 1949-51; was founder and chairman, music department, Drew Univ., 1952-72; professor, North Texas State Univ., 1972-   .
WORKS: Chamber music: piano trio, 1948; chamber symphony for 12 instruments, 1949; Piano: Sinfonia, 1947; Fantasia, 1957.
Department of Music
North Texas State University
Denton, TX 76203

*NEWMAN, ALFRED
b. New Haven, Conn., 17 Mar. 1901; d. Hollywood, Calif., 17 Feb. 1970. Studied with Sigismund Stojowski, Rubin Goldmark, and George Wedge in New York; with Arnold Schoenberg in Los Angeles. He gave his first concert at age 7; later was vaudeville pianist and conductor; conducted George White's Scandals and Gershwin shows on Broadway; went to Hollywood in 1930 and was music director for film companies to 1960. His

(NEWMAN, ALFRED)
film scores received 8 Academy awards and 36 other nominations.
WORKS: Film scores: Street scene; Hunchback of Notre Dame; Gunga Din; The hurricane; The prisoner of Zenda; Wuthering Heights; The bluebird; The song of Bernadette; How green was my valley; The razor's edge; Gentlemen's agreement; All about Eve; Love is a many splendored thing; and many others.

NEWMAN, ANTHONY
b. Los Angeles, Calif., 12 May 1941. Studied with Leonard Stein in Los Angeles; Leon Kirchner in Boston; and with Luciano Berio in New York. He received an ASCAP award, 1971. He has been on the faculty, Juilliard School, 1967-   ; and at State Univ. Coll., Purchase, N. Y., 1971-   .
WORKS: Keyboard: Chimaeras I and II, harpsichord; Habitat, organ; Barricades, organ; Bhajebochstlannanas, organ.
42 Clapboard Ridge Road, Danbury, CT 06810

NEWMAN, THEODORE S.
b. New York, N. Y., 18 June 1933. Studied with Vittorio Giannini and Vincent Persichetti, Juilliard School. His awards include the Edward B. Benjamin prize, 1958, 1959, 1960; Guggenheim fellowship, 1961; Gretchinaninoff Memorial prize, 1963; Elizabeth Sprague Coolidge prize, 1963; McCollin award, 1964.
WORKS: Ballet: Cain, for Harkness Ballet; Orchestra: Toccata; Fantasy; organ concerto; Discourse; Fragments; Band: Suite for band; Chorus: Alleluia, with brass and timpani.
240 West 14th St., New York, NY 10011

NEWMAN, WILLIAM S.
b. Cleveland, Ohio, 6 Apr. 1912. Studied with Herbert Elwell at Cleveland Inst. of Music; with Arthur Shepherd at Western Reserve Univ., Ph. D. 1939; musicology with Eric Hertzmann and Paul H. Lang, Columbia Univ., 1940, and at several libraries in Europe. He held a Guggenheim fellowship for research on sonata literature, 1960-61. He taught in Cleveland public schools; was in the Army Air Force, 1942-45; has been on the music faculty, Univ. of North Carolina, 1945-   , professor, 1955-   ; has given many piano recitals and appeared as soloist with major orchestras; is author of several important books on musicology and many articles in music journals.
WORKS: Theatre: an operetta, 1936; Orchestra: An American tragedy, overture, 1940; little symphony, 1940; Chamber music: piano sonata, 1929; cello sonata, 1935; string quartet, 1937; also band pieces.
Department of Music
University of North Carolina
Chapel Hill, NC 27514

NIBLOCK, JAMES
b. Scappoose, Ore., 1 Nov. 1917. Studied at Washington State Univ., B. A., B. Ed.; Univ. of Pennsylvania; Colorado Coll., M. A.; Univ. of Iowa, Ph. D.; composition with Roy Harris and Paul Hindemith. He was a private teacher and

(NIBLOCK, JAMES)
member, Beaumont String Quartet, 1948-62; concertmaster, Lansing Symphony Orchestra, 1961-62; professor and chairman, department of music, Michigan State Univ., 1962-   .
WORKS: Orchestra: Trigon, string orch.; Band: La folia; Soliloquy and dance; Triptych for brass and percussion; numerous unpublished works for orchestra, chamber groups, and voice. He is author of the book, Music for the high school chorus.
215 Elizabeth St., East Lansing, MI 48823

*NICHOLS, ALBERTA
b. Lincoln, Ill., 3 Dec. 1898; d. Hollywood, Calif., 4 Feb. 1957. Studied at Louisville Cons.; also with Alfred Calzin and George Copeland. She composed scores for Broadway shows Gay Paree and Angela; special material and songs for vaudeville, radio, musical commercials.

NICKERSON, CAMILLE
b. New Orleans, La., 30 Mar.   . Studied piano with her father and with Rene Salomon in New Orleans; at Oberlin Cons., B. M., M. M. She is a member of Pi Kappa Lambda; received 2 awards from Nat. Asso. of Negro Musicians, 1937, 1962. She was faculty member, Howard Univ., 1926-62, now professor emeritus.
WORKS: Chorus (Creole songs): Go to sleep; Dear, I love you so; Mister banjo; Mam'selle Zi Zi; Suzanne, Bel femme; Suzanne; and Christmas everywhere; The women of the U.S.A.; Interracial hymn; A precious lullaby; Songs: When love is done; Lizette.
1712 16th St., N.W., Washington, DC 20009

NIEMACK, ILZA
b. Charles City, Iowa, 8 Apr.   . Studied with Felix Borowski, Rubin Goldmark, Francis Pyle, Mario Castelnuovo-Tedesco. She was faculty member, Iowa State Univ., 1935-   , professor 1970-73, now professor emeritus.
WORKS: Orchestra: 2 piano concertos; Chamber music; 7 violin sonatas; Barcarolle for piano; many short pieces for violin; songs.
602 Lynn Ave., Ames, IA 50010

NIERENBERG, ROGER
b. New York, N. Y., 14 June 1947. Studied privately with Elie Siegmeister, 1961-65; with Milton Babbitt, Peter Westergaard, Edward T. Cone, Charles Wuorinen, Princeton Univ., B. A. with high honors 1969; Mannes Coll. of Music, 1971; Aspen School, 1971; also studied conducting, piano, trumpet, and viola. His awards include New York State Regents scholarship, 1965; Woodrow Wilson Nat. fellowship, 1969. He taught at Mannes Coll. of Music, 1971; has been on faculty, Queens Coll. CUNY, 1973-   ; director of Bands, Columbia Univ., 1973-   ; assistant conductor, Queens Symphony Orchestra, 1973-   .
WORKS: Chamber music: 2 songs for voice and string quartet, 1965; 3 songs for voice, flute, viola, piano, percussion, 1968; 2 short piano pieces, 1968; Short piece for bassoon and piano, 1969; Chorus: Motet, a cappella, 1966; Fire, flood and olive-tree, with piano and percussion,

(NIERENBERG, ROGER)
1967; Cantata for tenor, chorus, and chamber orch., 1969; Film score: College daze, 1970.
40 West 53rd St., New York, NY 10019

NIGHTINGALE, JAMES F.
b. Grantspass, Ore., 11 May 1948. Studied with Aurelio de la Vega, California State Univ. at Northridge, candidate for M. A. 1973. He is a private teacher and free-lance performer.
WORKS: Wind ensemble: Vicissitudes, accordion and winds; 2 inventions, brass sextet; Chamber music: Sketches, string quartet; Fragment, horn and accordion; Aquarian inventions, accordion.
6511 Rhea Ave., Reseda, CA 91335

NIGHTINGALE, MAE WHEELER
b. Blencoe, Iowa, 30 Dec. 1898. Studied at Univ. of California, Los Angeles; Univ. of Southern California; Fresno State Coll.; Westminster Choir Coll. She received the Mancini award for distinction in music teaching, California Music Educators Asso. and Kimber Found. She taught privately 1919-23; then in public schools, 1923-59; was music training teacher, Univ. of California, Univ. of Southern California, and Los Angeles State Coll., 1926-59.
WORKS: Operettas: Ride em cowboy; Queen of the sawdust; many published original works and arrangements for chorus, especially for young singers.
Box 300 Star Route
Mountain Center, CA 92361

*NIKOLAIS, ALWIN
b. Southington, Conn., 25 Nov. 1912. Played piano for silent movies; then studied dance. He composes electronic ballet scores, does the choreography and stage directing; became co-director, Henry Street Playhouse, New York in 1949; established the Nikolais Dance Theatre at the Playhouse in 1956. His theatre piece, Scenario was performed there in Feb. 1971; Cross-fade, on 5 Feb. 1974.
c/o Space for Innovative Development, Inc.
344 West 36th St., New York, NY 10018

NILES, JOHN JACOB
b. Louisville, Ky., 28 Apr. 1892. Studied with Edgar Stillman Kelley, Cincinnati Cons.; at Univ. and Cons. of Lyons, and Schola Cantorum, France; and at Transylvania Univ. His awards include a citation, Nat. Fed. of Music Clubs; honorary doctorates from Cincinnati Cons., Univ. of Kentucky, Univ. of Louisville, Transylvania Univ., Episcopal Theological Seminary in Kentucky; research grant, Nat. Endowment for the Humanities. He has taught briefly at Curtis Inst., Univ. of Missouri at Kansas City, Eastman School, Juilliard School, and elsewhere, but has been chiefly composer and concert artist, touring the U.S., Great Britain, and Europe. He is a noted authority on American folk music, especially of the Southern Appalachians, and has made his own dulcimers and lutes for authenticity in performance.

NILES, JOHN JACOB

(NILES, JOHN JACOB)
WORKS: Chorus: Black oak tree; Carol of the Polish Grenadiers; Death of Thomas a Beckett; I never had but one love; Oh waly waly; Our lovely lady singing; Rejoice all men; The silent stars; Turtle dove; Venezuela; I wonder as I wander; Black is the color of my true love's hair; many more original choral works and songs, and over 1000 arrangements of folk music.
Boot Hill Farm, RFD #7, Lexington, KY 40502

NIN-CULMELL, JOAQUIN
b. Berlin, Germany, 5 Sep. 1908; U.S. citizen 1951; son of Cuban composer, Joaquin Nin. Studied at Schola Cantorum, Paris, piano diploma 1930; with Manuel de Falla in Granada, Spain, 1930-34; and with Paul Dukas at Paris Cons. He is a corresponding member, Royal Acad. of Fine Arts of San Fernando, Madrid; and was Creative Arts Inst. fellow, 1965-66. He toured Europe, Cuba, and the U.S. as concert pianist, 1934-40; was professor, Williams Coll., 1940-50; professor, Univ. of California, Berkeley, 1950-   .
WORKS: Orchestra: piano concerto, 1946; Chamber music: Tres impresiones, piano, 1931; piano sonata, 1934; piano quintet, 1938; Dos canciones, voice and piano or string quartet; Chorus: Dedication mass.
Music Department, University of California
Berkeley, CA 94720

NIX, THEO M.
b. Comanche, Okla., 1 Dec. 1910. Studied with Bela Rozsa, Tulsa Univ.; with Philip Greeley Clapp and Philip Bezanson, Univ. of Iowa, Ph. D. He has been music director in public schools and colleges; professor and chairman, Fine Arts Division, Northeastern State Coll., 1952.
WORKS: Orchestra: Suite of dances; symphony; Chamber music: quintet for flute and strings; quartet on B A C H; many works for solo instruments.
804 Janet, Tahlequah, OK 74464

NIXON, ROGER
b. Tulare, Calif., 8 Aug. 1921. Studied with Arthur Bliss, Ernest Bloch, and Roger Sessions, Univ. of California, Berkeley, Ph. D. 1952; and privately with Arnold Schoenberg. He received the Phelan award, 1950; ASCAP awards, 1969-73; Ostwald award, 1973; and commissions. He taught at Modesto Jr. Coll., 1951-59; has been professor, San Francisco State Univ., 1960-   .
WORKS: Opera: The bride comes to Yellow Sky, Eastern Illinois Univ., 20 Feb. 1968; Orchestra: Air for strings, 1953; violin concerto, 1956; Mooney's Grove suite, 1964; Elegiac rhapsody, viola and orch., 1967; viola concerto, San Francisco, 29 Apr. 1970; Band: Prelude and fugue, 1961; Reflections, 1964; Fiesta del Pacifico, 1966; Nocturne, 1966; Elegy and fanfare-march, 1967; Centennial fanfare-march, 1970; A solemn processional; Chamber music: 3 piano preludes, 1947; string quartet, 1949; 4 duos, flute and clarinet, 1966; 4 duos, violin and viola, 1966; Nocturne, flute and piano, 1967; Chorus: Firwood, 1953; Now living things, 1960; The wine of astonishment, 1960; To the evening star, 1961;

(NIXON, ROGER)
The wind, 1962; Summer rain, 1964; By-by-baby, lullaby, 1965; Ditty, 1966; Love's secret, 1967; Songs: 6 moods of love, cycle for soprano and piano, 1950.
2090 New Brunswick Drive
San Mateo, CA 94402

NOEHREN, ROBERT
b. Buffalo, N. Y., 16 Dec. 1910. Attended Inst. of Musical Art, New York, and Curtis Inst. of Music; studied composition with Paul Hindemith. He was instructor, Davidson Coll., 1946-49; professor and university organist, Univ. of Michigan, 1949-   .
WORKS: Organ: Fugue; Fantasia: Homage to Hindemith; sonata; also piano pieces, songs, choral works, string trio.
815 Oakdale Road, Ann Arbor, MI 48105

NOHE, BEVERLY
b. East Rochester, N. Y., 24 Sep. 1935. Studied at Eastman School of Music, B. A. 1959. She was choir director-organist in East Rochester, 1967-73; has taught at Rochester School for the Deaf, 1967-   .
WORKS: Chamber music: Playground, flute, violin, and cello; Poème capricieuse, clarinet and piano; many sacred choral works.
110 Worthing Terrace
East Rochester, NY 14445

NOLTE, ROY E.
b. Louisville, Ky., 25 July 1896. Attended business school; studied organ and piano privately; was self-taught in composition. He won the Loranz Publishing Company Internat. Anthem Competition, 1927, with Lift up your heads. He was contributing editor, Volunteer Choir, 1928-57.
WORKS: Chorus: 28 choir cantatas including: Hosanna; King all glorious; The cross of redemption; Dawn of Christmas; Star of the silent night; many anthems; piano and organ pieces.
272 Pennsylvania Ave., Louisville, KY 40206

NOON, DAVID
b. Johnstown, Pa., 23 July 1946. Studied with Karl Kohn, Pomona Coll., B. A. 1968; at New York Univ., M. A. 1970; with Mario Davidovsky and Yehudi Wyner, Yale Univ., M. M. A. 1972; with Darius Milhaud and Charles Jones, Aspen School, 1969, 1971. He has received 2 BMI student composer awards, 1967, 1970; 2 Young Musician Found. awards, 1968, 1971; first prize at Aspen Festival, 1969; Composers' Forum award, 1971; Woods Chandler prize, 1971; John Day Jackson prize, 1972; Harriet Gibbs Fox prize, 1972; ASCAP award, 1973. He has been instructor, Northwestern Univ., 1973-   .
WORKS: Ballet: Labyrinth, chamber orch.; Ai, Ai; Orchestra: Tango 1940, string orch.; Berceuse seche; Chamber music: Quatre chansons, alto and chamber group; Inflections, piano, prepared piano, harpsichord, harp, vibraphone; Introduction, dirge, and frolic, winds; Duo, 2 violas; concerto for cello, 11 winds, harpsichord, piano; Fratricide, music for a pantomime;

(NOON, DAVID)
Fantasy, violin and piano 4-hands; Cadenzas, violin alone; Motets and monodies, woodwind trio; 6 chansons, soprano and chamber group; Da capo, piano; sonata, clarinet, prepared piano, vibraphone; Song and toccata, solo trombone; Chorus: Cantata for 8-part choir and instrumental octet; Psalm, tenor, 6-part solo choir, flute, cello, piano.
1563 Elmcroft Ave., Pomona, CA 91767

NORDEN, HUGO
b. Providence, R. I., 31 Dec. 1909. Studied with John Sebastian Matthews in Providence; with Howard R. Thatcher in Baltimore; at Univ. of Toronto, B. M. 1943, D. M. 1948; and violin with Hugo Kortschak and Felix Winternitz. He was faculty member, Boston Cons., 1943-45; professor, Boston Univ., 1945- ; music editor, Arthur P. Schmidt Company, 1943-58.
WORKS: Orchestra: symphony, 1948; Chorale, ennead, and fugue, string orch.; Chamber music: 2 violin sonatas; Passacaglia, horn and piano; string quartet; many small works for solo instruments and chamber groups; choral works. He is also author of: The technique of canon; Fundamental harmony; Fundamental counterpoint; Form: The silent language; and a translation from the Danish of Chorale harmonization in the church modes.
11 Mendelssohn St., Roslindale, MA 02131

*NORDEN, NORRIS LINDSAY
b. Philadelphia, Pa., 24 Apr. 1887; d. Philadelphia, 3 Nov. 1956. Studied with Cornelius Rybner, Columbia Univ., B. M. 1910, M. A. 1911; also with Max Spicker and Franklin Robinson. He was organist in New York, Brooklyn, and Philadelphia; conducted the Mendelssohn Club in Philadelphia, 1916-36.
WORKS: Orchestra: Thanatopsis, with chorus, 1922; Te Deum, with chorus, 1923; Silver plume, symphonic poem, 1924; Charity, with chorus, 1928; The white swan, symphonic poem.

NORDENSTROM, GLADYS (Mrs. Ernst Krenek)
b. Pokegama, Minn., 23 May 1924. Studied with Ernst Krenek, Hamline Univ. and Univ. of Minnesota.
WORKS: Orchestra: El Greco phantasia, string orch.; Elegy for Robert F. Kennedy; Chamber music: piano sonata; Variations for piano; Rondo, flute and piano; Palm Springs sextet, winds; Electronic: Signals from nowhere, organ and tape; Blocks and beans, tape.
623 Chino Canyon Road, Palm Springs, CA 92262

NORDOFF, PAUL
b. Philadelphia, Pa., 4 June 1909. Studied at Philadelphia Cons., B. M. 1927, M. M. 1932; with Olga Samaroff and Rubin Goldmark, Juilliard School; Combs Coll. of Music, B. M. in music therapy, 1960, honorary D. M. 1958. He received 2 Guggenheim fellowships, 1933, 1935; Columbia Univ. Bearns prize, 1933; Pulitzer grant, 1940; Ford Found. grant, 1954; and many commissions. His faculty positions included Philadelphia Cons., 1938-43; Michigan State Coll., 1945-46;

(NORDOFF, PAUL)
professor, Bard Coll., 1949-58; research and work in music therapy, Univ. of Pennsylvania, 1961-67; lecturing fellow, American-Scandinavian Found., 1967-68, 1973; senior music therapy consultant and supervisor of music therapy research, Child Study Center, Philadelphia, 1969- .
WORKS: Opera: The masterpiece, 1 act, Philadelphia, 24 Jan. 1951; The sea-change; Ballet: Every soul is a circus, 1939; In pursuit of folly; Tally ho, 1944; Theatre: music for Romeo and Juliet; Antony and Cleopatra, 1948; St. Joan; Orchestra: suite, 1940; violin concerto, 1940; 2 piano concertos; Winter symphony, 1954; Tranquil symphony; Chamber music: 2 string quartets; 2 song cycles; dance sonata for flute and piano; Chorus: secular mass, chorus and orch., 1934; The sun, cantata with eurhythmic ballet, 1945; Psalm 23, speaking and singing choruses, piano and bells; many songs; piano pieces. He co-author with Clive Robbins of Music therapy for handicapped children, 1967; Music therapy in special education, 1971; Therapy in music for handicapped children, 1971; and books of children's songs and play songs.
Chester Springs, PA 19425

NORTH, ALEX
b. Chester, Pa., 4 Dec. 1910. Studied with Bernard Wagenaar, Juilliard School; with A. Veprik, Moscow Cons.; with Aaron Copland and Ernst Toch. His honors include a Guggenheim fellowship; Composers and Lyricists Guild award for film score to Cleopatra, 1963; Laurel awards for film scores, 1956, 1957, 1966, 1967, 1969; Golden Globe award for Shoes of the fisherman, 1969; 11 Academy award nominations.
WORKS: Opera: Hither and thither of Danny Dither, children's opera; Ballet: Streetcar named desire; American Lyric, 1937; Daddy Long Legs; Mal de siecle; Wall Street ballet; Theatre (musicals): 'Tis of thee; Queen of Sheba; The great campaign; Orchestra: Rhapsody for piano and orch., 1941; Revue, clarinet and orch., Benny Goodman, soloist, Leonard Bernstein, conductor, New York, 20 Nov. 1946; 3 symphonies, 1947, 1968, 1971; 3 symphonic suites from film scores; Holiday set, 1948; Chamber music: woodwind quintet; woodwind trio; string quartet; Chorus (cantatas for chor. and orch.): Morning star, 1947; Negro mother, 1948; Film scores: Streetcar named desire, 1951; Death of a salesman, 1952; Member of the wedding; The rose tattoo, 1955; The unchained melody; The bad seed; The rainmaker; Spartacus, 1960; Cleopatra; The agony and the ecstasy; Who's afraid of Virginia Woolf, 1966; 2001, a space odyssey; Once upon a scoundrel; many others; Television scores: Billy Rose show; Playhouse 90; Nero Wolfe; I'm a lawyer; F. D. R. series; Africa; Silent night; The man and the city.
630 Resolano Drive
Pacific Palisades, CA 90272

NORTON, SPENCER
b. Anadarko, Okla., 3 Oct. 1909. Studied with Howard Hanson and Bernard Rogers, Eastman School of Music; with Ildebrando Pizzetti, Roberto

NORTON, SPENCER

(NORTON, SPENCER)
Casiraghi, Ferrucio Calusio, in Milan, Italy.
He received a Rockefeller grant; Ford Found.
grant; and commissions. He has been on the faculty, Univ. of Oklahoma, 1934-   , professor in
1973.
WORKS: Orchestra: Dance suite, 1939;
Venite, jubilate, motet for chorus and orch.,
1950; Solstice, 1951; Partita for 2 pianos and
orch., 1959; Te Deum, chorus and orch., 1965;
various smaller works for piano, organ, chamber
groups, etc.
Box 2063, Norman, OK 73069

NOSSE, CARL E.
b. North Irwin, Pa., 8 Jan. 1933. Studied at
Tarkio Coll., B. A.; U.S. Naval School of Music;
Duquesne Univ., M. M.; with John Boda and
Carlisle Floyd, Florida State Univ., D. M. 1973;
also with Klaus Pringsheim, Leo Sowerby, and
Leon Stein. He received a grant to study with
Nadia Boulanger at a seminar in Potsdam, N. Y.;
named Outstanding Young Man of the Year, 1969.
He taught in public schools, 1954-68; has been
instructor, Florida State Univ., 1972-   .
WORKS: Orchestra: Music for orchestra;
Set for small orchestra and percussion ensemble;
Richard Cory ballet, chamber orch. and small chorus; Band: Perspectives; Chamber music: piano
trio; Four eleven, woodwind quartet; Tripartite,
flute, cello, piano; suite for piano; Electronic:
Jurasic, tape; Serialization, tape; The forgotten,
percussion, narrator, and tape; many published
choral works.
2000 North Meridian Road #322
Tallahassee, FL 32303

NOTT, DOUGLAS D.
b. Yakima, Wash., 27 Feb. 1944. Studied with
Paul Creston, Robert Panerio, John De Merchant,
Central Washington State Coll., M. M. 1970. He
was graduate assistant, Central Washington State
Coll., 1969-70; director of bands and instructor
in composition, Yakima Valley Coll., 1970-   .
WORKS: Orchestra: Concerto in one movement,
saxophone and orch., 1972; Adagio and fugue, 1973;
Band: Rhapsodic song, saxophone and band, 1970;
Anagrams, a suite, 1970; Cascade, overture, 1973;
Fugue in Dorian, 1973; Voice: Obligation, chorus,
1971; Hymn for morning, soprano and piano, 1973.
211 Cleman Ave., Yakima, WA 98902

NOVAK, WILLIAM
b. Oceanside, N. Y., 31 Jan. 1952. Studied with
Joel Chadabe, State Univ. of New York at Albany.
He won an award in the State Univ. of New York
composers festival, 1972. He was assistant
director, electronic music studios, State Univ.
of New York, Albany, 1972-74.
WORKS: Electronic: Steppin' out, 1971;
Strange bedfellows, 1972; Set-up instructions,
1972; Automatic shoes, 1973; Sounds of the studio,
1973; Beaten bedfellows, 1973.
328-A Hudson Ave., Albany, NY 12207

NOVY, DONALD A.
b. Oak Park, Ill., 23 Apr. 1932. Studied with
Anthony Donato and Robert Delaney, Northwestern

(NOVY, DONALD A.)
Univ. He has been public school music teacher,
1957-   , Denver, 1958-   .
WORKS: Wind ensemble: Sonatina for brass.
2940 South Marion St., Englewood, CO 80110

NOWAK, ALISON
b. Syracuse, N. Y., 7 Apr. 1948. Studied with
Vivian Fine, Lou Calabro, and Henry Brant,
Bennington Coll., B. A. 1970; with Mario Davidsky,
Jack Beeson, and Charles Wuorinen, Columbia Univ.,
M. A. 1972. She received the Rappaport prize at
Columbia Univ. for a string trio, 1971.
WORKS: Opera: Diversion and division, 1-act
chamber opera, text by composer; Orchestra:
Quid pro quo; Chamber music: quintet, for flute,
violin, bassoon, guitar, piano; string trio.
310 West 107th St., New York, NY 10025

NOWAK, GERALD C.
b. Detroit, Mich., 16 Apr. 1936. Studied at
Trenton State Coll., B. S., M. A.; privately
with Lucien Cailliet. He has been associate
professor, Bucks County Community Coll.,
1968-   ; and is editorial consultant for a
music publisher.
WORKS: Band: Suite for woodwind quintet
and band; Olympic fanfare and march; Primarily
percussion; At the summit.
R.D. 1, Broad Acres Estates
Flemington, NJ 08822

NOWAK, LIONEL
b. Cleveland, Ohio, 25 Sep. 1911. Studied with
Quincy Porter, Roger Sessions, Herbert Elwell,
Cleveland Inst. of Music. He was music director,
Humphrey-Weidman Dance Company, 1938-42; professor, Converse Coll., 1942-46; conductor, Spartanburg Symphony Orchestra, 1942-46; professor,
Syracuse Univ., 1946-48; professor, Bennington
Coll., 1948-   .
WORKS: Modern dance scores: On my mother's
side, 1939; Flickers, 1941; House divided, 1943;
Story of mankind, 1945; Orchestra: piano concertino, 1944; Concert-piece for kettle-drums
and strings; Chamber music: Suite for 4 wind
instruments, 1945; sonata for solo violin, 1950;
Fantasia for 3 instruments, 1951; quartet for
oboe and strings, 1952; Suite for clarinet,
cello, piano, 1953; piano trio, 1954; Chorus:
Wisdom exalteth, a cappella, antiphonal chorus;
many solo songs and piano pieces.
Bennington College, Bennington, VT 05201

NOWAK, ROBERT
b. Bennington, Vt., 11 Apr. 1949. Studied with
Warren Benson and Samuel Adler, Eastman School
of Music; with Donald Erb, Cleveland Inst. of
Music. He was cellist with the National Ballet,
1973-74.
WORKS: Orchestra: cello concerto, performed
by Cleveland Orchestra with composer as soloist,
1972; Chamber music: Suite for solo flute, New
York, 8 May 1973; Fantasia, violin and piano.
1628 19th St., N.W., Washington, DC 20009

NUERNBERGER, LOUIS DEAN
b. Wakefield, Neb., 5 Jan. 1924. Studied with
Ross Lee Finney, Univ. of Michigan; with
Bernhard Heiden, Indiana Univ., D. M.; with Nadia
Boulanger in France; with Cesar Bresgen,
Mozarteum, Salzburg, Austria. He held Fulbright
scholarships, 1954-56. He was assistant professor, Berea Coll., 1959-64; professor, Oberlin
Cons., 1964-   .
WORKS: Chorus: Magnificat quinti toni,
a cappella; Time present--Die Erde bleibt--Lux
perpetua, double motet, a cappella; Song of
Simeon, with soloists, a cappella; Reflections
on the mortality of man, soprano solo, men's
chorus, shawns, sackbuts, lute and percussion;
Organ: 3 pieces.
27 Colony Drive, Oberlin, OH 44074

NUNLIST, JULI
b. Montclair, N. J., 6 Dec. 1916. Attended Barnard Coll., B. A. 1940; studied with Vittorio
Giannini, Nicolas Flagello, Ludmila Ulehla, Manhattan School of Music, B. A. 1961, M. A. 1964.
Her piano works won first prize in an Olivet
Coll. contest, 1962; a song cycle was selected
for performance at Univ. of Kansas, 6th annual
symposium of contemporary American music, 1972.
She was faculty member, Akron Univ., 1970-73;
music director, Nat. Regional Ballet Asso. conferences, 1968, 1969, 1972; faculty member, Connecticut Coll. American Dance Festival, 1971;
chairman, Fine Arts Department, Hathaway Brown
School, Shaker Heights, Ohio, 1972-   .
WORKS: Orchestra: Platero and I, symphonic
suite on Juan Ramon Jimenez's poems; song cycle
on Rilke text, baritone and orch.; Chamber music:
string quartet; 3 songs from Prieres dans
l'Arche; Chorus: Spells, choral cycle; Piano:
Lento and presto, 1961; Piece in serial style.
Topping Lane Rd., R. D. #3
Chagrin Falls, OH 44022

NUNN, THOMAS E.
b. San Antonio, Tex., 10 May 1946. Studied with
Lothar Klein and Hunter Johnson, Univ. of Texas;
with Isaac Nemiroff, State Univ. of New York at
Stony Brook.
WORKS: Chamber music: Fragments of stone,
mixed ensemble; Concert for flute, viola, harp,
percussion; septet, mixed ensemble; Elisions I,
II, III, for 2 pianos and/or 2 percussionists.
P. O. Box 651, Port Jefferson, NY 11777

NUROCK, KIRK
b. Camden, N. J., 28 Feb. 1948. Studied with
Vincent Persichetti, Roger Sessions, Luciano
Berio, Juilliard School, B. M., M. M.; with
Rayburn Wright, Eastman School of Music; with
Michael Czajkowski, New York Univ., Electronic
Music Laboratory; jazz composition with John La
Porta. He received the Elizabeth Sprague
Coolidge prize; Abraham Ellstein and Duke
Ellington scholarships. He has been music direc-
tor, Ensemble Studio Theatre, 1970-   ; founder
and director, Natural Sound Workshop, 1971-   ;
composer-in-residence, Vermont Summer Theatre
Festival, 1973.

(NUROCK, KIRK)
WORKS: Theatre: incidental music for Sunday dinner, by Joyce Carol Oates, 1970; A dream
out of time, Irving Bauer, 1970; has composed
for orchestra, chamber groups, piano, tape; for
the Tonight Show and Merv Griffin Show on television; the Kathryn Posin Dance Group; and for
the Natural Sounds Workshop. The Workshop ensemble uses no instruments and no amplification,
only vocal and body sounds complemented by movement and spacial elements. Night, for natural
voice and body sounds, performed at the WBAI
Free Music Store, New York, 10 Jan. 1973, was
favorably reviewed by John Rockwell in the New
York Times as "most effective effort indeed,
full of counterpointed babblings and moanings and
aspirated rhythms."
143 West 21st St., New York, NY 10011

NYQUIST, MORINE A.
b. Axtell, Neb., 29 Mar. 1909. Studied with
Allan Willman, Univ. of Wyoming, B. A. 1952,
M. A. 1955. He taught in Nebraska public
schools, 1928-35; was supervisor of education
and arts projects, Nebraska Federal Works Agency,
1935-43; welfare and recreation director, American Red Cross, 1943-46; music teacher, Wyoming
public schools, 1946-55; director of bands and
music education, Huron Coll., 1955-57; Texas
Lutheran Coll., 1957-   , associate professor
in 1972. He has published works for band, instrumental groups, and chorus.
Box 3476, Texas Lutheran College
Seguin, TX 78155

NYGUIST, ROGER THOMAS
b. Rockford, Ill., 11 July 1934. Studied organ
with Oswald Ragatz, Indiana Univ., D. M. He
was instructor, Southwestern Coll., Kan.,
1957-58; assistant professor-organist, Univ. of
California, Santa Clara, 1962-67, associate
professor-organist, chairman of music department,
1967-   .
WORKS: Organ: Adagio for organ.
Music Department, University of California
Santa Clara, CA 95053

OAK, KILSUNG
b. Korea, 7 May 1942; to U.S. 1968. Studied with
Stefan Wolpe, Long Island Univ.; with Vladimir
Ussachevsky and Chou Wen-chung, Columbia Univ.
He received the Rappaport prize in chamber music,
1972; and fellowships at Yale Summer School,
1972, Yaddo, 1973, and Columbia Univ., 1973.
WORKS: Chamber music: Invocation, 1970;
trio for 2 violins and piano, 1971; duo for violin and piano, 1972; Amorphosis, percussion
ensemble, 1973.
431 Riverside Drive, New York, NY 10025

OAKES, RODNEY HARLAND
b. Rome, N. Y., 15 Apr. 1937. Studied with
David Ward-Steinman, San Diego State Univ.,
B. A. 1960, M. A. 1966; with Robert McBride,
Univ. of Arizona; and with Anthony Vazzana,
Univ. of Southern California, D. M. A. 1973.
His awards include Celia Buck grant, 1966; com-
missions from Pittsburgh Diocese, 1969, Hanover

OAKES, RODNEY HARLAND

(OAKES, RODNEY HARLAND)
School District, Ashland, Va., 1970. He was on
the staff, Univ. of Southern California, 1971-72;
Los Angeles Harbor Coll., 1972-   .
   WORKS: Chamber music: Song for 2 voices,
soprano and alto and piano; Six by six, indefinite number of players; Introspectrum in 6 refractions, indefinite number of players plus
audience; Variations on 18th century hymn tune,
organ and brass; Chorus: Mass, chorus and
strings, 1966; You are the God, sopranos and
basses with organ, 1970; The primrose; Seeker of
truth, chorus and band.
   500 Prospect Blvd., Pasadena, CA 91103

OBRECHT, ELDON
   b. Rolfe, Iowa, 9 June 1920. Studied with Philip
Greeley Clapp, Univ. of Iowa, Ph. D. He has been
faculty member, Univ. of Iowa, 1947-   , professor, 1967-   .
   WORKS: Orchestra: 3 symphonies; Chamber
music: sonatas for string bass, horn, clarinet,
piano; Pantomimes, woodwind quintet; Triptych,
brass trio; Contrasts, oboe and piano; Lloyd
Jones settings for voice and piano; Diversions I
and II for doublebass alone; Night piece, flute
and clarinet; Canzona for organ; sonata for 4
bassoons.
   School of Music, University of Iowa
   Iowa City, IA 52242

O'BRIEN, EUGENE
   b. Patterson, N. J., 24 Apr. 1945. Studied with
Robert Beadell, Univ. of Nebraska; with Bernd
Alois Zimmermann in Cologne, Germany; John Eaton,
Indiana Univ.; and with Iannis Xenakis, Center
for Mathematical and Automated Music, Indiana
Univ. He received a Fulbright grant to Germany,
1969; BMI awards, 1968, 1970; Prix de Rome of the
American Acad., 1971-73. He has been faculty
member, Cleveland Inst. of Music, 1973-   .
   WORKS: Orchestra: symphony, 1969; cello
concerto, 1969-71; Chamber ensemble: Elegy for
Bernd Alois Zimmermann, 1970; Lingual, 1971;
Dédales, 1972-73, Koussevitzky Found. comm.
   42 Parkview Drive, Painesville, OH 44077

O'BRIEN, KATHARINE E.
   b. Amesbury, Mass. 10 Apr. 1901. Studied at
Bates Coll., A. B.; Cornell Univ., A. M.; Brown
Univ., Ph. D.; piano and composition with Warner
Hawkins in New York. She has received honorary
doctorates from Univ. of Maine and Bowdoin Coll.
She was chairman of mathematics department, New
Rochelle Coll., 1925-36; and at Deering High
School, 1940-71; was lecturer in mathematics,
Univ. of Maine, 1962-73, various years at Brown
Univ.
   WORKS: Chorus: When I set out for Lyonnesse,
Hardy text; Star of Bethlehem, text by composer.
She has published a book on mathematics, Se-
quences, 1966, many articles on mathematics; a
book of poems, Excavation and other verse, and
many poems in periodicals.
   130 Hartley St., Portland, ME 04103

*OCHSE, ORPHA CAROLINE
   Chaconne for organ. She has also published a
book, The history of the organ in the United
States, Bloomington, Ind., 1975.

*ODEGARD, PETER S.
   Sonatina, oboe and piano.

OEHLER, DALE DIXON
   b. Springfield, Ill., 10 Jan. 1941. Studied at
Northwestern Univ., B. A.; with Richard Hervig,
Univ. of Iowa, M. A., candidate for Ph. D.
   WORKS: Chamber music: Dimensions for flute;
Film scores: Streets of San Francisco; Mod
squad.
   4298 Bakman Ave., North Hollywood, CA 91602

OGDON, WILBUR L. (WILL)
   b. Redlands, Calif., 19 Apr. 1921. Studied with
Ernst Krenek, René Leibowitz, and Roger Sessions.
He received a Fulbright award, 1952; Creative
Arts fellowships, Univ. of California, 1969,
1973. He was assistant professor, Univ. of
Texas, 1947-50; associate professor, Illinois
Wesleyan Univ., 1955-65; music director, KPFA,
Berkeley, 1962-64; director of music communications, Univ. of Illinois, 1965-66; professor,
Univ. of California, San Diego, 1966-   .
   WORKS: Chamber music: Palindrome and varia-
tions, string quartet, 1960; By the Isar, soprano, flute, and doublebass, 1969; Un tombeau
de Jean Cocteau, soprano, clarinetist/mime,
pianist/conductor, and 15 instruments, 1972.
   482 15th St., Del Mar, CA 92014

*O'HARA, GEOFFREY
   b. Chatham, Ontario, 2 Feb. 1882; U.S. citizen
1919; d. St. Petersburg, Fla., 31 Jan. 1967.
Studied organ with Homer Norris; received honorary D. M., Huron Coll., 1947; citation award of
merit, 1948. In 1913 he was appointed instructor in native Indian music by the Secretary of
the Interior; taught at Columbia Univ., 1936-37;
Huron Coll., 1947-48.
   WORKS: Operettas: Peggy and the pirate,
1927; Riding down the sky, 1928; The count and
the co-ed, 1929; The smiling sixpence, 1930;
Lantern land, 1931; Harmony Hall, 1933; The princess runs away, 1934; Our America, 1934;
Puddinhead the first, 1936; The Christmas
thieves, 1943; Songs: K-K-K-Katy; Give a man a
horse he can ride; There is no death; numerous
other extremely popular songs.

*OHLSON, MARION
   b. Jersey City, N. J., 28 July. Has published
Now is the triumph, Easter anthem; other choral
works; piano pieces; songs.
   320 Fairmont Ave., Jersey City, NJ 07306

*OLDBERG, ARNE
   b. Youngstown, Ohio, 12 July 1874; d. Evanston,
Ill., 17 Feb. 1962. Studied piano with his
father and at 6 played Haydn symphonies in duet
form; studied with Middelschulte in Chicago;
with Rheinberger in Munich. He received a Nat.
Fed. of Music Clubs prize in 1911; taught at
Northwestern Univ., 1899-1941.

(OLDBERG, ARNE)
WORKS: Orchestra: 5 symphonies; 2 piano
concertos; horn concerto; Paola and Francesca,
1908; Academic overture, 1909; 2 rhapsodies;
violin concerto, 1933; The sea, symphonic poem,
1934; many chamber works; piano pieces.

OLDFIELD, WILLARD ALAN
b. Kimball, Neb., 27 Sep. 1935. Studied with
Lukas Foss, Henry L. Clarke, and Roy Harris,
Univ. of California at Los Angeles; with Nadia
Boulanger in Paris; with Merrill Ellis, Martin
Mailman, and William Latham, North Texas State
Univ., Ph. D. 1969. He was part-time teacher,
North Texas State Univ., 1966-69; associate pro-
fessor, Southern Illinois Univ., Carbondale,
1969-   .
WORKS: Orchestra: 3 units; Proportions;
Festive music; Chamber music: Dialogue for tim-
pani and brass quintet; Solos for woodwind quin-
tet; woodwind trio; Chorus: Mass, with piano,
bass, and percussion; Multi-media: Colors, for
tape, projections, and dancers.
School of Music, Southern Illinois University
Carbondale, IL 62903

*OLDS, GERRY
b. Cleveland, Ohio, 26 Feb. 1933. Studied at
Cleveland Inst. of Music; Chicago Cons., M. A.
1957.
WORKS: Orchestra: Short symphony, 1956;
violin concerto, 1957; Toccata for strings, 1958;
symphony in one movement, 1958; piano concerto,
1960; Chamber music: wind quintet, 1958; string
trio, 1959; Theme and variations in the style of
a suite, viola and cello, 1959.

*OLDS, WILLIAM BENJAMIN
b. Clinton, Wis., 3 June 1874; d. Los Angeles,
Calif., 10 Jan. 1948. Studied at Beloit Coll.,
B. A., honorary D. M.; Oberlin Cons.; American
Cons. His academic posts included Grinnell Coll.;
Illinois Coll.; James Milliken Univ.; dean, music
department, Univ. of Redlands, 1925-42; super-
visor, adult choruses, Los Angeles Bureau of
Music, 1943-48. His works include an opera, The
feathered serpent; choral works; and songs.

OLIVE, JOSEPH P.
b. Israel, 14 Mar. 1941; U.S. citizen 1961.
Studied with Ralph Shapey, Univ. of Chicago. He
has been engaged in research on speech and acoustics, Bell Laboratories, Murray Hill, N. J.,
1969-   .
WORKS: Chamber music: ABC, unaccompanied
violin; Suspended dynamics, percussion quartet;
Electronic: Speculum, for large chamber ensemble
and 4-track tape; Study #3, clarinet and tape;
Studies #4, #5, #6, for tape, all composed with
the help of the "Groove" program at Bell
Laboratories.
765 Longhill Rd., Gillette, NJ 07933

OLIVER, HAROLD
b. Easton, Md., 15 Sep. 1942. Studied with
Norman Grossman and Stefan Grove, Peabody Cons.;
with Mel Powell, Yale Univ.; Donald Martino at
Tanglewood; Milton Babbitt, Peter Westergaard,

(OLIVER, HAROLD)
J. K. Randall, Princeton Univ., Ph. D. His
awards include composition prize, Yale Univ.,
1966; Margaret Grant Memorial prize, Tanglewood,
1968; Cooperative Program in the Humanities
grant, Duke Univ., 1971; Martha Baird
Rockefeller Fund award, 1971. He was visiting
assistant professor, Duke Univ., 1970-72; assistant professor, Queens Coll., CUNY, 1972-   .
WORKS: Orchestra: Concerto for orchestra
and chamber ensemble, 1972; Chamber music:
Another spring, tenor and piano; piano etude;
woodwind quintet; violin sonata; Discourses,
for clarinet; Reflections for a Pierrot Lunaire
instrumental ensemble, 1968; The Kraken, tuba
and percussion.
29 Brookdale Rd., Glen Cove, NY 11542

*OLIVER, MADRA EMOGENE
b. Three Rivers, Mich., 28 Oct. 1905. Studied
at Univ. of Michigan, B. S. M.; Claremont Coll.,
M. A.; Oberlin Coll.-Cons. She is a private
teacher and organist; has published choral works,
songs, piano pieces and organ works.

OLIVER, RICHARD
b. Passaic, N. J., 9 Jan. 1927. Studied at
Montclair State Coll., A. B.; with Frederick
Werle, Normand Lockwood, Columbia Univ., A. M.;
with Nadia Boulanger in France. He was named
in 100 Outstanding Alumni, Montclair State Coll.,
1960; has received many commissions. He was
music director in private schools, 1953-62;
director of bands, public schools, Chappaqua,
N. Y., 1962-   .
WORKS: Orchestra: Fantasy, 1969; Band:
Irish legend; A tale of strange lands; Spectrum,
accordion and band, 1965; Chamber music: Suite
for violin and piano, 1954; Ballade, violin and
piano, 1964; Toccata, piano; Chorus: My Johnny
is comin' for me; Gooding carol; Masters in this
hall; many arrangements for band.
1946 Glen Rock St.
Yorktown Heights, NY 10598

OLIVEROS, PAULINE
b. Houston, Tex., 30 May 1932. Studied with
Paul Koepke, Univ. of Houston, 1951; privately
with Robert Erickson in San Francisco, 1952-60.
Her awards include the Pacifica Found. national
prize, 1961; Gaudeamus prize for best foreign
work, Bilthoven, Holland, 1962; research grants,
Univ. of California, 1968-70, 1969-70, 1971;
faculty fellowship in Project for Music Experiment, 1973. With Morton Subotnick and Ramon
Sender, formed the San Francisco Tape Music Center, 1961; became director of the Center when it
moved to Mills Coll., 1966; was appointed to the
faculty, Univ. of California, San Diego, 1967.
Ms. Oliveros early adopted the practical habit
of writing for available instruments, a habit
that later developed into composing with parti-
cular players in mind and fitting the work to
the personality. Theater piece for a trombone
was written for Stuart Dempster; The wheel of
fortune for William O. Smith; and Aeolian music
for the Aeolian Chamber Players, whom she had
never met, but who sent a group photograph of

OLIVEROS, PAULINE

(OLIVEROS, PAULINE)
themselves then later replaced the pianist with
a man totally unlike his predecessor in appear-
ance and personality. According to a review of
the work's Bowdoin Coll. performance (May, 1969),
the parts fit all the players well except the
pianist, though the piano part "would have been
a beautiful vehicle for the man in the
photograph."
WORKS: Chamber music: Variations for sextet,
1960; Trio for flute, piano, and page turner,
1961; Trio for trumpet, accordian, string bass,
1961; Outline, flute, percussion, string bass,
1963; Duo for accordion and bandoneon, with possible mynah bird obligato, see saw version, 1964;
Apple box orchestra, 10 performers, 1964; Night
jar, viola d'amore, 1968; Doublebasses at 20
paces, 1968; The wheel of fortune, theatre piece
for clarinet solo, 1969; Aeolian partitions,
theatre piece for chamber ensemble, 1969; Chorus:
Sound patterns, 1961; Meditation on the points
of the compass, 1970; XII sonic meditations for
group work over a long period of time, 1971;
Electronic: Time perspectives, 4-channel tape,
1961; Pieces of eight, wind octet and tape, 1965;
Rock symphony, tape, 1965; Mnemonics III and IV,
tape, 1965; Theater piece for trombone player,
with garden hose instruments and tape, 1966; Bog
road with bird call patch, tape and live electronics, 1970; Multi-media: 7 passages, tape,
mobile and dancer, 1963; Five, trumpet and dancer,
1964; Light piece for David Tudor, 1965; Before
the music ends, tape and dancer, 1965; Cat o' nine
tails, mimes and tape, 1965; Hallo, Halloween
piece for tape, instruments, mimes and lights,
1966; Festival house, orch., mimes, lights, films,
slides, 1968; AOK, accordion, 8 country fiddlers,
conductors, tape, 1969; Postcard theater, 1972;
Phantom fathom, an evening ritual, mixed media
events including meditation and an exotic pot-
luck dinner, Long Beach, 19 July 1972.
Department of Music
University of California/San Diego
La Jolla, CA 92037

OLSEN, A. LORAN
b. Minneapolis, Minn., 7 Oct. 1930. Studied at
Grinnell Coll., B. A. 1951; with Francis Pyle,
Drake Univ., M. M. 1955; with Philip Bezanson,
Univ. of Iowa, Ph. D. 1960; also with Gaetano
Comelli in Japan, 1952; Nadia Boulanger in France,
1954. He received the Steiner award, Grinnell
Coll., 1951; first prize Iowa Young Composers
contest, 1956; first prize Wisconsin State Fair
Young Composers contest, 1960. He was instruc-
tor, Luther Coll., 1955-57; teaching assistant,
Univ. of Iowa, 1957-58; faculty, Wisconsin State
Univ., 1958-60; Hastings Coll., 1960-65; assis-
tant to full professor, Washington State Univ.,
1965- .
WORKS: Dance: Dream of a primitive; The
alternative; Theatre: music for Midsummer's
night's dream; Orchestra: piano concertino;
Setting for chamber orch. and tape; Chamber music:
Soupe d'onions gratines, saxophone and piano;
woodwind trio; quintet for brass and piano; 4
Haiku, soprano and chamber ensemble; Chorus:
Could ye not watch; Confitemini Domino; Exultate

(OLSEN, A. LORAN)
justi in Domino; O bread of life; As on the
first day; Great and wonderful are thy deeds,
men's voices; Fire and ice; Song of joy; Piano:
sonatina; 2 Japanese folk songs; Study for
piano and tape recorder; Prelude and toccata on
A. H.; and 2 organ preludes.
Music Department
Washington State University
Pullman, WA 99163

*O'MEAGHER, HUGH
Studied at Peabody Cons., B. M. 1964. His works
include Concerto for harpsichord, percussion,
and orch., 1956; Concerto grosso for harpsichord,
flute, string quartet, 1967; 4 preludes for
piano, 1951; Variations on Oh dear, what can the
matter be?, piano, 1951.

O'NEAL, BARRY
b. New York, N. Y., 9 June 1942. Studied with
Gardner Read and Hugo Norden, Boston Univ.,
B. A. 1964. He was music librarian, Associated
Music Publishers, 1964-66; music salesman,
1966- .
WORKS: Orchestra: Skunk hour, tenor and
orch., 1965; Visionary landscape, no. 1, 1969;
Band: Passacaglia; Chamber music: piano quin-
tet, 1965; string quartet, 1968-70; Chorus:
Grain of sand, 1968; Lord have mercy, 1973;
Nativitie, 1973; Organ: Our vines have tender
grapes, 1970.
10 Nosband Ave., White Plains, NY 10605

*O'PRESKA, JOHN
b. 1945. Studied at North Texas State Univ.,
B. M. 1968. He has published a cello sonata;
Elegy, cello and piano; Mist, flute and piano.

ORE, CHARLES WILLIAM
b. Winfield, Kan., 18 Dec. 1936. Studied with
Theodore Beck, Concordia Coll., Seward, Neb.,
B. S. 1958; with Myron Roberts, Univ. of Ne-
braska; with Thomas Matthews, Northwestern Univ.,
M. M. 1960. He was assistant professor,
Concordia Teachers Coll., Ill., 1961-66; asso-
ciate professor, Concordia Teachers Coll.,
Seward, Neb., 1966- .
WORKS: Organ: 11 compositions for organ,
1971.
158 Faculty Lane, Seward, NB 68434

O'REILLY, JOHN SAMUEL
b. Walden, N. Y., 25 Nov. 1940. Studied with
Robert Washburn and Arthur Frackenpohl, State
Univ. of New York at Potsdam; and at Columbia
Univ. He received ASCAP awards, 1972, 1973,
1974; and numerous commissions. He taught in
public schools, 1962-72; was instructor, Nassau
Community Coll., 1972-73; editor and composer,
Alfred Publishing Company, 1973- .
WORKS: Orchestra: Heather's theme; Band:
Kings go forth; Kaleidoscope; Stratford overture; Music for the cinema; concerto for trumpet
and winds; Chamber music: 3 episodes for percussion; solos for the percussionist; Metropolitan brass quintet; Chorus: White ships and
whales, with chamber orch.
29 Murray Place, Merrick, NY 11566

ORLAND, HENRY
b. Saarbruecken, Germany, 23 Apr. 1918; U.S.
citizen 1944. Studied at Univ. of Strasbourg,
France; Northwestern Univ., B. M., M. M., Ph. D.;
and conducting privately with Nikolai Malko and
Bruno Walter. He received the Chicago Music
Critics award, 1952; Fromm Found. grant, 1956;
awards from City of St. Louis and Bach Society,
1964, 1965; Internat. Library of Contemporary
Music, Fontainebleau, France, 1969; MacDowell
award, 1972; Delius prize, 1973. He was teaching
assistant, Northwestern Univ., 1949-59; chairman
of theory-composition, St. Louis Inst. of Music,
1960-63; chairman, music department, Florissant
Valley Coll., 1963-   .
    WORKS: Opera: Man under glass, music drama;
Orchestra: Song of songs (symph. no. 2); Ode,
epitaph and dithyramb (symph no. 3); Ariadne,
episode and Psyche (symph. no. 4); bassoon concerto; concerto for flute and English horn; Ini-
tial; Pré-1-ét-ude, string orch.; Chamber music:
string trio; Chorus: Peace, a cappella; Tower
of famine, women's voice a capella; other chamber
and choral works; art songs on German, French,
and English texts.
    21 Bon Price Terrace, St. Louis, MO 63132

*ORNSTEIN, LEO
b. Kermenchug, Russia, 11 Dec. 1892; to U.S.
1907. Entered St. Petersburg Cons. at age 9;
studied with Percy Goetschius at New England
Cons.; with Bertha Fiering Tapper, Inst. of Musical Art, New York. He made his New York debut
as pianist in 1911; was soloist with all major
orchestras in the U.S.; gave many recitals in
the U.S. and Europe. In 1974 he gave all his
music manuscripts to the Yale Univ. Library.
    WORKS: Orchestra: Anger, peace, joy, 3
moods, 1914; The fog, symphonic poem, 1915;
piano concerto; Lysistrata, a suite, 1933; symphony, 1934; Impressions of Chinatown; Marche
funebre; 5 songs for voice and orch.; Pantomime;
Dance of the fates; Nocturne; concerto for 2
pianos; Chamber music: Nocturne, clarinet and
piano; Suite in classic style, flute and clarinet; Ballade, saxophone and piano; string quartet; piano quintet; violin sonata; cello sonata;
4 piano sonatas; Wild man's dance, piano; many
piano pieces; songs. See: The futurist music
of Leo Ornstein, by Vivian Perlis, Music Lib.
Asso. Notes, June 1975, 735-750.
    North Conway, NH 03860

OROWAN, THOMAS F.
b. New York, N. Y., 15 Nov. 1940. Studied at
Juilliard School; with William Sydeman and Peter
Pindar Stearns, Mannes Coll. of Music, B. S.
1965; with Gardner Read, Boston Univ., M. M.
1967, further study with Hugo Norden. He received a Phi Mu Alpha Sinfonia award, 1967; and
commissions. He was music editor, Allyn and
Bacon, 1969-71.
    WORKS: Orchestra: Serenade for strings,
1966; Band: Fanfare for brass, 1962; Chamber
music: trio for 2 trombones and tuba, 1962;
Kingspark nocturne, 4 winds, 1963; trio for
viola, clarinet, bassoon, 1963; Voyages, clarinet and guitar, 1963; 5 short dialogues, trombone

(OROWAN, THOMAS F.)
and piano, 1963; March, brass quintet, 1964;
suite for solo flute, 1964; sonata, 3 winds and
piano, 1964; string quartet, 1965; Pastorale,
oboe and piano, 1966; woodwind trio, 1966;
Presto, horn and piano, 1966; duo for 2 trumpets,
1966; suite for clarinet and piano, 1966; Piano:
suite, 1962; Nocturne, 1962; Images, animals and
Mr. Smith, 1962; Shindig, 2 pianos, 1963; sonatine, 1964; A piano parody, 1964; Prelude, 1964;
Reverie, 1965; Scherzino, 1966; Songs: The
grizzly bear, Housman text, 1970; City climates,
1970.
    82 Naples Rd., Brookline, MA 02146

ORREGO-SALAS, JUAN A.
Santiago, Chile, 18 Jan. 1919; to U.S. 1961.
Studied at Univ. of Chile, B. A. 1938; Catholic
Univ. of Santiago, architect diploma 1943; com-
position with Humberto Allende and Domingo Santa
Cruz, Nat. Cons., M. A. 1942; musicology at Co-
lumbia Univ., 1944-45; with Randall Thompson,
Princeton Univ., 1945-46; with Aaron Copland at
Tanglewood, 1946; Univ. of Chile, Ph. D. 1953.
His many awards include Rockefeller Found. grant,
1944; Guggenheim fellowships, 1945, 1954; Olga
Cohen Memorial award, 1956, 1959; Internat. Soc.
for Contemporary Music award, 1949; Chilean Contemporary Music Festival prize, 1948, 1950,
1952; Wechsler Found. award; 1954; Louisville
Orchestra award, 1955; Inter-American Music
Council, 1957; Koussevitzky Found., 1960; Kindler
Found., 1958; Cornell Univ., 1965; Coolidge
Found., 1971; Eastman School of Music, 1972;
honorary doctorate, Univ. of Chile, 1971; membership, Acad. of Fine Arts, Chile, 1971. He
was lecturer, Catholic Univ. of Santiago,
1942-43; music faculty, Univ. of Chile, 1943-49,
professor, 1949-61; chairman, music department,
Catholic Univ. of Chile, 1959-61; music critic
and editor, 1950-61; director, Latin American
Music Center, and professor, Indiana Univ.,
1961-   .
    WORKS: Opera-oratorio: El retablo del rey
pobre, 1952; Ballet: Juventud, 1948; Umbral del
sueño, 1951; The tumbler's prayer, 1960; Theatre:
music for the play Versos de ciego; 1961; Orchestra: Cantata de navidad, soprano and orch.,
1946; Escenas de Cortes y Pastores, 1946;
Obertura festiva, 1948; 4 symphonies, 1949, 1954,
1961, 1966; piano concerto, 1950; Serenata
concertante, 1954; Jubilaeus musicus, 1956; Concerto a tre, violin, cello, piano and orch.,
1962, Washington, D.C., May 1965; Volte, piano,
15 winds, harp and percussion, Rochester, N. Y.,
Dec. 1971; Band: Psalms for reciter and wind
symphony, Pittsburgh, July 1962; Concerto for
wind symphony, 1964; Chamber music: violin sonata, 1945; sonata a duo, violin and viola, 1945;
Songs in 3 movements, voice and string quartet,
1945; Canciones castellanas, soprano and 8 instruments, 1948; Cantos de advenimiento, voice,
cello and piano, 1948; Concerto da camera, woodwind quartet, 2 horns, harp and strings, 1952;
suite for solo bandoneon, 1952; sextet, clarinet,
string quartet, piano, 1954; Duo concertante,
cello and piano, 1955; Pastorale and scherzo,
violin and piano, 1956; 2 divertimientos for

331

ORREGO-SALAS, JUAN A.

(ORREGO-SALAS, JUAN A.)
woodwind trio, 1956; string quartet, Washington, D.C., Apr. 1958; Garden songs, voice, flute, viola and harp, 1959; concertino for brass quartet, 1963; Sonata a quattro, flute, oboe, harpsichord, contrabass, 1964; piano trio, 1966; Quattro liriche brevi, saxophone and piano, 1967; Mobili, viola and piano, 1967; A greeting cadenza for William Primrose, Bloomington, Ind., 1 Nov. 1971; Words of Don Quixote, baritone and chamber ensemble, 1971; Esquinas, solo guitar, 1971; Serenata, flute and cello, 1972; Sonata de estio, flute and piano, 1972; Presencias, 3 winds, 3 strings, and harpsichord, 1972; Chorus: Romances pastorales, a cappella, 1945; Romance de Don Gato, male voices a cappella, 1946; Canticos de navidad, women's or children's voices, 1948; Alboradas, women's voices, harp, piano, percussion, 1965; America, no en vano invocamos tu nombre, cantata for soprano and baritone soloists, male chorus, orch., Ithaca, N. Y., May 1966; 3 madrigals, a cappella, 1967; Missa, in tempore discordiae, tenor solo, chorus and orch., 1969; Piano: 2 suites, 1946, 1951; Variaciones y fuga sobre un pregón, 1946; Diez piezas simples, 1951; sonata, 1967.
Latin American Music Center, School of Music
Indiana University
Bloomington, IN 47401

*OSBORNE, WILLSON
b. 4 Apr. 1906. 2 ricerari for brass ensemble; Soliloquy, unaccompanied clarinet; Fantasy, unaccompanied flute.

*OSGOOD, HENRY OSBORNE
b. Peabody, Mass., 12 Mar. 1879; d. New York, N. Y., 8 May 1927. Studied in Boston and in Europe. From 1914 he was associate editor of the Musical Courier. He composed choral works and songs.

*OSSEWAARDE, JACK H.
Chorus: A paean of praise; Hosanna to the son of David; Sing we merrily; Organ: Magnificat and nunc dimittis; Improvisation for a requiem.

OSTERGREN, EDUARDO AUGUSTO
b. Sao Paulo, Brazil, 24 Apr. 1943; to U.S. 1967. Studied at Cons. Dramatico de Sao Paulo, B. M. 1963; with Lloyd Pfautsch, Southern Methodist Univ., M. M. 1968; at Indiana Univ., D. M. candidate, 1973. He was choir conductor, Univ. of Sao Paulo at Sao Carlos, 1965-67; professor, Ursuline Acad., Dallas, 1968-69; conductor, North Carolina State Univ. Symphony Orchestra, Raleigh, 1970-   .
WORKS: Chamber music: Sonata in 3 centuries, cello and piano, 1967; string quartet, 1974; Chorus: Psalm 146, 1969; Organ: Benedicamus Domino, 1971.
165 Pineland Circle, Raleigh, NC 27606

OSTERLING, ERIC
b. Hartford, Conn., 21 Mar. 1926. Studied at Ithaca Coll., B. S.; Univ. of Connecticut; and Hartt Coll. of Music. He has received several

(OSTERLING, ERIC)
commissions for band pieces. He has been high school music director, Portland, Conn., 1948-   .
WORKS: Band: First symphony; Adventurous night suite; Symphonic chorale; Beguine for youth; Tall cedars; Nordic overture; and many more band pieces.
16 Ridge Road, Cromwell, CT 06416

OSTRANDER, LINDA WOODAMAN
b. New York, N. Y., 17 Feb. 1937. Studied with Joseph Wood and Richard Hoffmann, Oberlin Coll., B. M. 1958; with Alvin Etler, Smith Coll., M. A. 1960; Ben Johnston, Univ. of Illinois, 1964-65; with Gardner Read, Boston Univ., D. M. A. 1972. She received full scholarships at Oberlin and Smith Coll.; Settie Lehman Fatman prize, 1960; Radcliffe Inst. scholar, 1963, 1964; fellowship, Univ. of Illinois, 1964-65; Gilchrist-Potter prize, Oberlin Coll., 1965-66; teaching fellowship, Boston Univ., 1969-72; commissions from Music in Maine, 1968; Main State Educational Television, sponsored by Nat. Endowment for the Arts, 1969; Arizona State Univ. Brass Choir, 1973. She was lecturer, Adelphi Suffolk Coll., 1961-63; faculty member, Southampton Coll., 1963-64; music consultant, Lesley Coll., 1972-73; assistant professor, Bunker Hill Community Coll., 1973-   .
WORKS: Orchestra: 2 suites; Quiet music; 2 concerti grossi, 1958, 1969; Chamber music: violin sonata, 1956; Variations, string quartet, 1958; piano trio, 1961; Game of chance, for any small ensemble, 1967; Fun 'n games, string quartet, 1968; string trio, 1971; Rounds, brass quintet, 1972; Cycle for six, 6 instruments, 1972; Multi-media: Tarot, saxophone, reciter, dancer, slides, lights, tape, 1973; Montage, slide show with music, 1973; also choral and vocal works, piano pieces.
48 Atwood Road, Southboro, MA 01772

*OSTRANSKY, LEROY
Songs for Julia, baritone and orch., Seattle Symphony, 3 Oct. 1973.
School of Music, University of Puget Sound
Tacoma, WA 98416

*O'SULLIVAN, PATRICK
b. Louisville, Ky., 23 Aug. 1871; d. Los Angeles, 18 Mar. 1947. Studied piano with Harold Bauer in Paris; with Scharwenka in Berlin; composition with Wilhelm Berger in Berlin. He taught at Louisville Cons., 1915-39; composed orchestral works; Epithalamium, chorus and string quartet; 65 Irish melodies for voices.

OTT, JOSEPH
b. Atlantic City, N. J., 7 July 1929. Studied with Walter Ihrke, Univ. of Connecticut, B. A. 1960; with Roy Harris, Univ. of California, Los Angeles, M. A. 1965; with Hans Sachsse in Munich, Germany. He received first prizes in Internat. Competition for Symphonic Composition, Trieste, Italy, 1963; Atwater Kent contest, 1964; Wisconsin Composers contest, 1966, 1968 (4 categories); American Music Center grants, 1964, 1968, 1969;

(OTT, JOSEPH)
ASCAP awards, 1968-73; Bennington Conference
scholarships, 1967, 1969; and many commissions.
He was director, dance department, George Washington Univ., 1960-63; teaching assistant, Univ.
of California, Los Angeles, 1963-65; assistant
professor, Milton Coll., 1965-72; composer-in-
residence, Kansas State Teachers Coll.,
1972-   .
  WORKS: Orchestra: Premise for orchestra;
Free variations; Matrix VI; Band: Mini laude;
Slide piece no.1; Wind ensemble: Suite for 6
tubas; Suite for 8 trombones; Chamber music:
quartet for percussion; Encore set, brass trio;
Toccata for brass quintet; Suite for flute quartet; 5 pieces for flute and clarinet; 2 ricer-
cares for percussion; Toccata, trombone and
piano; Matrix III and V, chamber orch.; Matrix
IV, piano trio; viola sonata; quartet for solo
alto saxophone; Electronic: Matrix VII, brass,
percussion and tape; Aeolian harp, chamber ensemble and tape; Timbres, brass quintet and tape;
also choral works and numerous unpublished works.
  1002 Exchange St., Emporia, KS 66801

OUDAL, ROBERT D.
  b. Minneapolis, Minn., 11 Jan. 1930. Studied
with Robert Delaney and Anthony Donata, Northwestern Univ.; with Paul Fetler, Earl George, and
Dominick Argento, Univ. of Minnesota. He was
music director, Suomi Coll., 1954-55; public
schools, Lakeville, Minn., 1956-57; department
chairman, Rochester, Minn., 1958-   .
  WORKS: Orchestra: Festival overture; March
for orchestra; Symphonet for strings; Chorus:
Sing, men and angels sing!, with brass, percussion and organ; Stopping by woods on a snowy
evening.
  3405 18th Ave., N.W., Rochester, MN 55901

OVANIN, NIKOLA
  b. Sisek, Yugoslavia, 25 Nov. 1911; U.S. citizen
1956. Studied with Herbert Elwell, Cleveland
Inst. of Music, B. M. 1939; with Arthur Shepherd,
Western Reserve Univ., B. S. 1941; with Ernst
Krenek, Hamline Univ., B. A., M. A. 1947; with
Bernard Rogers and Howard Hanson, Eastman School
of Music, Ph. D. 1969. He held a scholarship
at Cleveland Inst., 1938; received awards, Nat.
Composers' Clinic, Akron, 1942; Spokane Music
Festival, 1948; Fed. of Music Clubs, Milwaukee,
1954; Roth Competition, Nat. School Orch. Asso.,
1966. He held faculty positions at public and
private schools, 1941-42, 1956-62; Whitworth
Coll., 1947-48; San Jose State Coll., 1949-51;
Wisconsin State Coll., Eau Claire, 1953-55; New
York City Schools, 1962-   .
  WORKS: Orchestra: 3 symphonies, 1939, 1946,
1969; Pleiades, suite, 1954; Poem for string
orch., 1965; Hatikvah variations, 1965; Band:
Prelude moderne, 1947; Chamber music: Journey
ever softly unto Sandanda, string trio; Larghetto,
violin, clarinet, cello; cello sonata; Flute
suite, flute and piano; Dance suite, alto saxophone, dancer, percussion, 1971; Chorus: Suddenly there are flowers, women's voices; Songs:
Come with me, soprano and piano; Star stream,

(OVANIN, NIKOLA)
soprano and piano; Piano: Earth and Venus; 2
piano pieces.
  400 Central Park West, Apt. 18-T
  New York, NY 10025

*OVERTON, HALL
  b. Bangor, Mich., 23 Feb. 1920; d. New York,
N. Y., 24 Nov. 1972. Taught himself to play
piano by ear and began to compose in high school;
studied at Chicago Musical Coll.; with Vincent
Persichetti, Juilliard School, B. S. 1951; privately with Wallingford Riegger and Darius
Milhaud. He received commissions from
Koussevitzky Found., 1955; Walter Trampler, 1960;
Louisville Symphony, 1962; New and Newer Music
Series, Lincoln Center, 1971. He was a noted
jazz pianist; taught at Juilliard School,
1960-72; visiting professor at Yale Univ. 1972.
  WORKS: Opera: The enchanted pear tree,
opera buffa based on Boccaccio's Decameron,
produced at Juilliard, 7 Feb. 1950; Pietro's
petard, 1963; Huckleberry Finn, libretto by
Judah Stampfer, Juilliard, 20 May 1971; Ballet:
Nonage, 1951; Orchestra: 2 symphonies, 1955,
1962; concerto for violin and strings, 1958;
Dialogues, chamber orch., 1964; Pulsations, 1971;
Sonorities, Los Angeles, Oct. 1972; Chamber
music: string trio; 3 string quartets, 1950,
1954, #3, New York, 17 Mar. 1974; viola sonata,
1960; songs; piano pieces.

OWEN, BLYTHE
  b. Bruce, Minn., 26 Dec. 1898. Studied with
Max Wald, Louis Gruenberg, Chicago Musical Coll.,
B. M. 1941; with Albert Noelte, Northwestern
Univ., M. M. 1942; with Bernard Rogers, Howard
Hanson, Eastman School of Music, Ph. D. 1953;
and with Nadia Boulanger, Fontainebleau, France,
1949. She is a life fellow, Internat. Inst. of
Arts and Letters, Switzerland; received 6 Mu Phi
Epsilon biennial awards, 1942, 1951, 1953, 1955,
1957, 1961; Delta Omicron award, 1946; first
prize, Lakeview Musical Society, 1950; first
prize, Musicians Club of Women, Chicago, 1959;
2 Mu Phi Epsilon special merit citations, 1967;
first prize, American Pen Women, Chicago Chapter,
1953; Univ. of Maryland award, 1957; Composers'
Press award, 1957. Her faculty positions include
Cosmopolitan School of Music, 1943-61; Northwestern Univ., 1944-50; Chicago Teachers Coll.,
1947-50; Roosevelt Univ., 1950-61; Walla Walla
Coll., 1961-65; Andrews Univ., 1965-   .
  WORKS: Orchestra: State Street, a suite,
1946; symphony, 1947; piano concerto, 1953; Concerto grosso for strings, oboe, horns, bassoon,
1961; Chamber music: Sonata fantaisie, cello
and piano, 1940; piano quintet, 1944; violin
sonata, 1946; woodwind trio, 1950; 2 string
quartets, 1944, 1951; trio for flute, clarinet,
piano, 1959; piano trio, 1962; 2 inventions for
woodwinds, 1964; quartet, piano and string trio,
1963; Concert piece, bassoon and harpsichord,
1967; Sarabande and gigue, 4 tubas, 1969; Chorus:
Let God arise, 1944; Go, lovely rose, 1944; Festival te deum, 1951; Awake, O Zion, women's trio
with piano and trumpet, 1952; Blessed be the God
and Father, with soprano and instruments, 1950;

OWEN, BLYTHE

(OWEN, BLYTHE)
Hearken unto me, 1957; An Indian prayer, women's chorus, flute, drums, mixed chorus, 1970; Piano: Sonatina in A, 1939; sonata no.1, 1948; Toccata, 1950; Serially serious, 3 pieces, 1971; also songs and organ pieces.
115 Kephart Lane, Berrien Springs, MI 49103

*OWEN, HAROLD J.
b. 1931. Studied with Halsey Stevens, Univ. of Southern California, D. M. A.; is associate professor, Univ. of Oregon.
WORKS: Chamber music: 12 concert etudes for clarinet; Fantasies on Mexican tunes, 3 trumpets and piano; Chorus: Metropolitan bus, cantata, with piano 4-hands; Organ: Overture dans le style Francais.
Department of Music, University of Oregon Eugene, OR 97403

OWEN, JERRY MICHAEL
b. Gary, Ind., 6 June 1944. Studied with Donald H. White, DePauw Univ., 1962-64, 1966-68; with Richard Hervig and Peter Lewis, 1969-73. He was instructor, DePauw Univ., 1968-69; Coe Coll., 1969-73.
WORKS: Orchestra: Symphon, Eastman School Festival of American Music, 1967; Music for string orch., Eastman School Festival, 1968; Chamber music: 3 piano sonatas, 1966, 1967, 1968; string quartet, 1967; Haiku set, mezzo soprano, 1968; 3 notions, trombone and piano, 1971; Dialog, solo viola, 1973; Variations for 2 tubas and piano, 1973; Chorus: 3 settings of Frost poems, 1970; Electronic: Tetrabstraction I and II, tape recorder, 1970, 1971; Music after times of war, percussion, voices, and tape, 1972.
2427 Bever Ave., S.E., Cedar Rapids, IA 52403

OWEN, RICHARD
b. New York, N. Y., 11 Nov. 1922. Studied with Vittorio Giannini in New York.
WORKS: Opera: A fisherman called Peter, 1 act; A moment of war; Mary Dyer, Boston; Songs: I saw a man pursuing the horizon, Crane text; There were many who went in huddled procession, Crane text; The impulse, Frost text; Till we watch the last low star, Bynner text; Patterns, Amy Lowell text.
21 Claremont Ave., New York, NY 10027

PACE, ROBERT JOSEPH
b. Daytona, Fla., 15 Dec. 1949. Studied with Francis Judd Cooke, Alexander Goehr, and Donald Martino, New England Cons.; briefly with Angelo Paccagnini in Italy. He held a full scholarship at the New England Cons.
WORKS: Chamber music: piano trio; Sonnage for cello; Fantasy for piano; Italian songs.
Box 79, West Chatham, MA 02669

PACKALES, JOSEPH
b. New York, N. Y., 28 Mar. 1948. Studied with Samuel Adler, Eastman School of Music. He received the Howard Hanson prize, 1968. He has been director, New Arts Ensemble, 1971- ; artist-in-residence and chairman, music department, Belknap Coll., 1973- .

(PACKALES, JOSEPH)
WORKS: Chamber music: piano sonata in the form of 11 fragments; Solemn music, chamber ensemble; Songs: Cassandra's monologue from Agamemnon; Kenneth Patchen songs.
102 Lakeland Estates, RFD 2 Laconia, NH 03246

PACKER, GEORGE LEONARD
b. Philadelphia, Pa., 28 Oct. 1945. Studied with Henri Lazarof, Leon Kirchner, and John Vincent, Univ. of California, Los Angeles; with Henri Pousseur, Liege, Belgium. He received the Atwater Kent award, 1970; Gus Kahn award, 1971; Fulbright fellowship, 1972. He has been assistant professor, East Carolina Univ., 1973- .
WORKS: Orchestra: Time two, string orch., 4 horns, percussion, 1971; Reflections, Liege, Belgium, 12 June 1973; Chamber music: string quartet, 1972; Chorus: When spring returns and Heal, hardy air, 2 madrigals, 1971.
1108 East 10th St., Greenville, NC 27834

PADWA, VLADIMIR
b. Krivyakino, Russia, 8 Feb. 1900; U.S. citizen 1949. Studied at Cons. in Berlin, Petrograd, Leipzig; with Ferruccio Busoni, Michael Zadora, Paul Juon. He has received awards from New York Madrigal Society; Musical America; Peabody Cons.; annual ASCAP awards 1968-73. He was co-founder and faculty member, State Cons., Tallin, Estonia, 1919-21; co-founder and member, First Piano Quartet, 1941-50; chairman, piano department, New York Coll. of Music, 1945-68; associate professor of music education, New York Univ., 1968- .
WORKS: Ballet: Tom Sawyer, with optional narration; Theatre: music for Goethe's Faust, a cappella choir; Ondine by Giradoux; Noah, play by Obey; Peter Pan; Pied Piper; The nightingale; A nice place to live, book by Alec Benn; Eagle, book by Jack Selby, 1969; Orchestra: symphony; Solitude; symphony for string orch.; Partita, soprano and chamber orch.; Concerto for 2 pianos and string orch.; Ballads 1 and 2, woodwinds and strings; Suite for winds and percussion; Serenade for string orch.; Band: Saints in borrowed styles, variations on When the saints come marching in, also for brass quintet; Chamber music: 3 string quartets; concertino for alto saxophone and guitar; violin sonatina; Sonata-fantasia, violin and piano; cello sonata; clarinet sonata; clarinet sonatina; many short instrumental pieces; Chorus: Concerto for choir, percussion and piano; 4 songs in the style of spirituals; Ballad of the common man; This is the day; He giveth more; Piano: 24 preludes; Variations; 3 sonatas; Crescendo, suite; sonatina; many short piano pieces; many songs.
736 Riverside Drive, New York, NY 10031

*PAIK, NAM JUNE
b. Seoul, Korea, 20 July 1932. Studied in Tokyo and in Germany; an extreme avant garde composer who spends much of his time on the West Coast.

*PALANGE, LOUIS SALVADOR
b. Oakland, Calif., 17 Dec. 1917. Studied with Wesley La Violette at Univ. of California, Los Angeles, 1936. In his naval service during World War II, he conducted the Naval Training Station Orchestra, San Diego; has founded and conducted many orchestras in the Los Angeles-San Diego area.
WORKS: Orchestra: Evangeline, 1945; 2 symphonies, 1946, 1968; violin concerto, 1950; Hollywood panorama, 1952; Romantic piano concerto, 1954; Poker deck ballet suite, 1960; Overture domesticana; Band: Symphony in steel; Chamber music: Classical trio, flute, violin, viola, 1950.

PALANZI, RICHARD BRUNO
b. Framingham, Mass., 30 Oct. 1951. Studied with Stuart Smith, Lowell State Coll.; with Randall McClellan, Hampshire Coll.; with Gordon Mumma and David Behrman at Chocorua, N. H.
WORKS: Multi-media: Concrete piece I, tape and sound location modulator; Anti-ballistic musik I, K'an, The abyss, for winds, live electronics and video display, 1971; For bubble people, tape, intermedia environment and dance, 1972; Shapes and bridges, tape, intermedia environment and dance, 1972; Anti-ballistic musik, var. II, Requiem for Amchitka, winds, percussion, duodecaphonic computer output, live electronics and dance, 1973; After subways of Tanzou, tape, endless tape loop, percussion, video display, 1973; Past tense, winds, percussion, crosscut saws, electro-resonant objects, cybersonic media events, 1973.
84 Bethany Road, Framingham, MA 01701

*PALMER, ROBERT M.
b. Syracuse, N. Y., 2 June 1915. Studied with Howard Hanson, Eastman School of Music, B. M. 1938, M. M. 1939; with Roy Harris, 1939; with Aaron Copland at Tanglewood, 1940. His awards include a scholarship at Tanglewood; Guggenheim fellowship, 1952; MacDowell fellowship, 1954; commissions from League of Composers; American Acad. of Arts and Letters; Dmitri Mitropoulos; Coolidge Found. He taught at Univ. of Kansas, 1940-43; was visiting composer, Illinois Wesleyan Univ., 1954; professor, Univ. of Illinois, 1955-56; composer-in-residence, 1943-   , professor, 1956-   , Cornell Univ.
WORKS: Orchestra: Poem, violin and orch., 1938; concerto for small orch., 1940; symphony, 1939-42; concerto for orch., 1943; chamber concerto, violin, oboe, and strings, 1949; Memorial music, 1957; Wind ensemble: Choric songs and toccata; Nabachodonosor, brass ensemble and chorus, 1964; Chamber music: 2 string trios, 1937, 1942; piano sonata, 1938; concerto for 5 instruments, 1942; many other chamber works; choral works; piano pieces.
Department of Music, Cornell University
Ithaca, NY 14850

PALOMBO, PAUL M.
b. Pittsburgh, Pa., 10 Sep. 1937. Studied with Charles K. Hoag, Indiana Univ. of Pennsylvania; Robert Hall Lewis, Peabody Cons.; Bernard Rogers

(PALOMBO, PAUL M.)
and Howard Hanson, Eastman School of Music, Ph. D. He received a Rockefeller award, 1965; American Festival of Music awards, 1967, 1968; Howard Hanson prize, 1969. He taught in Baltimore County public schools, 1962-69; has been faculty member Coll.-Cons. of Music, Univ. of Cincinnati, 1969-   , associate professor, director, electronic music studio, 1970-   , acting head of composition, theory, and musicology, 1973.
WORKS: Chamber music: Metatheses, flute, oboe, harpsichord, doublebass, 1971; Ritratti anticamente, viola and piano, 1972; Montage, violin and piano, 1972; Electronic: Proteus, ballet for orch. and tape, 1969; Miniatures, organ and tape, 1969; Morphosis, ballet, 1970; Sonos I, tape and harpsichord, 1972; Sonos III, tape and double bass, 1973.
234 Glenmary Ave., Cincinnati, OH 45220

PALTRIDGE, JAMES GILBERT, JR.
b. Albany, Calif., 28 June 1942. Studied privately with Robert Erickson in Berkeley, 1959; with Roman Haubenstock-Ramati in Vienna, 1961; with David Sheinfeld in San Francisco, 1960, 1962-64. He has been copyist and head of audio production, Buffalo Productions, Inc., San Francisco, 1970-   .
WORKS: Theatre: music for The dyscolos by Menander, 1960; J.B. by MacLeish, 1964; Chamber music: sonatina, flute and piano, 1958; Variations, woodwind trio, 1961; 6 poems of Emily Dickinson, voice and chamber ensemble, 1961; violin duo, 1962; If I told him, reciter and wind ensemble, 1973; Chorus: Prayer, Rilke text, double chorus a cappella, 1967.
869 Shotwell St., San Francisco, CA 94110

*PANERIO, ROBERT M.
Jubiloso won the 1975 Ostwald award for band composition.
Central Washington State College
Ellensberg, WA 98926

*PANETTI, JOAN
Studied at Peabody Cons.; received BMI student composer awards, 1966, 1967; Morse fellowship at Yale, 1969. She is assistant professor, Yale Univ.; has toured Europe as pianist. Her published works include a piano concerto; Cavatina for piano; 3 songs for medium voice.
School of Music, Yale University
New Haven, CT 06520

*PAPALE, HENRY
A choral miscellany; Rock a' my soul, chorus with clarinet and temple blocks.

PAPE, LOUIS WAYNE
b. Centuria, Wis., 26 Feb. 1939. Studied at Univ. of Wisconsin-River Falls, B. S. 1961; Indiana Univ., M. M. 1968, candidate for Ph. D., 1973. He taught piano, Concordia Coll., St. Paul, 1961-63; assistant professor, Dakota State Coll., 1968-   .
WORKS: Chorus: Winter I, 1969; Electronic: The tiger, soprano, piano, and tape recorder,

PAPE, LOUIS WAYNE

(PAPE, LOUIS WAYNE)
1970; Spring flood victims--in memorium, tape, instruments and voices, 1972.
210 North Harth Ave., Madison, SD 57042

PARCHMAN, GEN LOUIS
b. Cincinnati, Ohio, 2 May 1929. Studied at Cincinnati Cons., B. M. 1956, M. M. 1956. He received annual ASCAP awards, 1963-73; many commissions. He was bassist, Cincinnati Symphony Orchestra, 1958-67; jazz bassist, Cincinnati Jazz Trio, 1970-73; is pop arranger for various groups and author of novels and other books.
WORKS: Orchestra: violin overture, 1959; Elegy, 1960; 2 symphonies for strings, 1960, 1962; 12 variations, 2 pianos and orch., 1960; 2 concertos for percussion ensemble, 1961, 1962; Adagio for strings, 1962; symphony no.3, 1962; symphony for brass and percussion, 1962; Little fugue, 1962; Winsel overture, 1962; timpani concerto, 1963; concerto for 2 pianos, 1963; marimba concerto, 1964; Dramatic overture, 1965; History of music, narrator and orch., 1965; symphony for chorus and orch., 1967; Study for orch., 1967; percussion concerto, 1967; 6 symphonies for percussion ensemble, 1967-73; concerto for soprano and orch., 1972; Band: symphony, 1964; Chamber music: piano trio, 1961; Elegy for 2 pianos, 1963; sonata for woodwind quintet, 1966.
23 Parchman Place, Cincinnati, OH 45217

*PARENTEAU, ZOEL
b. Northampton, Mass., 9 Apr. 1883; d. Englewood, N. J., 14 Sep. 1972. Studied with faculty members of Smith Coll.; and with Ernest Bloch. He was arranger for David Belasco, Charles Dillingham, Florenz Ziegfeld, and Victor Herbert; conductor for touring companies. He wrote scores for the musicals The amber express and Follow the girl; anthems and songs.

*PARK, STEPHEN
b. Austin, Minn., 23 Sep. 1911. Studied at Univ. of Nebraska, B. A.; with Ross Lee Finney, Univ. of Michigan, M. M.; at Tanglewood; with Darius Milhaud, Aspen School. He taught in public schools, 1929-36; at Univ. of Michigan; was associate professor and composer-in-residence, Univ. of Tampa, 1939-71; minister of music, Univ. Christian Church, Tampa.
WORKS: Chamber music: Pastorale, flute and strings; Suite for clarinet and strings, 1953; Pavanne, 2 violins; Suite for flute and piano, 1957.

PARKER, ALICE
b. Boston, Mass., 16 Dec. 1925. Studied at Smith Coll., B. A. 1947; with Robert Shaw, Julius Herford, and Vincent Persichetti, Juilliard School, M. S. 1949. She received annual ASCAP awards, 1968-73. She taught at Meadowbrook School, 1968; Aspen Festival School, 1970-71; Blossom Festival School, 1969-73.
WORKS: Opera: The martyrs' mirror, a church opera; Chorus: An Easter rejoicing; A sermon from the mountain: Martin Luther King; The feast of the ingathering; more than 300 published choral and vocal works and chamber music.
801 West End Ave., New York, NY 10025

*PARKER, CHARLES CHRISTOPHER (CHARLIE, YARDBIRD, or BIRD)
b. Kansas City, Mo., 29 Aug. 1920; d. New York, N. Y., 12 Mar. 1955. Was a virtuoso saxophonist whose improvisations on his instrument became legendary in his own time. His published compositions include Anthropology; Yardbird suite; and Ornithology.

*PARRIS, HERMAN M.
b. Ekaterinoslav, Russia, 30 Oct. 1903; to U.S. 1905. Studied at Univ. of Pennsylvania, B. M. 1921; and at Jefferson Medical Coll., Md., M. D. 1926. Except for Army service in World War II he has engaged in private medical practice in Philadelphia along with a prolific career in composition.
WORKS: Orchestra: 4 symphonies; 8 piano concertos; violin concerto; Hospital suite; Hebrew rhapsody; Rhapsody #2, Heart; Lament for string orch.; Chamber music: 4 string quartets; 22 piano sonatas; 2 violin sonatas; viola sonata; cello sonata; Images for brass octet; Woodwind miniatures; Suite for violin and viola; Suite for piano and strings; Fantasy for quintet; also choral works; songs.

PARRIS, ROBERT
b. Philadelphia, Pa., 21 May 1924. Studied with Peter Mennin, Juilliard School, 1946-48; with Aaron Copland at Tanglewood, 1950; and with Arthur Honneger in Paris, 1952-53. He has been associate professor, George Washington Univ., 1963- .
WORKS: Orchestra: symphony, 1952; piano concerto, 1954; Concerto for 5 kettledrums and orch., 1955; viola concerto, 1956; violin concerto, 1959; trombone concerto, 1964; Chamber music: sextet for brass, 1948; Night, baritone, clarinet and string quartet, 1951; quintet for woodwinds and strings, 1957; The raids: 1940, soprano, violin and piano, 1960; Lamentations and praises, chamber ensemble and percussion, 1962; violin sonata; viola sonata; 2 string quartets; 2 string trios; trio for clarinet, cello, piano; sonatinas for flute, oboe, clarinet, horn, bass; The book of imaginary beings, chamber ensemble and percussion, 1972; Chorus: Walking around, chamber cantata for men's voices, clarinet, violin, piano, Washington, D.C., 20 May 1973.
3307 Cummings Lane, Chevy Chase, MD 20015

*PARRISH, CARL
b. Plymouth, Pa., 9 Oct. 1904; d. Valhalla, N. Y., 27 Nov. 1965. Studied at Harvard Univ., Ph. D. 1924. He taught at Wells Coll.; Westminster Choir Coll.; Pomona Coll.; and from 1955 was professor, Vassar Coll. He wrote choral works, chamber music, song cycles, piano pieces.

PARTCH, HARRY
b. Oakland, Calif., 24 June 1901; d. San Diego, 3 Sep. 1974. Was self-taught in music. From 1925 he designed and built instruments to accommodate his own musical dramatic forms and to encompass his 43-tone-to-the-octave scale. For his work in building and adapting a great number

(PARTCH, HARRY)
of instruments he received awards and grants from Carnegie Corp. of New York, 1934; Guggenheim Found., 1943, 1944, 1950; Univ. of Wisconsin, 1944; Fromm Found. and Univ. of Illinois, 1956; Univ. of Illinois, 1959; Pasadena Art Museum, 1965; Thorne Music Fund, 1966, 1968; Nat. Inst. of Arts and Letters, 1966; San Francisco Art Inst., 1966; World Music Congress, 1968; Cassandra Found., 1970. Included in his exotic instruments are 2 chromelodeons, 3 kitharas, 4 marimbas, 2 harmonic canons, cloud-chamber bowls, adapted viola and guitars. The new instruments and the new notation devised for their use were not innovations for innovation's sake, but an expedient in expressing his music. "I am not an instrument builder," Partch said, "but a philosophic music-man seduced into carpentry."

WORKS: Theatre: Oedipus, music drama to his own translation of Sophocles' Oedipus Rex, Oakland, Calif., 14 Mar. 1952; Even wild horses, dance music for an absent drama, 1953; The bewitched, a dance satire, 1955; Revelation in the courthouse, musical tragedy, 1960; Water, water, an American ritual, 1962; Chamber music: 17 lyrics by Li Po, 1930-33; U.S. highball, a musical account of a transcontinental hobo trip, 1943; The letter, a depression message from a hobo friend, 1943; The wayward, an American collection, 1946-55; 11 intrusions, 1949-50; Plectra and percussion dances, 1949-52; Cloud-chamber music, 1950; 8 hitchhiker inscriptions from a highway railing at Barstow, California, 1956; Daphne of the dunes, 1958; And on the 7th day petals fell on Petaluma, 1964; Delusion of the fury, 1965-66; Films: Music studio--Harry Partch, 1958; Rotate the body, 1961; The dreamer that remains, 1972. Partch explained his philosophy and musical system in the 2nd edition of his book, Genesis of a music, New York, 1973.

PARTHUN, PAUL R.
b. Milwaukee, Wis., 1931. Studied with Leo Sowerby, American Cons.; at Univ. of Minnesota, Ph. D. He has received awards from Wisconsin Fed. of Music Clubs, 1950; Nat. Fed. of Music Clubs, 1951; Nat. Endowment for the Arts, 1974, for New Ojibwa songs for orchestra. He is professor, Bemidji State Coll.

WORKS: Band: Whispering Wisconsin, 1956; Chamber music: Fountain of Bandusia, soprano and chamber ensemble, 1950; Black orchid, flute, clarinet, cello, piano, 1951; Chorus: Blessing of St. Francis, solo voice, mixed chorus, male chorus, organ, 1966; Blessing of St. Francis, women's voices, 1968; Ave verum corpus, 1968; Adoramus te Christe, 1969; Aaronic benediction, 1973.

Star Route, La Porte, MN 56461

PASATIERI, THOMAS
b. New York, N. Y., 20 Oct. 1945. Studied with Vittorio Giannini and Vincent Persichetti, Juilliard School, D. M. A. (the first doctorate given by Juilliard); with Darius Milhaud at Aspen, Col. His awards include a scholarship at Juilliard, 1961; Richard Rodgers scholarship; Marion Freschi prize; Brevard Festival prize for

(PASATIERI, THOMAS)
orchestral music; Aspen Festival prize, 1965; George A. Wedge prize; Irving Berlin fellowship for music theater; commissions from Nat. Educational Television, 1971; Juilliard School, 1973; Baltimore Opera, 1973; Houston Grand Opera Company; and others.

WORKS: Opera: The women, La divina, Padrevia, triptych of 1-act operas, 1966; Calvary, 1-act, text by Yeats; The black widow, based on Dos Madres by de Unamumo; The trial of Mary Todd Lincoln, NET 1972; Signor Deluso, after Moliere's Sganarelle; The seagull, after Chekhov, Houston, Tex., 5 Mar. 1974; Ines de Castro, commissioned for presentation in Baltimore in 1976; Voice: Heloise and Abelard, for soprano and baritone, 1971; Rites of passage, mezzo soprano and chamber orch., Ft. Lauderdale, Fla., 19 Mar. 1974; Far from love, soprano and 4 instruments, Dickinson text; Album of songs on American poets; Piano: Cameos; 2 sonatas.
500 West End Ave., New York, NY 10024

*PASHLEY, NEWTON H.
O Lord, support us, chorus.
6675 Heartwood Drive, Oakland, CA 94611

PASQUET, JEAN
b. New York, N. Y., 31 May 1896. Studied with T. Tertius Noble in New York; also piano with Ossip Gabrilowitsch; and organ and orchestration. He held a William Mason scholarship for 5 years, received ASCAP awards. He was church organist, choral conductor, lecturer; education director, Aeolian Company.

WORKS: Over 400 published works for chorus, organ, piano.
714 South Stewart St., Winchester, VA 22601

PATTERSON, ANDY J.
b. Gordon, Tex., 20 Feb. 1929. Studied with William J. Marsh, Texas Christian Univ.; with Arnold Schoenberg in Los Angeles; with Ernst von Dohnanyi and John Boda, Florida State Univ. He won first prize in the Texas Composers Guild contest, 1969; has received many commissions; Abilene Alumni Chapter, Sigma Alpha Iota commission for a band work, 1973. He was graduate assistant, Texas Christian Univ., 1948-49, instructor, 1949-51, 1953-56; member, U.S. Army Band, 1951-53; graduate assistant, Florida State Univ., 1956-58; assistant professor, Georgia Teachers Coll., 1958-59; professor and head of composition department, chairman, graduate studies in music, Hardin-Simmons Univ., 1959- ; at Florida A&M Univ., 1967-68.

WORKS: Orchestra: symphony; Band: Suite for concert band; Sonics for symphonic band; Chamber music: woodwind quintet; sonatas for all orchestral instruments; many choral works; piano and organ pieces.
School of Music, Hardin-Simmons University
Abilene, TX 79601

PATTERSON, DAVID NOLTE
b. St. Louis, Mo., 22 Jan. 1941. Studied with Olivier Messiaen and Nadia Boulanger in Paris; with Leon Kirchner at Harvard Univ. and at

PATTERSON, DAVID NOLTE

(PATTERSON, DAVID NOLTE)
Tanglewood; piano with Luise Vosgerchian at
Harvard Univ. He received the New York Musicians
Club prize, 1970; commission from Washington Univ.
Madrigal Singers, 1973. He was composer-in-
residence, Lewis and Clark Inst., St. Louis,
1968; teacher, Shady Hill School, Cambridge,
1971-73; instructor, Wellesley Coll., 1971-73;
instructor, Univ. of Massachusetts, Boston,
1973-   ; church organist, Lexington, Mass.,
1970-73.
    WORKS: Chamber music: Differences, for 6
voices and an instrument, 1962; Shard, solo
flute, 1967; Chantier, violin and piano, 1970;
The celery flute player, a series of piano
pieces, 1972; Piece for 9 instruments, 1973;
Pied beauty, 12 voices with percussion, 1973.
    25 Sacramento St., Cambridge, MA 02138

*PATTERSON, FRANKLIN PEALE
    b. Philadelphia, Pa., 5 Jan. 1871; d. New
Rochelle, N. Y., 6 July 1966. Studied at Univ.
of Pennsylvania and in Munich; was an editor for
Musical Courier. He wrote 2 grand operas and 3
shorter operas, receiving the Chamber Opera
Guild prize in 1918 and the David Bispham medal
in 1925.

*PATTERSON, PAUL
    Wind trio, 1968; Intersections, chamber ensemble,
New York, 29 Apr. 1973.

*PATTISON, LEE
    b. Grand Rapids, Wis., 22 July 1890; d. Claremont,
Calif., 22 Dec. 1966. Studied piano and composition at New England Cons. and in Berlin; toured
with Guy Maier in duo piano recitals. His compositions included Told in the hills, piano suite,
and Florentine sketches for piano.

PAUL, BARBARIE
    b. New York, N. Y., 27 July 1945. Studied with
Ludmila Ulehla, Billy Taylor, and Charles
Wuorinen, Manhattan School of Music; with Jacob
Druckman and Hall Overton, Juilliard School; at
Tanglewood, 1972; also at Dalcroze School, Inst.
of Vocal Arts, Rhodes Acad.; dramatic and musi-
cal theatre, with Herbert Berghof; piano with
Hall Overton, Roland Hanna, Leonid Hambro,
Joseph Prostakoff, and William Ferruccio. Her
awards include Tanglewood fellowship, 1972;
multi-media commission, Walnut Street Theatre,
Philadelphia, 1972; Lehman Engel's BMI Musical
Theatre Workshop, 1973-   . She is founder and
director, Barberie Paul Musical Theatre, 1973.
    WORKS: Chamber music: O'wind, string quar-
tet and mezzo soprano; Circle of the world, soprano, chamber ensemble; A silent world, Where
shall we go, 2 songs for baritone and piano;
Electronic: Interplay, flute, piano, tape; A
song of earth and sky, chorus and tape; 2 songs
for trumpet, with piano and electric piano;
Multi-media: Celebration '72, theatrical concert; The land, theatre piece for baritone, 1969;
In the vast space of world, theatre piece, mezzo
soprano; Time, concrete/electronic ballet; Earth
pulse, concrete/ electronic cantata to be danced;
Departure, theatre piece for brass quintet; The

(PAUL, BARBARIE)
mass, concrete tape, live percussion, New York,
8 Dec. 1973; also songs in folk idiom and rock.
    382 Central Part West, New York, NY 10025

*PAULUS, STEPHEN
    b. Minnesota, 1949. Studied with Paul Fetler,
Univ. of Minnesota, B. M., M. M. He was co-
founder and co-director, Minnesota Composers
Forum.
    WORKS: Theatre: Pact, dance suite for
clarinet, piano, and 2 dancers; Chorus: 3 Chinese poems; Lift up your hearts; Snow had fallen,
Christ was born; Alleluia, He is risen; also
songs.

PAYNE, FRANK LYNN
    b. Asheville, N. C., 29 Nov. 1936. Studied with
Bruce Benward, Alexander King, Univ. of Arkansas;
with Samuel Adler, Merrill Ellis, William Latham,
North Texas State Univ. He won an Internat.
Tuba Ensemble composition contest; received a
commission from the Society for Commissioning
New Music. He was instructor, Texarkana Jr.
Coll., 1961-65; doctoral fellow, North Texas
State Univ., 1965-67; assistant professor, Okla-
homa City Univ., 1967-   .
    WORKS: Orchestra: Thymele; Wind ensemble:
Concerto for brass quintet and wind ensemble;
Chamber music: Toccata for 3 flutes; quartet
for tubas; Images I and II, oboe and piano; Con-
cert suite for trumpet and trombone.
    1316 N.W. 21st St., Oklahoma City, OK 73106

*PAYNE, JOHN
    b. New York, N. Y., 23 May 1941. Studied at
Brown Univ., B. A. 1962; has played in jazz
bands; specializes in electronic music, theatre
events, audience happenings, etc.

PAYNE, WILLIAM McGUIRE
    b. Winchester, Va., 3 Oct. 1943. Studied with
Robert Barrow and Paul Turok, Williams Coll.,
1962-65; David Simon, New York, 1965-66; with
Chou Wen-chung, Jack Beeson, and Harvey
Sollberger, Columbia Univ. 1966-68. He was
awarded the Hutchison fellowship in composition
at Williams Coll.
    WORKS: Ballet: Alice in Wonderland, flute,
clarinet, piano, 1964; Process, musique concrete,
1965; Orchestra: Velocities, 1969; Band:
Entities, 1970; Chamber music: 2 songs on poems
of Robert Lowell, 1967; Eleuthera, string octet,
oboe, flute, and clarinet, 1968; Counting piece,
oboe, cello, piano, 1969; Counting piece no.2,
saxophone and piano trio, 1970; Piano: Prelude
and inventions, 1965; Theme and variations, 1965;
Night Ruppert, 1966; 3 movements for piano, 1967.
    315 Sterling Place, Brooklyn, NY 11238

*PEARSON, ROBERT
    Band: Caprice; Minuteman; Watergate; Concert
piece for winds and percussion.
    1 Glengariff Road, Massapequa Park, NY 11762

PEASLEE, RICHARD C.
    b. New York, N. Y., 13 June 1930. Studied at
Yale Univ., B. A.; with Vincent Persichetti,

(PEASLEE, RICHARD)
   Vittorio Giannini, Bernard Wagenaar, and Henry
Brant, Juilliard School, B. S.; privately with
Nadia Boulanger and William Russo. He composes
for theatre and films and for concert performance.
   WORKS: Theatre: music for Marat Sade; Midsummer night's dream; Orghast; Oedipus; Boccaccio,
a musical; Songs of love and war, musical; The
serpent; Terminal; Indians; Orchestra: October
piece for rock group and symphony; Jazz: Stonehenge; Chicago concerto; Film scores: Marat Sade;
Tell me lies; Where time is a river.
   90 Riverside Drive, New York, NY 10024

PECK, RUSSELL
   b. Detroit, Mich., 25 Jan. 1945. Studied at
Eastman School of Music, 1962-63; with Leslie
Bassett and Ross Lee Finney, Univ. of Michigan,
B. M. with high distinction 1966, M. M. 1967,
D. M. A. 1972; with Gunther Schuller and Aaron
Copland at Tanglewood. He held fellowships for
all study, 1962-71, including Tanglewood and
Bennington Conference; received Nat. Fed. of
Music Clubs prize, 1960; BMI student awards,
1965, 1967, 1969; Koussevitzky prize, 1965; Composers' Forum, New York concert, 1969; Gaudeamus
prize, Netherlands, 1971; many commissions. He
has been composer, pianist, actor, filmmaker
with multimedia groups ONCE, The Great Society,
PORK, and Contemporary Directions Ensemble; was
professional resource person, Lincoln Center,
1967-69; Ford Found. composer-in-residence, public schools, Merrick, N. Y., 1967-69; with Indianapolis Symphony Orchestra and City of
Indianapolis, 1971-   .
   WORKS: Orchestra: Song of mankind, orch.
and choirs, for Indianapolis sesquicentennial,
1971; The emperor's new concerto, 1972; Who killed
Cock Robin?, 1973; Band: American epic, 1972;
Chamber music: Automobile, for Ars Nova Quartet,
1965; 1 db, doublebass, 1969; Lion's breath, percussion, Los Angeles, 10 Dec. 1973.
   4031 Clarendon Road, Indianapolis, IN 46208

PEEK, RICHARD M.
   b. Mason, Mich., 17 May 1927. Studied with Owen
Reed, Michigan State Univ.; with Harold W.
Friedell and Normand Lockwood, Union Theological
Seminary, New York. He received a commission,
Charlotte Chapter, American Guild of Organists.
He has been organist and choirmaster, Covenant
Presbyterian Church, Charlotte, N. C., 1952-   .
   WORKS: Chorus: Stations on the road to free-
dom, cantata; St. Stephen, cantata; Now glad of
heart be everyone; Organ: Church sonata for
organ; and more than 100 published works for
chorus and organ.
   1621 Biltmore Drive, Charlotte, NC 28207

PEERY, ROB ROY
   b. Saga, Japan, 6 Jan. 1900, of American parents;
d. Dayton, Ohio, 18 Sep. 1973. Studied at Midland Coll., B. A. 1920; at Oberlin Cons., B. M.
1925; privately with Rubin Goldmark, 1928-29; at
Union Theological Seminary, New York, 1928-29.
He received awards from Etude magazine, 1923;
Ohio State, 1925; Homiletic Review, 1926; Dartmouth prize, 1930; Franklin prize, 1938; honorary

(PEERY, ROB ROY)
doctorates, Midland Coll., 1938; Wittenberg Coll.
He was violinist, Omaha Symphony, 1920-21; organist, 1923-65; faculty member, Lenoir-Rhyne Coll.,
1922-23; Catawba Coll., 1926-28, 1929-31; publications manager, Theodore Presser Company,
1932-49; associate editor, Lorenz Publishing
Company, 1950-65.
   WORKS: Chorus: America, my wondrous land;
God shall wipe away all tears; Slumber on; The
Lord is my shepherd; This be my song; A star in
the sky; The wondrous star; and many more works
for chorus, organ, violin, orchestra. He was
also author of several musical text books.

PELLEGRINI, ERNESTO P.
   b. Flushing, N. Y., 23 Nov. 1932. Studied with
Vittorio Giannini, Peter Mennin, and Vincent
Persichetti, Juilliard School, B. S. 1957, M. S.
1961; with Philip Bezanson and Richard Hervig,
Univ. of Iowa, Ph. D. 1971. He received 2nd
prize in a Sosland contest for a string quartet,
1961; IBM graduate fellowship, 1968. He was faculty member, Knoxville Coll., 1962-68, 1969-71;
Univ. of Iowa, 1968-69; Ball State Univ.,
1971-   .
   WORKS: Orchestra: 7 statements in 3/4 time,
1963; Chamber music: string quartet, 1961; Piano
variations, 1968; Fantasia per organo, 1971;
Music for 16 instruments and percussion, 1971;
Divertimento a sette, 1973.
   2116 Wellington Drive, Muncie, IN 47304

PELLEGRINO, RONALD
   b. Kenosha, Wis., 11 May 1940. Studied with
James Ming, Lawrence Univ., B. M. 1962; with
Rudolph Kolisch, Robert Crane, and Hilmar
Luckhardt, Univ. of Wisconsin, M. M. 1965, Ph. D.
1968. In school he majored in composition and
woodwinds, but also studied privately on piano,
guitar, percussion, trumpet, and cello. His
awards include the Uilas fellowship, Univ. of
Wisconsin; Nat. Endowment for the Humanities
grant in support of work on the book, Thinking
for the electronic music synthesizer, 1973;
research grants, Oberlin Cons., 1971, 1972. He
was assistant professor and director, electronic
music studio, Ohio State Univ., 1968-70; Oberlin
Cons., 1970-73; since 1973 has been giving concerts, workshops and lectures in Berkeley, Calif.
   WORKS: Electronic: Markings, for stereo
tape, soprano and timpani, commissioned by Dena
Madole, choreographer, 1969; S and H explorations,
clarinet and ARP 2600 synthesizer, 1972; Electronic film scores: This is Milwaukee, NET documentary, 1968; Too, 16-mm film and tape, 1971;
Paths, 1972; Figured, 16-mm film and quadrophonic
tape, 1973; Cries, 16-mm film and quadrophonic
tape, 1973.
   2327 Prince St., Berkeley, CA 94705

*PELOQUIN, C. ALEXANDER
   b. 1918. Has composed for chorus: Songs of
Israel, psalms for the liturgical year; Shout
for joy; The bells, Poe text, chorus, 2 pianos,
2 contrabasses, percussion; Missa á la samba;
Christ, the light of the nations; Song of David,
1965; Mass for joy, 1966; Festival mass, 1966;

PELOQUIN, C. ALEXANDER

(PELOQUIN, C. ALEXANDER)
May the Lord bless you, 1968; Love is everlasting, 1969; Organ: Contemplation.
Department of Music, Boston College
Newton, MA 02167

PELZ, WALTER L.
b. Chicago, Ill., 30 Dec. 1926. Studied with Paul Fetler and Dominick Argento, Univ. of Minnesota, Ph. D. He received a choirmaster certificate, American Guild of Organists, 1960; commission from The Lutheran Hour; many other commissions for choral works. He taught in public schools, 1948-62; was minister of music, Christ Church Lutheran, Minneapolis, 1962-67; graduate assistant Univ. of Minnesota, 1967-69; assistant professor and composer-in-residence, Bethany Coll., Lindsborg, Kan., 1969-   .
     WORKS: Chamber music: violin sonata; string quartet; trio for flute, cello, piano; suite for viola, cello, piano; Chorus: Who shall abide, flute, guitar, voices, Show me thy ways, oboe, guitar, voices, 1968; A day of rejoicing, 1969; Genesis to a beat, cantata for 4 choirs, orch., tape recorder, and audience, Lindsborg, Kan., 21 Nov. 1970; A wedding blessing, solo voice, 1973.
     211 Normal St., Lindsborg, KS 67456

PENGILLY, SYLVIA
b. London, England, 23 Mar. 1935; to U.S. 1957. Studied with James Waters, Kent State Univ.; with Paul M. Palombo, Coll.-Cons., Univ. of Cincinnati, candidate for D. M. A. 1973. She was instructor, Kent State Univ., 1971-73.
     WORKS: Chamber music: The windhaven, voice and piano; quartet for violin, viola, cello, bass; 3 songs of Emily Dickinson, voice and piano; Degrees of entropy, wind ensemble; Electronic: Canon for 40 voices, tape.
     7085 East Glenmeadow Lane
     Cincinnati, OH 45237

PENINGER, JAMES DAVID
b. Orangeburg, S. C., 27 Dec. 1929. Studied at Coll. of Charleston, B. S. 1951; with Gilbert Carp and Roger McDuffie, Converse Coll., B. M. 1957, M. M. 1959. He has been public school music teacher, 1958-   ; minister of music Spartansburg churches, 1958-   ; lecturer, Wofford Coll.
     WORKS: Voice: more than 100 published songs and anthems.
     133 Clemson St., Spartansburg, SC 29302

*PENN, ARTHUR A.
b. London, England, 13 Feb. 1875; to U.S. 1903; d. New London, Conn., 6 Feb. 1941. Wrote comic operas, musicals, and such popular songs as Smilin' through; The magic of your eyes; Carissima; The lamplit hour; Sunrise and you; et al.

PENN, WILLIAM A.
b. Longbranch, N. J., 11 Jan. 1943. Studied with Robert Mols, Henri Pousseur, Mauricio Kagel, Allen Sapp, State Univ. of New York at Buffalo; with H. Owen Reed, Michigan State Univ., Ph. D. 1971; with Wayne Barlow and Rayburn Wright, Eastman School of Music. He received composition

(PENN, WILLIAM A.)
awards, State Univ. of New York, 1963, 1966; Michigan State Univ. graduate scholar award, 1968, composition award, 1970; annual ASCAP awards, 1970-   ; American Music Center grant, 1973. He was teaching fellow, State Univ. of New York, 1964-67, and at Michigan State Univ., 1967-70; assistant professor, Eastman School, 1971-   ; composer-in-residence, theatre department, Michigan State Univ., 1969-72; arranger for various groups; editor and writer on music.
     WORKS: Theatre (musicals): The pied piper of Hamlin, 1969; At last, Olympus!, 1969; The boy who cried, "Wolf," is dead, 1971; The canticle, 1972; incidental music for many plays; Orchestra: Spectrums, confusions, and sometime-moments beyond the order of destiny, 1969; symphony, 1971; Designs, winds, jazz quintet and percussion, 1972; Band: Ultra mensuram, 3 brass quintets, 1971; Niagara, 1678, 1973; Inner loop, stage band, 1973; Chamber music: Invocation and pavanne, solo violin, 1967; trio for violin, clarinet, piano, 1967; string quartet, 1968; Untitled composition #1, any instrumental combination, 1970; 4 portraits, cello solo, 1970; Guernica, violin solo, 1970; Chamber music I, viola and piano, 1971; Chamber music II, cello and piano, 1972; And among the leaves we were passing, Moog synthesizer, 1972; 3 essays, tuba. 1973; Multi-media: Apocalypse IV, actor, men's chorus, chamber orch., tape, and rebec or violin, 1969; War's peace, speaker, percussion, piano, cello, harmonica, slide projectors and film clips, 1970; Idiom III, tape and films, 1970; 5 glasses of absinthe, brass, jazz quintet, percussion, voices, speakers, tape, dancers, visual projections, 1972; also some songs and pieces called Freak music.
     Eastman School of Music, Rochester, NY 14604

*PENNARIO, LEONARD
b. Buffalo, N. Y., 9 July 1924. Studied piano with Guy Maier, Isabelle Vengerova; composition with Ernst Toch and Lucien Cailliet; made his debut as piano soloist with the Dallas Symphony, 1936; has been soloist with all major U.S. orchestras and has given recitals throughout the U.S. and Europe.
     WORKS: Piano: piano concerto; Midnight on the Newport Cliffs; March of the lunatics; Variations on the Kerry dance; also transcriptions for piano.

*PENNINGTON, JOHN
Apollo, aleatoric piece for band.

*PEPE, CARMINE
Violin sonata, 1965.
116 East 92nd St., New York, NY 10028

PERERA, RONALD C.
b. Boston, Mass., 25 Dec. 1941. Studied with Leon Kirchner and Randall Thompson, Harvard Univ.; and with Gottfried Koenig, Utrecht Univ. He received the Francis Boott prize at Harvard, 1961, 1962, 1966; John Knowles Paine traveling fellowship, 1967; Paderewski Fund award, 1972; ASCAP award, 1972. He was lecturer, Syracuse Univ.,

(PERERA, RONALD C.)
1968-69, instructor, 1969-70; visiting professor
and director, electronic music studio, Dartmouth
Coll., 1970-71; assistant professor and director,
electronic music studio, Smith Coll., 1971-   .
WORKS: Chorus: The garden hymn; The Lord's
prayer; Did you hear the angels song?; Mass,
with orch.; Voice: Apollo circling; 3 poems of
Gunther Grass, mezzo-soprano and chamber ensemble, commissioned by Goethe Inst., Cambridge,
Mass., 19 Nov. 1974; Piano: a suite; Electronic:
Evolutions; Alternate routes; Improvisation for
loudspeakers; Dove sta amore, soprano and tape;
Reverberations, organ and tape; Reflex, viola
and tape.
114 Wharf Lane, Yarmouth Port, MA 02675

*PERKINS, JOHN MacIVOR
b. St. Louis, Mo., 2 Aug. 1935. Studied at Har-
vard Univ., B. A. magna cum laude 1958; New
England Cons., with high honors 1958; with Arthur
Berger, Harold Shapero, and Irving Fine, Brandeis
Univ., M. F. A. 1962; with Nadia Boulanger in
Paris; with Roberto Gerhard and Edmund Rubbra in
London. He held the Sheldon fellowship, 1958-59;
Woodrow Wilson fellowship, 1959-61. He taught
at Univ. of Chicago, 1962-64; Harvard Univ.,
1965-70; has been associate professor and chairman, music department, Washington Univ.,
1970-   .
WORKS: Opera: Divertimento, chamber opera,
1958; Orchestra: Fantasy, intermezzo and variations, 1961; Music for orchestra, 1964; Chamber
music: Canons for 9 instruments, 1957; 3 miniatures for string quartet, 1960; Variations for
flute, clarinet, trumpet, piano, percussion,
1962; Caprice, piano, 1963; Music for 13 players,
1964; Music for brass, 1965; Voice: 3 studies
for chorus, 1958; 8 songs, 1956-62.
14 Kingsbury Place, St. Louis, MO 63155

*PERKINSON, COLERIDGE-TAYLOR
b. New York, N. Y., 1932. Studied at Manhattan
School of Music, B. A. 1953, M. M. 1954; at
Tanglewood; at Salzburg Mozarteum; and at Neder-
land Radio Union in Hilversum. His awards include a commission from the Ford Found. and a
grant, New York State Council on the Arts, 1974.
He was associate conductor, Symphony of the New
World, 1965.
WORKS: Theatre: music for Song of the
Lusitanian bogey; God is a guess what?; Man better man; Orchestra: viola concerto; Sinfonietta
#1 for string orch., New York premiere, composer
conducting, 8 Apr. 1973; Grass, piano, strings,
percussion; Chamber music: Blues form for violin,
New York, Feb. 1972; Film scores: The McMasters,
1970; Together for days, 1972.
755 West End Ave., New York, NY 10025

PERLE, GEORGE
b. Bayonne, N. J., 6 May 1915. Studied with
Wesley La Violette at DePaul Univ.; and privately
with Ernst Krenek. He received a Guggenheim fellowship, 1966; and commissions. He was faculty
member, Univ. of Louisville, 1949-57; Univ. of
California at Davis, 1957-61; Queens Coll., CUNY,
1961-   ; visiting professor, Yale Univ.,

(PERLE, GEORGE)
1965-66; Univ. of Southern California, summer
1965; Tanglewood, 1967; State Univ. of New York
at Buffalo, 1971-72.
WORKS: Orchestra: 2 symphonies; Rhapsody,
1954; 3 movements for orchestra, 1960; 6 bagatelles, 1965; cello concerto, 1966; Songs of
praise and lamentation, chorus and orch, dedicated to the memory of Noah Greenberg, New York,
19 Feb. 1975; Band: Solemn procession, 1947;
Chamber music: sonata for viola solo, 1942; 3
sonatas for clarinet solo, 1943; Hebrew melodies
for solo cello, 1945; string quintet, 1958; 3
wind quintets, 1959, 1960, 1967; 6 string quartets, 1960-69; Monody I, solo flute, 1960;
Monody II, doublebass solo, 1962; Serenade I,
viola and chamber orch., 1962; 3 inventions for
bassoon, 1962; Solo partita, violin and viola,
1965; Serenade II, chamber ensemble, 1968; Sonata
quasi una fantasia, clarinet and piano, 1972;
Piano: Little suite, 1939; 6 preludes, 1946;
2 sonatas, 1950, 1964; Toccata, 1969.
114 82nd Rd., Kew Gardens, NY 11415

*PERLMAN, GEORGE
Elegy and habañera, violin and piano.

*PERPESSA, HARIALAOS
Symphony #1; The 7th seal, symphony.
319 East 73rd St., New York, NY 10021

*PERRON, KURT
Fall '68, piano; Love'69, electronic tape.

*PERRY, JULIA
b. Akron, Ohio, 25 Mar. 1924. Studied at Westminster Choir Coll., M. M.; Juilliard School;
at Tanglewood; with Nadia Boulanger in Paris,
and Luigi Dallapiccola in Florence. Her awards
include 2 Guggenheim fellowships; Boulanger
Grand Prix; Nat. Inst. of Arts and Letters award,
1964; ASCAP award, 1969. She conducted a series
of concerts in Europe under the sponsorship of
the U.S. Information Service.
WORKS: Orchestra: Stabat mater, voice and
string orch., 1951; Short piece for orchestra,
1952; violin concerto; Chamber music:
Homunculus, C. F., percussion ensemble, 1960;
Pastorale, string quartet and flute.
564 Euclid Ave., Akron, OH 44307

PERRY, ZENOBIA POWELL
b. Okfuskee County, Okla., 3 Oct. 1914. Studied
privately with Cortez Reece; at Northern Colorado
Univ.; with Alan Willman and Darius Milhaud,
Univ. of Wyoming; further study with Milhaud
under a study grant by Univ. of Wyoming. She
was faculty member, Arkansas Agricultural,
Mechanical, and Normal Coll., 1946-55; teacher
and composer-in-residence, Central State Univ.,
1955-   .
WORKS: Orchestra: Ships that pass in the
night, 1953; Band: Prelude and danse, 1968;
Chamber music: piano sonatina, 1962; clarinet
sonatina, 1963; string quartet no. 2, 1964;
Atmospheres, song cycle for soprano and piano,
1972; 4 mynyms for 3 players, flute, clarinet,
piano, 1973; Chorus: Suite on poems of Thomas

PERRY, ZENOBIA POWELL

(PERRY, ZENOBIA POWELL)
Hardy; Mass in F-sharp, soprano and baritone soli, 1969.
1267 East Turner Place
Wilberforce, OH 45384

PERSICHETTI, VINCENT
b. Philadelphia, Pa., 6 June 1915. Studied with Russell King Miller, Combs Cons., B. M. 1935; conducting with Fritz Reiner, Curtis Inst.; piano with Olga Samaroff, Philadelphia Cons., M. M., D. M. His many awards include in part 3 Guggenheim fellowships; Columbia Records award; Nat. Inst. of Arts and Letters grant; Nat. Found. on the Arts and Humanities grant; Juilliard publication award; Symphony League award; honorary doctorates from Combs. Coll., Bucknell Univ., Baldwin-Wallace Coll.; Brandeis Creative Arts award, 1975; numerous commissions from major orchestras, foundations, etc. He was chairman, composition department, Combs Coll., 1938-40; Philadelphia Cons., 1941-61; and on faculty, Juilliard School, 1947-   .
WORKS: Orchestra: piano concertino, 1941; 9 symphonies, 1942-1973; Dance overture, 1942; Fables, narrator and orch., 1943; The hollow men, trumpet and string orch., 1944; Serenade no. 5, 1950; Fairy tale, 1950; piano concerto, 1962; Stabat mater, chorus and orch., 1963; Te Deum, chorus and orch., 1963; Introit for strings, 1964; The Pleiades, chorus, trumpet, string orch., 1967; The creation, soli, chorus, orch., 1969; Sinfonia: Janiculum, 1970; Night dances, 1970; A Lincoln address for narrator and orch., 1972; Band: Divertimento, 1950; Psalm, 1952; Pageant, 1953; Symphony for band, 1956; Serenade for band, 1960; Bagatelles for band, 1961; Chorale prelude: So pure the star, 1962; Masquerade, 1965; Chorale prelude: Turn not thy face, 1966; O cool is the valley, 1971; Parable IX, 1972; Chamber music: Serenade no. 1, 10 winds, 1929; 4 string quartets, 1939, 1944, 1959, 1972; Suite for violin and cello, 1940; solo violin sonata, 1940; Concertato for piano and string quartet, 1940; Fantasy, violin and piano, 1941; Serenade no. 3, piano trio, 1941; Pastoral, woodwind quintet, 1943; Vocalise, cello and piano, 1945; Serenade no. 4, violin and piano, 1945; King Lear, septet for woodwind quintet, timpani, piano, 1948; Serenade no. 6, trombone, viola, cello, 1950; harpsichord sonata, 1951; solo cello sonata, 1952; piano quintet, 1954; Little recorder book, 1956; Serenade no. 9, soprano and alto recorders, 1956; Serenade no. 10, flute and harp, 1957; Infanta Marina, viola and piano, 1960; Serenade no. 12, solo tuba, 1961; Serenade no. 13, 2 clarinets, 1963; Masques, violin and piano, 1965; Parables I-XI, chiefly for various solo instruments, 1965-72; Do not go gentle, organ, pedals alone, Boston, 18 Nov. 1974; Chorus: Magnificat, 1940; 3 canons for voices, 1947; 2 cummings choruses, 1948; Proverb, 1948; 2 cummings choruses for women's voices, 1950; Hymns and responses for the church year, 1955; Seek the highest, 1957; Song of peace, male chorus, 1959; Mass, a cappella, 1960; Spring cantata, for womens' voices, 1963; Winter cantata, women's voices, flute and marimba, 1964; 4 cummings choruses, 1964; Celebrations for chorus

(PERSICHETTI, VINCENT)
and wind ensemble, 1966; Love, women's voices a cappella, 1971; and many songs.
Hillhouse, Wise Mill Rd.
Philadelphia, PA 19128

PERSKY, STANLEY L.
b. New York, N. Y., 28 May 1941. Studied with Mark Brunswick and Paul Turok, City Coll. of New York; with Mel Powell and Gunther Schuller, Yale Univ.; with Milton Babbitt, Earl Kim, and Peter Westergaard, Princeton Univ. He was lecturer, City Coll. of New York, 1965-66, 1967-72, assistant professor, 1972-   .
WORKS: Chamber music: Sextet, 3 woodwinds and string trio, 1965; On walls, soprano and chamber ensemble, 1966; Composition from a graphic design, 11 instruments, 1967; Symbiosynthesis, chamber ensemble and tape, 1972.
11 Vassar Place, Scarsdale, NY 10583

*PETERS, WILLIAM FREDERICK
b. Sandusky, Ohio, 9 Aug. 1876; d. Englewood, N. J., 1 Dec. 1938. Studied at Leipzig Cons.; was theatre violinist, concert violinist; music director of Maude Adams productions.
WORKS: Opera: The purple road; Iole, operetta; Film scores: Way down east; Orphans of the storm; When knighthood was in flower; Little old New York.

PETERSEN, MARIAN F.
b. Salt Lake City, Utah, 4 July 1926. Studied with Leroy J. Robertson, Univ. of Utah, Ph. D. She has been faculty member, Univ. of Missouri, 1966-   , professor, 1972-   .
WORKS: Opera: The wife of Usher's well, a mini-opera; Chorus: The revelation, a cantata.
L12 Route #1, Lake Lotawana, MO 64063

PETERSON, MELODY
b. Oak Park, Ill., 5 Feb. 1942. Studied with Richard Hoffmann and Walter Aschaffenburg, Oberlin Coll. She won first prize, North Carolina Fed. of Music Clubs contest, 1967. She was a private teacher, 1965-69; part-time instructor, Oberlin Coll. Cons., 1968-69; music journalist, Los Angeles Times, 1970-   .
WORKS: Chamber music: Twice five for two, violin and cello, 1967; Monuments, baritone voice, 1972; Keyboard: Variations on an original theme, 2 pianos, 1958; Prelude and toccata, 1963; Prelude and postlude, organ, 1967.
303 South Ave., 57, Los Angeles, CA 90042

*PETERSON, WAYNE
b. 1927. Has received a Fulbright grant for study in London and commissions.
WORKS: Orchestra: Exaltation, dithyramb and caprice; Free variations; Chamber music: Phantasmagoria, flute, clarinet, contrabass; Metamorphoses, woodwind quintet; Music of the vineyards, string quartet, 1974; Chorus: Earth, sweet earth; Who is so dark of heart.
Department of Music
San Francisco State College
San Francisco, CA 94132

PETHEL, JAMES
    b. Gainesville, Ga., 24 Dec. 1936. Studied at
Carson-Newman Coll.; with Philip Slates, George
Peabody Coll.; and at North Texas State Univ.
He received a Nat. Defense Education Act grant.
He has been associate professor, Carson-Newman
Coll., 1962-   ; organist, First Baptist Church,
Morristown, Tenn., 1966-   .
    WORKS: Chamber music: piano sonata; string
quartet; Chorus: I hear America singing, male
voices and brass; anthems, vocal solos, and organ
pieces.
        Route 2, Jefferson City, TN 37760

PEYTON, MALCOLM C.
    b. New York, N. Y., 12 Jan. 1932. Studied with
Roger Sessions and Edward T. Cone, Princeton
Univ., B. A. 1954, M. F. A. 1956; also with
Wolfgang Fortner and Aaron Copland. He received
a Woodrow Wilson fellowship, 1955; Fulbright fellowship, 1956. He was faculty member at Princeton Univ., 1960-61; New England Cons., 1965-   .
    WORKS: Orchestra: The Blessed Virgin com-
pared to the air we breathe, chorus and orch.,
Boston, 14 Mar. 1974.
        390 Walden St., Cambridge, MA 02138

PFAUTSCH, LLOYD
    b. Washington, Mo., 14 Sep. 1921. Studied at
Elmhurst Coll., B. A. 1943, honorary D. M. 1969;
at Union Theological Seminary, M. Th., M. S. M.
1948. He has received annual ASCAP awards,
1961-   ; numerous commissions. He was visiting
professor, Univ. of Illinois, 1946-47; professor
of voice and choral director, Illinois Wesleyan
Univ., 1948-58; professor and choral director,
Southern Methodist Univ., 1958-   .
    WORKS: Chorus: A day for dancing, a masque
for chorus, woodwinds and dancers; Gloria, with
3 trumpets and percussion; God with us, cantata
for chorus, organ, flute, and trumpet; Israel at
the Red Sea, cantata for chorus, organ and flute;
more than 200 shorter choral publications.
        3710 Euclid Ave., Dallas, TX 75205

PFEIFFER, JOHN F.
    b. Tucson, Ariz., 29 Sep. 1920. Studied at
Bethany Coll., Lindsborg, Kan.; and at Univ. of
Arizona, Tucson. He has been a record producer
since 1949.
    WORKS: Electronic: Electronomusic - 9
images, 1965.
        R. D., Flanders, NJ 07836

PFEIL, CLIFFORD I.
    b. Rock Island, Ill., 27 Nov. 1931. Studied at
American Cons.; with Barney Childs and Robert
McBride, Tucson, Ariz.; with H. Owen Reed, Michigan State Univ. He was instructor, Oakland Univ.,
1968-72, assistant professor, 1972-   .
    WORKS: Orchestra: Clear and distant views
of rivers and streams, for orch. and audience;
Chamber music: Devices for breaking and entering,
piano solo; Ruth Ann's horse, cello and amplifier;
Dr. Clifford Pfeil, his piece, lute duet.
        12 Niagara, Pontiac, MI 48053

PFISCHNER, JAN. See McNEIL, JAN PFISCHNER

PHELPS, NORMAN F.
    b. Beaver Dam, Wis., 27 Apr. 1911. Studied with
Cecil Burleigh, Univ. of Wisconsin; with Philip
Greeley Clapp, Univ. of Iowa. He received an
Arthur Jordan Found. grant. He was faculty
member, Jordan Cons., Indianapolis, 1935-49;
Ohio State Univ., 1949-   , professor,
1972-   .
    WORKS: Orchestra: Dramatic overture, 1946;
Noel, Phantasy for orch., 1948; symphony, 1949;
Summer rhapsody, 1954; Band: 2 pieces, 1960;
Chamber music: brass quartet, 1940; horn sonata,
1947; oboe sonata, 1951; Film scores: University
story, Ohio State Univ. documentary; The Ostrock
story for NASA.
        683 Overlook Drive, Columbus, OH 43216

PHETTEPLACE, JON
    b. Fullerton, Calif., 4 Feb. 1940. Studied cello
and composition with Pietro Grossi in Florence,
also worked there in electronic music; cello with
Gaspar Cassado, Pablo Casals, and Andre Navarra
at Acad. Chigiana, Siena, Italy. He was consultant, RCA Records, New York, 1964; co-founder
of Musica Elettronica Viva, Rome, 1966; instructor and archive staff worker, Univ. of California,
San Diego, 1969-72, 1973-74.
    WORKS: Theatre: music for Woyzeck by George
Buchner, 1967; Electronic: Paesaggio naturale,
tape and video recorders; No. 1, 1965, for 8-
track tape, 1967; Displacement, amplified cello
and 3 performers, 1967; 3 plus 4, tape, 1968;
Sound City, performer and tapes, 1973.
        224 Sunset Drive, Encinitas, CA 92024

PHILLIPS, ARTHUR A.
    b. New York, N. Y., 21 Sep. 1918. Studied with
Louis Teicher and David McKay Williams, Juilliard
School, diploma. He is an associate, American
Guild of Organists, and AGO choirmaster;
Licentiate Teacher, and Fellow, Trinity Coll. of
Music, London. He has been organist and choir-
master in the New York area, 1943-   , St.
Albans Congregational Church, Long Island,
1971-   .
    WORKS: Organ: Choral, variations, canon
and fugue in c.
        537 West 141st St., New York, NY 10031

*PHILLIPS, BARRE
    b. San Francisco, Calif., 1934. Has played bass
with Don Ellis, Jimmy Giuffre, Archie Shepp,
Peter Nero, George Russell, and others.
    WORKS: Chamber music: Journal violone,
contrabass, 1968; Chorus: Bucket of water,
chorus and piano; The return of Odysseus, chorus
and orch.

PHILLIPS, BURRILL
    b. Omaha, Neb., 9 Nov. 1907. Studied with Edwin
Stringham, Denver Coll. of Music; with Edward
Royce, Bernard Rogers, Howard Hanson, Eastman
School of Music, B. M., M. M. He held 2 Guggen-
heim fellowships, 1942, 1961; was Fulbright
lecturer in American music, Univ. of Barcelona,
Spain, 1960. He was faculty member, Eastman

PHILLIPS, BURRILL

(PHILLIPS, BURRILL)
School of Music, 1933-49; professor, Univ. of
Illinois, 1949-64; visiting professor, Eastman
School, 1965-66, Juilliard School, 1968-69,
Cornell Univ., 1972-73.
WORKS: Orchestra: Selections from McGuffey's
Reader, 1934; Concert piece, bassoon and strings,
1940; Scherzo; piano concerto, 1942; Tom Paine
overture, 1947; Scena, small orch.; Triple con-
certo, viola, cello, piano, orch.; Return of
Odysseus, baritone, reader, chorus, orch., 1957;
La Piñata, small orch.; Band: Fantasia; Chamber
music: cello sonata, 1948; 2 piano sonatas; 2
string quartets; organ sonata, 1964; Canzona III,
for 7 instruments and poem, 1964; sonata for
violin and harpsichord, 1966; quartet for oboe
and strings; Chorus: Canzona V, with solo piano.
Branchport, NY 14418

PHILLIPS, CHARLES ALLEN
b. Port Huron, Mich., 12 July 1940. Studied at
Sherwood Music School, 1960-62; Wayne State Univ.,
B. A. 1966, M. A. 1972, both degrees in humanities. He taught public schools, 1966-70; has
been general salesman and piano specialist,
1971-   ; part-time English instructor, St.
Clair Community Coll., 1971-   .
WORKS: Chamber music: suite for flute and
piano; 8 bagatelles, piano; piano sonatina;
Chorus: Psalm 117, a cappella; Songs; In
memoriam, cycle for soprano; The Lord is my shepherd, soprano and organ.
817 Lincoln Ave., Port Huron, MI 48060

PHILLIPS, D. VALGENE
b. Butler, Okla., 29 Sep. 1935. Studied with
Harold Johnson and Robert Aichele, California
State Univ., San Jose, B. A. 1957, M. A. 1966;
privately with Fred Fox, Hayward, Calif. He
taught in public schools, San Jose, 1957-67;
has been associate professor, California State
Univ. at Humboldt, 1967-   .
WORKS: Wind ensemble: Stanzas; Kerana; 2
stanzas for St. Stephen's Day, brass choir; Chamber music: Lullabic digressions, woodwind quintet; A três, violin, horn, piano; √441, oboe and
horn; Litanie and traquenard, bassoon and
strings.
1397 Whitmire Ave., McKinleyville, CA 95521

*PHILLIPS, DONALD
Concerto in jazz, piano and orch.

*PHILLIPS, HARRY G.
The princess and the frog prince, children's
opera, Univ. of Alabama, Mar. 1970.

*PHILLIPS, PETER
b. 1930. Concerto grosso, jazz combo and
chamber orch.; Band: Continuum; Gothic suite;
Round trip, divertimento for band; Chamber music:
Music for brass quintet; sonata for string bass,
1964.
Whole Earth Studies, New York University
Washington Square, New York, NY 10003

*PHILLIPS, ROBERT
Sonatina for 2 pianos, New York premiere, 9 Feb.
1971, with the composer at one of the pianos.

PHILLIPS, VIVIAN D.
b. Colby Kan., 9 Mar. 1917. Studied with Harry
Cooper, Ottawa Univ., Kan.; with Hagbard Brase,
Bethany Coll., Lindsborg, Kan.
WORKS: Chamber music: Nocturne, string
quintet; Shades of Papa Haydn, string quintet;
Repose, chamber orch.; Voice: Wedding service,
organ and voice; Music for trial liturgy, organ
and voice; Prayer, vocal trio; He is risen,
chorus; Songs: The look; To Electra; Day is
done; The fog; The sky is low; Amare; Why fear
death?; The pasture; An assessment of my figure;
and others.
116 North Harrison, Shawnee, OK 74801

*PIASTRO, JOSEF (BORISSOFF)
b. Kerch, Crimea, 17 Feb. 1889; U.S. citizen
1926. Was concertmaster, Los Angeles Philharmonic, and a teacher in Los Angeles. His
Crimean rhapsody for violin and piano, 1920,
was orchestrated and performed by the San Francisco Symphony in 1938.

PICCOLO, ANTHONY
b. Teaneck, N. J., 4 Nov. 1946. Studied with
Earle Brown, Peabody Cons.; piano with Konrad
Wolff, conducting with Laszlo Halasz. He was
assistant conductor, Peabody Art Theatre, Baltimore, 1964; chorus master, Baltimore Comic Opera,
1965-67; instructor, Hawthorne School, Washington, 1969-71; instructor, Beauvoir, National
Cathedral, Washington, 1971-73; instructor, St.
Agnes School, Alexandria, Va., 1973.
WORKS: Chamber music: Found in Machaut's
chamber, tenor, flute, guitar, cello, 1968;
When Bathyllos to the dancers played, flute,
guitar, percussion, 1973; Chorus: Introitus,
boys' and men's choir, string orch., 1963; A
song of the forest, boys' chorus and orch., commissioned by Texas Boys' Choir, 1968; also church
music and incidental music to plays.
3030 Wisconsin Ave., N. W.
Washington, DC 20016

PICK, RICHARD S.
b. St. Paul, Minn., 20 Oct. 1915. Studied
violin, piano, and guitar privately in Chicago.
He is director, Chicago School of Music; and
director, classical guitar, De Paul Univ.
WORKS: Guitar: Autumn day suite; Baca and
fiesta day; 9 preludes; Film score: People
along the Mississippi, Encyclopedia Britannica
film; many method books for guitar.
9136 Sheridan Ave., Brookfield, IL 60513

*PIETRICH, ROGER T.
Choral variations on Ah, Holy Jesus, a cappella.

PIETSCH, EDNA FRIDA
b. Milwaukee, Wis., 7 May 1894. Studied piano
and violin in Milwaukee; composition with
Bernard Dieter, Chicago Cons. She received many
awards in annual contests sponsored by Wisconsin
State Fair and Wisconsin Fed. of Music Clubs.
She taught composition, Wisconsin Cons., 1942-66.

(PIETSCH, EDNA FRIDA)
WORKS: Orchestra: 2 piano concertos; viola concerto; Fantasy for orchestra, performed by Chicago symphony in 1942 and 1946; 5 oriental impressions; Chamber music: string quartet; piano quintet; woodwind quintet; suite for harp; Woodland fantasy, flute and piano; Piano: sonata; 5 poems; many works for chamber groups, chorus, duo piano, etc.
3522 West Kilbourn Ave., Milwaukee, WI 53208

PIKE, ALFRED
b. Chester, Pa. 11 Oct. 1913. Studied with Vincent Persichetti, Philadelphia Cons., D. M. 1953; privately with Henry Cowell; at Univ. of Pennsylvania, 1950-51. He was faculty member, Philadelphia Cons., 1950-53; professor, St. John's Univ., 1953- .
WORKS: Orchestra: Oasis, symphonic poem, 1948; Invention for orchestra, 1964; Sinfonietta for strings, 1967; Chamber music: 2 string quartets, 1950, 1954; Chorus: Psalm 96, 1960.
10220 Farragut Rd., Brooklyn, NY 11201

PIKET, FREDERICK
b. Instanbul, Turkey, 6 Jan. 1903; U.S. citizen, 1946; d. Bayside, N. Y., 28 Feb. 1974. Studied at the Vienna State Acad.; with Franz Schreker, Musikhochschule, Berlin. He won the Mendelssohn award in Berlin, 1930. He was faculty member, New York Coll. of Music, 1961-68; New York Univ., 1968-71; Hebrew Union Coll., New York, 1963-74; music director, Free Synagogue, Flushing, N. Y., 1955-74.
WORKS: Opera: No stars tonight, Lincoln Center, 1972; Orchestra: Curtain raiser to an American play, 1948; The funnies, suite; piano concerto; violin concerto; saxophone concerto; concerto for orch.; symphony; Band: Variations on a nursery tune; Chamber music: Prelude and triple fugue for woodwinds, 1930; piano sonata; Chorus: If thou must love me, a cappella; Sea charm, a cappella; High holiday cycle; The three festivals; In the end, cantata, with soli and chamber orch., Lincoln Center, New York, Dec. 1973.

*PILHOFER, PHIL
3 pieces for jazz quartet and chamber orch.

PILLIN, BORIS WILLIAM
b. Chicago, Ill., 31 May 1940. Studied with John Vincent, Univ. of California, Los Angeles, A. B. 1964; with Robert Linn, Univ. of Southern California, A. M. 1967; and with Leon Stein. His awards include a Woodrow Wilson fellowship, 1964; ASCAP award, 1973. He was vice president, Western International Music, Inc., 1970-73.
WORKS: Orchestra: symphony, 1964; Chamber music: string quartet, 1965; clarinet sonata, 1965; Scherzo, woodwind quartet, 1968; Duo for percussion and piano, 1971; 3 pieces for double-reed septet, 1972; Suite for flute, oboe, clarinet, and organ, 1973; cello sonata, 1973; Chorus: So gehst du nun, 1970; Organ: Fugue, 1969.
4913 Melrose Ave., Los Angeles, CA 90029

*PIMSLEUR, SOLOMON
b. Paris, France, 19 Sep. 1900; to U.S. 1903; d. New York, N. Y., 29 Apr. 1962. Studied at Columbia Univ., M. A. in literature 1923; composition with Rubin Goldmark; was a concert pianist. He wrote orchestral works, chamber music, many piano pieces, and a choral work, 2 songs for mixed voices.

PINKHAM, DANIEL
b. Lynn, Mass., 5 June 1923. Studied with Walter Piston, Archibald T. Davison, and Aaron Copland, Harvard Univ., A. B. 1944; with Arthur Honegger and Samuel Barber at Tanglewood; privately with Nadia Boulanger, organ with Carl Pfatteicher and E. Power Biggs; harpsichord with Putnam Aldrich and Wanda Landowska. He received a Fulbright fellowship, 1950; Ford Found. fellowship, 1962. He was visiting lecturer, Harvard Univ., 1957-58; is conductor, Cambridge Festival Orchestra; music director, King's Chapel, Boston; faculty member, New England Cons.
WORKS: Opera: The garden of Artemis, chamber opera; Orchestra: Divertimento, oboe and strings; piano concertino, 1949; 2 symphonies, 1960, 1963; Signs of the zodiac, narrator and orch., text by David McCord, 1964; violin concerto, 1968; Chamber music: Concertante, violin and harpsichord soli, strings and celesta, 1954; Concerto for celesta and harpsichord soli, 1955; Cantilena and capriccio, violin and harpsichord, 1956; Concertante II, violin and strings, 1957; Duet for recorder and harpsichord; Eclogue, flute, harpsichord and handbells, 1965; Etude for clarinet; Prelude, epigram and elegy, winds and percussion; Concertante, organ, celeste, percussion; Concertante, brass quartet, organ percussion; Prelude, adagio, chorale, brass quintet; brass trio, 1970; Chorus: Elegy, a cappella, 1947; 2 madrigals, 1955; Wedding cantata, 1956; Christmas cantata, 1957; Canticle of praise, with soprano solo, brass, percussion; Jonah, with 3 soli and orch.; Ascension cantata, with winds and percussion; many shorter choral works; Electronic: Aspects of the Apocalypse, tape alone; The other voices of the trumpet, tape, organ and trumpet; Safe in their alabaster chambers, voice and tape; many works for tape with chorus, solo instruments, and ensembles; works for organ, including 2 sonatas for organ and strings.
150 Chilton St., Cambridge, MA 02138

PISK, PAUL AMADEUS
b. Vienna, Austria, 16 May 1893; U.S. citizen 1941. Studied at Vienna Cons., diploma; with Arnold Schoenberg, Univ. of Vienna, Ph. D. He received the Grand Prize, City of Vienna, 1927; honorary degree, Univ. of Vienna, 1969; many U.S. awards and commissions. He was professor, Univ. of Redlands, 1937-50; Univ. of Texas, 1950-63; and Washington Univ., St. Louis, 1963-72.
WORKS: Ballet: American suite, 1948; Orchestra: Requiem for baritone and orch., 1942; Suite of American folksongs, 1944; Passacaglia, 1944; Bucolic suite, string orch., 1946; Rococo suite, violin and orch., 1953; Baroque chamber

PISK, PAUL AMADEUS

(PISK, PAUL AMADEUS)
concerto, violin and orch., 1953; 3 ceremonial rites, 1958; Chamber music: 3 violin sonatas, 1921, 1927, 1937; 3 sonnets, voice and string quartet, 1936; piano trio, 1939; suite for 4 clarinets, 1940; 4 beasts, Belloc text, voice and string quartet, 1942; woodwind quartet, 1945; flute sonata; clarinet sonata, 1947; suite for oboe and piano, 1947; brass quartet, 1951; Keyboard: organ sonata; Nocturnal interlude, piano, 1957.
2724 Westshire Drive, Los Angeles, CA 90068

*PISTON, WALTER HAMOR
b. Rockland, Me., 20 Jan. 1894. Graduated from art school, 1914, then studied piano and violin seriously; composition with Archibald T. Davison at Harvard Univ. B. A. summa cum laude 1924; with Nadia Boulanger and Paul Dukas in Paris, 1924-26. His many awards include the John Knowles Paine fellowship, 1924-26; Guggenheim fellowship, 1934; New York Music Critics' Circle award, 1945; Pulitzer prizes, 1948, 1961; honorary doctorate, Harvard, 1953; membership in Nat. Inst. of Arts and Letters, American Acad. of Arts and Letters, American Acad. of Arts and Sciences; and commissions for almost all of his long list of compositions. He served in the U.S. Navy in World War I; joined the faculty at Harvard Univ., 1926, professor, 1944-60. Only his major works are listed below.
WORKS: Ballet: The incredible flutist, 1938; Orchestra: Concerto for orchestra, 1934; 8 symphonies, 1938-64; 2 violin concertos, 1940, 1960; viola concerto, 1957; concerto for 2 pianos, 1959; Lincoln Center Festival overture, 1962; Capriccio for harp and strings, 1963; Variations for cello and orch., 1965; clarinet concerto, 1966; Fantasy, violin and orch., Milwaukee Symphony, 14 Apr. 1973; concerto for string quartet and orch., 1974, commissioned for the 50th anniversary of the Portland, Maine, Symphony; many chamber works, including 5 string quartets, 1933-1962; piano trio, 1935; violin sonata, 1939; piano quintet, 1949; woodwind quintet, 1956; string sextet, 1964; piano quartet, 1964; etc.
127 Somerset St., Belmont, MA 02178

PLAIN, GERALD
b. Sacramento, Ky., 30 Nov. 1940. Studied with Philip Slates, Butler Univ.; with Leslie Bassett, Ross Lee Finney, Eugene Kurtz, and Niccolo Castiglioni, Univ. of Michigan. He received the Rome Prize fellowship for 1974.
WORKS: Orchestra: Arrows; Chamber music: Raccoon song, cello solo; 3-sec, piano; Electronic: Golden Wedding, tape; aCHATtaNOOgaCHOO, alto flute, guitar, doublebass, and tape; Showers of blessings, clarinet and tape; Soft and semi-sweet modulation, voices and tape; Ripsnorter, tape alone.
9045 LaCrosse Ave., Skokie, IL 60076

*PLANCHART, ALEJANDRO E.
Divertimento for percussion trio.
School of Music, Yale University
New Haven, CT 06520

PLESKOW, RAOUL
b. Vienna, Austria, 12 Oct. 1931; to U.S. at an early age. Studied at Juilliard School; Queens Coll., B. A. 1954; Columbia Univ., M. A. 1958; privately with Stefan Wolpe. His awards include Martha Baird Rockefeller awards, 1971, 1973; first prize, Bowdoin Chamber Music contest, 1972; commission, New York State Council on the Arts; $3000, American Acad. of Arts and Letters, 1974. He has been faculty member, C. W. Post Coll., Long Island Univ., 1961-   , professor and chairman, music department, 1972-   .
WORKS: Orchestra: 2 movements for orchestra; Chamber Music: Movement for flute, cello, and piano; sextet: 3 woodwinds, piano trio; 2 pieces for flute and piano; Crossplay, 3 woodwinds, violin, piano, percussion; Music for flute, bass, piano, percussion; Music for 7 players; Bagatelles, violin solo, 1968; Bagatelles, viola, flute, piano; 3 bagatelles with contrabass; Movement for oboe, violin, piano, 1966; Movement for 9 players, 1967; For 5 players and baritone, text by Wolpe; Duo for cello and piano; Per vege viene, violin and piano, Cambridge, Mass., 27 Feb. 1973; 3 movements for quintet, New York, 10 Dec. 1971; 3 songs, tenor, string trio, 2 clarinets, piano; 2 songs on Latin fragments, soprano and piano; Piano: Music for 2 pianos; Piece for piano; 3 short pieces; 3 bagatelles.
C. W. Post College, P.O. Greenvale, NY 11548

PLESNICAR, DAVID
b. Cleveland, Ohio, 19 Oct. 1942. Studied at Mannes Coll. of Music; Cleveland Inst. of Music; and Case Western Reserve Univ. He is director, South Side Branch, Cleveland Music School Settlement. His keyboard compositions include 7 canons with prelude for harpsichord.
279 East 214th St., Euclid, OH 44123

PLETTNER, ARTHUR
b. New York, N. Y., 15 Nov. 1904. Studied at Bavarian State Cons., Wuenzburg, Germany; with Albert Stoessel, Bernard Wagenaar, Juilliard School; with Ernest MacMillan and Healey Willan, Univ. of Toronto, M. B., D. M. He received a Moravian anthem award for God is our trust; commission, American Guild of Organists. He played in orchestras and theatres in New York, 1924-37; was Juilliard professor of music, Univ. of Tennessee, Chattanooga, 1937-73.
WORKS: Theatre: music for The singing Christmas tree; Orchestra: symphony; Chamber music: Manhattan toccata, violin and piano; Barn dance for strings; Appalachia, string quartet; Chorus: Away in a manger; Fanfare for Christmas Day; Communion service in D; Organ: 12 short hymn tune meditations; Fumaroles 1970; Impromptu sacre et profane.
105 Druid Drive, Signal Mountain, TN 37377

*PLOYHAR, JAMES D.
The bugler rocks, band; 1836: A new land-a new nation, band; and other band pieces.
2308 11th St., Fargo, ND 58102

POLIFRONE, JON J.
b. Durand, Mich., 10 Jan. 1937. Studied with
H. Owen Reed, Michigan State Univ. with Nadia
Boulanger in Paris; with Ernst von Dohnanyi,
Carlisle Floyd, and John Boda, Florida State
Univ. He received the Hinman Creative Research
award; Michigan State Honors award; Redlands
Univ. composition award; Florida State Univ.
assistantship; California quadrennial Arts award;
Indiana Laus Tibi Deo award; Composer of the Year,
Society for American Composers, 1968, 1971. He
was instructor, Jordan Coll. of Music, Butler
Univ., 1961-63; associate professor and composer-
in-residence, Indiana State Univ., 1963-   .
    WORKS: Opera: Kentucky story; Wicked Sam
and the devil, a madrigal opera; Ballet:
Triptychos, ballet for chorus and orch.; Orchestra: piano concerto; violin concerto, 1972; Chorus: Canticles for Christmas, with soloists and
orch.; Psalms for chorus and percussion; Multimedia: Colors, for slides, dancers, tape, chorus,
and orch.; also chamber works, sonatas, song
cycles, piano works.
    927 Ridge Road, Terre Haute, IN 47803

POLIN, CLAIRE
b. Philadelphia, Pa., 1 Jan. 1926. Studied with
Vincent Persichetti, Philadelphia Cons., D. M.
1955; also with Peter Mennin, Juilliard School;
Lukas Foss and Roger Sessions at Tanglewood;
flute privately with William Kincaid. She received awards, Delta Omicron Internat. contests,
1953, 1959; Leverhulme fellowship, 1968-69;
Georgia State Univ. Brass Symposium, internat.
award, 1970; Rutgers Univ., research-creative
writing grant, 1973-74. She was faculty member,
Philadelphia Cons., 1955-64; associate professor,
Rutgers Univ., 1959-   .
    WORKS: Orchestra: 2 symphonies; Wind ensem-
ble: Cader Idris, brass quintet; Journey of
Owain Hadoc, brass quintet and 10 percussion;
Chamber music: flute sonata; Structures, solo
flute; Summer settings, solo harp, 1966; Serpen-
tine, solo viola; O, Aderyn Pur, flute, saxophone, and tape; Procis, flute and tuba;
Makimono I, violin, cello, piano, flute, clarinet,
Philadelphia, 14 Oct. 1973; Multimedia: Infinite,
soprano, alto saxophone, chorus, narrator, dancer.
    374 Baird Road, Merion, PA 19066

POLLAK, WILLIAM THOMAS
b. Philadelphia, Pa., 22 Dec. 1900. Attended
Columbia Univ., A. B., A. M.; Univ. of Toronto,
B. M., D. M.; studied with A. Madeley Richardson
and Rubin Goldmark and Albert Steossel, Juilliard
School. He held a Victor Baier fellowship in
church music, Columbia Univ.; Juilliard fellowship in composition; is an associate, American
Guild of Organists. He was professor and dean,
New York Coll. of Music, 1943-68; associate professor, New York Univ., 1968-69; organist and
choirmaster in various churches in New York area,
St. Catherine of Sienna Church, Franklyn Square
Long Island, 1970-   .
    WORKS: Orchestra: symphony; Chorus: Missa
solemnis in g, with soli and orch.; Mass in honor
of St. Benedict, male choir; Organ: accompaniment

(POLLAK, WILLIAM THOMAS)
    for John Marbeck's English Mass (1551 A.D.);
many other liturgical works.
    9 Melrose Lane, Douglaston, NY 11363

POLLOCK, ROBERT EMIL
b. New York, N. Y., 8 July 1946. Studied with
Claudio Spies, Swarthmore Coll., B. A.; with
Edward T. Cone, Peter Westergaard, Jacques-
Louis Monod, J. K. Randall, Milton Babbitt,
Robert Helps, Princeton Univ., M. F. A.
He received the Composers' String Quartet
award, 1970; MacDowell fellowship; Guggenheim
fellowship.
    WORKS: Opera: The nose, chamber opera,
after Gogol, 1973; Chamber music: Movement and
variations, string quartet, 1967; Septet, 3
winds, 3 strings, trombone, 1968; 2 duos for violin and piano, 1969, 1970; 3 short pieces, bassoon and prepared piano, 1969; wind trio, 1969;
trio for clarinet, violin, and cello, 1972, New
York, 6 Apr. 1974; wind quintet, 1973; Songs:
Song cycle on poems of Stephen Crane, soprano
and piano, New York, 14 Jan. 1974; many songs
and piano pieces.
    103 Mariner Lane, Long Beach T., NJ 08008

POOLER, MARIE
b. Wisconsin, 22 Apr. 1928. Studied at St. Olaf
Coll., B. M.; at California State Coll. at
Fullerton, M. A. She taught at Shimer Coll.,
1949-51; in public schools, 1957-67; at Long
Beach City Coll., Calif., 1971-   .
    WORKS: Chorus: numerous songs, hymns, and
anthems for adult and junior choirs.
    2801 Engel Drive, Los Alamitos, CA 90720

POPE, CONRAD
b. Corona, Calif., 21 Nov. 1951. Studied with
Malcolm Peyton and Donald Martino, New England
Cons., B. M. 1973 with honors; with Gunther
Schuller at Tanglewood. He received a Leonard
Bernstein fellowship to Tanglewood, 1971;
George W. Chadwick medal, 1973; Fulbright-Hays
grant, 1973; his cello sonata was chosen to
represent the U.S. at the 8th Biennale de Paris,
1973. He was co-director of Music: Here and
Now, Boston Museum of Fine Arts, 1971-73.
    WORKS: Orchestra: symphony, 1973; Chamber
music: string trio, 1970; Joys, baritone and 13
instruments, 1971; Sonata for violoncello alone,
Boston, 12 May 1973.
    Music Department, Princeton University
    Princeton, NJ 08540

*PORTER, COLE
b. Peru, Ind., 9 June 1892; d. Santa Monica,
Calif., 15 Oct. 1964. Attended Yale Univ., B. A.
1913; Harvard Law School; Harvard School of
Music; studied with Vincent d'Indy, Schola
Cantorum, Paris. He joined the French Foreign
Legion in 1916, becoming a French officer during
World War I. After the war he returned to the
U.S. and devoted full time to composing musical
comedies for stage and films.
    WORKS: Musical comedies: See America first,
1916; Hitchy koo, 1919; 50 million Frenchmen,
1929; The New Yorkers, 1930; Gay divorcee, 1932;

PORTER, COLE

(PORTER, COLE)
Anything goes, 1934; Jubilee, 1935; Red, hot and blue, 1936; Leave it to me, 1938; Dubarry was a lady, 1939; Panama Hattie, 1940; Let's face it, 1941; Something for the boys, 1943; Mexican hay-ride, 1944; Kiss me, Kate, 1948; Out of this world, 1950; Can-can, 1953; Silk stockings, 1955; Songs: Begin the beguine; It's de-lovely; Love for sale; Night and day; I love Paris; Don't fence me in; Wunderbar; In the still of the night; You're the top; What is this thing called love?; I've got you under my skin; and many others; Film scores: Born to dance; Rosalie; Broadway melody of 1940; You'll never get rich; Something to shout about; The pirate; High society; Les girls.

PORTER, ELLEN JANE LORENZ. See LORENZ, ELLEN JANE

*PORTER, HUGH
A rose breaks into bloom, organ.

*PORTER, QUINCY
b. New Haven, Conn., 7 Feb. 1897; d. Bethany, Conn., 12 Nov. 1966. Studied with David Stanley Smith and Horatio Parker, Yale Univ., B. M. 1921; violin with Lucien Capet, composition with Vincent d'Indy in Paris; with Ernest Bloch in New York. His awards included the Steinert and Osborne prizes; Guggenheim fellowship, 1929-31; Elizabeth Sprague Coolidge medal, 1943; Pulitzer prize, 1954. He was violinist in theatre orches-tras; faculty member, Cleveland Inst. of Music, 1922-32; professor, Vassar Coll., 1932-38; dean New England Cons., 1938-42, director, 1942-46; professor, Yale Univ., 1946-65.
    WORKS: Orchestra: Ukrainian suite for strings, 1925; Suite in c, 1926; Poem and dance, 1932; 2 symphonies, 1938, 1964; Music for strings, 1941; Fantasy on a pastoral theme, organ and strings, 1942; viola concerto, 1948; Fantasy, cello and small orch., 1950; The desolate city, baritone and orch., 1950; Concerto concertante, 2 pianos and orch., 1954; New England episodes, 1958; Chamber music: 10 string quartets, 1923-65; 2 violin sonatas, 1926, 1929; In monasterio, string quartet, 1927; Little trio, flute, violin, viola, 1928; clarinet quintet, 1929; Suite for viola alone, 1930; piano sonata, 1930; Quintet on a childhood theme, flute and strings, 1940; 6 miniatures for piano, 1943; horn sonata, 1946; 4 pieces for violin and piano, 1947; string sex-tet on Slavic folk tunes, 1947; duo for violin and viola, 1954; duo for flute and harp, 1957; Daydreams, piano, 1957. Mrs. Porter gave her husband's complete papers and music manuscripts to the Yale University Library in 1974.

POTTEBAUM, WILLIAM G.
b. Teutopolis, Ill., 30 Dec. 1930. Studied at Quincy Coll., B. S.; with Hermann Reutter in Stuttgart, Germany; with Wayne Barlow, Howard Hanson, Bernard Rogers, Eastman School of Music; with Myron Schaeffer, Univ. of Toronto. He won first place in the American Music in the Univ. contest, 1966. He was instructor in public schools, 1955-61; teaching assistant, Eastman

(POTTEBAUM, WILLIAM G.)
School, 1961-62; associate professor, State Univ. Coll., Brockport, 1963- .
    WORKS: Theatre: electronic music for Midsummer night's dream; The American dream; Beauty and the beast; Orchestra: Concerto for orchestra; Toccata for orchestra; Chorus: 2 Masses; Psalms 8, 22, 83, 97, 150, children's voices; Film score: How the animals got their names; works for band, solo instruments, piano.
    Department of Music, State University College Brockport, NY 14420

POTTENGER, HAROLD
b. Aurora, Mo., 21 Nov. 1932. Attended Univ. of Missouri, B. S. 1954; Univ. of Wichita, M. M. E. 1958; Indiana Univ. D. M. E. 1969. He was pub-lic school teacher, 1956-65; associate professor and head, music department, Southwest Baptist Coll., 1965-68; associate professor, U.S. Internat. Univ., 1968-70; associate professor, band director, Bradley Univ., 1970- .
    WORKS: Band: Suite for band; Chamber music: Remembrance, flute and piano; Portrait, piano; also choral compositions and arrangements.
    2611 West Barker, Peoria, IL 61604

*POUHÉ, JOSEPH FRANK
Pantomime, 1-act opera, Opera Orchestra of New York, 10 May 1971.
    220 West 98th St., New York, NY 10025

*POWELL, FELIX
Is associate professor and head, electronic studio, Univ. of Maryland, Baltimore County. His Cisterns II for tape and piano received its New York premiere at the Composers Theatre, 28 Mar. 1974.
    4 Ruby Court, Arbutus, MD 21227

*POWELL, JOHN
b. Richmond, Va., 6 Sep. 1882; d. Charlottesville, Va., 15 Aug. 1963. Studied at Univ. of Virginia; with Theodor Leschetizky and Karl Navratil in Vienna; made debut as pianist in Berlin, 1907. He was also an amateur astronomer and discovered a comet.
    WORKS: Opera: Judith and Holofernes; Or-chestra: Rapsodie negre, piano and orch., after Conrad's Heart of Darkness, 1918; In old Vir-ginia, overture, 1921; 2 piano concertos; violin concerto; Natchez on the hill, 3 dances, 1932; A set of 3, 1935; Virginia symphony, 1951; Cham-ber music: 2 violin sonatas; 3 piano sonatas; 2 piano suites; In the hammock, 2 pianos, 8 hands.

POWELL, LAURENCE
b. Birmingham, England, 13 Jan. 1899; U.S. citi-zen 1939. Studied at Birmingham and Midland Inst. School of Music; with Granville Bantock, Univ. of Birmingham, B. M. 1922 with first class honors; at Univ. of Wisconsin, M. A. 1926. He held a scholarship at Univ. of Birmingham, 1920; won first prize, Texas Composers Guild contest, 1948. He was instructor, Univ. of Wisconsin, 1924-26; associate professor, Univ. of Arkansas, 1926-34; head, music department, Little Rock

(POWELL, LAURENCE)
Junior Coll., 1933-39; conductor, Little Rock
Symphony, 1936-39; organist-choirmaster,
1939-   , St. Francis Cathedral, Sante Fe, N. M.,
1951-68; Our Lady of Victory Church, Victoria,
Tex., 1968-   .
    WORKS: Orchestra: 2 symphonies; Variations
for orch.; Penny overture; County fair; Concertino for English horn and small orch.; The ogre
of the northern fastness; Keltic legende; Chamber
music: string trio; 2 string quartets; Trio
sonatas, recorders and piano; Canticle, soprano,
recorder and piano; violin sonata; viola sonata,
cello sonata; Chorus: The Santa Fe Trail, symphonic ballad for chorus, narrator and orch.;
Mass in honor of St. Andrew.
    1112 Manor Drive, Victoria, TX 77901

*POWELL, MEL
    b. New York, N. Y., 12 Feb. 1923. Studied piano
with Nadia Reisenberg; composition with Paul
Hindemith, Yale Univ., B. M. 1952. His honors
include the Sigma Alpha Iota award, 1956;
Koussevitzky commission, 1957; Guggenheim fellowship, 1960; Nat. Inst. of Arts and Letters grant,
1963. He played in theatre and dance orchestras;
taught at Mannes Coll. of Music and at Queens
Coll.; joined the faculty at Yale Univ., 1958,
was chairman of composition and director of the
electronic music studio, 1961-72; dean, California Inst. of the Arts, 1972-   .
    WORKS: Band: Capriccio; Chamber music:
Divertimento, violin and harp, 1955; Divertimento
for 5 winds, 1956; piano trio, 1956; Filigree
setting, string quartet, 1959; Haiku setting,
1960; Etude, piano, 1963; Improvisation, piano,
clarinet, viola, 1963; 2 prayer settings, tenor,
oboe, viola, cello, violin, 1963; Electronic:
2 electronic settings, 1961, 1962; Events, 1963.
    California Institute of the Arts
    Valencia, CA 91355

POWELL, MORGAN
    b. Graham, Tex., 7 Jan. 1938. Studied with
Samuel Adler, North Texas State Univ.; with
Kenneth Gaburo, Univ. of Illinois. He received
a best composition award, Intercoll. Jazz Fes-
tival, Notre Dame Univ., 1961; faculty fellowships, 1968, 1972; Fromm Found. scholarship to
Bennington Conference, 1971; ASCAP awards,
1971-73; grant from Center for Advanced Study,
Univ. of Illinois, 1972-73. He was instructor,
North Texas State Univ., 1961-63; faculty member,
Berklee Coll. of Music, 1963-64; instructor to
associate professor and associate, Center for
Advanced Study, Univ. of Illinois, 1966-   .
    WORKS: Wind ensemble: Music for brass and
percussion; Darkness II, brass quintet and percussion; Jazz: Reflections; Moonbag; Sirhmrej;
Music for jazz ensemble; Birdmerchant; Chamber
music: Midnight realities, solo tuba; Blueberry
blue, piano; 3 songs for 2 violins and soprano;
Chorus: Loneliness, with instruments; Music for
a Protestant religious service; Zelanski medley,
with instruments.
    Music Bldg., University of Illinois
    Urbana, IL 61801

POWELL, ROBERT J.
    b. Benoit, Miss., 22 July 1932. Studied with
Helen Gunderson, Louisiana State Univ.; with
Alec Wyton, Harold Friedell, Seth Bingham,
Union Theological Seminary, New York. He is a
fellow, American Guild of Organists. He was
music director, St. Paul's School, Concord, N. H.,
1965-68; assistant organist-choirmaster at Cathedral of St. John the Divine, 1957-58; St.
Paul's Episcopal Church, Meridian, Miss.,
1958-64; Christ Church, Greenville, S. C.,
1968-   .
    WORKS: Chorus: Of the Father's love begot-
ten, cantata; Hosea, Come sing; Joyfully sing;
numerous other anthems; Organ: 15 chorale preludes; 5 voluntaries; 2 sets of Psalm preludes;
Introduction and passacaglia.
    Christ Church, P.O. Box 10228
    Federal Station, Greenville, SC 29603

POWERS, GEORGE
    b. Kokomo, Ind., 31 May 1917. Studied with Leo
Sowerby, American Cons., B. M.; with Roger
Sessions, Juilliard School; with Alec Rowley,
Trinity Coll., London; with Seth Bingham, Union
Theological Seminary, New York, S. M. D. He is
a fellow, American Guild of Organists. He was
faculty member, American Cons., 1946-48; Guilmant
Organ School, New York, 1965-66; Union Theological Seminary, School of Sacred Music, 1958-73;
organist-choirmaster, 1940-   ; St. Mark's In-
the-Bouwerie, Manhattan, 1955-72.
    WORKS: Chorus: Ah, my soul, a cappella;
Benedictus es, Domine; Create in me; Christ, our
passover; Come, great spirit; Keyboard: From my
sketchbook, piano suite; Ballade, piano; Scherzo,
organ; Interlude, organ.
    91 Christopher St., New York, NY 10014

*POWERS, MAXWELL
    b. Cleveland, Ohio, 4 Feb. 1911. Studied at
Cleveland Inst. of Music, B. M., M. M.; received
an honorary D. M., Cincinnati Cons. He has
been faculty member, Greenwich House Music School,
New York, 1945-   .
    WORKS: Orchestra: 2 piano concertos; sym-
phonic poem; an overture; Chamber music: string
quartet; violin sonata; cello sonata.

POZAR, CLEVE F. (name legally changed from Robert F.
Pozar)
    b. Virginia, Minn., 8 Aug. 1941. Studied at
Univ. of Michigan; composition with Bill Dixon
in New York; drums with Alan Dawson, Boston.
He has been percussionist for numerous theatri-
cal productions at Univ. of Michigan theatre,
Charles Theatre, Boston, Milwaukee Repertory
Theatre; with Bob James Trio, Bill Dixon Ensemble;
and for dance groups.
    WORKS: Jazz ensemble: Cosmic peace; Magis-
trate Lousvart; Echo Africa; Nancy's small world;
Good golly, Miss Nancy; Film scores: Implosion;
Louise Nevelson for Whitney Museum.
    125 Green St., Cambridge, MA 02139

POZDRO, JOHN W.
    b. Chicago, Ill., 14 Aug. 1923. Studied with
Robert Delaney, Northwestern Univ., B. M. 1948,

POZDRO, JOHN W.

(POZDRO, JOHN W.)
M. M. 1949; with Howard Hanson, Bernard Rogers, Alan Hovhaness, Eastman School of Music, Ph. D. 1958. His awards include citations, Kansas Fed. of Music Clubs, 1964, 1969; ASCAP awards, 1966-73; first prize, Roth Orchestra Composition contest, 1972; Delius prize for piano preludes, 1974; Ford Found. commission for 3rd symphony, 1960. He was instructor, Iowa State Univ., 1949-50; faculty, Univ. of Kansas, 1950-   , professor and chairman of theory and composition, 1961-   .
WORKS: Orchestra: 3 symphonies, 1949, 1957, 1959; A cynical overture, 1953; Rondo giocoso, string orch., 1964; Waterlow Park, 1972; Chamber music: 3 piano sonatas, 1946, 1963, 1964; quintet for winds and piano, 1947; 2 string quartets, 1947, 1948; sextet for flute and strings, 1948; woodwind quintet, 1951; Trilogy, clarinet, bassoon, trumpet, piano, 1960; Carillon: Landscape II, 1970.
Department of Music, University of Kansas
Lawrence, KS 66044

PRENDERGAST, ROY MARTIN
b. Canal Zone, Panama, 23 Feb. 1943. Studied with Peter Sacco, San Francisco State Coll.; with Frederick Beyer, Greensboro Coll.; and with Jack Jarrett, Univ. of North Carolina at Greensboro, where he has been instructor, 1972-   .
WORKS: Theatre: Pumpernickel ice cream, musical, 1968; How Miss Henry got that way, musical, 1972; Orchestra: piano concerto, 1971; Variations on a theme by Scriabin, a cello concerto, 1972; Chorus: Body poems, 1973; Film score: Step ahead, documentary film, 1973.
1505 Lafayette Court, Greensboro, NC 27408

PREOBRAJENSKA, VERA N.
b. San Francisco, Calif., 27 Apr. 1926. Studied at San Francisco State Univ., B. A. 1953; at Bernadean Univ. Las Vegas, Nev., M. A. 1972, Ph. D. 1973; studied with Ernst von Dohnanyi, Darius Milhaud, Frederick Jacobi, Ernest Bloch, Roger Sessions, Alexander Tcherepnin, Dmitri Shostakovitch. She was music editor for Skye Music Services; writer, arranger, orchestrator for commercial song writing, 1949-   ; teaching assistant and classroom pianist for ballet and modern dance, Univ. of California, Berkeley, 1965-68; appointed chairman, music department, Coll. of Fine Arts, Bernadean Univ., Las Vegas, 1973-   .
WORKS: Theatre: Concept of the egg, dance-comedy score, 1956; Hebraic rhapsody, ballet score for orch., 1968; Chorus: Holy Communion, 1960; Christmas prayer, 1962; Prayer to the guardian angel, 1966; The Lord's prayer, 1967; The creed, 1969; The creation, cantata, 1971.
5423 Ygnacio Ave., Oakland, CA 94601

PRESS, JACQUES
b. Tbilisi, Russia, 27 Mar. 1903; to U.S. 1926. Studied at a conservatory in Tbilisi; with Nadia Boulanger in Paris, 1924-25; orchestration with Leo Zeitlin. He has received 8 ASCAP awards. He was staff arranger and composer, Roxy and

(PRESS, JACQUES)
Capitol Theatres and NBC Radio, 1927-37; motion picture studios in Hollywood, 1938-50; music director and composer for television programs in New York, 1950-70.
WORKS: Orchestra: Hasseneh, symphonic suite; Wedding dance; Prelude and fugue in jazz; Jig-jag; Disconcerto, piano and orch.; Russian gypsy dance; Israeli festival march; Spanish interlude, a ballet, 1941; Chamber music: Polka coloratura, for 2 harps. Many of his orchestral works were introduced and recorded by Arthur Fiedler and the Boston Pops.
588 West End Ave., New York, NY 10024

PRESSER, WILLIAM
b. Saginaw, Mich., 19 Apr. 1916. Studied at Univ. of Michigan, M. M.; with Bernard Rogers, Burrill Phillips, Gardner Read, and Roy Harris, Eastman School of Music, Ph. D. His awards include the Rochester Religious Arts Festival award; Syracuse Univ. Festival of Arts award; 2 Composers Press publication awards; 2 Nat. School Orchestra Asso. awards; annual ASCAP awards, 1966-73. He taught at Buena Vista Coll., 1940-42; Florida State Univ., 1946-47; Florence State Coll., 1947-50; West Texas State Coll., 1950-51; Music and Arts Inst. of San Francisco, 1951-53; associate professor, Univ. of Southern Mississippi, 1953-   .
WORKS: Opera: The whistler, chamber opera for soprano, baritone, string quartet, piano; Orchestra: symphony no.1; concerto for tuba and strings; concerto for tenor saxophone and chamber orch.; Band: symphony no.2; Chamber music: trombone sonata; suite for brass quartet; Prelude and dance for flute; Rondo for piccolo and piano; Chorus: Annunciation and magnificat, chorus and winds; Voice: Songs of death, mezzo soprano, string quartet; numerous triadic, college-level works for band and orchestral instruments, chorus, and solo voice.
211 Hillendale Drive, Hattiesburgh, MS 39401

*PRESTON, JOHN E.
The coming American, chorus and organ.

*PREVIN, ANDRE
b. Berlin, Germany, 6 Apr. 1929; U.S. citizen 1948. Studied at Berlin Cons.; Paris Cons.; and with Mario Castelnuovo-Tedesco in Los Angeles. His awards include the Berlin Film Festival award, 1955; Academy award, 1963; Screen Composers Asso. award. He was an arranger for MGM at 17; served in the U.S. Army, 1950-52; was jazz and concert pianist and conductor; taught at Univ. of California at Los Angeles, 1957-58; conducted Houston Symphony, 1967-68; music director, London Symphony, 1968-1975; music director, Pittsburgh Symphony, 1976-   .
WORKS: Ballet: Invitation to the dance; Orchestra: Overture to a comedy, 1960; guitar concerto; Portrait for strings; Chamber music: string quartet; flute quintet; cello sonata; Impressions, piano; Film scores: It's always fair weather; Bad day at Black Rock, 1955; The subterraneans, 1960; Two for the seesaw, 1962.
Pittsburgh Symphony Orchestra
600 Pennsylvania Ave., Pittsburgh, PA 15222

*PRICE, FLORENCE B.
b. Little Rock, Ark., 9 Apr. 1898; d. Chicago, Ill., 3 June 1953. Studied with Benjamin Cutter, George W. Chadwick, Frederick Converse, New England Cons.; at American Cons.; Chicago Musical Coll.; also with Arthur Andersen. She received the Wanamaker award in 1925 for her symphony. She taught at Shorter Coll. and at Clark Univ.; was soloist with the Chicago Symphony playing her own works.
WORKS: Orchestra: Symphony in e, 1925, Chicago, 1932; piano concerto; violin concerto; symphonic poem; Concert overture on Negro spirituals; The wind and the sea, chorus and orch.; Lincoln walks at midnight, chorus and orch.; Rhapsody, piano and orch.; Chamber music: piano quintet; Negro folk songs in counterpoint, string quartet; Moods, flute, clarinet, piano; organ sonata; Passacaglia and fugue, organ.

PRICE, JOHN E.
b. Tulsa, Okla., 21 June 1935. Studied with O. Anderson Fuller, Lincoln Univ., A. B. 1957; with Bela Rozsa at Tulsa Univ., M. M. 1963; with Robert Wykes, Harold Blumenfeld, and Paul Pisk, Washington Univ., St. Louis, 1967-68. He received a commission from Community of Artists, Miami, 1972; was selected as exchange scholar, Phelps-Stokes Fund and the Asso. of Univ. and Research Inst., to lecture in the Caribbean, 1974. He began to compose at the age of 6; was vocal coach and composer, Karamu Theatre, Cleveland, 1957-59; served in U.S. Army, 1959-61; has been assistant professor and composer-in-residence, Florida Memorial Coll., 1964-   , chairman of Fine Arts, 1973-   .
WORKS: Theatre: music for 14 plays including Risible visible, 1957; Death of a salesman, 1958; Fairy tale wood, 1959; Candy man Beechum, 1962; Orchestra: Scherzo for clarinet and orch., 1957; Chamber music: Forsight of time and the universe, speaker, clarinet, trumpet, drums, 1955; brass quartet, 1956; Impulse and deviation, solo cello, 1958; duet for horn and trombone, 1959; Piece and deviation, viola and piano, 1962; quartet for violin, viola, horn, bassoon, 1962; trombone sonata, 1968; trio for clarinet, horn, trombone, 1968; numerous works for solo voice, chorus, chamber groups, and piano.
15800 N.W. 42nd Ave., Miami, FL 33054

PRICE, MILBURN
b. Electric Mills, Miss., 9 Apr. 1938. Studied with Halsey Stevens, Univ. of Southern California; also conducting at Baylor Univ. He was lecturer, Univ. of Southern California, 1966-67; faculty member, Furman Univ., 1967-   , chairman, music department, 1972-   .
WORKS: Chorus: Meditation on the nativity, a choral service; many published choral works.
Department of Music, Furman University
Greenville, SC 29613

PRICE, PAUL WILLIAM
b. Fitchburg, Mass., 15 May 1921. Studied at New England Conservatory, diploma; Cincinnati Cons., M. M.; percussion with George Carey and Fred Noak. He received an award from Nat. Asso.

(PRICE, PAUL WILLIAM)
of American Composers and Conductors for "outstanding contribution to American music." He was conductor of the Manhattan Percussion Ensemble for a State Department-sponsored tour of the Near East, 1967-68; was member, American Symphony Orchestra; percussion lecturer and clinician; president and editor, Music for Percussion, Inc.; has held faculty posts at Univ. of Illinois, Boston Univ., Ithaca Coll., Newark State Coll.; percussion teacher, Manhattan School of Music, 1957-   , coordinator, percussion department, 1970-   .
WORKS: Percussion: Inventions for 4 percussion players, 1947; 12 solos for timpani, 1951; Exhibitions for snare drum; 6 bass drum solos; percussion method books.
470 Kipp St., Teaneck, NJ 07666

PRIESING, DOROTHY
b. Nantucket, Mass., 31 July 1910. Studied at Columbia Univ., B. S., M. A.; with James Friskin, Howard Brockway, and Rubin Goldmark, Juilliard School; with Nadia Boulanger at Fontainebleau. At Juilliard she received the Coolidge prize in composition and the Seligman prize in fugue. She was instructor, Columbia Univ., 1936-39; Juilliard School, 1936-39, 1942-47; associate professor, Montclair State Coll., 1953-   .
WORKS: Band: Invocation; Chamber music: violin sonata; Pieces for piano; Chorus: Now is the caroling season; Noel; Wonder of the darksome night; Wild swans, women's voices; Children's carol; Voice: Songs on poems of James Joyce.
42 Llewellyn Road, Montclair, NJ 07042

*PRINCE, ROBERT
b. 1929. New York export: Op. jazz, orch., 1958.

PRIOLO, CHRISTOPHER
b. Plainfield, N. J., 12 Oct. 1949. Studied with Peter Racine Fricker and Thea Musgrave, Univ. of California, Santa Barbara. He won 2nd place in a contest sponsored by the Santa Barbara Music Society. He was student teacher, Univ. of California, Santa Barbara, 1973-74.
WORKS: Orchestra: Magnificat, orch., chorus, soloists; Chamber music: woodwind trio, 1969; Poème II, voice and piano; sextet, winds, strings, harp; duet for cello and harp; Prelude and fugue, 2 pianos; piano variations; Scherzo for harp.
958 Garcia Road, Santa Barbara, CA 93103

PRITCHARD, ROGER
b. Prestbury, England, 18 Feb. 1940; to U.S. 1963. Studied with Anthony J. Gnazzo, Mills Coll.; with Alden Jenks, San Francisco Cons.
WORKS: Chamber music: High lines, voice and bell; Death piece #98.4; Electronic: Crimond II, tape; Church music II, voice and tape; Single finger exercise, tape.
1333 Bonita Ave., Berkeley, CA 94709

PROCTER, LELAND
b. Newton, Mass., 24 Mar. 1914. Studied with Bernard Rogers, Howard Hanson, Eastman School of Music,

PROCTER, LELAND

(PROCTER, LELAND)
B. M.; with Spencer Norton, Univ. of Oklahoma, M. M.; with Walter Piston at Harvard Univ. He received a grant from the Ford Found. Fund for the Advancement of Education for study at Harvard Univ. He was head of music department, Southwestern State Coll., Okla., 1939-43; faculty member, New England Cons., 1946-58; mechanical designer, various companies in Boston and Springfield area, 1958-   .
WORKS: Opera: Eve of crossing, 1-act; Orchestra: symphony no.1; suite for string orch.; Moby Dick (symphony no.2), orch. and chorus; Chamber music: piano quintet; 2 string quartets; Fantasy, flute and piano; clarinet sonata; 3 chorale preludes, organ and oboe; Chorus: Canticle of the sun, cantata; 3 songs of service.
1 South Road, Hampden, MA 01036

*PROSTAKOFF, JOSEPH
b. Kokand, Central Asia, 1911; to U.S. 1922. Studied piano with Abby Whiteside; composition with Mark Brunswick and Karol Rathaus; teaches piano and is a free-lance editor. His compositions include 2 bagatelles for piano.

PROTO, FRANK
b. Brooklyn, N. Y., 18 July 1941. Is self-taught in composition. He has been composer and arranger with the Cincinnati Symphony Orchestra, 1966-   .
WORKS: Orchestra: doublebass concerto, 1969; Fantasy on the Bach C-minor Partita, jazz quintet and orch., 1970; saxophone concerto, 1971; concerto in one movement for violin, doublebass and orch., 1972; Outdoor overture, 1973; Casey at the bat, narrator, tape and orch., 1973; Chamber music: string trio; octet for woodwind quintet, percussion, bass and soprano voice; doublebass quartet; duet for violin and doublebass; doublebass sonata.
6265 Dawes Lane, Cincinnati, OH 45230

*PROULX, RICHARD
Has published for chorus: Advent anthem; The just man shall flourish; Behold, now, the house of God; and organ pieces.

PROVENZANO, ALDO
b. Philadelphia, Pa., 3 May 1930. Studied with Peter Mennin, Juilliard School, B. S. 1956, M. S. 1957. He held scholarships at Juilliard 1952-57. He taught in public schools, 1957-64; at Eastman School of Music, 1964-69; Juilliard School, 1969-70; City Coll. of New York, 1971-   . He is also composer-arranger-conductor for recordings, films, television, dance groups, etc.
WORKS: Opera: The cask of amontillado, 1968; Ballet: Malocchio, dance in 1 scene; Chamber music: Essay, string quartet; Recitation, violin and piano; woodwind quintet; Film scores: Jacktown, jazz score; 4 documentaries; also choral works, songs, piano pieces.
429 Burning Tree Road, Cherry Hill, NJ 08034

*PTASZYNSKA, MARTA
Sonospheres, performed at Composers Theatre, New York, May 1974.

PULLEN, MRS. CLAUDE E. See DUNGAN, OLIVE

*PURSELL, WILLIAM
b. 1926.   Studied at Peabody Cons. and at Eastman School of Music. He held the Boise composition scholarship at Peabody, 1944-47; received the Benjamin award in 1953 for Christ looking over Jerusalem.

PURSWELL, PATRICK W.
b. Ft. Sill, Okla., 1 July 1939. Studied with Frederick Goossens, Univ. of Alabama, 1957-63; with Kenneth Gaburo, Burrill Phillips, and Ben Johnston, Univ. of Illinois, 1963-65; with Richard Hervig, Univ. of Iowa, 1967-69. He was a member, Univ. of Chicago Contemporary Chamber Players, 1965-66; member, Center for New Music, Univ. of Iowa, 1966-71.
WORKS: Orchestra: symphony, 1959; Chamber music: woodwind quintet, 1957; piano sonata, 1958; violin sonata, 1960; quartet for bassoon and string trio, 1962; sonata for solo flute, 1962; Proxmit, cello and piano, 1963; "it" grew and grew, flute solo, 1964.
3126 Federal, Alliance, OH 44601

*PURVIS, RICHARD
b. San Francisco, Calif., 1915. Studied at Peabody Cons.; Curtis Inst.; Royal School of Music, London. He was organist-choirmaster in Philadelphia; bandmaster, U.S. Army, in World War II; then settled in San Francisco as organist-choirmaster. He has published many works for chorus and for organ.

PUSINA, JAN
b. Los Angeles, Calif., 5 Aug. 1940. Studied with Jean-Claude Eloy and William Denny, Univ. of California at Berkeley. He received the Niccola De Lorenzo composition prize, Univ. of California, Berkeley, 1968; was commissioned exhibitor, The Exploratorium, San Francisco, 1973. He was instructor, Merritt Coll., Oakland, 1969; East Bay Music Center, Richmond Calif., 1973.
WORKS: Chamber music: Divergence, ensemble of 6, 1969; Electronic: Kama, 3 percussion ensembles, solo instrument, and tape, 1968; Tape compositions, no. 1-6, 1970-73; Cultural train, live tape performance of environmental sounds, 1973; Sum tones and difference tones, flute and electronics, 1973.
1535 Berkeley Way, Berkeley, CA 94703

PUSZTAI, TIBOR
b. Budapest, Hungary, 23 Dec. 1946; U.S. citizen 1973. Studied with Robert Cogan, Alexander Goehr, and Gunther Schuller, New England Cons., artist's diploma 1970. He received the Lincoln Center Young Artist award, 1965; Koussevitzky composition prize, 1970; Frank Huntington Beebe Found. grant, 1973. He was faculty member and assistant to Gunther Schuller, New England Cons., 1970-73; faculty, Berkshire Music Center, 1973.
WORKS: Chamber music: Labyrinths, piano; Interactions, horn and percussion; Canticle, 2 horns, 3 clarinets; Silence plus seven, mixed ensemble; One farewell, bass-baritone and mixed

(PUSZTAI, TIBOR)
ensemble; Nocturnes, soprano and mixed ensemble;
Requiem profana, mezzo soprano, tenor, mixed
ensemble; Vertere in fugam avis paradisium, flute
and percussion, Boston, 30 Apr. 1973.
c/o New England Conservatory
290 Huntington Ave., Boston, MA 02115

*PUTSCHE, THOMAS
b. Scarsdale, N. Y., 1929. Studied with Milton
Babbitt, Aaron Copland, Arnold Franchetti, and
Vittorio Giannini. In addition to being an
assistant professor, Hartt Coll. of Music, he is
a member of Friends and Enemies of Modern Music
and the Internat. Society for Contemporary Music,
and an occasional music critic for the Hartford
Courant. His compositions include Cat and the
moon, a 1-act chamber opera on a play by W. B.
Yeats.
Hartt College of Music
University of Hartford
West Hartford, CT 06117

PYLE, FRANCIS JOHNSON
b. South Bend, Ind., 13 Sep. 1901. Studied at
Oberlin Coll., A. B.; with George F. McKay, Univ.
of Washington, M. A.; with Howard Hanson, Bernard
Rogers, Herbert Elwell, and Burrill Phillips,
Eastman School of Music, Ph. D. He received 2
Sigma Alpha Iota awards, 1955; his many commis-
sions include those from Central Coll., 1957;
Lycoming Coll., 1964; Drake Univ., 1965, 1972;
Vennard Coll., 1968; Univ. of Wichita, 1969; Iowa
Arts Council, 1970; Iowa Music Teachers Asso.,
1971, 1974. He was faculty member, Central Washington State Coll., 1929-37; professor and chairman, theory and musicology, Drake Univ., 1937-72,
emeritus, 1972-   ; orchestra director, Central
Coll., 1972-73; orchestra director and professor,
San Jacinto Coll., Pasadena, Tex., 1973-74.
WORKS: Orchestra: symphony, 1940; Old river
tune and clambake, 1945; Frontier sketches, string
orch., 1 1950; Pictures for Suzanne, string orch.,
1955; Overture to The Magic Fishbone, 1957; From
the southwest, suite, 1959; harp concerto, 1970;
3 Psalms, with chorus, brass choir, optional
tape, 1971; sinfonietta, chamber orch., 1971;
Wind ensemble: Greetings suite, 1949; Edged
night, with solo flute, 1952; Far dominion, 1963;
horn concerto, 1964; Concerto giubilante, organ,
winds, percussion, 1965; trumpet concerto, 1965;
Theme and dialogues, 1970; Pasadena '71, 1971;
symphony, 1972; Fanfare, 1972; Chamber music:
Currier and Ives, woodwind trio, 1955; trio for
flute, cello, piano, 1956; clarinet sonata 1959;
woodwind quintet, 1959; Sonata for 3, clarinet,
piano, and percussion, 1960; violin sonata, 1964;
concerto for harp and piano, 1969; flute sonata,
1970; bassoon sonata, 1973; Chorus: Now is the
hour of darkness past, double choir, 1959; Te
Deum, double choir, winds, percussion, 1962;
Full stature, 1968; I have chosen thee, 1968;
Canticle of the sun, with brass sextet, 1970;
Psalm 145, 1972; Piano: 2 sonatas, 1969; suite
for piano 4 hands; songs, works for accordion.
1535 41st St., Des Moines, IA 50311

*QUARLES, JAMES THOMAS
b. St. Louis, Mo., 7 Nov. 1877; d. Saugus, Calif.,
4 Mar. 1954. Studied with Widor in Paris;
taught at Cornell Univ., 1903-23; was professor,
Univ. of Missouri, 1923-43; composed the Univ.
of Missouri Alma mater, anthems, organ works,
songs.

QUEEN, VIRGINIA
b. Dallas, Tex., 25 Oct. 1921. Studied at American Cons. and Univ. of Colorado. She has been
associate professor, Ouachita Baptist Univ.,
1946-   .
WORKS: Chorus: Let thy holy spirit come
upon us, women's voices, 1961; Piano: Adagio
and scherzo; 3 vagaries; many works in
manuscript.
Ouachita Baptist University
Arkadelphia, AR 71923

QUESADA, VIRGINIA
b. Bayside, N. Y., 11 Feb. 1951. Studied with
Joel Chadabe at State Univ. of New York at
Albany.
WORKS: Electronic: God commercial, tape
and film, 1972; Women's lip, tape and film,
1972; Roller rink, tape alone, 1973.
R.D. #1, Johnston Road
Slingerlands, NY 12159

QUILLING, HOWARD L.
b. Enid, Okla., 16 Dec. 1935. Studied with
Ingolf Dahl, Robert Linn, and Ernest Kanitz,
Univ. of Southern California; with Lehman Engel,
BMI Music Theater Workshop. He was public
school band, orchestra and choir director unitl
appointment as associate professor, California
State Coll., Bakersfield, 1971-   ; music
director, St. Francis Church, 1973-   .
WORKS: Theatre: music for Danton's death,
1972; The wild duck, 1972; Tiny Alice, 1973;
Orchestra: Overture, 1966; Fantasy on The wayfaring stranger, 1967; piano concerto, 1969;
symphonia, chamber orch., 1971; Band: Intermezzo, 1967; Introspections, 1968; suite for
alto saxophone and wind orch., 1970; symphony
for winds and percussion, 1973; Chamber music:
quintet for clarinet and strings, 1958; piano
sonatina, 1962; string quartet, 1966; 2 violin
sonatas, 1969, 1971; quartet for winds, 1969;
2 piano sonatas, 1957, 1970; Fantasy, violin
and piano, 1972; Chorus: A song in celebration
of sacred love, triple chorus and wind orch.,
1972; Mass for St. Francis, 1973; Songs: 17
years old, a cycle, 1969; 3 songs from the
Finnish, 1957.
3001 Harmony Drive, Bakersfield, CA 93306

QUINN, J. MARK (James J.)
b. Chicago, Ill., 30 Apr. 1936. Studied with
Leon Stein, DePaul Univ. He received the
Ostwald award, American Bandmasters' Asso., 1959;
special citation, American Acad. of Television
Arts and Sciences, 1966. He has been associate
professor of humanities, Loop Coll., City Coll.
of Chicago, 1965-   , chairman, humanities and
art departments, 1968-   ; free-lance performer,
1958-   .

QUINN, J. MARK

(QUINN, J. MARK)
WORKS: Theatre: <u>Requiem for a slave</u>, ballet-opera for 2 solo singers, mixed choir, orch., WITW, Chicago, Mar. 1967; <u>Clash of kings</u>, ballet for winds, brass, percussion, 1968; <u>Ritual-D</u>, ballet for expanded jazz orch., WITW, Chicago, Nov. 1971; Orchestra: <u>Lament</u>, 1959; <u>Tale of a square dance</u>, 1963; Band: <u>Revolt in red</u>, 1956; <u>Portrait of the land</u>, 1958; <u>Chorale of the winds</u>, 1959; <u>Symphonic variants</u>, 1960; <u>Testament of battle</u>, 1959; <u>Soliloquy for a noble one</u>, 1961; <u>Credo, 1961</u>; <u>Varsomna-I</u>, 1973.
11473 South Homan Ave., Chicago, IL 60655

QUINTIERE, JUDE
b. Paterson, N. J., 9 Oct. 1939. Studied at New York Univ., B. M.; Columbia Univ., M. A.; electronic music with Gershon Kingsley, The New School. She was coordinator, creative arts, Tombrock Coll., 1968-73; lecturer, Coll. of St. Elizabeth, 1967-   ; lecturer, Fairleigh Dickinson Univ., 1973-   .
WORKS: Chamber music: <u>Lines and spaces</u>, for 4 instruments; <u>Tolerance 1966</u>, for 9 instruments, 1966; Electronic: <u>Elegy for City Hall</u>, magnetic tape, 1973; <u>The wheel</u>, soprano, alto, flute, saxophone, horn, cello, Moog synthesizer, New York, 30 Apr. 1973.
47-49 Greene St., New York, NY 10013

*RABINOF, SYLVIA
b. New York, N. Y., 10 Oct.   . Attended New York Univ.; studied with Ignace Paderewski, Rudolf Serkin, Albert Stoessel, Bernard Wagenaar, Philip James, and Georges Enesco; received an honorary D. M. from Lincoln Memorial Univ. She conducted the Morley Singers, 1942-44; toured as solo pianist and in duo concerts with her husband, Benno Rabinof, violinist.
WORKS: Operetta: <u>Hamlet, the flea</u>, children's operetta; Orchestra: <u>Carnival</u>, tone poem for chorus and orch.; Concert variation on <u>Turkey in the straw</u>; Suite for chamber orch.; Chorus: <u>Deluge</u>, cantata; Piano: <u>Gastronomic suite</u>.
33 Riverside Drive, New York, NY 10023

*RACHMANINOFF, SERGEI VASSILYEVICH
b. Oneg, Novgorod, Russia, 1 Apr. 1873; U.S. citizen 1943; d. Beverly Hills, Calif., 28 Mar. 1943. Studied at St. Petersburg Cons.; piano with Siloti, composition with Taneyev and Arensky, Moscow Cons., graduating in piano in 1891, in composition in 1892 and winning the gold medal for his 1-act opera, <u>Aleko</u>. His <u>Prelude in C# minor</u>, one of the best known piano pieces in the world, was also written in 1892. In 1909 he gave 26 recitals in the U.S.; returned to America in 1918 and eventually settled in California. His many works include 3 operas; 3 symphonies; 4 piano concertos; <u>The isle of the dead</u>, symphonic poem; <u>Rhapsody on a theme of Paganini</u>, piano and orch.; a cello sonata; choral works; and many works for piano solo and for 2 pianos.

RACKLEY, LAWRENCE
b. Media, Ill., 10 Sep. 1932. Studied with Robert Mills Delaney, Northwestern Univ.; with Bernard Rogers and Howard Hanson, Eastman School

(RACKLEY, LAWRENCE)
of Music. He was assistant professor, Central Michigan Univ., 1957-63; associate professor, Kalamazoo Coll., 1963-   .
WORKS: Orchestra: symphony; <u>Confluences</u>; <u>Discourse, soliloquy and concourse</u>, cello and orch.; Chamber music: chamber concerto for piano and 7 winds; <u>Divertimento</u>, 4 winds and strings; <u>Exchanges</u>, string bass and 3 tape recorders; Chorus: Cantata, with tenor solo and organ.
116 South Dartmouth, Kalamazoo, MI 49007

RAFFMAN, RELLY
b. New Bedford, Mass., 4 Sep. 1921. Studied at Dartmouth Coll., B. A. 1947; with Henry Brant, Columbia Univ., M. A. 1949; with Bernhard Heiden, Indiana Univ. He received the Ernest Bloch award, 1958; Ella Cabot Lyman Trust grant, 1962; commissions from After Dinner Opera Company; Illinois Wesleyan Univ.; churches. He was instructor, Southwest Missouri State Coll., 1949-50; faculty member, Clark Univ., 1954-   , chairman, music department, 1954-71, music and fine arts, 1971-72, visual and performing arts, 1972-   , Jeppson professor, 1969-   .
WORKS: Opera: <u>Midas</u>, 1964; Theatre: music for <u>The good woman of Setzuan</u>, 1972; Chamber music: <u>Diversion for 3 celli</u>, 1951; woodwind quintet, 1967; Chorus: <u>The friendly beasts</u>, 1956; <u>Triptych</u>, 1957; <u>Alleluia</u>, 1957; <u>I care not for these ladies</u>, 1959; <u>Fye on sinful fantasy</u>, 1959; <u>Sonnet XXX</u>, 1959; <u>Come be my love</u>, 1959; <u>In the beginning</u>, 1958; <u>The secular masque</u>, 1960; <u>Shall I compare thee</u>, 1961; <u>The passionate pilgrim</u>, 1962; <u>Farewell, thou art too dear</u>; <u>Jubilate deo</u>, 1966; <u>Psalm IV</u>, 1967; <u>Matins</u>, 1970; <u>Sweet was the song</u>, 1970; <u>The 3 ravens</u>, 1970; <u>Virtue</u>, 1970.
209 Lovell St., Worcester, MA 01603

RAHN, JOHN
b. New York, N. Y., 26 Feb. 1944. Studied with Milton Babbitt and Benjamin Boretz, Princeton Univ. He was lecturer, Univ. of Michigan, Ann Arbor, 1973-74.
WORKS: Band: <u>Deloumenon</u>, 1970; Chamber music: woodwind quintet, 1969; <u>Epithalamium</u>, piano, 1968; trio for clarinet, cello, piano, 1972; <u>Peanut butter defies gravity</u>, soprano and piano, 1973; Chorus: <u>Hos Estin</u>, with instrumental ensemble, 1971.
343 North Hagadorn, South Lyon, MI 48178

RAKSIN, DAVID
b. Philadelphia, Pa., 4 Aug. 1912. Studied with William F. Happich in Philadelphia; with Harl McDonald, Univ. of Pennsylvania, M. B.; with Isadore Freed in New York; and with Arnold Schoenberg in Hollywood. Since 1935 he has been composer-conductor for radio and television, for theatre, for major film studios, for recordings, symphony and chamber music concerts, ballet; lecturer and writer. He is adjunct professor, Univ. of Southern California and faculty member, USC Center for Urban Affairs; on music faculty, Univ. of California, Los Angeles; member, State Department Advisory Panel on

(RAKSIN, DAVID)
International Copyright. He was president, Composers and Lyricists Guild, 1962-70, on Board of Governors, 1970-   .
WORKS: Ballet: Inspiration; Mother Goose-Step; Theatre: Feather in your hat, multimedia, 1942; If the shoe fits, musical; The wind in the willows, musical; music for Noah; Mother Courage; The prodigal; The Chinese wall; Volpone; Film scores: more than 100, including Laura, Forever Amber; Force of evil; The secret life of Walter Mitty; Suddenly; Separate tables; Smoky; Al Capone; The bad and the beautiful; The redeemer; Will Penny; What's the matter with Helen; Madeline; The unicorn in the garden; The soldier; Television shows: more than 300 including Ben Casey, The breaking point; Report from America, USIA series. His adaptations of pieces from his film and television scores for orchestra have been performed by almost all major orchestras in the U.S. and many abroad.
12017 Pacoima Court, Studio City, CA 91604

*RALEIGH, STUART
Maledictions, wind ensemble, 1970.
Department of Music, Syracuse University
Syracuse, NY 13210

RAMEY, PHILIP
b. Chicago, Ill., 12 Sep. 1939. Studied at Internat. Acad. of Music, Nice, France, 1959; with Alexander Tcherepnin, privately, then at DePaul Univ., B. A. 1962; with Jack Beeson, Columbia Univ., M. A. 1965. He held 4 fellowships to the MacDowell Colony, 1969, 1971-72, 1974.
WORKS: Orchestra: Concert suite for piano and orch., 1962; Seven, they are seven, incantation for bass-baritone and orch., 1965; Orchestral discourse, 1967; piano concerto, 1969; Chamber music: sonata for 3 unaccompanied timpani, 1961; Cat songs for soprano, flute, piano, 1962; Music for brass and percussion, 1964; Capriccio for percussion, 1966; Night music for percussion, 1966; Toccata breva for percussion 1967; Commentaries, flute and piano, 1968; string quartet, 1970; clarinet sonata, 1971; Suite for violin and piano, 1971; Piano: 4 sonatas, 1961, 1966, 1968 (2); Epigrams, 1967; Doomsday fragments, 1970; Fantasy, 1972; Leningrad rag, 1972; Night song, 1973.
307 East 60th St., New York, NY 10022

RAMSIER, PAUL
b. Louisville, Ky., 23 Sep. 1927. Studied at Univ. of Louisville, B. M.; piano with Beveridge Webster, Juilliard School, M. M.; with Alexei Haieff, Ernst von Dohnanyi, New York Univ., Ph. D. He received fellowships from Huntington Hartford Found., MacDowell Colony, Yaddo; and annual ASCAP awards. He was faculty member, New York Univ., 1967-72; Ohio State Univ., 1972-73.
WORKS: Opera: The man on the bearskin rug, 1-act; Ballet: Leaf in the wind, 1954; 6 dance diversions, 1957; Pied piper, 1964; Theatre: The dancing princesses, musical for children, 1967; Orchestra: Sonata for orchestra, 1954; Divertimento concertante on a theme of Couperin,

(RAMSIER, PAUL)
contrabass and orch., 1965; Chamber music: Night songs, string quartet and soprano; Fiery dragon, narrator and chamber ensemble, 1960; Chorus: The moon and the sun; Wine (Riddle); Eden; Film score: Turkey, documentary; Multimedia; Celebrations, tape and dancer, 1973.
210 Riverside Drive, New York, NY 10025

RAN, SHULAMIT
b. Tel Aviv, Israel, 21 Oct. 1949; to U.S. 1966. Studied with Paul Ben Haim and Alexander U. Boscovitz in Israel; with Norman Dello Joio, Mannes Coll. of Music. She received a Ford Found. publishing and recording grant, 1969. She was musician-in-residence, St. Mary's Univ., Nova Scotia, 1972-73; assistant professor, Univ. of Chicago, 1973-   .
WORKS: Orchestra: Concert piece for piano and orch.; Chamber music: O the chimneys, voice ensemble and tape, 1969; Hatzv: Israel eulogy, voice and ensemble; 3 fantasy pieces for cello and piano.
1455 North Sandburg Terrace
Chicago, IL 60610

RANDALL, J. K.
b. Cleveland, Ohio, 16 June 1929. Studied with Herbert Elwell, Cleveland Inst. of Music; at Columbia, Harvard and Princeton Univ.; also with Alexei Haieff and George Thaddeus Jones; piano with Leonard Shure. He received a Fromm Found. commission, 1965, for Mudgett. He has been professor, Princeton Univ., 1958-   .
WORKS: Chamber music: Improvisation on a poem by e. e. cummings, voice and chamber ensemble, 1961; Electronic: Quartets in pairs, 1964; Mudgett: monologues by a mass murderer, 1965; Lyric variations for violin and computer, 1967; music for the film, Eakins, 1972.
52 Gulick Rd., Princeton, NJ 08540

*RANDEGGER, GUISSEPPE ALDO
b. Naples, Italy, 17 Feb. 1874; to U.S. 1900; d. New York, N. Y., 30 Nov. 1946. Gave piano recitals in southern U.S.; taught at Hamilton Coll. and at Belmont Coll.; then privately in New York. His works include a 1-act opera, The promise of Medea, and songs.

*RANEY, JAMES
b. Louisville, Ky., 1927. Has published 4 pieces for string quartet, guitar and contrabass; and 4 pieces for 5 guitars.

RAPH, ALAN
b. New York, N. Y., 3 July 1933. Studied with Vincent Jones, New York Univ.; at Columbia Univ. Teachers Coll.; and with Nadia Boulanger at Fontainebleau. He is instructor, Columbia Teachers Coll., 1969-   ; and at New York Univ., Long Island Univ., and Hebrew Arts School; leader of The 7th Century, contemporary instrumental ensemble, and The Chamber Brass Players.

RAPH, ALAN

(RAPH, ALAN)
WORKS: Ballet: Trinity; Sacred grove on Mt. Tamalpais; Chamber music: Caprice, bass-trombone solo; Hossana, chamber ensemble; Canzona, chamber ensemble.
756 7th Ave., New York, NY 10019

RAPHLING, SAM
b. Fort Worth, Tex., 19 Mar. 1910. Studied with Rudolph Ganz, Chicago Musical Coll.; with Leonid Kreutzer in Berlin. He held a Huntington Hartford fellowship; won first prize, American Composers Circle contest; first prize, Chicago Council of Women contest. He taught at Chicago Musical Coll., 1937-45; performed as piano soloist with Chicago Symphony Orchestra, 1940-44, under Toscanini, Rachmaninoff, and Frederick Stock.
WORK: Opera: President Lincoln, Peter Bees, Johnny Pye and the fool-killer, 1-act operas on Hawthorne stories; Liar-liar, children's opera; Orchestra: 4 piano concertos; trumpet concerto; timpany concerto; suite for strings; Ticker-tape parade, overture; Abraham Lincoln walks at midnight; Cowboy rhapsody, violin and orch.; Rhapsody, for oboe, trumpet and strings; Minstrel rhapsody, piano and orch.; Band: Involvement; Chamber music: Warble for lilac time, flute and strings; 3 violin sonatas; horn sonata; oboe sonata; 2 saxophone sonatas; Pastoral, oboe and piano; Lyric prelude, bass clarinet and piano; Dance suite, 2 trumpets; Duograms, 2 oboes; Prelude and toccata, flute and bassoon; Little suite, brass sextet; Playthings of the wind, flute solo; Chorus: The bells; Sayings from The people, yes; Fugue on "money:" Piano: 24 etudes; 5 sonatas; 2 sonatinas; Square dance, piano 4-hands; American album, 2 pianos; and many songs.
2109 Broadway, New York, NY 10023

*RAPLEY, FELTON
Though I speak with the tongues of men and angels, baritone solo, chorus and organ.

*RAPOPORT, EDA
Chant Hebraique, cello and piano; woodwind quintet; works for solo voice and strings, instruments and piano.

*RARIG, JOHN
Introduction and march, clarinet and piano.
3911 Berry Drive, North Hollywood, CA 91604

*RASBACH, OSCAR
b. Dayton, Ky., 2 Aug. 1888. Studied piano with Leschetizky, theory with Hans Thornton in Vienna. He was piano recitalist, accompanist and teacher. His works included 2 operettas, Dawn boy and Open house; and songs, Trees, text by Joyce Kilmer; Mountains; A wanderer's song; The look; Laughing brook; and piano pieces.

RASELY, CHARLES W.
b. Easton, Pa., 26 Apr. 1921. Studied with Vittorio Giannini, Juilliard School; and at Syracuse Univ., B. M. He is music director, public schools; church music director; music director, Oneida Little Theater.

(RASELY, CHARLES W.)
WORKS: Theatre: Snoop, Doop, 'n Oscar, operetta; Everybody sings, musical; Chorus: The church's one foundation; Psalm 23, the lamb; To see a world in a grain of sand; The woods of Penn.
333 Leonard St., Oneida, NY 13421

RASELY, THOMAS E.
b. Easton, Pa., 9 Jan. 1951. Studied with Walter S. Hartley, State Univ. Coll. at Fredonia, N. Y. He is public school music teacher, North Syracuse, N. Y.
WORKS: Band: Concert overture; Chamber music: Sonatina and adagietto, tenor saxophone; Chorus: 2 songs of hope; Skipping stones; Childhood is a good time; Songs: Birth; Poem.
167 Cotswold Court, Liverpool, NY 13088

*RATHAUS, KAROL
b. Tarnopol, Poland, 16 Sep. 1895; to U.S. 1938; d. New York, N. Y., 21 Nov. 1954. Studied in Berlin and Vienna; taught in Berlin, Paris, London; was on faculty, Queens Coll., New York, 1940-54. He composed an opera; a ballet; 3 symphonies; other orchestral works; 5 string quartets; 4 piano sonatas; many other chamber works.

*RATNER, LEONARD GILBERT
b. Minneapolis, Minn., 30 July 1916. Studied with Arnold Schoenberg at Univ. of California, Los Angeles; musicology at Univ. of California, Berkeley, Ph. D. 1947; composition privately with Ernest Bloch and Frederick Jacobi. He received a Guggenheim fellowship, 1962; has been faculty member, Stanford Univ., 1947-   .
WORKS: Opera: The necklace; Orchestra: Harlequin overture; symphony; Chamber music: 2 string quartets; violin sonata; cello sonata; piano sonata; Serenade for oboe, horn, quartet. He is author of Music: The listener's art, 1957; and Harmony, structure and style, 1962.
Department of Music, Stanford University Stanford, CA 94305

*RAUSCH, CARLOS
Para Gerardo (Phonos II), New York, 4 Feb. 1974.
305 Riverside Drive, New York, NY 10025

RAUSCHENBERG, DALE E.
b. Youngstown, Ohio, 13 Jan. 1938. Studied with Orlando Vitello, Youngstown Univ., B. M. E.; with Juan Orrego-Salas, Indiana Univ. M. M. He was timpanist, Youngstown Philharmonic, 1957-59; assistant professor of percussion, Towson State Coll., 1966-   ; percussionist with Baltimore Symphony and Morris Mechanic Theater, 1966-   .
WORKS: Percussion ensemble: Discussion; What?; Landscape.
29 Othoridge Rd., Lutherville, MD 21093

RAUSCHER, HENRY. See: HUMPHREYS, HENRY S.

*RAY, DON BRANDON
b. Santa Maria, Calif., 7 June 1926. Studied with John Vincent, Univ. of California, Los Angeles, B. A. 1948; with Ernest Kanitz, Univ.

356

(RAY, DON BRANDON)
of Southern California; also studied conducting and has been active as a conductor in California. He has composed incidental music to plays, anthems, etc.

*RAYMOND, LEWIS
b. Newark, N. J., 3 Aug. 1908; d. Burbank, Calif., 1956. Studied with Felix Deyo and Bernard Wagenaar, New York Coll. of Music; was organist and pianist in silent film theatres; Army Air Force bandsman in World War II; then staff arranger for radio station WOR and for Broadway musicals. His compositions include a string quartet; Chorale in Gregorian style, clarinet choir; Divertimento, 3 flutes; Short suite for brass; Design, horn and piano.

RE, PETER
b. New York, N. Y., 17 Mar. 1919. Studied with Vittorio Giannini, Juilliard School; with Paul Hindemith, Yale Univ. He received the Maine State Commission on Arts and Humanities award, 1973; commissions from Kappa Gamma Psi, Portland (Me.) Symphony, and Bangor Symphony. He has been professor, Colby Coll., 1951- ; conductor and music director, Bangor Symphony Orchestra, 1963-73; director Colby Coll. summer School of Music, 1963-72.
WORKS: Orchestra: Variations on airs by Supply Belcher; A Maine profile; Festive overture, Bangor, 21 Oct. 1973; Chamber music: 2 string quartets; Chorus: 2 madrigals.
19 Merrill Ave., Waterville, ME 04901

READ, GARDNER
b. Evanston, Ill., 2 Jan. 1913. Studied with Howard Hanson and Bernard Rogers, Eastman School of Music, B. M. 1936, M. M. 1937; with Ildebrando Pizzetti in Italy and Jan Sibelius in Finland, 1938-39; with Aaron Copland at Tanglewood, 1941; conducting with V. Bakaleinikoff and Paul White. He held scholarships for all study at Eastman School; 4 MacDowell fellowships; Cromwell Traveling fellowship, 1938-39; Tanglewood fellowship, 1941; Huntington Hartford fellowships, 1960, 1965. His many awards include first prize, New York Philharmonic Society contest, 1937; 2 Juilliard publication awards, 1938, 1941; first prize, Paderewski Fund competition, 1943; Composers Press publication award, 1948; co-winner in Pennsylvania Coll. for Women contest, 1950; numerous awards for choral and chamber works; special State Department grants to lecture on American music in Mexico, 1957, 1964; honorary doctorate, Doane Coll., 1962; and many commissions from major orchestras and other groups. He was head, composition, St. Louis Inst. of Music, 1941-43; Kansas City Cons., 1943-45; Cleveland Inst. of Music, 1945- 48; professor, Boston Univ., 1948- , chairman, theory and composition, 1950-52; guest instructor, Simmons Coll., 1951; Harvard Univ. extension courses, 1957-58; visiting professor, Univ. of California, Los Angeles, 1966. His works have been performed by all major U.S. orchestras, frequently with the composer conducting.

(READ, GARDNER)
WORKS: Opera: Villon, 3-act, 1967; Theatre: music for 11 plays, including Hedda Gabler, 1947; The shoemaker's prodigious wife, 1956; Maxwell Anderson's The golden six, 1958; Ibsen's Brand, 1961; Sister Gretchen's Pilate, 1961; Orchestra: 3 symphonic suites - The painted desert, 1933, Sketches of the city, 1933, Pennsylvania, 1947; Fantasy, viola and orch., 1935; 4 symphonies, 1936, 1942, 1946, 1958, #4, premiere, Cincinnati Symphony, 30 Jan. 1970; Prelude and toccata, 1937; The golden journey to Samarkand, chorus, soloists, orch., 1939; Night flight, 1942; First overture, 1943; cello concerto, 1945; Temptation of St. Anthony, 1947; Sound piece, brass and percussion, 1949; Toccata giocosa, 1953; The prophet, narrator, chorus, soloists, orch., 1960; Sonoric fantasia, violin and orch., 1965; Chamber music: suite for string quartet, 1935; 6 intimate moods, violin and piano, 1937; piano quintet, 1945; Sonata brevis, violin and piano, 1948; string quartet, 1957; Sonoric fantasia, no. 1, celesta, harp, harpsichord, 1958; Los dioses aztecas, percussion ensemble, 1959; Hex-static, chamber group, Harvard, Mass., 25 Jan. 1974; Keyboard: Passacaglia and fugue, organ, 1936; suite for organ, 1939; Sonata da chiesa, piano, 1945; many choral works and songs. He is author of Thesaurus of orchestral devices, 1952, reprint: Westport, 1969; and Music notation - A manual of modern practice, 1963, revised edition, Boston, 1969; numerous articles published in music journals.
47 Forster Rd., Manchester, MA 01944

READ, THOMAS LAWRENCE
b. Erie, Pa., 3 July 1938. Studied at Oberlin Cons., B. M. 1960; with Francis Judd Cooke, New England Cons., M. M. 1962; with Benjamin Lees, Peabody Cons., D. M. A. 1971; all degrees in violin. He received first prize, New England Cons. alumni contest, 1961; Nat. Fed. of Music Clubs contest, 1963. He was assistant professor, West Chester State Coll., 1965-67; assistant professor, Univ. of Vermont, 1967-72, associate professor, 1972- .
WORKS: Theatre: music for Marlowe's Dr. Faustus, Renaissance instruments and percussion, 1973; Wind ensemble: Isochronisms, brass and percussion, 1972; Chamber music: string trio, 1960; sonata for violin solo, 1960; cello sonata, 1961; Song of sorrow, dance music, chamber ensemble and soprano, 1963; Combination 23-20, violin and piano, 1965; Concatenations, flute and piano, 1967; Pastorale, viola, winds, percussion, 1968; quintet for trombone and string quartet, 1971; Chorus: Te Deum, with soloists, brass and organ, 1973.
69 Morse Place, Burlington, VT 05401

REALE, PAUL
b. New Jersey, 3 Feb. 1943. Studied with Chou Wenchung, Columbia Univ.; with George Crumb and George Rochberg, Univ. of Pennsylvania. He received awards from Nat. Society of Arts and Letters, 1969; Creative Arts Inst., 1972. He has been assistant professor, Univ. of California, Los Angeles, 1969- .

REALE, PAUL

(REALE, PAUL)
WORKS: Chamber music: Late telophase, flute, clarinet, cello, piano, 1971; The mysterious death of the magic realist, viola, cello, harpsichord, guitar, 1972; Terry's piece, 1973; Chorus: Alleluia and Sequence, women's voices, 1973.
22125 Gault St., Canoga Park, CA 91303

RECK, DAVID
b. Rising Star, Tex., 12 Jan. 1935. Studied with Paul Pisk, Univ. of Texas; George Rochberg, Univ. of Pennsylvania; and with Thirugokarnam Ramachandra Iyer, Central Coll. of Karnatic Music, Madras, India. He received a Rockefeller Found. grant, 1968; Guggenheim fellowship, 1970; commissions from Koussevitzky Found., Fromm Found., and others. He has been instructor, New School for Social Research, New York, 1966- .
WORKS: Chamber music: Number 2, for 12 players, 1965; 5 studies for tuba alone; 5 readings on poems by e. e. cummings, speaker, 3 percussionists, and friend, 1972; Chorus: Song of the masked dancers, on an Apache text, 3-part boys choir and instruments, 1973; Multimedia: Blues and screamer, for blues band and film, 1966; Metamusic, for 5 players, tape, film and slides.
99 Whittridge Rd., Summit, NJ 07901

REED, ALFRED
b. New York, N. Y., 25 Jan. 1921. Studied at Baylor Univ., B. M. 1955, M. M. cum laude 1956; with Vittorio Giannini, Juilliard School; also with Paul Yartin on a 4-year scholarship. He received the Luria prize, 1959; honorary doctorate, Internat. Cons. Lima, Peru, 1968. He was staff composer-arranger, Radio Workshop, New York, 1938-42; U.S. Army Air Force, 1942-46; composer-arranger for radio and television, 1948-53; conductor, Baylor Univ. Symphony Orchestra, 1953-55; editor, Hansen Publications, 1955-66; professor, Univ. of Miami, 1966- ; guest conductor of youth bands, 1966- .
WORKS: Orchestra: Rhapsody for viola and orch., 1959; A festival prelude; Titania's nocturne, string orch.; The pledge of allegiance; In memoriam, an elegy for the fallen; Band: Might and majesty, Biblical suite; Greensleeves, a fantasy; Rahoon, rhapsody for clarinet and band; Song of Threnos; Nordic trilogy; Jubilant overture; Punchinello; Chamber music: 5 dances for clarinets; Scherzo fantastique, contrabass, clarinet, piano; Ballade, alto saxophone and piano; Variations on London Bridge is falling down, brass quintet; Fantasy, woodwind choir; Chorus: The prophecy; Cathedral chorus; Tears, idle tears; A sea dirge; Choric song; more than 200 published works for orchestra, band, chorus, solo and ensemble groups.
1405 Ancona Ave., Coral Gables, FL 33146

REED, H. OWEN
b. Odessa, Mo., 17 June 1910. Studied with Helen Gunderson, Louisiana State Univ., B. M. with distinction 1934, M. M. 1936, B. A. (French) 1937; with Howard Hanson and Bernard Rogers, Eastman School of Music, Ph. D. 1939; with Bohuslav Martinu and Roy Harris. His awards include a Guggenheim fellowship, 1948; Composers Press

(REED, H. OWEN)
symphonic award, 1949; Huntington Hartford Found. fellowship, 1960; Michigan State Univ. Distinguished Faculty award, 1962; George Romney and Greater Michigan Found. citation, 1963; Helene Wurlitzer Found. fellowship, 1967; Michigan State Univ. research grant, 1967; annual ASCAP awards; and many commissions. He has been faculty member, Michigan State Univ., 1939- ; professor and chairman of composition, 1959- .
WORKS: Theatre: The masque of the red death, ballet-pantomime, 1936; Peter Homan's dream, folk-opera in 2 acts, 1955; Earth trapped, Indian spirit legend, chamber opera, 1960; Orchestra: Evangeline, 1938; symphony no. 1, 1939; overture, 1940; Symphonic dance, 1942; cello concerto, 1949; overture for strings, 1961; La fiesta mexicana, orchestra version, 1964; The turning mind, 1968; Band: Spiritual, 1947; Missouri shindig, 1951; Theme and variations, from the Beethoven string quartet, Op. 18, No. 5, 1954; La fiesta mexicana, 1949; Renascence, 1959; Che-Ba-Kun-Ah, Road of souls, band and string quartet, 1959; The touch of the earth, with chorus and soloists, 1971; For the unfortunate, band and tape, 1972; Chamber music: piano sonata, 1934; string quartet, 1937; Scherzo, clarinet and piano, 1947; Wondrous love, tenor and woodwind quintet, 1948; Symphonic dance, piano and woodwind quintet, 1954; Chorus: A psalm of praise, a cappella, 1939; 2 tongue twisters, 1950; Michigan morn, from Peter Homan's dream, 1955; Ripley Ferry, women's voices and wind septet, 1958; A tabernacle for the sun, oratorio for chorus, speaking chorus of men's voices, contralto, and orch., 1963; Living solid face, chorus and chamber ensemble, Cincinnati, 7 Feb. 1975. He is also author of the music text books: A workbook in the fundamentals of music, 1947; Basic music, 1954; Basic music workbook, 1954; co-author of: Basic contrapuntal technique, 1964; Scoring for percussion and the instruments of the percussion section, 1969.
Music Department, Michigan State University East Lansing, MI 48823

REICH, BRUCE
b. Chicago, Ill., 15 Sep. 1948. Studied with Robert Linn and Halsey Stevens at Univ. of Southern California; with Robert Middleton at Harvard Univ.; and with Penderecki at Yale Univ. He received an Epstein Memorial Found. grant, 1961-70; Helen S. Anstead award, 1970; NDEA Title IV fellowship, 1970-73. He was staff member, Univ. of Southern California, 1970-72; 1973- .
WORKS: Chamber music: piano sonata, 1969; string quartet, 1971; Movements for chamber ensemble, 1972; concerto for piano and chamber ensemble, 1973; Chorus: Cantata, with brass and percussion, 1970; Songs: What is man, baritone, 1968; 3 songs for mezzo-soprano, 1969; Songs of time, mezzo-soprano and chamber ensemble, 1973.
1440 Veteran Ave., Los Angeles, CA 90024

REICH, STEVE
b. New York, N. Y., 3 Oct. 1936. Studied at Cornell Univ., B. A. 1957 with honors in

(REICH, STEVE)

philosophy; composition at Juilliard School, 1958-61; with Darius Milhaud and Luciano Berio, Mills Co., M. A. 1963; African drumming in Ghana, 1970; Balinese gamelan in Seattle, 1973. He was awarded an Inst. for Internat. Education grant for study in Ghana, 1970; an invitation by German Academic Exchange Program to be artist-in-residence, 1974; his instrumental ensemble has received grants from New York State Council on the Arts, Nat. Endowment for the Arts, and Martha Baird Rockefeller Fund. He has been composer-performer with his own group, 1966-   .

WORKS: It's gonna rain, tape, 1965; Come out, 1966; Piano phase, 2 pianos, 1967; Violin phase, 4 violins or violin and tape, 1967; Pendulum music, microphones, amplifiers, and speakers, 1968; Four organs, 4 electric organs and maracas, 1970, Boston, 8-9 Oct. 1971; Phase patterns, 4 electric organs, 1970; Drumming, for tuned drums, marimbas, glockenspiels, mixed voices, whistling, and piccolo, 1971; Clapping music, for 2 performers clapping, 1972; 6 pianos, 1973; Music for mallet instruments, voices and organ, commissioned by Radio Bremen, 1973.

423 Broadway, New York, NY 10013

*REICHERT, JAMES A.

b. Toledo, Ohio, 12 May 1932. Studied at Oberlin Cons., B. M. ; Eastman School of Music, M. M.; at Tanglewood. For several years he was music director for CBS-TV: then producer for Gotham Recording Corporation. In 1972 he received an ASCAP award for incidental music to The effect gamma rays on man-on-the-moon marigolds, the 1971 Pulitzer prize play. He has also composed with Tod Dockstader an electronic work, Omniphony I.

REID, JOHN WILLIAM

b. Port Arthur, Tex., 23 Sep. 1946. Studied with Samuel Adler, Eastman School of Music, B. M. 1968; with David Diamond, Philip Batstone, Charles Eakin, Cecil Effinger, Univ. of Colorado, M. M. 1972. He was bassoonist with the NORAD band, 1968-72.

WORKS: Orchestra: Symphonic movements, 1971; Band: Overture; Chamber music: horn sonata; quartet for bassoon and strings; woodwind trios; string quartet; suite for brass; saxophone sonata; movement for clarinet alone; wind octet; 2 woodwind quintets.

Box 4038, Boulder, CO 80302

REIF, PAUL

b. Prague, Czechoslovakia, 23 Mar. 1910; U.S. citizen 1943. Studied with Richard Strauss, conducting with Bruno Walter and Franz Schalk, violin with Erica Morini, Vienna Acad. of Music; at the Sorbonne, Paris, Ph. D. in music history. He received a MacDowell fellowship; 2 American Music Center grants; annual ASCAP awards; and commissions. He served in U.S. Army Intelligence Corps, 1942-45, awarded Croix deGuerre and Purple Heart; has composed for films in Sweden, Austria, France, and the U.S.

WORKS: Opera: Portrait in brownstone, 1965; Mad Hamlet; Curse of the mauvais air, chamber opera; Orchestra: Fanfare and fugato; Philidor's

(REIF, PAUL)

defense, a musical chess game; Birches, tenor and orch., 1965; Eulogy for a friend, string orch. and percussion; Pentagram, piano and orch.; Chamber music: Wind spectrum, woodwind quintet; Banter, flute and piano, 1966; brass quintet, 5 divertimenti for 4 strings; Chorus: Triple City, with brass, 1963; Requiem to war, with percussion, 1963; Letter from a Birmingham jail, Martin Luther King text, 1965; Songs: The circus; 5 finger exercises, text by T. S. Eliot; Monsieur le Pelican, 1960; Reverence for life, 1960; Kaleidoscope, with woodwind quintet, text by composer; 4 songs on words of Kenneth Koch.

57 West 58th St., New York, NY 10019

REILLY, JACK

b. Staten Island, N. Y., 1 Jan. 1932. Studied with Ludmila Ulehla and Nicolas Flagello, Manhattan School of Music, B. M. and M. M. E. 1958; also with Hall Overton, Joseph Maneri, Lennie Tristano, George Russell, and Ali Akbar Khan. He held scholarships at Manhattan School, 1957-58, and with Ali Akbar Khan; was artist-in-residence, Molde School of Music, Norway, 1971. He taught at Berklee Coll. of Music, 1962; was music director, David Frost's TW3, 1965; lectured at schools in U.S., Canada, and Norway; member of the composition grant, Nat. Endowment for the Arts; faculty member, Turtle Bay Music School, 1970-72; New School for Social Research, 1972-   .

WORKS: Orchestra: Suite for orchestra; Allelujah, chorus and orch.; piano concerto; Liturgical jazz: Jazz requiem, chorus, jazz quintet, string orch., New York, 17 Nov. 1968; Mass of involvement; Requiem mass; Rag to raga; Chamber music: string trio; suite for woodwinds; In memoriam-Ben Webster; Rhapsody, piano and jazz trio; Suite for my ladies; Suite for my masters; The light of the soul; Piano: 2 suites; 2 sonatas.

66 West 12th St., New York, NY 10011

*REISER, ALOIS

b. Prague, Czechoslovakia, 4 Apr. 1884. Studied at Prague Cons.; with Antonin Dvorak, Univ. of Prague, D. M. He received the Elizabeth Sprague Coolidge prize, 1918; NBC prize; Pittsburgh Arts Society prize; New York Philharmonic prize. He toured Europe and the U.S. as cellist in the Bohemian Trio; played cello in the Pittsburgh Symphony; conducted at Prague Opera House and the Diaghliev Ballet Russe on its U.S. tour, 1918; conducted at Strand Theatre, New York, 1918-29; then was music director for Warner Bros. in Hollywood. His works include light operas; a symphony; Slavic rhapsody for orch., 1931; cello concerto; 1933; Erewhon for orch., 1936; chamber music and songs.

REPPER, CHARLES

b. Alliance, Ohio, 3 Jan. 1886. Studied with Walter Spalding and William C. Heilman, Harvard Univ., B. A., Phi Beta Kappa. He was composer for the Allegheny Coll. centennial pageant, 1915, and the Lexington, Ky., 150th anniversary pageant, 1925; on editorial staff, Boston Music Company and C. C. Birchard Company, Boston; private piano and theory teacher.

REPPER, CHARLES

(REPPER, CHARLES)
WORKS: Operettas: The dragon of Wu Foo;
Penny buns and roses; Chorus: Candle lights of
Christmas; Far away isles; Flags flying; Gardens
by the sea; It cannot be a strange countree;
Never an end; To a madonna; Songs: Carmencita;
The circle of the keys; In the garden of the
world; Where lilacs blow; many piano pieces.
780 Boylston St., 9K, Boston, MA 02199

*RETI, RUDOLF
b. Uzice, Yugoslavia, 27 Nov. 1885; to U.S. 1938;
d. Montclair, N. J., 7 Feb. 1957. Studied at
Vienna Cons., Ph. D. He was one of the founders
of the Internat. Society for Contemporary Music
at Salzburg, 1922. From 1938 he was pianist and
teacher in Montclair, N. J. He composed an opera,
Ivan and the drum; a ballet-opera, David and
Goliath, 1935; piano concerto, 1948; a string
quartet; piano pieces and songs. He was author
of 2 books: The thematic process in music, 1951;
and Tonality-atonality-pantonality, 1958.

RETZEL, FRANK
b. Detroit, Mich., 11 Aug. 1948. Studied with
Ruth Shaw Wylie, Harold Laudenslager, and James
Hartway, Wayne State Univ., B. M., candidate for
M. M. 1973. He received the Paul Paray award,
1971; Harold Laudenslager award, 1973. He has
been organist and music director, 1971-   ; St.
Dennis Church, Royal Oak, Mich., 1973-   .
WORKS: Chamber music: 2 pieces for piano,
1969; Mobile structures for 5 instruments, 1970;
Cables 87, soprano and 7 instruments, text by
Thomas Merton, 1971; 24 modules, 11 instruments,
1972; Dreams of Aesop, mezzo-soprano and piano,
text by Diane Leigh Vogt, 1973; Laminar flow, 7
instruments and percussion.
12901 East 7-Mile Road, Detroit, MI 48205

*REVICKI, ROBERTO
Random thoughts and Songs of praise, both for
women's chorus.

REX, HARLEY
b. Lehighton, Pa., 29 Mar. 1930. Studied at
Mansfield State Coll., B. S.; with Wallace Berry
and George Burt, Univ. of Michigan, M. M. 1962,
D. M. A. 1971; saxophone with Sigurd Rauscher and
Larry Teal. He was saxophonist and arranger,
U.S. Army Band, 1954-62; professor, Sam Houston
State Univ., 1962-   ; saxophonist, Houston
Symphony Orchestra, 1965-73; conductor, Houston
Municipal Band, 1966-   .
WORKS: Band: Preludio and movendo, saxo-
phone and band; Camminando; Andante and briliante,
saxophone and band; Saxophone rhapsody; Chamber
music: Shenandoah, saxophone quartet; Quartet
#1, Beethoven-Rex, clarinet quartet.
Route 5, Box 243, Huntsville, TX 77340

REYNOLDS, CHARLES HEATH
b. Patterson, La., 5 June 1924. Studied at Univ.
of Southwestern Louisiana; with Helen Gunderson,
Louisiana State Univ. He received awards in
Lafayette Madrigal Singers contest; Louisiana All-
State Band contest, 1967. He is faculty member,
Southwestern Louisiana Univ.

(REYNOLDS, CHARLES HEATH)
WORKS: Orchestra: piano concerto; Band:
Acadiana suite; symphony; Atchafalaya suite; A
quartet of pieces; Songs from an unwritten show;
Piano: In homage to Prokofiev; Variations on a
Lourdes hymn; also pieces for solo wind instru-
ments and piano.
610 Wilson St., Apt. 6
Lafayette, LA 70501

REYNOLDS, ERMA
b. Laurel, Miss., 25 Mar. 1922. Studied with
Donal Michalsky, California State Univ., Fullerton. She is a private teacher.
WORKS: Orchestra: Passacaglia, for string
orch.; No dance, suite for small orch.; Chamber
music: violin sonata; Exile, piano suite for
modern dance; March and lament for brass;
Capricci, clarinet and piano.
710 Casa Blanca Drive, Fullerton, CA 92632

REYNOLDS, GEORGE B.
b. St. Albans, Vt., 23 Dec. 1951. Studied with
Hubert C. Bird, Keene State Coll.
WORKS: Chamber music: Piece for solo clarinet; woodwind quartet; Le cyclope, baritone horn
and piano; Chorus: Shorts from the Bible, sacred
cantata for young voices, organ, and 2 trombones;
Songs: I shall go back, soprano; song set on
selected poems of e. e. cummings, soprano.
R. F. D. #2, Alburg, VT 05440

REYNOLDS, ROGER
b. Detroit, Mich., 18 July 1934. Attended Univ.
of Michigan, B. S. in engineering, 1957; then
studied composition with Ross Lee Finney and
Roberto Gerhard, Univ. of Michigan, M. M. 1961;
also with Gerhard at Tanglewood. His awards
include the Koussevitzky Internat. Recording
award, 1970; Nat. Inst. of Arts and Letters award;
Fulbright, Guggenheim, Rockefeller, and Inst. of
Current World Affairs fellowships. He has been
professor, Univ. of California, San Diego,
1969-
WORKS: Orchestra: The wedge, chamber orch.,
1961; Graffiti, 1964; The lies of the land, 1964;
Quick are the mouths of earth, chamber orch.,
1965; Threshold, 1967; Chamber music: Sky,
cycle on Haiku poems, soprano and instrumental
ensemble, 1960; Acquaintances, flute, doublebass,
piano, 1961; Mosaic, flute and piano, 1962;
Ambages, flute solo, 1965; string quartet; 4
etudes for woodwind quartet; 2 woodwind quintets;
Chorus: The emperor of ice cream, 8 voices, percussion, piano, doublebass, 1962; Masks, with
orch., Herman Melville text, 1965; Blind men,
with brass, percussion, piano, Melville text,
1966; Piano: Epigram and evolution, 1959; Fantasy for pianist, 1964; Electronic: A portrait
of Vanzetti, narrator, winds, percussion, tape,
1963; ...between..., chamber orch. and electronics, 1968; Traces, piano, flute, cello, 6 tapes,
electronics, 1969; I/0, ritual for 23 performers
(9 female vocalists, 9 male mimes, clarinet, 2
flutes, 2 technicians who manipulate and distri-
bute the sound electronically) 1969; Compass,
voices, instruments and electronics; Multimedia:

(REYNOLDS, ROGER)
Ping, instruments, electronics, slides, tapes, 1969.
Music Department
University of California at San Diego
La Jolla, CA 92037

REYNOLDS, VERNE
b. Lyons, Kan., 18 July 1926. Studied at Cincinnati Cons., B. M. 1950; Univ. of Wisconsin, M. M. 1961; Royal Coll. of Music, London, 1953-54. He received a Fulbright grant, 1953; Louisville Orchestra award, 1955; Los Angeles Horn Club award, 1955; ASCAP awards; and commissions. He played horn, Cincinnati Symphony Orchestra, 1947-50; Rochester Philharmonic Orchestra, 1959-68; Eastman Brass Quintet, 1961-   ; was faculty member, Univ. of Wisconsin, 1950-53; Indiana Univ., 1954-59; professor, Eastman School of Music, 1959-   .
WORKS: Orchestra: violin concerto, 1951; Saturday with Venus, overture, 1953; Chamber music: Theme and variations, brass choir; Music for 5 trumpets, 1957; 48 etudes for horn, 1959, transcribed for trumpet, 1970; Short suite for 4 horns; Partita, horn and piano, 1961; flute sonata, 1962; Suite for brass quintet, 1963; 3 elegies, oboe and piano; Serenade, horn and strings, 1966; tuba sonata, 1968; Concertare I, brass quintet and percussion, 1968; Concertare II, trumpet and strings, 1968; Concertare III, woodwind quintet and piano, 1969; horn sonata, 1970; violin sonata, 1970; Concertare IV, brass quintet and piano, 1971; Scenes, winds and percussion, 1971; 4 caprices, clarinet and piano, 1972; piano sonata, 1972; Chorus: The hollow men, baritone, male choir, brass, percussion, 1954.
Eastman School of Music, Rochester, NY 14604

*RHEA, RAYMOND
b. Littleton, Colo., 28 Dec. 1910; d. Texas. Studied at Denver Univ.; Northwestern Univ., B. M., M. M.; Univ. of Texas. He was church choir director and from 1936 a voice teacher in schools.
WORKS: Chorus: She walks in beauty, Byron text; Songs: Let my soul rise in song; Let music fill the skies; Echo noel; Hail our redeemer; O Lord most glorious; With singing heart.

RHOADS, WILLIAM E.
b. Harvey, Ill., 5 Aug. 1918. Studied at Univ. of Michigan, B. M. E. 1941, M. M. E. 1942. He served in the U.S. Army, 1942-46; taught in public schools, 1946-53; was faculty member, Univ. of New Mexico, 1953-73; chairman, music department, 1973-   .
WORKS: Band: Scottish rhapsody; 3 baladas; Puerto Alegre; Mazatlan; Latin elegy; Lament and march; Gentle ballad; Pete's bossa nova; many transcriptions for band and solo wind instruments.
2901 Las Cruces, N.E., Albuquerque, NM 87110

*RHODES, PHILLIP
b. North Carolina, 6 June 1940. Studied with William Klenz and Iain Hamilton at Duke Univ.; with Mel Powell and Donald Martino, Yale Univ. His numerous awards and commissions include a

(RHODES, PHILIP)
Ford Found. grant, 1969, and a $3000 grant, Nat. Inst. of Arts and Letters, 1974. He taught at Amherst Coll.; was professional-in-residence, City of Louisville, 1969; composer-in-residence, Kentucky State Arts Commission, 1972. His compositions include Lament of Michal, soprano and orch.; 3 pieces for band; 3 pieces for unaccompanied cello; Autumn setting, soprano and string quartet, 1969; Kyrie for women's chorus.

RICCI, ROBERT J.
b. New York, N. Y., 25 Apr. 1938. Studied with Donald Keats and David Epstein, Antioch Coll.; with Quincy Porter and Elliott Carter, Yale Univ., M. M.; with Scott Huston and Jeno Tackacs, Univ. of Cincinnati, Coll. Cons., D. M. A. He received the Bradley-Keeler Memorial scholarship, Yale Univ.; NDEA fellowship, Univ. of Cincinnati; Rockefeller Found. commission, 1967; John A. Hoffman composition prize, Univ. of Cincinnati, 1967. He was instructor, Antioch Coll., 1956-57; director of theory, Villa Maria Inst. of Music, Buffalo, 1964-66; lecturer, Univ. of Cincinnati, 1967; associate professor, Western Michigan Univ., 1968-   .
WORKS: Orchestra: symphony; Jazz ensemble: U. B.; Chamber music: string quartet; clarinet sonata; brass trio; woodwind quintet, 1967; 6 bagatelles, piano; trumpet sonata; 2 songs for soprano and piano, 1967. He is co-author with Robert Fink of A lexicon of 20th century music, New York, 1974.
928 Wheaton Ave., Kalamazoo, MI 49008

RICE, DOUGLAS
b. Seattle, Wash., 24 Mar. 1942. Studied with John Cowell and Lockrem Johnson, Cornish School, B. M. 1969. He was instructor, Helen Bush School, 1966-69; Cornish School, 1970, 1973; Bellevue Community Coll., 1969-   ; vice president and editor of guitar publications, Puget Music Publications, Inc., 1971-   .
WORKS: Chamber music: Divertimento no.1, guitar; Sonata concertante, flute and guitar; 2 guitar sonatas; 2 perpetual motions, guitar; Elegy, guitar.
410 East Roy St., Seattle, WA 98102

RICE, THOMAS N.
b. Washington, D.C., 6 Feb. 1933. Studied at Catholic Univ. and at Chapel Hill, N. C. He received a MacDowell fellowship, 1959.
WORKS: Opera: Fully clothed in armor, chamber opera; Orchestra: timpani concerto; violin concerto; overture, 1970; Chamber music: string quartet; Fantasy, clarinet and piano; duo for flutes; brass quintet.
7008 Ocean Front, Virginia Beach, VA 23417

*RICH, GLADYS
b. Philadelphia, Pa., 26 Apr. 1892. Studied at New England Cons.; Univ. of Utah, B. A.; New York Univ., M. A.; with Harvey Gaul and Edward Shippen Barnes. She was public school music supervisor, Newcastle, Pa., 1928-33; music director, State Teachers Coll., Clarion, Pa., 1933-38. She has published several operettas, many cantatas, and songs.

RICHARD, EDMUND

*RICHARD, EDMUND
Hudson River sketches, piano.

*RICHARDS, HOWARD L., JR.
b. Detroit, Mich., 2 Nov. 1927. Studied at Univ.
of Michigan; Rollins Coll., B. A., B. M.; Florida
State Univ., M. M. He wrote musicals in college;
was on the staff of Columbia Records; then
computer-programer for IBM. He has published 2
choral works on texts of James Joyce: Rain and
Who goes among the greenwood.

RICHARDS, STEPHEN
b. New York, N. Y., 9 May 1935. Studied with
Philip James, New York Univ.; with Jack Beeson,
Henry Cowell, and Otto Luening, Columbia Univ.;
with Eric Werner, Hebrew Union Coll. He has
been cantor, Syosset, N. Y., 1968-69; Rochester,
N. Y., 1969-71; Indianapolis Hebrew Congregation,
1971-   ; was music director, United American
Hebrew Congregations Arts Festival, 1971; music
consultant, Hebrew Union Coll., Cincinnati,
1972-   .
    WORKS: Jewish liturgical music: Ki Lekach
Tov; Songs about Passover; Psalms 137, 150, 98;
The ballad of Ruth.
    6731 Woodmere Court, Indianapolis, IN 46260

RICHARDSON, DARRELL ERVIN
b. Columbia, S. C., 17 Sep. 1911. Studied at
Univ. of South Carolina, B. S.; dentistry at
Univ. of Tennessee, D. D. S. 1950; music theory,
violin and trombone as electives, but largely
self-taught in composition. He was commissioned
to compose Carolina Regina for the South Carolina
300th anniversary, 1970. He was arranger and
composer in Hollywood in the 1930s; then after
military service during World War II took up
dentistry.
    WORKS: Orchestra: symphony, 1966; Varia-
tions on a 4-tone melody, 1969; Carolina Regina,
1970; Elegy, string orch., 1972; Chamber music:
Introduction, fugue, and variations, woodwind
quintet, 1969; 2 string quartets; Chorus: Crown
him lord of all; Behold thy son beloved; That
Easter morn; and songs.
    2829 Stratford Road, Columbia, SC 29204

RICHARDSON, LOUIS S.
b. Brooklyn, N. Y., 15 Oct. 1924. Holds a
doctorate in music but is self-taught in composition. He received a State Univ. grant in 1964;
has been associate professor, State Univ. Coll.,
Fredonia, N. Y., 1958-   .
    WORKS: Chamber music: piano sonata; violin
sonata; viola sonata; Theme and variations, cello
and piano; Theme and variations, saxophone and
piano; bassoon sonata; Voice: 4 Elizabethan
songs, a cappella chorus; 3 psalms for baritone
and piano; 4 songs of death, soprano, flute,
viola, and piano.
    401 Chestnut St., Fredonia, NY 14063

RICHARDSON, SHARON
b. Houston, Tex., 3 Aug. 1948. Studied with
Merrill Ellis, North Texas State Univ.
    WORKS: Orchestra: Serenade, viola and orch.;
Band: Fanfare and march; 3 statements for tuba

(RICHARDSON, SHARON)
quartet; many pieces for small ensembles and
solo instruments.
    10910 Gulf Freeway, Apt. 253
    Houston, TX 77034

RICHENS, JAMES W.
b. Memphis, Tenn., 7 Oct. 1936. Studied with
Raymond Haggh, Memphis State Univ.; with Bernard
Rogers, Louis Mennini, Samuel Adler, and Wayne
Barlow, Eastman School of Music, M. M. He was
named 1970 Composer of the Year by the Tennessee
Music Teachers Asso. He was public school
teacher, 1961-65; assistant professor, Memphis
State Univ., 1966-   .
    WORKS: Ballet: Escape to morning; Orches-
tra: Sonambulisms; Portrait of a city, commissioned for 150th anniversary of Memphis; Fanfare
for orchestra; Band: Prelude and dance, clarinet and band; Fantasia on Battle Hymn of the
Republic; Chicano!; Chamber music: piano sonata;
string quartet.
    5665 Buxbriar Ave., Memphis, TN 38101

RICHMOND, THOMAS L.
b. Kalamazoo, Mich., 5 Feb. 1935. Studied at
Western Michigan Univ., B. M. 1957; with H. Owen
Reed, Michigan State Univ., M. M. 1965, Ph. D.
1970. He has been associate professor, Concordia
Coll., Moorhead, Minn., 1967-   .
    WORKS: Orchestra: Portrait, chamber orch.;
Incantation and dance; Orchensem, 1970; Chamber
music: 2 movements, alto saxophone and string
trio; Chorus: A song of praise; Songs: Check,
text by James Stephens.
    1202 South 6th St., Fargo, ND 58102

RICHTER, MARGA
b. Reedsburg, Wis., 21 Oct. 1926. Studied with
William Bergsma and Vincent Persichetti,
Juilliard School, B. S., M. S.; also piano with
Rosalyn Tureck. She has received annual ASCAP
awards, 1966-   ; Nat. Endowment for the Arts
award, 1969; and commissions. She was instructor,
Nassau Community Coll., 1971-73.
    WORKS: Ballet: Abyss, 1964, The servant,
1968, Bird of yearning, all 3 commissioned and
performed by the Harkness Ballet; Orchestra:
Concerto for piano, violas, cellos and basses;
Landscapes of the mind I, piano and orch.;
Lament, string orch.; Aria and toccata, viola
and strings; Variations on a sarabande; 8 pieces;
Chamber music: Suite for violin and piano; Landscapes of the mind II, violin and piano; Suite
for solo viola; Soundings, harpsichord; clarinet
sonata; Passacaglia, organ; string quartet;
Chamber piece, woodwind quartet, viola, cello,
bass; Landscapes of the mind III, piano trio;
Chorus: Psalm 91, a cappella; 3 songs of madness
and death, a cappella; 3 Christmas songs, children's chorus and 2 flutes or piano; Songs:
Transmutation, 8 songs to Chinese texts; 2 Chinese songs; She at his funeral, Hardy text;
Piano: sonata; Fragments; Variations on a theme
by Latimer, piano 4-hands; Melodrama, 2 pianos.
    3 Bayview Lane, Huntington, NY 11743

RICHTER, MARION MORREY
b. Columbus, Ohio, 2 Oct. 1900. Studied at Ohio
State Univ., B. A. Phi Beta Kappa 1921; at
Juilliard School, graduated 1929; Columbia Univ.,
M. A. 1933, Ed. D. 1961. She held fellowships
at Juilliard, 1925-29; citations for work in
American music, 8th U.S. Army in Korea, 1969,
New Jersey Fed. of Music Clubs. She taught piano,
Morrey School, 1917-22; Hechscher Found.,
1923-28; Columbia Teachers Coll. Summer School,
1929-52; Juilliard Summer School, 1934-52; has
toured widely as pianist and lecturer in the
U.S., England, Mexico, the Orient, and Russia.
WORKS: Opera: Distant drums; Orchestra:
The waste land, tone poem after T. S. Eliot;
Band: Timberjack overture; Chamber music:
Sonata for trio, piano trio; Chorus: Sea chant,
women's voices; This is our camp, cantata play
for children; Piano: Prelude on a 12-tone row.
31 Bradford Road, Scarsdale, NY 10583

*RIDDLE, NELSON
b. Oradell, N. J., 1 June 1921. Played with
many noted dance bands then formed his own orchestra. He was music director, Capitol Records,
1951-62, and of Reprise Records, 1963-   ; has
been guest conductor at Hollywood Bowl.
WORKS: Brass ensemble: Cross country suite,
1958; Three-quarter suite, 1962; Theme and variations, 1971.

*RIEGGER, WALLINGFORD
b. Albany, Ga., 29 Apr. 1885; d. New York, N. Y.,
2 Apr. 1961. Studied with Percy Goetschius and
Alwin Schroeder, Inst. for Musical Art, B. M.
1907; then at Berlin Hochschule für Musik. He
received the Paderewski prize, 1922; Coolidge
prize, 1924; honorary D. M., Cincinnati Cons.,
1925; New York Music Critics' Circle award,
1948; membership in Nat. Inst. of Arts and Letters, 1953; Koussevitzky commission, 1953. He
conducted opera and symphony orchestras in Germany, 1915-17; returned to the U.S. and taught
at Drake Univ., 1918-22; Inst. of Musical Art,
1924-25; Ithaca Cons., 1926-28; from 1929 lived
in New York City.
WORKS: Orchestra: American polonaise, 1923;
Rhapsody, 1931; Fantasy and fugue for organ and
orch., 1931; Dichotomy, 1932; Scherzo, 1933;
Passacaglia and fugue; 4 symphonies, 1935, 1946,
1948, 1957; Canon and fugue, 1939; Music for orchestra, 1951; Dance rhythms, 1953; Romanza,
1953; Overture, 1956; Preamble and fugue, 1956;
Quintuple jazz, 1959; Variations, violin and
orch., 1959; Chamber music: La belle dame sans
merci, 4 solo voices and chamber orch., 1924;
Study in sonority, 10 violins or multiples of
10, 1927; Suite for solo flute, 1929; 3 canons,
woodwind quartet, 1930; Divertissement, flute,
harp, cello, 1933; Music for brass choir; woodwind duos; 2 string quartets; Whimsy, cello and
piano; violin sonatina; piano quintet, 1950;
brass nonet, 1951; concerto for piano and woodwind quintet, 1953.

RIEPE, RUSSELL
b. Metropolis, Ill., 23 Feb. 1945. Studied with
Will Gay Bottje, Southern Illinois Univ.; with

(RIEPE, RUSSELL)
Warren Benson, Wayne Barlow, and Samuel Adler,
Eastman School of Music. He received Woodrow
Wilson fellowship, 1967; NDEA Title IV fellowship for study at Eastman School, 1967-70;
Howard Hanson prize, 1972. He was teaching
assistant, Eastman School, 1969-72; assistant
professor, Southwest Texas State Univ.,
1972-   .
WORKS: Orchestra: Child dying, voice and
orch.; Symphonic fantasy; Incidental music for
strings; Chamber music: Divertimento, woodwind
quartet; Chorus: Cancionetas, chamber choir;
Electronic: Les Heures; also multiple-piano
arrangements.
2700 North LBJ Drive, #125
San Marcos, TX 78666

RIETI, VITTORIO
b. Alexandria, Egypt, 28 Jan. 1898, of Italian
parents; U.S. citizen 1944. Studied with
Frugatta, Respighi, and Casella in Italy, but
is largely self-taught. He received the New
York Music Critics award, 1954; Nat. Inst. of
Arts and Letters grant, 1972. He was faculty
member, Peabody Cons., 1948-49; Chicago Musical
Coll., 1950-53; Queens Coll., 1955-60; New York
Coll. of Music, 1960-64.
WORKS: Opera: Don Perlimplin, 1-act, 1944;
The pet shop, 1-act; Ballet: Waltz Academy,
1944; Night shadow; Bacchus and Ariadne, 1948;
Native dancers; Orchestra: 5 symphonies; 3
piano concertos; 2-piano concerto; 2 cello concertos; violin concerto; triple concerto; concerto for harpsichord and chamber orch., New
York, 16 Jan. 1973; Chamber music: 4 string
quartets; octet; piano quartet; harpsichord
sonata, New York, 16 Jan. 1973; Sonata à cinque,
New York, 16 Jan. 1973; piano trio, New York,
18 Jan. 1973 (these performances were in honor
of the composer's 75th birthday); also 2-piano
music, piano pieces, songs, choral music.
1391 Madison Ave., New York, NY 10029

RIGGINS, HERBERT L.
b. Augusta, Ga., 24 Apr. 1948. Studied at Emory
Univ.; with Charles Moon, California State Univ.
at Humboldt, B. A. magna cum laude; with Ronald
Lo Presti, Arizona State Univ., M. M. 1973. He
is instructor, Arizona State Univ., 1973-   .
WORKS: Chamber music: string quartet;
suite for 3 horns; suite for bassoon; Voice:
The silver swan, chorus; 3 haiku, mezzo-soprano
and piano.
Department of Music, Arizona State University
Tempe, AZ 85282

RILEY, ANN MARION
b. New Richmond, Wis., 28 Apr. 1928. Studied
with Nadia Boulanger in Fontainebleau; with
Alexander Tcherepnin in Nice; Jean Catoire in
Paris. She received a composition prize at the
Acad. Internat., Nice, 1961. She was assistant
professor, Scolastica Coll., Duluth, 1958-72;
faculty member, Music Center of Lake County,
Waukegan, Ill., 1973-   .
WORKS: Chamber music: quintet; Piece for
viola and piano; concerto for piano and brass;

RILEY, ANN MARION

(RILEY, ANN MARION)
Creation, song for soprano, clarinet, piano;
Piano: Patterns, 1961; Moon suite.
2727 Westwood Drive, Apt. 3B
Waukegan, IL 60085

RILEY, DENNIS
b. Los Angeles, Calif., 28 May 1943. Studied
with Cecil Effinger and George Crumb, Univ. of
Colorado; with Thomas Fredrickson, Ben Johnston,
and Robert Kelly, Univ. of Illinois; Richard
Hervig and Donald Jenni, Univ. of Iowa. He received BMI awards, 1966, 1967; Joseph Bearns
prize, 1968; President's award, Univ. of Colorado,
1962; Ford Found.-MENC composer fellowship,
1965-67; Creative Arts fellowship, Univ. of
Illinois, 1967-68; Dows fellowship, Univ. of
Iowa, 1969-71; Guggenheim fellowship, 1972-73.
He was music writer, Rocky Mountain News, Denver,
1963-65; composer-in-residence, Rockford, Ill.,
Public Schools, 1965-67; assistant professor,
California State Univ., Fresno, 1971-   .
    WORKS: Orchestra: Theme and variations,
1965; Concertante music III, viola and orch.,
1973; Chamber music: Variations II, string trio,
1967; Concertante music II and III, chamber ensembles, 1970, 1972; Variations III, viola alone,
1972; Chorus: Liebeslied, 1964; Elegy for Sept.
15, 1945, Rilke text, 1965; Cantata II, 1966;
Beata viscera, 1967; Cantata III: Whispers of
heavenly death, 1968; Electronic: The fragility
of the flower unbruised penetrates space, tape,
1970; songs and piano pieces.
    854 West Rialto, Clovis, CA 93612

RILEY, JAMES R.
b. Shreveport, La., 2 Sep. 1938. Studied with
Samuel Adler, North Texas State Univ., M. M.;
with Hunter Johnson and Kent Kennan, Univ. of
Texas, D. M. A. He received 2nd prize, Creative
Writing for Television competition, 1970. He
was instructor, Univ. of Texas, 1965-68; assistant professor, Mississippi State Univ., 1968-70;
associate professor, Wichita State Univ.,
1970-   .
    WORKS: Orchestra: 4 scenes for orchestra;
Wind ensemble: Suite for brass choir; 4 essays
for brass quintet; Chamber music: Textures,
trombone and piano; Dialogue, trumpet and
percussion.
    2716 North Pershing, Wichita, KS 67220

RILEY, JOHN
b. Altoona, Pa., 17 Sep. 1920. Studied with
Wayne Barlow and Bernard Rogers, Eastman School
of Music, B. M. 1951; with Arthur Honegger in
Paris, 1952-53; with Quincy Porter, Yale Univ.,
M. M. 1955. He received a Fulbright grant,
1952; Tamiment award, 1954. He was cellist in
San Antonio Symph., 1947-49, Rochester Phil.,
1949-51, Oklahoma City Symphony, 1951-52; New
Haven Symphony, 1953-62; Connecticut Symphony,
1953-56; has been instructor, Central Connecticut
State Coll., 1971-   .
    WORKS: Orchestra: Rhapsody for cello and
orch., 1951; Apostasy, 1954; Fantasy, oboe and
strings, 1955; Sinfonietta, 1955; Chamber music:
2 string quartets, 1954-1959; Divertimento,

(RILEY, JOHN)
woodwind quintet; Chamber music, song cycle on
text of James Joyce, tenor and piano trio; other
chamber works and songs.
    107 Golf St., Newington, CT 06111

*RILEY, TERRY
b. Colfax, Calif., 25 June 1935. Studied with
Seymour Shifrin, William Denny, Robert Erickson,
Univ. of California, Berkeley, M. A. 1961; also
with Pran Nath in San Francisco and in India,
1970. He has taught at Mills Coll., 1972-   .
    WORKS: Ballet: Genesis 70, 1970; Orchestra:
In C, aleatory piece in C major, 1964; Chamber
music: Spectra for 6 instruments, 1959; string
trio, 1961; Poppy Nogood and the phantom band,
organ, saxophone, percussion, electronic equipment, 1966; Rainbow in curved air, same as above,
1968.
    Department of Music, Mills Coll.
    Oakland, CA 94613

RINEHART, JOHN
b. Pittsburgh, Pa., 17 Mar. 1937. Studied with
Harold Miles, Kent State Univ.; Quincy Porter,
Yale Univ.; Marcel Dick and Donald Erb, Cleveland
Inst. of Music; with Ronald Pellegrino, Ohio
State Univ. He received the first Bloch Memorial
award, ASCAP, 1960; Osburn fellowship, Ohio State
Univ.; Yale scholarship. He taught at Cleveland
Inst. of Music, 1960-63; Heidelberg Coll.,
1963-   .
    WORKS: Chamber music: Capriccio, piano
trio, 1966; Variations, solo cello, 1967; Chorus:
4 odes, 1965; Credo; Piano: sonata, 1959; Suite
for piano, 1960; Electronic: Geomanteia, 4-
channel tape, 1969; Motims, piano and tape, 1973.
    15 South Monroe St., Tiffin, OH 44883

*RINEHART, MARILYN
O Thou who cometh from above, chorus.

*RINGO, JAMES
b. St. Louis, Mo., 4 Mar. 1926. Studied with
Vittorio Giannini and Frederick Jacobi, Juilliard
School, B. S. 1949; with Darius Milhaud and
Olivier Messiaen in Paris; at Mills Coll., M. A.
1951. In 1969 he received the ASCAP-Deems
Taylor award for his writings on music. His
compositions include 5 pieces from Le Trésor
d'Orphée for string orch., 1948; string trio,
1949; sonata for cello alone, 1950; 2 books of
Portraits for piano, 1951, 1954.

*RINKER, ALTON
b. Tekoa, Wash., 20 Dec. 1907. Was a singer
with Paul Whiteman's Rhythm Boys and others.
His compositions include 2 choral works, American poets' suite and Song portrait of birds;
many popular songs.

RIPPER, THEODORE W.
b. Coraopolis, Pa., 1 Aug. 1925. Studied with
Nikolai Lopatnikoff, Carnegie Inst. of Technology, B. F. A. 1947, M. F. A. 1948. He was organist, Univ. of South Dakota, 1948-49; faculty
Carnegie Inst. of Technology, 1949-55; organist,
Atlanta, Ga., 1955-65; First Methodist Church

(RIPPER, THEODORE W.)
Decatur, 1965-   ; instructor, Millikin Univ.,
1967-
   WORKS: Chorus: <u>Now quit your care</u>; <u>I'll
praise my maker</u>; Songs: <u>O love divine</u>; <u>What hast
thou done?</u>; Organ: 3 pieces; <u>Dance/carol</u>; Suite
for organ.
   32 Sickles Drive, Decatur, IL 62521

RITCHIE, TOM VERNON
   b. Lawrenceville, Ill., 3 July 1922. Studied
with Russell H. Miles and J. Robert Kelly, Univ.
of Illinois; with Leo Sowerby in Chicago. He
has held faculty posts at Culver Military Acad.,
1947-48; Midland Coll., 1949-54; Indiana Univ.,
1954-56; Drury Coll., 1956-62; Wichita State
Univ., 1962-65; Northeast Missouri State Univ.,
1965-   .
   WORKS: Chorus: <u>Ode to music</u>, male voices
and instruments; <u>Let us now remember heroes</u>,
with brass and percussion; Songs: 16 art songs
including <u>A Lincoln triptych</u>.
   Northeast Missouri State University
   Kirksville, MO 63501

RIVARD, WILLIAM H.
   b. Lewiston, Idaho, 31 Aug. 1928. Studied with
John Cowell, Leroy Ostransky, Univ. of Puget
Sound; with John Boda and Ernst von Dohnanyi,
Florida State Univ.; with Philip Bezanson and
Richard Hervig, Univ. of Iowa, on a graduate
fellowship. He was instructor, Univ. of Missouri,
1954-56; assistant professor, Northern Arizona
Univ., 1958-59; professor, Central Michigan Univ.,
1959-   .
   WORKS: Orchestra: <u>Concerto-sinfonia</u>, small
orch.; <u>Philosophical hautboy</u>, oboe and strings;
<u>Overture to War of the comedians</u>; Band: <u>Capric-
cio concitato</u>; Wind ensemble: <u>3 Biblical scenes</u>,
brass choir; Chamber music: <u>Arioso and scherzo</u>,
chamber ensemble; trombone sonata.
   Music Department, Central Michigan University
   Mt. Pleasant, MI 48858

RIVERA, RONALD M.
   b. New Orleans, La., 4 Sep. 1949. Studied with
Russell Smith at Louisiana State Univ.; electronic music in Boston and at the Workshop in
New Music, Chocorua, N. H.
   WORKS: Electronic: <u>Piefisher enters the
magic land of Quazoll</u>, 1973.
   48 Brighton Ave., #11, Boston, MA 02134

*RIZO, MARCO
   b. Havana, Cuba, 30 Nov. 1916. Studied with
Pedro San Juan, Nat. Cons. Havana; at Juilliard
School, B. S.; with Castelnuovo-Tedesco, Univ.
of California, Los Angeles; and at Los Angeles
Cons.; received an honorary D. M., Havana Univ.
He is piano soloist and gave a recital of his
own works in Town Hall, New York, in 1940. In
World War II he was in USAF Special Services;
then became arranger and orchestrator for films
in Hollywood.
   WORKS: Orchestra: <u>Broadway concerto</u>, New
York, 14 Jan. 1973; Piano: <u>Spanish suite</u>; <u>Suite
campesina</u>; <u>Toccata-zapateo</u>; many popular songs.

ROBB, JOHN DONALD
   b. Minneapolis, Minn., 12 June 1892. Studied
with Horatio Parker and Paul Hindemith, Yale
Univ., B. A.; with Nadia Boulanger and Darius
Milhaud in Paris; with Milhaud at Mills Coll.,
M. A.; with Roy Harris at Juilliard School. His
awards include a Rockefeller Found. teaching
fellowship in biology in China, 1915; first prize
for a piano composition, Nat. Composers Forum,
Chicago, 1947; annual ASCAP awards, 1960-   ;
commission, St. Louis Symphony Orchestra for his
3rd symphony, 1961; Smith Mundt grant as visiting
professor, Nat. Cons., El Salvador, 1962; Nat.
Endowment for the Arts copying grant, 1968;
$10,000 Rockefeller Found. grant for preparation
of a book on Hispanic Folk Music of New Mexico
and the Southwest, 1970; New Mexico Fed. of
Music Clubs concert of his works, 1970; Albuquerque Music Club concert of his works and John D.
Robb Day proclaimed by City Commission, 19 Feb.
1971. He is a lawyer as well as composer, and
author, and after serving in the U.S. Army in
World War I, he practiced law in New York,
1922-41; appointed professor, head of music
department, and acting dean, Univ. of New Mexico,
1942-45, dean of Coll. of Fine Arts, 1946-57;
professor and dean emeritus, 1957-   .
   WORKS: Theatre: <u>Little Jo</u>, opera, 1947-49;
<u>Delgadina</u>, ballet, 1951; incidental music for
<u>Piers Plowman</u>, 1956; <u>Joy comes to Deadhorse</u>,
musical play, 1956; <u>Dontaro</u>, chamber opera after
the Japanese, 1961; Orchestra: 3 symphonies,
1947, 1952, 1962; piano concerto, 1950; viola
concerto, 1953; <u>Matachines dance</u>, 1956; <u>Free
variations on 2 themes, Recollections of Iran</u>,
1960; <u>Fantasia on Christmas songs from Los
Pastores</u>, guitar and orch., 1964; Chamber music:
2 string quartets, 1932, 1964; 2 violin sonatas,
1936, 1972; violin sonatina, 1936; piano sonata,
1937; Suite for flute and viola, 1938; <u>The lepre-
chauns</u>, violin and piano, 1940; <u>Variations on a
chromatic line</u>, horn and piano, 1957; <u>Miniature
suite</u> for brass, 1963; <u>Little suite</u> for 4 double-
basses, 1965; 2 pieces for guitar solo, 1966;
<u>I am very old tonight</u>, soprano, oboe, piano,
1968; <u>Tears</u>, soprano, oboe, piano, 1971; Chorus:
<u>The palace at Calah</u>, 1954; <u>Bless the Lord</u>, 1963;
<u>Make a joyful noise</u>, 1963; <u>Touchstones of lib-
erty</u>, 1965; Christmas cantata on New Mexican
themes, 1972; many songs and piano pieces: Electronic: <u>Improvisation</u>, 1957; music for <u>Faerie
Queen</u> (KNME-TV), 1958; <u>Spatial serenade</u>, 1965;
<u>4 nature poems</u>, 1965; <u>Fantasy of echoes</u>, 1965;
<u>3 caprichos</u>, 1965; <u>Music for a pantomime</u>, 1965;
<u>Polyrhythmic variations</u>, 1966; <u>Sonatina 1967</u>,
for the unprepared piano, 1967; <u>Rhythmania</u>,
1968; <u>Green mansions</u>, 1968; <u>Transmutations</u>, orch.
and electronic instruments, 1968; <u>The golden hand</u>,
1970; <u>Space odyssey</u>, orch., electronic instruments, 1971; <u>Adagio and toccata</u>, chamber orch.
and tape, 1971; <u>Afterbeats</u>, 2 electronic etudes,
1972.
   2819 Ridgecrest Drive, S.E.
   Albuquerque, NM 87108

ROBBINS, DANIEL
   b. New Orleans, La., 4 Nov. 1947. Studied with
Leon Dallin, Gerald Strang, Ronald Sindelar,

ROBBINS, DANIEL

(ROBBINS, DANIEL)
    California State Univ., Long Beach, B. M. 1970;
with Ramiro Cortes, Ellis Kohs, Robert Linn,
Univ. of Southern California; privately with
Morris Ruger and Miklos Rozsa. He won first
place awards in composition, Southwestern Youth
Music Festival, 1964, 1965, 1968. He was teaching assistant, Long Beach City Coll., 1966-67,
staff member 1974-   ; private teacher,
1968-   .
    WORKS: Orchestra: Movement for violin and
orch., 1966; Suite for orchestra, 1968; Wind ensemble: Piece for brass choir, 1967; Chamber
music: Air for cello and piano, 1964; Suite for
flute and piano, 1965; Richard Cory, voice and
piano, 1965; Theme and variations, string quartet, San Diego, 12 Feb. 1967; cello sonata, 1969;
piano sonata, 1971; woodwind trio, 1972.
    3296 Julian Ave., Long Beach, CA 90808

ROBBINS, DAVID PAUL
    b. New York, N. Y., 18 July 1946. Studied with
Leslie Bassett, George Balch Wilson, Eugene
Kurtz, and Jack Fortner, Univ. of Michigan. He
was assistant professor, Pacific Lutheran Univ.,
1970-73; visiting lecturer, Univ. of Michigan,
1973-74.
    WORKS: Orchestra: Kabop, chamber orch.,
1968; Intersect, 1971; Chamber music: Sport,
theater piece for 10 players, 1969; Biggie,
cello and percussion, 1972; Momentum, brass
quintet and percussion, 1972; Chorus: Fall back
10 yards and contrapunt, with organ and percussion, 1971; John 3:16, choir and tape.
    c/o Pacific Lutheran University
    Takoma, WA 98447

*ROBERTS, EDWIN
    The hunting of the snark, children's opera,
libretto from Lewis Carroll text, New York,
Oct.-Nov. 1971.

ROBERTS, GERTRUD KUENZEL
    b. Hastings, Minn., 23 Aug. 1906. Studied with
Carlyle Scott, Univ. of Minnesota; piano with
many teachers including Julia Elbogen in Vienna.
She has taught piano since 1931; piano and harp-
sichord in Honolulu, 1946-   ; concert pianist
and harpsichordist.
    WORKS: Theatre: background harpsichord
music for Yerma by Lorca; Thieves carnival by
Anouilh; Alice in wonderland by Le Gallienne;
Orchestra: Elegy for John F. Kennedy; harpsi-
chord concerto; Songs: Every man doth dwell;
Yerma's lullaby; Harpsichord: Chaconne; Triptych;
Homage to Couperin; Charlot suite; Passacaille;
Das Kleine Buch der Bilder; Fantasie after Psalm
150; 3 bagatelles; Waltz for 2 harpsichords;
Piano: 12 time-gardens, 12 pieces on different
gardens in Hawaii.
    4723 Moa St., Honolulu, HI 96816

ROBERTS, MYRON J.
    b. San Diego, Calif., 30 Jan. 1912. Studied at
Univ. of Pacific, B. M. 1935; Union Theological
Seminary, M. S. M. 1937. He taught at School of
Sacred Music, Union Theological Seminary, 1937-40;
Union Junior Coll., Roselle, N. J., 1938-40; pro-
fessor, Univ. of Nebraska, 1940-74.

(ROBERTS, MYRON J.)
    WORKS: Chorus: O Lord, we beseech thee;
The storm on Lake Galilee; Organ: Prelude and
trumpetings; Nova; In memoriam; Homage to
Perotin; Dialogue; Five for organ and marimba;
Three for organ and 2 horns.
    School of Music, University of Nebraska
    Lincoln, NB 68508

ROBERTSON, DONNA NAGEY
    b. Indiana, Pa., 16 Nov. 1935. Studied at
Indiana Univ. of Pennsylvania, B. S. 1957; Eastman School of Music, M. M. She received Nat.
Fed. of Music Clubs award for a string quartet,
1960; 3 North Carolina Fed. of Music Clubs
awards, 1964, 1965, 1967. She has been associate
professor, Mars Hill Coll., 1958-   ; editor of
Music Now, 1973-   ; organ recitalist.
    WORKS: Chamber music: Prelude and fugue
for piano; trio for violin, oboe, harpsichord;
Recitation with 5 reflections, trombone and
piano; Nocturne, trombone and tenor; Chorus:
2 motets; No single thing abides, double chorus;
Voice: 4 Gaelic songs.
    Box 223, Mars Hill, NC 28754

ROBERTSON, DUNCAN D.
    b. Huron, S. D., 15 Aug. 1940. Studied with
William Critser, 1954-65. He is a research
engineer.
    WORKS: Chamber music: Divertimento for 9
winds, 1969; Organ: 2 soliloquies, 1969; Prelude, fugue, and epilogue, organ and 2 horns,
1971.
    Box 185, Mellette, SD 57461

ROBERTSON, EDWIN C.
    b. Richmond, Va., 26 Nov. 1938. Studied with
David Davis, Univ. of Virginia; with John Boda,
Florida State Univ. He was choral conductor,
Univ. of Richmond, 1968-69; assistant professor,
Univ. of Montevallo, 1971-   .
    WORKS: Chamber music: piano trio; quartet
for flute, clarinet, marimba, doublebass; movement for brass quintet; Trumpet reflection; Chorus: Sing my fair love good morrow; Golden
slumbers; 2 Psalms for choir and string orch.
    Town and Country Apts. # 10
    Montevallo, AL 35115

ROBERTSON, HUGH STERLING II
    b. New York, N. Y., 19 Jan. 1940; d. Bedford,
N. Y., 15 Nov. 1973. Studied with William Russo
in New York; Richard Hoffmann, Oberlin Cons.;
Henri Dutilleux, Ecole Normale, Paris, License
de composition, 1970; Nadia Boulanger, Paris,
1964-73. His awards include the Biennale in
composition for a violin sonata commissioned and
performed by Orchestra Radio-Tevision Francais,
1969; Lili Boulanger prize, 1971; Prince Pierre
of Monaco award, 1973; first prize in composition, Fontainebleau Cons., 1973. He was the
grandson of Fedor Chaliapin.
    WORKS: Opera: The atheist; Orchestra:
symphony; Chamber music: trio, clarinet, viola,
piano; piano trio; string quartet; quintet for
winds, strings, harp; quintet for winds and
strings; harp quintet; saxophone quintet; organ

(ROBERTSON, HUGH STERLING, II)
sextet; guitar sonata; Divertimento for guitar and cello; Chorus: 2 Baptist Masses; Cantata, with soloists and orch.; Songs: Ode for Ben Jonson, tenor, 1962; Epitaph on an army of mercenaries, tenor, 1967; Recitative on King Richard II, baritone; Spring from Love's labour's lost, baritone; Curfew, mezzo soprano and chamber orch.; Mais ces oiseaux, tenor and chamber orch.; Piano: Waltz; Etude; 3 pieces; sonata for 2 pianos; Wedding prelude; Variations; harpsichord suite; Film score: The wheel of ashes (Peter Goldman).

*ROBERTSON, LEROY
b. Fountain Green, Utah, 21 Dec. 1896; d. Salt Lake City, Utah, 25 July 1971. Studied with George Chadwick and Frederick Converse, New England Cons., diploma 1923; with Carl Busch, Ernest Bloch, Hugo Leichtentritt and Ernst Toch in Europe; at Univ. of Utah, M. A. 1932; Univ. of Southern California, Ph. D. 1954. His awards included the Endicott prize, 1923; Society for Publication of American Music award, 1936; New York Music Critics Circle awards, 1944; Utah Inst. of Fine Arts prize, 1945; and the Reichold award of $25,000, 1947. He was professor and chairman, music department, Brigham Young Univ., 1925-48; professor and chairman, music department, Univ. of Utah, 1948-62.
WORKS: Orchestra: Overture Emin, 1923; Prelude, scherzo, ricercare, 1940; Rhapsody, piano and orch., 1944; Punch and Judy, overture, 1945; Trilogy, 1947; violin concerto, 1948; cello concerto; piano concerto, 1966; Chamber music: piano quintet, 1938; string quartet, 1940; American serenade, string quartet, 1944; Fantasia, organ; Chorus: The Book of Mormon, oratorio, 1953; Come, come, ye saints; Hatikva; From the crossroads; The Lord's prayer.

ROBINSON, EARL
b. Seattle, Wash., 2 July 1910. Studied at Univ. of Washington, B. M. 1933; and with Aaron Copland. He received a Guggenheim fellowship, 1940. He wrote incidental music for plays in the Federal Theatre in New York, 1934; has been recitalist throughout the U.S. and Europe; since 1943 has lived in California.
WORKS: Theatre: Sandhog, folk opera; Ballet: Bouquet for Molly; Band: Soul rhythms; Cantatas: Ballad for Americans, 1939; Battle hymn; The lonesome train; Tower of Babel; The town crier; In the folded and quiet yesterdays, with narrator and orch.; Preamble to peace; Film scores: California; A walk in the sun; The romance of Rosy Ridge; Man from Texas; The Roosevelt story.
3937 Bledsoe, Los Angeles, CA 90066

*ROBINSON, KEITH
Visions, the quaint and triumphant, trumpet, New York, 11 Dec. 1971.
135 East 17th St., New York, NY 10003

ROBINSON, RICHARD
b. Chicago, Ill., 12 July 1923. Studied with Leo Sowerby, American Cons.; with Karel Husa and Robert Palmer, Cornell Univ. He received the

(ROBINSON, RICHARD)
Georgia Composers award, 1953; Piedmont Arts Festival award, 1967; was co-winner, first prize, Dartmouth Internat. Electronic Music competition, 1970. He was violinist, Atlanta Symphony Orchestra, 1952-73; director, Atlanta Electronic Music Center, 1968- ; program director, Ambience, a weekly electronic music program WREK-FM, Atlanta, 1971-72.
WORKS: Orchestra: 3 haiku for soprano and orch., 1967; Chamber music: woodwind trio, 1953; Electronic: Ambience, Mosaic, quadrasonic electronic piece, 1972; Alea, 1971; Voices, 1973.
3065 Brook Drive, Decatur, GA 30033

ROCHBERG, GEORGE
b. Paterson, N. J., 5 July 1919. Studied at Montclair State Teachers Coll.; Univ. of Pennsylvania, M. A.; Mannes School of Music; with Rosario Scalero, Curtis Inst. His many awards include Gershwin award, 1952; 2 Guggenheim awards; Fulbright fellowship; American Acad. in Rome fellowship; Prix d'Italia; ISCM Internat. Chamber Music award; Naumberg Chamber Music award; Nat. Endowment for the Arts grant; and commissions. He taught at Curtis Inst., 1948-54; was publications director, Theodore Presser Company, 1951-60; professor, Univ. of Pennsylvania, 1960- , chairman, music department, 1960-68.
WORKS: Orchestra: Night music, 1949; 3 symphonies, #1 1949-55, #2 1958, #3 for soloists, chamber chorus, double chorus, orch., New York, 24 Nov. 1970; Sinfonia fantasia, 1956; Waltz serenade; Time-span, 1960; Imago mundi, commissioned by Baltimore Symphony, Baltimore, 8 May 1974; violin concerto, commissioned by the Pittsburgh Symphony, premiere, 4 Apr. 1975; Band: Apocalyptica; Wind ensemble: Black sounds; Chamber music: Dialogues, clarinet and piano; 3 string quartets; piano trio; Serenata d'estate, chamber ensemble; La bocca della verita, violin or oboe and piano; Caprice variations, violin solo; 12 bagatelles, piano, 1952; 2 piano sonatas; Fantasia, violin and piano, 1955; Duo concertante, violin and cello, 1955-59; clarinet sonata, 1958; Contra mortem et tempus, flute, clarinet, viola, piano, 1965; Tableaux, soprano and 11 players, 1968; Electrikaleidoscope, New York, 19 Dec. 1972; Songs: 4 songs of Solomon, soprano; William Blake songs, soprano and chamber ensemble; 11 songs with text by Paul Rochberg, for mezzo soprano; also choral works and piano pieces. He is author of the book: The hexachord and its relations to the 12-tone row, 1955.
285 Aronimink Drive, Newton Square, PA 19073

*ROCHEROLLE, EUGENIE R.
Pastorale and parade, band.

RODBY, JOHN LEONARD
b. Wahiawa, Oahu, Hawaii, 14 Sep. 1944. Studied with Leonard Berkowitz and Aurelio de la Vega, California State Univ., Northridge, B. A. 1966; privately with Albert Harris and Donal Michalsky. He was pianist with Si Zentner Orch., 1963, Don Ellis Orch., 1967; musical director, Dinah Shore, 1968- , Tiny Tim, 1968-70, Dinah Shore TV

RODBY, JOHN LEONARD

(RODBY, JOHN LEONARD)
Show, 1970 and 1973-   , Burl Ives TV Special,
1972, Burt Reynolds TV Special, 1973.
WORKS: Orchestra: Variations for orch.,
1969; Festivals, 1970; saxophone concerto, 1971;
Concerto for 29, 1973; Chamber music: alto saxophone sonata, 1965; quintet for piano, viola,
horn, clarinet, cello, 1966; quintet for clarinet, cello, viola, guitar, celeste, 1972; Chorus:
Chorale, 1964; 3 poems by R. J. Foster, choir
and piano, 1967; Piano: sonata in 1 movement,
1968; 5 etudes, 1970.
5351 Penfield Ave., Woodland Hills, CA 91364

RODBY, WALTER
b. Virginia, Minn., 7 Sep. 1917. Studied at
Northern Iowa Univ., B. A. 1940; Teachers Coll.,
Columbia Univ., M. A. 1947; Trinity Coll. of
Music, London, 1946. He was director of vocal
music in public schools, Moville, Iowa, 1941-42;
Joliet, Ill., 1948-49; chairman, Division of
Fine Arts, Flossmoor, Ill., 1959-73. He led the
Homewood-Flossmoor High School Choir on a concert
tour of Europe and the Soviet Union, 1970, of
Europe, 1973. Since 1953, he has been choral
editor and written a monthly column for The
School Musician Magazine.
WORKS: Chorus: more than 125 published
choral compositions and arrangements.
819 Buell Ave., Joliet, IL 60435

*RODER, MILAN
b. Osijek, Slavonia, 5 Dec. 1878; U.S. citizen
1920; d. Hollywood, Calif., 23 Jan. 1956. Studied at the Vienna Cons.; was opera, operetta,
and orchestra conductor in Europe; from 1914 a
film composer in Hollywood.
WORKS: Opera: Jelka; Round the world,
comic opera; Orchestra: 4 symphonic sketches;
Rondo capriccioso; Moto perpetuo; Vindobona,
suite; also piano pieces; songs.

*RODGERS, JOHN
b. Bonham, Tex., 24 Mar. 1917. Studied at
Southern Methodist Univ., B. M.; North Texas
State Univ., M. M.; Union Theological Seminary,
M. S. M. He was organist, choir director, and
teacher; editor, H. W. Gray Company.
WORKS: Chorus: A little carol; Of the
Father's love begotten; Oh praise the Lord; The
sky can still remember.

*RODGERS, MARY
b. New York, N. Y., 11 Jan. 1931. Daughter of
Richard Rodgers, studied at Wellesley Coll.
WORKS: Theatre: Davy Jones locker, for a
marionette show; Feathertop, television score;
3 to make music; Once upon a mattress; The mad
show; Albums for children: Children's introduction to jazz; Some of my best friends are children; Ali Baba.
115 Central Park West, New York, NY 10023

*RODGERS, RICHARD
b. Hammels Station, Long Island, N. Y., 28 June
1902. Studied at Columbia Univ. and Juilliard.
His many awards include 7 honorary doctorates;
special Pulitzer award for Oklahoma, 1944;

(RODGERS, RICHARD)
Donaldson award for Carousel, 1945, Allegro,
1948, South Pacific 1949, Pal Joey, 1952;
Pulitzer prize for South Pacific, 1950;
Antoinette Perry award for South Pacific, 1950,
The king and I, 1952, No strings, 1962; Columbia
medal of excellence, 1949; Columbia Coll. award,
1952; Columbia's Alexander Hamilton medal, 1956;
Christopher award for The king and I, 1956;
Emmy award for Winston Churchill: The valiant
years, 1962; U.S. Navy distinguished public service award for the score to the film, Victory at
sea, 1953; membership in the Nat. Inst. of Arts
and Letters; and a Salute to Richard Rodgers,
Imperial Theatre, New York, Mar. 1972. Among
his other highly successful musicals were: The
girl friend, 1926; A Connecticut Yankee, 1927;
On your toes, 1936; Babes in arms, 1937; I married an angel, 1938; The boys from Syracuse,
1938; By Jupiter, 1942; Me and Juliet, 1953;
Pipe dream, 1955; The flower drum song, 1958.

RODRIGUEZ, ROBERT XAVIER
b. San Antonio, Tex., 28 June 1946. Studied
with Kent Kennan and Hunter Johnson, Univ. of
Texas, B. M. 1967, M. M. 1969; with Nadia
Boulanger at Fontainebleau; with Halsey Stevens
and Frederick Lesemann, Univ. of Southern California, D. M. A. 1974. His awards include
Brackenridge scholarship, 1964, 1965; Phi Mu
Alpha scholarship, 1965; Julia Klumpke scholarship, Cons. Americaine, 1969, 1970; 3 Alchin
scholarships, 1969-71; Young Musicians Found.
award, 1970; McHugh award, 1971; Prince Pierre
de Monaco composition award, 1971; 2 Rockefeller
performance grants, 1967, 1968; Nat. Endowment
for the Arts grant, 1973. He was instructor,
Univ. of Texas, 1968-69; instructor, Univ. of
Southern California, 1970-   .
WORKS: Orchestra: Adagio for small orch.,
1967; piano concerto, 1968; Lyric variations,
oboe, 2 horns, string orch., 1970; Canto, soprano, tenor, piano, orch., 1973; Favola concertante, concerto for violin and cello, based
on story of Psyche and Eros, Los Angeles, 14
June 1975; Chamber music: 2 piano trios, 1970,
1971; saxophone sonata in 1 movement, 1973;
Chorus: 2 Latin motets, 1969; Cantata on texts
from Isaiah, soloists, chorus, orch., 1972.
Raymondale Drive, 325-G
South Pasadena, CA 91030

ROFF, JOSEPH
b. Turin, Italy, 26 Dec. 1910; U.S. citizen 1964.
Studied with Healy Willan, Leo Smith, Ernest
MacMillan, Univ. of Toronto, B. M., M. A., D. M.
1948. He is a fellow of Trinity Coll., London,
England; received ASCAP awards, 1972, 1973. He
is composer-in-residence and lecturer, St.
Joseph's Coll., Brooklyn, N. Y.
WORKS: Operetta: Lady of Mexico, 1963;
Orchestra: Niagara; 3 fragments for strings;
Reverie; Chorus: more than 700 published works
for church and school choirs.
101 Greene Ave., Brooklyn, NY 11238

*ROGERS, BERNARD
b. New York, N. Y., 4 Feb. 1893; d. Rochester,
N. Y., 24 May 1968. Studied with Percy
Goetschius, Inst. of Musical Art, 1919-21; with
Ernest Bloch in Cleveland; Nadia Boulanger in
Paris; and Frank Bridge in London. His honors
include the Loeb prize, 1920; Pulitzer fellow-
ship, 1921; Guggenheim fellowship, 1927-29;
David Bispham medal 1931; Juilliard commission,
1947; Ditson prize, 1948; commissions from
Koussevitzky Found. and Louisville Orch.;
Fulbright grant, 1953; honorary doctorates, 1959,
1962; Ford Found. grant, 1960; Lillian B.
Fairchild award, 1962; commissions from Methodist
Youth Conf., 1963; American Wind Symphony, 1964;
membership in Nat. Inst. of Arts and Letters.
From 1929 he was on the faculty of the Eastman
School of Music.
    WORKS: Opera: The marriage of Aude, 1931;
The warrior, 1947; The veil, 1950; Ballet: The
colors of war, 1939; Orchestra: The faithful,
1918; To the fallen, 1919; Adonais, 1927; Prelude to Hamlet, 1928; 4 symphonies, 19--, 1930,
1937, 1948; 3 Japanese dances, 1933; 5 fairy
tales, 1935; The supper at Emmaus, 1937; Fantasy,
flute, viola and orch., 1938; Soliloquy, bassoon
and strings, 1938; The song of the nightingale,
1940; The dance of Salome, 1940; The plains,
1941; Invasion, 1943; Characters from Hans
Christian Andersen, 1945; In memory of Franklin
Delano Roosevelt, 1946; Amphitryon, overture,
1947; Leaves from the tale of Pinocchio, 1950;
The silver world, flute, oboe, strings, 1950;
Dance scenes, 1953; Variations on a song by
Moussorgsky, 1960; Apparitions; Chorus: The
raising of Lazarus, with soloists and orch., 1928;
The exodus, sacred poem, with soloists and orch.,
1932; The passion, oratorio, 1944; Light of man,
oratorio, 1964; Dirge for 2 veterans, Whitman
text; Psalm 114; also chamber music.

ROGERS, EARL. See ROSENBERG, EMANUEL

*ROGERS, EDDY
b. Norfolk, Va., 23 Sep. 1907; d. Denver, Colo.,
8 Oct. 1964. Studied at Royal Cons., Naples,
Italy, A. M., D. M.: and with Rubin Goldmark.
He was concert violinist in the U.S. and Europe;
staff conductor, NBC, New York.
    WORKS: Opera: Nella: Orchestra: Impromptu
for moderns; Town and country dance; Commodore
Maury march; Chamber music: Andante appassionato,
string quintet; and songs.

ROGERS, ETHEL TENCH
b. Newark, N. J., 21 Feb. 1914. Studied piano
and organ privately. She taught piano and organ
in Plainfield, N. J. and was church music director; has also taught piano and organ classes,
Univ. of Missouri, Kansas City.
    WORKS: Chorus: 4 cantatas; 150 anthems;
Keyboard: 62 books of organ pieces, for piano
and organ, piano solo, and 2 pianos.
    5700 Reinhardt Drive
    Shawnee Mission, KS 66205

ROGERS, JOHN E.
b. Dallas, Tex., 20 Feb. 1938. Studied at Univ.
of Georgia; with Halsey Stevens and Elliott
Carter, Yale Univ.; with Roger Sessions and
Milton Babbitt, Princeton Univ., M. M. 1964.
His awards include BMI student awards; Composers
Forum performance, New York. He was instructor,
Bowdoin Coll., 1964-67; assistant professor,
1967-72, associate professor and director of
electronic music studio, Univ. of New Hampshire,
1972-   .
    WORKS: Chamber music: Rotational arrays,
woodwind quintet; trio for flute, cello, piano;
Electronic: Electronic study; Canonic struc-
tures (computer generated sound).
    7 Bartlett Road, Durham, NH 03824

ROGERS, SUSAN WHIPPLE
b. Dallas, Tex., 15 Aug. 1943. Studied with
Lloyd Taliaferro, Univ. of Texas, Arlington;
with Rule Beasley, Centenary Coll. of Louisiana;
privately with Edward Kozak. She held scholarships for study at Univ. of Texas and Centenary
Coll. She has been a private horn instructor,
1960-   ; arranger for publishers, 1970-72.
    WORKS: Chamber music: Suite for horn and
piano; trio for horn, clarinet, piano; Pentatonic
suite for piano.
    1600 San Saba, Bossier City, LA 71010

*ROGERS, WILLIAM KEITH
6 short preludes on a tone row, piano.

*ROHE, ROBERT KENNETH
b. New York, N. Y., 22 Aug. 1916. Studied at
Cooper Union School of Fine Arts; bass with
Fred Zimmerman. He played bass with the Nat.
Orch. Asso., under Leon Barzin; with the New
York City Center Orch.; NBC Symphony; New Orleans
Philharmonic, 1944-   , assistant conductor,
1961-   ; instructor at Loyola Univ. His com-
positions include a ballet, Land of bottle; and
Mainescape for orch., 1966.

*ROHLIG, HARALD
Has published many works for organ.
    Huntingdon Coll., Montgomery, AL 36106

ROLLIN, ROBERT
b. New York, N. Y., 16 Feb. 1947. Studied with
Mark Brunswick, City Coll. of New York; with
Robert Palmer, Karel Husa, Elliott Carter,
Cornell Univ.; with Donald Erb and Mario
Davidovsky at Bennington, Vt. He received the
Lado award, 1968; Rockefeller grant, 1972;
Cornell Univ. Faculty research grant, 1972. He
was director, Ithaca Civic Opera, 1970-71;
assistant professor, and resident composer,
Otterbein Coll., 1972-73; assistant professor,
North Central Coll., 1973-   .
    WORKS: Orchestra: 7 sound images; Band:
Aquarelles, commissioned by Cornell Wind Ensem-
ble; Chamber music: 2 pieces for solo flute;
Thematic transformation for string quartet.
    322 East Van Buren Ave.
    Naperville, IL 60540

ROMBERG, SIGMUND

*ROMBERG, SIGMUND
b. Szeged, Hungary, 29 July 1887; U.S. citizen 1912; d. New York, N. Y., 9 Nov. 1951. Studied engineering in Bucharest; then music with Joseph Heuberger in Vienna. He was a cafe pianist in New York; staff composer for the Schuberts, 1913-19, 1921-24; composed more than 70 operettas.
WORKS: Operettas: The blue paradise; Maytime; Monte Cristo, Jr.; Blossom time; The rose of Stamboul; The student prince; The desert song; My Maryland; The new moon; Up in Central Park; also many songs and film scores.

ROMITI, RICHARD A.
b. Woonsocket, R. I., 6 Sep. 1940. Studied with Hugo Norden, John Goodman, and Gardner Read, Boston Univ. He won an undergraduate award in composition, 1971.
WORKS: Orchestra: Concerto for accordion and chamber orch.; Chamber music: Permutations, accordion; 4 pieces for accordion; string quartet; Fantasy for flute and piano. The composer says the accordion works are for instruments with a chromatic free-bass button, left-hand system.
563 Pulaski Blvd., Bellingham, MA 02019

RONSHEIN, JOHN
b. Cadiz, Ohio, 17 Feb. 1927. Studied with Francis Judd Cooke, New England Cons.; with Luigi Dallapiccola in Florence, Italy. He received the Dows award at the Univ. of Iowa. He was faculty member, Newton Junior Coll., 1965-66; New England Cons., 1966-67; assistant to associate professor, Antioch Coll., 1967-   .
WORKS: Songs: Easter-wings, 1964, and Bitter-sweet, 1969, both on texts from George Herbert's The Temple (1633), for mezzo-soprano and vibraphone.
313 Pleasant St., Yellow Springs, OH 45387

ROOBENIAN, AMBER. See HARRINGTON, AMBER ROOBENIAN

ROREM, NED
b. Richmond, Ind., 23 Oct. 1923. Studied at Curtis Inst.; at Tanglewood, 1946, 1947; with Bernard Wagenaar at Juilliard, M. S. 1948; privately with Virgil Thomson. His awards include the Gershwin Memorial prize, 1948; Fulbright fellowship, 1951; Guggenheim fellowship, 1957; Nat. Inst. of Arts and Letters grant, 1968; Lili Boulanger prize; Prix de Biarritz; Eurydice Choral prize; commissions from Ford Found., 1962; Lincoln Center, 1965; Koussevitzky Found., 1966; New York City Opera Company, 1965. He lived in Paris, 1949-58; was composer-in-residence, Univ. of Buffalo, 1959-60; Univ. of Utah, 1966.
WORKS: Opera: A childhood miracle, 1952; The robbers, text by composer; Miss Julie, 1965; Bertha, 1-act, 1968; 3 sisters who are not sisters, 1-act, 1969; Fables, 4 very short operas, 1970; Orchestra: Absalom, voice and orch., 1947; 3 piano concertos, 1948, 1950, 1969; 6 Irish poems, voice and orch., 1950; Lento for strings, 1950; 3 symphonies, 1950, 1955, 1958; Design for orchestra, 1953; 6 songs for high voice and orch., 1953; Poèmes pour la paix, voice and orch., 1956; Sinfonia for winds, 1957; Pilgrims, string orch., 1958; Eagles, 1958; Ideas for easy orchestra,

(ROREM, NED)
1961; Lions, 1963; Water music for violin, clarinet and orch., 1966; Sun, soprano and orch., 1967; Chamber music: Mourning scene from Samuel, voice and string quartet, 1947; 2 string quartets, 1947, 1950; violin sonata, 1949; Mountain song, piano trio, 1949; Sicilienne, 2 pianos, 4-hands, 1950; 4 dialogues for 2 voices and 2 pianos, 1954; 11 studies for 11 players, 1960; trio for flute, cello and piano, 1960; Lovers - A narrative in 10 scenes, harpsichord, oboe, cello, percussion, 1964; Some trees, soprano, mezzo, bass-baritone, piano, 1968; Gloria, soprano, mezzo, piano, 1970; Ariel, soprano, clarinet, piano, 1971; Day music, piano and violin, 1971; Night music, violin and piano, 1972; Last poems of Wallace Stevens, soprano, cello, piano, 1973; Solemn prelude, 11 brass, 1973; Chorus: 2 Psalms and a proverb, with string quartet, 1963; Lift up your heads, with brass quartet, 1963; Laudemus tempus actum, with orch., 1964; Letters from Paris, with orch., 1966; Canticle of the Lamb, 1971; Canticles, Set I and Set II, 1971-72; 3 motets, 1973; Little prayers, soprano, bass, chorus and orch., Sioux Falls, S. D., 20 Apr. 1974; Song cycles: 3 incantations from a marionette tale, 1948; Flight for heaven, 1950; Cycle of holy songs, 1950; King Midas, a cantata in 10 scenes, 1961; Poems of love and the rain, 1963; Hearing, 1966; War scenes, 1969; some 50 more published songs and 125 unpublished songs; more choral works, keyboard works. He is author of the books: The Paris diary, 1966; New York diary, 1967; Music from inside out, 1967; Music and people, 1968; Critical affairs, a composer's journal, 1970; received ASCAP-Deems Taylor award, 1971.
c/o Boosey and Hawkes
30 West 57th St., New York, NY 10019

ROSE, GRIFFITH W.
b. Los Angeles, Calif., 18 Jan. 1936. Studied with Isadore Freed, Hartt Coll. of Music; with David Kraehenbuehl, Yale Univ.; Nadia Boulanger at Fontainebleau; Wolfgang Fortner and Karlheinz Stockhausen in Germany; and Pierre Boulez in Basel.
WORKS: Chamber music: Salpinx, trumpet and 2 pianos, 1961, New York, 27 Sep. 1966; Complaintes, 2 texts by Jules Laforgue, for soprano, chamber ensemble, Freiburg, Germany, 6 Dec. 1964; Bluebeard, baritone, brass sextet, string quartet, Atlanta, Ga., 17 Feb. 1968; Crescendo, interlude, and 5 variations, for 11 brasses, string quartet, 2 pianos, Atlanta, Ga., 3 Mar. 1973; Concerto for viola and chamber ensemble, New York, 11 May 1974, commissioned by and performed under auspices of Composers Theatre.
Domaine de la Licorne, Route de Toulon
83170-Brignoles, France

ROSEN, JEROME
b. Boston, Mass., 23 July 1921. Studied with William Denny and Roger Sessions, Univ. of California at Berkeley; with Darius Milhaud in Paris, 1949-51. He received a Guggenheim fellowship; Fromm Found. award; Ladd prize; San Francisco Composers Forum award. He was instructor, Univ.

(ROSEN, JEROME)
of California, Berkeley, 1951-52; instructor through professor, Univ. of California at Davis, 1952- .

WORKS: Opera: Calisto and Melibea; Orchestra: saxophone concerto; clarinet concerto; Chamber music: string quartet; sonata for clarinet and cello; Elegy for solo percussion; Petite suite, clarinet quartet; 5 pieces for violin and piano; Chorus: 3 songs for chorus and piano.

Department of Music
University of California, Davis, CA 95616

ROSENBERG, EMANUEL (Earl Rogers)
b. New York, N. Y., 2 Apr. 1910. Studied composition with Herbert Elwell, Normand Lockwood, and Max Helfman. He won the Stockbridge School competition with a choral piece, 1955. He has taught voice and allied subjects, Cleveland Inst. of Music, Juilliard Summer and Extension School, YMHA Music School, New York, Queens Coll.

WORKS: Chorus: The night; O Lord of lords; Hail and farewell; From the Psalms; Evening song; 2 Friday Evening Services; Songs: The complete misanthropist; also folksong arrangements and children's songs.

920 Riverside Drive, New York, NY 10032

ROSENBOOM, DAVID
b. Fairfield, Iowa, 9 Sep. 1947. Plays piano, violin, viola, trumpet, drums; studied composition with Gordon Binkerd and Salvatore Martirano, electronic and computer music with Lejaren Hiller, Univ. of Illinois; experimental psychology, New York Univ. He was Edmund J. James scholar, Univ. of Illinois; received a Rockefeller fellowship, 1967; commissions from New Percussion Quartet; Drama Department, State Univ. of New York, Buffalo; New York State Council on the Arts; Columbia Univ.; Electric Circus Found.; Biome; York Univ.; The Canada Council; Electric Stereopticon. He was creative associate, Centre for Creative and Performing Arts, SUNY, Buffalo, 1967; artistic coordinator for Electric Ear series in mixed media, Electric Circus, New York, 1968-69; president and co-founder, Neurona Company, New York, an R&D firm that developed new techniques for electronic music synthesis, 1969; lecturer, 1968, coordinator for computer and electronic media, 1970, graduate research assistant, 1971, New York Univ.; consultant to Nippon-Gakki Company, Tokyo, New York City Board of Education, and American Asso. for the Advancement of Science, 1971; affiliate producer, David Lucas Associates, Inc., 1972-   ; assistant professor, director, Electronic Media Studios and Laboratory of Experimental Aesthetics, coordinator, Division of Interdisciplinary Studies, York Univ., 1972-   . His research in Toronto has resulted in new methods of relating brain activity to investigations of aesthetics, several advances in the electronic technology involved, and to the development of a new curriculum of studies in these fields. He is author of many papers on research on alpha brain waves and biofeedback.

WORKS: Orchestra: Contrasts, violin and orch., 1963; Caliban upon Setebos, 1966; Chamber music: septet for strings, brass, piano, 1964;

(ROSENBOOM, DAVID)
sextet, bassoon, flute, string quartet, 1965; trio for clarinet, trumpet, string bass, 1966; Pocket pieces, flute, viola, alto saxophone, percussion, 1967; Multimedia: The thud, thud, thud of suffocating blackness, instruments, tape, lights, slides, 1966-67; Urbouri, tape and film, 1968; And come up dripping, oboe and computer, 1968; How much better if Plymouth Rock had landed on the pilgrims, instruments and electronics, 72 hours long, of which 18 hours have been performed in a New York loft, 1969; Biofeedback techniques with audience participation: Ecology of the skin, 1970; Homuncular homophony; Portable gold and philosophers' stones. Mr. Rosenboom writes: "The coming decades will see the rise of communal art and the making of more meaningful relationships among man, his natural environment, and the entire energy-information web. Cybernetics and the theory of systems will manifest themselves in rituals concerned with organisms and their information and energy exchanges with the environment."

Department of Music, York University
Downsview, Ontario, Canada

*ROSENMAN, LEONARD
b. Brooklyn, N. Y., 7 Sep. 1924. Studied with Roger Sessions, Luigi Dallapiccola, and Arnold Schoenberg; held the Crofts fellowship for study at Tanglewood.

WORKS: Orchestra: violin concerto; concertino, piano and winds; Foci for 3 orchestras; Threnody on a song of K. R., a set of variations on a melody written by his wife, 1971; Chamber music: piano sonata; 6 Lorca songs; Film scores: East of Eden; Cobweb; Rebel without a cause; Edge of the city; The Chapman report; The savage eye.

23160 Mariposa de Oro St., Malibu, CA 90265

ROSENTHAL, DAVID
b. Berkeley, Calif., 4 Sep. 1952. Studied with Thomas Simons, New York; with Leonard Stein, Los Angeles. He was teaching assistant, California Inst. of the Arts, 1972-74.

WORKS: Chamber music: Music for flute and 3 percussionists, 1971; Music for piano and percussion, 1972; quintet for flute, trumpet, contrabass, percussion, 1972; quartet, flute, piano, percussion, 1973.

Route 3, Box 124D, Saugus, CA 91350

*ROSENTHAL, IRVING
Partita, horn solo; 3 Rennaissance madrigals, brass quintet.

ROSENTHAL, LAURENCE
b. Detroit, Mich., 4 Nov. 1926. Studied with Bernard Rogers and Howard Hanson, Eastman School of Music, M. M.; Nadia Boulanger in Paris; conducting at the Mozarteum in Salzburg. He received an Emmy award for music for the television documentary film, Michelango: The last giant, 1966; his film score for Becket was nominated for an Academy award. He was chief composer, 1st Documentary Film Squadron, U.S. Air Force, 1951-55.

ROSENTHAL, LAURENCE

(ROSENTHAL, LAURENCE)
WORKS: Ballet: The wind in the mountains,
1965; Theatre: music for Rashomon, 1958; A
patriot for me, 1969; Orchestra: Ode; Horas;
Overture; 4 Orphic tableaux, Ford Found. commission, 1965; Film scores: A raisin in the sun,
1960; Requiem for a heavyweight, 1961; The miracle worker, 1962; Becket, 1964; The comedians,
1967; Television scores: The power and the glory,
1961; Michelangelo: The last giant, 1966; many
other film, theatre, and television scores.
441 Buena Vista Road, New City, NY 10956

*ROSKOTT, CARL
b. 1953. Studied at Peabody Cons.; and New
England Cons. He received a Nat. Fed. of Music
Clubs junior composer award, 1969; conducted his
own compositions and standard symphonic works,
Eastern Music Festival Camp, Guilford Coll.,
N. C., 1969; conducted performance of his Reso-
lutions by the New England Cons. Repertory Orchestra, 29 Mar. 1972. Genesis for string trio,
woodwind quartet, trumpet, trombone, and piano
was performed by Boston Musica Viva, 10 Oct.
1972.

*ROSNER, ARNOLD
Studied at New York Univ., B. A. in mathematics;
and at State Univ. of New York at Buffalo, M. M.,
Ph. D. in music. He is faculty member at Brooklyn Coll. and Wagner Coll. His works include
Fantasia quasi una toccata, brass and percussion,
1965; cello sonata, 1968; A Mylai elegy for
orchestra, 1971.

*ROSS, ORVIN
At the gate of the year, chorus and organ.

ROSS, WALTER
b. Lincoln, Neb., 3 Oct. 1936. Studied with
Robert Beadell, Univ. of Nebraska, B. A. 1960,
M. M. 1962; with Karel Husa and Robert Palmer,
Cornell Univ., D. M. A. 1966; with Alberto
Ginastera in Buenos Aires, 1965. He received
the Vreeland award, Univ. of Nebraska, 1962;
Organization of American States fellowship, 1965;
Center for Advanced Studies fellowship, Univ. of
Virginia, 1971-72. He was assistant professor,
State Univ. Coll., Cortland, N. Y., 1966-67;
assistant professor, Univ. of Virginia, 1967-73;
associate professor, 1973-   .
WORKS: Orchestra: Concerto for brass quin-
tet and orch.; trombone concerto, New York, 12
May 1975; Band: tuba concerto; Chamber music:
Cryptical triptych, trombone and piano; 5 dream
sequences, percussion quartet and piano; Elec-
tronic: Midnight variations, tuba and tape,
1971.
Music Department, University of Virginia
Charlottesville, VA 22903

*ROSSINI, CARLO
b. Osimo, Italy, 3 Mar. 1890; U.S. citizen 1929.
Was ordained priest, 1913; studied at the
Pontifical Inst. of Music, Rome, M. M. He was
organist-choirmaster in Pittsburgh, 1923-50;
spent the next decade in Italy, returning to
New York in 1961.

(ROSSINI, CARLO)
WORKS: Chorus: 22 masses; 10 volumes of
choral compositions and arrangements of
liturgical music; etc.

ROSSITER, DAVID KENSETT
b. Summit, N. J., 23 Feb. 1952. Studied at
Oberlin Coll., 1971-72; with James Niblock,
Michigan State Univ., 1972-74; with Behrman,
Mumma, Tudor and Eastman at Chocorua, N. H.,
1973.
WORKS: Voice: Tuning up, an exercise in
group meditation, 1973; Electronic: Elephants
are, tape, 1972; Sringara, tape, 1973; Condemned
to wires and hammers, 6 players, 10 oscillators,
piano, tape, electronics, 1973.
300 Beal St., East Lansing, MI 48823

*ROTH, ROBERT N.
Improvisation on The infant king, organ.

ROTHGARBER, HERBERT
b. Brooklyn, N. Y., 7 Apr. 1930. Studied at
New York Univ., B. S., doctoral studies; Hunter
Coll., M. A.; composition with Wallingford
Riegger and Bernard Wagenaar. He has been public
school music teacher, Oceanside, N. Y.,
1957-   ; also private piano and composition
teacher.
WORKS: Chamber music: trio for flute,
clarinet, piano; trio, 2 trumpets and tuba; Dialogue, tuba and piano; Interplay, bassoon and
piano; piano pieces; 2 operas for children's
voices.
89 Ann Drive South, Freeport, NY 11520

ROTHSTEIN, ARNOLD
b. Yonkers, N. Y., 1923. Studied with Hugo
Kauder and Jacob Dymont, New York.
WORKS: Voice: Ani Maamin (Credo), voice
and piano, 1959; Music for the high holy days,
2-part setting, Vol. I, 1963; Vol. II, 1964;
The village fiddler, children's cantata, 1963,
NBC-TV 24 Jan. 1965; The last penny, children's
cantata, 1972.
29 Rellim Drive, Glen Cove, NY 11542

ROUSE, CHRISTOPHER
b. Baltimore, Md., 15 Feb. 1949. Studied with
Richard Hoffmann and Randolph Coleman, Oberlin
Coll., B. M. 1971; privately with George Crumb
in Philadelphia, 1971-73; with Robert Palmer,
Cornell Univ., 1973. He received a BMI composition award, 1973. He was teaching assistant,
Cornell Univ., 1973.
WORKS: Orchestra: Concerto for 4 chamber
ensembles, 1970; Kabir Padalavi, soprano and
orch., 1972; Chamber music: trio, 1971; Love
songs, 1973.
125 Coddington Road, Apt. A-11
Ithaca, NY 14850

ROUSSAKIS, NICOLAS
b. Athens, Greece, 14 June 1934; to U.S. 1950.
Studied with Otto Luening, Henry Cowell, Jack
Beeson, Columbia Univ., B. A. 1956, M. A. 1960;
with Ralph Shapey and Ben Weber; with Philipp
Jarnach, Hamburg, Germany, 1961-63; and on

(ROUSSAKIS, NICOLAS)
scholarship from the City of Hamburg, with Boulez, Berio, Ligeti, and Stockhausen at Darmstadt during the summers of 1962, 1963. Other awards include a Fulbright grant, 1961-63; fellowships at Mac-Dowell Colony, Yaddo, and Ossabaw Island, 1963-68; Nat. Inst. of Arts and Letters grant, 1969. He has been doctoral candidate and instructor, Columbia Univ., 1968-

WORKS: Chamber music: harpsichord sonata, 1967; 6 short pieces for flute, 1969; Helix, cello and piano, New York, 14 Dec. 1970; concertino for percussion and woodwinds, New York, 19 Mar. 1973; brass quintet, New York, 17 Dec. 1973; Chorus: Night speech, chorus and instruments, 1968.

225 West 86th St., P.H. 2F
New York, NY 10024

*ROVICS, HOWARD
b. 1936. Cybernetic study #1, flute and piano; Cybernetic study #2, clarinet, bassoon, piano; 3 studies for piano, 1964-66; March funèbre, clarinet and strings, New York premiere, 31 Jan. 1971; Events, piano, premiere, New York, 7 Nov. 1971; Look, friend, at me, oboe and piano, 1973; Piece for cello, piano, tape, 1973.
Manhattan School of Music, New York, NY 10027

ROXBURY, RONALD
b. Fruitland, Md., 4 Dec. 1946. Studied with Stefan Grove and Earle Brown, Peabody Cons., M.M. 1969; privately with Richard Rodney Bennett. He received Nat. Fed. of Music Clubs awards, 1965, 1966, 1968, 1969. He was vocal soloist, Cathedral of Mary Our Queen, Baltimore, 1969-72.

WORKS: Chamber music: Designs for 3 flutes, 1968; Aria for Fred, cello and piano; Haiku, guitar solo; Preludes for accordion; sonatina for flute and harpsichord; Le werewolf s'amuse, wolf-man and percussion; Quasimodo at wit's end, flute, guitar, doublebass; Graffiti, chamber ensemble; Ecstasies for Mi-Go, 14 guitars, 9 cellos; Brouhaha, 2 pianos 7-hands; piano sonata, 1968; Cancrizan, 2 pianos; Chorus: Motets for voices and chamber ensemble; 3 motets a cappella; Les derniers cris, with piano 4-hands and percussion, 1970; Multimedia: Ghazels for belly dancer and chamber ensemble; Requiem for Bill Null, chorus, mezzo soprano, theatrical devices, instruments; A movable feats, chorus, flute, guitar, multimedia, audience.
895 West End Ave., New York, NY 10025

ROY, KLAUS GEORGE
b. Vienna, Austria, 24 Jan. 1924; U.S. citizen 1944. Studied with Frederick C. Schreiber in Vienna; musicology with Karl Geiringer, Boston Univ., B. M. 1947; composition with Walter Piston, musicology with Davison, Kinkeldey, and Merritt, Harvard Univ., M. A. 1949. His many awards include the Arthur Shepherd composition prize, 1960; grant for an opera, 1957; Cleveland Arts Prize, 1965; Ohio Arts Council grant, 1973; numerous other grants and commissions. He was instructor and librarian, School of Fine and Applied Arts, Boston Univ., 1948-57; contributing music critic, Christian Science Monitor, 1950-57; director of

(ROY, KLAUS GEORGE)
publications and program book editor, Cleveland Orchestra, 1958- .

WORKS: Opera: Sterlingman, 1-act opera, television premiere, Boston, 1957; Theatre: music for Twelfth night, 1973; Wind ensemble: Tripartita, 11-part brass choir, 1949; Chamber music: trombone sonata, 1951; string trio, 1956; 2 rhapsodic pieces, viola and piano, 1957; Serenade, solo violin, 1957; duo for flute and clarinet; Chorus: St. Francis' canticle of the sun, a cappella with solo viola, 1951; 3 songs of praise, a cappella, 1952; Lie still, sleep becalmed; 3 folksongs, 1955; Songs: Holiday, soprano and piano; A song for Mardi Gras, medium voice and piano; piano pieces.
2528 Derbyshire Road
Cleveland Heights, OH 44106

*ROYCE, EDWARD
b. Cambridge, Mass., 25 Dec. 1886; d. Stamford, Conn., 7 July 1963. Studied at Harvard Univ., B. A. 1907; and at Stern Cons., Berlin. He was chairman, music dept., Middlebury Coll., 1913-15; faculty, Ithaca Cons., 1916-21; Eastman School of Music, 1923-47. His compositions included 2 tone poems, The fire bringers and Far ocean; songs, piano pieces.

ROYER, PAUL H.
b. Mt. Jackson, Va., 3 Sep. 1922. Studied at Westminster Choir Coll.; with Felix Labunski, Cincinnati Coll. of Music; with Bernhard Heiden and Thomas Beversdorf, Indiana Univ. He was staff member, Cincinnati Coll. of Music., 1947-50; Huron Coll., 1951-68; professor, South Dakota State Univ., 1968- , composer-in-residence, 1972.

WORKS: Orchestra: flute concerto; Band: Fanfare festiva; Prairie poem; Chamber music: Fantasy 69, violin and piano; Chorus: Sing unto the Lord; Psalm 150, with percussion.
337 Lincoln Lane South, Brookings, SD 57006

ROZSA, BELA
b. Kecskemet, Hungary, 14 Feb. 1905; U.S. citizen 1926. Studied with Percy Goetschius and Howard Brockway, Inst. of Musical Art, New York; Juilliard School; with Philip Greeley Clapp, Univ. of Iowa, Ph. D.; privately with Arnold Schoenberg. He won the Seligman prize, 1927, 1928; NBC Internat. Chamber Music prize, 1937. He was staff member, NBC, New York, 1929-38; on faculty, Baylor Univ., 1938-42; Iowa Wesleyan Univ., 1942-45; professor, Univ. of Tulsa, 1945- .

WORKS: Orchestra: Ibis, a symphony; Chamber music: piano sonata; 2 string quartets; piano quartet; piano quintet; violin sonata.
University of Tulsa, Tulsa, OK 74104

ROZSA, MIKLOS
b. Budapest, Hungary, 18 Apr. 1907; U.S. citizen 1945. Studied with Herman Grabner, Leipzig Cons.; at Leipzig Univ. and at Trinity Coll. of Music, London. He received the Francis Joseph prize of the City of Budapest, 1937, 1938; Acad. awards for film scores in Hollywood, 1945, 1948,

ROZSA, MIKLOS

(ROZSA, MIKLOS)
1959. He was faculty member, Univ. of Southern California, 1945-65.
WORKS: Orchestra: concerto for string orch., 1944; violin concerto, 1955; concert overture, 1956; piano concerto; cello concerto; Tripartita; Double concerto for violin and cello and orch., commissioned by Jascha Heifetz and Gregor Piatigorsky, 1964; Chamber music: Kaleidoscope, piano, 1946; sonata for 2 violins; string quartet; piano sonata, 1948; Sinfonia concertante, violin, cello, and orch.; Chorus: To everything there is a season, 1946; The varieties of life; Psalm 23; Film scores: El Cid; Quo vadis; King of Kings; Spellbound, 1945; A double life, 1948; Ben Hur, 1959.
c/o William Morris Agency
151 El Camino, Beverly Hills, CA 90212

*RUBINSTEIN, BERYL
b. Athens, Ga., 26 Oct. 1898; d. Cleveland, Ohio, 29 Dec. 1952. Studied piano with his father and with Alexander Lambert; toured the U.S. as a child prodigy, 1905-11; then studied in Berlin and Vienna. He joined the faculty of the Cleveland Inst. of Music, 1921; became director in 1932.
WORKS: Opera: The sleeping beauty, 1938; Orchestra: Scherzo, 1927; piano concerto, 1936; Piano: 32 etudes; 3 dances; Whirligig; and transcriptions.

RUCCOLO, JAMES S.
b. Akron, Ohio, 3 Feb. 1943. Studied at Eastman School of Music; with Clifton Williams, Univ. of Texas; with Grant Fletcher, Arizona State Univ.; and with Robert Muczynski, Univ. of Arizona, D. M. A. He received an award, Nat. Fed. of Music Clubs contest, 1969. He was associate professor, music program director, artist-in-residence, Prescott Coll., 1971-74.
WORKS: Orchestra: Movements for orch., 1967; Chamber music: Toccata for piano; Quiet is the night, soprano and piano; Rapsodia grossa, string quartet and piano; clarinet sonata.
242 South Arizona Ave., Prescott, AZ 86301

RUDHYAR, DANE
b. Paris, France, 23 Mar. 1895; U.S. citizen 1926. Studied at the Sorbonne and briefly at the Paris Cons., but is mostly self-taught in music. His awards include a $1000 prize from the Los Angeles Philharmonic Orchestra, 1922, for Soul fire (1919); a month devoted to broadcasting his works over KPFA, Berkeley, Calif., including music, interviews, comments, poems, and a complete reading of Rania: an epic narrative. Daniel Chenneviere came to the U.S. in 1916 for the performance of 2 orchestral works, Poèmes ironiques and Vision végétale, at the New York Metropolitan Opera on 4 Apr. 1917. He remained in this country, soon dropping his family name and eventually settling in Hollywood, alternating with New York, Chicago, and later Santa Fe. His extraordinary creative energy has produced over 30 books and booklets (from Claude Debussy, Paris 1913, poetry, novels, science fiction, to The astrological houses, 1972), about 3 dozen

(RUDHYAR, DANE)
paintings, numerous articles and lectures, and his musical compositions.
WORKS: Orchestra: To the real, 1920-28; The surge of fire, Los Angeles, 22 Oct. 1925; Sinfonietta, 1927; Ouranos, chamber orch.; Thresholds, 1954 (unorchestrated in 1972); Chamber music: 3 melodies, flute, cello, piano, 1919; 3 poems, violin and piano, 1920; 5 stanzas, string ensemble, 1927; piano quintet, 1950; Solitude, string quartet, New York, 17 Mar. 1951; Piano: Mosaics, a tone cycle, 1918; 9 tetragrams, 1920-1967; 3 paeans, 1925; 4 pentagrams, 1924-26; Granites, 1929; Syntony, 1968.
Box 636, San Jacinto, CA 92383

RUDIN, ANDREW
b. Newgulf, Tex., 10 Apr. 1939. Studied with Kent Kennan, Clifton Williams, Paul Pisk, Univ. of Texas; with George Rochberg, Univ. of Pennsylvania; also with Henry Weinberg, Ralph Shapey, and Karlheinz Stockhausen. He has been assistant professor, Philadelphia Musical Acad., 1965-   .
WORKS: Opera: The innocent, Philadelphia, 19-21 May 1972; Ballet: View, 1973; Chamber music: Remembering Ferruccio, for 9 players, 1973; Film scores: Spherics, NET-TV, July 1972; Electronic: Tragoedia, synthesizer; Il giuoco, tape and film.
Philadelphia Musical Academy
313 South Broad St., Philadelphia, PA 19907

*RUDNITSKY, ANTIN
b. Luka, Galicia, 7 Feb. 1902; to U.S. 1937. Studied with Artur Schnabel and Franz Schreker, Univ. of Berlin, Ph. D. 1926. He conducted opera in Russia and Poland, 1927-37; settled in New York as pianist, conductor, composer.
WORKS: Opera: Doubush, 1937; Ballet: Storm over the west, 1932; Orchestra: 3 symphonies, 1936, 1941, 1942; cello concerto, 1942; also chamber works.

RUDOW, VIVIAN ADELBERG
b. Baltimore, Md., 1 Apr. 1936. Studied with Jean Ivey, Peabody Cons., B. M. 1960. She was winner in the electronic music division, Annapolis Fine Arts Festival contest, 1972. She was on the piano faculty, Peabody Preparatory Department, 1958-59.
WORKS: Electronic: The oak and the reed, dance piece, 1972; The lion and the hares, 1972; music for The Trojan women, 1972; Changing space, dance piece, 1973; Syntheticon and Lies, dance pieces, 1974; music for Best of friends, 1974.
2424 Diana Road, Baltimore, MD 21209

*RUFTY, HILTON
b. Richmond, Va., 1909. Studied at Univ. of Richmond; Hampdon-Sydney Coll.; and Univ. of Virginia. He has been organist-choirmaster, St. Stephen's Church, Richmond, 1936-   ; associate professor, Univ. of Richmond, 1946-   . His compositions include the operetta, The 12 dancing princesses.
Univ. of Richmond, Richmond, VA 23173

*RUGER, MORRIS HUTCHINS
b. Superior, Wis., 2 Dec. 1902. Studied with
Seth Bingham, Columbia Univ., B. A. 1924; with
Andre Bloch in Paris, 1925-26; Northwestern Univ.,
1930; Juilliard School, 1934. From 1945 he was
on the staff of the Los Angeles Cons.
WORKS: Opera: Gettysburg, 1938; Orchestra:
violin concerto; Chamber music: piano quintet;
piano sonata; 2 piano suites; also choral works.
5999 Rancho Mission Road, San Diego, CA 92109

RUGGIERO, CHARLES H.
b. Bridgeport, Conn., 19 June 1947. Studied at
New England Cons.; B. M.; with H. Owen Reed, Michigan State Univ. He held scholarships at the New
England Cons. and at Michigan State Univ. He has
been performing percussionist and teacher,
1963-   ; was graduate assistant, Michigan State
Univ., 1971-73; instructor in theory and jazz,
1974-   .
WORKS: Chamber music: Dance music, chamber
ensemble, 1972; Electronic: The prima donnas,
electronic and percussion, 1973; other chamber
music and pieces for jazz ensemble
18 Plum St., Fairfield, CT 06430

*RUGGLES, CARL
b. Marion, Mass., 11 Mar. 1876; d. Bennington,
Vt., 24 Oct. 1971. Began violin study at age 6,
played for President Cleveland at 9; studied with
Walter Spalding and John Knowles Paine, Harvard
Univ. He was elected to membership in the Nat.
Inst. of Arts and Letters, 1954; received the
Koussevitzky international recording award, 1966.
He founded the Winona, Minn. Symphony, 1912, and
was its conductor to 1917; was active with Edgard
Varese in the Internat. Composers and the Pan
American Asso. of Composers, 1922-33; was instructor in modern composition, Univ. of Miami,
1937-47; then retired to Vermont and devoted himself chiefly to painting in oils and watercolors.
WORKS: Opera: The sunken bell (was accepted
for performance by the New York Metropolitan Opera,
but when it was suggested that the bell could be
made of papier-maché instead of being cast,
Ruggles withdrew the score in scorn and later de-
stroyed it); Orchestra: Men and angels, 5 trumpets and a bass trumpet, 1922, revised for brass
and strings and renamed Angels, 1929; Portals,
string orch., 1925; Men and mountains, symphonic
suite, 1924-35; Vox clamans in deserto, 1929,
voice and orch., Juilliard School, 24 Apr. 1974;
Sun-treader, after Browning, 1932; Organum,
1945-46; Piano: Polyphonic compositions for 3 pianos, 1940; Evocations, 4 chants for piano, 1945.

*RUGOLO, PETER
b. Sicily, Italy, 25 Dec. 1915; U.S. citizen 1933.
Studied at San Francisco State Coll., B. A. 1937;
at Mills Coll., M. A. 1941. His awards include
Nat. Acad. of Arts and Sciences award; TV Emmy
award; prize for outstanding achievement in
music composition for In defense of Ellen McKay,
a program in NBC's The bold ones - The lawyers'
series. He served in the U.S. Army, 1941-44; was
composer for Stan Kenton, 1945-51; for MGM Studios, 1954-57; for television, 1957-   .
WORKS: Chamber music: Petite suite, clarinet and piano; Offbeat, flute, clarinet, horn;
Television scores: Thin man, 1959; Thriller,

(RUGOLO, PETER)
1960; General Electric Theatre, 1960-61; Check-
mate, 1961; Ichabod and me, 1961; Alfred Hitch-
cock, 1960-63; The untouchables, 1962-63; The
Virginian, 1963.

*RUNKEL, KENNETH ELDON
b. Lisbon, Iowa, 10 June 1881. Studied at McGill
Univ., B. M., Lic., ACCO; with Frank Wright in
New York. He is a fellow of Trinity Coll. of
Music, London, and of the American Guild of Organists. He held his first position as organist in
Lisbon, Iowa in 1895 and retired from Flagler
Memorial Presbyterian Church, St. Augustine, Fla.,
in 1967 after 10 years as organist and choir
master.
WORKS: Chorus: Israel out of Egypt, cantata, with organ, 2 pianos, timpani, Baylor
Univ., 8 Mar. 1925; The good Samaritan, cantata,
1934; more than 85 published choral works. He
was a pioneer in the use of multiple choirs.
1313 Lincoln St., Apt. 206, Eugene, OR 97401

RUSH, LOREN
b. Fullerton, Calif., 23 Aug. 1935. Studied with
Robert Erickson, San Francisco State Coll., B. A.
1947; with Andrew Imbrie, Seymour Shifrin,
William Denny, and Charles Cushing, Univ. of Cal-
ifornia at Berkeley, M. A. 1960; at Stanford
Univ., D. M. A. 1973. He was George Ladd Prix
de Paris scholar, 1960-62; received the Rome
Prize fellowship, 1969-71; Inst. of Arts and Letters award, 1971; Guggenheim fellowship, 1971;
Prince Pierre de Monaco composition award, 1971;
and commissions. He has played bassoon in the
Oakland Symphony, contrabass in the Richmond
Symphony, also plays piano, percussion and Japanese koto. He has been a member of the Stanford
Computer Music Project, 1973-   .
WORKS: Orchestra: The cloud messenger,
Rome, July 1971; I'll see you in my dreams, for
amplified orch. and tape, San Francisco, Aug.
1973; Chamber music: 5 Japanese poems, soprano
and chamber ensemble, 1959; Serenade, violin and
viola, 1960; string quartet, 1961; Nexus 16,
chamber orch., 1964; Dans le sable, soprano,
speaker, 4 altos, 15 instruments, 1968, Rome,
Sep. 1970; Piano: Hexahedron, 1964; Oh, Susanna,
1970; soft music, HARD MUSIC, for 3 amplified
pianos, 1969-70.
37 Terrace Ave., Richmond, CA 94801

*RUSSELL, ALEXANDER
b. Franklin, Tenn., 2 Oct. 1880; d. Dewitt, N. Y.,
24 Nov. 1953. Studied with George Parker and
William Berwald, Syracuse Univ., B. A., honorary
D. M.; with Leopold Godowsky, Harold Bauer, and
Charles-Marie Widor in Europe. He was director
of the Wanamaker Concerts, New York, 1910-17;
professor, Princeton Univ., 1917-35.
WORKS: Chorus: In memory of Princeton men
fallen in World War I; Songs: Sunset; The sacred
fire; In fountain court; Lyric from Tagore; Expectations; Puer redemptor; and piano pieces.

RUSSELL, ARMAND KING
b. Seattle, Wash., 23 June 1932. Studied with
George McKay and John Verrall, Univ. of Washington; with Bernard Rogers and Howard Hanson,
Eastman School of Music. He received annual

RUSSELL, ARMAND KING

(RUSSELL, ARMAND KING)
ASCAP awards, 1966-73. He was associate professor, North Dakota State Coll., 1958-61; visiting professor, Eastman School, summers, 1959-64,
1972; professor, Univ. of Hawaii, 1961-   ,
chairman, music department, 1965-71.
WORKS: Orchestra: Harlequin concerto,
doublebass and orch.; Band: Theme and fantasia;
Symphony in 3 images; Chamber music: 2nd concerto for percussion; percussion sonata; Ballade
with epitaphs, for 2 voices and percussion; Particles, saxophone; many other instrumental and
vocal compositions.
3296 Huelani Drive, Honolulu, HI 96813

RUSSELL, CRAIG H.
b. Los Alamos, N. M., 3 Apr. 1951. Studied guitar at the Univ. of New Mexico and in Cervera,
Spain. He was guest lecturer, Univ. of New
Mexico, 1973-74.
WORKS: Theatre: Zapatera, musical comedy,
Univ. of New Mexico, 26-28 Apr. 1973; Orchestra:
concerto for piano, orch., and double chorus,
Albuquerque, 8 Feb. 1973; symphony, 1973; Jazz
ensemble: Relationship; Chamber music: quintet
for guitar, flute, string trio.
1165 41st, Los Alamo, NM 87544

RUSSELL, GEORGE
b. Cincinnati, Ohio, 23 June 1923. Attended
Wilberforce Univ. High School, 1940-43; studied
composition with Stepan Wolpe, 1949. His honors
include Outstanding Composer award, Metronome
Magazine, 1958; Downbeat Magazine composer award,
1961; Nat. Endowment for the Arts award, 1969;
2 Guggenheim fellowships, 1969, 1972; several
recording awards. He is author of The Lydian
chromatic concept of tonal organization, 1953,
and taught this method privately in New York,
1953-68; at the School of Jazz, Lenox, Mass.;
Festival of the Arts, Jyvaskyla, Finland, under
auspices of USIA; at Oslo, Norway, Lund, Sweden,
and Vaskilde Summer School, Denmark; New England
Cons., 1969-   . The George Russell Sextet performed at President Kennedy's Internat. Jazz Festival, 1962, at many other international jazz
festivals in Scandinavia and Western Europe, and
has toured extensively in the U.S. and abroad.
WORKS: Ballet: The chromatic universe,
1963; The net, 1968; Jazz ensemble: New York,
N. Y., 1958; The outer view, 1963; Othello ballet
suite, 1968; Electronic sonata for souls loved by
Nature, 1969; Listen to the silence, with choir,
1971; Now and then, 1973; Big city blues, 1973.
71 Martin St., Cambridge, MA 02138

*RUSSELL, JOHN
Has published for chorus: The dark hills; Merry
the green; Walk this mile in silence.
Department of Music, Vermont College
Montpelier, VT 05601

*RUSSELL, ROBERT
Has published chamber music: Places, suite for
piano 4-hands; Pan, flute and piano; trumpet
sonatina; Scherzo, clarinet and piano; Abstract
#1, 2 clarinets; Abstract #2, 2 trumpets or 2
horns; woodwind quintet; sextet for percussion,
Composers Theatre, New York, Feb. 1972.

*RUSSELL, WILLIAM
b. 1905. 3 dance movements, 1933; 3 Cuban pieces,
1939; Fugue; all for percussion and piano.
Department of Music, University of Miami
Coral Gables, FL 33124

RUSSO, JOHN
b. Trenton, N. J., 16 Jan. 1943. Studied with
Louis Cheslock, Peabody Cons., 1961-63; with
Matthew Colucci, Curtis Inst. of Music, B. M.
1967; with Clifford Taylor, Temple Univ., M. M.
1969. He held full scholarship at Curtis Inst.
and a graduate assistantship at Temple Univ.
He has been woodwind instructor, Widener Coll.,
1969-   ; Beaver Coll., 1972-   ; and is performing artist at Combs Coll. Franklin Concerts.
WORKS: Chamber music: 4 pieces for clarinet solo; Elegy for oboe; Meditations, woodwind
trio; clarinet sonata, 1964; Toccata for piano,
1970; Lo schifoso, bassoon solo, 1971.
3 West Ashland Ave., Glenolden, PA 19036

RUSSO, WILLIAM
b. Chicago, Ill., 25 June 1928. Studied with
Lennie Tristano, 1944-47; with John J. Becker
and Karel Jirak, Roosevelt Univ., B. A. 1955.
His awards include Musician of the Year award,
Metronome Year Book, 1957; Koussevitzky award,
1959; commission by Yehudi Menuhin and Lord
Astor, 1962; Illinois Arts Council commission,
1968. He was founder and director of Experiment
in Jazz, Chicago, 1947-50; trombonist, composer-
arranger, Stan Kenton's band, 1950-54; conducted
his own orchestra, 1958-61; was musical director,
London Jazz Orch., 1962-65; instructor, Manhattan
School of Music, 1959-61; School of Jazz, Lenox,
Mass., 1957-60; visiting professor, Peabody
Cons., 1969-71; adjunct professor, Antioch Coll.,
1971-72; director, Columbia Coll. Center for
New Music, Chicago, 1965-75; composer-in-
residence, City and County of San Francisco,
1975.
WORKS: Opera: John Hooten, 1961; The island,
1963; The rival; The land of milk and honey;
Antigone, 1967; Aesop's fables, rock opera, 1970;
Joan of Arc, chamber opera, 1970; Orchestra:
symphony no.1, 1957; symphony no.2, Titans, New
York, 19 Apr. 1959; cello concerto, 1962, Baltimore, 24 Feb. 1970; 3 pieces for blues band and
orchestra, Chicago, July 1968; The world of
Alcina; Band: Concerto grosso, 1960; Brookville,
tone poem, 1961; Jazz orchestra: English suite,
1955; The 7 deadly sins, 1960; English concerto,
violin and jazz orch., Bath, England, Festival,
June 1963; Fugue for jazz orch.; In memoriam,
with chorus and 2 solo voices, Los Angeles, Mar.
1966; America 1966, concerto grosso for jazz
orch.; Chorus: The Civil War, rock cantata,
San Antonio, 7 Apr. 1968; David, rock cantata,
1968; Liberation, rock cantata, 3 soloists,
chorus, dancers, rock band, 1969; Songs of celebration, soloists, chorus, orch., Baltimore, 21
Feb. 1971. He is author of 2 books: Composing
for the jazz orchestra, Univ. of Chicago Press,
1961; Jazz: Composition and orchestration, ibid.,
1968.
c/o City of San Francisco, City Hall
San Francisco, CA 94102

RUSSOTTO, LEO
  b. New York, N. Y., 25 May 1896. Attended Columbia Univ. and Juilliard School; studied with
Rubin Goldmark, Mortimer Wilson, and Abraham W.
Lilienthal. He received ASCAP awards, 1963,
1964. He was director of radio activities, Roxy
Theatre, 1927-31; staff pianist and choral director, NBC and ABC, 1931-43; associate conductor
and choral director, St. Louis Municipal Opera,
1944; associate conductor of Oklahoma on its
European tour, 1955.
      WORKS: Orchestra: Arioso, viola and orch.;
Novelette and poem, viola and orch.; Chant sans
paroles, cello and orch.; Humoreske, violin and
orch.; Reverie; Air de ballet; Concerto classico,
xylophone and orch.; many songs.
      219 West 81st St., New York, NY 10024

*RYDER, ARTHUR HILTON
  b. Plymouth, Mass., 30 Apr. 1875; d. Newton,
Mass., 18 July 1944. Studied with Walter Spalding
and John Knowles Paine, Harvard Univ.; was church
organist and choirmaster in the Boston area. He
wrote many songs, and in 1935 devised a new system of harmony which he taught in Boston.

*RYDER, NOAH F.
  b. Nashville, Tenn., 10 Apr. 1914; d. Norfolk,
Va., 17 Apr. 1964. Studied at Hampton Inst.,
B. S.; Univ. of Michigan, M. M. He received the
Navy's War Writers prize for a choral work, 1944.
He was public school music supervisor, 1935-36;
on faculty, Palmer Memorial Inst.; conductor,
Hampton Inst. Choir and head of theory, 1941-44;
from 1947 was director of music, Virginia State
Coll., Norfolk.
      WORKS: Chorus: Sea suite for male voices;
Haul away, mateys, we're almost home, 1944;
Piano: 5 sketches.

RYNEARSON, PAUL
  b. Long Beach, Calif., 12 Dec. 1945. Studied
with Alan Chaplin, California Inst. of the Arts;
with Dorrance Stalvey, Claremont Graduate School;
and with Ellis Kohs, Univ. of Southern California.
He was instructor, California Inst. of the Arts,
1968-69; and at Polytechnic School, Pasadena,
1970-71.
      WORKS: Chamber music: 11 contemporary flute
etudes, 1968; Geometriphon, flute, 1969.
      P. O. Box 441, Malibu, CA 90265

RZEWSKI, FREDERIC
  b. Westfield, Mass., 13 Apr. 1938. Studied at
Harvard Univ., B. A. magna cum laude 1958; and
at Princeton Univ., M. F. A. 1960. He was
Woodrow Wilson fellow, 1958-59, teaching fellow,
1959-60, Princeton Univ.; Fulbright fellow in
Italy, 1960-62; Ford Found., fellow, artist-in-
residence, West Berlin, 1963-65; creative associate, Center for the Creative and Performing
Arts, SUNY, Buffalo, 1966; Fromm fellow, Tanglewood, 1969; received commissions from New York
State Council on the Arts and Berliner Festspiel,
1972. Both as concert soloist and as member of
Musica Elettronica Viva he has earned a reputation as a phenomenal pianist for contemporary
music. His teaching posts include instructor,

(RZEWSKI, FREDERIC)
  Cologne, Germany, 1964, 1965, 1970; New Lincoln
School, New York City, 1972-73; Turtle Bay Music
School, New York, 1973; and a 3-week course in
collective composition, Chocorua, N. H., 1973.
      WORKS: Orchestra: Nature morte, 1964;
Drums and guns, 1973; Chamber music: sonata for
2 pianos, 1959; Poem for piano, 1959; octet, 1961;
Selfportrait, Composition for 2 players, Speculum
Dianae, 3 improvisational structures for 1, 2,
and 8 players, 1964; Spacecraft, improvising
group, 1965; Les moutons de Panurge, for melody
instruments, 1969; Coming together and Attica,
for speaker, bass instrument, and ensemble, 1972;
Second structure, for improvising musicians,
1972, performed by composer at piano and a Moog
synthesizer, Chicago, 16 Feb. 1973; Voice:
Requiem, chorus and instruments, 1963; Work songs
and Love songs, prose texts, 1968; Jefferson,
voice and piano, 1970; Electronic: Zoologischer
Garten, tape, 1965; Impersonation, for 2 vocalists, 4 tape recorders, 8 loudspeakers, photo-
electric mixer, 1967; Falling music, amplified
piano and tape, 1971. He is author of many
articles on contemporary music.
      780 Riverside Drive, New York, NY 10032

SACCO, JOHN CHARLES
  b. New York, N. Y., 11 July 1905. Studied at
Mannes School of Music; with Seth Bingham,
Douglas Moore, Columbia Coll., B. A., M. A.; and
with Deszo D'Antalffy. He was music director,
Paper Mill Playhouse; Starlight Musicals, Indi-
anapolis; associate music director, St. Louis'
Municipal Theatre; toured nationally with many
Broadway shows; editor, choral department,
G. Schirmer, Inc., New York.
      WORKS: Songs: Brother Will, Brother John;
Maple candy; Rapunzel; The spelling of Christmas;
The bells ring out for Christmas; and others.
      175 West 79th St., New York, NY 10024

SACCO, P. PETER
  b. Albion, N. Y., 25 Oct. 1928. Studied at New
York Univ. School of Education, B. S.; Eastman
School of Music, M. M. 1954, D. M. A. 1958. His
awards include grants from American Music Center,
1969; Nat. Endowment for the Arts, 1968; San
Francisco State Coll., 1967; annual ASCAP awards,
1966-72. He is professor, San Francisco State
Coll.
      WORKS: Opera: Mr. Vinegar, chamber opera,
1967; Orchestra: Introduction and allegro;
Classical overture; 3 meditations; 3 symphonies;
piano concerto; violin concerto, 1969; Band:
Suite for band; 4 sketches on Emerson essays;
work for trumpet and band; Make haste O God to
deliver me, chorus and band; Chamber music:
clarinet quintet; Study for brass and percussion;
Recitative, aria and eulogy, viola and piano;
Requiem, Nov. 22, 1963, wind quintet; Tuba mirum,
solo tuba; Elegia, flute and cello; 3 Psalms for
brass quintet and voice; Romance, clarinet and
piano; Fantasy, tuba and piano; Chorus: Behold
the fowls of the air; Awake O shepherds; The
snowstorm; Truly my soul waiteth upon God; The
moth; The squirrel; Daybreak; and others; Piano:

SACCO, P. PETER

(SACCO, P. PETER)
2 sonatas, 4 sonatinas; many songs and works for small ensembles.
933 9th Ave., San Mateo, CA 94402

*SACKS, STUART
b. Albany, N. Y., 28 Feb. 1941. Studied with Hugo Norden at Boston Univ. His Poeme for violin and piano and Saul for voice, oboe, percussion, and strings, were performed on CBS-TV, 11 Apr. 1965. He has composed orchestral works.

SAFANE, CLIFFORD JAY
b. New York, N. Y., 13 Feb. 1947. Studied with Edgar Curtis, Union Coll., Schenectady, N. Y., 1967-70; with Gregory Levin, Franklin Morris, Earl George, and Howard Boatwright, Syracuse Univ., 1970-72; David Del Tredici and Joyce Mekeel, Boston Univ., 1972-73. He received the Johan B. Hoffman award at Union Coll., 1967, 1968. He held a teaching fellowship at Syracuse Univ., 1971-72; is a member of the Levin Ensemble for New Music.
WORKS: Chamber music: 170 Winthrop St., for human whistle; Uevey 1971, solo alto saxophone, 1971; Canon for the New Year; Whispers and cries, alto saxophone and string quartet, 1974; Electronic: Electric Trane, Moog synthesizer and alto saxophone, 1973.
2294 Baylis Ave., Elmont, NY 11003

SAFRAN, ARNO M.
b. New York, N. Y., 27 Aug. 1932. Studied at New York High School of Music and Art; with Isadore Freed and Arnold Franchetti, Hartt Coll. of Music; with Irving Fine, Brandeis Univ.; with Aaron Copland at Tanglewood, 1952, 1953; Temple Univ., candidate for D. M. A. in 1974. He received Hartt publication award, 1953; BMI student awards, 1954, 1955; and commissions. He was public school music teacher, 1958-65; assistant professor, Trenton State Coll., 1965-71, associate professor, 1971-   .
WORKS: Orchestra: symphony, 1954; Music for orchestra, 1954; Serenade, chamber orch., 1955; 3 symphonic statements, 1962; Toccata for strings, 1968; Chamber music: 3 pieces for solo violin, 1953; string quartet, 1956; wind quintet, 1958; piano sonata, 1966; clarinet sonata, 1967; Voice: Music for Orpheus, cantata, 1969; Olessi songs, 1971.
30 Bayberry Road, Trenton, NJ 08618

*SAHL, MICHAEL
b. Brookline, Mass., 2 Sep. 1934. Studied at Amherst Coll., B. A. 1955; with Roger Sessions, Milton Babbitt, Princeton Univ., M. F. A. 1957; with Israel Citkowitz; and with Luigi Dallapiccola in Florence, Italy, on a Fulbright scholarship, 1957-58. He began to experiment with electronic tape while in Florence; remained in Europe to 1963. Back in the U.S. he played bass guitar in night clubs; performed his own works at State Univ. of New York, Buffalo, on a composer-pianist grant; was house musician, Lincoln Center Repertory Company, 1966; composed for films and television.

(SAHL, MICHAEL)
WORKS: Orchestra: symphony, WBAI Big Band, New York, 12 May 1973; Chamber music: Ensemble, 1965; Buell's piece, double bass, 1966; Electronic: Mitzvah for the dead, violin and tape, 1966-67; Electric circus, 1968; Tropes on the Salve Regina; electric violin concerto, New York, 21 Apr. 1974.
82 East 3rd St., New York, NY 10028

ST. CLAIR, RICHARD
b. Jamestown, N. D., 21 Sep. 1946. Studied with Leon Kirchner and Earl Kim, Harvard Univ., Ph. D. candidate, 1974; privately with Avram David, 1972-74. He has received Harvard Univ. prizes for piano pieces chamber and choral music. He was piano instructor, New England Cons., 1969-70; teaching fellow, Harvard Univ., 1973-74.
WORKS: Band: Amen concerto 1972, 2 pianos and band, 1972; Chamber music: Piano piece, 1967; cello sonata, 1969; piano sonata, 1970; Chorus: Yonder, a cappella, 1972; Mass, with soloists and orch., 1973.
295 Harvard St., Apt. 1-A
Cambridge, MA 02139

SALKOV, ABRAHAM A.
b. Rochester, N. Y., 17 Apr. 1921. Studied at Eastman School of Music in his early years; with Joseph Leonard in Los Angeles; received advice from Mario Castelnuovo-Tedesco. He was cantor, Temple Beth Am, Los Angeles, 1951-61; cantor, Chizuk-Amuno Congregation, Baltimore, 1961-   .
WORKS: Liturgical: Ovinu Malkenu, cantor and organ; S'firah, cantor and organ; El Hayeladim B'Yisrael, children's choir; L'Zeykher Olom, cantor, choir, string orch.; Hallel Y'Rushalmi, cantor, choir, harp, strings, brass, timpani, percussion.
2601 Manhattan Ave., Baltimore, MD 21215

SALTHOUSE, GRAHAM
b. Buxton, Derbyshire, England, 7 May 1941; to U.S. 1966. Studied at Royal Marines School of Music; and at Juilliard School. He played trumpet, Royal Marines Band, 1957-63; with various bands in London and Singapore, 1963-66.
WORKS: Wind ensemble: Statement for brass quintet.
112 East 90th St., New York, NY 10028

*SALZEDO, CARLOS
b. Arcachon, France, 6 Apr. 1885; U.S. citizen 1923; d. Waterville, Me., 17 Aug. 1961. Graduated from Paris Cons., winning the first prize in harp and piano. He was concert pianist and harpist in Europe; solo harpist with the New York Metropolitan Opera; organized annual harp festivals in the U.S.; helped organize the Internat. Composers Guild, 1921, and U.S. section of the Internat. Society for Contemporary Music, 1923; taught at Inst. of Musical Art, New York; established and headed the harp department, Curtis Inst., 1924; organized the Salzedo Harp Colony at Camden, Maine, 1931.
WORKS: Orchestra: The enchanted isle, harp and orch., 1919; Chamber music: 4 preludes to the afternoon of a telephone, 2 harps, 1921;

(SALZEDO, CARLOS)
sonata for harp and piano, 1922; Preambule et jeux, harp, 4 winds, 5 strings, 1929; Chanson dans le nuit, harp solo; Concert variations on O Tanenbaum; many other works for harp solo and in combination with other instruments or voice.

SALZMAN, ERIC
b. New York, N. Y., 8 Sep. 1933. Studied with Otto Luening, Vladimir Ussachevsky, Jack Beeson, Columbia Univ., B. A. with honors 1954; with Roger Sessions and Milton Babbitt at Princeton Univ., M. F. A. 1956; with Goffredo Petrassi in Rome, in Darmstadt, Germany, on a Fulbright scholarship, 1956-58. He was music critic, New York Times, 1958-62, New York Herald Tribune, 1962-66; music director, WBAI-FM, 1962-63, 1968-71; assistant professor, Queens Coll., CUNY, 1966-68; artistic director, QUOG Music-Theatre, 1970- .
WORKS: Opera: Voices, a cappella radio opera on Biblical texts, WBAI, Dec. 1971; Orchestra: Inventions for orchestra, 1958; Night dance, 1959; Chamber music: Suite on American Indian themes, violin and piano, 1953; piano suite, 1955; flute sonata, 1956; string quartet, 1957; Partita, solo violin, 1958; Voice: cummings set, voice and orch. or piano, 1953; On the beach at night, voice and piano, 1956; In praise of the owl and the cuckoo, soprano, guitar, chamber ensemble, 1964; Helix, voices, percussion, clarinet, guitar, 1972; Electronic: Foxes and hedgehogs, verses and cantos for 4 solo voices, instruments, and sound systems, 1967; Larynx music, voice and tape, 1967; Queens collage, tape, 1966; Wiretap, Rockgarden, tape pieces, 1968; Strophe and antistrophe, harpsichord and tape, 1972; Multimedia: Feedback, environmental work with multi-channel spatial audio-visual elements, instruments, voices, theatre, dance, indefinite length, 1968; The Peloponnesian War, full evening dance-mime-music-theatre work, 1968; The nude paper sermon, 1969; Can man survive?, 1969; Ecolog, 1971; Mirrors, 1972; Saying something, 1972; Biograffiti, 1973. He published a book, Twentieth century music, 1967.
QUOG Music Theatre
550 Broadway, New York, NY 10012

*SAMINSKY, LAZARE
b. Odessa, Russia, 8 Nov. 1882; U.S. citizen 1926; d. Port Chester, N. Y., 30 June 1959. Studied with Rimsky-Korsakov and Liadov. From 1924 he was music director, Temple Emanu-El, New York. His works include 4 operas, 2 ballets, 5 symphonies, and many other works in all genres.

SAMPSON, DAVID CHARLES
b. Charlottesville, Va., 26 Jan. 1951. Studied with Myron Fink, Curtis Inst. of Music; privately with Harold Boatrite and Karel Husa. He played trumpet in the Eastern Music Festival Orchestra, 1971; Colorado Philharmonic, 1972, 1973.
WORKS: Chamber music: The skein, song cycle for soprano; Exploitations, piano; Piece for brass quintet; 3 pieces for piano; Elegy, viola and piano.
Box 37, Star Route, Morrison, CO 80465

SAMSON, VALERIE BROOKS
b. St. Louis, Mo., 16 Oct. 1948. Studied with Hugo Norden, Boston Univ., B. A.; with Andrew Imbrie and Olly Wilson, Univ. of California, Berkeley, M. A. She was radio programmer-announcer, WTBS, Cambridge, Mass., 1969-70; was music director, Picchi Youth Orch., Oakland, Calif., 1971-72.
WORKS: Chamber music: duet for oboes, 1972; quartet for flute, clarinet, viola, cello, 1973; Encounter, chamber orch., 1973.
425 Hyde St., Apt. 43
San Francisco, CA 94109

*SAMUEL, GERHARD
b. Bonn, Germany, 20 Apr. 1924; U.S. citizen 1945. Studied with Howard Hanson, Eastman School of Music, B. M. 1945; with Serge Koussevitzky at Tanglewood; with Paul Hindemith, Yale Univ., M. M. 1947. He received the Haupt award, 1947; Fulbright fellowship, 1949; ASCAP award, 1972. He was conductor of the Oakland Symphony Orchestra, 1954-70; and associate conductor, Los Angeles Philharmonic Orchestra, 1970- . His published compositions include Looking at Orpheus for electric harpsichord, electric organ, harp, percussion and strings.
6603 Whitley Terrace, Los Angeles, CA 90028

*SANDBERG, MORDECAI
b. Rumania, Mar. 1897; to U.S. 1940; d. Toronto, Ont., 28 Dec. 1973. Studied in Vienna, then settled in Jerusalem to 1938. His works include 2 symphonies, 2 oratorios, chamber works, piano pieces, and a musical setting of the complete Book of Psalms. He planned to set the entire Bible.

*SANDERS, ALMA M.
b. Chicago, Ill., 13 Mar. 1882; d. New York, N. Y., 15 Dec. 1956. Studied at Chicago Musical Coll. She composed the scores for the musicals Tangerine; Elsie; The chiffon girl; The houseboat on the Styx; and many songs.

SANDERS, ROBERT
b. Chicago, Ill., 2 July 1906; d. Delray Beach, Fla., 29 Dec. 1974. Studied at Bush Cons., B. M. 1924, M. M. 1925; with Ottorino Respighi on a fellowship at American Acad. of Rome, 1925-29. His honors include a New York Philharmonic award for Little symphony in G, 1937; Guggenheim fellowship, 1954-55. He held faculty posts at Chicago Cons., 1929-38; Meadville Theological School, 1930-38; Chicago Univ., 1937-38; Indiana Univ., 1938-47; professor, Brooklyn, CUNY, 1947-72.
WORKS: Ballet: L'Ag'ya, 1944; Orchestra: Saturday night, 1933; Scenes of poverty and toil; Choreographic suite, 1935; violin concerto, 1936; 2 little symphonies, 1937, 1953; Symphony in A, 1955; Band: symphony, 1943; Chamber music: piano trio, 1925; string quartet, 1929; cello sonata, 1931; The imp, clarinet quartet, 1941; brass quintet, 1942; Rhapsody, woodwind quartet, 1943; trombone sonata, 1945; suite for brass quartet, 1949; Scherzo and dirge, 4 trombones, 1949; Fugue on a noel, woodwind quartet, 1949;

SANDERS, ROBERT

(SANDERS, ROBERT)
Square dance, trumpet and piano; horn sonata;
brass trio; clarinet sonata; Chorus: When
Abraham went out of Ur, a cappella; An American
psalm, women's voices and chamber ensemble, 1945;
The mystic trumpeter, baritone, chorus and orch.,
1947; A celebration of life, soprano, chorus and
orch., 1956; Chanson of the bells of Oseney; Out
of the cradle; When lilacs last in the dooryard
bloomed; A hymn of the future; Song of myself,
cantata, 1970. He was co-editor of Hymns of the
spirit, Boston, 1953; and a contributor to Celebration of life, Boston, 1964.

SANDIFUR, ANN E.
b. Spokane, Wash., 14 May 1949. Studied with
Charles Bestor, Willamette Univ.; Paul Creston,
Central Washington State Coll.; Stanley Lunetta,
Eastern Washington State Coll.; Alden Jenks,
San Francisco Cons.; Robert Ashley, Mills Coll.;
and at Chocorua, N. H. She received an award in
a Mu Phi Epsilon contest; grant from Nat. Center
for Experiments in Television, San Francisco.
She was contributing journalist for EAR, 1973;
director, first women's concert in Bay Area,
1973.
    WORKS: Chamber music: suite for oboe;
Pre-natal; Electronic: Bridging space; P.P.G.;
Big belly; Sequence II; Jona one.
    5291 Belvedere St., Oakland, CA 94601

*SANDOVAL, MIGUEL
b. Guatemala City, 22 Nov. 1903; U.S. citizen
1925; d. New York, N. Y., 24 Aug. 1953. Studied
with Eduardo Trucco; was accompanist for Rosa
Ponselle, Beniamini Gigli, Grace Moore, and other
noted singers. He wrote for films and radio;
was staff pianist, conductor, and composer, CBS
New York, 1941-49; general director, Guatemala
City national radio station.
    WORKS: Orchestra: Recuerdos en un paseo,
symphonic poem; Spanish dance, violin and orch.;
piano pieces and songs.

SANDRESKY, MARGARET VARDELL
b. Macon, Ga., 28 Apr. 1921. Studied with father,
Charles Vardell, Salem Coll., B. M. 1942; with
Howard Hanson, and Bernard Rogers, Eastman School
of Music, M. M. 1944; with Kurt Hessenberg in
Frankfurt, Germany, 1955-56. She held a Fulbright
scholarship for study in Germany; received several commissions. She was instructor, Oberlin
Cons., 1944-46; head of organ department, Salem
Coll., 1950-55; head of organ department, North
Carolina School of the Arts, 1965-67; associate
professor, Salem Coll., 1968-   .
    WORKS: Orchestra: Sinfonietta; Song for a
peaceful valley; Nicole and Roland; The 3 Marys;
Brief assemblance; Chamber music: 7 Japanese
drawings, woodwind quintet; 2 pieces for recorder
and 2 violas; piano trio; Chorus: King of glory,
King of peace; Jericho, cantata; Windows, cantata;
Songs: My soul doth magnify the Lord, soprano;
2 Italian songs; Organ: Overture to The common
glory.
    2820 Reynolds Drive, Winston-Salem, NC 27104

*SANJUAN, PEDRO
b. San Sebastian, Spain, 15 Nov. 1886; U.S. citi-
zen 1947. Studied with Joaquin Turina. Before
coming to the U.S. he divided his time between
Spain and Cuba; organized the Havana Symphony
Orchestra in 1926; was appointed professor,
Converse Coll., 1942; conducted the Spartansburg,
S. C., Symphony and festivals.
    WORKS: Orchestra: Rondo fantastico on a
Basque theme, 1926; Castilla, 1927; La macumba,
ritual symphony, 1945; Symphonic suite, 1965.

SAPERSTEIN, DAVID
b. New York, N. Y., 6 Mar. 1948. Studied with
Jacob Druckman, Juilliard Preparatory Division;
summer courses with Elliott Carter, Vincent
Persichetti, Walter Piston, Dartmouth Coll.;
with Milton Babbitt, Earl Kim, James K. Randall,
Princeton Univ., B. A. 1969; with Arthur Berger,
Seymour Shifrin, Martin Boykan, Harold Shapero
at Brandeis Univ. He received BMI student
awards, 1961, 1963, 1964; Samuel Wechsler award,
Brandeis Univ., 1970. He was affiliated with
Brooklyn Coll., CUNY, 1972-73.
    WORKS: Chamber music: wind quintet, 1963;
Fantasia, clarinet and piano, 1963; brass quartet, 1966; Variations for 8 players, 1969; Music
for solo flute, 1970; sextet, woodwind and string
trios, 1970, revised 1973; Antiphonies, percussion ensemble, 1972; Piano: Catacombs, 1961;
3 etudes, 1967; Bagatelle, 1969; 4 piano pieces,
1971-73; Electronic: Composition for violin and
tape, 1968.
    1290 Ocean Drive, Apt. 2-H
    Brooklyn, NY 11230

SAPIEYEVSKI, JERZY
b. Lodz, Poland, 20 Mar. 1945; to U.S. 1967.
Studied at the State Cons., Gdansk, Poland; and
at Catholic Univ. of America. He received a
first prize in composition in Poland, 1966;
Koussevitzky fellowship for Tanglewood, 1968;
and was finalist in the internat. competition
for conductors, Besancon, France, 1971. He was
composer and conductor for Polish Radio, 1964-66;
faculty member, Catholic Univ., 1970-73; American Univ., 1971-72; Univ. of Maryland,
1972-   ; music director, Reston Summer
Festival, 1973.
    WORKS: Orchestra: Moon worms, female cho-
rus and string orch.; Surtsey, string orch.;
Sinfonia Americana; Band: concerto for viola
and winds; Morpheus, wind symphony, 1973; Chamber music: Music number 17, percussion quartet;
Quinpulsatone, piano quintet.
    c/o SESAC
    10 Columbus Circle, New York, NY 10019

*SAPP, ALLEN DWIGHT
b. Philadelphia, Pa., 10 Dec. 1922. Studied with
Walter Piston and Edward Burlingame Hill, Harvard
Univ., A. B. 1942, A. M. 1949; further studies
with Archibald T. Davison, Irving Fine, Arthur T.
Merritt, Randall Thompson, Aaron Copland, and
Nadia Boulanger. He served as Army cryptanalyst,
1943-48; then joined the faculty at Harvard; in
1972 was professor, State Univ. of New York at
Buffalo. His works include several orchestral

(SAPP, ALLEN DWIGHT)
pieces; 2 violin sonatas; viola sonata; 4 piano sonatas; piano trio; string quartet, string trio; choral works; songs.
> Department of Music
> State University of New York
> Buffalo, NY 14214

SAPP, GARY J.
b. Abilene, Tex., 11 May 1944. Studied at Univ. of Hawaii; with Martin Mailman, William Latham, Samuel Adler, and Merrill Ellis, North Texas State Univ.; privately with Masahiko Sato in Japan. He was composer-arranger, Air Force Band of the Far East, 1966-70; composer-in-residence, Dallas Independent School District, 1973-74; instructor in music, Skyline Center, Dallas, 1973-74.
WORKS: Theatre: Uto, chamber opera on Japanese Noh drama, 4 soloists, dancer, chorus, chamber ensemble; Comedy of errors, musical comedy, co-composer; Chamber music: Shimo, flute, piano, soprano; Kwaidaj, 5 trumpets, 3 percussion; Erste Sonata fur Klavier.
> 822 Centerville Road, #135
> Garland, TX 75041

SARGENT, PAUL
b. Bangor, Me., 30 Mar. 1910. Studied piano at Eastman School of Music, B. M. 1931; Ecole Normale de Musique, Paris, diploma 1948; with John Mokrejs in New York, 1940-45. His studies in Paris and New York were on scholarships. He was accompanist for many noted singers, 1940-55.
WORKS: Songs: XXth century; River road; Stopping by woods on a snowy evening; Manhattan joy ride; 3 A.M.; Hickory Hill; Piano: Promenade; Night song; The sea; a suite.
> 408 64th St., New York, NY 10021

SATEREN, LELAND B.
b. Everett, Wash., 13 Oct. 1913. Studied at Augsburg Coll.; with Donald Ferguson, Univ. of Minnesota, M. A.; research in choral music and techniques in Europe, 1937, 1966, 1970. He received honorary doctorates from Lakeland Coll., 1965; Gettysburg Coll., 1965. He was school music director, 1935-38; director of music, Univ. of Minnesota Radio Station, KUOM, 1940-43; chairman of music department, professor, and choir director, Augsburg Coll., 1950- .
WORKS: Chorus: some 300 published choral works.
> Augsburg College, Minneapolis, MN 55404

SAUCEDO, VICTOR
b. Colton, Calif., 20 July 1937. Studied at Univ. of Southern California, B. A.; with Boris Kremenliev and Roy Harris, Univ. of California, Los Angeles, Ph. D.; with Karlheinz Stockhausen in Germany; and at the Darmstadt Summer School. He held a Sherwood Music School scholarship; California State fellowship; doctoral opportunity fellowship; Chancellor's research assistantship. He taught in Los Angeles schools, 1966-69; Long Beach City Coll., 1970; California State Univ., Dominguez Hills, 1970-71, at Los Angeles, 1971; Southwestern Coll., 1971- .

(SAUCEDO, VICTOR)
WORKS: Orchestra: Isocentonization for 4 orch.; Chamber music: Piano music III; string trio; Ecosahedron, for solo cello; Voice: The hollow men, baritone and chamber ensemble; ReJoyce, improvisatory work for voice and 4 instruments; Homage, solo voice, piano, percussion, and trombone; Electronic: Crossing; Multimedia: Philologia comica, for saxophone, dancer, tape, slides, and lights.
> 1866 Loyola Court, Chula Vista, CA 92010

*SAUSSY, TUPPER
Natchez trace, chorus, rock group, orch. performed by Nashville Symphony Orchestra, 13 Feb. 1971.

SAYLOR, BRUCE
b. Philadelphia, Pa., 24 Apr. 1946. Studied with Hugo Weisgall and Roger Sessions, Juilliard School, B. M. 1968, M. S. 1969; independently in Rome, 1966-67; with Goffredo Petrassi and Franco Evangelisti in Rome, 1969-70; at City Univ. of New York, candidate for Ph. D., 1970- . He held scholarships at Juilliard School, 1965-69, teaching fellowship 1968-69; received the Gretchaninoff prize, 1965, 1968; Nat. Soc. of Arts and Letters awards, 1968; Marion Freschel prize, 1968; Fulbright grant, 1969-70; ASCAP awards, 1971, 1972, 1973; Santa Fe Music Critics Asso. fellowship, 1973. He was lecturer, Queens Coll., CUNY, 1970-73, instructor, 1973-74; associate conductor, Queens Coll. Choir, 1970-72, conductor, Women's Glee Club, 1973, Contemporary Wind Ensemble, 1972, guest conductor, Opera Workshop, 1973. He is also music critic and author of articles for many music journals.
WORKS: Theatre: music for Victims of amnesia, wind quartet, 1968; Orchestra: Cantilena, string orch., 1965; To autumn and To winter, Blake texts, chorus and orch., 1968; Notturno, piano and orch., 1969; Conductus, winds, strings, and percussion, 1970; Chamber music: Suite for viola solo, 1967; Duo for violin and viola, 1970; Voice: Jesu, Thou joy of loving hearts, chorus and organ; 5 songs from Whispers of heavenly death, soprano and string quartet, 1965-67; 3 collects, soprano and organ, 1968; Lyrics for soprano and violin, 1971; Keyboard: Ricercare and sinfonia, organ, 1965, 1969; 5 short piano pieces, 1965-67; Ricercare for piano, 1972.
> 120 Riverside Drive, New York, NY 10024

SAYLOR, RICHARD
b. Reading, Pa., 6 Aug. 1926. Studied with Leland Smith, Stanford Univ.; with Arnold Fish in New York; with George Driscoll, Ithaca Coll. He received an award, Phi Mu Alpha contest; Steinman Arts Festival commission, 1968; Smithsonian Inst. fellowship to India, 1968-69. His academic posts include Xavier Univ., La., 1957-59; St. Lawrence Univ., 1959-68; California State Coll., San Bernardino, 1969-
WORKS: Orchestra: Symphony 1966; Either/or; Band: Ampersand; Prelude for band; Ballata; Prisoner of war; Electronic: Music for Rosmersholm; Music for Macbeth; Textures.
> 3880 Camellia Drive, San Bernardino, CA 02404

SCALERO, ROSARIO

*SCALERO, ROSARIO
    b. Moncalieri, near Turin, Italy, 24 Dec. 1870;
to U.S. 1919; d. Settimo Vittone, Italy, 25 Dec.
1954. Studied in Genoa, London, and Vienna;
taught in France and Italy until coming to the
U.S. He was head of composition, Mannes School,
New York, 1919-28; then joined faculty at Curtis
Inst. His compositions include a violin concerto,
chamber music, and songs.

SCARMOLIN, A. LOUIS
    b. Schio, Italy, 30 July 1890; U.S. citizen 1914;
d. Wyckoff, N. J., 13 July 1969. Came to the
U.S. as a boy of 10 and graduated from New York
Coll. of Music in 1907. His many honors include
an award for In retrospect, a quintet, American
Soc. of Ancient Instruments, 1938; 1st prize for
O wisest of men, in national contest for unveil-
ing statue of Benjamin Franklin, Philadelphia,
1938; 1st place for 2 Symphonic fragments for
orch., Nat. Composers Clinic, Chicago, 1944;
award for Credo for chorus and Tribal dance for
band, Fellowship of American Composers, Detroit,
1946; award for Night--A poem for orchestra,
Women's Symphony Orchestra of New York, 1947;
1st prize for The 2 cuckoo clocks, piano, Composers Press, 1947. After serving in the U.S. Army,
1917-19, he was music director of the Union City,
N. J. School System, 1919-49; also organist,
conductor, and accompanist for many leading
artists.
    WORKS: He composed for orchestra, varied
chamber groups, band, piano, organ, choral groups.
His more than 600 published works include the
opera, The interrupted serenade, performed in
Union City, N. J., 26 May 1974; Orchestra: Overture on a street vendor's ditty, 1938; Dramatic
overture, 1938; Mercury overture, 1939; Band:
Reuben and Rachel sight-seeing in New York, 1945;
Mexican Holiday, 1946. He left more than 1000
manuscripts yet to be submitted to publishers.
In September 1973 nearly 400 published works
were presented to the Coll. of St. Elizabeth,
Convent Station, N. J., by his widow, Aida
Balasso Scarmolin of Wyckoff, N. J. The music
library of the Univ. of Iowa has received a similar gift. The composer's letters and manuscripts
are to be added to the collections as released
by publishers.

*SCAVARDA, DONALD
    b. 1928. Matrix for clarinetist, 1962; Land-
scape journey, clarinet and piano, 1964.

SCELBA, ANTHONY J.
    b. New Jersey, 12 Feb. 1947. Studied double bass
with David Walter, Manhattan School of Music,
B. M., M. M., M. M. E.; and at Juilliard School,
candidate for D. M. A., the first to be admitted
to the doctoral program with a major in performance on double bass; largely self-taught in
composition. His awards and scholarships have
been for performance on the double bass. He
has been principal bassist, New Jersey Symphony
Orchestra, 1969- ; bassist, American Symphony
Orchestra, 1971; Lake George Opera Festival,
1974; faculty member, preparatory division, Manhattan School of Music, 1969-   .

(SCELBA, ANTHONY J.)
    WORKS: Chamber music: Double-bass trios,
1969, Passacaglia, for string quintet, 1970,
New York, 17 May 1972; Romantic, string quintet,
1972, New York, 18 Feb. 1974; Innocence and
sophistication, violin and contrabass, New York,
26 Nov. 1973; Fantasia, double bass and piano,
1974.
    110 Van Buren St., Passaic, NJ 07055

SCHACK, DAVID
    b. Fort Wayne, Ind., 16 Sep. 1947. Studied with
Richard Wienhorst, Valparaiso Univ., B. M. 1969;
at Indiana Univ., M. M. 1970; electronic music
with Raymond Haggh, Univ. of Nebraska, 1972. He
has been faculty member, Concordia Teachers Coll.,
Seward, Neb., 1970-   .
    WORKS: Chamber music: woodwind quintet;
brass quintet; brass quartet; Chorus: Salvation
unto us has come; The Lord is my shepherd; O
dearest Jesus; settings of the Mass, choir,
organ, handbells, woodwind quintet; Keyboard: 9
chorale preludes for organ; suite for organ; 3
movements for 2 pianos.
    427 North 3rd, Seward, NB 68434

*SCHAD, WALTER
    b. Brooklyn, N. Y., 24 Aug. 1889; d. New York,
N. Y., 16 Feb. 1966. Studied at Juilliard School
and New York Coll. of Music; played clarinet
under Victor Herbert and John Philip Sousa; was
on music research staff at NBC; editor and
arranger for music publishers; also private
teacher. His works include an opera, Plango;
orchestral pieces, Samson and A legendary hero;
and a piano trio.

*SCHAEFER, WILLIS H.
    Ballada for band.

SCHALIT, HEINRICH
    b. Vienna, Austria, 2 Jan. 1886; U.S. citizen
1946. Received the Austrian State award for
composition, 1906; 2 Eistedfod Festival awards
for chamber music, 1912, 1913 (in Wales). He
was organist in Munich, Germany, 1926-33; in
Rome, 1934-38; Rochester, N. Y., 1940-43;
Providence, R. I., 1943-48; Hollywood, Calif.,
1949-50.
    WORKS: Liturgical: Sabbath Eve liturgy,
1952; Hadrat Kodesh (The beauty of holiness),
1960; Psalm of brotherhood, chorus and organ;
Songs: Visions of Yehuda Ha-Levi, cycle for
high voice and piano, 1970.
    R.R. 5, Box 347, Evergreen, CO 80439

*SCHAUM, JOHN W.
    b. Milwaukee, Wis., 27 Jan. 1905. Studied at
Milwaukee State Teachers Coll.; Marquette Univ.,
B. M. 1931; Northwestern Univ., M. M. 1934. He
is a private piano teacher and has published
piano teaching methods and many books of collected piano pieces; also Mountain concerto for
piano; and songs.

*SCHELLING, ERNEST HENRY
    b. Belvidere, N. J., 26 July 1876; d. New York,
N. Y., 8 Dec. 1939. Was a child prodigy on the

(SCHELLING, ERNEST HENRY)
piano, playing at the Philadelphia Acad. of Music at age 4; then studied in Paris with several teachers, ending with Ignace Paderewski in Switzerland, 1898-1902. He returned to the U.S. in 1905 and devoted his time to conducting and composing.
WORKS: Orchestra: Suite fantastique, 1907; Legende symphonique, 1913; Symphonic variations, piano and orch., 1915; violin concerto, 1916; A victory ball, 1923; Morocco, symphonic tableau, 1927; a symphony; also chamber works and piano pieces.

SCHERER, BARRY
b. New York, N. Y., 10 Sep. 1949. Studied with Louise Talma and Ferdinand Davis, Hunter Coll., CUNY, A. B. cum laude 1972; New York Univ., 1973-   . He received a scholarship at Hunter Coll., 1972; graduate fellowship, New York Univ., 1973. He was staff member, Lake George Opera Festival, 1969, 1970.
WORKS: Opera: The prisoner of Jollern or Righteousness triumphant, 2-act, performed in concert, New York Metropolitan Opera House, 13 June 1971; Delizia or The gypsy's malediction, 2-act with ballet; librettos for both operas by composer; Chorus: How beautiful upon the mountains, with tenor solo and organ.
104-20 Queen's Blvd., Forest Hills, NY 11375

SCHIAVONE, JOHN SEBASTIAN (REV.)
b. Los Angeles, Calif., 27 Mar. 1947. Studied with Matt Doran, Mount St. Mary's Coll., Los Angeles. He won 2nd place, Archdiocese of Los Angeles competition for Parish Mass in honor of the Holy Family.
WORKS: Liturgical: Mass in praise of God the Holy Spirit; Mass in praise of Christ the High Priest; a number of choral anthems and motets.
870 West 8th St., San Pedro, CA 90731

SCHICKELE, PETER
b. Ames, Iowa, 17 July 1935. Played bassoon in the Fargo-Moorhead Orchestra and studied theory with its conductor, Sigvald Thompson; then studied at Swarthmore Coll., A. B. 1957; with Vincent Persichetti and William Bergsma at Juilliard School, M. S. 1960; also with Roy Harris. He received the Elizabeth Tow Newman Contemporary Music award, 1964; and commissions from Smith Coll., 1960, 1961; Fargo-Moorhead Symphony Orchestra, 1961, 1963; Juilliard Dance Department, 1964; Philadelphia Art Alliance, 1965; Juilliard Repertory Project; Louisville Orchestra, 1968; St. Louis Symphony, 1970, 1972. He held a teaching fellowship at Juilliard, 1957-60; was Ford Found. composer-in-residence, Los Angeles high schools, 1960-61; faculty member, Swarthmore Coll., 1961-62; Aspen Music School; Extension division, Juilliard School, 1963-65. He was co-founder in 1959 of Composers Circle, and in 1967 of The Open Window, a group which played in and wrote for a wide range of projects including the music and lyrics for Oh! Calcutta!, other shows, films, and even a television commercial. He has toured widely in the U.S. conducting and

(SCHICKELE, PETER)
performing in his "P.D.Q. Bach" and "Professor Schickele" pieces.
WORKS: Orchestra: Serenade, 1959; A zoo called Earth, with taped narration, 1970; Requiem Mantras, rock group and orch., 1972; 3 strange cases, narrator, Ogden Nash texts, 1972; 3 girls, 3 women, with male singer-pianist, 1972; Chamber music: Sequiturs, solo cello, 1959; string trio, 1960; Aspendicitis, 3 flutes, 2 trombones, 2 contrabasses, drums, 1961; 3 scenes for 5 instruments, 1965; Windows, violin, flute, guitar, 1966; Summer trio, flute, cello, piano, 1966; Gardens, oboe and piano, 1968; Chorus: The birth of Christ, 1960; On this plain of mist, women's voices, 1961; After spring sunset, 1961; The last supper, women's voices, 1965; Voice: Songs for baritone, bassoon, trombone, 1958; The flow of memory, mezzo-soprano and chamber ensemble, 1963; Piano: Little suite for Josie, 1957; 4 pieces, 1957; 3 sonatinas, 1957, 1958, 1964; Presents, Book I, 1960, Book II, 1972; A garland of rags, 1973; Film scores: The crazy quilt, 1965; Funnyman, 1967; 3 riddle films and Where the garbage goes, for Sesame Street, 1969; Silent running, 1971; P.D.Q. Bach works: Concerto for Horn and Hardart; Gross concerto for diverse flutes; Pervertimento, for bagpipes, bicycle, balloons, strings; Concerto for piano vs. orchestra; Hansel & Gretel & Ted & Alice, opera funnia for bargain counter tenor/harpsichord, beriberitone/calliope, piano; The art of round ground, 3 baritones discontinuo; Prof. Schickele works: The unbegun symphony; Eine Kleine Nichtmusik; Last tango in Bayreuth, 4 bassoons; Chaconne à son goût, orch.
193 St. John's Place, Brooklyn, NY 11217

SCHIFFMAN, HAROLD
b. Greensboro, N. C., 4 Aug. 1928. Studied at Univ. of North Carolina, Chapel Hill; with Roger Sessions privately in New Jersey and at Univ. of California, Berkeley; with Ernst von Dohnanyi and John Boda, Florida State Univ. He has been on the faculty, Florida State Univ., 1959-   .
WORKS: Orchestra: symphony, 1961; Prelude and variations, chamber orch., 1970; Chamber music: string quartet, 1951; Pentalogue, violin and piano, 1963; Divertimento, wind quintet, 1969; Musica battuta, percussion ensemble; Allegro con spirito di San Niccolo, wind quintet; Holiday fanfares, trumpet or horn trio; Piano: sonata, 1951; Variations for 2 pianos, 1966.
2304 Don Andres Ave., Tallahassee, FL 32304

*SCHIFRIN, LALO BORIS
b. Buenos Aires, Argentina, 21 June 1932; to U.S. 1958. Studied with Juan Carlos Paz in Buenos Aires; with Olivier Messiaen in Paris. He represented Argentina at the 1955 Internat. Jazz Festival in Paris; formed his own jazz group on his return to Buenos Aires; came to the U.S. as arranger for Xavier Cugat; since 1964 has been film and television composer in Hollywood.
WORKS: Ballet: Jazz Faust, 1963; Orchestra: Suite for trumpet and brass orch., 1961; Tunisian fantasy; The ritual of sound, 15 instruments, 1962; Jazz: Gillespiana, brass ensemble; Jazz

SCHIFRIN, LALO BORIS

(SCHIFRIN, LALO BORIS)
suite on mass texts; Dionysos; Mount Olive; Study in rhythm; The web; Mima, progressive jazz suite for piano; Rock requiem, 1971; Pulsations, for electric keyboard, jazz band, and orch., 1971; Film scores: The liquidator; The fox; The Cincinnati Kid; I love my wife; theme for TV's Mission impossible (2 Grammy awards); The rise and fall of the 3rd Reich, 1968.

*SCHILLINGER, JOSEPH
b. Kharkov, Russia, 31 Aug. 1895; to U.S. 1928; d. New York, N. Y., 23 Mar. 1943. Studied at St. Petersburg Cons.; taught in Kharkov and Leningrad. On coming to the U.S. he taught at the New School for Social Research and at Columbia Univ.; later established himself as a private teacher using his own mathematical system of composition. His pupils included many noted composers. His method was published posthumously as The Schillinger system of composition, New York, 1946, and The mathematical basis of the arts, New York, 1947.
    WORKS: Ballet: The people and the prophet; Orchestra: March of the Orient, 1926; First airphonic suite, theremin and orch., 1929; North Russian symphony; The twelve, symphonic cantata; Piano: Symphonic rhapsody; other piano pieces.

SCHIMMEL, WILLIAM
b. Philadelphia, Pa., 22 Sep. 1946. Studied with Lotta Hertlein and Paul Creston, Neupauer Cons., Philadelphia; with Elliott Carter, Vincent Persichetti, Roger Sessions, Hugo Weisgall, Juilliard School, M. S. He received Rogers and Hammerstein scholarship, 1969-70. He has been assistant professor, Brooklyn Coll., 1971-   ; teacher of literature and materials of music, Juilliard School, 1973-   .
    WORKS: Orchestra: Concerto for 3, accordion, bass, and percussion, 1968-69; Portrait no.1, after a painting by Joan Miro, 1969; Mass for chorus and orch., 1973; Chamber music: Tithonus, chamber ensemble, New York, 2 Apr. 1974; Keyboard: Motor piece, for free-bass accordion, 1972; Kingdom trilogy, 1971-73, which includes Kerygma for organ, Parousia, for accordion, Kingdom for piano.
    242 East 89th St., 2D, New York, NY 10028

SCHINDLER, ALLAN
b. Stamford, Conn., 15 May 1944. Studied with Ralph Shapey, Univ. of Chicago; with Joseph Wood and Edwin Dugger, Oberlin Coll. He was instructor, Ball State Univ., 1969-72; assistant professor, Boston Univ., 1972-   .
    WORKS: Chamber music: string sextet; Blues for the children of light, 8 instruments; 2 movements for chamber ensemble; Electronic: Cirrus, flute, cello, percussion and tape.
    10 Franclaire Drive, Boston, MA 02132

SCHINSTINE, WILLIAM J.
b. Easton, Pa., 16 Dec. 1922. Studied percussion with George Hamilton Green in New York; Eastman School of Music, B. M. 1945; Univ. of Pennsylvania, M. M. E. 1952. He was percussionist, Rochester Philharmonic, 1945; Nat. Symphony Orchestra,

(SCHINSTINE, WILLIAM J.)
1946-47; Pittsburgh Symphony, 1947-48; San Antonio Symphony, 1949-51; taught in Pottstown public schools, 1952-73; heads his own percussion school, 1973-   .
    WORKS: Band: March to the battle of jazz; Tympendium; Tympolero; Pennsylvania sketches; Miracle overture; numerous pieces for solo percussion instruments and percussion ensembles; teaching methods for percussion.
    614 Woodland Drive, Pottstown, PA 19464

SCHLABACH, ERROL WEISS
b. Canton, Ohio, 31 Aug. 1942. Studied with Marcel Dick, Cleveland Inst. of Music. He received annual ASCAP awards, 1970-73. He was arranger-composer, U.S. Navy Band, Washington, D.C., 1966-70; Sunshine Pops Orchestra, Orlando, Fla.; U.S. Marine Band, Washington, 1973.
    WORKS: Band: Swiss moods; Clarinet rhapsody, for clarinet, harp and band; many compositions for jazz and stage bands.
    5539 Columbia Pike, #319
    Arlington, VA 22204

*SCHLEIN, IRVING
b. New York, N. Y., 18 Aug. 1905. Studied at City Coll. of New York, B. A.; Brooklyn Coll. of Pharmacy, Ph. G.; Juilliard School; New York Coll. of Music; with Douglas Moore, Columbia Univ.; also on scholarship with Aaron Copland, Roy Harris, Wallingford Riegger, and Roger Sessions. He has been accompanist for singers, pianist for musicals, and public school music teacher.
    WORKS: Orchestra: Dance overture; Chamber music: sonatina for viola d'amore, New York, 16 Feb. 1973; piano pieces.

SCHMIDT, DIANE LOUISE
b. Seattle, Wash., 23 Nov. 1948. Studied accordion, Univ. of Puget Sound, B. M.; composition with William O. Smith and Robert Suderburg, Univ. of Washington, doctoral candidate 1973. She has held accordion and composition scholarships; was winner of the World Accordion Competition, Mozarteum, Salzburg. She has toured widely in Europe and the U.S. as accordion soloist.
    WORKS: Accordion: Theme and variations; 2 contemporary fugues.
    1436 South 129th, Seattle, WA 98168

SCHMIDT, WARREN F.
b. Milwaukee, Wis., 26 Apr. 1921. Studied organ at Univ. of Michigan; Univ. of Chicago; and in Frankfurt, Germany. He received a university scholarship; faculty fellowship; Fulbright fellowship. He has been professor of organ and theory, Wartburg Coll., 1950-   .
    WORKS: Organ: Fantesienne and fughetta; Thanksgiving suite; 3 pieces; Chorale fantasia.
    321 3rd Ave., N.E., Waverly, IA 50677

SCHMIDT, WILLIAM
b. Chicago, Ill., 6 Mar. 1926. Studied with Max Wald, Chicago Musical Coll.; with Halsey Stevens and Ingolf Dahl, Univ. of Southern California, B. M., M. M. with honors. He received a DuPont

(SCHMIDT, WILLIAM)
Band Composition award. He has been president,
Western International Music, Inc., and WIM
Records.
WORKS: Band: Concerto breve, brass and
band, 1957; The Natchez trace; Sakura variations;
Chorale, march, and fugato; Brass quintet: 3
suites; Concerto for piano; Music for scrimshaw,
with harp; Spiritual fantasy, with organ; Variations on a negro folksong; 7 variations on a hexachord; Chamber music: Spirituals, cello and
percussion; Vendor's call, piano with clarinet
choir; viola sonata, 1959; Allegro breve, organ;
Prelude and fugue, woodwind trio; Variations on
a whaling song, clarinet and piano; Ludus Americana, narrator and percussion, 1971; Rhapsody,
clarinet and piano; Septigrams, flute, piano,
piano, percussion, 1956; The percussive rondo,
percussion quartet, 1957; saxophone sonata; saxophone sonatina; Serenade, tuba and piano; Suite
for 4 saxophones; Variations for horn quartet.
2859 Holt Ave., Los Angeles, CA 90034

*SCHMINKE, OSCAR EBERHARD
b. New York, N. Y., 12 Dec. 1881; d. Liberty,
N. Y., 22 Feb. 1969. Was a practicing dentist;
composed chamber music, piano pieces, songs.

SCHMUTZ, ALBERT DANIEL
b. Halstead, Kan., 11 Oct. 1887. Studied at
Bethel Coll., Newton, Kan.; Inst. of Musical Art,
Wichita, Kan.; Chicago Cons., B. M., M. M.; and
with Ernst von Dohnanyi in Kansas City. He was
head, music department, Bethel Coll., Newton,
Kan.; professor, Kansas State Teachers Coll.;
taught at Nat. Music Camp, Interlochen, Mich.,
1948-52 and 1968-72.
WORKS: Band: Ballade symphonique; Chamber
music: saxophone sonata; clarinet sonata; quintet for clarinet and strings; string quartet;
woodwind trio; Divertimento, horn quartet; Fantasy sketch, brass sextet; Chorus: Song for
evening; Stopping by woods on a snowy evening;
From darkling; Keyboard: organ sonata; 7 psalms
without words, organ.
1413 Telegraph Ave., Stockton, CA 95204

*SCHNEIDER, EDWARD FABER
b. Omaha, Neb., 3 Oct. 1872; d. Santa Clara,
Calif., 1 July 1950. Studied with Xavier
Scharwenka in New York; with Hans Barth in Berlin.
He taught privately in San Francisco, then at
Mills Coll.
WORKS: Orchestra: In autumn time, 1913;
Sargasso Sea, 1922; Fires of wisdom; Thus spake
the deepset stone, 1938; songs; piano pieces.

*SCHOENBERG, ARNOLD
b. Vienna, Austria, 13 Sep. 1874; U.S. citizen
1940; d. Brentwood, Calif., 13 July 1951. Studied
with Alexander von Zemlinsky in Vienna, but was
largely self-taught. On coming to the U.S. he
taught first at the Malkin Cons. in Boston; was
appointed professor, Univ. of Southern California
in 1935, then at Univ. of California, Los Angeles,
1936. He retired from both positions in 1944,
but continued to teach private classes and to
compose. Schoenberg's influence on modern music

(SCHOENBERG, ARNOLD)
through the introduction of the 12-tone scale
has been revolutionary. His Style and idea,
a collection of essays, was published in 1951.
Only a few of his major works are listed below.
WORKS: Opera: Die gluckliche Hand, music
drama to his own libretto, 1910-13; Moses and
Aaron, opera to his own libretto, 2 acts completed 1932, the full work never finished; Orchestra: Verklarte Nacht, written for string
sextet, 1899, arranged for string orch., 1917;
revised, 1943; Ode to Napoleon, speaker, strings,
piano, 1942; Chorus: Gurre-Lieder, soloists,
chorus, orch., 1901; De profundis, a cappella,
1951; many chamber works.

*SCHOENFIELD, PAUL
Rock sonata for cello and piano, New York, 28
Feb. 1974.
Department of Music, University of Toledo
Toledo, OH 43603

SCHOETTLE, ELMER
b. Kansas City, Mo., 16 July 1910; d. Houston,
Tex., 11 Sep. 1973. Studied with Walter Piston,
Harvard Univ.; at George Peabody Coll., Nash-
ville, Tenn., B. A.; with Bernard Rogers and
Howard Hanson, Eastman School of Music, M. M.,
Ph. D. He received the Charles Ives award,
Texas Fed. of Music Clubs, Houston. He taught
at Fisk Univ., 1944-50; Univ. of Oklahoma,
1953-55; Northeast Missouri State Coll., 1955-57;
Univ. of Houston, 1957-73.
WORKS: Orchestra: Fantasy for string orch.;
Chamber music: sonatina for percussion; Flight,
tenor voice, clarinet, piano; quartet for piano
and strings; quartet for oboe and strings; piano
trio; violin sonata; Fantasie variations for
woodwinds; Chorus: The fear of the Lord.

SCHONTHAL, RUTH
b. Hamburg, Germany, 27 June 1924; U.S. citizen
1956. Studied at Stern Cons., Berlin; Royal
Acad. of Stockholm; with Manuel Ponce and Paul
Hindemith, Yale Univ., B. M. Her string quartet
received the Delta Omicron 3rd internat. award.
She has been a private teacher and in 1973
joined the faculty of Adelphi Univ.
WORKS: Ballet: The transposed heads, also
an orchestral suite from the ballet; Chamber
music: string quartet; cello sonata; violin
sonata; Voice: 9 lyric-dramatic songs on texts
by Yeats, mezzo-soprano and chamber orch.;
Totensange, soprano and piano; Piano: 5 sonatas;
Klange aus der Jugend, prepared piano; Miniatures; Miniscules.
12 Van Etten Blvd., New Rochelle, NY 10804

SCHOOLEY, JOHN HEILMAN
b. Nelson, Pa., 8 Feb. 1943. Studied at Mansfield State Coll., B. S. 1965; with Richard
Stoker, Royal Acad. of Music, London, certificate 1966; with Gregory Kosteck, East Carolina
Univ., M. M. 1968; with Charles Jones, Aspen,
Col.; and with Howard Boatwright in Vevey, Switz.
He received a Rotary Found. fellowship and Ellen
Stoeckel fellowship to Yale Summer School. He
was instructor, Eastern Kentucky Univ., 1968-70;
assistant professor, Fairmont State Coll., 1970-73.

SCHOOLEY, JOHN HEILMAN

(SCHOOLEY, JOHN HEILMAN)
WORKS: Orchestra: Concertino for winds and percussion; Dance scenes, 1967; Chamber music: Partita, brass quartet, 1966; 3 dances for woodwind trio, 1968, revised 1972; Serenata, tuba and piano, 1970; Vocalise for soprano and piano, 1970; Chorus: Lines to Ralph Hodgson Esquire, for girls' choir, 1973; Responses for the contemporary church, 1973.
1138 Bell Run Road, Fairmont, WV 26554

SCHRADER, BARRY
b. Johnstown, Pa., 26 June 1945. Studied at Univ. of Pittsburgh, B. A. 1967, M. F. A. 1970; with Morton Subotnick, California Inst. of the Arts, 1971. He won an award in the first Internat. Electronic Music Contest at Bourges, France, 1973. He has been on the music faculty, California Inst. of the Arts, 1971-   .
WORKS: Film scores: (electronic) Labyrinth, 1970; How to make a woman, 1971; Death of the red planet, 1972; Cowboys and Indians, 1972; Heavylight, 1973; Electronic: Serenade, 1969; Apparitions, 1970; Celebration, 1971; Bestiary, 1972-   ; Multimedia: Elysium, harp, dancers, lights, tape, 1971. He also composed an outdoor sound environment for Otto Piene's Sky Ballet, 1970.
School of Music
California Institute of the Arts
Valencia, CA 91355

*SCHRAMM, HAROLD
b. Chicago, Ill., 3 July 1935; d. Studied with Rudolf Ganz and Karel Jirak, Chicago Musical Coll., B. M., M. M.; held fellowships at Tanglewood, MacDowell Colony, Bennington Composers Conf., All India Radio. He was composer and arranger, Australian Broadcasting Commission, 1960-61; gave lecture recitals in the Far East and the U.S.
WORKS: Opera: Shilappadikaram; Orchestra: Invocation for strings; Mogul set, string orch.; Chamber music: Partita, 2 trumpets; Song of Tayumanavar, soprano and flute; Chorus: Alarippu, speaking chorus and percussion; India: a choral poem, on folksongs of India; Canticle, an aleatory setting to the composer's own text; Piano: Bharata sangita; Natyamalika, a suite; Vertical construction.

*SCREIBER, FREDERICK C.
b. Vienna, Austria, 13 Jan. 1895; U.S. citizen 1945. Studied at Vienna Acad. of Music and Vienna Univ. He was teacher and opera conductor in Vienna; from 1939, organist-choirmaster in New York.
WORKS: Orchestra: 9 symphonies; 2 violin concertos; cello concerto; Concerto grosso; The beatitudes, symphonic trilogy for chorus and orch., 1950; The intangible, oratorio, chorus and orch.; also chamber music; choral works, organ and piano pieces.

SCHROEDER, WILLIAM A.
b. Brooklyn, N. Y., 24 Apr. 1921. Studied with Max Wald, Chicago Musical Coll.; with Anthony Donato, Northwestern Univ. He held an Oliver Ditson scholarship, Chicago Musical Coll., 1942; received the Faricy award, Northwestern Univ.,

(SCHROEDER, WILLIAM A.)
1959. He taught at Peabody Cons., 1949-51; Judson Coll., 1952-56; Henderson State Teachers Coll., 1959-61; Wartburg Coll., 1961-65; Del Mar Coll., 1965-   ; at Nat. Music Camp, Interlochen, Mich., 1965-   .
WORKS: Wind ensemble: Invention and fugue; Prologue, canon, and stretto; March, antiphonal and triumphant, 2 brass choirs; Chamber music: Of moon and winds, song cycle for voice, string quartet, piano; string quartet; Age - The beauty of time, mezzo-soprano and woodwind quintet; Chorus: Canticle of praise, with brass quintet and timpani.
4413 Bluefield Drive
Corpus Christi, TX 78413

SCHROTH, GODFREY
b. Trenton, N. J., 7 Jan. 1927. Studied with Edwin Hughes and Paul Creston in New York; at Columbia Univ., M. A. He received the Lado Found. chamber music award, 1959; New Jersey Council on the Arts composition grant, 1972. He was lecturer, St. Joseph's Coll., 1956-61; director of music, St. Mary's Cathedral, Trenton, 1959-   .
WORKS: Orchestra: Symphonic fantasy; Fantasy scherzo; Rocky Mt. serenade, 1972; Chamber music: piano quintet, 1959; Chorus: Rod of Jesse; Vesper prayer; This is the day; The eyes of all; A ballad of Christmas; Organ: 2 suites; Meditation songs.
261 Lookout Ave., Hackensack, NJ 07601

*SCHRYOCK, BUREN
b. Sheldon, Iowa, 13 Dec. 1881; d. San Diego, Calif., 20 Jan. 1974. Conducted the San Diego Symphony, 1913-20; the San Diego Opera Company, 1920-36. His works include 5 operas, to his own librettos; a symphony; chamber music; piano pieces.

SCHUBEL, MAX
b. Bronx, N. Y., 11 Apr. 1932. Studied at New York Univ., B. A. 1953; privately with Charles Haubiel, 1952-53; at City Coll. of New York, 1957-58; with Frank Martin in Holland, 1964. He held scholarships at New York Univ. and for study with Haubiel; 2 MacDowell fellowships, 1969, 1972; received 2 Noble Found. awards, 1969, 1973; Ford Found. grant 1971; American Music Center grant, 1973; Nat. Endowment for the Arts $1500 grant, 1974. Since 1949 he has worked at various jobs - in record stores, for recording companies, free-lance woodworking and masonry and other jobs related to construction. In 1966 he was cofounder of Opus One, a recording company.
WORKS: Ballet: Insected surfaces, 1965-66, Univ. of Utah, 6-13 Apr. 1967; Orchestra: Specters and Sheldrakes, Wellesley, Mass., 11 Apr. 1965; Fracture, 1969; Overfeed, Young People's Symphony Orch., Springfield, Mass., 26 Jan. 1974; Chamber music: Omphaloskepsis, solo cello, 1964; Etudes, solo cello, 1965; Gigantica, double bass solo, 1965; Supercool, solo viola, 1965; Elegy, flute and cello, 1965; 4 duets, violin and cello, Quashed culch, flute and bass, 1966; Son of quashed culch, flute, cello, bass, 1967; Environmental music, flute, bass, percussion, 1966;

(SCHUBEL, MAX)

Spacewalk and choralic playpiece, piano, 1966; Exotica, cello and harpsichord, 1967; Joyeux noel, cello and piano, 1967; High ice, string quartet no. 2, Kohon Quartet, WNYC-TV, 3 Jan. 1968; Charismata, string quartet no. 3, with tape, 1968; Quashed culch the pyure, flute and harpsichord, 1969; Christmas treat, cello and harpsichord, 1969; Zones, flute, brass quintet, percussion, and actress, New York, 14 May 1972; Safety factor, flute, bass clarinet, bass trombone, contra bassoon, baritone saxophone, New York, 11 Feb. 1973.

Box 604, Greenville, ME 04441

*SCHULÉ, BERNARD

b. 1909.   Resonances, brass ensemble, 1962.

SCHULLER, GUNTHER

b. New York, N. Y., 22 Nov. 1925. Began study as a boy soprano at St. Thomas Choir School and soon added the study of composition, flute, and French horn to his curriculum. He started composing at age 12 and at the same time made such progress on the horn that he held a position as horn player with the Ballet Theatre Orchestra at age 16. His many honors include Nat. Inst. of Arts and Letters award, 1960; Brandeis Creative Arts award, 1960; 2 Guggenheim fellowships; Darius Milhaud award for score of film Yesterday in fact, 1964; honorary doctorate, Colby Coll., 1969; Alice M. Ditson conducting award, Columbia Univ., 1970; Rogers and Hammerstein award, 1971; and numerous commissions. He was solo horn player, Cincinnati Symphony, 1943-44; with Metropolitan Opera Orchestra, 1944-59; taught at Manhattan School of Music, 1950-63; was music director, 1st Internat. Jazz Festival, 1962; acting head, composition department, Berkshire Music Center, 1963-65, artistic co-director, 1969-   ; associate professor, Yale Univ., 1964-66; president, New England Cons., 1966-   .

WORKS: Opera: The visitation, after Franz Kafka, 1966, first American performance, San Francisco, 1967; The fisherman and his wife, children's opera, Boston, 8 May 1970; Variants, New York, 4 Jan. 1961; Orchestra: horn concerto, Cincinnati Symphony with composer as soloist, 1944; cello concerto, 1945; symphony for brass and percussion, 1949; Dramatic overture, 1951; Threnos, oboe and orch.; Composition in 3 parts; Concertino, jazz quartet and orch., 1959; 7 studies on themes of Paul Klee, 1959; Spectra, 1959; 5 bagatelles; American triptych; Contrasts, 1961; piano concerto, 1962; symphony, 1964; Diptich, brass quintet and orch., Boston, 31 Mar. 1967; Triplum, New York, 28 June 1967; double-bass concerto, New York, 27 June 1968; Journey into jazz, narrator, jazz quintet, orch.; Band: Study in textures; Meditation; Lines and contrasts, 16 horns; Concert jazz: Abstractions; 12 by 11, 1955; Variations on a theme by John Lewis; Transformations, 1957; Densities 1, 1962; Night music, 1962; Chamber music: suite for woodwind quintet, 1945; cello sonata, 1946; 2 string quartets; oboe sonata; Fantasia concertante, 3 oboes and piano, 1947; Fantasia concertante, 3 trombones and piano, 1947; quartet for 4 double-basses, 1947; trio, oboe, horn, viola,

(SCHULLER, GUNTHER)

1948; quintet for 4 horns and bassoon, 1949; 5 pieces for 5 horns, 1952; double quintet, woodwinds and brass; Recitative and rondo, violin and piano, 1953; quartet for flute and strings, 1953; Contours, chamber orch., 1956; woodwind quintet, 1958; Fantasy quartet, 4 cellos, 1958; Conversations, jazz quartet and string quartet, 1959; Music for brass quintet, 1961; Fantasy, for harp; Concerto da camera, 1971; Chorus: Psalm 98, cantata, Atlanta, June 1966; The power within us, oratorio, Atlanta, Mar. 1972. He is author of 2 books: Horn technique, New York, 1962; and Early jazz: Its roots and musical development, New York, 1968.

c/o New England Conservatory
290 Huntington Ave., Boston, MA 02115

SCHULTZ, RALPH C.

b. Dolton, Ill., 23 June 1932. Studied with Herman Spier and Rossetter Cole in Chicago; with Ross Lee Finney, Univ. of Michigan; Marcel Dick, Cleveland Inst. of Music; and with Seth Bingham, Union Theological Seminary, New York, S. M. D. He was church music director in Cleveland, 1954-61; chairman, music department, professor, Concordia Coll., Bronxville, N. Y., 1961-   ; music director, Village Lutheran Church, Bronxville, 1967-   ; lecturer in conducting, Union Theological Seminary, 1968-71.

WORKS: Orchestra: Intelligent man, a suite; Chorus: Let us all work with gladsome voice, with orch.; Lutheran chorale mass, with orch.; To Him be glory, with orch.; O sing unto the Lord a new song; Sing for joy, with instruments.

6 Concordia Place, Bronxville, NY 10708

SCHUMACHER, STANLEY E.

b. Indianapolis, Ind., 9 Aug. 1942. Studied with Philip Slates, Jordan Coll., Butler Univ., B. M. 1964; M. M. 1966; with Marshall Barnes, Herbert Brun, and David Behrman, Ohio State Univ., Ph. D. candidate 1974.

WORKS: Chamber music: Symmetries, for 4 instruments, 1968; Beat me daddy, 8 to a bar, trombone, piano, string bass, 1969; Dialogue, 3 narrators and trombone, 1970; Musography I, 2 clarinets, 3 trombones, 1972.

4928 Arbor Village Drive, Apt. C
Columbus, OH 43214

SCHUMAN, WILLIAM

b. New York, N. Y., 4 Aug. 1910. Left the School of Commerce, New York Univ. to study harmony with Max Persin and counterpoint with Charles Haubiel; attended Teachers Coll., Columbia Univ., B. S. 1935; M. A. 1937; studied conducting at the Mozarteum, Salzburg, 1935; composition with Roy Harris, Juilliard School, 1936-38. His many honors include 2 Guggenheim fellowships; the first Pulitzer Prize in music, 1943; Koussevitzky Found. award; Music Critics Circle of New York award; Columbia Univ. Bicentennial award, 1954; first Brandeis Creative Arts award in music, 1957; Nat. Inst. of Arts and Letters award; Gold Medal of Honor for music, Nat. Arts Club; 20 honorary doctorates; MacDowell Medal, 1971; election to American Acad. of Arts and Letters, 1973.

SCHUMAN, WILLIAM

(SCHUMAN, WILLIAM)
He was faculty member, Sarah Lawrence Coll., 1936-45; director of publications, G. Schirmer, Inc., 1945-52; president of Juilliard School, 1945-62; president of Lincoln Center, 1962-69.

WORKS: Opera: The mighty Casey, a baseball opera, 1952; Ballet: Undertow - Choreographic episodes, 1945; Voyage for a theatre; Night journey, 1947; Judith - Choreographic poem, 1949; The witch of Endor; Orchestra: 9 symphonies, 1936-1969; American festival overture, 1939; Newsreel, suite, 1941; Prayer in time of war, 1942; piano concerto, 1942; William Billings overture, 1943; Circus overture, 1944; violin concerto, 1947; Credendum - An article of faith, 1955; New England triptych, 1956; A song of Orpheus, fantasy for cello and orch., 1961; Variations on America, orchestral version of original organ work by Charles Ives, New York, 21 May, 1964; To thee old cause, oboe and orch.; In praise of Shahn--Canticle for orchestra, 1969; Concerto on old English rounds for solo viola, women's chorus and orch., 1973, Boston, 29 Nov. 1974; Band: George Washington Bridge, 1950; Chester overture, 1956; When Jesus wept-Prelude for band, 1956; Chamber music: Amaryllis variations for string trio (3 women's voices ad lib); 4 string quartets, 1936, 1937, 1939, 1950; Quartettino, 4 bassoons, 1939; Voyage, a cycle of 5 pieces for piano; 3 piano moods; Chorus: 4 Canonic choruses, 1933; Choral etude, 1937; Prologues, chorus and orch., 1957; Prelude for voices, 1939; Mail order madrigals; Requiescat, 1942; A free song, 1942; Holiday song, 1942; Carols of death; Declaration chorale; Te Deum, 1944; Truth shall deliver, 1946; The Lord has a child, 1957; Film scores: Steeltown; The earth is born, 1957.
929 Park Ave., New York, NY 10028

*SCHUMANN, WALTER
b. New York, N. Y., 8 Oct. 1913; d. Minneapolis, Minn., 21 Aug. 1958. Studied law and music, Univ. of Southern California. He served in the Army Air Force in World War II; was music director, This is the army, New York; conducted Voices of Walter Schumann.

WORKS: Theatre: John Brown's body, opera, 1953; Three for tonight, musical; Film scores: The night of the hunter; Television themes: Dragnet, Emmy award, 1955; Steve Canyon.

*SCHUYTEN, ERNEST EUGENE EMILE
Antwerp, Belgium, 7 Nov. 1881; to U.S. 1915. Graduated from Brussels Cons., 1900. He founded the New Orleans Cons. in 1919; was dean, Coll. of Music, Loyola Univ., 1932-52, while keeping his affiliation with the conservatory. His compositions include a piano concerto, violin concerto, a symphony, chamber works, choral works and songs.

SCHWADRON, ABRAHAM A.
b. Brooklyn, N. Y., 25 Dec. 1925. Studied with Walter Ihrke, Univ. of Connecticut; with Hugo Norden, Boston Univ. He taught in Connecticut public schools, 1953-59; was chairman, music department, Rhode Island Coll., 1959-68; professor, Univ. of Hawaii, 1968-69; professor, Univ. of California, Los Angeles, 1969- .

(SCHWADRON, ABRAHAM A.)
WORKS: Chamber music: Short suite, clarinet and trombone; other published chamber music and choral pieces.
11361 Elderwood St., Los Angeles, CA 90049

SCHWANTER, JOSEPH
b. Chicago, Ill., 22 Mar. 1943. Studied with Benard Dieter, Chicago Cons. Coll., B. M. 1964; with Alan Stout and Anthony Donato, Northwestern Univ., M. M. 1966, D. M. 1968. His awards include the Faricy award, 1965; BMI student awards, 1965, 1966, 1967; Bearns prize, Columbia Univ., 1967; Charles Ives scholarship, Nat. Inst. of Arts and Letters, first recipient, 1970; Creative Artists Public Service grant, New York State Council on the Arts, 1973. He was teaching fellow, Northwestern Univ., 1966-68; faculty member, Chicago Cons. Coll., 1967-68; assistant professor, Pacific Lutheran Univ., 1968-69; Ball State Univ., 1969-70; Eastman School of Music, 1970- .

WORKS: Orchestra: Sinfonia brevis, 1963; concertino for alto saxophone and 3 chamber ensembles, 1964; August canticle, 1968; Modus caelestis, 12 flutes, 12 strings, percussion, piano, celeste, 1972; Wind ensemble: Canticle of the evening bells, 1974; Chamber music: piano sonatina, 1962; Pastorale for winds, 1963; Nonet, piano and chamber ensemble, 1965; Diaphonia intervallum, chamber ensemble, 1965; Entropy, saxophone, clarinet, cello, 1967; Chronicon, bassoon and piano, 1967; Enchiridion, violin and piano, 1968; Consortium I, flute, clarinet, string trio, 1970; Consortium II, chamber ensemble, 1971; In aeternum II, organ, 1972; In aeturnum for cello and 4 players, Harvard Univ., 27 Feb. 1973; Shadows I, for piano quartet, 1973; Elixir, chamber ensemble, Cambridge, Mass., 25 Feb. 1975.
21 Overbrook Road, Rochester, NY 14624

SCHWARTZ, ELLIOTT
b. Brooklyn, N. Y., 19 Jan. 1936. Studied with Otto Luening and Jack Beeson, Columbia Univ., M. A. 1958; privately with Paul Creston; with Henry Brant, Chou Wen-chung, Hugh Aitken, Stefan Wolpe, Edgard Varese at Bennington Composers Conference. He has received annual ASCAP awards, 1965- ; 2nd prize, Gaudeamus Internat. Music Week, Netherlands, 1970; Maine State award, 1970; American Music Center award, 1970; Ford Found. travel/research grants, 1969, 1971, 1972; Nat. Endowment for the Arts grants, 1967, 1974. He was instructor, Univ. of Massachusetts, Amherst, 1960-64; assistant professor, Bowdoin Coll., 1964-69, associate professor, 1969- ; visiting lecturer, Trinity Coll., London, 1967, and Univ. of California, Santa Barbara, 1970.

WORKS: Orchestra: Magic music; Texture, chamber orch., 1966; Island, 1970 prize; Band: Memorial, 1963; Voyage; Chamber music: Concert piece for 10 players, 1965; Soliloquies, flute, clarinet, violin, piano, 1965; Essays, trumpet and trombone, 1966; Arias no. 1-5, various duets; flute sonata; oboe sonata; Dialogue no. 1, double bass solo; Trireme, bassoon and piano; Miniconcerto, flute, oboe, and string trio, 1969;

(SCHWARTZ, ELLIOTT)
Graffiti, violin and cello; Septet, 5 instruments, piano, speaker/singer; Decline and fall of the sonata, Bowdoin Coll., 10 Apr. 1973; Electronic: Options I, trombone solo, percussion and tape optional; Options II, clarinet solo, percussion and tape optional; Dialogue no. 2, clarinet and tape; Interruption, woodwind quintet with tape loop; Music for Napoleon and Beethoven, trumpet, piano, 2 tapes, assistant, 1970; Music for Prince Albert, piano, 2 tapes, assistant, 1970; 3 islands, chamber ensemble, with ostinato accompaniment of British weather reports on tape, 1970. He is author of Electronic music: A listener's guide, New York, 1973.
5 Atwood Lane, Brunswick, ME 04011

SCHWARTZ, FRANCIS
b. Altoona, Pa., 10 Mar. 1940. Studied with Vittorio Giannini, Juilliard School, B. S., M. S.; conducting with Dietfried Bernet in Vienna. He has been professor, Univ. of Puerto Rico, 1966-   , chairman, music department, 1971-   .
WORKS: Orchestra: Prayer for Puerto Rico, orch, and girl's voice, 1972; Chamber music: Homage to an obscenity, percussion and narrator, 1968; Time-light, flute and piano, 1969; Transfigured day, oboe and piano, 1969; My name is Caligula...What's yours, narrator and entire audience, 1970; My eyebrows are not bushy, violin or viola solo, 1971; Chorus: Antigone, piano, flute, violin, soprano, chorus, 1967; Piano: Variations on a North American folksong, 1963; Pregón #1, 1966; Electronic: Suicide, voice, flute, percussion, tape, 1972; The tropical trek of Tristan Trimble, orch., tape and narrator, 1973; Toothache #1, tape and narrator, 1973; Multimedia: Auschwitz, tape, aromas, lights, dancers, 1968. He is co-author with Dr. Maria Luiza Muñoz of El mundo de la musica, Puerto Rico, 1974.
2021 Cacique St., Santurce, PR 00911

SCHWARTZ, JULIE
b. Washington, D.C., 17 Apr. 1947. Has studied with Ron Nelson, Hall Overton, and Jacob Druckman; with Julius Eastman, Frederic Rzewski, Gordon Mumma at New Music in N. H., 1973. She received a Nat. Fed. of Music Clubs junior award for a piano composition, 1962. She has taught at The Arts Center, Albany, N. Y., 1973-   .
WORKS: Chamber music: Matrix I, winds and strings; Breathpace, solo oboe; Homespun, vocal quartet, strings, percussion; Rounds, chamber ensemble; And so do I like to bang and tootle?, flute and percussion; In return, string quartet.
112 Manning Blvd., Albany, NY 12203

SCHWARTZ, MARVIN R.
b. Bronx, N. Y., 4 Feb. 1937. Studied with Luigi Dallapiccola, Leo Kraft, Felix Salzer, Saul Novack at Queens Coll., B. A. 1957; with Irving Fine, Harold Shapero, Arthur Berger, Brandeis Univ., M. F. A. 1959; at Jewish Theological Seminary, D. S. M. 1964. He received the Ernest Bloch Memorial award, 1961; MacDowell fellowship, 1962. He has been chairman, music department, Queensborough Community Coll., 1969-   , associate professor, 1971-   ;

(SCHWARTZ, MARVIN R.)
adjunct assistant professor, Queens Coll., CUNY, 1970-71, adjunct associate professor, 1971-   .
WORKS: Opera: Look and long, 2-acts, after Gertrude Stein, commissioned and premiered by After Dinner Opera Company, 1972; Orchestra: In memoriam, Fredric Kurzweil, chorus, soloists, chamber orch., 1971; Ruth, chorus, soloists, orch., 1967; Chamber music: Tal, baritone and organ; Scherzo, violin and piano, 1963; 3 canons of love, bass-baritone and string trio, 1971; Threes and twos for three, alto flute, clarinet, bassoon, 1971.
166-10 75th Ave., Flushing, NY 11366

*SCHWARTZ, PAUL
b. Vienna, Austria, 1907; to U.S. 1938. Studied at Vienna State Acad. of Music, diploma and master's degree in composition; with Ernst Krenek and Franz Schmidt, Univ. of Vienna, Ph. D. 1933. He was chairman, music department, Bard Coll., 1938-47; chairman, music department, Kenyon Coll., 1947-   , also professor of church music.
WORKS: Chamber opera: The experiment, 1956; Orchestra: Overture to a Shakespeare comedy, 1948; Variations on an Ohio folk tune, 1952; Chamber music: string quartet, 1936; violin sonata, 1941; concertino for chamber orch., 1937, revised 1947; chamber concerto for 2 pianos, 1944; Vienna baroque suite, clarinet choir; Little trio, violin, viola, piano; Chorus: Fog, Sandburg text, Serenade, Hillyer text.
Department of Music, Kenyon College Gambier, OH 43022

*SCHWARTZ, STEPHEN
b. 1948.   Was a student at Carnegie Inst. of Technology when he composed the musical show Godspell.

SCHWARZ, IRA PAUL
b. Sheldon, Iowa, 24 Feb. 1922. Studied at the U.S. Naval School of Music, 1942; at Morningside Coll., A. B. 1952; Univ. of South Dakota, M. A. 1954; with Philip Bezanson, Univ. of Iowa, Ph. D. 1961; also with Thaddeus Jones and Nadia Boulanger. He served in Navy bands, 1941-47; taught in public schools, 1948-51; held academic posts, Univ. of South Dakota, 1955-58; State Univ. of Iowa, 1958-61; Minot State Coll., 1961-65; Northeast Missouri State Univ., 1966-68; Univ. of Southern Mississippi, 1968-70; has been professor and chairman, music department, State Univ. Coll., Brockport, N. Y., 1970, acting dean, Faculty of Fine Arts, 1972-73; has conducted many local bands and orchestras.
WORKS: Opera: The wedding; Wind ensemble: Montage, winds and percussion; Chamber music: string quartet, 1960; woodwind quintet, 1960; Chorus: Abraham and Isaac, cantata, 1967. He is author of A brief source book for humanities and related arts, 1971; co-author of Teaching the related arts, 1973.
P. O. Box 115, Brockport, NY 14420

SCHWERDTFEGER, E. ANNE (formerly SR. M. ERNEST, O.P.)
b. Galveston, Tex., 1 Feb. 1930. Studied with Arthur Hall, Dominican Coll., Houston; with

SCHWERDTFEGER, E. ANNE

(SCHWERDTFEGER, E. ANNE)
Clifton Williams, Univ. of Texas; with Carl Hager
Univ. of Notre Dame. She taught at Dominican
Coll., Hoston, 1958-72, was head, music department, 1962-72.
WORKS: Orchestra: Exaudi Domine, string
orch., 1959; Christus rex, chamber orch., 1960;
symphony in one movement, 1963; Chamber music:
Modal suite, harp and tuba, 1960; Variations on
an Irish air, 6 harps, 1962; Chorus: Amo
Christum, 1957; Hymn of St. Francis, 1961; Mass
in honor of St. Martin de Porres, 1965; 2 pieces
on texts by Tagore, 1969; Piano: Toccatina, 1962;
Modal suite, 1965; Charivari, 1966.
via Giovanni Stanchi 7, Rome, Italy

SCIANNI, JOSEPH
b. Memphis, Tenn., 6 Oct. 1928. Studied at
Southwestern at Memphis, B. S. 1949; with Bernard
Rogers and Howard Hanson, Eastman School of Music,
M. M. 1953, D. M. A. 1959. His awards include
the Benjamin award at Eastman, 1958; UNICO award,
1961; 4 awards for jazz performance; ASCAP
awards, 1971, 1972, 1973; Nat. Council on the
Arts awards, 1970, 1971, 1972. He was teaching
assistant, Eastman School, 1957-58; private
teacher, 1959-   ; faculty member, New York Coll.
of Music, 1965-68; New York Univ., 1968-71;
associate professor, Staten Island Community
Coll., CUNY, 1971-   ; led the New York Univ.
Jazz Ensemble, 1968-70.
WORKS: Orchestra: Sinfonia breve, 1958;
Adagio cantabile; Wind ensemble: Court Square,
1957; Air for band; Jazz orch: Big orange;
Alligator pear; Granite rock; Gaza strip;
Florence in July; Red Phantom rides again; Chamber
music: Lament for solo flute, 1962; Chorale and
fugue, for brass quartet; Piano: Man running,
8 pieces; 4 movements; Electronic: Horizon south,
bass and electronic mutations; Film score:
Another time, another place. He is author of
Sound of rock, New York.
400 2nd Ave., Apt. 11D
New York, NY 10010

*SCIAPIRO, MICHEL
b. Odessa, Russia, 6 Apr. 1891; to U.S. in youth;
d. New York, N.Y., 3 Mar. 1962. Studied violin
with Hugo Heermann and Otakar Sevcik; was concert
violinist at 5; soloist with Berlin Philharmonic,
Vienna Konzert Vereins Orchestra; was member of
the Arnhem Symphony; organized his own orchestra.
His works included Fantasy for string quartet;
many violin pieces and songs.

SCLATER, JAMES STANLEY
b. Mobile, Ala., 24 Oct. 1943. Studied with
William Presser, Univ. of Southern Mississippi;
with Hunter Johnson, Univ. of Texas, D. M. A.
He was winner, Southern Regional composition
contest, College Band Directors Nat. Asso., 1972.
He was part-time instructor, Univ. of Texas,
1967-69; music librarian, Austin Public Library,
1969-70; assistant professor, Mississippi Coll.,
1970-   ; principal clarinetist, Jackson
Symphony Orchestra, 1971-   .
WORKS: Orchestra: symphony; Band: Variations on Gone is my mistris; Requiescat in pace;

(SCLATER, JAMES STANLEY)
Visions, 1973; Chamber music: woodwind trio;
Suite for clarinet and piano; brass quintet,
1972.
709 East Leake, Clinton, MS 39056

*SCOTT, F. WAYNE
Rondo giocoso, brass ensemble.
Department of Music, Univ. of Colorado
Boulder, CO 80302

*SCOTT, JOHN NEWHALL
b. Portland, Ore., 11 May 1907; d. 25 July 1963.
Studied at Univ. of Washington. He was pianist
in dance bands, theatre, films, and radio. His
compositions include the film score for My darling Clementine and songs.

*SCOTT, JOHN PRINDLE
b. Norwich, N. Y., 16 Aug. 1877; d. Syracuse,
N. Y., 2 Dec. 1932. Studied at Oberlin Cons.
and privately. He was a vocal soloist and
teacher and composed many songs.

*SCOTT, ROBERT W. (BOBBY)
b. Mt. Pleasant, N. Y., 29 Jan. 1937. Studied
with Eduard Moritz; is a pianist and arranger
with dance bands. His works include the musical,
Dinny and the witches; music for the play, A
taste of honey; and quintet for horn and strings,
New York, 5 May 1974.

SCOTT, STEPHEN
b. Corvallis, Ore., 10 Oct. 1944. Studied with
Homer Keller, Univ. of Oregon, B. A.; with Paul
Nelson and Gerald Shapiro, Brown Univ., M. A.
1969. He has been instructor to assistant professor, Colorado Coll., 1969-   .
WORKS: Orchestra: Variations on an American
folk tune; Chamber music: Baby Ben, for 10
instruments; The Dee Wright Observatory, 2
pianos, 8-hands; Electronic: 5 Ferlinghetti
poems, narrator, instruments, tape; Suspended
animation, instruments and tape recorders;
Glacier music, woodwind quintet and tape recorders.
Music Department, Colorado
Colorado Springs, CO 80903

*SCOTT, TOM (THOMAS JEFFERSON)
b. Campbellsburg, Ky., 28 May 1912; d. New York,
N. Y., 12 Aug. 1961. Studied violin with his
uncle; composition later with George Antheil in
Los Angeles; and with Harrison Kerr and
Wallingford Riegger.
WORKS: Opera: The fisherman, 1936; Orchestra: Song with dance, 1932; Plymouth Rock, 1938;
Hornpipe and chantey, 1944; symphony, 1946;
From the sacred harp, 1946; Johnny Appleseed,
1948; Lento, saxophone and strings, 1953; Binorie
variations, 1953; Chamber music: 2 string quartets, 1944, 1956; Emily Dickinson suite, violin
and harp, 1955; Chorus: Ballad of the harp
weaver, narrator, chorus, string quartet, 1946;
Go down death; Creation, chorus and ensemble.

*SCOTT-HUNTER, HORTENSE
Studied at Peabody Cons. Her chamber operas,
Pelleas and Melisande and Harlequin in search

(SCOTT-HUNTER, HORTENSE)
of his heart were presented the New York Opera
Workshop, 1959; Maid of the mist, a ballet, was
performed in Baltimore, Sep. 1956; other works
include incidental music for The little world of
Kim Hai, 1959; Ad Te Domine, levavi, cantata,
1960; Love song, 1961.

SCOVILLE, MARGARET
b. Pasadena, Calif., 3 May 1944. Studied with
William Kothe, Ramon Fuller, Lejaren Hiller,
Morton Feldman, State Univ. of New York at
Buffalo.
WORKS: Chamber music: 4 fragments from
Empedocles, soprano, flute, piano; Ephemerae,
violin, 2 violas, cello; Time out of mind,
2 percussionists; Electronic: Electric Sunday,
magnetic tape; Number 9 (untitled), tape;
13 ways of looking at a blackbird, chamber
ensemble and tape.
467 West Delavan, Buffalo, NY 14213

*SEAGER, GERALD
The marriage of the grocer of Seville, 1-act
opera, Ohio State Univ., Columbus, Feb. 1971.

SEAMAN, EUGENE I.
b. New York, N. Y., 23 Oct. 1925. Studied with
Marion Bauer and Philip James, New York Univ.;
with Fritz Mahler and Carl Friedberg, Juilliard
School; at Pope Pius X School of Liturgical
Music; piano privately with the Lhevinnes and in
France and Germany. He was faculty member,
Adelphi Univ. and Queens Coll., 1967-69; staff
pianist, American Ballet Theatre, 1969-71;
partner in Seaman Concert Management, 1971-   .
His compositions include concertos, chamber music,
piano works; his chamber music has been performed
frequently in Carnegie Recital Hall and Town
Hall, New York.
1697 Broadway, New York, NY 10019

SEAR, WALTER
b. New Orleans, La., 27 Apr. 1930. Studied with
George Rochberg, Curtis Inst. of Music; with
Thaddeus Jones, Catholic Univ.; and with Otto
Luening, Columbia Univ. He received the Sosland
Chamber Music award. He was part-time faculty
member, Mannes Coll. of Music, 1967-72; Trenton
State Coll., 1970-72; owns and operates an
electronic music studio and is performer on
low brass.
WORKS: Orchestra: 2 symphonies; Chamber
music: 3 string quartets; sonata for unaccompanied tuba; and film scores. He is author of
The new world of electronic music, New York, 1972.
235 West 46th St., New York, NY 10036

*SEARCH, FREDERICK PRESTON
b. 1899; d. Published a string quartet and a
string sextet.

SEARS, ILENE HANSON
b. Crookston, Minn., 31 Aug. 1938. Studied with
Bernhard Heiden and Thomas Beversdorf, Indiana
Univ. She was piano instructor, Salem Coll.,
Winston-Salem, N. C., 1967-68; instructor in theory

(SEARS, ILENE HANSON)
and piano, Winston-Salem State Univ., 1968-   .
WORKS: Chamber music: piano sonatina;
cello sonata; Chorus: 3 Christmas carols.
136 Rosedale Circle
Winston-Salem, NC 27102

*SEAVER, BLANCHE EBERT
b. Chicago, Ill. 15 Sep. 1891. Studied with
her father and others; received the Jane Addams
award from Rockford Coll.; was named Woman of
the Year by the Los Angeles Times, 1964. Her
works include a Pontifical mass and many songs.
20 Chester Place, Los Angeles, CA 90007

*SEAVER, HARRY A.
b. Albany, N.Y., 20 Jan. 1909. Studied at
Harvard Univ., B. A. 1933.
WORKS: Chamber music: flute sonatina;
Heaven storming rhapsody, 2 pianos, 1932; violin
sonata, 1936; 3 Irish poems, cello and piano,
1936; piano quintet, 1936.

*SEAWELL, BRENT
Scope, tympany concerto.

SEBESKY, GERALD J.
b. Perth Amboy, N. J., 8 Sep. 1941. Studied at
Manhattan School of Music, B. M., M. M.; with
Chou Wen-chung, Columbia Univ., diploma; with
Robert Lincoln and Stefan Wolpe. He received a
New Jersey State Council on the Arts grant and
a Phi Mu Alpha composition award. He has taught
in New Jersey public schools, 1964, Edison
Township Schools, 1969-   .
WORKS: Band: Passacaglia and interlude;
Structures VII; Chamber music: brass quintet
no. 2; Montage for woodwinds; many published
works for band, stage band, and chorus.
584 Jacques St., Perth Amboy, NJ 08861

*SECUNDA, SHOLOM
b. Alexandria, Russia, 23 Aug. 1894; U.S. citizen
1918; d. New York, N. Y., 13 June 1974. Studied
at Cooper Union, 1912-13; Columbia Univ., 1913-
14; Inst, of Musical Art, 1914-19; with Ernest
Bloch on a scholarship. He was named a fellow,
Internat. Inst. of Arts and Letters, 1961.
During World War I he was a Navy band arranger;
was also music critic for the Jewish Daily
Forward; lecturer at Hunter Coll.; composed for
opera, burlesque, musical comedy, and for radio
and television.
WORKS: Opera: Sulamith, 1925; some 50
operettas; Orchestra: 3 symphonic sketches;
If not higher, oratorio, soloists, chorus, orch.;
chamber music; Jewish liturgical works; and songs,
including the very popular Bei mir bist du schoen.

*SEEGER, CHARLES LOUIS, JR.
b. Mexico City, Mex., 14 Dec. 1886. Studied at
Harvard Univ., A. B. 1908. He taught at Univ.
of California, 1912-19; Inst. of Musical Art,
1921-33; New School for Social Research, 1931-35;
was assistant to the music director, Fed. Music
Project, WPA, 1938-40; chief, music division, Pan
American Union, 1941-53. He was married to

SEEGER, CHARLES LOUIS, JR.

(SEEGER, CHARLES LOUIS, JR.)
Ruth Crawford, the composer. Though chiefly a musicologist, he composed music for the pageants Derdra, 1914, and The queen's masque, 1915; an overture; violin sonata; and songs.

*SEEGER, RUTH CRAWFORD. See CRAWFORD-SEEGER, RUTH

*SEGALL, BERNARDO
b. Campinas, Brazil, 4 Aug. 1911. Studied piano with Alexander Siloti and composition with Lazare Saminsky in New York; received an honorary degree from Sao Paulo Cons.; has been concert pianist from age 9.
WORKS: Ballet: As I lay dying; Domino furioso; The wall; Desperate heart; And dreams intrude; Theatre: music for Camino real; Skin of our teeth; The sound and the fury; Film scores: Congolaise; Hope is eternal; The luck of Ginger Coffey; also songs.
23155 Mariposa de Oro
Malibu, CA 90265

*SEIBERT, BOB
Medusa's head, concert march for band; Concert Jazz: A roarin' borealis; Jazz suite, 8 brass, 5 saxophones; Theme and variations in jazz.

SEIDEL, RICHARD D.
b. Reading, Pa., 4 Aug. 1925. Studied at Lebanon Valley Coll., B. S.; Philadelphia Cons., M. M. cum laude; Montclair State Coll., M. A.; composition with Harry Robert Wilson. He was director, high school choral music, 1958-67; director, Lutheran Choral Society, 1965-67; chairman, Division of Fine Arts, Centenary Coll. for Women, 1967- .
WORKS: Chorus: Christmas lullaby, women's voices; Go lovely rose; Psalm 23; 2 sets of songs for children.
8 George Ave., Wyomissing, PA 19610

SELBST, GEORGE
b. New York, N. Y., 21 Feb. 1917. Studied at Juilliard School; New York Coll. of Music; and with Jacob Weinberg, Manhattan School of Music. He was director of music and curriculum for exceptional children, Suffolk County, N. Y., Board of Cooperative Educational Services, 1957-65; public school music teacher, Islip, N. Y., 1965- ; conductor, Islip Symphony Orchestra, 1965- .
WORKS: Orchestra: symphony; violin concerto; Chamber music: sonatas; sonatinas; Liturgical: Hebrew requiem; organ preludes; works commissioned by Rodof Sholom Temple, Youngstown, Ohio; other sacred and secular works.
96 C Enfield Court, Ridge, NY 11961

*SELETSKY, HAROLD
Has published a string quartet and has had various works performed in New York.

SELIG, ROBERT
b. Evanston, Ill., 1939. Studied with Anthony Donato, Northwestern Univ., B. M. 1961, M. M. 1962; with Irving Fine, Brandeis Univ., 1962; Halsey Stevens, Univ. of Southern California,

(SELIG, ROBERT)
1963; Gardner Read, Boston Univ., 1966-68; privately with Donald Martino and Ernst Krenek; and at Tanglewood, 1966, 1968, 1972. He was awarded performance of his first symphony, Big Ten Contemporary Music Symposium, 1962; scholarships at Northwestern Univ., 1962, Brandeis Univ. 1962; BMI grant, 1963; Boston Univ. grant for study at Tanglewood, 1966; Fromm Found. grant, 1968; Tanglewood fellowship, 1968; Guggenheim fellowship, 1972. He was assistant composer, United Artists Music Company, 1964-66; teaching fellow, Boston Univ., 1966-68; faculty member, New England Cons., 1968- .
WORKS: Opera: Chocorua, Tanglewood, 2 Aug. 1972; Orchestra: Chicago: 3 portraits of a city, chamber orch.; Athena, for mezzo soprano and string orch., 1962; 2 symphonies, 1962, 1969; Mirage, trumpet and string orch., Tanglewood, 1968; Rhapsody for flute, violin, bass clarinet solos and orch.; Chamber music: violin sonata, 1960; 3 songs to texts of D. H. Lawrence, bass-baritone, winds, piano, Tanglewood, 22 July 1966; string quartet; woodwind quintet; The 3 seasons of autumn, voice, flute, cello, percussion, Boston, 2 Feb. 1973; Chorus: Mist in the valley, text by Millay, chorus and orch., 1971.
New England Conservatory of Music
290 Huntington Ave., Boston, MA 02115

*SELLECK, JOHN
Migrations, New York, 14 Jan. 1974; Ichinen Sangen, New York, 22 Feb. 1974.

SEMEGEN, DARIA
b. Bamberg, Germany, 27 June 1946; U.S. citizen 1957. Studied with Samuel Adler, Eastman School of Music; with Bulent Arel, Yale Univ.; Vladimir Ussachevsky, Columbia Univ.; with Witold Lutoslawski, Warsaw Cons., 1968-69. Her awards include 2 MacDowell fellowships; BMI awards, 1967, 1969; Mu Phi Epsilon composition prize, 1968; Fulbright grant, 1968; Woods Chandler prize, Yale Univ., 1970, 1971. She was staff technician, Columbia-Princeton Electronic Music Center, 1972; lecturer in composition and electronic music, State Univ. of New York at Stony Brook, 1973- .
WORKS: Orchestra: Triptych for orchestra, 1966; Chamber music: Quattro, flute and piano, 1967; Jeux des quatres, clarinet, trombone, cello, piano, 1970; Music for violin solo, 1973; Voice: Lieder auf der Flucht, soprano and 8 players, 1967; Dans la nuit, baritone and chamber orch., 1969; Electronic: Composition no. 1, 1972, received the Internat. Society for Contemporary Music award, 1975.
421 West 118th St., New York, NY 10027

SEMMLER, ALEXANDER
b. Dortmund, German, 12 Nov. 1900; U.S. citizen 1930. Studied piano with Joseph Pembaur, composition with Gustav Jenner; musicology at Universities of Marburg, Berlin, and Munich. He was a concert pianist at age 15, touring Europe and the U.S.; was pianist with CBS Symphony, then staff conductor at CBS in the 1940s; as special consultant to U.S. State Department, he was

(SEMMLER, ALEXANDER)
American administrator, music department, RIAS West Berlin; presented concerts and lectures in Mexico on invitation of Mexican Cultural Ministry, 1953-54; in New York, 1955-70, was music director, TRF Music, Inc., and Pantoscope Records. In retirement he is working on a book, Atonal melody writing.
WORKS: Chamber music: piano trio, 1964; Chorus: The owl and the pussy cat; also works for orchestra, chamber groups, solo instruments, voice, etc.
21 Millstream Road, Woodstock, NY 12498

*SENDREY, ALBERT RICHARD
b. Chicago, Ill., 26 Dec. 1900. Studied with his father, Alfred Sendrey in Leipzig; at Trinity Coll., London; also with John Barbirolli and Albert Coates. He was arranger for film companies in Paris and London, 1935-44; then in Hollywood.
WORKS: Opera: Bohème-A-go-go, rock opera, 1971; Orchestra: Oriental suite, 1935; 3 symphonies; piano concertino; Toccata and fugue; Chamber music: 2 string quartets; Divertimento for cello; duo for horn and viola; viola sonata.

*SENDREY, ALFRED
b. Budapest, Hungary, 29 Feb. 1884, permanently to U.S. in 1940. Conducted opera in Chicago, 1911-12, New York, 1913-14, Berlin, 1914-15, Vienna, 1915-16, Leipzig, 1918-24; then conducted orchestras in Leipzig, 1924-32; went to Paris in 1933, to U.S. in 1940; became a teacher in Los Angeles. His compositions include a 1-act opera; orchestral pieces; works for solo instruments; choral music.

*SEREBRIER, JOSE
b. Montevideo, Uruguay, 3 Dec. 1938; to U.S. 1950. Received 2 Guggenheim fellowships for composition; has been a conductor as well as composer from a very early age.
WORKS: Orchestra: symphony, 1957; Partita for orchestra; Poema elegiaco, 1963; Colores magicos, harp and orch., with color lighting, 1971; Chamber music: violin sonata, 1954.

SERLY, TIBOR
b. Losonc, Hungary, 25 Nov. 1900; U.S. citizen 1909; came to the U.S. as a very young child; studied violin and composition in New York, then returned to Budapest to study on scholarship with Zoltan Kodaly and Bela Bartok at Royal Acad. of Music, violin with Hubay, graduated with highest honors as composer and performer. He was violist with the Cincinnati Symphony, Philadelphia Orchestra, and NBC Symphony. He has developed new techniques for string instruments and for composition. He completed and orchestrated Bartok's viola concerto and 3rd piano concerto, and transcribed for orchestra the Mikrokosmos suite and other early piano pieces of Bartok, and was the first conductor to record several Bartok compositions. He has been guest and composer-conductor with many major orchestras in the U.S. and Europe.
WORKS: Orchestra: viola concerto, 1929; 2 symphonies, 1931, 1932; 6 dance designs, 1934;

(SERLY, TIBOR)
Transylvania suite, chamber orch., 1935; Sonata concertante, string orch., 1936; Pagan city, symphonic poem, 1938; Ballet Mishchianza, 1937; Ex-machina ballet, 1943; Elegy, 1945; Bartok viola concerto, 1948; Rhapsody, viola and orch., 1948; concerto for 2 pianos, 1952; trombone concerto, 1953; Fun with the instruments of the orchestra, 1954; Lament for string orch. (Homage to Bartok), 1958; concerto for violin and wind symphony, 1958; Symphonic variations, audience and orch., 1956; string symphony, 1956; Little Xmas cantata, audience and orch., 1957; American fantasy of quodlibets, 1959; concertino 3 times 3, piano and chamber orch., 1965; Chamber music: violin sonata, 1923; string quartet, 1924; Innovations, strings and 2 harps, 1933, revised for string quartet and harp, 1968; sonata for solo violin, 1947; trio for clarinet, violin, piano, 1950; Chorale for 3 harps, 1967; Canonic prelude, 4 harps, 1967; Stringometrics, violin and harp, 1968; Canonic fugue, for 10 strings, 1972; Bi-modals, 2 recorders, 1973; Fantasy on a double quodlibet, 3 harps or 3 groups, 1973; Voice: 4 songs from James Joyce's Chamber music, 1926; Strange story, mezzo-soprano and orch., 1927; Consovowels no. 1, solo soprano, 1968, no. 2, soprano and clarinet, 1970, no. 3, soprano and clarinet, 1971; Piano: sonata, 1946; suite for 2 pianos, 1946. He is author of the book, A second look at harmony, New York, 1965.
1328 18th Ave., Apt. 211
Longview City, WA 98632

*SESSIONS, ROGER HUNTINGTON
b. Brooklyn, N. Y., 28 Dec. 1896. Studied at Harvard Univ., A. B. 1915; with Horatio Parker, Yale Univ., B. M. 1917. His many awards include 2 Guggenheim fellowships, 1926-28; Damrosch fellowships in Rome, 1928-31; Naumberg Found. award, 1949-50; New York Music Critics Circle award, 1950; 5 honorary doctorates, 1958-71; membership in American Acad. of Arts and Sciences, Internat. Society for Contemporary Music, Nat. Inst. of Arts and Letters and the Inst.'s gold medal, 1961. He has taught at Smith Coll.; Cleveland Inst. of Music; Boston Univ.; New Jersey Coll. for Women; Princeton Univ., 1935-45, 1953-65; Univ. of California, Berkeley, 1945-52; Juilliard School, 1972-   ; and was visiting composer, Univ. of Iowa, 1971.
WORKS: Opera: The trial of Lucullus, 1946; Montezuma, 1947; Orchestra: The black maskers, suite, 1923; 8 symphonies, 1927-68; violin concerto, 1935; Scherzino and march, 1938; Idyll of Theocritus, soprano and orch., 1954; piano concerto, 1956; Divertimento, 1960; Rhapsody for orch., Baltimore, 18 Mar. 1970; concerto for viola and cello, New York, 5 Nov. 1971; Chamber music: 3 piano sonatas, 1930, 1946, 1965; 2 string quartets, 1936, 1950; From my diary, piano, 1940; duo for violin and piano, 1942; sonata for violin solo, 1953; string quintet, 1958; Chorus: Turn, O libertad, 1943; Mass in celebration of the 50th anniversary of Kent School, 1955; Psalm 140, 1963; 3 choruses on Biblical texts, for chorus and chamber orch., Amherst Coll., 8 Feb.

SESSIONS, ROGER HUNTINGTON

(SESSIONS, ROGER HUNTINGTON)
1975, on the occasion of a weekend festival high-
lighting Session's contribution to American
music.

SEVERY, VIOLET CAVELL
b. Pasadena, Calif., 26 May 1912. Studied with
W. B. Olds and Wayne Bohrnstedt, Univ. of Redlands,
B. M., M. M.; with Juan Orrego-Salas, Indiana
Univ.; John Barnes Chance, Univ. of Kentucky;
privately with Frances Marion Ralston. She has
been assistant professor, Morehead State Univ.,
1956-   .
WORKS: Chorus: Psalmotet, for chorus, boy
soprano, baritone, organ and plucked instrument,
commissioned by Music Teachers Nat. Asso. and
Kentucky Music Teachers Nat. Asso., 1970; other
works for woodwind quintet, string orch., flute,
oboe, and voice.
UPO 834, Morehead State University
Morehead, KY 40351

SEVITZKY, FABIEN
b. Vyshny Volotchek, Russia, 30 Sep. 1893; U.S.
citizen 1928; d. Miami, Fla., 3 Feb. 1967. Studied at St. Petersburg Cons., Russia; and at De
Pauw Univ., D. M. His awards include 3 honorary
doctorates, Illinois Wesleyan Univ., Indiana
Univ., and Butler Univ.; Cavalier Order de Boyaca,
Colombia, S. A. He was founder and conductor
of the Philadelphia String Chamber Sinfonietta,
1925; conductor, Philadelphia Grand Opera, 1927-
28; Pennsylvania Opera Company, 1928-30; Peoples
Symphony Orchestra, Boston, 1932-35; Indianapolis
Symphony, 1937-55; San Diego Summer Symphony,
1949-52; Indianapolis Symphonic Choir, 1937-55;
Univ. of Miami Symphony, 1959-65; Greater Miami
Philharmonic, 1965-66, music consultant, 1966-67;
also guest conductor of orchestras throughout
the U.S., Canada, Europe, South and Central
America, and Havana.
WORKS: Orchestra: Nocturne; Overture to an
opera; Chamber music: Chanson triste, violin and
piano; Nocturne, double bass and piano; Voice:
Christmas bells; My prayer; also many transcriptions for orchestra.

SEYFRIT, MICHAEL EUGENE
b. Lawrence, Kan., 16 Dec. 1947. Studied with
John Pozdro and Edward Mattila, Univ. of Kansas;
with Vincent Persichetti, Juilliard School;
Halsey Stevens, Robert Linn, and Anthony Vazzana,
Univ. of Southern California. His awards include
BMI student award; Phi Mu Alpha contemporary
music award; Nat. Inst. of Arts and Letters,
Charles E. Ives scholarship; Henry H. Bellamann
Found. award; Nat. Fed. of Music Clubs award.
He has been lecturer, California State Univ.,
Fullerton, 1973-   .
WORKS: Theatre: music for As you like it,
1971; Twelfth night, 1972; Orchestra: Windfest,
symphony no. 1 for winds, 1968; Peace, symphony
no. 2 for winds, 1969; Dichroism, symphony no. 3,
chamber orch., 1970; Chamber music: Winter's
warmth, bass voice, chamber ensemble, 1970;
Similes, oboe and cello solos with 3 flutes, alto
flute 4 percussion, 1970; Shadows and the night
wind, clarinet, alto flute, marimba, timpani,

(SEYFRIT, MICHAEL EUGENE)
1970; Brass rings, brass quintet, 1971; Continuum, vacuum, residuum, clarinet, English horn,
cello, prepared piano--6 hands, 1971; For one,
alone, clarinet solo, 1972; Portal, woodwind
quartet, 1973; Piano: Variegations, 1972;
Interactions, 1972.
440 South Veteran Ave., #107
Los Angeles, CA 90024

*SEYMOUR, JOHN LAURENCE
b. Los Angeles, Calif., 18 Jan. 1893. Studied
with Fannie Charles Dillon; at Univ. of California, Los Angeles, B. A., M. A., Ph. D.; with
Vincent d'Indy in Paris and with Pizzetti in
Italy. He was head of the drama department,
Sacramento Junior Coll., 1926-50. He received
the Bispham medal in 1935 for his opera, In the
Pasha's garden. His works include 5 other
operas; 4 operettas; ballets; piano concerto;
chamber music.

SHACKELFORD, RUDY
b. Newport News, Va., 18 Apr. 1944. Studied
with Milton Cherry, Virginia Commonwealth Univ.;
with Gordon Binkerd, Univ. of Illinois, D. M. A.;
and with Luigi Dallapiccola, George Rochberg,
Vincent Persichetti. He received an award, Ohio
State Univ. composition contest, 1969; 2 fellowships at Yaddo, 1972, 1973; MacDowell fellowship,
1974. He taught at Shenandoah Cons., 1972.
WORKS: Chamber music: Intaglio Stravinsky,
harpsichord, bass, 6 instruments, Dallas, 6 Oct.
1973; Cantata I on poems of Denise Levertov.
soprano and chamber ensemble; Cantata II, on
text by Dylan Thomas, tenor and string trio;
Keyboard: Nocturne, piano with recitation of
poem by Samuel Beckett, 1966, revised 1973;
Sonata for organ, 1969; Trio sonata 1970, organ,
Diferencias, organ; Berg im Nebel/Berg im Spiegel,
piano, 1971; Le tombeau de Stravinsky, harpsichord, 1971; songs and choral works.
Severn Post Office
Glouscester County, VA 23155

SHACKFORD, CHARLES REEVE
b. New York, N. Y., 18 Apr. 1918. Studied with
Paul Hindemith, Yale Univ., B. A. 1941, M. M.
1944; with Walter Piston, Harvard Univ., Ph. D.
1954. He was Atherton fellow at Harvard, 1947-49;
received Wyman Fund research grant, 1949; American Acad. of Arts and Sciences grant, 1955; Ford
Found. fellowship, 1961; several commissions.
His academic posts include Bennett Junior Coll.,
1944-46; teaching fellow, Harvard Univ., 1949-50;
lecturer, Wellesley Coll., 1952-53; research
fellow in acoustics, Harvard Univ., 1954-56;
music director, School of Nursing, Newton, Mass.,
1956-62; associate professor and chairman, music
department, Wilson Coll., 1962-65; visiting professor, Connecticut Coll., 1965-66, professor,
1966-   , chairman, 1969-72; director, Belmont
(Mass.) Community Chorus, 1955-59; organist and
choir director, Boston area, 1953-62.
WORKS: Orchestra: Serenade, piano and
chamber orch. 1942; Fantasy on Vysehrad, 2 pianos
and orch., 1969; Band: Overture concertante,
1973; Chamber music: trio for oboe, violin,

394

(SHACKFORD, CHARLES REEVE)
viola, 1942; string trio, 1947; duo for 2 clarinets, 1948; duo for horn and cello, 1949; Fantasy, cello and piano, 1951; woodwind trio, 1952; Toccata, brass sextet, 1967; sonata for viola solo, 1970; quintet for clarinet, horn, string trio, 1973; works for chorus and solo voice. He has published articles in music journals.
1611 Connecticut College
New London, CT 06320

SHAFFER, SHERWOOD
b. Beeville, Tex., 15 Nov. 1934. Studied with Bohuslav Martinu and Vittorio Giannini, Curtis Inst. of Music, B. M.; with Giannini, Manhattan School of Music, M. M. He won the Outstanding Educators of America award, 1972. He was faculty member, Manhattan School, 1962-65; chairman, theory department, North Carolina School of the Arts, 1965-   .
WORKS: Orchestra: Concertante, cello and orch., 1962; Rhapsody, double bass and orch., 1967; Chamber music: Cassation, violin and cello, 1964; cello sonata, 1965; double bass sonata, 1965; violin sonata, 1966; Serenade, oboe and horn; Sacra hora, soprano, baritone, viola, and cello, 1967; Variations, viola and cello, 1968; Berceuse and galliard, guitar, 1969; 4 quatrains, percussion, 1970; Faces of time, chorus and chamber ensemble, 1970.
133 Woodbriar Road, Winston-Salem, NC 27106

SHAHAN, PAUL W.
b. Grafton, W. Va., 2 Jan. 1923. Studied at Fairmont State Coll., B. M.; with Weldon Hart, West Virginia Univ., M. M.; with Roy Harris, Peabody Coll., M. E.; and with Kent Kennan, Bernard Rogers, Howard Hanson, Eastman School of Music. He received the Thor Johnson award, 1952; and many commissions. He taught in the Grafton, W. Va. public schools, then was staff arranger, WSM, Radio-TV, Nashville, 1951-52; has been choir director in various churches; associate professor, Murray State Coll., 1957-   .
WORKS: Opera: The Stubblefield story, 1963; Orchestra: 3 portraits for orchestra, 1950; 2 symphonic miniatures, 1953; Soliloquy, trumpet and strings, 1953; Morocco, 1954; Band: concerto for string bass and band, 1953; Spring festival, 1955; Holiday in Spain, 1959; The fountain head, 1963; The Lincoln heritage trail, 1966; A splash of splendour, 1966; Mosaics in motion, 1968; Wind ensemble: Spectrums, brass choir, 1952; Leipzig towers, brass choir, 1955; The Stadtpfier suite, brass, 1957; The City of David, brass and organ, 1956; Chamber music: The solemn sea, tuba and piano, 1960; Seascape, tuba and piano, 1960; Chorus: Sing, rejoice unto the Lord, 1960; How excellent are thy works, 1962; Psalm 150, 1963.
He has published articles in music journals.
Murray State College, Murray, KY 42071

SHAKARIAN, ROUPEN
b. Cairo, Egypt, 12 Mar. 1950; U.S. citizen 1965. Studied with John Verrall and William Bergsma, Univ. of Washington. He received the Brechemin

(SHAKARIAN, ROUPEN)
Family scholarship in Seattle; Calouste Gulbenkian scholarship, Lisbon, Portugal.
WORKS: Orchestra: harpsichord concerto no. 2, 1972; Chamber music: 3 movements for solo cello, 1972; Fantasy, violin and piano; 5 Renaissance poems, soprano and chamber orch.; Concertante, chamber ensemble; Chorus: Christmas cantata, choir and chamber orch.
7725 2nd N.E., Seattle, WA 98115

*SHAPERO, HAROLD SAMUEL
b. Lynn, Mass., 29 Apr. 1920. Studied with Nicolas Slonimsky, Malkin Cons., Boston; with Walter Piston, Harvard Univ., B. A. magna cum laude 1941; with Paul Hindemith at Tanglewood; with Nadia Boulanger in Cambridge, Mass.; and with Ernst Krenek. His awards include the American Prix de Rome, 1941; Gershwin prize, 1946; Bearns prize, 1946; Guggenheim fellowship, 1946-48; Fulbright research grant, 1961-62; and commissions. He has been professor, Brandeis Univ., 1952-   .
WORKS: Ballets: Pocahontas; The minotaurs; Orchestra: 9-minute overture, 1941; Serenade for string orch., 1945; symphony for classical orch., 1948; The travelers, 1948; concerto for orch., 1951-58; Credo, 1955; Partita, piano and orch., 1960; Jazz combo: On Green Mountain, 1958; Chamber music: 3 pieces for 3 pieces, woodwind trio, 1938; trumpet sonata, 1939; string quartet, 1940; 4-hand piano sonata, 1941; violin sonata, 1942; 3 amateur sonatas for piano, 1944; Chorus: The defense of Corinth, men's voices with piano 4-hands; Emblems, men's voices.
9 Russell Circle, Natick, MA 01760

SHAPEY, RALPH
b. Philadelphia, Pa., 12 Mar. 1921. Studied violin with Emanuel Zetlin, composition with Stefan Wolpe. His many awards include Frank Huntington Beebe award for Europe, 1953; MacDowell fellowships, 1956, 1957, 1958; selection of his clarinet concerto with Copland's Piano fantasy as the 2 works to represent the U.S. at the Internat. Society for Contemporary Music Festival, Strasbourg, France, 1958; Italian Government grant, 1959-60; Brandeis Creative Arts award, 1962; Edgar Stern Family Fund award, 1962; Copley Found. award, 1962; Nat. Inst. of Arts and Letters award, 1966; Who's Who citation, 1966; Naumberg recording award, 1966; and many commissions. He served in the U.S. Army, 1942-45; was assistant conductor, Philadelphia Nat. Youth Administration Symphony Orchestra, 1938-42; active as conductor of new music, 1950-64; faculty member, Univ. of Pennsylvania, 1963-64; professor, Univ. of Chicago, 1964-   , music director, Contemporary Chamber Players, of the Univ. of Chicago, 1964-   .
WORKS: Orchestra: Fantasy, 1951; symphony no. 1, 1952; Challenge - The family of man, 1955; Ontogeny, 1958; violin concerto, 1959; Rituals, 1959; Chamber music: 6 string quartets, 1946, 1949, 1951, 1953, 1958, 1963; piano quintet, 1947; violin sonata, 1950; oboe sonata, 1952; quartet for oboe and string trio, 1952; cello sonata, 1953; concerto for clarinet and chamber

SHAPEY, RALPH

(SHAPEY, RALPH)
ensemble, 1954; piano trio, 1955; duo for viola and piano, 1957; Rhapsodie, oboe and piano, 1957; Evocation, violin, piano and percussion, 1959; Soliloquy, narrator, string quartet, percussion, 1959; Movements, woodwind quintet, 1960; De profundis, solo contrabass and instruments, 1960; Five, violin and piano, 1960; Discourse for 4 instruments, 1961; Piece, violin and instruments, 1962; Convocation for chamber group, 1962; Chamber symphony, 10 solo players, 1962; brass quintet, 1963; Configurations, flute and piano, 1965; string trio, 1965; Partita, violin and 13 players, 1966; Poeme, viola and piano, 1966; For solo trumpet, 1967; Partita-fantasy, cello and 16 players, 1967; Reyem, flute, violin, and piano, 1967; Cantata, soprano, tenor, bass, narrator, chamber orch., percussion, 1951; Walking upright, 8 songs for female voice and violin, 1958; This day, female voice and piano, 1960; Dimensions, soprano and 23 instruments, 1960; Incantations, soprano and 10 instruments, 1961; Songs of ecstasy, soprano, piano, percussion and tape, 1967; Piano: sonata, 1946; 3 essays on Thomas Wolfe, 1949; suite, 1952; Sonata - variations, 1954; Mutations no. 1, 1956, no. 2, 1966; Form, 1959; Birthday piece, 1962; Seven, piano 4-hands, 1963; Deux, 2 pianos; Film score: Hidden sounds (Skriveni Zvuci) for a 1972 Yugoslav film, American premiere, Wheaton Coll., Norton, Mass., 26 Apr. 1974.
    5835 South University Ave.
    Chicago, IL 60637

*SHAPIRO, NORMAN R.
b. 1930. The fish. The seagull, The termite, 3 songs on Ogden Nash texts.

*SHARAF, FREDERIC
Episode for piano.

SHARLIN, WILLIAM
b. New York, N. Y., 7 Jan. 1920. Studied with Vittorio Giannini, Manhattan School of Music, M. M. 1949; with Eric Werner, Hebrew Union School of Sacred Music, New York, B. S. M. 1951. He held a fellowship at Hebrew Union Coll., Cincinnati, 1951-54; has been cantor, Leo Baeck Temple, 1954-   ; adjunct professor and department chairman, Hebrew Union Coll., Los Angeles, 1955-   .
    WORKS: Liturgical: Shalom Aleychem; Mi Barechev; May the time not be distant, women's voices; Service of inauguration, cantor, male chorus, brass ensemble, harp, guitars, organ, 1972.
    3580 Multiview Drive, Los Angeles, CA 90068

SHATIN, JUDITH
b. Boston, Mass., 21 Nov. 1949. Studied with Robert Moevs, Douglass Coll., Rutgers Univ., 1967-71; at Juilliard School, 1972-74; also with Hall Overton, Otto Luening, and Milton Babbitt. She has received the Julia Carlie Memorial prize; Abraham Ellstein award; and Aspen Music Festival awards, 1971, 1972. She was a teaching fellow at Juilliard School, 1972-74.

(SHATIN, JUDITH)
    WORKS: Orchestra: Chrysalis, 1973; Chamber music: Grave music, soprano, string trio and bass; Tombeau des morts, viola, cello, string bass, harp, piano; Limericks for solo flute; Passages, solo viola; Legends, flute, oboe, cello, percussion.
    365 West End Ave., Apt. 1104
    New York, NY 10024

*SHATTO, CHARLES
Poem for organ.
    2544 Pine St., San Francisco, CA 94101

SHAUGHNESSY, ROBERT MICHAEL
b. Worcester, Mass., 24 Sep. 1925. Studied with Paul Creston in New York; with Hugo Norden in Boston; cello with Bedrich Vaska. He was assistant professor, Massachusetts State Coll. at Lowell, 1957-65; professor, Southampton Coll., Long Island Univ., 1965-   .
    WORKS: Chamber music: Concertino for tuba and strings; Dances from the enchanted garden; duo for recorder and guitar; Suite for strings; Etudes for guitar; The bacchae, violin and cello, 1970; Bolotowsky, flute and string quartet.
    179 Hampton Road, Southampton, NY 11968

SHAW, ARNOLD
b. New York, N. Y., 28 June 1909. Attended Columbia Univ., M. A., but is self-taught in music. He was named Nevada composer of the year, 1973, and commissioned by the Nevada Music Teachers Asso. and the Music Teachers Nat. Asso. He was an executive of New York music publishing companies, 1941-66; lectured on Schillinger System of composition at Juilliard School, 1945; taught at Fairleigh Dickinson Univ., 1964-65; lectured at Univ. of Nevada and Univ. of Oklahoma, 1970-71.
    WORKS: Voice: Sing a song of Americans, texts by Rosemary and Stephen Vincent Benet, 1941; Piano: Mobiles, 10 graphic impressions for piano, 1966; Stabiles, 12 images for piano, 1968; Plabiles, 12 songs without words, 1971; Waltzes for now, 1974; The mod moppet, 7 nursery ripoffs for piano, 1974.
    2288 Gabriel Drive, Las Vegas, NV 89109

SHAW, CLIFFORD
b. Little Rock, Ark., 19 Sep. 1911. Studied with Frederic A. Cowles in Louisville, but is largely self-taught in composition. He received a citation from the Kentucky Fed. of Music Clubs for outstanding contributions to the cultural life of Kentucky by his compositions. He has been staff member in the music department of radio and television station WAVE, Inc., Louisville, 1933-   .
    WORKS: Songs: The lamb, text by Blake; Romance; Piano: Valentine; Vienna fragment; A London fragment; Love in springtime; Third Street rhumba; Manhattan bacarolle; also works for orchestra, band, chorus, many songs, and 2 ballets.
    Hampton Hall Apts. #82
    209 York St., Louisville, KY 40203

SHAW, DAVID FERGUSON
b. Woonsocket, R. I., 22 Jan. 1926. Studied with Francis Judd Cooke, New England Cons., B. M. cum laude; at Boston Univ., M. M. E.; with Arthur Honneger in Paris; at Assumption Coll., M. M.; at workshops with Milton Babbitt, Emerson Meyers, Virginia Hageman, and Jonathan Weiss. He held a Ditson scholarship at New England Cons.; represented the Cons. at a Juilliard School symposium, 1952; had works performed at Southern Music Educators Conference, Mobile, 1969. He teaches electronic music and theory, Fairfax High School, Fairfax, Va.
    WORKS: Band: Introduction and dance, with electronics; Chorus: 4 Marian tableaux; Alleluia; Psalm 98; O Lord, My God; On that night; Lux fulgebit, with tape; 4 Blake poems; 3 Haiku poems; Noel Bearmais; Venez divin messie; Celebrons naissance; Missa brevis, Te Deum.
    3507 North Ottawa St., Arlington, VA 22213

SHAW, JAMES R.
b. Philadelphia, Pa., 27 Aug. 1930. Studied with Robert McBride, Univ. of Arizona, M. M. He taught in public schools, 1953-63; assistant professor, Glassboro State Coll., 1963-   .
    WORKS: Chorus: Rock-a-my-baby; Beautiful day; 4 horizons on text of Amy Lowell; Applause contours; many art songs.
    450 Lake Ave., Pitman, NJ 08071

*SHAW, MARTIN
O Christ, who holds the open gate, chorus.

SHEFF, ROBERT NATHAN
b. San Antonio, Tex., 1 Jan 1945. Studied privately with Otto Wick, Frank Hughes, and Raymond Moses in San Antonio. He received a BMI student composer award for a piano sonata, 1962. He began playing in jazz and rock groups at an early age; participated as composer and performer in the ONCE festivals and concerts at Ann Arbor, Mich. 1962-70; organized Everybody wins, a 12-hour open concert event for all musicians in the community; was pianist, organist, vocalist, and composer for several pop groups; has been instructor, Mills Coll., and technician, Center for Contemporary Music of Mills Coll., 1970-   . His works are chiefly for electronic equipment with verbal scores and graphics, requiring audience participation and from a few hours to a few days for performance.
    1940 Channing Way, Berkeley, CA 94613

SHEINFELD, DAVID
b. St. Louis, Mo., 20 Sep. 1910. Studied with Ottorino Respighi in Rome; conducting with Pierre Monteux in Hancock, Me. He received an award from American Music Center; commissions from Philadelphia Chamber Symphony, Pittsburgh Symphony, Oakland Symphony, San Francisco Chamber Music Society, San Francisco Symphony, 1971. He was violinist, San Francisco Symphony, 1945-71.
    WORKS: Orchestra: 4 etudes; Confrontations; Time warp; Chamber music: Memories of yesterday and tomorrow, for 3 players; Elegiac sonorities, organ.
    1458 24th Ave., San Francisco, CA 94122

SHEINKMAN, MORDECAI
b. Tel-Aviv, Israel, 30 May 1926; U.S. citizen at birth. Studied at St. John's Coll., Annapolis, Md.; with Boris Blacher in Berlin; with Wolfgang Fortner, in Detmold, Germany. He was assistant professor, Kirkland Coll., 1968-72; assistant professor of humanities, Richmond Coll., CUNY, 1972-   ; director, opera workshop, Manhattanville Coll., 1969-71; visiting lecturer and conductor, university orchestra, Princeton Univ., 1973-74.
    WORKS: Orchestra: Passi; piano concerto; Serenade, string orch.; Chamber music: Divertimento, clarinet, trumpet, trombone, harp; violin sonata; songs.
    11 Riverside Drive, New York, NY 10023

SHEPARD, JEAN ELLEN
b. Durham, N. C., 1 Nov. 1949. Studied with Stefan Grove and Robert Hall Lewis, Peabody Cons., candidate for master's degree, 1973. She has received the Gustav Klemm composition award and 2nd prize in a Mu Phi Alpha Sinfonia contest.
    WORKS: Chamber music: To a child dancing, narrator, flute and percussion; various chamber music pieces.
    1008 River St., Jacksonville, NC 28540

*SHEPHERD, ARTHUR
b. Paris, Idaho, 19 Feb. 1880; d. Cleveland, Ohio, 12 Jan. 1958. Studied with George W. Chadwick and Percy Goetschius, New England Cons. He received the Paderewski prize and 2 Nat. Fed. of Music Clubs prizes. He conducted the Salt Lake Symphony, 1897-08; was faculty member, New England Cons., 1908-17; served in the U.S. Army, 1917-19; assistant conductor, Cleveland Orchestra, 1920-26; professor, Western Reserve Univ., 1927-50.
    WORKS: Orchestra: 4 overtures; Fantaisie humoresque, piano and orch., 1918; 2 symphonies, 1927, 1940; Choreographic suite, 1931; Fantasy on Down East spirituals, 1946; violin concerto, 1947; Theme and variations, 1952; Band: Hilaritus; Chamber music: 2 piano sonatas, 1907, 1929; 2 violin sonatas, 1914, 1927; 3 string quartets, 1927, 1935, 1936; piano quintet, 1940; Praeludium salutatorum, woodwind quartet and string trio, 1942; Divertimento, woodwind quintet, 1943; Chorus: Song of the sea wind, 1915; He came all so still, 1915; Deck thyself, my soul, 1918; Ballad of trees and the master, 1935; Song of the Pilgrims, cantata, 1937; Invitation to the dance, 1937; Grace for gardens, 1938; Build thee more stately mansions, 1938; Psalm 42, 1944; Drive on, 1946; and songs.

SHERE, CHARLES
b. Berkeley, Calif., 20 Aug. 1935. Studied at Univ. of California, Berkeley; with Luciano Berio, Mills Coll.; and with Robert Erickson, San Francisco Cons. He was music director, KPFA-FM, 1964-67; music and art critic, KQED-TV, 1967-   ; music and art critic, Oakland Tribune, 1972-   .
    WORKS: Orchestra: piano concerto, 1964; Night music, 1967; From calls and singing, 1968; Chamber music: Fratture, chamber ensemble, 1966; Ces desirs du quatuor, 1965; Screen: quartet #3,

SHERE, CHARLES

(SHERE, CHARLES)
for 4 to 6 strings, 1969; Handler of gravity,
organ, 1971; Dates, soprano and chamber ensemble,
1972; Parergon to wind quintet, for solo flute,
1973.
1824 Curtis St., Berkeley, CA 94702

*SHERMAN, ELNA
b. Mass.; d. For an oriental bazaar, suite for
3 recorders; other published chamber music.

SHERMAN, ROBERT WILLIAM
b. Mich., 17 Jan, 1921. Studied with H. Owen
Reed, Michigan State Univ.; with Bernard Rogers,
Eastman School of Music. He has been head, music
department, Ball State Univ., 1968-   .
WORKS: Ballet: 7 ages of man; Chamber
music: wind quintet; septet for flute, clarinet,
bassoon, string quartet; quintet for clarinet and
strings; 13 additional ways of looking at a
blackbird, soprano and piano; tenor saxophone
sonata; trio sonata, violin, saxophone, piano;
Dichromes, trumpet and cello.
3730 University Ave., Muncie, IN 47304

*SHIELDS, ALICE
b. 1943.   Studied at Columbia-Princeton electronic music center where she composed The transformation of Ani on texts from the Egyptian Book
of the Dead, 1970.
125 West 70th St., New York, NY 10023

SHIFRIN, SEYMOUR J.
b. New York, N. Y., 28 Feb. 1926. Studied privately with William Schuman, 1942-45; Columbia
Univ., B. A. 1947, M. A. 1949; with Darius
Milhaud in Paris, 1951-52. His awards include
Seidl fellowship, 1947-48; Bearns prize, 1950;
Fulbright fellowship, 1951-52; Fromm Found.
award, 1953; Nat. Inst. of Arts and Letters
grant, 1957; Brandeis Univ. Creative Arts award,
1959; Copley Found. award, 1961; Boston Symphony
Orchestra Horblit award, 1963; 2 Koussevitzky
Internat. Recording awards, 1970, 1972; Naumburg
award, 1970; and many commissions. He was lecturer, Columbia Univ., 1949-50; lecturer, Coll.
of the City of New York, 1950-51; faculty member,
Univ. of California, Berkeley, 1952-66; professor, Brandeis Univ., 1966-   .
WORKS: Orchestra: Music for orchestra,
1948; Chamber symphony, 1953; 3 pieces for orch.;
Chamber music: cello sonata, 1948; 5 string
quartets, 1949, 1962, 1966, 1967, 1972; Serenade
for 5 instruments, 1954; Concert piece for solo
violin, 1959; In eius memoriam, chamber ensemble,
1968; duo for violin and piano, 1969; Chorus: A
medieval Latin lyric, a cappella, 1954; Cantata
to Sophoclean choruses, chorus and orch., 1958;
Give ear, O ye heavens, 1959; Odes of Shang,
with piano and percussion, 1963; Chronicles, 3
male soloists, chorus and orch., 1970; Songs:
2 early songs, soprano, 1947; No second Troy,
soprano, 1953; Spring and fall, soprano, 1953;
Satires of circumstance, mezzo-soprano and 6
instruments, 1964; and piano pieces. He has
published articles in music journals.
Department of Music, Brandeis University
Waltham, MA 02154

*SHILKRET, NATHANIEL
b. New York, N. Y., 1 Jan. 1895. Studied at
Bethany Coll., and with Pietro Floridia. He
played clarinet in New York orchestras; was music
director, Victor Talking Machine Company, 1916;
organized the Victor Salon Orchestra for recordings and for radio concerts; in 1935 went to
Hollywood.
WORKS: Orchestra: Skyward, symphonic poem,
1928; trombone concerto, 1942; other orchestral
pieces; violin pieces; and the Biblical cantata,
Genesis, for which he composed one movement and
commissioned one movement each from Castelnuovo-
Tedesco, Milhaud, Stravinsky, Tansman, and Toch.

SHINBROT, MARK S.
b. Los Angeles, Calif., 7 July 1945. Studied
with Roger Chapman, Daniel Lentz, Thea Musgrave,
and Peter Racine Fricker, Univ. of California,
Santa Barbara. He held a summer fellowship,
1972. He did film scoring for Rex Fleming Productions, Santa Barbara, 1969.
WORKS: Chamber music: Tojurno, viola, oboe,
clarinet; Sketches for piano; 2 sets of songs:
Selections and The olden days; incidental music
and music for children's films.
515 Masefield Drive, Pleasant Hill, CA 94523

SHINDO, TAK
b. Sacramento, Calif., 11 Nov. 1922. Studied
with Robert MacDonald, Los Angeles City Coll.; at
California State Univ., Los Angeles, B. A. 1952;
with Miklos Rozsa and Halsey Stevens, Univ. of
Southern California, M. A. 1970. He has been
faculty member, California State Univ., Los Angeles, 1965-   ; conductor, composer, arranger for
Columbia Broadcasting System; composer, arranger,
technical advisor, film studios in Hollywood and
the Daiei Studio, Tokyo, 1949-   .
WORKS: Chamber music: Impressions, piano
trio; Autumn rain; many smaller works in ethnic
music, Japanese children's songs, jazz, etc.
816 Hyperion Ave., Los Angeles, CA 90029

SHINN, RANDALL
b. Clinton, Okla., 28 Sep. 1944. Studied with
Paul Zonn and Ben Johnston, Univ. of Illinois.
WORKS: Chamber music: Serenade for brass
quintet; quintet for horn and strings; Songs of
our climate, soprano and chamber ensemble; woodwind quintet; 2 songs for tenor, clarinet and
piano; Ceremonial fanfare, brass trio; 3 folksongs for winds, percussion and piano.
Music Building, University of Illinois
Urbana, IL 61801

*SHIRLEY, DONALD
b. Kingston, Jamaica, B.W.I., 1927. Entered
Leningrad Cons., at age 9; earned the Ph. D. at
Harvard Univ. He has been piano soloist with
major orchestras in the U.S. and Europe. His
Legacy for string orchestra was given its premiere in New York, 3 Dec. 1973.

*SHORES, RICHARD
b. Rockville, Ind., 9 May   . Studied at
Indiana Univ., B. M.; Eastman School of Music,
M. M.; conducted the Indianapolis Little

(SHORES, RICHARD)
   Symphony, 1942-46; was composer and arranger,
NBC and WGN, Chicago to 1958, when he went to
Hollywood as composer for film and television
background scores. He has published Mulholland
suite for 2 flutes, clarinet, and piano.

SHORT, GREGORY NORMAN (GREG)
   b. Toppenish, Wash., 14 Aug. 1938. Studied piano
with Lonnie Epstein at Juilliard School, 1956-57;
composition with William O. Smith, Univ. of Washington, 1966-67; with Homer Keller, Monte Tubb,
and Harold Owen, Univ. of Oregon, B. M. 1971,
candidate for D. M. A. 1974. His awards include
a composition award, Eugene (Ore.) Women's Choral
Society, 1970; NDEA fellowship, Univ. of Oregon,
1971-74. He has been a private teacher of piano
in Seattle and Eugene, 1959-   ; taught piano at
Cornish School, Seattle, 1964-69, and at Highline
Community Coll., Midway, Wash., 1967-69.
   WORKS: Orchestra: Adagio for double string
orch., 1967; symphony no. 1, 1968; Hobbit preludes, orch. with Renaissance consort, organ,
electronic tape, 1966-   ; Band: concerto for
band, 1972; Wind ensemble: From dust we came,
with rock band, folksinger, jazz improvisation,
Renaissance consort, and tape, 1972; symphony
no. 2, brass choir and percussion, 1973; Chamber
music: Concerto for piano, winds, electric guitar, percussion, 1965; woodwind quintet, 1972;
Chorus: A craydle hymn, double choir and organ,
1965; A welcome carol, women's voices, a
cappella, 1970; Songs: Earth's miracles, soprano
and piano, 1966-71; The pilgrim, soprano, piano,
percussion, 1972; The peaceful lier, texts by
Kenneth Pachen, for solo baritone voice, 1973;
Piano: 3 sonatas, 1958, 1960, 1972; Dozen etudes
for piano, 1965-71; other piano pieces.
   1728 Ferry St., Apt. 7, Eugene, OR 97401

*SHORTALL, HARRINGTON
   b. Chicago, Ill., 1895. Studied at Harvard Univ.
and with Nadia Boulanger in Paris. He taught in
Chicago; from 1946 at the Chicago Theological
Seminary.
   WORKS: Orchestra: Symphonia brevis, 1937;
Wealth of variations for Thomas Jefferson's pro-
posed orchestra of artisans, 1942; Chorus: Choral memorial, 1935, won the Westminster choir
award, 1936; Hymns for Uncle Sam's nephews and
nieces, 1944; and chamber works.

*SHRADER, DAVID LEWIS
   b. Columbia, Mo., 3 May 1939. Studied at Univ.
of Iowa, B. A. 1961, M. A. 1963; with Homer
Keller, Univ. of Oregon, D. M. A. 1969. He was
instructor, Univ. of Oregon, 1964-69; associate
professor, Univ. of Washington, 1969-74; chairman, music department, Illinois State Univ.,
1974-   . His published works include Sea and
tympathy for timpani.
   Music Department, Illinois State University
   Norman, IL 61761

SHREVE, SUSAN E.
   b. Detroit, Mich., 24 Nov. 1952. Studied at
Wayne State Univ.; Bordeaux Cons., France. Her
piano concerto received an award, Mu Phi Epsilon
contest, 1973.

(SHREVE, SUSAN E.)
   WORKS: Orchestra: piano concerto, 1971;
cello concerto, 1974; Chamber music: saxophone
sonata, flute sonata.
   16760 Pierson, Detroit, MI 48219

SHULMAN, ALAN
   b. Baltimore, Md., 4 June 1915. Studied with
Louis Cheslock, Peabody Cons.; with Bernard
Wagenaar at Juilliard School; also cello with
Felix Salmond, Emanuel Feuermann, composition
with Paul Hindemith. He received scholarships
from the New York Philharmonic and Juilliard
School; annual ASCAP awards, 1961-   . He was a
charter member, NBC Symphony, 1937-42, 1948-54;
co-founder and cellist, Stuyvesant String Quartet,
1938-52; cellist, Philharmonia Trio, 1963-69;
participated in chamber music festivals at Mt.
Desert Island, Me., 1969-72, at Newport, R. I.,
1973.
   WORKS: Orchestra: Theme and variations,
viola and orch., 1940; cello concerto, 1948;
Waltzes, 1949; Laurentian overture, 1951;
Popocatepetl, symphonic picture, 1952; Chamber
music: Top brass, brass ensemble, 1947; suite
for solo cello, 1950; suite for solo viola;
Suite miniature, cello octet, 1956; numerous
shorter works for piano, chamber groups, etc.
   Powder Mill House
   6 Fountain Terrace, Scarsdale, NY 10583

SHULZE, FREDERICK B.
   b. Portland, Ore., 25 Aug. 1935. Studied with
Jack C. Goode, Wheaton Coll., Ill.; at Northwestern Univ., M. M.; Univ. of Washington, D. M.
A. in organ. He won first prize in a hymn tune
contest, Nat. Church Music Fellowship, 1958. He
was assistant professor, Cascade Coll., 1960-68;
associate professor, Taylor Univ., 1970-   .
   WORKS: Band: Meditation; Chorus: The Lord
is my shepherd; O clap your hands; Walk together
chillin; Psalm 98; Electronic: Music for tape
recorder and orch.
   Taylor University, Upland, IN 46989

SHURTLEFF, LYNN RICHARD
   b. Vallejo, Calif., 3 Nov. 1939. Studied with
Merrill Bradshaw, Brigham Young Univ.; at
Indiana Univ.; and at Vienna Acad. of Music. He
held a graduate fellowship at Brigham Young Univ.,
and a Ferdinand Grossman fellowship for Vienna.
He has been associate professor, Univ. of Santa
Clara, 1966-   .
   WORKS: Orchestra: 2 symphonies; Dialogues,
chamber orch.; Charlie Brown suite, jazz trio and
chamber orch.; Chorus: For the first manned moon
orbit, chorus and chamber orch.; Sing unto the
Lord a new song, choir and jazz trio; O be joyful,
choir and 2 timpani; Echoes from Hungry Mountain,
a cappella; Quietness, chorus and orch.; Organ:
Concert piece.
   University of Santa Clara
   Santa Clara, CA 95053

SIBBING, ROBERT
   b. Quincy, Ill., 9 Feb. 1929. Studied with
Philip Greeley Clapp, Univ. of Iowa; with Robert

SIBBING, ROBERT

(SIBBING, ROBERT)
Kelly and Hunter Johnson, Univ. of Illinois. He has been associate professor, Western Illinois Univ., 1968-   .
WORKS: Chamber music: sonatas for tuba, cello, flute, alto saxophone, soprano saxophone, and a suite for alto saxophone and piano.
R.R. 4, Macomb, IL 61455

SIEG, JERRY PAUL
b. Bonifay, Fla., 17 Sep. 1943. Studied with William Hoskins, Jacksonville Univ.; with Carlisle Floyd, Florida State Univ. He has been instructor, Cumberland Univ., 1967-   .
WORKS: Chamber music: brass quintet; 2 brass quartets; suite for oboe and trumpet; Chorus: 3 psalms; 3 vocal quartets for chorus; Songs: 3 songs for mezzo-soprano; Dew, for 2 baritones.
Rt. 1, Box 45-A, Williamsburg, KY 40769

SIEGEL, BENJAMIN
b. Poland, 17 Feb. 1919; U.S. citizen 1926. Studied with Max Helfman and Henry Fried, Hebrew Union Coll., School of Sacred Music; and at American Theatre Wing. He was music director, YMHA, Washington Heights, N. Y., 1945-50; cantor, Temple Israel, Great Neck, N. Y., 1950-   .
WORKS: Liturgical: Friday evening Chassidic service; Friday evening children's service; Entreat me not to leave thee; numerous single religious compositions.
16 Millbrook Court, Great Neck, NY 11021

SIEGEL, HENRY
b. Cleveland, Ohio, 6 May 1906. Studied with Samuel Baldwin, City Coll. of New York; with Kurt Roger, Henry Cowell, and Hall Overton in New York; with Darius Milhaud in Aspen, Col. He has been a high school instructor in history and music, 1930-70; played violin and viola in several university and community orchestras, 1956-73.
WORKS: Orchestra: March of the immigrants, Redwood City, Calif., 13 Dec. 1972; Keyboard: Prelude and fugue, organ; Scherzo, piano, New York, 7 Nov. 1970; songs and choral works for high school productions.
1560 Willow Road, #406
Palo Alto, CA 94304

*SIEGEL, NORMAN
Who stole the crown jewels, children's opera, Cubicolo Theatre, New York, Dec. 1970.

*SIEGEL, PAUL
b. New York, N. Y., 8 Dec. 1914. Studied at Brooklyn Coll., B. A.; New York Univ., M. A.; with Josef Marx at Vienna Acad. of Music. Since 1953 he has been a music publisher.
WORKS: Orchestra: Symphonic diary; One world symphony; 4 symphonic songs; Autumn concerto; Ballet Nijinsky; Between 2 worlds, concerto; and songs.

SIEGMEISTER, ELIE
b. New York, N. Y., 15 Jan. 1909. Studied with Seth Bingham, Columbia Univ., B. A. 1927; with

(SIEGMEISTER, ELIE)
Wallingford Riegger, 1926; with Nadia Boulanger in Paris, 1927-31; conducting with Albert Stoessel at Juilliard School. His honors include 10 ASCAP awards; Ford Found. recording grant; commissions from Nat. Endowment of the Arts, Nat. Gallery, Penn. Fed. of Music Clubs, American Wind Symphony, and Shreveport Symphony. He was director, American Ballad Singers, 1940-47; professor and composer-in-residence, Hofstra Univ., 1949-   ; music director, Pro Arte Symphony, 1966-67.
WORKS: Opera: Darling Corie, 1-act, 1952; Miranda and the dark young man, 1-act, 1955; The mermaid in lock no. 7, 1-act, 1958; The plough and the stars, 3-act, 1963-69; Theatre: Doodle Dandy of the USA, play with music, 1942; Sing out, sweet land, musical, 1944; Orchestra: American holiday, 1933; Strange funeral in Braddock, 1935; Ozark set, 1943; Prairie legend, 1944; Wilderness road, 1944; Western suite, 1945; Funnybone Alley, 1946; Lonesome Hollow, 1946; Sunday in Brooklyn, 1946; Summer night, 1947; 5 symphonies, 1947 (revised 1972), 1950, 1957, 1970, 1971; From my window, 1949; Divertimento, 1953; clarinet concerto, 1956; flute concerto, 1960; Theater set, 1960; Dick Whittington and his cat, 1966; 5 fantasies of the theater, 1967; The face of war, with baritone solo, text by Langston Hughes, 1968; A cycle of cities, chorus, dancers, orch., Wolf Trap Festival, Vienna, Va., 8 Aug. 1974; Chamber music: 3 string quartets, 1935-68, 1960, no. 3, on Hebrew themes, Elkins Park, Pa., May 1974; 4 violin sonatas, 1951-59, 1965-70, 1965, 1971; Improvisation, ballad, and dance, solo accordion, 1963; Fantasy and soliloquy, solo cello, 1964; American harp, solo harp, 1966; sextet for brass and percussion, 1965; Chorus: Abraham Lincoln walks at midnight, 1937; A tooth for Paul Revere, narrator, 4 principals, chorus, orch., 1945; The new colussus, 1949; Christmas is coming, with narrator and piano or orch., 1957; This is our land, 1961; In our time, 1965; I have a dream, on text of Martin Luther King, Jr., with baritone, narrator and piano or orch., 1967; Piano: Theme and variations no. 1, 1932, no. 2, 1967; American sonata, 1944; sonata no. 2, 1964; On this ground, 1971; many songs, band pieces, and shorter instrumental works. He was editor (with Olin Downes) of A treasury of American song, New York, 1940, 2nd printing 1962; and author of Work and sing, New York, 1944; Invitation to music, Irvington-on-Hudson, 1961; Harmony and melody (2 vol.), Belmont, Calif., 1965-66; The new music lover's handbook, Irvington-on-Hudson, 1970.
56 Fairview Ave., Great Neck, NY 11023

SIENNICKI, EDMUND J.
b. Cleveland, Ohio, 11 Apr. 1920. Studied with Herbert Elwell in Cleveland; at Kent State Univ., B. S. E.; Teachers Coll., Columbia, M. A.; bassoon in New York and San Francisco. He received prizes, Nat. School Orch. Asso. contests, 1959, 1962; 2 grants from Martha Holden Jennings Found.; Ohio Music Education Asso. commission; 2 MacDowell fellowships, 1964, 1965. He is music teacher, Cleveland Public Schools; bassoonist, Parma Civic Orchestra.

(SIENNICKI, EDMUND J.)
WORKS: Orchestra: Park Avenue hoedown; Ballade, bassoon and orch.; Dorian sketch; Band: Scherzo; Marziale e danza; Brazilian holiday; Chamber music: Let me tell it, clarinet trio; Vicarswood, woodwind trio; Allegro and Diversion, woodwind quintet; Journey, bassoon and percussion; many other works for school orchestras and bands. He has published 4 educational books for woodwinds.
3315 Dellwood Drive, Parma, OH 44134

SIFLER, PAUL J.
b. Yugoslavia, 31 Dec. 1911; U.S. citizen 1937. Studied with Leo Sowerby and Robert Sanders in Chicago. He has been choral conductor in New York; organist and choir master at several churches and synagogues; in 1973 at St. Thomas Episcopal Church, Hollywood, Calif.
WORKS: Orchestra: piano concerto; Suite for strings; Chamber music: Marimba suite; also anthems, organ works, piano pieces.
3947 Fredonia Drive, Hollywood, CA 90028

*SILBERTA, RHEA
b. Pocahontas, Va., 19 Apr. 1900; d. New York, N. Y., 6 Dec. 1959. Studied at Juilliard School; was pianist, concert singer, and vocal coach. Her works include The nightingale and the rose, orch., narrator, soloists, chorus; and Fantaisie ballade, piano.

SILLIMAN, A. CUTLER
b. Delhi, N. Y., 8 June 1922. Studied at Northwestern Univ.; with Louis Mennini, Bernard Rogers, and Allen McHose, Eastman School of Music, Ph. D. He received a commission from the Erie Philharmonic Orchestra, 1963. He was assistant professor, Ashland Coll., 1947-49; professor, State Univ. Coll., Fredonia, N. Y., 1949-   .
WORKS: Orchestra: Toccata; Band: Fantasy on Nun Komm, der Heiden Heiland; Variations; Wind Ensemble: Festival fanfare, brass choir; Chamber music: woodwind quintet; 5 trios for trumpet, horn, and trombone; Chorus: Sonnet, chorus and brass choir.
State University College, Fredonia, NY 14063

SILSBEE, ANN L.
b. Cambridge, Mass., 21 July 1930. Studied with Irving Fine, Radcliffe Coll., A. B. 1951; with Earl George, Syracuse Univ., M. M. 1969. She was instructor, State Univ. Coll. Cortland, N. Y., 1970-71; visiting lecturer, Cornell Univ., 1971-73.
WORKS: Chamber music: Only the cold bare moon, song cycle on 8 Chinese prose poems, soprano, flute, piano; Mirages, bass voice, cello and quarter-tone harpsichord; Phantasy, oboe and harpsichord; Chorus: Prometheus, dramatic cantata for solo bass voice, chorus, chamber ensemble, and prepared tape.
117 Northview Road, Ithaca, NY 14850

*SILVER, FREDERICK (FRED SILVERBERG)
b. New York, N. Y., 30 Mar. 1936. Studied at Boston Univ., B. M.; Juilliard School, B. S., M. S. He received the Rodgers and Hammerstein

(SILVER, FREDERICK)
scholarship; Freschi prize; Gretchaninoff prize; and commissions.
WORKS: Theatre: For heaven's sake, musical; Chorus: Before the paling of the stars, Rossetti text; and songs.

SILVER, SHEILA J.
b. Seattle, Wash., 3 Oct. 1946. Studied with Erhard Karkoschka in Stuttgart, Germany, 1969-71; with Arthur Berger, Seymour Shifrin, Harold Shapero, Martin Boykan, Brandeis Univ. 1971-74; with Jacob Druckman at Tanglewood, 1972. She received the Prix de Paris from Univ. of California at Berkeley, 1969; Irving Fine Memorial fellowship, Brandeis Univ., 1972-74.
WORKS: Chamber music: Quarthym, solo alto recorder, 1971; Ode to Julius, 2 pianos and percussion, 1972; Passtense, 12 instruments, 1973.
1 Fayette St., Cambridge, MA 02139

SILVERMAN, FAYE-ELLEN
b. New York, N. Y., 2 Oct. 1947. Studied with William Sydeman, Mannes Coll. of Music; with Otto Luening, Barnard Coll., B. A. cum laude 1968; with Leon Kirchner and Lukas Foss, Harvard Univ., A. M.; with Jack Beeson and Vladimir Ussachevsky, Columbia Univ., candidate for D. M. A., 1973. She received an award, Stokowski composition contest, 1961; Regents scholarship and teaching fellowships. She taught piano, clarinet, and theory in various schools, 1968-72; was instructor, New York Community Coll., 1972-73; teaching assistant, Columbia Univ., 1972-   ; associate editor, Current Musicology, 1972-   .
WORKS: Orchestra: Madness, narrator and orch.; Chamber music: 3 movements for saxophone alone; In shadows, soprano, guitar, clarinet; Chorus: For showing truth, women's voices.
c/o Seesaw Music Corp.
177 East 87th St., New York, NY 10028

SILVERMAN, STANLEY
b. New York, N. Y., 5 July 1938. Studied at Boston Univ., B. A.; Columbia Univ., B. A.; with Leon Kirchner, Darius Milhaud, Henry Cowell, Mills Coll., M. A.; and with Roberto Gerhard. His awards include Rockefeller grant, 1964; Guggenheim fellowship, 1966; Fromm Found. grants, 1968, 1971; Martha Baird Rockefeller grant, 1970; OBIE award, 1970; Nat. Opera Inst. award, 1971; Koussevitzky Found. commission, 1972; Drama Desk award, 1973. He was faculty member, Berkshire Music Center, 1962-68; music consultant, Stratford Nat. Theater of Canada, 1969; music director, Repertory Theater, Lincoln Center, 1965-73.
WORKS: Opera: Elephant steps, 1968; Dr. Selavy's magic theatre, 1972; Orchestra: Planh, chamber concerto; Chorus: A midsummer night's show, with instruments, 1971, New York, 16 May 1973; Oedipus, with instruments, 1972; Canso, 1964; also 20 theatre scores.
262 Central Park West, New York, NY 10024

*SIMEONE, HARRY
b. Newark, N. J., 9 May 1911. Is a conductor and arranger. His published works include an opera,

SIMEONE, HARRY

(SIMEONE, HARRY)
The emperor's new clothes; and 2 choral works, All the world's a stage and We are the music makers.

*SIMMONS, HOMER
b. Evansville, Ind., 6 Aug. 1900. Studied at Univ. of Southern California, B. A.; piano with Homer Grunn and Ignace Paderewski; composition with Ottorino Respighi, Nadia Boulanger, and Gordon Jacob. He has given piano recitals in Europe and the U.S.
WORKS: Opera: Red Riding Hood; Orchestra: Phantasmania, piano and orch., 1929; California nights, piano and orch.; Impressions Basques; Chamber music: Panels from a lacquered screen, voice and string quartet; 2 string quartets; Piano: Stairways; Alice in Wonderland, suite, 2 pianos; The old Dutch clock; Lyra Davidica, 2 pianos and string quartet; Evenings in old Vienna, 2 pianos and string quartet; Scherzino.

*SIMONDS, BRUCE
b. Bridgeport, Conn., 5 July 1895. Studied at Yale Univ., B. A. 1917, B. M. 1918, M. A. 1938; Schola Cantorum, Paris, 1919-24; Matthay School, London, 1920-21. He was concert pianist; joined Yale Univ. faculty, 1921, professor, 1938, dean, Yale School of Music, 1946-54. His published works include 2 organ pieces, Dorian prelude and Prelude on Iam sol recedit igneus; and Habanera for violin and piano.

SIMONS, NETTY
b. New York, N. Y. Studied at Juilliard School; with Stefan Wolpe, New York Univ. She received a scholarship at Juilliard; Ford Found. recording/publication award. She taught piano and theory, 3rd Street Settlement School, 1928-33, was voice coach, 1930-33; produced and scripted radio broadcasts for American Composers Alliance, 1966-71.
WORKS: Opera: Bell witch of Tennessee, 1-act, 1958; Theatre: Buckeye has wings, 1 to any number of players, 1971, New York, 11 Mar. 1974; Too late - The bridge is closed, 1 to any number, color coded, 1972; Puddintame, 1 to any number, color coded, text of limericks, 1972; Orchestra: Piece for orchestra, 1949; Pied piper of Hamelin, with narrator, 1955; Lamentations #1, 1961, #2 1966; Variables (may also be performed by any 5 instruments or multiples of 5), 1967; Scipio's dream, 1968; Illuminations in space, viola and orch., 1972; Chamber music: Duo for violin and cello, 1939; Set of poems for children, narrator and chamber group, 1949; string quartet, 1950; quartet for flute and strings, 1951; 2 violin sonata, 1954; Diverse settings, soprano and chamber group, 1959; Circle of attitudes, solo violin, 1960; Facets #1-4, varying small ensembles, 1961-62; 3 Trialogues for mezzo-soprano, baritone, viola, texts of Dylan Thomas, 1963, 1968, 1973; Time groups #2, 3 winds, string quartet, double bass, 1964; Design groups #1, 1-3 percussionists, graphics score, 1966; Design groups #2, duo for any 2 high and low pitched instruments, 1968; Silver thaw, 1-8 players, graphics score, 1969; 2 dot, for 2 pianos, 1970;

(SIMONS, NETTY)
Wild tales told on the river road, clarinet and percussion, 1973; The great stream silent moves, piano, harp, percussion, 1973; piano pieces; songs.
374 South Mountain Road, New City, NY 10956

SIMONS, THOMAS
b. New York, N. Y., 22 Apr. 1943. Studied with Luciano Berio at Juilliard School and in Italy. He held an Italian Government scholarship, 1968; received a Martha Baird Rockefeller grant, 1970. He was instructor, of piano, Princeton Univ. 1969-71; instructor, Oberlin Coll. Cons., 1971-74.
WORKS: Chamber music: Cantata, soprano, chamber ensemble, 1965; Piece for organ, 1966; Fields, 3 woodwinds, viola, cello, harp, piano, percussion, 1967; Binary reflexion, percussion and piano, 1971; Penetration, solo flute, 1972; Movement for marimba, 1972; Mirror, percussion, 1973.
143 West College, Oberlin, OH 44074

**SIMPSON, GEORGE ELLIOTT
b. Orange, N. J., 1 Nov. 1876; d. Kansas City, Mo., 8 Oct. 1958. Studied composition with Carl Busch in Kansas City, 1894-1900; with Jadassohn and Reinecke in Leipzig, 1900-03. He taught in Kansas City and Texas. His compositions included a symphony, 12 tone poems, 4 overtures, many piano pieces and songs.

SIMS, EZRA
b. Birmingham, Ala., 16 Jan. 1928. Studied at Birmingham Cons., 1945-58; with Quincy Porter, Yale Univ., 1950-58; with Darius Milhaud and Leon Kirchner, Mills Coll., M. A. 1955. He was awarded a Guggenheim fellowship, 1962; and has recieved many commissions. He is cataloguer and programmer, Loeb Music Library, Harvard Univ. He uses quarter and one-sixth tones in many of his compositions, and contributed an article on microtones to the Harvard Dictionary of Music, 2nd ed.
WORKS: Ballet (all tape, tape collage, or musique concrete): Masque, 1955; Antimatter, 1968; McDowell's fault, 1968; Alec, 1968; A frank overture, 4 indented interludes, and a coda, 1969; Lion at the door, a cappella song, 1969; Warts and all, 1969; Real toads, 1970; More overture and another interlude, 1970; Prince Metternich, In memoriam, 1970; Summer piece: homage to Gene Krupa, 1970; Elina's piece, 1970; ...including the ..., 1970; Interlope, 1970; 5 Toby minutes plus 49.5", 1971; Ground cover, 1972; Theatre: music for The Trojan women, 1955; The ticklish acrobat, 1957; Cat's cradle: music to The Sacrament according to the Books of Bokonon, 1969; Chamber music: Chamber cantata on Chinese poems, tenor and chamber ensemble, 1954; cello sonata, 1957; string quartet, 1959; Sonate concertanti, 'demountable octet', comprising 5 sonatine for oboe, viola, cello, double bass, and 5 sonate for string quartet; Cantata III, mezzo-soprano and percussion, 1962; octet for strings, in sixth-tones, 1964; From an oboe quartet, oboe and string trio, 1971; Study, violin, viola or cello or any 2 voices, 1973;

(SIMS, EZRA)
Variations, oboe and string trio, 1973; Electronic tape: Commonplace book or Salute to our American Container Corp., 1969; Tango variations, 1971; Museum piece, 1972; Wall to wall, 1972; 30 years later, 1972; Where the wild things are, 1973.
1168 Massachusetts Ave., Cambridge, MA 02138

SIMUTIS, LEONARD J.
b. Brooklyn, N. Y., 29 May 1920. Studied with Leon Stein, De Paul Univ. He received an award in an international competition for Lithuanian composers, 1948. He was lecturer, De Paul Univ., 1951-56, head, graduate music education, 1966-70; assistant professor, Chicago Teachers Coll., 1951-62; professor, Chicago State Univ., 1962-   .
WORKS: Ballet: Polish wedding; Chorus: A spring morning, women's voices; Ancestral dirge, with baritone solo, 1948; Cease O storm, women's chorus and baritone, 1949; Songs: The land I left behind, baritone and piano, 1951; I remember, baritone and piano, 1953.
3551 West 98th St., Evergreen Park, IL 60642

SINZHEIMER, MAX
b. Frankfurt/Main, Germany, 20 June 1894; U.S. citizen 1944. Studied with Walter Braunfels, Univ. of Munich; with Philipp Wolfrum, Univ. of Heidelberg, Ph. D. 1920. He was conductor at opera houses in Darmstadt, Mannheim, and Frankfurt/Main; music director at synagogues and churches in New York and Chicago; organist-choirmaster, St. Andrew's Lutheran Church, Chicago, 1959-   ; faculty member, American Cons., 1947-   .
WORKS: Orchestra: Sinfonia after instrumental music of Salomone Rossi, performed by Chicago Symphony Orchestra, 1944; Chorus: The song of Mary; Psalm 128; many anthems and psalm settings; organ preludes, etc.
5741 West Addington St., Chicago, IL 60634

*SIR, NEIL
Has had works performed at the Washington Square Music Society concert, New York Univ., 12 Mar. 1973; and at the Concert of New Music, New York Univ., 5 Apr. 1973.
Music Department, University of New Hampshire
Durham, NH 03824

SIWE, THOMAS
b. Chicago, Ill., 14 Feb. 1935. Studied with Hunter Johnson and Robert Kelly, Univ. of Illinois. He was percussionist with the Univ. of Chicago Contemporary Chamber Players, 1963-68; assistant professor, Univ. of Illinois, 1969-   .
WORKS: Percussion: Duet for snare drum and timpani; sextet for percussion ensemble; Othello music; In the greenhouse.
School of Music, University of Illinois
Urbana, IL 61801

*SIX, HERBERT L.
All cats turn gray when the sun goes down, jazz opera, New York, 21 May 1971.
Music Department, University of Missouri
Kansas City, MO 64111

*SKJEVELAND, HELGE
b. Provo, Utah, 1950. Received a BMI award in 1973 for Anamorphosis for orch.

SKOLNIK, WALTER
b. New York, N. Y., 20 July 1934. Studied with Bernhard Heiden and Thomas Beversdorf, Indiana Univ.; with Goffredo Petrassi, Tanglewood, 1956. He received a Ford Found.-MENC grant for composer-in-residence, Shawnee Mission Kan., School District, 1966-68. He was instructor, St. Paul's Coll., 1964-65; assistant professor, Youngstown State Univ., 1969-70.
WORKS: Orchestra: Capriccio; clarinet concerto, Indiana Univ., Oct. 1968; Diptych; trumpet concertino; Passacaglia; Band: Chorale fantasia; Quixotic rhapsody, New York, May 1973; Toccata festiva, Seattle, Mar. 1968; Chamber music: sonatina for alto saxophone, 1962; flute, sonatina, 1965; Serenata notturna, flute and string trio; Divertimento, saxophone quartet; Pastorale, woodwind quintet; trumpet sonata, 1971; Concert music, brass choir, timpani, percussion, 1973; Chorus: Historical limericks; Hodie Christus natus est; The old man in the tree; Piping down the valleys wild; Song for all seas, all ships, Univ. of Kansas, 10th Annual Symposium of Contemporary Music, May 1968; The sparrow song; 3 nonsense songs of Edward Lear; Zoological studies; and others.
3975-A Sedgwick Ave., Bronx, NY 10463

SLADEK, PAUL
b. Vienna, Austria, 18 Jan. 1896; U.S. citizen 1912. Studied violin and viola, Vienna Cons., in the U.S. with Albert Spalding and Leopold Auer; composition with Caspar Koch. He was presented with a violin and a scholarship by the Vienna Public School; twice won the Composers Press publication award, 1954, 1959. He was head of the violin department, Duquesne Univ., 1940-56.
WORKS: Orchestra: Menuet pompadour, 1954; The old clock, 1959; Chamber music: many published pieces for violin or viola and piano.
5108 Bayard St., Pittsburgh, PA 15232

*SLATER, NEIL
Again D. J., opera on Don Juan theme, Bridgeport, Conn., 5 May 1972.
Music Department
University of Bridgeport, CT 06602

SLATES, PHILIP M.
b. Canton, Ohio, 24 Sept. 1924; d. Indianapolis, Ind., 1966. Studied with Bernard Rogers and Howard Hanson, Eastman School of Music; with Burrill Phillips, Univ. of Illinois, D. M. A. 1961. His awards included Bennington Composers Conference fellowship, 1955; first prize, Ohio Univ. Chamber Opera contest, 1956; Southern Fellowship Fund award, 1958; Ford Found. grant, 1959. He taught at George Peabody Coll., 1961-64; was professor, Jordan Coll. of Music, Butler Univ., 1964-66.
WORKS: Opera: Pierrot of the minute, 1-act; Double bill: The candle and The bargain, to the composer's libretto; Ballet: 2 religious dance

SLATES, PHILIP M.

(SLATES, PHILIP M.)
dramas, Pieta and Kanon for Easter; Orchestra: Commentary and summary; Variations for orchestra; 2 symphonies; Band: 5 intaglios; Rituals; Gothic overture; Chamber music: many works for small ensembles, solo instruments, duets; Chorus: And there shall come forth; Kyrie and gloria; Reconciliation; Early rising; 4 nature sketches; Soft music for the birth of Christ; Tolite meum jugum.

SLAWSON, WAYNE
b. Detroit, Mich., 29 Dec. 1932. Studied with Leslie Bassett and Ross Lee Finney, Univ. of Michigan, D. M. A. He was assistant professor, Yale Univ., 1967-72; associate professor, Univ. of Pittsburgh, 1972-   .
WORKS: Orchestra: Motions; Chamber music: Limits, for string quartet; Electronic: Wishful thinking about winter, computer synthesized tape; Much, electronic, concrete, and computer music (with Robert Morris).
Music Department, University of Pittsburgh Pittsburgh, PA 15260

SLEETH, NATALIE
b. Evanston, Ill., 29 Oct. 1930. Studied with Hubert Lamb, Wellesley Coll., B. A. 1952; Organ at Northwestern Univ.; with Lloyd Pfautsch, Southern Methodist Univ., 1969. She was church organist, Glencoe, Ill., 1952-54; church music secretary, Highland Park United Methodist Church, Dallas, 1968-   .
WORKS: Chorus: Jazz gloria, with 3 trumpets, double bass, bongo drums; Hallelujah; Gaudeamus hodie; Feed my lambs; Fa la la fantasie, a cappella; and many others.
7439 Colgate Ave., Dallas, TX 75225

SLOCUM, WILLIAM BENNETT
b. Grand Junction, Colo., 17 Dec. 1936. Studied horn, Univ. of New Mexico, B. F. A., M. M.; at Juilliard School, Aspen Music School, Berkshire Music Center; but had no formal training in composition. He played first horn, Buffalo Philharmonic Orch., 1960-63; Cleveland Orch., 1966-68; taught at Univ. of Wyoming, 1963-66; Cleveland Inst. of Music, 1966-   ; Youngstown State Univ., 1972-   .
WORKS: Chamber music: woodwind quintet, 1967; 7 lyric pieces for clarinet solo, 1969; Variations for horn solo, 1971; 5 songs for baritone, piano, viola, clarinet, and horn, 1971; Ambivalence for trumpet, 2 horns, percussion, 1972.
317 Redondo Road, Youngstown, OH 44504

SLONIMSKY, NICOLAS
b. St. Petersburg, Russia, 27 Apr. 1894; U.S. citizen 1931. Studied piano with his aunt, Isabelle Vengerova, composition with Vassili Kalafati and Maxmilian Steinberg, St. Petersburg Cons. He came to the U.S. in 1923; was professor, Eastman School of Music, 1923-25; secretary to Serge Koussevitzky in Boston, 1925-27; founder and conductor, Boston Chamber Orchestra, 1927-34; conductor, Harvard Univ. Orchestra, 1928-30; later presented premieres of works by Charles Ives, Edgard Varese, Henry Cowell, Carl Ruggles,

(SLONIMSKY, NICOLAS)
Wallingford Riegger, and other American composers of that period in Europe, South America, and the U.S. He was instructor of the Russian language, Harvard Univ., 1946-47; lecturer in music, Univ. of California, Los Angeles, 1964-67. He is perhaps best known for his work in musicology as author of Music since 1900, 1937, 4th edition, New York, 1970; Music of Latin America, 1945; The road to music, 1947; Thesaurus of scales and melodic patterns, 1947; A thing or two about music, 1948; and Lexicon of musical invective, 1953. He was editor of Oscar Thompson's International cyclopedia of music and musicians, 1946-58; and of Baker's Biographical dictionary of musicians, 1958-71. He is on the editorial board of the Encyclopedia Britannica and has contributed to the Britannica Year Book, Grove's Dictionary of music and musicians, and other publications. In 1962-63 he lectured in Russia, Poland, Yugoslavia, Bulgaria, Rumania, Greece, and Israel under the auspices of the U.S. State Department.
WORKS: Ballet: Prince goes a-hunting, Rochester, N. Y., Mar. 1925; Orchestra: Overture on an ancient Greek theme, in the Greek enharmonic mode, for strings tuned in quarter-tones, trumpet and percussion, Hollywood Bowl, July 1933; 4 simple pieces, Boston Pops Orch., July 1941; My toy balloon, calls for 100 toy balloons to be exploded at the final sforzando, Boston Pops, 14 July 1942; Chamber music: Moto perpetuo, violin and piano, 1936; 4 Russian melodies, clarinet and piano, 1937; Little suite, 3 woodwinds, percussion typewriter, and cat's meow, 1941; suite for cello and piano, 1950; Piano: Studies in black and white, uses consonant counterpoint on the white keys for the right hand, on the black keys for the left hand, 1928; Silhouettes Ibériennes, 1934; Russian nocturne, 1942; Yellowstone Park suite, 1951; Moods, 1963; 50 minitudes, 1973; Voice: 5 advertising songs, 1925; Impressions, 1927; Garden songs, 1928; Gravestone at Hancock, N. H., 1945; Möbius strip tease, a perpetual canon for soprano and tenor with piano nonobligato, Univ. of California, Los Angeles, 5 May 1965.
10808 1/2 Wilshire Blvd.
Los Angeles, CA 90024

SMART, GARY L.
b. Cuba, Ill., 19 Dec. 1943. Studied with Yanis Xenakis, Bernhard Heiden, and Roque Cordero, Indiana Univ., B. M. in piano, M. M. in piano and composition; Cologne Univ., Germany. In 1973 he was composer-in-residence, City of Anchorage, sponsored by the Contemporary Music Project, Music Educators Nat. Conference.
WORKS: Orchestra: Variations for woodwinds and orchestra, 1970; Aurora borealis, orch., electronic tape, piano, 1971; Sundog music, 1973; Chamber music: Mobile 1969, for 9 woodwinds, percussion, and 2 pianos.
1218 F Street, Anchorage, AK 99502

SMILEY, PRIL
b. Lake Mohonk Lake, N. Y., 19 Mar. 1943. Studied with Henry Brant, Louis Calabro, Vivian Fine

(SMILEY, PRIL)
at Bennington Coll. She received an award in
the First Internat. Electronic Music competition,
Dartmouth Arts Council, 1968. She has been composer, Columbia Princeton Electronic Music Center, 1963-   , instructor, 1965-   ; electronic
music consultant, Lincoln Center Repertory
Theatre, 1968-
      WORKS: Electronic: music for 19 major
theatre productions in New York, Tanglewood,
Cleveland, Baltimore, Cincinnati; Eclipse, 1967;
Kolyosa, 1970; music for 2 television documentaries and 4 independent films.
      601 West 113 St., New York, NY 10025

*SMIT, JOHANNES
      b. New Jersey, 1913; d. Memphis, Tenn. Studied
with Peter Mennin and Howard Hanson, Eastman
School of Music, Ph. D. 1953. He was chairman,
theory division, music department, Memphis State
Univ., in 1966-69, at least. His published
works include a trio for flute, cello, piano.

SMIT, LEO
      b. Philadelphia, Pa., 12 Jan. 1921. Received a
scholarship to study piano with Isabelle Vengerova
at Curtis Inst., 1930-32; studied composition
with Nicolas Nabokov, 1935. His awards include
a Guggenheim grant, 1950; Fulbright grant, 1950;
Boston Symphony Orchestra Merit award, 1953; New
York Critics Circle award, 1957; and commissions.
He made his piano debut in Carnegie Hall, New
York, 1939, toured the U.S. 1940, Europe 1953-55.
His faculty posts include Sarah Lawrence Coll.,
1947-49; head, piano department, Univ. of California, Los Angeles, 1957-63; Slee Professor of
Composition, State Univ. of New York at Buffalo,
1962, professor of music, 1963-   . In 1967-68
he toured 16 Latin American countries for the
U.S. State Department.
      WORKS: Ballet: Virginia sampler, New York,
4 Mar. 1947; Orchestra: The Parcae, overture,
1951, Boston, 16 Oct., 1953; Capriccio, string
orch., 1958; symphony no.1, Boston, 1 Feb. 1957;
symphony no.2, New York, 10 Feb. 1966; piano
concerto, Buffalo, Nov. 1968, composer as soloist;
4 Kookabana marches, Istanbul, 1973; Caedmon,
Buffalo, Dec. 1972, composer conducting;
Copernicus, chorus and orch., commissioned by
Nat. Acad. of Sciences, 1973; chamber works;
piano pieces.
      39 Dorchester Road, Buffalo, NY 14222

*SMITH, ANITA
      b. New York, N. Y., 19 Dec. 1922. Studied with
Karol Rathaus on scholarship at Queens Coll.
      WORKS: Chamber music: violin suite; Homage
to Gershwin; Perambular funiculi; Songs: 3 settings of Carl Sandburg texts; 3 concert songs on
Lindsay texts.

SMITH, BRANSON
      b. Pine Village, Ind., 21 Dec. 1921. Studied
with Newell Long, Indiana Univ.; with Kurt
Fredercik, Univ. of New Mexico; Champ Tyrone,
Highlands Univ. He received and award, Arizona
Fed. of Music Clubs, 1969. He has been a public
school music teacher in Indiana, New Mexico, and
in 1973 in Tucson, Ariz.

(SMITH, BRANSON)
      WORKS: Ballet: Legends of Superstition
Mountain, 1972; Orchestra: Concertpiece for
orch., 1959; Theme and mutations, 1960; Lyrical
statement for strings, 1967; Band: Tikvat noar,
clarinet and band, 1970; Chamber music: string
quartet, 1967; woodwind quintet, 1968; viola
sonata, 1969; Chorus: Ecumenical cantata, 1964;
Imagination, text from Walden, 1968; Piano:
Caper for pianoforte, 1968; 5 pieces for young
people, 1970.
      1944 East 3rd St., Tucson, AZ 85719

SMITH, CARY
      b. Pleasant View, Va., 1 Jan. 1934. Studied at
American Univ.; San Francisco State Univ.; and
with Aurelio de la Vega, California State Univ.
at Northridge. He received a composition prize
at Northridge, 1969. As an operatic baritone
he has sung in many U.S. companies, including
the San Francisco Opera Company; is staff member,
California State Univ., Northridge.
      WORKS: Chamber music: Studies for small
orch., 1968; duet for flute and piano, 1968;
Frammenti, string quartet, 1969; Interplay,
winds, percussion, and bass, 1969; Changes, for
flutes, brass, bass, electric bass, timpani,
1970; Chorus: Mass, for brass, percussion,
organ, solo violin and choir, 1969.
      7529 Remmet Ave., Canoga Park, CA 91303

SMITH, CHARLES WARREN
      b. Palmerton, Pa., 5 Sep. 1936. Studied with
Allan Willman, Univ. of Wyoming; with Walter Kob,
New York Univ.; with Wayne Barlow, Eastman
School of Music; at George Peabody Coll., doctoral candidate in 1973. He received an American Guild of Musical Artists award in
composition and flute performance, 1958. He
taught in public schools, 1958-68; at Madison
Coll., 1968-69; Wake Forest Univ., 1969-   .
      WORKS: Band: Suite for band; The harmonica
player; Jubilee; Fanfare and fantasia; Piece,
brass and percussion; Chamber music: Adagio and
allegro, flute, clarinet, piano; Chorus: Te
Deum; I will publish the name of the Lord; O
sing unto the Lord; So, we'll go no more a'roving;
Behold, the tabernacle of God; The worm; Piano:
Suite contemporain; 2 pieces for children; Quartal piece; Reflections.
      1509 South Hawthorne Road
      Winston-Salem, NC 27103

SMITH, CLAUDE T.
      b. Monroe City, Mo., 14 Mar. 1932. Studied at
Central Coll., Fayette, Mo.; and at Univ. of
Kansas. He has received many commissions. He
is public school music teacher in Chillicothe,
Mo.
      WORKS: Orchestra: Fanfare and celebration,
1973; Band: Sonus ventorum, 1970; Variations,
baritone horn and band, 1971; Overture romantique, 1971; Rhapsody, trombone and band, 1971;
Concert dance and intermezzo, 1972; Prelude-
variations, 1972; Credence, 1973; also works for
small wind ensembles, chorus.
      1505 Hickory Drive, Chillicothe, MO 64601

SMITH, CLIFFORD

*SMITH, CLIFFORD
b. Oregon, 1945. Metanimasque; Lux-hymn eidola; Myst XXIII; Mystery-elan phantasmata, Book CXVII; all for piano, were performed at Carnegie Recital Hall, New York, 20 May 1975.

*SMITH, DAVID STANLEY
b. Toledo, Ohio, 6 July 1877; d. New Haven, Conn., 17 Dec. 1949. Studied with Horatio Parker, Yale Univ., B. A. 1900, B. M. 1903; and in Munich and Paris. He was on the Yale faculty 1916-46, dean, Yale School of Music, 1920-46; conductor, New Haven Symphony, 1920-46.
WORKS: Orchestra: 4 symphonies, 1905, 1917, 1930, 1938; The fallen star, chorus and orch., received Paderewski prize, 1909; Impressions, 1916; Fete galante, with flute solo, 1921; Sinfonietta, string orch., 1931; A satire, 1933; Epic poem, 1935; Requiem, with solo violin, 1939; Credo, symphonic poem, 1941; 4 pieces for string orch., 1943; The apostle, symphonic poem, 1944; many chamber music pieces, choral works, and songs.

SMITH, G. ALAN
b. Wilwaukee, Wis., 4 Aug. 1947. Studied with John Downey, Univ. of Wisconsin-Milwaukee; with Alvin Epstein, Lloyd Pfautsch, Carlton R. Young, Southern Methodist Univ. He received an award in a Phi Mu Alpha contest, 1968. He has been music director in various churches in Milwaukee, 1968-71; in Plano, Tex., 1971-73.
WORKS: Orchestra: An eastern rainbow; The devil and the blacksmith; Chamber music: 7th Webster's: 7th study, dance suite, chamber ensemble; By night on my bed, soprano and 3 flutes; Sing with me now, soprano, flute, piano; The wedding, string quartet with baritone; Chorus: Canine commandments; O sacred head now wounded; Make a joyful noise unto the Lord; Revelation revolution; A psalm of thanksgiving; Songs: Concerns, cycle for soprano; But the greatest of these, soprano and wind ensemble; Good evening, Miss Pruitt, soprano and tenor; Multimedia: Imagination dead imagine, instrumental ensemble, tape, dancers, lights, and narrator, based on a Beckett monologue.
3621 McFarlin Blvd., Dallas, TX 75205

SMITH, GLANVILLE
b. St. Cloud, Minn., 28 June 1901. Has published pieces for organ: A Christmas wreath; preludes, interludes, and amens.
Cold Spring, MN 56320

SMITH, GREGG
b. Chicago, Ill., 21 Aug. 1931. Studied at Univ. of California, Los Angeles, B. A., M. A.; composition privately with Leonard Stein, conducting with Fritz Zweig. His awards include a Ford Found. grant for conducting; 3 Grammy awards for recordings of the complete choral works of Charles Ives by the Gregg Smith Singers, a group he founded and conducts. He was associate professor, Ithaca Coll., 1965-68; director of choral music, State Univ. of New York, Stony Brook, 1968-72; director of choral music, Peabody Cons., 1969-75; associate professor, Barnard Coll.,

(SMITH, GREGG)
1974-   ; toured Europe, 1958, USSR, 1961; conducted premiere of Stravinsky's Requiem canticles at Princeton Univ.
WORKS: Opera: Aesop's fables; Chorus: Bible songs for young voices; Beware of the soldier; Landscapes, T.S. Eliot text; Nature and spirit, R. W. Emerson texts; Babel, chorus or solo quartet, 5 speaking groups, piano 4-hands, Biblical text; Folksongs, soprano and chamber ensemble, New York, 20 Jan. 1974; Magnificat, commissioned and performed by Laurel (Md.) Oratorio Society, 7 Dec. 1974; numerous arrangements of choral works.
171 West 71st St., New York, NY 10023

*SMITH, HALE
b. Cleveland, Ohio, 29 June 1925. Studied with Marcel Dick, Cleveland Inst. of Music, M. M. 1952. His awards include commissions from the Thorne Fund, 1971, and BMI, 1972. He was associated with Karamu House, Cleveland in 1955; editor and consultant for music publishers, 1959-   ; faculty member, C. W. Post Coll., 1968-70; associate professor, Univ. of Connecticut, 1970-   .
WORKS: Orchestra: In memoriam - Beryl Rubinstein, chorus and chamber orch., 1953; Contours, 1962; Music for harp and orchestra, 1967; Faces of jazz, 1968; Rituals and incantations, Houston, Tex., 7 Sep. 1974; Band: Expansions; Somersault; Take a chance, aleatoric episode; Chamber music: 3 brevities, solo flute; Epicedial variations, violin and piano, 1956; Evocations, piano; Songs: Beyond the rim of day, 3 songs to texts of Langston Hughes; The valley wind, soprano; By yearning and Be beautiful, 2 songs performed New York, 30 Apr. 1974.
Department of Music
University of Connecticut
Storrs, CT 06268

SMITH, JERRY NEIL
b. Lefors, Tex., 20 Feb. 1935. Studied with Kent Kennan, Univ. of Texas.; with Herbert Elwell, Eastman School of Music. He received 3 research and creativity awards and a summer research grant, Univ. of Colorado; and commissions. He taught in public schools, 1956-59; was faculty member, Univ. of Southwest Louisiana, 1959-60; Univ. of Florida, 1961-64; Univ. of Colorado, 1964-72; and head, music department, Univ. of Northern Iowa, 1972-   .
WORKS: Orchestra: Proclamation; Essay for young Americans; Band: Epilog for band; Fanfare and celebration.
Department of Music
University of Northern Iowa
Cedar Falls, IA 50613

SMITH, JOHN SHAFFER
b. Hamlin, Tex., 10 June 1913. Studied with Joseph Schillinger and Rudolf R. A. Schramm, New York Univ. He received a commission from the San Angelo Symphony Society, 1960, for Texas suite; 2 awards, Contemporary Music Festival, San Jose State Coll., 1961. He has been composer-arranger for dance orchestras, radio, television,

(SMITH, JOHN SHAFFER)
1937-   ; was conductor, Roxy Theatre Orch.,
New York, 1946-50; instructor, New York Univ.,
1948-52; director, composition studies, Hartnett
Nat. Music Studios, 1952-57.
WORKS: Orchestra: Tone poem; trumpet concerto; One mood, trombone and orch.; Texas suite,
1960; Band: Rendicion; Chamber music: quintet,
oboe and strings; Rondo for brass sextet; Chronol-
ogy, brass quintet; and songs.
5052 Berkeley Ave., Westminster, CA 92683

SMITH, JULIA
b. Denton, Tex., 25 Jan. 1911. Studied at North
Texas State Univ., B. A.; piano with Carl
Friedberg and Lonny Epstein, Juilliard School;
composition with Rubin Goldmark, Frederick
Jacobi, Bernard Wagenaar, on a fellowship; with
Vincent Jones, Virgil Thomson, Marion Bauer, New
York Univ., M. A. Ph. D. Her awards include
Sigma Alpha Iota, Texas Music Teachers Asso.,
Nat. Fed. of Music Clubs, ASCAP awards; 2 Martha
Baird Rockefeller grants; Ford Found. publishing-
recording grant; honorary member of Girl Scouts,
USA, for opera Daisy, based on life of Juliette
Gordon Low; commissions from CBS and Opera Guild
of Miami, Fla. She was faculty member, Juilliard
School, 1940-42; founder and head, music educa-
tion department, Hartt Coll. of Music, 1940-45;
free-lance composer-pianist-lecturer, 1945-   .
WORKS: Opera: Cynthia Parker, 1939; The
stranger of Manzano; The gooseherd and the goblin;
Cockcrow, 1964; The shepherdess and the chimney-
sweep; Daisy, Miami, 3 Nov. 1973; Orchestra:
Episodic suite; American dance suite; Hellenic
suite; Folkway symphony; piano concerto; Band:
Remember the Alamo; Sails aloft, overture; Chamber music: piano sonatina; Characteristic suite,
piano; Episodic suite, piano; Nocturne and Festival piece, viola and piano; Cornwall, piano
trio; string quartet; choral works and songs.
She is author of Aaron Copland, His work and contribution to American music, New York, 1955;
Master pianist--Carl Friedberg, Phil. Lib., 1963;
Directory of American women composers, NFMC, 1970.
417 Riverside Drive, New York, NY 10025

*SMITH, KENT
Toccata for organ.

SMITH, LANI
b. Cincinnati, Ohio, 9 June 1934. Studied with
John Larkin, Felix Labunski, Scott Huston, Univ.
of Cincinnati Coll. Cons., B. M., M. M. He received the Columbia Univ. Bearns composition
prize; Chapel Choir Conductors Guild anthem contest award; Martin Dumler award, Univ. of Cincinnati. He has been organist and choirmaster,
1955-   ; private teacher, 1959-66; composer,
arranger, editor, Lorenz Publishing Company,
1967-   .
WORKS: Ballet: A Christmas carol, 2-act,
based on Dickens' story, 1973; Orchestra: Prelude and scherzo, for brass, strings, timpani,
commissioned by Thor Johnson, 1957; also more
than 200 published choral and organ works, and
5 folk-rock musicals.
903 McCleary, Apt. D, Dayton, OH 45406

*SMITH, LELAND C.
b. Oakland, Calif., 6 Aug. 1925. Studied with
Darius Milhaud, Mills Coll., 1941-43; with Roger
Sessions, Univ. of California, Berkeley, M. A.
1948; with Olivier Messiaen in Paris, 1948-49.
He has held teaching posts at Univ. of California, Berkeley, Mills Coll., Univ. of Chicago;
joined the faculty at Stanford Univ., 1958,
professor, 1968-   . His works include Santa
Claus, an opera on a libretto by e.e. cummings,
1955; a symphony, 1951; concerto for orch., 1956;
numerous works for chamber groups; and songs.
3732 Laguna Ave., Palo Alto, CA 94302

*SMITH, MELVILLE
b. 1898.   3 songs to Sandburg texts.

SMITH, RICHARD HARRISON
b. Erie, Pa., 23 Aug. 1937. Studied with Morten
Luvaas, Allegheny Coll.; with Paul Christiansen,
Concordia Coll., Moorhead, Minn. He was minister of music, Olivet Lutheran Church, Fargo,
N. D., 1962-69; choral director, Oak Grove
Lutheran High School, Fargo, 1967-69; choral
director, Jamestown Coll., 1969-   .
WORKS: Chorus: War poem; Except our God
build a house; Fanfare and processional; The
babe and the cross.
319 6th Ave., Northeast, Jamestown, ND 58401

*SMITH, RUSSELL
b. Tuscaloosa, Ala., 23 Apr. 1927. Studied at
Eastman School of Music; with Otto Luening and
Douglas Moore, Columbia Univ., B. S. in music,
M. A.; with Aaron Copland at Tanglewood, 1947.
His awards include the Seidl fellowship in theat-
rical composition, Columbia Univ., 1951; special
award, Gershwin Memorial contest, 1954;
Guggenheim fellowship, 1955. He is associate
professor, State Univ. in New Orleans.
WORKS: Opera: The unicorn in the garden,
Thurber text; Orchestra: Can-can and waltz;
Tetrameron, 1957; piano concerto #2; Chorus:
Gloria and service in G; Set me as a seal,
women's voices; 3 songs from Emily Dickinson,
women's voices; Organ: 3 chorale preludes.
Department of Music, State University
New Orleans, LA 70122

SMITH, STUART S.
b. Portland, Me., 16 Mar. 1948. Studied with
Edward Diemente and Edward Miller, Hartt Coll.
of Music; with Salvatore Martirano, Univ. of
Illinois, candidate for D. M. A., 1973. He
taught percussion, Hartt Coll. of Music,
1970-73.
WORKS: Chamber music: Gestures I, II, III,
piano; One for Syl, solo vibraphone; Poems I, II,
III, 5 brake drums and narrator; A fine old tra-
dition, 2 pianos, alto saxophone; One for two, organ and alto saxophone; One for
J.C., saxophone and bassoon; A gift for Bessie,
bassoon, piano, violin, percussion; Mute, alto
saxophone; Legacy variations, any 3 melody instruments; To all of those, organ and tape;
2 for 4, percussion quartet; Here and there a
flower frozen, short wave radio, piano, and any
melody instrument.
813 North Willis St., Champaign, IL 61820

SMITH, WARREN STORY

*SMITH, WARREN STORY
   b. Brookline, Mass., 14 July 1885; d. Framingham,
Mass., 15 Oct. 1971. Studied at the Faelten
Pianoforte School, Boston; taught there 1908-19;
was faculty member, New England Cons., 1922-58;
assistant music critic, Boston Evening Transcript,
1919-24; music editor, Boston Post, 1924-53. His
works for orchestra include Romance, 1916; A
caravan from China comes, voice and orch., 1916;
Andante cantabile, 1920; also many songs and
piano pieces.

SMITH, WILLIAM OVERTON
   b. Sacramento, Calif., 22 Sep. 1926. Studied
with Darius Milhaud, Mills Coll.; with Roger
Sessions, Univ. of California, Berkeley, M. A.;
at Juilliard School; with Ulysse Delecleuse,
Paris Cons. His awards include the Prix de Paris,
1951-53; Prix de Rome, 1957; Guggenheim fellowships, 1961, 1962; American Acad. of Arts and
Letters award, 1972. He has held faculty posts
at Univ. of California, Berkeley, 1953-54; San
Francisco Cons., 1954-55; Univ. of Southern California, 1955-57, 1958-60; Univ. of Washington,
1966-   ; is virtuoso clarinetist.
      WORKS: Orchestra: Concerto for jazz soloist
and orch.; Quadri, jazz quartet and orch.; Chamber music: suite for clarinet, flute, trumpet,
1947; Serenade, flute, violin, trumpet, clarinet,
1947; Schizophrenic scherzo, clarinet, trumpet,
saxophone, trombone, 1947; clarinet sonata, 1948;
Concertino, trumpet and jazz group, 1948; quintet,
clarinet and string quartet, 1950; string quartet, 1952; Capriccio, violin and piano, 1952;
suite for violin and clarinet, 1952; Divertimento,
jazz group, 1956; concerto for clarinet and jazz
combo, 1957; trio, clarinet, violin, piano, 1957;
quartet, clarinet and piano trio, 1958; 5 pieces
for clarinet alone, 1958; Elegy for Eric, jazz
combo, 1964; Mozaic, clarinet and piano; Variants,
clarinet solo; Multimedia: Quadrodram, clarinet,
trombone, piano, percussion, dancer, film, 1970.
      School of Music, University of Washington
      Seattle, WA 98105

*SMOLANOFF, MICHAEL
   Vercingetorix, 1-act opera.
      Rutgers, The State University
      Camden, NJ 08102

SMOLOVER, RAYMOND
   b. Russia, 15 Jan. 1921; to U.S. 1922. Attended
Carnegie Inst. of Technology and Columbia Univ.
Teachers Coll. He has been cantor and music
director, 1949-   ; executive director, American
Conference of Cantors, 1968-74.
      WORKS: Folk/rock services: Where the rain-
bow ends, interfaith service; Edge of freedom;
Gates of freedom.
      10 Crest Lane, Scarsdale, NY 10583

SNOW, MARY McCARTY
   b. Brownsville, Tex., 26 Aug. 1928. Studied
with Anis Fuleihan, Indiana Univ.; with Burrill
Phillips, Univ. of Illinois. She received a
grant from Texas Technological Univ. to compose
a work based on arid and semi-arid land cultures.

(SNOW, MARY McCARTY)
She was instructor, Texas Technological Univ.
1967-69.
      WORKS: Theatre: electronic scores for
Marat-Sade; Indians; The Bacchae; Chamber music:
5 monodies for clarinet; Electronic: Mandora,
violin and tape; Hieroglyphs, instruments and
tape (Texas Tech. Univ. grant).
      2808 25th, Lubbock, TX 79410

SNYDER, RANDALL
   b. Chicago, Ill., 6 Apr. 1944. Studied with
Lavern Wagner, Quincy Coll.; with Hilmar
Luckhardt, Burt Levy, and Les Thimmig, Univ. of
Wisconsin. He won first prize, Eastern Illinois
Univ. wind ensemble composition contest. He was
instructor, Univ. of Wisconsin, 1973-74.
      WORKS: Orchestra: Concerto for bassoon and
chamber orch., 1971; Hegemony, piano and orch.,
1973; Wind ensemble: Variations, 1971; Chamber
music: quintet for saxophone and string quartet; 7 epigrams, saxophone and piano.
      2514 Gregory St., Madison, WI 53701

SNYDER, THEODORE
   b. New York, N. Y., 27 Nov. 1924. Studied with
William Bergsma and Vincent Persichetti,
Juilliard School; with Aaron Copland at Tanglewood; with Bernard Rogers and Wayne Barlow,
Eastman School of Music, D. M. A. He received
a Crofts award for study at Tanglewood; and an
award from the American Society of Women's Music
Clubs. He was faculty member, Hampton Inst.,
1955-60; Luther Coll., 1963-65; associate professor, State Univ. Coll. at Brockport,
1970-   .
      WORKS: Orchestra: 4 variations; St.
Nicholas, for pantomime, chorus, and orch.;
Chamber music: quartet for piano and winds;
Chorus: 2 Ascension Day choruses.
      3 Rundel Park, Rochester, NY 14607

*SODERLUND, GUSTAVE FREDERIC
   b. Goteberg, Sweden, 25 Jan. 1881; to U.S. 1916.
Studied piano in Sweden and in the U.S. with
Josef Lhevinne. He taught at Univ. of Kansas,
1919-27; Eastman School of Music, 1928-52. He
composed a symphonic poem, Svithiod; chamber
music, and piano pieces.

*SOKOLOFF, NOEL
   b. 1923.   Epithalamium, violin and piano.

SOLLBERGER, HARVEY
   b. Cedar Rapids, Iowa, 11 May 1938. Studied
with Eldon Obrecht and Philip Bezanson, Univ.
of Iowa; with Jack Beeson and Otto Luening,
Columbia Univ., M. A. 1964. His awards include
the Bearns prize, 1963; Fromm Found.-Berkshire
Music Center commission, 1964; American Acad. of
Arts and Letters award, 1965; Koussevitzky commission, 1966; special citation, American
Internat. Music Fund, 1967; and 2 Guggenheim
fellowships, 1969, 1973. He has been faculty
member, Columbia, 1965-   , (in 1973, assistant
professor on leave); faculty, Manhattan School
of Music, director of Contemporary Ensemble,

(SOLLBERGER, HARVEY)
1972- ; co-director, Group for Contemporary
Music, 1962- .
WORKS: Theatre: music for Sophocles'
Antigone, male speaker or speaking chorus with
electronic music, 1966; Chamber music: Grand
quartet for flutes, 1962; 2 pieces for 2 flutes,
1962; Solos for violin and 5 instruments, 1962;
Chamber variations for 12 players and conductor,
1964; Impromptu for piano, 1968; Divertimento,
flute, cello, piano, 1970; Iron Mountain song,
trumpet and piano, 1971; As things are and become,
string trio, 1972; The two and the one, cello
and 2 percussionists, 1972; string quartet, New
York, 19 Mar. 1973; Riding the wind, New York,
14 Jan. 1974.
R. D. 1, Cherry Valley, NY 13320

SOLOMON, MELVIN
b. Richmond, Va., 3 Jan. 1947. Studied bassoon
with William Polisi, Juilliard School, B. M.,
M. M. He received 5 grants, Dance in Education
Fund, Westchester County, N. Y.; and many commissions. He was composer-in-residence, Univ.
of Vermont, 1969-73, and at Steffi Nossen School
of the Dance, 1969-73; teacher, YMHA of Mid-
Westchester Music School and Central Music School,
Yonkers, N. Y., 1973- .
WORKS: Ballet: The waxing of the woodbine,
1969; Lona, 1969; The garden of Earthly delights,
1972; The best things, 1972; Orchestra: The
Martian chronicles; Concertino; Concerto for
bassoon and strings, 1973; Chamber music: Etudes
to spring, bassoon solo, 1970; Poeme for cello,
1971; Chorus: Revelations, for 100 voices, organ
and harp.
5214 Wythe Ave., Richmond, VA 23226

SOMER, AVO
b. Tartu, Estonia, 27 June 1934; U.S. citizen
1956. Studied musicology at Univ. of Michigan,
Ph. D. 1963; participated in Karlheinz
Stockhausen's 'Ensemble', Darmstadt, Germany,
Aug. 1967. He has been faculty member, Univ. of
Connecticut, 1961- , professor, 1973- .
WORKS: Chamber music: Trio variations,
string trio, 1965; Concertino, chamber ensemble,
Bennington Composers' Conference, 28 Aug. 1964;
Refrains, flute, clarinet, percussion, piano,
New York, 13 Apr. 1966; Winter music, string trio,
1967; Elegy II, piano quintet, New York, 27 Jan.
1970; Chorus: Cantata no.4, women's voices,
Toronto, Ont., 15 Mar. 1959; Vilemees, a cappella,
Boston, Mass., 24 Apr. 1960.
115 Northwood Road, Storrs, CT 06268

*SONDHEIM, STEPHEN JOSHUA
b. New York, N. Y., 22 Mar. 1930. Studied at
Williams Coll., B. A. 1950; and with Milton
Babbitt, Princeton Univ. Composer, lyricist,
and librettist, he wrote the music for Girls of
summer, 1956; Invitation to a march, 1961; music
and lyrics for A funny thing happened on the way
to the forum, 1962; Anyone can whistle, 1964; A
little night music, 1972; and lyrics for
Bernsteins's West Side story, 1957; Styne's
Gypsy, 1959; and Rodgers' Do I hear a waltz?, 1965.
246 East 49th St., New York, NY 10017

SONGER, LEWIS A.
b. Evansville, Ind., 4 Sep. 1935. Studied with
Will Gay Bottje, Southern Illinois Univ.; with
Roy Harris, Indiana Univ.; with Francis
Buebendorf, Univ. of Missouri at Kansas City.
He received a Huntington Hartford fellowship,
1963; Buebendorf award for chamber music. He
has held faculty posts at Cottey Coll., Mo.,
1960-63; Westminster Coll., Pa., 1965-68; East
Tennessee State Univ., 1968- .
WORKS: Orchestra: Symphony no.2; piano
concerto; Wind ensemble: Foothills and mountains; Chamber music: cello sonata; Octet-nova;
Crab canon for 3 percussionists; Chorus: Great
art thou, O Lord; A prayer with psalm.
1515 Chickees St., Johnson City, TN 37601

*SONNECK, OSCAR GEORGE THEODORE
b. Jersey City, N. J., 6 Oct. 1873; d. New York,
N. Y., 30 Oct. 1928. Was a noted musicologist
who was named first chief of the music division,
Library of Congress, 1902-17. In 1917 he joined
the staff of G. Schirmer Company, music publishers in New York, becoming vice president in
1921. His compositions include a symphonic movement for small orchestra; string quartet;
Romance and rhapsody, violin and piano; songs,
piano pieces.

SOOMIL (LEWIS) STEPHAN
b. Bremerton, Wash., 21 June 1940. Studied with
Joseph Wood, Oberlin Coll.; with Darius Milhaud
and Luciano Berio, Mills Coll.; with John
Vincent, Univ. of California, Los Angeles. He
received the Paul M. Henry award, Mills Coll.,
1965; Atwater Kent 2nd prize and Alex Stordahl
award, Univ. of California, 1970. He has been
accompanist and composer, UCLA dance department,
1972- .
WORKS: Chamber music: Theme and variations,
piano, 1964, chamber ensemble, 1973; Winter song,
soprano and 9 instruments, 1968; Entropy, 2
pianos, 1968; Shadows, 6 horns, 1972; Electronic:
Toward Phoenicia, tape, 1967; Strata, 5 instruments and tape, 1967; Sensations of the swan, 3
instruments and tape-delay system, 1968; Isle of
Wight, tape, 1970; Sidon, tape, 1972; Mojave,
tape using live and electronic sounds, 1972.
849 Dickson St., Venice, CA 90291

SORCE, RICHARD
b. Passaic, N. J., 29 July 1943. Studied with
Ludmila Ulehla, Manhattan School of Music; with
Joseph Scianni and J. Willard Roosevelt, New
York Coll. of Music; and with John Gilbert and
Michael Czajkowski, New York Univ., B. S., M. A.
He held a graduate scholarship at New York Univ.
He was a private teacher, 1962-72; public school
music teacher, 1971-73.
WORKS: Band: Alleluia, band and chorus;
Fantasia for brass; Chamber music: 2 fugues for
3 brass; Theme and variations, woodwinds; 2 in-
ventions for woodwinds; Chorus: Spring and fall,
to a young child, women's voices; Turn back O
man; piano pieces and songs.
715 McCoy Road, Franklin Lakes, NJ 07417

SORENSON, JOHN ROGER

SORENSON, JOHN ROGER
b. Pasadena, Calif., 8 May 1945. Studied with
Matt Doran, Mount St. Mary's Coll., Los Angeles;
and with Donal R. Michalsky, California State
Univ., Fullerton. He won a graduate composition
award, Music Associates, California State Univ.,
Fullerton, 1973. He has been public school
music teacher, 1970-   .
WORKS: Chamber music: Trio concertato,
violin, viola, bass clarinet, 1972; 3 reflections for guitar; Etude for 5 instruments, 1973;
Intermission piece for 2 clarinets; Songs for
soprano and guitar, 1973; Celestial, for 3 wind
groups, 1973; 3 pieces for free-bass accordion,
1973; Chorus: 13 ways of looking at a blackbird,
small chorus and chamber ensemble, 1972; Piano:
sonata, 1970.
2965 East Jackson Ave., #76
Anaheim, CA 92806

*SOSNIK, HARRY
The dogmas of the quiet past, band; Starward, a
space processional for band.

SOUERS, MILDRED
b. Des Moines, Iowa, 26 Feb. 1894. Studied with
Francis J. Pyle, Drake Univ.; and with Marion
Bauer in New York. She won a first prize for a
choral work, Nat. Fed. of Music Clubs. She was
accompanist, lecture-recitalist, and coach.
WORKS: Chorus: Winter nocturne; Songs:
April weather, The immortal; Piano: Impromptu;
Passacaglia; Bar and technique melodies for the
dance studio; numerous other published works for
voice, organ, piano, and solo instruments.
4230 Ingersoll Ave., Des Moines, IA 50312

SOULE, EDMUND FOSTER
b. Boston, Mass., 4 Mar. 1915. Studied with
Harl MacDonald, Univ. of Pennsylvania, B. M.
1939, M. A. 1946; with Richard Donovan, Yale
Univ., B. M. 1948; at Eastman School of Music,
Ph. D. 1956; Univ. of Denver, School of Librar-
ianship, M. L. S. 1966. He received the Frances
Osborne Kellogg prize for fugue writing, 1947.
He has held faculty posts at Milton Acad., Mass.,
1948-49; Washington State Univ., 1949-51,
1961-65; Salem Coll., W. Va., 1955-58; Univ. of
the Pacific, 1958-61; music librarian, Univ. of
Oregon, 1966-   .
WORKS: Chamber music: Serenade for alto
saxophone and piano, 1964; brass quintet; 6 trumpet duets; 3 flute duets; saxophone quartet; Fanfare, 11 brass instruments; Canzona, 7 brass
instruments; brass trio; many choral works,
songs, and piano pieces.
5399 Bailey Hill Road, Eugene, OR 97405

SOUTHALL, MITCHELL B.
b. Rochester, N. Y., 30 Aug. 1922. Studied at
Langston Univ., B. A. 1946; with Philip Greeley
Clapp, Univ. of Iowa, M. A. 1947, M. F. A. 1948,
Ph. D. 1949. He was cited for Outstanding Service to Langston Univ., 1946; was graduate
assistant, Univ. of Iowa, 1947-49; received
teaching awards, 1955, 1971. He has held faculty posts at Langston Univ. 1949-53; Lane Coll.,
1953-56; Southern Univ.; Texas Coll.; Mississippi

(SOUTHALL, MITCHELL B.)
Valley State Coll.; Rust Coll.; assistant professor, Univ. of Tennessee at Martin, 1972-   .
WORKS: Chorus: In silent night, 1955;
75th anniversary, for Lane Coll., 1955; Piano:
Romance, 1940; Elf dance, 1940; Impromptu in d,
1941; Impromptu militaire, 1942; numerous unpublished works and published arrangements.
P. O. Box 631, Martin, TN 38237

SOUTHERS, LEROY WILLIAM, JR.
b. Minot, N. D., 13 July 1941. Studied with
Anthony Vazzana, Halsey Stevens, Ingolf Dahl,
Robert Linn, Ellis B. Kohs, Univ. of Southern
California, B. M. magna cum laude 1963, M. M.
1965, D. M. A. candidate 1973. He received the
Alchin scholarship; Helen Amstead award; Ford
Found.-MENC grant for composer-in-residence in
public schools, Kenosha, Wisc., 1966-68; Nat.
Found. on the Arts grant, 1968. He was instructor, Los Angeles Acad. of Performing Arts,
1968-69; lecturer, Univ. of Southern California,
1969-72, instructor, 1972-   .
WORKS: Orchestra: Concerto for string bass,
1967; The ghosts of the buffaloes, chorus and
orch., 1968; Band: Essay for band, 1964; Concerto for 4 horns, euphonium, and wind ensemble,
1967; Study for band, 1968; New variations on a
17th century song, 1967; Chamber music: Concert
piece for chamber ensemble, 1965; Symphony for
chamber ensemble, 1967; Concerto for trombone
and chamber ensemble.
3708 West Victory Blvd., Burbank, CA 91505

*SOWANDE, FELA
b. Nigeria, 1905. Is a faculty member, Univ. of
Pittsburgh. His published works include Joyful
day, Nostalgia, Akinia, from African suite, chorus and orch.
6236 5th Ave., Apt. B
Pittsburgh, PA 15232

*SOWERBY, LEO
b. Grand Rapids, Mich., 1 May 1895; d. Port
Clinton, Ohio, 7 July 1968. Studied with Arthur
Olaf Andersen, American Cons., M. M. 1918. He
was the first recipient of the American Prix de
Rome, 1921-24; other awards include an honorary
D. M., Univ. of Rochester, 1934; Pulitzer prize,
1946; fellow, Trinity Coll., London, 1957; fellow, Royal School of Church Music, Croydon, England, 1963. He served in the U.S. Army, 1917-19;
was faculty member, American Cons., 1925-62;
organist, St. James Episcopal Church, Chicago,
1927-62; director, Coll. for Church Musicians,
Nat. Cathedral, Washington, D.C., 1962-68.
WORKS: Orchestra: Comes autumn time, overture, 1916; Irish washerwoman, 1916; From the
northland, 1923; King Estmere, 2 pianos and
orch., 1923; Money musk, 1924; Prairie, symphonic
poem, 1929; 4 symphonies; 3 piano concertos; 2
cello concertos; 2 organ concertos; many chamber
works; Chorus: Vision of Sir Launfal, 1926;
Canticle of the Sun, chorus and orch., 1945;
Christ reborn, oratorio, 1953; The throne of God,
1957.

*SPALDING, ALBERT
b. Chicago, Ill., 15 Aug. 1888; d. New York,
N. Y., 26 May 1953. Studied violin in Europe;
made his American debut as violinist with the
New York Symphony in 1908. Thereafter he made
annual tours in the U.S. and many in Europe. He
composed violin concertos, a violin sonata,
string quartet, suite for violin and piano,
piano pieces, and songs. He also published an
autobiography, Rise to follow, New York, 1944;
and an imaginative biography of Tartini, A fiddle, a sword, and a lady, New York, 1953.

*SPEAKS, OLEY
b. Canal Winchester, Ohio, 28 June 1874; d. New
York, N. Y., 27 Aug. 1948. Was a church and
concert baritone and composer. His highly popular songs included On the road to Mandalay, 1907;
Morning, 1910; Sylvia, 1914; The prayer perfect;
When the boys come home, 1918.

SPEARS, JARED
b. Chicago, Ill., 15 Aug. 1936. Studied with
Maurice Weed, Northern Illinois Univ., B. S. E.;
with Blythe Owen and Irwin Fischer, Cosmopolitan
School of Music, B. M., M. M.; with Anthony
Donato and Alan Stout, Northwestern Univ., D. M.
He received the Faricy creative music award,
1966; first prize Phi Mu Alpha international
contest, 1967; many commissions. He was public
school music teacher, 1958-65; teaching assistant, Northwestern Univ., 1965-67; associate
professor, Arkansas State Univ., 1967- .
    WORKS: Band: March for moderns, 1965; Col-
location, winds and percussion, 1968; Kimberly
overture, 1969; 3 cameos, 1970; Pidgeon Cove
legend, 1970; Chatham, 1970; Prologue and pageant,
1971; Neologue, 1973, Triolog, 1973; Chronolog,
1973; many works for small brass ensembles; choral pieces.
    205 Driver (Box 4N)
    State University, AR 72467

SPECTOR, IRWIN
b. New Jersey, 11 Jan. 1916. Studied with Nadia
Boulanger, Paris; with Philip James, Marion Bauer,
Charles Haubiel, Laszlo Kun, and Harold Morris
in New York. He was instructor, Monmouth Coll.,
1942-48; professor, Illinois State Univ.,
1948- ; visiting professor, Univ. of Kansas,
1968-69.
    WORKS: Orchestra: Fantasy, violin and
orch.; Rhapso-concerto, cello and orch.; Chamber
music: Pieces in 3, piano; Songs of love and
music, voice and 4 instruments; other works for
orchestra, chamber groups, piano, voice.
    903 West College Ave., Normal, IL 61761

*SPELLER, FRANK N.
A triptych of praise and thanksgiving, organ.

*SPELMAN, TIMOTHY MATHER
b. Brooklyn, N. Y., 21 Jan. 1891; d. Florence,
Italy, 21 Aug. 1970. Studied with Walter R.
Spalding and Edward Burlingame Hill, Harvard
Univ., 1909-13; with Courvoisier in Munich.
After World War I he alternated residence in
Italy and New York.

(SPELMAN, TIMOTHY MATHER)
    WORKS: Opera: The sunken city, 1930;
Courtship of Miles Standish, 1943; Theatre:
Snowdrop, 4-act pantomime, 1911; La magnifica,
1-act music drama, 1920; also works for orchestra, chorus, and chamber music.

SPENCER, JAMES HOUSTON
b. Malone, N. Y., 28 July 1895; d. Adrian,
Mich., 3 Sep. 1967. Studied with George
Whitefield Chadwick, New England Cons., diploma
1919. His awards include the Mary Cromwell
grant for study in Europe, 1938; 3 MacDowell
fellowships; first prize, Detroit News composition contest; first prize, Chicago Tribune contest; membership in American Guild of Organists;
honorary doctorate, Adrian Coll. He was chairman, music department, Adrian Coll., 1921-65;
organist and choirmaster, various churches in
Ann Arbor, Toledo, Detroit.
    WORKS: Opera: Song of Solomon, Adrian,
Mich., 1937; Orchestra: 2 symphonies, subtitled American dance fantasy and American folk
symphony; Fiddler of the northern lights, a tone
poem, 1967; Chamber music: Nativity, andante
pastorale, woodwind sextet and piano; Rustic
suite, string quartet; Pandean sketches no.1 and
2, flute and piano; piano trio; Piece for piano
and strings; Organ: Chinese boy and bamboo
flute; Symphonesque; Choral communion; many
songs and piano pieces.

*SPENCER, S. REID
b. Baltimore, Md., 30 July 1872; d. Brooklyn,
N. Y., 28 July 1945. Studied at Northwestern
Univ., then taught there, 1895-1900. He founded
his own music school in Brooklyn in 1927. He
composed piano and organ pieces and church music.

*SPENCER, VERNON
b. Durham, England, 10 Oct. 1875; d. Los Angeles,
Calif., 9 Jan. 1949. Graduated from Leipzig
Cons., 1897. He was director, Cons. of Music,
Nebraska Wesleyan Univ., 1903-11; then taught
in Los Angeles. He composed many songs and
piano pieces.

SPENCER, WILLIAMETTA
b. Marion, Ill., 15 Aug. 1932. Studied with
Ernest Kanitz, Univ. of Southern California;
with Tony Aubin, Ecole Normale, Paris. She received a Fulbright scholarship to Paris; 4
first prizes, Mu Phi Epsilon national composition
contests; Southern California Vocal Asso. award
for choral composition, 1968. She has been associate professor, Rio Hondo Coll., 1966- .
    WORKS: Chamber music: Adagio and rondo,
oboe and piano; Chorus: At the round Earth's
imagined corners; Death be not proud; Missa
brevis; Nova, nova ave fit ex Eva; 4 madrigals
to poems of James Joyce; 3 Christmas madrigals;
In excelsis gloria, men's voices; Past 3 O'clock,
men's voices; Tyrley, tyrlow, men's voices.
    6430 South Pierce, Apt. 7
    Whittier, CA 90601

SPERRY, DON R.

SPERRY, DON R.
b. Dallas, Tex., 17 Feb. 1947. Studied with
James Brody, Thomas Wirtel, James Richards,
Margaret Wheat, East Texas State Univ.; with
Gene Cho, Martin Mailman, Robert Ottman, William
Latham, Dale Peters, North Texas State Univ.
WORKS: Orchestra: 2 symphonies, 1972, 1973;
Chamber music: Sonata for 3; Canonic duets,
violin and cello; Piece for 4; septet; trio;
Thinking (Thoughts of you), solo flute, strings,
guitar, 1970; Uncertain faces, soprano, chamber
orch.
2835 Villa Creek, Apt. 153
Dallas, TX 75234

SPIALEK, HANS
b. Vienna, Austria, 17 Apr. 1894; U.S. citizen
1931. Studied with Felix Weingartner and M.
Spohr, Vienna Cons.; with Alexander Glazunov,
Moscow Cons. He was arranger and editor for New
York music publishers, 1927-47; also arranged
more than 100 Broadway musicals.
WORKS: Theatre: Heavenly light, musical
play; Orchestra: The tall city; Sinfonietta;
Manhattan watercolors; To a ballerina; piano concerto; also piano pieces and chamber works.
145 West 86th St., New York, NY 10024

SPIEGEL, LAURIE
b. Chicago, Ill., 20 Sep. 1945. Studied at Shimer
Coll., A. B. 1967; independent study at Oxford
Univ. and private study with J. W. Duarte, London,
1967-68; privately with Michael Czajkowski in New
York; 1969-71; guitar at Juilliard School,
1969-72; privately with Jacob Druckman, 1972-73,
with Emmanuel Ghent, 1973-74; with Druckman at
Brooklyn Coll., M. A. 1974. She has been guitar
instructor, Bucks County Community Coll.,
1970-   , instructor in electronic music,
1971-   ; assistant to director of electronic
music, Aspen Music Festival, 1971-   , instructor,
1972-   ; resident visitor, Bell Telephone Research Laboratories, for composing with the
GROOVE system, 1973-74; and under a Rockefeller
grant, junior research fellow, Inst. for Studies
in American Music, 1973-74.
WORKS: Theatre: music for The library of
Babel by Paul Ahrens, New York, May 1972; The
house of Bernarda Alba, Bucks County, BC3 Theatre,
Dec. 1972; White devil by John Webster, Bucks
County, April-May 1973; The clinic by Robert
Goldman, New York, Nov. 1973; Film scores; educational films, commercials, and experimental
films; Electronic: Harmonic spheres, 1971; Return to zero, 1971; Orchestras, 1971; Raga, 1972;
Sediment, 1972; Sunsets, 1973; Purification,
1973; also multimedia shows presented in New York.
331 East 89th St., New York, NY 10028

SPIEGELMAN, JOEL W.
b. Buffalo, N. Y., 23 Jan. 1933. Studied with
Irving Fine, Harold Shapero, Arthur Berger,
Brandeis Univ., with Nadia Boulanger, Paris Cons.,
1956-60. He was recipient of a French Government
fellowship; Ingram Merrill award, 1967, 1968;
grant for travel to USSR, U.S.-Soviet Cultural
Exchange; American Philosophical Society grant;
ASCAP awards, 1967-73. He taught at Longy School

(SPIEGELMAN, JOEL W.)
of Music, 1961-62; Cummington School of the Arts,
1961-62; Brandeis Univ., 1961-66; has been
chairman, music department, Sarah Lawrence Coll.,
1966-   .
WORKS: Chamber music: Fantasy, string quartet, 1963; Kousochki, piano 4 hands; Chamber
music, for piano, strings and percussion; Chorus:
V'haavtah, sacred service for reader, cantor,
chorus and tape; Phantom of the opera, women's
voices with self accompaniment by crotales and
wind chimes; Electronic: The 11th hour, electronic symphony; Multimedia: Daddy, chamber
work for actress, soprano, flute, oboe, ARP
synthesizer, conga drums.
40 Harbor Road, Westport, CT 06880

*SPIER, HARRY R.
b. Boston, Mass., 7 Nov. 1888; d. New York,
N. Y., 20 Jan. 1952. Was accompanist and choral
director, and organist, Church of the Atonement,
New York. His compositions included pieces for
flute and piano, piano, choral works, and songs.

SPIES, CLAUDIO
b. Santiago, Chile, 26 Mar. 1925; U.S. citizen
1966. Studied at New England Cons., 1942-46;
with Nadia Boulanger, Longy School of Music,
1943, 1945; with Harold Shapero, Irving Fine,
Walter Piston, Harvard Univ., 1947-53. He received the Ingram Merrill award, 1966; Brandeis
Univ. Creative Arts award, 1967; Nat. Inst. of
Arts and Letters award, 1969. He was instructor,
Harvard Univ., 1953-57; lecturer, Vassar Coll.,
1957-58; Swarthmore Coll., 1958-70; assistant
to full professor, Princeton Univ., 1970-   .
WORKS: Chamber music: Tempi, for 14 instruments, 1962; Impromptu, piano, 1963; Times 2,
2 horns; 3 intermezzi, piano; Vio piacem, viola
and keyboard, 1965; Chorus: Animula vagula,
blandula, 1964; Verses from the Book of Ruth,
women's voices; In paradisum; Songs: 3 songs on
poems of May Swenson, 1969; 7 Enzensberger Lieder,
1972.
117 Meadowbrook Drive, Princeton, NJ 08540

*SPINDLE, LOUISE COOPER
b. Muskegan, Mich., 1 Jan. Studied at Chicago
Musical Coll. Her works include Southlands
suite for orchestra; choral pieces, and songs.

SPINO, PASQUALE J.
b. Newark, N. J., 7 July 1942. Studied with
Vaclav Nelhybel in New York; with Paul Fetler
and Dominick Argento, Univ. of Minnesota. He
was teaching assistant, Univ. of Minnesota,
1965-67; his symphony #1 was selected for performance at Indiana State Univ. Contemporary
Music Festival, 1973. He is a public school
music teacher.
WORKS: Orchestra: Symphonic movement for
string orch.; symphony #1; Band: Theme and variations; Jubilation; Fanfare, chorale, and march;
Chamber music: cello sonata; suite for piano;
saxophone quartet; brass quintet; trombone quartet; Chorus: A prophecy, with tenor and baritone
solos, brass, percussion; Lament, with tenor
solo, violin and piano; A patch of old snow;

(SPINO, PASQUALE J.)
    Nothing gold can stay; other pieces for woodwind
and brass ensembles.
    313 Gordon Ave., Williamstown, NJ 08094

SPIVAK, JOSEPH
    b. Brookline, Mass., 15 Oct. 1948. Studied with
Charles Dodge, Charles Wuorinen, Jack Beeson,
Columbia Univ. He was director, Columbia Com-
posers, 1969-72; music director, Shaker Village
Work Group, 1971; founding member, The Composers
Ensemble, 1971-   ; tape editor, Vanguard Record-
ing Society, 1972-   .
    WORKS: Orchestra: Thesis for orchestra;
Chamber music: 6 canonic pieces for 2 flutes;
Quartet for solo piano; trio for flute, cello,
piano; Weekend music; Prelude for guitar; Trio
for no dogs aloud; Chamber duet.
    201 West 89th St., New York, NY 10024

SPIZIZEN, LOUISE
    b. Lynn, Mass., 24 Aug. 1928. Studied at Vassar
Coll., A. B.; with Wallingford Riegger; with
Robert Erickson, Kenneth Gaburo, Wilbur Ogdon,
Univ. of California at San Diego, M. A. She
received a Vassar Coll., prize in composition for
a dance score; 2 commissions, Westport Madrigal
Singers. She was music director, The Interplayers,
1949-50; Dorothea Spaeth Dancers, 1950-52; private teacher and performer, 1959-   ; instructor,
San Diego Community Coll., 1972-   ; instructor,
Univ. of California, San Diego, 1969-   .
    WORKS: Ballet: Birthday of the Infanta,
modern dance score; Theatre: music for The silver tassie by Sean O'Casey, 1949; Chorus: Weary
with toil; liturgical setting for Reformed Jewish
service, women's voices and organ; 3 games for
10 players, with string quintet.
    925 Havenhurst Drive, La Jolla, CA 92037

SPONG, JON
    b. Des Moines, Iowa, 5 Dec. 1933. Studied with
Francis Johnson Pyle, Drake Univ. He has been
faculty member, Washington State Univ., 1959-60;
Drake Univ., 1961-66; Univ. of Missouri, 1966-69;
Angelo State Univ., 1970-71; organist-choirmaster,
First United Methodist Church, Des Moines,
1971-   .
    WORKS: Organ: Scenes from the life of
Christ; Christmas pastorales; Organ music for
joyous occasions; Contemplation and celebration.
    1300 Woodland, Apt. 311
    Des Moines, IA 50309

SPRATLAN, LEWIS
    b. Miami, Fla., 5 Sep. 1940. Studied with Mel
Powell, Gunther Schuller, Yehudi Wyner, Yale
Univ., B. A., M. M.; with Roger Sessions, George
Rochberg, Donald Martino at Tanglewood. He received the Gertrude Robinson Smith, the Miner D.
Crary, and the Amherst Coll., Trustee-Faculty
fellowships. He was assistant professor, Pennsylvania State Univ., 1968-70; assistant professor, Amherst Coll., 1970-   .
    WORKS: Orchestra: 2 pieces for orchestra,
1970; Dance suite, 1973; Chamber music: Serenade,
for 6 instruments, 1969; Diary music I, for 10

(SPRATLAN, LEWIS)
players, 1971; Summer music for 5 instruments,
1972; 3 Plath songs, 1972.
    23 Orchard St., Amherst, MA 01002

SPRAYBERRY, ROBERT JONES
    b. Decatur, Ala., 7 Dec. 1952. Studied with
Frank Carroll, Centenary Coll.; with Kenneth
Klaus, Louisiana State Univ. He received awards
for his scores to Romeo and Juliet and The serpent; commissions from Parish Playhouse, Shreveport, and Baton Rouge Little Theatre. He is
composer-in-residence, Marjorie Lyons Playhouse,
Shreveport.
    WORKS: Theatre: music for Romeo and Juliet;
Bury my heart at Wounded Knee; The brick and the
rose; The serpent; The glass menagerie; Anne of
a 1000 days; Piano: Dance suite; Fugue; Passacaglia; also a fugue for percussion.
    3046 Fritchie Drive, Baton Rouge, LA 70809

SPRING, GLENN E., JR.
    b. Hot Springs, Ark., 19 Apr. 1939. Studied
with Perry Beach, La Sierra Coll.; with Ralph
Guenther, Texas Christian Univ.; with John
Verrall and Robert Suderberg, Univ. of Washington, D. M. A. 1972. He received a commission,
Washington State Arts Commission. He was violinist, Fort Worth and Columbia Symphonies,
1962-65; concert-master, Walla Walla Symphony,
1966-   ; Instructor, Otterbein Coll., 1965;
associate professor, Walla Walla Coll.,
1966-   .
    WORKS: Orchestra: Shapes, a short symphony,
Walla Walla Symphony, 26 Feb. 1974; Chamber
music: trio for flute, viola and piano, 1970;
Chorus: Christmas lullaby, 1965; Missa brevis,
with 2 pianos and timpani, 1968, revised 1972.
    1059 Brickner, College Place, WA 99324

*SPROSS, CHARLES GILBERT
    b. Poughkeepsie, N. Y., 6 Jan. 1874; d. Pough-
keepsie, 23 Dec. 1962. Was organist and accompanist in the New York area. He composed 5
cantatas; chamber works, and over 200 songs.

SPRUNG, DAVID R.
    b. Jersey City, N. J., 24 Oct. 1931. Studied
with Vittorio Rieti and Luigi Dallapiccola,
Queens Coll., CUNY: with Roger Sessions and
Milton Babbitt, Princeton Univ. He received the
Joseph Dillon Memorial prize for his piano trio;
and the Karol Rathaus Memorial prize. He was
principal horn, Pittsburgh Symphony, 1961-63,
Chautauqua Symphony, 1961-   ; co-principal
horn, San Francisco Opera, 1973-   ; assistant
professor, Wichita State Univ., 1963-68; Sonoma
State Coll., 1966-70; associate professor, California State Univ., Hayward, 1970-   .
    WORKS: Orchestra: Prelude for orchestra;
Chamber music: string quartet, 1959; piano trio;
Music for Gail, horn and piano; Fantasy for
piano; Chorus: Psalm 8, women's voices; I hear
the noise of many waters; Song cycle: The tower
of David.
    5600 Snake Road, Oakland, CA 94611

STABILE, JAMES
    b. Brooklyn, N. Y., 28 May 1937. Studied with
Vittorio Giannini, Nicolas Flagello, Ludmila
Ulehla, Manhattan School of Music; with John B.
MacMillan, Nyack Coll.; conducting at Univ. of
Southern California. He was assistant professor,
The King's Coll., 1964-67; Nyack Coll., 1965-67;
visiting lecturer, free-lance composer, arranger,
conductor, California, 1967-   .
    WORKS: Orchestra: piano concerto; Rockland
overture; Pacific Coast overture; Suite for chamber orch.; Chamber music: Suite for brass quartet; Suite for brass ensemble; Ballade for
vibraphone; tuba sonata; The greatest of miracles,
piano; Chorus: St. Paul oratorio; Christmas cantata; Film scores: The lost generation, television film; Tokyo crusade; Chicago--City with a
vision; CBS television special.
        787 North Woodlawn Drive
        Thousand Oaks, CA 91360

STAFFORD, JAMES E.
    b. Summerville, La., 20 Aug. 1933. Studied with
James Hanna, Southwestern Louisiana Univ.; with
Kenneth Klaus, Louisiana State Univ. He has
been associate professor, East Tennessee State
Univ., 1965-   .
    WORKS: Chamber music: Quintet for flute,
violin, cello, horn, piano, 1969; Synesthesia
for brass; Chorus: Mass for brass and voices
according to the Book of Common Prayer; The time
of singing, 1967.
        P. O. Box 2615
        East Tennessee State University
        Johnson City, TN 37601

STAHL, HOWARD M.
    b. New York, N. Y., 18 Sep. 1948. Studied with
Frederick Piket, Hebrew Union Coll., School of
Sacred Music. He has been cantor, Congregation
Beth Emeth, Albany, N. Y., 1972-   .
    WORKS: Chorus: Ma'agal Chozer (Circle with-
out end), a rock-folk service for choir, guitars,
piano, drums, flute, 1972.
        8-2 Woodlake Road South, Albany, NY 12203

*STAHL, WILLY
    b. New York, N. Y., 1896; d. 1963. Graduated
from the Vienna Cons., 1913. He played viola in
the New York Symphony and the St. Paul Orchestra;
taught in Hollywood, Calif. His compositions
include Dead forest, tone poem, 1932; and chamber
music.

*STAHLBERG, FRITZ
    b. Ketzin, Germany, 7 June 1877; to U.S. 1899.
Was violinist in the Pittsburgh Symphony, 1900-08;
New York Symphony, 1908-29, and assistant conductor, 1912-29; then was head of music division
for MGM studios in Hollywood. He composed 2
symphonies, a symphonic suite, violin pieces,
and songs.

*STAIRS, LOUISE E.
    b. 1892. Was organist, conductor and teacher.
She composed cantatas and songs.

STALVEY, DORRANCE
    b. Georgetown, S. C., 21 Aug. 1930. Attended
Cincinnati Coll. of Music, M. M. 1955, but is
self-taught in composition. He received the
Prince Ranier III de Monaco composition prize,
1961. He has been faculty member, Immaculate
Heart Coll., 1963-72, associate professor,
1972-   ; taught at Pomona Coll., 1968-69;
executive director, Monday Evening Concerts,
1971-   .
    WORKS: Chamber music: 5 little pieces,
piano, 1957; string trio, 1960; Movements and
interludes, chamber ensemble, 1964; Changes,
piano, 1966; Celebration, brass and percussion,
1967; Points-lines-circles, chamber ensemble,
1968; PLC-Extract, clarinet solo, 1968; PLC-
Abstract, doublebass solo, 1972; Sequent I, 4
groups of 4 instruments, 1973, New York, 12 Jan.
1975; Electronic: Togethers I, guitar and tape,
1970; Togethers II, percussion and tape, optional
film, 1970; Togethers III, clarinet and tape,
optional slides, 1970; Fitan, 2-channel tape,
1971; Multimedia: Conflicts, instruments, chorus, dancers, tape, visuals, 1970; In time and
not, instruments, chorus, dancers, actors,
visuals, tape, staging, 1970.
        2145 Manning Ave., Los Angeles, CA 90025

STANLEY, HELEN (Mrs. Denby Gatlin)
    b. Tampa, Fla., 6 Apr. 1930. Studied with Hans
Barth and Ernst von Dohnanyi, Cincinnati Cons.,
B. M. 1951; Florida State Univ., M. M. 1954;
Muskingum Coll., B. S. 1961. Her awards include
a graduate fellowship, Florida State Univ.; C.
Hugo Grimm prize for Night piece; Florida State
Music Teachers Asso.-Music Teachers Nat. Asso.
award, 1972; and commissions. She has been
violist, El Paso Symphony; music director, Ballet
Center, El Paso; lecturer, School of Broadcasting, Jones Coll., 1965-66; Jacksonville Univ.,
1962-67; free-lance lecturer, composer, pianist,
1967-   .
    WORKS: Ballet: Birthday of the infanta;
Orchestra: symphony no. 1; Night piece, women's
chorus and orch.; Chamber music: trombone sonata; string quartet; woodwind quintet; brass
quartet; Overture, brass and timpani; Piece for
horn, percussion, piano; 2 pieces for wind soloist and piano; Songs: Credo; The isle; Piano:
sonatina; etudes; Modal suite; Electronic:
Lunar encounter, operetta, tape score; Electronic prelude; duo-sonata, tape and piano;
Rhapsody, tape and orch., Gainesville, Fla.,
12 Nov. 1972.
        1768 Emory Circle South
        Jacksonville, FL 32207

STANTON (Stankunas), JOSEPH
    b. Lithuania, 1 Nov. 1906; U.S. citizen 1955.
Studied in Kaunas, Lith., at Sao Paulo Cons.,
Brazil; and at Sao Paulo Inst. of Music, M. M.
1948. He taught in public schools in Sao Paulo
for 12 years and at the Inst. of Music; organist
and teacher, St. Patrick's Church, Elizabeth,
N. J., and privately, 1953-   .
    WORKS: Chorus: Mass in D; Mass in E-flat;
Keyboard: piano sonata; preludes and postludes

(STANTON, JOSEPH)
for organ; about 100 Lithuanian songs transcribed for solo voice, duets trios, and chorus.
1043 Applegate Ave., Elizabeth, NJ 07202

STARER, ROBERT
b. Vienna, Austria, 8 Jan. 1924; U.S. citizen 1957. Began playing piano at age 4 and was accepted at the Vienna State Acad. of Music at 13; in 1938 continued studies at Jerusalem Cons.; graduate study on scholarship at Juilliard School, diploma 1949. His awards include 2 Guggenheim fellowships; Fulbright post-doctoral research grant; many commissions. In World War II he volunteered for service in the British Royal Air Force; is on faculty at Juilliard School, and professor, Brooklyn Coll., CUNY.
WORKS: Opera: The intruder, 1 act, 1956; Pantagleize, 3 acts, Brooklyn Coll., 7 Apr. 1973; Ballet: The dybbuk, Berlin Festival, 1960; Samson agonistes; Phaedra; Holy jungle, New York, 22 Apr. 1974; Orchestra: Dalton set; 3rd Street overture; 3 symphonies, 1948, 1951, 19 ; 3 piano concertos, 1948, 19 , no. 3, Baltimore, 9 Oct. 1974; concertino for 2 voices or instruments, 1948; Prelude and dance, 1949; Concerto à tre, clarinet, trumpet, trombone, and strings; 1954; concerto for viola, strings, percussion, 1959; Mutabilii, variants for orch., 1965; concerto for violin and cello and orch., 1968; Prelude and rondo giocoso; 6 variations with 12 notes; Chamber music: Elegy for strings; Dialogues, Clarinet and piano; Little suite, violin and piano; woodwind quartet; many choral works, songs, piano pieces.
c/o MCA, 445 Park Ave., New York, NY 10022

STARKS, HOWARD F.
b. Erie, Pa., 1 Mar. 1928. Studied at Pennsylvania State Univ., Indiana Univ. of Pennsylvania, and at Southern Baptist Theological Seminary. He has been minister of music at various churches, 1954- .
WORKS: Chorus: Come, gracious Lord; Rise up, O men of God; Everywhere, everywhere, Christmas tonight; and some 30 more published choral works.
1857 Westmoreland Ave., Florence, SC 29501

STAUFFER, DONALD W.
b. Canton, Ohio, 30 July 1919. Studied at Eastman School of Music, B. M. 1941, M. M. 1942; Catholic Univ., Ph. D. in music education 1954. He received the Silver Medal, Swedish March Music Society; citation of excellence, Nat. Band Asso.; Orpheus award, Phi Mu Alpha Sinfonia. He served in the U.S. Navy, 1942-73, from tuba and doublebass player to commander and leader, U.S. Navy Band, 1969-73; associate professor, Birmingham Southern Coll., 1973- .
WORKS: Band: Fugue 'n swing; Canine capers suite; Moods modal; Deliberation suite; Eine kleine Deutsche suite; U.S.S. Kennedy march; Ch' chamba Latin fantasy. He is author of 2 books on band instruments and technique: Intonation deficiencies of wind instruments, Washington,

(STAUFFER, DONALD W.)
D.C., 1954; A treatise on the tuba, Rochester, N. Y., 1942, 1962.
Birmingham Southern College
Birmingham, AL 35204

STEARNS, PETER PINDAR
b. New York, N. Y., 7 June 1931; son of Theodore Stearns; studied with Leonard Stein and Miklos Rozsa in Los Angeles; with Bohuslav Martinu, Mannes Coll. of Music. He has been faculty member, Mannes Coll. of Music, 1957- , chairman of composition department, 1961-73; was assistant professor, Yale Univ., 1964-65.
WORKS: Orchestra: 1st little symphony, WNYC, New York, 18 Feb. 1952; Toccata, 1952, New York, 17 Feb. 1954; piano concerto, 1952, WNYC, New York, 16 Feb. 1956; 6 symphonies, 1953, 1956, 1956, 1957, 1961, #6; Capriccio in piccolo, 1954, Stuttgart, 7 June 1957; violin concerto, 1957; Passacaglia, 1958; Interlude for strings, WNYC, New York, 12 Feb. 1959; Reminiscence, strings and piano, WNYC, New York, 15 Feb. 1960; Chamber music: 5 string quartets, 1950, 1951, 1955, 1958, 1960, #5, New York, 17 Feb. 1962; 3 canzone, 2 clarinets and bassoon, 1953; New York, 12 Oct. 1957; duo for clarinet and bassoon, Hannover, Germany, 6 June 1958; Serenade for 15 winds, New York, 16 Apr. 1959; 3 pieces for clarinet and piano, 1958; 3 short pieces, bassoon and piano, 1959; septet for 3 winds, string trio and bass, 1959; 5 short pieces for oboe, clarinet, bassoon, 1961; Chamber set, 1959, New York, 17 Feb. 1962; many choral works; about 100 songs; piano and organ works.
Sherman, CT 06784

*STEARNS, THEODORE
b. Berea, Ohio, 10 June 1880; d. Los Angeles, Calif., 1 Nov. 1935. Studied at Oberlin Cons. and at Wurzburg Cons. He received the Bispham medal, 1925; Guggenheim fellowships, 1927-28. He was music critic in New York, 1922-26; was appointed to the faculty at Univ. of California, Los Angeles, 1932.
WORKS: Theatre: Snowbird, opera-ballet, 1923; Atlantis, lyric drama, 1926; Orchestra: Tiberio, symphonic poem; 2 orchestral suites.

STEELE, LANNY
b. Houston, Tex., 30 Dec. 1933. Studied with Samuel Adler, North Texas State Univ.; with Ross Lee Finney, Leslie Bassett, George B. Wilson, Univ. of Michigan, M. M. He was Rackham Scholar at Univ. of Michigan; won first place award, Contemporary Music Festival, Sam Houston State Univ., 1966; received Nat. Endowment for the Arts commission, 1971. He was instructor and director of jazz studies, North Texas State Univ., 1963-64; lecturer, East Michigan Univ., 1965-66; assistant professor, director of jazz ensembles, and composer-in-residence, Texas Southern Univ., 1968- ; director, SuM Concerts, Inc., Houston.
WORKS: Orchestra: III for J at 3, 1967; Jazz ensemble: Intersection, chamber orch and jazz ensemble, 1967; Ghetto, 1970; Thunderbird, concerto for alto saxophone, 1970; Space City blues, concerto grosso for 4 soloists, 1971;

STEELE, LANNY

(STEELE, LANNY)
Thelonius, 1971; 3rd Ward Vibration Society, concerto grosso; New York triptych, concerto grosso
for 3 soloists; Chamber music: piano sonata,
1963; string quartet, 1964; Fantasy, clarinet and
piano, 1965; concertino for 5 woodwinds, 1966;
Spacewalk, flute alone, 1968.
      2709 Robinhood, Houston, TX 77002

*STEELE, PORTER
      b. Natchez, Miss., 12 Dec. 1880; d. 1966. Studied
with Horatio Parker at Yale Univ.; also studied
law and was admitted to the bar in New York in
1905. He composed piano pieces and songs.

STEFFEN, FREDERICK JOHN
      b. Tilden, Neb., 18 Feb. 1949. Studied with
Warren Benson and Samuel Adler, Eastman School of
Music. He received first prize in composition,
Rochester Religious Arts Festival, 1968, 1969,
1970; Louis Lane award, 1971. He was departmental
assistant, Valparaiso Univ., 1971-73.
      WORKS: Orchestra: Variations for orchestra;
horn concerto; Chorus: Whither shall I go; Psalm
118; For me to live is Christ; Take this song, a
contemporary hymn; Songs: Aaron's benedition;
Piano: sonata.
      1101 Evans Ave., Apt. 4A
      Valparaiso, IN 46383

STEIN, ALAN
      b. Chicago, Ill., 22 Jan. 1949. Studied with
Thomas Fredrickson, Thomas Wirtel, Robert Kelly,
Univ. of Illinois. He held a summer fellowship,
Univ. of Illinois, 1973. He has been instructor,
Univ. of Illinois, 1971-73, lecturer, 1973-74.
      WORKS: Opera: A dove in the rainbow, 1 act,
based on story of Noah, Urbana, Ill., 13 Dec.
1973; Chamber music: Quintessence I, 5 trombones;
Piano, soprano, 3 pianos and tape; Ternion, 12
percussionists; No trumpets, no drums, flute trio;
Chorus: An afterthought, a cappella; The most
precious gift, a cappella; Mozart, 1935, chorus
and orch.
      524 Drexel Ave., Glencoe, IL 60022

*STEIN, HERMAN
      b. Philadelphia, Pa., 1915. Sour suite for wood-
wind quintet.
      3787 Amesbury Road, Los Angeles, CA 90027

STEIN, LEON
      b. Chicago, Ill., 18 Sep. 1910. Studied with Wes-
ley La Violette, De Paul Univ., B. A. 1931, M. M.
1935, Ph. D. 1949; also composition with Leo
Sowerby and Eric Delamarter; conducting with
Frederick Stock and Hans Lange. He was winner
an American Composers' commission, 1950; co-winner,
Midland Found. nat. contest, 1955. He served in
the U.S. Navy, 1944-45; was faculty member, instructor to professor, De Paul Univ., 1931-   ,
chairman of composition and theory and director,
graduate division, School of Music, 1948-66, dean,
School of Music, 1966-   .
      WORKS: (first performance dates are Chicago
unless otherwise noted) Opera: Deirdre, 1 act,
18 May 1957; The fisherman's wife, St. Joseph,
Mich., 10 Jan. 1955; Ballet: Exodus, 29 Jan.

(STEIN, LEON)
1939; Doubt, 21 Jan. 1940; Orchestra: Prelude
and fugue, 30 June 1936; Passacaglia, 1936, 1
Sep. 1942; Sinfonietta for string orch., 1938,
Grand Rapids, Mich., 9 Feb. 1941; violin concerto, 1939, 3 Dec. 1948; 3 symphonies, #1, 1940,
2 Dec. 1951, #2, 1942, New York, 18 Feb. 1951,
#3, 1950, 22 Nov. 1953; 3 Hassidic dances, 1941,
13 Apr. 1942; Triptych on 3 poems of Walt Whitman, 1943, 29 Mar. 1949; Great Lakes suite,
1944; Symphonic movement, 1950; A festive overture, 1950; The Lord reigneth, cantata, chorus
and orch., 1953, 20 Jan. 1956; Rhapsody for
flute, harp and string orch., 1954, 8 Nov. 1955;
Adagio and rondo ebraico, 1957; Then shall the
dust return, 1971; Chamber music: Suite for
string quartet, 1930; sonatine for 2 violins,
1931, 3 Oct. 1939; Adagio and dance, piano trio,
1931; violin sonata, 1932; 5 string quartets, #1,
12 Dec. 1933, #2, 29 Apr. 1963; #3, 1964, 22 May
1967, #4, 1965, 13 Nov. 1966, #5, 1967, 5 Apr.
1968; woodwind quintet, 31 Mar. 1937; trio for
trumpets, 20 Jan. 1953; quintet for saxophone
and string quartet, 10 Feb. 1958; sextet for saxophone and woodwind quintet, 23 Feb. 1959; trombone quartet, 1960; sonata for violin alone,
1960; quartet, 2 trumpets, 2 trombones, 1960;
trio for violin, saxophone, piano, 1961; suite
for saxophone quartet, 1965; 11 solo sonatas for
various instruments, 1968-70; suite for woodwind
quintet, 1970; also choral works and piano pieces.
He is author of The racial thinking of Richard
Wagner, New York, 1950, and Musical forms--The
study of structure and style in music, Evanston,
Ill., 1962, and of many articles in music journals.
      School of Music, De Paul University
      Chicago, IL 60604

STEINBROOK, DAVID HERMAN
      b. Philadelphia, Pa., 3 Oct. 1941. Studied with
George Rochberg and Henry Weinberg, Univ. of
Pennsylvania; with Roger Sessions, Milton Babbitt,
and Earl Kim, Princeton Univ. He received a
Woodrow Wilson fellowship. He was instructor,
Princeton Univ., 1966-69; instructor and assistant
professor, Swarthmore Coll., 1970-   .
      WORKS: Chamber music: Sonnet 73 of
Shakespeare, soprano and chamber ensemble, 1965,
revised 1958; 5 compositions for piano, 1972;
Sonnets to Orpheus, 1-9, by Rilke, soprano and
piano trio, 1973.
      317 North Chester Road, Swarthmore, PA 19081

STEINER, FREDERICK
      b. New York, N. Y., 24 Feb. 1923. Studied at
Institute of Musical Art, New York; on scholarship, with Normand Lockwood, Oberlin Cons., B. M.
1943. He has been free-lance composer and conductor in radio, television, and films, 1943-   ;
music director of radio and television programs.
      WORKS: Wind ensemble: Tower music, brass
and percussion; Chamber music: Pezzo Italiano,
cello and piano; 5 pieces for string trio; woodwind quintet; string quartet; songs for soprano
and string quartet; Film scores: The man from
Del rio, 1956; Run for the sun, 1956; Time limit;
Television scores: The shrimp, 1953; Country

(STEINER, FREDERICK)
doctor, 1954; Miss Pepperdine, 1955; Playhouse 90 films, 1956; Perry Mason series, 1957; Navy log, 1957; Secret mission, 1958; and others.
4455 Gable Drive, Encino, CA 91316

STEINER, GITTA
b. Prague, Czech., 17 Apr. 1932; U.S. citizen 1941. Studied with Elliott Carter and Vincent Persichetti, Juilliard School, B. M. 1967, M. S. 1969; with Gunther Schuller at Tanglewood. Her awards include the Abraham Ellstein scholarship at Juilliard; Gretchaninoff award, 1966; Marion Freschi award, 1966, 1967; Tanglewood fellowship, 1967; Composers' Forum concert, New York; ASCAP award, 1972; and commissions. She has been teaching privately 1960-   ; was instructor, Brooklyn Cons., 1968-71.
WORKS: Orchestra: Suite for orch., 1958; violin concerto, 1963; Tetrark, string orch., 1965; piano concerto, 1967; Chamber music: Suite for flute, clarinet, bassoon, 1958; brass quintet, 1964; Fantasy, clarinet and piano, 1964; Jouissance, flute and piano, 1965; Movement for 11, 1966; Refractions, violin solo, 1967; percussion quartet, 1968; string quartet, 1968; 3 pieces for solo vibraphone, 1968; 5 pieces for trombone; 4 bagatelles for vibraphone, 1969; trio for piano and 2 percussionists, 1969; duo for horn and piano, 1970; duo for cello and piano, 1971; Percussion music for 2, 1971; Chorus: 4 choruses of Emily Dickinson; 5 choruses, 1965; 5 poems, 1970; 4 settings, 1970; 4 choruses, 1972; Songs: 3 songs by James Joyce; 3 poems, 1960; Pages from a summer journal, 1963; 2 songs, 1966; Concert piece for 7, #1 and 2, soprano and chamber ensemble, 1968; Interludes, 1968; trio for voice, piano, percussion, 1971; Piano: 3 pieces, 1961; sonata, 1964; Fantasy piece, 1966. She is author of the texts of many of her songs and choral works.
71-81 244th St., Douglaston, NY 11362

STEINER, MAX (Maxilian Raoul Walter)
b. Vienna, Austria, 10 May 1888; U.S. citizen, 1920; d. Los Angeles, 28 Dec. 1971. Studied at Vienna School of Technology and the Imperial Acad. of Music; with Robert Fuchs, Hermann Grädener, and Gustav Mahler. At age 15 he won the Academy's gold medal for the astonishing feat of completing the 8-year course in one year. At 16 he wrote book, lyrics and music for a musical comedy, The beautiful Greek girl, which opened at the Orpheum Theatre in Vienna with the composer conducting and ran for a year. He was also proficient on the doublebass, violin, piano, organ, and trumpet. He spent 8 years in London as composer and conductor, 1906-14; came to New York and spent 15 years as orchestrator and conductor on Broadway, 1914-29; then went to Hollywood and started a 36-year career in film composing. He soon won his first Academy award for The informer, 1935, followed by awards for Now, voyager and Since you went away; 18 Academy nominations; 8 first place Laurel awards, 1949-60; Officier de l'Academie Francaise; Cinema Exhibition Congress medal--Brussels; World Cinema Congress medal, 1936; Italian medal, 1936; Golden

(STEINER, MAX)
Globe award, 1937; Cinema Exhibition award--Vienna, 1948; Wisdom Award of Honor, 1966; the Max Steiner Music Society was formed in 1965 and has become a worldwide organization.
WORKS: Film scores: Of his 300 film scores some of the most notable are The life of Emile Zola; Jezebel; Four daughters; Gold is where you find it; Dark victory; The old maid; We are not alone; The letter; Virginia City; All this and heaven too; Sergeant York; Casablanca; Arsenic and old lace; The corn is green; Mildred Pierce; The adventures of Mark Twain; Saratoga trunk; Life with father; The treasure of the Sierra Madre; The voice of the turtle; Key Largo; Johnny Belinda; Adventures of Don Juan; The fountainhead; The flame and the arrow; The glass menagerie; Battle cry; Helen of Troy; Marjorie Morningstar; John Paul Jones; A summer place; Cash McCall; Dark at the top of the stairs; and Gone with the wind, a score of 192 minutes of music in 222 minutes of film.

*STEINERT, ALEXANDER LANG
b. Boston, Mass., 21 Sep. 1900. Studied at Harvard Univ., A. B. 1922; with Charles Martin Loeffler in Boston; with Koechlin and d'Indy in Paris; and in Rome on the American Prix de Rome, 1927-30. He was opera conductor in New York and Los Angeles.
WORKS: Orchestra: Nuit meridionale, 1926; Leggenda sinfonica, 1930; piano concerto, 1935; Air Corps suite, 1942; Flight cycle, 1944; Rhapsody, clarinet and orch., 1945; The nightingale and the rose, speaker and orch., 1950; also chamber music and film scores.

STEINKE, GREG A.
b. Fremont, Mich., 2 Sep. 1942. Studied at Oberlin Cons., B. M. 1964; with Paul Harder and H. Owen Reed, Michigan State Univ., M. M. 1967, Ph. D. 1973; with Richard Hervig, Univ. of Iowa, M. F. A. 1971; with Ross Lee Finney, Dartmouth Congregation of the Arts; Donald Erb and Mario Davidovsky, Bennington Composers' Conference. His awards include Michigan Fed. of Music Clubs prize, 1966; BMI award, 1968; Univ. of Maryland grants, 1969, 1970; Nat. Gallery of Art performance, 1972; Bennington scholarship, 1972; several commissions, 1968-72. He was private teacher of oboe and oboist in various orchestras, 1963-65; instructor, Michigan State Univ., 1965-66, 1972-73; Univ. of Iowa, 1966-67; Univ. of Idaho, 1967-68; Univ. of Maryland, 1968-72; professor, California State Univ., Northridge, 1973-   .
WORKS: Theatre: Right on!, musical review, 1970; incidental music for many plays, 1967-   ; Orchestra: In memoriam, 1965; Music for bassoon and orchestra, 1967; Chamber music: woodwind trio, 1962; 23rd psalm, oboe and choir, optional harp and strings, 1962; sonata for oboe, oboe d'amore, English horn, 1963; Music for string quartet, 1964; A music for oboe, contrabass, percussion, 1967; The lay of the love and death of Cornet Christopher Rilke, reciter and chamber group, 1969; 7-4-3, dancers and chamber ensemble, 1969; Music for percussion ensemble and

STEINKE, GREG A.

(STEINKE, GREG A.)
conductor, 1972; A flight of virtuosity, 6 hand-clappers, 1972; Music for 3, oboe, guitar, percussion, 1972; Tricinium, alto saxophone, trumpet, piano, 1972; Aero-cordo-phonics, solo saxophone, 1973; 4 desultory episodes, oboe and tape, 1973; songs and piano pieces.
16663 Superior St., Sepulveda, CA 91343

*STENBERG, JORDAN
b. Fresno, Calif., 31 May 1947. Studied with Robert Moran at San Francisco Cons.; with Robert Ashley at Mills Coll. He is in the forefront of avant garde composers and has also experimented with composition to encourage plant growth.

STEPHENS, CHARLES COLE
b. Charleston, S. C., 6 Feb. 1938. Studied with H. Owen Reed, Paul Harder, and Roy Niblock, Michigan State Univ. He received first prize, Richmond Professional Inst. competition, 1967; performances at Willamet Chamber Music Festival and Premieres of New Music, Michigan State Univ. He was head of music, Holly, Mich. school systems, 1961-64; teaching assistant, Michigan State Univ., 1965-69; chairman, music department, St. Clair County Coll., 1969-74.
WORKS: Ballet: 12 tones, 3 movement ballet; Orchestra: States of mind; 900,000 days, symphony for choir, rock band, tape and orchestra; Chorus: Christmas mass, choir and jazz-rock band; Hatteras, choir and 2 harps; Psalm 96; Symphony for winds, tape and speaking chorus.
2009 Riverside Drive, Apt. H
Port Huron, MI 48060

STEPHENSON, MARK
b. Provo, Utah, 26 Oct. 1950. Studied briefly with Myron Fink and Matthew Colucci, Curtis Inst. of Music, but is largely self-taught. He was bassist with Concerto Soloists of Philadelphia, 1968-71.
WORKS: Chamber music: doublebass sonata, 1970; Concertpiece for bass and strings, 1971; Emily Dickinson songs, 1971; Nocturne for piano, 1971; Cavatina for strings, 1973.
4522 Spruce St., Philadelphia, PA 19139

STEPLETON, JAMES IRVIN
b. Muncie, Ind., 28 Apr. 1941. Studied with H. Owen Reed, Michigan State Univ.; and with Morris Knight, Ball State Univ. He won an award in the Mario Castelnuovo-Tedesco first internat. contest for a guitar composition; and first prize, chamber opera division, Nat. Contest for New Music for Worship, 1969. He is assistant professor and chairman of theory and composition, Augustana Coll., Sioux Falls, S. D.
WORKS: Opera: For those who will say yes, chamber opera; Chamber music: Intermezzo, violin and cello; Serenade, solo guitar; wind quintet; Proem and roundelay for saxophone quartet; Polarities, bass clarinet and piano.
Department of Music, Augustana College
Sioux Falls, SD 57102

STEPPER, MARTIN PAUL
b. Bronx, N. Y., 11 Jan. 1948. Studied with Earl George and Franklin Morris, Syracuse Univ., B. M., summa cum laude, 1970; with Myron Fink, Curtis Inst. of Music, M. M. 1973. He held full scholarships at Syracuse Univ. and at Curtis Inst.; received a Phi Kappa Lambda award, 1969. He was instructor, Paterson, N. J., public schools, 1970-71; area adult school, Morris County, N. J., 1970-71; private teacher, 1969-74.
WORKS: Orchestra: piano concerto, 1973; Chamber music: violin sonata, 1968; woodwind quintet, 1970; Serenade, chamber ensemble, 1971; Rhapsody for clarinet, 1972; piano sonata, 1972; string quartet, 1973.
19 Park Ave., Haskell, NJ 07420

STERN, ALFRED BERNARD
b. Boston, Mass., 6 Dec. 1910. Studied clarinet and theory with Paul Mimart in Boston; and at the Univ. of California, Berkeley. He received several ASCAP awards and a Children's Theatre Award for music, 1967. He was music director, WCOP-Radio, Boston, 1935-36; music director and board chairman, Actors Ensemble, Berkeley; music director, East Bay Children's Theatre, 1965-73; choral director, Berkeley school system; has had special music assignments, Univ. of California to compose revues and incidental music.
WORKS: Theatre: incidental music and songs for After the rain; Death of a salesman; Mother of us all; Skin of our teeth; and others; many children's musicals and songs.
1430 Grizzly Peak Blvd., Berkeley, CA 94708

STERN, MAX
b. Valley Stream, N. Y., 31 Mar. 1947. Studied with Samuel Adler and Bernard Rogers, Eastman School of Music, B. M. 1969; with Alexander Goehr, Yale Univ.; electronic music with Bulent Arel in New York. His awards include a MacDowell fellowship and a Ford Found. grant. He taught at 3rd Street Music School Settlement, 1971-72; doublebass, theory composition, privately; played doublebass, Rochester Philharmonic, 1968-69; New Haven Symphony and Bridgeport Symphony, 1969-70; Nat. Orch. Asso., and Radio City Music Hall, 1970-72.
WORKS: Opera: The philosophy lesson, after Moliere, 1968; Ballet: Galumph; Orchestra: Sonnet; Chamber music: Sonnet and dance, doublebass; piano sonata, 1967; string sextet, 1968; string quartet, 1972.
156 West 72nd St., New York, NY 10023

STERN, ROBERT
b. Paterson, N. J., 1 Feb. 1934. Studied with Louis Mennini, Kent Kennan, Wayne Barlow, Bernard Rogers, Howard Hanson, Eastman School of Music, Ph. D.: with Lukas Foss, Univ. of California, Los Angeles. His awards include the Edward B. Benjamin first prize, 1956; 3 MacDowell fellowships, 1967, 1969, 1972. He taught at Hochstein Memorial School and Eastman School, 1961-62; Hartford Cons., 1962-64; was visiting composer and director of electronic music, Hampshire Coll., 1970-71; is associate professor, Univ. of Massachusetts, Amherst.

(STERN, ROBERT)
WORKS: Ballet: Fort Union, 1960; Orchestra: In memoriam Abraham, string orch., 1956; Credo, 1957; symphony, 1961; Hazkarah, cello and orch.; Carom, orch. and tape, commissioned by Springfield, Mass., Symphony; string quartet; Fragments, flute, clarinet, harpsichord; Music for horn and soprano; Terezin, soprano, cello, piano; Adventures for one, percussion; Fantasy piece, piano; A little bit of music, for 2 clarinets; Night scene, violin, piano, and electronic sounds; also songs.
136 West St., Amherst, MA 01002

*STERNE, COLIN
b. 1921. Gentle Lady, My love is in a light attire, 2 songs to texts of James Joyce.

STERNKLAR, AVRAHAM
b. Trieste, Italy, 21 Oct. 1930; U.S. citizen 1956. Studied with Paul Ben Haim in Israel; with Vittorio Giannini, Juilliard School; also piano with James Friskin and Edward Steuerman at Juilliard. He was music correspondent for the Israel Broadcasting Station, 1949-53, while a student at Juilliard; on faculty, YMHA, Lexington Avenue, New York, for a year; has been active as performer, teacher, and composer.
WORKS: Chamber music: sonatas for piano, violin, clarinet, cello; piano sonatinas and suites, including A promise fulfilled based on paintings by the composer's mother; 2 piano works; choral music and songs.
P. O. Box 7, Plainview, NY 11803

STEUERMANN, EDWARD
b. Sambor, Poland, 18 June 1892; U.S. citizen 1944; d. New York, N. Y., 11 Nov. 1964. Studied piano with Vilem Kurz in Poland, 1904-10; with Ferruccio Busoni in Switzerland and Berlin, 1911-12; composition with Arnold Schoenberg in Berlin, 1912-14. His piano debut at age 11 was followed by extensive concert appearances and tours in Europe, America, and Israel; he is credited with the first performances of all Schoenberg's piano works, chamber music with piano, and his piano concerto (NBC Symphony, 1944). He received the Schoenberg Medal, highest honor of the Internat. Society for Contemporary Music, Salzburg, 1952, for "activities in promoting and deepening general understanding for contemporary musical works." Other awards include an honorary doctorate, Philadelphia Musical Acad., 1962; honorary membership, Royal Acad., Florence, Italy.
WORKS: Orchestra: Variations for orchestra, 1958; Music for instruments, 1960; Suite for chamber orchestra, 1964; Chamber music: 7 waltzes for string quartet, 1946; piano trio, 1954; Improvisation and allegro, violin and piano, 1955; Toccata and aria, flute and piano, 1955, unfinished; Diary, string quartet, no.2, 1961; Dialogues, violin solo, 1963; Piano: sonata, 1926, revised 1954; Evening song, 1938; Spring song, 1939; suite for piano, 1952; other piano pieces, choral works, and songs.

*STEVENS, BERNARD
2 improvisations on folk songs, brass quintet.

*STEVENS, GLENN
b. Chesaning, Mich., 26 July 1899. Studied at Chicago Musical Coll.; violin with Leopold Auer and Eugene Ysaye. He was violinist with Isham Jones' orchestra and others; conducted his own orchestra. He composed an opera, The Legend of Tucumcari, from which Indian lullaby for violin and piano has been published.

STEVENS, HALSEY
b. Scott, N. Y., 3 Dec. 1908. Studied with William Berwald, Syracuse Univ.; with Ernest Bloch, Univ. of California. His honors include publication awards from Middlebury Coll. Composers' Conference, 1946, Society for Publication of American Music, 1949, Nat. Asso. of Wind and Percussion Instructors, 1954; Guggenheim fellowships, 1964, 1971; Nat. Inst. of Arts and Letters citation and grant, 1961; honorary doctorate, Syracuse Univ., 1966; Nat. Fed. of Music Clubs awards, Friends of Harvey Gaul and Phi Mu Alpha-Sinfonia awards; many commissions.
He was associate professor, Dakota Wesleyan Univ. 1937-41; professor and director, Coll. of Music, Bradley Univ., 1941-46; faculty member, Univ. of Southern California, 1946-   , chairman, composition department, 1948-   , professor, 1951-   , composer-in-residence, 1972; visiting professor at many colleges and universities; program annotator, Los Angeles Philharmonic, 1946-51; Phoenix Symphony, 1947-48; Coleman Chamber Concerts, 1967-   .
WORKS: Theatre: music for Sheridan's The Rivals, 1961; Orchestra: 2 symphonies, 1945; A Green Mountain overture, 1948; Triskelion, 1953; Adagio and allegro, for strings, 1955; The ballad of William Sycamore, chorus and orch., 1955; Sinfonia breve, 1957; 5 pieces, 1958; Symphonic dances, 1958; A testament of life, chorus and orch., 1959; Magnificat, chorus and orch., 1962; cello concerto, 1964; Threnos: In memoriam Quincy Porter, 1968; concerto for clarinet and strings, 1969; double concerto for violin, cello, strings, Los Angeles, 4 Nov. 1973; Band: 11 Ukrainian folksongs, 1957; Chamber music: flute sonatina, 1943; violin sonatina, 1944; 2 piano trios, 1945, 1954; Suite for clarinet and piano, 1946; quintet, flute, string trio, piano, 1946; violin sonata, 1947; Intermezzo, cadenza, and finale, cello and piano, 1949; string quartet no.3, 1949; bassoon sonata, 1949; viola sonata, 1950; horn sonata, 1953; Sonatina giocosa, doublebass and piano, 1954; Suite for solo violin, 1954; trumpet sonata, 1956; septet for woodwinds and strings, 1957; cello sonatina, 1957; sonata for solo cello, 1958; trio for winds and/or strings, 1959; suite for viola and piano, 1959; violin sonatina no.3, 1959; bass tuba sonatina, 1960; cello sonata, 1965; trombone sonata, 1965; Divertimento for 2 violins, 1966; Melodic studies for clarinet, 1966; 12 studies for solo bassoon, 1968; oboe sonata, 1971; 12 studies for solo oboe, 1972; Dittico, alto saxophone and piano, 1972; Quintetto Serbelloni, for woodwinds, 1972; many choral works and songs.
9631 2nd Ave., Inglewood, CA 90305

STEWART, DAVID N.

*STEWART, DAVID N.
Guitar sonata; quintet.

STEWART, DONALD G.
b. Sterling, Ill., 8 Jan. 1935. Studied with
Bernhard Heiden and Roy Harris, Indiana Univ.,
B. M. 1960; with Gunther Schuller, Manhattan
School of Music. He has played clarinet with
many jazz orchestras with the Florida Symphony,
Birmingham Symphony, Vermont Symphony; is founder-
member, Boehm Quintette; librarian, Brooklyn
Philharmonic.
WORKS: Orchestra: Opener, 1964; The 200-
bar passacaglia, 1972; piccolo concerto, 1973;
Chamber music: string quartet, 1962; Life-
slices, flute and piano, 1967; brass quintet,
1968; duets for flute and clarinet, 1969; Concert duet for flute and bass clarinet, 1971; The
tattooed desert, low male voice and chamber
ensemble, 1973.
Box 65, Tunbridge, VT 05077

STEWART, FRANK GRAHAM
b. La Junta, Colo., 12 Dec. 1920. Studied with
Bernard Rogers, Eastman School of Music, B. M.
1942; with Roger Sessions, Colorado Coll.,
M. A. T. 1968; with H. Owen Reed, Michigan State
Univ., Ph. D. 1971. He received a scholarship
for summer study with Roger Sessions, 1939;
Ditson fellowship, 1946-47; and a research grant
for study of the music of the Choctaw Indians,
1972. He taught at Colorado State Univ.,
1967-68; Univ. of Missouri at Columbia, 1968-69;
was graduate assistant, Michigan State Univ.,
1969-71; assistant professor, Mississippi State
Univ., 1971-   .
WORKS: Opera: To let the captive go, chamber opera, 1971, New York, 5 Mar. 1974; Orchestra: accordion concerto, 1952; Band: Scene,
1970; Chamber music: Phantom train of Marshall
Pass, narrator, winds, percussion, 1970; Characteristics, brass quintet, 1973; Chorus: English
as she is taught, chorus and percussion, 1969.
Box 5261, Mississippi State University
Starkville, MS 39762

STEWART, HASCAL VAUGHAN
b. Darlington, S. C., 17 Feb. 1898. Studied at
Winthrop Coll., A. B. and postgraduate work;
Teachers Coll., New York; composition privately
with Gustave Weigl. She was on the music faculty,
Winthrop Coll., 1921-22.
WORKS: Songs: Sleep to wake; As a promise;
Threshold of Christmas; Overtones; Mary in Chris-
tendom; many songs and piano pieces.
P. O. Box 197, Carmel, CA 93921

*STEWART, KENSEY D.
The tide rises, the tide falls, chorus; Alleluia,
chorus.

*STEWART, RICHARD
Prelude for organ and tape, 1972.

STEWART, ROBERT
b. Buffalo, N. Y., 6 Mar. 1918. Studied at
American Cons., M. M. E. 1947, M. M. in violin,
1950, M. M. in composition 1950. He received a

(STEWART, ROBERT)
MacDowell fellowship, 1956; 2 awards, Georgia
State Coll. Symposium for Contemporary Music for
Brass, 1966, 1972; several commissions. He
taught in Chicago area schools, 1938-41; composed
music for radio shows On target and Meet your
Navy while in naval service, 1941-45; taught
theory and violin, American Cons., 1945-53;
professor, Washington and Lee Univ., 1954-   .
WORKS: Orchestra: Requiem for a soldier;
Prelude for strings; Wind ensemble: Divertissement, brass choir; Music for brass no.4; Hydra
III, brass and percussion; 2 brass quintets;
duos for brass choirs; Hydra IV, brass quintet
band; Chamber music: concerto for horn and chamber orch.; Fantasia, viola and chamber orch.;
Hydra, winds, strings, piano; Mystic, for contrabass; 3 pieces for woodwind quintet; 3 string
quartets; 2 ricercari, woodwind quintet and
strings; Heart attack, tuba and percussion; 3
trios for various ensembles; duo for violin and
piano.
Department of Music and Drama
Washington and Lee University
Lexington, VA 24450

STEWART, ROBERT J.
b. Albany, N. Y., 22 Apr. 1932. Studied with
Thomas Canning, Eastman School of Music; with
Henri Lazarof and Roy Harris, Univ. of California,
Los Angeles; and with Richard Hervig, Univ. of
Iowa, Ph. D. He is associate professor, California State Univ. at Fullerton.
WORKS: Chamber music: string quartet; violin trio; Canto I and II, clarinet and piano;
Rondeau for 2 pianos; Tears, contralto, horn,
clarinet, strings; Virelai, flute, viola, bass,
harpsichord; also works for orchestra, band,
brass ensembles, mixed ensembles, chorus, solo
voice, piano.
5641 Mountain View, Yorba Linda, CA 92686

*STIDFOLE, ARTHUR
Solitaire, solo flute.

STILL, WILLIAM GRANT
b. Woodville, Miss., 11 May 1895. Studied at
Oberlin Cons.; with George W. Chadwick, New England Cons.; and with Edgard Varese in New York.
He learned to orchestrate by playing many instruments, among them violin, cello and oboe, in
professional orchestras, and by orchestrating
for W. C. Handy, Don Voorhees, Sophie Tucker,
Willard Robison, Paul Whiteman and Artie Shaw.
For several years he was arranger and conductor
for the Deep South Hour on CBS and WOR. His
many honors include Guggenheim and Rosenwald
fellowships; 2nd Harmon award, 1927; honorary
M. M., Wilberforce Coll., 1936; honorary doctor-
ates, Howard Univ., 1941, Oberlin Coll., 1947;
Bates Coll., 1954; Univ. of Arkansas, 1971,
Pepperdine Univ. 1973, New England Cons., 1973,
Peabody Cons., 1974; Cincinnati Symphony Orches-
tra award, 1944; citation from Nat. Asso. for
American Composers and Conductors, 1949; Phi
Beta Sigma award, 1953; Freedoms Found. award,
1953; prize offered by U.S. Committee for the
U. N., Nat. Fed. of Music Clubs and Aeolian

(STILL, WILLIAM GRANT)

Music Found. for his orchestral work, The peaceful land, 1961; citations from Los Angeles City Council and County Board of Supervisors, 1963; and many important commissions. He was the first black man to conduct a major symphony orchestra in the U.S., Los Angeles, 1936, and in the Deep South, New Orleans, 1955.

WORKS: Opera: Blue steel, 1935; Troubled island, 1938, New York, 1949; A bayou legend, 1940, Jackson, Miss., 15 Nov. 1974; Costaso, 1949; Mota; The pillar; Minette Fontaine; Highway I, U.S.A., 1-act, Miami, 13 May 1963; Ballet: La guiablesse, 1927; Sahdji, 1930; Lenox Avenue, 1937; Miss Sally's party, 1940; Orchestra: Darker America, 1924; From the Black Belt, 1926; Africa, a suite, 1930; Afro-American symphony, 1931, revised 1969; Dismal swamp, 1935; Kaintuck', with piano solo, c. 1935; symphony in g, 1937; And they lynched him on a tree, with narrator, contralto, and 2 choruses, c. 1939; Plain-chant for America, with baritone soloist or chorus, c. 1940; Old California, 1941; Pages from Negro history, a suite, 1943; Poem, 1944; Festive overture, 1944; symphony #3, 1945; Archaic ritual, 1946; Wood notes, 1947; symphony #4, 1949; symphony #5; A deserted plantation, suite; Danzas de Panama, for strings, New York premiere, 9 Jan. 1971; The American scene, a set of 5 suites; Little red schoolhouse, suite; Patterns; The peaceful lands, c. 1961; Preludes; From a lost continent, with chorus; Psalm for the living, with chorus; Ennanga, with solo harp; Christmas in the Western World, strings and chorus; Band: From the delta, 1945; To you, America!, 1952; Chamber music: Suite for violin and piano; Pastorela, violin and piano, 1946; 5 Little folk suites from the Western Hemisphere, string quartet; Chorus: Caribbean melodies, with solo voices, piano, and percussion, 1941; Songs of separation, a suite; The voice of the Lord, Psalm 29; 3 rhythmic spirituals; From the hearts of women, 4 songs.

1262 Victoria Ave., Los Angeles, CA 90019

STILLER, ANDREW PHILIP

b. Washington, D.C., 6 Dec. 1946. Studied with Robert Crane, Univ. of Wisconsin, B. A. in zoology 1968; with Morton Subotnick, Univ. of Maryland, 1969; with Allen Sapp, Lejaren Hiller, Morton Feldman, State Univ. of New York at Buffalo, M. A. 1971, Ph. D. 1974. He was graduate assistant, Center for the Creative and Performing Arts, SUNY at Buffalo, 1971-73.

WORKS: Chamber music: quintet for bass instruments, 1966; 13 ways of looking at a blackbird, speaker, bass clarinet, small orch., 1967; Ctenophores, chamber ensemble, tapes, 1967; Cathouse sonata, piano, 1967; Electronic construction, 1968; Magnification, 1-65 instruments, 1968; Peel me another grape, Pocahontong, 20 random instruments, 1968; The Frammisstani Embassy in Ulan Bator, string quintet, 1969; Pithekoprakta, 6 trombones, 1969; The planets, various ensembles, 1969; Cadres and communes, solo woodwind or voice, 1970; Stiller's folly, 53 woodwinds, 1971; Dance of death, bone instruments and dancer, 1971; Fibrillation, woodwind

(STILLER, ANDREW PHILIP)

quintet, 1972; Keep me hi and I'll ball you forever, 17 brass, 1972; Musica Ungetutscht, solo instrument and continuo, 1972; Pierrot Solaire, low voice and keyboard, 1972; The Kennedy Center cannot hold, 8 winds, celeste, and basso, with N. Osterreich, 1973.

419 Crescent Ave., Buffalo, NY 14214

*STILLMAN, MITYA

b. Ilyintza, Russia, 27 Jan. 1892; to U.S. c 1918; d. New York, N. Y., 12 Apr. 1936. Studied with Gliere at the Kiev Cons. He was posthumously awarded a first prize for his 7th string quartet. He was violist in the Detroit Symphony; then in the Hartmann String Quartet; from 1928 was first violist with the CBS Symphony.

WORKS: Orchestra: Dnieprostroy, symphonic poem; Cyprus, for strings, woodwinds, percussion; Yalta suite; Chamber music: 8 string quartets; string trio; 4 songs for mezzo soprano, flute, harp, string quartet.

STOCK, DAVID FREDERICK

b. Pittsburgh, Pa., 3 June 1939. Studied with Nikolai Lopatnikoff, Carnegie Inst. of Technology, B. F. A. 1962, M. F. A. 1963; with Arthur Berger and Alexei Haieff, Brandeis Univ.; and with Aimee Vaurebourg-Honegger, Ecole Normale de Musique, Paris. He received fellowships for Tanglewood, 1964, Bennington Composers Conference, 1966-67, and the NDEA fellowship for Brandeis Univ., 1966-68; Samuel Wechsler award, 1967; Guggenheim fellowship, 1974. He was faculty member, Cleveland Inst. of Music, 1964-65; graduate assistant, Brandeis Univ., 1966-68; faculty, New England Cons., 1968-70; faculty, Antioch Coll., 1970-   , chairman, music department, 1971-   .

WORKS: Theatre: music for Ghost sonata; Othello; House of Bernada Alba, Scotch'n'soda, musical comedies; Orchestra: Divertimento, 1957; Capriccio for small orch., 1963; symphony in 1 movement, 1963; Chamber music: quintet for clarinet and strings, 1966; FLASHBACK, chamber ensemble, 1968; 3 pieces for violin and piano; Triple play; Serenade for 5 instruments; NORO, game piece; SCAT, soprano and 4 instruments, 1970; string quartet; Film score: Evolution of a shadow.

137 West Davis St., Yellow Springs, OH 45387

*STOCK, FREDERICK

b. Jülich, Germany, 11 Nov. 1872; U.S. citizen 1919; d. Chicago, Ill., 20 Oct. 1942. Studied with his father, a band master, and at the Cologne Cons. His many awards included election to the Nat. Inst. of Arts and Letters, 1910; honorary doctorates from Northwestern Univ., 1915, Univ. of Michigan, 1924, Univ. of Chicago, 1925; Chevalier, Legion d'Honneur, 1925; Bruckner Society of America medal, 1939. He was violinist in the Cologne Municipal Orchestra, 1891-95; first violist, Chicago Symphony Orchestra, 1895-01, assistant conductor, 1901-05, conductor, 1905-42. He composed a symphony, a violin concerto, overtures, chamber music, and songs. His violin concerto was performed by Efrem Zimbalist

STOCK, FREDERICK

(STOCK, FREDERICK)
with the composer conducting the Chicago Symphony, 3 June 1915.

*STOCKHOFF, WALTER WILLIAM
b. St. Louis, Mo., 12 Nov. 1887; d. St. Louis, 1 Apr. 1968. Was largely self-taught in composition.
WORKS: American symphonic suite (an orchestration of his piano suite, To the mountains); 5 dramatic poems for orch., 1943; Piano: a sonata; Metamorphoses.

STOEPPELMANN, JANET
b. St. Louis, Mo., 5 Dec. 1948. Studied at Univ. of South Florida, M. M. 1973; with Jocy de Oliveira in Tampa.
WORKS: Chamber music: Sindhura, solo harp, 1973; Chorus: Seashore of endless worlds, female voices, 1971; Tollite jugum meum, motet, 1971; 3 Japanese haiku concerning butterflies, female chorus, 1972; Trisagion, 1972; Parallax, 1973; Multimedia: Metallon, 4-channel tape, miked tam tams, percussion and sculpture, 1972; The Great Wall of China, after Kafka, 4-channel tape and narrator, 1973.
920 N.W. 186th Drive, Miami, FL 33169

*STOESSEL, ALBERT
b. St. Louis, Mo., 11 Oct. 1894; d. New York, N. Y., 12 May 1943. Studied with Willy Hess and August Kretzschmar at Berlin Hochschule; made his American debut as violinist with the St. Louis Symphony in 1915. He was director of the New York Oratorio Society, 1921-43; chairman, music department, New York Univ., 1923-30; director, opera department, Juilliard School, 1930-43; from 1925 conducted the Worcester, Mass., music festivals.
WORKS: Opera: Garrick, produced at Juilliard School, 1937; Orchestra: Hispania suite, 1921; Cyrano de Bergerac, symphonic poem, 1922; Concerto grosso for strings and piano, 1935; Chamber music: Suite antique, 2 violins and piano, 1922; violin sonata; violin pieces; also choral works, songs, and piano pieces.

*STÖHR, RICHARD
b. Vienna, Austria, 11 June 1874; to U.S. 1938; d. Montpelier, Vt., 11 Dec. 1967. After receiving a doctorate in medicine in 1898, he began the study of music at the Vienna Cons., then taught there. He taught at Curtis Inst. of Music, 1939-41; and at St. Michael's Coll., Winooski, Vt., 1941-50.
WORKS: Orchestra: 4 symphonies; Vermont suite, premiered by the Vermont State Symphony Orchestra in 1954; also many chamber works, songs, piano pieces.

STOKES, ERIC
b. Haddon Heights, N. J., 14 July 1930. Studied with James Ming, Lawrence Coll.; with Carl McKinley, New England Cons.; and with Paul Fetler, Univ. of Minnesota. His awards include Montalvo Found. fellowships, 1957, 1958; Shevlin fellowship, Univ. of Minnesota, 1959-60; MacDowell fellowship, 1962; McMillin Fund grant, 1969;

(STOKES, ERIC)
Ford Found. grant, 1969-70; Martha Baird Rockefeller grant, 1969-70. He has been faculty member, Univ. of Minnesota, 1969-   .
WORKS: Opera: Horspfal, Minneapolis, 15 Feb. 1969; Orchestra: A Center Harbor holiday, 1963; 3 sides of a town, Minneapolis, 27 Oct. 1964; Gnomic commentaries, Minneapolis, 17 June 1965; Sonatas, Naarden, Holland, 11 July 1970; On the Badlands - parables, St. Paul, 3 June 1972; The continental harp and band report, Minneapolis, 5 Mar. 1975; Chamber music: Smoke and steel, tenor and chamber orch., Boston, 14 May 1958; Expositions on themes of Henry David Thoreau, chamber ensemble, 1970; Eldey Island, flute and tape, 1971; Of the mountains, of the past, the shifting lights call to remembrance the music, 1972; 5 verbs of Earth encircled, chamber orch., 1973; Lampyridae, a summer nocturne, Minneapolis, 9 Aug. 1973; also choral works and music for plays.
1611 West 32nd St., Minneapolis, MN 55408

*STOKOWSKI, LEOPOLD
b. London, England, 18 Apr. 1882; U.S. citizen 1915. Studied at Queen's Coll., Oxford; and at the Royal Coll. of Music, London; also in Paris and Munich. His many honors include the Bok award of $10,000 for public service to Philadelphia; fellow, Royal Acad. of Music, London; Chevalier, Legion of Honor, France; Order Polonia Restituta, Poland; several honorary doctorates. He was organist at St. James Church, Piccadilly, in 1900; organist and choir director, St. Bartholomew's Church, New York, 1905-08. In 1909-12 he was conductor of the Cincinnati Symphony Orchestra; then led the Philadelphia to 1938, bringing it to a peak of performance and giving American premieres of many contemporary works. He organized the All-American Youth Orchestra and with it toured the U.S., South America, and Canada, 1940-42; then led a succession of orchestras ending with the Houston Symphony, 1955-60; was co-founder and director of the American Symphony, 1962-   . He appeared in the films: The big broadcast of 1939, 100 men and a girl, and Disney's Fantasia, for which he also supervised the music.
WORKS: Orchestra: a symphony; Spring, chorus and orch.; 2 violin concertos; 3 piano concertos; also choral works; organ pieces; and many transcriptions for orchestra, especially of works by Bach.

STOLTZE, ROBERT H.
b. Spokane, Wash., 21 Jan. 1910. Studied with Rudolph Ganz, Louis Gruenberg, Max Wald, Karel Jirak, and John Becker in Chicago. He received a Ganz scholarship; awards from Friends of New Music and Danforth Found.; composer of the year award and a grant, Oregon Music Teachers Asso., 1971. He was professor, Lewis and Clark Coll., 1946-73.
WORKS: Orchestra: Symphonic variations, chamber orch., 1960; Band: Melodic symphony, 1970; Chamber music: flute sonata, 1961; 2 butterflies and a lion, flute, viola, guitar, 1961; suite for 2 pianos, 1965; violin sonata,

(STOLTZE, ROBERT H.)
1966; cello sonata, 1969; piano sonata, 1971; White butterflies, flute, guitar, chamber orch., 1973.
9938 S.W. Terwilliger Blvd.
Portland, OR 91219

*STONE, DWIGHT DONALD
Interlude on Veni Emmanuael, organ; Introduction, air, and dance, 4 recorders.

STONE, MALCOLM A.
b. Hollywood, Calif., 5 Aug. 1934. Studied with S. R. Beckler, Mary Bowling, and Lucas Underwood, Univ. of the Pacific; and at California State Univ. at Sacramento. He was named composer of the year at Univ. of the Pacific, 1962. He was high school music education director, 1963-69; director of theatre arts, Lodi High School, 1969-72; music director, Columbia Theatre, Univ. of the Pacific, 1964.
WORKS: Chamber music: Little sonnet, oboe and piano; Chorus: Psalm 23; Psalm 120; Night plane; Kyrie Eleison; 3 little surprises; Invocation; Songs: Lament of the forgotten; many unpublished works.
5954 Echo, Stockton, CA 95207

STONE, WILLIAM C.
b. Harrisburg, Pa., 10 Jan. 1921. Studied with Burrill Phillips, Allen McHose, and Wayne Barlow at Eastman School of Music, M. M. He was music director, Reinhardt Coll., Ga., 1951-55; assistant professor, Pfeiffer Coll., 1955-61; associate professor, Campbell Coll., 1961-   .
WORKS: Chamber music: string quartet in 1 movement; Songs: Prayer, to composer's own text; Teach me, Lord; Piano: Fantasy; Nocturne; Misty night; sonatina, 1 movement; Theme and variations; Passacaglia.
Box 395, Buies Creek, NC 27506

*STOUFFER, PAUL M.
b. Chambersburg, Pa., 21 Feb. 1916. Studied at Peabody Cons.; Univ. of Pennsylvania, B. A., M. A.; taught in public and private schools in Philadelphia; has been director of music education, Springfield, Pa., schools, 1958-   .
WORKS: Orchestra: concertino for 2; Canzone; Christmas dance pantomime; Band: Song of the troubadour; Ti-teeka-tah; Chamber music: clarinet quartet; Toccata for trumpets; Toccata for clarinets; 2 violin sonatas; also choral works.

STOUT, ALAN
b. Baltimore, Md., 26 Nov. 1932. Studied at Johns Hopkins Univ.; with Henry Cowell, Peabody Cons.; at Univ. of Copenhagen; with John Verrall, Univ. of Washington; privately with Wallingford Riegger and Vagn Holmboe. His awards include an Illinois Sesquicentennial commission for symphony no.2, 1968; Chicago Symphony Orchestra 80th anniversary commission for symphony no.4, 1971; Methodist Church, Board of Education grant; Danish Government grant, 1954-55; and other commissions. He has been on the faculty, School of Music, Northwestern Univ., 1963-   ; guest

(STOUT, ALAN)
professor, Johns Hopkins Univ., 1968, Musikhögskolan, Stockholm, 1972.
WORKS: Orchestra: 4 symphonies; Movements for violin and orch.; George Lieder, baritone and orch.; 3 hymns for orch., Baltimore, 27 Sep. 1972; Wind ensemble: Die Engel for soprano, brass and percussion; Pulsar for brass and timpani; Pieti for brass; Chamber music: 10 string quartets; cello sonata, 1966; Music for oboe and piano; Music for flute and harpsichord; Suite for flute and percussion; Toccata for alto saxophone and percussion; Keyboard: Study in densities and durations for organ; Organ chorales; Toccata and lament for harpsichord.
2600 1/2 Central St., Evanston, IL 60201

STOVER, FRANKLIN HOWARD
b. Sacramento, Calif., 5 Nov. 1953. Studied at California State Univ., Sacramento. He was winner of the 1973 California Composers Symposium, Sacramento, for Prelude to a symphony, 1969.
WORKS: Chamber music: Canto, flute alone, 1968; Essays and etudes, clarinet alone, 1969; Metal, percussion ensemble, 1970; Estrattos, 2 pianos and live electronic sounds, 1973; 4 arcanums, woodwind quintet and guitar, 1974.
5417 Earnell St., Carmichael, CA 95608

STOVER, HAROLD
b. Latrobe, Pa., 26 Nov. 1946. Graduated in organ at Juilliard School. He has been organist-choirmaster, Second Presbyterian Church, New York, N. Y., 1968-
WORKS: Keyboard: Piano variations, 1968; Te decet hymnus deus in Sion, organ, 1970; Incantation, piano, percussion, and speaking voice, 1971; 3 nocturnes, organ, 1972; Music in praise at the close of day, organ and treble voices, 1973.
235 West 102nd St., New York, NY 10025

STRAIGHT, WILLARD
b. Ft. Wayne, Ind., 18 July 1930. Studied with Everett Anderson, Univ. of Kansas, 1947-51, B. M.; with Vittorio Rieti and Rudolph Ganz, Chicago Musical Coll., 1951-55; piano with various teachers, including Ganz and Mieczslaw Horszowski in New York. He is assistant conductor, Littel Orchestra Society of New York; concert pianist, and accompanist.
WORKS: Theatre: Toyon of Alaska, opera; The Athenian touch, musical; Orchestra: Development for orchestra; piano concerto; Structure for orchestra; Chamber music: piano quintet, woodwind quintet; Piece en forme, cello and piano; 3 developments, flute, violin, cello; choral works, songs, piano pieces.
127 West 79th St., New York, NY 10024

STRANDBERG, NEWTON
b. River Falls, Wis., 3 Jan. 1921. Studied with Anthony Donato, Northwestern Univ.; with Henry Cowell, Columbia Univ.; and with Nadia Boulanger, American Art School, Fontainbleau, France. He received the Faricy award; Birmingham Symphony award; Birmingham Festival of Arts award; first prize, Oregon Coll. of Education national contest.

STRANDBERG, NEWTON

(STRANDBERG, NEWTON)
He was faculty member, Denison Univ., 1947-49;
Samford Univ., 1950-67; Sam Houston State Univ.,
1967-   .
WORKS: Orchestra: Amenhoten III, Trinite;
Sea of Tranquility; Band: Xerxes; Kinetic thea-
ter; Magnificat; Processional; Picasso; Ping-
pong; Chamber music: sonata for 2 pianos; Can-
tata profana; 3 string quartets; Chorus:
Augustine, with winds; Benecitus, 2 choirs, drum,
chimes, piano; Canticle, with orch.; Keyboard:
Planh, piano; Sanna sanna heySanna hosanna!,
organ.
Sam Houston State University
Huntsville, TX 77340

STRANG, GERALD
b. Claresholm, Alberta, Canada, 13 Feb. 1908;
U.S. citizen. Studied at Stanford Univ., A. B.
1928; with Charles Koechlin, Arnold Schoenberg,
and Ernst Toch, Univ. of Southern California,
Ph. D. 1948. He was teaching assistant to
Schoenberg, 1936-38; taught at Long Beach City
Coll., 1938-58; was professor, San Fernando Valley State Coll., 1958-65; professor, California
State Coll. at Long Beach, 1965-69, chairman,
music department, 1965-68; lecturer in electronic
music, Univ. of California, Los Angeles,
1969-   . He worked in the engineering department, Douglas Aircraft Company, 1942-45; has
been consultant in building design and acoustics,
1950-   ; worked in electronic and computer
music, Bell Telephone Laboratories, N. J., 1963,
1969.
WORKS: Orchestra: Intermezzo, 1937; 2 symphonies, 1942, 1947; concerto grosso, 1951; cello
concerto, 1951; Chamber music: Mirrorrorrim,
piano, 1931; sonatina for clarinet alone, 1932;
Percussion music for 3 players, 1935; 3 pieces
for flute and piano, 1937; Divertimento for 4
instruments, 1948; violin sonata, 1949; sonata
for flute alone, 1953; Variations for 4 instruments, 1956; Electronic: Compusitions 2-10,
tape computer music, 1963-72; Synthion 1 and 2,
tape synthesis. He is author of articles on
acoustics and on computer music.
6500 Mantova St., Long Beach, CA 90815

STRANGE, ALLEN
b. Calexico, Calif., 26 June 1943. Studied with
Donal Michalsky, California State Univ. at
Fullerton; with Pauline Oliveros, Robert Erickson,
Kenneth Gaburo, Univ. of California, San Diego.
He received a Fullerton Friends of Music award,
1965; Univ. of California Regents fellowship,
1967-68; San Jose Found. grant in electronic
music, 1970. He was instructor, Indiana Univ.
of Pennsylvania, 1969; assistant professor, California State Univ., San Jose, 1969-   ; co-
founder of Biome, a new music ensemble special-
izing in electronic music.
WORKS: Orchestra: Western connection;
Charms, string orch.; Band: Rockytop screamers
and further scapes; Star salon strikers and
sliders last orbit, amplified string trio and
percussion; Dirt talk, version 2, organ, violin,
percussion; Switchcraft, bass, flute, and engineer; the doug Meyers (') playing flute, solo

(STRANGE, ALLEN)
flute; Chamberpiece, flute, clarinet, violin,
guitar; Chorus: Rainbow rider, 4 choruses;
Electronic: 2 by 2, tape; Propagation and decay
of resonant particles, live electronics; Skags,
4 electronically processed voices; Domino, tape;
Dirt talk, version 1, tape; Multimedia: Mora
speculum, 4 actors and tape; And still another
story concerns, tape and projectors; Palace,
violin, tape, projectors; No dead horses on the
moon, tape and projectors; Vanity Faire, narrator, 3 music boxes, tape. He is author of
Electronic music: Systems, techniques and con-
trols, Dubuque, Iowa, 1972, and of various articles in music journals.
California State University
San Jose, CA 95114

STRASSBURG, ROBERT
b. New York, N. Y., 30 Aug. 1915. Studied with
Carl McKinley and Frederick Converse, New Eng-
land Cons., B. M. 1939; with Paul Hindemith at
Tanglewood, 1940; Walter Piston and Igor
Stravinsky, Harvard Univ., M. A. 1941; with
Mario Castelnuovo-Tedesco, Univ. of Judaism, Los
Angeles, D. F. A. 1970. He received a Boston
Symphony scholarship to Tanglewood, 1940; Har-
vard fellowship, 1940-41; Nat. Inst. of Arts
and Letters award; MacDowell fellowship, 1946.
His faculty posts include Brooklyn Coll.,
1947-50; Univ. of Miami, Hillel House, 1958-60;
Univ. of Judaism, 1961-   , assistant dean,
1961-63; assistant to associate professor,
California State Univ., Los Angeles, 1966-   .
WORKS: Opera: Chelm, comic folk opera,
1956; Orchestra: The patriarchs, string orch.,
1946; Sinfonietta in G; Festival of lights
symphony; Tropal suite, string orch., 1967;
Chorus: Psalm 117; Whitman cantata, Look back
unto this day; many liturgical works; Piano:
Torah sonata, 1950; Variations, Hunting the
deer; many chamber works, songs, incidental
music for plays, etc.
3335 Rowena Ave., Los Angeles, CA 90027

STRAUSS, GEORGE R.
b. Cleveland Heights, Ohio, 19 Nov. 1951. Studied with Paul Cooper and Ellsworth Milburn, Cincinnati Coll.-Cons.
WORKS: Orchestra: 2 symphonies, 1973, 1974;
Chamber music: Theme with variations, flute,
violin, cello, 1970; Travesty, winds, brass,
harp, timpani, 1972; To the victims of Scioto
Street, string quartet, piano, percussion, film,
1972; K. 299 revisited, flute and harp, 1973;
Songs: Die Kindheit, soprano and piano, 1971;
Program notes, soprano and bass-baritone, a
cappella, 1973; Piano: Perspectives, prepared
piano, 1972.
Box 8211, Aspen, CO 81611

*STRAVINSKY, IGOR
b. Oranienbaum, Russia; U.S. citizen 1945; d.
New York, N. Y., 6 Apr. 1971. Studied law at
Univ. of St. Petersburg; then studied music
privately with Rimsky-Korsakov. He was a member of the American Acad. of Arts and Letters;
received the Internat. Sibelius award, 1963.

(STRAVINSKY, IGOR)
He also received many commissions from Sergei Diaghilev, ballet impresario, and wrote some of his most noted works to be presented by Diaghilev at the Ballets Russes in Paris. Stravinsky settled in the U.S. after the fall of France in 1939.
WORKS: Opera: Le rossignol, 1914; Mavra, 1-act, 1922; Renard, 1-act, 1922; Oedipus Rex, opera-oratorio, 1927; The rake's progress, 1951; Ballet: The firebird, 1910; Petrouchka, 1911; The rite of spring, 1913; The soldier's tale, 1918; Pulcinella, 1919; Les noces, 1923; Apollon musagete, 1927; Le baiser de la fée, 1928; Persephone, 1934; Jeu de cartes, 1936; Orpheus, 1948; Agon, 1957; Orchestra: Symphony of psalms, chorus and orch., 1930; violin concerto, 1931; Dumbarton Oaks concerto, 1938; Circus polka, 1942; 3 symphonies, 1907, 1940, 1945; other orchestral works; many chamber works; choral pieces; songs; piano pieces.

*STRAYHORN, WILLIAM (BILLY)
b. Dayton, Ohio, 29 Nov. 1915; d. New York, N. Y., 30 May 1967. Studied music in Pittsburgh; from 1939 was lyricist, arranger, composer and collaborator with Duke Ellington. Some of his own songs were Tapioca; Lush life; Take the A train; Passion flower; Overture to a jam session.

STREET, TISON
b. Boston, Mass., 20 May 1943. Studied with Leon Kirchner and David Del Tredici, Harvard Univ. He received a Naumberg recording award, 1972; Nat. Inst. of Arts and Letters award, 1973; Rome Prize, 1973. He has been a visiting lecturer, Univ. of California, Berkeley.
WORKS: Chamber music: string trio; Variations, flute, guitar, cello; string quartet, 1972; string quintet, 1973; Chorus: 3 sacred anthems; So much depends.
56 Fletcher Road, Belmont, MA 02178

*STRICKLAND, LILY TERESA
b. Anderson, S. C., 25 Jan. 1887; d. Hendersonville, N. C., 6 June 1958. Studied at Converse Coll., Litt. B., honorary D. M.; with Percy Goetschius at Juilliard School. She traveled in the Far East, 1920-30.
WORKS: Operetta: Jewels of the desert; Orchestra: Himalayan sketches; Oasis, 1942; Sketches from the Southwest; Songs: Mah Lindy Lou; Here in the high hills; My lover's a fisherman; At eve I hear a flute; also choral works, piano suites.

*STRICKLAND, WILLIAM
A flower given to my daughter, Joyce text; Ione, dead this long year, Pound text; She weeps for Rahoon, Joyce text; 3 songs for medium voice.

*STRICKLAND, WILLY
The trumpet shall sound!, narrator and orch., performed, New York, 4 Feb. 1971.

*STRILKO, ANTHONY
b. 1931. Tranquil music for organ; Music for oboe alone; many songs and choral works published.

*STRINGFIELD, LAMAR
b. Raleigh, N. C., 10 Oct. 1897; d. Asheville, N. C., 21 Jan. 1959. Studied with Georges Barrere and Percy Goetschius, Inst. of Musical Art. He received the Pulitzer award, 1927. He organized the Inst. of Folk Music, Univ. of North Carolina, 1930; was conductor, North Carolina Symphony, 1932-35; Knoxville Symphony Orchestra, 1946-47; Charlotte Symphony Orchestra, 1948-49.
WORKS: Opera: The mountain song; Carolina charcoal, musical folk drama, 1952; Orchestra: Indian legend, 1923; From the southern mountains, suite, 1927; A negro parade, 1931; The legend of John Henry, 1932; Moods of a moonshiner, 1934; Mountain dawn, 1945; About Dixie, 1950; also chamber music.

*STRINGHAM, EDWIN JOHN
b. Kenosha, Wis., 11 July 1890; d. Chapel Hill, N. C., 1 July 1974. Studied at Northwestern Univ. and Cincinnati Cons.; with Ottorino Respighi, Royal Acad. of Music, Rome, 1929 on a scholarship. His other awards include an honorary D. M., Denver Coll. of Music, 1928; Cromwell fellowship to Germany, 1936. He taught at Denver Coll. of Music, 1919-29; Columbia Univ., 1930-38; Juilliard School, 1930-45; and Queen's Coll., CCNY, 1948-46.
WORKS: Orchestra: The phantom, 1916; Visions, 1924; The ancient mariner, 1928; 3 pastels, 1928; symphony, 1929; 2 nocturnes, 1931, 1938; Fantasy on American folk tunes, violin and orch., 1942; also chamber music; choral works; and songs.

STRINI, TOM
b. St. Louis, Mo., 14 Nov. 1949. Studied with James Woodward and Alan Oldfield, Southern Illinois Univ.; with Malcolm Arnold, Shawnigan Lake Inst. of the Arts, Vancouver Island, B. C. He received the Mark Gerdelman award, 1972-73 graduate assistantship, Southern Illinois Univ.
WORKS: Orchestra: Prelude and fugue, string orch.; Nocturne, string orch.; Orchestra music; Chamber music: Night soliloquy, guitar; Study in scherzo style, guitar; Annabel Lee, tenor and guitar; Socrates, upon hearing his sentence, baritone and piano; string quartet.
27 University Heights, Carbondale, IL 62901

STRINGER, ALAN
b. El Paso, Tex., 15 Jan. 1938. Studied with William Wood, Univ. of New Mexico. He has been organist at various churches, in 1973, First Congregational Church, Albuquerque.
WORKS: Theatre: 3-D, 3-tiered wedding cake, musical in 3 acts; Chamber music: 2 hymns in rock style, saxophone and organ; On seeing at night the first blossoms of spring, handbells and piano; Ostinato, bells and organ; Chorus: Prayer for the Great Family, with piano, organ, tape; Woe unto them who join house to house, with piano and percussion; Songs: Under the war shadow, song cycle; Anti-religious songs, a cycle; piano and organ pieces.
8640 Horacio Place, N. E.
Albuquerque, NM 87111

STROUD, RICHARD
b. Dunsmuir, Calif., 26 Jan. 1929. Studied with William Billingsly, Univ. of Idaho; and at California State Univ. at Humboldt. He is director of bands, Eureka City Schools, Calif.
WORKS: Wind ensemble: Articulations, for brass; Application for band; The brass ring, 5 quintets; Chamber music: Sketch for 4 woodwinds; Thumbnail sketches, trumpet trio; quintet for percussion and clarinet; Capriccio, wind quartet; Tubantiphon, 2 tubas.
131 Huntoon, Eureka, CA 95501

*STRUKOFF, RUDOLF STEPHEN
b. Rostov on Don, Russia, 18 July 1938. Studied at Andrews Univ., B. M. 1960; with H. Owen Reed, Gomer Jones, and Paul Harder, Michigan State Univ., M. M. 1964, Ph. D. 1970. He was instructor, Michigan State Univ., 1963-64; professor, Indiana State Univ., 1966-69; associate professor, Andrews Univ., 1969-   . His published works include Childhood sketches, a 7-song cycle for mezzo soprano.
Music Department, Andrews University
Berrien Springs, MI 49104

STRUNK, STEVEN
b. Evansville, Ind., 7 Mar. 1943. Studied with Rouben Gregorian, Boston Cons.; with Luciano Berio and Vincent Persichetti, Juilliard School, D. M. A. 1971. He received Juilliard's Gretchaninoff Memorial prize in composition, 1966, 1967, 1970. He was instructor, Florida State Univ., 1967-69; assistant professor and chairman of theory and composition, Eastern New Mexico Univ., 1971-73; assistant professor, Catholin Univ., 1973-   .
WORKS: Orchestra: Transformations, for 30 solo strings; Geometrics; Chamber music: Quartet II, clarinet, vibraphone, marimba, piano; Conticuere omnes, 5 sopranos and chamber orch.; Episodes, flute and piano.
10402 Hemley Lane, Silver Spring, MD 20902

STUART, HUGH M.
b. Harrisburg, Pa., 5 Feb. 1917. Studied at Oberlin Cons.; Univ. of Michigan; Columbia Univ.; and Rutgers Univ. He was public school music teacher and supervisor from 1940; in East Orange, N. J., 1948-74; also lecturer, clinician, and guest conductor at colleges and universities throughout the U.S.
WORKS: Band: Manhattan vignettes; Somerset sketches; and numerous published educational works for band, ensemble groups and solo instruments.
304 Wellesley Drive, S. E.
Albuquerque, NM 87101

STUCKY, STEVEN EDWARD
b. Hutchinson, Kan., 7 Nov. 1949. Studied with Richard Willis, Baylor Univ., B. M. 1971; with Karel Husa, Robert Palmer, Burrill Phillips, Cornell Univ., M. F. A. 1973. He received the American String Teachers Asso. award, 1965; Nat. Fed. of Music Clubs, awards, 1969, 1970, 1971.
WORKS: Orchestra: Prelude and toccata, 1969; symphony, 1972; Chamber music: 4

(STUCKY, STEVEN EDWARD)
bagatelles, string quartet, 1969; duo for viola and cello, 1969; Movements, cello quartet, 1970; Divertimento, clarinets, piano, percussion, 1971; quartet for clarinet, viola, cello, piano, 1973; Chorus: Nature, like us, 4 Dickinson poems, 1971; Songs: 3 songs, soprano, clarinet, viola, piano, 1969; Schneemusik, soprano and piano, 1973.
c/o Manuscript Publications
5362 Kootenai St., Boise, ID 83705

STUESSY, JOSEPH
b. Houston, Tex., 14 Dec. 1943. Studied at Southern Methodist Univ.; with Samuel Adler, Wayne Barlow, and Bernard Rogers, Eastman School of Music, M. M. He was assistant professor, Texas Woman's Univ., 1969-73; assistant professor, Southern Methodist Univ., 1973-   .
WORKS: Opera: Does the pale flag advance?, 2-act, 1972; Orchestra: piano concerto; Diology; Invasions; Chamber music: Improvisational suite, trumpet.
2768 North Hillbrier, Plano, TX 75074

STURCHIO, FRANK G.
b. Orsara di Puglia, Italy, 27 Oct. 1894; U.S. citizen 1943; d. 14 Aug. 1971. Studied at San Pietro A. Majella Cons., Italy; and Our Lady of the Lake Coll., San Antonio, B. M. He played with concert bands of Sousa, Pryor, LaMonica, and Moses; organized and directed bands in Wauchula, Ft. Myers, and West Palm Beach, Fla., and St. Mary's Univ., San Antonio, Tex., for 18 years.
WORKS: Band marches: La Fiorentina; King Cane; Cotton Bowl; Into the wind; Fiesta Flambeau; Lone Star; Everglades sugar; numerous other unpublished compositions.

*STYNE, JULE
b. London, England, 31 Dec. 1905; U.S. citizen 1916. Was piano soloist with the Chicago Symphony at age 9; studied at Chicago Musical Coll.; Northwestern Univ. He led dance bands in Chicago and New York, then went to Hollywood as composer of musical comedies and film scores.
WORKS: Musical comedies; High button shoes; Gentlemen prefer blondes; Two on the aisle; Peter Pan; Bells are ringing; Say darling; Gypsy; Do re mi; Funny girl; Fade out-fade in; Film scores: Anchors aweigh; West Point story; Don't fence me in; Pink tights; My sister Eileen; Living it up; and many songs.

SUBOTNICK, MORTON
b. Los Angeles, Calif., 14 Apr. 1933. Studied on his own in Los Angeles; with Leon Kirchner and Darius Milhaud, Mills Coll., M. M. He has held teaching posts at Mills Coll., 1959-66; New York Univ., 1966-69; Univ. of Maryland, 1968-69; Univ. of Pittsburgh, 1969-70; California Inst. of the Arts, 1969-   where is also director of electronic music.
WORKS: Orchestra: Play!#2; Lamination #1; Chamber music: The tarot; Play!#1, 1964; Play! #4; Misfortune of the immortals; 2 serenades; 2 butterflies, Los Angeles, 17 Apr. 1975;

(SUBOTNICK, MORTON)
Electronic: Serenade #3, 4 instruments and tape; Serenade #4, piano and electronic sounds, 1966; Silver apples of the moon; The wild bull, 1968; Touch, 1969; Sidewinder; Prelude #4, piano and tape; 4 butterflies.
11355 Farlin St., Los Angeles, CA 90049

SUCHY, GREGORIA KARIDES
b. Milwaukee, Wis., 14 Nov. Studied with Anthony Donata, Northwestern Univ.; Alexander Tcherepnin, De Paul Univ.; Rudolph Ganz, Chicago Musical Coll.; and with Ralph Shapey, Univ. of Chicago. Her awards include Wisconsin Fed. of Music Clubs awards, 1960, 1961, 1962, 1964, 1966, 1967; research grants, Univ. of Wisconsin, 1960, 1963, 1965, 1968; faculty fellowship, Univ. of Wisconsin-Milwaukee, 1967. She taught in Milwaukee schools, 1943-44; was instrumental teacher, Northwestern Cons., 1944-47; professor, Univ. of Wisconsin-Milwaukee, 1947-
WORKS: Ballet: Skins and exposures, electronic score; Orchestra: Suite on Greek themes, 1961; Greek rhapsody, 1962; Symphonic piece with trumpet and piano obbligato, Milwaukee, 14 Dec. 1972; Chamber music: string quartet, 1966; Chorus: A Christmas carol; Songs: Greek maxims, 12 songs for soprano; Piano: A fantasy, Circle dance in 7/8; Sousta; 3 lovers, for 2 pianos; Mother Goose rhymes in 12-tone; Mo-Goose revisited.
2601 East Newton Ave., Milwaukee, WI 53211

SUCOFF, HERBERT
b. New York, N. Y., 18 Jan. 1938. Studied at Juilliard School and Queens Coll.; privately with Stefan Wolpe. He has been lecturer, C. W. Post Coll., 1968- ; composer-in-residence, Craftsbury Chamber Players, Vermont, 1968- ; director, SeaCliff Chamber Players, 1970- ; director, Nassau County Chamber Music Workshop, 1972- .
WORKS: Chamber music: 3 string quartets; quartet for flute, oboe, cello, harpsichord; 3 pieces for violin and piano; duo for violin and cello; trio for piano, cello, clarinet; Chorus: Cantata, with narrator and chamber ensemble.
4 Irving Place, Sea Cliff, NY 11579

SUDERBURG, ROBERT
b. Spencer, Iowa, 28 Jan. 1936. Studied with Paul Fetler, Earl George, Univ. of Minnesota; Richard Donovan, Quincy Porter, Yale Univ.; and with George Rochberg, Univ. of Pennsylvania. He received the Helen Dusa prize, 1959; BMI award, 1962; Halstead award, 1963; Houston Symphony/Rockefeller Found. award, 1967; ASCAP award 1967; Guggenheim fellowship, 1968; III Festival of Music of Spain and America award, 1970; Hindemith Found. award, 1971. His faculty posts have included Albertus Magnus Coll., 1959-60; Bryn Mawr Coll., 1960-61; Univ. of Pennsylvania, 1961-63; Philadelphia Musical Acad., 1963-66; visiting professor, Brooklyn Coll., 1971-72; professor, Univ. of Washington, 1966- .
WORKS: Orchestra: Orchestra music I-III, 1969, 1971, 1973; Within the mirror of time, piano concerto, 1974; Chamber music: Chamber music I, violin and cello, 1967; Chamber music II, string quartet, 1967; Chamber music III, trombone and piano, 1972; Solo music, violin, 1972; Chorus:

(SUDERBERG, ROBERT)
Concert mass, 1960; Cantata I, with orch., 1963; Cantata II, with orch., 1964; Composition on traditional carols, with brass and congregation, 1965; Choruses on poems of Yeats, with wind orch., percussion, 1966; also piano pieces.
School of Music, University of Washington Seattle, WA 98100

*SUESSE, DANA
b. Kansas City, Mo., 3 Dec. 1911. Studied with Alexander Siloti, Rubin Goldmark, and Nadia Boulanger; won prizes in Nat. Fed. of Music Clubs composition contests at age 9 and 10; made debut as pianist with Paul Whiteman's orchestra and received commissions from Whiteman.
WORKS: Theatre: The man who sold the Eiffel Tower, musical; Orchestra: Symphonic waltzes, piano and orch.; 2-piano concerto; Young man with a harp, suite; Jazz concerto; American nocturne; Concerto in rhythm; and songs.

SUITOR, M. LEE
b. San Francisco, Calif., 4 Feb. 1942. Studied with Wayne Bohrnstedt, Univ. of Redlands; privately with Joseph Goodman, New York; consultations with Alec Wyton and Robert W. Jones. He was organist-choirmaster, First Presbyterian Church, and lecturer, State Univ. of New York, Binghamton, 1969-73; organist-choirmaster, St. Luke's Episcopal Church, Atlanta, Ga., 1973- .
WORKS: Chorus: Poverty; other published anthems; chamber music, pieces for organ, etc.
3589 Kingsboro Road, N.E., Atlanta, GA 30319

SULLIVAN, TIMOTHY
b. Clifton Springs, N. Y., 1 Sep. 1939. Studied with Ned Rorem and Virgil Thomson, Univ. of Buffalo; with Yehudi Wyner, Bulent Arel, Hall Overton, Yale Univ. At Yale he received the Frances Kellogg Osborne prize and the Henry and Amanda Noss prize. He has been assistant professor, Nazareth Coll., of Rochester, 1966- .
WORKS: Chamber music: Toccata, cantata, and fanfares, for chamber ensemble, soprano, male voices, 1966; Electronic: Musaic, a classical studio tape piece, 1971; Children of the city, chamber ensemble, tape, male voices, 1973.
97 South Washington St., Rochester, NY 14608

SUMERLIN, MACON D.
b. Rotan, Tex., 24 Oct. 1919. Studied with Edwin Young, Hardin-Simmons Univ., B. M. 1940; with Bernard Rogers and Herbert Elwell, Eastman School of Music; Kent Kennan and Anthony Donata, Univ. of Texas, M. M. 1947; and with Merrill Ellis, North Texas State Univ., D. M. He received a Texas Guild of Composers award, 1951. He was assistant professor, Hardin-Simmons Univ., 1947-51; associate professor and composer-in-residence, McMurry Coll., 1952- .
WORKS: Ballet: Masquerade; Orchestra: 5 symphonies; Band: Fanfare, andante, and fugue; Suite for brass choir; Chamber music: violin sonata; piano sonata; organ sonata; Chorus: I am music, a cantata.
Department of Music, McMurry College Abilene, TX 79605

SUMMERLIN, EDGAR

*SUMMERLIN, EDGAR
Evensong, a jazz liturgy for chorus; Bless this world, for chorus, baritone solo, narrator, brass, organ, jazz trio, projectors, written on a grant from the New York Council on the Arts and presented at Vassar Coll., 8 Nov. 1970.
City College of CUNY, New York, NY 10031

*SUMMERS, STANLEY
Allegro breve, 4 clarinets.
1729 Jenner, Lancaster, CA 93534

*SUMNER, SARAH
Studied violin with Paul Stassevitch in New York; composition with Irving Fine and Walter Piston, Harvard Univ.; with Nadia Boulanger in Paris on a Fulbright scholarship. Her Songs for soprano, woodwind quartet, piano, received its premiere in Chartres, France, 1973, and its American premiere in Philadelphia, 14 Oct. 1973.
751 Millbrook Lane, Haverford, PA 19041

SUNDSTEN, JOHN
b. Munsala, Finland, 11 Oct. 1899; U.S. citizen 1918. Studied with Per Olsson, Judson W. Mather, Boyd Wells, and Elie Robert Schmitz. From 1917 to 1954 he served as organist and music director in churches of Tacoma and Seattle; was musical coordinator and conductor of Seattle's Scandinavian Music Festival, 1951-71; for 40 years was director, Runeberg Singing Societies; for 10 years of the Svea Male Chorus; private teacher of piano and organ, 1971- . He toured the Scandinavian countries as choral conductor and guest concert pianist, receiving numerous awards for his service to Scandinavian culture. In 1962 he was awarded the Knighthood of the Finnish Lion by the President of Finland, and the Royal Order of Vasa by the King of Sweden.
WORKS: Orchestra: Festival overture; Basso ostinato; Gunderkin, with narrator; Orientale #2; Out West; Oriental teahouse; 4 Nordic dances; Song cycles: Thoughts from the life of Job; The poet, text of 15 century Korea; The tryst, 15th century Korean text; Sea-drift, Whitman text; many piano pieces and arrangements.
2212 Everett Ave. East, Seattle, WA 98102

*SUR, DONALD
b. Honolulu, Hawaii, 1935, of Korean parents. Studied with Seymour Shifrin, Univ. of California, Berkeley; with Earl Kim and Roger Sessions, Princeton Univ.; with Colin McPhee, Univ. of California, Los Angeles; and again with Earl Kim at Harvard Univ., where he earned his Ph. D. In 1965 he received a Ford Found. grant for study of Asian music. By frugality and because of the favorable rate of exchange he was able to study in Seoul for 5 years. He has been assistant professor at Massachusetts Inst. of Technology, 1968- ; began teaching a course in non-Western music in 1970; and established MIT's Center for Asian Music which opened in 1974. He was invited to attend the Brussels Conference on New Music Notation in 1975.
WORKS: Chamber music: Katana II, chamber ensemble, 1962; Sleep walkers ballad, on Lorca text, soprano and chamber ensemble, 1962; Piano

(SUR, DONALD)
fragments, 1966; Intonation, chamber ensemble, 1966; Red dust, for 30 Korean percussion instruments, is the early morning part of a larger projected composition that would last all day, 1967; Intonation before Sotoba Komachi, revised version performed, Cambridge, Mass., 10 Feb. 1975.
84 Wendell St., Cambridge, MA 02138

SURINACH, CARLOS
b. Barcelona, Spain, 4 Mar. 1915; U.S. citizen 1959. Studied at Municipal Cons., Barcelona; conducting with Eugen Papst in Cologne; composition with Max Trapp in Berlin. His honors include the 1966 Arnold Bax composition medal of Great Britain; Spanish Knight Commander of the Order of Isabella I of Castile with Cross, 1972; numerous commissions. After his studies in Berlin he was conductor, Orquestra Filarmonica, Barcelona, and of Gran Teatro del Liceo Opera House, 1944-47; moved to Paris in 1947, and to U.S. in 1950. He was visiting professor, Carnegie-Mellon Univ., 1966-67.
WORKS: Ballet: Acrobats of God; Agathe's tale; Apasionada; Celebrants; Cordoba; David and Bath-Sheba; Embattled garden; Feast of ashes; Hazana; Los renegados; Ritmo jondo; La sibila; Venta quemada; Orchestra: Concertino for piano, strings, and cymbals; Concerto for orchestra; Doppio concertino for violin, piano, and orch.; Drama jondo, 1965; Fandango; Feria magica, Louisville, Ky., 14 Mar. 1956; Hollywood carnival; Madrid 1890; Melorhythmic dramas, Detroit, Aug. 1966; Passacaglia symphony; Sinfonia chica; Sinfonietta flamenca, 1953; Symphonic variations; symphony no. 2; transcriptions for orchestra from the piano suite, Iberia, of Albeniz; Wind symphony: Paeans and dances of heathen Iberia; piano concerto, Minneapolis, 13 Nov. 1974; Chamber music: Tres cantos bereberes, flute, oboe, clarinet, viola, cello, and harp, 1952; Flamenco cyclothymia, violin and piano; Flamenquerias, 2 pianos, 1952; Pavana and rondo, for accordion; piano quartet; Prelude of the sea, accordion; guitar sonatina; Tientos, harp or piano, English horn, timpani, 1953; piano sonatina; Chorus: Songs of the soul; Cantata of Saint John, with percussion, 1963; many works for voice and orchestra and voice and piano.
440 East 59th St., New York, NY 10022

SUSA, CONRAD
b. Springdale, Pa., 26 Apr. 1935. Studied with Nikolai Lopatnikoff, Carnegie Mellon Univ., B. M. cum laude; with William Bergsma and Vincent Persichetti, Juilliard School. He was recipient of the George Gershwin Memorial scholarship; 2 Benjamin awards; Marion Freschl award; Gretchaninoff composition prize; and a Ford Found. fellowship to be composer-in-residence for the city schools in Nashville. He then became field director of the Educational Department, Lincoln Center, New York.
WORKS: Theatre: Transformations, on texts of Anne Sexton's book of the same name, written for the Minnesota Opera Company, Minneapolis, 5 May 1973; Orchestra: Eulogy, string orch.;

(SUSA, CONRAD)
Love-in, ballet after Handel; Pastorale, string quartet with double string orch.; Chamber music: Serenade for a Christmas night, organ, harp and vibraphone; Chorus: The birds, Belloc text; A lullaby carol; 2 Marian carols; 3 mystical carols; 2 rock carols; 3 George Herbert settings; 6 Joyce songs; Discovery and praises--An invocation; Songs; Serenade no. 5, oboe, cello, 2 percussions, 2 solo tenors; Hymns for the amusement of children, mezzo-soprano and piano.
c/o E. C. Schirmer Co.
112 South St., Boston, MA 02111

*SUTCLIFFE, JAMES
b. Soochow, China, 1929; U.S. citizen 1957. Came to the U.S. in 1948 to study at Juilliard School and Eastman School of Music. In 1959 he was faculty member director of the opera workshop, Duquesne Univ. His Gymnopédie was recorded by the Eastman Orchestra.

SUTHERLAND, BRUCE
b. Florida. Studied with Halsey Stevens and Ellis Kohs, Univ. of Southern California. He received an award, Louis Moreau Gottschalk contest, 1970; Music Arts award, Stairway of the Stars, 1973.
WORKS: Orchestra: Allegro fanfara, 1970; Chamber music: string trio; saxophone quartet; quintet for flute, clarinet, and piano trio; Notturno, flute and guitar; Prelude and fugue, 2 pianos; Chorus: Green grass, 1973.
2336 Pier Ave., Santa Monica, CA 90406

SUYCOTT, FORREST D.
b. Granite City, Ill., 2 Nov. 1922. Studied with Philip Greeley Clapp and Philip Bezanson, Univ. of Iowa; with Jacques Ibert at Tanglewood. He was director of bands, Western Illinois Univ., 1955-68, dean, Coll. of Fine Arts, 1968- .
WORKS: Orchestra: Prelude and variations, Chamber music: contrabass sonata; brass sextet; quintet for mixed ensemble.
R. F. D. #1, Macomb, IL 61455

SVOBODA, TOMAS
b. Paris, France, 6 Dec. 1939; U.S. citizen 1971. Studied with Miloslav Kabelac, Prague Cons., B. A. 1959; with Vaclav Dobias, Prague Acad. of Music, 1962-64; with Ingolf Dahl, Univ. of Southern California, M. M. 1969. He began to compose at a very early age. His first symphony was performed by the Prague Symphony Orchestra in 1957 and he was invited to study with Nadia Boulanger in Paris in 1963. Other honors include the Helen S. Anstead award, 1967, and various commissions. He was teaching assistant in Prague, 1959-64; was church organist and private teacher in Los Angeles, 1967-69; has been assistant professor, Portland State Univ., 1970- .
WORKS: Orchestra: 3 symphonies, 1957, 1962, 1966; 3 pieces for orchestra, 1966; Reflections, 1968; Sinfonietta, a la Renaissance, 1972; A child's dream, children's choir and orch., for 50th anniversary of Portland Junior Symphony Orchestra, 1973; Chamber music: Chorale and dance, brass quintet, 1966; Concertino for oboe,

(SVOBODA, TOMAS)
brass choir, 2 timpani, 1966; 2 epitaphs, string quartet, 1967; Divertimento for 7 instruments, 1967; XLIV sonnet of Michelangelo, alto voice and 11 instruments, 1967; Meditations, cello and piano, 1969; 3 movements, piano, harpsichord, percussion, 1971; Parabola, clarinet, piano, and string trio, 1971; Double octet, for 8 flutes and 8 cellos, 1971; Prologue, clarinet, harpsichord, percussion, 1972; duo for flute and oboe, 1972; Piano: Bagatelles, In a forest, 1965; 9 etudes in fugue style, 1966; sonata, 1967; sonata for 2 pianos, 1972; A quiet piece, 1973; also organ pieces.
4320 S. E. Oak St., Portland, OR 97215

SWACK, IRWIN
b. Cleveland, Ohio, 8 Nov. 1919. Studied with Herbert Elwell, Cleveland Inst. of Music; with Vittorio Giannini, Juilliard School; Normand Lockwood and Henry Cowell, Columbia Univ.; and with Gunther Schuller at Tanglewood on a Ford Found. fellowship. He has held teaching posts at Jacksonville State Coll., and at Louisiana Polytechnic Inst.
WORKS: Orchestra: Essay for orch.; Fantaisie concertante for strings; Chamber music: 2 string quartets; woodwind quintet; Psalm 8, tenor, trumpet, and strings; Dance episodes for 7 instruments; piano trio; piano sonata.
2924 Len Drive, Bellmore, NY 11710

SWAN, ALFRED JULIUS
b. St. Petersburg, Russia, 9 Oct. 1890; U.S. citizen 1954; d. Haverford, Pa., 2 Oct. 1970. Studied with Vassili Kalafati and Vyatcheslav Karatygin at the St. Petersburg Cons. He came to the U.S. in 1920 and taught at Univ. of Virginia, 1921-23; Swarthmore Coll. and Haverford Coll., 1926-59; Univ. of Aix-Marseilles, 1959-67; Temple Univ., 1965-70.
WORKS: Chamber music: 6 string quartets; 2 violin sonatas; piano sonatina; Chorus: 10 church canticles; many songs.

SWANN, JEFFREY
b. Williams, Ariz., 24 Nov. 1951. Studied with David Ahlstrom, Southern Methodist Univ.; with Darius Milhaud, Aspen Music Festival; and with Hall Overton, Juilliard School. His sextet won first prize at the Aspen Festival, 1967.
WORKS: Opera: Prometheus, text after Aeschelus; Orchestra: symphony no. 1, performed by Dallas Symphony; Sinfonia concertante, performed by Dallas Symphony, 1967; Chamber music: Arches, violin and cello.
1064 Barbara Ann, Hurst, TX 76053

*SWANSON, HOWARD
b. Atlanta, Ga., 18 Aug. 1907. Studied with Herbert Elwell, Cleveland Inst. of Music; with Nadia Boulanger in Paris on a Rosenwald fellowship. He also received the New York Music Critics Circle award, 1952; his songs were performed by Marian Anderson.

SWANSON, HOWARD

(SWANSON, HOWARD)
WORKS: Orchestra: 3 symphonies, 1945, 1948, 1970; Night music, small orch., 1950; Concerto for orch.; Chamber music: Suite for cello and piano, 1949; The cuckoo, piano; 7 songs.
81 Columbia St., New York, NY 10002

*SWEET, REGINALD
b. Yonkers, N. Y., 14 Oct. 1885. Studied with Friedrich Koch and Hugo Kaun in Berlin; then taught in Chautauqua and in New York City. His compositions include Riders to the sea, a 1-act opera; and chamber music.

SWENSON, WARREN ARTHUR
b. Okanogan, Wash., 27 Apr. 1937. Studied at Univ. of Washington. He was harpsichordist-pianist, Munich Chamber Opera, 1966; Bavarian Opera Stage, 1965-66; composer, School of the Arts, New York Univ., 1971-   ; organist and composer, Packer Collegiate Inst., 1972-   .
WORKS: Opera: The legend of Pecos Bill, folk opera, 1963; Theatre: Captain Peoplefox and his people, a musical, commissioned and broadcast by Bavarian Radio, 1964; Orchestra: viola concerto; Chorus: A festival mass; Requiem mass; other choral works and organ pieces.
216 East 7th St., New York, NY 10009

SWICKARD, RALPH
b. San Jose, Calif., 17 Nov. 1922. Studied with Leonard Ratner, Stanford Univ.; with John Vincent, Univ. of California, Los Angeles; with Vladimir Ussachevsky and Otto Luening, Columbia Univ. He was instructor, California State Univ., San Jose, 1970-71.
WORKS: Chamber music: 4 duets for flute and viola; string quartet, 1957; Chorus: Missa brevis, 1958; Electronic: Bagatelle no. 2, tape; Sermons of St. Francis, narrator and tape, 1968; Hymn of creation, narrator and tape, 1969. He was producer of the documentary film A visit with Darius Milhaud, 1956.
409 Bonhill Road, Los Angeles, CA 90049

*SWIFT, KAY
b. New York, N. Y., 19 Apr. 1905. Studied with Arthur E. Johnstone, Inst. of Musical Art; with Charles Martin Loeffler, New England Cons. She was staff composer at Radio City Music Hall for 2 years; was the first magazine radio columnist; chairman of music for the New York World's Fair, 1939; piano soloist with the New York Philharmonic at Lewisohn Stadium.
WORKS: Ballet: Alma mater; Theatre; Fine and dandy, musical comedy; Paris '90, musical comedy; One little girl, Campfire Girls' 50th anniversary show, 1960; Century 21, Seattle World's Fair, 1962; many songs, piano pieces.
400 East 59th St., New York, NY 10022

SWIFT, RICHARD
b. Middle Point, Ohio, 24 Sep. 1927. Studied with Leland Smith, Univ. of Chicago, M. A. 1956. His awards include the Rockefeller Found.-Louisville Symphony Young Composer award, 1955; fellowship, Inst. for Advanced Musical Studies, Princeton, 1959, 1960; fellowship, Inst. for

(SWIFT, RICHARD)
Creative Arts, 1966-67, 1972; MacDowell fellowship, 1971; Rockefeller Performing award, 1968; first prize, Composers String Quartet 2nd competition, 1973, with 121 scores submitted. He has been professor, Univ. of California, Davis, 1956-   , chairman, music department, 1963-71.
WORKS: Opera: Trial of Tender O'Shea, 1964; Orchestra: A coronal, 1956; piano concerto, 1961; Extravaganza, 1962; Tristia, 1968; violin concerto, 1968; symphony, 1970; Chamber music: Serenade concertante, piano and wind quintet, 1956; clarinet sonata, 1957; trio for clarinet, cello, and piano, 1957; Domains I, baritone and chamber ensemble; Eve, soprano and chamber ensemble; Carmina archilochi, soprano and chamber ensemble; Stravaganze, a group of 8 works for various ensembles or solo instruments; Prime, saxophone and chamber ensemble; 4 string quartets, #4, Composers String Quartet, Boston, 29 Mar. 1974; Chorus: Planctus, with chamber ensemble; Thanatopsis, with chamber ensemble.
Department of Music, University of California Davis, CA 95616

*SWING, RAYMOND GRAM
b. Cortland, N. Y., 25 Mar. 1887. Studied at Oberlin Coll. Cons. He has received honorary doctorates from 5 colleges, honorary M. A. from Harvard Univ., 1942. He was newspaper reporter 1906-22; became a news commentator in 1935. His violin sonata, 1928, was commercially recorded.

SWISHER, GLORIA WILSON
b. Seattle, Wash., 12 Mar. 1935. Studied with John Verrall, Univ. of Washington; Darius Milhaud, Mills Coll.; with Howard Hanson and Bernard Rogers, Eastman School of Music. She received a Woodrow Wilson fellowship, 1956-57; Capitol Choir contest award, 1961. She was instructor, Washington State Univ., 1960-61; Pacific Lutheran Univ., 1969-70; Shoreline Community Coll., 1969-   .
WORKS: Opera: The happy hypocrite; Orchestra: clarinet concerto; Yuki no Niigata, koto and orch.; Canción, flute and orch.; Band: The mountain and the island; Solo flute variations; Sado, flute and piano; Variations on an original theme, piano; Chorus: God is gone up with a merry noise; 2 faces of love.
7228 6th Ave. N. W., Seattle, WA 98117

SYDEMAN, WILLIAM T.
b. New York, N. Y., 8 May 1928. Studied with Roy Travis and Felix Salzer, Mannes Coll. of Music, B. S.; privately with Roger Sessions; with Arnold Franchetti, Univ. of Hartford, M. M. His awards include 2 Tanglewood fellowships; Pacifica Found. award, 1960; Nat. Inst. of Arts and Letters award, 1962; Boston Symphony Merit award, 1964; Koussevitzky Found. award; State Department exchange lectureship in Czechoslovakia, Rumania, and Bulgaria, 1966; and many commissions. He was on the composition faculty, Mannes Coll. of Music, 1959-70.
WORKS: Orchestra: Concert piece for chamber orchestra; Concert piece for horn and strings; Concertino for oboe, piano, strings, 1956;

(SYDEMAN, WILLIAM T.)
concerto for piano 4-hands and chamber orch.; double concerto for trumpet, trombone, band, and strings; In memoriam--John F. Kennedy, 1966; Music for viola, winds and percussion; Oecumenicus, a concerto for orch., 1966; Orchestral abstractions, 1958; Study for orchestra, no. 1 1959, no. 2 1964, no. 3 1965; Chamber music: The affections, trumpet and piano; Concerto da camera for viola; Concerto da camera for violin no. 1 1959, no. 2 1960, no. 3; Divertimento, woodwind trio and string quintet; 1957; many duos for various instruments and piano; Homage to L'histoire du soldat, 7 instruments; 7 movements for septet, 1958; Music for flute, viola, guitar, percussion; Music for low brass; quartet for flute, clarinet, violin, piano; quartet for oboe and string trio, 1961; quartet for violin, clarinet, trumpet, double bass, 1955; sonata for unaccompanied cello; string quartet, 1955; trios for varying instruments including flute, violin and double bass, 1958; Variations for oboe and piano; Variations for violin and piano; 2 woodwind quintets, 1955, 1961; Voice: The lament of Elektra, alto solo, chorus, chamber ensemble; Malediction, tenor, speaking actor, string quartet, and tape, New York, 5 Feb. 1971; Prometheus, cantata for 3 male soloists, female chorus, orch.; Songs for soprano, flute, and cello; many other chamber and vocal works.
P. O. Box 1176, Running Springs, CA 92382

SYVERUD, STEPHEN LUTHER
b. Prince Albert, Sask., 3 Mar. 1938. Studied with Roger Nixon, Alexander Post, and Wayne Peterson, San Francisco State Coll.; with Richard Hervig and Robert Shallenberg, Univ. of Iowa, D. M. A. He received the Clapp Composition award, Univ. of Iowa, 1968. He was assistant professor, Jackson State Coll., 1968-70; assistant professor, director of electronic music studio and contemporary music ensemble, Grinnell Coll., 1970-71; assistant professor, director, electronic music studio and co-director, contemporary music ensemble, Northwestern Univ., 1971-   .
WORKS: Chamber music: Vietnam II, clarinet, oboe, double bass, percussion; 4 pieces, clarinet and piano; Electronic: Vectors, percussion and tape; Reaction, clarinet and reverberators; Screaming monkeys, tape.
2717 Ewing Ave., Evanston, IL 60201

SZABO, BURT
b. Wellington, Ohio, 28 Dec. 1931. Studied with Norman Phelps, Ohio State Univ.; with H. Owen Reed, James Niblock, Paul Harder, Mario Castelnuovo-Tedesco, Michigan State Univ. He received performance awards from Redlands Univ. and the Dallas Symphony Orchestra. He was instructor, Western Michigan Univ., 1964-68; professor, Edinboro State Coll., 1968-71; professor, Florida Technological Univ., 1971-   .
WORKS: Orchestra: 2 pieces for orchestra; A forest hymn, tenor and orch; Jazz orchestra: 3 enigmas; Impressions; Diversions of Aves; Chamber music: Divertimentissimo for winds; Spring, 2 sopranos and woodwind ensemble; Foreboding, for tenor, piano, clarinet; Chorus: She

(SZABO, BURT)
is not fair; Rejoice and be merry; A farm picture, men's voices.
Dept. of Music, Florida Tech. University Orlando, FL 32816

*SZELL, GEORG
b. Budapest, Hungary, 7 June 1897; U.S. citizen 1946; d. Cleveland, Ohio, 30 July 1970. Studied composition with Josef B. Foerster and Max Reger. He was an early prodigy both as pianist and composer. At age 11 he performed his Rondo for piano and orchestra with the Vienna Symphony; at 17 conducted his own symphony and played the Beethoven Emperor Concerto with the Berlin Philharmonic. He was opera and orchestra conductor in Europe to 1939; conducted the New York Metropolitan Opera, 1942-46; the Cleveland Orchestra, 1946-70. His compositions include Theme and variations for orchestra, 1916; and Lyric overture, 1922.

*SZENDREI, ALADAR. See SENDRY, ALFRED

TAFFS, ANTHONY
b. London, England, 15 Jan. 1916; U.S. citizen 1954. Studied with Bernard Rogers and Herbert Elwell, Eastman School of Music. He has been professor, Albion Coll., 1949-   .
WORKS: Opera: Lilith; Noah; The 10 virgins; The summons; Chamber music: piano sonata; violin sonata; organ sonata; 3 string quartets; Chorus: The son of man, oratorio; A modern psalmody, oratorio; The Shulamite, cantata for soprano, tenor, chorus, small orch.; many church anthems and songs.
409 Brockway Place, Albion, MI 49224

TAGAWA, RICK M.
b. Los Angeles, Calif., 7 May 1947. Studied with Elliott Carter, Juillard School, 1967-71; also briefly with William Kraft, Alan Stout, and Luciano Berio. He received the George Gershwin Memorial award, 1969-71.
WORKS: Orchestra: Antoku Tenno, elegy to a 12th century Japanese emperor; Chamber music: Inspirations diabolique, percussion ensemble; Elegy, piano solo.
3414 West 52nd St., Los Angeles, CA 90043

*TAKACS, JENO
b. Siegendorf, Austria, 25 Sep. 1902; to U.S. 1952. Taught at Cincinnati Cons. and from 1955 was also visiting professor at the Geneva Cons. in the summers.
WORKS: Orchestra: 2 ballets; 2 piano concertos, 1932, 1947; Philippine suite, 1934; Antiqua Hungarica, 1941; Partita, guitar and orch., 1950; Folk dances of Burgenland, 1953; Chamber music: violin sonata, 1956; oboe sonata, 1957; trumpet sonata, 1958; piano pieces.

TALLARICO, PASQUALE
b. Italy, 25 Sep. 1891; U.S. citizen 1916; d. Wilton, N. H., 17 Jan. 1974. Studied theory and composition with Alfred J. Goodrich and Rubin Goldmark, piano with John Mokrejs and Rafael Joseffy, all in New York. He made his piano

TALLARICO, PASQUALE

(TALLARICO, PASQUALE)
debut in New York in Mar. 1913, and won a performance with the Chicago Symphony in 1914. He was head, piano department, Coll. of Music and Fine Arts, Indianapolis, 1917-20; faculty member, Peabody Cons., 1920-52; then retired to Wilton, N. H.

WORKS: Chamber music: The timid maiden, originally composed for violin later transcribed for cello, then for alto saxophone and played widely in all forms; many songs and piano pieces.

TALMA, LOUISE
b. Arcachon, France, 31 Oct. 1906. Studied at Inst. of Musical Art, New York, 1922-30; with Nadia Boulanger and Isidore Philipp, Fontainebleau, France, for 17 summers; New York Univ., B. M. 1931; Columbia Univ., M. A. 1933. Her many honors include Isaac Newton Seligman prize, 1927, 1928, 1929; Joseph H. Bearns prize, 1932; Stovall composition prize, 1938, 1939; Juilliard publication award, 1946; 2 Guggenheim fellowships, 1946, 1947; North American prize, 1947; French Government Prix d'Excellence de Composition, 1951; Fulbright research grant for 10 months in Rome to compose The Alcestiad, 1955-56; Koussevitzky Found. commission, 1959; Marjorie Peabody Waite award and citation, Nat. Inst. of Arts and Letters, 1960; Nat. Fed. of Music Clubs award, 1963; Nat. Asso. for American Composers and Conductors, 1963; Sibelius Medal from Harriet Cohen Internat. Awards, London, 1963; $7500 sabbatical leave grant, Nat. Endowment for the Arts, 1966; election to membership in the Nat. Inst. of Arts and Letters, 1974, the first woman composer to be chosen for NIAL. She taught at Manhattan School of Music, 1926-28; Fontainebleau School, summers 1936-39, the only American to teach there; faculty, Hunter Coll., 1928- , professor, 1952- .

WORKS: Opera: The Alcestiad, text by Thornton Wilder, 1955-58, Frankfurt, Germany, 1 Mar. 1962; Orchestra: Toccata for orchestra, 1944, Baltimore, 20 Dec. 1945; Dialogues, piano and orch., Buffalo, 12 Dec. 1965; A time to remember, chorus and orch., text from speeches of John F. Kennedy, New York, 11 May 1968; The tolling bell, baritone and orch., Milwaukee, 29 Nov. 1969 (nominated for Pulitzer Prize); Chamber music: Song and dance, violin and piano, 1951; string quartet, New York, 19 Feb. 1955; violin sonata, New York, 13 Feb. 1963; All the days of my life, tenor and chamber group, 1965, Washington, D.C., 25 Nov. 1966; 3 duologues, clarinet and piano, New York, 28 Mar. 1968; Summer sounds, clarinet quintet, 1969-73; Chorus: The divine flame, oratorio, chorus, soloists, orch., 1948, Cambridge, Mass., 14 Feb. 1950 (excerpts); Let's touch the sky, with woodwinds, New York, 24 Nov. 1952; La corona, 7 sonnets by John Donne, a cappella, 1955, New York, 19 Nov. 1964; Voices of peace, cantata, chorus and strings, Philadelphia, 10 Feb. 1974; Songs: Carmina Mariana, 2 sopranos and piano, 1943, New York, 21 Jan. 1946; Terre de France, cycle for soprano, New York, 27 Jan. 1946; Rain song, text by Garrigue, soprano and piano, 1973; Piano: Four-handed fun, piano 4-hands, 1939; sonata

(TALMA, LOUISE)
no.1, New York, 21 Jan. 1945; Alleluia in form of toccata, 1945; Pastoral prelude, 1949; 6 etudes, 1954; sonata no.2, 1955, New York, 13 Feb. 1959; Passacaglia and fugue, MacDowell Colony, 31 July 1962.
410 Central Park West, New York, NY 10035

TANCREDI, RALPH ANTHONY
b. Italy, 15 Jan. 1921; U.S. citizen 1934. Studied with Donal Michalsky, California State Univ. at Fullerton. He taught in public schools, 1966-67; at Mount San Antonio Coll., 1973- .
WORKS: Chamber music: Theme and variations, violin, cello and wind ensemble; 4 songs based on the Pentagon Papers, baritone and piano; Music for brass ensemble and percussion; string sextet; Divertimento, 2 clarinets and bassoon; Music for 5, clarinet, horn, trumpet, double bass, piano; Andante and allegro, 2 trumpets and piano; Chorus: Mass, with 2 clarinets and 2 bassoons.
917 Washington Ave., Pomona, CA 91767

TANENBAUM, ELIAS
b. Brooklyn, N. Y., 20 Aug. 1924. Studied at Juilliard School, B. S.; Columbia Univ., M. A.; composition privately with Dante Fiorillo, Bohuslav Martinu, Otto Luening, and Wallingford Riegger. He received a MacDowell fellowship. He is director of electronic music, Manhattan School of Music.
WORKS: Theatre: music for Notes from a dark street, CBS-TV production; Orchestra: Variations for orchestra, 1955; Chamber music: Structures, brass quintet; Electronic: Patterns and improvisations, brass quintet and tape; ARP art, 4 pieces for ARP synthesizer (Movements, Contrasts, Blue fantasy, For the 'Bird'); The families of Sonmy, chorus and tape, New York, 12 Nov. 1973.
30 Irving Place, New Rochelle, NY 10801

TANG, JORDAN CHO-TUNG
b. Hong Kong, 27 Jan. 1948; to U.S. 1969. Studied at Chung Chi Coll., Hong Kong; with Jan Bender and H. W. Zimmermann, Wittenberg Univ.; Marcel Dick, Cleveland Inst. of Music; with Ramiro Cortes and Vladimir Ussachevsky, Univ. of Utah. He received the Mary Paine Eudy scholarship, 1970, 1971; American Choral Directors Asso. of Ohio award, 1971; Beryl Rubenstein scholarship, 1971-72; Leroy Robertson Memorial award, 1973; Utah State Fair contest, 2nd prize 1973, first prize 1974; Univ. of Utah research fellowship, 1974. He was timpanist, Springfield (Ohio) Symphony, 1969-71; conductor, Chinese Chorus, Salt Lake City, 1972-73; assistant conductor, Univ. of Utah Symphony, 1973- ; and Utah Youth Orchestra, 1973- .
WORKS: Orchestra: Symphonic movement, chamber orch.; timpani concerto; Chamber music: string quartet; A little suite for woodwind quartet; Symbolism for organ; Piece for harp and cello; The world, solo voice; In a summer-house among the bamboos; Elegy, cello and strings; piano sonatina; Chorus: Psalm of praise, with

(TANG, JORDAN CHO-TUNG)
brass and timpani; Passio brevis, with soloists, instruments, and tape.
c/o Music Department, University of Utah
Salt Lake City, UT 84112

TANNER, JERRE EUGENE
b. Lock Haven, Pa., 5 Jan. 1939. Studied at Univ. of Northern Iowa; with Philip Bezanson, Univ. of Iowa, B. A. 1960, with Roger Nixon, California State Coll., San Francisco, M. A. 1970. He received a Huntington Hartford Found. award, 1964-65; Celia S. Buck award, 1966. He was acting lecturer, Univ. of Hawaii, Hilo Coll., 1966-67, instructor, Hilo Continuing Education and Community Service, 1970-
WORKS: Orchestra: Bartokiana; Le tombeau; Band: Suite; Grand prelude and fugue; Chamber music: Interlude no.1, for 17-string koto; Spring, solo flute; Adagio, flute and harp; Night, bassoon and percussion; Autumn, solo winds and strings; Hummingbirds, percussion ensemble; Fugue, string trio; Fugue, string quartet; many choral works and songs.
P. O. Box 1478, Kailua-Kona, HI 96740

TANNER, PAUL O. W.
b. Skunk Hollow, Ky., 15 Oct. 1917. Studied at Univ. of California, Los Angeles, B. A., M. A.; privately with Stefan Wolpe in New York and Roy Harris in Los Angeles. He has played trombone with Glenn Miller, Les Brown, and Tex Beneke orchestras; has been faculty member, Univ. of California, Los Angeles, 1958-
WORKS: Band: Concerto for 2 trombones and band; Aria for trombone and band; Chamber music: Imitation, 3 trombones; A study in texture, 4 trombones; Just Bach, 4 trombones; El cangrejo, 6 trombones; many more works for trombone, books, methods, etc.
969 Hilgard Ave., Los Angeles, CA 90024

TANNER, PETER H.
b. Rochester, N. Y., 25 June 1936. Studied with Robert Hall Lewis, Thomas Canning, Louis Mennini, Alan Hovhaness, Bernard Rogers, Eastman School of Music, B. M. 1958, M. M. 1959; Catholic Univ. of America, Ph. D. 1967. He played in the U.S. Marine Band, 1959-63; was assistant professor, Kansas State Univ., Manhattan, 1963-66; associate professor, Univ. of Wisconsin-Eau Claire, 1966-69; associate professor, Univ. of Massachusetts, Amherst, 1969-
WORKS: Orchestra: Concerto for timpani and brass; flute concerto; Introduction and allegro, piano and orch.; Chamber music: sonata for marimba with piano or wind ensemble; Diversions, flute and marimba; Andante, marimba and piano; Chorus: Sing for joy.
January Hills, Route 3, Amherst, MA 01002

TARANTO, VERNON ANTHONY, JR.
b. New Orleans, La., 16 Nov. 1946. Studied with Kenneth Klaus and Dinos Constantinides, Louisiana State Univ.
WORKS: Orchestra: Soliloquy, string orch., 1967; Band: Fantasie on an American folk song, clarinet and band; Chamber music: Study #1,

(TARANTO, VERNON ANTHONY, JR.)
brass trio; The middleland, song cycle for soprano and woodwinds; trio for flute, cello and piano, commissioned by USAF Chamber Players.
Box 343, Prairieville, LA 70769

TARLOW, KAREN ANNE
b. Boston, Mass., 19 Sep. 1947. Studied with Philip Bezanson, Charles Fussell, Robert Stern, and Frederick Tillis, Univ. of Massachusetts, Amherst; with Wolfgang Fortner in Germany. She received the Lebow Memorial scholarship, 1972.
WORKS: Chamber music: Lieblingstier, 3 solo voices, 4 woodwinds, and cello, 1969; Games for 3, oboe, piano, viola, 1970; The lowest trees have tops, 3 solo voices, chamber ensemble, 1972; 2 songs for voice and piano, 1972; Salvación de la primavera, women's voices, 1973; Music for wind quintet, 1973.
24 South Prospect St., Amherst, MA 01002

TATGENHORST, JOHN J.
b. East Liverpool, Ohio, 22 Aug. 1938. Studied with Marshall Barnes, Norman Phelps, and Donald E. McGinnis, Ohio State Univ.; with Billy May in Hollywood. He has been percussion instructor, Capital Univ., 1963- ; arranger for several universities, 1964- .
WORKS: Band: Tanglewood, an overture; Clarion textures; Montage; Cubano drums; and many works for marching band. He is author of The Slingerland elementary bell method, and co-author of The percussion.
2415 Buckley Road, Columbus, OH 43220

*TATTON, JACK MEREDITH
b. Leek, Staffordshire, England, 1 Nov. 1901; U.S. citizen 1939. Studied at King Williams Coll., Isle of Man; Cambridge Univ., B. A., M. A.; Royal Coll. of Music, London. He taught in schools, 1927-36; since then has raised cattle in Texas. He has composed Latin motets, 2 masses, and many songs.
Salt Creek Ranch, Refugio, TX 78377

TAUB, BRUCE J.
b. New York, N. Y., 6 Feb. 1948. Studied with Stanley Persky and Mario Davidovsky, City Coll. of New York; with Vladimir Ussachevsky, Jack Beeson, and Chou Wen-chung, Columbia Univ., candidate for D. M. A. in 1973. He is preceptor at Columbia Univ.; member of executive committee, American Society of University Composers.
WORKS: Orchestra: 6 pieces for orchestra, BMI award, 1972; Chamber music: quintet, New York, 9 Feb. 1973; times 3 and o sweet spontaneous earth, 2 songs of e. e. cummings, New York, 22 Feb. 1974.
c/o American Music Center
2109 Broadway, New York, NY 10023

TAUTENHAHN, GUNTHER
b. Lithuania, 22 Dec. 1938; U.S. citizen 1956. Studied at Caldwell Seminary, N. J.; is self-taught in composition. He won a Young Musicians award, 1958. He has developed a compositional style stressing the coloring of one note throughout a work; each instrument plays no more than 2

TAUTENHAHN, GUNTHER

(TAUTENHAHN, GUNTHER)
consecutive notes with great care being taken in the choice of timbre for each note. He has been a private teacher of piano and composition, 1968-   .

WORKS: Orchestra: Double bass concerto, 1968; violin concerto, 1969; concerto for bassoon and percussion, 1969; double concerto, 1969; viola concerto, 1969; trumpet concerto, 1970; Symphonic sounds #1, 1971; Chamber music: 5 bagatelles for string quartet, 1968; Exposition, piano, 1968; double bass suite, 1970; sonata for unaccompanied violin, 1971; Emotions of a note #1-3, violin and percussion.
1321 South Irena, Redondo Beach, CA 90277

TAXIN, IRA
b. New York, N. Y., 19 Apr. 1950. Studied with Joyce Barthelson and Ludmila Ulehla, Scarsdale, N. Y., 1966-68; with Hugo Norden, Gardner Read, Joyce Mekeel, Boston Univ., B. M. 1972; with Jacob Druckman and Donald Martino at Tanglewood, 1972, 1973; with Roger Sessions and Elliott Carter, Juilliard School, M. M. 1974. He held fellowships at Tanglewood; Irving Berlin fellowship at Juilliard, 1973-74; American Acad. of Arts and Letters, Charles E. Ives scholarship, 1974. Other awards include the Westchester Music Teachers Council award, 1968; Westchester Philharmonic Symphony award, 1968; Boston Univ. undergraduate award, 1970; BMI awards, 1972, 1973; Margaret Grant Memorial prize, 1972; Lado, Inc., prize, 1973; Phi Mu Alpha Sinfonia prize, 1973.

WORKS: Orchestra: Poem of meditations and gatherings, 1971; concerto for piano and chamber orch., 1972; Saba, 1974; Chamber music: trio for violin, trombone, piano, 1969; trumpet sonata, 1970; 3 movements for flute and piano, 1970; 4 poems from the Song of songs, 1970; string quartet, 1971; Piece for brass quintet, 1971; Chamber piece in 2 parts, 1972; brass quintet, 1973.
629 Kappock St., Riverdale, NY 10463

TAXMAN, BARRY
b. Rock Island, Ill., 14 May 1922. Studied with Quincy Porter and Paul Hindemith, Yale Univ., B. M.; at Univ. of Chicago, M. A. He was instructor, Music and Arts Inst. of San Francisco, 1953-55; accompanist, Juilliard School, 1960. He has composed 20 orchestral pieces; 400 works for instrumental groups; 50 vocal works; and 200 keyboard pieces.
2334 Cedar St., Berkeley, CA 94708

TAYLOR, CLIFFORD
b. Pennsylvania, 30 Oct. 1923. Studied with Nikolai Lopatnikoff, Carnegie-Mellon Univ., B. F. A. 1948; with Walter Piston, Paul Hindemith, Randall Thompson, A. Tillman Merritt, Irving Fine, Harvard Univ., M. A. 1950; at Tanglewood, 1950. He received first prize, Nat. Symphony Orchestra contest, 1955; first prize, Friends of Harvey Gaul contest, 1955; first prize, Rheta A. Sosland contest, Univ. of Missouri, 1963. He was faculty member, lecturer to associate professor, Chatham Coll., 1950-63; Temple Univ., 1963-   , professor, 1969-   ,

(TAYLOR, CLIFFORD)
chairman of composition 1964-   , director of electronic music, 1968-   .

WORKS: Orchestra: Theme and variations, 1955; Introduction and dance fantasy; Concerto grosso for string orch.; Chaconne; 2 symphonies; concerto for organ and chamber orch.; Sacred verses, chorus, soloists, orch.; Chamber music: violin sonata, 1955; Adagio and allegro, from woodwind quintet, revised 1958; string quartet, 1959; trio for clarinet, cello, piano, 1960; string quartet no.1, 1960; Concert duo, violin and cello, 1961; duo for alto saxophone and trombone; Movement for 3, piano trio, 1968; 5 poems for oboe and 5 brasses, 1971; piano sonata; piano suite; Electronic: Parabolic mirrors, tape; many choral settings and songs.
149 Fernbrook Ave., Wyncote, PA 19095

TAYLOR, CORWIN H.
b. Germantown, Ohio, 14 Oct. 1905. Studied with Sidney Durst and Carl Hugo Grimm, Cincinnati Coll. of Music, B. M., M. M.; at Univ. of Cincinnati, B. S., Ed. M., Ed. D. He taught in public schools, 1933-37; Wilmington Coll., 1935-37; Cincinnati Coll. of Music, 1937-42; was bandmaster, U.S. Coast Guard, 1942-45; faculty, Peabody Cons., 1945-50; Baltimore public schools, 1950-68; professor, Univ. of Maryland, 1968-   .

WORKS: Band: Curtis Bay march, 1943; U.S. Coast Guard march, 1945; Victory review march, 1946; Los campañeros, scherzo for 3 trumpets and band, 1950; Wind ensemble: Andante and scherzo, brass quartet, 1939; 3 novelties for 4 clarinets, 1942; Inscriptions in brass, suite for brass choir, 1964.
3450 Toledo Terrace, Hyattsville, MD 20782

*TAYLOR, (JOSEPH) DEEMS
b. New York, N. Y., 22 Dec. 1885; d. New York, 3 July 1966. Studied at New York Univ., B. A. 1906; privately with Oscar Coon, 1908-11. His many honors included commissions from the New York Metropolitan Opera, 1926, 1930; honorary music doctorates, New York Univ., 1927, Dartmouth Coll. and Univ. of Rochester, 1937, Cincinnati Cons., 1941, Syracuse Univ., 1944; Litt. D. Juniata Coll., 1931; member, Nat. Inst. and American Acad. of Arts and Letters. He held editorial positions with various publications, 1906-21; was music critic, New York World, 1921-25, New York American, 1931-32; editor Musical America, 1927-29; intermission commentator, New York Philharmonic radio broadcasts, 1936-43, and on other radio programs.

WORKS: Opera: The king's henchman, libretto by Edna St. Vincent Millay, 1927; Peter Ibbetson, 1931; Ramuntcho, 1942; The dragon, 1954; Theatre: The echo, musical comedy, 1909; Orchestra: The siren song, 1912; Through the looking-glass, suite for chamber orch., 1919, full orch., 1922; Jurgen, 1925; Fantasy on 2 themes, 1925; Circus days, jazz orch., 1925, full orch., 1933; Casanova, ballet music, 1937; Processional, 1941; Christmas overture, 1943; Elegy, 1945; Restoration suite, 1950; Chamber music: The portrait of a lady, 11 instruments, 1918; Lucrece, string quartet; A kiss in Xanadu, piano; Chorus: The

(TAYLOR, (JOSEPH) DEEMS)
chambered nautilus, chorus and orch., 1914; The highwayman, baritone, women's voices, orch., 1914. He was also author of the books: Of men and music, 1937; The well-tempered listener, 1937; Music to my ears, 1941; Some enchanted evenings: the story of Rodgers and Hammerstein, 1953; The one-track mind, 1957.

*TAYLOR, PRISCILLA
4 songs for chorus and piano, to her own texts.

TAYLOR, ROWAN
b. Ogden, Utah, 1 June 1927. Studied with Leroy Robertson, Leon Dallin, Carl Fuerstner, Crawford Gates, Brigham Young Univ.; with Lukas Foss and John Vincent, Univ. of California at Los Angeles. He is conductor of the West Valley Chamber Orchestra and the Los Angeles Pierce Coll.-Community Symphony Orchestra and Brass Ensemble. His compositions include an opera, an oratorio, a cantata, and 21 symphonies.
22544 Tiara St., Woodland Hills, CA 91364

TCHEREPNIN, ALEXANDER
b. St. Petersburg, Russia, 21 Jan. 1899; U.S. citizen 1958. Studied at St. Petersburg Cons.; composition with Paul Vidal and piano with Isidor Philipp, Paris Cons. Though he is the son of Nikolai Tcherepnin, he did not study formally with his father. His mother taught him how to write down his musical ideas and by the time he entered the St. Petersburg Cons. he had composed orchestral scores, operas, ballets, 5 piano concertos, 12 piano sonatas, and many vocal and chamber works. His awards include first prize, Schott's international composition contest; David Bispham award, American Opera Society; Glinka prize; Achievement award, Chevalier of Arts and Letters, French Ministry of Culture; election to the Nat. Inst. of Arts and Letters, 1974. In 1918 his family moved to Tbilisi, where Alexander entered the university. He had by this time become a virtuoso pianist and his concert tours included four trips to the Orient as well as Europe and America. He eventually settled in the U.S., taught at San Francisco Inst. of Music and Art, 1948; De Paul Univ., 1949-64.
WORKS: Opera: Ol-Ol, after Leonid Andreyev; Die Hochzeit der Sobeide, Hofmansthal text; The marriage, completion of Moussorgsky's opera on Gogol text; The farmer and the fairy, Aspen Col. 13 Aug. 1952; Ballet: Ajanta's frescoes, 1923; Training, 1935; Trepak, 1938; Der Fahrend Schuler mit dem Teufelbannen, 1938; Legende de Razine, 1941; Le dejeuner sur l'herbe, Lanner-Tcherepnin, 1945; Chota Roustaveli, 1945; La colline des fantomes, 1946; La femme et son ombre, 1947; Le gouffre; Orchestra: 6 piano concertos, 1919, 1924, 1932, 1947, 1963, 1965; Concerto da camera, flute, violin, and chamber orch., 1924; Georgian rhapsody, cello and orch., 1924; Mystere, cello and chamber orch., 1926; 4 symphonies, 1926, 1945-51, 1954, #4 Boston, 5 Dec. 1958; Magna mater, 1927; concertino for piano trio and string orch., 1931; Festmusik; Russian dances, 1933; Georgian suite, piano and strings,

(TCHEREPNIN, ALEXANDER)
1940; Evocation, 1948; Romantic overture; Symphonic march; Suite for orchestra, 1953; harmonica concerto, 1956; Polka; Divertimento; Symphonic prayer, 1960; Georgiana; The lost flute, narrator and orch., English translation of Chinese poems; The XII, narrator and orch., poem by A. Block; Serenade, string orch., 1964; Bagatelles, piano and strings; Sonatina, timpani and orch.; Chamber music: Ode, cello and piano, 1919; piano trio, 1925; 2 string quartets, 1925, 1926; piano quintet, 1927; duo for violin and cello; 3 cello sonatas; 12 preludes, cello and piano; violin sonata; Sonatine sportive, saxophone and piano, 1939; Andante, tuba and piano, 1939; trio for 3 flutes, 1939; flute quartet, 1939; trio for 3 trumpets; March for 3 trumpets, 1939; Elegie, violin and piano; Perpetuum mobile, violin and piano, 1945; Arabesque, violin and piano; Romance, violin and piano; Suite for solo cello, 1946; Partita, accordion; Suite for harpsichord, 1966; Sonata da chiesa, viola da gambe and organ, 1966; Tzigane and Invention for accordion; Cantatas: Nativity, soloists, chorus, string quintet, percussion; Vom Spass und Ernst, low voice and string orch., 1964; The story of Ivan the fool, with narrator, 1967; Musica sacra, Festival of Easter, Lourdes, France, 28 Apr. 1973.
170 West 73rd St., New York, NY 10023

TCHEREPNIN, IVAN
b. Issy-Les-Moulineaux, France, 5 Feb. 1943; U.S. citizen 1960. Studied first with his father, Alexander Tcherepnin; with Leon Kirchner, Harvard Univ., B. A. 1964, M. A. 1969; with Henri Pousseur and Karlheinz Stockhausen in Cologne, 1965-66; with David Tudor at Mills Coll. He received the Brookline Library prize, 1964; John Knowles Paine traveling fellowship, 1965; Harvard Univ. Knight prize, 1965; ASCAP award 1966. He was lecturer, San Francisco Cons., 1969-71, Stanford Univ., 1970-72; and has been assistant professor, Harvard Univ., 1972-   .
WORKS: Chamber music: 4 pieces from before, piano solo, 1962; Cadenzas in transition, piano, clarinet and flute, 1963; Work music, electric guitar, horn, cello and clarinet, 1965; Wheelwinds, for 9 winds, 1966; Rings, string quartet and electronics, 1966; Light music for 4 instrumental groups and electronics, 1968; Les adieux, 18 players, lights, and electronics, 1971.
111 Lake View Ave., Cambridge, MA 02138

TCHEREPNIN, SERGE A.
b. Issy-Les Moulineaux, France, 2 Feb. 1941; U.S. citizen 1960. Son of Alexander Tcherepnin, studied with Nadia Boulanger in Paris; with Leon Kirchner and Billy Jim Layton, Harvard Univ., B. A. 1964; graduate studies at Princeton Univ.; with Earle Brown, Karlheinz Stockhausen, Luigi Nono, and Pierre Boulez in various European cities. He was instructor in electronic media, School of Fine Arts, New York Univ., 1968-70; on composition faculty, California Inst. of the Arts, 1970-   .
WORKS: Chamber music: Inventions for piano, 1960; Kaddish, for instrumental ensemble and actor, text by A. Ginsberg, 1961; Morning after

TCHEREPNIN, SERGE A.

(TCHEREPNIN, SERGE A.)
piece, saxophone and piano, 1965; Electronic: Heaven, tape, 1966; Film, for actors, musicians, electronics and lights, 1967; The Serge-o-phone, an electronic music machine, 1973.
California Institute of the Arts
Valencia, CA 91355

TEITELBAUM, RICHARD
b. New York, N. Y., 19 May 1939. Studied with Alfred Swan, John Davison, Claudio Spies, Haverford Coll., B. A. 1960; Aspen Music School, 1957, 1960; with William Sydeman, Mannes School of Music; with Mel Powell, Yale Univ., M. M. 1964; with Goffredo Petrassi in Rome, and Luigi Nono in Venice; Wesleyan Univ., Ph. D. candidate, 1970-71. His awards include Bradley-Keeler scholarship, 1962-63; Greenwald Memorial prize, 1964; Horatio Parker scholarship, 1963-64; John Day Jackson prize, 1964; Ditson travel fellowship, 1964-65; graduate fellowship, Wesleyan Univ., 1969-70; NDEA fellowship, 1970-71. He was faculty member, California Inst. of the Arts, 1971-72; assistant professor, School of the Art Institute of Chicago, 1972-73; assistant professor, New York Univ., Toronto, 1973-   .
WORKS: Chamber music: Intersections for piano, 1963; string trio, 1964; Concerto da camera, for 14 instruments, 1966; Electronic: In tune, for amplified heart beats and brainwaves with Moog synthesizer, 1966; La mattina presto, tape, 1969; Border region, for film, tape, slides, and optigan, 1972. He has published many articles in music journals.
R. R. 1, Gilford, Ontario, Canada

*TEMPLAR, JOAN
Flute sonata.

*TEMPLETON, ALEC
b. Cardiff, Wales, 4 July 1909; U.S. citizen 1941; d. Greenwich, Conn., 28 Mar. 1963. Studied at the Royal Coll. of Music and Royal Acad. of Music, London. He made his U.S. debut as pianist in Chicago, 1936; performed on radio and on records; toured the U.S., Canada.
WORKS: Orchestra: Concerto grosso; Concertino lirico; Bach goes to town; Mozart matriculates; Mendelssohn mows them down; Gothic concerto, 1954; Chamber music: violin sonata; 2 piano sonatas; Pocket-size sonata, clarinet and piano; string quartet; trio for flute, oboe, piano; also choral works.

*TENNEY, JAMES
Stochastic quartet, electronic, 1963.
California Institute for the Arts
Valencia, CA 91355

TEPPER, ALBERT
b. New York, N. Y., 1 June 1921. Studied with Quincy Porter, Carl McKinley, and Francis Judd Cooke, New England Cons.; with Hans Gal, Univ. of Edinburgh; privately with Tibor Serly in New York. He held a Fulbright scholarship for study in Scotland. He was instructor, New England Cons., 1947-50; faculty member, Hofstra Univ.,

(TEPPER, ALBERT)
1952-   , chairman, music department, 1954-58, 1967-73, professor, 1967-   .
WORKS: Orchestra: Tent music; symphony for strings; concertino for oboe and strings; Band: Circus overture; Chamber music: string quartet, 1946; suite for clarinet and bassoon; Chorus: Cantata, with brass and percussion, 1969; For city spring, with orch.; 5 songs from the Catullus of William Hull.
36 Honeysuckle Road, Levittown, NY 11756

*TERHUNE, ANICE POTTER
b. Hampden, Mass., 27 Oct. 1873; d. Pompton Lakes, N. J., 9 Nov. 1964. Studied in Cleveland; with Coenen in Rotterdam; and with Edward M. Bowman in New York. She married the author, Arthur Payson Terhune in 1901.
WORKS: Opera: Hero Nero, 1904; The woodland princess, 1911; also several books of children's songs. In 1945 she published an autobiography, Across the line.

*TERRY, FRANCES
b. Connecticut, 1884. Published a violin sonata.

*TGETTIS, NICHOLAS
Piano sonatina; choral works.

*THATCHER, HOWARD RUTLEDGE
b. Baltimore, Md., 17 Sep. 1878; d. Baltimore, 21 Feb. 1973. Graduated from Peabody Cons.; received an honorary doctorate, 1973. He was organist, choirmaster, violist, conductor, and teacher in the Baltimore area; on the faculty at Peabody Cons., 1911-53.
WORKS: Opera: The double miracle, 1-act; The king's jester, operetta; Orchestra: Concert overture; Legend; Elegy, 4 cellos and orch.; viola concerto; violin concerto; clarinet concerto; Lyric suite, 1951; horn concerto, 1959; Chamber music: cello sonatina; Pastoral and rondo, 4 violins; string quintet; string quartet; piano quartet; suite for 3 violins; Petite suite, 2 violins and piano; Organ: Legend; Fantasy on Concord, 1958.

THAYER, FRED M.
b. Ithaca, N. Y., 19 Dec. 1941. Studied with Warren Benson and Gregg Smith, Ithaca Coll.; with Karl Korte and Ezra Laderman, State Univ. of New York at Binghamton; Robert Palmer and Marice Stith, Cornell Univ.; and with Samuel Dolin, Univ. of Toronto. He was winner in a student composer contest, State Univ. of New York at Potsdam. He was a Peace Corps volunteer as elementary music teacher in Colombia, S. A., 1963-65; taught in public school, Elmira, N. Y., 1967-71; director, Elmira Cantata Singers, 1969-71; director, Harpur Chorale, Binghamton, 1972-73.
WORKS: Opera: The tinker's wedding, 1-act chamber opera; Chamber music: duo for violin and cello; Adagio, oboe, violin, cello, double bass; The earth says May, song cycle for soprano, oboe, horn, cello.
1901 Danby Road, Ithaca, NY 14850

*THAYER, WILLIAM ARMOUR
   b. Brooklyn, N. Y., 5 Oct. 1874; d. Brooklyn,
9 Dec. 1933. Studied with Dudley Buck; was
organist in Brooklyn, 1893-1933; professor,
Adelphi Coll., 1907-33. He composed numerous
songs, including the well-known My laddie.

THEOBALD, JAMES CHESTER
   b. Winchester, Mass., 10 Mar. 1950. Studied
with Edward J. Miller, Edward Diemente, and
Alvin Epstein, Hartt Coll.; with Robert Lombardo
and Ramon Zupko, Chicago Musical Coll. He won
theory and composition awards at Hartt Coll.,
1973. He was public school teacher, 1971-72;
announcer WWUH-FM, Hartford, 1971-73.
   WORKS: Chamber music: Jabberwocky, narrator
and 5 instruments; Plane-5, 4 instruments;
Alternatives 720, percussion solo; Meditations,
cello and piano; Aftermath, brass and percussion;
Llousansa-5, string quartet and soprano; The
boowahjeddyfogiros, 5 instruments; Chorus:
Alleluia - amen; Open spaces; Something about
somebodies; Sagittarius, with chamber orch.
   26 Perry Street, New York, NY 10014

*THIELMAN, RONALD
   Chelsea suite, band; Overture odalisque, band.
   New Mexico State University
   University Park, NM 88003

THIEL-PHILLIPS, VIVIAN D. See PHILLIPS, VIVIAN D.

*THIMMIG, LESLIE
   b. Santa Maria, Calif., 1943. Studied with
John LaMontaine, Eastman School of Music, B. M.
1965; with Bulent Arel and Mel Powell, Yale
Univ., M. A. 1969. He was clarinetist with the
Eastman Wind Ensemble and Philharmonic, and
with the New Haven Symphony; and jazz saxophonist in Chicago and New York, and with his
quintet on a tour of Poland sponsored by the
U.S. State Department, 1963. His compositions
include 7 profiles for string quartet.
   School of Music, University of Wisconsin
   Madison, WI 53706

*THOMAS, ALAN
   Tender buttons, women's chorus, text by
Gertrude Stein.

THOMAS, ANDREW
   b. Ithaca, N. Y., 8 Oct. 1939. Studied with
Karel Husa, Robert Palmer, and Burrill Phillips,
Cornell Univ., B. A.; with Luciano Berio and
Elliott Carter, Juilliard School, M. S.,
D. M. A.; also studied with Otto Luening,
Robert Moevs, and Nadia Boulanger. He received
a Thorne Music Fund grant, 1973; commissions
from Da Capo Chamber Players and The Light
Fantastic Players. He has been faculty member,
Juilliard School, 1972-   ; director, Lenox
Arts Center Ensemble, 1973; general manager,
The Composers' Forum, 1973-   ; artistic
director, Notes from Underground, performing
ensemble for contemporary music, 1973-   .

(THOMAS, ANDREW)
   WORKS: Chamber music: 2 studies for
woodwind quintet; The roman de Fauvel, soprano,
percussion, and piano; Presidio 27, soprano
and brass quintet, 1970; Dirge in the woods, in
memory of Hall Overton, chamber ensemble, New
York, 11 May 1973.
   251 West 76th Street, New York, NY 10023

THOMAS, C. EDWARD
   b. Vineland, N. J., 19 Nov. 1935. Studied at
Wheaton Coll., Ill., B. M.: American Cons.,
M. M.; Univ. of Iowa, D. M. A. candidate 1972.
He has been associate professor, Bethel Coll.,
St. Paul, Minn., 1966-1974; executive director,
Afro-American Music Opportunities Asso., 1969-74;
president, Narthex Records, 1967-74.
   WORKS: Chorus: I have a dream, cantata;
A fantasy of carols; Sleep, holy babe; Joy to
the world.
   2909 Wayzata Boulevard
   Minneapolis, MN 55440

*THOMAS, HELEN
   b. East Liverpool, Ohio, 29 May   . Studied
at New England Cons. Her published works include
an operetta, Song of yesterday, and songs.
   105 West 55th St., New York, NY 10019

THOMAS, JOHN PATRICK
   b. Denver, Colo., 26 Mar. 1941. Studied with
Allan Willman, Univ. of Wyoming, 1959-61; with
Andrew Imbrie and Seymour Shifrin, Univ. of
California at Berkeley, 1961-66; with Darius
Milhaud and Charles Jones, Aspen School. He
received the Copley Found. award; Aspen Fromm
Found. prize; Theodore Presser Found. grant;
2 Alfred Hertz Found. fellowships; Di Lorenzo
composition prize; Fromm Found. fellowship to
Tanglewood. He was lecturer, 1966-67, assistant
professor, 1969-71, State Univ. of New York at
Buffalo; has performed widely in the U.S. and
abroad as a singer.
   WORKS: Orchestra: 1963; Chamber music;
Various objects disturb the water's surface,
string quartet, 1962; 4 poems of William Searle,
soprano and piano, 1963-65; Ostraka, brass
quintet, 1965; Canciones, bass-baritone and
clarinet, 1965-67; Last rites, counter-tenor and
guitar, 1971; Mignon, soprano and cello, 1973;
Keyboard: Pieces for Joan Gallegos, 2 pianos,
1963; Peniel, organ, 1967; 145 W. 85th Street,
piano, 1964-71.
   Box 406, 234 North Day Street
   Powell, WY 82435

*THOMAS, PAUL LINDSLEY
   Come, see the place, chorus, brass, organ;
Fanfare and alleluia, chorus and trumpets;
Variations on the Welsh hymn tune, Aberystwyth,
organ.

THOME, DIANE
   b. New York, N. Y., 25 Jan. 1942. Studied with
Darius Milhaud at Aspen, Colo.; with Roy Harris,
Inter-American Univ. of Puerto Rico; A. U.
Boscovitch in Israel; and with Milton Babbitt at
Princeton Univ. Her awards include

437

THOME, DIANE

(THOME, DIANE)
David Halstead award, Univ. of Pennsylvania;
Charles Ives award, Nat. Fed. of Music Clubs;
Nat. Society of Arts and Letters award; fellow-
ships at Columbia Univ., Univ. of Pennsylvania,
and Princeton Univ. She was pianist for the
Israel Dance Theatre, 1963-64; has taught piano,
Princeton Univ., 1971-   ; theory at Rutgers
Univ., 1973-   .
      WORKS: Electronic: January variations,
computer-synthesized tape; Polyvalence for
computer and instruments; Le berceau de miel,
string quartet, alto flute, voice, and tape.
      H305 Garden Court, 4631 Pine Street
      Philadelphia, PA 19143

THOME, JOEL
      b. Detroit, Mich., 7 Jan. 1939. Studied at
Eastman School of Music, B. M. 1960; conducting
certificate, Ecole International, Nice, France,
1960; with A. U. Boscovitch in Israel; with
George Rochberg, Univ. of Pennsylvania, M. M.
1967. He received the David Halsted prize,
1965; MacDowell fellowship, 1968; and many commissions. He was faculty member, Israel Acad.
of Music, Univ. of Tel-Aviv. 1961-64; teaching
fellow, Univ. of Pennsylvania, 1964-67; assistant
professor, Glassboro State Coll.; 1973, director-
conductor, Philadelphia Composers' Forum.
      WORKS: Ballet: Act without words no. 1,
adapted from Beckett, electronic score;
Magritte! Magritte!; 3 poems; Chamber music:
Prisms, solo piano, percussion and chamber
ensemble, 1964; In memoriam Ury, 1965; Multimedia: Circus, tape, 5 musicians, magician,
polarized light projections.
      H305 Garden Court, 4631 Pine Street
      Philadelphia, PA 19143

THOMPSON, DONALD BRYCE
      b. Chicago, Ill., 15 Oct. 1925. Studied with
Frank Cookson, Northwestern Univ.; with Halsey
Stevens, Ernest Kanitz, and Ingolf Dahl, Univ.
of Southern California, B. M. 1949, M. M. 1951,
M. S. 1971. He won 2nd prize in a Nat. Fed. of
Music Clubs contest. He has been member of the
technical staff, Space Division, Rockwell International, 1951-
      WORKS: Band: Partita; Intermezzo; 5 pieces
(with Halsey Stevens); Diptych for brass and
percussion; Chamber music: Trio concertato,
clarinet, horn, piano; 3 monologues for
trombone; trombone sonata; string quartet;
Allegro vivo, marimba and piano.
      12671 Chase Street, Garden Court, CA 92645

*THOMPSON, RANDALL
      b. New York, N. Y., 21 Apr. 1899. Studied at
Harvard Univ., A. B. 1920, M. A. 1922; American
Acad. in Rome, 1922-25; Univ. of Rochester,
D. M. 1933; with Ernest Bloch in New York, 1920-
21. His awards include Damrosch fellowship,
1922; Guggenheim fellowship, 1929-31; Elizabeth
Sprague Coolidge medal, 1941; Ditson award,
1944; Eastman School publication award; member
Nat. Inst. of Arts and Letters; and many
commissions. He was faculty member, Wellesley
Coll., 1927-29, 1936; Harvard Univ., 1929;

(THOMPSON, RANDALL)
guest conductor, Dessoff Choirs, New York,
1931-32; choral conductor, Juilliard School,
1931-32; professor, Univ. of California,
Berkeley, 1937-39; director, Curtis Inst.
1939-41; professor and department chairman,
Univ. of Virginia, 1941-45; professor, Princeton
Univ., 1945-48; professor, Harvard Univ.,
1948-65, department chairman, 1952-57.
      WORKS: Opera: Solomon and Balkis, 1942;
Theatre: music for The Grand Street follies,
1922; The straw hat, 1926; Orchestra: Pierrot
and Cothurnus, 1923; The piper at the gates of
dawn, 1924; 3 symphonies, 1930, 1932, 1949;
A trip to Nahant, fantasy, 1955; Jazz: Jazz
poem, piano and orch., 1928; Chamber music:
The wind in the willows, string quartet, 1924;
suite for oboe, clarinet, viola, 1940; string
quartet, 1941; Chorus: 5 odes of Horace, 1924;
Pueri Hebraeorum, women's voices, 1928; Rosemary,
women's voices, 1929; The peaceable kingdom,
1936; Tarantella, men's voices, 1937; The lark
in the morn, 1938; Alleluia, 1940; The testament
of freedom, men's voices, 1943; The last words
of David, with orch., 1949; The place of the
blest; Mass of the Holy Spirit, 1955; Ode to
the Virginian voyage, 1956; Requiem, 1928;
Frostiana, 1959; The mirror of St. Anne,
antiphonal setting of Isaac Watts text in inverse
contrary imitation; The nativity according to
to St. Luke, oratorio, 1961.
      22 Larch Road, Cambridge, MA 02138

*THOMPSON, VAN DENMAN
      b. Andover, N. H., 10 Dec. 1890. Studied at
Colby Acad.; Harvard Univ., 1908-09; New England
Cons., 1909-10. He received a Nat. Fed. of
Music Clubs prize, 1919; commission from the
Methodist Episcopal Church for the 150th
anniversary, 1934; D. M., De Pauw Univ. 1935;
was a fellow of the American Guild of Organists.
He was faculty member, Woodland Coll., 1910-11;
from 1911, professor, De Pauw Univ., chairman,
School of Music, from 1937. His compositions
include The evangel of the new world, oratorio,
1934; church anthems, organ and piano pieces.

THOMSON, MILLARD S.
      b. Hartford, Conn., 13 Aug. 1918. Studied at
Wesleyan Univ., B. A.; with Isadore Freed and
Arnold Franchetti, Hartt Coll. of Music,
M. M.; with H. Owen Reed and Paul Harder,
Michigan State Univ., Ph. D. 1964. He was
faculty member, Brown Univ., 1949-56; Michigan
State Univ., 1964-65; associate professor,
Plymouth State Coll., 1965-   .
      WORKS: Theatre: Give it a whirl, musical
play; Chamber music: Epitaph, violin and piano;
Meadow interval, song cycle; Shadows of autumn,
cantata; Introduction and dance, clarinet and
piano; Chorus: Break forth into joy, anthem.
      20 Avery Street, Plymouth, NH 03264

*THOMSON, VIRGIL
      b. Kansas City, Mo., 25 Nov. 1896. Studied at
Harvard Univ., A. B. 1922; with Nadia Boulanger
in Paris. His awards include Officer, Legion
of Honor, France; gold medal, Nat. Inst. of

(THOMSON, VIRGIL)
Arts and Letters; honorary doctorates, Syracuse
Univ., 1949, Rutgers Univ., 1956; membership
American Acad. of Arts and Sciences. He was
organist, King's Chapel, Boston, 1923-24; lived
in Paris for 10 years; was writer on music for
many publications; music critic, New York
Herald Tribune, 1940-54.
WORKS: Opera: 4 saints in 3 acts, text by
Gertrude Stein, 1934; The mother of us all,
Stein text, 1947; Lord Byron, 1970, Juilliard
School, 20 Apr. 1972; Ballet: Filling station,
1937; Orchestra: 2 symphonies, 1928, 1941;
5 suites; The Seine at night, 1948; Wheatfield
at noon, 1948; cello concerto, 1949; Fugues and
cantilenas; Sea piece with birds, 1952; 5 songs
for voice and orch., 1952; concerto for flute,
strings, percussion, 1954; The feast of love,
baritone and orch., 1964; Band: A solemn music
and a joyful fugue, 1949; Chamber music: Sonata
da chiesa, 5 instruments, 1926; 5 portraits for
4 clarinets, 1929; violin sonata, 1930; 4 portraits, violin and piano, 1931; 2 string
quartets, 1931, 1932; 4 piano sonatas; Serenade,
flute and violin; organ and piano pieces; Chorus:
Capital capitals; Masses; Medea; Scenes from the
Holy Infancy; Missa pro defunctis, 1960; Cantata
based on nonsense rhymes, Towson State Coll.,
Md., 18 Nov. 1973; Film scores: The plow that
broke the plains, 1939; The river, 1942;
Louisiana story, 1948; The goddess; Power among
men; Voyage to America, 1964. He is author of
the following books: State of music, 1939; The
musical scene, 1945; The art of judging music,
1948; Music right and left, 1951; Virgil Thomson,
an autobiography, 1967; American music since
1910, 1971.
222 West 23rd Street, New York, NY 10011

THOMSON, WILLIAM
b. Ft. Worth, Tex., 24 May 1927. Studied with
Bernhard Heiden, Indiana Univ., Ph. D. He
received awards from Nat. Fed. of Music Clubs
composer competition; Texas Composers; and was
Ford Found. composer-in-residence, 1960-61. He
was faculty member, Sul Ross State Coll., 1951-
60; Indiana Univ., 1961-69; Univ. of Hawaii,
1967-68; Case Western Reserve Univ. and Cleveland
Inst. of Music, 1969-73; professor, Univ. of
Arizona, 1973-   .
WORKS: Orchestra: Transformations; Fantasia
and dance, for clarinet and orch. (or piano);
Band: Permutations; Chorus: Desert seasons.
7421 Sabino Vista Drive, Tucson, AZ 85711

THORNE, FRANCIS
b. Bay Shore, N. Y., 23 June 1922. Studied with
Paul Hindemith at Yale Univ.; privately with
David Diamond in Florence, Italy. He has
received a Nat. Inst. of Arts and Letters award;
and Nat. Endowment for the Arts fellowship. He
was faculty member, Juilliard School, 1971-73;
executive director, Walter W. Naumburg Found.,
1969-72; executive director, Lenox Arts Center,
1972-   .
WORKS: Orchestra: 2 symphonies, 1961, 1964;
symphony in 1 movement, 1963; Elegy, 1963;
Fantasia for string orch., 1963; Burlesque

(THORNE, FRANCIS)
variations, 1964; Rhapsodic variations, piano
and orch., 1965; piano concerto, 1966; Lyric
variations; Gemini variations, viola, double
bass, orch., 1968; Solar plexus, electric
guitar and orch., 1968; Chamber deviation I,
clarinet, double bass, orch., 1968; Liebesrock,
1969; symphony #3, percussion and strings, 1969;
Antiphonies, wind and percussion, 1970; Song of
the Carolina Low Country, chorus and orch.,
Charleston, 13 Feb. 1971; Fanfare, fugue, and
funk; Chamber music: Songs and dances, 1969;
6 set pieces for 13 players; Chamber deviation
II, brass quintet, guitar, percussion, 1971;
trio, New York, 13 Feb. 1973; Voice: Songs of
the Great South Bay, soprano, New York, 8 May
1974.
116 East 66th Street, New York, NY 10021

THORNTON, WILLIAM
b. Birmingham, Ala., 31 July 1919. Studied with
Helen Gunderson and Joyce Michelle, Louisiana
State Univ., B. M. 1941, M. M. 1946; with Halsey
Stevens, Ingolf Dahl, and Roger Sessions, Univ.
of Southern California, Ph. D. 1953. His awards
include Nat. Fed. of Music Clubs, 1st prize;
Carolyn Alchin award; Western Composers award;
Composers of Louisiana award; Archives of Texas
Composers award; several commissions. He was
instructor, Univ. of Minnesota, 1955-56;
chairman, division of fine arts, Parsons Coll.,
1956-60; chairman, department of music, Trinity
Coll., 1960-   .
WORKS: Orchestra: Symphonic dance;
Introduction and dance; Festive music; Contrastes
Mexicanos; symphony no. 1; Serenade, winds and
percussion; Chamber music: violin sonatina;
cello sonata; 2 string quartets; harpsichord
sonata; piano sonata; Serenade, clarinet and
flute.
347 Sharon Drive, San Antonio, TX 78216

THREATTE, CHARLES
b. Atlanta, Ga., 15 Feb. 1940. Studied with
John Boda and Carlisle Floyd, Florida State
Univ.; with Darius Milhaud and Charles Jones,
Aspen, Colo. He received 1st prize, Florida
Composers League, 1960; prizes, Aspen Composers
contest, 1969, 1970, 1972. He was composer-in-
residence, Youth Experimental Opera Workshop,
Atlanta, Ga., 1970; choirmaster, Presbyterian
Church, 1973-74; adjunct instructor and
consultant, Rollins Coll., 1974.
WORKS: Orchestra: Processionals, 1970;
Symphonies of carols, Orlando, Fla., 10 Dec.
1971; Fantasy, Orlando, 2 May 1974; Wind
ensemble: 3 antiphonies for 2 brass choirs,
Aspen, Colo., 19 July 1973; Chamber music:
flute sonata, 1959; Introduction and scherzo,
brass quartet, 1965; Ode, horn and piano, 1967;
3 miniatures for flute alone, 1968; Fantasy,
flute, harp and viola, 1969; Prelude, ode, and
postlude, flute and harp, 1972; Serenade, flute,
oboe, bassoon, 1973; also works for chorus and
solo voice.
1530 Woodland Avenue, Winter Park, FL 32789

TIERNEY, HARRY AUSTIN

*TIERNEY, HARRY AUSTIN
b. Perth Amboy, N. J., 21 May 1890; d. New York,
N. Y., 22 Mar. 1965. Studied piano at Virgil
Cons., New York and for awhile was a concert
pianist; then turned to composing popular and
musical shows.
WORKS: Ballet: Prelude to a holiday in
Hong Kong; Musical comedies: Irene, 1919;
Ziegfeld follies, 1919, 1920, 1924; The Broadway
whirl; Up she goes, 1922; Kid boots, 1923; Rio
Rita, 1927; Royal vagabond; Songs:
M-I-S-S-I-S-S-I-P-P-I, 1916; If you're in love
you'll waltz, and many others.

*TIETJENS, PAUL
b. St. Louis, Mo., 22 May 1877; d. St. Louis,
25 Nov. 1943. Studied piano with Leschetizky,
and Bauer. He was soloist with the St. Louis
Symphony at 14; taught privately; was music
director, Maude Adams productions, 1916-19,
1930.
WORKS: Opera: The tents of the Arabs;
Theatre: The wizard of Oz; music for Barrie's
Kiss for Cinderella; Orchestra: Carnival;
Rustic Sketches; and songs.

TILLIS, FREDERICK C.
b. Galveston, Tex., 5 Jan. 1930. Studied at
Wiley Coll., B. A. cum laude 1949; with Philip
Bezanson, Univ. of Iowa, M. A. 1952, Ph. D. 1963;
with Samuel Adler, North Texas State Univ.,
summers, 1959, 1960. His awards have included
United Negro Coll. Fund Fellowships, 1961-62 and
1962-63; Danforth associateship, 1969; several
commissions. He served in the Air Force,
1952-56, band director, 1954-56; faculty posts
have included Wiley Coll., instructor, 1949-51,
assistant professor, director of instrumental
music, 1956-61, associate professor, chairman,
music department, 1963-64; professor, Grambling
Coll., 1964-67; professor, head of music department, Kentucky State Coll., 1967-69; associate
professor, director of jazz workshop, Univ. of
Massachusetts, Amherst, 1969-   ; consultant
and summer lecturer, Regis Coll.
WORKS: Orchestra: Designs for orchestra,
1963; Band: Overture to a dance, 1961; Celebration, 1966; Jazz ensemble: 1 dozen rocks, Inc.,
1971; Jazz metamorphosis, 1972; Blue stone
diferencia, 1972; Chamber music: quartet for
woodwinds and cello, 1952; string trio, 1961;
Phantasy, viola and piano, 1961; brass quintet,
1962; quintet for 4 woodwinds and percussion,
1962; Motions, trombone and piano, 1964; piano
trio, 1972; Seton concerto for trumpet, 1973;
also works for chorus, solo voice, keyboard
instruments and electronic tape.
55 Grantwood Drive, Amherst, MA 01002

*TIOMKIN, DMITRI
b. St. Petersburg, Russia, 10 May 1894; U.S.
citizen 1937. Studied at St. Petersburg Cons.
and St. Petersburg Univ. His many awards include
L. L. D., St. Mary's Univ.; Chevalier, French Legion of Honor; Hollywood Foreign Press Club
awards, 1952, 1954, 1956; Greater Los Angeles
Press Club award, 1959; Christopher award, 1959;
at least 3 Academy awards for film scores and

(TIOMKIN, DMITRI)
several nominations. He has been concert
pianist and conductor since 1919, composer of
more than 120 film scores.
WORKS: Film scores: Bridge of San Luis
Rey; Duel in the sun; Mr. Smith goes to
Washington; Corsican brothers; Portrait of
Jeannie; Lost horizon; Cyrano de Bergerac; Dial
M for murder; The moon and sixpence; High noon,
Academy award, 1952; The chameleon; The high
and mighty, Academy award, 1954; Wild is the
wind; Friendly persuasion; Giant; The old man
and the sea, Academy award, 1958.

TIPEI, SEVER
b. Bucharest, Romania, 1 Nov. 1943; to U.S. 1972.
Studied at the Bucharest Cons., M. A. 1967; Univ.
of Michigan, doctoral candidate, 1972-73. He
was music critic in Bucharest, 1964-71; then
went to Paris and joined GERM, an avant garde
group of composers and performers, and was very
active as a pianist performing contemporary
works. He has written articles on music theory.
WORKS: Chamber music: Stanzas, for 18 solo
strings, 1969; Translation, voice, clarinet,
prepared piano, 1970; Single tone, 5 musicians
playing the same tone, 1971; Make your own music,
for an amateur musician and an exotic wind
instrument, 1973; Chorus: Another little while,
16 solo voices, 1969; Piano: sonata, 1968;
also several film scores.
1403 East 5th Street, Royal Oak, MI 48067

TIPTON, CLYDE
b. Richmond, Va., 17 Aug. 1934. Studied at
Westminster Choir Coll., M. M.; with Roger
Sessions; and with Darius Milhaud at Aspen, Colo.
He is master of music, Lawrenceville Preparatory
School, N. J., and professor, Rider Coll.
WORKS: Opera: Aleatoric operatic scenes;
Medea; The forced marriage, on Moliere text;
Theatre: Indian summer, musical for the young;
Orchestra: Graduation music, processional and
progrediendum; Chamber music: In praise of,
5 brass, organ, and bells; Sound scheme for
strings; Span, violin, flute, cello; Chorale with
transparencies, string quartet; Chorus: Mod
magnificat, women's voices; Hodie; O little
town; And death shall have no dominion; 4
pounds, text by Ezra Pound.
44 Merritt Drive, Trenton, NJ 08638

TIPTON, JULIUS R. III
b. Memphis, Tenn., 4 Mar. 1942. Studied with
Charles Knox, Mississippi Coll., B. M. 1964;
with Kenneth Klaus, Louisiana State Univ.,
M. M. 1967; with William L. Hooper, New Orleans
Baptist Seminary, Ed. D. 1972. He has been
choral director, composer-in-residence, and
acting department chairman, Xavier Univ. of
Louisiana, 1972-   ; music director, Woodland
Presbyterian Church, New Orleans, 1969-   .
WORKS: Opera: Judas; Orchestra: Variazioni
da chiesa; Chorus: He is coming; Be thou my
vision; I am thine, O Lord; A song of praise;
God is our refuge and our strength; Hear, hear,

(TIPTON, JULIUS R. III)
O ye nations; A new song; Songs: Alas, and did
my savior bleed; Song of Christmas night.
171 Roselyn Park Place
New Orleans, LA 70114

*TIRCUIT, HEUWELL (ANDREW)
b. Plaquemine, La., 18 Oct. 1931. Studied at
Louisiana State Univ.; Northwestern Univ., M. M.
1964. He played drums from early boyhood; was
percussionist, U.S. Army bands, 1954-56; played
percussion in Japanese orchestras and wrote
music criticism for Japanese news papers, 1956-
63; then was music critic for the Chicago
American, later, the San Francisco Chronicle.
    WORKS: Ballet: The lonely people, 1950;
Argument, 1959; Orchestra: Manga, suite, 1959;
cello concerto, 1960; A singing of instruments,
1960; Knell, 27 solo flutes and percussion,
1962; Dance patterns, solo percussion and orch.,
1962; Chronological variations, 1963; a cycle
of 6 concertos, 1966-72; Fool's dance, solo
percussion and orch., 1967; percussion concerto,
1969; concerto for violin and 10 wind instruments, 1971; Chamber music: 2 string quartets,
1953, 1957; string trio, 1960; violin sonata,
1960; viola sonata, 1961; Erotica I, solo alto
flute, 1961; Cassation, cello and wind quintet,
1961; flute sonata, 1968; Erotica II, percussion
solo, 1970; Erotica III, solo cello, 1971;
Chorus: 3 cantatas, 1959, 1962, 1967.
    221 Longford Drive, San Francisco, CA 94101

TIRRO, FRANK PASCALE
b. Omaha, Neb., 20 Sep. 1935. Studied with
Robert Beadell, Univ. of Nebraska; with Anthony
Donata and Frank Cookson, Northwestern Univ.;
with Leonard B. Meyer, Univ. of Chicago. He
received the Ida Vreeland award, 1960; Nat. Fed.
of Music Clubs award, 1961; Harvard Univ. Villa
I Tatti fellowship, 1970-71; ASCAP awards, 1970,
1971, 1973. He was faculty member, Univ. of
Chicago, 1961-70; Univ. of Kansas, 1971-72;
assistant professor, Duke Univ., 1972-   ,
chairman, music department, 1974-   .
    WORKS: Ballet: Exorcise; Masque of the
red death; Orchestra: symphony, 1973; Chamber
music: Antiphonal suite, organ and brass;
clarinet sonata; Chorus: American jazz mass;
American jazz te deum; Sing a new song; Keyboard:
Church sonata for organ; Melismas for carillon.
    Department of Music, Duke University
    Durham, NC 27708

TITCOMB, EVERETT
b. Amesbury, Mass., 30 June 1884; d. Boston,
31 Dec. 1968. Was the first American to have
a composition performed at the Annual Festival
of Church Music in London, where in 1936 massed
choirs sang his I will not leave you comfortless
at the Chrystal Palace. He received an honorary
doctorate of music from Nashotah House Seminary
in 1954. His experiences as choir boy at 9,
church organist at 16, choirmaster at 18, led
to acceptance of the post of organist-choirmaster
at the Church of St. John the Evangelist, Boston,
in 1910, a position he held until retirement
in 1960. For a time he also served as music

(TITCOMB, EVERETT)
director of the Canterbury Choir at Trinity
Church, Boston, and taught courses in liturgical
music at Boston Univ. and the New England Cons.
    WORKS: About 150 published works for
choir and organ.

TITTLE, JOHN STEPHEN
b. Willard, Ohio, 20 May 1935. Studied with
Harold Miles, Kent State Univ.; Howard Whittaker,
Cleveland Music School Settlement; Hilmar
Luckhardt and Robert Crane, Univ. of Wisconsin,
M. M. He was teaching assistant, Univ. of
Wisconsin, 1966-69; assistant professor,
Dalhousie Univ., Nova Scotia, 1970-   .
    WORKS: Chamber music: string quartet,
1966; All things change, and yet do not, a cycle
of Chinese and Japanese poems for small choir,
flute, harp, cello, 1966; Morning music, horn
and percussion, 1967; Summer music, double bass,
marimba, percussion, 1968; Last song and dance
for Sita, for 16 players, 1968; Winter's not
forever, soprano, female speaker, 6 players,
1971; Moondance (curious), flute, oboe, piano,
percussion, 1972; It is there all the time,
double bass and harpsichord, 1972; This time/that
time, 4 brass, piano, percussion, 1973; Multimedia: ...his circle completed..., for 2 choirs,
2 speakers, small orch., optional dancers, projections, etc., 1968-72.
    Boutilier's Point, Halifax County
    Nova Scotia, Canada

*TOCH, ERNST
b. Vienna, Austria, 7 Dec. 1887; U.S. citizen
1940; d. Los Angeles, Calif., 1 Oct. 1964.
First studied medicine and philosophy, Univ. of
Vienna and Univ. of Heidelberg, Ph. D.; taught
himself music; later gave up medicine to become
piano teacher and composer. His awards include
the Mozart prize, 1909; Mendelssohn prize, 1910;
Austrian State prize, 4 times; Pulitzer prize,
1956; member, Nat. Inst. of Arts and Letters.
He was lecturer, New School for Social Research,
1934-36; professor, Univ. of Southern California,
1937-48; also taught privately and composed for
films.
    WORKS: Opera: The princess and the pea,
1927; Egon and Emilie, 1928; The fan, 1930;
Theatre: Enamoured Harlequin, puppet show,
1964; Orchestra: Pinocchio, a merry overture,
1936; Hyperion, 1948; 5 symphonies, 1950, 1951,
1955, 1957, 1964; Notturno, 1953; Peter Pan,
1956; Symphony for strings, 1964; 3 pantomimes,
1964; Chamber music: 13 string quartets; piano
quintet, 1938; many other chamber works; Chorus:
The water, oratorio, 1930; Bitter herbs, cantata
with soloists, narrator, and orch., 1941;
numerous piano works.

TODD, GEORGE BENNETT
b. Minneapolis, Minn., 31 May 1935. Studied
with Roger Sessions, Earl Kim, J. K. Randall,
Princeton Univ., M. M. He has been faculty
member, Middlebury Coll., 1965-   , associate
professor and chairman, music department,
1971-   .

TODD, GEORGE BENNETT

(TODD, GEORGE BENNETT)
WORKS: Chamber music: Haiku songs, soprano and chamber ensemble, 1968; Elisions, chamber group, 1969; Sequentials, for any large ensemble 1972.
R. D. 3, Middlebury, VT 05953

TOENSING, RICHARD
b. St. Paul, Minn., 11 Mar. 1940. Studied with Ross Lee Finney, Leslie Bassett, and George B. Wilson, Univ. of Michigan, D. M. A. He received B. M. I. student composer awards, 1963, 1964; Joseph Bearnes prize, Columbia Univ., 1965; and commissions. He was assistant professor and director of choirs, Upsala Coll., 1966-73; assistant professor, Univ. of Colorado, 1973-   .
WORKS: Band: Doxologies, 1965; Cornell Univ., Apr. 1971; For all the wild things; Chamber music: Homages, chamber orch., Chorus: Easter motet, with tape; 16-voice mass; Piano: Sycamore shade blue rag; All-Upsala banquet tablecloth wiping-up rag; Organ: Sounds and changes II and III; Doxologies II; several multimedia pieces.
600 Ithaca Drive, Boulder, CO 80303

TORCASO, ENRICO
b. New Kensington, Pa., 27 Nov. 1936. Studied with Joseph Wilcox Jenkins, Duquesne Univ., with Frank McCarty, Univ. of Pittsburgh. He has been teaching fellow, Univ. of Pittsburgh; instructor, Duquesne Univ.
WORKS: Orchestra: Introduction and allegro; Chamber music: Divertimento for octet, strings and woodwinds; Ellipse, brass quintet; Refractions, percussion, piano, cello.
1632 Victoria Avenue, Arnold, PA 15068

*TOURS, FRANK
b. London, England, 1 Sep. 1877; to U.S. 1904; d. Santa Monica, Calif., 2 Feb. 1963. Studied at the Royal Cons. in London. He was director of Broadway shows; then music director and composer for Paramount Music Corporation. He wrote musicals and songs, the latter including In Flanders Fields.

TOWER, JOAN
b. New Rochelle, N. Y., 6 Sep. 1938. Studied with Henry Brant and Louis Calabro, Bennington Coll., B. A.; with Otto Luening, Jack Beeson, and Chou Wen-chung, Columbia Univ., M. A., D. M. A.; with Darius Milhaud at Aspen, Colo.; and with Wallingford Riegger, Ralph Shapey, and Charles Wuorinen in New York. She was lecturer, C. W. Post Coll., Long Island Univ., 1968-71; visiting lecturer, Bard Coll., 1972-   ; pianist for the Da Capo Chamber Players.
WORKS: Chamber music: percussion quartet, 1963; Brimset, 1965; Movements for flute and piano, 1968; Prelude for 5 players, 1971; Breakfast rhythms, New York, 23 Feb. 1974.
545 West 111th Street, New York, NY 10025

TOWNSEND, DOUGLAS
b. New York, N. Y., 8 Nov. 1921. Graduated from High School of Music and Art, 1941; studied privately with Tibor Serly, Stefan Wolpe, and

(TOWNSEND, DOUGLAS)
Felix Greissle in New York; with Aaron Copland at Tanglewood, and with Otto Luening at Bennington. He held scholarships for Tanglewood, 1947, and for Bennington Composers Conference, 1949, 1950. In addition to his position as lecturer, Brooklyn Coll., 1958-   , he has been active as editor, arranger, musicologist, and composer.
WORKS: Opera: Lima beans, chamber opera, New York, 7 Jan. 1956; Orchestra: Fantasy for small orchestra, 1951; Adagio for strings, 1956; Symphony for string orch., New York, 29 Nov. 1958; Chamber symphony no. 1; Suite no. 1 for strings, New York, 8 Dec. 1973; Chamber music: Ballet suite, for 3 clarinets, 1956; Tower music, brass quintet, 1957; Dance, improvisation, and fugue, flute and piano; 8x8 variations on a theme of Milhaud; Chamber concerto no. 1, violin and string quartet, 1957; Chamber concerto no. 2, trombone and strings; 4 fantasies on American folk songs, piano 4-hands, 1957, later orchestrated; duo for violas, 1957.
172 East 4th Street, New York, NY 10009

TRACK, GERHARD
b. Vienna, Austria, 17 Sep. 1934; to U.S. 1958. Studied with Otto Siegl and Alfred Uhl, Vienna Acad. of Music. He received 2nd prize in the Austrian State Radio Network competition for sacred music, 1970. He was music director and conductor, Vienna Boys Choir, 1953-58; associate professor and conductor, St. John's Univ., Collegeville, Minn., 1958-69; music director, Metropolitan Youth Symphony, Minneapolis, 1958-69; music director and conductor, Pueblo Civic Symphony Asso., Colo., 1969-   .
WORKS: Orchestra: In dulci jubilo, overture; Festlisches spiel, piano and orch., 1955; Prelude, march and chorale, 1957; Hymnus, 1958; Chamber music: violin sonata; Chorus: Festive ordinary, chorus and orch.; The colors of spring: 7 stars of the Assiniboine, chorus and orch; Mass in honor of Queen of Peace, 1966; Organ: Festival prelude and fugue.
130 Baylor, Pueblo, CO 81005

*TRAFFORD, EDMUND
Introduction and allegro, clarinet and piano.

TRAVER, JAMES FERRIS
b. Valley Stream, N. Y., 28 May 1929. Studied with Felix Deyo, Frank Wigglesworth, and Hall Overton. He received awards at a Rochester Festival of the Arts and a Delius Festival. He is a businessman.
WORKS: Orchestra: Meditation on a sacred subject; From the New England Hills; Cape Cod sketches; Wind ensemble: 2 songs of the sea; A Keltic suite; Chorus: Praise the Lord our king; Christ, the Lord e'er reigneth; To the Lord thy praises sing; and many more.
92 North Pocono Road
Mountain Lakes, NJ 07046

TRAVIS, ROY
b. New York, N. Y., 24 June 1922. Studied with
Otto Luening, Columbia Univ., A. B. 1947, M. A.
1951; with Felix Salzer and Bernard Wagenaar,
Juilliard School, B. S. 1949, M. S. 1950.
His honors include the Gershwin award; Fulbright
fellowship; 2 appointments to Univ. of
California, Inst. for the Creative Arts; ASCAP
award 1972; Guggenheim fellowship, 1972. He
was instructor, Columbia Univ., 1952-53; Mannes
Coll. of Music, 1952-57; instructor to associate
professor, 1957-68, professor, 1968-   , Univ.
of California at Los Angeles.
     WORKS: Opera: The passion of Oedipus, 1965;
Orchestra: Collage for orchestra; piano
concerto; Symphonic allegro; Songs and epilogues;
Chamber music: Duo concertante, violin and
piano; African sonata, piano; Switched-on
Ashanti, for flute, African instruments, synthesizer; 5 preludes for piano.
     16680 Charmel Lane
     Pacific Palisades, CA 90272

*TREMBLAY, GEORGE
b. Ottawa, Ont., 14 Jan. 1911; to U.S. 1919.
Studied organ with his father and composition
with Arnold Schoenberg in Los Angeles.
     WORKS: Orchestra: 3 symphonies, 1940,
1946, no. 3 in one movement, 1949; Chamber music:
string quartet, 1936; 2 piano sonatas; 2 wind
quintets.
     22852 Crespi Street
     Woodland Hills, CA 91364

*TREVARTHEN, ROBERT RICHARD
Trombone sonata; sonata for 2 trumpets, horn,
trombone.
     Department of Music, Western Carolina College
     Cullowhee, NC 28723

*TRIGGS, HAROLD
b. Denver, Colo., 25 Dec. 1900. Studied at
Univ. of Chicago; with Rubin Goldmark at
Juilliard School; piano with Josef and Rosina
Lhevinne. In 1932 he toured the U.S. with
Vera Brodsky in a 2-piano team; has taught at
Columbia Univ.
     WORKS: Orchestra: The bright land, string
orch., 1942; Piano: 2 sonatas, 1951, 1953; 18
preludes.

*TRIMBLE, LESTER
b. Bangor, Wis., 29 Aug. 1923. Studied with
Nikolai Lopatnikoff, Carnegie Inst. of Technology;
with Darius Milhaud at Tanglewood and in Paris;
with Arthur Honegger in Paris. His awards
include the Wechsler commission at Tanglewood,
1959; Nat. Inst. of Arts and Letters award, 1961;
B. M. I. commission, 1971; and was first occupant
of the Composers' Cabin, Wolf Trap Farm, Vienna,
Va., 1973. He taught at Univ. of Maryland; at
Juilliard School, 1972-   ; was music critic
for The Nation; guest reviewer, New York
Herald Tribune; and has been general manager,
American Music Center.
     WORKS: Orchestra: symphony, 1951; violin
concerto, 1955; Closing piece, 1957; 5 episodes,
1961; In praise of diplomacy and common sense,

(TRIMBLE, LESTER)
1965; Chamber music: 2 string quartets, 1950-
1955; sextet for woodwinds, horn, piano, 1952;
Kennedy concerto, chamber orch., 1964; Solo
for a virtuoso, violin solo, 1971; Panels I,
chamber orch., Tanglewood, 7 Aug. 1973; Chorus:
4 fragments from Canterbury Tales, men's voices,
1958.
     98 Riverside Drive
     New York, NY 10024

*TROGAN, ROLAND
b. 1933.   5 nocturnes for piano; violin sonata,
1959; Seafarer, piano fantasy and cantata, 1966.
     76 Walbrooke Avenue
     Staten Island, NY 10314

*TROGEN, STANLEY
The wandering scholar, chamber opera, Portland,
Ore., 4 Dec. 1973; Andrew Jackson, Old Hickory,
opera commissioned by Premiere Productions,
Portland, Ore., for American Bicentennial 1976.

TROMBLY, PRESTON A.
b. Hartford, Conn., 30 Dec. 1945. Studied with
Charles Whittenberg, Univ. of Connecticut, B. M.;
with Bulent Arel and Mario Davidovsky, Yale
Univ., M. M. 1972; and with George Crumb at
Tanglewood. He received a B. M. I. student
composer award, 1970; Tanglewood fellowship,
1970; Yale Univ. awards; Bennington Composers'
Conference fellowship; Guggenheim fellowship,
1974. He was instructor, Vassar Coll., spring
1972; composer-conductor, Yale Repertory Theatre,
fall-winter 1972.
     WORKS: Chamber music: In memoriam: Igor
Stravinsky, for 4 woodwinds, solo violin, solo
double bass, 1971-72; 4 pieces, violin and cello,
1972; trio for flute, double bass, percussion,
1973; Electronic: Kinetics I and II, for tape
alone; Kinetics III, flute and tape, 1971.
     516 Orange Street, Apt. 25
     New Haven, CT 06511

*TROWBRIDGE, LUTHER
b. 1892.   Quietude, clarinet or English horn;
Alla marcia, trumpet.

TROXELL, JERRY
b. Maryville, Mo., 28 Dec. 1936. Studied with
Philip Bezanson and Richard Hervig, Univ. of
Iowa; with George B. Wilson and Leslie Bassett,
Univ. of Michigan. He was public school music
instructor, 1957-65; instructor, Northwest
Missouri State Univ., 1966; assistant professor,
Albion Coll., 1967-72; assistant professor,
Sangamon State Univ., 1973-   .
     WORKS: Orchestra: Metamorphic preludes,
1972; Chamber music: Scherzo, trombone and
piano, 1962; Tanka, soprano and instruments,
1972; Eve's diary, clarinet, violin, piano,
1973; Vibrance, alto saxophone and tape, 1974.
     1121 West Washington Street
     Springfield, IL 62702

TRUBITT, ALLEN R.
b. Chicago, Ill., 24 Aug. 1931. Studied with
Karel Jirak, Roosevelt Univ.; with Bernhard
Heiden, Indiana Univ. He received first prize,

TRUBITT, ALLEN R.

(TRUBITT, ALLEN R.)
Greenwood Press competition; first prize, Rice
Univ., 50th anniversary contest, 1962. He was
associate professor, Indiana Univ. of
Pennsylvania, 1957-64; Univ. of Hawaii, 1964-   ,
chairman, music department, 1971-   .
WORKS: Orchestra: symphony; overture in D,
1962; Band: Lingua franca; Chamber music:
string quartet; A posteriori, dance piece for
chamber orch.; Chorus: Bontsha the silent,
staged cantata; Carol of the bird; Snowflakes;
3 songs on the shortness of life; Songs:
Immortal autumn, a cycle.
Music Department, University of Hawaii
Honolulu, HI 96822

TRUDEAU, ALFRED H.
b. Providence, R. I., 25 Aug. 1906. Studied
organ with Rene Viau in Providence, 1923-26,
then was self-taught in composition, harmony,
etc. He received Nat. Fed. of Music Clubs awards,
1971, 1973. He is a minister.
WORKS: Chamber music: Holiday at the
Spanish Missions, piano; The lost mate, song
cycle; violin sonata; Salutations, violin and
piano, WNYC Radio, New York, Festival of
American Music, 21 Feb. 1972; Chorus: Mass in
honor of St. James; Organ: 6 pieces in different
styles; Suite on Marian themes; Toccata in F;
50 preludes; many works for piano, organ, strings,
woodwinds, voice, choir.
1818 Coal Place S.E.
Albuquerque, NM 87106

*TRUED, S. CLARENCE
b. Ceresco, Neb. 20 Apr. 1895. Studied at
Augustana Coll., B. M.; with Felix Borowski and
Percy Grainger, Chicago Musical Coll.; and with
Clarence Eddy in Chicago. He was piano soloist,
accompanist, and church organist.
WORKS: Band: The howitzer dinger; Chorus:
Cantorio, with soloist, narrator, and orch.;
Faith, hope, love; Now come to His table; On a
snowy evening; and piano pieces.

TRUESDELL, F. DONALD
b. Marysville, Kan., 14 Sep. 1920. Studied
with Ross Lee Finney, Univ. of Michigan, B. M.
1950, M. M. 1951, M. M. in piano 1952; with
Wayne Barlow, Eastman School of Music, D. M. A.
1960. He held a 1-year scholarship at Univ. of
Michigan and a fellowship for doctoral study
at Eastman School. He was faculty member,
Washington State Univ., 1952-58; professor and
chairman, music department, Coll. of William and
Mary, 1960-73.
WORKS: Orchestra: piano concerto, 1951;
Chamber music: string quartet, 1950; piano trio,
1960; 3 piano preludes; woodwind quintet.
College of William and Mary
Williamsburg, VA 23185

TRYTHALL, GILBERT
b. Knoxville, Tenn., 28 Oct. 1930. Studied
with David Van Vactor, Univ. of Tennessee, B. A.
1951; with Wallingford Riegger, Northwestern
Univ., M. M. 1952; with Robert Palmer, Cornell
Univ., D. M. A. 1960. He has received

(TRYTHALL, GILBERT)
commissions from Ford Found., American Music
Center, Knoxville Symphony, Nashville Symphony,
Georgia State Brass Ensemble, and the Music
Teachers Nat. Asso. He taught in public schools,
1950-53; was jazz pianist, U.S. Air Force,
1953-57; assistant professor, Knox Coll., 1960-
64; professor and director, electronic music
studio, George Peabody Coll. for Teachers,
1964-   .
WORKS: Orchestra: A solemn chant, string
orch.; First symphony, 1958; harp concerto;
Dionysia; Chroma I, with tape and 8 slide
projectors, Nashville, 9 Nov. 1970; Chamber
music: string quartet in one movement; The
music lesson, opera buffa in 1 act; brass
quintet; Metamorphosis, piano suite; flute
sonata; Electronic: Music for aluminum rooms,
tape; Nova sync, band and tape, Daytona Beach,
29 Apr. 1971; Pulsions, band and tape; The
electric womb, 8 tape cartridges; Multimedia:
The world, mother, apple pie, percussion, tape,
film slides; Echospace, brass, tape, films;
Programmatic sensorium I, taped music for a
translucent geodesic dome, audience reclined
inside dome, Nashville, 7 May 1971; also
electronic film scores. He is author of
Electronic music: Principles and practice,
New York, 1973, and many articles.
3902 Trimble Road, Nashville, TN 37215

TRYTHALL, RICHARD
b. Knoxville, Tenn., 25 July 1939. Studied
with David Van Vactor, Univ. of
Tennessee; with Roger Sessions, Princeton Univ.
His awards include Fulbright grant to Germany,
1963; Prix de Rome, American Acad. in Rome,
1964-67; Guggenheim fellowship, 1967; Naumburg
recording award, 1972; commissions from Fromm
Found./Berkshire Music Center and Dorian
Woodwind Quintet. Since 1968 he has been a
freelance composer-pianist in Italy; was member,
Center for the Creative and Performing Arts,
State Univ. of New York at Buffalo, spring terms,
1972, 1973.
WORKS: Orchestra: Composition for piano
and orchestra, 1965; Penelope's monologue,
soprano and orch., 1966; Costruzione per
orchestra, 1967; Continuums; Chamber music:
Coincidences, piano, 1969; Suite on music of
Domenico Scarlatti, harpsichord and tape;
Divertimento, woodwind quintet and tape;
Multimedia: Verse, for slides, film, tape.
Via 4 Novembre 96, Roma 00187, Italy

TUBB, MONTE
b. Jonesboro, Ark., 5 Nov. 1933. Studied at
Univ. of Arkansas; with Bernhard Heiden,
Indiana Univ., M. M. He was Ford Found.
Composer-in-residence, Atlanta, Ga., 1964-66.
He was assistant professor, Tarkio Coll., 1960-
64; associate professor, Univ. of Oregon,
1966-   .
WORKS: Orchestra: Discourse in 2 moods,
string orch., 1966; Concert piece, 1967;
Orchestra music, 1972; Band: Concert piece,
1967; Sutras, 1968; Soundprint 15, 1970; Wind
ensemble: 3 variations on a short tune, 1965;

(TUBB, MONTE)
Dialogue, 1966, Chamber music: piano sonata, 1958; string quartet, 1959; 5 Haiku, soprano and string quartet, 1965; Song for cello and piano, 1966; Earthmessage 5, cello and piano 4 hands, 1973; Chorus: In just spring, a cappella, 1962; Gloria, with 2 soli and orch., 1965; Agnus dei, a cappella, 1965; The proposal, a cappella, 1966; Libera me, girls' voices and piano, 1966; Soundpiece, for 36 voices, 1971; and songs.
School of Music, University of Oregon
Eugene, OR 97403

TUCKER, GREGORY
b. New Philadelphia, Pa., 12 Oct. 1908; d. Westport, Mass., 7 July 1971. Studied with Reginald Owen Morris and Rosario Scalero, Curtis Inst. of Music; later with Hanns Eisler and Wallingford Riegger; piano with Leo Ornstein and Eduard Steuermann. His awards included a Guggenheim fellowship, 1957-58, and commissions. He held faculty posts at Bennington Coll., 1933-46; Longy School of Music, 1946-70; instructor in piano, Harvard Coll., 1947-53; Wellesley Coll., 1948-53; professor, music department, Massachusetts Inst. of Technology, 1947-71.
WORKS: Theatre: Out of one happening, dance, 1939; Metropolitan daily, dance, 1939; The bridge, dance drama after Hart Crane, 1939; The king and the duke, dance drama after Mark Twain, 1940; The people, yes, dance drama after Carl Sandburg, 1943; Orchestra: concertino for piano and strings, 1958; Band: Centennial overture, 1961; Chamber music: Suite for violin and piano, 1958; concertino for piano and 11 instruments, 1958; wind quintet, 1963; trio for flute, cello, piano, 1964; Merwan songs, alto flute and piano, 1970.

*TUCKER, TUI ST. GEORGE
Music for bass recorder and narrator, performed, New York, 14 Jan. 1973; string quartet, New York, 6 Feb. 1974.
47 Barrow Street, New York, NY 10014

TUDOR, DAVID
b. Philadelphia, Pa., 20 Jan. 1926. Studied organ and theory with H. William Hawke in Philadelphia; piano with Irma Wolpe, composition with Stefan Wolpe in New York. He was piano instructor, Contemporary Music School, New York, 1948-51; instructor and pianist, Black Mountain Coll., 1951-53; conducted seminars, Internat. Summer School for New Music, Darmstadt, 1956, 1958, 1959, 1961; creative associate, State Univ. of New York at Buffalo, 1965-66; guest lecturer, Univ. of California at Davis, 1967; guest lecturer, Mills Coll., Tape Music Center, 1967-68; conducted seminars, Nat. Inst. of Design, Ahmedabad, India, 1969; is an outstanding performer of contemporary piano works.
WORKS: Electronic: Bandoneon factorial, programmed light, audio, video projection, New York, 14 Oct. 1966; Rainforest, Buffalo, 9 Mar. 1968; Video III (with Lowell Cross), Los Angeles, 10 May 1968; Video/laser I (with Lowell Cross) Mills Coll., 9 May 1969; 4 Pepsi

(TUDOR, DAVID)
pieces, Pepsi Pavilion, Expo '70, Osaka; Untitled, Bremen, Germany, 8 May 1972; Monobird, Munich, 30 Aug. 1972; Microphone, 1-9, Mills Coll., May 1973; Laser bird, Univ. of Iowa, 12-14 June 1973; Rainforest 4, group composition, New Music in New Hampshire, July 1973.
Gate Hill Road, Stony Point, NY 10980

TULL, FISHER
b. Waco, Tex., 1934. Studied with Samuel Adler, North Texas State Univ., B. M., M. M., Ph. D. His awards include 4 first prizes, Texas Composers Guild, 1965, 1968, 1970, 1972, 2nd prize 1970; 6 annual ASCAP awards, 1968-73; Ostwald award, American Bandmasters Asso., 1970; Nomination to Texas Composers Archives, Dallas Public Library, 1971; Piper Professor nominee, Sam Houston State Univ., 1973. He is director, department of music, Sam Houston State Univ.
WORKS: Band: Terpsichore, 1967; Toccata, 1969; Antiphon, 1970; Sketches on a Tudor psalm, 1972; Wind ensemble: Liturgical symphony, brass and percussion, 1960; Variations on an Advent hymn, brass and percussion, 1962; Soundings, brass and percussion, 1965; Jazz ensemble: 4 to go, 1960; Swing board, 1961; Chamber music: Exhibition, brass quintet, 1961; Canonical trilogy, 4 trumpets, 1961; Fantasie, oboe and piano, 1966; woodwind quintet, 1966; Diversion, 6 trombones, 1967; Scherzino, woodwind ensemble, 1968; sonatina, percussion ensemble, 1967; trio for trumpet, horn, trombone, 1967; Sketches for 5 brass, 1967; Erato, flute and piano, 1968; Lament, 4 horns and tuba, 1968; Concert piece, 4 trombones, 1968; Chorus: 3 choral poems, 1963.
Music Department, Sam Houston State University
Huntsville, TX 77340

*TURKIN, MARSHALL W.
Saxophone sonata.

*TURNER, CHARLES
b. Baltimore, Md., 25 Nov. 1921. Studied with Samuel Barber at Curtis Inst.; at Juilliard School; and with Nadia Boulanger. He served in the U.S. Navy in World War II; received an Italian Government fellowship in 1954.
WORKS: Ballet: Pastorale, 1957; Orchestra: violin concerto, 1940; Encounter, symphonic sketch, 1955; Chamber music: Serenade for Icarus, violin and piano, 1960.

*TURNER, GODFREY
b. Manchester, England, 27 Mar. 1913; to U.S. 1936; d. New York, N. Y., 7 Dec. 1948. Studied at Cambridge Univ. and with Nadia Boulanger in Paris. He won first prize, BMI contest, 1947. He taught at San Francisco Cons., 1938-43; was music editor, Boosey and Hawkes, New York, 1944-46; secretary, American Music Center, 1946-48.
WORKS: Orchestra: Trinity concerto, chamber orch.; viola concerto; Sonata concertante, piano and strings; Saraband and tango; Gregorian overture; Wind ensemble: Fanfare, chorale, and finale, brass.

TURNER, MILDRED COZZENS

TURNER, MILDRED COZZENS (Mrs. Huntington Turner)
b. Pueblo, Colo., 23 Feb. 1897. Studied at
Univ. of Wisconsin; was a public school music
supervisor, Mineral Point, Wis. Her published
compositions include the songs: Dalmatian
lullaby; Galaxy; Geisha.
45 East End Avenue, New York, NY 10028

*TURNER, MYRA BROOKS
b. Alabama. Has published a high school musical
with orch; many choral works and songs.

TURNER, THOMAS G.
b. Hamilton, Ohio, 30 Sep. 1937. Studied with
Kenneth Gaburo and Lejaren Hiller, Univ. of
Illinois; with Robert McBride, Univ. of Arizona;
with Eugene Weigel, Univ. of Montana; attended
Internat. Summer School for New Music, Darmstadt.
He was faculty member, Univ. of Idaho, 1962-65;
music critic for The (London) Times Educational
Supplement, 1966; on faculty, creative arts
department, Univ. of North Carolina at Charlotte,
1973- .
WORKS: Chamber music: viola sonata, 1960;
Modules and variables, guitar and piano, 1973;
Piano: Intermezzo, 1966; 6 variations; Arrows,
1973; also songs and choral music.
6205 King George Drive, Charlotte, NC 28213

TURNER, THOMAS SAMPLE
b. Corning, Iowa, 21 Apr. 1941. Studied with
Carl Bricken, Univ. of Chicago; with Philip
Greeley Clapp, Univ. of Iowa, Ph. D. 1941. He
has been faculty member, Univ. of Iowa,
1939- .
WORKS: Orchestra: 2 symphonies; Symphonic
suite, 1943; also an opera and various chamber
works, 1947-68.
School of Music, University of Iowa
Iowa City, IA 52243

TUROK, PAUL
b. New York, N. Y., 3 Dec. 1929. Studied with
Karol Rathaus, Queens Coll., B. A.; with Roger
Sessions, Univ. of California, Berkeley, M. M.;
and with Bernard Wagenaar at Juilliard School.
He received the Dillon prize; Hertz Traveling
Scholarship, Univ. of California; and a composer
residency, Villa Montalvo. He was associate
music director, KPFA, Berkeley, 1955-56; lecturer,
City Coll. of New York, 1960-63; visiting
professor, Williams Coll., 1963-64; music
reviewer, New York Herald-Tribune, 1964-65; Music
Journal, 1964- .
WORKS: Theatre: Scene: Domestic, chamber
opera; Youngest brother, ballet; Orchestra: symphony; violin concerto; Lincoln and liberty;
Chartres west; Homage to Bach; Great Scott!;
Joplin overture; Chamber music: 3 string
quartets; 3 wind quintets; brass quintet;
string trio; clarinet trio; sonatas for organ,
cello, harpsichord, horn; Songs: Evocations;
3 songs for soprano and flute; Piano: Transcendental etudes.
170 West 74th Street, New York, NY 10023

TURRIN, JOSEPH EGIDIO
b. Passaic, N. J., 4 Jan. 1947. Studied at
Eastman School of Music and Manhattan School of

(TURRIN, JOSEPH EGIDIO)
Music. He received a New Jersey State Council
of the Arts grant for 1976. In 1973 he taught
at Center for New Music, Columbia Coll.,
Chicago.
WORKS: Opera: Feathertop, chamber opera;
Orchestra: symphony in 2 movements; Elegy for
trumpet and strings; Band: tuba concerto;
March and choral for brass choir; Fanfare for 8
trumpets; Chamber music: Walden trio, flute,
cello, piano; Caprice, trumpet and piano;
clarinet sonata; Aeolus, flute and piano; also
piano pieces and songs.
96 Huron Avenue, Clifton, NY 07013

*TUSTIN, WHITNEY
b. Seattle, Wash. Studied at Univ. of Washington
and in Paris; works include Pastorale moderne,
scherzo, tarantella woodwind trio; 30 oboe duets.
Music Dept., Hofstra Univ., Hempstead, NY 11550

TUTHILL, BURNET
b. New York, N. Y., 16 Nov. 1888. Studied at
Columbia Univ., M. A. 1910; Cincinnati Coll. of
Music, M. M. 1935. He received honorary music
doctorates from Chicago Musical Coll., 1943, and
from Southwestern at Memphis, 1972. From 1910
to 1922, he kept music as an avocation and worked
as a businessman in New York then became general
manager of the Cincinnati Cons. and resumed the
study of music. After receiving his master's
in composition he became director of music at
Southwestern at Memphis, 1935, and director,
Memphis Coll. of Music, 1937, holding both
positions until retirement in 1959. He was
active as conductor, 1910-59. In 1919 he
founded the Society for Publication of American
Music and was its treasurer to 1949; in 1924,
he and Charles N. Boyd founded the Nat. Asso. of
Schools of Music, of which he was secretary to
1959. Since retirement he has compiled a list of
clarinet concertos and a list of clarinet sonatas
published by MENC, 1972-73; a list of quartets
and quintets for clarinet and strings, published
1974; and has written A history of the National
Association of Schools of Music-the first forty
years, and Recollections of a musical life,
1900-1974, also published 1974.
WORKS: Orchestra: Bethlehem, pastorale,
1934; Come seven, 1935; Laurentia, symphonic
poem, 1936; symphony, 1940; Big river, with
women's chorus and soprano, 1942; Elegy, 1946;
clarinet concerto, 1949; Rhapsody for clarinet
and chamber orch., 1954; concerto for string
bass and winds, 1962; saxophone concerto, 1965;
trombone concerto, 1967; Band: Overture brilliante, 1937; Suite for band, 1946; Rondo
concertante, 2 clarinets and band, 1961;
Fantasia, tuba and band, 1968; Chamber music:
Scherzo, 3 clarinets, 1909; Fantasy sonata,
clarinet and piano, 1932; Sonatina in canon,
flute and clarinet, 1933; piano trio, 1933;
clarinet quintet, 1935; Divertimento in classic
style, wind quartet, 1936; alto saxophone
sonata, 1939; oboe sonata, 1945; trumpet sonata,
1950; Family music, flute, 2 clarinets, viola,
cello, 1952; string quartet, 1953; quintet for
piano and 4 clarinets, 1957; 6 for bass, string
bass and piano, 1961; flute sonata, 1963;

(TUTHILL, BURNET)
1963; saxophone quartet, 1966; tenor saxophone sonata, 1968; 5 essays for brass quintet, 1969; Caprice for guitar, 1972; Tiny tunes for tuba, 1973; Chorus: Requiem, with 2 soli and orch., 1960; many shorter compositions for voice and instrumental groups.

295 Buena Vista Place, Memphis, TN 38112

*TWEEDY, DONALD
b. Danbury, Conn., 23 Apr. 1890; d. Danbury, 21 July 1948. Studied with William C. Heilman, Walter Spalding, and Edward Burlingame Hill, Harvard Univ.; with Percy Goetschius, Inst. of Musical Art, 1912. He was in the U.S. Army in World War I; taught at Eastman School of Music, 1923-27; at Hamilton Coll., 1937-38; and at Texas Christian Univ., 1943-46.

WORKS: Ballet: Alice in Wonderland, 1935; Orchestra: L'Allegro, symphonic study, 1925; 3 dances, 1925; Williamsburg suite, 1941; Chamber music: viola sonata, 1916; violin sonata, 1920; cello sonata, 1930; Chorus: Anthem for Lent, Out of the depths, 1942; and piano pieces.

TWOMBLY, MARY LYNN
b. New York, N. Y., 8 Jan. 1935. Studied with Meyer Kupferman, Sarah Lawrence Coll., 1952-54; with Vittorio Giannini, Manhattan School of Music, 1954-58; electronic music with Elias Tannenbaum, 1971-72. She received the Harold Bauer piano award, 1957; commissions from Little Orchestra Society, 1960. She was composer and conductor for films and records, Weston Woods Children's Library, 1966-67; participated in music workshops, Fairleigh Dickinson Univ., 1973.

WORKS: Opera: The Little match girl, for young voices, 1964; Who are the blind?, 1969; Ballet: Alice in wonderland, 1960; Orchestra: Symphonic statements, piano and string orch., 1971; Chorus: Songs of Christmas, 1964.

Old Route 202, Pomona, NY 10970

TYSON, MILDRED LUND
b. Moline, Ill., 10 Mar. Studied with Carl Beecher, Northwestern Univ., B. M.; and at Columbia Univ. She taught piano and voice at Pomona Coll.; was organist and choir director in Sidney, N. Y. Her published compositions include the songs: The lilacs are in bloom; One little cloud; Sea moods; Like barley bending; The Great Divide.

Unadilla, NY 13849

UBER, DAVID
b. Princeton, Ill., 5 Aug. 1921. Studied with Charles Gerhard and Alexander Hilsberg, Curtis Inst.; at Carthage Coll., A. B.; with Harold Morris and Harry Wilson, Columbia Univ., M. A., Ed. D. He received commissions from Johnson Wax Corporation and Carthage Coll., annual ASCAP awards, 1960-73. He has been solo trombonist, New York City Ballet Company Orchestra, 1958- ; professor, Trenton State Coll., 1959- ; musical director, Princeton Univ. Band, 1971- ; and was director of ensemble

(UBER, DAVID)
music, Interlochen Nat. Music Camp, 1960-65.
WORKS: Band: 4 episodes; When I can read my title clear; Odyssey; Symphonic sketches, 1 and 2; Panorama, with trombone solo; Brass choir: A Christmas festival of carols; Christmas in brass; Evolution; Gettysburg; Gloria in excelsis, 1970; The power and the glory, symphony; Liturgy; Symphonic fanfare; numerous other compositions and arrangements for woodwind, brass, and percussion ensembles.

31 Melville Road, Cranbury, NJ 08512

UDELL, BUDD
b. Grand Rapids, Mich., 4 Apr. 1934. Studied with Bernhard Heiden, Indiana Univ., with Paul Cooper, Univ. of Cincinnati, Coll.-Cons. He was composer-arranger, U.S. Navy Band, 1958-61; faculty member, West Virginia Univ., Creative Arts Center, 1963-70; Univ. of Cincinnati, Coll.-Cons., 1972- .

WORKS: Band: Freedom 7, 1962; Chamber music: 2 songs of Gerard Manley Hopkins, soprano, harp, clarinet, 1962; 4 miniatures, clarinet and piano, 1970; Allectation, clarinet, horn, cello, piano, percussion, 1972; Chorus: Judgment, with contralto solo, chamber orch., electronic tape, 1972.

566 Christmas Lane, Cincinnati, OH 45224

UDOW, MICHAEL WILLIAM
b. Detroit, Mich., 10 Mar. 1949. Studied with Thomas Frederickson, Edwin London, Herbert Brün, and Gordon Binkerd, Univ. of Illinois; with Paul Steg, Northern Illinois Univ.; and with W. Kotonski in Warsaw, Poland. He received a BMI student composer award; Fulbright-Hayes grant for study in Poland, 1972-73. He was principal percussionist, Santa Fe Opera, 1968-72; percussionist, New Orleans Philharmonic, 1971-72; founder and director, New Orleans Contemporary Chamber Players, 1971-72; charter member, Blackearth Percussion Group, 1971-73; lecturer, Northern Illinois Univ., 1973- .

WORKS: Chamber music: African welcome piece; Understanding, 6 unspecified instruments, percussion, tape recorder; 7 textural settings of Japanese poetry, chamber orch.; Acoustic composition #1 for 1-5 percussionists and tape; Acoustic study #1; American Indian children's poems, oboe, English horn, bassoon, piano.

104 Prospect, DeKalb, IL 60115

ULEHLA, LUDMILA
b. New York, N. Y., 20 May 1923. Studied at Manhattan School of Music, B. M. 1946, M. M. 1947. She has received annual ASCAP awards, 1968- ; and many commissions. She joined the faculty at Manhattan School in 1947, has been chairman of composition, 1971- ; is also professor, Hoff-Barthelson Music School, Scarsdale, N. Y., 1968- .

WORKS: Orchestra: 5 over 12; Michelangelo, a tone portrait, New York, 18 Feb. 1971; Songs: Sonnets from Shakespeare, voice and chamber orch., 1951; Time is a cunning thief, voice and piano; Gargoyles, soprano, piano, bassoon; also piano works.

120 Lee Road, Scarsdale, NY 10583

ULRICH, BARRY R.

*ULRICH, BARRY R.
   Suite for brass quartet, Fullerton, Calif.,
3 May 1969.

ULRICH, EUGENE J.
   Olmsted, Ill., 13 Dec. 1921. Studied with J.
Robert Kelly, Univ. of Illinois; with Bernard
Rogers, Howard Hanson, Wayne Barlow, Eastman
School of Music, Ph. D. He has been professor,
Phillips Univ., 1949- .
   WORKS: Chamber music: sonatina, flute solo;
baritone horn sonata; suite for unaccompanied
marimba; numerous other wind instrument solos,
percussion solos, etc.
   2610 East Pine, Enid, OK 73701

ULTAN, LLOYD
   b. New York, N. Y.; 12 June 1929. Studied with
Philip Bezanson, Univ. of Iowa; with Roger Goeb
and Henry Brant, Bennington Composers Conference.
He received a fellowship, Univ. of Iowa; scholarship to Bennington Conference; numerous commissions. He was chairman, music department,
Dickinson Coll., 1956-62; chairman, music
department, American Univ., 1962-   ; visiting
professor, Royal Coll., of Music, London, 1968-
69; guest lecturer, Cambridge Univ., 1969.
   WORKS: Chamber music: string quartet,
1964; piano sextet, 1970; bassoon sonata; piano
sonata, Fuschl am See; guitar quintet, guitar
with string quartet.
   10508 Tyler Terrace, Potomac, MD 20854

UNDERWOOD, LUCAS
   b. Salzburg, Austria, 22 Nov. 1902; U.S. citizen,
1945. Studied with H. W. von Waltershausen and
Siegmund von Hausegger, Acad. of Music, Munich,
Ph. D. He was a music critic in Hannover, 1930-
37; taught music at Margaret Hall School,
Versailles, Ky., 1939-46; was professor and
director of opera, Univ. of the Pacific, 1946-72;
musical director, Stockton Opera Asso.,
1968-   .
   WORKS: Opera: The holy night, Christmas
opera; Orchestra: Evening at the lake; German
rhapsody; Chorus: Missa brevis; Madrigals;
Piano: Variations; Passacaglia; many other
choral works and songs.
   13 Atherton Island, Stockton, CA 95204

UNDERWOOD, WILLIAM L.
   b. Greenwood, Miss., 9 Mar. 1940. Studied
with Johannes Smit, Memphis State Univ., B. M.,
M. A. 1966; with William P. Latham and Dika
Newlin, North Texas State Univ., D. M. A. 1970.
He taught theory and piano, North Texas State
Univ., 1968-70; has been professor, Henderson
State Coll., 1970-74.
   WORKS: Opera: A medicine for melancholy,
comic opera based on a Ray Bradbury story;
Orchestra: 2 symphonies, 1966, 1971; Chamber
music: 3 songs of e. e. cummings for soprano,
flute, and string quartet; numerous short works
for chorus and band.
   1219 Henderson, Arkadelphia, AR 71923

UNG, CHINARY
   b. Cambodia, 24 Nov. 1942; to U.S. 1964. Studied
with Jack Beeson, Chou Wen-chung, Mario
Davidovsky, and Vladimir Ussachevsky, Columbia
Univ.; with George Crumb at Tanglewood; and with
Bulent Arel. He received the Bronze Medal of
Honor for performing arts, Cambodia, 1962;
Premier Prix, Faculté de Musique, Univ. des
Beaux Arts, Cambodia, 1963; Margaret Grant
Memorial composition prize, Tanglewood, 1970;
Rapaport prize, Columbia Univ., 1971;
Koussevitzky Music Found. in the Library of
Congress award, 1973.
   WORKS: Orchestra: Anicea, 1970; Chamber
music: Tall wind, chamber ensemble, 1970.
   622 West 114th Street, New York, NY 10025

UNGER, LEIGH JAMES
   b. Milwaukee, Wis., 15 Oct. 1945. Studied at
Whittier Coll., B. A. with honors in piano 1967;
with Donal Michalsky, California State Univ. at
Fullerton, M. A. 1974; master classes in piano
with Rosina Lhevinne and Daniel Pollack. He
received the Bank of America achievement award
in science and mathematics, 1963; and numerous
awards for piano performance. He was teaching
assistant, Whittier Coll., 1965-67; accompanist,
Fullerton Junior Coll., 1970-71; member of piano
faculty, Univ. of Redlands.
   WORKS: Chamber music: Improvisation for
flute and piano, 1970; Songs: 3 songs for
baritone and piano, 1967; Song from Pomes
Penyeach, Joyce text, baritone and piano, 1969;
2 songs for soprano and piano, 1970; 12 love
songs, soprano, 1971; Piano: 6 preludes,
1967; 3 intermezzi, 1967; 3 studies, 1969;
Distractions to the contemplative, 1970; Suite,
1971.
   893 South Lemon, Anaheim, CA 92805

*USSACHEVSKY, VLADIMIR
   b. Hialar, Manchuria, 3 Nov. 1911; to U.S. 1930.
Studied at Pomona Coll., B. A. 1935; with
Howard Hanson and Bernard Rogers, Eastman School
of Music, Ph. D. 1939. He received an award
from the American Acad. of Arts and Letters,
1963, and in 1973 was elected to membership in
the Nat. Inst. of Arts and Letters. He was in
the U.S. Army in World War II; on the faculty
at Columbia Univ., 1947-72; at Univ. of Utah,
1972-   .
   WORKS: Orchestra: Theme and variations,
1935; Miniatures for a curious child, 1950;
piano concerto, 1951; Chamber music: piano
sonata, 1952; Chorus: Jubilee cantata, with
orch., 1938; Missa brevis, with soprano and
10 brass instruments; Electronic: Sonic
contours, tape and instruments, 1952; Underwater
valse, 1952; Incantation, tape, with Otto
Luening, 1953; Poem of cycles and bels, tape
and orch., with Luening, 1954; Piece for tape
recorder, 1955; Studies in sound, 1955;
Metamorphosis, 1957; Linear contrasts, 1958;
Improvisation, no. 4711, 1958; Wireless fantasy,
1960; Concerted piece, tape and orch., with
Luening, 1960; Of wood and brass, 1965; Computer

(USSACHEVSKY, VLADIMIR)
piece, 1968; Creation, chorus, orch., tape;
Rhapsodic variations, with Luening, New York,
29 Apr. 1973.
Department of Music, University of Utah
Salt Lake City, UT 84112

*VALENTI, MICHAEL
The pledge, opera, New York, 25 Mar. 1971.

*VALENTINE, ROBERT
Concerto for flute or oboe and strings.

VAN APPLEDORN, MARY JEAN
b. Holland, Mich., 2 Oct. 1927. Studied with
Bernard Rogers and Alan Havhaness, Eastman
School of Music, B. M. 1948, M. M. 1950, Ph. D.
1966. She received the Delta Kappa Gamma
international scholarship, 1959-60; was desig-
nated member, Texas Composers Hall of Fame with
manuscripts entered in the Archives, Dallas
Public Library; won awards in Mu Phi Epsilon
composition contests. She has been professor
and chairman, music literature and theory,
Texas Tech Univ., 1967-   .
WORKS: Orchestra: piano concerto, 1954,
Houston, 1973; Keyboard: Sonnet for organ, 1959;
9 piano pieces; 3 piano pieces.
Texas Tech University, P.O. Box 4239
Lubbock, TX 79409

*VAN CLEAVE, NATHAN
b. Bayfield, Wis., 8 May 1910. Writes for films
and radio. His works for orchestra include a
trumpet concerto; Fantasy for strings; American
holiday; Dances from Satanstoe; Daybreak serenade; Canzonetta.

VAN DER SLICE, JOHN
b. Ann Arbor, Mich., 19 Feb. 1940. Studied with
Armand Russell, Neil McKay, Ingolf Dahl, Univ.
of Hawaii; with Paul Zonn, Univ. of Illinois.
He was instructor, Univ. of Hawaii, Jan.-June
1970.
WORKS: Chamber music: For flute, 1969;
septet, 1969; piano sonata, 1970; Portions,
1970; Thesis, 1972; For koto, 1972.
1204 West Stoughton, Apt. 22
Urbana IL 61801

VAN DE VATE, NANCY H.
b. Plainfield, N. J., 30 Dec. 1930. Studied
piano at Eastman School of Music, 1948-49; at
Wellesley Coll., A. B. 1952; piano with Bruce
Simonds, Yale Univ., 1954; composition, Univ.
of Mississippi, M. M. 1958; at Florida State
Univ., D. M. 1968. Her awards include the
Rochester Prize scholarship and George Eastman
scholarship at Eastman School; Presser scholarship, 1949-52; grant from the French Government
for special study in French, 1950-52; Wellesley
Coll. Scholar; ASCAP awards, 1973-75; Delius
award for a brass quintet, 1975; residence
awards at Yaddo and Ossabaw Island (Ga.) Project;
and commissions. She was a private piano teacher,
1957-63; instructor, Univ. of Mississippi, 1960;
assistant professor, Memphis State Univ., 1964-
66; instructor, Univ. of Tennessee, 1967;

(VAN DE VATE, NANCY H.)
associate professor, Knoxville Coll., 1968-69,
lecturer, 1971-72.
WORKS: Opera: The death of the hired man,
chamber opera, 1960; Orchestra: Adagio for
orchestra, 1958; piano concerto, Univ. of
Houston, 1 Mar. 1969; Chamber music: Short suite
for brass quartet; woodwind quartet; viola
sonata; Variations, clarinet and piano; Lento
for piano; Chorus: Make a joyful noise unto the
Lord; How goes the night; An American essay,
with soloists, piano, percussion, Knoxville,
16 May 1972; Songs: Death is the chilly night;
Cradlesong; Loneliness; Lo-yang; Youthful age.
5610 Holston Hills Road, Knoxville, TN 37914

VANEUF, ANDRE. See COHEN, SOL B.

VAN HULSE, CAMIL
b. Sint Niklaas, Belgium, 1 Aug. 1897; to U.S.
1923. Studied with his father, Gustave Van
Hulse, the with Franz Lenaerts and Edward
Verheyden, Antwerp Cons., diploma in piano and
composition; with Arthur De Greef in Brussels.
He received 11 awards in composition contests;
Royal Medal in Antwerp; Order of Leopold; Order
of the Crown. He settled in Tucson, Ariz., as
organist and choirmaster, 1924-57; gave organ
and piano recitals in North and South America;
was conductor, Tucson Symphony Orchestra,
1928-30.
WORKS: Orchestra: Via crucis, oratorio for
orch., chorus, soloists, organ, and narrator; The
Belgian in U.S.A., for 40th anniversary of the
Tucson Symphony, 1968; Chamber music: Trio-
elegy, piano trio; woodwind quintet; In Christmas
mood, flute and organ; Aubade, flute and harp;
Chorus: The Beatitudes, cantata; Christmas
oratorio; Our glorious king, cantata; Twas in the
moon of wintertime, Christmas cantata; The
passion according to St. Luke, with organ and
narrator, Garden City, N. Y., 30 Mar. 1969;
numerous masses, anthems, and motets; Organ:
Saint Louis, Roi de France; Symphonia mystica;
Symphonia elegiaca; Jubilee suite; Christmas
rhapsody; Homage to Breughel, Phoenix, Ariz.,
20 Mar. 1970; many other works for organ; piano
pieces.
1029 North Euclid, Tucson, AZ 85719

VAN KATWIJK, VIOLA EDNA BECK (Mrs. Paul van Katwijk)
b. Denison, Tex., 26 Feb. 1894. Studied piano
with Richard Burmeister in Berlin; piano and
composition with Percy Grainger; also coached
with Paul van Katwijk. Her awards include 2
first prizes, Mu Phi Epsilon national contests,
1928, 1930; and 2 first place awards, San
Antonio Club contests for piano compositions.
She made her piano debut with the St. Louis
Symphony in Dallas, Tex; was on piano faculty,
Southern Methodist Univ., 1922-55.
WORKS: Songs: Winter valley, 1928; My
terrace, 1930; Piano: The jester; Gamelan;
Dusk on a Texas prairie; many unpublished
compositions for piano and voice.
4610 Wildwood Road, Dallas, TX 75209

VAN NOSTRAND, BURR

*VAN NOSTRAND, BURR
  Lunar possession manual, based on American
  Indian ceremonial dance, soprano and chamber
  ensemble, 1973, Boston, Mass., 2 Feb. 1975,
  American premiere.

VAN SLYCK, NICHOLAS
  b. Philadelphia, Pa., 25 Oct. 1922. Studied
  at Philadelphia Cons.; with Walter Piston,
  Harvard Univ., B. A., M. A.; piano with George
  Reeves. He won first prize in a Brookline
  Library competition with Chamber music for 2
  pianos. He was director, South End Music
  Center, Boston, 1950-62; director, Longy
  School of Music, Cambridge, 1960-   ; faculty,
  Harvard Graduate School of Education, 1965-68;
  conductor, Quincy Symphony, 1952-57; conductor,
  Merrimack Philharmonic Orchestra, 1968-   .
    WORKS: Chamber music: Passamezzo antico,
  brass quintet; Suite for harpsichord; cello
  sonata; Chorus: Rhythm rounds; Piano: Toccata;
  In 3 dimensions; Gardens of the west, 1973;
  Duo capriccioso, piano 4 hands, Boston WGBH,
  16 Oct. 1974; With 20 fingers, 3 volumes of
  piano duets; also symphonies, concerti, sonatas,
  choral and chamber works.
    1572 Massachusetts Avenue
    Cambridge, MA 02138

VAN VACTOR, DAVID
  b. Plymouth, Ind., 8 May 1906. Studied with
  Carl Beecher, Mark Wessel, Arne Oldberg, and
  Albert Noelte, flute with Arthur Kitti,
  Northwestern Univ., B. M. 1928, M. M. 1935; with
  Franz Schmidt, Vienna Acad., 1928-29; with
  Paul Dukas, Arnold Schoenberg, flute with Marcel
  Moyse, Paris 1931. His awards include the New
  York Philharmonic first prize of $1000 for
  Symphony no. 1, 1938; Fulbright research grant;
  Guggenheim fellowship, 1957; numerous commis-
  sions. He was flutist, Chicago Symphony
  Orchestra, 1931-43; taught at Northwestern
  Univ., 1936-43; was assistant conductor, Kansas
  City Philharmonic Orchestra, 1943-45; head of
  theory and composition, Kansas City Cons.,
  1943-45; professor, Univ. of Tennessee,
  1947-   . He made tours to South America for
  the State Department, one as member of a wood-
  wind quintet in 1941, then as guest conductor
  of orchestras in Rio de Janeiro and Santiago,
  Chile, in 1945, 1946, 1965.
    WORKS: Ballet: The play of words, 1931;
  Dance contrasts, 1961; Suite for orchestra on
  Chilean folk tunes, 1965; Brass octet, 1968;
  Orchestra: Chaconne, string orch., 1928;
  5 small pieces for large orch., 1929; flute
  concerto, 1932; Passacaglia and fugue, 1933;
  Overture to a comedy no. 1, 1934, no. 2, 1941;
  Concerto grosso for 3 flutes, harp and orch.,
  1935; 2 symphonies, 1937, 1958; Symphonic suite,
  1938; 5 bagatelles for strings, 1938;
  Divertimento, 1939; viola concerto, 1940;
  Variazioni solenne, 1941; Music for the Marines,
  1943; United Nations fanfare, 1944; Recitative
  and saltarello, 1946; Pastorale and dance, flute
  and strings, 1947; Prelude and march, 1950;
  violin concerto, 1950; Armed Forces medley,
  1951; Fantasia, chaconne, and allegro, 1957;
  Trojan Women suite, 1959; Suite for trumpet and

(VAN VACTOR, DAVID)
  small orch., 1962; Sinfonia breve, 1964;
  Louise, a requiescat for string orch., Knoxville,
  12 Oct. 1970; Sarabande and variations, brass
  quintet and strings, 1972; Suite for trumpet,
  piccolo and orch., 1972; Andante and allegro,
  alto saxophone and string orch., Muncie, Ind.
  16 Dec. 1973; Chamber music: 10 variations on a
  theme by Beethoven, flute and piano, 1929;
  quintet for flute and strings, 1932; Suite for
  2 flutes, 1934; Nachtlied, soprano and strings,
  1935; 2 string quartets, 1940, 1949; Divertimento
  for string trio, 1942; flute sonatina, 1945;
  Duettino, violin and cello, 1952; woodwind
  quintet, 1959; Economy band no. 1, trumpet,
  trombone, percussion, 1966; Economy band no. 2,
  horn, tuba, percussion, 1969; tuba quartet,
  Georgia State Univ., 22 Feb. 1971; Suite for 12
  solo trombones, Knoxville, 20 Feb. 1972; Chorus:
  Credo, with orch., 1941; 8 a capella choruses
  from The Shropshire lad, Housman, 1953; Christmas
  songs for young people, with orch., 1961; Walden,
  with orch., Knoxville, 16 May 1971; also band
  pieces and songs.
    2824 Kingston Pike, Knoxville, TN 37919

VARDELL, CHARLES GILDERSLEEVE, JR.
  b. Salisbury, N. C., 19 Aug. 1893; d. Winston-
  Salem, N. C., 19 Oct. 1962. Studied at Princeton
  Univ., A. B. 1914; Inst. of Musical Art, New
  York, diploma 1916; Eastman School of Music,
  M. A., Ph. D. He taught at Flora MacDonald
  Coll., 1919-23, dean, 1951-61; Salem Coll.,
  professor, 1923-28, dean, 1928-51; St. Andrew's
  Coll., 1961-62.
    WORKS: Orchestra: Carolinian symphony,
  performed by Philadelphia Orch.; Joe Clark steps
  out, 1933; Voice: Dark days or fair, song; The
  inimitable lovers, cantata, 1929; Song in the
  wilderness, 1947; Piano: Concert gavotte, 1924;
  Organ: Skyland, 1937.

VARDI, EMANUEL
  b. Jerusalem, Palestine, 21 Apr. 1917; U.S.
  citizen 1927. Studied with his father, then
  with Bernard Wagenaar, Juilliard School; with
  Nicolas Nabokov, Peabody Cons.; and with Tibor
  Serly in New York. He won silver medals for a
  film score for Lehigh Cement and one for
  American Express. He is principally a film
  composer including feature films, industrials,
  television films, and commercials. He is also
  violinist and violist.
    WORKS: Chamber music: Suite on American
  folk songs, violin or viola and piano; Concerto
  for solo horn, string quartet, 2 winds, keyboard,
  New York, 15 May 1974; Film scores: Once before
  I die, motion picture; Diary of Anne Frank,
  television special; Life study, feature; Devil's
  axe, electronic score.
    2 Wood Lane, Suffern, NY 10901

*VARESE, EDGARD
  b. Paris, France, 22 Dec. 1883; U.S. citizen
  1926; d. New York, N. Y., 6 Nov. 1965. Studied
  with Vincent d'Indy and Albert Roussel, Schola
  Cantorum, Paris; and with Charles-Marie Widor,
  Paris Cons. His honors include the Brandeis
  award, 1962; the first Koussevitzky Internat.

(VARESE, EDGARD)

recording award, 1963; MacDowell medal, 1965; was a member, Nat. Inst. of Arts and Letters, and fellow, Swedish Royal Acad. of Music. Varese founded the New Symphony Orchestra for the performance of new music, which gave its first concert in New York, 11 Apr. 1919. He was co-founder with Carlos Salzedo of the Internat. Composers' Guild, 1922; organized the Pan American Society for presentation of music of the Americas, 1926; conducted choruses and orchestras in the U.S. and Europe.

WORKS: Orchestra: Offrandes, voice and small orch., 1922; Integrales, small orch. and percussion, 1925; Ameriques, 1925; Arcana, 1927; Ionization, 41 percussion instruments and 2 sirens, 1931; Wind ensemble: Hyperprism, winds and percussion, 1923; Octandre, woodwind quartet, brass trio, double bass, 1924; Equatorial, bass voice, brass, organ, percussion, thereminovox, 1934; Chamber music: Density 21.5, flute solo, 1935; Chorus: Etude pour espace, with 2 pianos and percussion, 1947; Nocturnal, soprano, men's chorus, chamber orch. piano, percussion, 1961; Electronic: Deserts, winds, percussion, electronic sounds, 1954; Poeme electronique, for Brussels Exposition, 1958.

*VARS, HENRY

b. Warsaw, Poland, 29 Dec. 1902; to U.S. 1947. Studied at Warsaw Cons. He has composed for theatre, films, and radio.

WORKS: Orchestra: a symphony; symphonic suite; piano concerto; Chamber music: string quartet; violin sonata; piano sonata; piano preludes; and songs.

VAUCLAIN, CONSTANT

b. Philadelphia, Pa., 5 Aug. 1908. Studied with Rosario Scalero, Curtis Inst. of Music. He was on the faculty, Curtis Inst., 1939-63; associate professor, Univ. of Pennsylvania, 1947- .

WORKS: Ballet: Suite for youth, chamber ballet, 1952; Orchestra: April overture, 1940; Symphony in 1 movement, Philadelphia, 18 Apr. 1947; Symphony for strings and piano, 1948; Prelude to Endymion, 1949, Rochester, 4 May 1951; Narrative, 1958; Allegretto, string orch., Chicago, 10 May 1958; Chamber music: string quartet, 1955, Philadelphia, 3 May 1957; Suite for strings and piano, 1956; string quartet, New York, 8 Oct. 1965; Piano: 3 Degas, suite, 1950; sonatina, 1956; Organ: Motet on Psalm 11, Philadelphia, 10 Nov. 1962.

20 Old Gulph Road, Gladwyne, PA 19035

VAUGHAN, CLIFFORD

b. Bridgeton, N. J., 23 Sep. 1893. Studied with Henry Lang, Philadelphia Cons., also piano and organ. He received several ASCAP awards. He has been church organist in Philadelphia and Hollywood; was composer-conductor for Ruth St. Denis, Denishawn Dancers, Michael Fokine, Doris Humphrey, and Charles Weidman; composer-orchestrator for major film studios in Hollywood for 30 years.

WORKS: Orchestra: 4 symphonies; violin concerto; piano concerto; organ concerto; 30

(VAUGHAN, CLIFFORD)

Oriental translations for small orch.; Hindu Nautch dance; Chamber music: 2 string quartets; Violin concertante; Revery for harp; 6 preludes for piano; 2 voluntaries for organ; Chorus: The 10 Commandments, cantata; Queen Esther, oratorio; numerous other works for piano, organ, chamber groups, and liturgical music.

5830 1/2 Lexington Ave., Hollywood, CA 90038

VAUGHAN, RODGER

b. Delphos, Kan., 2 Feb. 1932. Studied with Ingolf Dahl and Halsey Stevens, Univ. of Southern California, M. M. He won the Kansas Centennial award, 1961, for best orchestral composition. He was faculty member, Wichita Univ., 1956-60; Univ. of Southern California, 1961-63; Upland Coll., 1963-65; California State Univ. at Fullerton, 1965-

WORKS: Orchestra: Centennial symphony; Overture to Dionysus; Quattro bicinie, clarinet and tuba; Quinte bicinie, viola and tuba; 3 songs for soprano and tuba; Chorus: Psalm 100; Psalm 121; Festival anthem; Christmas lullaby.

226 Borromeo, Placentia, CA 92670

*VAZZANA, ANTHONY

b. Troy, N. Y., 4 Nov. 1922. Studied at New York State Univ., B. S.; with Ingolf Dahl and Halsey Stevens, Univ. of Southern California, M. M., D. M. A. He received Alchin and Friends of Music scholarships and a Bennington Composers Conference fellowship. He taught in public schools, 1948-51; New York State Univ., Champlain, 1951-52; Cortland, N. Y., 1953-54; Danbury State Coll., 1954-57; Univ. of Southern California, 1959-

WORKS: Orchestra: symphony; Symphonic allegro; suite for chamber orch.; Chamber music: 2 pieces for clarinet; Incontri, violin and piano, 1972; Film scores: Tomorrow may be dying.

1228 21st St., Manhattan Beach, CA 90266

*VECSEI, DESIDER JOSEF

b. Budapest, Hungary, 25 Sep. 1882; to U.S. 1915; d. Hollywood, Calif., 1 Mar. 1966. Studied in Budapest and at the Vienna Cons. He was concert pianist in Europe and the U.S.; received a French Government award, Officer de l'Academie. He composed many songs and piano pieces.

VEGA, AURELIO DE LA

b. Havana, Cuba, 28 Nov. 1925; U.S. citizen 1966. Studied at De La Salle Coll., Havana, B. A.; Univ. of Havana, M. A. in humanities, Ph. D. in international law; Inst. Musical Ada Iglesias, Havana, Ph. D. in composition; privately with Frederick Kramer and Ernst Toch. His awards include the Virginia Colliers chamber music award, 1954; Andrew Mellon fellowship, 1964; Outstanding professor award, California State Univ. and Coll., 1971; Honor Distinction award, Atheneum of Buenos Aires, 1972; and commissions. He was music critic in Havana, 1950-59; professor, Univ. of Oriente, Santiago, Cuba, 1953-59, dean School of Music, 1954-59; guest professor, Central Univ., Cuba, 1963;

VEGA, AURELIO DE LA

(VEGA, AURELIO DE LA)
musical advisor, Nat. Inst. of Culture, Havana, 1965-69; guest professor, Univ. of Southern California, summer 1959; professor, California State Univ. at Northridge, 1959- .
WORKS: Orchestra: Overture to a serious farce, 1950; Elegy, string orch., 1954; Intrata, 1972; Chamber music: Legend of the Creole Ariel, cello and piano, 1953; Structures, piano and string quartet, 1962; Exametron, flute, cello, and percussion, 1965; Exospheres, oboe and piano, 1966; Antinomies, piano, 1967; Labdanum, flute, viola, vibraphone, Los Angeles, 30 Nov. 1970; Electronic: Vectors, tape, 1963; Interpolation; clarinet and tape, 1965; Tangents, violin and tape, 1973; Para-tangents, trumpet and tape, 1973.
California State University
Northridge, CA 91324

VELKE, FRITZ
b. Washington, D.C., 10 Sep. 1930. Studied with William Graves and G. Thaddeus Jones, Catholic Univ. of America. He received the Ostwald award, American Bandmasters Asso., 1962. He was trombonist, U.S. Air Force Band, Washington, 1953-57; instrumental music teacher, Fairfax County, Va., schools, 1957- ; conductor, Alexandria, Va., Citizens' Band, 1964-66; Conductor, Falls Church City Band, 1972- .
WORKS: Orchestra: Concerto grosso for brass sextet and orch.; Adagietto for strings; Band: Quartal piece; Concertino for band; Fanfare and rondo; Foray at Fairfax; Plaything; Capriccio; Chamber music: string quartet.
Box 9263, Alexandria, VA 22304

*VENÉ, RUGGERO
b. Lerici, Spezia, Italy, 12 Aug. 1897; to U.S. 1932; d. Italy, 18 Aug. 1961. Studied at Royal Cons. of Parma; with Nadia Boulanger in Paris; with Ottorino Respighi in Rome. He was conductor and choral coach in European theatres; in the U.S. taught at the Malkin Cons.; New England Cons.; Columbia Univ.; Washington Univ.; and Indiana Univ. His compositions include Rossaccio, symphonic poem; a string quartet; piano quintet.

VERCOE, BARRY LLOYD
b. New Zealand, 24 July 1937; to U.S. 1962. Studied at Univ. of Auckland; with Ross Lee Finney, Univ. of Michigan. He received the Philip Neil prize in composition, 1959; Ford grant in the MENC Contemporary Music Project, 1967-68. He was assistant professor, Oberlin Cons., 1965-67; visiting lecturer, Yale Univ., 1970-71; assistant professor and director, studio for experimental music, Massachusetts Inst. of Technology, 1971- .
WORKS: Orchestra: Metamorphoses, 1965; Digressions, for chorus, orch., and computer sounds, 1968; Chamber music: Setropy, clarinet and piano, 1964; Electronic: Synthesism for computer, 1970.
11 Round Hill Road, Lexington, MA 02173

*VERESS, SANDOR
b. Kolozsvar, Hungary, 1 Feb. 1907. Studied with Bela Bartok and Zoltan Kodaly. From 1947 he lived in Rome until appointment as professor, Bern Univ., Switzerland; joined the faculty at Peabody Cons. in 1965.
WORKS: Ballet: Terszili Katica, 1943; Orchestra: violin concerto, 1939; 4 Transylvanian dances, string orch., 1944; Threnos in memory of Bela Bartok, 1945; piano concerto; Sinfonia Minneapolitana, Minneapolis 12 Mar. 1954; concerto for double orchestra; Chamber music: 2 string quartets; woodwind trio; violin sonata; and songs.

VERNON, KNIGHT
b. Camden, N. J., 12 Dec. 1934. Studied with Ernst Bacon and David W. Johnson, Syracuse Univ., B. M. 1957; with Leslie Bassett, Univ. of Michigan, M. M. 1967. Awards include first prize, Nat. Asso. of Methodist Musicians, 1961; first prize, Rochester Festival of Religious Arts, 1968; copying grant, American Music Center, 1969; selection of a quintet for performance, Festival of Music, Rio de Janeiro, 1970; and commissions. He was church organist-choirmaster and public school music teacher, 1959-68; faculty member, Interlochen Arts Acad., 1968-72; left teaching in 1972 to undertake building harpsichords.
WORKS: Orchestra: In memoriam, with narrator, 1967, Interlochen Arts Acad., 18 Oct. 1970; Chamber music: Suite for brass and percussion; 1968; quintet for winds, 1969, Rio de Janeiro, 15 May 1970; Chorus: Haiku west, treble voices a cappella, 1966; They shall mount up with wings, a cappella, Rochester, N. Y., 5 May 1968; Swords into plowshares, a cappella, 1970; Piano: Sound structures, Ann Arbor, Mich., 25 Feb. 1964, was choreographed in 1969 as a solo modern dance entitled Alone.
525 White Pigeon St., Constantine, MI 49042

VERRALL, JOHN W.
b. Britt, Iowa, 17 June 1908. Studied with Reginald Owen Morris in London, 1929-30; with Zoltan Kodaly in Budapest, 1930-31; Donald Ferguson, Univ. of Minnesota, B. A. 1932; Aaron Copland at Tanglewood, 1938; Roy Harris at Colorado Coll., 1939; and with Frederick Jacobi, Juilliard School, 1945. His awards include a Guggenheim fellowship, 1948; Honolulu Acad. of Arts award, 1949; Seattle Centennial Opera award, 1952; D. H. Lawrence fellowship, Univ. of New Mexico, 1964; concert of his music, Univ. of Washington, 31 May 1973. He was associate professor, Hamline Univ., 1934-42; assistant professor, Mt. Holyoke Coll., 1942-46; editor, G. Schirmer and Boston Music Company, 1946-48; professor, Univ. of Washington, 1948-73, professor emeritus, 1973.
WORKS: Opera: The cowherd and the sky maiden, 1951; The wedding knell, 1952; Three blind mice, 1955; Orchestra: symphony, 1939; Portrait of man, 1940; Concert piece, strings and horn, 1941; violin concerto, 1947; Prelude and allegro for strings, 1948; Variations on an ancient tune, 1955; Dark night of St. John,

(VERRALL, JOHN W.)
1959; Suite for orch., 1959; piano concerto, 1959; viola concerto, 1968; Band: Passacaglia, 1958; Chamber music: 2 violin sonatas, 1939, 1963; trio for 2 violins and viola, 1941; 7 string quartets, 1941, 1942, 1948, 1948, 1952, 1956, 1961; 2 Serenades for wind quintet, 1944, 1950; violin sonata, 1950; piano quintet, 1953, Seattle, 6 Oct. 1955; violin sonata, 1956; cello sonatina, 1956; oboe sonata, 1956; viola sonatina, 1956; Nocturne, bass clarinet and piano, 1956, Indianapolis, 8 Feb. 1960; septet for winds, 1966; symphony for chamber orch., 1966; Nonette, wind quintet and string quartet, Seattle, 4 Mar. 1971; Brief elegy, clarinet solo, 1970; flute sonata, 1972; Chorus: Ah come, sweet death,, canon a cappella, 1947; Piano: 4 pieces, 1949; sonata, 1951; Sketches and miniatures, 1954; Autumn sketches, 1956; Preludes en suite, 1960; Prelude, intermezzo and fugue, 2 pianos, 1965; Organ: Canzona, 1965. His published books include Fugue and invention in theory and practice, 1966; Basic theory of scales, modes, and intervals, 1966.
    3821 42nd Ave. N. E., Seattle, WA 98105

VEYVODA, GERALD JOSEPH
b. Queens, N. Y., 30 Sep. 1948. Studied with Ruth Anderson, Hunter Coll., B. S. 1970, M. A. 1972. He received the Ethel Lippman Hurwitz award and the George M. Schuster award. He was lecturer, Hunter Coll., Feb.-June 1971.
    WORKS: Chamber music: Thru the looking glass, wind quintet, tape, mezzo-soprano; Into the artifice of eternity, wind quintet and tape; 1971; quartet for winds, 1970; Sonnet to science, text by Poe, soprano and chamber orch., 1971.
    18 Poplar Ave., Bronx, NY 10465

*VIERRA, M. L.
Out of the depths, chorus.

*VIGELAND, HANS
My faith, it is an oaken staff, chorus.

*VILLA, JOSEPH
Elegy Hebraique, mezzo soprano, New York, 30 Apr. 1973.

*VINCENT, HENRY BETHUEL
b. Denver, Colo., 28 Dec. 1872; d. Erie, Pa., 7 Jan. 1941. Studied organ in Ohio and Paris; was organ and choirmaster in Erie, Pa.
    WORKS: Opera: Esperanza, 1906; Indian days, operetta; Chorus: The prodigal son, oratorio, 1901; anthems; Songs: The garden of Kama, cycle; and organ pieces.

VINCENT, JOHN
b. Birmingham, Ala., 17 May 1902. Studied with George W. Chadwick, New England Cons., diploma 1926; George Peabody Coll., B. S. 1932, M. A. 1933; with Walter Piston, Harvard Univ., 1933-35; Ecole Normale de Musique, Paris, and with Nadia Boulanger privately, 1935-37; Cornell Univ., Ph. D. 1942. He received the John Knowles Paine Traveling fellowship, 1935-37; Guggenheim fellowship, 1964; many commissions, including

(VINCENT, JOHN)
Louisville Symphony, 1954, Eugene Ormandy, 1958, Contemporary Records, 1961, et al. He was head, music department, Western Kentucky Univ., 1937-45; professor, Univ. of California, Los Angeles, 1946-69, followed Schoenberg as chairman of music department, 1948-53; director, Huntington Hartford Found., 1953-65; president, California Inst. of the Arts, 1963-64; State Department conductor and lecturer in South America, 1964.
    WORKS: Opera: Primeval void, 1-act opera buffa to own libretto, 1969, Vienna, Austria, 14 May 1971; Theatre: music for The hallow'd time, play by Richard Hubler, 1954; Ballet: 3 Jacks, 1941, Los Angeles, 16 Mar. 1954; Orchestra: Suite for orchestra, 1932; Miracle of the cherry tree, 1944, voice and orch., Los Angeles, 2 Dec. 1947; I wonder as I wander, low voice, chorus, and orch., 1944; Soliloquy and dance, cello and orch., 1947; Symphony on a folk song, 1951; Nude descending the staircase, string orch., 1948; Symphony in D, Louisville, Ky., 5 Feb. 1955; The house that Jack built, narrator and orch. (from 3 Jacks), 1956; La Jolla chamber concerto, La Jolla, 19 July 1959; Symphonic poem after Descartes, Philadelphia, 20 Mar. 1959; Overture to Lord Arling, 1959; Consort for piano and strings, Dallas, 25 Apr. 1961; Benjamin Franklin suite, string orch. and glass harmonica obbligato, Philadelphia, 24 Mar. 1963; Rondo rhapsody, Washington, D.C., 9 May 1965; The phoenix, symphonic poem, Phoenix, Ariz., 21 Feb. 1966; Band: Nacre, 1973; Chamber music: string quartet, 1936, Princeton, N. J., 23 May 1938; woodwind trio, 1937; string quartet, Lexington, Ky., 8 Apr. 1967; Percussion suite, Los Angeles, 24 Apr. 1973; Chorus: 3 Grecian songs, 8-part chorus, 1936; Stabat mater, male voices with soprano solo, Chicago, 31 Mar. 1970; many other choral works and songs. He is author of Diatonic modes in modern music, 1951, revised and updated, 1973.
    c/o Music Department,
    University of California
    Los Angeles, CA 90024

*VIRIZLAY, MIHALY
b. Hungary; to U.S. 1957. Studied with Zoltan Kodaly, Franz Liszt Acad., Budapest. He received the Harriet Cohen Internat. award for cello, 1962. He has given many recitals on the cello and appeared with major orchestras; joined the faculty of Peabody Cons. as cello teacher in 1962; has been visiting professor at Indiana Univ., summers, 1966, 1967; and is principal cellist, Baltimore Symphony Orchestra. His compositions include an orchestral suite on The emperor's new clothes and a sonata for unaccompanied cello.

VIRKHAUS, TAAVO
b. Estonia, 29 June 1934; U.S. citizen 1955. Studied at Univ. of Miami; with Wayne Barlow, Bernard Rogers, and John LaMontaine, Eastman School of Music, D. M. A. 1967. He received the Howard Hanson prize, 1966; 2nd place in Phi Mu Alpha contest, 1959. He is director of music, Univ. of Rochester, River Campus; associate

VIRKHAUS, TAAVO

(VIRKHAUS, TAAVO)
professor, Eastman School of Music, 1966-   ;
a conductor, Opera Theater of Rochester,
1970-
WORKS: Orchestra: Overture to Kalevipoeg,
1957; French overture, 1965; violin concerto,
1966; Chamber music: miniature string quartet,
1957; Electronic: Contrasts and variables,
organ and tape, 1971.
15 Callingham Road, Pittsford, NY 14534

VLAHOPOULOS, SOTIREOS
b. St. Louis, Mo., 1 June 1926. Studied with
Virgil Thomson, State Univ. of New York; with
Roy Harris, Indiana Univ.; and at American Cons.
He was a public school music teacher, 1952-57,
1958-60; teaching assistant, Indiana Univ.,
1957-58; assistant professor, Rosary Hill Coll.,
1960-67, associate professor and composer-in-
residence, 1970-   .
WORKS: Orchestra: 5 ancient myths; The
Earth is an island, song cycle for soprano and
orch.; The moon pool, tone poem for strings;
Elegy, oboe and strings; Song of the red ruby,
9 instruments and strings; Chamber music: string
quartet; trio for 2 clarinets and bassoon; sonata
for solo cello; bassoon sonatina; duo for viola
and cello; Chorus: In memoriam, women's voices;
Songs cycles: The lights in the sky are stars,
for soprano; The poet is an unhappy creature,
for baritone; Songs of the unknown, for alto;
Piano: sonata, sonatina, etc.
4303 Wakefield Drive, Annandale, VA 22003

*VODERY, WILL HENRY BENNETT
b. Philadelphia, Pa., 8 Oct. 1885; d. New York,
N. Y., 18 Nov. 1951. Graduated from Univ. of
Pennsylvania. He was composer, arranger, band
master; arranged scores for more than 50 musical
comedies; wrote the music for The time, the place,
and the girl; wrote songs for The oyster man,
1910; was music superviser of the Ziegfeld
follies, 1911-32.

VOLLRATH, CARL PAUL
b. New York, N. Y., 26 Mar. 1931. Studied at
Stetson Univ., B. M., 1953; Teachers Coll.,
Columbia Univ., M. A. 1956; with Ernst von
Dohnanyi, Carlisle Floyd, John Boda, Florida
State Univ., Ed. D. 1964. He won first prize,
Florida Composers League, 1952. He was clarinetist, U.S. Military Acad. Band, 1953-56; music
consultant, Dade County Schools, Fla., 1956-58;
assistant professor, Troy State Univ., 1965-   .
WORKS: Opera: The quest, 1964; Theatre:
music for The king's own Christmas, 1962; The
cherry orchard, 1964; Orchestra: Piece for trombone and orch., 1952; War, voice and orch., 1952;
Heavenly beauty, voice, chorus, orch., 1952;
Short piece for orch., 1960; Band: Ulysses' return, 1951; Concert suite, 1955; Sinfonietta,
1960; Concert overture, 1968; Everyman's suite,
1973; Chamber music: 2 clarinet sonatas, 1959,
1969; quintet for winds, strings, and harpsichord,
1969; baritone horn sonata, 1969; Fantasy, viola
and piano, 1972; Kyriology for flute, 1973; many
pieces for various instruments and piano; songs;
piano pieces.
Troy State University, Troy, AL 36081

VON GUNDEN, HEIDI
b. San Diego, Calif., 13 Apr. 1940. Studied
with Matt Doran, Mount St. Mary's Coll.; with
Byong-kon Kim, California State Univ., Los
Angeles; and with Pauline Oliveros, Univ. of
California at San Diego. She was teaching
assistant, Univ. of California, San Diego,
1972-74.
WORKS: Chamber music: Triptych, organ,
harpsichord, and percussion; Fantasy, organ,
tape, mouth-blown pipes, clarinet, percussion;
Diathrosis, organ, harpsichord, 2 trombones,
2 accordions, piano, celeste; Chorus: Mass for
Pentecost, choir, resonating tubes, organ, tape,
projected score.
4115 Idaho St., San Diego, CA 92104

*VON WURTZLER, ARISTID
b. Budapest, Hungary, 20 Sep. 1925; U.S. citizen
1958. Studied with Zoltan Kodaly at Liszt Acad.,
Budapest. He was harpist with the Budapest Phil-
harmonic for 7 years; later with the Detroit
Symphony and New York Philharmonic; director,
New York Harp Ensemble; chairman, harp depart-
ment, Hartt Coll. of Music.
WORKS: Chamber music: Capriccio, harp;
Space odyssey, 4 harps; Modern sketches: Yester-
day/today/tomorrow, harp.
Hartt College of Music
University of Hartford
200 Bloomfield Ave., West Hartford, CT 06117

*VREE, MARION F.
Has published choral works. She teaches at Los
Angeles Pierce College, 6201 Winnetka Avenue,
Woodland Hills, CA 91364.

WADA, YOSHIMASA
b. Kyoto, Japan, 11 Nov. 1943; to U.S. 1967.
Studied with John Watts, The New School, New
York; privately with Pran Nath, LaMonte Young,
and Kocherlakota Paramjyoti in New York. He
received a Creative Arts Public Service grant,
1974. He specializes in long-tone harmonic works
for electronics and voice or instruments using
overtone series. The instruments used are large
horns up to 30 feet in length, which he builds
of steam fittings and plumbing materials.
WORKS: Multimedia: A-440, for pipe horns,
voice, tuning fork, and galvanized sheet, 1972;
50-gallon drum chant, solo voice inside 3 50-
gallon metal drums, amplified, 1972; Sundown
1080, for pipe horns, electronic drones, and
voice, 1973; Earthsound 2160, for pipe horns,
synthesizer, electronic drones, 1974. Though
not notated, his works are not aleatoric but
thoroughly rehearsed.
15 Greene St., New York, NY 10013

*WADE, JAMES
The martyred, opera based on novel by American-
Korean author Richard Kim, performed at Seoul,
Korea, 18 Apr. 1970.

*WADE, WALTER
b. 1926.   Arise, my love, chorus, Biblical text.
Department of Music, Memphis State University
Memphis, TN 38111

*WAGENAAR, BERNARD
b. Arnhem, Netherlands, 18 July 1894; U.S. citizen 1927; d. York, Me., 19 May 1971. Studied with his father, Dutch composer Johan Wagenaar; violin with Gerard Veerman. He received the first Ditson award from Columbia Univ., for his chamber opera; Society for Publication of American Music award, 1928; Eastman School publication award, 1929; many commissions. He was violinist in the New York Philharmonic, 1921-27, also played celeste, harpsichord, organ. He resigned from the Philharmonic to join the faculty at Juilliard School; also taught privately and conducted his own works.
WORKS: Opera: Pieces of eight, 2-act chamber opera, New York, May 1944; Orchestra: 4 symphonies, 1928, 1932, 1937, 1949; Divertimento, 1929; Sinfonietta, 1930; violin concerto, 1940; triple concerto, flute, harp, cello and orch., 1941; Concert overture, 1953; 5 tableaux, cello and orch., 1955; Chamber music: violin sonata, 1925; 4 string quartets; piano sonata; cello sonata; concertino for 8 instruments.

WAGNER, JOSEPH F.
b. Springfield, Mass., 9 Jan. 1900; d. Los Angeles, Calif. 12 Oct. 1974. Studied with Frederick Converse, New England Cons., diploma 1923; privately with Alfredo Casella in Boston, 1927; at Boston Univ., B. M. 1932; with Nadia Boulanger in Paris, 1934-35; also conducting with Pierre Monteux and Felix Weingartner in Europe. His awards include an honorary doctorate, Ithaca Coll.; Endicott prize, New England Cons.; Benjamin awards; Northern California Harpists Asso. award; fellowships at MacDowell Colony, Huntington Hartford Found., Montalvo Asso.; commissions from Eastern Illinois Univ. and Pepperdine Univ. He was assistant director of music and supervisor of instrumental music, Boston public schools, 1923-44; on faculty, Boston Univ., 1929-40; Hunter Coll., 1945-46; Brooklyn Coll., 1945-47; founder and conductor, Boston Civic Symphony Orch., 1925-44; conductor, Duluth Symphony, 1947-50; Nat. Symphony Orch. of Costa Rica, 1950-54; guest conductor of many orchestras in U.S. and Europe; faculty member, Los Angeles Cons., 1960-63; composer-in-residence and faculty member, Pepperdine Univ., 1963-72.
WORKS: Theatre: New England Sampler, 1-act opera; 3 ballets; Orchestra: 4 symphonies; 2 sinfoniettas; Northland evocation; Panorama; Rhapsody, clarinet, piano, strings, 1925; concertino, piano and orch.; A fugal triptych, 1941; concertino for harp and orch., 1947; A psalm of faith, soprano and orch.; Introduction and rondo, trumpet and orch.; Fantasy in technicolor, 1948; Introduction and scherzo, bassoon and strings, 1951; concerto for organ, brass, percussion, 1963; harp concerto, 1964; violin concerto; Band: Eulogy; American jubilee overture, 1946; Concerto grosso, 1949; Symphonic translations, 1958; A festive fanfare, brass and percussion, 1968; Merlin and Sir Boss, 1968; Chamber music: violin sonata; Rhapsody, clarinet and piano; clarinet sonatina; Serenade, violin, cello, oboe; 3 pastorales, oboe and piano, 1941; 3 moments musicals, string quartet; Theme and variations, violin, cello, flute, clarinet, 1950; Costa Rican pastoral, chamber

(WAGNER, JOSEPH F.)
orch.; Sonata of sonnets, voice and piano, 1961; Fantasy sonata, harp solo, 1963; Prelude and toccata, harp, violin, piano, 1964; Concert piece, violin and cello, 1966; 3 charades, brass quintet, 1968; 3 Browning love songs, voice and piano, 1970; Chorus: Gloria in excelsis, women's voices and chamber orch., 1925; David jazz, men's voices and jazz combo, 1934; The voice of the Lord, men's voices and orch., 1934; The story of a princess, with narrator and orch.; Under freedom's flag/Pledge of allegiance, 1940; Song of all seas, all ships, 1946; Ballad of brotherhood, 1947; Missa sacra, with soprano solo and orch.; American ballad set, 1963; Piano: 4 landscapes, 1936; sonata, 1946; and organ pieces.

*WAGNER, LEONARD
Fanfare, scherzo, and allegro, brass ensemble.

*WAGNER, THOMAS
b. Brackenridge, Pa., 24 Feb. 1931. Studied at Univ. of Pittsburgh; with James Friskin, Juilliard School; with Aaron Copland and Irving Fine at Tanglewood on scholarship. He is a concert pianist and has performed his own works in New York.
WORKS: Opera: The beggar; The crocodile; The wheat remains; Theatre: music for The lion in winter; Orchestra: Madrigal concerto; piano concerto; 2-piano concerto; Chorus; The girl with the little bean nose.
65 West 95th St., New York, NY 10025

WALCOTT, RONALD HARRY
b. Los Angeles, Calif., 13 May 1939. Studied with Richard Hoffmann, Oberlin Cons., B. A.; with John Vincent and Henri Lazarof, Univ. of California, Los Angeles, M. A., Ph. D. candidate in 1973; with B. Schaeffer and W. Kotonski in Poland. He received Atwater Kent awards in composition, 1965, 1966; Fulbright-Hays grant to Poland, 1962-65. He was teaching assistant and museum scientist, Univ. of California, Los Angeles, 1965-66, 1970-73.
WORKS: Chamber music: Fragments, percussion quartet; Generations, small ensemble; Variations for Oregon; Piece for piano; Relations, piano, clarinet, trombone, and cello.
5134 Angeles Crest Highway
La Canada, CA 91011

*WALD, MAX
b. Litchfield, Ill., 14 July 1889; d. Dowagiac, Mich., 14 Aug. 1954. Studied in Chicago and with Vincent d'Indy in Paris. He received 2nd prize in an NBC composition contest, 1932. From 1936 he was chairman, theory department, Chicago Musical Coll.
WORKS: Opera: Mirandolina, 1936; Gay little world, light opera, 1942; Orchestra: Retrospectives, 1926; The dancer dead, symphonic poem, 1932; Comedy overture, 1937; In praise of pageantry, 1946; Voice: October moonlight, song cycle for soprano and string quartet; Piano: 2 sonatas; other piano pieces.

WALDEN, STANLEY

WALDEN, STANLEY
b. 1932.   <u>Circus</u>, #3 from <u>3 views from the</u>
<u>open window</u>, for orchestra.
R. D. 3, Box 438
Hopewell Junction, NY 12533

*WALDMAN, ROBERT
<u>Saturday matinee</u>, chamber-opera musical, 1974.
NEA grant for American Bicentennial 1976.

*WALDROP, GIDEON WILLIAM
b. Haskell County, Tex., 2 Sep. 1919. Studied
at Baylor Univ., B. M. 1940; Eastman School of
Music, M. M. 1941, Ph. D. 1952. He received commissions from the San Antonio Symphony Society,
1958, 1963. He was conductor of the Shreveport
Symphony and faculty member, Centenary Coll.,
1941-42; served in the Army Air Force, 1943-45;
was conductor, Baylor-Waco Symphony and associate
professor, Baylor Univ., 1946-51; editor, <u>Review</u>
<u>of Recorded Music</u>, 1952-54; editor and general
manager, <u>Musical Courier</u>, 1954-58; on staff at
Juilliard School, 1961-   , dean, 1963-   .
WORKS: Orchestra: symphony, 1952; <u>From the</u>
<u>Southwest</u>, overture; <u>Prelude and fugue</u>; <u>Pressures</u>,
string orch.; Chamber music: trio for viola,
clarinet, harp, 1939; <u>Lydian trumpeter</u>, trumpet
and piano, 1946; also choral works and songs.
Juilliard School, Lincoln Center
New York, NY 10023

WALENSKY, DANA GRANT
b. Sioux City, Iowa, 24 July 1948. Studied with
G. Winston Cassler, St. Olaf Coll.; with Sister
Jane Klimisch, Mount Marty Coll.
WORKS: Orchestra: symphony; Chamber music:
<u>Lagrimoso</u>, brass ensemble; <u>Prelude and fugue</u>,
woodwind trio; <u>Fantasia (soldiers)</u>, piano; Chorus:
<u>O brother man</u>; <u>Choral fantasia</u>, with flute, oboe,
horn, and baritone horn.
302 North 22nd St., Omaha, NB 68102

*WALKER, DON
<u>Variations on the name of Ives</u>, orch.

WALKER, GEORGE
b. Washington, D.C., 27 June 1922. Studied at
Oberlin Coll., B. M. 1940; Eastman School of
Music, D. M. A.; his major teachers were Rudolf
Serkin and Rosario Scalero; and Nadia Boulanger
in Paris; also studied with Gregor Piatigorsky,
Gian-Carlo Menotti, and Robert Casadesus. His
many awards have included Fulbright, John Hay
Whitney, Guggenheim, Rockefeller, Nat. Endowment
for the Arts, MacDowell and Yaddo fellowships;
Harvey Gaul prize; Rhea Soslund prize; grants
from the Bok Found., and the Research Councils
of the Univ. of Colorado and Rutgers Univ. He
held faculty positions at New School for Social
Research, 1961; Dalcroze School of Music, 1960-61;
Smith Coll., 1961-68; Univ. of Colorado, 1968-69;
Rutgers Univ., Newark, 1969-   , professor,
1972-   ; piano faculty, Peabody Cons.,
1974-   .
WORKS: Orchestra: trombone concerto; a sym-
phony; <u>Variations for orchestra</u>; <u>Address for or-</u>
<u>chestra</u>, <u>Passacaglia</u> performed New York, 21 Oct.
1973, complete work, Baltimore, 16 Jan. 1974;

(WALKER, GEORGE)
<u>Spirituals</u>, Houston, 7 Sep. 1974; Chamber music:
2 string quartets, violin sonata; Chorus: <u>Stars</u>;
<u>Gloria--in memoriam</u>, women's voices; Piano: 2
sonatas; <u>Spatials</u>, <u>Spektra</u>; <u>Variations on a</u>
<u>Kentucky folk song</u>.
323 Grove St., Montclair, NJ 07042

WALKER, JAMES
b. Milwaukee, Wis., 13 Nov. 1937. Studied at
Univ. of Wisconsin; with Leon Kirchner, Billy
Jim Layton, and Roger Sessions, Harvard Univ.,
M. M. He received an award, Northwestern Inter-
nat. composition contest, 1966; a commission,
Ohio Music Educators Asso., 1973; fellowship,
Faculty Awards Program, State Univ. of New York,
1973-74. He was conductor, Harvard Wind Ensemble
and Bands, 1960-70, Freshman Glee Club, 1964-68,
Harvard Chorus, 1969; conductor, Chautauqua
School of Music Symphony, 1965-72, Chamber Sym-
phony, 1970-   ; associate professor, State
Univ. Coll. at Geneseo, 1972-   .
WORKS: Chamber music: <u>Recitative in tran-</u>
<u>sition</u>, saxophone quartet, 1966; violin sonata;
Chorus: <u>Jabberwocky</u>, with harpsichord, piano and
electronic sounds, Columbus, Ohio, Feb. 1974.
Music Department
State Univ. of New York, Geneseo, NY 14454

WALKER, MARK
b. Alamogordo, N. M., 5 June 1918. Studied with
Norman Phelps, Jordan Coll. of Music, Butler
Univ., B. M., M. M.; with Roy Will, Indiana Univ.,
Ph. D. He has received ASCAP awards and commis-
sions from Indianapolis Symphony, Columbus Sym-
phony, Ohio Music Educators Asso., Butler Univ.,
Ohio State Fair Orchestra, Luther Coll., Youngs-
town Symphony String Quartet. He was bandleader,
U.S. Army, 1943-46; associate professor, Butler
Univ., 1946-61; associate professor, Ohio State
Univ., 1961-68; professor, Youngstown State
Univ., 1968-   .
WORKS: Orchestra: <u>Butler centennial over-</u>
<u>ture</u>; <u>Variations on a given theme</u>; <u>The wharf</u>,
ballet score; <u>Ricercar</u>; Band: <u>Overture and</u>
<u>allegro</u>; <u>Overture in the Dorian mode</u>; <u>Jordan</u>
<u>rhapsody</u>; <u>Premiere rhapsody</u>, clarinet and band;
<u>Capricce</u>, bassoon and band; Wind ensemble;
<u>Sarabande and bouree</u>, brass choir; <u>Concert over-</u>
<u>ture</u>; Solo for clarinet and winds; Chamber music:
<u>Moods minor</u>, trumpet trio and piano; <u>4 violins</u>
<u>in concert</u>; duo for 2 violins; string quartet.
152 Wolcott Drive, Youngstown, OH 44512

WALKER, RICHARD
b. Illinois, 23 Jan. 1912. Studied at Bradley
Univ., but is largely self-taught in composition.
He was clarinetist and flutist in orchestras,
bands, and wind ensembles, 1935-65; private
teacher, 1946-71.
WORKS: Band: <u>Scythian overture</u>; <u>Danish</u>
<u>overture</u>; <u>Lyrical overture</u>; <u>Corybantes</u>; Chamber
music: <u>Badinerie</u>, brass quartet; <u>Rococo</u>, woodwind trio; <u>Falconry match</u>, brass trio; <u>Suite for</u>
<u>saxophones</u>; <u>Rondo scherzando</u>, clarinet trio;
<u>Aubade</u>, clarinet quartet; <u>Persian caprice</u>, clari-
net; <u>Petite rien</u>, flute; <u>Ballade</u>, alto saxophone.
325 Fullerton Parkway, Chicago, IL 60614

WALKER, ROBERT S.
    b. Cheltenham, Pa., 12 Oct. 1935. Studied with
Julius Hijman and Roy Harris, Philadelphia
Musical Acad.; with Clifford Taylor, Temple
Univ. He has been music teacher, Philadelphia
public schools, 1961-   .
    WORKS: Orchestra: symphony; Chamber music:
2 songs for soprano voice; Toccata for piano;
woodwind quintet; string quartet in 2 movements.
    1113 Stratford Avenue
    Melrose Park, PA 19126

WALLACE, KATHRYN
    b. Shawnee, Okla., 21 Oct. 1917. Studied at
Oklahoma Univ., B. F. A. 1938; with Warren M.
Angell, Oklahoma Baptist Univ., 1957-58.
    WORKS: Chorus: For the beauty of the
Earth; Be thou, O God, exalted; The Lord is
my shepherd; Piano: Moods; Tin soldier parade.
    1900 North Beard Street, Shawnee, OK 74801

WALSH, MICHAEL A.
    b. Camp LeJeune, N. C., 23 Oct. 1949. Studied
with Warren Benson and Samuel Adler, Eastman
School of Music, 1967-71.
    WORKS: Orchestra: Elegy, violin and orch.;
Herbstlied, violin and orch.; Medieval songs,
cycle for voice and orch.; Chamber music: piano
trio; Piano variations on a theme of Anton
Webern; string quartet in 1 movement; 7 Deutsche
Lieder, voice and piano.
    1 Regent Street, Rochester, NY 14607

*WALTER, BRUNO
    b. Berlin, Germany, 15 Sep. 1876; U.S. citizen
c. 1945; d. Beverly Hills, Calif., 17 Feb.
1962. Studied at Sterns Cons., Berlin; became
opera coach at the Cologne Municipal Opera at
age 17; then assistant conductor under Mahler
at the Hamburg State Theatre; became one of the
world's noted opera conductors. After settling
he was a frequent guest conductor at the New
York Metropolitan Opera; conducted the New York
Philharmonic, 1947-49.
    WORKS: Orchestra: 2 symphonies;
Siegesfahrt, soloists, chorus, orch.; Chamber
music: string quartet; piano quartet; piano
trio; many songs.

WALTER, SAMUEL
    b. Cumberland, Md., 2 Feb. 1916. Studied at
Boston Univ.; with Seth Bingham, Union Theological Seminary, New York; with Nadia Boulanger,
Fontainebleau, France. He was instructor,
Boston Univ., 1945-50, assistant professor and
university organist, 1950-55; instructor, Union
Theological Seminary, School of Sacred Music,
1957-65; lecturer, Douglass Coll., Rutgers Univ.,
1962-70, assistant professor, 1970, Voorhees
Chapel organist, 1964-   ; organist and choirmaster, Church of the Resurrection, New York,
1967-   .
    WORKS: Chorus: Blessed are the pure in
heart; Christ is the world's true light; Hearts
to heaven and voices raise; and many other
published choral works; Organ: 6 hymn tune
preludes, 1962; 9 compositions for organ, 1965;
Music for processions, 1966; Cardinal suite,

(WALTER, SAMUEL)
1966; Prelude on a Scandinavian hymn tune. He
is author of Basic principles of service playing,
1963; Music composition and arranging, 1965; and
articles in music journals.
    83 School House Lane
    East Brunswick, NJ 08816

WALTERS, HAROLD L.
    b. Gurdon, Ark., 29 Sep. 1918. Attended
Cincinnati Cons.; American Univ.; studied with
Nadia Boulanger in Paris. He received an honorary music doctorate, Washington Coll. of Music;
citation of excellence, Nat. Band Asso., 1973.
He was arranger, U.S. Navy Band, 1938-44; scored
many Broadway shows, radio, etc.; composer-
editor, Rubank Music Publishing Company,
1949-   .
    WORKS: over 1500 published works for
orchestra, band, chorus, instrumental ensembles,
and solos.
    4931 Pierce Street, Hollywood, FL 33021

*WALTERS, MICHAEL J.
    Studied with Warren Benson, Ithaca Coll., B. S.
1965, M. S.; with Clifton Williams, Univ. of
Miami, D. M. A. He was band director and teacher
in public schools before joining the faculty in
music education at the New England Cons. He
conducted the premiere of his Apparitions for
wind ensemble at the Conservatory, 19 Mar. 1974.

*WALTON, KENNETH E.
    b. Tulse Hill, London, England, 17 Feb. 1904;
U.S. citizen. Has published works for chorus:
Hush, my love; O lovely world of mine; Christmas
rhapsody; and songs.

*WARD, BEVERLY A.
    Benedictus es, Domine, chorus and organ.

*WARD, FRANK EDWIN
    b. Wysox, Pa., 7 Oct. 1872; d. Wolfboro, N. H.,
15 Sep. 1953. Studied at New York Coll. of
Music; with Edward MacDowell, Columbia Univ.,
1898-1903. He was associate professor at
Columbia Univ., 1909-19; organist and choirmaster, Church of the Holy Trinity, New York,
1906-46.
    WORKS: Orchestra: Ocean rhapsody; Chamber
music: 2 string quartets; other chamber works;
Chorus: The saviour of the world, Lenten cantata; The divine birth, Christmas cantata; also
anthems, songs, organ pieces.

*WARD, ROBERT EUGENE
    b. Cleveland, Ohio, 13 Sep. 1917. Studied with
Bernard Rogers and Howard Hanson, Eastman School
of Music, B. M. 1939; with Frederick Jacobi and
Albert Stoessel, Juilliard School; and with
Aaron Copland at Tanglewood. His many awards
include MacDowell fellowship, 1938; Juilliard
publication award, 1942; Ditson award, 1944;
American Acad, of Arts and Letters award, 1946;
Guggenheim fellowships, 1950, 1951; Pulitzer
prize, 1962; membership, Nat. Inst. of Arts
and Letters; honorary D. M., Peabody Cons, 1975.
He served in the U.S. Army, 1942-46; was music

WARD, ROBERT EUGENE

(WARD, ROBERT EUGENE)
editor and executive vice president, Galaxy Music Corporation and Highgate Press; president, North Carolina School of the Arts.

WORKS: Opera: Pantaloon, 3-acts, on Andreyev's play He who gets slapped, 1956; The crucible, 4 acts, 1961; The lady from Colorado, 2 acts, 1964; Orchestra: Fatal interview, soprano and orch., 1937; Ode, 1939; Yankee overture, 1940; Hushed be the camps today, chorus and orch., 1941; 4 symphonies, 1942, 1947, 1950, 1958; Adagio and allegro, 1943; Jubilation overture, 1946; Concert music, 1948; Night music, chamber orch., 1949; Jonathan and the gingery snare, 1949; Sacred songs for pantheists, soprano and orch., 1951; Festival overture; Divertimento, 1960; Hymn and celebration, 1962; Music for celebration, 1963; Let the word go forth, 1965; piano concerto; Band: Fantasia for brass choir and timpani, 1953; Fiesta processional; Prairie overture; Music for a great occasion, for the inauguration of Duke Univ. president, 18 Oct. 1970; Chamber music: violin sonata, 1950; Arioso and tarantella, viola or cello and piano, 1954; An abstract, clarinet and piano; many choral works, songs, piano pieces.

North Carolina School of the Arts
P. O. Box 4657, Winston-Salem, NC 27107

*WARD, RUSSELL
Preservation rock and Sand, man, both for concert jazz band.

*WARD, WILLIAM REED
b. Norton, Kan., 20 May 1918. Studied with Charles S. Skilton and Robert Palmer, Univ. of Kansas, B.M., B. M. E. 1941; with Bernard Rogers and Howard Hanson, Eastman School of Music, M. M. 1942, Ph. D. 1954. He received an award in the Nat. Arrangers contest, 1947. He was instructor, Colorado State Univ., 1942-44; assistant professor and head of composition, Laurence Coll., 1944-47; on faculty, San Francisco State Coll., 1947-   , department chairman, 1954-   , professor, 1959-   ; has also held posts as organist-choirmaster.

WORKS: Orchestra: 3 symphonies, 1938, 1947, 1954; Variations on a western tune, 1948; Chamber music: suite for woodwind quintet, 1954; Be thou my vision, organ; Chorus: Lullaby for a pinto colt, 1941; A vision of the world, 1955; Psalm 136, 1959; A psalm of praise, 1960; Fray Junipero Serra, The great walker, oratorio, 1960.

San Francisco State College
San Francisco, CA 94132

WARD-STEINMAN, DAVID
b. Alexandria, La., 6 Nov. 1936. Studied with John Boda, Florida State Univ., B. M. cum laude 1957; with Burrill Phillips, Univ. of Illinois, M. M. 1958, D. M. A. 1961; with Nadia Boulanger in Paris, 1958-59; also with Darius Milhaud, Wallingford Riegger, and Milton Babbitt. His honors include 4 BMI student composer awards; 2 Nat. Fed. of Music Clubs prizes; Phi Mu Alpha award; Sigma Alpha Iota American music award; Bearns prize of Columbia Univ.; Ernst von Dohnanyi award, Florida State Univ.; honorary

(WARD-STEINMAN, DAVID)
doctorate, Gracian Inst. of Montreal; Outstanding professor award, California State Colleges; Kinley Memorial fellowship, Univ. of Illinois. He was assistant professor, San Diego State Coll., 1961-65, associate professor, 1965-68, professor, 1968-70; visiting fellow, music department, Princeton Univ., 1970; Ford Found. composer-in-residence, Tampa Bay area, Fla., 1970-72; professor, California State Univ., San Diego, 1972-   .

WORKS: Opera: Tamar, 2-act opera; Ballet: These 3; Western Orpheus, San Diego, Feb. 1965; Rituals for dancers and musicians, 1971; Incidental music: The Oresteia; Joe Egg; The puppet prince, Sarasota, Fla., 1 July 1971; Orchestra; symphony, 1959; Concert overture; Concerto no. 2 for chamber orchestra, San Diego, Mar. 1963; Concerto grosso for combo and chamber orchestra; cello concerto, American premiere, Seattle, Dec. 1967; Prelude and toccata; Antares, with gospel choir and tape or synthesizer, Tampa, Fla., 22 Apr. 1971; Arcturus, with Putney synthesizer or tape, Chicago, June 1972; Band: Jazz tangents; Raga for winds; Gasparilla Day, 1971; Chamber music: Child's play, bassoon and piano; duo for cello and piano; Grant Park, baritone and chamber ensemble; Montage, woodwind quintet; brass quintet; 3 songs for clarinet and piano, 1957; The tale of Issoumbochi, for narrator, boy soprano, ensemble, Japanese fairy tale; Wedding music, soprano, woodwind quintet, organ; Putney 3, woodwind quintet, prepared piano, piano interior, Putney synthesizer and tape; Fragments from Sappho, soprano, flute, clarinet, piano, 1965; Chorus: The song of Moses, narrator, 4 soli, double chorus, San Diego, 31 May 1964; Piano: sonata, 1957; 3 miniatures; 3 lyric preludes; Elegy for Martin Luther King; sonata for piano fortified; Latter-day lullabies, 1972; Electronic: Now-Music for 4 tape recorders and dice; Vega, Putney synthesizer and tape; Riversong variations, Putney synthesizer and tape, 1973; Multimedia: Kaleidoscope, videotape for TV, sound/color film, for dancers, musicians, synthesizers, tape, and integral video-camera work; Nova (collage '72), sound/color film, synthesizer, tape, 1972.

9403 Broadmoor Place, LaMesa, CA 92041

*WARE, HARRIET
b. Waupun, Wis., 26 Aug. 1877; d. New York, N. Y., 9 Feb. 1962. Studied piano with William Mason in New York; with Sigismund Stojowski in Paris; composition with Hugo Kaun in Berlin.

WORKS: Operetta: Waltz for three; Orchestra: The artisan, symphonic poem, New York Symphony, 1929; Chorus: Sir Olaf, cantata, New York Symphony, 1910; Trees, choral cycle; Undine, choral cycle; Songs: Women's triumphal march, became the national song of the Fed. of Women's Clubs, 1927; Joy of the morning; The fay song; Boat song; The call of Radha; Stars; Sunlight; Waltz song; numerous songs and piano pieces.

WARE, JOHN MARLEY
b. Two Rivers, Wis., 6 July 1942. Studied
with Bernhard Heiden and Thomas Beversdorf; with
Kenneth B. Klaus, Louisiana State Univ. He
received a Ford Found. 3-year master's grant,
1963; his works were chosen 4 years for performance at Symposium of Contemporary Music for
Brass, Atlanta, Ga., 1967-70. He was instructor,
Huntington Coll., 1964-65; instructor, Univ. of
Tennessee, 1966-69; assistant professor, Middle
Tennessee State Univ., 1971-72; assistant
professor, Univ. of Wisconsin, Superior,
1972-   .
WORKS: Orchestra: concerto for trombone
and strings; Deploration, string orch.; Chamber
music: piano sonata, sonata for viola solo;
2 brass quintets; Fantasy, bassoon and piano;
Soundings, trombone and piano; Chorus: Loneliness, with brass and timpani; Organ:
Passacaglia; Fantasy.
1908 Weeks Avenue, Superior, WI 54880

WARFIELD, GERALD ALEXANDER
b. Fort Worth, Tex., 23 Feb. 1940. Studied
with Samuel Adler, North Texas State Univ.; with
Lukas Foss and Yannis Xenakis at Tanglewood;
with Milton Babbitt, Edward T. Cone, Earl Kim,
Peter Westergaard, and Godfrey Winham, Princeton
Univ. He received first prize in a contest of
the New Jersey Chapter, Nat. Society of Arts and
Letters, 1967; first prize, Arizona Cello
Society, 1973. He has been associate editor,
Index of New Musical Notation, New York Public
Library, 1973-   , and music catalog editor,
Educational Audio-Visual, 1975-   .
WORKS: Chamber music: Miniature, flute
and piano; 2 for 3, woodwind trio; Variations
and metamorphoses, cello ensemble, 1973, New
York, 24 Feb. 1975; Voice: A study of 2 pears,
song cycle, 1967; A noiseless, patient spider,
chorus.
114 West 71st Street, #A-2
New York, NY 10023

*WARGO, GEORGE A.
Was formerly on the faculty at Peabody Cons.
His string quartet was performed at the Nat.
Gallery, Washington, D.C., 22 Sep. 1946.
Department of Music, Pacific Union Coll.
Angwin, CA 94508

WARKENTIN, LARRY
b. Reedley, Calif., 14 Aug. 1940. Studied at
Tabor Coll., B. A. 1962; Fresno State Univ.,
M. A.; with Ingolf Dahl, Carl Parrish, and
Paul Pisk, Univ. of Southern California,
D. M. A. 1967. He received a Nat. Endowment for
the Arts summer grant, 1971; Bank of America
award, 1958; scholarship, Tabor Coll., 1958-62.
He was active as director and teacher of church
music, 1963-72; has been associate professor
and chairman, Humanities Division, Pacific Coll.,
1966-   .
WORKS: Orchestra: concertino for piano and
string orch., 1964: Chamber music: St. Paul on
Mars Hill, baritone and piano, 1960; 6 quatrains,
baritone and woodwind quintet, 1961; Chorus:
The word of God, with baritone solo and orch.,

(WARKENTIN, LARRY)
Fresno, 28 Apr. 1974; other works for chorus,
solo voice, and piano.
Pacific College, 1717 South Chestnut Avenue
Fresno, CA 93702

WARNE, KATHARINE MULKY
b. Oklahoma City, Okla., 23 Oct. 1923. Studied
with Darius Milhaud, Mills Coll.; with Bernard
Wagenaar, Juilliard School; and with Donald Erb,
Cleveland Inst. of Music. She received first
prize, Mills Coll. composition contest, 1944,
1945; full fellowship in composition at Juilliard
School; a first and a 2nd prize, Kansas Fed. of
Music Clubs contest, 1959; performance at Univ.
of Kansas symposium and Cleveland Contemporary
Arts Festival. She was instructor, Univ. of
Kansas, 1947-50, assistant professor, 1950-53,
1957-60.
WORKS: Chamber music: Apollo-Orion, chamber
orch.; Tetrad for percussion; Interplay, piccolo,
trumpet, cello; choral psalm settings, songs,
piano works.
15715 Chadbourne Road, Cleveland, OH 44120

*WARNER, RICHARD
5 spirituals for organ.
Department of Music, Kent State University
Kent, OH 44242

WARREN, ELINOR REMICK
b. Los Angeles, Calif., 23 Feb. 1906. Studied
piano and composition in Los Angeles; with
Clarence Dickinson in New York; with Nadia
Boulanger in Paris. Her awards include first
prize, Gedok Internat. Choral and Orchestral
competition, Germany; honorary music doctorate,
Occidental Coll.; Woman of the Year in Music,
Los Angeles Times, 1955; annual ASCAP awards,
1958-   ; selection along with Igor Stravinsky
and Walter Piston as an American composer to
participate in the first Los Angeles Internat.
Music Festival, 1961; many commissions. She
began composing at an early age and had compositions published by leading New York firms while
she was still in high school. She was also
an accomplished concert pianist and accompanist
for many well-known singers.
WORKS: Orchestra: Along the western shore;
The crystal lake; Suite for orchestra, 1954;
symphony in 1 movement; Singing Earth, with
soprano or tenor, Sandburg text; Sonnets for
soprano and string orch., Millay text; theme
for the Hollywood Bowl, 1959; Chorus: Transcontinental, with baritone solo and chamber
orch.; Abram in Egypt, with baritone solo and
orch., text from Dead Sea Scrolls and Book of
Genesis, 1961; Requiem, with 2 soli and orch,
1966; The harp weaver, with baritone and harp
soli and orch.; The sleeping beauty, 2 soli and
chamber orch.; The passing of King Arthur, 2 soli
and orch; many other choral works and songs.
154 South Hudson Avenue
Los Angeles, CA 90004

WARREN, HARRY
b. Brooklyn, N. Y., 24 Dec. 1893. Dropped out
of school at 16, joined a carnival as a drummer

WARREN, HARRY

(WARREN, HARRY)
and began to compose in his spare time. During
World War I he was assigned to the naval air
station at Montauk Point and continued to compose. After the war he became a rehearsal
pianist and song-plugger until teaming up with
Billy Rose in writing songs and Broadway musicals. In 1932 he went to Hollywood, where he
composed for films.
    WORKS: Stage scores: The laugh parade;
Crazy quilt; Film scores: 42nd Street; Gold
diggers, 1933, 1935, 1937; Roman scandals;
Weekend in Havana; Springtime in the Rockies;
Yolanda and the thief; Diamond horseshoe; That
night in Rio; and many others; Songs: Chattanooga choo-choo; Lullaby of Broadway; Atchison,
Topeka and the Santa Fe; 42nd Street; Shuffle
off to Buffalo; Don't give up the ship; Cheerful
little earful; Boulevard of broken dreams; I
found a million-dollar baby; She's a Latin from
Manhattan; Down Argentine way; and some 1000
others.
        c/o ASCAP, 1 Lincoln Plaza
        New York, NY 10023

WARREN, WILLIAM A.
    b. Toledo, Ohio, 8 Feb. 1952. Studied clarinet
at Eastman School of Music; with John Ferritto,
Wittenberg Univ. He has played clarinet,
Rochester Opera Theatre, 1968-70; Springfield
Civic Opera, 1970-   ; Springfield Symphony,
1973.
    WORKS: Band: Fantasy for woodwind doublers,
woodwind quartet and band; Chamber music:
Abstractions of a familiar melody, string orch.;
clarinet trio; Duo concertante, trombone and
piano; In memoriam Green Pen, cello and clarinet;
woodwind quintet; Ballad, alto clarinet and
piano; works for chorus and for solo voice.
        46 1/2 East Ward Street
        Springfield, OH 45504

WASHBURN, GARY SCOTT
    b. Tulsa, Okla., 14 Jan. 1946. Studied with
Neil McKay, Armand Russell, Ingolf Dahl, Joji
Yuasa, Morton Feldman, Univ. of Hawaii; with
Gardner Read, David Del Tredici, Joyce Mekeel,
Boston Univ. He received a Nat. Endowment for
the Arts grant; scholarships at Boston Univ. and
Univ. of Hawaii. He was faculty member, Owasso
High School, 1971; teaching assistant, Boston
Univ., 1972-73; on faculty, Univ. of Hawaii,
1970, at Hilo, 1973-
    WORKS: Orchestra: Geometric studies, orch.
and 3 percussion ensembles, 1970; Chamber music:
percussion sextet, 1969; Passacaglia, chamber
ensemble; Eight, wind sextet and percussion;
The breathless feather, viola solo; Zeitdehner,
viola and percussion; Tiabeoc, piano; Kaliapahoa,
double bass; Electronic: quintet, 2 saxophones,
2 percussion, tape, 1971; Godo, tape; Kokora,
piano and tape.
        335 Makani Circle, Hilo, HI 96720

WASHBURN, ROBERT
    b. Bouckville, N. Y., 11 July 1928. Studied
at State Univ. Coll. at Potsdam, B. S., M. S.;
with Bernard Rogers and Alan Hovhaness, Eastman

(WASHBURN, ROBERT)
School of Music, Ph. D.; with Darius Milhaud
Aspen Music School; with Nadia Boulanger in
Paris. He received a Danforth Found. grant,
1958; Ford Found. fellowship for composer
residency, Elkhart, Ind., 1959-60; MacDowell
fellowship, 1963; State Univ. of New York
fellowships, 1963, 1971, 1973. Between study
at Potsdam and Eastman he served 4 years in the
Air Force; then was appointed professor, State
Univ. Coll. at Potsdam, 1954-   ; has served
as guest composer at 9 universities and colleges.
    WORKS: Orchestra: symphony, 1959; Synthesis
for orchestra, 1960; St. Lawrence overture,
1962; 3 pieces for orch.; Suite for strings;
Sinfonietta for string orch., 1964; Serenade for
strings; Prologue and dance; North Country
sketch, 1969; Triplex; Chamber music: Suite for
woodwind quintet; 3 pieces for 3 woodwinds;
woodwind quintet; string quartet; Concertino
for woodwind and brass quintets; brass quintet;
Chorus: A child this day is born, with brass;
Scherzo for spring; 3 Shakespearean love songs,
men's voices; Now welcome summer; Praise the
Lord, with brass; Ode to freedom, with orch,
or band; Gloria, with brass; 5 songs for men's
voices; Earth song; Julilate Deo; Spring cantata;
also many band pieces.
        R. D. 4, Potsdam, NY 13676

WASON, ROBERT WESLEY
    b. Bridgeport, Conn., 25 July 1945. Studied
with Arnold Franchetti and Thomas Putsche, Hartt
Coll. of Music, M. M. 1969. He received a
composition award, Hartt Coll., 1967; commissions
from Carmel Central School District, N. Y., 1969,
Hartford Chamber Orchestra, 1974. He was
teaching assistant, Hartt Coll., 1967-69,
instructor, 1970-
    WORKS: Orchestra: 4 poems of Michelangelo,
with chorus and soloists, 1969; Prelude for
orchestra, 1970; Concerto for chamber orchestra
and jazz ensemble, Hartford, Aug. 1974; Chamber
music: Burn's songs, tenor and piano, 1972;
sonata for oboe solo, 1973; trio for clarinet,
viola, piano, 1974; Theme with variations, solo
guitar, 1974.
        90 North Granby Road, Granby, CT 06035

WATERS, EMORY WALLACE
    b. Hoboken, N. J., 30 Sep. 1947. Studied with
Philip Rhodes and Peter Westergaard, Amherst
Coll., B. A. 1969; with Donald Martino, New
England Cons., M. M. 1971; with Bruno Maderna,
Tanglewood, 1971. He held the E. P. Lay
fellowship at Amherst Coll.; his Antiphon was
chosen for performance at the 7th Internat.
Student Composer Symposium, Montreal, 1971.
He was instructor, Virginia State Coll.,
1971-73; assistant professor, Union Coll.,
Schenectady, N. Y., and conductor, Northeastern
New York Youth Orchestra, 1973-
    WORKS: Orchestra: Antiphon for double
chamber orch., 1969; 2 pieces for orch., 1973;
Chamber music: Variations for 4 players, flute,
oboe, viola, bassoon, 1971; 3 songs, soprano,
3 flutes, clarinet, piano, 1974; Electronic:
Rhymes and echoes, alto saxophone and tape, 1974.
        706 Union Street, Schenectady, NY 12305

WATERS, J. KEVIN (S. J.)
b. Seattle, Wash., 24 June 1933. Studied the John Verrall and George F. McKay, Univ. of Washington, D. M. A. 1970; with Roy Harris, Univ. of California, Los Angeles; with Bruno Bartolozzi and Niccolo Castiglione in Italy. He has received several commissions. He was lecturer, Univ. of Washington, 1968-69; assistant professor, Seattle Univ., 1969-   ; visiting professor, Gonzaga-in-Florence, Italy, 1970-71; founder and director, Seattle Univ. Fine Arts Ensemble, 1970-   .
    WORKS: Opera: The mask of Hiroshima, 1971; Orchestra: Ennistymon, a passacaglia, 1968; Chorus: Inversnaid, with 2 soprano soli and small orch., 1964; Mass of the American martyrs, 1965; Psalm of thanksgiving, 1967; Multimedia: A solemn liturgy, chorus, male and female cantors, brass band and percussion, dancers, San Francisco, 30 July 1973.
        Seattle University, Seattle, WA 98122

WATERS, JAMES
b. Kyoto, Japan, of American parents, 11 June 1930. Studied with Bernard Rogers, Eastman School of Music, Ph. D. 1967. He received the Louis Lane composition award, 1966. He was faculty member, Westminster Choir Coll., 1957-68; associate professor, Kent State Univ., 1968-   .
    WORKS: Orchestra: 3 holy sonnets of John Donne, bass-baritone and orch., 1966; concertino for string quartet and string orch., 1968; 3 songs of Louise Boghn, alto solo and orch., 1971; Wind ensemble: Concerto antifonale, brass and percussion, 1972; Chorus: Dirge, with instruments, 1972; Litanie, with instruments, 1973; 2 psalms.
        School of Music, Kent State University
        Kent OH 44242

*WATKINS, R. BEDFORD
b. Keiser, Ark., 27 July 1925. Studied at Southwestern at Memphis, B. M. 1949; with Gerald Kechley, Univ. of Michigan, M. M. 1951; with Philip Bezanson, Univ. of Iowa, Ph. D. 1966. He was teaching assistant, Southwestern at Memphis, 1949-50; piano instructor, Winthrop Coll., 1951-56; professor of piano and harpsichord, Illinois Wesleyan Univ., 1956-   .
    WORKS: Chamber music: 4 burlesques, violin and piano, 1962; Pentamerous suite, trumpet and piano, 1972.
        Department of Music
        Illinois Wesleyan University
        Bloomington, IL 61701

*WATSON, JAMES
Psalm 25 for chorus.

*WATSON, SCOTT
b. Florida. Studied at Peabody Cons., B. M. in piano 1946. His compositions include Gigue for piano quartet, 1951; So fades the lovely blooming flower, song, 1945; Weeping Mary, song, 1945.

WATSON, WALTER R.
b. Canton, Ohio, 13 Oct. 1933. Studied with Karl Ahrendt, Ohio Univ.; with Samuel Adler,

(WATSON, WALTER R.)
North Texas State Univ.; with Darius Milhaud, Aspen Music School. He received ASCAP awards, 1970, 1971, 1972; summer fellowships, Kent State Univ., 1968, 1970, 1972; first prize, U.S. Navy Band composition contest 1973. He was faculty member, Stephen F. Austin State Univ., 1961-1966; associate professor, Kent State Univ., 1966-   .
    WORKS: Band: Antiphony and chorale; Chamber music: Essay for flute; trombone sonatina; Chorus: 5 Japanese love songs, women's voices; Organ: Reflection; other works for orchestra; band, solo and ensemble instruments, chorus, and solo voice.
        1224 Fairview Drive, Kent, OH 44240

WATSON, WILLIAM CARL
b. Covington, Ky., 21 June 1934. Studied bassoon, Cincinnati Coll. of Music, 1954; at Univ. of Kentucky, B. M. 1957; composition with Kenneth Gaburo, Univ. of Illinois, M. M. 1958; with Hugo Norden, Boston Univ.; William Graves and Thomas Canning, West Virginia Univ., Ph. D. 1965. He was instructor, Hastings Coll., 1963-65; assistant professor and chairman of theory, Wichita State Univ., 1965-67; associate professor, Washington State Univ., 1967-   ; on leave from Washington State as lecturer, Chinese Univ. of Hong Kong, 1972-74.
    WORKS: Chamber music: Piece for bassoon and piano; Serenade for wind instruments, double bass, piano; 3 short pieces for wind quintet; A little dog of Yaumati, cello solo; 3 studies on Chinese tripods, flute, bassoon, harpsichord; Etudes on 6 notes, clarinet with optional piano.
        Music Department, Washington State University
        Pullman, WA 99163

WATTS, JOHN
b. Cleveland, Tenn., 16 July 1930. Studied with John Drueger and David Van Vactor, Univ. of Tenn., B. A. 1950; Cecil Effinger, Univ. of Colorado, M. M. 1953; with Burrill Phillips, Univ. of Illinois, 1955-56; Robert Palmer, Cornell Univ., 1958-60; and with Roy Harris, Univ. of California, Los Angeles, 1961-62. He held a Yaddo fellowship, 1964. He was faculty member, North Dakota State Coll., 1956-57; Internat. Inst. of Music, Puerto Rico, 1960-61; founder-director, Composers Theatre, 1964-   ; faculty member and music workshops coordinator, New School for Social Research, 1969-   ; adjunct associate professor, Staten Island Community Coll., 1971-72.
    WORKS: Theatre: music for Faust, 1973; 3 large works for children's theatre; Dance scores: Locrian; songandance; Still life; Margins; Perimeters, This is not a working number; glass and shadows, and others; Orchestra: Signals, soprano and orch.; Piano: sonata; Film scores: Daisies; War, a documentary; Electronic: Piano for Te, piano and 13 players with tape; Elegy to Chimney: In memoriam, 1972, for trumpet, ARP synthesizer and tape; WARP for brass quintet, ARP synthesizer and tape; Laugharne, soprano, ARP synthesizer and orch., New York, 10 May 1974.
        25 West 19th Street, New York, NY 10011

WATTS, MARZETTE
b. Montgomery, Ala., 3 Sep. 1938. Studied at
New York Univ.; and with Don Cherry and Ornette
Coleman. He received grants from Creative
Artists Public Service Program and Nat. Endowment
for the Arts. He was visiting artist, Wesleyan
Univ., 1972; recording engineer and owner,
Le Doux Sound, Inc., 1973-   .
    WORKS: Electronic: Piece for 2 synthesizers
and woodwinds, received CAPS award; all works are
jazz and/or electronic.
    27 Cooper Square, New York, NY 10003

*WATTS, WINTTER
b. Cincinnati, Ohio, 14 Mar. 1884; d. Brooklyn,
N. Y., 1 Nov. 1962. Studied at Juilliard School
and at the American Acad. in Rome, 1923-25. He
received the Loeb Prize, 1919; Pulitzer award,
1923; American Prix de Rome, 1923.
    WORKS: Opera: Pied Piper; Theatre: music
to Alice in Wonderland; Orchestra: Bridal overture, 1916; Etchings, suite, 1921; Young blood,
symphonic poem, 1923; Song cycles: Vignettes of
Italy; Wings of night; Like music on the water;
on poems by Sara Teasdale; and many separate
songs.

WAUGH, HARVEY RICHARD
b. Clarksville, Iowa, 13 Oct. 1902. Studied
at Grinnell Coll., B. A. 1924; with Leopold Auer
and Leon Sametini, Chicago Musical Coll.; at
Univ. of Iowa, M. A.; with Samuel Gardner,
Columbia Univ. He was graduate assistant,
Univ. of Iowa, 1929-30; assistant professor,
Iowa State Teachers Coll., 1930-33; chairman,
music department, Saint Cloud State Coll.,
1933-42, 1946-65; served in the U.S. Navy,
1942-45, principal arranger, Blue Jackets
Choir, Great Lakes, 1942-43.
    WORKS: Orchestra: O people of Sion,
with chorus; Theme and variations, string orch.;
Adagio on an English folk song, string orch.;
also choral works.
    413 Cloverleaf Park, Saint Cloud, MN 56301

*WAXMAN, DONALD
b. Steubenville, Ohio, 29 Oct. 1925. Studied
with Howard Thatcher and Elliott Carter, Peabody
Cons.; and at Juilliard School. He received the
Gustav Klemm prize, 1949; Guggenheim fellowship.
His works include A Paris overture for orchestra;
woodwind trio; Thomas Hardy choral cycle.

WAXMAN, ERNEST
b. New York, N. Y., 14 Oct. 1918. Studied with
Aaron Copland, Roy Harris, and Isadore Freed in
New York. He won 2nd place, Nat. Composers'
Congress contest, 1950; performance by New York
Philharmonic string section of Spoon River
rhapsody. He has been private piano teacher,
1930-   ; studio pianist, Columbia Broadcasting
System, 1945-58; music teacher, public school,
1960-   .
    WORKS: Orchestra: David and Goliath, with
narrator; Spoon River rhapsody, flute and
strings; Fanfare overture, 1950; concerto for
piano and strings; clarinet concerto; trumpet
concerto with chamber orch.; Chamber music:

(WAXMAN, ERNEST)
2 piano sonatas; 4 divertissements, clarinet
and piano; Capriccio, brass quintet; Voice:
5 songs set to Negro poetry.
    6146 Little Neck Road
    Little Neck, NY 11362

*WAXMAN, FRANZ
b. Konifsbutte, Germany, 24 Dec. 1906; U.S.
citizen 1940; d. Los Angeles, Calif., 24 Feb.
1967. Studied in Berlin and Dresden, and with
Arnold Schoenberg in Los Angeles, 1934. His
awards included Academy awards for scores to
films Sunset Boulevard, 1950, and Place in the
sun, 1951; award of merit, Nat. Asso. of American
Composers and Conductors, 1956.
    WORKS: Orchestra: Sinfonietta, 1950;
Fantasy on Carmen, violin and piano; Joshua,
oratorio, chorus and orch., 1959; Symphonic
fantasy on A mighty fortress is my God; Elegy
for strings; Film scores: Rear window; Crime
in the streets; Peyton Place; The spirit of
St. Louis; The nun's story; Cimarron; Taras
Bulba; and many others.

*WAYDITCH, GABRIEL
b. Budapest, Hungary, 28 Dec. 1888; to U.S.
1907; d. New York, N. Y., 28 July 1969. Studied
at the Budapest Acad. of Music. He wrote 14
operas to his own librettos, one of which takes
6 1/2 hours to perform.

WAYLAND, NEWTON HART
b. Santa Barbara, Calif., 5 Nov. 1940. Studied
with Daniel Pinkham, Francis Judd Cooke, and
David Barnett, New England Cons. He received
a Rockefeller grant as artist-in-residence,
WGBH-TV, Boston, 1969-70; commission from Cape
Cod Symphony Orchestra. He was faculty member,
New England Cons., 1966-70; music director,
Charles Playhouse, 1967-69; pianist, Boston
Symphony, 1967-   ; music director, Adventures
in Music, 1971-   ; music director, ZOOM,
1972-   ; conductor, Associate Artists' Opera,
1972-   .
    WORKS: Theatre: music for Beauty and the
beast; Pinocchio; Wind in the willows; Alice in
wonderland; The emperor's new clothes; Orchestra:
What's my thing?; Songs: 8 fatal songs, mezzo-
soprano with tenor saxophone or bassoon; The bat-
poet, cycle of 4 songs for mezzo-soprano, piano
and percussion; original songs for ZOOM: Zoom-
theme; Fannee-Doolee; Ubbi-dubbi; Flying, Men
from Mars, and others; 5 commercial songs, poems
by Anthony Kahn, for soprano, baritone, piano,
traps and bassoon or string bass; also scores
for several films shown on Educational Television Stations.
    Nashua Road, Groton, MA 01450

*WEAST, ROBERT
Trumpet sonata.
    Department of Music, Drake University
    Des Moines, IA 50311

*WEATHERS, W. KEITH
b. 1943. Prelude and fugue on Christ is risen.
    Department of Music, Biola College
    La Mirada, CA 90638

*WEAVER, JOHN
    Studied at Peabody Cons. He is director of
music, Madison Avenue Presbyterian Church, New
York; teaches organ at Curtis Inst. and Westminster Choir Coll. His works for chorus and
organ include Psalm 100 and Epiphany alleluia;
Toccata for organ.
        Curtis Institute of Music
        Philadelphia, PA 19103

WEAVER, MARY
    b. Kansas City, Mo., 16 Jan. 1903. Studied at
Smith Coll.; Ottawa Univ., B. A., B. M.; with
Rosario Scalero and Deems Taylor, Curtis Inst.
of Music. She taught piano, Univ. of Missouri,
Kansas City, 1946-57; Manhattan School of Music,
1957-70.
    WORKS: Chorus: All weary men; Kneel down;
When Jesus lay by Mary's side; Like doves de-
scending; Rise up all men; Songs: Cradle song;
The heart of heaven.
        7 East 14th Street, New York, NY 10003

WEAVER, POWELL
    b. Clearfield, Pa., 10 June 1890; d. Oakland,
Calif., 22 Dec. 1951. Studied with Percy
Goetschius and Gaston Dethier, Juilliard School;
with Pietro Yon in New York; with Ottorino
Respighi in Rome. He gave organ recitals in
Italy and on returning to the U.S. became
music director, B'nai Jehudah Temple, Kansas
City. He gave recitals in Mid-West and South;
was accompanist for many singers; head, music
department, Ottawa Univ.; organist-choirmaster,
First Baptist Church, Kansas City, 1937-51.
    WORKS: Orchestra: Plantation overture,
1925; The little faun, 1925; The vagabond, 1931;
Dance of the sand-dune crane, piano and orch.,
1941; Ballet suite; Fugue for strings; Ode for
piano and strings; Chorus: Boating song; Spirit
of God; The hummingbird; O God, our help in ages
past; Songs: Moon-marketing; The Abbot of Derry;
The night will never stay; Windy weather; also
chamber music including a violin sonata.

WEAVER, THOMAS
    b. Kansas City, Mo., 4 Oct. 1939. Studied at
Juilliard School and with Nadia Boulanger. He
has held faculty posts at Furman Univ.; Brevard
Music Center; Third Street and Henry Street
Settlement Schools; 1961-62; Univ. of Georgia,
1969-   .
    WORKS: Chamber music: Dialogues, flute
and clarinet; string quartet.
        146A Kentucky Circle, Athens, GA 30601

WEBB, ALLIENE BRANDON
    b. Palestine, Tex., 2 Jan. 1910; d. Dallas, Tex.,
16 Nov. 1965. Studied voice with Peter Tchach.
She was choir director and soloist, Park Cities
Baptist Church, Dallas, for 12 years.
    WORKS: Chorus: Father, teach me to pray;
He's walking with me; Hosanna to his name; My
father's prayer; The endless song; 'Twas the
night before Christmas; and songs.

WEBB, RICHARD
    b. Martins Ferry, Ohio, 24 June 1942. Studied
with Karl Ahrendt and Eugene Wickstrom, Ohio

(WEBB, RICHARD)
    Univ., M. M.; with Paul Cooper and Scott
Huston, Coll.-Cons., Univ. of Cincinnati. He
was assistant professor, East Tennessee State
Univ., 1965-68; teaching fellow, Univ. of
Cincinnati, 1968-71; associate professor, East
Tennessee State Univ., 1971-   .
    WORKS: Chamber music: Kaleidoscope,
string quartet, won 1964 Sphere award in compo-
sition; Chorus: Excerpts from Ecclesiastes,
with brass and organ; Organ: Psalm suite;
Tiento for Epiphany.
        915 Beech Drive, Johnson City, TN 37601

*WEBER, BEN BRIAN
    b. St. Louis, Mo., 23 July 1916. Studied at
Univ. of Illinois, and De Paul Univ. His awards
include Nat. Inst. of Arts and Letters, 1950;
2 Guggenheim fellowships, 1950, 1953; Fromm
Found. awards, 1953, 1955; Phoebe Ketchum Thorne
award, 1965; membership in Nat. Inst. of Arts
and Letters, 1971; and commissions.
    WORKS: Ballet: Pool of darkness, chamber
ensemble; Orchestra: Symphony on poems of
William Blake, baritone and 12 instruments, 1950;
violin concerto, 1954; Prelude and passacaglia,
1954; Rapsodie concertante, viola and orch.,
1957; piano concerto, 1961; Dolmen, an elegy,
1964; Sinfonia clarion, New York, 26 Feb. 1974;
Chamber music: Serenade, flute, oboe, cello,
harpsichord; 2 string quartets; 2 violin sonatas;
Concert aria after Solomon, soprano and chamber
ensemble; concerto for piano, woodwind quintet,
cello, 1950; Nocturne, flute, clarinet, cello;
2 dances, viola and piano; Sonata da camera,
violin and piano; Dance, cello solo; Nocturne,
flute and piano; clarinet concertino; Serenade,
string quartet and double bass; Chamber
fantasie, violin solo and 6 instruments, 1959;
Piano: Fantasia, 1945; Episodes; Humoresque,
c. 1963.

WEBER, JOSEPH
    b. Antioch, Calif., 31 July 1937. Studied with
Wendell Otey and Roger Nixon, San Francisco
State Coll. He received the Paul Masson composition prize, 1961.
    WORKS: Orchestra: symphony; Chamber music:
string quartet; Songs for voice, violin, clarinet, vibraphone; Portfolio I, violin and piano;
Portfolio II, trombone and piano; Portfolio III
for miscellaneous objects; Piano: 3 sonatas;
Canzone for 2 pianos.
        1336 38th Avenue, San Francisco, CA 94122

*WECK, FREDERICK
    4 choruses for unaccompanied voices, Nat. Gal-
lery of Art, Washington, D.C., 20 May 1973:
Crucifixus, Washington Oratorio Society, 17 May
1975.

WEED, MAURICE JAMES
    b. Kalamazoo, Mich., 16 Oct. 1912. Studied with
H. Owen Reed, Michigan State Univ.; with Edward
Royce, Burrill Phillips, Bernard Rogers, Howard
Hanson, Eastman School of Music. His awards
include Benjamin award, 1954; first prize, Nat.
Symphony Orchestra, 25th anniversary competition,
1955; Ostwald award, American Bandmasters Asso.,

WEED, MAURICE JAMES

(WEED, MAURICE JAMES)
1959; MacDowell fellowship, 1961; first prize, J. Fischer and Bros. contest, 1964; 5th Pedro Paz award, Olivet Coll., 1966. He was public school music supervisor, 1934-43; assistant professor, Ripon Coll., 1946-51; teaching fellow, Eastman School, 1951-54; head, music department, Northern Illinois Univ., 1954-61, professor, 1961-   .

WORKS: Orchestra: symphony, 1955; Symphonie breve; concertino, cello and orch.; Serenity, chamber orch.; The mountains, a suite; Band: Vestigia nulla retrorsum; Symphonic rondo; American spirit overture; Hopkins Park; Introduction and scherzo; Chamber music: string quartet; piano trio; Sept cinquains, song cycle, soprano and chamber group; Chorus: Psalm 71; Triptych for voices; Praise ye the Lord, 1966; The wonder of the starry night; Psalm 13; Keyboard: Little toccata, organ; Variations on a modal theme, piano.

326 Delcy Drive, DeKalb, IL   60115

WEEKS, CLIFFORD M.
b. New York, N. Y., 15 Apr. 1938. Studied at Berklee Coll. of Music, diploma, 1962; with Avram David, Boston Cons., B. M. magna cum laude 1963, candidate for M. M. 1973; studies at Boston State Coll. He was public school music teacher and band director, 1963-72; acting coordinator for instrumental music, Boston schools, 1972-   ; instructor, Nat. Center for Afro-American Arts, 1971-73; member, Advisory Board, Berklee Coll. of Music, 1973-   .

WORKS: Chamber music: Triptych, tuba and piano, Boston, 26 May 1963; jazz compositions and arrangements.

26 Fells Ave., Medford, MA   02155

WEGNER, AUGUST MARTIN III
b. Saginaw, Mich., 20 Feb. 1941. Studied with William Rivard, Central Michigan Univ.; with Richard Hervig, Univ. of Iowa, where he received the Philip Greeley Clapp composition award. He is assistant professor and department head, Univ. of Wisconsin at Parkside.

WORKS: Orchestra: Ice-nine, prepared piano and orch.; Chamber music: Concert music for euphonium and percussion; Movement for piano trio; Something for flute and piano; Chorus: Coney Island, 8 voices and 11 instruments.

CA 216, University of Wisconsin-Parkside
Kenosha, WI   53140

WEHR, DAVID A.
b. Mt. Vernon, N. Y., 21 Jan. 1934. Studied with David Stanley York and Warren Martin, Westminster Choir Coll.; with Clifton Williams, Univ. of Miami; Ph. D. in conducting and choral literature, 1971. He has received annual ASCAP awards, 1966-   . He was organist-choirmaster-carillonneur, Cathedral of the Rockies, Boise, Id., 1958-68; carillonneur, New York World's Fair, 1964; associate professor and director of choral groups, Eastern Kentucky Univ., 1971-   .

WORKS: Chorus: God is working his purpose out; Now alien tongues; Father, O hear us; All

(WEHR, DAVID A.)
ye mountains praise the Lord; We sing the birth was born tonight; numerous other published choral works.

Hillcrest Estates, Richmond, KY   40475

WEIDENAAR, REYNOLD
b. Grand Rapids, Mich., 25 Sep. 1945. Studied with Paul Harder, Michigan State Univ.; privately with Robert A. Moog and Vladimir Maleckar; with Donald Erb, Cleveland Inst. of Music, valedictory award, 1973. He was editor, Electronic Music Review, 1967-68; recording engineer, Audio Recording Studios and the Cleveland Orchestra, 1969-70; at Cleveland Inst. of Music, teaching fellow, 1970-72, recording engineer, 1970-   , coordinator of electronic music studio, 1970-   , faculty member 1972-   ; coordinator, Johnson Composers' Conference, 1972, 1973.

WORKS: Chamber music: sextet; Electric air; Electronic: Fanfare; Neon rainbow; The tinsel chicken coop.

592 Elm St., Painesville, OH   44077

*WEIGEL, EUGENE JOHN
b. Cleveland, Ohio, 11 Oct. 1910. Studied violin at Cleveland Inst. of Music; composition with Arthur Shepherd, Western Reserve Univ.; with Paul Hindemith, Yale Univ. B. M. 1946; viola with Hugo Kortschak. He was violist with the Walden String Quartet, artist in residence, 1947-56, chairman of theory department, Univ. of Illinois, 1950-56; then was named composer in residence and professor, Montana State Univ.

WORKS: Opera: The lion makers, 1953; The mountain child, 1958; Orchestra: Sonata for strings, 1948; Prairie symphony, 1953; Requiem mass, chorus and orch., 1956; Chamber music: clarinet quintet, 1946; woodwind quintet, 1949; 3 pieces for 4 trombones, 1953; many songs and piano pieces.

WEIGL, KARL
b. Vienna, 6 Feb. 1881; U.S. citizen 1943; d. New York, 11 Aug. 1949. Studied at Vienna Music Acad., graduated 1902; studied composition with Robert Fuchs and Alexander v. Kemlinsky; with Guido Adler, Vienna Univ., Ph. D. 1903. His awards include the Beethoven Prize in 1910 for a string quartet; Philadelphia Mendelssohn Club prize for an 8-part choral work, 1922; and the City of Vienna prize in 1924 for a symphonic cantata, World Festival. He was lecturer and teacher, Vienna Univ.; coach of the Vienna Opera, 1904-16, and assistant to Gustav Mahler, the conductor; then professor at the New Vienna Cons.; in the U.S. from 1938, he held teaching posts at Brooklyn Coll., Boston Cons., and Philadelphia Music Acad.

WORKS: Orchestra: 6 symphonies, no. 5 performed in New York, 1969; Music for the young, overture; Rhapsody, piano and orch.; Old Vienna, symphonic cycle; Summer evening music, string orch.; 3 intermezzi, string orch.; Chamber music: 8 string quartets, piano trio; viola sonata; choral works; pieces for cello; piano pieces.

WEIGL, VALLY (Mrs. Karl)
b. Vienna, 11 Sep. 1889; U.S. citizen 1944.
Studied composition with Karl Weugl, musicology
with Guido Adler, and piano at Vienna Univ.; at
Columbia Univ. Teachers Coll., M. A. 1953. She
was awarded Elk Found. fellowships, 1955, 1958;
licensed as music therapist by New York Asso. for
Music Therapy, 1959; Rockefeller recording grant,
1973. She has given lectures and concerts all
over the U.S. and Europe.
WORKS: Chamber music: Andante for strings,
ACA-BMI citation, 1945; New England suite, clarinet or flute, cello, piano; Nature moods, voice,
clarinet or flute; Dear Earth, voice, horn and
piano trio; Lyrical suite, chamber ensemble;
many songs, choral works, and vocal chamber
music.
55 West 95th St., New York, NY 10025

*WEILL, KURT
b. Dessau, Germany, 2 Mar. 1900; to U.S. 1935;
d. New York, 3 Apr. 1950. Studied with Albert
Bing in Dessau; with Humperdinck and Krasselt in
Berlin; later with Busoni in Berlin. Almost his
entire career was devoted to composition of stage
works.
WORKS: Theatre: The protagonist, opera on
play by George Kaiser, 1924; The royal palace,
opera on book by Ivan Goll, 1927; Mahagonny,
satirical opera, libretto by Bertolt Brecht,
1927; The threepenny opera, libretto adapted by
Brecht from John Gay, 1928; The silver lake,
opera on book by Kaiser, 1933; A kingdom for a
cow, musical play, 1935; Johnny Johnson, musical,
text by Paul Green, 1936; music for The eternal
road of Franz Werfl, 1937; Knickerbocker holiday,
musical on text of Maxwell Anderson, 1938; music
for The ballad of the Magna Carta, radio drama
by Maxwell Anderson, 1939; Lady in the dark,
musical, book by Moss Hart, 1941; One touch of
Venus, musical to text by S. J. Perelman and
Ogden Nash, 1943; Street scene, opera on texts
by Elmer Rice and Langston Hughes, 1947; Down in
the valley, folk opera, book by Arnold Sundgaard,
1947; Lost in the stars, opera, libretto adapted
by Maxwell Anderson from Alan Paton's Cry the
beloved country, 1949; Orchestra: 2 symphonies,
1921, 1933; Fantaisie, passacaglia and hymnus,
1923; Quodlibet, 1924; concerto for violin and
woodwinds; Chamber music: string quartet; chorus: Lindberg's flight, radio cantata, 1927; The
new Orpheus, cantata; Songs: Mack the knife;
September song; The saga of Jenny; and many
others.

WEILLE, F. BLAIR
b. Boston, Mass., 9 Nov. 1930. Studied piano at
New England Cons.; with Arthur Tillman Merritt
and Walter Piston, Harvard Univ., A. B. 1953;
with Otto Luening and Jack Beeson, Columbia
Univ., A. M. 1957. He received annual ASCAP
awards, 1967-71. He was staff member, ABC Command Records Division, 1960-69; Longine Symphonette Society, Dimension Records Division,
1969-   ; member, Board of Directors, Composers
Recordings, Inc., 1971-   .

(WEILLE, F. BLAIR)
WORKS: Orchestra: Short symphony; Chamber
music: Suite for brass quintet; Annabel Lee,
baritone and chamber orch.; Minneapolis-St. Paul,
popular song.
166 East 96th St., New York, NY 10024

*WEINBERG, HENRY
b. Philadelphia, Pa., 7 June 1931. Studied at
Univ. of Pennsylvania, B. F. A. 1952; with
Milton Babbitt and Roger Sessions, Princeton
Univ., M. F. A. 1961, Ph. D.; with Luigi
Dallapiccola in Florence, Italy. His honors
include Fulbright-Italian Government grants,
1961-62; Guggenheim fellowship; MacDowell Colony
fellowship; Fromm Found commission; Naumberg
award; Brandeis Creative Arts award. He was
instructor, Univ. of Pennsylvania, 1962-65;
assistant professor, Queens Coll., CUNY,
1965-72, associate professor, 1972-   .
WORKS: Chamber music: cello sonata, 1955;
Sinfonia, chamber orch., 1957; 2 string quartets,
1959, 1960-64; Cantus commemorabilis I, chamber
ensemble, 1966; Chorus: Vox in ramo, 1956;
Songs: 5 Haiku, 1958; song cycle, 1960.
Department of Music, Queens College, CUNY
New York, NY 11367

*WEINBERG, JACOB
b. Odessa, Russia, 5 July 1879; U.S. citizen
1934; d. New York, N. Y., 2 Nov. 1956. Studied
law at Univ. of Moscow; music at the Moscow
Cons. He toured as concert pianist, 1912-14,
1922-26; was professor, Odessa Cons., 1915-21;
professor and chairman of theory department, New
York Coll. of Music, 1927-37; faculty member,
Hunter Coll., 1937-56.
WORKS: Opera: The pioneers, 1925; Orchestra: piano concerto; Chorus: The Gettysburg
address, ode for chorus and orch., 1936; Isaiah,
oratorio, 1948; The life of Moses, oratorio,
1952; Sabbath liturgy, baritone, chorus and
organ; Chamber music: piano trio; suite for 2
pianos; string quartet; 2 violin sonatas.

*WEINBERGER, JAROMIR
b. Prague, Czechoslovakia, 8 Jan. 1896; U.S.
citizen 1948; d. St. Petersburg, Fla., 8 Aug.
1967. Studied at the Prague Cons. and with Max
Reger in Leipzig. He taught in Prague,
Bratislava, and Vienna; from 1939 he lived in
St. Petersburg, Fla.
WORKS: Opera: Schwanda, the bagpiper,
1927; The beloved voice, 1931; The outcasts of
Poker Flat, 1932; A bed of roses, 1934;
Wallenstein, 1937; Orchestra: Overture to a
puppet show; Overture to a cavalier's play;
Christmas; Czech songs and dances; Under the
spreading chestnut tree, 1939; The legend of
Sleepy Hollow; Song of the high seas, 1940;
saxophone concerto, 1940; Lincoln symphony,
1941; Czech rhapsody, 1941; The bird's opera,
1941; Band: Mississippi rhapsody; Prelude to a
festival; Homage to the pioneers; Organ: Religious and profane preludes; sonata; also chamber
music, choral works, and songs.

WEINER, LAWRENCE
b. Cleveland, Ohio, 22 June 1932. Studied with
Kent Kennan, Clifton Williams, Paul Pisk, Univ.
of Texas; with Juan Orrego-Salas, Indiana Univ.;
with John Butler, Alfred Reed, Univ. of Miami.
He received the Carl Owens composition award,
Univ. of Texas, 1955; Ostwald band composition
award, 1967; NDEA grant, 1971; and commissions.
He was public school music instructor, 1959-68;
assistant professor, Texas A & I Univ.,
1968-
    WORKS: Orchestra: Prologos synkretismos;
Elegy, string orch.; Quaternity, string orch.;
Commemoration overture, Corpus Christi, 26 Jan.
1974; Band: Daedalic symphony; 3rd symphony for
wind ensemble; Air; Benediction; Choral and
fugue; Cataphonics; Atropos; 3 fanfares; suite
for brass sextet; Chorus: Shenandoah; Psalm of
prayer and praise, with brass; Sing praise to
God; The sower.
    Department of Music, Texas A & I University
    Kingsville, TX 78363

*WEINER, LAZAR
b. Cherkassy, near Kiev, Russia, 27 Oct. 1897;
to U.S. 1914. Studied with Frederick Jacobi,
Robert Russell Bennett, and Joseph Schillinger
in New York. He was conductor of choral groups
in the New York area. He has written several
ballets; chamber music; the cantatas: Legend of
toil, 1933; Man in the world, 1939; Fight for
freedom, 1943; To thee, America, 1944; and
Yiddish art songs.
    310 West 97th St., New York, NY 10025

*WEINER, STANLEY
b. 1925.   Concerto for horn and strings; Homage to violinists, 7 caprices for unaccompanied
violin; sonata for violin solo; piano sonata,
1971.

WEINGARDEN, LOUIS
b. Detroit, Mich., 23 July 1943. Studied with
Miriam Gideon in New York; with Elliott Carter
at Juilliard School; at Columbia Univ.; and at
the Jewish Theological Seminary, New York. His
awards include the Prix de Rome; Guggenheim fellowship; Charles Ives scholarship, Nat. Inst. of
Arts and Letters; commissions from Fromm Found.,
New York State Endowment for the Arts, Denver
Symphony Orch.; National Endowment for the Arts
grant. He has been a partner in an architectural
and interior design firm, 1972-
    WORKS: Orchestra: Ghirlande, soprano and
orch.; piano concerto, Denver, 16 Feb. 1975;
Chamber music: Things heard and seen in summer,
piano trio; Fantasy and funeral music, 2 pianos
and percussion; cello sonata; Suite for violin
alone; Vox clamans in deserto, organ and brass;
Chorus: The sorrows of David, cantata for chorus, soli, and orch.; 3 short sacred songs,
women's voices a cappella.
    No. 1 West 72nd St., New York, NY 10023

*WEISGALL, HUGO
b. Czechoslovakia, 13 Oct. 1912; to U.S. 1920.
Studied with Louis Cheslock, Peabody Cons.; with
Rosario Scalero, Curtis Inst. of Music; privately

(WEISGALL, HUGO)
with Roger Sessions in New York; at Johns
Hopkins Univ., Ph. D. in German literature 1940.
His awards include the Bearns prize; Ditson
award; 3 Guggenheim fellowships; composer-in-
residence, American Acad. in Rome, 1966-67; Nat.
Inst. of Arts and Letters grant; honorary doctorate, Peabody Cons., 1973; elected to Nat.
Inst. of Arts and Letters, 1975. Following military service in World War II, he was cultural
attache at the American Embassy in Prague,
1946-47; held teaching posts at Juilliard School;
Pennsylvania State Univ.; Jewish Theological
Seminary, New York; Queens Coll., CUNY; W.-Alton
Jones professor, Peabody Cons., 1974-75.
    WORKS: Opera: Night, 1932; Lilith, 1934;
The tenor, 1950; The stronger, 1952; 6 characters in search of an author, 1956; Purgatory,
1958; Athaliah, 1963; 9 rivers from Jordan,
1968; Ballets: Quest, 1937; One thing is certain, 1938; Outpost, 1947; Chamber music: Fancies and inventions, from The Hebrides of Robert
Herrick, baritone and 5 instruments, Baltimore,
1 Nov. 1970; End of summer, tenor and chamber
ensemble, Baltimore, 17 Nov. 1974; choral works
and songs.
    Peabody Conservatory
    1 East Mt. Vernon Place, Baltimore, MD 21202

WEISLING, RAYMOND
b. Milwaukee, Wis., 13 Mar. 1947. Studied with
Barney Childs, Wisconsin Coll.-Cons.; at Univ.
of Wisconsin, Milwaukee; at California Inst. of
the Arts. He was awarded first prize, Kinetic
Theatre Program, Oregon Coll. of Education, 1970.
He was instructor in electronic music, Wisconsin
Coll.-Cons., 1972-73.
    WORKS: Orchestra: Last voyages to summer,
1970; Band: An original American cold-flow,
1970; Chamber music: Poon Lim...A night upon
the waves, for 7 winds, 1969; This for alto
flute, 1969; Night sky set, soprano and 6 players, 1970; Jupiter and Silvertree, bass flute
and 6 instruments, 1972; Electronic: Bluemound
pieces, 7 tape compositions, 1970-73.
    c/o California Institute of the Arts
    Valencia, CA 91355

*WEISS, ADOLPH A.
b. Baltimore, Md., 12 Sep. 1891; d. Van Nuys,
Calif., 21 Feb. 1971. Studied with Cornelius
Rybner at Columbia Univ.; with Adolph Weidig in
Chicago; at Univ. of California, Los Angeles;
and with Arnold Schoenberg in Berlin, 1925-27.
He received a Guggenheim fellowship 1931-32;
Nat. Inst. of Arts and Letters grant, 1955. He
was bassoonist in various orchestras; founded
the New Music Wind Quintet; conducted orchestras
in New York; was instructor, Los Angeles Cons.,
and bassoonist, Santa Clara and Ventura Orchestras.
    WORKS: Orchestra: I segreti, 1922; Ameri-
can life, scherzo jazzoso, 1929; The libation-
bearers, choreographic cantata, soloists, chorus,
and orch., 1930; Variations, 1931; Suite, 1938;
10 pieces for low instrument and orch., 1943;
trumpet concerto, 1952; Wind ensemble: Tone
poem, brass and percussion, 1957; Rhapsody for

(WEISS, ADOLPH A.)

4 horns, 1957; Vade mecum, 1958; Chamber music: 3 string quartets, 1925, 1926, 1932; Chamber symphony for 10 instruments, 1927; 12 piano preludes, 1927; Petite suite, woodwind trio, 1939; violin sonata, 1941; Passacaglia, horn and viola, 1942; Protest, 2 pianos, 1945; sextet, woodwind quartet, horn, piano, 1947; trio, clarinet, viola, cello, 1948; concerto for bassoon and string quartet, 1949; trio, flute, violin, piano, 1955; 5 fantasies, violin and piano, 1956.

*WEISS, EDWARD

Tania for band.

WELCHER, DAN

b. Rochester, N. Y., 2 Mar. 1948. Studied with Samuel Adler and Warren Benson, Eastman School of Music, B. M. 1969; with Ludmila Ulehla, Manhattan School of Music, M. M. 1972. He won first prize, First Internat. Gebrauchmusik for Recorders contest, 1970. He was 2nd bassoonist, Rochester Philharmonic Orchestra, 1968-69; bassoonist and arranger, U.S. Military Acad., 1969-72; instructor, Univ. of Louisville, 1972- ; principal bassoonist, Louisville Orchestra, 1972- ; head of composition department, Sewanee Summer Music Center, 1973.

WORKS: Orchestra: Pisces, symphony for bassoon and orch., 1968; Episodes for orchestra, 1971; flute concerto, Louisville, Apr. 1974; Band: Walls and fences, 5 tactile experiences for winds and percussion, 1970; Elizabethan variations for 4 recorders; Nocturne and dance, trumpet and piano, 1967; Black riders, 6 epigrams of Stephen Crane, soprano and 4 instruments, 1972.

1213 Dorsey Lane, Louisville, KY 40223

*WELLS, JOHN BARNES

b. Ashley, Pa., 17 Oct. 1880; d. Roxbury, N. Y., 8 Aug. 1955. Studied at Syracuse Univ. He was a singer with Victor Herbert's orchestra; church organist and choirmaster in New York; voice tutor at Princeton Univ. His compositions included the songs: The elfman; If I were you; The dearest place; The owl; The little bird; The lightning bug; etc.

WELLS, RONALD KENNETH

b. Pasadena, Calif., 18 Aug. 1926. Studied at Asbury Coll., A. B.; at Southern Baptist Theological Seminary, M. S. M. He has been minister in various churches, 1951-68; First Baptist Church, Spartanburg, S. C., 1968- .

WORKS: Theatre: Who is my neighbor?, sacred music drama; I wonder, song drama; Here comes tomorrow, song drama; also songs.

893 Ezell Blvd., Spartanburg, SC 29301

*WELLS, THOMAS

Had works performed at the Computer Arts Festival, New York, 3-4 Apr. 1973. His 11.2.72 for electronic tape was performed in New York, 22 Feb. 1974 at the 9th Annual Conference, American Society of University Composers.

Department of Music, University of Texas
Austin, TX 78712

*WELSH, WILMER HAYDON

Studied at Peabody Cons., diploma 1953 in organ. His works for organ include The song of songs, a religious dance, 1954; and Requiem, 1954; both performed at the Nat. Cathedral, Washington, D.C., in Oct. 1954.

Department of Music, Davidson College
Davidson, NC 28036

WELWOOD, ARTHUR

b. Brookline, Mass., 15 Feb. 1934. Studied with Hugo Norden and Gardner Read, Boston Univ.; with Quincy Porter and Mel Powell, Yale Univ. He received commissions from Hartford Civic Arts Festival, 1971, and Connecticut Commission on the Arts, 1973. He was visiting instructor, Univ. of Evansville, Ind., 1963-64; assistant professor, Central Connecticut State Coll., 1964- .

WORKS: Chamber music: Songs from the Chinese, tenor solo and chamber ensemble, 1968; Chorus: Polyphonies of the 11th and 12th centuries, arranged for soprano, chorus, chamber orch., and 'found' percussion (assorted, nondesignated instruments), 1972; Multimedia: Earth opera I, soloists, chorus, lights, dancers, 'found' instruments, spontaneous creation, performed for and with an audience of 1000, 1969; My father moved through dooms of love, a masque for soprano, chamber orch., chorus, slides, lights, and dancers, 1970; Manifestations V, masque for soprano, 25 musicians, 50 dancers, poetry readers, electronic tapes, and audience, 1971; Songs of war, nature, and the way, based on Tang Dynasty poetry, for mezzo-soprano, chamber ensemble, percussion, narrator, and 5 modern dancers, 1972. He is author of A primer for found music, a manual for creative music projects in the public schools.

32 Cambridge St., New Britain, CT 06051

WERLE, FLOYD E.

b. Billings, Mont., 8 May 1929. Studied at Univ. of Michigan. He has been chief of composition and arranging, U.S. Air Force Band, Washington, 1951- ; director of music, United Methodist Church, Rockville, Md., 1967- .

WORKS: Orchestra: Venite exultemus, Arlington, Va., 12 Mar. 1972; Band: Concert etude; 2 concertos for trumpet and band; Sinfonia sacra, rock combo and band; Partita for saxophones; The now faith.

5504 Aldrich Lane, Springfield, VA 22151

*WERLE, FREDERICK C.

Variations and fugue, brass ensemble; Sonata brevis #2, piano; Toccata, piano.

Mannes School of Music, New York, NY 10021

WERNER, ERIC

b. Vienna, Austria, 1 Aug. 1901; U.S. citizen 1944. Studied with Egon Kornauth in Vienna; with Franz Schreker and Ferruccio Busoni in Berlin. He received a Guggenheim fellowship for musicology in 1957. He is primarily a musicologist and author of several books on the

WERNER, ERIC

(WERNER, ERIC)
subject. He is professor emeritus, Hebrew Union Coll., New York and Cincinnati, and Tel Aviv Univ.
WORKS: Orchestra: Symphony requiem; also chamber music and liturgical compositions.
900 West 190th St., New York, NY 10040

WERNER, KENNETH. See HARMONIC, PHIL.

WERNICK, RICHARD
b. Boston, Mass., 16 Jan. 1934. Studied with Irving Fine, Harold Shapero, Arthur Berger, Brandeis Univ., B. A.; with Leon Kirchner, Mills Coll., M. A.; with Aaron Copland, Boris Blacher, Ernst Toch at Tanglewood. He has received Ford Found. grants and ASCAP awards. He is associate professor and chairman, music department, Univ. of Pennsylvania; director, Penn Contemporary Players.
WORKS: Chamber music: 2 string quartets; Cadenzas and variations for solo cello; Cadenzas and variations for solo violin; Divertimento, clarinet, bassoon, violin, cello; Stretti, clarinet, violin, viola, guitar; Voice: Kaddish requiem; Lyrics for soprano, percussion, contrabass; Haiku; A prayer for Jerusalem.
University of Pennsylvania
Philadelphia, PA 19104

WESCOTT, STEVEN DWIGHT
b. Minneapolis, Minn., 14 July 1950. Studied with Ronald A. Nelson, Minneapolis; with Dominick Argento and Paul Fetler, Univ. of Minnesota. He was teaching assistant, Univ. of Minnesota, 1973.
WORKS: Chorus: A gift of light; other choral anthems and organ music.
3332 Idaho Ave. South
St. Louis Park, MN 55426

*WESSEL, MARK E.
b. Coldwater, Mich., 26 Mar. 1894; d. 1973. Studied at Northwestern Univ., B. M. 1917, M. M. 1918; and with Arnold Schoenberg. He received a Guggenheim fellowship, 1931; Pulitzer scholarship. He taught at Northwestern Univ. and at Univ. of Colorado.
WORKS: Orchestra: Scherzo burlesque, piano and strings, 1926; Symphony concertante, horn, piano, orch., 1929; symphony, 1932; Holiday, 1932; Song and dance, 1932; 2 piano concertos; many chamber works; piano pieces.

WEST, GEORGE ADDISON
b. Hightstown, N. J., 11 Mar. 1931. Studied at Oberlin Cons.; with H. Owen Reed and Paul O. Harder, Michigan State Univ., M. A. 1962, Ph. D. 1971. He has received commissions for television, film background scores, concert and marching bands. He was arranger-composer, U.S. Air Force Band, Washington, 1954-57; professor, Stephen F. Austin State Univ., 1964-67; Univ. of Calgary, 1969-71; Madison Coll., 1971-   .
WORKS: Jazz ensemble: Jazz quartally, 4-movement suite; Chamber music: Largo and allegro, trombone and string quartet; and many jazz works.
212 Governor's Lane, Apt. 2
Harrisonburg, VA 22801

WEST, RICHARD M.
b. Yakima, Wash., 23 Nov. 1940. Studied at U.S. Navy School of Music, Washington, D.C.; at Oregon State Univ., B. S.; Univ. of Oregon, M. M. Ed. He taught in public schools, 1967-71; at Linn-Benton Community Coll., 1971-   .
WORKS: Chorus: Little Jesus, tiny Jesus boy; God created man; Songs: Brotherhood, cycle of 7 songs for voice and guitar.
1515 West 12th St., Albany, OR 97321

*WESTBROOK, HELEN SEARLES
b. Southbridge, Mass., 15 Oct. 1898; d. Chicago, c. 1965. Studied with Wilhelm Middleschulte and Adolf Weidig, American Cons., B. M. and gold medal. She was theatre organist; organ soloist with the Chicago Symphony; music director, Central Church, Chicago. She wrote many songs and organ and piano pieces.

WESTERGAARD, PETER
b. Champaign, Ill., 28 May 1931. Studied with Walter Piston, Harvard Coll., A. B. magna cum laude 1953; with Roger Sessions, Princeton Univ., M. F. A. 1956; with Darius Milhaud, Aspen Music School and in Paris; with Wolfgang Fortner in Germany. His awards include Harvard nat. scholarship, 1949-53; Francis Boote prize, 1953; John Knowles Paine traveling fellowship, 1953-54; Fulbright fellowship, 1956, 1957, guest lectureship, 1958; Columbia Univ. grant, 1963; Guggenheim fellowship, 1964-65. He was teaching assistant, Princeton Univ., 1955-56; instructor to assistant professor, Columbia Coll., 1958-66; associate professor, Amherst Coll., 1967-68; visiting lecturer, Princeton Univ., 1966-67, associate professor, 1968-71, professor, 1971-   , chairman, music department, 1974-   .
WORKS: Chamber opera: Charivari, 1953; Mr. and Mrs. Discobbolos, 1965; Orchestra: Symphonic movement, 1954; 5 movements for small orch., 1958; Noises, sounds and sweet airs, chamber orch., 1968; Band: Tuckets and sennets, 1969; Chamber music: Partita, flute, violin, harpsichord, 1953-56; Inventions, flute and piano, 1955; string quartet, 1957; trio for flute, cello, piano, 1962; Variations for 6 players, 1963; Cantatas: The plot against the giant, 1956; A refusal to mourn the death, by fire, of a child in London, 1958; Leda and the swan, 1961.
Department of Music, Princeton University
Princeton, NJ 08540

*WESTIN, PHILIP L.
Is founder and conductor of the California Wind Symphony of Los Angeles. His In memoriam - Ingolf Dahl, 1972, was performed, composer conducting, at the Los Angeles Music Center, 30 Oct. 1973.
19404 Galway Ave., Gardena, CA 90247

WETZEL, RICHARD D.
b. Pitman, Pa., 27 Dec. 1935. Studied at Indiana Univ. of Pennsylvania; Carnegie Mellon Univ.; Duquesne Univ.; Univ. of Pittsburgh, M. M. and Ph. D. in musicology; composition privately with Roland Leich. He has received

(WETZEL, RICHARD D.)
several commissions. He taught in public schools, 1957-62; was free-lance instrumentalist and teacher, 1962-69; music archivist, Old Economy Museum, 1967-70; associate professor of music history and literature, Ohio Univ., 1970- .

WORKS: Chamber music: Sonatine for double reeds, 2 oboes and 2 bassoons, 1973; Chorus: Mr. Man, folk-style anthem; Service for the Lord's Day; He is the way; God of our life; Organ: Theme and variations.
Box 206, Chesterhill, OH 43722

*WETZLER, HERMANN HANS
b. Frankfurt, Germany, 8 Sep. 1870; to U.S. 1892; d. New York, N. Y., 29 May 1943. Studied with Clara Schumann and Humperdinck in Frankfurt. He was church organist in New York, 1892-1905; also formed his own orchestra in New York; was opera conductor in Germany 1905-30; returned to the U.S. 1940. He composed an opera; orchestral works, chamber music, choruses, songs.

WETZLER, ROBERT PAUL
b. Minneapolis, Minn., 30 Jan. 1932. Studied at Thiel Coll., B. A. 1954; Northwestern Lutheran Theological Seminary, M. Div. 1957; and at Univ. of Minnesota. He received annual ASCAP awards, 1967-72. He was organist and choirmaster, 1953-68; director of publications, Art Masters Studios, Inc., 1960- , president, 1966- .
WORKS: Chorus: more than 70 published choral works.
2614 Nicollet Ave., Minneapolis, MN 55408

WHALEY, GEORGE BOYD
b. Altamount, Kan., 9 Mar. 1929. Studied with William Latham, Univ. of Northern Iowa; with Francis J. Pyle, Drake Univ. He was public school band director, 1957-70; teaching fellow, Univ. of Wyoming, 1970-71; associate professor and band director, Yankton Coll., 1971- .
WORKS: Orchestra: concerto for brass quartet and strings; Festive dances; 5 images; Band: The knight, death, and the devil; sonata for band; Contramusics; Toccata for brass, organ, timpani, percussion; symphony for band; Chamber music: Divertimento for horn and woodwind quintet; Chorus: 4 songs for chorus and winds; Serenade: 5 for mi'lady.
1001 Walnut, Yankton, SD 57078

WHATLEY, G. LARRY
b. Tallassee, Ala., 7 Feb. 1940. Studied with J. Frederic Goossen, Univ. of Alabama; with Bernhard Heiden and Roque Cordero, Indiana Univ., M. M. He has been faculty member, Brevard Coll., 1963- , associate professor, 1973- .
WORKS: Orchestra: Collage for orchestra, 1962; Variations for string orch., 1963; Symphonic overture, 1965; Palindrome, 1970; Band: Toccata for wind band, 1962; Festival prelude, 1967; Introit and alleluia, 1968; many marches; Chamber music: piano sonatina, 1960; trio for reeds, 1961; Music for organ and trumpet, 1961; quartet for violin, oboe, horn, piano, 1961; brass octet, 1962; woodwind quintet, 1964;

(WHATLEY, G. LARRY)
Contrasts, trombone and piano, 1965; string quartet, 1967; brass quintet, 1969; tuba sonata, 1970; Chorus: Psalm 100 and Psalm 23, 1960; Fairest Lord Jesus, 1961; O praise the Lord, 1965; 3 psalms, 1971; and songs.
Route 3, Box 38, Brevard, NC 28712

WHEAR, PAUL WILLIAM
b. Auburn, Ind., 13 Nov. 1925. Studied at Marquette Univ., B. S.; with Donald H. White, DePauw Univ., B. A., M. M.; with Gardner Read, Boston Univ.; with Wilfred Josephs in London; Wayne Barlow at Eastman School of Music; and at Western Reserve Univ., Ph. D. His awards include Summy-Birchard Oshkosh award, 1956; Youngstown Symphony prize, 1958; Henry Cowell prize, 1960; Nat. School Orch. Asso. prize, 1962; Nat. Asso. Coll. Wind and Percussion Instructors prize, 1964; Pedro Paz prize, 1966; Kent State Univ. prize, 1963; Huntington Hartford fellowship, 1965; Nat. Found. on the Arts award, 1968; Benedum Found. grant, 1970. He was director of instrumental music, Mount Union Coll., 1952-60; chairman, music department, Doane Coll., 1960-69; resident composer, Marshall Univ. 1969- ; conductor, Huntington Chamber orchestra, 1970- ; editor, Ludwig Music Publishers, 1967- .
WORKS: Orchestra: Proemion, symphonic poem, 1949; violin concerto, 1950; St. Joan, symphonic poem, 1951; Catharthis suite, 1967; A touch-tone telephone tune, 1969; symphony no. 2, The bridge, 1971; Sonnets from Shakespeare, baritone and orch., 1973; Band: Antietam, 1966; Wycliffe variations, 1968; symphony no. 1, Stonehenge, 1970; Of this time, with narrator, 1971; Chamber music: 3 string quartets; Pastorale lament, horn and piano, 1960; trombone sonata, 1961; Septsonics, 6 trombones and tape, 1972; Chorus: The 10 commandments, cantata, 1955; The seasons, oratorio with orch., 1965; Psalms of celebration, with orch., 1965; Joyful, jubilate, 1969; Hosanna, double chorus, a cappella, 1971; many shorter works in all categories.
524 Ninth Ave., Huntington, WV 25701

WHEELOCK, DONALD F.
b. Darien, Conn., 17 June 1940. Studied with Edgar Curtis, Union Coll., Schenectady, A. B. 1962; with Yehudi Wyner, Yale Univ., M. M. 1966; He was teaching assistant, Union Coll., 1962-63; instructor to assistant professor, Colgate Univ., 1966-69; assistant professor, Amherst Coll., 1969-74; also theory teacher, Smith Coll., 1973-74.
WORKS: Orchestra: Celebrations, soprano and orch., 1968, Colgate Univ., 2 Dec. 1969; Music for dance perhaps, chamber orch., 1971; 3 pieces for orchestra, 1971; Chamber music: Divertimento, flute, English horn, violin, cello, 1966; Suite for 10 instruments, 1967; sonata for solo cello, 1969; string quartet, 1969, Amherst Coll., 5 Nov. 1970; Serenade, soprano and 7 players, 1970; 4 songs, soprano and oboe, 1970; Suite for piano, 1971; quartet for brass, 1972; 10 bagatelles, oboe and string quartet, 1972; octet, 5 winds and piano trio,

WHEELOCK, DONALD F.

(WHEELOCK, DONALD F.)
1972; Divertimento no.2, violin, trumpet, clarinet, bassoon, 1972; string quartet no.2, 1973; 3
songs, soprano, flute, clarinet, violin, cello,
1973.
233 South Pleasant St., Amherst, MA 01002

WHIPPLE, R. JAMES
b. Philadelphia, Pa., 1 Dec. 1950. Studied with
Roland Leich and Leonardo Balada, Carnegie-
Mellon Univ., B. A. 1972; with David Del Tredici
and Gardner Read, Boston Univ., M. M. 1974. He
is a free-lance composer, arranger, bassoonist.
WORKS: Orchestra: oboe concerto; concertino,
bassoon and strings; Band: The epic concerto,
alto saxophone and band; Maroon and white salute;
Chamber music: Antics, piccolo and bassoon; La
démence, 2 clarinets; I heard a fly buzz when I
died, 2 pianos; Frolic for 4 'fags', 3 bassoons,
contrabassoon; A solemn psalm of Pittsburgh memories, clarinet, trombone, contrabassoon; and
church music.
1917 Edge Hill Road, Abington, PA 19001

WHITCOMB, ROBERT B.
b. Scipio, Ind., 7 Dec. 1921. Studied with
Felix Labunski, Cincinnati Coll. of Music; with
Bernard Rogers and Howard Hanson, Eastman School
of Music. He received a commission from Thor
Johnson, 1952; first prize, Nat. Asso. Coll.
Wind and Percussion Instructors, 1962; Western
Washington State Coll. grant, 1966. He has
taught at Culver Military Acad. 1948-49; Univ.
of Wyoming, 1950-52; New Mexico State Univ.,
1952-53; South Dakota State Univ., 1953-63;
Western Washington State Coll., 1963-68; chairman,
music department, Southwest Minnesota State Coll.,
1968-   .
WORKS: Orchestra: Variations, piano and
orch.; Band: Introduction and dance; Chamber
music: 3 piano sonatinas; organ sonata; cello
sonata, 1966; Suite, viola and piano; Fantasy
trio, viola, oboe, piano; 3 nocturnes, cello and
piano; Chorus: The mighty one; May God be gracious; March of the 3 kings, women's voices,
baritone, chamber ensemble; Sandburg seasons
(Timber moon, Winter weather, Spring grass, Summer stars).
309 A St., Marshall, MN 56258

WHITE, A DUANE
b. Wytheville, Va., 22 Nov. 1939. Studied with
Dwight Gustafson, Bob Jones Univ., B. S. 1961,
M. A. 1963; with Bruce Benward, Univ. of Wisconsin, Ph. D. in musicology 1971; private musicological research in Vienna, 1969. He held a Ford
Found. grant, Univ. of Wisconsin, 1968-69; and
was awarded a travel grant for European study
by the university. He was graduate assistant,
Bob Jones Univ., 1961-63, faculty member
1963-   ; teaching assistant, Univ. of Wisconsin,
1967-68, 1969-70.
WORKS: Theatre: music for Shakespeare's
The winter's tale; Chamber music: Suite for
flute and piano; Voice: The lines are fallen
unto me in pleasant places, chorus and soprano
solo; With rue my heart is laden, voice and piano.
2111 East North St., Greenville, SC 29607

*WHITE, CLARENCE CAMERON
b. Clarksville, Tenn., 10 Aug. 1880; d. New York,
N. Y., 30 June 1960. Studied at Howard Univ.
and at Oberlin Coll., graduated 1901. His many
awards included 2 Rosenwald fellowships; honorary M. A., Atlanta Univ.; honorary D. M.,
Wilberforce Univ.; Harmon Found. medal; David
Bispham medal, 1932; Benjamin award, 1954. He
taught at Washington Cons.; was guest artist
with Samuel Coleridge-Taylor in the U.S. and
London; conducted his own music studio in Boston,
1910-22; was chairman, music department, West
Virginia State Coll., 1924-31; director of music,
Hampton Inst., 1931-35.
WORKS: Opera: Ouanga, 1932; Ballet: A
night in Sans Souci; Orchestra: symphony, 1928;
Bandanna sketches; Piece for strings and timpani;
violin concerto; Elegy for orchestra, 1954; violin pieces.

WHITE, DONALD H.
b. Narberth, Pa., 28 Feb. 1921. Studied with
Vincent Persichetti, Philadelphia Cons.; with
Bernard Rogers and Howard Hanson, Eastman School
of Music, Ph. D. He has received 8 annual ASCAP
awards and many commissions. He has been professor, De Pauw Univ., 1947-   .
WORKS: Orchestra: Sagan, an overture, 1946;
Kennebec suite, 1947; cello concerto, 1952;
Divertissement no.2, string orch., 1968; A song
of mankind, 2 choirs, soloists and orch., 1971;
Band: Miniature set, 1957; Dichotomy, 1964;
Ambrosian hymn variants, 1965; Patterns, 1967;
Terpsimetrics, 1969; concertino for clarinet,
woodwind choir, percussion, 1971; concertino for
timpani, winds, percussion, 1972; Blue Lake
divertissement, 1972; Chamber music: trumpet
sonata, 1946; 3 for 5, woodwind quintet, 1958;
Diversions, brass sextet, 1964; Serenade no.3,
brass quartet, 1963; Divertissement no.1, clarinet choir, 1965; trombone sonata, 1966; Lyric
suite, euphonium and piano, 1970; Trio variations, piano trio, 1970; Suite hommage, bass
trombone, and piano, 1972; also choral works,
piano pieces.
R. R. 1, Fairway Drive
Greencastle, IN 46135

*WHITE, ELISE FELLOWS
b. Maine, 1873; d. 1933. Composed songs and
violin pieces.

WHITE, GARY
b. Winfield, Kan., 27 May 1937. Studied with
John Pozdro, Univ. of Kansas; with H. Owen Reed
and Paul Harder, Michigan State Univ., Ph. D.
1969. He held a graduate fellowship, Michigan
State Univ., 1966-67. He has been faculty member, Iowa State Univ., 1967-   , professor,
1973-   .
WORKS: Theatre: music for The egg, 1962;
Cyrano de Bergerac, 1963; Bury the dead, 1968;
Orchestra: Dramatic overture, 1961, Lawrence,
Kan., 7 May 1963; Prologue, 3 trumpets, timpani,
strings, 1964; symphony, 1969, Michigan State
Univ., 4 June 1971; Wind ensemble: 2 movements
for brass, 1963; Striations, winds and percussion, 1971; Chamber music: sonata for cello

(WHITE, GARY)
solo, Univ. of Kansas, 24 May 1961; woodwind quintet, 1961; string quartet, 1963; Chaconne for percussion, 1963; 2 movements for chamber ensemble, 1965; woodwind quintet, 1966; Strata, solo clarinet, 1968; Composition for piano, brass, percussion, 1970; Centrum, violin and tape, 1971; Chorus: A canticle from Daniel, with brass and percussion, 1967; Electronic: Music for a festival of light, computer and synthesized sound, 1972; also works for carillon.
39B Exhibit Hall, Iowa State University
Ames, IA 50010

WHITE, JOHN D.
b. Rochester, Minn., 28 Nov. 1931. Studied with Earl George and Paul Fetler, Univ. of Minnesota, B. A.; with Bernard Rogers and Howard Hanson, Eastman School of Music, M. A., Ph. D.; also with Nadia Boulanger and Ross Lee Finney. He received the Benjamin award, Eastman School, 1960; Nat. Fed. of Music Clubs award, 1962; first prize, Rochester Religious Arts Festival, 1963; annual ASCAP awards, 1965- . He was faculty member, Kent State Univ., 1956-63, associate dean, Graduate School, 1956-73; on faculty, Univ. of Michigan, 1963-65; dean, School of Music, Ithaca Coll., 1973- .
WORKS: Opera: The legend of Sleepy Hollow, 3-acts, 1961; Orchestra: symphony no.2, 1960; Dialogue concertante, cello and orch.; Folk elegy, cello and orch., 1962; concerto for cello and chamber orch., 1962; Chamber music: Variations, clarinet and piano; piano sonatina, 1954; Aria and double fugue, harpsichord, 1967; Chorus: 3 madrigals, with orch.; The monkey's sonnet; The passing of winter; The turmoil; Cantos of the year, with baritone solo and orch., 1968; Songs: The lamb and Cradle song, Blake texts; 3 James Joyce songs, 1964; Whitman music, mezzo-soprano, cello, piano, 1970.
School of Music, Ithaca College
Ithaca, NY 14850

WHITE, LOUIE L.
b. Spartanburg, S. C., 1 Aug. 1921. Studied with Pedro Sanjuan, Converse Coll.; with Ernst Bacon at Syracuse Univ. He received the Hyatt composition award, Spartanburg, S. C.; 2 awards, Church of the Ascension, New York. He was faculty member, Syracuse Univ., 1947-48; taught in a private school in New York, 1953-69; associate professor, Rutgers Univ., 1970- .
WORKS: Opera: Jephthah, chancel opera; Orchestra: harpsichord concerto; Chorus: Rejoice, Emanuel shall come, Christmas cantata; many works for chorus, piano, chamber orchestra and solo voice.
61 West 9th St., New York, NY 10011

WHITE, MICHAEL
b. Chicago, Ill., 6 Mar. 1931. Studied at Oberlin Coll.; Univ. of Wisconsin; Chicago Musical Coll.; and with Peter Mennin, Juilliard School. He has received 2 Juilliard fellowships; 3 Ford Found. fellowships; Guggenheim fellowship; ASCAP awards; Columbia Univ. chamber music prize. He was composer-in-residence, Seattle public

(WHITE, MICHAEL)
schools, 1961-62; instructor, Oberlin Cons., 1964-66; associate professor, Philadelphia Musical Acad., 1966- .
WORKS: Opera: The dybbuk, 1962; The metamorphosis; Alice; Orchestra: Fantasy for orchestra, 1957; Suite for orchestra, 1959; The diary of Anne Frank, soprano and orch., 1960; Gloria, chorus and orch., 1960; Prelude and ostinato, for string orch., 1960; Concerto antico for wind ensemble; Opposites, wind ensemble; Chorus: The passion according to a cynic; The first sabbath of spring; The ancient vespers; The prophet; Voice: Songs from the Japanese; A child's garden; A Bach trip.
7147 Ardleigh St., Philadelphia, PA 19119

*WHITE, PAUL TAYLOR
b. Bangor, Me., 22 Aug. 1895; d. Henrietta, N. Y., 31 May 1973. Studied composition with George W. Chadwick, violin with Felix Winternitz, New England Cons.; violin with Eugene Ysaya in Cincinnati; conducting with Eugene Goossens in Rochester; received an honorary D. M., Univ. of Maine. He was violinist, Rochester Philharmonic, 1924-29; associate conductor, Rochester Civic Orchestra, 1929-53, conductor from 1953; faculty member Eastman School of Music and conductor, Eastman Symphony from 1935; guest conductor of his own works with many orchestras including the Boston Pops.
WORKS: Orchestra: Variations, 1925; Mosquito dance; symphony, 1934; Pagan festival overture, 1936; Boston sketches, 4 spokes from the Hub, 1938; College caprice, 1939; Lake spray, 1939; Voyage of the Mayflower, chorus and orch.; Sea chanty, harp and strings, 1942; Lake Placid scenes, 1943; Idyll, 1944; Andante and rondo, cello and orch., 1945; Chamber music: Fantastic dance, woodwinds, 1922; 2 string quartets; violin sonata, 1926; 5 miniatures for piano.

WHITE, RUTH
b. Pittsburgh, Pa., 1 Sep. 1925. Studied with Nikolai Lopatnikoff, Carnegie-Mellon Inst.; privately with George Antheil in Los Angeles. She received first prize in composition, Nat. Society of Arts and Letters; Huntington Hartford Found. fellowship. She was supervisor, Univ. of California Demonstration School, Los Angeles, 1951-59; president, Rhythms Productions Records, 1955- ; vice president, Cheviot Corp., 1961- .
WORKS: Electronic: Pinions, 1968; 7 triumphs from the tarot cards, 1968; Flowers of evil, 1969; Short circuits, 1970; also film scores, multimedia works such as music for the San Diego Space Theater, educational phonograph albums, etc.
Whitney Bldg., Box 34485
Los Angeles, CA 90034

WHITE, RUTH EDEN
b. Florence, S. C., 25 Dec. 1928. Studied at Coker Coll. She has been church organist, 1947- , at Calvary Baptist Church, Florence, S. C., 1963- .

WHITE, RUTH EDEN

(WHITE, RUTH EDEN)
WORKS: Chorus: Have you heard?; Fill me, Lord, with all thy ways; Let praise fill the skies; other choral works, many with original texts.
1108 Brunwood Drive, Florence, SC 29501

WHITECOTTON, SHIRLEY
b. Aurora, Ill., 23 Sep. 1935. Studied with Jack Goode, Wheaton Coll.; also at Aspen Music School and at Northwestern Univ. She was a private voice teacher, 1960-73.
WORKS: Chorus: We have a king, cantata; Little known Scottish folk songs, Books I and II, Words of life; Christmas comes in the morning, cantata; Michael; Light; The lamb; God is watching; A Christmas carol, etc.
408 West Jefferson, Wheaton, IL 60187

*WHITHORNE (WHITTERN), EMERSON
b. Cleveland, Ohio, 6 Sep. 1884; d. New York, N. Y., 25 Mar. 1958. Studied piano in Cleveland, and after tours on the Chautauqua circuit as a boy pianist studied with Theodor Leschetizky, Robert Fuchs, and Artur Schnabel in Europe for several years. He was music critic in London, 1907-16; married Ethel Leginska in 1907, was her concert manager, 1907-09, divorced 1916; music editor in St. Louis, 1916-20; then settled in New York.
WORKS: Theatre: Sooner or later, ballet; music to O'Neill's Marco Millions, 1928; Orchestra: The rain 1913; The aeroplane, 1925; Saturday's child, to poems of Countee Cullen, soprano, tenor, and orch., 1926; New York days and nights, 1926; Poem, piano and orch., 1927; Fata morgana, 1928; 2 symphonies, 1929, 1936; The dream pedlar, 1931; violin concerto, 1931; Fandango, 1932; Moon trail, 1933; Sierra Morena, 1938; Chamber music: Greek impressions, string quartet; string quartet; piano quintet; The grim troubadour, voice and string quartet.

WHITMAN, JAMES K.
b. Oakland, Calif., 12 May 1946. Studied with Robert Gross, Occidental Coll.; with Richard Swift, Univ. of California at Davis; with Leo Smit and Lejaren Hiller, State Univ. of New York at Buffalo. He received the Elanor Remick Warren award, 1965; a commission from West German Radio, Cologne, 1973. He has been assistant at the electronic studio, West German Radio, Cologne, 1973-   .
WORKS: Theatre: Yuzuru, play with music for flute, clarinet, percussion and tape; Chamber music: Soldier in the groove, flute, violin, cello; Electronic: Pavasiya, chorus and tape; GGK, tape; Dance of Shiva, 4-channel tape.
Gereonswall 66, 5 Köln 1, West Germany

*WHITMER, THOMAS CARL
b. Altoona, Pa., 24 June 1873; d. Poughkeepsie, N. Y., 30 May 1959. Studied composition with William Wallace Gilchrist. He taught at Stephens Coll., 1897-1909; was director of music, Pennsylvania Coll. for Women, 1909-16; church organist in Pittsburgh, 1916-32; then taught privately in New York.

(WHITMER, THOMAS CARL)
WORKS: Opera: Oh, Isabel, 1951; Ballet: A Syrian night, 1919; Orchestra: Poem of life, piano and orch., 1914; Radiations over a 13th century theme, string orch., 1935; Chorus: When God laughed, a cappella, 1932; Supper at Emmaus, choral suite, 1939; Cantata after Walt Whitman, 1942; also chamber music, songs, piano pieces.

WHITNEY, C. MAURICE
b. Glens Falls, N. Y., 25 Mar. 1909. Studied at Ithaca Coll., B. S. 1932; New York Univ., M. A. 1939; and at Columbia Univ., New England Cons., Westminster Choir Coll., Williams Coll. His awards include first prize, Composer Press contest, 1949; citation for outstanding achievement, Ithaca Coll., 1951; John Hay fellowship, 1961; citation as Teacher-of-the-year, New York State Teachers Asso., 1966; honorary L. H. D., Elmira Coll., 1966. He taught in public schools, 1932-69; was visiting professor, Adirondack Community Coll., 1969-71.
WORKS: 136 works for orchestra, band, chorus, solo instruments and ensembles, mainly for school, college, and church use. He is author of Backgrounds in music theory.
1508 Danbury Drive
Sun City Center, FL 33570

*WHITNEY, ROBERT SUTTON
b. Newcastle-on-Tyne, England, 6 July 1904, of American parents. Studied at American Cons., 1922-28; conducting with Eric De Lamarter and Frederick Stock. His honors include the Ditson award for service to American music, 1951; honorary D. M., Univ. of Louisville, 1952; L. L. D., Hanover Coll., 1956. He made his debut as conductor with the Chicago Civic Orchestra in 1932; was conductor of the Louisville Orchestra, 1937-1974; dean, School of Music, Univ. of Louisville, 19 .
WORKS: Orchestra: Concerto grosso, 1932; symphony, 1936; Sinfonietta, 1939; Sospiri di Roma, chorus and orch., 1941; Concertino for orch., 1961.
2134 Alta Ave., Louisville, KY 40301

WHITNEY, RYAN LAYNE
b. Seattle, Wash., 1 July 1953. Studied privately with Lockrem Johnson in Seattle. He has received a BMI student composer award; first prize, Nat. Fed. of Music Clubs composition contest; various prizes in state contests.
WORKS: Piano: 6 burlescas; Tema con variazioni, 1969; sonata no.1.
37232 49th Ave. South, Auburn, WA 98002

WHITTAKER, HOWARD
b. Lakewood, Ohio, 19 Dec. 1922. Studied with Herbert Elwell and Ward Lewis, Cleveland Inst. of Music, B. M., conducting with Boris Goldovsky; with Herbert Elwell, Oberlin Cons. M. M. 1947; later at Eastman School of Music. He received a commission, Otterbein Coll., 1946; Fortnightly Musical Club award, 1948; Mendelssohn Glee Club award, 1953; fine arts award, Women's City Club of Cleveland, 1963. He has been director, Cleveland Music School Settlement, 1948-   . In

(WHITTAKER, HOWARD)
1968 he was appointed consultant to Vice President Hubert Humphrey and worked with the President's Council on Youth Opportunity.
WORKS: Orchestra: Fantasy on Ben Hamby melodies, 1946; Variations for orchestra, 1947; piano concerto, 1954; 2 murals for orchestra, 1958; Chamber music: 2 string quartets, 1947, 1948; violin sonatina, 1957; cello sonata, 1957; cello sonatina, 1969; violin sonata, 1970; Chorus: True repentance, 1953; Behold he cometh with clouds, cantata, 1953; Songs: The child in the garden, 1952; To song, 1952; This bread I break, 1955; Of time and the river, song cycle, 1956; This is the shape of the leaf, 1958; The dark chamber, 1958; Piano: 2 sonatas, 1954, 1960; Variations, 1958.
Berkshire Road, Gates Mills, OH 44040

*WHITTENBERG, CHARLES
b. St. Louis, Mo., 1927. Studied at the American Acad. in Rome and in Munich. He received a teaching grant for new music performance techniques, American Council of Learned Societies, 1962; 2 Guggenheim fellowships, 1963-65; Prix de Rome, 1965-66; and many commissions. He has been on the faculty, Univ. of Connecticut, 1966-   , associate professor, 1972-   ; has also been affiliated with the Columbia-Princeton electronic music center and the summer institute at Bennington Coll.
WORKS: Wind ensemble: Triptych for brass quintet, 1962; Chamber music: 3 pieces for clarinet solo, 1963; Conversations, unaccompanied double bass; Polyphony, unaccompanied trumpet; string quartet in one movement, 1965; Games of 5, woodwind quintet, 1968; Electronic: Electronic study II, tape and contrabass, 1962.
Department of Music, University of Connecticut Storrs, CT 06268

WHITTREDGE, EDWARD B.
b. Dorchester, Mass., 31 Jan. 1893. Studied organ with John Hermann Loud; theory at Boston Univ.; summer sessions at Westminster Choir School, Christiansen Choral School, and Fred Waring Workshop. He was admitted as fellow, American Guild of Organists, 1933. He was organist-choirmaster, Christ Church, Quincy, Mass., 1919-36; minister of music, Wollaston Congregational Church, 1936-69; director, Wentworth Inst. Glee Club, 1958-68.
WORKS: Chorus: Psalm 91, cantata; As it began to dawn; Lord speak to me; Surely He hath borne our griefs; The church's one foundation; numerous other published choral works.
789 Brook Road, Milton, MA 02186

WHITWELL, CRAIG MARTIN
b. Santa Rosa, Calif., 21 Apr. 1948. Studied with Higo Harada and Allen Strange, California State Univ. at San Jose; with Ralph Shapey and George Crumb, Univ. of Pennsylvania. He received the Eva Thompson Phillips award, 1970, 1971. He was lecturer in the Creative Associates program, California State Univ., San Jose, 1970-71.
WORKS: Chamber music: Episode, trombone and piano, 1969; Duo sonata, trombone and flute,

(WHITWELL, CRAIG MARTIN)
1969; Theme and variations in arch form, for 2 winds, 1970; Variations on a theme by Satie, 1971; Fantasy, 4 strings and oboe, 1972; Villanelle, brass quartet.
Box 607, Apt. A-12
3600 Chestnut St., Philadelphia, PA 19104

WICHMANN, RUSSELL G.
b. Appleton, Wis., 29 July 1912. Studied at Lawrence Univ., B. M. 1934; with Clarence Dickinson, T. Tertius Noble, and Edwin J. Stringham, Union Theological Seminary, S. M. M. 1936; Army Music School, 1944; with Arthur Honegger and Marcel Dupre in Paris, 1950-51; with Wayne Barlow and Allen McHose, Eastman School of Music, 1959-60. He received the Pittsburgh Arts Society award, 1937; alumni distinguished service award, Lawrence Univ., 1970. He has been minister of music, Shadyside Presbyterian Church, Pittsburgh, 1936-   ; assistant professor and organist, Univ. of Pittsburgh, 1936-46; Army bandleader, 1944-45; professor and head, music department, Chatham Coll., 1946-   ; conductor, Mendelssohn Choir of Pittsburgh, 1952-66.
WORKS: Chorus: Dayspring of eternity; Come thou, my light; O Lamb of God; I lift up my eyes; Bell carol; Psalm 100; Psalm 148; Psalm 150; The voice of God; God of our life; and others.
313 Dewey Ave., Edgewood Pittsburgh, PA 15218

*WICK, OTTO
b. Krefeld, Germany, 8 July 1885; to U.S. 1905; d. Austin, Tex., 9 Nov. 1957. Studied at Univ. of Kiel; New York Coll. of Music, Ph. D. He was conductor in New York, 1910-24; guest conductor in Europe; composer, arranger, conductor, NBC, New York, 1928-31; organized and conducted, New York Orch., 1931-35; with Southwest Festival Asso., San Antonio, 1938-42; dean, Univ. of San Antonio, 1939-46; then director, San Antonio Opera Company.
WORKS: Opera: The lone star; Matasuntha, music drama; Moon maid, light opera; For Art's sake, operetta; Orchestra: Suite for strings and harp; symphonic poem; Symphonic fantasy; Trilogy for orchestra; Chorus: Temple of Peshawar, cantata.

*WICKHAM, FLORENCE
b. Beaver, Pa., 1880; d. New York, N. Y., 20 Oct. 1962. Studied voice in Philadelphia and Berlin; sang at the New York Metropolitan Opera, 1909-12; then retired from the stage and devoted her time to composition. Her works included an operetta, Rosalynd, 1938; many published choral pieces, and songs.

WIDDOES, LAWRENCE L.
b. Wilmington, Del., 15 Sept. 1932. Studied with Bernard Wagenaar, Vincent Persichetti, and William Bergsma, Juilliard School, B. S., M. S. He received the Benjamin award at Juilliard; Society for the Publication of American Music award; Elizabeth Sprague Coolidge chamber music award; Contemporary Music Project, composer-in-

WIDDOES, LAWRENCE L.

(WIDDOES, LAWRENCE L.)
residence, Salem, Ore.; Bowdoin Coll. composition contest award. He has been faculty member, Juilliard School, 1965- .
WORKS: Orchestra: Morning music; Chamber music: 1000 paper cranes, guitar, viola, harpsichord, 1966; From a time of snow, flute, clarinet, viola, cello, piano; flute sonatina; Acanthus, harp and viola, New York, 11 May 1973; Love song, voice and piano; Aubade, chamber ensemble, New York, 19 Apr. 1974; Chorus: Sanctus; Pied beauty.
210 West 70th St., New York, NY 10023

WIDDOWSON, KENNETH WEST
b. Punxsutawney, Pa., 4 Nov. 1928. Studied at Duquesne Univ.; with Bernhard Heiden, Indiana Univ.; with Paul Cooper, Univ. of Michigan. He was educational director, Ludwig Music Publishing Company, 1961-62.
WORKS: Band: States War fantasy, 1955; Portrait of this old man, 1961; Phantom squadron, 1962; Valley Forge fantasy, 1967.
3203 Ward Ave., Trenton, MI 48183

WIENER, IVAN
b. New York, N. Y., 15 June 1933. Studied with Robert Starer, 1955-57, 1959; with Wallingford Riegger, 1957-58. He held the Frederick Jacobi scholarship, 1955-57. He was librarian and editor, Galaxy Music Corp., 1964-67; editor, Broude Brothers, Ltd., 1967- .
WORKS: Orchestra: Fantasie cincertante, double bass and orch.; symphony; concerto grosso, 5 solo instruments and strings; cello concerto; double bass concerto; Variations for orch.; Chamber music: Inventions for 2 alto recorders; 2 string trios; 3 segments, percussion ensemble; Chorus: love is more thicker than forget, e.e. cummings text; Requiem, chorus, soloists, orch.
556 Ave. Z, Brooklyn, NY 11223

WIENHORST, RICHARD W.
b. Seymour, Ind., 21 Apr. 1920. Studied at Valparaiso Univ., A. B.; with Leo Sowerby, American Cons., M. M.; with Nadia Boulanger at Fontainebleau; musicology at Albert Ludwige Univ., Germany; with Bernard Rogers and Howard Hanson, Eastman School of Music, Ph. D. He received a Danforth Found. award; Lilly Found. graduate study award. He was bandleader, U.S. Army, 1942-46; professor, Valparaiso Univ., 1947- .
WORKS: Chorus: Magnificat, chorus and orch.; Missa brevis, a cappella; The seven words of Christ from the cross; A nativity cantata, with flutes and strings; Psalm 150; Hear, O Lord; I know the thoughts I think; Lord, thine enemies roar.
103 Sturdy Road, Valparaiso, IN 46383

WIGGINS, ARTHUR M.
b. New York, N. Y., 18 Mar. 1920. Studied at U.S. Air Force Bandsman School of Music, Washington; is self-taught in composition. He was chief arranger, NORAD Band, Colorado Springs, 1959-65; chief arranger, Air Force bands in New York and Canal Zone, 1965 to retirement, 1973.

(WIGGINS, ARTHUR M.)
WORKS: Band: Intervale; The court jester; Ballet for jazz; Chamber music: Conversations for alto saxophone; Song and dance man, bass clarinet; Una mas, trumpet; The horn, for horn.
6875 Narrow Guage
Colorado Springs, CO 80911

WIGGINS, DONALD GLEN
b. Orlando, Fla., 22 Feb. 1943. Studied with Roger McDuffie, Converse Coll.; with Ben Johnston and Edwin London, Univ. of Illinois. He was faculty member, Converse Coll., 1967-70; voice instructor, State Univ. Coll., Fredonia, N. Y., 1972- .
WORKS: Theatre: music for Murder in the cathedral; also songs and an opera.
Route 1, Bowers Road, Cassadaga, NY 14718

WIGGINS, MARY
b. Indiana, Pa., 10 Feb. 1904. Studied composition privately with Gladys W. Fisher and Harvey B. Gaul; with Roland Leich, Carnegie-Mellon Univ. She received a Nat. Fed. of Music Clubs award, 1973. She has been a private piano teacher, 1924- ; organist, 1931- ; taught organ at Schenley High School, 1951-57; piano at Pittsburgh Musical Inst., 1959-62. She has composed for piano, organ, violin, bassoon, solo voice, chorus, and numerous piano teaching pieces.
1038 North Negley Ave., Pittsburgh, PA 15206

WIGGLESWORTH, FRANK
b. Boston, Mass., 3 Mar. 1918. Studied at Bard Coll., Columbia Univ., B. S.; Converse Coll., M. M.; composition with Otto Luening, Henry Cowell, and Edgard Varese. He received the Alice M. Ditson award; Nat. Inst. of Arts and Letters award; fellowship, American Acad. in Rome, 1951-54; 2 MacDowell fellowships. He was instructor, Columbia Univ., 1946-51; Queens Coll., 1954-55; faculty, New School for Social Research, 1954- , chairman, music department, 1967- ; composer-in-residence American Acad., 1969-70; senior composer-in-residence, Composers' Conference, 1973.
WORKS: Orchestra: New England concerto, violin and strings, 1941; 2 symphonies, 1957, 1958; 3 portraits for strings; Chamber music: Lake music, solo flute; duo for oboe and viola or clarinet; Chorus: Creation, with small orch., 1940; Jeremiah, with baritone solo and orch., 1942; Sleep becalmed, with orch., 1948. He has composed in all forms for both stage and concert except string quartet.
19 Downing St., New York, NY 10014

*WIGHAM, MARGARET
b. Minnesota. Has published a concerto for 2 pianos, other piano pieces.

WILCOX, JAMES H.
b. Bolton, England, 10 July 1916; to U.S. 1921. Studied with Arne Oldberg, Northwestern Univ.; at Univ. of Wisconsin; at Eastman School of Music, 1949-53; with Ernst von Dohnanyi, Florida State Univ., 1954-56. He was faculty member,

(WILCOX, JAMES H.)
Florida State Univ., 1954-56; professor and head, music department, Southeastern Louisiana Univ., 1963-70, dean, School of Humanities, 1970- .
WORKS: Band: Introduction and passacaglia, 1956; Chamber music: Heroic sketch, horn and piano, 1950; Concert piece, trumpet and piano, 1954; violin sonata, 1955.
105 College Drive, Hammond, LA 70401

*WILDER, ALEC
b. Rochester, N. Y., 16 Feb. 1907. Studied with Herbert Inch and Edward Royce, Eastman School of Music. He received the ASCAP-Deems Taylor award in 1974 for his book, American popular song - The great inventors, 1900-50.
WORKS: Opera: The lowland sea, 1951; Sunday excursion, 1953; Kittiwake Island, musical comedy, 1955; Ballet: Juke box, 1942; Orchestra: concerto for oboe, strings, percussion, 1957; Chamber music: 6 woodwind quintets, 1957-60; suite for brass quintet, 1959; cello sonata; 3 horn sonatas; trombone sonata; trumpet sonata; tuba sonata; sonata for horn, tuba, and piano; flute 1965; English horn sonata; bass trombone sonata, 1968; nonet for brass, 1969.

WILDING-WHITE, RAYMOND
b. Caterham, Surrey, England, 9 Oct. 1922; U.S. citizen. Studied at Massachusetts Inst. of Technology, 1940-42; at Juilliard School, 1948-49; privately with Jerzy Fitelberg in New York; with Francis Judd Cooke, New England Cons., B. M. 1951, M. M. 1957; with Aaron Copland, Jacques Ibert, and Luigi Dallapiccola at Tanglewood, 1950-51-52; at Boston Univ., D. M. A. 1961. His awards include the F. S. Croft award, 1951, 1952, at Tanglewood; Samuel Wechsler commission; New England Cons. New Music prize, 1959; Shepherd award, 1964; Cleveland Women's City Club award, 1967. He was producer and director, WGBH-FM-TV, Boston, 1951-56; production manager, Nat. Merchandising Corp., 1957-59; instructor, Archbishop Cushing Coll., 1958-59; assistant professor, Case Inst. of Technology, 1961-68; assistant professor, De Paul Univ., 1968- .
WORKS: Opera: The tub, chamber opera, 1952; The selfish giant, libretto from Oscar Wilde, 1952; Yerma, libretto from Garcia-Lorca by composer, 1962; Ballet: The trees, 1949; The lonesome valley, 1960; Theatre: Monday morning at the Gargoyle Works, action piece for 5 performers, 1968; Slinky, for one amplified performer, 1969; Bad news, a set of short Dada pieces, 1970; Orchestra: piano concerto, 1949; Even now, baritone and orch., 1954; Concertante, violin, horn, and strings, 1963; Chamber music: string quartet, 1948; piano sonata, 1950; 3 organ preludes, 1951; 2-piano sonata, 1953; violin sonata, 1956; Little suite for winds, 1958; Variations for chamber organ and string trio, 1959; 16 character sketches, piano studies, 1950-60; Monte Carlo suite no.1, for string quartet, 1962, no.2, for piano, 1962; trumpet sonatina, 1964; Metals, metallic constructions for audience participation, 1964; Counterpoints and events, 2 clarinets, 1965; 6 fragments for jazz ensemble, 1966; The children's corner, collage for any group of keyboard

(WILDING-WHITE, RAYMOND)
instruments and one singer, 1966; Haiku, soprano, tenor, various instruments, 1967; a group of 9 pieces all called Whatzit, for various performers, instruments, and/or tape, e.g., #7 for 24 live and 144 recorded harpsichords, 1967-73; Chorus: 3 Christmas carols, 1948; Psalm I, 1950; Space madrigals, 1950; Psalm II, 1951; Psalm III, 1951; 2 masses, 1954; The ship of death, with wind orch., 1956; Psalm 47, 1959; Paraphernalia - A regalia of madrigalia from Ezra Pound, 1959; 6 Bennington epitaphs, 1960; Psalm IV, 1962; Mexico City blues, male chorus and jazz combo, 1964; Laudamus viros gloriosos, male voices and brass, 1965; Silence, 3 or 5 performers, any voice, 1969; Psalm 137, for 24 solo voices, 1970; De profundis, large and small choruses, soloists, instrumental groups and tape, 1973; also songs, electronic and multimedia works. He is author of articles in music journals and of a forthcoming book: An outline of 20th century techniques.
715 South Ridgeland Ave., Oak Park, IL 60304

WILKINSON, SCOTT
b. Bement, Ill., 27 June 1922. Studied with Arthur Olaf Andersen, Univ. of Arizona; with Darius Milhaud, Mills Coll. and in Paris. He received a composition award at Mills Coll. He was on the editorial staff, Carl Fischer, inc., 1956-61, 1964-71; lecturer in theory, Univ. of New Mexico, 1971- .
WORKS: Chamber music: violin sonata; Chorus: Blessed are they; also band works.
518 Camino de la Sierra, N.E. Albuquerque, NM 87123

WILLEY, JAMES H.
b. Lynn, Mass., 1 Oct. 1939. Studied with Bernard Rogers and Howard Hanson, Eastman School of Music. He received first prize, Eastern Illinois Univ. contest, 1970. He was assistant professor, State Univ. Coll. at Geneseo, N. Y., 1966-74.
WORKS: Orchestra: violin concerto, 1972; Wind ensemble: Commentary II, winds and percussion, 1970; Voice: 3 Elizabethan lyrics, 1968; Gacelas, voice and piano, 1969.
25A Prospect St., Geneseo, NY 14454

*WILLIAMS, CLIFTON
b. Arkansas, 1923. Studied at Louisiana Polytechnical Inst.; with Helen Gunderson, Louisiana State Univ.; with Bernard Rogers and Howard Hanson, Eastman School of Music. He has received 2 Ostwald awards of the American Band Masters Asso.; and an honorary D. M., Nat. Cons. of Lima, Peru. He served in the Army Air Corps in World War II; joined the faculty at Univ. of Texas in 1949; became chairman of theory and composition, Univ. of Miami, 1966.
WORKS: Band: Trail scenes suite; Trilogy, suite; concertino for percussion and band; Symphonic dances; Fanfare and allegro; Dedicatory overture; Dramatic essay; The ramparts; and many other band pieces.
School of Music, University of Miami Coral Gables, FL 33124

WILLIAMS, DAVID H.

*WILLIAMS, DAVID H.
b. Caerphilly, Wales, 21 Nov. 1919. Studied at
Peabody Cons. and Columbia Univ. He has been
church organist-choirmaster in the New York area,
Conn., Vermont, and Tucson, Ariz.
WORKS: Chorus: Gloria; Take my life and let
it be, in calypso style; 3 Lenten scenes; Draw
nigh to Jerusalem; On the passion of Christ, cantata; To Zion Jesus came.
9020 Shadow Mountain Drive, Tucson, AZ 85704

*WILLIAMS, DAVID McKAY
b. Caernarvonshire, Wales, 20 Feb. 1887; to U.S.
as an infant. Studied with Vincent d'Indy, Louis
Vierne, and Charles-Marie Widor, Schola Cantorum,
Paris; and at King's Coll., Nova Scotia, D. M.
A festival service honoring his 85th birthday
was held at St. Bartholomew's Church, New York,
in 1972. He taught at David Mannes School; was
chairman, organ department, Columbia Univ.,
1920-24; and at Juilliard School, 1942-48;
organist-choirmaster, St. Bartholomew's Church,
New York, 1920-48. His compositions include an
opera, Florence Nightingale; an operetta, Enchanted waters; In the year that King Uzziah died
for chorus; many church anthems, etc.

WILLIAMS, DAVID RUSSELL
b. Indianapolis, Ind., 21 Oct. 1932. Studied
with Otto Luening, Jack Beeson, Henry Cowell,
Columbia Univ., B. A., M. A. 1956; with Howard
Hanson, Bernard Rogers, Wayne Barlow, Eastman
School of Music, Ph. D. 1965. He received the
Eastman School publication award. He was director of music, Windham Coll., 1959-62; assistant
professor, Eastman School of Music, 1965-   .
WORKS: Orchestra: In the still of the bayou;
concerto for piano 4-hands; Lullaby under the mag-
nolias; 5 states of mind; Air for oboe and strings;
Band: Sinfonia; Mt. Olympus march; St. Anthony
march; Suite for brass; Recitation, trombone
choir; Chamber music: Suite for clarinet, oboe,
piano; sonatina for harp and bassoon; clarinet
sonatina; Song and dance, violin and piano; Fanfare, brass quintet; Keyboard: 5 pieces for
harpsichord; 8 piano sonatas.
520 East Ave., Rochester, NY 14607

*WILLIAMS, DONALD
Silence spoke with your voice, chorus.

*WILLIAMS, FRANCES
b. Caernarvonshire, Wales, 4 June   ; to U.S.
at an early age. Studied at Cornish School of
Music, Seattle; with Rubin Goldmark and James
Friskin, Juilliard School. She joined the staff
at Harold Flammer, Inc., later became editor-in-
chief. She has published more than 300 choral
works and songs.
545 West End Ave., New York, NY 10024

WILLIAMS, HOWARD
b. Auburn, Calif., 25 June 1933; d. Durham, N. H.,
9 Feb. 1972. Studied with Seymour Shifrin,
Andrew Imbrie, Luigi Dallapiccola, Univ. of California, Berkeley, A. B. 1954, M. A. 1965. He
received the Alfred Hertz Memorial resident fellowship, Berkeley, 1962-63, traveling fellowship,

(WILLIAMS, HOWARD)
Paris, 1963-64; DeLorenzo composition prize,
1963; and a MacDowell fellowship, 1968. He was
graduate assistant, Univ. of California,
1958-63; instructor to associate professor, Univ.
of New Hampshire, 1965-72.
WORKS: Orchestra: 6 poems, tenor and orch.;
Chamber music: concertino for tuba, percussion,
and piano; clarinet sonata; string quartet; Chorus: Settings, women's voices; Piano: Cycle
for piano; 5 bagatelles; 3 movements.

WILLIAMS, JACK ERIC
b. Odessa, Tex., 28 Mar. 1944. Studied with
Ethelston P. Chapman, Odessa Jr. Coll.; with
Kurt Overhoff, Texas Tech Univ. He won first
place, Texas Manuscript Society contest, 1962;
first place, Texas Young Composers contest, 1963,
1964, 1965; first place, Nat. Grass Roots Opera
contest, 1965; and the Alice Lee Madrigal award,
1964. He has been music director, various summer theaters; and on a Tennessee Arts Commission
grant, composer-in-residence, McGavock High
School, Nashville, Feb.-May 1974.
WORKS: Opera: The hinge-tune, 1-act, 1964;
We gave him piano lessons, 1-act, 1970; Eyes at
Treblinka, musical drama, 1973; Chamber music:
oboe sonata, 1970; sextet, winds and piano, 1972;
Chorus: Stabat mater, 1971; Yerma, 1971; Sing
and play with nursery children, vol. I and II;
A very special person, 1972; With this rose I
thee wake; On the human condition, 1973.
4307 Elkins Ave., Nashville, TN 37209

WILLIAMS, JAY T.
b. Rochester, Minn., 31 Oct. 1941. Studied with
Iannis Xenakis, Indiana Univ. He was graduate
assistant, Indiana Univ., 1964-65, 1969-71;
piano technician, North Carolina School of the
Arts, 1971-   ; radio announcer and contemporary
music program producer, WFDA-FM, Winston-Salem,
1972; and, on a North Carolina State Arts Council
grant, guest lecturer, North Carolina School
System, 1972-   .
WORKS: Chamber music: Char-main, solo viola;
Electronic: Mean 82, tape; Apertures, tape;
Numerology I, tape; Numerology II, tape and trombone; Ayres out of mouthes, tape; Inside PHI,
tape; Recipe for Braille letters, tape, saxophone, and dancer.
2436 Patria St., Winston-Salem, NC 27107

*WILLIAMS, JEAN E.
Has published 5 piano concertos and many choral
works.
315 Northeast 41st Ave., Portland, OR 97208

*WILLIAMS, JOHN T.
b. Flushing, N. Y., 8 Feb. 1932. Studied piano
with Rosina Lhevinne at Juilliard School; composition with Mario Castelnuovo-Tedesco in Los
Angeles. He received a television Emmy award,
1971-72, for the score for Jane Eyre on NBC's
Bell System Family Theatre. His works include
Sinfonia for wind ensemble; Elegy for strings,
1966; chamber music and jazz.
333 Loring Ave., Los Angeles, CA 90024

WILLIAMS, KENNETH S.
b. Cleveland, Ohio, 3 Dec. 1920. Studied with Arthur Shepherd and Melville Smith, Western Reserve Univ., B. A., M. A. He was instrumental instructor in public schools, 1950-63; assistant professor, Houston Baptist Coll., 1967-69.
WORKS: Band: Salute ASBDA; Bold frontier; Vilabella.
8706 Willcrest Drive, Houston, TX 77072

*WILLIAMS, MARY LOU
b. Pittsburgh, Pa., 8 May 1910. Was pianist in dance orchestras and arranger for Benny Goodman, Louis Armstrong, Duke Ellington, Cab Calloway, and others. She appeared in Town Hall, New York; with the New York Philharmonic, 1946; toured Europe, 1952-54.
WORKS: Orchestra: The zodiac suite; Chorus: Black priest of the Andes, cantata; Anima Christi: Praise the Lord.

WILLIAMS, PATRICK M.
Bonne Terre, Mo., 23 Apr. 1939. Studied at Duke Univ., B. A.; with Rudolph Thomas, Columbia Univ.; and privately with George Tremblay in Los Angeles. He has been arranger for Count Basie, Skitch Henderson, Steve Lawrence, Shari Lewis, Jerry Vale, and others; composes chiefly for motion pictures and television.
WORKS: Orchestra: The silent spring, adagio for cello and strings; Jazz: Double concerto for concert band and jazz ensemble; And on the 6th day, fanfare for jazz orchestra; Television: themes for What's my line and Tonight show.
532 17th St., Santa Monica, CA 90406

WILLIAMS, RONALD
b. Hollywood, Calif., 14 Dec. 1947. Studied with Anthony Gnazzo, David Tudor, Alden Jenks in Berkeley, Calif. He was lecturer, San Francisco Cons., 1973; research assistant, Univ. of California, Los Angeles, 1973.
WORKS: Piano, Passacaglia; Electronic: Auscultation; Grains of wave, tape piece for earphones.
2435 Loma Vista, Pasadena, CA 91104

*WILLIAMS, SPENCER
b. New Orleans, La., 14 Oct. 1889; d. Flushing, N. Y., 14 July 1965. Played piano in night clubs in New Orleans, then Chicago, and in New York, 1913-32; lived in Paris and London to 1957, when he returned to New York. He composed very popular blues songs: Arkansas blues, 1919; Basin street blues, 1923; Mahogany Hall stomp, 1924, etc.

WILLINK, GEORGE PETER JOHN
b. Voorburg, Netherlands, 10 July 1947; U.S. citizen 1963. Studied with Champ B. Tyrone, New Mexico Highlands Univ.; with William F. Wood, Univ. of New Mexico. He was public school music teacher, Fort Sumner, N. M., 1969-71.
WORKS: Band: El abrigo, 1973; Wind ensemble: concertino for double brass quartet, 1970; 4 pieces for woodwinds, 1972; Opinions, 8 brasses, timpani, percussion, 1972; Chamber music: Triumph, trumpet and piano, 1966; Introspection,

(WILLINK, GEORGE PETER JOHN)
trombone and piano, 1972; Chorus: Fugue in a, with 2 pianos 4-hands, 1966; Grooks, with woodwinds and piano, 1973.
1705 Silver Ave., S.E.
Albuquerque, NM 87106

WILLIS, RICHARD
b. Mobile, Ala., 21 Apr. 1929. Studied at Univ. of Alabama, B. M.; with Wayne Barlow, Bernard Rogers, and Howard Hanson, Eastman School of Music, M. M., Ph. D. His awards include Sigma Alpha Iota awards, 1953, 1962; Bearns prize, 1955; Prix de Rome fellowship, 1956; 1st and 2nd place, Willamette Univ. Festival competition; 1st place, Birmingham Festival of Arts; Howard Hanson prize, 1964; Pedro Paz award, 1965; Society for Publication of American Music award, 1968; commission, Provincetown Symphony; Southern Fellowships Fund grant; Volkwein-ASBDA award, 1973. He was head of theory, Shorter Coll., 1953-63; professor and composer-in-residence, Baylor Univ., 1964-   .
WORKS: Theatre: The playground, dance-drama, 1956; And winter's end, masque for dancers, chorus, pianos, percussion; The search for meaning; Orchestra: 2 symphonies, 1953, 1964; piano concertino; Suite from The playground, 1965; Prelude and dance, small orch., 1955; Recitative and dance, flute and strings; Evocation, 1967; Band: Essay for band; Canto; Aria and toccata, 1969; Epode; Partita; Chamber music: 2 string quartets; violin sonatina; Concert-piece, viola and piano; flute sonata; clarinet sonatina; Soliloquy, flute and piano; trumpet sonatina; violin sonata; Toccatina for organ; Passaggi, brass quintet, piano, percussion; Chorus: 5 Elizabethan songs, with instruments; The drenched land; Unto Thee, O Lord; Song of Praise; O give thanks; Give unto the Lord; Remember; There was darkness.
1010 Southwood, Waco, TX 76710

WILLMAN, ALLAN ARTHUR
b. Hinckley, Ill., 11 May 1909. Studied at Knox Coll., B. M.; at Chicago Musical Coll., M. M.; privately with Albert Noelte, Rudolph Ganz, in Chicago; with Nadia Boulanger and Thomas de Hartmann in Paris. He received the Paderewski prize, 1935; American Composers fellowship, 1946. He has been on the faculty, Univ. of Wyoming, 1936-   , professor and chairman, music department, 1941-   ; visiting lecturer, Univ. of California at Berkeley, 1946; made many concert tours of European as pianist, one for the U.S. State Department in 1953.
WORKS: Orchestra: Solitude, symphonic poem, 1930, Boston, 20 Apr. 1936; Idyll, 1930; Chamber music: A ballade of the night, string quartet and voice, 1936; piano sonata; many works for voice and for piano solo.
Department of Music, University of Wyoming
Laramie, WY 82071

WILLMAN, REGINA HANSEN
b. Burns, Wyoming, 5 Oct. 1914; d. Portland, Ore., 28 Oct. 1965. Studied at Univ. of Wyoming, B. M. 1945; at Univ. of New Mexico, M. M. 1961;

WILLMAN, REGINA HANSEN

(WILLMAN, REGINA HANSEN)
privately with Darius Milhaud at Mills Coll. and
in Paris; with Roy Harris at Colorado Coll.; also
attended Univ. of California at Berkeley,
Juilliard School, the Sorbonne in Paris, and the
Cons. of Lausanne in Switzerland. She was twice
a resident composer, Wurlitzer Found., Taos,
N. M., 1956-57, 1960-61.
     WORKS: Ballet: The legend of the willow
plate, chamber orch.; Steel mill, 2 pianos;
Theatre: music for Euripides' Medea; Orchestra:
Design for orchestra I; Design for orchestra II,
Anchorage (Alaska) Symphony, May 1971; Chamber
music: Vocalise for equal voices and low strings;
First holy sonnet, John Donne, voice and string
trio; The little tailor, suite for piano; choral
pieces and other instrumental pieces.

*WILLSON, MEREDITH
     b. Mason City, Iowa, 18 May 1902. Studied at
Inst. of Musical Art, 1919; privately with Henry
Hadley and Georges Barrere. His honors include
honorary D. M., Parsons Coll., and Coe Coll.;
Litt. D., Indiana Inst. of Technology; first
annual Texas award to outstanding figure in musical life, 1958; Distinguished Iowan award, 1958;
Antoinette Perry award, New York Drama Critics
Circle award, Outer Circle award, Thespian Theatre award, all for The music man, 1958; for which
he wrote the book, lyrics and music.
     WORKS: Theatre: You and I, book, lyrics,
music, 1941; May the good Lord bless you and keep
you, lyrics and music, 1950; The music man, 1958;
The unsinkable Molly Brown, lyrics and music,
1960; Here's love, 1963; Orchestra: 2 symphonies,
1936, 1940; O. O. McIntyre suite, 1936; The
Jervis Bay, symphonic poem, 1942; Variations on
an American theme; Chorus: Anthem for the atomic
age; Ask not, speaking and singing chorus, narrator, piano or band, text from the Kennedy
inaugural address. He is author of the books:
What every young musician should know; Who did
what to Fedalia, novel; And there I stood with
my piccolo, 1948; The eggs I have laid, 1955;
But he doesn't know the territory, 1959.

WILSON, DONALD M.
     b. Chicago, Ill., 30 June 1937. Studied with
Karel Husa and Robert Palmer, Cornell Univ.,
M. A. 1962, D. M. A. 1965; with Gunther Schuller
at Tanglewood, 1963, 1964. His awards include
2nd place, Bearns prize, 1963; A. M. Drummond
award, 1964; Ohio Music Teachers Asso. award,
1970; MacDowell fellowship, 1972. He was manager,
Cornell Univ. Orchestras, 1960-64; staff member,
WRVR-FM, New York, 1964-65; music director,
WUHY-FM, Philadelphia, 1965-66, program director,
1966-67; faculty, Bowling Green State Univ.,
1967-   , associate professor, 1972-   ,
chairman of composition, 1973-   .
     WORKS: Orchestra: Dedication, string orch.,
1960; Band: Visions, chorus and band, 1970;
Chamber music: clarinet quintet, 1960-62; 5
Haiku, tenor and chamber ensemble, 1962; Doubles,
game-piece for 2 woodwinds vs. 2 strings, 1964;
Multimedia: 17 views, violin, narrator, and
slides, 1967; Space-out, rock cantata, soprano,
jazz band, tape and visuals, 1971; Electronic

(WILSON, DONALD M.)
     wedding, tape, with or without dancers, 1972.
          School of Music
          Bowling Green State University
          Bowling Green, OH 43403

WILSON, GALEN
     b. Emporia, Kan., 18 Sep. 1926. Studied with
Ernst Krenek, Los Angeles Cons.; with Darius
Milhaud, Music Acad. of the West, Santa Barbara;
with Lukas Foss and John Vincent, Univ. of California, Los Angeles, M. A.; with Halsey Stevens,
Univ. of Southern California, D. M. A. He was
public school music teacher, 1956-67; assistant
professor, Fullerton State Coll., 1967-68;
associate professor, California State Univ.,
San Diego, 1969-   ; jazz pianist, 1960-69.
     WORKS: Band: Variations; Wind ensemble:
Sonate harmonique, brass choir; Chamber music:
piano sonata; string trio; Fantasy for piano;
sonatina for brass quintet; Chorus: Mass in
honor of St. James; 5 English motets; Electronic:
Applications, tape.
          1567 Elm Ave., El Centro, CA 92243

*WILSON, GEORGE BALCH
     b. Grand Island, Neb., 1927. Studied with Ross
Lee Finney, Univ. of Michigan; at the Royal Cons.
in Brussels; American Acad. in Rome; and with
Nadia Boulanger and Roger Sessions. His awards
include a Fulbright fellowship; the Prix de Rome;
and an award and citation from the Nat. Inst.-
American Acad. of Arts and Letters, 1970. He
is professor and director of the electronic music
studio, Univ. of Michigan; also founder and director of Contemporary Directions, a university
concert series devoted to new music.
     WORKS: Chamber music: string quartet;
Concatenations, chamber ensemble, 1969; Electronic: Exigencies, tape, 1968.
          Department of Music, University of Michigan
          Ann Arbor, MI 48104

*WILSON, HARRY ROBERT
     b. Salina, Kan., 18 May 1901. Studied at Man-
hattan State Coll., B. S.; Columbia Univ., M. A.,
Ed. D.; with Rubin Goldmark and Albert Stoessel,
Juilliard School on a fellowship. He was public
school music teacher, 1921-32; faculty member,
New Coll., Columbia Univ., 1932-37; professor,
Columbia Teachers Coll., 1937-   , chairman,
music department from 1958.
     WORKS: Chorus: Upon this rock, oratorio,
with soloists and orch.; Sing-a-rama; Banners of
peace; Let our great song arise; Look to this
day; O brother man; Peace must come like a troubadour; A thing of beauty; The finger of God.

WILSON, KAREN
     b. Cincinnati, Ohio, 9 Jan. 1942. Studied with
Dwight Gustafson and Frank Garlock, Bob Jones
Univ.; with Roger Hannay, Univ. of North Carolina, Chapel Hill, M. M. 1972. She has been on
the faculty, Bob Jones Univ., 1966-69,
1972-   ; was graduate assistant, Univ. of
North Carolina, 1970-72. Her compositions include a piano sonatina.
          Box 34605, Greenville, SC 29614

*WILSON, MORTIMER
b. Chariton, Iowa, 6 Aug. 1876; d. New York,
N. Y., 27 Jan. 1932. Studied with Frederick
Gleason and Wilhelm Middelschulte, Chicago Cons.;
with Max Reger in Leipzig. He taught at Univ.
of Nebraska, 1901-07; at Atlanta Cons. and conducted the Atlanta Symphony, 1911-15; at Breneau
Coll., 1916-18; then taught privately in New
York.
     WORKS: Orchestra: 5 symphonies; From my
youth, suite; New Orleans overture; Overture
1849; My country, scenic fantasy; concerto grosso
for strings; Chamber music: 2 piano trios; 3
violin sonatas; violin pieces.

*WILSON, OLLY
b. St. Louis, Mo., 1937. Studied at Washington
Univ., B. M. 1959; electronic music at Univ. of
Illinois, M. M. 1960; and at Univ. of Iowa,
Ph. D. 1964. He received the Dartmouth Arts
Council prize, 1968; and a $3000 award from the
American Acad. of Arts and Letters, 1974. He
played double bass in the St. Louis Symphony and
the Cedar Rapids Symphony; has taught at Florida
A & M Univ.; West Virginia Univ.; Indiana Univ.;
Oberlin Cons.; and has been associate professor,
Univ. of California, Berkeley, 1972-   .
     WORKS: Orchestra: 3 movements for orch.,
1964; Akwan, Baltimore Symphony, Oct. 1973; Chamber music: Piece for 4, flute, trumpet, piano,
double bass; Chorus: Spirit song, soprano,
women's choir, chorus, orch., Oakland Symphony,
12 Mar. 1974; Songs: Wry fragments, tenor and
percussion, 1961; And death shall have no dominion, tenor and percussion, 1963; Chanson innocent,
contralto and 2 bassoons, 1965; Electronic:
Cetus, tape, 1967; In memoriam - Martin Luther
King, Jr., chorus and tape, 1968; Piece for piano
and electronic sound, 1971.
     Department of Music, University of California
Berkeley, CA 94720

WILSON, PHIL
b. Waltham, Mass. 19 Jan. 1937. Studied trombone
with William Tesson, New England Cons. He received the Wells Kerr music award when director,
music department, Phillips Exeter Acad.; has been
instructor in arranging and composition and chairman, trombone department, Berklee Coll. of Music,
1965-   .
     WORKS: Concert jazz: The Earth's children;
The left and the right; Buttercrunch; and other
jazz works.
     8 Hammond Road, Belmont, MA 02118

WILSON, RICHARD
b. Cleveland, Ohio, 15 May 1941. Studied with
Robert Moevs and Randall Thompson, Harvard Univ.,
B. A. magna cum laude 1963; with Moevs at Rutgers
Univ., M. A. 1966. He received the G. A. Knight
prize, 1963; F. H. Beebe award, 1963; Naumberg
fellowship at Harvard Univ., 1964; Vassar faculty
fellowship under Ford Found. Program, 1970; annual
ASCAP awards, 1970-73. He was assistant professor, Vassar Coll., 1966-70, associate professor,
1970-   .
     WORKS: Orchestra: Fantasy and variations,
large chamber orch., 1965; Initiation, 1970;

(WILSON, RICHARD)
Chamber music: Suite for 5 players, 1963; trio,
oboe, violin, cello, 1964; Music for violin and
cello, 1964; Music for solo flute; Concert
piece, violin and piano, 1967; string quartet,
1968; quartet for flutes, harpsichord, string
bass, 1969; Chorus: A dissolve, women's voices,
1968; Light in the spring poplars, double chorus, 1968; Soaking; Home from the range, 8-part
chorus; Can, 8-part chorus.
     8 Vassar Lake Drive, Poughkeepsie, NY 12601

*WINDINGSTAD, OLE
b. Sandefjord, Norway, 18 May 1886; to U.S.
1913; d. Kingston, N. Y., 3 June 1959. On
coming to New York organized and conducted the
Scandinavian Symphony Orchestra, 1913-1929; conducted the Brooklyn Symphony and other orchestras.
His compositions included a symphony, 1913; The
tides for orch., 1939; and a cantata, The bard
of Norway, 1929.

*WINESANKER, MICHAEL MAX
b. Toronto, Ont., 7 Aug. 1913. Studied with
Healey Willan, Univ. of Toronto, B. M. 1933; at
Trinity Coll., London, Licentiate in music, 1940;
Univ. of Michigan, M. A. 1941; Cornell Univ.,
Ph. D. 1944. He taught at Univ. of Texas,
1945-46; Texas Christian Univ., 1946-   ,
chairman of music department, 1956-   . His
compositions include a piano sonata, string quartet, and songs.
     Department of Music
     Texas Christian University
     Fort Worth, TX 76129

*WINHAM, GODFREY
Taught composition at Princeton Univ. His works
include Composition for orchestra.

*WINKLER, DAVID
b. New York, N. Y., 1949. Received a BMI student
composer award, 1972, for a piano quartet and a
concerto for clarinet and 6 players. Other
works include: Chamber concerto, performed Manhattan School of Music, 23 Apr. 1973; double
concerto, performed by Speculum Musicae, New
York, 6 Dec. 1973.
     26 West 23rd St., New York, NY 10010

WINKLER, PETER K.
b. Los Angeles, Calif., 26 Jan. 1943. Studied
with Darius Milhaud, Aspen Music School; with
Seymour Shifrin and Douglas Leedy, Univ. of California, Berkeley, A. B. 1964; with Earl Kim and
Milton Babbitt, Princeton Univ., M. A. 1966. He
received a junior fellowship, Harvard Univ. Society of Fellows. He has been assistant professor, State Univ. of New York at Stony Brook,
1971-   .
     WORKS: Chamber music: Etude for 2 horns,
1964; string quartet, 1967; Humoresque, piano,
1970; Ragtime grackle, for oboe, 1972; Do it!,
for 2 jazz pianists, 1973; 7 piano rags; Chorus:
Praise of silence, soprano, chorus, instruments
and tape, 1969; various works for theatre and
radio dramas.
     15 Bayview Ave., East Setauket, NY 11733

WINSLOW, RICHARD KENELM

*WINSLOW, RICHARD KENELM
    b. Indianapolis, Ind., 15 Mar. 1918. Studied at
Wesleyan Univ., B. A. 1940; Juilliard School,
B. S. 1947, M. S. 1949. He served in the U.S.
Navy, 1942-45; joined the faculty, Wesleyan Univ.,
1949, has been professor, 1958-   , department
chairman, 1972-   .
    WORKS: Opera: Sweeney agonistes, 1952;
Adelaide, 1955; Ikon, 1960; Theater song, 1960;
Alice, 1965; Chorus: Job, oratorio, 1964; The
last quarter moon; Against pride in clothes,
women's voices; Huswifery, women's voices; Home
from the range; Light in spring poplars.
        Department of Music, Wesleyan University
        Middletown, CT 06457

WINSOR, PHILIP G.
    b. Morris, Ill., 10 May 1938. Studied with Will
Ogdon, Illinois Wesleyan Univ.; with Robert
Erickson in San Francisco; Luigi Nono in Venice,
Italy; Salvatore Martirano, Univ. of Illinois;
and with Wayne Peterson, San Francisco State
Univ. His awards include the Prix de Rome; Ful-
bright fellowship; Tanglewood fellowship; Mills
Coll., Center for Contemporary Music fellowship;
Pacifica Found. Radio Directors award; Oregon
Arts Festival award, 1971. He was director of
the electronic music studio, Moorhead State Coll.,
1967-68; head, theory and composition, DePaul
Univ., 1968-   .
    WORKS: Chamber music: Melted ears, 2 pianos,
1967; Asleep in the deep, for 5 tubas; Multimedia:
Actions, for tape, trombone, 4 dancers, 1 actor;
Missa brevis for tape, dancer, and visuals.
        1431 West Hutchinson, Chicago, IL 60613

*WINTER, PAUL
Festival fanfare for brass.

WIRTEL, THOMAS
    b. St. Louis, Mo., 26 May 1937. Studied with
Bain Murray and Richard Hoffmann, Oberlin Coll.;
with Samuel Adler, North Texas State Univ., B. M.,
M. M. 1963; with Bernhard Heiden, Indiana Univ.,
D. M. 1969. His awards include a Rockefeller
grant for composer residency with the Dallas Symphony Orchestra, 1966-67; MacDowell fellowship,
1966; Fromm Found. prize; Nat. Endowment for the
Arts jazz grant, 1973; East Texas State Univ.
research grant, 1974. He was teaching assistant
and director of jazz bands, North Texas State
Univ., 1961-63; teaching assistant and director
of Jazz Ensemble II, Indiana Univ., 1963-66;
assistant professor, East Texas State Univ.,
1967-73, associate professor, 1973-   ; visiting
professor, Univ. of Illinois, 1970-71.
    WORKS: Orchestra: Concertino for orch.,
1967; Polarities, 1967; Chamber music: violin
sonata; Dualities, violin, piano, and electronic
sounds; Film scores: Patterns in jazz, USIA documentary of which he was the subject as well as
composer of the score.
        Music Department, East Texas State University
        Commerce, TX 75428

*WIRTH, CARL ANTON
    b. Rochester, N. Y., 24 Jan. 1912. Studied at
Eastman School of Music, B. M., M. M. He was

(WIRTH, CARL ANTON)
founder and director, Rochester Community Music
Program; conductor, Rochester Community Symphony;
founder and conductor, Rochester Chamber Opera;
in 1962 conducted Radio Republik Indonesia Symphony under sponsorship of U.S. State Department;
was founder, Composer Project, 1951, chairman
to 1959; served on executive board, American
Symphony Orch. League, 1955-57.
    WORKS: Orchestra: Ichabod Crane suite;
Idlewood concerto, alto saxophone and orch.;
Elegy on an Appalachian folksong; Jephthah, soprano, alto saxophone, string orch.; Chamber
music: Dark flows the river, alto saxophone and
piano; Portals: a prelude for organ.

WISE, BRUCE
    b. Detroit, Mich., 24 Aug. 1929. Studied with
Ross Lee Finney, Univ. of Michigan; with Wolfgang
Fortner, Freiburg, Germany, 1959-60, on a grant
from the German Government. He has held faculty
positions at Univ. of Michigan, 1961-62; Univ.
of Missouri, 1962-67; professor, Univ. of
Wisconsin-Oshkosh, 1967-   .
    WORKS: Orchestra: Patterns for orchestra,
1961; Variations, 1973; Chamber music: 4
pieces for piano, 1957; 2 pieces for piano and
chamber group, 1958; Songs of autumn, 1958;
Music for 3, 1963; duo for viola and piano, 1971;
string trio no. 2, 1972.
        Department of Music, University of Wisconsin
        Oshkosh, WI 54901

WISHART, BETTY ROSE
    b. Lumberton, N. C., 22 Sep. 1947. Studied with
Richard Bunger, Queens Coll., Charlotte, N. C.;
with Roger Hannay, Univ. of North Carolina,
Chapel Hill. She held a scholarship at Queens
Coll., 1966-69. She was graduate assistant,
Univ. of North Carolina, 1970-72; teacher of
piano, theory and composition, Kohinoor Music
Company, 1972-73; on staff, Argo Classical Records, 1973-   .
    WORKS: Chamber music: Experience, string
quintet; Memories of things unseen, chamber quartet; Shanti, voice and piano; Piano: Illusion
suite; Kohinoor sonata; Apprehensions;
Leukoplakia; Organ: Sounds.
        P. O. Box 236, Lenox Hill Station
        New York, NY 10021

*WITKIN, BEATRICE
Studied composition with Mark Brunswick, Roger
Sessions, and Stefan Wolpe; piano with Edward
Steuerman. Her awards include first prize in
High Fidelity magazine's electronic music con-
test for Glissines, 1970; ASCAP awards; Marth
Baird Rockefeller Found. commission; grants from
Rockefeller Found., Ford Found., and Nat. Endow-
ment on the Arts.
    WORKS: Chamber music: Interludes for flute,
1960; Duo for violin and piano, 1960-61, New
York, 18 Dec. 1962; Prose poem, on the story of
Adam and Eve by James T. Farrell, for soprano,
narrator, cello, horn, percussion, 1963-64; Con-
tour for piano, 1964; Parameters for 8 instruments, 1964; Chiaroscuro, cello and piano, 1968;
Triads and things, brass quintet, 1968; Breath

(WITKIN, BEATRICE)
and sounds, tuba and tape, 1970-71; Echology,
flute and tape, New York, 11 Feb. 1973.
885 West End Ave., New York, NY 10025

WOLF, KENNETH (Merrill K. Wolf, MD)
b. Cleveland, Ohio, 28 Aug. 1931. Studied with
Arthur Shepherd in Cleveland, 1941-43; with Paul
Hindemith, Yale Univ., 1944-45; piano with Bruce
Simonds, Artur Schnabel, and Rosina Lhevinne.
He is professor of neuroanatomy, Univ. of Massachusetts, Medical School, Worcester.
WORKS: Orchestra: 2 piano concertos; Chamber music: 2 sonatas for harpsichord or piano;
violin sonata; horn sonata; Concert variations,
woodwind quintet; 7 bagatelles, clarinet and
piano; Chorus: 3 ways of looking at a frog, a
cappella; Belloc's beasts, a cappella; Pieces for
Friday evening Jewish worship. Dr. Wolf describes
his neo-classical style of composition with a
quote from the New York Times: "Imagine Puolenc
mixed with Hindemith and some conscious 18th century archaisms."
84 Leeson Lane, Newton, MA 02159

*WOLFE, JACQUES
b. Botoshan, Rumania, 29 Apr. 1896; to U.S. 1898.
Studied with Percy Goetschius and James Friskin,
Juilliard School, graduated 1915. During World
War I he was clarinetist in an Army band; then
went to North Carolina to study Negro spirituals.
He was concert pianist and accompanist in New
York and taught in the public schools to 1947,
then settled in Miami as a photographer.
WORKS: Opera: John Henry, on Roark Brad-
ford's play, 1939; Mississippi legend; The tryst-
ing tree; Chamber music: Marine holiday, piano;
Prayer in the swamp, violin and piano; Serenade,
string quartet; Chorus: Psalm 67, with orch.;
Songs: De glory road; Gwine to hebb'n; Halleluja
rhythm; Shortnin' bread; The handorgan man;
Sailormen; and others.

*WOLFE, STANLEY
b. Brooklyn, N. Y., 7 Feb. 1924. Studied with
William Bergsma, Vincent Persichetti, Peter
Mennin, at Juilliard School, B. S. 1952, M. S.
1955. He received a Guggenheim fellowship, 1957;
Ditson award, 1961. He joined the faculty at
Juilliard School in 1955, became director of the
extension division in 1963; adjunct professor,
Lincoln Center campus of Fordham Univ.,
1969-   .
WORKS: Ballet: King's heart, 1956; Orchestra: 5 symphonies, 1954, 1955, 1959, 1965, 1970;
Lincoln Square overture, 1957; Canticle for
strings, 1957; Variations for orchestra, 1967;
Chamber music: Adagio, woodwind quintet, 1948;
3 profiles, piano; string quartet, 1961.
875 West End Avenue, New York, NY 10025

WOLFF, CHRISTIAN
b. Nice, France, 8 Mar. 1934; U.S. citizen 1947.
Studied piano in New York; composition informally
with John Cage, but is chiefly autodidact; classical languages, Harvard Univ., Ph. D. 1963. He
held a Ford Found. fellowship in the Mills Coll.
project, 1973. He was instructor and assistant

(WOLFF, CHRISTIAN)
professor, classics department, Harvard Univ.,
1962-70; associate professor, classics and music,
Dartmouth Coll., 1971-   ; lecturer Darmstadt,
August 1972.
WORKS: Orchestra: Burdocks, 1 or more orchestras, any instruments, 1971; Chamber music:
trio for flute, cello, trumpet, 1951; 9 for 9
instruments, 1951; For prepared piano, 1951; For
piano I, 1952; For pianist, 1959; duet II, piano
and horn, 1961; duo for violin and piano, 1961;
Summer, string quartet, 1961; For 5 or 10 players,
1962; In between pieces, any 3 performers, 1963;
septet, 1964; For 1, 2, or 3 people, any sound
sources, 1964; Electric spring, 2 recorders, electric guitar, bass guitar, trombone, 1965; Prose
collection, 10 short pieces, 1968-70; Snowdrop;
1970; Lines, string quartet, 1971; Accompaniments,
piano solo, 1972; Changing the system, chamber
ensemble, 1973.
104 South Main St., Hanover, NH 03755

*WOLFF, WERNER
b. Berlin, Germany, 2 Oct. 1883; to U.S. 1938;
d. Rüschlikon, Switz., 23 Nov. 1961. Was an
opera conductor in Germany; chairman, music
department, Tennessee Wesleyan Coll., 1938-43;
director and conductor, Chattanooga Opera Asso.,
1943-59; music critic, Chattanooga Daily Times,
1950-59. He composed symphonic works, chamber
music, songs, and piano pieces.

*WOLFORD, DARWIN
9 psalms for organ.
Department of Music, Ricks College
Rexburg, ID 83440

WOLKING, HENRY CLIFFORD, JR.
b. Orlando, Fla., 20 May 1948. Studied at
Berklee Coll. of Music; with Richard Bowles,
Univ. of Florida, B. M. E. 1970; with Martin
Mailman and William Latham, North Texas State
Univ., M. M. He received scholarships at Berklee
Coll. and Univ. of Florida; Phi Beta Kappa Creative Achievement award, 1970; 2nd place award,
Internat. Trombone Composition contest, 1973.
He was trombone soloist, Univ. of Florida symphonic and stage bands, 1968-70; trombonist with
numerous rock, soul, and jazz ensembles; assistant professor, Univ. of Utah, 1972-   .
WORKS: Band: 2 movements for large wind
ensemble; concerto for trombone and band; Time-
pieces; Chamber music: woodwind quintet; 3 movements for 3 trombones; Pictures from the gone
world, song cycle for soprano and piano;
Trahmbone, theatre piece for 2 sopranos, 2 altos,
4 trombones; Fantasy for string orch.; Slideworks
for 10; and numerous jazz compositions.
1349 Vine St., Salt Lake City, UT 84112

*WOLLNER, GERTRUDE PRICE
Studied at Hunter Coll. and New York Univ. She
has composed for chamber orchestra, quartet,
piano, dance, and theatre. Her music for Caesar
and Cleopatra was performed by the Civic Theatre
in Washington, D.C. She is author of Improvisation in music, Boston.
26 Clifton St., Belmont, MA 02178

WOLPE, STEFAN

*WOLPE, STEFAN
    b. Berlin, Germany, 25 Aug. 1902; U.S. citizen
    1944; d. New York, N. Y., 4 Apr. 1972. Studied
    at the Berlin Hochschule fur Musik, 1919-24;
    privately with Ferruccio Busoni, Anton Webern,
    and Herman Scherchen. His many awards included
    the Brandeis Univ. Creative Arts award; Nat.
    Inst. of Arts and Letters award, 1949; Rothschild
    Found. award, 1953; Fulbright fellowship, 1956;
    League of Composers-ISCM award, 1958; Fromm
    Found. award, 1960; Guggenheim fellowship, 1962;
    New York Music Critics Circle citation, 1963;
    member, Nat. Inst. of Arts and Letters;
    Koussevitzky Internat. Recording award, 1970.
    He taught at the Palestine Cons., 1934-38;
    Settlement Music School, Philadelphia, 1939-42;
    was music director and professor, Contemporary
    Music School, New York, 1948-52; Philadelphia
    Acad. of Music, 1949-52; Black Mountain Coll.,
    1952-56; Chatham Square Music School, New York,
    1957-63; C. W. Post Coll., Long Island Univ.,
    1957-70.
        WORKS: Opera: Schöne Geschichten, 1927;
    Zeus and Elida, 1927; Ballet: The man from
    Midian, 1942; Theatre: Strange stories, theatre
    piece, 1929; Orchestra: 5 symphonies; Piece for
    piano and 16 instruments, 1960; Chamber music:
    March and variations, 2 pianos, 1931; 10 songs
    from the Hebrew, 1938; oboe sonata, 1938; violin
    sonata, 1949; quartet for trumpet saxophone, per-
    cussion, piano, 1950; Enactments, 3 pianos,
    1950-53; percussion quartet; quintet with voice,
    baritone, horn, cello, harp, clarinet, piano,
    1958; Piece in 2 parts, flute and piano, 1960;
    Piece for 2 instrumental units, 1962; Piece in
    2 parts for violin alone, 1963; Chamber piece #1,
    14 instruments, 1964-65; Cantatas: The passion
    of man, 1929; On the education of man, 1930;
    About sport, 1931; Israel and his land, 1939;
    Unnamed lands, 1940.

*WOLTMANN, FREDERICK
    b. Flushing, N. Y., 13 May 1908. Studied at
    Brooklyn Polytechnic Inst. and Columbia Univ.;
    with Howard Hanson and Bernard Rogers, Eastman
    School of Music; with Ildebrando Pizzetti, Ameri-
    can Acad. in Rome, 1937.
        WORKS: Orchestra: Dance of the torch bear-
    ers, 1932; Poem, flute and orch., 1935; Rhapsody,
    horn and orch., 1935; Legend, cello and orch.,
    1936; Songs from a Chinese lute, voice and 33
    instruments, 1936; Songs for autumn, soprano,
    baritone, and orch., 1937; piano concerto, 1937;
    The pool of Pegasus, 1937; Scherzo for 8 winds,
    1937; From Dover Beach, 1938; The Coliseum at
    night, 1939; Solitude, 1942; From Leaves of
    grass, 1946; and songs.

WONG, BETTY ANNE (Siu Junn)
    b. San Francisco, 6 Sep. 1938. Studied with
    Morton Subotnick, Nathan Rubin, Colin Hampton,
    Mills Coll., B. A. 1960; with Pauline Oliveros,
    Robert Erickson, Kenneth Gaburo, Univ. of Cali-
    fornia, San Diego, M. M. 1971; Chinese music
    with David Liang, Lawrence Lui, and Leo Lew,
    1971-74. She held a teaching fellowship, a re-
    gents fellowship, and California State Scholar-
    ships, 1968-71. She has been a piano teacher,

(WONG, BETTY ANNE)
    1961-   ; consultant and composer, Performing
    Arts Workshop, San Francisco, 1966-68; co-manager
    and performer, Flowing Stream Ensemble, a multi-
    cultural, multi-racial performing group whose
    repertoire spans more than 25 centuries,
    1971-   ; consultant, Mission Childcare, San
    Francisco Unified Schools, 1972-73; instructor,
    and coordinator, Community Chinese Music Work-
    shops, a joint project with San Francisco Cons.
    under a Rockefeller grant, 1973-   .
        WORKS: Electronic: Submerged still cap-
    able, tape, 1969; Check one - People control the
    environment, People are controlled by the envi-
    ronment, tape, 1970; Quiet places in the environ-
    ment, tape, 9 performers and audience, 1971;
    Private audience with Pope Pius XII, tape and
    slides, 1971; Furniture music or 2-way stretch
    on a swivel chair, tape and visuals, 1971; and
    film scores.
        957 Filbert St., San Francisco, CA 94133

WONG, HSIUNG-ZEE
    b. Hong Kong, 24 Oct. 1947; to U.S. 1966.
    Studied at Univ. of Hawaii, 1966-68, courses
    with Ernst Krenek and Chou Wen-chung; California
    Coll. of Arts and Crafts, B. F. A. in industrial
    design 1972; electronic music with Robert
    Ashley and Leonard Klein, 1970; composition with
    Robert Sheff and Dane Rudhyar, Mills Coll., 1973.
    She received California Coll. of Arts and Crafts
    alumni scholarships, 1970-72. She has been a
    free-lance graphic designer, artist and illustra-
    tor, 1967-   ; initiated Hysteresis, a women's
    creative arts group at Mills Coll., 1973; per-
    forms with the Flowing Stream Ensemble.
        WORKS: Chamber music: Art songs/ballads,
    voice and guitar, 1964-72, parts performed,
    KPFK, Los Angeles, 6 Dec. 1973; The cry of wo-
    men in the wilderness, for piano, Chinese gong
    and amplified Zen bell, 1972; Piano ritual I,
    for piano-percussion, Chinese woodblock, opera
    gong, and voice, Oakland, Calif., 1 July 1973;
    Electronic: Maturity, taped piano improvisation,
    1972; Earth rituals, tape with chanting and
    sound improvisation, 1973; The sounding of the
    sane, tape with audience chanting, Oakland, 1
    July 1973; They move, don't they?, a sound cal-
    ligraphic score with visual slides, 1973.
        4021 Howe St., Apt. 6, Oakland, CA 94611

WOOD, DALE
    b. Glendale, Calif., 13 Feb. 1934. Studied at
    Occidental Coll.; composition at Los Angeles and
    Los Angeles City Coll. He won his first award
    at age 13 in a national hymn-writing contest;
    won a scholarship to Occidental Coll.; received
    annual ASCAP awards, 1968-73. He has held posts
    as church organist-choirmaster 1950-   ; at
    Episcopal Church of St. Mary the Virgin, San
    Francisco, 1968-   ; director of music, Cathe-
    dral School for Boys, San Francisco, 1973-   ;
    is contributing editor, Journal of Church Music;
    writes a monthly column for Music Ministry.
        WORKS: Chorus: A service of darkness; Come,
    gracious spirit; Let the whole creation cry;

(WOOD, DALE)

Christ is made the sure foundation; Jubilate deo;
The lamb; Sing for joy; and many other published
choral works.
22 Oak Road, Fairfax, CA 94930

WOOD, JOSEPH
b. Pittsburgh, Pa., 12 May 1915. Studied piano,
Inst. of Musical Art, New York, diploma, 1936;
with Bernard Wagenaar, Juilliard School, B. S.
1949; with Otto Luening, Columbia Univ., M. A.
1950. His awards include a Juilliard fellowship,
1936-40; first prize, Juilliard opera competition,
1942; Alice Ditson award, Columbia Univ., 1946;
Villa Montalvo residence, 1957; Huntington Hartford fellowship, 1960; 7 MacDowell fellowships;
H. H. Powers travel grants, Oberlin Coll., 1966,
1973; and many commissions. He was staff composer, Chekhov Theatre Studio, 1939-41; composer-
arranger, New York, 1941-50; U.S. Army, 1943-46;
faculty, Oberlin Coll. Cons., 1950-
    WORKS: Opera: The mother, 1942; Ballet-
oratorio: The progression; Orchestra: 3 symphonies, 1939, 1952, 1958; Poem for orchestra,
1950; concerto for viola and piano with orch.;
violin concerto; Chamber music: piano trio,
1937; viola sonata, 1938; string quartet, 1942;
violin sonata, 1947; piano quintet, 1956; choral
works, incidental music, etc.
    261 West Lorain St., Oberlin, OH 44074

*WOOD, RUSSELL
The emperor's new clothes, 1-act children's opera,
Chicago, 12 Feb. 1972.

WOOD, WILLIAM FRANK
b. San Francisco, Calif., 3 Aug. 1935. Studied
with James Adair, Sacramento State Coll.; with
Normand Lockwood, Univ. of Oregon; with Wolfgang
Fortner at Tanglewood; with Bernard Rogers, Wayne
Barlow, and Howard Hanson, Eastman School of
Music, Ph. D. He won first prize, Prague Spring
Internat. Composers Competition, 1966; has received commissions. He is associate professor,
Univ. of New Mexico.
    WORKS: Orchestra: symphony, 1966; Chamber
music: Night music, solo guitar and chamber
orch., 1968; 5 bagatelles for solo guitar; cello
sonata; violin sonata, 1973; other chamber works.
    Department of Music, University of New Mexico
    Albuquerque, NM 87106

WOODARD, JAMES P.
b. Rocky Mount, N. C., 21 Nov. 1929. Studied at
Univ. of North Carolina; Juilliard School;
Hochschule fur Musik, Munich; with Carlisle Floyd
and John Boda, Florida State Univ., D. M. He received the Olivet Pedro Paz prize, 1970, for a
partita. He was professor, Murray State Univ.,
1965-70; professor, Southern Illinois Univ.,
Edwardsville, 1970-   .
    WORKS: Orchestra: concerto for 2 pianos,
1965; Chamber music: duo for violin and cello,
1964; 5 sonnets of Shakespeare, baritone and
piano, 1967; Fantasies, flute and string quartet,
1972; piano sonatina, 1973.
    818 Randle St., Edwardsville, IL 62025

WOODBURY, ARTHUR
b. Kimball, Neb., 20 June 1930. Studied at Univ.
of Idaho, B. A. 1951, M. M. 1955; and at Univ.
of California at Davis, 1957-58. He attended
Univ. of Idaho on scholarship. He was lecturer,
Univ. of California, Davis, 1963-72; professor,
Univ. of South Florida, 1972-
    WORKS: Orchestra: symphony, 1958; Auto-
biography; Band: Introduction and allegro;
Chamber music: woodwind quartet, 1955; Remem-
brances, violin, saxophone, percussion, 1968;
Electronic: Patricia Belle, soprano, electronic
instruments, amplified chamber ensemble, 1968;
Recall, theatre piece, 1969; An evening of the
music of Neil Jansen, a put-on, for tape and
Moog synthesizer, 1969; Velox, computerized tape;
Hum, Moog synthesizer and tape; Werner
Vonbrawnasaurus Rex, for tape, synthesizers, and
instruments, 1970.
    13018 Leeds Court, Tampa, FL 33620

*WOOD-HILL, MABEL
b. Brooklyn, N. Y., 12 Mar. 1870; d. Stamford,
Conn., 1 Mar. 1954. Studied at Smith Coll. and
with Cornelius Rybner, Columbia Univ. She received awards from the Associated Glee Clubs of
the U.S. and Canada; Nat. League of American
Pen Women; a citation from the City of New York,
1953; Canadian Government commission for a vocal
work, The jolly beggars, for the Banff Festival
of 1928. She was founder of the Brooklyn and
New York Music School Settlements.
    WORKS: Ballet: The adventures of Pinocchio,
1931; Orchestra: The wind in the willows;
Courage; Fables of Aesop; Outdoor suite; From a
far country; chamber music; choral works; and
songs.

WOODWARD, HENRY LYNDE
b. Cincinnati, Ohio, 18 Sep. 1908. Studied at
Cincinnati Coll. of Music; with Walter Piston at
Harvard Univ., Ph. D.; with Nadia Boulanger in
Paris. He received a MacDowell fellowship, 1932.
He has held faculty posts at Cincinnati Coll. of
Music, 1929-33; Western Coll., 1933-38; 1939-42;
Vassar Coll., 1938-39; Carleton Coll., 1942-73,
professor emeritus, 1973-   ; summers at Cornell
Univ. and Union Theological Seminary, New York.
    WORKS: Orchestra: symphony; Chamber music:
3 violin sonatas; Suite for viola and piano;
Chorus: O clap your hands; Organ: Toccatina;
Easter alleluia; On 'Heinlein'.
    209 West University Drive
    Chapel Hill, NC 27514

WOOLF, GREGORY BUXTON
b. Seattle, Wash., 2 Jan. 1935; d. Nashville,
Tenn., 13 Jan. 1971. Studied at Tufts Univ.,
B. A.; Eastman School of Music, M. A., Ph. D. He
held faculty posts at Brockport State Coll., New
York, 1960-63; Tufts Univ., 1963-68; George
Peabody Coll., 1968-71.
    WORKS: Orchestra: tuba concerto; Chamber
music: clarinet sonata; string quartet; Chorus:
A time's passing, a cappella; A mass for All
Saints' Day, for quadruple chorus, organ, and
tape; also a musical play for children.

WOOLLEN, RUSSELL

*WOOLLEN, RUSSELL
b. Hartford, Conn., 7 Jan. 1923. Studied at
Pope Pius X School of Liturgical Music, New York;
with Nadia Boulanger and Nicolas Nabokov in Paris;
1949-51; and with Walter Piston at Harvard Univ.,
1953-55. After ordination as priest he taught
at Catholic Univ., later becoming professor at
Howard Univ. School of Music, and pianist with the
National Symphony Orchestra.
WORKS: Orchestra: symphony, 1957-58; Summer
jubilee overture, 1958; Chamber music: harpsichord suite; flute quartet; piano trio; Voice:
suite for high voice on poems of Gerard Manley
Hopkins; In martyrum memoriam, chorus and orch.,
Washington Oratorio Society, 17 May 1975.
School of Music, Howard University
Washington, DC 20001

*WOOLSEY, MARY HALE
b. Spanish Fork, Utah, 21 Mar. 1899; d. 1969.
Studied at Brigham Young Univ.; Univ. of Utah;
and at Columbia Univ. She held several editorial
positions and was author of a book, The keys and
the candle.
WORKS: Operettas: Starflower; The giant
garden; The happy hearts; The enchanted attic;
Neighbors in the house; many songs including
When it's springtime in the Rockies.

*WORK, JOHN WESLEY JR.
b. Tullahoma, Tenn., 15 June 1901; d. 1968.
Studied at Fisk Univ., B. A.; Columbia Univ.,
M. A.; Yale Univ., B. M.; and at Juilliard School
on a 2-year Rosenwald fellowship. He received
first prize, Fellowship of American Composers
contest for a cantata; many commissions. He
joined the faculty at Fisk Univ. in 1933; became
professor in 1943, later was chairman, music department; was conductor, Fisk Jubilee Singers,
1948-57.
WORKS: Orchestra: Picture suite of the
South; Yenvalou, suite for strings, 1955;
Taliafero; Night in the valley; Chamber music:
Nocturne, violin and piano; Piano: sonata;
Appalachian suite; Scuppernong suite; Concert
piece, 2 pianos; Variations on a theme; Finale,
Chorus: The singers, cantata, 1946; Issac Watts
contemplates the cross, choral cycle; many other
choral works and songs.

*WORK, JULIAN C.
b. Nashville, Tenn., 25 Sep. 1910. Attended Fisk
Univ. and studied music privately. He was
arranger for vaudeville; staff arranger for CBS
radio and later television.
WORKS: Band: Autumn walk; Stand the storm;
Driftwood patterns; Processional hymn; Portraits
from the Bible (Moses, Ruth, Shadrach, Meschach,
Abednego).

WORST, JOHN
b. Grand Rapids, Mich., 13 July 1940. Studied
with Marshall Barnes, Ohio State Univ., M. A.
1964; with H. Owen Reed, Michigan Univ.; and with
Leslie Bassett, Univ. of Michigan. He won an
award, Internat. Delius competition, 1971; commission, Michigan Music Teachers Asso., 1973. He
was assistant professor Calvin Coll., 1964-69,
1972-   .

(WORST, JOHN)
WORKS: Band: Song and march; Chamber music:
3 biblical chants, alto solo and chamber ensemble; Chorus: Spirit songs, with brass quintet
and 3 flutes; Jonah songs, with string quartet.
7181 McCords, Alto, MI 49302

*WORTH, AMY
b. St. Joseph, Mo., 18 Jan. 1888; d. 1967.
Studied music with Jessie Gaynor. She was piano
teacher, organist, and choir director. Her published choral works included Mary, the mother,
Christmas cantata; Christ rises; Sing of Christmas; He came all so still; many songs and piano
pieces.

*WRIGHT, KENNETH W.
b. Hastings, Neb., 1913. Studied at Hastings
Coll., A. B.; Eastman School of Music, M. A.
1939, Ph. D. 1941; also with Roy Harris; violin
with Michel Piastro. He joined the faculty at
Univ. of Kentucky in 1949.
WORKS: Opera: Call it square, chamber
opera; Orchestra: concerto for 2 violins; overture; Poem, oboe and string orch.; violin concerto; Dance mosaics.
Department of Music, University of Kentucky
Lexington, KY 40506

*WRIGHT, M. SEARLE
The green blade riseth, chorus.
Christ Church, 318 East 4th St.
Cincinnati, OH 45202

WRIGHT, MAURICE
b. Front Royal, Va., 17 Oct. 1949. Studied with
Paul Earls and Iain Hamilton, Duke Univ., B. A.
magna cum laude, 1972; with Charles Dodge,
Charles Wuorinen, Vladimir Ussachevsky, Mario
Davidovsky, Jacques Monod, Jack Beeson, Columbia
Univ., M. A. 1973. He received the Henry
Schumann prize, Duke Univ.; Delius Festival
award; Nat. Fed. of Music Clubs award; President's
fellowship at Columbia Univ.; 2 fellowships to
Bennington Conference. He was teaching assistant,
Columbia Univ., 1973-74.
WORKS: Orchestra: Progressions; Band:
Fantasy; Chamber music: Sonata exotica, trombone
and piano; organ sonata; Variations for piano;
Trichotomy, clarinet, cello, piano; 3 pieces;
trumpet, flute, viola; chamber symphony; Aulos,
oboe and chamber ensemble; Chorus: The swans,
with violin, cello, harpsichord; The winter wind,
with piccolo, tuba, piano; Mixed media: Dialogues: Music and... (with Paul Earls), New
York, 24 Feb. 1974; also pieces for carillon
and electronic compositions.
160 West 71st St., #4B, New York, NY 10023

WRIGHT, RAYBURN
b. Alma, Mich., 27 Aug. 1922. Studied with
Burrill Phillips and Bernard Rogers, Eastman
School of Music; at Juilliard School; with Henry
Brant and Otto Luening, Columbia Univ., Teachers
Coll. He received the Nat. Acad. of Television
Arts and Sciences Emmy nomination for his score
to the film, Saga 1492. He was staff arranger-
composer, Radio City Music Hall, 1950-59;

(WRIGHT, RAYBURN)
free-lance television-film composer, 1963-66; professor of jazz studies and contemporary media, Eastman School of Music, 1970-   .
WORKS: Orchestra: Regeneration, concerto for jazz quartet, rock ensemble, and orch.; Textures, percussion trio and orch.; Wind ensemble: Interfaces I, trombone choir and percussion ensemble; Film scores: Saga 1492; The world's girls; Soviet woman; Custer to the Little Big Horn; Cortez and the legend; Mrs. L. B. Johnson's visit to Washington, D.C.; The Blue and the Red Danube; The birth of Christ; Kitty Hawk to Paris: The heroic years.
Eastman School of Music
26 Gibbs St., Rochester, NY 14604

WUNSCH, ILSE GERDA
b. Berlin, Germany, 14 Dec. 1911. Studied piano in Berlin; piano with Rudolph Ganz, composition with Max Wald, Chicago Musical Coll., M. M. Her faculty posts include New York Coll. of Music, 1948-68; Stern Coll. for Women, Yeshiva Univ., 1960-64; associate professor of music education, New York Univ., 1968-   ; also organist and choir director, Temple Beth El, Cedarhurst, 1949-68.
WORKS: Voice: Young faith, a Sabbath evening and morning service in 2 books, 1956; Piano: 12 progressing tone plays, 33rd Annual American Music Festival, New York, 19 Feb. 1972.
67 West 68th St., New York, NY 10023

*WUORINEN, CHARLES
b. New York, N. Y., 9 June 1938. Studied with Otto Luening, Columbia Univ. His many awards include the New York Philharmonic young composers award, 1954; Lili Boulanger award, 1960; Bearns prize; Brandeis Creative Arts award; honorary doctorate, Jersey City State Coll.; American Acad. of Arts and Letters award; Koussevitzky Internat. recording award, 1970; Pulitzer prize, 1970; Guggenheim fellowship, 1972; commissions. He was on the faculty at Columbia Univ., 1946-71; has also taught at Princeton Univ.; New England Cons.; Univ. of Iowa; Manhattan School of Music; and Univ. of South Florida.
WORKS: Orchestra: 3 symphonies; piano concerto, 1966; Politics of harmony, 1971; concerto for amplified violin and orch., 1972, Tanglewood, 1973; Chamber music: chamber concerto, cello and 10 players, 1963; chamber concerto, flute and 10 players, 1964; Janissary music, percussion, 1966; duo, violin and harpsichord, 1967; Ringing changes, percussion ensemble, 1970; The long and the short, violin solo; string trio; string quartet; Variations for unaccompanied cello, 1970; Flute variations II, 1971; Variations for harp and string trio, 1973; movement for woodwind quintet, New York, 3 May 1973; On alligators, 8 players, New York premiere, 6 May 1973; Prelude and fugue for percussion; Grand Union, cello and 4 drums, Chicago, 5 Nov. 1973; Arabia felix, chamber ensemble, New York, 23 Feb. 1974; Fantasia, violin and piano, Baltimore, 6 Apr. 1975; Voice: Prayer of Jonah, chorus and strings, 1962; 1851: A message to Denmark Hill, baritone, flute, cello, piano, 1970; A song to the lute in

(WUORINEN, CHARLES)
musicke, voice and piano, 1970; Keyboard: Making ends meet, piano 4-hands; piano sonata, 1969; Into the organ pipes and steeples, organ; Harpsichord divisions; Electronic: Orchestral and electronic exchanges, 1965; Time's enconium, 1969, received Pulitzer prize.
680 West End Ave., New York, NY 10025

WYETH, ANN (Mrs. John W. McCoy, II)
b. Chadds Ford, Pa., 15 Mar. 1915. Studied piano and composition with Harl McDonald.
WORKS: Orchestra: Christmas fantasy, performed by Philadelphia Orchestra under Stokowski; other orchestral works, piano pieces, songs.
Chadds Ford, PA 19317

WYKES, ROBERT A.
b. Aliquippa, Pa., 19 May 1926. Studied with Cecil Effinger, Colorado Coll.; at Eastman School of Music, M. M. 1950; with Burrill Phillips, Univ. of Illinois, D. M. A. 1955. He received the Paderewski Prize commission for his piano quintet, 1959. He was flutist, Toldeo Symphony, 1950-52; St. Louis Symphony, 1963-65; faculty member, Bowling Green State Univ., 1950-52; Univ. of Illinois, 1952-55; professor, Washington Univ., 1955-   .
WORKS: Opera: The prankster, chamber opera; Orchestra: Density III, 1961; Horizons, 1964; Wave forms and pulses, 1964; The shape of time, 1965; Toward time's receding, New York premiere, 21 Jan. 1974; Chamber music: flute sonata, 1955; concerto for 11 instruments, 1956; 4 studies for piano, 1958; piano quintet, 1959; concertino for flute, oboe, piano and strings; Chorus: 4 American Indian lyrics, 1957.
Department of Music, Washington University
St. Louis, MO 63130

WYLIE, RUTH SHAW
b. Cincinnati, Ohio, 24 June 1916. Studied at Wayne State Univ., A. B. 1937, M. A. 1939; with Bernard Rogers, Eastman School of Music, Ph. D. 1943; with Arthur Honegger, Samuel Barber, Aaron Copland at Tanglewood, 1947. She held a doctoral fellowship at Eastman School; received Mu Phi Epsilon awards several times; Univ. of Missouri Creative Research awards; Wayne State Univ. awards; Huntington Hartford fellowship, 1952-53; MacDowell fellowships, 1954, 1956. She was faculty member, Univ. of Missouri, 1943-49; assistant to full professor, Wayne State Univ., 1949-69, head of composition department, 1960-69.
WORKS: Ballet: Facades, chamber ensemble, 1951; The ragged heart, chamber ensemble, 1961; Orchestra: Suite for strings, 1941; Suite for chamber orch., 1942; 2 symphonies, 1943, 1946; Holiday overture, 1951; concerto grosso, 7 solo woodwinds and string orch., 1952; Involution, 1967; clarinet concertino, 1968; Chamber music: 3 string quartets, 1942, 1944, 1956; viola sonata, 1952; flute sonata, 1960; 3 inscapes, chamber group, 1970; 5 occurrences, woodwind quintet, 1971; Incubus, chamber group, 1972; Piano: 2 sonatas; 5 preludes, 1955; Soliloquy for the left hand, 1966; Psychogram, 1968; also

WYLIE, RUTH SHAW

(WYLIE, RUTH SHAW)
works for solo voice and chorus and for improvisation chamber ensemble.
1251 Country Club Drive, Long's Peak Route
Estes Park, CO 80517

WYMAN, DANN CORIAT
b. Boston, Mass., 13 Nov. 1923. Studied violin and viola with Arthur Fiedler; attended Northeastern Univ. He has been a free-lance violinist, violist, and arranger with jazz and concert orchestras, 1946-   .
WORKS: Orchestra: Overture; Serenade for strings; Impressions; Chamber music: string quartet; Ode to the viola; Aloneness for solo viola; Song with no words, soprano, viola, harpsichord; The question, soprano and piano.
220 Hobart Road, Chestnut Hill, MA 02167

WYNER, YEHUDI
b. Calgary, Alberta, Canada, 1 June 1929; U.S. citizen at birth. Studied at Juilliard School; with Richard Donovan and Paul Hindemith, Yale Univ., A. B. 1950, B. M. 1951, M. M. 1953; with Walter Piston, Harvard Univ., M. A. His awards include the Rome prize; Alfred E. Hertz Memorial fellowship; Fulbright and Guggenheim fellowships; American Inst. of Arts and Letters grant; Brandeis Creative Arts award; commissions from Michigan Univ., Yale Univ., Fromm Found., Koussevitzky Found., Park Ave. Synagogue, Ford Found. He was visiting lecturer, Queens Coll., 1958-59; music director, Turnau Opera Asso., 1961-63; music director, Westchester Reform Temple, 1958-68; associate professor, Yale Univ., 1964-   , chairman, composition faculty, 1969-73; music director, New Haven Opera Society, 1968-   ; keyboard artist, Bach Aria Group, 1968-   .
WORKS: Theatre: music for Lowell's The old glory; Singer's The mirror; Orchestra: Da camera, piano and orch., 1967; Band: Canto cantabile, soprano and band; Chamber music: Dance variations, wind octet, 1953; Concert duo, violin and piano, 1956; Serenade for 7 instruments, 1958; 3 informal pieces, violin and piano, 1961; De novo, cello and small ensemble, New York, 2 Mar. 1971; Cadenza, clarinet and piano, New York, 6 Feb. 1973; Memorial music, soprano and 3 flutes; Piano: sonata, 1954; Partita; 3 short fantasies; liturgical works.
78 Lyon St., New Haven, CT 06511

WYTON, ALEC
b. London, England, 3 Aug. 1921; U.S. citizen 1968. Studied at Royal Acad. of Music; Oxford Univ., B. A. 1945, M. A. 1949. He was named fellow, Royal Coll. of Organists, 1942, choirmaster, 1946; American Guild of Organists, 1950; Royal Canadian Coll. of Organists, 1962; Royal Acad. of Music, 1964; Royal School of Church Music, 1965; received honorary music doctorate, Susquehanna Univ., 1970. He was organist and choirmaster, St. Matthew's, Northampton, organist and musical advisor, BBC, extra-mural lecturer, Cambridge Univ., 1946-50; organist and choirmaster, Christ Church Cathedral, St. Louis, 1950-54 and at Cathedral Church of St. John the

(WYTON, ALEC)
Divine, New York, 1954-   . His faculty positions include Union Theological Seminary, 1961-   ; head of organ department, Westminster Choir Coll., 1965-67; visiting professor, 1967-73. He has given organ recitals, lectures, and workshops in most major cities of the U.S. and England, and is author of articles in music journals.
WORKS: Chorus: Come Holy Ghost; Go ye, therefore; An endless alleluia; Sing joyfully to God; numerous other anthems, liturgical works, and compositions for organ, including Music for space, 2 organs, trumpet, percussion, and tape, New York, 21 Jan. 1973.
Cathedral Church of St. John the Divine
1047 Amsterdam Ave., New York, NY 10025

YANNATOS, JAMES
b. New York, N. Y., 13 Mar. 1929. Studied with Paul Hindemith and Quincy Porter, Yale Univ.; Ernst Bacon, Syracuse Univ.; Hugo Weisgall, Cummington School of the Arts; Nadia Boulanger in Paris; Luigi Dallapiccolo, New York; with Darius Milhaud, Aspen Music School; and with Philip Bezanson, Univ. of Iowa, Ph. D. He received a Ditson fellowship; Fulbright fellowship; and Univ. of Iowa fellowship. He was lecturer and assistant professor, Grinnell Coll., 1961-63; assistant professor, Univ. of Hawaii, 1964-69; lecturer, Harvard Univ., 1969-   .
WORKS: Opera: Silence bottle, children's opera; Rocket's red blare, Cambridge 6 May 1971; Orchestra: Fanfare and variations; Prieres dans l'arche, voice and orch.; Chamber music: 5 epigrams for string quartet; 3 settings of e. e. cummings.
9 Stearns St., Cambridge, MA 02138

YANNAY, YEHUDA
b. Timisoara, Roumania, 26 May 1937; to U.S. 1964, permanent resident 1972. Studied with A. U. Boscovitch, Israel Acad. of Music, diploma, 1964; with Arthur Berger and Harold Shapero, Brandeis Univ., M. F. A. 1966; Salvatore Martirano, Univ. of Illinois, 1968-70, D. M. A. 1974; with Elliott Carter, Ernst Krenek, Donald Martino, and Gunther Schuller at Tanglewood. His awards include a Fulbright fellowship; Wien Internat. scholarship; Koussevitzky fellowship; Univ. of Illinois fellowship and Research Board grant; Nat. Endowment for the Humanities grant; Univ. of Wisconsin Dean's Research grant; commissions from Israel Composers' Fund, Israel Music Festival; Brandeis Univ.; Milwaukee Symphony. He was teaching assistant, Brandeis Univ., 1965-66; dean, Israel Cons., 1966-68; teaching assistant, Univ. of Illinois, 1968-70; instructor, Univ. of Wisconsin, 1968-70; assistant professor, 1972-   ; founder and conductor, Music from almost yesterday, a contemporary performance group, and the Synth-in series for new instrumental music, theater, and live electronics.
WORKS: Theatre: Wraphap, for actress, amplified aluminum sheet and Yannachord, 1969; Houdini's 9th, for a doublebass and escape artist, 1969; Orchestra: Mirkamim, 1968; concerto for audience and orch., 1971; Chamber music: Spheres,

(YANNAY, YEHUDA)
soprano and 10 instruments, 1963; Permutations, solo percussion, 1964; Incantations, voice, keyboard, interior piano, 1964; Statement for flute, 1964; Interconnections, 14 instruments, 1965; Random rotated, 4 winds, 1965; Foregroundmusic, for 6 instruments and speaker, text after a poem by A. Ginsberg, 1965; 2 fragments, violin and piano, 1966; Mutatis mutandis, for 6 players, 1968; Per se, chamber concerto, violin and 7 instruments, 1969; Coloring book for the harpist, 1969; preFIX-FIX-sufFIX for bassoon, horn, cello, 1971; Squares & symbols, exits & traps, for piano and 1-3 winds or strings, 1971; BugPiece, with live insect notation, 1972; Chorus: Dawn, 1970; Departure, 9 voices and 5 instruments, 1972; Electronic: Coheleth, environment with mobile choir, microphones, wireless microphones, and voice-controlled filters, 1970.
4044 North Downer Ave., Milwaukee, WI 53211

YARDEN, ELIE
b. Philadelphia, Pa., 7 June 1923. Studied with Stefan Wolpe, Settlement School, Philadelphia. He received an Israel Composers' Fund grant, 1960; Van Leer Found. research grant for work at electronic music center, Hebrew Univ., Jerusalem, 1963-65; commission from Tel-Aviv Chamber Music Asso., 1963; Rockefeller recording grant, 1972. He was teacher of composition and theory, Rubin Acad. of Music, Jerusalem, 1958-60; Israel Acad. of Music, Tel-Aviv, 1960-65; associate professor, Bard Coll., 1967- ; lecturer, Vassar Coll., 1973- .
WORKS: Opera: Eros and Psyche, chamber opera, 1970; Orchestra: Prelude, passacaglia and fugue, 1958; Chamber music: 3 string quartets, 1949, 1956, 1965; Bagatelles for piano, 1957; 4 variations, cello quartet, 1957; Divertimento 1963, chamber ensemble; Suite 549 for piano, 1972.
Bard College, Annandale-on-Hudson, NY 12504

YARDUMIAN, RICHARD
b. Philadelphia, Pa., 5 Apr. 1917. Did not begin formal musical study until age 22, then studied harmony, counterpoint and piano in Philadelphia; his self education in composition was encouraged by Jose Iturbi and Leopold Stokowski; studied conducting with Pierre Monteux in Hancock, Me., 1947. His commissions include those from the Stringart Quartet, 1955; Edward B. Benjamin-Quiet Music Project, 1959; Princeton Theological Seminary, 1960; Rudolf Firkusny; Eugene Ormandy, 1961; Hollins Coll., 1964; Fordham Univ., 1964; Maryville Coll., 1969; William Kincaid, 1973. He taught piano privately for many years; is music director, The Lord's New Church, Bryn Athyn, Pa.; writes and edits the church hymnal; was cofounder of the Chamber Symphony of Philadelphia; has done extensive research into ancient and medieval modal systems and into regional American music through its various periods of development.
WORKS: Orchestra: Armenian suite, 1937, Philadelphia, 5 Mar. 1954; Symphonic suite, 1939; 3 pictographs, 1941; Desolate city, Philadelphia, 6 Apr. 1945; violin concerto, 1949, Philadelphia, 11 Nov. 1960; Cantus animae et cordis, string

(YARDUMIAN, RICHARD)
orch., Philadelphia, 17 Feb. 1956; piano concerto, Philadelphia, 3 Jan. 1958; Chorale-prelude on Veni, Sancte Spiritus, Philadelphia, 3 Mar. 1959; symphony no.1, Philadelphia, 1 Dec. 1961; symphony no.2, Philadelphia, 13 Nov. 1964; Chamber music: Monologue, violin solo, 1947; string quartet, 1955; untitled work for flute and strings, 1973; Chorus: Create in me a clean heart, 1962; Magnificat, 1965; Come, Creator spirit, a mass with orch., Philadelphia, 31 Mar. 1967; The story of Abraham, mixed media oratorio for chorus, orch., 5 soloists, with original paintings on 70-mm film in mural form by Andre Girard and shown on a screen suspended above the stage; the story is based on Genesis, Chapters 12-17, London, England, 4 May 1972; U.S. premiere, Maryville Coll., 18 May 1972; Piano: Chromatic sonata, 1946; and shorter piano pieces.
Bryn Athyn, PA 19009

YASUI, BYRON K.
b. Honolulu, Hawaii, 13 Dec. 1940. Studied with Armand Russell and Neil McKay, Univ. of Hawaii, B. M. E. 1965; with Anthony Donata, Alan Stout, and Richard Hillert, Northwestern Univ., M. M. 1967, D. M. A. 1972. He was instructor, Sherwood Music School, Chicago, 1970; instructor, Leeward Community Coll., Hawaii, 1970; assistant professor, Univ. of Hawaii, 1971- .
WORKS: Orchestra: symphony, 1970; Wind ensemble: Music for timpani and brass, 1972; Chamber music: brass quintet, 1966; Polarity I and II, woodwind quartet, 1970; Improvisations, guitar, harp, harpsichord, 1970; 5 movements for solo cello, 1973.
1820 Nuuanu Ave., Honolulu, HI 96817

YATES, RONALD L.
b. Michigan, 27 Apr. 1947. Studied with Donald Andrus and Gerald Strang, California State Univ., Long Beach, B. M. 1970, M. M. 1971; with Peter Racine Fricker and Edward Appleton, Univ. of California, Santa Barbara, Ph. D. 1973.
WORKS: Orchestra: Memoriam, contralto and orch.; A veil awave upon the waves, symphony; Chorus: L'hommage à Josquin; Motet for 16 voices; Missa brevis, double choir; chamber works and solo pieces.
2732 Loomis, Lakewood, CA 90714

YAVELOW, CHRISTOPHER JOHNSON
b. Cambridge, Mass., 14 June 1950. Studied with Gardner Read, David Del Tredici, Joyce McKeel, Hugo Norden, Boston Univ., B. M. 1972, M. M. 1974. He was awarded performance of 4 works at The Composers' Forum, New York, 1974; first prize, Shenandoah Coll. and Cons. Composition contest, 1973. He has been music copyist, 1972- ; accompanist, Boston Cons., 1973-74; director, Outstanding Artists Chamber Music Series, North Shore, 1973- .
WORKS: Chamber music: string quartet, 1971; clarinet quintet, 1972; Introspections, chamber group, 1972; sonata for 2 trumpets, 1972; Fanfare for 2 trumpets and timpani, 1973; Dimension 1, 3 winds and piano, 1973; Bisoliloquy, chamber group, 1973; Soneptua, string quartet, 1973;

YAVELOW, CHRISTOPHER JOHNSON

(YAVELOW, CHRISTOPHER JOHNSON)
Moments, woodwind trio, 1973; Songs: How has it escaped me?, 1971; The fantastic fooley bear, 1972; 4 songs of Sappho, 1973; The United States of America, 1973; Piano: Yavelovelations, 4-hands, 1972; I'll be seeing you, 1973; Multimedia: Green, 7 instruments and film, 1971; Sermon, chamber group and slide projections, New York, 9 Feb. 1974; An explanation of one mechanical man, theatre piece for cello and piano, Boston, 17 Nov. 1974; works for orchestra and for electronic tape.
93 Little Nahant Road, Nahant, MA 01908

YODER, PAUL V.
b. Tacoma, Wash., 8 Oct. 1908. Studied at Univ. of North Dakota, B. A. 1930, honorary D. M. 1958; with Albert Noelte, Northwestern Univ., M. M. 1941. He received the Edwin Franko Goldman award, American School Band Directors Asso.; Kappa Kappa Psi Distinguished Music award; and Nat. Band Asso. AWAPA award. He taught in public schools, 1930-36; free-lance composer and arranger of band music, 1936-   ; visiting professor, Troy State Univ., 1973.
WORKS: Band: More than 400 published original compositions for band and over 1000 transcriptions.
2808 Northeast Court
Fort Lauderdale, FL 33306

*YON, PIETRO ALESSANDRO
b. Settimo Vittone, Italy, 8 Aug. 1886; U.S. citizen 1921; d. Huntington, N. Y., 22 Nov. 1943. Studied at the Milan Cons. and Ste. Cecilia Acad. in Rome. He was organist in Rome, 1905-07; in New York, 1908-26; at St. Patrick's Cathedral, New York, 1926-43; was organ recitalist in the U.S. and Europe. His works include Concerto Gregoriano, organ and orch.; an oratorio, The triumph of St. Patrick; many liturgical works, organ and piano pieces, songs.

YORK, DAVID STANLEY
b. West Hartford, Conn., 25 June 1920. Studied with Paul Hindemith, Yale Univ.; at Westminster Choir Coll.; and with Thomas Beversdorf, Indiana Univ. He won 2nd prize, Schulmerich composition contest, 1947. He has been faculty member, Westminster Choir Coll., 1946-   , professor and director of admissions in 1973.
WORKS: Chorus: Once to every man and nation; Lord, make me thine instrument; Blessing and honor; To music; Psalm 150; O Lord, how excellent is thy name; The four freedoms; and many others; Organ: Divinum mysterium, with bells.
258 Washington Road, Princeton, NJ 08540

YORK, WALTER WYNN
b. Claremore, Okla., 6 Aug. 1914. Studied with Howard Hanson, Herbert Elwell, Edward Royce, Bernard Rogers, Eastman School of Music; also at Univ. of Oklahoma and Westminster Choir Coll. He received an Ellen Lyman Cabot Trust grant, 1964; fellowships at MacDowell Colony, 1958, 1959, 1961, 1964; Yaddo 1964; Huntington Hartford Found., 1961, 1969. He has held faculty posts at Indiana Univ. of Pennsylvania, 1950-54; Southern

(YORK, WALTER WYNN)
Connecticut State Coll., 1961-63; Olivet Coll., 1965-   .
WORKS: Opera: The Bostonians, 1974; Ballet: Chrysis; Orchestra: Rootabaga suite, for children and adults; Chamber music: Neo-Gothics, woodwind quintet; Chorus: The perennial philosophy, with soloists and orch., 1964; A collect for peace; Peter Gray.
413 Cottage, Olivet, MI 49076

YOSHIOKA, EMMETT GENE
b. Honolulu, Hawaii, 19 Mar. 1944. Studied with Ingolf Dahl, Halsey Stevens, Robert Linn, Ellis Kohs, Anthony Vazzana, Univ. of Southern California. He received Univ. of Southern California awards in composition, 1966, 1972; Amstead award, 1972. He was flutist with the Honolulu Symphony, 1960-61; flute instructor, State Univ. of New York at Albany, 1966-69; baritone saxophonist, Los Angeles Saxophone Quartet, 1969-72; faculty member, Univ. of Southern California, 1969-72.
WORKS: Band: Duo concertino, alto saxophone and band; Prologue, fugue, and epilogue; Intermezzo, oboe and band; Chamber music: Extase, trombone solo; Aria and allegro, saxophone quartet; Chorus: 2 S2, 16-part choir; In amber light.
1729 Bertram St., Honolulu, HI 96816

*YOUMANS, VINCENT
b. New York, N. Y., 27 Sep. 1898; d. Denver, Colo., 5 Apr. 1946. Studied engineering; served in the Navy in World War I; then became a song plugger and rehearsal pianist. He composed highly successful musical comedies such as: 2 little girls in blue, 1921; Wildflower, 1923; No, no, Nanette, 1924; A night out, 1925; Oh, please, 1926; Hit the deck, 1927; and the film score, Flying down to Rio, 1933.

YOUNG, GORDON ELLSWORTH
b. McPherson, Kan., 15 Oct. 1919. Studied at Southwestern Coll., B. M., honorary S. M. D., 1973; at Curtis Inst. of Music, 1944-46; organ with Alexander McCurdy and Joseph Bonnet. He has received annual ASCAP awards, 1968-   ; many commissions. He has served as organist in Tulsa, Philadelphia, Kansas City, Lancaster, Pa.; organist-choirmaster, First Presbyterian Church, Detroit, 1952-72; faculty member at various institutions, including Texas Christian Univ.
WORKS: Chamber music: Contempora suite, trumpet and piano; Detroit sketches, trumpet and piano; Triptych, cello and piano; Chorus: Missa exultate, Interlochen, 1964; some 200 other published choral works; Organ: Chorale preludes on 7 hymn tunes; 8 voluntaries on hymn tunes; Variations on an American hymn tune; Baroque suite; and numerous works for organ; songs.
669 Virginia Park, Detroit, MI 48231

*YOUNG, JANE CORNER
b. Athens, Ohio, 1916. Studied at Ohio Univ.; with Marcel Dick, Cleveland Inst. of Music; piano with Beryl Rubinstein and Arthur Loesser. She received the Cleveland Inst. Alumni award in composition, 1961. She is faculty member at

(YOUNG, JANE CORNER)
Cleveland Inst. and head of the music department at Hawthornden State Hospital. Her works include Essences for 2 violins, 1961; Dramatic soliloquy, piano, 1961.
20206 Wickfield Ave.
Warrensville Heights, OH 44122

YOUNG, LA MONTE
b. Bern, Idaho, 14 Oct. 1935. Studied at Univ. of California, Los Angeles, B. A. 1958; composition at Univ. of California, Berkeley, 1958-60; privately with Leonard Stein, 1955-56; Karlheinz Stockhausen, 1959; electronic music with Richard Maxfield, New School for Social Research, New York; Indian vocal music with Pran Nath in New York and New Delhi. His many awards include 2 grants, Nat. Inst. of Arts and Letters; 2 Guggenheim fellowships; Cassandra Found. grant; Cultural Found. grant, 1971; and an Experiments in Art and Technology grant for study in India, 1971 (for the last two, his wife, Marian Zazeela was co-recipient). He has been in the forefront of avant garde music since 1955 as composer, performer, instructor, writer, and lecturer. He edited an anthology (music, poetry, art), 1963; was director of a concert series at Yoko Ono's Studio, New York; and has been director, Theatre of Eternal Music, 1962-   .
WORKS: for brass, octet, 1957; for guitar, 1958; trio for strings, 1958; Vision, 11 instruments producing unspecified sounds, 1959; Untitled works, improvisations with live friction sounds produced by gong on cement, gong on wood floor, metal on wall, 1959-   ; Untitled works, improvisations within a specified structure for piano using a rhythmic-chordal drone style of the composer's invention, 1959-62; Poem for chairs, tables, benches, etc., for the objects named, which are pushed or pulled along the floor within a time structured for each performance according to a method described in the score, another version permits use of any sound sources, 1960; 2 sounds, 2 specific sounds, each recorded on its own reel of tape, 1960 (since 1964 this work has been used by Merce Cunningham for the dance Winterbranch); arabic numeral (any integer), for gong or piano, 1960; Composition 1960 #1-15, word scores involving various objects and activities: #2 consists of building a fire in front of the audience; #5 of releasing butterflies into the performance area; and the latest in the series The tortoise, his dreams and journeys, a continuing performance work initially for voices, strings, drones, with microphones, mixers, amplifiers, loudspeakers, and light projections: The obsidian ocelot, the sawmill, and the blue sawtooth high-tension line stepdown transformer refracting the legend of the dream of the tortoise traversing the 189/98 lost ancestral lake region illuminating quotients from the black tiger tapestries of the drone of the holy numbers, Oct. 1965.
P. O. Box 190 Canal St. Station
New York, NY 10013

YOUNG, MICHAEL E.
b. San Francisco, Calif., 25 June 1939. Studied with George F. McKay, John Verrall, and Greg Short, Univ. of Washington, B. A., M. A.; organ with Walter Eichinger and Edward Hansen. He was named associate, American Guild of Organists, 1965. He was church organist in Seattle, 1961-70; at Saints Peter and Paul Catholic Church, Vancouver, B. C., 1970-   .
WORKS: Chamber music: Suite for bassoon and piano; piano trio; Keyboard: 3 preludes and fugues for organ; 2 piano sonatas; Suite for harpsichord; Music for organ and brass; Sonata of joy for organ.
1425 West 38th Ave.
Vancouver 13, B.C. Canada

YOUNG, PHILIP H.
b. Greenville, S. C., 3 July 1937. Studied at North Greenville Coll.; Furman Univ.; and with John Boda, Florida State Univ. He received 2nd place, Broadman anthem competition, 1963; first place, Lorenz Publishing Company church music contest, 1965. He has been minister of music, First Baptist Church, Henderson, N. C., 1959-   .
WORKS: Chorus (cantatas): God with us, Emmanuel; Today the Prince of Peace is born; To David's town; Christ's sacrifice complete; also music for handbells.
First Baptist Church, Box 75
Henderson, NC 27536

YOUNG, ROBERT H.
b. Santa Cruz, Calif., 20 Apr. 1923. Studied at Otterbein Coll., B. M.; Northwestern Univ., M. M.; and at Univ. of Southern California, D. M. A. He was minister of music in various churches, 1952-62; faculty member, Baylor Univ., 1962-   , associate, vocal and keyboard divisions, professor of church music, chairman, voice department, director of Chamber Singers and Baylor Chorale, 1973.
WORKS: Chorus: All for love; Gabriel's message; O mortal man; When I survey the wondrous cross; Of the Father's love begotten; and others.
School of Music, Baylor University
Waco, TX 76703

*YOUNG, VICTOR
b. Bristol, Tenn., 9 Apr. 1889; d. Ossining, N. Y., 2 Sep. 1968. Studied at Cincinnati Coll. of Music; New York Univ.; piano with Isidor Philipp in Paris. He toured the U.S. and Canada as pianist and accompanist; was music director, Edison Phonograph Laboratory, made piano rolls and records; held various academic posts.
WORKS: Operetta: A happy week; Ballet: Charm assembly line; Orchestra: Scherzetto; Jeep; In the Great Smokies; A fragment, string orch.; songs and piano pieces; also scored early sound film, In old California.

*YOUNG, VICTOR
b. Chicago, Ill., 8 Aug. 1900; d. Palm Springs, Calif., 10 Nov. 1956. Studied violin at Warsaw Cons., then in Chicago. He was violinist and

YOUNG, VICTOR

(YOUNG, VICTOR)
arranger with Ted Fiorito; music director on radio in Chicago and New York; went to Hollywood in 1935 and composed many film scores including The uninvited; For whom the bell tolls; Samson and Delilah; The greatest show on Earth; Around the world in 80 days, received Acad. award, 1956; many popular songs.

*YOUNT, MAX
Manzanos I-IV and Waves, both for flute and harpsichord, performed, New York, 23 Mar. 1973, with the composer at the harpsichord.
Department of Music, Beloit College
Beloit, WI 53511

YOUSE, GLAD ROBINSON
b. Miami, Okla., 22 Oct. 1898. Studied at Stephens Coll.; and composition with Tibor Serly in New York. Her awards include nomination as one of 3 top-ranking women composers in Nat. Fed. of Music Clubs Parade of American Music, 1955; Alumnae achievement citation, Stephens Coll., 1955; Sigma Alpha Iota, Ring of excellence, 1956, citation 1967; Kansas Fed. of Music Clubs citations, 1963, 1968; Theta Sigma Phi Matrix award, 1965. She was composer-director, Jenkins Music Conferences, Kansas City, 1948-66.
WORKS: More than 200 published sacred and secular works for chorus and solo voice.
532 East 12th St., Baxter Springs, KS 66713

YTTREHUS, ROLV
b. Duluth, Minn., 3 Dec. 1926. Studied with Ross Lee Finney, Univ. of Michigan; Nadia Boulanger in Paris; with Roger Sessions and Milton Babbitt, Princeton, N. J.; with Aaron Copland at Tanglewood; with Goffredo Petrassi, St. Cecilia Acad., Rome. He received a Minnesota Fed. of Music Clubs award; Fulbright scholarship; Margaret Lee Crofts award; Italian Government scholarships. He was instructor, Univ. of Missouri, 1963-67; assistant professor, Purdue Univ., 1968; associate professor, Univ. of Wisconsin at Oshkosh, 1969- .
WORKS: Orchestra: Espressioni per orchestra, Rome 1962, American premiere, Boston, 13 May 1973; Chamber music: 6 Haiku, 1961; Music for winds, percussion, and viola, 1961; Music for winds, percussion, cello, and voices, Tanglewood, 1971; Sextet 1964-70, New York, 4 Mar. 1973; Angstwagen, soprano and percussion, 1973; quintet, for Da Capo Chamber Players, New York, 4 Feb. 1974.
874 Oak St., Oshkosh, WI 54901

ZABRACK, HAROLD
b. St. Louis, Mo., 30 June 1928. Studied with Rudolph Ganz and Max Wald, Chicago Musical Coll., B. M. in piano 1949, M. M. 1951; piano study, Freiburg, Germany, 1955-57; doctoral study in piano, Indiana Univ., 1958-59; composition with Nadia Boulanger, Fontainebleau, 1962. He received the Rudolph Ganz scholarship, 1946-49; many awards for piano performance; Fulbright scholarships, 1955, 1956; composition award for study at Fontainebleau; and commissions. He was instructor, Chicago Musical Coll., 1949-51; graduate assistant, Indiana Univ., 1958-59; associate professor, Webster Coll., 1962-65; has presented master

(ZABRACK, HAROLD)
classes in piano at a number of universities; concert pianist and teacher, 1952- .
WORKS: Orchestra: Symphonic variations, piano and orch., 1959; 2 piano concertos, 1964, 1965; Chamber music: 2 duets, viola and oboe, 1961; Song cycle on classical Greek texts, soprano; Fantasie, horn and organ; Piano: 2 sonatas, 1965, 1969; 5 piano contours; Scherzo: Hommage à Prokofieff.
155 West 68th St., New York, NY 10023

ZADOR, EUGENE
b. Bataszek, Hungary, 5 Nov. 1894; U.S. citizen 1944. Studied at Vienna Cons. and with Max Reger, Leipzig Cons., Ph. D. His awards include the Grand Prix of Hungary, 1934, and the Benjamin Prize, 1960. He was professor, Vienna Cons., 1922-38; New York Coll. of Music, 1939; then went to Hollywood as film orchestrator and arranger, 1940-61.
WORKS: Opera: Christoph Columbus, New York, 8 Oct. 1939; The virgin and the fawn, 1-act, Los Angeles, 24 Oct. 1964; The magic chair, 1-act, 1965; The scarlet mill, 1967; Revisor (Inspector General), after Gogol, 1928, premiere, Los Angeles, 11 June 1971; Orchestra: Czardas rhapsodic, 1939; Children's symphony, 1941; Pastorale and tarantella, 1941; Biblical triptych, 1943; Elegie and dance, 1953; Divertimento for strings, 1955; Fugue-fantasia, 1958; Suite for brass, 1961; Rhapsody, 1961; Christmas overture, 1961; Variations on a merry theme, 1963; The remarkable adventure of Henry Bold, with narrator, 1963; Triptych, 1964; 5 contrasts for orch., 1964; trombone concerto, 1966; Rhapsody, cimbalom and orch., 1968; Studies for orchestra, 1969; Fantasia Hungarica, double bass and orch., 1970; double bass concerto, 1971; accordion concerto, 1973; Chamber music: Suite for 8 celli, 1966; Music for clarinet and strings, 1969; woodwind quintet, 1972; Duo-fantasy, 2 celli, strings, harp, Riverside, Calif., 3 Dec. 1973; brass quintet, 1973; Chorus: Lonely wayfarer; 3 rondelles for women's voices; Scherzo domestico, 1961; Cantata technica, 1964; The judgment, 3 soli, women's chorus, 9 brass instruments. For earlier works see Baker and Groves.
249 South Arden Blvd., Los Angeles, CA 90004

*ZADORA, MICHAEL VON
b. New York, N. Y., 14 June 1882; d. New York, 30 June 1946. Studied with his father and at the Paris Cons.; later with Leschetizky and Busoni. He was concert pianist and teacher; composed songs and piano pieces.

*ZAHLER, NOEL
Flute sonata.

ZAIMONT, JUDITH LANG
b. Memphis, Tenn., 8 Nov. 1945. Studied piano and theory, Juilliard School, 1958-64; Long Island Inst. of Music, diploma, 1966; Queens Coll., B. A. magna cum laude 1966; Columbia Univ., M. A. 1968. She received scholarships for all study, 1958-68; MacDowell fellowship, 1971; Debussy scholarship for study in France, Alliance

(ZAIMONT, JUDITH LANG)
Francaise, 1971-72; Nat. Fed. of Music Clubs awards, 1963, 1964, 1968, 1970; Queens Coll. awards, 1965, 1966; Karol Rathaus Memorial prize, 1966; BMI award, 1966; Gold Medal 1st prize, Gottschalk competition, 1970; 2nd prize, Delius Composition contest, 1971. She has been accompanist and resident composer, Great Neck Choral Society, N. Y., 1967-71, 1972-   ; lecturer in musicology, New York City Community Coll., 1970-71; instructor in theory, Queens Coll., 1972-   ; private teacher and duo-piano recitalist, 1960-67.

WORKS: Orchestra: piano concerto, 1972; Chamber music: flute sonata, 1962; Experience, flute and piano, 1966; 2 movements for wind quartet, 1967; Grand tarantella, violin and piano, 1970; Capriccio, solo flute, 1971; trumpet sonata, 1971; trio for flute, viola, piano, 1971; Chorus: They flee from me..., with flute, 1966; Man's image and his cry, with 2 soli and orch., 1968; Canto II, 1970; The chase, on an original narrative poem, 1972; Songs: 4 songs for mezzo and piano, 1965; A solemn music, cycle for baritone, 1967; Coronach, cycle for soprano, 1970; Chant for solo voice and drone, 1970; Piano: City suite, 1961; Piano variations, 1965; Scherzo, 1969; Snazzy sonata, 4-hands, 1972; 12 preludes, 1973.
264-20 82nd Ave., Floral Park, NY 11004

ZAMBARANO, ALFRED P.
b. Naples, Italy, 24 Feb. 1885; U.S. citizen 1906; d. New Haven, Conn., 22 June 1970. Came to the U.S. as an infant, but returned to Italy to study at the Naples Cons., graduating in 1907. He played piano at the Providence Opera House, 1918-28; was baritone soloist with concert bands, 1918-30; taught in public schools in Rhode Island, Connecticut, and Massachusetts, 1930-65. His National Capitol March won first place in the national competition for a march to celebrate the sesquicentennial of Washington, D.C., in 1950.

WORKS: Band marches: The national capitol, 1950; Green thunderbolt; National unity; Bobcat march; Chamber music: Neopolitan tarantella, clarinet and piano; Friendship, trombone and piano; A valiant hero, tuba and piano; Elephant's frolic, tuba and piano; trumpet trio; and songs.

ZANINELLI, LUIGI
b. Raritan, N. J., 30 Mar. 1932. Studied with Gian Carlo Menotti, Bohuslav Martinu, Vittorio Giannini at Curtis Inst. of Music. He received the Steinway piano composition award, 1955; annual ASCAP awards, 1966-73; and numerous commissions. He was instructor, Curtis Inst., 1952-58; composition and theory teacher, New School of Music, Philadelphia, 1955-58; composer-conductor, RCA Italiana, Rome, 1964-66; director of music, Marymount Intonation School, Rome, Italy, 1966-68; composer-in-residence, Univ. of Calgary, Canada, 1968-73; composer-in-residence, Univ. of Southern Mississippi, 1973-   .

WORKS: Festa, march; Hymn and variations, with optional chorus; Margaret suite; Peg leg Pete, solo tuba and band; Puppet overture; Wind ensemble: Jubilate Deo, brass choir; Music for a

(ZANINELLI, LUIGI)
solemn occasion, brass and percussion; Chamber music: Arioso, flute, cello, piano; Dance variations, woodwind quintet; Designs for brass quintet; Dialogue, violin and piano; Musica drammatica, woodwind quintet and percussion; 3 children's dances, woodwind quintet; Canto lirico, trumpet and piano; Epitaph, flute, 2 pianos, strings, percussion; Piano: The enchanted lake, 4-act children's ballet; A lexicon of beasties, 26 pieces for student and teacher; 3Rs for dancing, music for labanotation; Fantasia; Film scores: Una moglie Americana, Italy, 1965; The visitor, Canada, 1973; and nearly 50 published choral works.
1216 Marie St., Hattiesburg, MS 39401

ZATMAN, ANDREW
b. Washington, D.C., 6 June 1945. Studied with John Vincent, Henri Lazarof, Roy Travis, Alden Ashforth, and Boris Kremenliev, Univ. of California, Los Angeles, M. A. He has been composer-in-residence, School of Music, Jewish Community Center of Greater Washington, 1971-   .

WORKS: Chamber music: woodwind trio, 1969; Suite for solo flute, 1971; flute sonata, 1972; Piano: 24 preludes, 1965; sonata #2, 1967; Variations on November leaves of Boris Kremenliev, 1969.
303 Congressional Lane, Rockville, MD 20852

*ZECKWER, CAMILLE
b. Philadelphia, Pa., 26 June 1875; d. Southampton, N. Y., 7 Aug. 1924. Studied with his father, Richard Zeckwer; composition with Dvorak and Scharwenka. He succeeded his father as director of the Philadelphia Musical Acad., 1917-24.

WORKS: Opera: Jane and Janette, 3-act; Orchestra: Swedish fantasy, violin and orch.; piano concerto; Sohrab and Rustum, symphonic poem, 1916; Chamber music: Serenade melancolique; piano trio; Chorus: The new day, cantata; other choral works, songs, piano pieces.

*ZEISL, ERIC
b. Vienna, Austria, 18 May 1905; to U.S. 1939; d. Los Angeles, Calif., 18 Feb. 1959. Studied at Vienna Acad. of Music; became professor at Vienna Cons. From 1939 he taught at the Los Angeles Cons.

WORKS: Opera: Leonce and Lena, 1937; Job, 1945-58; Ballet: Uranium 235; Jacob and Rachel; Orchestra: Little symphony, 1937; Passacaglia-fantasy, 1937; November, suite for chamber orch., 1940; Variations and fugue on Christmas carols; Cossack dance, 1946; Return of Ulysees, suite for chamber orch., 1948; Requiem concertante, with chorus; Requiem Ebraico, with chorus; Chamber music: 2 string quartets; violin sonata; cello sonata; Sonata barocca, piano, 1949; Brandeis sonata, violin and piano, 1950; Songs: Prayer for the United Nations, baritone and piano; 7 songs for soprano; Moon pictures, baritone.

ZERCHER, J. RANDALL
b. Mt. Joy, Pa., 9 Dec. 1940. Studied with Harold Moyer, Bethel Coll., Kan.; with Joseph

491

ZERCHER, J. RANDALL

(ZERCHER, J. RANDALL)
Goodman, Union Theological Seminary, New York,
M. M. He received 2 Thresher awards in composition, Bethel Coll., 1963, 1964. He was instructor, Bethel Coll., 1966-68; instructor, Hesston
Coll., 1968-   , chairman, music department,
1973-   .
WORKS: Chorus: My beloved spake, 1965; I
bind my heart this tide, 1969; Organ: Union,
a prelude, 1970; also Play-ground, a collaborative
musical drama.
Hesston College, Hesston, KS 67062

ZES, TIKEY A.
b. Long Beach, Calif., 27 Oct. 1927. Studied
with Gerald Strang, Long Beach, Calif.; with
Ingolf Dahl, Univ. of Southern California,
D. M. A. 1969. He received 2 Helen Anstead
awards at USC, 1963, 1969. He has been associate
professor, San Jose State Univ., 1964-   .
WORKS: Orchestra: French overture, 1963;
Chorus: Music for the divine liturgy of St. John
Chrysostom, 1966; 2 Greek folk songs, 1969;
Byzantine concert liturgy, chorus and orch.,
1969.
1523 Arata Court, San Jose, CA 95125

ZIFFRIN, MARILYN J.
b. Moline, Ill., 7 Aug. 1926. Studied at Univ.
of Wisconsin, B. M.; Columbia Univ., Teachers
Coll., M. A.; graduate work, Univ. of Chicago;
composition with Alexander Tcherepnin and Karl
Ahrendt. She received 2nd prize, Internat.
Society for Contemporary Music, Chicago Chapter
contest, 1955; Delius award, 1972; and commissions. She was assistant professor, Northeastern
Illinois State Coll., 1961-66; associate professor, New England Coll., 1966-   .
WORKS: Chamber music: XIII for chamber ensemble, Monadnock Music Center, 22 Aug. 1969;
Movement for clarinet and percussion, 1972; string
quartet, 1972; Haiku, song cycle for soprano,
viola, harpsichord; In the beginning, percussion,
quintet; sonata for organ and cello, Colby Coll.,
8 Mar. 1973; 4 pieces for tuba, Indiana Univ.
of Pennsylvania, 12 Apr. 1973.
P. O. Box 179, Bradford, NH 03221

ZILEVICIUS, JUOZAS
b. Plunge, Lith., 16 Mar. 1891; to U.S. 1929.
Studied at St. Petersburg Cons.; Warsaw Cons.
He was awarded the 3rd Order of Gedeminas by the
Lithuanian Government, 1935. He was professor,
Vitebsk Cons., 1919-20; director of arts,
Lithuania, 1922-24; director and professor,
Klaipeda Cons., 1924-29; director of music, St.
Peter and Paul Church, Elizabeth, N. J., 1929-60;
curator, Zilevicius Library of Lithuanian Musi-
cology, Chicago, 1960-   .
WORKS: Theatre: Lietuvaite, operetta;
Orchestra: symphony, Kaunas, Lith., 27 July,
1923, was first symphony composed by a Lithuanian;
Chamber music: string quartet; octet; Ausra,
violin and piano; variations and fugues for piano;
Chorus: Vytautas the Great, cantata.
2345 West 56th St., Chicago, IL 60636

*ZIMBALIST, EFREM
b. Rostov, Russia, 7 Apr. 1889; to U.S. 1911.
Studied with Leopold Auer, St. Petersburg Cons.;
made his debut as violinist in Berlin at 18;
toured Europe and the U.S. From 1929 he was on
the faculty at Curtis Inst. of Music, director,
1941-61.
WORKS: Opera: Landora, 1956; Orchestra:
Slavonic dances, violin and orch.; American rhapsody, 1936; violin concerto; Portrait of an
artist, symphonic poem, 1945; Chamber music:
Concert fantasy on Le Coq d'or, violin and piano;
violin sonata; string quartet; violin pieces;
songs.

*ZIMMERMAN, PHYLLIS
Alleluia for chorus.

*ZINDARS, EARL
b. 1927.   The brass square; quintet for brass.

ZINN, MICHAEL ALAN
b. New Haven, Conn., 23 Aug. 1947. Studied with
Walter Ihrke and Charles Whittenberg, Univ. of
Connecticut, B. M. 1969, M. A. 1971; with Paul
Harder and H. Owen Reed, Michigan State Univ.,
Ph. D. candidate 1974. He received a commission,
Connecticut Music Educators Asso., 1969. He
was research assistant, Univ. of Connecticut,
1965-71; teaching assistant, Michigan State
Univ., 1971-73; director, New Musical Arts Ensemble, 1973-74; production assistant and score
reader, WKAR-TV, East Lansing, Mich., 1973-74.
WORKS: Chamber music: Quartet for 6 instruments, proportional notation, 1971; Suspensions,
alto saxophone, bassoon, and vibraphone, 1973;
Yellow spring, soprano, flute, oboe, violin,
text by Rimenez; Electronic: Composition for
tape and orch., 1969; Spring storm, chamber ensemble and tape, 1972.
1204 C University Village
East Lansing, MI 48823

ZITO, TORRIE
b. Utica, N. Y., 12 Oct. 1933. Studied with
Vittorio Giannini, Manhattan School of Music.
He has been a free-lance composer-arranger in
popular music field, 1959-   .
WORKS: Band: Major Boogaloo march; La
fiesta de la roca; Brazilian fantasy; Journey
into the blue rock country; Holiday fanfare and
march; also stage band works.
140 East 83rd St., New York, NY 10028

ZONN, PAUL
b. Boston, Mass., 16 Jan. 1938. Studied with
Richard Hervig, Univ. of Iowa, M. F. A. 1966.
His awards include a Rockefeller grant to Center
for Performing and Creative Arts, Buffalo,
1966-67; Fromm fellowships at Tanglewood, 1967,
1968; Ford Found. grants, summers, 1968, 1969,
1970; Univ. of Illinois faculty fellowship,
summer 1971; and commissions. He was composer-
in-residence and conductor, Grinnell Coll.;
1967-70; assistant professor, Univ. of Illinois,
1970-72; associate professor and chairman,
composition-theory division, 1972-   .

(ZONN, PAUL)
WORKS: Orchestra: clarinet concerto; Chamber music: concerto for viola and 13 instruments; Cellomusic, solo cello; A child's garden of revolution, small ensemble; Chroma, oboe and piano; compositions for woodwind quartet; Divertimentos 1-3, for varying ensembles; Ernie's suite, chamber ensemble; Fantasie duo, 2 cellos; Grunge, solo flute; The justice variations, actor and 6 instruments; Liberata I-III, varying chamber ensembles; Melos, piano trio; One slow turn of the world, woodwind trio, double bass, percussion; wind sextet; oboe sonata; piano sonata; 2 string quartets; Well pursed, flute and piano; other shorter chamber pieces, vocal works, electronic compositions.
308 Pond Ridge Lane, Urbana, IL 61801

ZORKO, GEORGE MATTHEW
b. East Cleveland, Ohio, 7 May 1947. Studied with Normand Lockwood, Univ. of Denver; with Merrill Ellis, North Texas State Univ.
WORKS: Orchestra: Psalm; Chamber music: wind octet; Canonic fantasia, accordion; On guard, chamber orch. and accordion; Chorus: Missa, 32-voice choir and organ.
9040 Ranch Drive, Chesterland, OH 44026

ZUCKERMAN, MARK
b. Brooklyn, N. Y., 8 July 1948. Studied with George B. Wilson, Univ. of Michigan; Elie Yarden, Bard Coll.; with Milton Babbitt, J. K. Randall, Peter Westergaard, and Claudio Spies, Princeton Univ. He held the Whiting fellowship in the humanities at Princeton, 1973-74, and was research assistant in computer music, 1972-73.
WORKS: Chamber music: Retrogressive study, piano, 1970; Paraphrases, flute alone, 1971.
18 Tamara Drive, Roosevelt, NJ 08555

ZUKOFSKY, PAUL
b. Brooklyn, N. Y., 22 Oct. 1943. Studied with Bernard Wagenaar and Vincent Persichetti, Juilliard School, M. M. He made his professional debut on the violin with the New Haven Symphony at age 8; gave a Carnegie Hall recital at 13; has performed with many major orchestras; has excelled in presenting contemporary works for the violin in concert and on records. He has taught violin at the New England Cons., Swarthmore Coll., and at State Univ. of New York, Stony Brook.
WORKS: Orchestra: for orchestra, 1964; Chamber music: Variants, soprano, trumpet, violin, bass clarinet, 1960; 13 pomes, a prelude and a postlude, 2 speakers, 15 percussion players, 1962; for 3 mallet men and a percussion player, 1963; Catullus "fragmenta", soprano, alto, string trio, 1968.
Box 97, Port Jefferson, NY 11777

ZUPKO, RAMON
b. Pittsburgh, Pa., 14 Nov. 1932. Studied with Vincent Persichetti, Juilliard School; with Otto Luening, Columbia Univ.; and with Karl Schiske, Vienna Acad. of Music. He won first prize, Premio Citta di Trieste, Italy, 1965; had 2 compositions chosen for performance by St. Louis Symphony,

(ZUPKO, RAMON)
1966, 1967; and a composition chosen to represent the U.S. at the ISCM world festival, Basel, Switzerland, 1970. He was Ford Found. composer-in-residence, Lubbock, Tex., 1961-62, at Joliet Ill., 1966-67; assistant professor and director, electronic and experimental music laboratory, Roosevelt Univ., 1967-71; assistant professor and director, electronic and experimental laboratory, Western Michigan Univ., 1971-   .
WORKS: Orchestra: Centroids, 1966; Translucents, string orch., 1967; Radiants; Wind ensemble: Tangents, 18 brass instruments; Chamber music: Reflexions, 8 instruments; Winter '64, piano; La guerre, soprano and instruments, 1970; Metacycles, for modified voices; Spring sonata, modified piano sounds; Electronic: Voices, amplified soprano and tape; Trichromes, winds, tape, percussion; Multimedia: 3rd planet from the sun.
1540 North 2nd St., Route 1
Kalamazoo, MI 49009

ZUR, MENACHEM
b. Tel Aviv, Israel, 6 Mar. 1942; to U.S. 1969. Studied with William Sydeman, Mannes Coll. of Music; with Meyer Kupferman, Sarah Lawrence Coll.; Vladimir Ussachevsky and Mario Davidovsky, Columbia Univ. He received the ORR prize in Jerusalem, Israel, for his cantata. He has been teaching theory, Queens Coll., 1972-   .
WORKS: Theatre: A legend, theatre piece for female violinist and male pianist; Affairs, theatre piece for soprano, conductor, 8 musicians; Orchestra: concerto for singer and orch.; Chamber music: 3 pieces for bassoon and piano; Pictures, 3 celli and one double bass; Discussion, violin and clarinet; Fantasy for piano; concertino, woodwind quintet; cello sonata; Electronic: And there arose a mist, cantata for chorus, brass quartet, percussion, tape; other electronic pieces.
2736-A Independence Ave., Bronx, NY 10463

ZWEIG, ESTHER
b. New York, N. Y., 29 July 1906. Studied at Hunter Coll.; New York Univ.; Univ. of Vienna; Jewish Theological Seminary; instructors included Walter Damrosch and Kurt Weill. She received an award, Jewish Theological Seminary, 1927; certificate of merit, Univ. of Vienna. She taught choral music, Hebrew Schools of New York, 1927-37; directed Esther Zweig Ensemble, WEVD, New York, 1949-50.
WORKS: Chorus: The conquerors of Canaan, cantata; Songs: I close my eyes and dream; I sing to you, America.
2435 Haring St., #4E, Brooklyn, NY 11235

ZWILICH, ELLEN TAAFFE
b. Miami, Fla., 30 Apr. 1939. Studied with John Boda and Carlisle Floyd, Florida State Univ.; Elliott Carter and Roger Sessions, Juilliard School, D. M. A. candidate 1974. Her awards include 3 Florida Composers League student prizes; Rogers and Hammerstein scholarship; Elizabeth Sprague Coolidge chamber music prize; 2 awards of Marion Frescal prize at Juilliard.

ZWILICH, ELLEN TAAFFE

(ZWILICH, ELLEN TAAFFE)
    WORKS: Orchestra: Symposium; Chamber music:
violin sonata, written for her husband, Joseph
Zwilich, 1973-74; string quartet, 1974; Allison,
chamber ensemble, 1974; Impromptu for harp, 1974;
Songs: Einsame Nacht, cycle for baritone and
piano, 1971; Im Nebel, contralto and piano, 1972;
Trompeten, for soprano and piano.
    600 West 246th St., Riverdale, NY 10471

Addendum

*ADAM, CLAUS
b. Sumatra, 5 Nov. 1917; to U.S. 1931. Studied cello and composition in Germany and Austria; has taught cello at Juilliard School for many years; retired as cellist of the Juilliard String Quartet in 1974. His compositions include a cello concerto, 1973; piano sonata, 1952.
Juilliard School, Lincoln Center
New York, NY 10023

*AKIYOSHI, TOSHIKO
b. Dairen, Manchuria, 12 Dec. 1929. Studied at Dairen Music Acad.; on scholarship at Berklee School of Music; piano with Margaret Chaloff. She has been pianist in dance bands, soloist with the Japan Philharmonic Orchestra; with her husband formed the Toshiko Mariano Quartet. Her works include Jazz suite for strings and woodwinds (Mademoiselle award); My elegy; Silhouette; songs.

*ALEXANDER, JEFF
b. Seattle, Wash., 2 July 1910. Studied at Becker Cons. and with Joseph Schillinger.
WORKS: Orchestra: Yellow and brown; Chamber music: Suite for flute and strings; Divertimento, viola and piano; Film scores: The tender trap; The mating game; The gazebo; and others; has also composed for television.

*ASPER, FRANK W.
b. Logan, Utah, 9 Feb. 1892. Studied at New England Cons.; Boston Univ.; Univ. of Utah; honorary D. M., Bates Coll. He taught at the New England Cons., then at McCune School of Music and Art; was organist at Salt Lake City Tabernacle, conducted choir for broadcasts; gave concerts in U.S., Canada, Mexico, and Europe. His works include many sacred and secular pieces for organ.

*AXT, WILLIAM
b. New York, N. Y., 19 Apr. 1888; d. Ukiah, Calif., 12 Feb. 1959. Studied privately in Berlin. He was assistant conductor, Hammerstein Grand Opera Company, N. Y.; music director, Capitol Theatre, N. Y., 1919; head of MGM music department. His film scores included Grand Hotel; Parnell; The garden murder case; Reunion in Vienna; The thin man; Rendezvous; and others.

*BAROVICK, FRED
b. New York, N. Y., 28 June. Studied at Curtis Inst.; Univ. of Pennsylvania, Ph. D. He has been arranger for Hal Kemp, Kay Kyser, Mal Hallett, Vincent Lopez, Tommy and Jimmy Dorsey, and for Broadway shows, television, records, and educational films.
WORKS: Orchestra: Symphony for strings; Trombone quartet with symphony orchestra; Modern trombone solo with brass choir; The lost horizon; also popular songs.

*BASKERVILLE, DAVID
b. Freehold, N. J., 18 Aug. 1919. Studied at Univ. of California, Los Angeles, M. A., Ph. D. He has played in the Seattle Symphony and Los Angeles Philharmonic; was director, Westlake Coll. of Music, 1947-48; staff composer and arranger, NBC radio, Hollywood, 1949-50; taught at Univ. of California, 1951-56; has been music director, Robin Hood Band from 1957; on staff Paramount Pictures from 1957.
WORKS: Band: Grand entry swing march; Ventura overture; Moonride; Hollywood swing march.

*BENTER, CHARLES
b. New York, N. Y., 29 Apr. 1887; d. New York, 2 Dec. 1964. He was apprentice boy musician, U.S. Navy 1905; received an honorary D. M. from Columbia Univ. He organized the Navy Band in Washington, D.C. in 1919 and was its leader to retirement in 1942; was first to attain officer rank in the music branch of the Navy and was commissioned Lt. by act of Congress in 1923; was founder and officer in charge, Navy School of Music; conducted Metropolitan Police Dept. Band, Washington, to 1962. His many works for band include the marches: Irresistible; Lure of Alaska; Major Denby; Washington Times; Light cruisers; All hands; etc.

*BLACK, FRANK J.
b. Philadelphia, Pa., 28 Nov. 1896; d. Attended Missouri Valley Coll., honorary D. M.; studied piano with Rafael Joseffy. He made his debut as concert pianist at age 10; became theatre conductor in Philadelphia and New York; then conductor on radio; was general music director, NBC, 1932-48.

BLACK, FRANK J.

(BLACK, FRANK J.)
WORKS: Orchestra: <u>Bells at eventide</u>; <u>A sea tale</u>; Film scores: <u>White Cliffs of Dover</u>; <u>Murder of Lidice</u>.

*BLANCHARD, WILLIAM G.
b. Greencastle, Ind., 5 Sep. 1905. Studied at De Pauw Univ., B. M.; Univ. of Michigan, M. M.; also with Seth Bingham and Hugh Porter. He was church organist in Greencastle, 1919-27; school music supervisor, 1930-36; from 1936 he was on faculty, Pomona Coll. and associate professor, Associated Colleges. His works include church anthems and organ pieces.

*BOYLE, GEORGE F.
b. Sydney, Australia, 29 June 1886; to U.S. 1910; d. Philadelphia, Pa., 20 June 1948. Studied piano with Busoni, then toured as concert pianist and conductor in Australia, Germany, Holland, Great Britain. He taught at Peabody Cons.; Curtis Inst.; and Juilliard School.
WORKS: Operetta: <u>The black rose</u>; Orchestra: piano concerto; piano concertino; cello concerto; <u>Symphonic fantasie</u>; <u>Holiday overture</u>; Chamber music: violin sonata; viola sonata; cello sonata; piano sonata; <u>Ballade elegiaque</u> for piano trio; Chorus: <u>Pied Piper of Hamelin</u>.

*BUECHE, GREGORY A.
b. Tipton, Kan., 13 Feb. 1903. Studied with Gustave Soderlund and Charles Skilton, Kansas Univ., B. M.; with Rudolph Ganz and Olaf Andersen, Chicago Musical Coll., M. M. He taught in public schools in Kansas and Colorado, 1927-37; was head of music department, Colorado State Univ., from 1937 to retirement.
WORKS: Band: <u>Heritage</u>, with chorus: Chamber music: <u>Rondino</u>, flute and piano; <u>Prelude and chorale</u>, piano; <u>Vestiges</u>, piano; <u>Dollin' up Dolly</u>, piano.

*BUNCE, CORAJANE DIANE. <u>See</u> WARD, DIANE

*BURKE, JOHNNY
b. Antioch, Calif., 3 Oct. 1908; d. New York, N. Y., 25 Feb. 1969. Studied at Crane Coll.; and Univ. of Wisconsin. He was staff member at music publishers in Chicago and New York; then under contract to Paramount in Hollywood.
WORKS: Film scores: <u>Pennies from heaven</u>; <u>Double or nothing</u>; <u>Sing, you sinners</u>; <u>Road to Singapore</u>; <u>A Connecticut yankee in King Arthur's Court</u>; <u>Riding high</u>; and others; also stage scores and many songs.

*BUTLER, JACK H.
b. Augusta, Ga., 18 June 1924. Studied at Erskine Coll. and Univ. of South Carolina. He has taught in public schools and is church music director and piano teacher.
WORKS: Orchestra: <u>The Gettysburg address</u>, chorus and orch.; Piano: <u>Lonely as a star</u>; <u>The weary plowman</u>.
11 East Drive, Atlanta, GA 30305

*CAIN, NOBLE
b. Aurora, Ind., 25 Sep. 1896. Studied at American Cons., B. M.; Univ. of Chicago, M. A.; Friends Univ., B. A., honorary D. M.; Lawrence Coll., honorary D. M. He was founder of the Senn High School Chorus, Chicago and the Chicago A Cappella Choir; was choral director and producer, NBC, 1932-39; guest conductor at schools, colleges, and music festivals.
WORKS: Chorus: <u>Christ in the world</u>, oratorio; <u>Evangeline</u>; <u>The king and the star</u>; <u>Paul Revere's ride</u>; <u>Ode to America</u>; <u>Holy Lord God</u>, anthem; and many others; also arrangements of spirituals and folksongs. He is author of the book: <u>Choral music and its practice</u>.

*CALKER, DARRELL W.
b. Washington, D.C., 18 Feb. 1905; d. Malibu, Calif., 20 Feb. 1964. Studied at Univ. of Maryland, B. S.; and at Curtis Inst.
WORKS: Ballet: <u>Royal coachman</u>; <u>Quiet week</u>; <u>Decameron</u>; scores for Ballet Russe de Monte Carlo, Ballet Russe, and Sadlers Wells; Orchestra: <u>Penguin Island</u>; <u>Golden land</u>; Film scores: <u>Adventure Island</u>; <u>Bachelor's daughter</u>; <u>El Paso</u>; <u>Albuquerque</u>; <u>Geronimo</u>; <u>Savage drums</u>.

*CESANA, OTTO
b. Brescia, Italy, 7 July 1899; to U.S. as a boy. Studied with Julius Gold. He was staff composer and arranger for film studios in Hollywood; later arranger for Radio City Music Hall, New York, and for radio.
WORKS: Ballet: <u>Ali Baba and the 40 thieves</u>; Orchestra: 6 symphonies; 6 concertos (one each for clarinet, trumpet, trombone, piano, 2 pianos, 3 pianos); <u>Negro heaven</u>; also <u>Swing septet</u> and songs. He was author of several books on music theory.

*CHARKOVSKY, WILLIS
b. Chicago, Ill., 1 Mar. 1918. Studied with Felix Borowski and Leo Sowerby; De Paul Univ., B. M.; Northwestern Univ., M. M. He won a piano contest of the Society of American Musicians; made his professional debut as pianist in Chicago, 1936. He served in the Army in World War II; taught at Northwestern Univ., 1957; has been band and orchestra director, Univ. of Illinois; soloist with Grant Park Symphony from 1957. His works include a piano concerto; woodwind quintet; sonata for 2 pianos.

*CHASE, NEWELL
b. West Roxbury, Mass., 3 Feb. 1904; d. New York, N. Y., 26 Jan. 1955. Studied at Boston Univ.; Harvard Univ.; with Wallace Goodrich and Frederick Converse, New England Cons.; and with Tibor Serly. He was church organist, pianist, dance orchestra conductor; assistant conductor, Capitol Theatre, New York, 1924; solo pianist in the "Roxy Gang;" went to Hollywood in 1928 as composer and music advisor for films; served in the Air Force in World War II.
WORKS: Orchestra: <u>Concerto for Louise</u>; <u>Midnight in Mayfair</u>; <u>Tanglewood pool</u>; <u>Trickette</u>; <u>Classical satire</u>; <u>Bachette</u>; <u>In chiffon</u>; many popular songs.

*CHENETTE, EDWARD STEPHEN
b. London, Ky., 17 Aug. 1895; d. Bartow, Fla.,
10 Sep. 1963. Studied at High Park Cons., Des
Moines, Iowa, M. A.; Bush Temple Cons.; Societe
Academique, Paris. He was band conductor with
the Chautauqua Inst. to 1916, when the entire
band enlisted in the Canadian Expeditionary
Forces; conductor, Chicago Regimental Band and
Illinois State Legion Band; director of music,
Iowa State Coll.; then on faculty, Florida Southern Coll. He was author of books on band technique and composed many marches and other works
for band.

*CHERNIAVSKY, JOSEF
b. Russia, 31 Mar. 1895; to U.S. 1919; d. New
York, 3 Nov. 1959. Studied with Alexander
Glazounov and Rimsky-Korsakov, Imperial Cons.,
St. Petersburg; with Julius Klengel in Leipzig.
He toured the U.S. as theatre and concert con-
ductor; then was music director, WLW, Cincinnati.
His works included 3 operettas: Barnum; Music
drama; The dybbuk.

*COOPER, JOHN CRAIG
b. Kansas City, Mo., 14 May 1925. Studied at
Kansas City Cons.; Univ. of Missouri, B. A.,
M. A.; with Charles Jones, Mills Coll.; with
Nadia Boulanger, American Cons., Fontainebleau,
France; with Darius Milhaud, Aspen Inst.; also
with Ben Weber and Hans Neumann. His awards
include the Paulina award, Univ. of Missouri;
3 MacDowell fellowships; Alice Ditson grants.
He has taught piano at King's Coll., Briarcliff
Manor, N. Y.
    WORKS: Chamber music: Dialogues, woodwind
quintet; Elegy, piano; Chorus: Ah, sunflower;
Child of a day; Songs: Do not go, my love; Free
me from the bonds.

*COPPOLA, CARMINE (CARMEN)
b. New York, N. Y., 11 June 1910. Studied at
Manhattan School of Music, B. A., M. A.;
Juilliard Graduate School, M. M. He was first
flutist, Radio City Music Hall, 1934-36; Detroit
Symphony, 1936-41; NBC Orchestra, 1942-48; staff
arranger, Radio City Music Hall, 1948-56; opera
conductor, Brooklyn Acad. of Music, 1948-55.
    WORKS: Wind ensemble: Flute flight; Phantom
cavalry, woodwind quintet; Oboe fantasie; Danse
pagan.

*COX, RALPH
b. Galion, Ohio, 29 Aug. 1884; d. New York, N. Y.,
10 June 1941. Studied at Oberlin Cons.; Guilmant
Organ School; Wooster Univ. He was organist-
choirmaster in Greenwich, N. Y., and Orange,
N. J. His works include the songs: To a hill-
top; The road to spring; In a southern garden.

*CUPPETT, CHARLES HAROLD
b. Coquimbo, Chile, 25 June 1894. Studied at
Ohio Wesleyan Univ., B. S., Phi Beta Kappa. He
was organist and choirmaster; composer and conductor for commercial films.
    WORKS: Opera: Le baiser; Orchestra: piano
concerto; Indigo moon; Lament for the living,
suite for piano and orch.

*CURRY, W. LAWRENCE
b. Parnassus, Pa., 19 Mar. 1906; d. Pa., 28 Feb.
1966. Studied at Univ. of Pennsylvania, B. A.,
Phi Beta Kappa; Union Theological Seminary,
M. S. M., S. M. D. He was lecturer, Univ. of
Pennsylvania, 1931-38; instructor, Beaver Coll.,
1929-35, glee club conductor, 1935-59; chairman
of music department, 1935-66; minister of music,
First Methodist Church, Philadelphia, 1932-66;
conductor of various choral groups; editor and
music consultant.
    WORKS: Songs: Psalm of gratitude; God is
our refuge; Sing ye! Sing the savior's birth;
Lincoln speaks; many liturgical works.

*CUTTER, MURRAY
b. Nice, France, 15 Mar. 1902. His works include a ballet, The snow queen, and special
material for films.

*DARBY, KENNETH LORIN
b. Hebron, Neb., 13 May 1909. Studied with
Tibor Serly, Ernst Toch, Herman Hand, and
Victor Young. He founded The King's Men, male
quartet, 1929, and Ken Darby's Singers; was
writer, producer, music supervisor, and conductor for Walt Disney Studios. His works include
The lake, symphonic suite for orchestra; many
songs; and the film score, How the West was won.

*DARCY, THOMAS F., JR.
b. Vancouver, Wash., 7 May 1895; d. Studied at
Juilliard School and Army Bandmaster's School.
In World War I he was the youngest bandmaster in
the regular army; received many medals in his
army career; was commissioned Captain in 1953.
His works for band included The U.S. Army march;
March of the free peoples; An American overture.

*D'ARTEGA, ALFONSO
b. Silao, Guanajuato, Mexico, 5 June 1907.
Studied with Boris Levenson, Strassberger Cons.
He has been conductor for radio, theatre, rec-
ords, films, and concerts, including the Buffalo
Philharmonic, Stadium Symphony, Miami Symphony,
Symphony of the Air, St. Louis Symphony, New
London Symphony; and Radio-Television Italia in
Milan and Rome.
    WORKS: Orchestra: American panorama; Niag-
ara Falls; Fire and ice ballet; Romanesque
suite; and songs.

*DAVENPORT, DAVID N.
b. Richmond, Ind., 27 Sep. 1925. Studied at
Indiana Univ., B. A., M. A. He has been choral
conductor at festivals and guest conductor at
Hollywood Bowl. He has published many works for
chorus.
    3536 Woods Drive, Richmond, IN 47374

*DAVID, VINCENT (pseudonym)
b. Hudson Falls, N. Y., 19 Sep. 1924. Studied
at Juilliard School; at Columbia Univ.; and with
Wallingford Riegger. He was violin soloist with
symphony orchestras at age 12, later violinist
in symphony and dance orchestras. He received a
Ballet Society commission, 1947.

DAVID, VINCENT

(DAVID, VINCENT)
    WORKS: Orchestra: <u>Introduction and scherzo</u>;
<u>Oriental fantasy</u>; <u>Fantasia</u> for clarinet and cham-
ber orch.; <u>Reverie</u>; <u>An American portrait</u>; Chamber music: <u>Fantasia</u>, clarinet and piano; string
quartet; <u>Suite for unaccompanied violin</u>; <u>The</u>
<u>return</u>, voice and piano.

*DAVIDSON, HAROLD P.
    b. New York, N. Y., 19 July 1908. Studied at
Pomona Coll., B. A.; Claremont Coll., M. A.; and
at Univ. of Southern California. He has taught
in high school and at Claremont Coll.; has been
professor and chairman, music department, California State Polytechnic Univ., from 1936.
    WORKS: Songs: <u>Pardon for puns</u>; <u>Derby ram</u>;
<u>Love's delights</u>; <u>Miserere meus, Deo</u>.
    California State Polytechnic Univ.
    San Luis Obispo, CA 93401

*DAVIS, GENEVIEVE
    b. Falconer, N. Y., 11 Dec. 1889; d. Plainfield,
N. J., 3 Dec. 1950. Studied piano with Adolph
Frey, Syracuse Univ. She was pianist and vocal
soloist; her compositions were chiefly songs and
piano pieces.

*DAVIS, JOHN CARLYLE
    b. Cincinnati, Ohio, 31 Mar. 1878; d. Wyoming,
Ohio, 17 July 1948. Studied at Cincinnati Coll.
of Music and Harvard Univ.; received the Springer
Gold Medal. He was reporter on the Cincinnati
Post; founder and director, Wyoming Inst. of
Musical Art; church organist-choirmaster,
1904-17; inventor of improvements on the piano
and electric pipe organ.
    WORKS: Orchestra: violin concerto; <u>About</u>
<u>the world</u>, suite; <u>3 dances</u>, piano and orch.;
<u>Zira dances</u>; <u>Valse Vieux Carre</u>; and songs.

*DEACON, MARY CONNOR
    b. Johnson City, Tenn., 22 Feb. 1907. Studied
at East Tennessee State Coll.; also with Frank
LaForge, William Stickler, and Carl Deis. She
was church organist, 1936-42; taught at Royal
Cons., Toronto. Her published songs include
<u>Ocean lore</u>; <u>I will lift mine eyes</u>; <u>Beside still</u>
<u>waters</u>; <u>Your cross</u>; <u>Hear my prayer</u>; <u>Follow the</u>
<u>road</u>; <u>Call of the sea</u>.

*DECRESCENZO, VINCENZO
    b. Naples, Italy, 18 Feb. 1875; to U.S. 1903;
d. New York, N. Y., 13 Oct. 1964. Studied at
conservatories in Naples, Palermo, and Sicily.
He was accompanist for Caruso, Gigli, Schipa,
De Luca, Galli Curci, Albanese. He wrote many
songs.

*DEPPEN, JESSIE L.
    b. Detroit, Mich., 10 July 1881; d. Los Angeles,
Calif., 22 Jan. 1956. Studied with Adolph
Weidig and Leopold Godowsky, American Cons. She
made her debut as pianist in Steinway Hall, New
York, in 1896. Her compositions are chiefly
songs and piano pieces.

*DE SANTIS, EMIDIO
    b. Aquila, Italy, 18 May 1893; U.S. citizen
1921. He played clarinet in the Providence
Symphony, 1918-30, with various bands from 1918;
president of his own record and publishing company. His works include 3 clarinet concertos;
6 concertinos for orchestra; several military
marches.

*DIGGLE, ROLAND
    b. London, England, 1 Jan. 1887; to U.S. 1904;
d. Los Angeles, Calif., 13 Jan. 1954. Studied
music in London and Oxford. He was organist
and choirmaster in Wichita, Kan., and Quincy,
Ill., before going to St. John's Church, Los
Angeles in 1914.
    WORKS: Orchestra: <u>Concert overture</u>; <u>Fairy</u>
<u>suite</u>; <u>Legend</u>; <u>California suite</u>; <u>American fan-</u>
<u>tasy</u>; Chamber music: Trio for organ, violin,
harp; violin sonata; cello sonata; 2 string
quartets; <u>Sonata gothique</u>; organ pieces and hymn
tunes.

*DI JULIO, MAX
    b. Philadelphia, Pa., 10 Oct. 1919. Studied at
Univ. of Denver, B. M., M. M. E.; with Darius
Milhaud at Aspen School. He was trumpeter in
the Air Force band in World War II; then staff
arranger, KOA, Denver; has been guest conductor,
Denver Symphony; professor and chairman, music
department, Loretto Heights Coll., from 1946.
    WORKS: Opera: <u>Baby Doe</u>; Musical: <u>Boom</u>
<u>town</u>; Songs: <u>All the year 'round</u>, cycle; <u>Shep-</u>
<u>herds, awake</u>; <u>Little children, listen</u>.
    Loretto Heights College
    Denver, CO 80130

*DRUMMOND, DEAN
    <u>Suite</u> for clarinet.
    California Institute of the Arts
    Valencia, CA 91355

*DUARTE, JOHN W.
    b. 1919. <u>Variations on a Catalan folk song</u> for
guitar.

*DUDDY, JOHN H.
    b. Norristown, Pa., 19 Dec. 1904. Studied at
Temple Univ., B. M., M. A.; Philadelphia Musical
Acad.; Christian Church School; Westminster
Choir Coll.; Princeton Univ.; and with
H. Alexander Matthews. He was church organist
and teacher in various schools; chairman of
vocal department, Lutheran Theological Seminary,
Philadelphia. He has written many songs, organ
pieces, and choral works.

*DUDLEY, MARJORIE EASTWOOD
    b. S. Dak. Has written a piano concerto, a sym-
phony, string quartet, many works for chamber
groups and vocal solos.

*DU PAGE, RICHARD
    b. Kansas City, Mo., 10 Aug. 1908. Studied at
Washington and Lee Univ.; Vanderbilt Law School;
music with Rubin Goldmark, Aurelio Giorni, John
Erb, and Tibor Serly. He received a commission
from the Saratoga Spa Music Festival. He has

(DU PAGE, RICHARD)
been arranger for stage shows, dance orchestras, radio; conducted the Sperry (Gyroscope) Orchestra; was staff member, WOR, 1946-53.
WORKS: Orchestra: Polyrhythmic overture; Variations on an Irish theme; Prelude for harp and orch.; Prelude and blues for symphony orchestra; Symphonic song; In the valley of Morpheus; Afghanistan; and several suites for orch.

*EICHHORN, HERMENE WARLICK
b. Hickory, N. C., 3 Apr. 1906. Studied at Univ. of North Carolina, B. S. M.; and privately. She has been organist, Holy Trinity Episcopal Church, Greensboro, from 1926, and choirmaster from 1932; wrote music column for the Greensboro Daily News, 1928-51. Her works include 3 cantatas; Mary Magdalene; Song of the highest; First Corinthians.
1504 Kirkpatrick Place, Greensboro, NC 27408

*ELLIOTT, ALONZO
b. Manchester, N. H., 25 May 1891; d. Wallingford, Conn., 24 June 1964. Studied at Yale Univ., B. A.; Trinity Coll., Cambridge, England; Columbia Law School; with Nadia Boulanger, American Cons., Fontainebleau; and with Leonard Bernstein. He received the Joseph Vernon Prize in 1914.
WORKS: Opera: El chivato; Songs: There's a long, long trail a'winding; Bristol Eighth, Masefield text; Tulips; and many others.

*ELLSASSER, RICHARD
b. Cleveland, Ohio, 14 Sep. 1926. Studied at Oberlin Coll.; Baldwin-Wallace Coll., B. M.; New York Univ.; Boston Univ., School of Theology; Univ. of Southern California, School of Religion, M. Th. He received a Henry Levitt award; is life member, Internat. Inst. of Arts and Letters, Switzerland. He was organ soloist with a symphony orchestra at age 7; made New York debut in 1937; has given organ concerts in the U.S., Canada, Latin America, and Europe.
WORKS: Ballet: Greenwich Village; Orchestra: organ concerto; Chorus: The decalogue (10 anthems); Only the valiant.

*ENDERS, HARVEY
b. St. Louis, Mo., 13 Oct. 1892; d. New York, N. Y., 12 Jan. 1947. Studied at Washington Univ.; voice with David Bispham. He was baritone soloist in churches; also a banker.
WORKS: Chorus: To the Great Pyramids; Death in Harlem; Russian picnic; and songs.

*EPHROS, GERSHON
b. Serotzk, Poland, 15 Jan. 1890. Studied at Inst. of Jewish Music, Jerusalem; also with Hermann Spielter and Joseph Achron. He was cantor in the New York area, 1919-57; instructor, School of Sacred Music, Hebrew Union Coll., 1948-58.
WORKS: Chamber music: string quartet; Chorus: Children's suite, on poems of Bialik; Biblical suite, with soloist and orch.; Midnight penitential service, with soloist and orch.; Friday evening service; L'Yom Hashabbat; also a 5-volume Cantorial anthology; Album of Jewish folksongs.

*ERDODY, LEO
b. Chicago, Ill., 17 Dec. 1888; d. Los Angeles, Calif., 5 Apr. 1949. Studied violin with Joseph Joachim and Emanuel Wirth; composition with Max Bruch in Berlin. He was a film composer and conductor.
WORKS: Opera: Peasants' love; The terrible meek; and songs.

*ETTORE, EUGENE
b. New Bedford, Mass., 2 June 1921. He has won awards for accordion compositions. He is an instrumental consultant, Major Music School, Irvington, N. J., editor and arranger for music publishers.
WORKS: Accordion: Manhattan concerto; Pioneer concerto; Contrast; Prelude and scherzo; Concert etude No. 2, etc.
9 Millstone Drive, Box 210
Livingston, NJ 07039

*FARLEY, ROLAND
b. Aspen, Col., 17 Mar. 1892; d. New York, N. Y., 11 May 1932. Studied at State School of the Deaf and Blind, Colorado Springs; Royal Cons. of Leipzig. He composed many songs including Oh Mother, my love; The night wind; A lark went singing; At sunset; etc.

*FICHTHORN, CLAUDE L.
b. Reading, Pa., 7 June 1885. Studied at Missouri Valley Coll., B. A., Honorary D. M.; Columbia Univ., M. A. He was organist-choirmaster in Reading, Pa., and Kansas City, Mo.; then dean and professor, School of Music, Missouri Valley Coll., chairman of music department from 1947.
WORKS: Chorus: O saving victim, a cappella; In Judea's hills; The everlasting light; also sacred songs and organ pieces.

*FIELDS, IRVING
b. New York, N. Y., 4 Aug. 1915. Studied at Eastman School of Music. His compositions include An American forest, a symphony; and Latin American songs.

*FLICK-FLOOD, DORA
b. Cleveland, Ohio, 3 Aug. Studied at Sanster Music School; Baldwin-Wallace Coll; also with Sigismund Stojowski; held 5 piano scholarships. She gave concerts in the U.S. and Europe; taught in Cleveland public schools and at Tucker School. Her published works include Tango del Prado for band; choral works, songs, piano pieces.

*FORSYTH, CECIL
b. London, England, 30 Nov. 1870; to U.S. 1914; d. New York, N. Y., 7 Dec. 1941. Studied at Edinburgh Univ.; Royal Coll. of Music, London. He was an executive in a New York publishing firm to 1941.
WORKS: Comic opera: Westward Ho!; Cinderella; Orchestra: Chant Celtique, viola and orch.; viola concerto; Studies after Les Miserables; Ode to a nightingale.

FRANGKISER, CARL M.

*FRANGKISER, CARL M.
b. Loudonville, Ohio, 18 Sep. 1894; d. Lee's
Summit, Mo. Studied at Capito Coll. of Music,
B. M., M. M., D. M.; U.S. Band School. He was
an army band conductor in World War I; played
cornet in theatres and touring shows, and in the
Buffalo Bill, Sells-Floto, and Barnum and Bailey
circuses; conducted park concerts in Kansas City
area for 38 years; taught at Kansas City Cons.;
was music director and editor, Unity School of
Christianity from 1925.
WORKS: Band: The victorious; 3 Gates of
gold; Hickory hill; Transcendence; Dedication;
Stratosphere; Mightier than circumstance; and
others.

*FRANK, RENE
b. Mulhouse, Alsace-Lorraine, 16 Feb. 1910; to
U.S. 1947; d. Fort Wayne, Ind., 21 Mar. 1965.
Studied in Germany with Hermann Reuter, Wolfgang Fortner, Nikolai Lopatnikoff; Indiana Univ.,
M. M., D. M. He taught in the U.S. Army School
in Kyoto, Japan, 1946-47; then held faculty
posts at Pikeville Coll.; Fort Wayne Bible Coll.,
1951-65; Indiana Univ. Center, 1956-64.
WORKS: Opera: Call of Gideon, 1-act; Orchestra: 5 psalms, voice and orch.; Passion
symphony; Little suite; Chamber music; piano
sonatina; violin sonata; string quartet; Chorus:
The spite of Michal, cantata, Ernest Bloch award;
The prodigal son; And God came, Christmas oratorio; Songs: Triptych of heavenly love, song
cycle.

*FREED, WALTER
b. Spokane, Wash., 17 June 1903. Studied at
Univ. of Southern California on scholarship; won
a Paul Whiteman national contest for modern American music. He was theatre organist and teacher
of piano and organ.
WORKS: Ballet: The what-not shelf; Orchestra: Fiesta; Concerto in minature, piano and
orch.; and songs.

*FREEMAN, NED
b. Hallowell, Me., 27 Dec. 1895. Studied with
John Orth, Stuart Mason, and Philip Greeley
Clapp. He was pianist and arranger for theatre
and dance orchestras, radio, and films. His
works include Gallery, 12 sketches for orch.;
and songs.

*FREUDENTHAL, JOSEF
b. Leisa, Germany, 1 Mar. 1903; to U.S. 1936;
d. New York, N. Y., 5 May 1964. Studied in
Frankfurt and Munich. He lived in Palestine
before coming to the U.S.; founded Transcontinental Music Corp.
WORKS: Songs: The last words of David; Let
us sing unto the Lord; Precepts of Micah; A lamp
unto my feet; The earth is the Lord's.

*GEARHART, LIVINGSTON
b. Buffalo, N. Y., 31 Dec. 1916. Studied at
Grace Church Choir School; Curtis Inst. of Music;
with Nadia Boulanger and Darius Milhaud. He was
pianist in hotel and night club orchestras; on

(GEARHART, LIVINGSTON)
Fred Waring radio show, 1943-54; then associate
professor, State Univ. of New York at Buffalo.
WORKS: Chamber music: Suite for woodwinds;
Piano: Rhapsody for 2 pianos; American sketch;
Devil's dream; Dynamo.
Music Department
State University of New York
Buffalo, NY 14214

*GOLDSWORTHY, WILLIAM ARTHUR
b. Cornwall, England, 8 Feb. 1878; to U.S. 1887;
d. Studied organ with Samuel P. Warren in New
York. He was organist-choirmaster in New York
churches, at St. Mark's-in-the-Bouwerie,
1926-42.
WORKS: Opera: The Queen of Sheba; The
return of the star, music drama; The prophet,
oratorio; Organ: Majesty; Scherzo.

*GOLLAHON, GLADYS
b. Cincinnati, Ohio, 8 Apr. 1908. She has published sacred and secular songs including Our
Lady of Fatima.

*GOMEZ, VICENTE
b. Madrid, Spain, 8 July 1911; U.S. citizen
1943. Studied at Madrid Cons. Since the age
of 13 he has given guitar recitals in Spain,
Europe, North Africa, Cuba, Mexico, Venezuela
and the U.S.
WORKS: Guitar: Canción de la primavera;
Lamento gitano; Melody of Spain; El albaicin;
Carnival in Spain; La farruca; Granada arabe;
Film score: Blood and sand.

*GROSS, BETHUEL
b. Leavenworth, Kan., 7 Mar. 1905. Studied at
Washburn Coll., B. A., B. M.; Northwestern Univ.,
B. M., B. M. E., M. M., Ph. D.; Univ. of Chicago;
Loyola Univ. He has held faculty and administrative posts at Univ. of Akron, Illinois
Wesleyan Univ., Shurtleff Coll., De Paul Univ.,
Chicago Cons., Baker School of Fine Arts, Northwest School of Fine Arts, Loyola Univ. at Chicago; has been organist and music director in
Chicago churches from 1940.
WORKS: Orchestra: 6 organ symphonies; 2
symphonic poems; Chorus: The lost star; Reflec-
tions on Christmas, oratorio; 5 modal carols; 6
modernistic carols; and songs.

*GUMP, RICHARD
b. San Francisco, Calif., 22 Jan. 1906. Studied
at Stanford Univ.; California School of Fine
Arts; with Dominico Brescia. He joined the
staff of Gump's Retail Store in 1925, has been
president since 1947; under the pseudonym
Dr. Fritz Guckenheimer he organized the
Guckenheimer Sauer Kraut Band in 1948.
WORKS: Orchestra: 7 variations on an American theme; Polynesian impression; Chamber music:
clarinet quintet; violin sonata; piano sonata;
Cambodian impression for string quartet; oboe
sonata; Fantasia, piano 4-hands; Chorus: Gift
of December, cantata; and songs.

*HAACK, BRUCE C.
b. Alberta, Canada, 4 May 1932. Studied at Univ.
of Alberta, B. A. He has received commissions
from the New York Orpheum Symphony and the New
York Ballet Club. He founded the publishing
firm, Dimension 5.
WORKS: Stage scores: How to make a man;
The kumquat in the persimmon tree; Ballet: The
constant she; Les etapes; Orchestra: Windsong;
Sweet Adeline; Piano: Mass for solo piano.

*HAEUSSLER, PAUL
b. Ravena, N. Y., 13 July 1895. Studied with
Felix Deyo, Brooklyn Cons. He was organist,
Ainslee Street Presbyterian Church, Brooklyn,
for 25 years. His works include sacred songs
and choral pieces.

*HAJOS, KARL
b. Budapest, Hungary, 28 Jan. 1889; d. Hollywood,
Calif., 1 Feb. 1950. Studied at Budapest Acad.
of Music. He settled in Hollywood in 1928 as a
film composer.
WORKS: Operetta: The black Pierrot; The
red cat; Natja; White lilacs; America sings;
Orchestra: Phantasy, piano and orch.; Rhapsody
in waltz time; and many film scores.

*HALPERN, LEON
b. New York, N. Y., 15 May 1908. Studied at
Damrosch Cons.; Juilliard School; and with Howard
Brockway. His works include the ballet, Angels
and prejudices.

*HANDY, GEORGE (GEORGE JOSEPH HENDLEMAN)
b. Brooklyn, N. Y., 1920. His instrumental compositions include New York suite and 3 quartets for
the New York Saxophone Quartet, 1964-65. He has
also written popular songs.

*HARPER, MARJORIE
b. St. Paul, Minn., 26 Apr.   . Studied with
Rubin Goldmark and Alexander Lambert. She has
published anthems, songs, and piano pieces.
146 Belmont Ave., Jersey City, NJ 07304

*HARRIS, EDWARD C.
b. Elizabeth, N. J., 16 Feb. 1899. Attended
East Liberty Acad., Pittsburgh; studied music
privately. He was accompanist to Lawrence
Tibbett and Georges Enesco; music critic on the
San Francisco Bulletin, 1928-29; has made concert tours in Canada, Australia, New Zealand,
Africa, South America; was church organist,
Plymouth, Mass., 1943-46; was private voice
teacher. He composed many songs and piano
pieces.

*HARRIS, JERRY WESELEY
b. The Dalles, Ore., 21 Oct. 1933. Studied at
Lewis and Clark Coll., M. A.; Univ. of Oregon,
D. Ed. He has been head of the music department,
Sunset High School, Beaverton, from 1956; violist
in Portland Symphony and Portland Chamber Orchestra; director of church music; editor, Oregon
Music Educators Journal, from 1958. He has written many sacred choruses.

*HEATON, WALLACE
b. Philadelphia, Pa., 31 Jan. 1914. Studied at
West Chester State Coll.; Philadelphia Musical
Acad., B. M., M. M.; composition with Stefan
Wolpe; received honorary D. M., Combs Coll. of
Music. He organized the music department of
Drexel Technological Inst. and became professor
and department chairman. He has taught also
at Philadelphia Musical Acad.; Crozer Theologi-
cal Seminary; and privately; is church organist
in the Philadelphia area.
WORKS: Chorus: Great among nations; Fes-
tival piece; God, my king.
Music Department, Drexel University
Philadelphia, PA 19104

*HEYWARD, SAMUEL EDWIN, JR.
b. Savannah, Ga., 26 Mar. 1904. Studied music
at the New England Cons. He was a singer and
played viola in symphonies and chamber groups.
WORKS: Chamber music: Suite for violin;
Chorus: Ballad for Harry Moore; Cradle to
grave; The love cycle.

*HIGGINSON, JOSEPH VINCENT
b. Irvington, N. J., 17 May 1896. Studied at
Manhattan Coll. of Music; New York Univ., B. A.,
M. A.; Juilliard School; Pius X School of Litur-
gical Music; with Percy Goetschius, Marion Bauer,
Albert Stoessel, Philip James, and Charles
Haubiel. He was organist-choirmaster, St.
Catherine of Alexander, Brooklyn; managing edi-
tor, Catholic Choirmaster; taught at Pius X
School and in private schools. His works in-
clude Magdalen, a tone poem for orchestra; and
sacred songs.

*HILLEBRAND, FRED
b. Brooklyn, N. Y., 25 Dec. 1893; d. New York,
N. Y., 15 Sep. 1963. Studied at Juilliard
School. His works include an opera, Southland;
and operetta, The swing princess; stage and
television scores; and songs.

*HOFFELT, ROBERT O.
b. Springfield, Mo., 1920. Studied at Illinois
Wesleyan Univ., B. M., 1942; with Francis J.
Pyle, Drake Univ., M. M. Ed. 1946. He was faculty member, Drake Univ., 1946-49; Michigan
State Normal Coll., 1949-57; Jacksonville Univ.,
1958-64; manager of music resources, Abingdon
Press, from 1964. His published works include
Not alone for mighty empire for male chorus.
c/o Abingdon Press
201 Eighth Ave. South, Nashville, TN 37202

*HOFFMANN, ADOLF G.
b. Cincinnati, Ohio, 30 May 1890; d. Studied
at Cincinnati Coll. of Music; with Adolf Brune
and Adolf Weidig; received the Springer Medal.
He was cellist in string quartets, Chicago Symphony, and Chicago Grand Opera Company, orchestra manager, cellist, arranger, and conductor,
Chicago Theatre, 1921; staff member WGN and
WGN-TV from 1934; faculty member, De Paul Univ.
and American Cons.
WORKS: Orchestra: a symphony; Chicago
Theatre of the Air theme; Chamber music: Prelude

HOFFMANN, ADOLF G.

(HOFFMANN, ADOLF G.)
and fugue, string quartet, harp, celeste; Suite for bassoon and piano; string quartet.

*HOLLANDER, RALPH
b. Brooklyn, N. Y., 9 Nov. 1916. Studied at Juilliard School; Manhattan Coll. of Music, M. A. He has been concert violinist in the U.S. and Europe; soloist with the Longine Symphonette.
WORKS: Orchestra: Galmud, tone poem; Elegie for strings; Chamber music: Gitana, violin and piano; Psalms of David I and II, violin and speech chorus.

*HOLLER, JOHN
b. New York, N. Y., 13 Jan. 1904. Studied organ with Norman Coke-Jephcott, David Williams, and Charles Banks. He was organist-choirmaster, St. Mark's Church, New York; associate editor with a music publishing firm. He has composed sacred choral works.

*HOLMES, G. E.
b. Baraboo, Wis., 14 Feb. 1873; d. Chicago, Ill., 10 Feb. 1945. Studied music privately. He taught at Prior's Cons., Danville, Ill., and at Vandercook School of Music, Chicago. His published works included many band marches and songs.

*HOVDESVEN, E. A.
b. Lyon County, Minn., 4 May 1893. Studied at St. Olaf Coll., B. A., B. M.; Juilliard School; Toronto Univ., D. M.; Fontainebleau Cons. He is Associate, Royal Coll. of Organists, England, and Fellow, Canadian Coll. of Organists. He has toured as concert and theatre organist; taught at St. Olaf's Coll.; Mercersberg Acad., Pa.; North Texas State Univ.; Warburg Coll.; retired in 1963.
WORKS: Orchestra: organ concerto; symphony; also many choral works and organ pieces.

*JOHNSON, JAMES P.
b. New Brunswick, N. J., 1 Feb. 1891; d. New York, N. Y., 17 Nov. 1955. Studied music privately. He made his professional debut in 1904; played in theatres, night clubs, films; formed own band and toured Europe; was accompanist to Bessie Smith, Ethel Waters, and others.
WORKS: Opera: Dreamy kid; De organizer, folk opera; Operetta: The husband; Kitchen opera; Ballet: Sefronia's dream; Manhattan street scene; Orchestra: Symphonic Harlem; Symphony in brown; African drums; piano concerto; Mississippi moon; Yamacraw, negro rhapsody; Symphonic suite on St. Louis Blues; City of steel; and popular songs.

*JONES, DAVID HUGH
b. Jackson, Ohio, 25 Feb. 1900. Studied at Guilmant Organ School; American Cons., Fontainebleau; with T. Tertius Noble, Henri Libert, Marcel Dupre, Andre Bloch, Charles Widor; Washington and Jefferson Coll., D. M.; Beaver Coll., D. M. He was organist in Ohio and New York, 1917-26; was chairman, organ department, Westminster Choir Coll., Dayton, 1926-29; chairman,

(JONES, DAVID HUGH)
composition, Westminster Choir Coll., Ithaca, 1929-32; and in Princeton, N. J., 1932-51; director of music, Princeton Theological Seminary, 1947-51, professor from 1951; visiting professor in Cuba, 1955-56. He has composed many anthems and sacred songs.

*JONES, STEPHEN OSCAR
b. New York, N. Y., 12 July 1880; d. Studied at the New York German Cons. He was arranger for Broadway musicals.
WORKS: Orchestra: Rondo a la breve; Rondo appassionato; Alaska overture; Serenade and valse; Top brass; Chamber music: string quartet; String sonata; Chorus: Evensong, male voices; and songs.

*JOUARD, PAUL E.
b. Mt. Vernon, N. Y., 28 May 1928. Studied at Yale Univ., B. M., M. M.; with Percy Grainger and Clarence Adler, Juilliard School. He is concert pianist; and has been conductor, Lake Placid Club Orchestra from 1949.
WORKS: Piano: Prelude and fugue; Modal variations on a French air; Sonata romantica; Playland suite.

*KEMPINSKI, LEO A.
b. Ruda, Germany, 25 Mar. 1891; to U.S. 1908; d. Hampton, Conn., 25 May 1958. Studied at Breslau Univ.; with Percy Goetschius at Juilliard School. He was church organist in Philadelphia; music director in theatres; editor for a music publishing firm.
WORKS: Orchestra: Victory concerto, piano and orch.; also many marches, songs, music for films and radio.

*KINDER, RALPH
b. Stalybridge, England, 27 Jan. 1876; to U.S. 1881; d. Bala, Pa., 14 Nov. 1952. Was organist in Bristol, R. I.; in Philadelphia, 1899-37; then in Whitemarsh, Pa. He composed numerous organ pieces, anthems, and songs.

*KLEINMAN, ISADOR I.
b. New York, N. Y., 25 Jan. 1913. Held a Damrosch scholarship for study of violin and viola, 1920-30. He played in theatre orchestras; Roxy Theatre Orchestra, 1946-49; American Symphony, 1954; from 1958 with Little Orchestra Society.
WORKS: Orchestra: Musical offering; Suite for strings; Tel Aviv, tone poem; violin concerto; viola concerto.

*KLENZ, WILLIAM
Songs: Walk the silver night, Bevington text; Hush, Robert Nathan text.
Department of Music
State University of New York
Binghamton, NY 13901

*KRANCE, JOHN P., JR.
b. Bridgeport, Conn., 25 June 1935. Studied on scholarship at Eastman School of Music, B. M. He has been staff member at radio stations in

(KRANCE, JOHN P., JR.)
Rochester and Washington, D.C.; was in U.S. Army, 1955-58; editorial assistant, MPHC, 1958-59; then became music director, WPAT, Paterson, N. J.
WORKS: Orchestra: Epitaphs; Signatures and fanfares; Prelude to Christmas; Band: Scenario; Symphonic fanfares; Dialogue for trumpet and band; Chamber music: Metamorphosis, chamber ensemble.

*KRANE, SHERMAN M.
b. New Haven, Conn., 18 Nov. 1927. Studied at Hartt Coll. of Music, B. M., M. M.; Michigan State Univ., Ph. D. He has taught in private and public schools; at Hartt Coll.; Michigan State Univ.; was visiting lecturer, Experimental Coll., Virgin Islands; became music director, Bernard Horwich Jewish Community Center, Chicago.
WORKS: Opera: The giant's garden; and film scores.

*LACKEY, DOUGLAS M.
b. Sacramento, Calif., 10 Aug. 1932. Studied at Univ. of California, Los Angeles.
WORKS: Drum and coco, percussion sextet; also film background scores and music for commercial films.

*LANGE, ARTHUR
b. Philadelphia, Pa., 16 Apr. 1889; d. Washington, D.C., 7 Dec. 1956. Studied music privately. He was arranger for dance orchestras and musicals in New York; head of music department, MGM, 1929; music director for other film studios; organized and conducted Santa Monica Symphony, 1947-56.
WORKS: Orchestra: a symphony; Symphonette romantique; Symphonette spirituelle; Water whispers suite; etc.; film scores; songs.

*LANGENDOEN, JACOBUS C.
b. The Hague, Neth., 3 Feb. 1890. Studied at the Netherlands Royal Cons.; cello with Joseph Malkin and Isaac Moisel. He was cellist in The Hague Orchestra, 1908-10; Royal Opera, 1914-17; with Boston Pops Orchestra, 1920-62.
WORKS: Orchestra: Improvisations; Puppet, trumpet and orch.; Variations on a Dutch theme.

*LANGENUS, GUSTAVE
b. Malines, Belgium, 6 Aug. 1883; to U.S. 1910; d. Commack, N. Y., 30 Jan. 1957. Studied at Malines Music School; Royal Cons., Brussels. He toured with Sousa's Band in Europe; played clarinet in orchestras in England; then in New York Symphony; New York Philharmonic; NBC Symphony; with the Perole Quartet and Budapest Quartet; was co-founder of the New York Chamber Music Society; taught at Juilliard School, Dalcroze School; and elsewhere; was guest band conductor. His compositions include Swallows flight, for flute, clarinet and orch.; and many pieces for small ensembles.

*LEFEVERE, KAMIEL
b. Malines, Belgium, 24 Nov. 1888. Studied at Belgian Acad. of Fine Arts; Internat. Carillon School, Belgium. He became assistant

(LEFEVERE, KAMIEL)
carilloneur at the school; then carilloneur in England, France, Holland; in Cohasset and Gloucester, Mass., 1924-30; from 1927 in New York City. He was author of 2 books: Bells over Belgium and Carillons and singing towers in the U.S. and Canada. He composed many works for carillon.

*LEONARDI, LEONID
b. Moscow, Russia, 27 July 1901; to U.S. 1923; d. Studied with Maurice Ravel, Vincent d'Indy, Nadia Boulanger, Paris Cons.; also with Anton Rubinstein. He made his debut as pianist at the Imperial Court at age 9; toured Europe in recitals. In the U.S. he was music director in New York and St. Louis theatres; conductor for musicals, films, radio in New York; in World War II music director, 11th Naval District, San Diego.
WORKS: Theatre: Song of the forest, lyric drama; Orchestra: The song of America; Blue Ridge rhapsody, piano and orch.; Freedom's plow, narrator and orch.; Chamber music: Manhattan vignettes, for woodwinds; and piano pieces.

*LEVAN, LOUIS
b. Russia, 15 Sep. 1906. Studied violin with Leopold Auer in New York. He organized and conducted the New York Student Symphony. His compositions include 3 violin concertos, 4 violin sonatas; and songs. He is author of The foundation of the violin.

*LOBODA, SAMUEL
b. Coy, Pa., 21 May 1916. Attended Indiana (Pa.) State Teachers Coll., B. S.; Army Music School. He was army officer and band leader; then executive officer, Army Music School.
WORKS: Band: For God and country, official American Legion march; The screaming eagles; The 101st Airborne march; Chorus: Lift up your heads; The story of the stranger.

*LOHOEFER, EVELYN (pseudonym)
b. Clinton, N. C., 28 Dec. 1921. Studied at Univ. of North Carolina, B. S.; on scholarship at Bennington Coll.; with Sigismund Stojowski, Norman Lloyd, and Vittorio Giannini at Juilliard School. She was accompanist for a USO dance tour of Europe, 1944; assistant to Norman and Ruth Lloyd, College School of Dance, New London, Conn., 1954-59; then private teacher in New York and Washington.
WORKS: Ballet: Shakers; Pony tails; Madeline and the bad hat; Modern fantasy; Conversation piece.

*LOVINGWOOD, PENNMAN, SR.
b. 25 Dec. 1895. Attended Samuel Huston Coll.; Temple Univ. He was church soloist, 1928-32; member of W. C. Handy's group, 1930; organized the Drum and Bugle Corp in Englewood, N. J. in 1942. He has received the Wanamaker prize and the Griffith Music Found. Silver-bronze medal.
WORKS: Opera: Menelik; Evangeline and Gabriel; and songs.

McCLEARY, FIONA

*McCLEARY, FIONA
b. Sanderstead, Surrey, England, 29 Jan. 1900;
U.S. citizen 1932. Studied with Myra Hess,
Harriet Cohen, Ralph Vaughan Williams, Arnold
Bax, Royal Acad. of Music; and at Matthay Piano
School, London. She has given piano recitals
throughout the U.S. Her compositions are for
piano and for small instrumental groups.

*MacFAYDEN, ALEXANDER
b. Milwaukee, Wis., 12 July 1879; d. Milwaukee,
6 June 1936. Studied at Chicago Musical Coll.;
received honorary D. M. from Chicago Cons. He
was a concert pianist; taught at Wisconsin Coll.
of Music and Chicago Cons. The Wisconsin Fed.
of Music Clubs established the MacFayden Memorial
piano competition. He composed many songs.

*McGRAW, CAMERON
b. Cortland, N. Y., 28 Apr. 1919. Studied at
Middlebury Coll., B. A.; Cornell Univ., M. A.;
with Robert Palmer, Roy Harris, and Hunter
Johnson. He taught in private schools, 1943-46;
New York State Coll. of Education, 1947-49;
Cornell Univ., 1950-52; was co-director,
Jenkintown (Pa.) Music School, 1954; member of
2-piano team from 1951.
WORKS: Chorus: These things shall be; 3
French noels; Piano: Almanac; Structures and
designs; Tunes for dessert; Pet silhouettes.

*MACHAN, BENJAMIN A.
b. Cleveland, Ohio, 11 Sep. 1894; d. Woodbury,
Conn., 14 Feb. 1966. Studied piano and composition with his father and made his debut as piano
soloist with the Cleveland Symphony at 5. After
army service in World War I he formed a jazz
band in Paris; on returning to New York he wrote
for films and radio.
WORKS: Orchestra: American concerto, violin and orch.; American suite; Rhapsody in jazz;
Nutmeg suite; Connecticut hymn; many songs; Film
scores: We, the people, documentary; Seeds of
destiny, won Academy award, 1944.

*McKAY, FRANCIS HOWARD
b. Harrington, Wash., 7 Mar. 1901. Studied at
Washington State Coll.; Eastman School of Music;
Univ. of Washington, B. A., M. A.; Northeast
Missouri State Coll.; Univ. of Southern California. He has taught in public schools and colleges in Ketchikan, Alaska from 1955.
WORKS: Orchestra: American sketch; 2 prom-
enades; Woods in April; also pieces for band,
wind ensemble, and chorus.

*McNEIL, JAMES CHARLES
b. Columbia, S. C., 24 Sep. 1902. Studied at
Univ. of Southern California; Chicago Univ.,
B. M.; Chapman Coll., M. M.
WORKS: Orchestra: Judith; Mojave; South
Carolina suite; In the mist; Suite for strings;
also song cycles, cantatas.

*MAINENTE, ANTON EUGENE
b. Paterson, N. J., 5 Nov. 1889; d. Auburn, Me.,
18 Aug. 1963. Studied at New England Cons.,
where he later taught. In Boston he also con-

(MAINENTE, ANTON EUGENE)
ducted opera and played flute in the Boston Pops
Orchestra. During World War I, he taught at the
AEF Bandleaders School; later at Gould Acad.;
Hebron Acad.; formed Mainente School of Music,
1921.
WORKS: Orchestra: Symphony America; Impres-
sions of an afternoon; Reminiscences.

*MAIORANA, VICTOR E. (VICTOR LAMONT)
b. Palermo, Italy, 20 July 1897; to U.S. as a
child; d. New York, N. Y., 18 Oct. 1964. He was
a theatre organist and editor in a music publishing firm. His works for orchestra included
Reflections on the lake; Legend of the canyon.

*MARAIS, JOSEF
b. Sir Lowry Pass, South Africa, 17 Nov. 1905;
U.S. citizen 1945. Studied at South African Coll.
of Music on scholarship; Royal Acad. of Music,
London. He was violinist in the Capetown Symphony; translated Afrikaans folksongs; with his
wife, Miranda, gave vocal concerts; worked with
Office of War Information in Voice of America
broadcasts.
WORKS: Opera: Tony Beaver; Orchestra:
Africana suite; Voice: 14 songs from the veld;
The bangalorey man, for children; many other
songs.

*MARRYOTT, RALPH E.
b. Jamesburg, N. J., 15 Apr. 1908. Attended
Peddie School. He has been minister of music,
director of school music, choral director, and
organist in Jamesburg from 1926. His works
include an organ suite and many sacred songs.

*MAURICE-JACQUET, H.
b. St. Mande, France, 18 Mar. 1886; d. New York,
N. Y., 29 June 1954. Studied at Paris Nat. Cons.
She made her piano debut at 9; toured Europe as
pianist and conductor; founded Union des Femmes
Artistes Musiciennes, Paris; was accompanist to
Grace Moore; taught at School of Vocal Arts,
New York; Acad. of Vocal Arts, Philadelphia;
American Cons. of Music, Drama, and Dance, New
York. Her awards included the French Legion of
Honor and a commission from the French Ministry
of Fine Arts.
WORKS: Opera: Romanitza; Messaoula; Oper-
etta: Le poilu; La petite dactyl; Ballet: Les
danses des chez nous; Orchestra: American sym-
phony; Chorus: The mystic trumpeter.

*MERETTA, LEONARD V.
b. Keiser, Pa., 5 Sep. 1915. Studied at Ernest
Williams School of Music; Univ. of Michigan,
M. M. He played trumpet with Major Bowes group;
has toured as trumpet soloist; taught in public
schools; at Univ. of Michigan, 1941-45; has been
professor and director of bands, Western Michigan Univ. from 1945.
WORKS: Band: Tioga; Men of might; also
pieces for small wind ensembles.
Department of Music
Western Michigan University
Kalamazoo, MI 49001

*MERRIFIELD, NORMAN L.
  b. Louisville, Ky., 19 Nov. 1906. Studied at
Northwestern Univ., B. M. Ed., M. S.; Indiana
Univ.; Jordan Coll. of Music; Army Band School;
Trinity Coll. of Music, London; Michigan State
Coll. He taught at Fisk Univ., 1927-28; was
dean of music, Florida A&M Coll., 1932-34; was
an army bandmaster in World War II; head of music
department, Crispus Attucks High School, Indianapolis, 1932-42 and from 1946. His compositions include a symphony and choral arrangements.

*MILLIGAN, ROY HUGH
  b. New Rochelle, N. Y., 4 Sep. 1922. Studied
at Ernest Williams School of Music, Brooklyn;
at New York Univ., B. S., M. A. He has been
school band instructor from 1946; at East Islip,
N. Y., since 1955. His works for band include
the award winning March Sherwood.

*MITCHELL, RAYMOND EARLE
  b. Milwaukee, Wis., 31 May 1895; d. Studied
with Carl Eppert; on scholarship at Marquette
Univ. He was music critic and editor for the
Hollywood Citizen-News and Musical Courier,
1929-35.
  WORKS: Orchestra: Dusty road; Pastorale
suite; Childhood scenes; Danae's garden; and
songs.

*MONELLO, SPARTACO V.
  b. Boston, Mass., 29 June 1909. Studied with
Edward Burlingame Hill, Walter Piston, Aaron
Copland, Harvard Univ., B. A., M. A.; Univ. of
Grenoble, France; on scholarship at Kenyon Coll.;
with Roger Sessions; and at Columbia Univ.,
D. Ed. He received 2 Hartford Found. fellow-
ships. He was civilian instructor in the Air
Force in World War II; has taught at William and
Mary Coll. and Univ. of California. His works
include Lament for orch. and a symphony for
strings.

*MONTGOMERY, BRUCE
  b. Philadelphia, Pa., 20 June 1927. Studied at
Bethany Coll., B. F. A.; Univ. of Pennsylvania.
He received 2 Univ. of Pennsylvania commissions;
was music director for the University; glee club
director for Special Services in Korean War; was
conductor on a European tour sponsored by the
American Friends Service Comm.
  WORKS: Opera: John Barleycorn; Theatre:
The amorous flea; Spendthrift; Chorus: Make a
joyful noise, cantata; Let us now praise famous
men; 3 haiku.

*MUSOLINO, ANGELO
  b. New York, N. Y., 6 Dec. 1923. Studied with
his father and with Josef Schmid. He taught at
Brooklyn Cons., 1953-56; has since been private
teacher and freelance arranger. His works include a violin sonata and Fugata for piano.

*NATHAN, ROBERT
  b. New York, N. Y., 2 Jan. 1894. Attended
Phillips Exeter Acad. and Harvard Univ. A noted
poet and author, he has also composed a violin
sonata; Dunkirk for orch.; and musical settings
for poems of Walt Whitman.

*NORMAN, THEODORE
  b. Montreal, P.Q., 14 Mar. 1912; U.S. citizen.
Studied in Europe; also with Adolph Weiss and
Willy Hess. He played violin in the Los Angeles
Philharmonic, 1935-42; formed string quartet;
gave a guitar concert of his own works, Paris,
1956; has taught guitar in California.
  WORKS: Ballet: Metamorphosis; Guitar:
Exit; Mobile; two 12-tone pieces. He is author
of a book, The classical guitar.

*OLMSTEAD, CLARENCE
  b. Minneapolis, Minn., 11 July 1892. Studied at
Univ. of Minnesota.
  WORKS: Orchestra: Serenade; Time, voice
and orch.; and songs.

*OLSON, ROBERT G.
  b. Pelican Rapids, Minn., 29 May 1913. Studied
at Univ. of Minnesota, B. A.; Eastman School of
Music, M. A.; Cite Univ. Paris. He has taught
at Bemidji Coll.; Northwood School, Lake Placid;
St. Louis Inst. of Music; Foothill Coll.; was
editor-in-chief for Summy-Birchard for 10 years.
His works include Suite in brief for 2 pianos
and choral pieces.

*PARRY, ROLAND
  b. Ogden, Utah, 7 May 1897. Studied at Weber
Coll., B. A., M. A., and was professor there
from 1935. He received a commission for the
choral work, All faces west. Other works include A child is born for chorus, and songs.

*PAUL, DORIS A.
  b. Upland, Ind., 16 Aug. 1903. Studied at Taylor
Univ., B. A., B. M. Ed.; Northwestern Univ.;
Univ. of Michigan, M. M.; with Fred Waring and
Olaf Christiansen. She has taught in public
schools; at Taylor Univ.; Iowa State Teachers
Coll.; Univ. of Denver.
  WORKS: Chorus: Christmas bells; Thou art
my lamp; Remember now thy creator; 38 introits
and responses.

*PAXTON, GLENN G., JR.
  b. Winnetka, Ill., 7 Dec. 1921. Studied with
Max Wald, Chicago Musical Coll.; at Princeton
Univ., B. A. He received 2 CBS commissions.
  WORKS: Ballet: Postures; Orchestra: The
quiet city; Piano: 4 characteristic pieces;
also stage scores, television scores, and songs.

*PERL, LOTHAR
  b. Breslau, Germany, 1 Dec. 1910. Studied in
Germany. He is pianist and accompanist; has
taught at Los Angeles City Coll. and at Adelphi
Coll.; has composed and conducted for films and
television.
  WORKS: Piano: Dance suite; 4 American
variations on a theme by Paganini.

*PLUMBY, DONALD
  b. Martins Ferry, Ohio, 8 Nov. 1919. Studied at
Univ. of Kentucky. His compositions include
Picture of a hunt, a duo for violin, or flute or
oboe and cello or bassoon; and songs.

POCHON, ALFRED

*POCHON, ALFRED
b. Yverdon, Switzerland, 30 July 1878; U.S. citizen 1928; d. Lutry, Switz., 26 Feb. 1959. Studied violin with Cesar Thomson. He organized the Flonzaley Quartet in 1903 and was second violinist until the quartet disbanded in 1929; organized the Stradivarius Quartet in New York; was director of the Cons. of Lausanne, Switz., 1941-57. His compositions include pieces for string quartet and Passacaglia for viola.

*PORTNOFF, MISCHA
b. Berlin, Germany, 29 Aug. 1901. Studied with his father at Stern Cons., Berlin; Royal Acad. of Stockholm. He conducted his own studio in Brooklyn; composed stage scores and many works for piano.

*PORTNOFF, WESLEY (brother of Mischa Portnoff)
b. Simferopol, Russia, 13 Feb. 1910; d. New York, N. Y. Studied with his father at Stern Cons. in Berlin. He conducted orchestras in the Scandinavian countries for 5 years.
    WORKS: Orchestra: violin concerto; Chamber music: Tempo of Manhattan, suite for violin; also stage scores and ballets.

*RAGLAND, ROBERT OLIVER
b. Chicago, Ill., 3 July 1933. Studied at Northwestern Univ., B. S.; American Cons., B. A., M. A.; with Alexander Tcherepnin and William Russo. He served in the U.S. Navy, 1953-55; is pianist and arranger for dance bands; has scored films in the U.S. and Europe; also television scores.
    WORKS: Orchestra: 12 symphonies; Overture 1861; Chamber music: string quartet; and songs.

*RAPTAKIS, KLEON
b. Andros, Greece, 25 May 1905. Studied at Juilliard School; Columbia Univ. He served in the U.S. Army in World War II; from 1952 has had his own music school.
    WORKS: Orchestra: 3 symphonies; The hero; Chamber music: Sonata for strings; 2 piano sonatas; piano quintet; Voice: Book of Greek songs and dances, including a music history of Greece.

*RASLEY, JOHN M.
b. Davenport, Iowa, 20 Jan. 1913. Studied music privately. He has been director of church choirs and other choral groups from 1941; associate editor and staff composer, Lorenz Music Publishers from 1956.
    WORKS: Chorus: The miracle of Bethlehem, cantata; and sacred songs.

*REDDICK, WILLIAM J.
b. Paducah, Ky., 23 June 1890; d. Detroit, Mich., 18 May 1965. Studied at Cincinnati Coll. of Music; Cincinnati Univ.; with Clarence Adler, Ernest Hutcheson, Rudolph Ganz, and Oliver Denton. He was pianist, organist, accompanist, choral director; was music director, New York Opera Company for 5 years; Chautauqua for 12 summers; taught at Brooklyn Music School, etc.; was founder and music director of the Ford

(REDDICK, WILLIAM J.)
Sunday Evening Hour on radio, 1936-46. His compositions include Espanharlem for chorus; Love in a cottage, a song cycle; and other songs.

*REED, ROBERT B.
b. Philadelphia, Pa., 25 Mar. 1900; d. Studied with Hugh Clark, H. Alexander Matthews, Robert Elmore; Univ. of Pennsylvania, B. M. He was organist-choirmaster, Radnor, Pa., 1925-32, 1942-48; then on staff, Library of Congress.
    WORKS: Chorus: The incarnate word, a Christmas pageant; The Easter story, cantata; Shadow march; The Arkansas traveler, male voices; and songs.

*RIESENFELD, HUGO
b. Vienna, Austria, 26 Jan. 1879; to U.S. 1907; d. Hollywood, Calif., 10 Sep. 1939. Studied on scholarship at Vienna Cons. and at Vienna Univ. He was violinist, Imperial Opera House; Vienna Philharmonic; Mozart Festival, Salzburg, 1904; Bayreuth Festival; concertmaster, Manhattan Opera Company, 1907-11; Century Opera Company, New York, 1915; managing director of 3 New York theatres, 1919-25; music director, Hollywood studio, 1928-30.
    WORKS: Operetta: Merry martyr; Orchestra: Symphonic epos; Chopin ballet; Dramatic overture; Balkan rhapsody; Etchings of New York; Children's suite; American festival overture; and songs.

*ROBINSON, EDWARD
b. New York, N. Y., 28 Jan. 1905; d. New York. Studied on a fellowship with Seth Bingham at Columbia Univ., B. A., M. A. He was music critic, Columbian Daily Spectator; editor and publisher, Fortnightly Music Review, 1928-29; columnist and drama critic, 1934-38; accompanist and piano teacher.
    WORKS: Piano: Chillmark suite; Gay Head dance; The storekeeper's daughter; Variations on a theme by Beethoven; Songs: Stop, look and listen; A child's introduction to science, a song cycle.

*ROSEMONT, WALTER LOUIS
b. Philadelphia, Pa., 16 Aug. 1895; d. Studied at Univ. of Pennsylvania. He was opera and orchestra conductor in the U.S. and Europe; music editor for publishers; foreign correspondent for magazines; teacher.
    WORKS: Orchestra: Troilus and Cressida; Over hill and dale; Fughetta; Regrets in a garden; Scene orientale; Bird ballet; The prophetess; also songs and music for travel films.

*ROTTURA, JOSEPH JAMES
b. Rochester, Pa., 11 Apr. 1929
    WORKS: Chorus: Ballad of Jesse James; The beatitudes; Christmas on the trail; Missa simplex; Overture for voices; We sing of America.

*RUBENS, HUGO
b. New York, N. Y., 1 Apr. 1905; d. He was organist and pianist in film theatres.
    WORKS: Orchestra: Carnegie Hall concerto; Scotland Yard suite; Love's labor lost, overture; and songs.

*RUSCH, HAROLD W.
b. Wabeno, Wis., 14 Oct. 1908. Attended Lawrence Univ.; studied music privately. He received commissions from Univ. of Wisconsin and Thor Johnson. He was public school music supervisor; author of books on instrumental and vocal techniques.
WORKS: Orchestra: trilogy of 3 suites: Menominee sketches, La nouvelle France, Colonial scenes; Band: Levee dance; Camptown drummer; Victory chant; Apostle Islands overture; many marches.

*RYTERBAND, ROMAN
b. Lodz, Poland, 2 Aug. 1914. Studied music in Poland, Switzerland, and at Northwestern Univ. He has been organist, choir director, and pianist in Europe, Africa, and the U.S.; was music director, CKVL radio, Montreal; faculty member, Chicago Cons. Coll.
WORKS: Orchestra: Rhapsody; Toccata for harpsichord and chamber orch., commissioned by Northwestern Univ.; Chamber music: piano sonata; sonata for violin and harp; 2 sonatas for contralto, flute and harp; Chorus: Jubilate Deo.

*ST. CLAIR, FLOYD J.
b. Johnstown, Pa., 4 Feb. 1871; d. Cleveland, Ohio, 23 Aug. 1942. Attended Curry Coll. He was cornetist, band director, and church organist; editor and arranger for music publishers. His works were chiefly marches and other band pieces.

*SALTA, MENOTTI
b. Perugia, Italy, 23 July 1893; U.S. citizen 1936. Studied at Verdi Cons., Milan. He was conductor and arranger for film theatres in New York, 1928-34; with CBS 1928-29; NBC 1930-34; Radio City Music Hall, 1939-40.
WORKS: Ballet: Mirage; Orchestra: Nocturne; Nostalgic serenade; 4 characteristic dances; also piano pieces.

*SAUTER, EDWARD ERNEST
b. Brooklyn, N. Y., 2 Dec. 1914. Studied with Stefan Wolpe, Bernard Wagenaar, Louis Gruenberg at Juilliard School; attended Columbia Univ. He is conductor, arranger, and film composer.
WORKS: Orchestra: Concerto for jazz band; Focus; and songs.

*SAVINO, DOMENICO
b. Taranto, Italy, 13 Jan. 1882; U.S. citizen 1914. Studied at Naples Cons. He was director of a record company, 1915-25; editor for a music publisher; film composer.
WORKS: Orchestra: a symphony; piano concerto; Overture fantasy; Vesuvian rhapsody; Madrilena; Panorama; and songs.

*SAXTON, STANLEY
b. Fort Plain, N. Y., 5 Aug. 1904. Studied at Syracuse Univ., B. M., M. M.; with Charles Widor, Marcel Dupre, Nadia Boulanger at Fontainebleau. He has received commissions; was pianist, organist, choral conductor; professor, Skidmore Coll., from 1928.

(SAXTON, STANLEY)
WORKS: Orchestra: piano concerto; Mohawk suite; Skidmore suite; also choral works and organ pieces.

*SCHAEFER, HAROLD HERMAN
b. New York, N. Y., 22 July 1925. Studied with Mario Castelnuovo-Tedesco and Henry Brant, High School of Music and Art. He has received commissions from the United Nations for a 10th anniversary work, Ballad of an ancient hope; from the Nat. Asso. for Retarded Children for Their world is limited; from Joseph Eger for Overture to the blues; and from Daniel Nagrin for Bop song. He is pianist, accompanist, and arranger as well as composer.

*SCHERER, FRANK HERBERT
b. New York, N. Y., 5 Dec. 1897. Studied with T. Tertius Noble and Rosario Scalero. His works include Contemplation of the cricifixion, an oratorio; and Good Friday requiem, a cantata.

*SCHOLIN, C. ALBERT
b. Jamestown, N. Y., 24 May 1896; d. Brentwood, Mo., 22 Dec. 1958. Studied at American Cons., B. M., M. M. He was pianist, organist and teacher; founded music publishing company in St. Louis. His works included Suite for orchestra; Pastorale for organ; a cantata and many anthems.

*SCHOOP, JACK
b. Zurich, Switzerland, 31 July 1909. Studied in Paris and Berlin; with Alfred Cortot, Robert Casadesus; Artur Schnabel, Paul Dukas, Paul Hindemith, and Arnold Schoenberg. He received a commission for the Swiss Government for a work for the 1939 Exposition. He was concert pianist; accompanist to his sister Trudi Schoop; in World War II formed the Schoop Company and toured with the USO.
WORKS: Comic opera: The enchanted trumpet; Ballet: Maria del Valle, dance drama; Marche ballet; Orchestra: Fata Morgana; Everything new, 1939; Wishing tree, musical fantasy.

*SCHROEDER, WILLIAM A.
b. Brooklyn, N. Y., 10 Nov. 1888; d. Wilton, Conn., 20 Apr. 1960. Attended Brooklyn Polytechnic Inst.; studied with Roy Harris and Rubin Goldmark. He was bandmaster in World War I; composed for Navy shows; then for the Broadway stage.
WORKS: Orchestra: The Emperor Jones; Rhapsody; Miniature, piano concertino; And God walked the plains, with narrator; Ballet on an Irish theme; Jack and the bean stalk.

*SCHUYLER, PHILLIPA DUKE
b. New York, N. Y., 22 Aug. 1932; d. Da Nang, Vietnam, 9 May 1967. Attended a convent school; studied piano privately. She made her debut with the New York Philharmonic at age 14; made 3 world tours under the auspices of the U.S. State Department; was guest artist at independence celebrations in Leopoldville, Ghana, Madagascar; played command performances for

SCHUYLER, PHILLIPA DUKE

(SCHUYLER, PHILLIPA DUKE)
Emperor Haile Selassie, King and Queen of Malaya, and Queen Elizabeth of Belgium. She was author of Who killed the Congo?; Jungle Saints; Kingdom of dreams.
WORKS: Rumpelstiltskin, received Wayne Univ. award; Manhattan nocturne, Detroit Symphony Orch. prize; White Nile suite.

*SELMER, KATHRYN LANDE
b. Staten Island, N. Y., 6 Nov. 1930. Studied at Eastman School of Music and at Juilliard School. She has been singer and composer for NBC's Birthday House and Captain Kangaroo. Her works include the children's operas: Shoemaker and the elf; The princess and the pea; The princess who couldn't laugh; and songs.

*SHIELDS, LEROY
b. Waseca, Minn., 2 Oct. 1898; d. Ft. Lauderdale, Fla., 9 Jan. 1962. Studied at Univ. of Chicago; Columbia Univ.; received honorary D. M., Chicago Musical Coll. He toured as concert pianist; conducted extensively for radio, records and films, and for symphony orchestras.
WORKS: Orchestra: Union Pacific suite; Gloucester, tone poem; The great ball; many popular songs.

*SHURE, RALPH DEANE
b. Chillisquaque, Pa., 31 May 1885. Studied at Oberlin Coll., B. M. He held academic posts at Central Univ. of Iowa, 1907-09; Clarendon Texas Coll., 1909-19; Pennsylvania State Teachers Coll., 1919-21; American Univ. 1921-25; was music director, Mt. Vernon Place Methodist Church, Washington, D.C., 1921 to retirement.
WORKS: Orchestra: 5 symphonies; Chorus: 75 anthems; also organ and piano works.
8 Pine Ave., Takoma Park, MD 20012

*SIEGEL, ARSENE
b. Lyons, France, 26 Nov. 1897; U.S. citizen 1926. Studied privately in France; on scholarship with Felix Borowski at Chicago Musical Coll.; American Cons.; and with Heniot Levey. He was organist for radio stations and film theatres.
WORKS: Chamber music: Pasquinade, saxophone and piano; Sanctuary, received Nat. Composition Clinic prize for a piano work; Mirage, piano; The Windy City, piano suite; The hour of worship, organ; also anthems and songs.

*SINATRA, RAY
b. Gergenti, Italy, 1 Nov. 1904; U.S. citizen. Studied with Wallingford Riegger, Joseph Schillinger, Percy Grainger, and Albert Stoessel. He gave a recital at Symphony Hall, Boston, at age 13. He was organist in Boston theatres; pianist in dance orchestras; then scored films in Hollywood. His works include Central Park ballet and a piano concerto.

*SINGLETON, ALVIN
Studied at Juilliard School and Yale Univ., M. M. He has lived in Graz, Austria for some years; his Be natural for string trio won an award at Darmstadt, 1974. Other works include: A

(SINGLETON, ALVIN)
seasoning, 1971, blues piece for voice, flute, alto saxophone, trombone, bass, percussion, to his own text, the instrumentalists also have speaking parts; Argoru I for piano; Argoru II for cello; Argoru III, virtuoso piece for flute solo, 1971, Kwitana, 1974, concerto for piano, bass, percussion and an ensemble of string trio and woodwind trio, and a brass ensemble of 2 trumpets and 2 trombones.

*SKORNICKA, JOSEPH E.
b. Birch Creek, Mich., 13 Feb. 1902. Studied at Univ. of Wisconsin, B. E.; Northwestern Univ., M. A.; Oregon State Univ., Ed. D. He taught in Milwaukee schools from 1922; was head of music education and conductor of the Milwaukee Civic Orchestra from 1959. His compositions include pieces for orchestra and for band.

*SNYDER, WILLIAM
b. Park Ridge, Ill., 11 July 1916. Studied at De Paul Univ.; Chicago Cons., B. M.; American Cons., M. M.; also with Leo Sowerby and Moriz Rosenthal. He is pianist on radio and with dance bands.
WORKS: Orchestra: Seamist; Concerto for a summer night; Amber fire; Chorus: The 10 commandments.

*SODERO, CESARE
b. Naples, Italy, 2 Aug. 1886; to U.S. 1906; d. New York, N. Y., 16 Dec. 1947. Studied at Royal Cons., Naples. He conducted opera in England; on radio; Metropolitan Opera, 1942-43; conducted Mendelssohn Glee Club 12 seasons; was music director for a record company.
WORKS: Ballet: Ombre Russe; Orchestra: Preludio appassionata, violin and orch.; Nocturne, oboe and orch.; Chamber music: string quartet; Valse scherzo, woodwinds; Morning prayer, woodwinds; Invocation, cello and piano.

*SOLITO DE SOLIS, ALDO
b. Castrovillari, Italy, 25 May 1905; U.S. citizen. Studied at the Verdi Cons., Milan, Gold Medal; and at Leipzig Cons. He has been concert pianist in Europe, South American and in New York. He has composed many works for piano and songs.

*SOMOHAMO, ARTURO
b. San Juan, Puerto Rico, 1 Sep. 1910. Studied with Belen Salgado, Rafael Marquez, Louis Watts, Alexander Borovsky, and Bogumil Sykora. He was concert pianist in Central and South America; founded and conducted Philharmonic Orchestra of Puerto Rico; has been guest conductor in Europe.
WORKS: Orchestra: Haitian souvenirs; Puerto Rican rhapsody; Variations humoresque; Recuerdos; Caribbean rhapsody; Fiesta en San Juan; etc., and songs.

*SORRENTINO, CHARLES
b. Sicily, Italy, 13 Aug. 1906. Studied on scholarship at Manhattan School of Music; with Franz Kneisel, Maximilian Pilzer, Mario Corti,

(SORRENTINO, CHARLES)
and Vittorio Giannini. He was composer and
arranger for CBS 1931-60.
WORKS: Orchestra: Ameresque; Illusion,
voice and orch.; Chorus: Salem witches; Hummingbird; Home is best.

*SPRATT, JACK
3 miniatures for woodwind trio.
199 Sound Beach Ave., Box 277
Old Greenwich, CT 06870

*STANTON, ROYAL W.
b. Los Angeles, Calif., 23 Oct. 1916. Studied
at Univ. of California, Los Angeles, B. E., M. A.
Taught music in public schools, 1939-50; was
choral director, Long Beach City Coll., 1950-61;
from 1961, chairman, Fine Arts Division, Foothill Coll. He has composed songs and choral
works.

*STEELE, HELEN
b. Enfield, Conn., 21 June 1904. Attended
Wellesley Coll., B. A.; studied music privately.
She was voice teacher and accompanist for
singers.
WORKS: Voice: America, our heritage; The
legend of Befana; Duerme; Lagrimas.

*STEINER, GEORGE
b. Budapest, Hungary, 17 Apr. 1900; d. U.S.
Studied at Budapest Acad. of Music; was violinist in opera and symphony orchestras; gave
recitals in Europe. In the U.S. he has been composer for radio, television, and films. His
works include Rhapsodic poem for viola and orch.;
Serenade sarcastique, violin and cello.

*STEININGER, FRANK K. W.
b. Vienna, Austria, 12 June 1906; to U.S. 1935.
Studied music with Josef Marx. He was theatre
conductor in Vienna, Berlin and London; then in
Hollywood, New York, Pittsburgh, and Los Angeles.
WORKS: Operetta: Song without words; Centennial spectacle, for Topeka, Kan.; also film
scores and many songs.

*STONE, GREGORY
b. Odessa, Russia, 20 July 1900; to U.S. 1923.
He has been conductor and pianist in Latin America; film composer.
WORKS: Violin: Dolina; Hora in suoni
harmonici; Hora spiccata; Hora burlesca.

*STOTHART, HERBERT
b. Milwaukee, Wis., 11 Sep. 1885; d. Los Angeles,
Calif., 1 Feb. 1949. Studied at Milwaukee
Teachers Coll.; Univ. of Wisconsin; and in
Europe. He taught in public school, then at
Univ. of Wisconsin. From 1929 he was in Holly-
wood; wrote film scores; became general music
director for MGM.
WORKS: Pageant: China; Chorus: Voices of
liberation, cantata; Film scores: The good earth;
Romeo and Juliet; Mutiny on the Bounty; Mrs.
Miniver; The green years; The picture of Dorian
Gray.

*STOUGHTON, ROY SPAULDING
b. Worcester, Mass., 28 Jan. 1884; d. Allston,
Mass., 1 Feb. 1953. He was editor for a music
publisher.
WORKS: Ballet: The spirit of the sea; The
vision of the Aissawa; Cantatas: Esther; The
woman of Sychar; The resurrection and the life;
The wind of the west; many organ works and songs.

*STRAUSS, JOHN
b. New York, N. Y., 28 Apr. 1920. Studied at
Yale Univ., M. M.; Dalcroze School of Music,
certificate. He is composer and conductor for
films and television.
WORKS: The accused, opera-monologue for
television; Song cycle on Lorca texts; Car 54
where are you?, television theme.

*TAYLOR, LIONEL L.
b. Provo, Utah, 23 Mar. 1916. Studied at California School of the Arts, B. A., M. M. He
was an Army bandleader in World War II; instructor, Los Angeles Cons., 1947-54; arranger for
radio television, 1955-60; then instructor, Los
Angeles City Coll. His works include Incident
at the river, a cantata; other choral works and
songs.
Los Angeles City College
855 North Vermont Ave.
Los Angeles, CA 90029

*TAYLOR, TELFORD
b. Schenectady, N. Y., 24 Feb. 1908. Studied at
Williams Coll., B. A., M. A., L. L. D.; Harvard
Univ., L. L. B. He is a lawyer in New York City;
was assistant to the United States Chief of
Counsel at the Nuremberg war crimes trials in
1945; in 1946 became Chief of Counsel; was tech-
nical advisor and narrator for the television
play, Judgment at Nuremberg. He was author of
Sword and swastika, 1952, and Grand inquest:
The story of congressional investigations, 1955.
He has conducted his own works at Central Park
Mall, N. Y.
WORKS: Band: Italia eterna; Farewell to
the cavalry; 50 stars on the field of blue.

*THOMAS, CHRISTOPHER
b. Bristol, England, 7 Mar. 1894; U.S. citizen
1939. Studied on scholarship at Royal Coll. of
Music, London; teachers included Malcolm Sargent
and Percy Goetschius. He was church organist
and teacher in schools and colleges in England
and, following service in the British Army in
World War I, in churches and schools in the U.S.
From 1958 he was music director at St. Peter's
Church, Charlotte, N. C.
WORKS: Chamber music: Little prelude and
fugue, piano; Scottish suite, violin and piano;
and choral works.

*TREHARNE, BRYCESON
b. Merthyr Tydfil, Wales, 30 May 1879; to U.S.
1927; d. New York, N. Y., 4 Feb. 1948. Studied
on scholarship at Royal Coll. of Music, London;
received honorary D. M. from McGill Univ. He
taught at Univ. of Adelaide, 1900-11; spent 2
years in a German prison camp in World War I;

(TREHARNE, BRYCESON)
was lecturer at McGill Univ., 1923-27; editor for Boston Music Company and Willis Music Company from 1928.
WORKS: Operetta: The toymaker; Abe Lincoln; A Christmas carol; Chorus: Song of Solomon, oratorio; The banshee; Again in unison we stand; Song's eternity; Mount your horses; and songs.

*TRINKAUS, GEORGE J.
b. Bridgeport, Conn., 13 Apr. 1878; d. Ridgewood, N. J., 19 May 1960. Studied at Yale Univ.; was music editor in New York.
WORKS: Opera: Wizard of Avon; Orchestra: 2 symphonies; symphonietta; several overtures; Rhapsody, violin and orch.; 5 suites; Band: several overtures and other pieces; songs.

*VOLLINGER, WILLIAM
Compositions include 2 chamber operas; some 200 songs to his own texts; Little picture musics, 8 short instrumental pieces.
21 Ruckman Road
Woodcliff Lake, NJ 07675

*WALLS, ROBERT B.
b. Idaho, 24 Dec. 1910. Studied at Minnesota State Coll., B. E.; Univ. of North Dakota, M. S.; He taught in public schools in Minnesota and in Valley City, N. D.; at Univ. of Idaho, 1940-47; has been professor, Oregon State Univ., from 1947.
WORKS: Chorus: The names of Oregon, with narrator; Shallow Brown; Willow wind; Choral tune-ups.
Department of Music, Oregon State University
Corvallis, OR 97331

*WARD, DIANE (Corajane Diane Bunce)
b. Jackson, Mich., 10 Jan. 1919. Studied at Michigan State Univ., B. A., M. A.; Univ. of Michigan; and at American Cons. She is singer, actress, writer for radio and television, and public school teacher.
WORKS: Opera: Visiting the Bancrofts; The little dipper, operetta; Chorus: 2 poems.

*WARNER, PHILIP
b. Chicago, Ill., 6 Nov. 1901. Studied at American Cons., B. M.; Northwestern Univ., M. M. He taught at American Cons.; Sherwood Music Schools; Northwestern Univ.; was accompanist for singers; pianist on radio. He has received the Kimball award and the Sinfonia Nat. Contest prize.
WORKS: Orchestra: Sinfonietta; Sarabande-chaconne; Youth overture; Green mansions; The lake at dawn; Chamber music: Valse caprice, saxophone; Cuban skies, piano; choral works and songs.

*WEINSTEIN, MILTON
b. Cohoes, N. Y., 26 Apr. 1911. Studied with Joseph Schillinger and Tibor Serly. He is arranger for dance bands; composer and arranger for radio, television, educational films.
WORKS: Orchestra: Astrological suite; trumpet concerto.

*WHITFORD, HOMER
b. Harvey, Ill., 21 May 1892. Studied at Oberlin Coll., B. M.; Harvard Univ.; and at Fontainebleau. He was associate professor, Dartmouth Coll.; church organist in Cambridge, Mass. for 21 years; conductor of choral groups. His works include numerous choral pieces, church services and technical books for organ.

*WILD, EARL
b. Pittsburgh, Pa. Studied piano with Selmar Jansen. He has performed with major orchestras of the U.S. and in many music festivals. His compositions include a piano concerto and Revelations, an Easter oratorio, 1962.

*WRAGG, RUSSELL
b. Waukee, Iowa, 14 Aug. 1919. Attended Stanton Military Acad.; studied composition privately with Henry Holden Huss. He was pianist in night clubs and orchestras; organized All-Out Concerts in World War II; was co-founder of a piano school to which he returned after the war. His compositions include many piano pieces and songs.

*YELLIN, GLEB
b. Russia, 1 Mar. 1901. Studied in Leningrad and Berlin and with Reinhold Gliere. He was composer, conductor, and arranger with NBC, 1935-47; music director for Billy Rose productions; then composer and conductor for Marlene Dietrich on radio and television.
WORKS: Orchestra: Symphonic fantasy on eastern themes; Nocturne appassionata, violin and orch.

*YOUNG, ROLANDE MAXWELL
b. Washington, D.C., 13 Sep. 1929. Studied at Catholic Univ.; with Harold Bauer at Manhattan School of Music; with Vittorio Giannini at Juilliard School. She made her debut as pianist in Town Hall, New York in 1953.
WORKS: Little acorns, piano; and songs.

*ZISKIN, VICTOR
b. New York, N. Y., 18 Mar. 1937. Studied with Walter Piston and Tillman Merritt at Harvard Univ.; also with Isabella Vengerova, Jean Casadesus, Leonard Bernstein, Roger Sessions, Nadia Boulanger, and Kay Swift. He was the first Harvard freshman to write Hasty Pudding shows; has received the Damon Runyan Memorial Found. commission and an American Jewish Congress award for his off-Broadway stage score, Young Abe Lincoln; performed his own works in Carnegie Hall, 1959-1960.
WORKS: Ballet: Ballet for street urchins; Harlequin ballet; Aubade; Orchestra: San Francisco rhapsody, piano and orch.; On the borders of Israel; Civil War suite; Piano: Allegro pour piano; Suite for piano in 5 parts; and songs.

Women Composers

The # indicates that the composer so-marked will be found in the addendum.

#Akiyoshi, Toshiko
Allitsen, Frances
Alter, Martha
Altman, Adella C.
Amacher, Maryanne
Anderson, Beth
Anderson, Ruth
Babits (Patrick), Linda
Bahmann, Marianne
Bail, Grace Shattuck
Ballaseyus, Virginia
Ballou, Esther Williamson
Bampton, Ruth
Barkin, Elaine
Barnett, Alice
Barthelson, Joyce
Bartlett, Floy
Bassett, Karolyn Wells
Bauer, Marion
Bean, Mabel
Beaton, Isabella
Beaumont, Vivian
Beck, Martha (Carragan)
Behrend, Jeanne
Bell, Lucille Anderson
Bellamy, Marian
Bellerose, Sister Cecilia
Bellman, Helen M.
Bennett, Claudia
Bennett, Wilhelmina
Bentley, Berenice Benson
Berckmann, Evelyn
Bish, Diane
Bitgood, Roberta
Blake, Dorothy Gaynor
Bley, Carla
Blood, Esta
Boesing, Martha
Bolz, Harriett Hadlock
Bond, Victoria
Bonds, Margaret
Boozer, Patricia
Borroff, Edith
Boykin, Helen
Bradley, Ruth
Brandt, Dorothea (Nelson)
Branning, Grace
Branscombe, Gena
Bringuer, Estela
Britain, Radie
Britton, Dorothy Guyvor
Brock, Blanche Kerr
Brockman, Jane E.
Brogue, Roslyn
Brouk, Joanna
Brown, Clemmon May
Brown, Elizabeth Bouldin
Brown, Elizabeth Van Ness

Brush, Ruth J.
Buchanan, Annabel M.
Buckley, Dorothy Pike
#Bunce, Corajane Diane,
  See: Ward, Diane
Burke, Loretto
Burt, Virginia
Bush, Grace E.
Butler, Lois
Byers, Roxana
Caldwell, Mary E.
Calvin, Susan
Caperton, Florence
Carno, Zita
Carreau, Margaret
Chance, Nancy
Chertok, Pearl
Clarke, Rebecca
Clarke, Rosemary
Coates, Gloria K.
Cobb, Hazel
Cole, Ulric
Coolidge, Peggy Stuart
Cooper, Rose Marie
Couper, Mildred
Cowles, Cecil Marion
Cowles, Darleen
Crane, Helen
Crane, Joelle Wallach
Crawford, Dawn C.
Crawford, Louise
Crawford-Seeger, Ruth
Crews, Lucile
Crisp, Barbara
Curran, Pearl Gildersleeve
Dallam, Helen
Daniels, Mabel
#Davis, Genevieve
Davis, Jean Reynolds
Davis, Katherine K.
Davis, Margaret W.
Davis, Mary
#Deacon, Mary Connor
Decevee, Alice
Del Riego, Theresa
Denbow, Stefania
#Deppen, Jessie L.
Deyo, Ruth Lynda
Diamond, Arline
Diemer, Emma Lou
Diller, Saralu
Dillon, Fannie Charles
Dittenhaver, Sarah L.
Dlugoszewski, Lucia
Donahue, Bertha Terry
Donaldson, Sadie
Dortch, Eileen Wier
Drennan, Dorothy

Dretke, Leora N.
Droste, Doreen
#Dudley, Marjorie Eastwood
Dumesnil, Evangeline Lehman
Dungan, Olive
Dunn, Rebecca W.
Du Page, Florence
Dushkin, Dorothy
Dvorkin, Judith
Eagles, Moneta
Eakin, Vera
Edwards, Clara
Edwards, Jessie B.
Efrein, Laurie
#Eichhorn, Hermene W.
Eilers, Joyce Elaine
Eisenstein, Judith K.
Eisenstein, Stella Price
Elliott, Marjorie R.
Emig, Lois Myers
Endres, Olive P.
Escot, Pozzi
Ezell, Helen Ingle
Fairlie, Margaret
Feldman, Joann E.
Ferris, Joan
Fine, Vivian
Finley, Lorraine Noel
Firestone, Idabelle
Fischer, Edith
Fisher, Doris
Fisher, Gladys W.
Fishman, Marion
Fleming, Shari Beatrice
#Flick-Flood, Dora
Forman, Joanne
Forster, Dorothy
Foster, Fay
Fowler, Marje
Franco, Clare J.
Frank, Jean Forward
Freitag, Dorothea
Frumker, Linda
Fryxell, Regina Holman
Fuchs, Lillian
Fuller, Jeanne Weaver
Galajikian, Florence Grandland
Gardner, Mildred
Garwood, Margaret
Gebuhr, Ann
Genet, Marianne
Gentemann, Sister Mary E.
George, Lila Gene
Gessler, Caroline
Ghiglieri, Sylvia M.
Gideon, Miriam
Gilbert, Pia
Gilbertson, Virginia

Women Composers

Glanville-Hicks, Peggy
Glaser, Victoria
Glen, Irma
Glick, Henrietta
Glickman, Sylvia
Godwin, Joscelyn
Goetschius, Marjorie
#Gollahon, Gladys
Golson, Florence
Goodsmith, Ruth
Gould, Elizabeth
Gray, Judith
Gresham, Ann
Grimes, Doreen
Gudauskas, Giedre
Gulesian, Grace Warner
Haban, Sister Teresine M.
Hadden, Frances Roots
Hahn, Sandra
Hall, Frances
Halpern, Stella
Harkness, Rebekah
#Harper, Marjorie
Harrington, Amber Roobenian
Harris, Ethel Ramos
Hays, Doris Ernestine
Hayward, Mae Shepard
Hazen, Sara (Evans)
Heinrich, Adel Verna
Henderson, Rosamond
Hier, Ethel Glenn
Hoffmann, Peggy
Hoffrichter, Bertha C.
Hokanson, Dorothy Cadzow
Hokanson, Margrethe
Housman, Rosalie
Howe, Mary
Hoy, Bonnie
Hsu, Wen-Ying
Hughes, Mother Martina
Hull, Anne
Hunkins, Eusebia
Hytrek, Sister Theophane
Ivey, Jean Eichelberger
Jambor, Agi
James, Dorothy
Jessye, Eva
Johnson, Harriett
Jolley, Florence Weaver
Jones, Sister Ida
Jordan, Alice
Kamien, Anna
Kavasch, Deborah
Kayden, Mildred
Kendrick, Virginia
Kessler, Minuetta
Kettering, Eunice Lee
Kinscella, Hazel Gertrude
Klimisch, Sister Mary Jane
Kolb, Barbara
Kreiss, Hulda
Kruger, Lily Canfield
Lambert, Cecily
Lang, Edith
Larson, Elizabeth
Lathrop, Gayle Posselt

Latiolais, Jayne
Laufer, Beatrice
Leahey, Mary Weldon
Lefever, Maxine
Leginska, Ethel
Leonard, Grace
Levy, Lauren
Lipscomb, Helen
Lloyd, Caroline
Lockshin, Florence L.
#Lohoefer, Evelyn
Lorenz, Ellen Jane
Love, Loretta
Lu, Yen
Lucke, Katharine E.
Luckman, Phyllis
Lutyens, Sally Speare
#McCleary, Fiona
McCollin, Frances
MacDonald, Catherine
McIlwraith, Isa
McKinney, Mathilde
McLain, Margaret Starr
McLaughlin, Marian
McLean, Priscilla
McLin, Lena
McMillan, Ann
McNeil, Jan
McPherson, Frances Marie
Madsen, Florence J.
Mageau, Sister Mary Magdalen
Mamlok, Ursula
Mana-Zucca (Zuckermann, Augusta)
Manning, Kathleen Lockhart
Marcus, Adabelle Gross
Marshall, Jane
Marth, Helen Jun
Masoner, E. L. (Betty)
#Maurice-Jacquet, H.
Maxwell, Jacqueline Perkinson
Mekeel, Joyce
Meloy, Elizabeth
Meneely, Sarah
Merriman, Margarita L.
Middleton, Jean B.
Mikulak, Marcia
Miller, Joan
Mishell, Kathryn Lee
Monk, Meredith
Montgomery, Merle
Moore, Mary Carr
Moore, Maurine Ricks
Moscovitz, Julianne
Munger, Millicent
Munger, Shirley
Musgrave, Thea
Musser, Clare
Mustillo, Lina
Newlin, Dika
Nichols, Alberta
Nickerson, Camille
Niemack, Ilza
Nightingale, Mae
Nohe, Beverly
Nordenstrom, Gladys
Nowak, Alison

Nunlist, Juli
O'Brien, Katherine
Ochse, Orpha Caroline
Ohlson, Marion
Oliver, Madra Emogene
Oliveros, Pauline
Ostrander, Linda
Owen, Blythe
Panetti, Joan
Parker, Alice
Paul, Barberie
#Paul, Doris A.
Pengilly, Sylvia
Perry, Julia
Perry, Zenobia P.
Petersen, Marian F.
Peterson, Melody
Phillips, Vivian D.
Pietsch, Edna Frida
Polin, Claire
Pooler, Marie
Preobrajenska, Vera N.
Price, Florence B.
Priesing, Dorothy McLemore
Ptaszynska, Marta
Queen, Virginia
Quesada, Virginia
Rabinof, Sylvia
Ran, Shulamit
Rapoport, Eda
Reynolds, Erma
Rich, Gladys
Richardson, Sharon
Richter, Marga
Richter, Marion Morrey
Riley, Ann
Rinehart, Marilyn
Roberts, Gertrud
Robertson, Donna N.
Rocherolle, Eugenie R.
Rodgers, Mary
Rogers, Ethel Tench
Rogers, Susan Whipple
Rudow, Vivian Adelberg
Samson, Valerie Brooks
Sanders, Alma M.
Sandifur, Ann E.
Sandresky, Margaret V.
Schmidt, Dianne
Schonthal, Ruth
Schwartz, Julie
#Schuyler, Phillippa Duke
Schwerdtfeger, E. Anne
Scott-Hunter, Hortense
Scoville, Margaret
Sears, Helen
Sears, Ilena H.
Seaver, Blanche E.
#Selmer, Kathryn Lande
Semegen, Daria
Severy, Violet C.
Shatin, Judith
Shepard, Jean
Sherman, Elna
Shields, Alice
Shreve, Susan

512

WOMEN COMPOSERS

Silberta, Rhea
Silsbee, Ann
Silver, Sheila J.
Silverman, Faye-Ellen
Simons, Netty
Skjeveland, Helge
Sleeth, Natalie
Smiley, Pril
Smith, Anita
Smith, Julia
Snow, Mary Helen McCarty
Souers, Mildred
Spencer, Williametta
Spiegel, Laurie
Spindle, Louise Cooper
Spizizen, Louise
Stairs, Louise E.
Stanley, Helen
#Steele, Helen
Steiner, Gitta
Stewart, Hascal V.
Stoeppelmann, Janet
Strickland, Lily Teresa
Suchy, Gregoria
Sumner, Sarah
Swift, Kay
Swisher, Gloria Wilson
Talma, Louise
Tarlow, Karen Anne

Taylor, Priscilla
Templar, Joan
Terhune, Anice Potter
Terry, Frances
Thomas, Helen
Thome, Diane
Tower, Joan
Tucker, Tui St. George
Turner, Mildred C.
Turner, Myra Brooks
Twombly, Mary Lynn
Tyson, Mildred Lund
Ulehla, Ludmila
Van Appledorn, Mary J.
Van de Vate, Nancy
Van Katwijk, Viola Beck
Von Gunden, Heidi
Vree, Marion F.
Wallace, Kathryn F.
Ward, Beverly A.
#Ward, Diane (Bunce)
Ware, Harriet
Warne, Katharine
Warren, Elinor Remick
Weaver, Mary
Webb, Alliene Brandon
Weigl, Vally
Westbrook, Helen Searles

White, Elise Fellows
Wickham, Florence
Wiggins, Mary
Wigham, Margaret
Williams, Frances
Williams, Jean E.
Williams, Mary Lou
Willman, Regina Hansen
Wilson, Karen
Wishart, Betty Rose
Witkin, Beatrice
Wollner, Gertrude Price
Wong, Betty
Wong, Hsiung-Zee
Wood-Hill, Mabel
Woolsey, Mary Hale
Worth, Amy
Wunsch, Ilse
Wyeth, Ann
Wylie, Ruth Shaw
Young, Jane Corner
#Young, Rolande Maxwell
Youse, Glad Robinson
Zaimont, Judith Lang
Ziffrin, Marilyn J.
Zimmerman, Phyllis
Zweig, Esther
Zwilich, Ellen Taeffe